A GUIDE TO
Intra-state Wars

This book is dedicated J. David Singer, the founder of the Correlates of War Project, and to all those who so selflessly worked on the project in the hope that we can prevent war by understanding it.

SAGE | 50 YEARS

SAGE was founded in 1965 by Sara Miller McCune to support the dissemination of usable knowledge by publishing innovative and high-quality research and teaching content. Today, we publish more than 850 journals, including those of more than 300 learned societies, more than 800 new books per year, and a growing range of library products including archives, data, case studies, reports, and video. SAGE remains majority-owned by our founder, and after Sara's lifetime will become owned by a charitable trust that secures our continued independence.

Los Angeles | London | New Delhi | Singapore | Washington DC

A GUIDE TO Intra-state Wars

AN EXAMINATION OF CIVIL, REGIONAL, AND INTERCOMMUNAL WARS, 1816–2014

JEFFREY S. DIXON
Texas A&M University–Central Texas

MEREDITH REID SARKEES
Global Women's Leadership in International Security (GWLIS)

SAGE reference | CQPRESS

Los Angeles | London | New Delhi
Singapore | Washington DC

SAGE | CQPRESS

Los Angeles | London | New Delhi
Singapore | Washington DC

FOR INFORMATION:

CQ Press
SAGE Publications, Inc.
2455 Teller Road
Thousand Oaks, California 91320
E-mail: order@sagepub.com

SAGE Publications Ltd.
1 Oliver's Yard
55 City Road
London, EC1Y 1SP
United Kingdom

SAGE Publications India Pvt. Ltd.
B 1/I 1 Mohan Cooperative Industrial Area
Mathura Road, New Delhi 110 044
India

SAGE Publications Asia-Pacific Pte. Ltd.
3 Church Street
#10-04 Samsung Hub
Singapore 049483

Editorial Assistant: Jordan Enobakhare
Developmental Editor: Carole Maurer
Production Editor: Tracy Buyan
Copy Editor: Pam Schroeder
Typesetter: Hurix Systems Pvt. Ltd.
Proofreader: Lawrence W. Baker
Indexer: Sylvia Coates
Cover Designer: Rose Storey
Marketing Manager: Teri Williams

Printed in the United States of America.

ISBN 978-0-8728-9775-5

SFI Certified Sourcing
www.sfiprogram.org
SFI-00453

15 16 17 18 19 10 9 8 7 6 5 4 3 2 1

Contents

Tables and Figures

TABLES

FIGURES

Acknowledgments

This work was started with the support and encouragement of J. David Singer, and we mourn that he did not live to see its completion. Singer's vision and commitment to the quantitative study of war created the Correlates of War Project (COW), which is now one of the most influential and enduring data-gathering projects in world politics. Singer and Melvin Small, the original project historian, established a framework and coding rules for the study of war that has guided the COW Project and much of the wider scholarship about war for more than fifty years. Singer was a rare academic who valued equally his research, his teaching, and his political activism. His eagerness to mentor students and colleagues brought an eclectic group of scholars into the fold of the COW community, and the expansion of the project, and its prodigious output, would not have been possible without the enthusiasm and tremendous teamwork of this group. The entire COW Project is also indebted to Phil Schafer, whose relentless data gathering has formed the bases of numerous data sets. COW's survival and continued existence are also due in great measure to the leadership of its subsequent directors, Stuart Bremer, Scott Bennett, Paul Diehl, and Zeev Maoz, the current COW director.

David Singer and Mel Small were the authors of the first two COW war handbooks (*The Wages of War* and *Resort to Arms*), while the third, *Resort to War*, was written by Meredith Reid Sarkees and Frank Whelon Wayman. This book constitutes the fourth in the sequence. It also is being published as part of the Correlates of War book series established by CQ Press. CQ Press staff Andrea Pedolsky, Editorial Director, and Doug Goldenberg-Hart, Senior Acquisitions Editor, originally helped us frame this work and provided encouragement in working toward its completion. Similarly, the book would not have been finished without the patience and flexibility of James Brace-Thompson, previously Executive Editor of SAGE Reference, and Carole Maurer, Senior Developmental Editor, who gently prodded and cajoled us to stop researching and begin writing.

In addition to our collective gratitude to the COW community and to SAGE, each of us, as coauthors, wants to express our thanks to those who have helped us individually in this endeavor. Jeffrey Dixon would like to acknowledge the contributions of research assistants Breann Crane (for work on Latin America), Tara Braas Passini (for work on a few wars in the Middle East), and Kevin Tomaszewski (for citations, formatting, and helpful assistance on some cases in the Middle East and Asia/Oceania). During the early stages of the project, the support of Richard Stoll was essential, and some of the earliest Spanish-language data on Latin American civil wars was gathered by Rosa Sandoval-Bustos, with funding from the

National Science Foundation. Katharine Dixon provided patient support throughout most of the project. Finally, we would like to thank coauthor Meredith Sarkees for her guidance early in the project and attention to detail during the writing process.

Meredith Reid Sarkees especially is indebted to and grateful for the dedicated research assistance of Jon Kotaska, who was so skilled at tracking down sources and information concerning some of the more obscure wars. Invaluable research assistance also was provided by Amy Frame, Christine Sarkees, Kerrie Sarkees, Carol Reid, and John R. Sarkees. Lois P. Reid and John R. Sarkees provided much-needed and appreciated editing assistance. Meredith also would like to thank Gediminas Vitkus for his insightful and thought-provoking discussions of the coding of the Forest Brethren war and for his willingness to share his own research on the topic. His research was also key in the coding of the war in Ukraine. Similarly, Meredith is grateful for the assistance of Jorge A. Restrepo in alerting her to the data-gathering efforts of CERAC, and for compiling summary Colombian fatality data. The history of the COW project was significantly improved by the comments and suggestions of Zeev Moaz, Paul Diehl, James Lee Ray, and Richard Stoll, and our exchanges brought back many fond memories of David Singer. Throughout this long endeavor, David Singer and Diane Macaulay epitomized graceful hosts as they provided Meredith with a welcoming place to stay during her visits to Ann Arbor to peruse the University of Michigan archives. Their counsel and encouragement did much to restore her soul. Meredith will never be able to adequately thank them for their influence on her life. Most importantly, Meredith is eternally grateful to John R. Sarkees, who truly understands the magnitude of effort that this book has entailed. He bore the many costs of this work with grace and an optimism that it would one day be finished. Finally, Meredith would like to thank Jeff Dixon, whose stalwartness, meticulous adherence to coding rules, and dedication to this project are the keys to its success.

Foreword

Wars have been one of the earliest and most persistent collective human endeavors. Many other collective rituals have come and gone, but the practice of mass bloodshed has been a permanent feature of humankind for millennia. Political, economic, social, and technological changes over the course of history have shaped and reshaped warfare. But its main features remain constant. The characteristics of the phenomenon we call *war* have remained the same since the dawn of civilization: organized groups of (typically) men, equipped with instruments that are capable of causing severe physical damage, engage in a series of sustained violent clashes that result in large number of fatalities.

While these characteristics seem to be fixed, the nature of warfare has undergone dramatic changes over time. The Correlates of War (COW) project, as the first chapter of this book documents, was born out of an intellectual desire to understand both the nature of these changes and the factors that cause individuals, groups, and states to engage in warfare. In contrast to other attempts to do the same—and there were quite a few at the time—the project's aim was to develop a science of conflict and peace, firmly grounded in systematic, empirical analysis. One of the first prerequisites of such an approach is the collection of quantifiable data on the phenomena under study. Again, as the first chapter of the book shows, the project evolved, expanded, and diversified. Yet, the fundamental philosophy of the application of scientific methods via the systematic testing of quantitative data on political, social, and economic factors related to war and peace remains the backbone of the project.

One of the key changes in the character of warfare was the relative decline of large-scale warfare between and among nations and the relative rise in the number and severity of organized warfare within states. The project's founder and first director, J. David Singer, was one of the first to recognize this trend and to appreciate its importance. Therefore the second book that provided a systematic description of wars—*Resort to Arms* (1982)—devoted significant space to the study of a data set on civil wars. The third round of data collection on wars by Sarkees and Wayman—*Resort to War* (2010)—further expanded on this effort, providing systematic data on various intra-state wars and non-state (or communal) wars. The current volume focuses on various types of war within states, thus adding an important layer of data to the existing compilations of war data collected by the COW project.

One of the most important features of the book you are about to read—which applies to most COW data sets—is that it enables us to trace changes, dynamics, and evolution in intra-state wars over time. There is a glaring absence of systematic data and scientific analysis in the myriad debates in the scholarly literature and public discourse about the changes in the frequency, intensity, and nature of warfare in general and intra-state wars in particular. In part, the unscientific (or, as J. David Singer liked to call it, "prescientific") nature of this debate was due to the absence of longitudinal data on these issues. With the current volume and the attendant data that are publicly available—the paucity of data on intra-state warfare can no longer serve as an excuse. Thanks to the Herculean efforts of Meredith Sarkees and Jeff Dixon, the raw facts about the changes in the number, severity, location, and participation in intra-state warfare are here; it is now the time for the scientific community to use these data in an effort to understand the nature of these changes and the factors that caused them.

An important tradition pioneered by the COW project in international relations—a tradition that by now has diffused to a large number of scholars engaged in data-based analysis of international processes—is to provide a transparent and detailed explication of the underlying logic of data collection, clear operational definitions of the basic concepts and variables, and a systematic description of the major trends in the data. This is the cornerstone of our ability to replicate analyses and to build cumulative knowledge on war. This book continues this tradition. Anyone wishing to better understand intra-state wars—what they are, what kinds exist, how they start, how they end, when and where they have occurred—would need to consult this book.

Although this book was written by political scientists, and although its focus is on the political aspects of intra-state wars, it is an essential resource for other social scientists interested in economic, social, political, or even cultural evolution. Sociologists who want to understand the causes and consequences of social stratification would need to consult this book. Economists who wish to understand the economic sources and consequences of warfare will need to use these data. Cultural and religious scholars who wish to understand the implications of cultural and religious divisions within societies would have to examine whether and how divergent groups within societies (perhaps divided along cultural, ethnic, or religious fault lines) choose to resort to warfare to resolve their grievances.

The Latin adage *si vis pacem, para bellum* (if you want peace, prepare for war) has long been a leading line in the study of political-military strategy. The philosophy of the COW project has paraphrased this adage into *si vis pacem, studium bellum* (if you want peace, study war). This book emerges out of an intellectual passion that rests on the belief that understanding problems is an essential stage in attempts at finding solutions. The study of war—at least within the COW tradition—is related closely to the study of peace. It is not only my hope but my firm belief that this book will contribute to our ability to devise strategies to increase peace and stability in societies that have or are experiencing internal war. Moreover, the study of intra-state wars that relies on the data provided by this book may well help improve the quality of life, human rights practices, justice, and equality in these societies.

Zeev Maoz, University of California, Davis
Director, Correlates of War Project

Preface

I was skeptical when I hired on in 1964 as the "historian" on a project filling up with political scientists eager to quantify virtually any activity having to do with international diplomatic and military interactions. I did have some interest in social science, as my dissertation involved public opinion and foreign policy, but when it came to numbers, I was, as Dave Singer would accurately contend, "preoperational." Needless to say, I learned a lot about the folks across the interdisciplinary wall, while I think I was of assistance to some of them who could not find Tuscany on a map or whose historical references went back only as far as the Korean War. They, of course, helped me to see how history could be more than a series of unrelated anecdotes. Along the way, they were amused by those same anecdotes at the legendary weekly seminars. The main problem I encountered working on the project at the start was one of data-quality control. COW was omnivorous, eager for whatever data I could provide and not always as interested as I was in their provenance. More importantly, I found myself often playing the role of historical grand pooh-bah, pointing out that certain kinds of data were simply unavailable or, especially, that even when we had accurate data sets, some fanciful indicators that easily could be developed did not have face validity.

On the other hand, I think I was of some assistance in constructing surrogate variables for complicated historical processes that did not do violence to history and that could be aggregated and analyzed with our then-primitive tools in a meaningful way. Speaking of primitive tools, it would have been so much easier to begin COW in the present time, with the vast resources of the Internet available in multiple languages. We had to do it the old way in libraries with dusty tomes such as our perennial favorite, the *Almanach de Gotha*, which is so little used now that one has to file special requests to retrieve it from storage. At the least, most of those tomes were more reliable than some of the seemingly authoritative information we might pluck from the Internet today. Indeed, I frequently have to tell students engaged in historical research with me that they should go the library to perform most of their work. When informed, some ask, "Where is the library?" Many of the political science students working as assistants on the project learned their way around the stacks, especially in the D, or Eurocentric, area. I enjoyed working on the COW team because almost all historians do their work alone. When I was an undergraduate, I looked forward to the time when I would be in a history department, talking with colleagues about our mutual research. Alas, although we share our ideas with one another at seminars and brown bags, most of us are too busy with our own work to take a serious interest in our counterparts' work and generally do not have the expertise in narrow subdisciplines to offer more than theoretical and stylistic commentary. Of course, working on an ever-growing team meant the need for larger grants. I was concerned about the amount of time COW people spent discussing, planning, and writing grant proposals every two years or so.

One role that I played with some gusto was as the official respondent to Karl Deutsch. Deutsch, a brilliant polymath who knew a good deal about history, came into town periodically as COW's most distinguished consultant. On occasion, it was my task gently to challenge his memory or facts when he lectured confidently to COW political scientists about an obscure nineteenth-century Middle European war. It was difficult competing with him because his charming Middle-European accent lent authenticity to his account.

Despite some interest in quantification among economic and social historians in the 1960s and 1970s, most were not impressed with the work I did with COW. Leading two lives, I generally was careful to leave numbers out of my writing in modern American history. Once, when I included two figures depicting the opinion–policy relationship during the Vietnam War era, a colleague in an otherwise friendly review wondered why I needed to use them.

More interesting, perhaps, my work with COW social scientists has taught me to begin my articles and books with lengthy methodological introductions and to insist that my students do likewise. And for this I am most grateful to my more scientifically oriented colleagues. Although explicit concern about coding rules may seem elementary to most other scholars, many accomplished historians still pay little attention to how they go about their business. Even though political science is the softest of the sciences and history is the hardest of the humanities, the twain still do not meet. Over the years I have been gratified to see how many students who worked on COW have achieved prominence in their disciplines. It is also rewarding to witness the vast number of scholars outside of the project who have used and continue to use some of the data that I had a hand in developing.

This important new volume will surely add to the utility of COW for the next generation of social scientists interested in trying to understand the problem of war in modern society. In *Wages of War*, David Singer and I focused upon inter-state and extra-state wars. A major advance in *Resort to Arms* was the addition of civil wars. There we also laid out a war typology of internal war that encouraged further data gathering on regional and communal violence. It is gratifying to see that Dixon and Sarkees have continued this work.

Melvin Small, Distinguished Professor of History Emeritus, Wayne State University and original historian for the Correlates of War Project

About the Authors

Jeffrey S. Dixon received his BA in International Relations and Political Science/History from Concordia College in Moorhead, Minnesota. He received his PhD in Political Science from Rice University in Houston, Texas, writing his dissertation on the consequences of third-party military intervention on civil war outcomes. He has published articles on the causes of civil wars, how civil wars end, and the duration of civil wars. He is currently Distinguished Graduate Faculty and Associate Professor of Political Science at Texas A&M University–Central Texas and co-host of the Correlates of War Civil War Dataset.

Meredith Reid Sarkees is a long-time affiliate of the Correlates of War (COW) Project, having worked with COW founder J. David Singer for many years. She has served as host or co-host of the datasets on inter-state, extra-state, intra-state, and non-state wars for over twenty years and has published a number of articles about the trends in warfare. A handbook on all of the COW wars, *Resort to War 1816–2007*, was written by Sarkees and Frank Whelon Wayman. Sarkees also co-edited *Advancing Peace Research: Leaving Traces, Selected Articles by J. David Singer* with Jody Lear and Diane Macaulay as a testament to the significance of the COW project and Singer's work. Sarkees's other research area focuses upon women's leadership and the status of women in both academia and the realm of international relations. She co-authored with Nancy E. McGlen a groundbreaking study of the women serving in American foreign policy institutions, *Women in Foreign Policy*. Sarkees currently serves as president of Global Women's Leadership in International Security (GWLIS).

Introduction

What Is War and Why Do We Study It?

It is hard to overstate the importance of studying war, especially because, as noted political scientist Karl W. Deutsch concluded, "Nothing less than this—the understanding of war and the possible ways to its abolition—is on the agenda of our time."[1] War is an activity that has widespread ramifications, touching virtually every aspect of human life in one way or another; yet despite the horrendous loss of life caused by war and the monumental costs it incurs, the practice of war has endured. Views on war range from overwhelmingly negative—as a problem to be solved, an anachronism to be abolished, or a crime to be punished—to enthusiastically supportive, as bringing forth the best in human behavior, as a means of confronting evil (even if only in utilitarian terms), or as a potentially interesting adventure.[2] Consequently, there are a variety of reasons why people study the phenomenon of war: historians may wish to understand one particular historical event; military strategists may want to learn how to conduct war more effectively; political theorists may desire to conceptualize war as part of an overall philosophical view of the nature of humankind; psychologists may seek to understand the origins of war in human biology or psyche; international relations scholars may want to conceptualize war as a tactic of international or world politics; institutionalists may want to examine ways in which the international community can develop laws or institutions to legislate or control the practice of war; pacifists may study war in terms of preventing decisions to go to war; optimists may wish to examine patterns of war to see evidence of human progress; environmentalists may wish to examine the environmental impacts of war and/or the role of environmental issues as causes of war; and behaviorists may study war to determine whether scientific methodologies can increase our understanding about the patterns of war and the factors that contribute to its onset. Though research in these areas has different foci and asks fundamentally different questions, it all has contributed to our understanding of what Hillman refers to as our "Terrible Love of War."[3]

A number of attempts to define war have been generated in the realm of philosophy. Even though Thomas Hobbes, Immanuel Kant, and John Locke represented competing normative positions concerning war (Hobbes representing realism, with Kant and Locke reflecting liberalism), they commonly viewed war as a broad set of omnipresent characteristics that described the human condition. Hobbes argued that war was not merely a behavior but a fundamentally natural relationship among actors (which might be individuals or states):

> Hereby it is manifest, that during the time men live without a common Power to keep them all in awe, they are in that condition which is called Warre; and such a warre, as is of every man, against every man. . . . For Warre, consisteth not in Battell onely, or the act of fighting, but in a tract of time, wherein the Will to contend by Battell is sufficiently known: . . . So the nature of War, consisteth not in actuall fighting; but in the known disposition thereto, during all the time there is no assurance to the contrary.[4]

Similarly, Kant's *Metaphysics of Morals* stated, "This non-rightful condition is a condition of war (of the right of the stronger), even if it is not a condition of actual war and actual attacks being constantly made (hostilities)," though states are bound to leave it if they can do so, through mechanisms that resemble international law or a federation of nations.[5] Locke similarly described the overarching nature of war, yet he argued that war was not a natural state of affairs, contrasting the state of nature with the state of war. For Locke, war involves deliberate design: "The state of war is a state of enmity and destruction," and declaring by word or action a design upon another's life puts one in a state of war.[6] Notably, Locke rejected the notion that anarchy is by definition a state of war, but the lack of a common power does give one a right to war in defense of one's natural rights.[7]

Rejecting the expansive views of war, Rousseau presented an explicitly statist view of war in his *Social Contract,* which seems to foreclose the possibility of "civil war" as such:

> War, then, is not a relation between men, but between states; in wars, individuals are enemies wholly by chance, not as men, not even as citizens, but only as soldiers; not as members of their country, but only as its defenders. In a word, a state can have as an enemy only another state, not men, because there can be no real relations between things possessing different intrinsic natures.[8]

Clausewitz, who combined a philosophical perspective with a more explicit discussion of military tactics, had several definitions of war. He combined behavior and intent by claiming, "War is thus an act of force to compel our enemy to do our will."[9] Yet he also expanded on the statist approach by describing war as the behavior of political communities: "When whole communities go to war—whole peoples, and especially civilized peoples—the reason always lies in some political situation, and the occasion is always due to some political object. War, therefore, is an act of policy."[10] Detractors have claimed that this description of war as a continuation of politics seems to normalize the practice of war. Orend has continued the political focus in his discussions of war, for example, in his assertion that "war should be understood as an actual, intentional, and widespread armed conflict between political communities."[11] Though he excluded phenomena such as gang fights explicitly, he expanded the conception of political communities to allow for civil war: "War is a phenomenon which occurs only between political communities, defined as those entities which either are states or intend to become states."[12]

The statist focus in definitions of war also has been common in the realm of international law, which primarily focuses upon states' obligations under international law. Yet even here, the meaning of war has been contested: "When we get to international law, we find that there is no binding definition of war stamped with the *imprimatur* of a multilateral treaty in force. What we have is quite a few scholarly attempts to depict the practice of States and to articulate, in a few choice words, an immensely complex idea."[13] Despite this lack of an authoritative definition, there are a number of elements common to virtually all legal definitions of war. The first of these is again statist—the notion that war is waged by sovereign states and that any other violence is not real war. Halleck's 1885 treatise on the law of war defended a then-common definition of war as "a contest between states, or parts of states, carried on by force."[14] A second common aspect of legal definitions of war is—unsurprisingly—legalism. Some cynics have argued that by trying to delineate lawful war from unlawful violence, legal definitions frequently have legitimized the practice. Oppenheim's (1906) classic treatise on international law addressed this conundrum by emphasizing that "war is not inconsistent with, but a condition regulated by, international law."[15] He defined war as "the contention between two or more States through their armed forces for the purpose of overpowering each other and imposing such conditions of peace as the victor pleases."[16] Like Halleck, Oppenheim essentially denied the existence of civil war as a distinct form of war because a state fighting insurgents would not create a state of war in a legal sense. Yet he allowed that the American civil war was "real war" because it featured states of some form on each side.[17] In addressing Oppenheim's work, Dinstein identified four requirements in Oppenheim's definition of war: contention between at least two states; use of armed force by those states; a purpose of overpowering the enemy and imposing peace on the victors; and an implied condition of symmetrical and diametrically opposed goals.[18] In accepting the first requirement, Dinstein argued that "Oppenheim was entirely right in excluding civil wars from this definition" because there is "no single corpus of law applicable to armed conflicts."[19] As he had objections to the other requirements, Dinstein offered a modified definition of war:

> War is a hostile interaction between two or more States, either in a technical or a material sense. War in the technical sense is a formal status produced by a declaration of war. War in the material sense is generated by the actual use of armed force, which must be comprehensive on the part of at least one party to the conflict.[20]

This emphasis on "comprehensive" use of force suggests a third element to legal definitions of war (in addition to statism and legalism); yet scholars' understanding of "comprehensiveness" has varied, and Greenwood grouped them into two perspectives: the subjective and the objective. The subjective school defined a war in terms of the view of the participants—war exists when they consider themselves to be in a state of war.[21] The objective school relied on a checklist of criteria that must be met for war to exist, though these criteria also could be used to deny the existence of a state of war, as in Korea and Vietnam.[22] Delupis concluded that while the subjective understanding remains relevant, changing state practices has led to increased emphasis on objective criteria.[23] Though most legal definitions of war have relied on these three elements (statism, legalism, and some substantial use of armed force), they are far from value neutral, and each of these elements contains normative assumptions. The first assigns rights to states—regardless of any evaluation of the state itself in regard to its treatment of its citizens. States are the primary actors of interest, and individuals are largely invisible to international law, and thus actions of individuals, as in a civil war, are addressed only in an ad hoc manner outside the general legal meaning of a state of war. Similarly in terms of legalism, the line between lawful and unlawful is not value neutral: the use of force against the state is held to be illegitimate, whether it represents organized military resistance to a tyrannical state or the violence of a mob. In the same vein, the emphasis on "comprehensiveness" can deny the status of "warfare" to states without the capacity to engage in the large-scale use of force. As Aron concluded, "European public international law has never taken the outlawing of war as its object or principle. . . . In short, it legalized and limited war, it did not make it a crime."[24]

There have been, however, those who have argued that discussions about war should adopt a more explicitly normative approach, incorporating the valuation of war as presumptively undesirable and making some distinctions about the levels and types of violence. This can be seen within international law by the Kellogg-Briand Pact that famously outlawed war. Others have rejected Clausewitz's view of war as part of normal politics. For instance, Midlarsky argued that war is "a failure of normal power (political) relations, such that force (coercion), in the form of political violence, results. . . . War is, then, not the 'continuation of political relations' but their termination in the onset of extreme coercion.[25] Such conceptions about the undesirability of war were at the heart of the nineteenth- and twentieth-century peace movements. Jane Addams, founder of the Women's Peace Party, was derided for her rejection of the idea that war could be righteous.[26] Similarly, the Women's Peace Union was initially dismissed as it sought to outlaw war. Such normative approaches to war (particularly those espoused by women) were derided by realist political scientists and policy makers as naïve, irrational, and unpatriotic; these negative valuations have been seen by feminist theorists as reflecting the gendered, masculinized, patriarchal perspectives that have dominated the study of international relations and war. In contrast, feminist theories propose new perspectives that put less emphasis on military issues and more emphasis on a broader definition of security that includes the elimination of physical, structural, and ecological violence.[27] Thus the conceptions of insecurity and war need to be significantly expanded to encompass violence in the interconnected international, national, and family realms.[28]

There have been a number of efforts to bring together the descriptions on war from some of these various perspectives; in the appendices of his *A Study of War*, Wright summarized the analyses of war by economists, political scientists, and social psychologists prior to World War II; Small and Singer edited international war anthologies in 1985 and 1989;[29] in 2001 Goldstein did a masterful job in using the framework of gender to examine war from biological and sociological perspectives;[30] Sarkees provided a brief overview of some of the discussions of war in the fields of religion, psychology, philosophy, the new wars literature, and some behavioral studies;[31] Vasquez provided a useful review of the various definitions of war as they are used in international relations in *The War Puzzle*;[32] and, specifically in terms of civil war, Newman and DeRouen recently have published a handbook that assembles articles representing a number of the theoretical and methodological debates.[33] However despite, or maybe because of, this plethora of scholarship on war, a difficulty that remains is that there is not one commonly accepted definition of what we mean when we use the term *war*.

The Need for Systematic, Scientific Studies of War

The behavioral or scientific study of war that emerged in the mid-twentieth century initially encompassed both a normative view of war as undesirable and an expansive definition of war. As Deutsch wrote in 1965, much of this work, often referred to as peace research, was based on the tenet that "war, to be abolished, must be understood. To be understood, it must be studied."[34] In this endeavor, the behavioralists faced a number of challenges: as Bouthoul noted, presenting an exhaustive definition of war "would assume a perfect knowledge of this phenomenon. We are far from that.[35] The difficulties derived from having a plethora of views about, and definitions of, war were cited by one of the founders of peace research using statistical studies of war, Quincy Wright.

> To different people war may have very different meanings. To some it is a plague which ought to be eliminated; to some, a mistake to be avoided; to others, a crime which ought to be punished; and, to still others, it is an anachronism which no longer serves any purpose. On the other hand, there are some who take a more receptive attitude toward war and regard it as an adventure which may be interesting, an instrument which may be useful, a procedure which may be legitimate and appropriate, or a condition of existence for which one must be prepared.[36]

Wright, who began his study of war in 1926, initially utilized a general definition of war as "violent contact of distinct but similar entities," which he then augmented with elements of the definitions from four realms of study: legal, sociological philosophical (ideological), and psychological to produce a definition of war as "a state of law and form of conflict involving a high degree of legal equality, of hostility, and of violence in the relations of organized human groups; or, more simply, the legal condition which equally permits two of more hostile groups to carry on a conflict by armed force."[37] Wars were thus characterized by four elements: "(1) military activity, (2) high tension level, (3) abnormal law, and (4) intense political integration."[38] Claiming that the previous analyses of war by some of the aforementioned narrow perspectives had highlighted certain aspects of war while missing others, Wright assembled an impressive amount of information about wars. The goals of social science, he claimed, were to be both practical and theoretical and to center attention upon factors that could be isolated and measured in an attempt to examine "what war has been in the past, what it is in the present, and what it may be in the future."[39]

A similar approach was adopted by Lewis F. Richardson, who aimed to apply statistical methodologies to identify persistent patterns in war.[40] Both Wright and Richardson wanted to examine a broad array of factors that could be seen as related to the causes of war. Yet, as Wright admitted, any such delineation is artificial in that "a war, in reality, results from a total situation involving almost everything that has happened to the human race up to the time the war begins."[41] To make a study feasible, however, one must then extract the variables that seem most promising based on historical examination of what war has been in the past. Each of these variables should be measurable. The work of Wright and Richardson marked what Singer and Small referred to as a turning point in the study of war, which laid the foundation of the scientific and quantitative study of war.[42] Wright described the scientific method in terms of the isolation of a problem, the establishment of standards of measurement, and the elimination of personal biases. In terms of the study of war, that specifically means that the researchers must separate themselves from their own wishful thinking about war, and though it is impossible ultimately to exclude in the ways available in the physical sciences, one must do one's best to reduce them.[43]

Thus the scientific study of war has in some sense a split personality. Its founding was very much within a normative framework: referred to as peace research, it was based on the normative position that war is undesirable. Yet, its methodology attempted to be value free, supported by the sense that policy makers had been making decisions based on personal biases and ideologies rather than facts. Thus peace research fits within the rubric of critical research, which has as its dictum that the "point of knowledge is not just to understand the world, but to try to change it for the better."[44] Yet its methodologies and results have been critiqued as in fact biased by feminist theorists such as Sylvester.[45] Though some quantitative studies eschew an explicit normative position, it was within this bifurcated space that a number of the studies of war developed, including Correlates of War (COW) and the Uppsala Conflict Data Program (UCDP). Though the scientific study of war has grown significantly over the past seventy years, there are still huge gaps in our understanding of war. Furthermore, competing methodologies and definitions, coupled with contradictory findings, have contributed to the tendency of policy makers to decide upon issues of war and peace on the basis of wishful thinking rather than facts. Thus as the world faces a number of complex wars, scientific studies of war critically are needed.

Notes

1. Deutsch, 1965, xi.
2. Wright, 1965, 3.
3. Hillman, 2004.
4. Hobbes, 1651.
5. Kant, 1996, 114–15.
6. Locke, 1980, 14.
7. Ibid., 15.
8. Rousseau, 1968, 56.
9. Clausewitz, 1993, 83.
10. Ibid., 98.
11. Orend, 2006, 2.
12. Ibid., 2.
13. Dinstein, 2005, 4–5.
14. Halleck, 1885, 150.
15. Oppenheim, 1906, 56.
16. Ibid., 56.
17. Ibid., 58–59.
18. Dinstein, 2005, 5.
19. Ibid., 6.
20. Ibid., 15.
21. Greenwood, 1987.
22. Delupis, 2000, 8.
23. Ibid., 14.
24. Aron, 1973, 99.
25. Midlarsky, 1975, 1.
26. LeFebvre, 1996, 37.
27. Tickner, 1992, 22–23.
28. Ibid., 58.

29. Small and Singer, 1989.
30. Goldstein, 2001.
31. Sarkees, 2010.
32. Vasquez, 1993.
33. Newman and DeRouen, 2014.
34. Deutsch, 1965, xii.
35. Bouthoul, 1962, 37.
36. Wright, 1965, 3.
37. Ibid., 8–13.
38. Ibid., 685.
39. Ibid., 16, 21.
40. Richardson, 1960, xxxv.
41. Wright, 1965, 17.
42. Singer and Small, 1972, 4.
43. Wright, 1965, 683–84.
44. Jackson, 2014, 80.
45. Sylvester, 2002, 167.

CHAPTER ONE

The Correlates of War Project

A History of the Correlates of War Project

This kind of research may help to liberate all who are, in one way or another, prisoners of war. . . . If we pick our research questions with courage, address them with imagination and rigor, and write them up with clarity and forthrightness, those of us in the world politics and peace research community may just make that modest difference between human survival and thermonuclear Armageddon.

—J. David Singer[1]

The Correlates of War Project (COW), which continues as the longest-running research program in the study of international relations, was launched by J. David Singer in 1963.[2] Singer had been introduced to behavioral methodology during a postdoctoral program at Harvard University, and while in Cambridge he met Karl Deutsch, who would become an influential voice in the COW project. Subsequently Singer moved to the University of Michigan in 1958 to teach in a temporary capacity in the political science department and to work with the Center (and *Journal*) for Research on Conflict Resolution, headed by Kenneth Boulding and Robert Angell. Though Singer had reservations about the term *peace research* because of its predominantly psychological focus, he considered the center to be "near irresistible in both normative and epistemological terms," and he remained involved with the center until its dissolution.[3] Singer's association with the center contributed to the ending of his contract with the political science department, and he subsequently accepted a position at the Naval War College for 1960. Luckily, prior to his departure from Ann Arbor, Singer had given a talk at the Mental Health Research Institute (MHRI), which was at that time working on an integrated theory of human behavior. Though dominated by biological and neurological scientists, MHRI wanted to include social scientists as well and thus offered Singer a full-time research position that would begin upon his return. He also continued his work with the Center for Research on Conflict Resolution, and when the center received its first major outside funding from the Carnegie Corporation, Singer applied for, and received in 1963, a grant for a two-year pilot study titled "The Correlates of War." Singer conceived of the COW Project as a continuation of the endeavor to systematically and scientifically describe and understand war begun by Quincy Wright and Lewis Fry Richardson.[4] COW also was anchored securely in the dictum of peace research that "war, to be abolished, must be understood. To be understood, it must be studied."[5] Singer's commitment to the behavioral science approach also was fueled by overt policy goals as well. He felt that both the study and practice of world politics had "suffered too long under the influence of those who offered sweeping generalizations on the basis of a few selected cases, presenting 'theories' without a trace of reproducible evidence, and proposed policies that rested on meager speculation or the conventional wisdom of a particular and provincial time and place."[6] Thus, Singer hoped that the scientific approach to the study of war would enable him to make a difference in the policy realm as well.[7]

The 1963 grant enabled Singer to bring other researchers to the COW project, and his first goal was to recruit an open-minded historian as a research assistant. He soon hired Melvin Small, who was at the time a graduate student in American diplomatic history at Michigan, as the project's historian. Singer and Small then began to chart the steps for a scientific study of war. Singer decided that the first task of the project would be to define operationally the key variables. A goal was to improve upon the earlier data-gathering projects through the consistency, accuracy, and reproducibility of its data. The approach they adopted was a combination of deductive and inductive reasoning. Identifying the key variables was initially deductive: some variables were selected based on their importance in existing theories of world politics as a goal of the project was to compare some of the widely accepted theoretical notions about war (especially those of realism or realpolitik) to the historical evidence.[8] Other variables emerged inductively from the historical records themselves. Thus Singer described the project's overall approach: "The project is far from atheoretical, but it certainly has proceeded without the framework of a fully articulated formal model."[9] From 1963 to 1964, Singer continued planning the initial phases of the COW project while accepting a Fulbright Scholarship in Oslo, where he assisted in establishing the Peace Research Institute. Meanwhile in Ann Arbor, Small threw himself into the task of identifying and devising coding rules for the key variables, which he hoped came as close as possible to historical reality. He and two assistants began gathering information for two data sets: international wars and diplomatic recognition.

Singer returned to Michigan in the fall of 1964 with half-time positions at the political science department and MHRI. This period was what Singer referred to as the "golden age" of the world politics program at Michigan, lasting until the late 1970s, which brought a number of talented graduate students into the program and to working with COW.[10] A second grant from the Carnegie Corporation (1965–1967) enabled the project to hire five part-time assistants and to significantly expand its data-gathering operations. Singer's work within MHRI was instrumental in the framing of the COW Project: MHRI had been created to try to build a unified system of explanation of human behavior, and Singer's adoption of the systems approach influenced the early trajectory of COW. Singer and Small conceived of wars taking place within a global structure of five nested systems: the global system, the international system, the interstate system, the central system, and the major power system.[11] The primary war participants were the geopolitical entities with the capabilities, status, and willingness to engage in interactions among the members of the interstate system, referred to as "states." Singer and Small saw this distinctive period of interactions as emerging after the Congress of Vienna, when the end of the Napoleonic wars marked what they saw as a clear transition to the modern state system.[12] Thus they utilized 1816 as the project's base year from which data on wars would be gathered. Initially dividing this temporal domain into two periods, 1816–1919 and 1920–1965, would also provide a time frame that was long enough to measure some of the significant changes in the structure of the system.[13] Utilizing the diplomatic recognition data as one of the key markers of system membership, Singer and Small identified the population of states within their temporal domain, which was published in 1966 as "The Composition and Status Ordering of the International System 1815–1940."[14] Subsequently, Singer, Small, and Bruce Russett expanded this list to include other entities that either had not qualified for interstate system membership or were part of the broader international system in the twentieth century.[15] Thus much of COW's early work focused on system-level analyses and only later shifted to substate levels.

With the potential war participants now identified, Singer and Small developed a general typology of wars that was based on the experiences confronting the members of the interstate system. Their three basic types of war were: (1) inter-state (or intra-systemic) wars that were between or among states or members of the interstate system; (2) extra-state (initially referred to as extra-systemic) wars that were between a state and a non-state entities outside the state's borders; and (3) civil wars that involved conflicts between the national government and another group within a state. In explaining wars, three central variables that were derived from the realpolitik paradigm were the capabilities, commitments, and contiguities of states.[16] The primary outcome variable was of course war and more specifically the frequency, severity, and magnitude of international war across the system. The severity of a war was measured in terms of battle-connected deaths, and here Singer and Small adopted procedures that differed from earlier compilations in that they excluded civilian fatalities.[17] They also established a threshold of 1,000 combatant deaths to differentiate war from other forms of less-severe conflict.[18] Gathering fatality statistics was one of Small's great frustrations with his work with COW. For most wars there are no accurate battle death statistics; such fatality numbers—or even hints at such numbers—are scattered throughout disparate sources. Small noted that "military historians are frequently satisfied when they can describe a battle as bloody or can assert that casualties ran in the thousands."[19] Yet such information was not sufficient for COW purposes, forcing Small and Singer to devote significant effort, examining multiple sources to produce guesstimates and rounded fatality numbers. Small was specifically troubled by the ways in which people used this data. He felt that many scholars unaffiliated with the project were so driven by the desire for "ready-made cheap data" to test a model that they "cared little about the true meaning of the numbers they were using."[20]

With these preliminary stages complete, Singer and Small were able to focus on the primary task of COW, identifying all of the international wars that occurred after 1816. They also developed a data set concerning the alliance behavior between and among system members.[21] In 1968, David Singer edited a volume, *Quantitative International Politics*, which included both discussions of the quantitative method and some of the early statistical findings.[22] Singer and Small's contribution to the book was their article, "Alliance Aggregation and the Onset of War, 1815–1945," which utilized the war and alliance data sets. The empirical findings in this book demonstrated what Singer felt was the progress that was being made in transitioning the study of war from prescientific to scientific work.[23] Evidence of the growing importance of quantitative research also can be seen in the 1969 volume edited by James Rosenau, *International Politics and Foreign Policy*, in which five of the articles were written or coauthored by Singer.[24] That same year, Small and Singer also released an updated version of the alliance data.[25] The first COW war handbook, *The Wages of War, 1816–1965: A Statistical Handbook*, was published by Singer and Small in 1972, and it included lists of all of the inter-state and extra-state wars.[26] The data on each war included variables for battle deaths, start and end dates, initiators, and the victors. From these data, it was possible to compute fundamental information such as the percentage of war initiators who won, magnitudes of wars (measured by nation-months or the total of the number of states multiplied by the length in months of their war participations), duration, severity (battle-connected deaths), and intensity (fatalities per nation-month, per capita, etc.).

During the early years (1963–1967), COW was supported by the Center for Research on Conflict Resolution, MHRI, and the Carnegie Foundation. Such support enabled COW to provide subsidies to graduate students to assist in the arduous task of data gathering. COW benefitted significantly from the growing coterie of scholars affiliated with the project, and Singer specifically mentioned Karl Deutsch, Bruce Russett, George Kraft, Bernard Mennis, Marcia Feingold, Vilma Ungerson, Warren Phillips, Michael Wallace, Larry Arnold, Tim Pasich, Urs Luterbacher, John Stuckey, Hugh Wheeler, Stuart Bremer, Susan Jones, Ann Clawson, and Marsha Stuckey for their contributions to the data in *The Wages of War*.[27] Projects of this magnitude needed sizable support to pay for the data managers, graduate assistants, secretarial support, and computer resources; yet COW found it difficult to secure adequate funding for its type of scientific research. Thus Singer developed a process of educating and mentoring students (who generally had fellowship support elsewhere), whereby they would be introduced to quantitative research and then gradually integrated into the work of COW rather than providing regular fellowship support directly. Though there was an obvious cost to the project in relying primarily on volunteer labor, Singer was especially proud of his mentoring, concluding that the greater good of educating future social scientists was worth the trade-off.[28] From the late 1960s through the 1980s, COW's funding sources shifted to an increased emphasis on outside grants, and Small was concerned about the loss in productivity for the project entailed in the commitment of time and resources in continually working on grant proposals.[29] Though COW continued to be supported by MHRI, new sources of funding or support were Wayne State University, the National Science Foundation (1967–1976 and 1978–1983), and the Harry Frank Guggenheim Foundation (1978–1979).

Meanwhile, in addition to the existing data on system members, wars, and alliances, the COW project also was interested, additional correlates of war, that is to say, the other elements that might be associated with war. Thus, following Singer's dictum that "data are made, not born,"[30] additional data sets were developed that tapped into these potential correlates. In this endeavor, Singer established an atmosphere of intellectual pluralism: many of the data sets were developed as parts of graduate student dissertations, and Singer provided encouragement and support, even though he might not have considered the data a priority. One of the new data sets (released in 1970), which was largely the work of Michael Wallace, was the Inter-governmental Organization (IGO) data that captured states' memberships in IGOs.[31] The project also devoted considerable energies, including those of John Stuckey, James Lee Ray, and Stuart Bremer (who also served as the project's data manager), to gathering data on the national material capabilities of states, which initially included data on military expenditures, military personnel, energy consumption, iron and steel production, total population, and urban populations for the major powers in the system at five-year intervals.[32] From these data, each state's share of the overall system capabilities (or power) could be computed.[33] This allowed, further, an analysis of the structure and polarity of the international system. Small and Singer also released the data set on states' diplomatic representations in 1973.[34]

By the late 1970s, the quantitative study of international politics was stalling. In 1976, Hoole and Zinnes identified four major data-gathering projects and provided structured evaluations of each: COW was the only one to survive.[35] However, that year, Singer and Small published a paper (written with the assistance of James Lee Ray, Zeev Maoz, Bruce Bueno de Mesquita, and Ric Stoll) containing what they considered to be a minor research finding, that democracies rarely fight one another.[36] This finding subsequently has been identified as one of the most significant findings in quantitative international politics;[37] it stimulated interest in quantitative studies and launched a virtual cottage industry of research on the democratic peace, including studies by COW affiliates Bruce Russett and Stuart Bremer, among others.[38] On the other hand, Singer remained skeptical of the democratic peace arguments,[39] as did other members of the COW community, including Errol Henderson.[40] Furthermore, the proliferation of COW data led to numerous studies and publications (a 1982 COW bibliography included more than eighty publications utilizing COW data);[41] and in 1979 and 1980, three anthologies were published, bringing together some of this work.[42] In addition, COW affiliates Stuart Bremer and Thomas Cusak moved on to the Wissenshaftszentrum in Berlin, where Bremer directed (1976–1988) the GLOBUS computer simulation project. One characteristic of COW that distinguished it from some of the other data projects was its willingness to freely share its data with scholars outside the project, and by 1982, Small and Singer estimated that more than one hundred scholars had been given COW data in either the punch card or magnetic tape formats available at that time.[43]

The second war handbook for the project was published in 1982 as *Resort to Arms: International and Civil Wars, 1816–1980*.[44] Here Small and Singer (with the collaboration of Robert Bennett, Kari Gluski, and Susan Jones) not only updated the data on inter-state and extra-state war but also included new data on civil wars (the civil war data set had been created by Bennett and Jones). Those who assisted in the data gathering involved in the project were: Cindy Cannizo, Mike Champion, Charles Gochman, Tom Keselman, Russell Leng, Zeev Maoz, Brad Martin, Michael Mihalka, Alden Mullins, Judy Nowack, Mark Small, Ned Sabrosky, Richard Stoll, John Thomas, Michael Wallace, and Peter Wallensteen; and production support for the book was provided by Virginia Corbin, Sarajane Miller Small, and Mary Macknick.[45]

In 1985, Small and Singer published an edited volume *International War: An Anthology and Study Guide* (a second edition was published in 1989), which encompassed articles about the various ways in which war had been studied.[46] This book not only included Small and Singer's discussion of international warfare, but it also presented an article by Gochman and Maoz that described a major advance in the project, the development of the Militarized Interstate Dispute (MID) data set.[47] MIDs are conflicts among states that entail a sequence of interstate interactions that include at least one of fourteen types of military acts, grouped as threats, displays, or uses of force (categories developed by Ric Stoll).[48] Work on the MID data, facilitated by Dan Jones and Ric Stoll, had consumed much of the project's attention in the late 1970s and early 1980s. Stoll's creation of a number of the MID variables led him to say that "you live by your coding rules and you die by your coding rules," a phrase that Singer was fond of repeating. The MID data set has been used widely and has been instrumental in the "steps to war" approach adopted by John Vasquez and Paul Senese.[49]

Meanwhile, work continued on the national material capabilities data, which Singer described in 1987 in "Reconstructing the Correlates of War Dataset on Material Capabilities of States, 1816–1985."[50] The late 1980s also saw the emergence of numerous other data sets focused on international behavior, including two closely related to COW: the Behavioral Correlates of War (BCOW) Project led by Russell Leng and the Long Range Analysis of War (LORANOW) created by Claudio-Cioffi Revilla.[51] However, the lack of adequate funding for data development hindered scientific research. This situation led to the creation of the Data Development for International Research (DDIR) at the Merriam Laboratory for Analytic Political Research at the University of Illinois at Urbana-Champaign, which aimed to integrate some of the existing data. DDIR received funding from the National Science Foundation, which enabled it to support eleven projects partially, including COW for 1986–1989 and four other projects linked to COW.[52] At the beginning of the 1990s, a number of anthologies brought together some of the published articles utilizing COW data. In 1990 alone there were three collections: Gochman and Sabrosky edited *Prisoners of War? Nation-States in the Modern Era*; Singer and Diehl published *Measuring the Correlates of War*; and Singer edited *Models, Methods, and Progress: A Peace Research Odyssey*. That same year a comparison of COW to other data sets was prepared by Claudio Cioffi-Revilla and published as *The Scientific Measurement of International Conflict*. In 1992 Vasquez and Henehan edited *The Scientific Study of Peace and War: A Text Reader*, which included articles from other scientific studies plus Vasquez's article that synthesized some of COW's findings.[53] In 1993 a comprehensive list of the vast array of empirical studies using COW data was presented by Brian Gibbs and J. David Singer.[54]

However, in the late 1980s and early 1990s, data gathering in Ann Arbor declined as many of the COW affiliates focused their efforts at their new institutions and as outside funding for COW dried up (Singer received a grant from the US Institute for Peace in 1988–1990 and his last grant from the National Science Foundation in 1992–1994). At Michigan, the dedicated efforts of Phil Schafer contributed to the updates to the System Membership data set and war datasets; and Singer, Dan Jones, and Stuart Bremer continued work on the MID data, though Bremer had moved to the University of Binghamton. Gary Goertz served as data manager for the project in 1986–1988, and Diane Macaulay and Ricardo Rodriguez briefly assumed the position as the project's data manager in the early 1990s. In the fall of 1993, Meredith Reid Sarkees accepted Singer's invitation to spend a sabbatical year with COW, and she assumed the role as data manager for all the COW data sets (a position she held for the next seven years). Initially Sarkees worked with repairing and restructuring some of the COW data on the Michigan mainframe to distribute them to research scholars and DDIR. She then was tasked with restoring some of the data sets that had not been utilized recently (such as the IGO, diplomatic representation, alliance data, and the beginnings of a cultural data set), which sometimes meant tracking down mothballed equipment to read the old computer tapes and punch cards.[55] Sarkees ultimately reformatted the alliance data from the original dyadic format that merely coded the highest level of commitment into one that had the alliance as the primary unit of analysis and (with the help of students at Niagara University) expanded the capability data set to annual figures for all states. Participating in Singer's weekly seminars, she worked with COW colleagues including Singer, Small, Phil Schafer, Dan Jones, Errol Henderson, Paul Williamson, Frank Wayman, Volker Krause, Robert Packer, Paul Huth, Sheldon Levy, Jeffrey Dixon, and Anthony Perry (as well as visitors including Stuart Bremer, Dan Geller, Zeev Maoz, Ric Stoll, Claudio Cioffi-Revilla, and Paul Hensel) on revisions of the war typology and some of the new coding rules that were adopted in 1995.[56] The ramifications of these new rules as well as the resultant new versions of the inter-state, extra-state, and intra-state data sets through 1997 were presented by Sarkees, Wayman, and Singer.[57] The next year, Geller and Singer brought together many of the findings on war in *Nations at War: A Scientific Study of International Conflict.* As interest in, and research about, the role of territory as a correlate of war increased, one of the major accomplishments of COW during this period was the development of the new territorial change data set, created by Jaroslav Tir, Philip Schafer, Paul Diehl, and Gary Goertz.[58] The related Territorial Contiguity data set was released in 2002.[59]

As Singer was moving toward retirement, Stuart Bremer was chosen as the next director of the COW project, a position he held from 1998 to 2002. Sarkees and Bremer converted all of the COW data sets to an Access format and moved the data sets from the University of Michigan mainframe to Pennsylvania State. This transfer of the mantle of leadership of the project was celebrated in March 2001 by a conference at Penn State discussing the future study of war. Bremer shifted the governing structure of COW from a fluid, loose council of scholars affiliated with the project who convened during the annual meetings of the International Studies Association and the American Political Science Association to a small, elected COW advisory board. One of Bremer's major contributions to the project was his development of a new data host process, whereby each of the COW data sets would be assigned to a host or hosts who would be responsible for maintaining and updating the data. Another of his endeavors was the expansion of the MID data v. 3.0 through a three-year multi-university initiative supported by the National Science Foundation. The primary investigators for the project were Scott Bennett, Stuart Bremer, Paul Diehl, Dan Geller, Doug Gibler, Paul Hensel, Chuck Gochman, Zeev Maoz, Glenn Palmer, Brian Pollins, Jim Ray, Pat Regan, and Ric Stoll, though numerous additional researchers contributed to the data gathering.

After Bremer's untimely death, Scott Bennett served as interim COW director from 2002 to 2004. During that period, Gibler and Sarkees released the new alliance data updated to 2000 in 2004,[60] and a new version of the MID data was released.[61] Also in 2004, Paul Diehl assembled a number of articles utilizing COW data in *The Scourge of War.* The following year, Diehl was chosen as the new COW director, and Bennett assumed the new position of associate director. The project continued to expand, with the additions of the Trade data set, developed by Katherine Barbieri, Oman Keshk, and Brian Pollins in

2009,[62] and the World Religion data set by Zeev Maoz and Errol Henderson in 2010.[63] A further innovation within the project was the launching of the COW books series published by CQ Press. The first book in the series was a two-volume work concerning alliances written by Douglas Gibler as *International Military Alliances, 1648–2008.* The second book in the series was the third COW handbook on war, *Resort to War, 1816–2007* by Meredith Reid Sarkees and Frank Whelon Wayman. The third book was *Handbook of International Rivalries,1494–2010* by William R. Thompson and David R. Dreyer. This current book on intra-state wars is the fourth in the series.

J. David Singer died on December 28, 2009. At the time of his death, he was working with Jody B. Lear, Diane Macaulay, and Meredith Reid Sarkees on an anthology to bring together abbreviated versions of articles, written by Singer alone or with his colleagues, that Singer felt illustrated his intellectual evolution "From Bombs and Rockets to Peace Science." This collection was published in 2012 as *Advancing Peace Research: Leaving Traces, Selected Articles by J. David Singer.* The COW project is undoubtedly one of the most significant traces that Singer has left behind.

In 2012, Zeev Maoz was elected as the new COW director. The system of assigning the individual data sets to the responsibility of data hosts has continued, and as of 2014, the data sets and their hosts are as follows:

- International Alliances: Doug Gibler, University of Alabama
- Intergovernmental Organizations: Timothy Nordstrom, University of Mississippi; John Pevehouse, University of Wisconsin; Meg Shannon, Florida State University
- Territorial Change: Paul Diehl, University of Illinois
- Direct and Colonial Contiguity: Paul Hensel, University of North Texas
- Interstate and Extra-state War: Meredith Sarkees, Global Women's Leadership in International Security (GWLIS); Frank Wayman, University of Michigan-Dearborn
- Intra-state War: Jeffrey Dixon, Texas A&M University–Central Texas; Meredith Sarkees, GWLIS
- Cultural: Errol Henderson, Penn State University; Zeev Maoz, University of California–Davis
- Militarized Interstate Disputes: Glenn Palmer, Penn State University
- National Material Capabilities Data: Michael Greig, University of North Texas; Andrew Enterline, University of North Texas
- Diplomatic Data: Resat Bayer, Koc University
- System Membership: Volker Krause, Eastern Michigan University; Phil Schafer, University of Michigan
- Trade: Katherine Barbieri, University of South Carolina; Omar Keshk, The Ohio State University

The descriptions of the data sets and the data are available at the COW Web site, www.correlatesofwar.org.

The COW Definition of War and Its Key Variables

David Singer saw himself as a peace scientist, one who was comfortable with the dictum of critical research that the "point of knowledge is not just to understand the world, but to try to change it for the better."[64] As noted above, COW was founded by Singer on the principle that if one wants to promote peace, or reduce the incidence of future wars, one has to examine the history of prior wars.[65] Though Singer saw his project as building upon the scientific approach to the study of war adopted by Quincy

Wright and Lewis Frye Richardson, he also wanted to be able to improve upon their work through the consistency, accuracy, and reproducibility of COW's coding rules and its data. As described in the introduction, there have been myriad attempts to define *war.* Many were quite expansive, meaning that any situation involving tension, contention, and conflict could be deemed to be war. Even Wright's definition of war included a fairly broad scope of behavior. In contrast, Singer and Small wanted to have a fairly limited definition of war specifically differentiating war from conflict in general and one consisting of elements that could be consistently quantified. A detailed description of the steps Singer and Small followed can be found in *The Wages of War* and *Resort to Arms,* so only their final decisions will be presented here. Furthermore, there have been some refinements and revisions in the coding rules over the years so that the COW definitions and coding rules described here are the current versions.[66]

Singer and Small began with the sense that "we must define war in terms of violence. Not only is war impossible without violence (except of course in the metaphorical sense), but we consider the taking of human life the primary and dominant characteristic of war."[67] Yet even defining war as violence that takes human life would be too broad as both the conceptions of violence and death need to be refined further. Following Wright's thinking (described in the introduction) of war as conflict by armed force of organized human groups,[68] Singer and Small identified two key elements—*sustained combat* by *organized armed forces.* They followed Richardson, however, in rejecting Wright's requirement of a legal status for the combatants as well as criteria describing the objectives of the participants and the political consequences of the war.[69] They also retained the emphasis that Richardson placed in his classification scheme on the number of deaths (not casualties that include those wounded) that occur on both sides of the war.[70] In his study, Richardson used a logarithm to base ten of the total number of deaths to measure the magnitude of each conflict, and he included in his data set of wars those conflicts that entailed more than 317 deaths (magnitude 2.5).[71] However, Singer and Small broke with Richardson over three points: his inclusion of civilian deaths; his omission of deaths due to wounds and disease; and the 317 threshold.[72] They decided to focus upon only the deaths of military personnel, or combatants, and to include not only those who died in combat but also those "who subsequently died from combat wounds or from diseases contracted in the theater of war (termed *battle-related deaths* or *battle-deaths*)."[73] Singer and Small then examined a distribution of conflict fatalities to determine what magnitude or number of deaths constituted war, and they ultimately decided on a threshold of 1,000 deaths within a year as the level of hostilities that differentiate war from lower levels of conflict. Thus their overarching definition of war was: sustained combat, involving organized armed forces, resulting in a minimum of 1,000 battle-deaths (of combatants) within a year (a twelve-month period from the start date). This definitional inclusion of sustained combat thus excludes instances of one-sided violence, such as massacres of civilians. The threshold of 1,000 deaths as a key feature of war has proven to be empirically significant in describing wars, and variations of it have been adopted by an assortment of other war data-gathering projects, including UCDP.

Definitions of Key Variables

The Temporal Domain

As noted previously, one of the first major decisions of the project was establishing the temporal domain for its research. Wright had gathered data on wars since 1480, while Richardson examined wars from 1820 onward. Singer and Small chose to go back to the Congress of Vienna because they saw the end of the Napoleonic wars as marking a clear transition to the modern state system (or interstate system).[74] Thus they began gathering data from 1816 onward, which they also felt would provide a time frame that was long enough to measure some of the significant changes in the structure of the system.

The interstate system consisted of the political entities that had sufficient resources to "play a moderately active role in world politics, to be a player more than a pawn, and to generate more signal than noise in the system."[75] Membership in the interstate system was based on criteria of population, territory, independence, sovereignty, and diplomatic recognition, and members were referred to as *states*. The importance of states will be addressed further below in terms of the COW typology of war.

COW also needed to code the temporal domain of each war or, specifically, its start and end dates. Singer and Small adopted the following coding:

> Each war's *opening date* is that of the formal declaration, but only if it is followed immediately by sustained military combat. If hostilities precede the formal declaration and continue in a sustained fashion up to and beyond that latter date, the first day of combat is used. Even in the absence of a declaration, the sustained continuation of military incidents or battle, producing the requisite number of battle deaths, is treated as a war, with the first day of combat again used for computing duration.[76]

The war then continues until its termination or as long as there is sustained military combat resulting in 1,000 battle-related deaths per year. Thus, coding the end date of a war is not always clear-cut and can be related to the difficulties in ascertaining levels of conflict through fatality figures. The end date may be the date of an armistice or cease-fire agreement as long as conflict does not resume thereafter. If there is a delay between the cessation of military action and the armistice or if the armistice fails to halt the hostilities, then the end date is the day that most clearly demarcates the close of sustained military conflict. The date of the final peace treaty would not be used unless it coincided with the end of combat.[77] However, wars (especially civil wars) may not necessarily end through a cease-fire or an agreement of any sort but may instead peter out as the rebels cease fighting or retreat to fight another day. In such cases a judgment has been made about the date at which the last sustained combat took place that contributed to 1,000 battle-related deaths within a year. In essence, a war ends if (a) there is a truce or other agreement that ends combat for a year or more; (b) if the apparent defeat of one side (absent a formal surrender or truce) ends combat for one year or more; or (c) if a twelve-month period passes without 1,000 battle-deaths. In the last case, the termination date for the war is the last day in which it can be said that 1,000 battle-deaths were suffered during the previous twelve months.[78] There must be clear evidence that fighting has shrunk to this level. If we have only an overall total fatality figure for multiple years, and we cannot find how many died within a particular twelve-month period, unless we have specific evidence of a lull, we continue to classify the conflict as a war as continuing as there are on average 1,000 battle deaths per year. The start and end dates that are reported in the individual war histories that follow are in effect the earliest start date and the latest end date for the war. Each war participant can have differing start and end dates depending upon when it entered and left the war.

A war's duration generally is calculated by subtracting the start date from the end date, resulting in a measurement of the war's duration in months or days. One exception to this procedure concerns wars in which there is a break in the fighting. Small and Singer specifically considered the cessation of hostilities arising out of a truce, a temporary cease-fire, or an armistice agreement. In general, if the fighting stopped for thirty days or less, no break in the war was coded; however, if there were a cessation of hostilities resulting from such an agreement that endured for more than thirty days, this break was marked by essentially ending participation (end date 1) and then resuming the war on a second start date. This break then led to a reduction in the war's overall duration measure equal to the length of the interruption.

> To illustrate, the three-week truce (December 19, 1933 to January 8, 1934) arranged by the League of Nations during the Chaco War is not counted as a break, and the war is treated as if it had run continuously for the three years from June 15, 1932, through June 12, 1935, for a duration of 35.9 months. On the other hand, because a formal truce lasted for two of the total six months between the onset and termination of the Second Schleswig-Holstein War (February 1, through August 20, 1864), that war is treated as having a duration of only 3.6 months.[79]

Such a break can last up to a year in length. If hostilities resume after more than a year of a cessation of hostilities, the original war will be coded as having ended, and a new war will be coded.

Temporary cessations of hostilities that result from causes other than specific agreements are treated differently. In wars, there are periods when the level of violence drops for a time and then rises again. For instance, fighting may be halted informally during a rainy season only to resume when weather conditions improve. In a sense, these breaks in fighting are not the same. Truces, cease-fires, and armistice agreements represent a commitment to end hostilities, at least on some level, whereas temporary lulls in the fighting do not. Thus, temporary lulls in the fighting are not recorded as breaks in the fighting; however, should such a lull last for more than a year and there are not 1,000 battle-related fatalities within that year, the war will be coded as having ended. Should the hostilities resume after that point, a new war will have begun.

As noted previously, the following descriptions of the war present overall war start and end dates; however, within the data sets themselves, each individual war participant is described in terms of the dates that it entered and left the war. Frequently, participants join an ongoing war at a later date, while in other multi-participant wars, one party may be defeated or just withdraw from the war before the others. In such cases, the entity's active participation period (start date to end date) delineates the period of its own forces' involvement in sustained military combat. Relatedly, for wars that require participants to be members of the interstate system, a state may be included as a war participant only for the period during which it is a system member. For example, Baden, Bavaria, and Württemberg entered the Franco-Prussian War of 1870–1871 on the first day (July 19, 1870). Even though they had troops in active combat during the entire war (until 1871), their war participation is coded as ending in November 1870, when they became integrated into the new German empire and thus ceased to be independent system members.

Battle-related Deaths

As described previously, Singer and Small began with a requirement that a conflict had to cause a minimum of 1,000 battle-related deaths within a twelve-month period for it to be considered a war. Battle-deaths were those suffered by the combatants and included deaths from direct combat, wounds, and disease. The battle-deaths were suffered not only by the armed forces of the war participants but also by persons fighting on their behalf. For example, in terms of wars involving states, battle-death figures include not only personnel of the system member but native troops from the colonies, protectorates, and dominions who fought alongside them.[80]

Gathering fatality figures is probably the most difficult and complicated element of data gathering on wars: many historical accounts of war contain only vague generalizations about battles that resulted in severe (or light) casualties; authors frequently incorrectly utilize the terms *deaths* and *casualties* interchangeably; many sources report only total death figures, combining deaths of civilians and combatants; frequently the size of the armed forces is unknown, as are its losses (especially for wars conducted in remote locations); and there are also wide differences in fatality numbers among sources. Probably more significant, however, is the reality that war fatalities represent valuable and contestable political information. States often have an incentive to minimize their own losses in battle to protect themselves from criticism for failure or as an incentive to inflate their deaths to garner international sympathy and support. Conversely, states also may downplay the fatalities they caused their opponent so that they do not appear to be excessively bloodthirsty, or they may inflate the opponent's fatalities as a way of proving the efficacy of their own military campaign. Even though finding fatality statistics is somewhat easier today due to the growing number of nongovernmental agencies with resources devoted to gathering statistics on the costs of war, governments also have displayed their ability to utilize technology as a means of concealing war fatality figures. COW attempts to overcome these difficulties by conducting fairly extensive research on each war and then evaluating conflicting numbers in terms of other information, for instance, the sizes of the armed forces involved. Sometimes, information on fatalities from individual battles can be aggregated into total battle-deaths. In many cases, where sources provide only casualty numbers (rather than fatalities), COW has adopted a calculation of fatality estimates by using the historically observed ratio of three wounded for every one killed in combat.[81] Thus if a total casualty figure is available, it is divided by four to estimate battle-deaths. However, as Singer and Small noted, in many cases COW is reduced to producing guesstimates of battle-related deaths. They tried to emphasize the inaccuracy of most fatality estimates by generally rounding figures up to the nearest hundred, and in the three bloodiest wars, they initially rounded the total battle-deaths to the nearest million.[82] Though subsequent research has in some cases located new battle-death figures, Small and Singer's caution is still valid: "Despite these multiple cross-checks and a large dose of skepticism at every turn, we must reemphasize the fact that our battle death figures are only estimates."[83] The figures can best be seen as general guides concerning the relative magnitude of the costs of war participation.

The Initiator and the Outcome of the War

The final variables that apply generally to all wars are those of the war initiator and the winner of the war. In determining which combatant was the war initiator, Small and Singer were merely determining which party started the war, not which party precipitated or was responsible for the war. They relied on the consensus of historians to classify the initiator as the actor whose battalions made the first attack in strength on their opponent's armies or territories.[84] They emphasized that this was not in any way a moral judgment: "As our language should make very clear, we are not labeling any government the 'aggressor' in these wars, or trying to reach a firm, data-based conclusion as to which participant 'caused' the war, whether by action, threat, or other provocation."[85] This distinction is important for scholars seeking to utilize COW's MID data set (which has slightly different coding) to examine the stages in conflict escalation. Though in most cases the initiator was one party, it could be several combatants that acted in concert in the initial attack, as in the Boxer Rebellion, in which Japan, the United Kingdom, Russia, France, and the United States are coded as the initiators. Determining the initiator also can be tricky if one side enters the other's territory without having to fight initially.

Small and Singer had no operational indicators for determining the side that was victorious in the war. Instead of developing complex schemas for weighing the relative benefits attained in a war, they admitted merely to following the consensus among the acknowledged specialists in deciding which side "won" each war.[86] In terms of coding the individual combatants as winners or losers, they treated "every nation that qualified as an active participant on the victorious side as a 'victor,' regardless of its contribution to that victory or the costs it sustained; the same holds for all those that fought on the vanquished side in these inter-state wars."[87] Since, as noted above, it is possible for a war participant to enter and leave a war in several instances, a combatant could be coded as an ultimate winner despite its complete defeat in an earlier stage of the war, for example, Poland and Belgium in World War II. Similarly, a participant who switches sides in the war can have two separate participant records and two separate outcome determinations, both as a winner and a loser, for instance, Italy in World War II. As the project began to gather more information on intra-state wars in particular, it became clear that there were more outcomes that merely winning, losing, or ending in a tie. Thus, several new outcome codes have been developed. Though this variable may continue to evolve, at this point, the following outcome codes are being used: 1 = Side A wins; 2 = Side B wins; 3 = compromise (a solution is reached in which both sides gain something); 4 = war is transformed into another category; 5 = war is ongoing; 6 = stalemate (fighting ceases without an agreement); 7 = conflict continues but at below war-level fatalities.

The COW Typology of War

Though Singer and Small had rejected the inclusion of statism within their definition of war, they were very much focused upon states, and they based all of their data sets, including those on war, on the states, or members of the interstate system. Though many people see the terms *state*, *nation-state*, and *countries* as synonymous, Singer and Small established a comprehensive scheme into which different types of actors were organized. They conceived a view of world politics based on five nested systems, or a nested hierarchy of five major levels of analysis or systems: (1) The most comprehensive is the global system, which is composed of all humankind and all the worldwide groupings that people have formed (from informal to regimented) and need not have an international or political focus. (2) The next, more-restricted level is the international system, made up of all the geopolitical units and a plethora of existing subnational and extranational groupings, including nonterritorial entities, or non-state actors. (3) The primary level for Singer and Small was the interstate system, which is composed of territorial entities that satisfied the criteria of system membership, referred to as *states*; within the interstate system are two systems of a more restricted nature—(4) the central system and the (5) major power system.[88] The current data set State System Membership List (2011) is available at the COW Web site: www.correlatesofwar.org.

The interstate system was seen by Singer and Small as a particular phenomenon that was defined both in temporal fashion and by the characteristics of its members. In particular, the interstate system was seen as a distinctive set of relations that emerged among relevant actors after the end of the Congress of Vienna: with the November 20, 1815, signing of the Treaty of Paris, the so-called concert system, or Singer and Small's interstate system, was launched. The distinguishing characteristic of this system was the recurring international interactions between and among the interstate system members. COW notes that interstate system members are in essence a subset of what people commonly refer to as countries, in that COW requires that states must interact with one another within the broader international system. Thus membership in this interstate system was not meant to encompass all global actors, nor all sovereign entities, but only those that actively participated in the interstate system.[89] The actors that participated in the system, or were eligible to be considered system members (or members of the interstate system), were referred to as *states*, and they were those who were "large enough in population or other resources to play a moderately active role in world politics, to be a player more than a pawn, and to generate more signal than noise in the system," and which were "sufficiently unencumbered by legal, military, economic, or political constraints to exercise a fair degree of sovereignty and independence."[90] The COW initial criteria for coding system membership were succinctly summarized by Bremer:

The defining criteria are as follows:

a) Between 1816 and 1919 a geopolitical entity is a state if its population is at least 500,000 and it receives accredited diplomatic missions (at the chargé d'affaires level or higher) from Britain and France.

b) After 1919 a geopolitical entity is a state if it is a member of the League of Nations or the United Nations or its population is at least 500,000 and it receives accredited diplomatic missions (at the chargé d'affaires level or higher) from two major powers.[91]

As Singer and Small began to examine a number of complex cases both in terms of system membership and wars, they utilized two additional criteria for system membership, more specifically, independence and sovereignty. For instance, loss of membership in the system was strictly a function of loss of sovereignty and independence, through a member being occupied, conquered, annexed, or federated with others.[92] Similarly if a state's legitimate government went into exile or was replaced by a puppet regime, the entity was treated as experiencing the occupied status and thus was no longer a system member. Any change in an entity's status that did not last for one month or more was not included.[93] States also could interact in the broader international system with non-state entities, which includes both geopolitical or territorial entities (such as colonies, or countries that are in the process of state formation or have not attained diplomatic recognition) as well as non-territorial entities (such as intergovernmental or nongovernmental organizations, like rebel forces or terrorist organizations). Such entities would be the non-state participants in extra-state wars (described next).

Who Is Fighting Whom?

Singer and Small then developed their typology of war based on the members of the interstate system, or states, and the determination of who is fighting whom. Wars between or among states are inter-state wars; wars between a state and a non-state entity outside its borders are extra-state wars; wars within a state are intra-state wars; and wars not involving states and not taking place within state borders are non-state wars. Once the war participants have been identified, the question of who is fighting whom devolves into describing the war in a way that identifies the primary combatants. For instance, if there are multiple participants on a side in a war, the classification of the war type will be coded based upon a determination of which party is doing the bulk of the fighting. Though COW originally merely relied upon the judgment of historians to make this decision, a more specific definition of the party that is doing the bulk of the fighting is the party on each side that is causing the greatest number of battle-deaths.[94]

Consequently, COW has a comprehensive typology of war (sustained combat between or among armed forces involving substantial casualties of at least 1,000 deaths per year [or a twelve-month period]) that has four primary categories and nine specific war types.[95]

- I. Inter-state wars (war type 1)
- II. Extra-state wars
  - A. Colonial—conflict with colony (war type 2)
  - B. Imperial—state versus non-state (war type 3)
- III. Intra-state wars
  - A. Civil wars
    - 1. For central control (war type 4)
    - 2. Over local issues (war type 5)
  - B. Regional internal (war type 6)
  - C. Intercommunal (war type 7)
- IV. Non-state wars
  - A. In non-state territory (war type 8)
  - B. Across state borders (war type 9)

Describing Inter-state War

Since Singer and Small were primarily interested in inter-state war, this is the most straightforward of the categories of war. Specifically, at least one sufficiently active participant on each side of the war must be a state or member of the interstate system. Thus inter-state war is war in which the regular armed forces of a state that qualifies as a member of the interstate system engage in sustained combat with the forces of one or more other members of the interstate system resulting in 1,000 battle-related deaths (among all the state participants) per year (or twelve-month period). Any individual interstate system member qualifies as a war participant through either of two alternative criteria: sustaining a minimum of 100 fatalities or having a minimum of 1,000 armed personnel engaged in active combat.[96] The focus on states as the primary actors does not exclude other actors from being involved in the war as well. States frequently have been assisted in war not only by other state participants but also by partisans, rebel groups, non-state autonomous entities, and their colonies or possessions. Though these actors do not have individual records in the inter-state data set, the battle-related deaths for a system member include not only the deaths among its own uniformed military personnel but also actors who fought on the government's behalf such as national guard, police, and the "native troops from the colonies, protectorates, and dominions who fought alongside them."[97]

As indicated previously, when describing the initiator of a war, Small and Singer were merely determining which party started the war. In terms of inter-state wars, this generally means identifying which state's forces crossed the border into its opponent's territory first. Examining conflict escalation was one of the motivations for the development of the COW MID data set (MIDs can range from mere displays of force to combat resulting in fewer than 1,000 battle-deaths). For each MID, an initiator is also coded, and it is important to note here that the initiator of the inter-state war and the initiator of the MID are not necessarily the same state.

Describing Extra-state War

Extra-state wars are those in which a member of the interstate system is engaged in sustained combat outside its borders against the forces (however irregular) of a political entity that is not a member of the state system.[98] In addition, there must be at least 1,000 battle-deaths per year. The subcategories of extra-state wars are these:

1. Colonial War (or State vs. Dependent Non-state Actor): The member of the interstate system engages in sustained combat against the forces of a political entity that is geographically outside the internationally accepted boundaries of the state and that is a dependency, colony, protectorate, mandate, or otherwise under its suzerainty or control and not merely within a claimed sphere of influence.

2. Imperial War (State vs. Independent Non-state Actor): A member of the system is engaged in sustained combat outside its borders with the forces of an independent non-state entity. The adversary might be an independent political entity that does not qualify for system membership because of serious limitations on its independence, a population insufficiency, or a failure of other states to recognize it as a legitimate member. One by-product of the imperial-colonial terminology is that it obscures the fact that extra-state wars can be fought against non-territorially identified entities as well: such as pirates, an international terrorist organization, or the private army of a multinational corporation. The non-state entities would need to have an organized armed force capable of engaging in sustained combat. Such entities frequently are referred to as

Non-state Armed Groups (NSAs). To be considered a war participant, such non-state entities would need to commit a minimum of 100 armed troops to sustained combat or suffer a minimum of twenty-five battle-related deaths.[99]

Describing Intra-state War

An intra-state war is sustained combat between or among organized armed forces taking place within the territorial boundaries of a state system member and leading to 1,000 battle-related deaths per year. There are three types of intra-state wars (note: these will be discussed in more detail in Chapter 2):

1. Civil Wars: The bulk of the fighting on one side of the war has to be conducted by the national government of an interstate system member, and there has to be effective resistance by both sides.[100] In other words, civil war is sustained military conflict within the territory of the state "pitting the central government against an insurgent force capable of effective resistance."[101]
2. Regional Wars: These occur within the boundaries of an interstate system member; however, neither of the major war participants (who are conducting the bulk of the fighting on each side) is a system member: what gives them a distinct identity is that the major combatant on one side of the war is a local or regional government (not the national government). The armed forces on this side of the war would be regional (similar to the New York State National Guard) and would include all those who enter the conflict in the name of that government, from regional military forces to local police and citizens.
3. Intercommunal Wars: These wars occur within the boundaries of a member of the interstate system, but neither of the major war participants (who are conducting the bulk of the fighting on each side) is a system member or a regional or local government.

Describing Non-state War

The final category of war in the COW typology is that of non-state war, or wars between two (or among possibly more) combatants, none of which is a member of the COW interstate system. What distinguishes this category from the previously discussed intra-state, non-state war types (regional and intercommunal) is that wars do not take place within the boundaries of a particular system member. We have identified two subcategories of non-state wars based on the location of the war: in non-state territory, combat takes place in territory that is not part of the territory of a member of the interstate system; across state borders involves wars that take place across the borders of existing states but do not involve the state or regional governments in the conflict.

Internationalized Wars and War Transformations

COW classifies wars based on who is fighting whom in terms of the identification of the participants as state members or non-state actors and a decision about who is doing the bulk of the fighting. Thus changes would have to be made should there be an alteration in the value of either of these measures. COW has two ways through which it accomplishes this: through internationalized wars and war transformations. Wars can involve more than the standard two-party conflict, and if additional parties join a war, it changes the nature of war to some degree. However, the fundamental nature of an inter-state war between two system members does not significantly change when one (or more) additional states join in the conflict because the war remains one among system members: thus the war is merely coded as internationalized. The same procedure is followed for extra-state, intra-state, and non-state wars when an outside actor joins the war but does not alter the fundamental description of the primary participants: such wars are classified as internationalized. A state intervener must qualify as a war participant either by committing more than 1,000 troops to the conflict or by suffering 100 battle-deaths, whereas a non-state intervener would need to commit a minimum of 100 armed troops to sustained combat or suffer a minimum of 25 battle-related deaths.[102]

However, there are two general circumstances under which COW has decided that there is sufficient significant change to cause a shift in war classification. The more common form of shift takes place when a state intervener takes over the bulk of the fighting from one of the original war participants. It thus replaces one of the parties as the major combatant, transforming the war's classification. The need for a change in classification is linked to COW's principle of the mutual exclusivity of wars, whereby a war involving the same participants should not appear simultaneously in more than one war classification. If, for example, a state intervenes on either side in an extra-state war between a state and a colony and plays a minor role, the war remains an extra-state war and becomes merely internationalized. However, if the outside intervener takes over the bulk of the fighting from one of the original participants, the original war must end, and a new war begins. For example, in a civil war, if the intervener takes over the bulk of the fighting from the initial state, the war becomes a new extra-state war between the intervener state and a non-state actor outside the intervener's territory. However, if the intervener takes over the bulk of the fighting on behalf of the rebels, the intra-state war ends, and a new inter-state war begins. Such interventions are becoming more common in intra-state wars, whereby outside states intervene in internationalized civil wars. If a major combatant decides to withdraw from a conflict and the conflict continues with other parties, that specific war may end, and the conflict may be classified as a different type of war based on the categorization of the war participants. For instance, in the 1980s, the USSR was involved in an extra-state war in Afghanistan against the *mujahideen*. When the Soviet troops withdrew, the extra-state war ended, though the conflict continued as a civil war when the Afghan government then took over the bulk of the fighting in its conflict with the *mujahideen*. Probably the most well-known example that demonstrates transformations would be the Vietnam War, which started out as a civil war in 1960 between the government of South Vietnam and the National Liberation Front (also known as the Viet Cong); it was transformed into an internationalized civil war with the involvement of the United States in 1961; and in 1965, the United States fundamentally altered the type of conflict when it started bombing North Vietnam, ending the intra-state war and starting an inter-state war between two system members, which each took over the bulk of the fighting from its ally, South Vietnam on one side and North Vietnam on the other. The most complex set of transformations has taken place in Afghanistan, which over the past thirty years has experienced a series of wars, beginning with an intra-state war, followed by an extra-state war, transformed by the withdrawal of the USSR into intra-state war, transformed again by the intervention of the United States and its allies into an inter-state war, which then became an extra-state war after the defeat of the Taliban government.

Our discussion now shifts to the focus of this book: a more detailed examination of intra-state wars.

Notes

1. Singer, 1990, 26–27.
2. An interview with Singer about the origins of COW can be found at https://scar.gmu.edu/parents-of-field/david-singer.
3. Singer, 1990, 11–12.
4. Wright, 1965; Richardson, 1960.
5. Deutsch, 1965, xii.
6. Singer, 1990, 15.
7. Singer's personal story can also be found in Singer, 2012, 1–16.
8. Singer, 1990, 19.
9. Ibid., 18.

10. Singer, 2012, 9; and Singer, 1989, 222.
11. Singer and Small, 1966, 236–82.
12. Singer and Small, 1972, 20.
13. Singer, 1990, 14.
14. Singer and Small, 1966, 236–82.
15. Russett, Singer, and Small, 1968, 932–51.
16. Singer, 1990, 15.
17. Singer and Small, 1972, 48.
18. Ibid., 30, 35.
19. Small, 1990, 30.
20. Ibid., 30.
21. Small and Singer, 1969, 257–82.
22. Singer, ed., 1968b.
23. Ibid., 10.
24. Rosenau, 1969.
25. Small and Singer, 1969, 159–90.
26. Singer and Small, 1972.
27. Ibid., v.
28. Singer, 1990, 21–23.
29. Small, 1990, 32.
30. Singer, 1982, 9.
31. Wallace and Singer, 1970, 239–87.
32. Singer, Bremer, and Stuckey, 1972, 19–48.
33. Ray and Singer, 1972, 403–37.
34. Small and Singer, 1973, 577–99.
35. Hoole and Zinnes, eds., 1976.
36. Singer and Small, 1976, 49–69.
37. Maoz, 1997.
38. Russett, 1994; Bremer, 1992, 309–41.
39. Sarkees, 2013, 259–284.
40. Henderson, 2002.
41. Small and Singer, 1982, 367–72.
42. Singer, ed., 1979b; Singer, ed., 1980; Singer, ed., 1979a.
43. Small and Singer, 1982, 16.
44. Ibid.
45. Ibid., 13.
46. Small and Singer, eds., 1989.
47. Gochman and Maoz, 1985, 27–36.
48. Stoll, 1977; Gochman and Maoz, 1985, 28–29.
49. Vasquez, 1987, 343–70; Senese and Vasquez, 2008.
50. Singer, 1987, 115–32.
51. Leng and Singer, 1988; Cioffi-Revilla, 1991, 603–29.
52. Merritt and Zinnes, 1990.
53. Vasquez, 1987, 343–70.
54. Gibbs and Singer, 1993.
55. Sarkees, 1995, 4, 8.
56. Sarkees, 2000, 123–144.
57. Sarkees, Wayman, and Singer, 2003, 49–70.
58. Tir, Schafer, Diehl, and Goertz, 1998.
59. Stinnett, Tir, Schafer, Diehl, and Gochman, 2002, 58–66.
60. Gibler and Sarkees, 2004.
61. Ghosn, Palmer, and Bremer, 2004, 133–54.
62. Barbieri, Keshk, and Pollins, 2009, 471–91.
63. Maoz and Henderson, 2013.
64. Jackson, 2014, 80.
65. Singer, 1976; Lear, Macaulay, and Sarkees, 2012, 122; Sarkees and Wayman, 2010, 6.
66. For more a more detailed discussion of the changes, see Sarkees, 2010a, 39–73; and Sarkees, 2000, 123–44.
67. Small and Singer, 1982, 205–206.
68. Wright, 1965, 8–13.
69. Small and Singer, 1982, 37–38.
70. Richardson, 1960, 5.
71. Ibid., 6.
72. Small and Singer, 1982, 69–70.
73. Ibid., 71.
74. Singer, 1990, 14.
75. Small and Singer, 1982, 39.
76. Ibid., 66.
77. Ibid., 66.
78. Wording from Dixon, 2003.
79. Small and Singer, 1982, 66.
80. Singer and Small, 1972, 48–49.
81. Dupuy, 1990, 48–49.
82. Small and Singer, 1982, 75.
83. Ibid., 73.
84. Ibid., 194.
85. Ibid., 194–95.
86. Ibid., 182.
87. Ibid., 182.
88. For a complete description, see Singer and Small, 1966, 236–82; Russett, Singer, and Small, 1968, 932–51; Singer and Small, 1972, 19–24; Sarkees and Wayman, 2010, 14–19.
89. As some critics rightly have pointed out, many scholars have utilized the system membership list without much thought about what it was designed to capture.
90. Singer and Small, 1972, 20.
91. Bremer with Ghosn, 2003, 24.
92. Singer and Small, 1966, 247–49.
93. Sarkees and Wayman, 2010, 18.
94. Sarkees, 2010a, 53–54.
95. Ibid., 46; Sarkees, 2011; Sarkees, 2000, 128.
96. For a discussion of the rationale, see Sarkees, 2010a, 61–62; Small and Singer, 1982, 185.
97. Small and Singer, 1982, 71.
98. Ibid., 52.
99. Sarkees, 2010a, 64.
100. Small and Singer, 1982, 210.
101. Ibid., 216.
102. Sarkees, 2010a, 64.

CHAPTER TWO

The Study of Intra-state War

Why Are Intra-state Wars Important?

Within the last twenty years, there has been an explosion in the study of intra-state, predominantly civil, war among peace researchers, historians, political scientists, supporters of intergovernmental organizations, and quantitative scholars. After having been relegated to the sidelines for so long by the priority given by both academics and policy makers to the study of inter-state and great-power war, the importance of civil wars is being recognized, and they have become a focal point for both in-depth historical studies and

FIGURE 2.1 Intra-state War Onsets and Internationalized Intra-state War Onsets per Decade

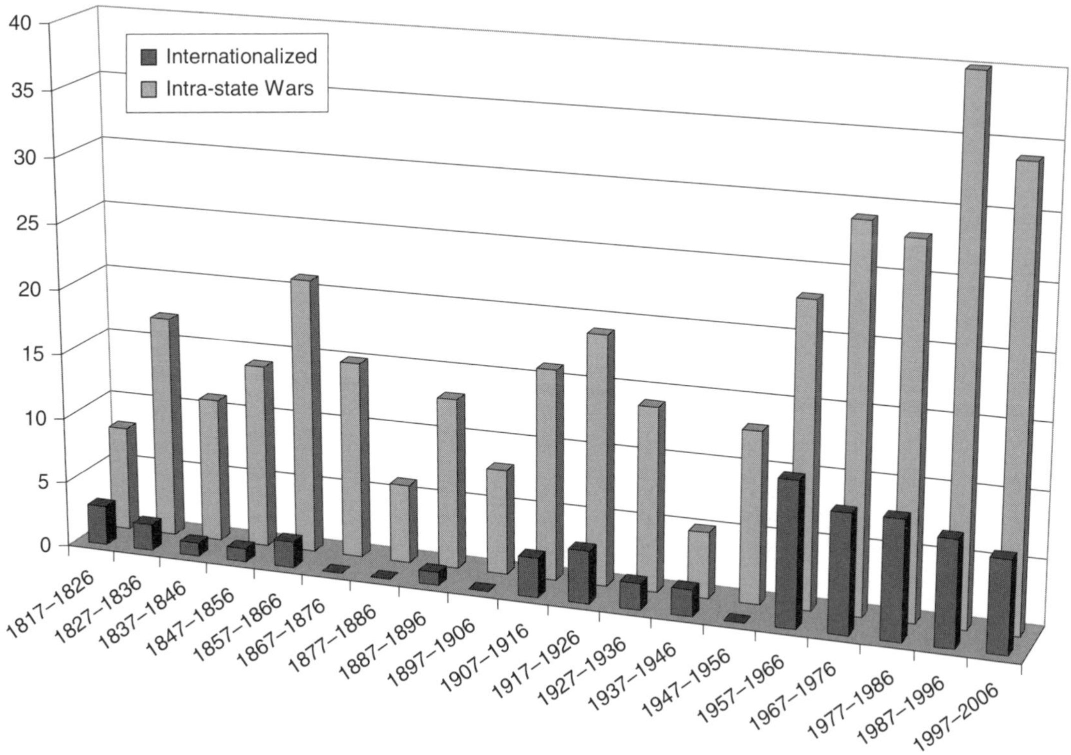

Source: Sarkees, Meredith Reid. "Patterns of Civil Wars in the Twenty-first Century: The Decline of Civil War?" In *The Routledge Handbook of Civil Wars,* edited by Edward Newman and Karl DeRouen Jr., Figure 19.16, p. 253. London: Routledge, 2014. Reprinted with permission.

large-scale data-gathering efforts. There are a number of reasons for this sense that intra-state wars are becoming increasingly important. A recent analysis of the COW intra-state war data (v. 4.0) demonstrated that there has been a significant increase in both the number of intra-state wars and the proportion of those wars that are internationalized by outside intervention (see Figure 2.1).

Relatedly, analyses of a composite of all COW war data has noted the increasing percentage of all war onsets that can be attributed to intra-state wars, in the vicinity of 80 percent.[1] That fact, coupled with the relative constancy in war onsets by decade over time since 1816, has led some to argue that what we are experiencing is a substitutability of warfare through which states eschew inter-state wars while currently preferring to intervene in the civil wars of others.[2] Some have highlighted the importance of intra-state wars due to the all-too-common violence against civilians during civil wars or to argue that what we are seeing is a proliferation of ethnic or "new" wars.[3] Others have argued that the interest in civil wars is necessitated by the fact that civil wars currently pose a significant threat to peace and development because of the longer duration of civil wars[4] and the pattern of civil war recurrence or an enduring cycle of violence that has been called "the Conflict Trap."[5] Also important has been the fact that the increasing tendency of states to intervene in intra-state wars has been matched by the growing activism of intergovernmental and nongovernmental organizations, which have expanded their efforts both to provide humanitarian aid and to promote efforts at conflict resolution.[6]

The growing importance of intra-state (predominantly civil) wars and the vast array of research on civil wars prompted Newman and DeRouen to compile a recent volume that brings together scholarship representing some of the major themes in civil war research: methodological debates; causes of civil wars; the nature and impact of civil wars; the international dimensions; and the termination or resolution of civil wars.[7] Despite this plethora of research on war, there are, as Newman has recently noted, still significant gaps in our knowledge about war and about intra-state war in particular.[8] Some of these gaps are the result of the significant cleavages in the field over general understandings of civil war, definitions of civil war, methodologies of study, and interpretations of trends. The entire concept of civil war is problematic: there is no one commonly accepted definition of a civil war; many scholars utilize the terms *intra-state war* and *civil war* as synonymous; and there needs to be more exploration of the variations of experience within the category of intra-state war.[9] In the study of civil wars, the methodological gap between quantitative and qualitative approaches seems as wide as ever, and even within the quantitative approach, there are differing interpretations of the trends in civil wars. For instance, while Sarkees emphasizes that intra-state war onsets are at historically high levels, others, like the *Human Security Report*, highlight a downward trend both in international wars since 1967 and in civil wars within the last 20 years, since the end of the Cold War.[10]

To address some of these issues, Newman and DeRouen, along with Clayton, encouraged the utilization of a more mixed methods research approach, combining scientific and historical studies that examine a few specific variables across multiple cases studies.[11] This is in essence the approach that we have adopted here. Though our work is firmly grounded in the scientific study of large-scale data sets, the major portion of this book is devoted to providing brief historical descriptions of each war in an attempt to provide a context to the limited number of variables we highlight. We hope that this framework will help examine the nature of, and different types of experiences within, the arena of intra-state war.

How COW Intra-state Wars Are Defined and Categorized

As described in Chapter 1, the COW typology of war is based on the identification of the war participants, or who is fighting whom. The primary focus is upon state members of the interstate system that emerged in 1816. Wars are categorized by the experience of states: inter-state wars are between or among states; extra-state wars are between a state and a nonstate entity outside its borders; intra-state wars take place within the borders of the state; and non-state wars involve non-state actors not within state borders. Within the COW war typology, all classifications of war share the same basic definition of war that focuses upon three primary elements: sustained combat, organized armed forces, and 1,000 battle-related deaths. Thus war is sustained combat between or among organized armed forces, leading to 1,000 battle-related deaths (of combatants) per year (or twelve-month period starting from the war onset). The element of sustained armed combat requires that there be effective resistance offered by both sides to a conflict, thus massacres are not considered as war. This criterion, combined with the focus on organized armed forces, means that civilian fatalities also are not included in determining whether combat should be considered a war. To be a war, there must 1,000 battle-related deaths per annum between or among the war participants, or combatants. The coding rules for the wars' start and end dates, the battle-deaths, the identification of the participants, the composition of the armed forces, the initiator, and the outcome are all the same for intra-state wars. However, these elements do play out somewhat differently in intra-state wars as compared to other war categories, and so they will be addressed in greater detail here.[12]

Battle-related Deaths

Within all intra-state wars, the war threshold is the same, at 1,000 battle-related deaths (of combatants) within a twelve-month period from the start of the war. Determining the number of battle-related deaths is the most difficult aspect of coding COW wars: many historical accounts don't include specific fatality numbers; available fatality numbers may or may not include civilian fatalities; and historians frequently use the term *casualties* as a synonym for deaths, whereas others use the term in a more technical sense, including both those who were killed and those who were wounded. These problems are amplified in wars involving non-state actors, such as extra-state, intra-state, and non-state wars, where battle-death figures are less available and less reliable. Determining battle-related deaths for non-state armed groups and excluding civilian fatalities can be particularly difficult in wars in which it can be harder to distinguish combatants (who may or may not wear uniforms) from civilians. Governments also may have vested interests in over-reporting or undercounting fatalities (especially those of civilians) for political reasons. For instance, a government may try to conceal the intentional or unintentional killing of civilians by claiming that they were combatants, or they may exaggerate the killing of civilians as a means of delegitimizing the opposition. Furthermore, in intra-state wars, governments have greater control over media access to conflict zones and thus are more able to control reporting about fatalities. One welcome by-product of the increased interest in intra-state wars is the emergence of a number of new research efforts and data-gathering projects that have provided valuable information on disaggregating fatality statistics (like CERAC concerning deaths in Colombia and the Lithuania's National War Experience in the Nineteenth and Twentieth Centuries project).[13] For an example of difficulties in determining fatality figures for just one war, see the exchange between Gediminas and Sarkees about the coding of the Forest Brethren War, COW Intra-state War #723.[14]

Dates and Duration

Similarly, in discussing war duration, the definitional issues also become somewhat more complex for intra-state wars. Coding the start date of intra-state wars is harder because intra-state wars do not involve the relatively visible event of armed forces crossing an international border. Declarations of war are also less common, and initial combat may take place in remote areas where reporting or record keeping is not available. Similarly, determining the end date of an intra-state war is also more complicated because intra-state wars frequently encompass periods when combat waxes and wanes (perhaps during the agricultural seasons) or when combat just fades away rather than being ended by a peace treaty or agreement. COW's requirement of 1,000 battle-related deaths (among combatants) per twelve-month period and the related ending of a war when that level of combat is not sustained mean that the coder must identify the last date of significant combat as the end of the war. COW's decision to code wars as continuing only as long as the threshold of 1,000 battle-related deaths per year is maintained frequently contrasts with other data-gathering projects that continue wars for long periods when combat is fairly light.

War Participants

Intra-state wars take place within the territorial boundaries of a state member of the interstate system, yet the war participants are combinations of states and non-state actors (or non-state entities [NSEs]) that need not even include the state as a primary participant (unlike inter-state and extra-state wars). As will be described in the classifications of intra-state war, only the category of civil war requires that one of the primary war participants must be a state system member fighting against a non-state actor. The regional and intercommunal wars involve primary participants that are both non-state entities. Like the non-state actors in extra-state wars, the non-state actors in intra-state wars can be either territorially based geopolitical units (GPUs) or actors that are not territorially identified but have an organized armed force capable of engaging in sustained combat. Such entities are frequently referred to as non-state armed groups (NSAs). In intra-state wars (unlike extra-state wars), the GPUs have to be internal to the state and thus are frequently geopolitical or regional subunits, like provinces, departments, or American states. In determining whether an NSE is a GPU or an NSA, a key factor is whether the non-state entity has a government with sovereignty over a defined territory: if so, it is a GPU. Thus, for example, in the war for the secession of Texas from Mexico (Intra-state War #527), the participants are listed as Mexico and Texas (as opposed to the Texas secessionists) because the Texans had created a government structure.

Identifying the non-state participants in intra-state wars can be difficult for a number of reasons, generally related to a lack of information. Non-state armed groups may be of relatively recent origin, and/or their need for secrecy when confronting the government may mean that there is little generally known about the organization or its activities. In such cases, intra-state war participants frequently have been described as conglomerates or aggregates, such as rebels, rather than as specific armed groups. To be considered a war participant, such non-state entities would need to commit a minimum of 100 armed troops to sustained combat or suffer a minimum of twenty-five battle-related deaths.[15] The difficulty in identifying non-state participants is linked to the issue of how to code armed combat by multiple actors within a state: Is there a single intra-state war, or are there multiple simultaneous wars? In general, COW categorizes wars as encompassing and mutually exclusive (not coding as two wars conflict between or among the same participants at the same time). It is more difficult to distinguish separate wars when they take place within the confines of a state. For example, in coding civil war, the coder must decide whether combat reflects (a) a single civil war involving many non-state armed groups opposed to the central government or (b) several simultaneous civil wars, each characterized by the same government fighting a different non-state armed group. In making this determination, the primary determinant of the coding is the degree of coordination between or among the various non-state entities. For instance, if a state is facing combat with a variety of non-state armed groups who are coordinating their opposition, it will be coded as one single civil war. If, on the other hand, the state is facing combat against multiple non-state armed groups that are operating in geographically distinct regions and are not coordinating their operations, then the conflict will be coded as multiple wars (assuming that all the other criteria for a war are met). The key difficulties with this categorization are of course identifying all of the non-state armed groups involved in the war and then determining how much coordination existed between or among them. Though it is relatively easy to recognize evidence of coordination—common command structures, frequent meetings or communication among group leaders, or joint offensives—it is much more difficult to measure the absence of such coordination. Consequently, we are in essence utilizing negative coordination criteria. In instances in which a state is engaged in combat with multiple non-state armed groups, each of which is operating in a distinct geographic area, multiple wars will be considered to exist unless there is specific evidence of more than trivial coordination and cooperation between or among the armed groups. The difficulty in applying this rule can be seen in cases where conflict in different geographic regions is consolidated (the Russian civil war), while other conflicts were coded as separate conflicts (Ethiopian civil war).[16]

Interventions and Transformations

A final issue that complicates the coding of intra-state wars is that of war interventions and war transformations. As described in Chapter 1, a war is internationalized when an outside actor intervenes in a war but does not fundamentally change the classification of the primary war participants, or who is fighting whom. Whether the fundamental nature of the war should change or not is determined by which parties are doing the bulk of the fighting. If the type of participants or their relative roles in the war change or if the intervener replaces one of the parties as the major combatant (or takes over the bulk of the fighting), the classification of the war must change to reflect the reality of who is fighting whom. The original war thus ends, and a new war, with a different classification, is created. Such interventions occur more often in the extra-state and intra-state war categories and specifically within the category of civil wars, or wars between the central government and a rebel group. To reiterate, if the outside state intervener is fighting on the side of the rebels and then takes over the bulk of the fighting, the civil war ends, and the conflict is transformed into an inter-state war between the intervener and the original state government. If the outside state is intervening against the rebels on the side of the government and takes up the bulk of the fighting, the civil war ends, and the war becomes an extra-state war between the state intervener and a non-state actor outside the intervener's territory.

Intra-state War Categories

As already noted, COW has clear definitional differences between intra-state and civil wars: intra-state wars are all of those that take place within the recognized territorial borders of the state, while civil wars are a subset of intra-state wars that require the participation of the system member government. As described in Chapter 1, COW intra-state wars are divided into three categories, again depending upon who is fighting whom: civil wars require that the government of the state must be a war participant (War Types 4 and 5); regional wars involve the government of a subunit against a non-state actor (War Type 6); and intercommunal wars involve two nongovernmental actors (War Type 7). Each of these categories will be described in more detail next.

Civil Wars

For COW, civil wars involve the government of the state against a non-state actor within its borders. This is the largest of the three subcategories of intra-state war. However, coding these wars can sometimes be complicated. On occasion, just determining who the government is is not clear, for instance, in cases of rival entities claiming the right to govern all or part of a state. In such cases, Small and Singer defined *the government* as those forces that were at the start of the war in de facto control of the nation's institutions, regardless of the legality or illegality of their claim.[17] They did not, however, specifically define what was meant by the "nation's institutions." Yet in terms of civil wars, they noted that the control of the nation's institutions need not necessarily include control of the armed forces as the armed forces might be the combatants in a war against the government. Thus we have further refined the *nation's institutions* as the institutions of governance: whichever party begins the war in possession of the institutions of government (parliament, the palace, etc.) may be termed the government. When each side controls an institution (e.g., Chile's Congressist rebellion, which pitted the president against Congress), then the executive or monarch's faction is termed the government. Thus, control of the nation's institutions need not necessarily include control of the armed forces. Although a government generally can expect its armed forces to defend it, in a civil war that pits the government against armed forces, the government must rely on civilian combatants or other branches of the civilian or military infrastructure that remain loyal.[18] Consequently, within the category of civil war, Small and Singer also included in the general category of the government, or on the side of the government, or the armed forces of the national government, all those—from national military forces to local police and citizens—who enter the conflict in the name of that government.[19] It should be emphasized that determining which party is the government is not dependent on diplomatic recognition. Although diplomatic recognition of the state (or membership in the United Nations) is a requirement for an entity to be a member of the inter-state system, that is not a *de jure* recognition (or approval) of a specific government. Thus it is possible for one party to be considered by COW as the government of a state due to its control of the national institutions, while another party may be recognized diplomatically by other states, or even retain a United Nations seat (as was the case when the Northern Alliance retained the UN seat for Afghanistan, despite the fact that the Taliban government was in control in Afghanistan).

When defining civil wars, Small and Singer also began to describe the other participants in the civil war. Unlike the category of extra-state wars in which the characteristics of the non-state actors involved are relatively undefined (unless it is already a colony, dependency, or occupied territory), the requisite condition of a civil war is that the government is fighting against an internal insurgent force capable of "effective resistance." Small and Singer developed a two-part definition of effective resistance:

> [A] violent episode of sustained military combat shall be considered a civil war if (a) both sides are initially organized for violent conflict and prepared to resist the attacks of their antagonists, or (b) the weaker side, although initially unprepared, is able to inflict upon the stronger opponents at least five percent of the number of fatalities it sustains.[20]

The effective resistance criterion was specifically utilized to differentiate civil wars from massacres. The application of these two alternative criteria is similar to the two alternative means by which a state can be considered a war participant (committing 1,000 armed troops to combat or suffering 100 fatalities). The primary requirement is that each participant must have an organized armed force capable of engaging in sustained combat; however, application of this criterion alone would eliminate as civil wars such cases in which the non-state actor perhaps is not initially well organized but relatively soon develops an armed organization. For example, the 1923 Agrarian Rising in Bulgaria initially was not considered to be a COW civil war due to organizational concerns, but it was later added to the civil war list (through the application of criterion b) when it became clear that the peasants became nominally organized and armed. In terms of practical applications, in situations of war-level combat between the state's government and a non-state actor, COW assumes for purposes of war inclusion or exclusion that both sides were capable of effective resistance unless there is evidence that indeed one side suffered more than 20 battle-deaths for every one suffered by its opponent. It should be noted that even in this instance, if the historical sources concur on organization, then the non-state actor will be included as a war participant—the 20:1 ratio is merely a fallback for instances where organization cannot be established any other way.

Small and Singer also considered a number of alternative ways in which to categorize the non-state actors in civil wars. Two possibilities were to categorize the rebels by differing degrees of organization by indicating a range of organizational abilities from the disciplined military to the untrained rebellious masses; alternatively one could categorize participants in terms of the types of weapons they used. Such distinctions often have been used to differentiate civil wars from insurrections and riots. Small and Singer ultimately rejected such a classification as unreliable. However, as noted in Chapter 1, a subsequent decision was adopted for specific non-state actors to be considered war participants; they must either commit 100 armed personnel to combat or suffer twenty-five battle-related deaths. Additional data gathering concerning the non-state participants in civil wars is an innovation of this new version of the data and will be discussed further.

Just as Small and Singer rejected classifying civil wars by the types of weapons or tactics used (overt vs. covert or conventional military vs. guerrilla), they also initially rejected categorizing civil wars by the purposes and goals of the rebels. Requests from scholars, however, led COW to reconsider the issue. Despite the difficulty of ascertaining the objectives of political protagonists or most other entities, COW nonetheless concluded that motives and goals are the most relevant criteria for differentiating the various forms that civil war might take. COW adopted a minimalist categorization of the objectives of the non-state participants, and in version four of the data, civil wars were grouped into two categories based on the apparent motives of the non-state actors: (1) conflicts for control of the central government (War Type 4) or (2) conflicts over local or regional interests (War Type 5).[21] In Category 1, for central control, the insurgent forces seek to overthrow the existing national regime and replace it with one that is more receptive to their material, cultural, or psychic interests. But at the more-restricted local, provincial, or regional level, in Category 2, the insurgents fight to modify the national regime's treatment of this particular region or group of people, to replace the local regime with a friendlier one, or to secede from the larger statewide political system to set up their own regime. In trying to make this distinction between local as distinct from central government or statewide objectives, not only do we recognize the ambiguities and uncertainties involved in the behavior of the different elements that make up the insurgency, but also we must recognize that their objectives are far from constant. These will change as the insurgent coalition changes in its composition and in the relative power of its constituent groups and also as the fortunes of war fluctuate. It is this changeable nature of objectives that has dissuaded the project from trying to subdivide civil wars further.

Regional Wars

Regional wars (War Type 6) are intra-state wars in that they occur within the boundaries of an interstate system member, though the system member government is not a participant in the war. In virtually all respects, regional intra-state wars function like civil wars, but what gives them their distinct identity is that the major combatant on one side of the war is a local or regional government (not the national government). The armed forces on this side of the war would be regional (similar to the New York State National Guard); however, as with civil wars, the side of the local or regional government would include all those who enter the conflict in the name of that government, from regional military forces to local police and citizens.

The key difficulty in identifying these wars, and in differentiating them from civil wars, is in determining the purpose for which the regional government is fighting. If the regional government is fighting against a non-state actor for local issues, including the perpetuation of the regional government itself, then the war would be a regional intra-state war. On the other hand, a regional or local government also could be merely a participant in a civil war involving the national government. A regional government could fight alongside or in the name of the national government in a civil war opposing a non-state actor seeking local autonomy or independence. Conversely, the regional government could be a participant in a civil war against the national government if the regional government itself is seeking autonomy or independence.

Intercommunal Wars

The third category of intra-state wars is intercommunal war (War Type 7). Intercommunal wars are intra-state wars in that they occur within the boundaries of a member of the interstate system. However, in intercommunal wars, the major war participants (who are conducting the bulk of the fighting on each side) are non-state actors, not the system member or a regional or local government. This type of warfare, between nongovernmental forces within a state, is obviously not new, and many scholars have become interested in what they call *ethnic conflict*. We consider this terminology, and many of the purported explanations of ethnic conflict, to be misguided, so that term has not been adopted by COW and will not be used here.[22] However, intercommunal wars are becoming more common as advanced weapons technology boosts the probability that conflicts between or among non-state actors will reach the requisite battle-death threshold for war.

Innovations in This Update

The intra-state war data set is the war set that has undergone the most changes since it was released as the civil war dataset by Small and Singer in 1982.[23] By 2010, the intra-state war data set had grown from Small and Singer's 106 wars to 335 wars.[24] This version of the data now includes 413 wars, almost a 22 percent increase. Not only has the data been updated by adding wars that began between 2007 and 2014 (to encompass the period 1816–2014), but historical research utilizing many of the recent war case studies also had uncovered or identified a number of additional intra-state wars.

However, the major innovation in this war handbook and the affiliated version of the data set is that we have gathered significant amounts of data on the non-state participants in each war. In cases where the non-state actor is an aggregate, we have attempted to disaggregate the collective description and to specify each of the non-state armed forces that meets the individual conditions for war participation (again, non-state entities need to commit a minimum of 100 armed troops to sustained combat or suffer a minimum of twenty-five battle-related deaths).[25] Needless to say, a key difficulty with this endeavor is, of course, identifying all of the non-state armed groups involved in the war. Wars frequently involve multiple groups, some more organized and larger than others, thus just gathering enough information not only to identify all the combatants but also to ensure that they meet the criteria for a war participant can be challenging. For instance, dozens of non-state actors fought inside Russia's borders between 1917 and 1922 (see Chapters 5 and 7). The process of opening up the collective grouping of the rebels precipitated a more-detailed investigation of whether these multiple groups were in fact working together in one war or whether it would be more accurate to conceptualize them as fighting separate wars. While it is relatively easy to recognize evidence of coordination, such as common command structures, frequent meetings, communication among non-state group leaders, or joint offensives, it is much more difficult to measure the absence of such coordination. Consequently, we are in essence utilizing negative coordination criteria. In instances in which a state is engaged in combat with multiple non-state armed groups, each of which is operating in a distinct geographic area, multiple wars will be considered to exist unless there is specific evidence of coordination and cooperation between or among the non-state actors. Similarly, rebel groups that consistently fight each other cannot be said to be coordinating their behavior. Moreover, it also should be noted that distinct civil wars will be coded if they occur within different states (against different state governments), even though there may be links among the non-state armed groups.

There have been several additional innovations in the data about each war. Once the participants have been identified, data was gathered on the armed forces of each participant. In terms of the state, the "Total System Member Military Personnel" are those that have been defined as the military personnel in the COW National Material Capabilities dataset.[26] To this has been added information on "Theater Armed Forces." For the system member, that number refers to the portion of its military personnel that were (as far as it is known) utilized in the war. If that number is the same as the Total System Member Military Personnel, then no additional information is reported here. However, that number can be either lower or higher if: the state only utilizes a portion of its military for the war (e.g., if conflict is in a remote location); the state government is disserted by or is being attacked by elements of its military personnel; or the state relies upon additional armed forces from its police, regional national guards, or non-state armed groups (such as pro-government militias). The Theater Armed Forces category is where we also report the armed forces available to the non-state actors. Available data is reported on these figures at several points through the war.

We also have attempted to provide more specific battle-death figures for each of the war participants. As noted in Chapter 1, gathering battle-death figures is the most difficult part of coding wars. So much of the data is missing (or not yet found), and the quality of much that has been reported is of questionable accuracy, that we are providing merely what we consider to be our best "guesstimates." Since it is more common to find references to total deaths in a war, we provide a variable of total combatant deaths. This figure also may represent our attempts to aggregate fatality information from individual battles. We also have tried to code battle-deaths for each of the individual war participants. Examples of how some of these calculations have been derived are presented in Tables 7.2 and 7.3.

As already noted, this war handbook constitutes a mixed-method approach to the study of intra-state war: it provides quantitative measures of the war experience of the participants; plus it provides a brief case study of each war, including discussions of its antecedents, a history of the war itself, and a section on its outcomes. The case study generally also includes a "Coding Decisions" section in which we describe the rationale for some of the variable codings and any anomalies about the war. The arrangement of these case studies within this handbook reflects another innovation of this work. Unlike previous COW war handbooks (*Wages of War*, *Resort to Arms*, and *Resort to War*) that presented the information about the wars primarily in chronological order, here we have adopted a regional approach. Each of the wars has been coded as taking place within one of six regions (North America, South America, Europe, the Middle East and North Africa, Asia and Oceania, and sub-Saharan Africa). These regions are based on the contemporary definitions of these terms. There are a number of system members whose territories may span two regions, such as Russia and the earlier Ottoman Empire. Wars are grouped on the basis of the geographical location of where they took place, thus bi-regional states may have wars that can be found in two regions. This procedure varies from the process utililized for the foundational data set of the COW Project, the State System Membership List. That data set and the subsequent war data sets coded states and wars as being within six slightly different regions: the Western Hemisphere, Europe, the Middle East and North Africa, Asia, sub-Saharan Africa, and Oceania. On occasion, intra-state wars were coded as being fought in the COW region in which the state was coded as existing in the system membership list (rather than the geographic location of the actual fighting). Thus readers may notice a shift in regional grouping of some intra-state wars (e.g., from the Middle East to Europe or Europe to Asia). The remainder of this book will constitute the description of each of the intra-state wars. The chapter for each region will begin with a list of the intra-state wars in that region, and a complete list of all the intra-state wars can be found in the Appendix.

Notes

1. Ibid., 245; Sarkees, 2010c, 565.
2. Sarkees, Wayman, and Singer, 2003.
3. Kalyvas, 2006; Kaufman, 2001; Kaldor, 1999.
4. Walter, 1999, 1.
5. Collier et al., 2003.
6. Crocker, Hampson, and Aall, eds., 2005; Anderson, 1999; Goodhand, 2006.
7. Newman and DeRouen, eds., 2014.
8. Newman, 2014, 9.
9. Newman and DeRouen, 2014, 7.
10. Sarkees, 2014, 255; Human Security Project, 2011, 19, 61.
11. Newman and DeRouen, 2014, 9; Clayton, 2014, 28–40.
12. Small and Singer, 1982, 210–20; Sarkees, 2009; Sarkees, 2010b, 337–41.
13. CERAC (Centro de Recursos para el Análisis de Conflictos), 2008; Gediminas, 2014.
14. Gediminas, 2012, 515–27; Sarkees, 2012, 528–38.
15. Sarkees, 2010a, 64.
16. Dixon and Sarkees, 2005, 13–14.
17. Small and Singer, 1982, 213.
18. Ibid., 214.
19. Ibid., 213.
20. Ibid., 215.
21. Sarkees, 2009.
22. Sarkees, 2001.
23. Small and Singer, 1982, 203–91.
24. Sarkees, 2010b, 337.
25. Sarkees, 2010a, 64.
26. Correlates of War Project, 2010.

CHAPTER THREE

Intra-state Wars in North America

Below is the list of the intra-state wars that took place in North America. Each war will then be described individually with the pertinent basic data provided.

TABLE 3.1 List of Intra-state Wars in North America

(Continued)

TABLE 3.1 **List of Intra-state Wars in North America** (Continued)

Individual Descriptions of Intra-state Wars in North America

INTRA-STATE WAR #520

First Mexican War of 1832 (aka Mexican Civil War or First Federalist Revolt)

Participants: Mexico versus Liberals.
Dates: January 2, 1832, to December 23, 1832.
Battle-related Deaths: Armed Forces of Mexico (Government Army)—1,400; Liberal militias (Rebel Army)—1,000.[1] (See Coding Decisions.)
Initiator: Liberals.
Outcome: Liberals win.
War Type: Civil for central control.
Total System Member Military Personnel: *Armed Forces of Mexico* (Government Army): 25,000.[2] Its actual strength was only 19,667 (initial); 25,000 (peak).[3]
Theater Armed Forces: *Liberals or Federalist Alliance* (Rebel Army): 1,400 (initial); 7,000 (peak).[4]

Antecedents: Mexico achieved its independence from Spain in 1821 (Extra-state War #304). Subsequently, Mexico continued to be plagued by a series of factional conflicts between federalists and centralists (or liberals and conservatives). In general, federalists favored a dispersal of power among the states and regions, while centralists favored strengthening the central government to prevent the disintegration of the country. Initially a Mexican empire was established, lasting only till 1823, when a republic was created by two heroes of Mexico's War of Independence, Gen. Antonio López de Santa Anna and Guadalupe Victoria (the revolutionary name of Manuel Félix Fernández), who served as its first president. Factional strife continued, as did conflict with indigenous groups (including the Mexico–Yaqui Indian War of 1825 to 1827, Non-state War #1509). At the end of January 1829, President Gómez Pedraza was forced into exile, and Vicente Guerrero assumed the presidency, unwisely agreeing that Anastasio Bustamante would remain as vice president. Meanwhile, Spain's King Ferdinand VII ordered the formation of an army in Cuba that was, on July 6, 1829, sent to invade Mexico in an attempt to restore Spanish rule (Extra-state War #317). The defeat of the Spanish by a Mexican army led by General Santa Anna (governor of the state of Veracruz) made Santa Anna into a national hero. The fact that President Guerrero, an uneducated *mestizo*, was in power angered the conservative elites, including the army, and a revolt in December 1829 brought Bustamante to power. Bustamante's government was in essence a conservative dictatorship, beholden to the military that had put him in power, which increasingly aroused opposition in the liberal regions (including Zacatecas, Durango, San Luis Potosí, Oaxaca, and Guerrero). This 1832 war began when Santa Anna led a rebellion against President Bustamante calling for the restoration of the deposed Pedraza.

Narrative: In anticipation of the 1832 presidential election, a number of President Bustamante's opponents joined Santa Anna in an antigovernment or federalist alliance. Santa Anna began the war on January 2, 1832, by seizing the Veracruz garrison and the custom duties that had been collected there. Santa Anna engaged the first Mexican forces sent against him in several skirmishes, and the first major combat of the war occurred on February 24, when Santa Anna's forces ambushed a government column. On March 3, Santa Anna's army clashed with government forces led by Generals José Maria Calderón and José Antonio Facio at Tolome, and Santa Anna's outnumbered force suffered more than 450 rebel casualties, including 32 officers. After this reverse, Santa Anna fell back to his base of support at Veracruz and reinforced his troops to a strength of about 2,500 men. The government troops followed, and from April 12, a protracted and deadly siege of Veracruz resulted. By May 13, the government had lost a thousand soldiers in the siege, mostly due to yellow fever, to which Santa Anna's local forces were immune. Losing about fifteen soldiers each day to disease, the government finally lifted the siege.

Meanwhile, others sympathetic to Santa Anna, including some of the Northern provinces, also raised rebellions in April and May. On June 3, 1832, Gen. Esteban Moctezuma, leading a militia from the state of Zacatecas, attacked a government army under Gen. Pedro Luciano Otero at Poza de las Carmelos. Otero was defeated and killed, while Moctezuma seized the nearby town of San Luis Potosi.[5] By June 13, the government agreed to an armistice. However, the talks foundered and rebel attacks resumed, becoming nearly constant in August and September. Bustamante personally marched out of Mexico City with an army of 4,000 to quash the rebellion. On September 17, he defeated Moctezuma's forces at El Gallinero Pass (near San Luís Potosi) in an engagement that produced heavy losses on both sides, including 1,000 to 2,000 rebel casualties. Meanwhile, on September 29 in the Battle of San Augustin del Palmar, Santa Anna captured Puebla (located on the road east of Mexico City). Bustamante then backtracked to intercept Santa Anna's army, which was by then threatening Mexico City. When Santa Anna learned of Bustamante's location, he chose to move north to meet him rather than occupy the capital, while leaving behind a small force to maintain a siege of the capital.

Meanwhile, Pedraza had returned from exile, arriving in Mexico sometime in October, and the rebels began constructing a parallel government. Two major battles followed: on December 6, the bloody Battle of Rancho Posadas was fought to a stalemate. Bustamante then went for Santa Anna's headquarters at Casa Blanca, where his force was repulsed a day later. Although an armistice was signed on December 11, 1832, intermittent clashes continued until both sides reached an agreement to end the war.

Termination and Outcome: On December 23, both sides signed a formal peace agreement, the Pact of Zavaleta, calling for amnesty, a caretaker government by Pedraza, and presidential elections. Bustamante resigned, and Pedraza reoccupied the presidency for three months. The elections were held and on April 1, 1833, Santa Anna was elected president with Valentin Gómez Farías as vice president. They created a liberal and anticlerical regime. Ultimately Farías's severe anticlerical measures persuaded Santa Anna to stage a conservative coup, with the support of the clergy, in 1834, and his victory served to consolidate his position as dictator. Opposition to his regime rose in the north, where the states of Jalisco, Neuvo León, San Luís, Zacatecas, and Coahuila (which then included Texas) rebelled (Intra-state War #525.5). Overall, the 1832 war was merely the first in a series of governmental changes and revolts that were to plague Mexico for the next twenty-two years, with the presidency changing hands thirty-six times and Santa Anna serving as president eleven times.

Coding Decisions: Mexico is coded as becoming a member of the COW interstate system in 1831, thus wars involving Mexico prior to that time are not included in the intra-state war category (like the Mexico–Yaqui Indian War of 1825 to 1827 (Non-state War #1509). Calculating the number of battle-deaths for this war is difficult because some statistics (all of the disease deaths on the rebel side and those of the government after May 13) are unavailable. Moreover, confusion results when some of the sources use the term *casualties* to indicate the number killed, while others use it to refer to both the killed and the wounded. With these caveats in mind, we interpret the sources as saying that more than 1,220 died on the government side (1,000 of them from disease), plus there were 400 additional combatant deaths by both sides; thus 1,400 is the most reasonable figure for the government. For the liberals, adding up known losses gives a total of 780, plus some share of additional deaths suffered by both sides, so 1,000 is a reasonable figure.

Sources: Archer (2000); Bravo Ugarte (1962); Calcott (1964); DePalo (1997); Fehrenbach (1973); Fowler (2000a); Fowler (2007); Green (1987); Hu-DeHart (1984); Jaques (2007); Krauze (1997); Marley (1998); Meyer, Sherman, and Deeds (2003); Parkes (1966); Scheina (2003a); Schlarman (1951).

INTRA-STATE WAR #525.5
Zacatecas Rebellion of 1835 (aka Second Federalist Revolt)

Participants: Mexico versus Zacatecas Militia.
Dates: May 11, 1835, to May 14, 1835.
Battle-related Deaths: Zacatecas militia: [ ]; Armed Forces of Mexico: [ ]; Total Combatant Deaths: 1,000.
Initiator: Zacatecas militia.

Outcome: Mexico wins.
War Type: Civil for central control.
Total System Member Military Personnel: *Armed Forces of Mexico*: 25,000[6]; Total *Zacatecas militia*—17,000.[7]
Theater Armed Forces: Armed Forces of Mexico: 3,500 to 4,000 for this expedition; Zacatecas militia—5,000.[8]

Antecedents: In 1832, Gen. Antonio López de Santa Anna (then the governor of Veracruz) led a rebellion against the conservative regime of President Anastasio Bustamante (Intra-state War #520). During this war, Santa Anna was aided by a number of regional army garrison commanders, including Governor Francisco García Salinas, who headed the powerful Zacatecas militia. As a result of the war, Bustamante resigned, and former president Gómez Pedraza was returned to power as a caretaker for three months until elections could be held. On April 1, 1933, Santa Anna was elected president with Valentin Gómez Farías as vice president. However, Santa Anna soon turned over the presidency to Gómez Farías, while he returned to Veracruz. Gómez Farías immediately began to institute liberal reforms, specifically targeting the powers and privileges of the Church and the military. The anticlerical measures in particular antagonized the upper class, and when a cholera epidemic broke out, the Church was quick to portray it as punishment against Mexico's impious regime.[9] Military garrisons in Morelia and Tlálpam led uprisings in May and June 1833 in support of the Church and the military. On June 2, Santa Anna led a force of 1,500 troops to subdue the rebels. During this foray, Santa Anna purportedly was captured by rebels who apparently anticipated that Santa Anna would join their cause. Santa Anna was able to escape and return to the capital, whence he gathered another army and launched a second offensive that defeated the rebels at Guanajuato on October 8. However, Santa Anna became increasingly sympathetic to the growing antiliberal sentiments and to the military's opposition to the government's attempts to reduce the power of the military. Though he was technically still Mexico's president, in April 1834, Santa Anna launched a "holy revolution" to remove Gómez Farías from power. After assuming control on April 24, 1834, Santa Anna repealed the anticlerical legislation and abolished the congress.

Narrative: In 1835, a new congress took office that contained a combination of centralists and federalists, yet it overturned many of the federalist reforms and adopted those proposed by Santa Anna. Santa Anna's policies were not universally popular, especially among his former liberal or federal allies in the outer regions such as Querétaro, San Luís Potosí, Guanajuato, and Jalisco. The more remote areas generally were immune from government control and had developed their own local leadership or chieftains, who maintained local militias. One of the largest and best armed of the state militias was that of Zacatecas, led by Governor Francisco García Salinas, who had aided Santa Anna in the 1832 war. Yet, by 1835, Santa Anna's view was that the regional militias were a danger to the nation, and one of the military reforms proposed by the new congress aimed at creating a professional standing Mexican army and limiting the size of the militias. The federalist states were not disposed to lose this degree of autonomy, and Juan Alvarez began to organize a federalist opposition to Santa Anna. Though some of the states merely condemned Santa Anna's growing centralism, the northern state of Zacatecas decided to rebel once again. Governor Francisco García mobilized his militia, raised an army of 5,000, and had them construct fortifications. Santa Anna marched his army of 3,500 men against his former ally. Santa Anna lured the Zacatecas militia into a trap, and in several hours of heavy fighting near Guadalupe, the Mexican army crushed the poorly armed rebels, killing thousands.[10] Santa Anna punished Zacatecas harshly, allowing the army to loot the regional capital for two days and seizing 20 percent of the state's territory to create a new state of Aguascalientes. Santa Anna's army then went on a triumphal march through the region before returning to the capital.

Termination and Outcome: Santa Anna's victory in this war served to consolidate his conservative rule. Gómez Farías and many of the other liberals fled the country. Some went on to Texas to aid the revolutionary movement there (Intra-state War #527). The dominance of conservative rule was formalized in April 1836, when the congress replaced the federalist Constitution of 1824 with the conservative Seven Laws.

Coding Decisions: We have found very little adequate information on the fatalities of this war. Most of the sources talk about heavy fighting and a crushing rebel defeat. Fehrenbach refers to the deaths of thousands, though some of these may have been civilian deaths during the looting of the capital. Thus as a best guess, we are coding 1,000 total battle deaths, with the vast majority being experienced by the rebel forces.

Sources: Archer (2000); DePalo (1997); Fehrenbach (1973); Parkes (1966); Scheina (2003a).

INTRA-STATE WAR #527
Texan War of 1835 to 1836 (aka Texas Independence)

Participants: Mexico versus Texas.
Dates: October 2, 1835, to April 20, 1836.
Battle-related Deaths: Mexico—1,500; Texas—700.[11] (See Coding Decisions.)
Initiator: Texas.
Outcome: Texas wins.
War Type: Civil for local issues (secession).
Total System Member Military Personnel: Armed Forces of Mexico: 25,000.[12]
Theater Armed Forces: Armed Forces of Mexico: 3,500 (initial), 8,000 (peak), 2,000 (final).[13] Texas Secessionists (Rebel Army): 300 (initial), 1,200 (peak), 1,000 (final).[14]

Antecedents: At the time of Mexican independence (Extra-state War #304 in 1817 to 1818), Texas was a sparsely populated and poorly administered region of Mexico. The Mexican government adopted policies to encourage immigration to settle Texas, especially by Americans. By the 1830s, settlers from the United States far outnumbered the native Mexicans (approximately 25,000 US colonists with their 5,000 slaves vs. 7,800 Mexicans). Thus the government of Mexico began to restrict further immigration and to assert its control in the region. When the more liberal government of Gen. Antonio López de Santa Anna and Vice President Valentin Gómez Farías came to power in 1832 (Intra-state War #520), the shift initially encouraged the Texans to pursue their goal of greater autonomy as a state within a Mexican federal system (rather than its existing status as an appendage of the state of Coahuila). At that point, the Texans themselves were split, with the majority belonging to the peace camp, which favored autonomy within Mexico, while the newer settlers generally favored outright independence or union with the United States. In 1833, the Texans drafted a state constitution, and Stephen Austin was sent to Mexico City, where he presented the constitution and a list of the Texans' grievances to Santa Anna. Austin was arrested, imprisoned, and ultimately detained for two years.

In the interim, Santa Anna (switching ideological sides) launched a conservative rebellion against Gómez Farías, removing him from office. By the end of May 1835, Santa Anna had defeated the major liberal opposition to his rule (Intra-state War #525.5), proclaimed himself dictator of Mexico, abolished the Constitution of 1824, and ordered troops to be sent to Texas to maintain order. With the more moderate Austin detained in Mexico, the pro-independence faction, or "War Dogs," increased in influence in Texas. Consequently, on June 30, 1835, Texans led by William Barrett Travis began the process of forcing Mexican troops out of Texas and assaulted Mexican troops at Anahuac, forcing their surrender. The move for independence was further fueled by the arrivals in Texas of Stephen Austin and Lorenzo de Zavala, who had been involved in the earlier Federalist opposition to Santa Anna. An informal alliance emerged between the Texans and the Mexican Federalists. Committees in support of Texan independence sprang up throughout the United States, funneling arms and volunteers to the Texan cause. In September, Santa Anna sent 500 reinforcements under the command of his brother-in-law, Brigade Gen. Martín Perfecto de Cós, to maintain order in Texas. Tensions continued to rise as Texas pushed for independence.

Narrative: The centralist faction in Mexico, concluding that only greater central control could prevent the disintegration of the country, began to reassert control over Texas. The first armed engagement of the war occurred on October 2, 1835, when eighty Mexican troops were sent to Gonzales to repossess an old cannon. They were attacked and dispersed by a militia of 150 Texans led by John W. Moore. The initial Texas strategy was to force the army of General Cós out of Texas. The Texan army grew in strength as it marched to San Antonio (or San Antonio de Béxar or Béjar), where most of the Mexican troops were garrisoned. The Texans did not yet have enough strength to attack San Antonio, but they scored several small victories in the outlying areas.

By October 20, the rebels numbered 450 men, and under the leadership of Austin, they laid siege to San Antonio. During the siege, they fought their first real battle at Concepcíon Mission on October 28, where the ninety-two men commanded by Col. James Bowie and Capt. James W. Fannin routed a Mexican force of 275 to 400 men led by General Cós. Though the Texans now had 1,000 men, they were still too few and they lacked cannons needed for a direct attack, so the siege of San Antonio continued.

In November, Texan leaders meeting at Felipe de Austin declared their loyalty to the Mexican Constitution of 1824, a measure designed to appeal to the liberals in Mexico. However, they asserted their right to secede, and by November 12, the Texans had created a provisional government, with the radical Henry Smith as president and Sam Houston as commander of army. The Texans also requested help from the United States, and though America officially remained neutral, volunteers and private aid made their way into Texas. The Texans also tightened their grip on San Antonio. Finally, a reinforced Texan contingent attacked the town, which fell after five days of combat from December 5 to 9, 1835. The 1,100 Mexican troops under General Cós had taken refuge in the Mission San Antonio de Valero (the Alamo), which was then occupied by the Texans as Cós withdrew toward Loredo. In late 1835, Santa Anna prepared to lead personally an expedition against the rebels. He gathered 8,000 to 10,000 men into the Army of Operations and began a march northward to Texas. Disease was rampant among the poorly provisioned government columns; by the time Santa Anna reached Texas, he had only 6,018 men, including reinforcements he gathered along the way. Desiring to avenge Cós's defeat, Santa Anna planned a two-pronged attack against the Alamo. Texan leader Sam Houston, misreading the goal of the Mexican advance, planned to gather the small detachments of Texan forces nearer to Austin. In January 1836, Houston ordered James Bowie to lead a group of thirty men to destroy the Alamo and withdraw. However, Bowie and a number of other Texan commanders chose to ignore Houston's directives and decided to fortify the fort instead. Mexican troops reached the Alamo, defended by 183 men (including David Crockett and the Tennessee Mounted Volunteers), on February 23, 1836. For several days the Mexicans bombarded the fort with artillery, and finally, on March 6, the Mexicans stormed the Alamo from all four sides. All the Texan troops were lost, while the Mexican suffered seventy-eight battle-deaths, though more also subsequently died from their wounds.

Though the loss of the Alamo was not strategically significant, it had widespread political ramifications, solidifying the sentiments in favor of Texan independence. After the Alamo, Santa Anna dispersed his army to pursue the rebels, which caused many settlers to flee in what became known as the "Runaway Scrape." It also reduced the Texans' hope for a negotiated settlement. In early 1836, a group of fifty Texan emissaries had been sent on an expedition to create an alliance with the Mexican Federalists against Santa Anna. However at San Patricio on February 27, 1836, virtually the entire 50-man force was captured or killed by a 400-man Mexican contingent led by Mexican general José Urrea. Subsequently, a group of Texans meeting in Washington, D.C., declared complete independence on March 2, 1836, elected David G. Burnet as president and Lorenzo de Zavala as vice president, and reaffirmed Sam Houston as the commander of the army.

Santa Anna continued his advance by dividing his army into four parts: one group remained in San Antonio; the other three were to move eastward (one to the north, one in the center, and one to the south), confronting rebel forces while marching to reunite near San Filipe de Austin. Santa Anna assigned the southern route to his most competent commander, General Urrea. Urrea defeated rebel forces in a string of battles, including the Battle of Coleto Creek, on March 18, 1836. After suffering heavy loses, the Americans under James Fannin surrendered unconditionally on March 20. Despite Urrea's requests for clemency, Santa Anna then ordered that all the Texans (approximately 390 men) be executed on March 27 in what also became known as the Golidad Massacre. Sam Houston's forces were the only organized resistance remaining. Houston used his movement eastward to rebuild his army, and once it reached 800 men, Houston turned to confront the Mexicans. On April 20, Santa Anna and about 1,000 soldiers encountered Houston's small force near the San Jacinto River outside New Washington, and they skirmished throughout the day. The Mexicans were later reinforced by the arrival of troops under the command of General Cós, increasing the Mexican army to 1,500 troops. Santa Anna kept his men up all night awaiting an attack by Houston, but Houston waited until the following afternoon to attack and caught Santa Anna's men unprepared. The battle on April 21, 1836, lasted only eighteen minutes, but Houston's men continued to slaughter government soldiers for hours. The rebels suffered only 8 fatalities, while 650 of Santa Anna's men were killed and 730 taken prisoner.[15]

Termination and Outcome: Gen. Santa Anna fled from the battle of San Jacinto, and on the following day, April 22, 1836, he was apprehended, dressed as a private, by a small group of Texans. Santa Anna was taken to meet Houston (who had been wounded in the battle). After several hours of negotiations, Santa Anna agreed to sign an order for all Mexican troops to evacuate Texas, which marked the end of the war. General Cós was captured on the April 24. Santa Anna remained a captive, and on May 14, 1836, at Velasco, Texas, he and David G. Burnet (the interim president of the Republic of Texas, Lone Star Republic) signed two documents, known as the Treaties of Velasco, which officially concluded the war and began the process of recognizing Texan independence. The new government of President José Justo Corro disavowed any commitments made by Santa Anna. The Republic of Texas was recognized by the United States, Britain, France, the Netherlands, and Belgium. In 1837, Santa Anna was allowed to return to Mexico. Mexico did not formally recognize Texas's status and ultimate annexation by the United States until the Treaty of Guadalupe Hildago, which ended the Mexican–American War in 1848 (Inter-state War #7).

Coding Decisions: As noted in Chapter 2, when determining whether the non-state participant in the war is a geopolitical unit (GPU) or a non-state armed group (NSA), an indicative element is whether the GPU has developed a government structure. In this case, Texas had created a provisional government on whose behalf the army was acting. Thus Texas is coded as the war participant (e.g., in contrast to coding the Texas secessionists as the primary actor).

As per most wars, there are varying estimates of battle-related deaths. For instance, at the second battle at the Alamo, Mexican deaths have been reported as between 78 and 1,500. For the Mexican government, we estimate 1,500 battle-deaths. Texan battle-deaths have been estimated at 314, though nearly another 400 prisoners taken by the government were executed after their capture, producing an estimated total of 700 Texan deaths. This produces a figure of 2,200 total battle-deaths, which still may be an underestimate, given the heavy losses to disease suffered by the central government

Sources: Alessio Robles (1945–1946); Archer (2000); Axelrod (2007); Bancroft (1885); Calcott (1936); Callcott (1964); Clodfelter (1992, 2002); Davis (2004); DePalo (1997); Fowler (2000a); Frost (1882); Jacques (2006); Marley (1998); Meyer and Beezley (2000); Meyer, Sherman and Deeds (1999); Phillips and Axelrod (2005); Priestley (1926); Scheina (2003a); Schlarman (1950/1951); Stephenson (1921).

INTRA-STATE WAR #532.5

Tampico Revolt of 1838 to 1839 (aka Tamaulipas Campaign or Third Federalist Revolt)

Participants: Mexico versus Military (federalist) Rebels led by Gen. José Urrea and Gen. José Antonio Mejía.
Dates: May 1838 to June 5, 1839.
Battle-related Deaths: Mexico—900; Rebels—800. (See Coding Decisions.)
Initiator: Military Rebels led by Gen. José Urrea.
Outcome: Mexico wins.
War Type: Civil for central control.
Total System Member Military Personnel: Government of Mexico: 25,000.[16]
Theater Armed Forces: Mexico: 3,200 (Canalizo—1,100, Valencia—1,600, and Federal Military—500); Rebels: [ ].

Antecedents: One result of the Mexican defeat in the Texan War of 1835 to 1836 (Intra-state War #526) was Gen. Antonio López de Santa Anna's loss of the Mexican presidency. Santa Anna had been captured by the Texans in 1836 at the Battle of San Jacinto, though by November of that year, he was released from custody and allowed to go to the United States, where he offered to try to negotiate a compromise over Texas. Because Santa Anna was no longer an official government representative, the United States rejected his proposal. Meanwhile, in Mexico, Anastasio Bustamante (who had served as president from 1830 to 1832 and had been ousted by a revolt that led to the election of Santa Anna and Valentin Gómez Farías as president and vice president in 1832; see Intra-state War #520) was recalled from exile, was reelected president, and took office on April 19, 1837, supposedly for an eight-year term. Santa Anna was allowed to return to his hacienda, Manga de Clavo, in Veracruz. However, it would not be long before Santa Anna would reenter the political fray, and his successes would lead him to be hailed as "the Hero of Tampico, Veracruz, and Acajete."[17]

Bustamante had been elected on the basis of a conservative platform that promised to regain Texas and restore law and order by creating a strong central government. However, when the promises were not fulfilled, an opposition grew among a wide spectrum of political groups, from conservative groups and the Mexican military to the liberal federalists. Outbreaks of resistance occurred in the states of Jalisco, San Luis Potosi, Coahuila, and Tamaulipas, which included the port of Tampico.

Narrative: After having served in the war of Texan Independence (Intra-state War #527 from 1835 to 1836), Gen. José Urrea was appointed to the position of the commandant general of the distant Northwest state of Sonora. Feeling underappreciated as he had not been named governor as well, Urrea led an army into the neighboring state of Sinaloa to increase support for the federalist cause. Bustamante responded by sending an army under General Paredes against Urrea. The two forces met at Mazatlán (in Sonora) in May 1838, where Urrea's army was defeated. Urrea fled southward to Durango and then eastward to the coastal state of Tamaulipas to continue the rebellion in the port city of Tampico. Bustamante countered by sending Gen. Valentín Canalizo's division of 1,100 troops to confront the rebels at Tampico. On November 30, Canalizo attacked but was beaten back, losing 500 soldiers.

At the same time, Bustamante was facing an additional threat posed by the French in what would be called the Pastry War of 1838 (not a war under the COW criteria). The French government had submitted a claim to Mexico on behalf of a pastry chef whose goods had been taken by a group of Mexican soldiers in 1828. The bill was resubmitted in 1838, and when it was not paid, France dispatched two naval fleets to blockade the ports of Veracruz and Tampico. The French bombardment of Veracruz began on November 27, 1838. Being nearby when French forces landed, Santa Anna offered his services to the Mexican army and was able to rally the troops to repulse the invaders. During the confrontation, Santa Anna's leg was injured so severely that it had to be amputated, and public sympathy restored Santa Anna's popularity. Santa Anna had himself carried on a litter into the capital, arriving on February 17, 1839.

Meanwhile, at Tampico, Urrea joined forces with Gen. José Antonio Mejía, who had been part of the federalist opposition to Santa Anna in 1834 and 1835. Returning from exile, Mejía landed in Tampico on January 3, 1839, and became the second in command of the rebel forces. Bustamante took personal command of the government forces confronting the federalist rebels. On March 18, 1839, Bustamante appointed Santa Anna as interim president, and the next day, he left to join Gen. Mariano Arista, who was assembling an army at San Luís Potosí (north of the capital) to advance eastward against Tampico. In April, before Bustamante and Arista could get to Tampico, Generals Urrea and Mejía left a rebel contingent under Gen. Ignacio Escalada in Tampico, marched southward to seize the fortress at Puebla, which was eighty miles east of Mexico City, and controlled the road from the capital to Veracruz. Santa Anna quickly mobilized 500 troops from the Federal District and 1,600 troops from the Puebla garrison under General Valencia to confront the rebels. Santa Anna had himself carried on his litter to join the government forces at Puebla, and his arrival persuaded the garrison not to defect to the rebels. On May 3, 1839, the armies met near Acajete, where Valencia defeated Mejía's force in heavy fighting in which 600 Mexicans died, including General Mejía, who was executed on Santa Anna's orders. Meanwhile General Arista had moved eastward and besieged the rebels at Tampico. General Urrea fled from Puebla back to Tampico to join Escalada's forces. The rebels were severely outnumbered as the city was attacked by a government force of 3,000. The rebels finally surrendered to General Arista's army on June 5, 1839. Urrea fled again and was not apprehended until October of that year.

Termination and Outcome: The government's victory at Acajete reinforced Santa Anna's reputation as a national hero. Though he remained in office for several months, Santa Anna soon tired of the political demands in the capital and once more retired to his hacienda. Bustamante reclaimed the position of president, though challenges to his administration continued to arise. Urrea languished in prison until 1840, when his supporters affected his escape.

Coding Decisions: We have been able to find only a few mentions of battle-deaths for this war: government losses of 500 at Tampico and total combatant deaths of 600 at Acajete. Figures have not been found for two other major battles: Mazatlán and the second battle of Tampico. Thus our best guess of total battle-deaths is 900 sustained by Mexico and 800 for the rebel forces.

Sources: DePalo (1997); Estep (2013); Jaques (2007); Moseley (1991); Scheina (2002); Scheina (2003a).

INTRA-STATE WAR #541
Triangular Revolt of 1841 (aka Federalist Revolt)

Participants: Mexico versus Military Rebels.
Dates: August 31, 1841, to October 6, 1841.
Battle-related Deaths: Mexico—700; Military Rebels—500.
Initiator: Military Rebels.
Outcome: Military Rebels win.
War Type: Civil for central control.
Total System Member Military Personnel: Government of Mexico: 20,000;[18] Loyalists Mexican forces were 17,000.[19]
Theater Armed Forces: Government of Mexico: 1,000 (initial); 3,500 to 4,500 (peak).[20]
Military Rebel forces: Parades began with 700[21] (initial total of Paredes, Cortázar, and Juvera was 2,200)[22] with Valencia: 1,200, Santa Anna: 1,500[23] and peak united rebel forces: 9,000.[24]

Antecedents: After his victory over the military rebellion in 1839 (Intra-state War #532.5), General Santa Anna served as president for several months but soon retired once more to his estate, leaving Anastasio Bustamante as acting president. Bustamante's tenure continued to be tumultuous due to the widespread resentment about Bustamante's centralist constitution, the failure to regain Texas, and the general lack of economic progress. A Federalist revolt occurred in 1840, when Gen. José Urrea (who had escaped from prison) joined Valentine Gómez Farías in a federalist *pronunciamento.* On July 15, 1840, the federalists seized Mexico City and briefly captured Bustamante, though the revolt ended with the rebels accepting exile. Revolts also took place in the southern states of Yucatán and Tabasco. Mexico's need to raise funds led to increasing taxes on property owners and businesses, and their resentment about the increasing financial demands precipitated this war. In January 1841, civic leaders in the west-central state of Jalisco petitioned the congress to abolish taxes on foreign goods. Disgruntled Guadalajara merchants also sent appeals to Santa Anna and Gen. Parades y Arrillaga, the state's preeminent caudillo, urging them to organize the opposition to Bustamante. Paredes began talks with Gen. Gabriel Valencia (Bustamante's chief of staff) and Santa Anna against the president. Paredes acted first by issuing his *pronunciamiento* of Guadalajara on August 8, 1841, which described his plans for a new government. Parades gathered an army of 1,100 men, and leaving two companies to guard the city, he and his contingent of 700 men began to march from Guadalajara eastward toward Guanajuato (northwest of Mexico City.)

Minister of War Juan Nepomuceno Almonte summoned the loyalist generals to the capital. On August 24, Santa Anna entered the fray from the eastern state of Veracruz through a letter to Minister of War Almonte in which he accused Bustamante of betraying the 1824 Constitution. On August 27, Santa Anna gave orders to stop the Veracruz customs house from sending collected duties to the capital, and he then travel northward toward Perote, where an army of 1,500 men awaited him.

Narrative: On August 31, General Valencia joined the rebellion, taking control of Mexico City's *Cuidadela* arsenal and its 1,200-man army. Bustamante, surprised by the defection of his once-loyal ally, led a column toward the *Cuidadela.* Military cadets marched to join Valencia, while loyalist troops occupied buildings around the palace. The next day, September 1, 1841, Valencia turned the guns of the *Cuidadela* barracks against the palace. Bustamante began to organize the defense of the regime. On September 4, 1841, Valencia issued a *pronunciamento* against the government, outlining the evils practiced by the government and the resolution of the military to act for the common good. The proclamation described the actions that Generals Santa Anna, Parades, Pedro de Cortázar, and Julián Juvera were talking in support of the rebellion. In the capital, the government had established a semicircular line around the palace, while the rebels had advanced from the *Cuidadela*, seizing strategic buildings. Heavy bombardment began between the forces.

This was basically a war between conservative centralist groups because many of the rebels ultimately favored a military dictatorship led by Santa Anna. The movement spread rapidly as regional *caudillos* announced support for General Valencia, who was still in command of Mexico City's garrison. On September 9, Santa Anna began his march to the capital, gaining reinforcements and seizing the fortress at Puebla along the way. He also issued his Plan of Perote (written on September 9 but published in pamphlet form as an open letter to Bustamante on September 13) in which he justified the rebellion as necessary to restore a strong central government. The period of September 10 to 14 was marked by an increasing number of defections of military leaders to the side of the rebels. In the capital, some of the junior officers stood with the president; the two military factions split the capital, and their artillery exchanges destroyed palaces and killed hundreds of civilians.

Bustamante crafted a compromise to create a new tripartite executive, consisting of Bustamante, Nicolás Bravo (president of the government council), and Santa Anna. The offer was communicated to the three primary rebel leaders on September 13 but was not accepted. So that Bustamante could personally take command of the loyalist forces, he turned over executive power to interim president Javier Echeverría on September 23, 1841. Bustamante, with the support of Gen. Valentín Canalizo and Minister of War Almonte, was making gradual progress against the rebels in the capital. On September 19, Bustamante ordered General Torrejon, who had been restraining Santa Anna near Puebla, to return with his 900 troops to the capital. Bustamante placed himself in command of the united armies (now numbering 3,500–4,000 men). Bustamante then divided his forces, and he marched out of the capital on September 20 to meet Parades, while Almonte moved against Santa Anna. The initial round of talks between the loyalist and rebel leaders produced no agreement. On September 28, the rebel trio issued the Plan of Tacubaya (*Bases de Tacubaya*), which called for Santa Anna to assume power provisionally. On October 1, 1841, the government declared its opposition to the Plan of Tacubaya.

From October 2 to 4, the level of conflict in the capital rose, with canons bombarding the city and heavy street fighting. Much of the old city was severely damaged. Santa Anna withdrew to the outskirts of Piedad a la Viga, where there were bloody skirmishes with Bustamante's troops, and the loyalists were routed on October 3, 1848. Bustamante began to realize the weakness of his position: he returned to the capital, left 100 men to guard the palace, and withdrew his army to Guadalupe.

Termination and Outcome: On October 5, rebel soldiers surrounded the palace and allowed the government troops to surrender. Santa Anna and Bustamante met at Punta del Río on October 5, and Santa Anna offered Bustamante a chance to surrender. On October 6, Bustamante accepted the *Bases de Tacubaya* and resigned. Santa Anna entered the capital on October 7, becoming interim president on October 9, 1841. A new constituent congress was elected, dominated by federalists who wanted to curtail the power of central government and the army. Santa Anna once again handed over power to an interim president, Nicolás Bravo, who was tasked with dissolving the congress on December 19, 1842. A revised constitution, the *Bases Orgánicas*, adopted on June 13, 1843, kept Santa Anna as president but restricted his dictatorial powers somewhat. Gradually the military was persuaded to rebel against Santa Anna. His erstwhile ally General Paredes revolted on November 1, 1844, and Santa Anna was deposed on December 16, 1844. Eventually Santa Anna was given amnesty and fled to exile in Havana in May 1845. His exile did not last long, and in December 1846, Congress once again appointed Santa Anna as president. However, Mexico's loss in the Mexican–American War of 1846 to 1847 (Inter-state War #7) again led to Santa Anna's exile.

Coding Decisions: We have been unable to locate any real fatality statistics for this war. The journal of Madame Fanny Calderón de la Barca, the wife of the first Spanish ambassador to Mexico, includes numerous descriptions of heavy cannonading and fighting during the war. Costeloe refers to "many casualties" from the cannon fire (similar to the 1840 war with 700 deaths), though this war was longer. This war also involved significant conflicts outside the city. Thus, our best guess for this war is that there were 1,200 battle deaths, with 700 suffered by the government and 500 by the rebels.

Sources: Archer (2000); Calderón de la Barca (1843); Costeloe (1988); DePalo (1997); Fehrenbach (1973); Fisher and Fisher (1970); Fowler (2000b); Fowler (2007); Fowler (2012); Lynch (1992); Meyer, Sherman, and Deeds (2003); Moseley (1991); Robinson (1847); Scheina (2002); Scheina (2003a); Vazquez-Gomez (1997).

INTRA-STATE WAR #545
Mayan Caste War phase 1 of 1847 to 1848

Participants: Mayans versus Yucatán.
Dates: January 15, 1847, to August 16, 1848.
Battle-related Deaths: Yucatán: [ ]; Mayans: [ ].
Total Deaths: Combatants and civilians: 100,000. (See Coding Decisions.)
Initiator: Mayans.
Outcome: Transformed into Intra-state War #553.
War Type: Regional Internal.
Theater Armed Forces: Armed forces of Yucatán: National Guard: 17,000 (peak)[25] aided by American mercenaries: 250 peak; Mayans with Yaqui allies: 40,000 to 50,000 (peak).[26]

Antecedents: Caste wars are defined as regional uprisings of Indian villagers directed at the expulsion or elimination of non-Indian authorities. In Mexico, these large-scale revolts took place in both the northern and southern regions. The Mayan Caste war was "the bloodiest uprising by a native people of the Americas since the original European conquests in the sixteenth century."[27] It is divided here into two distinct phases and two wars due to the nature of the participants. In the first phase, the Mayans are fighting against the Yucatán government, and in the second, the conflict pits the Mayans against the government of Mexico.

One of the vestiges of Spanish rule over Mexico was the development of a stratified society with the *peninsulares*, or those of Spanish descent born in Spain, at the peak; followed by the *criollos*, those of Spanish descent born in Mexico; the *mestizos* of mixed European and native ancestry; and *indios*—or Indians. The term *ladinos* also was used as a collective word to refer to those of Spanish culture. The wars in the Yucatán have their roots in two conflicts: (1) between the Yucatán *ladinos* and the central government of Mexico and (2) Maya Indians (who suffered under the repressive caste system) against the *ladinos*.

After Mexico became independent of Spain (Extra-state War #304), the Mexican Empire disintegrated into independent states. The first Republic of Yucatán was declared on May 29, 1823, though it joined the Federal Republic of the United Mexican States on December 23, 1823, with a special status as the Federated Republic of Yucatán. The Yucatán was one of the states that favored a federal form of government structure. As President Santa Anna shifted from his earlier support of federalism to creating a more centralized government, the ruling class of Yucatán resented its loss of autonomy (in 1835 the status of Yucatán had been changed to a department), increased tariffs, and the recruitment of Yucatecans to fight against the rebellion in Texas (Intra-state War #527, 1835 to 1836).

Consequently, Santiago Imán y Villafaña, a *criollo* and son of a wealthy family, began a movement to gain the Yucatán's independence from Mexico. Imán created a government in Tizimín, and on May 2, 1839, Imán launched a liberal rebellion against the central government of Mexico. With the aid of the Mayans, who constituted 75 to 80 percent of the population, the rebels defeated the remaining Mexican troops at Campeche in June 1840. Yucatán declared its independence on October 1, 1841, with Santiago Méndez Ibarra as its governor. After General Santa Anna seized power from President Bustamante in early October 1841 (Intra-state War #541), he sent Andrés Quintana Roo to persuade Yucatán to rejoin Mexico. When Yucatán refused, Santa Anna began to take steps to reestablish Mexican control over the Yucatán (which is an extra-state conflict). On August 26, 1842, a small Mexican force landed, and Yucatán was able to raise an army of 6,000 by again appealing to the Mayans. Ultimately, the Mexicans offered to withdraw if favorable terms could be negotiated. In the treaty of December 1843, Yucatán ultimately rejoined Mexico on the government's terms, as a department, on January 1844.

After Gen. Joaquín Herrera staged a coup against Santa Anna in December 1844, relations between Mexico and Yucatán continued to deteriorate, and on January 1, 1846, Yucatán's assembly in Mérida declared its independence from Mexico. The department's Mexican-appointed governor, José Tiburcio López, resigned. The Yucatán assembly then elected Miguel Barbachano as provisional governor. In the meantime, Mexico's President Herrera had been overthrown by Gen. Mariano Paredes, and Mexico became embroiled in the Mexican–American War

(Inter-state War #7). The war led to growing demands for the return of Santa Anna, and on his way back from exile in Cuba, Santa Anna stopped in Yucatán to talk with Governor Barbachano. He offered generous terms if Yucatán would rejoin Mexico. Barbachano agreed, and the Yucatán legislature ratified this decision at the end of October 1846.

This agreement was not universally popular. The *ladino* citizens of the southwest areas around Campeche revolted against the Yucatán government at Mérida (in the north of the peninsula) on November 2, 1846. The Campeche rebels chose Domingo Barret as their leader. Barret was able to secure the allegiance of the Yucatán Light Battalion and the Sixteenth Battalion of Campeche, which marched against the Yucatán government in Mérida under the leadership of Antonio Trujeque. The Mayans had become convinced that having their own territory was necessary to retain their way of life. Thus the Campeche rebels were able to assemble an army of approximately 600 *indios* (mostly Mayans with some Yaqui) to march against Mérida. However, on November 26, under pressure from former governor Santiago Méndez, who had not supported the revolt, the rebels rescinded their independence proclamation and returned back to Campeche.

Narrative: A new independence proclamation was issued in Campeche on December 8, 1846, and this time, with Santiago Méndez supporting the rebels, civil conflict against the Yucatán government spread. In January 1847, the rebels (*ladino* and Mayan) under the command of Col. Antonio Trujeque and Juan Vázquez set up an ambush outside of Peto to trap the Barbachanista army. As the rebels attacked, the government army fled or surrendered. This victory reinforced the Mayan sense of the efficacy of their armed interventions. Meanwhile, at Tabi, a Barbachano unit assassinated local Mayan leaders in what has been described as the "first race-based atrocity."[28] Three days later, on January 15, 1847, the Mayan troops (about 66 percent of this 2,000-strong rebel force) under Colonel Trujeque attacked the city of Valladolid. Though the attack had begun as a military advance, at one point, the *degüello* was sounded, meaning "attack without quarter," and the Mayans began attacking the *ladinos* throughout the city. This marks a shift in the leadership of the revolt from the *ladinos*-led Campeche militia to the Mayans and thus really signals the start of the Mayan Caste War.

The violence in Valladolid continued for six days, during which at least eighty-five civilians were killed. On January 18, a rebel force, led by the newly appointed Lt. Bonifacio Novela, attacked the Yucatán garrison at Sisal. Meanwhile, Barbachano, who was trapped in the capital city of Mérida, surrendered on January 22, 1847, and then fled to Havana. Barret began the process of trying to consolidate the Yucatán government, which moved to Mérida on June 23. The Mayan revolt spread to the interior, including Mayan attacks on individual *ladino* haciendas and towns, and hundreds of *ladinos* were killed in their major settlements. Gradually the *ladino* rebels withdrew from the conflict and in some cases assisted the government fighting against their former Mayan allies. The Mayans were now increasingly organized as never before under the leadership of Jacinto Pat and Cecilio Chi. The Yucatán government sought to bring together the earlier competing factions. Both the Mayans and other forces engaged in attacks against civilians.

In December 1847, the Mayans continued their advance eastward and began to encircle Valladolid. The government's 2,500-soldier garrison at Ichmul resisted the Mayan siege from December 5, 1847, to February 6, 1848, leading to 1,000 Yucatán battle-deaths.[29] That month, an attempt at mediation between Barbachano and Jacinto Pat was sidelined by an attack of 2,000 Mayans against Chancenote (near Valladolid), in which the majority of the residents were slaughtered and the Mayans lost 1,500. The Mayans continued their victories in February and March. After the fall of Ichmul, the Mayans, who had a growing number of recruits, split their forces into regional groups, with the southern group under Jacinto Pat heading to Peto, while the 15,000 Mayans under Cecilio Chi besieged Valladolid (and its 1,500 soldiers). Valladolid was abandoned by its *ladino* population (of 10,000) on March 19, 1848. By March 25, the Yucatán government was facing total military collapse. The Yucatán government under Méndez sought aid from three foreign powers—Spain, Britain, and the United States—offering sovereignty over Yucatán in exchange. Though Yucatán did receive some supplies from the Spanish in Cuba, no significant assistance was approved by the United States, though a group of 250 American mercenaries did fight for Yucatán for several months. Méndez finally resigned on March 27 in favor of Barbachano, his former rival, with whom the Mayans were willing to negotiate. Babachano had two priests conduct the peace talks, and they came to terms with Mayan leader Jacinto Pat. On April 23, 1848, the governor of Yucatán ratified their agreement in the Treaty of Tzucacab in Ticul, though other Mayan leaders, including Cecilio Chi, rejected the terms.

Fighting continued, and May 1848 saw further government losses as the Mayans advanced along a long front around the capital, Mérida. In the southwest, on May 20, 1848, the local government forces withdrew inside the walls of Campeche, where they were able to withstand numerous assaults. On May 26, the Yucatán garrison at Ticul was overrun, and most of its 1,800 defenders were killed. That was quickly followed by the collapse of Yucatán garrisons at Izamal in the east (on May 28) and Balcalar (on May 28). By the end of the month, the Mayans occupied 80 percent of the peninsula and had driven most of the *ladinos* into the towns of Mérida and Campeche. When the Mayans were on the verge of capturing Mérida, they halted their advance, though the reason for the retreat is a matter of contestation among scholars. This gave the Yucatán government time to rebuild its forces. Mexico was now free of its war with the United States (Inter-state War #7) and was able to begin supplying the Yucatán government with arms. The Yucatán government forces then went on the offensive in June, recapturing Ticul on June 7, 1848, and forcing the Mayan troops to retreat. Further advances in July allowed the Yucatán government to regain control of almost half the territory it had lost.

Termination and Outcome: However, by mid-1848, it had become clear to the Yucatán government that it had been unable to defeat the Mayans and that it needed the assistance of the Mexican government to continue the war. On August 17, 1848, Governor Barbachano again affirmed that Yucatán was part of Mexico and asked for direct assistance. This marks the end of the first phase of the Mayan Caste War (this regional internal war), as the primary combatant on one side shifted from the government of a regional subunit (Yucatán) to that of the central Mexican government. When the fighting resumed, it was thus a new civil war (Intra-state War #553).

Coding Decisions: We follow rebel leader Colonel Trujeque in starting the Caste War with the Mayan attack on Valladolid in January 1847, though other scholars (including Clodfelter and Alexander) use July 30, 1847, as the start date.

The coding of this intra-state war as a Regional Internal War (War Type 6) is based on the determination of the major combatants in the conflict and their status at the time of the start of the war. In January 1846, the department of Yucatán declared its independence from Mexico, and COW has coded Yucatán as an autonomous entity at this point. If the Caste War had begun then, it would have been a non-state war. However, the decision to rejoin Mexico was ratified by the Yucatán legislature on October 1846, and the Yucatán was once again part of Mexico when the war began in January 1847. As the war took place inside the boundaries of Mexico, it is an intra-state war, and because Yucatán was clearly the major war participant, operating in its own interests and with its own armed forces, the war is coded as a Regional Internal War. This war ends when the Mexican government takes over the bulk of the fighting against the Mayans, which begins the second phase of the conflict (Intra-state War #553), which is classified as a civil war.

The only specific battle-death figures we located were for a couple of the major battles (Ichmul and Valladolid). Thus, while there are no specific estimates of total battle-deaths (of combatants), the scale of the killing was enormous as the result of disease, famine, and the large number of attacks on civilians by both sides. Dumond estimates that between 1846 and 1851, 100,000 people from Yucatán died.[30] Clodfelter suggests a higher figure of 147,000 people that had died by 1850.[31] Scheina notes that the population of the Yucatán declined by 247,000 persons between 1846 and 1850.[32] Because we have been unable to devise any way to calculate the battle-deaths of the combatants for the two sides, we are merely reporting the estimate of 100,000 total deaths to indicate the magnitude of the war.

Sources: Alexander (2004); Angel (1993); Clodfelter (2002); Coatsworth (1988); Dumond (1997); Fitchen (1979); Ortega (1988); Reed (2001); Rugeley (1996, 2009); Scheina (2003a).

INTRA-STATE WAR #553

Mayan Caste War phase 2 of 1848 to 1855 (aka Mayan Revolt)

Participants: Mexico, with the *ladino* forces of Yucatán, and American mercenaries versus Yucatán Mayans.

Dates: August 17, 1848, to March 4, 1855.
Battle-related Deaths: Armed Forces of Mexico: [ ]; *ladino* forces of Yucatán: [ ]; American mercenaries: 220 to 420;[33] Mayans, aka *Cruzob* (Rebel Army): [ ]. (See Coding Decisions.)
Initiator: Mexico.
Outcome: Mexico wins.
War Type: Civil for local issues.
Total System Member Military Personnel: Armed Forces of Mexico: 21,000[34]; a total of Mexican armed forces and the *ladino* forces of Yucatán were 24,500 (initial); 43,000 (final).[35]
Theater Armed Forces: Armed Forces of Mexico: 279 (initial—1,850);[36] combined with the *ladino* forces of Yucatán and *hidalgo* Indian allies: 15,000 (initial);[37] 17,000 (in 1849);[38] *indios*: 11,684 peak;[39] American mercenaries: 938.[40] Mayans, aka *Cruzob* (Rebel Army) and Yaqui Indian allies: 30,000 (prewar); 14,000 (initial); 80,000 (peak); 12,000 (final).[41]

Antecedents: This conflict was viewed by Yucatán *ladinos* (inhabitants of Spanish culture) less as a war between rival governments and more as a race war (hence its name) between the ruling *ladinos* and the native Mayan *indios*. The Mayans rebelled against their treatment under the *ladino*-controlled Yucatán government. The resulting conflict caused horrific fatalities among the combatants and the civilian population. It endured at war level for eight years and then at lower combat levels for another forty-six years.

This was the second phase of the Mayan Caste War. The first phase (Intra-state War #545 of 1847 to 1848) was a regional war of the Mayans against the government of a regional subunit, the Mexican province of Yucatán. When the Yucatán officials realized that they could not defeat the revolt, they asked for the assistance of the Mexican government on August 17, 1848, thus ending Yucatán's move toward independence. The Mexican government was now in a position to provide significant assistance. In the Mexican–American War (Inter-state War #7), Mexico had lost one-third of its territory to the United States, which through the treaty of Guadalupe Hidalgo (February 2, 1848), provided $15 million in compensation. Mexico utilized a portion of those funds to buy guns and ammunition that it shipped to Campeche to assist in the fight against the Mayans. From that point, the Yucatán government was then fighting with and on behalf of the Mexican government, and the war was thus transformed into this war, a civil war of the central government against an internal armed group (civil for local issues, or War Type 6). Heavy fighting resumed and lasted for another six and a half years.

Narrative: The day after the agreement with Mexico, Yucatán's governor José Tiburcio López Barbachano launched military campaigns in the northern sector of the peninsula, both eastward and toward the south. The *ladino* government of Yucatán was able to reorganize and rearm its army with assistance from the Mexican government. Under the leadership of Gen. Sebastian Lopez de Llergo, the army recruited about 10,000 *hidalgos*, or loyal Indians, to help fight the Mayan rebels. The government army faced several Mayan forces, one of them 9,000 strong. In the northern sector, the government forces were able to dislodge the rebels near the northeastern city of Valladolid. However, in the east-central region, the rebels were more successful. On September 8, 1848, Yaxcabá, which was under the control of the Yucatán government, was attacked by a Mayan force led by Cecilio Chi, Vanancio Pec, Florentino Chan, Crescencio Poot, and Cosme Damián Pech. The Mayan army captured the city, and the government troops retreated. However, such rebel successes were short-lived.

In 1848, the Yucatán governor had offered Yucatán sovereignty to Spain, Britain, or the United States to present a Mayan victory. Though none of the foreign powers accepted, the Yucatán government did receive assistance from American mercenaries under the leadership of Capt. George White, who landed at Sisal (on the northern coast) in October 1848. The American preference for frontal assaults against Mayan positions meant that 220 to 420 Americans were killed in their first few battles. Most of the remaining Americans returned home by November, though 140 of them stayed and participated in conflicts around the southern city of Bacalar. The Yucatecan government launched an offensive in November 1848 to drive the Mayans out of the towns they had captured in 1847, and the Yucatán forces retook Tizimín on November 3. Meanwhile, south of the capital, approximately 5,000 Mayans loyal to Jacinto Pat besieged government forces at Tekax from October 6 till it was abandoned to government troops in December. December 1848 marked a series of government successes. On December 25, government forces succeeded in retaking Valladolid and by the end of the month had succeeded in recapturing most of the territory it had lost. The Mayans retreated further south and east, which would become their strongholds. That period also saw the death of one of the preeminent, most committed Mayan leaders, Cecilio Chi.

In early 1849, the Mayans attacked the central towns of Tihosuco, Saban, and Tituc, but by May, the government captured the southern port of Bacalar, cutting off the supply of foreign gunpowder to the Mayans from the bordering British Honduras (now Belize). At this point, the lines of a stalemate began to emerge. The general government strategy (developed by General Llergo) was to encircle the Mayans and gradually fortify or destroy the jungle that sheltered them. While the government forces were able to seize towns, they had great difficulty penetrating the dense jungles of the east, where the Mayans were able to retreat to relative safety when outnumbered. A second of the original Mayan leaders, Jacinto Pat, was assassinated in September 1849, and the Mayan rebels became fragmented, with leadership now being claimed *inter alia* by José María Barrera, Venancio Pec, and Florentino Chan. At the end of the year, Governor Barbachano sent priests as a peace delegation to the Mayan leaders. The Mayan leaders proposed thirteen conditions for ending the rebellion; however, the government's army (now numbering 17,000) felt that the rebels were almost defeated and was not willing to settle.

The government of Mexico dispatched Gen. Manuel Micheltorena to develop a new strategy to win the war. Micheltorena arrived in April 1850, when the fragmented rebels were more difficult to subdue. The Mayan forces had grown into columns of a thousand each, which would unite periodically and then disperse. Micheltorena formalized the strategy already in use of the *línea*, that is, a front from Tizimin in the northeast then southward and westward. The government forces would attempt to push the rebels back to the jungles eastward. However, in the jungle, the conflict became a war of attrition. The Mayans retreated further toward the jungle in the east and created a new base at Chan Santa Cruz (Cruz Chen), which became the focal point of the resistance. One of the Mayan commanders was José María Barrera, who had been one of Jacinto Pat's field commanders. As he led his band into the forest, they stopped by a tree into which a cross had been carved. It was there that the spiritual movement that revitalized the Mayans was born. One of Barrera's band was Juan de La Cruz Puc, who heard voices coming from the tree, and he was transformed, he claimed, so that he spoke as the Cross. One of the commandments of the Cross was that the Mayans would win the war. Those who responded to the message (or the followers of the Speaking Cross) came to be called the *Cruzob*, and they proved to be the hard core of the Mayan revolt. The *Cruzob*, believing that they had immunity from bullets, attacked the Yucatán army at Kampocolche on January 4, 1851.

The war continued, with each side winning engagements but unable to make strategic progress. Micheltorena was replaced on May 15, 1851, by Mexican Gen. Rómulo Díaz de la Vega. He devised a defensive strategy that relied more on Mexican troops. A major Mexican offensive began on February 19, 1852, that consisted of dividing the army into five columns: one that advanced to the northeast, three that advanced toward the center, and the final one, led by General Vega, that advanced southward to Chan Santa Cruz and then on to Bacalar. The army succeeded in seizing Chan Santa Cruz, and the army's advance was seen as a major success. However, as the Mexican offensive continued south, the Mayans attacked in Kampolche, Tekax, and Tepich. Nonetheless, the war was taking a toll on both sides, and ten Mayan commanders approached the British in British Honduras to serve as mediators in peace negotiations in August and September 1853. A peace treaty was signed on September 16, 1853, between the rebels, now referred to as the *Pacificos del Sur* and the Yucatán government. The agreement did split the *Pacificos*, who represented 25 percent of rebels, from the majority.

The *Cruzob* were still a potent fighting force and attacked into the Cocomes in 1853. The Mayans defeated several government expeditions in April to June 1854 and in early 1855.

Termination and Outcome: In late 1854, Santa Anna recalled Governor Vega to assist in suppressing a rebellion in Mexico, and the military campaign in Yucatán began to wind down, though it remained at war-level fatalities till March 1855. The government declared an "official" end to the war on March 4, 1855. The war ended with no decisive results and in a sense was a stalemate because a large group of

Maya remained free of government control. Yet, the war is coded as a Mexican victory because the effort to drive *ladinos* out of the province and achieve autonomy for all of the Yucatán Mayans failed. By the time the war "officially" ended, the "free" Mayans had been reduced from 100,000 to only 40,000. Limited conflict did continue at below-war levels, as did conflict between the liberal and conservative factions in Yucatán. Resistance to the central government finally ended in 1901 (see Intra-state War #639), and some scholars like Clodfelter use 1901 as the end date of the Caste War. In 1858, the state of Yucatán was divided, creating a separate state of Campeche, and in 1902, Yucatán lost the territory that is now the state of Quintana Roo.

Coding Decisions: In terms of the numbers of Mayans, aka *Cruzob* (Rebel Army) and Yaqui Indian allies involved, the estimate for initial strength combines estimates for two different Mayan forces in late 1848. The estimate for final strength is derived from the total number of Mayans in resistance and assumes that the proportion of them who were active combatants remained the same.[42]

In terms of battle-deaths overall, there were 200,000 to 300,000 fatalities, but we cannot determine how many of them qualify as battle-deaths.[43] Just between 1846 and 1851, the total population of Yucatán declined by 40 percent or more than 205,000 individuals.[44]

Sources: Angel (1993); Angel (1997); Bodart (1916); Caplan (2001); Cayley (1856); Clodfelter (1992, 2008); Dumond (1997); Ellis (1976), Godechot (1971); Hamnett (1999); Marley (1998); Parkes (1966); Reed (1964); Reed (2001); Robertson (1952); Rugeley (2009); Scheina (2003a).

INTRA-STATE WAR #558
Puebla War of 1855 to 1856 (aka Plan of Zacapoaxtla)

Participants: Mexico versus Conservative Military.
Dates: December 11, 1855, to March 21, 1856.
Battle-related Deaths: Mexico: 200; Conservative Military: 1,000. (See Coding Decisions.)
Initiator: Military.
Outcome: Mexico wins.
War Type: Civil for central control.
Total System Member Military Personnel: Armed Forces of Mexico: 26,000.[45]
Theater Armed Forces: Mexico: 16,000 (peak); Conservative rebels: 6,000[46] plus 1,000 in Querétaro.

Antecedents: By means of the federalist Triangular Revolt in 1841 (Intra-state War #541), Antonio López de Santa Anna became president of Mexico by overthrowing President Anastasio Bustamante. Santa Anna was then deposed in turn on December 16, 1844, by a military revolt. However, continuing conflict in Mexico, including the buildup to the Mexican–American War of 1846 to 1847 (Inter-state War #7), led to Santa Anna's recall and resumption of the presidency, yet Mexico's loss in that war contributed to Santa Anna being exiled once again. It also was a factor in the founding of the Conservative Party in 1838 by Lucas Alamán. In 1852, another military coup and an appeal from Alamán returned Santa Anna to the presidency, now representing the conservative faction in Mexican politics, which favored a centralized government, and support for the army and the church. Alamán's death in June 1853 removed any restraining influence on Santa Anna.

Santa Anna's primary opposition was from the liberals (or federalists) who favored a more decentralized government structure and a society that was more democratic and secular. Under the federal regimes, many of Mexico's provinces had exercised a great deal of autonomy, generally under the leadership of local strongmen or *caudillos.* One such *caudillo* was Juan Alvarez of the southern state of Guerrero. In February 1854, Alvarez declared himself in opposition to the central government and launched what was known as "the Federalist Revolt" or the "Revolution of Ayutla." Alvarez soon was joined by neighboring provinces of Michoacán, Mexico, Morelos, and Oaxca. While leading to few military battles (this is not considered a war by COW), the growing opposition persuaded Santa Anna to flee into exile in August 1855. Alvarez assumed power and launched what would be known as the Reform period. Though the liberals had come to power with Alvarez, they were split into extreme and moderate factions over the extent of change desired in existing government entities. Gen. Ignacio Comonfort began his tenure as the new minister of war with a restructuring of the army that slashed the number of national garrisons and instead transferred resources to the National Guard, or provincial militias. The more extreme faction, or *puros*, objected that these reforms were insufficient to reduce the power of the army. On November 22, 1855, a second major reform measure, known as Ley Juárez (proposed by Minister of Justice Benito Juárez), created equality of all citizens before the law, eliminating the special privileges enjoyed by the military and the clergy. The conservatives objected to these measures, and several (including Antonio Haro y Tamariz and Javier Miranda, the canon of the Puebla cathedral) began conspiring against the government. On December 2, 1855, army generals Tomás and López Uraga issued plans (Plan of the Sierra Gorda and Plan of Tolimán, respectively) calling for a return to conservative rule and Santa Anna to power. President Alvarez, who did not want to deal with the emerging conflict, resigned, appointing Comonfort as president.

Narrative: As Comonfort took office, on December 11, 1855, he was greeted with an additional series of uprisings, most of which were suppressed quickly. However, one that began in the town of Zacapoaxtla (located in the Puebla Sierra), constituted this war. Parish priest Ortega y Garciá had gathered the local conservative leaders, and crowds began both rioting and fortifying conservative positions. Reputedly, the crowd contained soldiers, under the command of conservative general Francisco Güitián, who were disguised as *paisanos*. The local garrison was able to restore order. In a proclamation dated the next day (December 12, 1855), the rebel leaders declared an opposition to the liberal laws and support of the privileges of the clergy. The government responded by sending two cavalry units against the rebels, but the soldiers defected, going over to the side of the conservatives, as did an infantry column on December 24, 1855.

Meanwhile, in Mexico City, the government searched the house of Antonio Haro and found a document, "El Plan del Llano del Rodeo," which included a defense of the church and suggestions for restoration of the Mexican monarchy. The government arrested Haro on January 2, 1856, but he was able to escape on January 5 and joined the rebels, who immediately chose him as their leader. An additional defection of 1,500 men led to a significant growth in the rebel force (to 4,000–6,000) gathering in the Sierra. The rebels shifted to a direct attack against the army garrison at the city of Puebla. The city had both a strategic location (east of Mexico City on the road to Veracruz) and a largely conservative population. The Mexican garrison at Puebla held out for a week (January 17, 1856–January 23, 1856) before surrendering. The rebels (perhaps unwisely) let the Mexican troops under the leadership of Gen. Juan B. Traconis depart. General Traconis and the remains of his garrison established a base on the bridge at Rio Frio, which prevented the rebels from advancing on the capital. The states of Guanajuato, Querétaro, Veracruz, Zacatecas, Oaxaca, and Morelos all sent troops to the capital. Comonfort was able to organize a new army that included regular army soldiers paired with these newer forces. Meanwhile, conservative uprisings in favor of the rebel Plan of Zacapoaxtla in del Valle, Yulancingo, Pachuca, Chalchicomula, and Huehuetla were defeated by the National Guard. A number of the rebels from these conflicts fled to join the rebel army at Puebla.

Finally on February 23, 1856, Comonfort led his army toward Puebla, incorporating Traconis's troops at Rio Frio along the way. Comonfort established his headquarters at San Martín Texmelucan, only 21 miles from Puebla. Since many of the government's troops were untested, the plan was to advance slowly toward Puebla. In initial skirmishing, the rebel forces retreated gradually. However, on March 8, the rebels, organized in five columns, launched an early-morning attack at Ocotlán. The rebels succeeded in advancing in the middle of the front while being forced to retreat on their right flank. During the fierce fighting, there had been heavy casualties, especially among the rebels, who lost five times as many men as did the government.[47] The rebels sought a cease-fire, and Comonfort and Haro discussed terms of surrender. The rebels utilized the truce to withdraw to Puebla, and the government forces followed them, first by moving toward San Juan Hill, where they could establish a battery to bombard the city. Heavy fighting broke out on March 10. Meanwhile, government troops under Gen. Rosas Landa captured the Cholula Gate; President Comonfort's troops entered the city from the south. The day ended with the rebels abandoning San Juan Hill and the remaining 2,600 rebels retreating within the city. During the next few days, the government consolidated its position while trying to persuade the rebels to surrender.

Termination and Outcome: On March 14, the government's final assault began, and by March 17, the rebels had been reduced to 2,100, while the government army had received reinforcements, bringing it up to 16,000.[48] There was an armistice from March 20 to March 21 for religious holidays, during which rebel leader Haro resigned and was replaced by Gen. Carlos Oronoz. Oronoz surrendered unconditionally to Comonfort, ending the war. Haro escaped into exile. The conflict between these two factions—liberals and conservatives—would reignite again in the Reform War of 1858 to 1861 (Intra-state War #561).

Coding Decisions: We have not found any references to fatalities in the skirmishes in Zacapoaxtla or the surrounding states in support of the Plan of Zacapoaxtla nor for the skirmishing leading up to the battle at Ocotlán or in the later siege and seizure of Puebla. The only figures seem to be for the battle at Ocotlán, though there is disagreement among scholars about these. Fowler mentions rebel losses of 800, including 119 dead and 400 desertions.[49] Broussard describes much heavier fighting at Ocotlán in which the 6,000 rebels were reduced to 2,600, or rebel losses of 3,400.[50] Fowler's percentage of fatalities (15 percent) of the 3,400 yields at least 510 rebel fatalities at Ocotlán. Broussard also describes 500 rebel losses at Puebla, where the opportunities for desertion would have been lower. As we round up for the earlier battles, we estimate 1,000 rebel battle-deaths, and if the rebel deaths were five times those of the government (as Broussard suggests), that would mean approximately 200 government fatalities.

Sources: Broussard (1979); Fehrenbach (1973); Fowler (2000a, 2000b); Fowler (2012); Hamnett (1999); Hamnett (2001); Meyer and Beezley (2000); Parkes (1966); Vanderwood (2000).

INTRA-STATE WAR #561
Mexican Reform of 1858 to 1861 (aka War of the Reform or Three Years War)

Participants: Mexico versus Liberals (Constitutionalists).
Dates: February 14, 1858, to January 1, 1861.
Battle-related Deaths: Liberals (Constitutionalists), aka Rebel Army: [ ]; Armed Forces of Mexico: [ ]. (See Coding Decisions.)
Initiator: Liberals.
Outcome: Liberals win.
War Type: Civil for central control.
Total System Member Military Personnel: Armed Forces of Mexico: 26,000 (initial-peak).[51]
Theater Armed Forces: Liberals (Constitutionalists), aka Rebel Army: 10,000 (prewar), 10,000 (initial), 25,000 (peak), less than 8,000 (final).[52]

Antecedents: The Mexican liberals (or federalists or constitutionalists) came to power in 1855 and withstood a number of rebellions by the disenchanted conservative military (including Intra-state War #558) in which the conservative challenge to the liberal military reforms in Mexico was defeated. The liberals then continued their program, *La Reforma.* Many of the liberal leaders in the new government had been served as liberal state governors, including Benito Juárez, a Zapotec Indian who had served as governor of Oaxaca and who was appointed as minister of justice when the liberals under President Juan Alvarez came to power in August 1855. In November 1855, Juárez sponsored a new law, the *Ley Juárez,* which stripped the military and clergy of some of their privileges. In June 1856, President Ignacio Comonfort (who had assumed office in December 1855 and was known as a moderate within the liberal faction) succeeded Alvarez as president. A new law was promulgated (known as the *Ley Lerdo*), which confiscated Church property, in an attempt to reduce the Catholic Church's economic power. The Church responded by threatening to excommunicate anyone who bought the property at auction. In 1857, a new Constitution expanded personal freedoms and omitted any mention of Catholicism as the state religion, again prompting Church threats of excommunication.

The conservatives, led by Gen. Félix María Zuloaga, launched a revolt on December 17, 1857, ostensibly in Comonfort's name. They dissolved Congress and arrested Juárez (who recently had been named chief justice of the supreme court and thus first in line to the presidency). They initially proclaimed the Tacubaya Plan, which called for suspension of the liberal 1857 Constitution. The Church signaled its approval by saying that those who adhered to the plan would be free from the threat of excommunication. Comonfort used his authority to free Juarez, who promptly established an alternative government at Guanajuato and rallied eleven of the Mexican states (mostly northern) to the liberal—now termed *Constitutionalist*—cause. Conservative general José de la Parra led a mutiny specifically against Comonfort on January 15, 1858; Comonfort resigned and fled; and General Zuloaga was installed as president on January 21. Mexico now had two rival governments—one conservative (which was in control of the institutions of the central government and is thus considered the government here) and one liberal, each of which was prepared to resort to arms. Each government first tried to woo individual states using political and economic promises. Juárez also was able particularly to recruit Indians to the liberal side, though Tomás Mejia was an Indian general who came down from the sierra to join the conservative army on February 11, 1858. Mejia would become a key figure in sustaining the conservative cause in the future.

Narrative: Fearing recapture by government forces, Juárez proceeded further west from Guanajuato to Guadalajara, where he established a government and tried to rally the army to his side. Though Juárez had the support of the liberal northern states in principle, the governors were hesitant to commit their state militias to a united liberal army. On February 14, 1858, a force of 5,400 government troops began an advance on the rebellious states (which marks the start of the war). The first real battle of the war was that of Salamanca (located east of Guadalajara) on March 10, 1858. Government troops under the command of Luis Osollo, aided by generals Miguel Miramón and Tomás Mejia, attacked liberal forces led by Anastasio Parodi and Leanardo Valle. The liberal constitutionalist forces were easily overcome. Soon thereafter, the garrison of Guadalajara mutinied, going over to the conservative government side. Juárez fled to Panama. However, the constitutionalists regrouped. In late April 1858, Constitutionalists under General Degollado besieged Guadalajara. Juárez and his cabinet returned to Mexico on May 4, arriving at the eastern port of Veracruz, and were welcomed and restored to office by Governor Manuel Gutiérrez Zamora. Here the liberals were more able to receive outside assistance, and gradually, state governors from Guanajuato, Jalisco, Michoacán, Veracruz, Coahuila-Neuvo ta León, and others ordered their militias to join the liberal cause.

That spring, the liberals were able to go on the offensive, besieging Mexico's important gulf port of Tampico. The siege was lifted when an army under General Mejía dashed from his base in the northern sierra to relieve the city on May 15. The period that followed was one of relative parity in terms of victories by each side. However, the government was unpopular and controlled only those places where it left heavy garrisons. On September 21, 1858, the liberals scored a minor victory at Las Cuevitas, while the government won a major battle at Ahualulco de los Pintos on September 29.

Facing increasing opposition, Zuloaga finally resigned on December 23, after a coalition of centrists succeeded in winning the loyalty of troops in Mexico City. However, instead, by December 29, a military junta was formed under the leadership of reactionary general Miguel Miramón. Zuloaga was nominally retained as president but had little authority. General Miramón won a series of victories against the Constitutionalists, and by the end of 1858, the liberals seemed to be losing the war.

However, in fighting in early 1859, the liberals recaptured many of the cities lost in December. The government's offensive against Veracruz went forward on March 3, 1859, involving 5,000 government soldiers against about 3,000 liberal defenders. Malaria began to take a toll on the advancing soldiers, and Miramón called off the operation on March 29. Liberal armies harried Miramón as he retreated toward Mexico City, arriving on April 9. After Miramón's return, the combined government armies under Márquez and Mejía went on the offensive on April 11, defeating rebels at Tacubaya and inflicting heavy casualties.

Meanwhile, a representative from the United States, Robert MacLane, arrived in Veracruz, recognized Juárez's government in April 1859, and began to send supplies to the liberals. Meanwhile, Miramón's conservative government received covert financing from Spain. Miramón had determined another major offensive, and on November 13, his forces advanced northwest from the capital to confront the liberals near Querétaro. The government won a substantial victory over 7,000 liberals, and since July, the liberals had lost nearly 10,000 men. Miramón then returned to Mexico City but set out against Veracruz on February 9, 1860. His siege of the city began on March 6 but was ultimately stymied by American intervention. Miramón abandoned the siege for lack of supplies. By June, the liberals were able to retake the offensive almost everywhere. However, as the Constitutionalists gathered their forces for a joint attack on Mexico City, Miramón struck first, defeating a liberal force at Toluca. On December 8, Miramón led a force of 8,000 eastward against a liberal force at San Miguel Calpulalpan. Miramón underestimated the size of the liberal army, and on December 22, he attacked a liberal army of 16,000 soldiers. Elements of Miramón's forces began to flee, which soon turned the battle into a wholesale rout. Miramón was forced to flee back to Mexico City.

Termination and Outcome: The government now asked for terms of capitulation, but the rebels insisted on unconditional surrender. On December 24, most government ministers and officials, including Miramón, fled. On January 1, 1861, the liberal army, now 25,000 strong, entered the capital. On January 11, Benito Juárez returned as president. The outcome of the war was a complete military victory by the liberal rebels. The cost of the war had been horrific in terms of fatalities and money. In July 1861, the Mexican government's decision on a moratorium of its debt repayments led to intervention by foreign powers (Inter-state War #40, Franco-Mexican War of 1862 to 1867).

Coding Decisions: We have found no complete estimate or breakdown of the battle-deaths for this war. Estimates of deaths range from 2,000 to 70,000. We have found no conclusive evidence upon which to make an estimate.

Sources: Bancroft, Nemos, Savage, and Peatfield (1886); Bouthoul and Carrère (1978); Clodfelter (1992); Davis (1968); Hamnett (2001); Jaques (2007); Jensen (1953); Kohn (1999); Marley (1998); Meyer and Beezley (2000); Meyer, Sherman, and Deeds (2003); Miller (1985); Richardson (1960).

INTRA-STATE WAR #572
US Civil War of 1861 to 1865

Participants: United States of America versus Confederate States of America.
Dates: April 12, 1861, to May 11, 1865.
Battle-related Deaths: United States of America: 360,000; Confederacy: 258,000. (See Coding Decisions.)
Initiator: Confederate States of America.
Outcome: United States wins.
War Type: Civil for local issues (secession).
Total System Member Military Personnel: Armed Forces of the United States of America: 217,000 (pre-secession).[53]
Theater Armed Forces: Armed Forces of the United States of America (Government Army): 25,000 (prewar, initial); 1,063,000 (peak, final).[54] Armed Forces of the Confederate States of America (Rebel Army): 23,000 (prewar); 60,000 (initial); 463,891 (peak); 174,223 (final).[55]

Antecedents: Dating back to the origins of the United States, there were divisions between the northern and southern states concerning their understandings of the role of government: the industrial preponderance of the northern states generally meant that they favored a stronger central government than did the southern states. The issue that soon dominated all others was slavery. Large slaveholders formed a powerful political bloc, resistant to anything that might lead to abolition. Meanwhile, the abolitionist movement, begun by the Quakers, became a national movement in the 1830s. The rapid territorial expansion of the United States made it increasingly difficult to reassure northerners who worried about the growing power of the slave states. The Kansas–Nebraska Act of 1854 left the fate of slavery to be determined by popular sovereignty in all new territories. During the election of 1860, the economic issues that had divided the political parties paled in significance compared to the intra-party differences over the expansion of slavery. When Abraham Lincoln was elected president on a platform that opposed the expansion of slavery, Southern states began to secede. Southern militias seized most central government (Union) arms depots and forts in the South without armed resistance.

By February 1861, more than 3,000 government troops in Texas defected to the secessionist cause. Together with at least 19,000 militia of the seven states that had seceded (South Carolina, Mississippi, Florida, Alabama, Georgia, Louisiana, and Texas), this provided the South with an armed force of 22,000 before the war. By comparison, the government forces were no more than 25,000 strong. That month, the secessionists formally founded the Confederate States of America with its capital in Montgomery, Alabama. They demanded the surrender of federal fortifications guarding southern ports, and turned back federal ships that tried to bring supplies to Fort Sumter at Charleston, South Carolina. Lincoln's government initially decided to plan an evacuation; however, by April 6, Lincoln had changed his mind and authorized a resupply expedition. When informed of this decision, the government of the Confederates States, under the leadership of President Jefferson Davis, ordered Brigadier Gen. P. G. T. Beauregard, who commanded the troops at Charleston, to demand the immediate evacuation of the fort. On April 10, 1861, Beauregard dispatched a mission to the fort, demanding its surrender, which marks the start of the war. When the Union forces refused, the Confederates began bombarding the fort early on the morning of April 12. The fort surrendered the next day, and the troops were evacuated.

Narrative: The bombardment of Fort Sumter fueled increasing movements toward secession. On April 15, Lincoln issued a proclamation calling up 75,000 volunteers, mostly from state militias. By this time, the Confederacy had 60,000 enrolled. The first battle-deaths occurred on April 19, when a group of Massachusetts volunteers was attacked by armed civilians in Baltimore, suffering four killed. A struggle for the border states ensued, and Delaware and Maryland soon were occupied by Union forces. In Kentucky, the American government tolerated collaboration with the Confederacy to avert outright secession.

As each side consolidated its position, there was remarkably little fighting, and Southerners were confident that Great Britain would intervene on the side of the Confederacy. The first major battles were fought in July 1861, by which time the government army numbered more than 186,000. Aside from a few incidents in Maryland, all of the thirty-five recorded engagements in the war prior to July 21 occurred in Missouri or Virginia. The rebels moved their capital to the latter in May, establishing Richmond as the hub of the Confederacy, against which the Union would launch repeated and costly assaults over the next four years.

Rather than recounting each major battle, we confine ourselves to describing the general outline of the campaigns. In general, the Confederacy was strongest in the East and weakest in the West. The initial Union strategy was the "Anaconda Plan," which called for economic strangulation of the South by blockade. On land, the campaigns of 1861 consisted largely of probing attacks by the North that were repelled by the South. The first major battle occurred in the East, when a government force thrust toward the rebel capital and was routed at Bull Run (also known as Manassas Junction).

In the center, the Confederacy invaded the border state of Kentucky, provoking a strong pro-Union response in the population. Further west, the Confederacy was driven largely from Missouri. In Indian Country (now Oklahoma), the Union had pulled forces back after losing a quarter of the army in Texas. The Confederacy took advantage of the opportunity, allying itself to the slaveholding tribes, especially the Cherokee. The Confederates soon annexed the territory, and pro-Union tribes or factions were pushed north into the new state of Kansas in December 1861. In the far West, a small number of Confederate troops from Texas advanced into the southern part of New Mexico Territory, losing many to disease but annexing the southern parts of the territory.

As 1862 opened, the Union Army was 600,000 to 700,000 strong, while the rebels numbered about 376,000. The most fluid area of the war was the West, where the Union made strong progress during the year. In the East, the Union succeeded in checking rebel advances but otherwise made little progress. The most intense fighting in the West was the campaign for the Mississippi River. The government campaign made great progress during the year as Union forces moved downriver after advancing through Missouri. Meanwhile, Union forces also advanced upriver, first capturing New Orleans—the largest city of the Confederacy—and then taking the Louisiana capital of Baton Rouge. They were finally stopped at Vicksburg, Alabama. Meanwhile, the Union was moving in on Tennessee. While one Union force (led by Gen. Ulysses S. Grant) steamed up the Tennessee River, another advanced deep into the state from Nashville. The two pincers were to meet at Corinth, just south of the Tennessee–Mississippi border. However, the rebels attacked Grant's force at Pittsburg, landing near the small church of Shiloh. The government won the battle, the pincers met, and Corinth was taken.

Though the mountainous eastern regions of both Kentucky and Tennessee were controlled by the rebels at the beginning of the year, the Confederates were soon forced to fall back and abandon most of Kentucky. The process of indecisive but bloody offensives and counteroffensives was most pronounced in the states of Virginia and Maryland. The main Union campaign in the first half of the year was an attempt to advance up the Virginia Peninsula (between the James and York rivers) and capture Richmond from the southeast. While the advance was slow, it made steady progress as the rebels fought delaying actions and retreated toward Richmond. One month later, the rebels struck back. In the "Seven Days" battles, the forces defending Richmond (renamed the Army of Northern Virginia and now led by Gen. Robert E. Lee) succeeded in pushing the Union Army of the Potomac, led by Gen. George McClellan, back to the James River, from which they were evacuated in August to defend Washington. As the Peninsular Campaign drew to a close, Union armies again tried a thrust straight to Richmond. The 1862 effort met the same fate as the 1861 effort; Union forces were once again routed at the Second Battle of Bull Run (Manassas). This time, the Confederate armies followed up their successes by invading the North. They advanced into Maryland, and troops under Gen. Stonewall Jackson captured vast stores of arms and ammunition at the federal arsenal of Harper's Ferry on September 15, before advancing northward to Sharpsburg (northwest of Washington). General Lee arranged the army along Antietam Creek, and on September 17, General McClellan's forces attacked. The bloody Battle of Antietam was the deadliest single-day engagement of the war. The Confederate advance was halted, and when McClellan declined to press his advantage, the rebels were allowed to retreat. In less than a year, the Confederacy had lost a substantial amount of territory: its "Arizona Territory" west of Texas; its holdings in Missouri and Kentucky; most of Tennessee; significant parts of Mississippi, Louisiana, Arkansas, and Indian Territory; and coastal islands or ports in North Carolina, South Carolina, Alabama, Florida, and Texas. Union strength had increased to an average of 777,623 soldiers during the last nine months of the year; the same average for the rebels was only 424,018.

While unofficial peace efforts had been carried on throughout the war, they all foundered on Confederate President Jefferson Davis's insistence that recognition was a prerequisite to negotiation. In addition, the Confederate states rejected calls for the voluntary, federally funded, and gradual elimination of slavery. Following Antietam, Lincoln used the Union's improved military position to threaten to end slavery altogether. On January 1, 1863, he followed through on his promise and declared slaves in all areas not under Union control to be free.

The general pattern of warfare of the earlier years was repeated in 1863, although the fighting was more intense. There were three main fronts in 1863—the Trans-Mississippi area; eastern Tennessee and Georgia; and the East—to capture Richmond. By the end of the year, Vicksburg had surrendered, and the Union had cut the Confederacy in two, seizing a large strip of territory through Louisiana, Mississippi, Alabama, and Tennessee. However, the rebels had their greatest successes in the East. On May 6, the Union's Army of the Potomac was driven back across the Rappahannock River by rebel general Robert E. Lee and the Army of Northern Virginia (which was less than half of the Union Army's size). The rebels followed up their victory by invading the North: the rebels moved up the Shenandoah Valley, captured Sharpsburg, Maryland, and by late June had taken Mechanicsburg and threatened Harrisburg, the capital of Pennsylvania. Union forces moved in a line roughly parallel to Lee's advance, and they probed for an opportunity to turn west and cut off Lee's forces, eventually concentrating near Gettysburg, Pennsylvania. This concentration of forces presented Lee with the opportunity to destroy the Union army in the North, and from July 1 to July 3, the two armies clashed in the bloodiest battle of the war. The rebel assaults failed on the last two days, and they fled southward, escaping annihilation only because of the sluggishness of the Union pursuit. From 1862 to 1863, spectacular cavalry raids were conducted behind enemy lines by Confederate generals Nathan Bedford Forrest and Jeb Stuart and Union colonel Benjamin Grierson. Both sides also faced rebellions by indigenous peoples during the war, including a major uprising by the Dakota in Minnesota in 1862 (Intra-state War #577).

As 1864 opened, Union forces had advanced along virtually the entire front. While rebel strength remained roughly constant at 463,000 soldiers, the Union's armed forces continued to grow, surpassing the 1 million mark. A Confederate military victory and foreign intervention on their behalf were virtually out of the question after Gettysburg, so rebel hopes generally rested on inflicting enough casualties and delaying the Northern advance long enough to turn the bulk of the Northern population against the war. The American presidential election of 1864 provided a virtual referendum on the war because it pitted Lincoln against respected military commander Gen. George McClellan, an advocate of ending the attempt to coerce the South into rejoining the Union.

With the Mississippi Valley under Union control, the central objectives of the government were to split the Confederacy again by driving through Georgia to the Atlantic and to destroy Lee's Army of Northern Virginia. It completely achieved the first and made progress on the second. Around Chattanooga, about 100,000 Union troops under Gen. William Tecumseh Sherman mounted an offensive against up to 64,000 Confederates defending Georgia. Beginning on May 7, Sherman used his numerical superiority to turn rebel positions, forcing them to fall back southward for more than two weeks and eighty miles before making successful stands at New Hope Church and Pickett's Mill. As a result, a long and exposed Union salient jutted into Georgia. The Confederacy lacked the personnel to both mount serious attacks against the base of the salient and to defend Atlanta; it chose the latter course of action. Unable to take the city by frontal assault, Sherman attempted to cut the city's last rail lines of supply. In a series of battles, the Confederates failed to outflank the government, to dislodge it from its positions around Atlanta, or to defend the railways successfully. Suffering from heavy casualties (more than one-third of their in-theater forces) and in danger of encirclement, the rebels destroyed anything that might be of value to the Union army. They then withdrew from Atlanta, which was occupied by Sherman's forces on September 2.

Unable to halt the Union advance, Hood at last resolved on the strategy of attacking the salient in the hope that it might force the Union to pull back into Tennessee. On September 29, Hood's army crossed the Chattahoochee River west of Atlanta, then advanced more than thirty miles into Sherman's rear. Hood led 38,000 men north into Tennessee, aiming for the critical rail junction of Nashville. He launched a disastrous attack on fortified Union troops at Franklin. The numerically superior Union forces attacked the rebel lines after two weeks, crushing Hood's army. Sherman had initially pursued Hood northward, but once the rebels turned west into Alabama, he began his own offensive southeast from Atlanta and advanced all the way to the sea, taking Savannah on December 21. The Confederacy was now divided in three.

While the government was less successful in the East, it made more progress than in previous years. The Virginia front remained relatively calm until May 3. On that night, Grant sent 118,700 Union soldiers across the Rapidan River against its 63,900 defenders, beginning the Forty Days campaign. Two days later, another 30,000 government troops landed at Bermuda Hundred just fifteen miles from Richmond. Lee counterattacked two days later in the 140 square-mile Wilderness, inflicting a severe defeat on the Union. Despite losing 17,666 men against only 7,750 rebel casualties, Grant shifted eastward and continued the offensive. From May 5 to May 18, the government lost more than 50,000 troops in Virginia, including 14,000 deserters. Grant continued his drive on Richmond. When he reached the crossroads of Cold Harbor, just over ten miles northeast of the Confederate capital, his initial attacks failed to make headway. Unable to capture Richmond at an acceptable cost, the front stagnated for the rest of the year. Lee ordered one of the most audacious offensives of the war, another invasion of the North by only 10,000 infantry and 4,000 cavalry. Led by Gen. Jubal Anderson Early, the rebels crossed the Potomac River into Maryland just north of the Valley then turned southeast to march on Washington. Grant hurriedly dispatched 5,000 men to defend the capital. By the time he reached the District of Columbia's borders on July 11, Early had perhaps 13,000 men to face the 9,643 soldiers defending the capital. The timely arrival of an entire corps from Petersburg ended whatever chance Early had of taking the heavily fortified city, and he retired the next day. By the end of the year, Early's forces had been driven more than 100 miles away from the Potomac.

Lincoln handily defeated McClellan in the November 1864 election, running on a "National Union Party" ticket with prowar Democrat Andrew Johnson. The election of 1864 also resulted in a huge legislative majority for Lincoln. As 1865 opened, the rebels had lost any chance for peace on Confederate terms, given Lincoln's reelection, the huge Republican majorities in Congress, and the deteriorating situation on the battlefield. Congress forwarded a constitutional amendment abolishing slavery to the states in January. The Confederate Army had shrunk to about 160,000 to 180,000, while the Union had an army of nearly a million (one-third of them reserves) and another hundred thousand in other armed services. The stalemate on the Petersburg–Richmond front continued into the new year, and Grant turned to Sherman for assistance. Sherman turned north from Savannah and marched into the Carolinas. Under Gen. John Schofield, about 30,000 Union soldiers in North Carolina pushed southward to link up with Sherman. Schofield defeated a rebel army of 30,000 under Gen. Joseph Eggleston Johnston at Bentonville from March 19 to March 20. By this time, Sheridan's forces had completed their Shenandoah Valley campaign and were ready to attack Lee's rear. From March 29 to March 31, 1865, Sheridan hit the westernmost trenches of the rebels near Dinwiddie Courthouse. The next day, at Five Forks, the rebels finally broke. Lee was forced to abandon Petersburg and march westward, and the rebels relocated their capital to Danville, on the border of Virginia and North Carolina. Effective resistance more or less collapsed throughout the South during the first week of April. Grant advanced in parallel with Lee.

By this time, the Confederacy consisted of isolated pockets, none of which were strong enough to stand up to a major Union attack. The Army of Northern Virginia, reduced to 12,500 effectives, mounted its last attack on April 9; it was almost immediately halted by Union reinforcements. Later that day, Lee surrendered his forces at Appomattox Courthouse on the promise that his men would not be prosecuted for treason. Most rebel forces either surrendered or simply went home after hearing news of Lee's defeat. On April 14, 1865, President Lincoln was shot, dying the next day. On April 18, Sherman and Johnston reached a negotiated settlement to the war. A general truce immediately entered into effect until the agreement was ratified by both sides' presidents. The terms were so generous that the new American president, Andrew Johnson, rejected them. Most rebels surrendered, but one more engagement was fought. On May 11, a small force of Union soldiers attacked Confederate encampments near Palmetto Ranch in Texas.

Termination and Outcome: The last Confederate forces surrendered in May, and the last Confederate-ally American Indian tribe, the Cherokee, surrendered in June. Because the surrenders were negotiated on the battlefield and addressed only military issues, the outcome of the war was a military victory by the government. President Johnson issued an amnesty on May 29, although it established many more exclusions than the surrender agreements reached with Lee and other Confederate commanders. Despite the limited nature of the amnesty, only one person was executed after the war—the commander of the Confederacy's notorious prisoner-of-war camp at Andersonville. The Thirteenth Amendment abolishing slavery was ratified in December 1865.

Coding Decisions: We code the United States of America with 360,000 battle-deaths. The Confederate States of America had about 258,000 battle-deaths. The total was 618,000, which includes the 30,218 Union soldiers and 25,976 Confederate soldiers who died in captivity.[56] Small and Singer initially coded a total of 650,000 battle deaths, though that figure included some civilian deaths.

Sources: Axelrod (2007); Barrett (1963); Bodart (1916); Carrère (1972); Catton (1952a, 1952b, 1953); Clodfelter (2002, 2008); Dumas and Vedel-Peterson (1923); Dyer (1959); Escott, Powell, Robertson, and Thomas (1993); Foote (1986a, b, c); Hunt (2002a, b); Keleher (2008); Livermore (1957); Marley (1998); McPherson (2008); Michno (2003); Morris (1970); Nofi (1995), Perre (1962); Phisterer (1868); Reid (1999); Smithsonian Institution (2011).

INTRA-STATE WAR #577

Sioux–Minnesota War of 1862 (aka Minnesota–Dakota War or Dakota War)

Participants: Santee Sioux versus Minnesota Armed Forces, organized militias, and settlers and irregulars.

Dates: August 17, 1862, to September 29, 1862.

Battle-related Deaths: Santee Sioux: 608; Minnesota regiments: 113;[57] militias and settlers: 400.

Initiator: Santee Sioux.

Outcome: Minnesota, militias, and settlers win.

War Type: Regional Internal.

Theater Armed Forces: Minnesota armed forces: 3 companies of Fifth Minnesota Volunteers,[58] or 795 men[59] in 4 forts (initial); 4,000 (peak). Organized militias, settlers, and irregulars: 3,000 (peak).

Santee Sioux (with Winnebago and Yankton participants): 1,300 (initial at Lower Agency);[60] 4,000 (peak).

Antecedents: The Sioux Wars of 1854 to 1890 was one of the six major conflicts between the United States and Native Americans that began between 1840 and 1860.[61] Fighting between settlers and Sioux in 1854 and 1857 set the stage for the Sioux uprising in Minnesota in 1862. This war, one of the bloodiest Native American uprisings, also became a precipitant of the wider conflict between the United States and the Plains Indians that lasted for almost thirty years and cost 20,000 casualties.[62]

There were three major clans of the Sioux, and the Dakota (or Santee) remained in the southwestern half of the state of Minnesota. As settlers, many from northern Europe, entered the area, the demand for Indian land grew, and in 1851, the Dakota ceded much of their land to the United States in exchange for two reservations along the Minnesota River (the Upper Sioux Agency and the Lower Agency) and payments of $3 million in money and supplies to be paid out annually over fifty years. The Sioux did not fare well in the bargain: life on the reservations was difficult, the promised government annuities were often late, and when they arrived, significant portions were used to pay the traders for credits that had been issued. Security for the settlers had been provided by four United States Army forts in the region. However after 1861, the Civil War had led to the recall of the US forces, and the forts were then manned by three companies of the Fifth Minnesota Volunteers.

In 1862, the Santee Sioux were in a difficult situation. Lack of food was exacerbated by the failure of the annuity payments to arrive in June. In July, some of the younger warriors formed a secret society called the "Soldiers Lodge," which soon numbered 5,000 to 6,000 members, to discuss a possible revolt. The situation was further aggravated by opportunistic traders, including Andrew Myrick, who refused to extend further credit for food with the comment that the Sioux could "eat grass" instead. In August, 550 lodge members broke into the warehouse and took flour that was stored there. Believing that the situation had been stabilized, Agent Thomas Galbraith gathered a group of volunteers for the Civil War, calling them the Renville Rangers, and they set out on August 13 for Fort Snelling.

Narrative: On August 17, 1862, four young Sioux warriors decided to take some eggs from a nearby homestead, where the Sioux killed five settlers. The four warriors returned to the reservation seeking the backing of the tribe for war against the settlers. Before dawn on August 18, the Lower Agency tribes met at the house of Little Crow, the most prominent of the Santee leaders. Little Crow was opposed to the war but was soon persuaded by the younger warriors that the Sioux should attack the next day. However, later that day, 200 to 300 Sioux engaged in fighting at the trading post, killing 20 of the settlers, including trader Myrick, who was discovered with grass stuffed in his mouth. The conflict soon spread throughout the southwestern corner of Minnesota, from Iowa northwest to Fort Abercrombie in the Dakota Territory. Though some of the Native Americans warned the settlers to flee or sheltered them, a large number joined in attacking the trading posts and farms along the Yellow Medicine River in the Upper Agency on the evening of the August 18. By the next day (August 19), the first of 40,000 settlers had begun to flee their homes.

Over the next six weeks, there were two major thrusts of the Sioux campaign: direct attacks on established military forts and raiding party attacks on settlers' farms to gain provisions. These raids entailed massacres of unarmed civilians, and hundreds were killed and taken into captivity. As news of these attacks spread, a pattern emerged in which the settlers would leave their farms and gather at one of the larger buildings or a nearby town where fortifications could be built for defense. In these endeavors, the settlers would organize themselves either into loose group of irregulars or more formalized local militias, both of which operated as combatants on their own or in conjunction with the Minnesota armed forces. Some of the settlers also fled into the military forts and participated in combat in the defense of the fort. It is these elements of armed conflict that constitute the COW war.

After the attack on the Lower Agency, some of the workers fled to Fort Ridgely. The fort had only 76 soldiers. Upon hearing of the uprising at the Lower Agency, the fort's commander, Capt. John Marsh, organized a relief column of 46 men who headed toward the agency. They were ambushed by 100 Santee at Redwood Ferry, and 24 of the troops, including Marsh, were killed. Fifteen of the survivors straggled back to the fort, and its new nineteen-year-old commander, Lieut. Thomas P. Gere, sent appeals for assistance to Minnesota Governor Alexander Ramsey. Meanwhile 250 refugees entered the fort—and 25 of the men joined in the fort's defense.

On the morning of Tuesday, August 19, 300 Sioux gathered to discuss battle plans. Against Little Crow's advice to attack weakened Fort Ridgeley, the younger warriors decided to attack the largest town in the vicinity, New Ulm. This decision allowed a company of 50 men of the Fifth Minnesota volunteers, 50 Renville Rangers, and 50 citizen volunteers to reinforce Fort Ridgely, raising the total to 180 defenders. The 1,000 inhabitants of New Ulm, warned of the advancing Sioux, built barricades manned by two militia units consisting of 40 men. On the afternoon of August 19, the advance party of 100 to 200 Sioux attacked New Ulm. The next day, 300 to 400 Sioux warriors under Little Crowe attacked Fort Ridgeley; however the fort's cannon fire forced them to withdraw. The Sioux then besieged the fort, while Little Crow appealed to the bands in both the Upper and Lower Agencies for support. On August 22, 800 Sioux began a coordinated attack against the fort from all sides. During the five-hour struggle, the Sioux were able to enter the fort's stables, capture some of the fort's livestock, and set fire to most of the fort's buildings before being driven back by the artillery. After receiving the fort's appeal, Governor Ramsey appointed Col. Henry Hastings Sibley to take charge of the 400 men of the Sixth Minnesota at Fort Snelling and to go to Fort Ridgeley's aid. Sibley moved slowly, waiting for further recruits before finally arriving to relieve to Fort Ridgely on August 28.

During the pause in the fighting at New Ulm, several surrounding communities dispatched groups of armed volunteers to assist in its defense. These militias and irregulars, now numbering more than 300, chose Judge Charles E. Flandrau as their commander. On August 23, 650 Sioux launched a pincer movement attack on New Ulm. In heavy fighting, the Sioux advanced into the town. The settlers burned forty outlying buildings and built new barricades before the Sioux withdrew. During the battle, at least 26 of the citizen soldiers were killed as well as a large number of Sioux. Fearing another attack, Flandrau and the 2,500 citizens decided to evacuate New Ulm.

The Sioux headed northwest, where they split into two groups: Little Crow with 110 warriors moved northward, and Gray Bird with 350 to 500 warriors moved to plunder settlements south of the Minnesota River. Meanwhile, Colonel Sibley's 940 fresh recruits and 400 volunteer cavalrymen led by Col. Sam McPhail arrived at Fort Ridgely. On August 31, a detail of about 170 men were dispatched to the Lower Agency as a burial detail. The soldiers set up camp near Birch Coulee, with wagons and horses arranged in a horseshoe configuration around the perimeter, framing the tents in the middle. In the early morning of September 2, Gray Bird sent 200 of his warriors to surround and attack the camp. The soldiers were taken by surprise, and soon almost half were killed or seriously wounded. The remaining Sioux joined in besieging the camp. At Fort Ridgely, Colonel Sibley heard the sounds of the battle and dispatched a relief detail of 200 men, followed by a second force of 1,000 men. As the relief columns advanced on September 3, the Sioux withdrew.

Meanwhile, Little Crow had lost the leadership of most of his band. Yet he engaged in several skirmishes near Forrest City with 75 soldiers led by Capt. Richard Strout. Receiving reinforcements, Little Crow routed Strout's men in the brief Battle of Acton. Fighting also took place further west, along the Minnesota border with the Dakota Territory at Fort Abercrombie, which was manned by 80 men of Company D of the Fifth Minnesota Infantry and local settlers. The fort was besieged for six weeks by 400 Upper Santee (Sissetons), Yankton, and Yanktonais. Attacks on September 3 and September 6 were driven back by artillery fire. A relief column of 450 men arrived on September 23, and there were subsequent battles on September 25 and 29.

Back at Fort Ridgely, Colonel Sibley finally was ready to undertake Governor Ramsey's plan to either exterminate the Sioux or to drive them out of Minnesota. Sibley took most of the fort's 1,619 men, plus 38 Renville Rangers and 44 citizen volunteers, and marched northwest along the Minnesota River before camping near Wood Lake. About 1,200 Sioux under Little Crow met Sibley's column on September 23, and charges by the Third Regiment, the Renville Rangers, and the artillery persuaded the Sioux to abandon the battlefield. The Battle of Wood Lake was considered a major Minnesotan victory. Little Crow and 100 warriors fled northward to Canada.

Termination and Outcome: COW codes this war as ending as of September 29, 1862, with the last attack on Fort Abercrombie. Sibley's advance continued, and more than 2,000 Sioux surrendered to his forces. Sibley created a military commission to try the Sioux for crimes, and 307 were sentenced to death. The condemned were moved to Camp Lincoln at South Bend. Though Sibley favored immediate executions, the list of the condemned was sent to President Lincoln, who commuted the death sentences of all but 38, who were hung at Mankato on December 26, 1862, in the largest mass execution in US history. Little Crow, who had fled to Canada, returned to Minnesota, where he was killed by settlers on July 3, 1863.

Coding Decisions: The decision to include this war was difficult, primarily because the characteristics of this war make its coding complicated and because COW's specific coding rules at times differ from the ways in which historians have described the war. For instance, in terms of the end date of this war, we have coded September 29, 1862, as the ending of sustained combat, while others describe the war as lasting until 1864 or 1865. The period of 1863 to 1865 primarily included the massacres of civilians, and though the loss of life was significant, these periods do not qualify as war under COW coding rules.

The coding of this conflict as a Regional Internal war hinges on two key interrelated decisions concerning: (1) the identity of the major combatants and (2) the calculation of battle deaths. Because the American Civil War had led to the withdrawal of most of the regular US Army forces from Minnesota, security was being provided primarily by Minnesota under the command of Governor Ramsey. These Minnesota state forces conducted the bulk of the fighting on one side, making this a Regional Internal war. Minnesota forces were also aided by local militias and groups of irregulars, or settler volunteers, who planned and coordinated the defense of towns and engaged in combat with the Sioux. In such instances, these militia and volunteer irregulars also must be considered combatants and their deaths included in battle-death calculations. As noted in Chapter 2, combatants need not be initially prepared for war as long as they are able to subsequently inflict battle-deaths.[63] COW's conceptualization of some of the settlers as combatants differs from many accounts that portray the settlers merely as innocent victims.

The related, though more difficult, question is whether there were 1,000 battle deaths in this conflict. For COW, the fatalities of civilian noncombatants are not included as battle-related deaths: yet, the deaths of the settler combatants would be considered battle-deaths, and it is difficult to disentangle the two. Estimates of the number of settlers killed during this war range from 500 to 2,000, most of whom are described as innocent victims of massacres. Rev. Alexander Berghold (writing in 1891) and Judge Flandrau saw a figure of 1,000 deaths as likely.[64] If we start with the 1,000 settler deaths, we next need to determine how many of these were combatant deaths. The evidence is fairly clear that the majority of settler deaths were of civilian noncombatants. Clodfelter mentions that 400 settlers were killed in the first few days.[65] As these deaths would have taken place before the settlers could have organized to resist, the settlers killed likely would not have been combatants. If we take an estimate of 1,000 settlers killed and exclude 600 or so who may have been massacred throughout the war, then we have a rough estimate of 400 settlers who died as combatants, either as irregulars or in local militias. The deaths of the Minnesota Volunteers were documented more often. Clodfelter records 113 soldiers killed by the Santee.[66]

Determining the number of Sioux deaths is also a matter of conjecture as eyewitnesses reported that the Sioux often removed the bodies of those killed from the field. Keenan estimates that 150 Sioux were killed.[67] Koblas records more than 100 Sioux deaths at Fort Ridgely, yet Clodfelter suggests that 100 Sioux were killed in each of the two major engagements of Fort Ridgely and New Ulm.[68] The Sioux also attacked Fort Abercrombie, Birch Coolie, and Wood Lake, and as they were attacking entrenched positions, one would assume that their fatalities might exceed those of the defenders. Sioux deaths also occurred in some of the smaller engagements and rescue missions that often refer to the deaths of 5 to 20 Sioux each. Thus an initial figure of 400 Sioux deaths seems plausible. COW also includes in the category of battle-deaths those deaths that occur in the wave of killing that can be a reaction to victory and the deaths of those who subsequently die of wounds or diseases contracted in the war theater.[69] Consequently, we follow a number of authors, including the hangings of the 38 Sioux on December 26, 1862. The remaining prisoners were later transferred to prison in Mankato and then in Iowa. Of these prisoners, 120 died during their confinement (which also would be battle-deaths).[70] Clodfelter also included a figure of 300 (of the 1,318 non-condemned) Sioux who died of disease at Fort Snelling in the winter of 1862 and 1863.[71] Since this group included an undetermined number of combatants and noncombatants, we only include an estimate of 50 deaths as battle related. Thus we have calculated an estimate of 608 Sioux deaths for this war.

Sources: Axelrod (2007); BCI Eclipse (2005); Berghold (2007); Board of Commissioners (2005); Carley (1961); Christgau (2012); Clodfelter (1992, 1998, 2008); Collins (2006); Flandrau (1890); Folwell (1924); Heard (1864); Jaques (2007); Keenan (2003); Kessel and Wooster (2005); Koblas (2006); Kohn (1999); Minnesota Historical Society (2005); Oehler (1959); Richardson (1960).

INTRA-STATE WAR #587
Queretaro War of 1867

Participants: Mexico aided by French, Austrian, Hungarian, and Belgian volunteers versus Liberals.
Dates: February 6, 1867, to June 21, 1867.
Battle-related Deaths: Mexico: 1,500; Liberals: 1,000; French, Austrian, Hungarian, and Belgian volunteers: 300.[72] (See Coding Decisions.)
Initiator: Liberals.
Outcome: Liberals win.
War Type: Civil for control of central government.
Total System Member Military Personnel: Armed Forces of Mexico: 33,000.[73]
Theater Armed Forces: Mexican Imperial Army, aka Imperialists: 20,000 (prewar); 17,000 (after initial desertions); 17,000 (peak), 4,000 (final). French, Austrian, Hungarian, and Belgian volunteers (non-state intervener for government), participating from February 6 to May 15: 1,500 (initial, peak); 1,200 (final). Army of the Mexican Republic, aka Republicans or Liberals (Rebel Army): 60,000 (prewar, initial); 100,000 (peak, final).[74]

Antecedents: This brief war took place after the end of the Franco-Mexican War (Inter-state War #40). The war between France and the liberal Mexican government of Benito Juarez began in 1862 over the failure of the Mexican government to repay its foreign debts, though France also was desirous of extending its influence in the Western Hemisphere. In 1864, the French installed Austrian Archduke Maximilian as the emperor of Mexico. Juarez's government fled northward, and fighting continued between his army and that of France, which was aided by the conservatives in the Mexican army that supported Maximilian. Desiring to rid France of an expensive and unpopular war, Napoleon announced that France would withdraw from the war, and French forces were withdrawn by February 5, 1867, thereby ending the inter-state war. Maximilian was urged to return to Europe, yet he refused to abdicate. This civil war is coded as beginning the next day because the bulk of the fighting against Juarez's forces was henceforth conducted by the Mexican Imperialist Army of Maximilian, aided by foreign volunteer regiments (chiefly Belgian, Austrian, and Hungarian). Emperor Maximilian was then in control of the institutions of government and thus is considered to be the government of Mexico.

Narrative: Emperor Maximilian felt betrayed by the withdrawal of the French forces from his fight against the Republican Army of former liberal president Benito Juarez, who was attempting to unseat him. His Imperial Army, under the leadership of generals Miguel Miramón and Tomás Mejia (veterans of the Mexican Reform War against the liberals, Intra-state War #561) faced advances by the rebel army, and there were fourteen reported engagements in February. Key cities that were held by government forces included Pueblo, Queretaro, Mexico City, and Veracruz. Republican armies, which were augmented by continuing defections of government troops, moved against all but the last of these. In an attempt to block the republican advance, an Imperial force under General Miramón seized the central city of Zacatecas (northwest of the capital). On February 12, at nearby San Jacinto, Miramón was routed by a Republican army led by Gen. Mariano Escobedo. Following the battle, the Republicans executed more than 100 Imperial prisoners. Escobedo then advanced southward toward Querétaro, 160 miles northwest of Mexico City. Maximilian, hoping to confront the rebels away from the capital, personally led the bulk of the government army to Querétaro. What was to have been a decisive offensive instead turned into a siege as lethargy on the Imperial side allowed Republican reinforcements to arrive and besiege the town.

During the last days of February, Maximilian consolidated his position with reinforcements so that he had 20,000 men led by Miramón and Mejia. Two major assaults on Querétaro by the Republicans failed, with heavy losses for the rebels, though the city was besieged from March 6 to May 14, 1867. Meanwhile Gen. Leonardo Márquez and 1,100 cavalry proceeded to Puebla, where a government garrison of 2,500 under Gen. Manual Noriega was threatened by a large rebel force under Gen. Porfirio Díaz. Warned of Márquez's imminent arrival, Díaz immediately stormed the town on April 2, resulting in 2,000 government casualties (including the execution of Noriega and 74 officers) and only 1,000 rebel casualties. Díaz then moved to intercept Márquez, inflicting a crushing defeat at San Lorenzo on April 10, with 300 government troops killed. Márquez's force was reduced by two-thirds by the time it limped back into Mexico City, pursued by Díaz.

From April 12 to May 3, the government forces at Queretaro attempted six attacks on the Republican forces besieging the town. Typhus and starvation threatened the populace and the government troops. The Republican forces eventually took the city by means of simple bribery—they promised one of the garrison commanders (Col. Dom Miguel Lopez) a substantial amount of money if he allowed them entrance. During the early hours of May 15, the rebels steadily infiltrated the city. When the alarm was finally sounded, only a handful of troops remained loyal to Maximilian. Maximilian, Miramón, and Mejia surrendered when it became clear that further resistance was futile.

The government was now reduced to isolated forces in Mexico City and Puebla. In Mexico City, General Márquez, aided by an Austrian-Hungarian garrison under Count Carlos Khevenhuller, continued to hold out. After Maximilian was captured on May 15, the volunteers considered their war to be over, and they retired to their citadel while informing Republican General Díaz that they would take no further part in hostilities. Although the garrison of Mexico City was reduced at that point to between 4,000 and 5,000, it repeatedly attacked its besiegers. The last major attack by the besieged government forces was at La Pieta, where after a sharp engagement, the wounded were left to die on the field.

Termination and Outcome: Maximilian, Miramón, and Mejia were tried by the Republicans and executed on June 19. Once word of Maximilian's execution reached the capital, its residents turned against Márquez. His forces began to desert en masse, and on June 21, he disguised himself and fled Mexico City. Díaz began to bombard the city's defenses, and almost immediately flags of surrender appeared. This was the last armed action of the war; Veracruz surrendered without a fight on June 27.

The outcome was an unconditional surrender by the government and the restoration of the republic under Juarez. Unfortunately, conflict did not end, and regional insurrections soon broke out against the liberal government of Juarez.

Coding Decisions: Information concerning the battle-deaths for this war is sketchy at best. We have found documentation for only 2,015 battle-deaths, but the sheer number of battles for which we lack data suggests that the real toll was much higher, as does the fact that there was a typhus epidemic at Queretaro.

Sources: Alec-Tweedie (1906); Clodfelter (1992); Echenique (1894); Frost (1882); Gilmore (1964); Hamnett (2001); Jaques (2007); Marley (1998); Martin (1914); *New York Times* (1868–1871); Pérez (1901); Phillips and Axelrod (2005); Rondon Marquez (1944); Scheina (2003a, b); Stevenson (1899); Thomson and LaFrance (1999).

INTRA-STATE WAR #592

Guerre des Cacos of 1868 to 1869 (aka Guerre de Salnave)

Participants: Haiti versus *Cacos* (black peasants).
Dates: November 19, 1868, to December 18, 1869.
Battle-related Deaths: Haiti: [ ]; black peasants (*Cacos*): [ ].
Initiator: Black peasants (*Cacos*).
Outcome: Black peasants (*Cacos*) win.
War Type: Civil for central control.
Total System Member Military Personnel: Armed Forces of Haiti: 4,000.[75]
Theater Armed Forces: Armed Forces of Haiti: 3,000 (final). Black peasants (*Cacos*): [ ].

Antecedents: In the 1830s, Haiti controlled the entire island of Hispaniola. From 1844 to 1845, an independence movement by Santo Domingo was successful in expelling the Haitians from the East, creating the Dominican Republic (Non-state War #1531). Strained relations between the two sectors remained, leading to armed conflict in 1849 and a second war in 1855 (Non-state War #1538). From 1847 to 1859, Haiti was ruled by its last emperor Faustin Soulouque, who was overthrown in a revolt led by Nicholas Fabre Geffrard. Subsequently, a Haitian republic was created with Geffrard as its president. President Geffrard was faced with the conflict between the black (90 percent) and mulatto (10 percent) populations, and his regime confronted fifteen coup attempts in eight years. In 1865 a group of 250 mulattos led by a dark northerner, Major Sylvain Salnave, tried to topple the Geffrard government. Geffrard abdicated in March 1867, fleeing to exile in Jamaica. A provisional government was established under the collective leadership of Salnave, Gen. Victorin Chevallier, and Gen. Jean Nissage-Saget. The collective leadership did not last long. Within weeks, Salnave was elected president of Haiti (May 1867—taking office on June 14, 1867), and the two and a half years of his rule were some of the most disastrous in Haiti's history.

By October 1867, Salnave was in turn challenged by an uprising led by Gen. Leon Montas. Salnave used his actions as the justification to suspend the constitution on April 22, 1868, declaring himself president for life with unlimited authority. This usurpation of power led to a widespread rebellion by the *Cacos*, who were generally black peasants. Though the conflict frequently has been portrayed primarily in racial terms, the various participants were not in fact so distinctly divided, and the *Cacos* military leaders were propertied individuals of both colors. Similarly, though Salnave had been aligned with mulatto interests, his forces also included the *piquets*, who were blacks resentful of the propertied class.

For the next year, the conflict was characterized by infrequent, brief attacks with few fatalities. A number of Salnave's, former allies, including Nissage-Saget, joined the opposition. Gradually, the rebels gained ground both in the North and the South, and Salnave's forces in the capital of Port au Prince were besieged. Salnave, who in general had the support of the United States, purchased two ships in New York and began a successful naval campaign in September 1868, both against rebel ships and by bombarding coastal rebel strongholds.

Narrative: Salnave's fortunes changed when the *piquets* of the South were persuaded to support the government, and their intervention converted the insurrection into a civil war.[76] In November, 2,000 *piquets*, under the leadership of General Geronimo surrounded the city of Jacmel (on the southeast coast). Their attack on the garrison there on November 19, 1868, was repulsed, with 300 *piquets* killed, including the general.[77] A subsequent government attack on December 9 was also repulsed, with significant fatalities on both sides. By the end of 1868, Haiti was in effect divided into three territories. In September, Jean Nissage-Saget was proclaimed as the leader of the Republic of the North (with its capital at St. Marc), where he was aided by generals Nord Alexis and Pétion Faubert. The state of the South (or the Meridional state) had its capital at Les Cayes under the leadership of Gen. Michel Domingue. In the relative middle was the republic controlled by Salnave.

As 1869 began, the number of rebels was increasing, and Salnave's basic strategy was to try to first reconquer the South and to regain control of the coastal ports. He continued his naval attacks along the south coast, and Aquin surrendered on January 20, 1869. This in conjunction with *piquet* activities around Jacmel enabled Salvane to encircle Gen. Domingue in Les Cayes. The siege of the *Cacos* at Les Cayes began on February 4, 1869, with heavy naval bombardment and savage assaults by the *piquets*. The city was besieged. On June 12, Salnave's troops bombarded Les Cayes for forty-eight hours then landed 800 men to attack the fort. Though the government troops were briefly in possession of the fort, the rebels regrouped and regained the fort, killing or capturing more than one-half of Salnave's forces.[78] The siege lasted for nine months, and Salnave's forces only withdrew on October 31, when they retreated to Port au Prince.

The government's prospects suffered a further blow in July, when the rebels obtained two new ships in the United States. On September 14, 1869, two fleets engaged in the most drawn-out naval battle of the war near Port-de-Paix (on the northern coast). The fight ended as a draw off Le Borgne, though eighteen rebels were killed. The rebel ships retreated to Acut for repairs, and the government's *Pétion* had to tow the *Salnave* into Cap-Haitien. The naval battle was another turning point in the war because Salnave, who had had great success in attacks by sea, was now land bound. Government-controlled ports could not receive provisions from the capital, and they began to surrender. In contrast, the rebels had one remaining ship, the *Artibonite*, and they began a number of seaborne attacks, which were successful in recapturing many of the towns: General Alexis captured Fort St. Michel and Fort Liberté along the north coast, and Miragoane, along the southern peninsula, fell to the *Cacos* at the end of October. Meanwhile, Salnave purchased one more warship, renamed as *Terreur*, but a second purchase, an ironclad named *Atlanta*, sank in December 1869 before arriving in Haiti. In October, the rebels lost thirty-four men in a failed assault on Cap-Haitien. The city was on the verge of surrendering later that month. The city fell to Nissage-Saget on November 14, 1869, when the rebels also seized the ship the *Pétion*. The remainder of the North gradually fell into rebel hands. Salnave decided to focus his efforts in the South, and concentrated his army against Jacemel. However, on November 4, one of Selvane's commanders there, Secretary of War Gen. Victorin Chevallier, took his entire army over to the side of the *Cacos*.

Termination and Outcome: Salnave began to prepare his last stand at Port-au-Prince. In December, the rebels, utilizing the three rebel ships, transported as many *Cacos* as possible to the capital. This amounted to a *Cacos* army of 1,200, under generals Brice and Boisrond-Canal, to confront Salnave and 3,000 government troops.[79] On December 18, 1869, the rebels snuck into the harbor, captured the government ship *La Terreur*, and turned its guns against the palace. Ultimately one-third of the capital was destroyed, and an estimated 500 people were killed.[80] Surviving the gunfire, Salnave and a few loyal confederates fled the city, which marks the end of the war. On December 27, 1869, a provisional government was established with Jean Nissage-Saget as president and Michel Domingue as vice president. Salnave escaped into the Dominican Republic. On January 10, 1870, Salnave was captured and returned to Haiti. On January 15, a revolutionary tribunal in Port-au-Prince found Salnave guilty of treason, and he was executed immediately.

Coding Decisions: Given the long periods of armed conflict at low fatality levels, determining the start date of this war entailed identifying the point at which armed conflict would lead to more than one thousand battle-related deaths within the subsequent twelve-month period. In the previous version of the intra-state war data set, we had coded this war as starting in February 1869 with the siege of Les Cayes.[81] However, Heinl and Heinl noted that it was the intervention of the *piquets* that converted the insurrection into a civil war.[82] With information indicating that 300 *piquets* died in the assault on November 19, 1868, we have altered the start date accordingly.

To this point, we have been unsuccessful in locating specific data on the numbers of troops involved and the numbers of combatants killed in the war. There are multiple references to heavy fighting with significant costs, and some scholars have noted that prisoners taken by both sides were routinely shot. Based on these reports, plus the large number of battles, and the reporting of 752 deaths in just three engagements, we have concluded that this conflict entailed more than the requisite thousand combatant fatalities to be considered a war. However, we are hesitant to make any estimates of the actual numbers of battle-deaths.

Sources: Clodfelter (2002); David (1968); Gorman (2002); Hazard (1873); Heinl and Heinl (1978); Heinl and Heinl (2005); Leger (1970); Rippy (1940); Rotberg (1971); Sarkees (2010a, b, c); Skidmore and Smith (2004); *The New York Times* (1868–69); Tinker (1928).

INTRA-STATE WAR #602
Díaz Revolt of 1876 (aka Tuxtepec Rebellion)

Participants: Mexico versus Díaz-led Rebels.
Dates: January 15, 1876, to November 23, 1876.
Battle-related Deaths: Mexico: 1,900; Tuxtepecanos (Rebel Army): 1,200.
Initiator: Rebels.
Outcome: Rebels win.
War Type: Civil for control of the central government.
Total System Member Military Personnel: Armed Forces of Mexico: 22,000.[83]
Theater Armed Forces: Armed Forces of Mexico: 70,000 (prewar); 70,000 (initial); 92,500 (peak—adds mobilized National Guard to the regular armed forces).[84] Tuxtepecanos (Rebel Army): 2,000 (initial); 14,000 (peak); 16,000 (final).[85]

Antecedents: José de la Cruz Porfirio Díaz Mori found his profession as a soldier in the Mexican–American War of 1846 to 1848 (Inter-state War #7). He sided with the liberals in the fight against Antonio López de Santa Anna in 1855 and in the Mexican Reform War of 1858 to 1861 (Intra-state War #561). Díaz also gained renown in his support of liberal President Benito Juárez in the war against the French (Inter-state War #40) and the subsequent Queretaro War of 1867 (Intra-state War #587). At the conclusion of the war, Díaz resigned his military command, and gradually he became disenchanted with the Juárez government. In the Mexican presidential election of 1871, President Juárez defeated two contenders, including Díaz. Seeing the election results as fraudulent, Díaz staged the la Noria insurrection during 1871 and 1872 against the increasingly unpopular president. The rebels lost every battle, and they essentially were defeated on March 2, 1872, at La Bufa in Zacatecas. The rationale for the revolt vanished with Juarez's untimely death on July 18, 1872. He was succeeded by Sebastián Lerdo de Tejada, who offered the rebels amnesty and new elections.

Narrative: In 1875, when Lerdo appeared ready to run for another term, Díaz went to the United States to organize a rebellion, espousing the causes of federalism and free elections. His co-conspirator, Gen. Fidencio Hernandez, announced the revolt against the government through the Plan of Tuxtepec in Ojitlan, Oaxaca, on January 15, 1876. Hernandez immediately led a force of 2,000 Mexican Indians against the capital of the state. On January 27, Hernandez won a minor victory at San Felipe del Agua. The following day, his forces entered the city of Oaxaca unopposed, and he incorporated much of its garrison into his army, proclaiming Díaz as its commander. The revolt spread rapidly, and in February, the revolutionary plan was adopted by generals in Jalisco, Puebla, Vera Cruz, Nuevo Leon, Yucatán, San Luis Potosí, and Guerrero.

Many of the revolts were soon brought under control, but the Sierra Madre and much of Oaxaca remained firmly in rebel hands. In Oaxaca, Hernandez and 4,000 rebels attacked 1,000 federal troops led by Gen. Ignacio Alatorre on February 18 at Cerro del Jazmin. Though the government forces initially retreated to Yanhuitlan, their counteroffensive routed the rebels, who suffered nearly 900 killed against 600 government battle-deaths. Meanwhile, *serraño* (highland) forces organized in the West. At first they numbered only 300, but by early March, the union of several smaller forces created a rebel army of 2,000. The government launched an offensive into the Western Sierra, inflicting a string of defeats on the rebels throughout April and May.

Attempting to salvage the situation in the North, Díaz entered Mexico on March 22 with 40 followers, who soon increased to 800. On April 2, he took Matamoros (on the northeastern border), establishing a supply line to Brownsville, Texas, which enabled him to import rifles. He also recruited volunteers from Texas, with up to 800 joining his army. Now swollen to between 2,000 and 2,600 men, his army advanced, winning an engagement on April 7. However, when Lerdo sent 6,000 troops against him, Díaz retreated to New Orleans.

Díaz's exit prompted many rebels in the northeast to abandon the fight. By the middle of May combined rebel forces in the northeast were reduced to about 1,300. Battles became much smaller affairs, with the government winning most of them. At the Battle of Icamole on May 20, rebels suffered heavy losses in a defeat by government troops from Monterrey led by Gen. Carlos Fuero. Further south, the Oaxacan rebels numbered about 4,000 in May. On May 28, the troops led by Hernandez fought the Battle of San Juan Epatlan at Puebla against approximately the same number of government troops under generals Ignacio Alatorre and Diódoro Corella. The battle was fierce, with 150 rebels and 130 government soldiers killed (including Corella). Subsequently, the rebels were forced to disperse their troops into small units. However, they gained a temporary respite as 4,000 rebels joined the cause in Puebla, though they were defeated quickly. In Queretaro (north of the capital), an entire column of 1,500 rebels was ambushed and dispersed at Ajuchitlán on May 31, with 60 killed. From June 16 to June 18, rebels attacked government forces at Tulancingo Pachuca but were defeated. This general pattern—formation of rebel groups and largely unsuccessful attacks on government positions in the South—continued for several months.

Presidential elections were held in June and July, though the results were a matter of dispute. In July, Díaz sailed from New Orleans to Veracruz, whence he made his way to Oaxaca. The Oaxacan rebels were badly in need of leadership since General

Hernandez had been captured by government forces on July 18. The intensity of combat decreased for several months as the government dealt with the electoral crisis. Eventually, an electoral commission declared Lerdo reelected. The results invigorated the rebellion. In the North, more than 3,000 rebels took Tula on October 24. In Oaxaca, Díaz assembled 4,000 troops for an offensive against the government. The most significant consequence of the announcement, however, was the formation of a new rebel movement. The president of the supreme court, Jose Manuel Iglesias, asserted that under the constitution, the lack of a quorum made Lerdo's reelection illegal and that, therefore, he was the legal president of Mexico. Iglesias left Mexico City for Salamanca, where 3,000 soldiers defected from the government to his movement. He published his manifesto on October 28, calling himself and his supporters "Legalists." The Legalist movement grew rapidly from its base in the state of Guanajuato, with government soldiers defecting in Queretaro and San Luis Potosi. As it is not clear that they engaged in any sustained combat, they are not considered war participants.

Termination and Outcome: Alarmed by the growing strength of the Legalists, Díaz negotiated an agreement with Legalist representatives known as the Convention of Acatlán. When Iglesias vetoed the agreement, Díaz decided to act quickly. His troops engaged government forces led by General Alattore on November 16 at Tecoac in Puebla. The arrival of additional rebel forces under Gen. Manuel Gonzales secured a decisive victory. Lerdo's government fled, and Díaz (now commanding between 12,000 and 16,000) marched into Mexico City unopposed on November 23. The outcome was an unconditional rebel victory. Díaz broke off negotiations with the Legalists and proclaimed himself president on November 28, 1876. Díaz gained the support of Legalist governors, and from December 15 to December 30, about 9,000 Legalists defected to Díaz. On January 2, Iglesias went into exile. On May 12, 1877, Díaz was elected president, and his long dictatorship lasted until the Third Mexican War in 1910 (Intra-state War #652).

Coding Decisions: Kohn refers to the entire period of 1871 to 1877 as one war; however, COW coding rules require sustained combat with a minimum of 1,000 battle-deaths per annum, which does not occur until 1876. Díaz estimated that there were 1,900 government battle-deaths. Simply adding together known battle fatalities produces a total of 3,100 battle-deaths (which may be an underestimate). However, subtracting 1,900 from 3,100 produces an estimate of 1,200 rebel battle-deaths.

Sources: Alec-Tweedie (1906), Bancroft, Nemos, Savage, and Peatfield (1888); Clodfelter (2002, 2008); Garner (2001); Hart (2002); Jaques (2007); Kohn (1986); Marley (1998); Payno (2010); Perry (1978).

INTRA-STATE WAR #611

Haitian Civil War of 1883 to 1884 (aka Miragoane Drama)

Participants: Haiti versus Liberals.
Dates: March 27, 1883, to January 8, 1884.
Battle-related Deaths: Armed Forces of Haiti: 2,400; Liberals: 400. (See Coding Decisions.)
Initiator: Liberals.
Outcome: Haiti wins.
War Type: Civil for control of the central government.
Total System Member Military Personnel: Armed Forces of Haiti: 7,000 (prewar, initial, peak, final).[86]
Theater Armed Forces: Armed Forces of Haiti: 6,828 (prewar, initial, peak, final).[87] Liberal Rebels (Rebel Army): 163 (initial); 400 (peak); 150 (final).

Antecedents: In Haiti, national and liberal adherents had confronted one another throughout the nineteenth century. Their clashes often turned into racial massacres as the nationalists (or reactionaries) were primarily *noirs* (blacks) and the liberals (or republicans) were primarily the multiracial *mulâtres* elites. Sylvain Salnave assumed the presidency in March 1867 but was deposed and executed during the Guerre des Cacos of 1868 to 1869 (Intra-state War #592). Two of the leaders of the rebellion then assumed leadership of the republic, Jean Nissage-Saget as president and Michel Domingue as vice president. Nissage-Saget served the full four years of his term, followed by a period of turmoil before Domingue assumed the presidency in 1874. Within two years, he was succeeded by Pierre Théoma

Boisrond-Canal, another of the generals in the *Cacos* war. Boisrond-Canal's administration was marked by heightened disputes between the National and Liberal parties in the House of Representatives. Liberal leader Jean-Pierre Boyer-Bazelais played an instrumental role in the riots that broke out in June 1879. Though the rebellion was crushed (sending Boyer-Bazelais into exile), Boisrond-Canal resigned the next month. Nationalist Lysius Salomon (who had served in the government of Emperor Faustin I) returned from exile in Europe on August 18, 1879, to assume the presidency. Salomon made clear his determination to restore order: he declared martial law in the capital, made hundreds of arrests, sentenced many to death, and seized hostages to ensure compliance among the exiles. Relatively soon, the liberal elite began to plan a coup, and they succeeded in obtaining an American steamer, the *Tropic*, to transport a small revolutionary force of exiled Haitian rebels from Jamaica and Cuba into the country.

Narrative: On March 23, 1883, the *Tropic* departed the island of Inagua (north of Haiti) with seventy Haitian exiles. At sea the next day, it rendezvoused with the *Albo*, a British ship traveling from Jamaica with liberal Jean-Pierre Boyer-Bazelais and another twenty rebels. On March 27, 1883, the ninety-two exiles landed on Haiti's southern peninsula, where they were joined by another seventy local rebels. The rebels easily seized the garrison at the town of Miragoane, located on the coast west of the capital of Port-au-Prince, and about a thousand government troops were sent against them. The rebels won the first skirmishes, forcing the government to resort to a siege, with the port of Miragoane blockaded by the Haitian Navy. The war began to spread. On April 13, some of the *Cacos* of the North rebelled, though they were defeated quickly. The rest of the major fighting took place on the southwestern peninsula, west of Port-au-Prince. On May 27, the town of Jérémie joined the rebellion. Government assaults on Jérémie failed, and the government tried to enforce a blockade of the entire tip of the peninsula.

The inability of the rebels to supply their forces may have saved the government. On July 22, a force of forty-four rebels succeeded in taking the town of Jacmel to the southeast, less than twenty-five miles from the capital. As additional towns joined the rebellion, the government was forced to mount an offensive. On August 2 and 3, an attack by 800 *piquets* allied to the government failed to take Jacmel, with heavy losses. A second attempt on September 17 also failed. On September 22, a group of liberal students assassinated Haitian Gen. Pénor Benjamin in a failed coup attempt. In response, a mob composed mainly of government soldiers and poor *noirs* (blacks) went on a riotous killing spree in Port-au-Prince. The city's business district was destroyed, and 4,000 citizens, mostly *mulâtres*, were killed. This massacre appears to have broken the will of the liberals.

By October, hunger and disease were severe at Miragoane. Rebel leader Boyer-Bazelais died on October 27. In mid-November, Salmon's newly purchased ship, *Dessalines*, caught and critically damaged the rebel ship *La Patrie*, further harming the rebels' supply lines. The government tightened its siege of rebel-held towns and bombarded Jérémie and Jacmel from November 19 to November 21. By December, most rebels in Miragoane were dead from hunger or disease. On December 5, they asked for terms of surrender but were rebuffed by the government. Jérémie fell to a government assault around Christmas, and Jacmel was taken five days later. On January 8, 1884, the rebels remaining in Miragoane broke out but were killed in combat or executed, marking the end of the war.

Termination and Outcome: The outcome was a government victory. The end of the war was followed by a bloodbath. Forty-seven rebels were executed at Jacmel after being promised amnesty, and at least 150 of those who fled from Miragoane were captured and executed. President Salomon remained in office. Revolts in Port-au-Prince in 1887 and Cap-Haitien in 1888 finally persuaded Salomom to resign and to return to Paris.

Coding Decisions: The peak number of rebel combatants was estimated by extrapolating backward from the final rebel strength at Miragoane (150 as the majority of rebels in the town died before then. Accordingly, there must have been more than 300 rebels in Miragoane. There were 44 rebels in Jacmel and an unknown but likely similar number in Jérémie, yielding a total of about 400.

Estimates of battle deaths vary widely. Contemporary accounts speak of hundreds up to 7,000 killed.[88] Rodman says that the rebels "accounted for" 8,000 of the 13,000 government soldiers facing them, but both numbers appear to be exaggerations because the entire government army was smaller than 7,000 men. The number of rebels was always small, though disease took a high toll from both sides. Moreover, the number of rebels executed was probably higher than the number killed in battle.[89] Finally, a massacre in Port-au-Prince killed 4,000 people, nearly all of them civilians. Considering all estimates, we accept the figure of 7,000 total deaths but subtract the 4,000 known civilian deaths and 200 executions to reach a maximum total of 2,800 battle-deaths. As far as we can determine, every rebel died. During the sieges, about 100 rebels died—53 at Miragoane and 45 elsewhere. Because about 200 were executed, 100 are unaccounted for, giving us an estimate of 400 rebel battle-deaths.[90] Thus the estimates of battle deaths are: armed forces of Haiti, 2,400 and liberals, 400.

Sources: Annual Register of Word Events (1758–); Appleton's Annual (1886); Atherley-Jones and Bellot (1907); Clodfelter (2008); Heinl (1996); Heinl and Heinl (1978, 2005); Jackson (1999); Rodman (1954).

INTRA-STATE WAR #635
Second Yaqui War of 1899 to 1900

Participants: Mexico versus Yaqui Indian Rebels.
Dates: July 21, 1899, to January 18, 1900.
Battle-related Deaths: Armed Forces of Mexico: 80; Yaqui Indian Rebels: 1,100.
Initiator: Yaqui Indians.
Outcome: Mexico wins.
War Type: Civil for local issues.
Total System Member Military Personnel: Armed Forces of Mexico—33,000.[91]
Theater Armed Forces: Armed Forces of Mexico: 1,000 (peak, including 82 Yaqui Auxiliary).[92] Yaqui Indian Rebels: 400 (initial);[93] 3,000 (peak).

Antecedents: The Yaqui Indians generally lived in what became the far northwestern Mexican state of Sonora. The Spanish had been lured to the area by the presence of silver, and they began the process of seizing Yaqui land. In the eighteenth century, the Yaqui saw themselves as independent of Spanish rule, and they allied with the nearby Mayo in an attempt to drive the Spanish out. The Yaqui maintained their resistance to outside domination after Mexico gained its independence. Juan Ignacio Jusacamea, later know as Juan Banderas, attempted to create an Indian military confederation among the western Indian tribes. The Yaqui resisted Mexican attempts to draft Yaqui to fight against the Apache, precipitating the Mexico–Yaqui Indian War of 1825 to 1827 (Non-state war #1509).[94] The war ended as a compromise with the Yaqui gaining some autonomy.

The Mexicans continued seizing Yaqui lands, with the result that some of the Yaqui were dispersed, while others were sold into slavery, some to plantations in Oaxca and Yucatán. In 1868, Yaqui leader Cajeme (José Maria Leyva) led a revolt, which was subdued by a major Mexican expedition in 1877. During the 1880s the Mexican elites continued seizing Yaqui land and began selling the land to the wealthy *criollos* and foreigners, leading to another revolt, led by Cajeme and Tetabiate from 1885 to 1886. Cajeme's followers were sold as slaves to plantations in Quintana Roo, where most of them died.

Mexico began a comprehensive plan for the recolonization of the Yaqui lands along the Rio Yaqui. The plan encouraged both new settlers and formerly displaced Yaqui to adopt farming on distributed plots of land, which conflicted with Yaqui communal land ownership. Renewed resistance broke out in 1892 and from 1894 to 1895. In 1896, Mexican Col. Francisco Peinado ended the conflict through negotiations. An agreement, the Peace of Ortiz, which included a commitment of Yaqui obedience to the Mexican government, was signed on May 15, 1897, by Tetabiate and Gen. Luis E. Torres. General Torres recruited a number of the former Yaqui guerrillas, including Tetabiate and José Loreto Villa, to serve as officers in the Mexican auxiliary troops and distributed parcels of land to encourage the Yaqui to take up farming along the Río Yaqui.

Narrative: Yaqui resistance grew as white colonists increased and Mexican soldiers did not leave. Torres ordered the two former Yaqui guerrillas, Tetabiate and Villa, to capture the new leaders of the Yaqui resistance. Thereupon Tetabiate and his men rebelled, returning to the mountains, while Villa remained with General Torres. On July 21, 1899, the Yaqui chiefs demanded that all Mexicans leave

Sonora (the start of this war). The Yaqui assassinated the nephew of General Torres and attempted to kill Villa as well. The position of the Yaqui differed from earlier periods of conflict: many had left the mountains and returned to lands along the river, where they had been able to stockpile weapons. The rebels were able to field large forces of 500 to 1,000 men in areas along the river and caught the Mexicans by surprise. Torres responded, gathering troops from the Torin and Potam garrisons to fight the rebels along the Río Yaqui. The Yaqui thus faced both seasoned Mexican troops and the Yaqui auxiliary forces commanded by Villa and Julian Espinosa. Consequently, in most of these engagements, the Yaqui did not fare well, suffering a high number of casualties. In September 87 Yaqui rebels were killed at Bahueca. Consequently, the rebels began to break into smaller contingents and retreat to their strongholds in the Sierra de Bacatete. In January 1900, the Mexican government sent reinforcements to this campaign. Gen. Lorenzo Torres planned an assault on a rebel army under Pablo Opodepe that had taken refuge in stronghold on the Mazocoda plateau. On January 18, Torres's 1,000 men were able to scale the cliffs and defeat the rebels in bloody fighting. The bodies of more than 400 rebels were found on the battlefield, and others had thrown themselves off the cliffs into the canyon to avoid capture. In the Mexican victory, the government forces lost 54 killed. An additional 900 captives (many noncombatants) died during a forced march into captivity. This major engagement marks the end of the war.

Termination and Outcome: This war is a Mexican victory. The government launched another campaign later in 1900; however, the number of rebels had declined, and the skirmishes (which continued into 1904) were relatively small. In one of these, Tetabiate was killed by government forces led by Loreto Villa. To further the policy of intimidating the Yaqui, the government ramped up their policy of sending captured Yaquis abroad or to other parts of the country. There are reports that 8,000 Yaquis were sold as slaves to plantations in the Yucatán. This mistreatment made the Yaqui willing participants in the Third Mexican War of 1910 to 1914 (Intra-state War #652) and The Fourth Mexican War of 1914 to 1920 (Intra-state War #673). A final Mexican excursion against the Yaqui took place in from 1926 to 1927.

Coding Decisions: Col. Garcia Peña calculated that 920 rebels perished in the battles of this war.[95] Clodfelter reported that 1,000 were killed in the battle at Mazacoda alone, with another 87 at Bahueca.[96] Scheina and Clodfelter estimate that 1,800 captives were seized at Mazocoda, with half dying in the subsequent march to captivity. Hu-Dehart puts the numbers at 1,000 captives and 834 survivors; however, she refers to the captives as including the wounded rebels, while Clodfelter refers to them as noncombatants.[97] Thus a figure of 1,100 Yaqui deaths seems reasonable if we assume that of the captives, 100 may have been rebels who died of their wounds. The only Mexican fatality figure we have located is the 54 (or 56) who died in the final battle. Because we know that some were killed in the earlier attacks of the war, a total figure of 80 seems a reasonable best guess.

Sources: Clodfelter (2002); Hu-DeHart (1984); Marley (1998); Scheina (2003a); Spicer (1980).

INTRA-STATE WAR #637

Quintana Roo War of 1899 to 1901

Participants: Mexico versus Mayan *Cruzob*.
Dates: October 1899 to May 4, 1901.
Battle-related Deaths: Armed Forces of Mexico: 2,000.[98] *Cruzob* (Rebel Army): [ ].
Initiator: Mexico.
Outcome: Mexico wins.
War Type: Civil for local issues (autonomy).
Total System Member Military Personnel: Armed Forces of Mexico: 33,000 (prewar, initial, peak, final).[99]
Theater Armed Forces: Armed Forces of Mexico including Yucatán National Guard: 1,000 (initial); 4,000 (peak).[100] *Cruzob* (Rebel Army): 3,000 (initial);[101] 2,200 (peak);[102] 800 (final).[103]

Antecedents: The name of this war refers to the region in which the fighting took place. After the Caste Wars of 1847 to 1855 (Intra-state Wars #545 and #553), the state of Yucatán (site of the fighting) was subdivided, creating a separate Campeche in the West in 1858 and the territory of Quintana Roo along the eastern coast in 1902, which was named after Andrés Quintana Roo, who had been sent in 1841 by General Santa Anna to encourage Yucatán to reincorporate with Mexico.

The Caste Wars had entailed a revolt primarily by the Mayan Indians, or *indios*, against the *ladinos*, or those of Spanish culture to achieve autonomy for all of the Yucatán Mayans. In this the Mayans failed; however, during the course of the war, many of the *ladinos* had fled westward toward Campeche, while the Mayans dominated in the East. The wars took a terrible toll on the Mayans, who were reduced in number from 100,000 to only 10,000 by 1895. During the war, a spiritual movement was founded by Juan de La Cruz Puc, who was transformed when he heard voices coming from a cross carved in a tree. Those who responded to his message (or the followers of the Speaking Cross) came to be called the *Cruzob*, and they proved to be the hard core of the Mayan revolt. The *Cruzob* main town was established at Chan Santa Cruz in 1850, in the southeastern Yucatán, and after the end of the war, it became a free Mayan state that was recognized as a de facto independent nation by the United Kingdom from the late 1850s through 1893. This status was not recognized by Mexico. As the Yucatán became increasingly richer due to increased demand for timber and *henequen*, which is used in making rope, the Mexican government became more interested in reasserting control over the area. During this period, Mexico had revived the practice of shipping *indios* captured in the conflict with the Yaqui to northwest Mexico to work on the Yucatán *henequen* plantations (Intra-state War #635). Agricultural concerns, first established on the northeastern tip of Yucatán, began expanding toward the *Cruzob*-controlled areas of the southeast, prompting a resumption of hostilities between the *Cruzob* and the Yucatán in 1886.

Subsequently the *Cruzob* leaders had approached the officials in British Honduras with the request to join the British colony. Britain and Mexico had come into conflict over logging in the region but were desirous of entering into a treaty with one another. The British began the project of the demarcation of the border between Mexico (Yucatán) and British Honduras, even though the Mexicans wanted to postpone the agreement pending the completion of a military campaign against the *Cruzob* rebels. The signing of the Mexican–British treaty on July 3, 1893, precipitated a flood of *Cruzob* refugees into British Honduras. After the treaty was ratified in July 1897, Mexico attempted to persuade the *Cruzob* to submit to Mexican control peacefully while prohibiting arms sales to the *Cruzob* from British Honduras.

In 1896, the leadership of Chan Santa Cruz had passed to Felipe Yama, who initially favored a pacific resolution of the conflict, as did Mexican president Porfirio Díaz. However, *Cruzob* hesitance was fueled by their opposition to a trans-Yucatán railroad, which would both further agricultural expansion and provide a means to send federal troops to engage in the pacification campaign. By February 1898 the railroad was almost completed from the capital of Mérida southeast to Peto. To protect the railroad, a Yucatán militia detachment of 150 men was sent to the nearby town of Ichmul, which had been the site of one of the Mayan victories in the Caste War. By June 1899, the railroad had reached Tihosuco, formerly one of the Mayan strongholds.

Narrative: In 1898, President Díaz, seeking a Yucatán governor willing to undertake a joint federal state pacification campaign against the *Cruzob*, appointed Gen. Francisco (Pancho) Cantón, who had earlier participated in the fight against the Mayans. In addition to the Yucatán militia already assigned to the railroad, three federal battalions under the leadership of Gen. Ignacio A. Bravo arrived on September 15, 1899. The next month, Angel Ortiz Monasterio arrived in Mérida as the commander of a fleet of six Mexican ships, and planning was underway for military expeditions should peaceful tactics fail. In an attempt at a pacific solution, in October 1899, a British delegation had a meeting with the central Mayan leadership at Santa Cruz Chico, though Felipe Yama declined to attend. The meeting was unproductive. The war started with the advance of Bravo's troops southward from Ichmul to Saban and into the territory of Chan Santa Cruz. The first major *Cruzob* attack occurred at Okop on December 27 and 28, 1899. Though the *Cruzob* suffered casualties, the attack had little impact on Bravo's forces. However, the Mexican government used this incident of what they referred to as rebel-initiated hostilities to inform the British that Mexico was no longer willing to participate in peace negotiations. A second attack by the *Cruzob* on the Saban-Okop road in February 1900 was repelled by a force of 200 Mexican soldiers at a cost of 20 Mexican casualties to 12 rebel deaths. The Mexicans continued to advance, and in April they forced the rebels out of Santa María. That same month, the governor of British Honduras received letters from *Cruzob* leaders Felipe Yama and León Pat claiming that it was the Mexicans who had started the war and asking Britain to intervene.

Bravo continued to advance to the southeast and began systematically to deforest the area held by the *Cruzob*, depriving them of the ability to wage guerrilla warfare. The Mexicans also established a station called Sombrerete (later named Zaragoza) on the Caribbean coast at the Mexican border with British Honduras, where troops and supplies could be unloaded. By January, the forces there numbered about 1,000 under the command of Gen. Rosalino Martínez. Through the first part of 1900, Bravo's troops continued to slowly advance until the summer rains stalled their advance and disease began to take a toll. Meanwhile, rebel uprisings in the northeast led to an increase in the number of rebels moving to San Antonio Muyil.

At the beginning of 1901, Bravo's forces (halfway to Santa Cruz) concentrated on a new offensive toward the rebel capital. The Mexicans, armed with more modern weapons, easily were able to repel the rebel guerrilla attacks. In the next few months, the government fought two major battles and twenty-two skirmishes against a rebel force of only 1,000 to 1,500 men, which quickly declined to 800 due to combat, desertions, starvation, and an epidemic of mumps. In February, the new commandant at Sombrerete, Gen. Jose María de la Vega, led a 500-strong force against the southern rebel stronghold at Bacalar, forcing the rebels to retreat. Vega captured Bacalar on March 20, 1901, and then advanced northward, reaching Nohpop, only sixteen kilometers from Santa Cruz, by April. The success of the Mexican two-pronged advances prompted many of the rebels to abandon the fight and flee to British Honduras, some killing *Cruzob* leader Felipe Yama in the process. When Bravo entered Santa Cruz on May 4, 1901, it was deserted. Bravo established his new headquarters there, and when he was visited a month later by Governor Cantón, the governor renamed the town Santa Cruz de Bravo.

Termination and Outcome: The war ended as an unconditional victory for the government, though some rebels had merely withdrawn and continued random attacks. In September, Brigadier Gen. Victoriano Huerta arrived from Veracruz with an additional 500 soldiers to launch a new attack against the rebels at Chunpom. The Mexicans took control of the land and forced the Mayans into near slavery under a system of fifty plantations. In November 1901, the Mexican government proposed detaching eastern Yucatán and creating a separate federal district, Quintana Roo, in order to maintain direct control. The proposal was approved in April 1902. Quintana Roo was reconfigured as part of Yucatán in 1915 but was separated again, becoming Mexico's newest state in 1974.

Coding Decisions: The government expedition suffered more than 2,000 deaths, "mostly due to disease and deprivation."[104] Rebel battle-deaths, while heavy, are unknown.

Sources: Dumond (1997); Perry (1978); Robins (2005); Scheina (2003a, b); Weinberg (2000); Wells and Joseph (1996).

INTRA-STATE WAR #649
Bluefields Insurrection of 1909 to 1910

Dates: October 10, 1909, to August 20, 1910.
Participants: Nicaragua versus Estradistas.
Battle-related Deaths: Nicaragua: [ ]; *Estradistas*: [ ]; Total Combatant Deaths: 1,192.
Initiator: Estradistas.
Outcome: Estradistas win.
War Type: Civil for control of the central government.
Total System Member Military Personnel: Armed Forces of Nicaragua: 4,000 (prewar); 4,000 (initial); 4,000 (peak).[105]
Theater Armed Forces: Estradistas (Rebel Army): 2,000 (prewar); 2,000 (initial); 4,500 (peak).[106]

Antecedents: José Santos Zelaya came to power in Nicaragua's 1891 Liberal Revolution with a nationalist agenda for economic development and adopted a policy of granting foreign concessions in return for capital. These concessions frequently involved acrimony between Nicaragua and European investors. Zelaya particularly alienated the residents (both foreign and domestic) of Mosquitia, or the Mosquito Coast, which had been a British protectorate from 1655 to 1860. It remained an autonomous entity until Zelaya's government incorporated the resource-rich area in 1894, ultimately renaming the region the Zelaya Department. In 1899, the government suppressed a major revolt there, financed by Anglo-American business leaders.

Nicaraguan–American relations were strained further by the American assumption of the Panama Canal project in 1904 and by the related American desire to hinder moves by Zelaya's government to create a Nicaraguan alternative. Zelaya's government also posed a challenge to American designs by its moves to revive the Central American Confederation, which precipitated two inter-state wars in 1906 and 1907 (Inter-state Wars #88 and #91). In the later war, Nicaragua was successful in overthrowing the conservative government in Honduras, and American mediation in the Washington Conference of 1907 reflected the growing American opposition to the Zelayan regime.

The Nicaraguan liberals began to fragment into "authentic" liberals and *probonos*, who benefited from Zelaya's largesse. In 1909, labor unrest increased considerably, and in August, the "authentic" liberals denounced Zelaya and split the party at its national convention. That year, two events precipitated the eventual civil war. First, Zelaya invaded El Salvador seeking regime change, and though the invasion was quickly repelled, Zelaya continued to supply El Salvador's liberal rebels with arms. Second, in May 1909, a major strike occurred on banana plantations in Bluefields, the capital of the Mosquitia region (Zelaya Department), in protest of higher taxes imposed by the government and the increase in fees charged by United Fruit, which had a government-granted monopoly on banana transportation via the Bluefields Steam Company. The strike dragged on through the summer.

In July, Juan Estrada, an alienated Zelayalista, informed the American consul that he could overthrow the government successfully with $50,000 and 2,000 rifles. He had a strong following in the Bluefields area, and he claimed he could mobilize the support of its 2,000-strong garrison rapidly for an insurrection.

Narrative: On October 10, 1909, Juan Estrada proclaimed a revolt against Zelaya in Bluefields. The first operation of the war was his seizure of "the Bluff" overlooking Bluefields Lagoon. He immediately set up an independent government on the Mosquito Coast and then appointed conservative general Emiliano Chamorro to lead the revolution in the West. From the onset, the rebellion was an alliance of convenience between "authentic" liberals and the Conservative Party. Rebel military forces consisted of the regional garrison, black Creoles from the region under Willie Lowis, and American volunteers. Although the rebellion was "conservative," few Nicaraguan conservatives took part in it. The rebellion was financed by Manuel Estrada Cabrera, the president of Guatemala, a political ally of the United States and longtime regional rival of Zelaya. While there is no evidence of direct involvement by the US government in the initial revolt, American merchants sold merchandise to the rebels.

The rebels steadily increased in number, occupying San Juan del Norte and the lake town of San Carlos without resistance. On October 14, Zelaya sent a force against Bluefields, which advanced about fifty miles into the Zelaya region before being routed at Rama. In the South, Zelaya's forces marched on Castillo Viejo, where they engaged Chamorro's army on October 22. The government lost about 100 soldiers killed in the engagement, but historians disagree about who won the battle. It is clear that the government won the campaign in the South, defeating the rebels in battles on November 6 and 10. The United States found a pretext for armed intervention when two Americans and one Frenchman were captured while trying to mine the San Juan River. All three were tried, and the two Americans were executed. The United States broke diplomatic relations with Nicaragua on December 1, 1909, and landed Marines in Bluefields. Realizing the danger that American intervention posed, Zelaya resigned as president on December 16 and fled Nicaragua a week later. Zelaya's resignation did not stop the fighting. The rebels continued their advance from Ram, and from December 20 to December 21, the bloody Battle of Recreo was fought between the two sides near Managua. The use of modern machine guns and obsolete tactics generated high casualties: of 4,000 government soldiers engaged, more than 400 were killed. The defeat was devastating to the government.

Zelaya appointed José Madriz as his successor, and Madriz immediately offered Estrada a generous peace agreement. Though the United States continued to favor Estrada, six weeks of negotiations following Zelaya's resignation made it clear that Estrada had lost the leadership of the rebellion to Chamorro and the conservatives. By January 17, 1910, the rebels had columns of 1,600, 1,500, and 1,000. Three fierce engagements were fought at La Garita and Santa Clara. Despite the heavy losses, the rebel army increased to 4,500 men by the end of January. In February, Chamorro again struck west toward Managua. On February 18, the two sides met again at Chino, and four days later the rebels suffered a decisive defeat near Tisma. A rebel attack at Tipitata, about ten miles from the capital, was catastrophic for the rebels, reducing their army to only 150 effectives. Chamorro retreated to Bluefields, arriving there with four aides in late April.

At that point, the rebels also lost Guatemalan assistance, and the number of American volunteers had fallen to 50. By May, the government recaptured Chili in a bloody battle that involved nearly 8,000 troops on both sides. The rebels were reduced to a shrinking perimeter around the city of Bluefields itself. The United States declared Bluefields to be a neutral zone, where no fighting would be permitted, in effect, providing the rebels a safe base of operations. As the government army approached Bluefields, the United States landed 200 marines to secure the town on May 19, 1910. Another 150 American volunteers sailed to reinforce the rebels. Five days later, the first unit of actual Nicaraguan conservatives arrived. By May 31, the government had reoccupied the Bluff but was unable to advance. On that same day, another 200 American marines landed in the city and cleared out the forces of both sides in the suburbs. The number of marines deployed eventually reached 700.

Demoralization set in among the government soldiers as they realized that they could not defeat the rebellion without fighting the United States. In mid-June, the conservatives pushed the government forces away from Bluefields in a costly engagement. By the end of the month, the rebels controlled most of the countryside surrounding Bluefields. By July, the rebels launched another offensive against Managua. Only late in the month did the government attempt to defend a strategic position, at the Battle of Comalopa, which turned out to be the last battle of the war. Government forces simply fled from rebel advances. Madriz resigned the presidency and left the country on August 20, 1910, appointing José Estrada as president.

Termination and Outcome: The outcome was a rebel victory. José and Aurelio Estrada continued the functions of government until their brother Juan Estrada arrived on August 29, 1910, immediately assuming the presidency. From October 27 to 30, 1910, the United States negotiated the Dawson Pact with the leaders of the rebellion. The pact called for elections, abolished certain concessions, and offered the good offices of the United States to secure a loan for the new government. The result was a mixed liberal–conservative provisional government.

Coding Decisions: In terms of war participants, despite its dominant role in the conflict, the United States is not coded as a war participant as its forces (less than 1,000) never actually participated in combat. There is a paucity of information on battle-deaths for this war. Teplitz cites at least 1,192 deaths, which we cite here for total combatant deaths.[107]

Sources: Rice (1995); Scheina (2003a, b); Teplitz (1973), Woodward (1993).

INTRA-STATE WAR #652
Third Mexican War of 1910 to 1914 (aka Mexican Revolution)

Participants: Mexico versus Liberals and Radicals, aided by the United States.
Dates: November 20, 1910, to June 6, 1911, August 26, 1911, July 19, 1914. (See Coding Decisions.)
Battle-related Deaths: Mexico: 90,000; liberals and radicals: 60,000; the United States: 22.
Initiator: Liberals and radicals.
Outcome: Liberals and radicals win.
War Type: Civil for control of the central government.
Total System Member Military Personnel: Armed Forces of Mexico: 30,000 (prewar); 31,000 (initial); 57,000 (peak); 30,000 (final).[108]
Theater Armed Forces: First Phase—Armed Forces of Mexico: 14,000 (prewar, initial); 18,000 (peak). There is no final estimate because many units switched to the rebels in the closing weeks of the war.[109] Revolutionary Army: at least 2,000 (initial); 40,000 (peak, final). It should be noted that the rebel army essentially doubled in the last few weeks of the war as previous supporters of the government signed on to the revolution.[110]

Second Phase—Armed Forces of Mexico: 31,000 (prewar); 45,000 (postcoup); 150,000 (peak); 150,000 (final).[111] Zapatistas (Rebel Army): 3,000 (prewar, initial); 15,000 (peak); 15,000 (final).[112] Orozquistas (Rebel Army), participating from March 23, 1912, until February 27, 1913: 6,000 (prewar, initial, peak); 3,000 (final).[113] Vasquistas (Rebel Army), participating until fall 1912: [ ]. Constitutionalists (Rebel Aggregate), participating from March 7, 1913, to July 15, 1914: 3,700 (initial—counts Sonora and Coahuila units only); 41,000 (peak, final). The peak and final estimates include units under Carranza and Villa only.[114] United States of America (Pro-rebel Intervener), participating from April 21, 1914, to July 15, 1914: 5,800 (initial);[115] 7,000 (final).[116]

Antecedents: Porfirio Díaz had ruled Mexico as a dictator since seizing power in 1876 (Intra-state War #602). By 1908 he was approaching eighty years of age and expected to run for his eighth term of office. Because many believed he would die in office, a political battle developed for the vice presidency. The leading candidates were the unpopular vice president, Rámon Corral, and Manuel Reyes, governor of Nuevo León and a former minister of war. He formed the pro-Díaz, moderately liberal Democratic Party to advance his views, and the *Reyista* movement quickly captured support from those who had formed the base of previous, unsuccessful, liberal parties.

The chief non-liberal opponents of the regime were the indigenous population, who like the Yaqui, had suffered the loss of communal lands during the Porfirian era (see Intra-state War #635) as the government secured land for foreign (frequently American) business. In 1908, Emilio Zapata launched an insurrection in Anenecuilco that was immediately suppressed. In late 1909, Zapata organized peasants to seize disputed land, which he redistributed in May 1910, inaugurating a campaign of seizures and redistributions that developed into open rebellion later that year.

On the presidential front, Díaz was unable to choose his successor. When Reyes undertook a military mission in Europe, the leadership of much of the liberal movement shifted to wealthy businessman Francisco Ignacio Madero González and his Anti-reelectionist Party, opposed to the reelection of Díaz. Madero was nominated to oppose Díaz for the presidency, and given Díaz's reluctance to allow a fair election, he also began to plan for an armed insurrection. Díaz had Madero and 5,000 to 6,000 of his supporters imprisoned before voting began. Díaz "won" the election and released Madero on bail, after which Madero fled to the United States on October 7, 1910. He drafted a document (the Plan of San Luis Potosí) declaring the election as null and void, calling for a "legal" revolution to restore the constitutional liberties denied by the regime, and affirming Madero as president. It set 6 p.m. on November 20 for the planned revolt. In the meanwhile, Madero made contacts with potential revolutionaries and purchased arms in New York.

Narrative: Mexico would be convulsed by war for the next ten years, leading to the deaths of about 1.5 million persons.[117] This first section of the overall period of rebellion lasted almost four years, and had three phases—the anti-Díaz revolts, the anti-Madero revolts, and the anti-Huerta revolts. In the first of these, the government preempted the urban revolt on November 18 by raiding the houses of known liberals. On November 20, 1910, a widely dispersed and disparate set of rebel groups began attacking government forces, starting this war.

Only the handful of risings in the countryside had any appreciable effect. In the North, a notable Maderista was Pascual Orozco in Chihuahua, who first attacked government officials affiliated with Díaz and then proceeded to seize the town of Guerrero on November 30, 1910. Other revolutionaries in the Sierra included Pancho Villa (José Doroteo Arango Arámbula), who joined a band led by Castulo Herrera in a successful attack on a train loaded with federal forces. Herrera appointed Villa as his second in command, yet Villa soon gained control of the rebel group. Villa then joined forces with Orozco, and together they decided to fight a pitched battle at Cerro Prieto on December 11, 1910. In fierce fighting, the rebels were repulsed, persuading them that they were still more suited for guerrilla warfare.

Further south, other risings succeeded in establishing bases in the mountains of Durango and Sinaloa. Ramón Iturbe was one of these revolutionaries who shifted from warfare in the Sierra to war in lowlands as his numbers grew. Zapata's forces united with other Morelos rebels and endorsed Madera. Initially Díaz had offered the rebels a truce; however, he soon decided that a military victory was necessary to restore faith in his regime. He sent a

5,000-soldier army under Gen. Juan Hernández to Chihuahua, which produced government victories at Cerro Prieto and Ciudad Guerrero but soon suffered 200 killed in an ambush at the canyon of Galindes Vinata. By early 1911, rebels controlled the mountains, and the government controlled the lowlands. As the rebels moved toward the lowlands, they gained the support of Calixto Contreras and 4,000 Ocuila Indians in February 1911.

Madero personally crossed into Mexico on February 14, 1911, but his 600 troops were defeated by the government at Casas Grandes on March 6. Seeking to reaffirm his leadership of the revolution, he formally appointed Orozco and Villa to positions within his Revolutionary Army. On April 14, Zapata officially was designated as Madero's representative in the state of Morelos (south of the capital). The government's near-monopoly on machine guns and artillery enabled it to defeat much larger rebel forces, inflicting severe casualties. Nonetheless the rebels continued to make progress around the country. By April there were more than 18,700 rebels. The sheer geographical scope of the rebellion forced the government to disperse its best troops, making it increasingly difficult to maintain superiority on every front.

In April, Madero besieged Ciudad Juárez. Rebels led by Villa and Orozco stormed the city, which fell on May 10. On May 13, 1911, Zapata's force of 4,000 attacked 400 government troops at Cuautla, and few government troops survived. The rebel victory enshrined Zapata's reputation while also finally persuading Díaz of the precariousness of his position. On May 21, Madero agreed to the Treaty of Cuidad Juárez, which provided that Díaz and Vice President Corral would resign by the end of May to be replaced by a caretaker regime that would hold free elections. The end of the Díaz regime came on May 25, when Díaz resigned and fled the country. The fighting continued until June 6, when Madero also entered Mexico City. He assumed the presidency on November 6, 1911.

Unfortunately, the resulting peace turned out to be short-lived, and the two-month pause in the fighting delineates the two phases of this war. The second phase of the revolt began during the term of the interim president, León de la Barra, who was fundamentally opposed to the radical elements of the revolution. Rebels like Zapata did not recognize the authority of the interim government, and consequently the president relied heavily on conservative Gen. Victoriano Huerta in attempts to disarm and pacify the South. Following a massacre of former agrarian rebels in Puebla, Emilio Vasquez Gomez resigned his government post and began plotting a new rebellion. On August 23, 1911, he entered Mexico from the United States, and his supporters proclaimed him president. Meanwhile, President de la Barra sent Huerta with a force of 1,500 infantry and 600 cavalry to disarm the Zapatistas. By August 26, Zapata's forces were besieged and actively fighting Huerta's army at Yautepec, which marks the revival of the war. Disheartened by Madero's lack of support, Zapata and 1,500 men returned to attack federal forces in Morelo.

Thus, by the time that Madero took office in November, he already faced two armed rebellions: the Vazquista revolt in the North and the Zapatista rebellion in the South. His moderate plan of reform was insufficient to pacify the radicals but prompted a backlash from conservatives. Madero also vacillated between attempts to make peace with Zapata, and efforts to defeat the ongoing insurrections. On November 28, 1911, Zapata released his Plan of Ayla, which repudiated Madero, demanded significant land reform, and announced his support of former Madero ally, Pascual Orozco, as the legitimate president. The Vazquista revolt was defeated in late 1911 but reignited in Chihuahua in February 1912. Also in the north, Orozco launched a rebellion with 8,000 soldiers on March 2, 1912, and initially allied himself with Zapata. The first major battle on this front occurred on March 23, 1912, when the rebels routed a federal army of 6,000 men at Rellano. Orozco's success gave him almost complete control of Chihuahua, where he established his new government. Orozco's army continued to advance, defeating the 300 men led by Pancho Villa at Parral on April 2. Villa had remained loyal to Madero, and after his defeat, Villa was invited to join the regular army at Torreón, where he assisted Huerta in hunting down Orozquistas (until Huerta had him arrested in June). The rebels' capital at Chihuahua City fell to Huerta's forces on July 8, after which Orozco moved his capital to Ojinaga and pursued guerrilla warfare.

Opposition to Madero on the right continued to spread, encompassing Felix Díaz, the nephew of the former dictator Porfirio Díaz, who led an unsuccessful revolt in Veracruz. In February 1913, a group of twenty-two generals (who had the active support of American ambassador Henry Lane Wilson) decided to act against Madero. A violent stretch of the war known as *La Decena Trágica* (The Tragic Ten Days) began on February 9, 1913. Gen. Manuel Mondragon led a group of military cadets who released Felix Díaz and Manuel Reyes from prison and attempted to seize the National Palace, where Reyes was killed. Díaz succeeded in occupying the citadel and establishing defensive positions, and 1,500 to 2,000 soldiers defected to his side. Huerta was again recalled and placed in command of government forces, and an artillery battle ensued. American ambassador Wilson secretly arranged for Huerta to overthrow Madero. On February 18, Huerta had Madero arrested and later shot. Huerta and Díaz (now reduced to only 400 troops) reached an agreement that enabled Huerta to become president on February 19, 1913.

Once it became clear that Huerta had installed himself as a reactionary dictator, further revolts erupted: in Coahuila and Sonora (aided by several thousand Yaqui Indian) in the northwest; by Zapatistas in the south; Carranza's "Constitutionalists" in the northeast; Villa in Chihuahua; and smaller rebellions elsewhere. Huerta responded by tackling the best-coordinated forces first, sending an expedition into Sonora, where they stopped in May and engaged in the Battle of Hacienda Santa Rosa, in which half of the government forces were killed, wounded, or taken prisoner. A second government expedition of 4,000 soldiers suffered a similar fate. Pancho Villa easily defeated an Orozquista force at Nuevas Casas Grandes in June. Rebel forces continued to grow from 8,000 in March to more than 17,000 in August. Nonetheless, they remained heavily outnumbered as government forces reached about 75,000. Subsequent government expeditions in the North were defeated by Villa in October and November 1913, with heavy government losses.

By 1914, the government's army had increased to between 80,000 and 100,000 but seemed to be losing on every front. In January, Pancho Villa drove the 5,000-strong government army into a refugee camp in the United States. Villa purchased large quantities of arms and ammunition from the United States and on March 25 sent 16,000 against 10,000 federal troops to Torréon. Bitter fighting lasted until government forces evacuated the city on April 3.

At this point, the United States intervened when a minor incident in Tampico on April 9, 1914, gave the United States a pretext to act against Huerta. Informed that a German ship, the *Ypiranga*, was due to arrive at Veracruz with a shipment of weapons for the Mexican government, US president Woodrow Wilson ordered a naval squadron to seize the wharf. Initially 700 US Marines landed on April 21 and were fired upon by forces of the local garrison (killing four Americans). American Rear Adm. Frank Friday Fletcher decided to expand his mission from seizing the wharf to seizing the city. An additional 3,000 marines and a navy regiment were landed, and three warships bombarded the city. American forces of 3,300 sailors and 2,500 marines seized the port, cutting off Huerta's foreign supply lines. In all, the Mexican government lost 126 killed; the Americans suffered 22 fatalities.[118]

By May, Huerta was losing the war. Villa's 23,000 troops advanced on the government position at Zacatecas, northwest of the capital. The 12,000 government troops established defensive positions; however, the rebels stormed Zacatecas from all sides on June 22 in what turned out to be the bloodiest battle of the campaign. At least 6,000 government soldiers were killed, along with 1,000 rebels and numerous civilians.[119] The various rebel armies converged on Mexico City, inflicting defeats on government troops. A peace conference held near Niagara Falls, New York, faltered over President Wilson's insistence on Huerta's removal. Huerta decided to resign on July 15, fleeing the country. Huerta's successor, Francisco Carbajal, unsuccessfully offered terms to Carranza and Villa.

Termination and Outcome: The war continued for a few days as rebel forces raced to be the first to occupy the capital. Zapata seized Milpa Alta (near the capital) on July 19, which seems to be the last major fighting and thus marks the end date of the war. The outcome was an unconditional military victory for the rebels (Constitutionalists). Carranza was sworn in as president. Carranza quickly dashed Zapata's hopes of change by rejecting his land reform program on September 5. Villa also declined to accept Carranza's authority, and the former allies of this war would become adversaries in the next phase of the Mexican Revolution (Intra-state War #673). US troops finally left Veracruz on November 23, 1914.

Coding Decisions: The Mexican Revolution originally was treated by Small and Singer as one civil war from 1910 to 1920, while others have divided it into four separate phases. Here it is divided into two distinct wars, the Third and Fourth Mexican Wars (Intra-state Wars #652 and #673). This division is based upon information describing the more-than-three-month cessation of hostilities from July 1914 until November 1914 and the change in the primary war participants, which under general COW coding rules marks the beginning of a new war. Furthermore, this war is coded as having a break in the fighting between June 6, 1911, and August 26, 1911, after the rebels temporarily had won and Madero assumed the presidency. Because the break in the hostilities lasted longer than a month and less than a year, it is coded as an interruption in the war rather than the start of a new war.[120]

Deciding upon accurate battle-death figures is complicated. The fatality levels in the war were horrific, with estimates hovering in the 1 to 1.5 million range for the entire period of 1910 to 1920; however, the vast majority of these were civilian deaths. In trying to determine the number of fatality figures for combatants, we began with three general findings concerning deaths during the entire ten-year period: (1) Krauze concluded that 250,000 lives were lost in combat and 750,000 were lost to hunger and disease;[121] (2) Gonzáles Navarro reported 300,000 deaths due to combat;[122] and (3) McCaa concluded that there were 350,000 excess male deaths.[123] As COW includes both deaths in combat and deaths by disease among the combatants, the 250,000 figure is probably low. Conversely, as the excess male deaths figure includes male civilians and combatants, it may be too high. Therefore, we have concluded that the 300,000 figure seems plausible for total combatant deaths. McCaa also reported annual crude death rates that seem to indicate that there is a relative parity of the death rates between the two periods of 1910 to 1914 and 1915 to 1920,[124] thus we are estimating 150,000 total combatant deaths for each of Wars #652 and #673. This seems plausible in terms of Clodfelter's conclusion that a conservative estimate of battle-deaths for just the period of February 1913 to August 1914 would therefore be about 85,000, but that the true figure was probably substantially higher.[125]

To further allocate the deaths to the government and rebel forces, we created a chart of the fatalities in the major battles. Though the data is very incomplete, it did provide us with a general trend that indicates that 60 percent of the battle-deaths were suffered by the government forces and 40 percent by the rebels. Thus we estimate that the Mexican armed forces suffered 90,000 deaths and the rebels suffered 60,000 combatant deaths. To these numbers we also report the 22 deaths suffered by the Americans.

Sources: Atkin (1969); Boot (2002); Camín and Meyer (1993); Clodfelter (2008); Cumberland (1968); Jensen (1953); Knight (1986); Krauze (1997); Marley (1998); McCaa (2003); McHenry (1962); McLynn (2000); Meyer (1967); Phillips and Axelrod (2005); Scheina (2003b); Vanderwood (1976); Wright (1965).

INTRA-STATE WAR #658
Cuban Black Uprising of 1912

Participants: Cuba versus Partido Independiente de Color.
Dates: May 20, 1912, to July 18, 1912.
Battle-related Deaths: Cuba: 50; Partido Independiente de Color: 1,000.
Initiator: Partido Independiente de Color.
Outcome: Cuba wins.
War Type: Civil for local issues.
Total System Member Military Personnel: Armed Forces of Cuba: 5,000 (prewar, initial, peak, final).[126]
Theater Armed Forces: Armed Forces of Cuba (which consisted of the Permanent Army and the Rural Guard): 2,000 (initial in the Oriente);[127] 8,000 (peak—5,000 plus 3,000 armed militia); or 10,455 (peak).[128] Partido Independiente de Color: 1,200 (initial);[129] 10,000 (peak).[130]

Antecedents: Despite the end of slavery in Cuba in 1880, lacks (or Afro-Cubans) were still discriminated against in Cuban society and politics. Blacks had participated in the Cuban wars (Extra-state War #404 and Inter-state War #70) in the hopes that the establishment of the Cuban Republic would recognize their service with improved living conditions and enhanced political participation. Soon after assuming office in 1902, Cuba's first president, Tomás Estrada Palma, faced the August Revolution, which prompted the United States to send in troops to restore order. The United States then appointed Charles Edward Magoon as the new governor, a position that lasted from 1906 to 1909.

During this period, the blacks had aligned themselves politically with the Liberal Party. However, black disenchantment with the lack of improvement led them to split with the liberals in 1907 and to create the *Agrupacion Independiente de Color* under the leadership of Evaristo Estenoz. In 1908 this group became the *Partido Independiente de Color* (PIC). With the support of the PIC, the liberal candidate José Miguel Gómez was elected, taking office in January 1909. However soon thereafter (on February 14, 1910), the government adopted the Morúa Law, which prohibited the establishment of political parties along racial lines (aimed against the PIC). In April 1910 President Gomez had Estenoz arrested and briefly imprisoned, and in May, he decided that the PIC needed to be disbanded. Estenoz was arrested again on September 22, 1910.

At the beginning of 1912, Cubans began preparing for the presidential election. The Liberal Party represented a majority; however, blacks were 34 percent of the electorate, so both the Liberal and Conservative Parties wanted to secure their support. Yet the black population was still less than pleased about its situation, and political agitation increased. In the face of the growing harassment of PIC, Estenoz appealed to the United States to intervene. Failing to get US support, in April 1912, Estenoz warned that the blacks in Cuba would take up arms to defend their liberty.

Narrative: PIC political demonstrations were planned to begin throughout the country on May 20, 1912, the tenth anniversary of Cuban independence. Government troops began arresting members of the PIC indiscriminately on May 18, 1912, in Havana, the central city of Santa Clara, and the northern sector of the eastern province of Oriente. Estenoz fled the city of Santiago de Cuba; blacks began taking up arms, and their attacks mark the start of the war. The most intensive activities of the war took place in the eastern province of Oriente, where the proportion of blacks was highest and where the terrain was suitable for guerrilla warfare. Rebels began attacking foreign plantations, bridges, and telegraph stations and exchanging shots with members of the Rural Guard. At that point, Estenoz and Gen. Pedro Ivonet were leading groups of 500 and 700 rebels. As the blacks began to develop a pattern of guerrilla warfare in the mountains, the Cuban government began sending more troops to the Orientate. Blacks from Haiti, the Dominican Republic, and Jamaica began to enter Cuba to aid the rebels. Seeing the expanding conflict, thousands of whites organized local militias and volunteered to go to the Oriente and Santa Clara to fight on behalf of the government. For instance, the National Council of Veterans soon had 2,000 troops in Santa Clara. White militias were formed throughout the country, and within the next week, militias in the central cities of Cienfuegos and Sagua la Grande claimed to have killed a number of rebels.

On May 27, President Gómez sent Major General Monteagudo to the Oriente, where the government's forces now totaled more than 5,000. Both the government forces and the local militias went on the offensive. The rebels (numbering as many as 10,000) broke into smaller bands and retreated to the mountains, though Estenoz and his force of 800 men did capture La Maya.

June 1912 marked an increase in both rebel activity and government repression measures against the rebels and all blacks throughout the island. Estenoz abandoned La Maya, and the rebels retreated, pursued by government forces, which ultimately surrounded and attacked the rebel camp, killing 100 rebels. The army then conducted mass executions of rebels and captured black civilians. Civil unrest was also growing in Havana, where blacks with suspected ties to the rebels were attacked by white militias (now numbering more than 1,100 men in Havana). Gómez finally understood that the United States would intervene if the rebellion were not brought under control. General Monteagudo expended offensives to crush the rebellion, leading to considerable bloodshed. US president Taft ordered nine warships to stand by at Key West, and on June 9, two American cruisers were dispatched, and 570 marines landed at Carmanera in Guantánamo. Another four warships arrived, and soon the United States had landed more than 1,000 troops in the Oriente, supposedly only for protection.

General Monteagudo divided his army and the militia volunteers into smaller groups (of about 150 each) that were dispersed throughout the Oriente, where they engaged rebel forces and suffered numerous casualties. They responded by executing rebel prisoners, and large numbers of black civilians were massacred. These government atrocities prompted another appeal by the rebels for US intervention to protect the rights of blacks, though the United States still declined to act. Ultimately, there was little that the rebels could do to stop the advancing government forces, and rebels began to surrender.

Termination and Outcome: On June 25 troops led by Monteagudo decimated the rebel group led by

Ivonet near Micara, and again the government followed its victory by massacring civilians. In a battle on June 27 between the Cuban army and forces led by Estenoz, Estenoz was killed, along with another 150 rebels. In the following weeks, the rebellion subsided as rebel leaders were killed while resisting capture. On July 18, 1912, Pedro Ivonet was seized by government forces and shot while supposedly trying to escape, which marks the end of the war. The war was a victory for the government. American actions in sending troops to protect economic interests while abandoning its support for the rights of blacks contributed to the decades of Cuban anti-Americanism that would contribute to the Cuban Revolution of 1958 to 1959 (Intra-state War #745).

Coding Decisions: Though the United States sent armed forces into Cuba during this war, it did not actively engage in armed conflict and thus is not coded as a war participant. Determining the combatant battle deaths is complicated by the guerrilla nature of most of the combat and the extensive killings of civilians. Estimates of the total number of blacks killed range from 3,000 to 6,000.[131] Cuban governmental sources claim that 2,000 rebels were killed while only 16 of the government's troops died.[132] These figures seem a bit high in terms of the number of rebel deaths and low for the government deaths, given the number of engagements that are described. We have concluded that a figure of 50 deaths on the government side and 1,000 deaths among the rebels seem plausible.

Sources: Clodfelter (2002); Fermoselle (1987); Gerome (1997); Helg (1995); Nodal (1986).

INTRA-STATE WAR #673

Fourth Mexican War of 1914 to 1920 (aka Constitutionalist-Conventionist War)

Participants: Mexico (Constitutionalists) aided by the United States versus Conventionists.
Dates: November 3, 1914, to July 28, 1920.
Battle-related Deaths: Mexico: 90,000; Conventionists: 60,000; United States: [ ].
Initiator: Conventionists.
Outcome: Mexico and the United States win.
War Type: Civil for control of the central government.
Total System Member Military Personnel: Armed forces of Mexico: 31,000 (prewar); 30,000 (initial); 200,000 (peak); 120,000 (final).[133]
Theater Armed Forces: Constitutionalist Army, aka Carrancistas (Government Army): 60,000 (after initial defections); 200,000 (peak); 100,000 (final).[134] Conventionists (Rebel Army), participating against the government until May 31, 1915, and against both Villa and the government from January 16, 1915, to May 31, 1915: 90,000 (prewar, initial); 10,000 (after split with Villa). The 90,000 figure consists of forces led by Villa (40,000), Zapata (25,000), and other Conventionist armies (25,000).[135] Villistas (Rebel Army), participating from January 16, 1915, when Villa broke with the Conventionists: 40,000 (initial); 50,000 to 100,000 (peak); 759 (final). These figures include the Yaqui rebels, who normally allied themselves with Villa.[136] Zapatistas (Rebel Army), participating from January 16, 1915, to April 10, 1919: 20,000 (initial, peak).[137] Felicistas (Rebel Aggregate), participating from November 14, 1914, to July 28, 1930: 33,000 (peak); including the Oaxacan autonomists: 25,000.[138] Pelaez-led Forces (Rebel Army), participating from late 1914: 5,000 (peak).[139] Obregón-led Rebels (Rebel Army), participating from April 15, 1920: 110,000 (peak). United States of America (Pro-Government Intervener), participating from March 15, 1916, to June 21, 1916: 4,800 (initial); 12,000 (peak, final),[140] and participating from June 15, 1919, to June 1, 1919: 3,600.[141]

Antecedents: Following the bloody struggle to defeat President Huerta in the first phase of the Mexican Revolution (Intra-state War #652), Venustiano Carranza entered Mexico City on August 20, 1914, and began governing under the title of first chief of the constitutional revolution the next day. The Mexican Army was effectively dissolved and replaced by Carranza's Constitutionalist forces, led by Gen. Álvaro Obregón. However, Carranza's regime precipitated divisions among the former rebel allies as the radicals, including Emilio Zapata, became dissatisfied with Carranza's moderate program. Meanwhile, in Sonora former governor Jose Maria Maytorena attempted to regain control by expelling Obregón supporters. Three former rebel allies—Obregón, Pancho Villa, and Maytorena—met on August 29 to settle their differences precipitating from Villa's attempt to execute Obregón. Gradually, control of Mexico was divided as the three former rebel factions split: Carranza and Obregón controlled from Mexico City to the northeast; Villa dominated in the north-central region; and Zapata was dominant in the South. In compliance with an agreement between Carranza and Villa that had kept Villa allied with the Constitutionalists, Carranza called a convention of revolutionary leaders to be held on October 1 in Mexico City. However, Villa balked at sending delegates. The convention was held but was boycotted by the Villistas and Zapatistas. A second meeting on October 10, the Aguiscalientes Convention, saw the formation of a Villista–Zapatista alliance (though neither of the leaders attended). The major figure of the convention was Obregón. The convention constituted itself as the sovereign authority, electing Gen. Eulalio Gutiérrez as an interim president (supported by Obregón). Carranza rejected the convention's authority to do so under the existing constitution. Thus there were two groups claiming to be the government of Mexico. Since at the time of the outbreak of the war Carranza's administration controlled most of the national institutions, Carranza is coded as representing the government of Mexico at this point. After failing to persuade Carranza to resign, Gutiérrez appointed Villa to subdue the resistance. When faced with the choice of supporting Villa or Carranza, Obregón chose the latter. This split thus led to the alternative naming of the upcoming war as pitting the Constitutionalists (under Carranza) versus the Conventionists (led by Villa and Zapata).

Narrative: Villa's army went in pursuit of Carranza's army, and the two forces met at Parral (in Chihuahua) on November 3, when the Constitutionalists claimed to have defeated the Villistas, inflicting considerable losses. The convention declared Carranza to be a rebel on November 10, and Zapata declared war against Carranza two days later. Both factions, Constitutionalist and Conventionist, mobilized their forces and sought to secure the loyalty of uncommitted generals. In Oaxaca, a group of Felicistas (conservative supporters of Felix Díaz) had ruled since July. On November 14, Constitutionalist general Luis Jiménez Figueroa seized control of Oaxaca City, but was forced to withdraw, and was killed at Tehuacán on December 2. Other Felicista bands sprang up around Veracruz, rallying landholders against the Carranza regime. As the Constitutionalist government continued to disintegrate, Mexico was divided further factionally into four layers: Villistas in the North, a set of Carrancista forces in the middle, Zapata just south of Mexico City, and the Felicistas in the southernmost states.

Initially the national campaign was a nearly bloodless one; as Villa marched south, towns fell to him without resistance. Carranza and Obregón made no attempt to fight for Mexico City, and Carranza reestablished his government at the port of Veracruz, which provided him access to American arms and control of the customs house. The Conventionists entered the capital, with Villa and Zapata arriving together on December 6. They formed a loose alliance; however, there were deep ideological and personality differences between the two. The two rebel leaders had met on December 4 at Xochimilco and agreed that neither one was fit to be president; that Eulalio Gutíerrez was not ultimately acceptable; and that each should dominate in his own region. Gutíerrez in essence broke apart the Conventionist alliance by gathering a force of 10,000 troops, fighting his way out of the capital against Villa, renouncing the presidency, and joining Carranza.

At the beginning of 1915, the Conventionists controlled most of Mexico. However, the Constitutionalists took advantage of the divides among the rebels, and Obrégon first moved to retake Puebla. Obregón, in command of 12,000 troops, defeated the Zapatistas at Tecamalchaco then occupied Puebla City on January 5, 1915. In the West, 9,000 Carrancistas attacked the 10,000 Villista defenders of Guadalajara on January 17, and after two days of fighting, the Constitutionalists occupied the city. Villista and Zapatista abandoned the capital, which was occupied by Obregón on January 28. Obregón continued his advance to confront Villa in the North, and the bloodiest phase of the war began here on April 6, 1915, when 22,000 Villistas attacked Obregón's 11,000 men. Villa attempted frontal assaults against entrenched defenders, and over two days, the unsuccessful assault cost Villa 1,800 battle-deaths against only 557 Carrancista fatalities. By April 15, Villa had lost another 4,000 killed, and his forces had been routed. The armies met again at Trinidad, where they engaged in a thirty-eight-day battle starting on April 29, 1915, which has been described as "Villa's Waterloo."[142] A series of assaults from June 1 to June 5 cost Villa 8,000 to 10,000 casualties. Carrancista losses were about a third as large, including Obregón, who lost his right arm. Obregón continued to defeat Villista throughout July, and Villa and 12,000 demoralized troops retreated to the Northwest to establish defensive positions in Sonora.

Meanwhile, around the capital, government forces under Pablo González pursued and defeated a Zapatista force of 6,000 on July 30. On October 19, 1915, the United States and a number of other countries recognized Carranza as the de facto government of Mexico. The recognition was militarily important because it caused the United States to immediately cut off arms supplies to Villa. Villa continued his retreat toward Sonora, suffering defeats at the city of Agua Prieta from November 1 to 3, 1915, and at the Sonoran capital, on November 18. As most of his army surrendered to Obregón, Villa retreated to the mountains with only 200 core supporters.

Advancing on all fronts, the Constitutionalists also had decided to retake the southern state of Oaxaca from its Felicista rulers, and Santa Cruz fell on November 8, 1915. In contrast to the bloody fighting of 1915, 1916 was dominated by smaller campaigns against Zapata, Villista guerrillas, and Felicistas. Villa, frustrated by the United States' recognition of Carranza and its refusal to supply arms to the rebels, decided to provoke the United States. Villa formed a unit of 400 men that raided the American border town of Columbus on March 9, defended by 350 members of the Thirteenth Cavalry. Villa's troops killed 18 Americans (8 civilians and 10 soldiers) at the cost of more than 100 of his own men. The attack triggered an invasion by 4,800 American troops on March 15, eventually increasing to 12,000 in what was known as the "Punitive Expedition" to capture or kill Pancho Villa.

The American expedition was led by Brigadier Gen. John J. "Black Jack" Pershing, who had built his military reputation in the Philippines. Pershing divided his 4,800 men into "flying columns" that were to search for Villa. Though the Americans had had some successes, their expedition did not halt the Mexican raids into the United States, several of which occurred in May and June 1916. Attempts by the Carranza government to force the withdrawal of US forces (now at 10,000 men) heightened tensions between the two allies, leading to several clashes between their troops. On June 21, an American reconnaissance mission of 84 men was routed by 400 Carrancista soldiers at Carrizal with 12 American and 30 Mexican battle-deaths. This defeat caused the United States to halt its advance, although its troops would not withdraw until early in 1917.

Further south, a Carranza army pursued its offensives against Zapata's base of Morelos. In May, most of the region had been conquered. Fifteen hundred prisoners were sent to Mexico City for future deportation to plantations in the Yucatán. By mid-June, the Zapatista "capital" of Tlaltizapán was captured. Yet a July 1916 counteroffensive by Zapatistas nearly wiped out two federal garrisons in Morelos. In October he mounted a major offensive, winning the Battle of Xochilmo on the fourth. By December, the government had lost 7,000 troops in Morelos (out of 30,000), either dead or hospitalized from disease. By January 1, 1917, most towns in Morelos were back in Zapatista hands.

The year 1917 opened with the government in control of most of the country, while Zapata continued to pose a serious threat. In the fall of 1916, Carranza had convened a constitutional convention, and the new constitution contained some popular land and labor reforms. When Carranza promulgated the new constitution in January 1917, he announced that he would not implement some of the reforms, which prompted a split with Obregón (who supported the constitution). Obregón resigned as minister of war, returning to Sonora, where he cornered the market on chickpeas.

Felix Díaz was the only major rebel actually to gain strength during 1917. He allied with Manuel Pelaez, who brought 6,000 troops to the Felicista army, which peaked at about 20,000.

There was a dramatic decline in the fighting in 1918, but deaths increased. Starvation, an epidemic of typhus, and the deadly Spanish flu killed up to 300,000 people and decimated the armies of all sides. Notwithstanding these losses, the government made some advances during the year against the armies of Zapata and Felix Díaz. By 1919, the government was running out of rebels willing to fight. On April 10, Zapata was lured to a meeting with a government commander and was killed. Pancho Villa had renewed large-scale combat against the government in March. When he attacked the border town of Ciudad Juárez on June 15, an American soldier was killed by a stray bullet. American artillery began to pound Villa's position, and 3,600 American troops crossed the border to pursue Villa. Villa's forces were attacked and dispersed by a federal relief column. The deaths of many Felicista commanders weakened the movement, which disintegrated into hostile factions.

The major threat to the government was now political rather than military. The war, the regime's harsh methods, and war taxes had made the Carranza regime unpopular throughout much of the country. Carranza announced Ignacio Bonillas, a civilian, as his nominee for the forthcoming 1920 presidential elections. Obregón and Pablo González also declared their candidacies. The break between Carranza and Obregón became a military struggle. The first armed clash occurred on April 15, 1920. Obregón called for a revolt at Chilpancingo on April 20. Obregón attracted allies from across the political spectrum. Carranza once again abandoned Mexico City, aiming to establish his government at Veracruz with 10,000 followers. After a series of skirmishes, Carranza was caught and killed on May 20, 1920, by a Pelaez associate, Adolfo Herrero.

Termination and Outcome: Felipe Adolfo de la Huerta Marcor was appointed interim president, and many of the former rebels reached peace agreements with the new government. However, negotiations between the government and Villa were difficult, especially after Obregón raised the bounty on Villa's head and set a trap for Villa. Consequently, Villa's forces undertook a march across a 700-mile desert from Chihuahua into Coahuila, where it seized the town of Sabinas. Caught by surprise, de la Huerta decided to offer Villa more generous peace terms. De la Huerta and Villa reached an agreement on July 28, 1920, whereby Villa agreed to demobilize his 759 remaining soldiers in exchange for pay and land. This agreement marked the end of the revolution. In the subsequent presidential election, Pablo González withdrew his candidacy, leaving the field clear for Obregón, who was elected president, taking office on December 1, 1920.

Coding Decisions: The war is coded as a victory for the Mexican government in the sense that the rebels were not able to defeat the government militarily and that Obregón considered himself to be the legitimate successor to Carranza. However, in a broader sense, the Mexican Revolution brought about an expansion of citizen's rights and many of the social reforms espoused by the rebels.

The fatality levels during the entire period of the revolution were horrific, with estimates hovering in the 1 to 1.5 million deaths range from 1910 to 1920. As described in the Coding Decisions section of the antecedent of this war (Intra-state War #652), we are estimating 150,000 total combatant deaths for each of the Intra-state Wars #652 and #673, with government forces suffering 90,000 deaths and the rebels 60,000 battle-deaths in each war.

Sources: Atkin (1969); Boot (2002); Camín and Meyer (1993); Caplan (2001); Clodfelter (2008); Cumberland (1968, 1972); Jaques (2007); Jensen (1953); Knight (1986); Koth (2002); Krauze (1997); Marley (1998); Matthews (2007); McCaa (2003); McHenry (1962); McLynn (2000); Phillips and Axelrod (2005); Scheina (2003b); "Villa Force" (1914); Wright (1965).

INTRA-STATE WAR #695

De La Huerta Rebellion of 1923 to 1924 (aka Delahuertista Rebellion)

Participants: Mexico versus Huerta-led Rebels.
Dates: December 4, 1923, to May 10, 1924.
Battle-related Deaths: 7,000 Mexicans died in this war.[143]
Initiator: Huerta-led Rebels.
Outcome: Mexico wins.
War Type: Civil for control of the central government.
Total System Member Military Personnel: Armed Forces of Mexico: 85,000 (prewar); 66,000 (initial); 52,000 (final).[144]
Theater Armed Forces: Armed Forces of Mexico: 55,000 (prewar); 30,000 (after initial defections);[145] plus more than 18,000 *agraristas* (supporters of land reform). *Delahuertistas* (Rebel Aggregate): 25,000 (initial);[146] 50,000 (peak). An estimated 24,000 conservative civilians also joined the revolt as armed combatants.

Antecedents: At the end of the ten-year period of war referred to as the Mexican Revolution (Intra-state Wars #652 and #673), Felipe Adolfo de la Huerta Marcor (not to be confused with the former dictator Victoriano Huerta) was selected by the congress as the interim president of Mexico. De la Huerta was the former governor of the northwest state of Sonora and had participated with Álvaro Obregón in the April 1920 Plan of Agua Prieta against the presidency of Venustiano Carranza. De la

Huerta remained in office until Obregón was elected and took office as president on December 1, 1920. De la Huerta then served as finance minister. Obregón had campaigned on a platform to rebuild the country while at the same time making it attractive to business interests. However, Obregón's pragmatic administration also engendered opposition, including that of the Catholic Church, whose prerogatives had been limited in the 1917 Constitution. Obregón did not, however, share the more strident anticlerical views of his minister of the interior, Plutarco Elías Calles. Obregón's policies were decidedly *agrarista* (supportive of land reform) in keeping with Mexico's 1917 Constitution and his co-optation of the former Zapatista land reform program. His support of land reform fueled opposition from those who would be disadvantaged by it, including foreign companies and the landed elite (in 1923, 114 elite families still held 25 percent of Mexico's land).[147] A number of generals also aligned themselves with the landowners, including Guadalupe Sánchez, Enrique Estrada, who served as Obregón's secretary of war from December 1920 to March 1922, and Fortunato Maycotte. These three generals—Sánchez, Estrada, and Maycotte—conspired against Obregón for more than a year, and Obregón was probably aware of the fact. Rather than precipitate a conflict that he might lose, he incrementally reduced their authority while simultaneously staffing areas that seemed safe with people he knew personally so that when rebellion came, he would have secure base areas.

Significant political jockeying was prompted by the upcoming 1924 presidential elections. One contender was former interim president and Finance Minister Adolfo de la Huerta, the candidate of the National Cooperativist Party (PNC), who had the support of Generals Sánchez, Estrada, and Maycotte. Obregón supported his minister of the interior, Plutarco Elías Calles, who was viewed as a radical by landowners, the Church, conservatives, and de la Huerta. When Pancho Villa, an ally of de la Huerta, denounced any attempts by Obregón to impose the unpopular Calles, Obregón and Calles conspired to have Villa assassinated on July 20, 1923.

On November 26, armed *agraristas*, proclaiming their support for Calles, seized control of Coyol in Veracruz and warned that they would be forced to resort to arms if the abuses of peasants continued. De la Huerta, realizing that he might not win a rigged election, supported the moves by the generals to oppose Obregón.

Narrative: The first general to break with the government was Gen. Romulo Figueroa in the southern coastal state of Guerrero, who pronounced his opposition on November 30, 1923. By December 3, government columns were said to be converging on his position at Iguala. A barracks revolt the next day marks the start of the war. The army split almost evenly, with 25,000 troops going over to de la Huerta and 30,000 staying to support Obregón. At the outbreak of hostilities, General Maycotte rushed to Mexico City requesting arms and money to fight the rebels. However, instead of attacking Figueroa, Maycotte returned to his political base in Oaxaca. Within days, the military authorities in six states had declared against the government. Sanchez joined the rebellion on December 6 with 12,000 soldiers. De la Huerta finally proclaimed his revolt on December 7, after fighting was already underway. Many of the former Villistas came to his side.

Obregón personally assumed control of the government forces. He avoided major offensive operations for some time as the rebellion quickly spread around Mexico. Both Calles and Obregón had been part of the Sonoran element of the Mexican Revolution, and the government quickly established its control of the northern states. However, the government faced rebels on three main fronts: East, South, and West. De la Huerta initially established a provisional government at Veracruz. From Veracruz, rebels advanced toward the state of Puebla, taking the city without a fight on December 15. The government organized defenses in Mexico City, but the rebels failed to take the capital. About 10,000 government troops attacked Puebla's 4,500 defenders later that month, routing them in a battle that claimed 700 Delahuertista lives. Other fronts posed less urgent threats.

In mid-December, another wave of rebellions broke out, mostly in southern states: Campeche, Chiapas, Tabasco, Yucatán, and Oaxaca. The revolt in Oaxaca was the most significant, for it was there that General Maycotte finally declared for the rebellion. He declined to endorse de la Huerta, however, and instead proposed a plan for a military triumvirate to be composed of himself, Estrada, and Sanchez. By late December, the bulk of the armed forces and most governors had sided with either Obregón or de la Huerta. De la Huerta was able to lure more than 26,000 soldiers to his side. While 80 percent of officers remained loyal, he was still able to turn enough of them to his side, and in the end, more than 100 generals fought for de la Huerta. In addition, de la Huerta won the loyalty of the landed class (*hacendados*), who added 24,000 armed civilians to his forces.

The government retained the loyalty of 35,000 soldiers and was able to quickly mobilize the *agraristas*. Eighteen thousand of them fought for Obregón in Veracruz alone. The forces were therefore nearly equal: 50,000 rebels against somewhat more than 53,000 pro-government troops. However, supplies were unequal; the United States readily sold arms to Obregón while withholding them from de la Huerta. It also sent naval forces to prevent any Delahuertista blockade and even allowed 2,000 government soldiers to pass through American territory to attack rebels in the Northeast. By January 1924, the government was able to use American-supplied aircraft to attack and disable the rebels' supply trains. Moreover, the revolt was poorly coordinated, allowing the government to face and destroy one rebel army at a time. However, by January 3, 1924, the rebels controlled more than half of the country.

The government mounted two major campaigns—one to the East and one to the West. On the eastern front, government forces advanced toward Esperanza in the state of Puebla. Sanchez had to face them alone, and on January 28, the Battle of Esperanza resulted in a decisive government victory, causing 400 rebel deaths. Sanchez retreated while the government, aided by *agraristas*, advanced into Veracruz. Córdoba fell on February 4, prompting de la Huerta to move his provisional government south from Veracruz to Frontera, on the Yucatán peninsula. The port of Veracruz fell on February 11, and *agraristas* were now in control of most of Veracruz.

In the West, Estrada had advanced into Michoacán and besieged its capital, Morelia, which fell on January 23. Estrada turned to face the federal troops at his rear. Both armies gathered troops at Ocatlán, where Estrada's 1,900 troops entrenched themselves. After almost two weeks of preparation, 6,000 government soldiers launched a frontal assault on February 9 and dislodged the rebels at a cost of 400 to 2,000 army fatalities. Estrada tried to salvage the situation, but after a few skirmishes, his forces melted away. By the end of February, Jalisco and Michoacán were both in the hands of the government, and Estrada had fled the country.

The government now turned its attention to the South. Shifting forces from the other fronts, it created a formidable force against Maycotte and other rebels who had taken refuge there. In the end, there were few engagements in this campaign. Romulo Figueroa was the first to surrender. De la Huerta fled to the United States on March 12. On March 22, Sanchez was cornered at San Francisco de las Peñas (now known as Cardel); he was killed and his forces were defeated. In Hidalgo, the rebels had retreated to Pazuelos, where they were surrounded and defeated on April 21, 1924, losing 74 killed. Maycotte was cornered in Oaxaca, captured on May 10, and shot on May 12.

Termination and Outcome: There was a bloody wave of reprisals following the government victory. Obregón ordered every rebel officer above the rank of major to be shot. At least fifty-four generals were executed. Calles was elected president, assuming office on December 1, 1924. Because Calles was elected with popular support, he began his administration with attempts at land reform and promoting citizen's rights. He is also known for creating the Partido Nacional Revolucionario (PRN), which ultimately became the Partido Revolucionario Institucional (PRI), which governed Mexico until 2000. However, his anticlerical measures prompted the devastating religious backlash in 1926 (Intra-state War #701). In 1928, Obregón was elected as Calles's successor.

Sources: "Agrarians Seize" (1923); Brewster (1999); Brewster and Brewster (2007); Carriedo (2005); Clodfelter (1992, 2008); England (2008); Gonzales (2002); Haber, Razo, and Maurer (2003); Hansis (1979); "Has Fortified" (1923); Henderson (1998); Jensen (1953); Koth (2002); Krauze (1997); Machado (1972); Marley (1998); McLynn (2000); Quintana (2007); "Rebels Defeat Federals" (1923); "Revolt in Mexico" (1923); Scheina (2003b).

INTRA-STATE WAR #696
Honduran Conservative War of 1924

Participants: Honduras versus Conservatives, aided by Revolutionary Liberals.
Dates: February 7, 1924, to April 28, 1924.
Battle-related Deaths: Honduras: 2,000; Conservative and Liberal Rebels: 1,000.
Initiator: Conservatives.
Outcome: Conservatives win.
War Type: Civil for central control.

Total System Member Military Personnel: 3,000 (prewar, initial, peak, final).[148]

Theater Armed Forces: Armed Forces of Honduras and liberal militias: 3,000 (prewar); 6,000 (peak); 1,300 to 1,400 (final).[149] Coalition of Conservatives and Revolutionary Rebels (Aggregate): 500 (prewar); 6,000 (initial); 10,000 (peak, final). Consisting of *Carista* Nationalists (Rebel Army): 500 (prewar); 2,000 (initial); 5,000 (peak, final)[150] and Revolutionary Liberals (Rebel Army): 4,000 (initial—2,000 in Ferrera's "private army" of Honduran Indians and 2,000 in Tosta's private force); 5,000 (peak, final).[151]

Antecedents: After the dissolution of the Mexican Empire, Honduras became part of the Central American Confederation (United Provinces of Central America) along with Costa Rica, El Salvador, Guatemala, and Nicaragua in 1825. Ideological splits between the conservative and liberal regimes led to the dissolution of the confederation in 1840 (Non-state War #1528). The conflict between the nationalists (conservatives) and liberals played out within Honduras as well, and this war was one of seventeen armed conflicts to emerge there from this divide between 1920 and 1923.

In 1919, liberal general Rafael López Gutiérrez launched an insurrection against President Francisco Bertrand, a representative of the nationalist and conservative National Party. Bertrand had refused to allow an open election for the presidency, and the intervention of the United States led to Bertrand's resignation. López Gutiérrez became president the following year. US involvement was in large part determined by the role that the American United Fruit Company played in Honduras and throughout the region. To protect these economic interests, the United States would continue its policy of intervention in Honduras (militarily intervening six times by 1925).

López Gutiérrez assumed the presidency in 1920 and under US pressure had agreed to allow an open presidential election in 1923. The conservative factions, united in the National Party of Honduras (PNH), nominated Gen. Tiburcio Carías Andino. The Liberal Party of Honduras (PLH), however, was unable to unite behind a single candidate, supporting both Policarpo Bonilla and Juan Angel Arias. In the three-way race, Carías received a plurality of the votes. With no candidate receiving a majority, the liberal congress was supposed to select the winner, but it simply refused to do so. In January 1924, López Gutiérrez announced his decision to remain in office pending new elections.

Narrative: On January 30, 1924, conservative general Carías, with the support of United Fruit, declared himself to be the legitimate president and left the capital to amass arms for a revolt. A second opposition group was led by revolutionary liberals Vicente Tosta (in San Juancito) and Gregorio Ferrera (in La Esperanza). The first engagement of the war occurred on February 7, 1924, when a *Carista* force was defeated by government troops near Jacaleapa (along the border with Nicaragua). Despite the defeat, about 2,000 plantation workers hastened to join the *Caristas*, and by February 9, Carias was reported to have mustered 5,000 men. On February 9, Carias personally led his force in an advance on the capital. The government easily defeated the rebels on February 20 at Alauca. Carias fled to Nicaragua, where the country's government assisted in rearming and reorganizing his army. In the meantime, the forces under Tosta and Ferrera continued the fight. Though divided geographically, Tosta and Ferrera coordinated operations. Tosta's force, about 2,000 strong, took Comayagua (northwest of the capital) after a battle from February 21 to February 22 and a week later defeated government forces at San Pedro Sula after three days of fighting. As Tosta continued moving north, approaching La Ceiba (on the northern coast), the United States landed a force of between 50 and 100 marines to protest American interests but did not intervene in the fighting. A battle between the rebels and government forces took place on February 28, and after several engagements, the government troops withdrew from La Cieba on March 3.

After La Ceiba, the United States played a larger role in the conflict. At Puerto Cortes, marines landed on March 4, established a neutral zone, and proceeded to disarm the government soldiers. The government abandoned the city two days later, and the marines re-embarked. Meanwhile, Ferrera's forces routed government troops at Zambrano (in the West near the Guatemala border) on March 4 and advanced on the capital on March 9. The following day, a seventy-two-hour armistice was negotiated. During the armistice, President Gutierrez died of a diabetic coma (on March 10), and a council of ministers assumed control of the government's war effort. Carias had reentered the country, and at this point, the rebel groups controlled most of the countryside. Although the government controlled only a few thousand troops, it hoped that Carias, Tosta, and Fererra would turn against each other.

The expiration of the armistice marked the resumption of the fighting and the beginning of the Siege of Tegucigalpa, a six-week period of near-daily battles around the capital (to April 28, 1924), which caused terrible fatalities. Meanwhile, on March 17, the remnants of government forces in the North were driven into Guatemala by Tosta. Though the rebels were unable actually to capture the city, on March 24, the rebel factions led by Tosta, Ferrera, and Carias were able to agree to cooperate against the government and on the composition of a future provisional government.

The liberal government attempted to lift the siege by raising counterrevolutions in the rear of the rebel armies. On March 30, *Policarpistas* (supporters of José Policarpo Bonilla Vasquez, the founder of the Liberal Party) proclaimed themselves against the rebel alliance, raised an army, and advanced on the capital. This force was defeated by Fererra at the Battle of Cerro de Hule on April 7. Fighting intensified around Tegucigalpa, with 125 killed on April 9 alone. One counterrevolutionary force of 600 reached Tegucigalpa to reinforce the government's 700 to 800 defenders on April 20. The United States proposed an armistice, which was accepted by the government on April 19 and by the rebels on April 21. Negotiations for a peace settlement, facilitated by American diplomat Sumner Welles (former minister to the Dominican Republic) were held on a ship in the port of Ampal from April 23 to April 28. Nonetheless, fighting continued. Arms supplied by the United Fruit Company and Cumayel Fruit Company reached the rebels on April 24, and the government lost most positions dominating Tegucigalpa by April 27. The following day, April 28, 1924, the capital fell to the combined rebel armies, now 10,000 strong, marking the end of the war.

Termination and Outcome: Despite the military victory of the rebels, the Welles negotiations attempted to create a government that would qualify to be recognized under the terms of the General Treaty of Peace and Amity of 1923 among the Central American countries and the United States. Thus, under the Pact of Ampala, General Vicente Tosta was installed as provisional president (ruling from April 30, 1924, to February 1, 1925), based upon his promise to appoint a bipartisan cabinet. He appointing a cabinet composed almost entirely of conservatives and nationalists, with the exception of Ferrera. Carias's dream was crushed by the declaration that the 1923 treaty prohibited any leader of the recent revolution to be recognized as president. Ferrera raised a revolt against the new government from August to October 1924, which was defeated. In the presidential election in December 1924, the liberals did not nominate a candidate, while the nationalists nominated Miguel Paz Barhona, who was elected and ruled from February 1, 1925, to February 1, 1929. Ultimately, Carias did come back to win the presidential election in 1932 and ruled Honduras for sixteen years (February 1, 1933, to January 1, 1949).

Coding Decisions: Though the United States played a significant role in this war, it did not meet the criteria to be considered a war participant (one thousand combatants or one hundred battle-deaths).

We have found no detailed fatality figures for this war. At the time, it was reported that about 3,000 people had died in the war,[152] and as the vast majority of these would have been combatants, we are utilizing that figure to represent total combatant deaths. In addition, we have found no description of the allocation of the fatalities suffered by the government or the rebels. However, at the time, the *New York Times* reported that the government had suffered 1,000 fatalities in the fighting around Tegucigalpa alone, so we are estimating overall 2,000 government and 1,000 rebel deaths.[153]

Sources: *Dallas Morning News* (1924); Jaques (2007); Lafeber (1993); Merrill (1995); Munro (1974), *New York Times* (1924, February 5, February 9, February 28); O'Brien (1999), Ross (1969); Stearns (2001).

INTRA-STATE WAR #701
Cristeros Revolt of 1926 to 1929 (aka *La Cristiada*)

Participants: Mexico versus *Cristeros*
Dates: August 29, 1926, to July 17, 1929.
Battle-related Deaths: Mexico and *Agraristas*: 55,000;[154] *Cristeros* (Rebel aggregate): 35,000.[155]
Initiator: *Cristeros*.
Outcome: Compromise.

War Type: Civil for central control.
Total System Member Military Personnel: 64,000 (prewar, initial); 74,000 (peak); 70,000 (final).[156]
Theater Armed Forces: Armed Forces of Mexico: 79,759 (peak).[157] *Agraristas* (Pro-government Aggregate): 20,000 (peak). *Cristeros* (Rebel aggregate): 20,000 (initial);[158] 50,000 (peak, final).[159]

Antecedents: During the ten-year period of war referred to as the Mexican Revolution (Intra-state Wars #652 and #673), the moderately liberal congress had enacted the Revolutionary Constitution of 1917 that promoted an expansion of personal rights and strong anticlerical measures intended to guarantee the supremacy of state over church. The government was divided in its views of the constitution, with then-president Venustiano Carranza opposing some of its measures, while Minister of War Álvaro Obregón supported it, mostly on land reform issues. As a result of the war, Carranza was forced from office, and Obregón subsequently was elected president, taking office on December 1, 1920. The relatively pragmatic Obregón did not enforce a number of the constitution's provisions. Obregón did not share the more strident anticlerical views of his minister of the interior, Plutarco Elías Calles. However, in 1923 Obregón announced that he would support Calles in the upcoming presidential election. Conservative elements (including Felipe Adolfo de la Huerta Marcor and senior military officers, generals Guadalupe Sánchez, Enrique Estrada, and Fortunato Maycotte) launched a revolt against Calles's nomination in December 1923 (Intra-state War #695). Calles helped coordinate the government's successful campaign against the conservatives, and after the opposition had been defeated on the battlefield, Calles ran for and was elected president in late 1924. Initially Calles espoused a pragmatic agenda of economic programs and expansion of public education (which subsequently enabled him to create the broad-based political party, *Partido Nacional Revolucionario* [PNR] in 1929). However, as Calles began to enforce the anti-Church provisions of the 1917 Constitution, he was met by growing opposition.

Support for Calles could be found within the *Confederación Regional de Obreros Mexicanos* (CROM, or the Regional Confederation of Mexican Workers) and the *Partido Laboral Mexicano* (the Mexican Labor Party). Resistance to the anticlerical policies was coordinated by the National League for the Defense of Religious Liberty (LNDLR), formed in 1924, and included: the *Unión Popular* (UP, the Popular Union Party), the Catholic Labor Confederation (CLC), and the Mexican Association of Catholic Youth (ACJM). By April 1925, priests were refusing to comply with any civil laws that were not in agreement with Church laws, challenging the government's authority over the Catholic populace. When the Catholic Church condemned the 1917 Constitution in early 1926, the government began dismantling Church-run social services. It then created a penal code, "Calles's Law," that specified harsh sanctions for violators of the laws. As the government began enforcing requirements that religious leaders register with the government, Church officials responded by suspending religious services on July 31, which put believers in danger of mortal sin because they could not receive any of the religious sacraments provided by the institutional Church.

Narrative: Civil violence began on August 12, 1926, in Los Altos, Jalisco (northwest of the capital). Meanwhile, the *Cristeros* (those invoking the name of Jesus Christ) began to organize for direct warfare: the LNDLR formed a war committee under the leadership of René Capistrán Garza and began to both purchase weapons and recruit soldiers. The *Cristeros* initially were based in the states northwest of the capital (Jalisco, Guanajuato, Colima, and Michoacán), and their initial plan was to drive federal authorities from the region, though the LNDLR also had visions of overthrowing the central government. The war started on August 29, 1926, at Huejuquilla and Valparaiso, where armed *Cristero* rebels ambushed a government unit. The war became a savage one in which guerrillas on horseback attacked a newly modernized army, though the *Cristeros* sometimes had an advantage in terrain that was not suited to mechanized warfare.

The rebellion began to spread, and within six months, the LNDLR appointed military leaders in virtually all the surrounding western states, where the rebellion firmly became established. Initially there was no generally recognized leadership or coordination among rebels groups, so victories like the destruction of a government garrison at Colotlán had little strategic value. In November, the rebels successfully attacked a government train, and such attacks would soon become centerpieces of rebel strategy.

On January 1, 1927, LNDLR simply proclaimed itself the leadership of the rebellion.

At the beginning of 1927, there were only 3,000 rebels fighting in fourteen different areas, potentially facing 64,000 Mexican soldiers. However, the rebel forces grew rapidly, with 20,000 to 30,000 insurgents by the end of the year. Many women participated in the revolt, often fighting in all-female units and disregarding the limits the LNDLR attempted to place on their participation. Over the course of the war, the Mexican Army remained between 60,000 and 70,000 strong, though its inability to contain the rebellion led the government to seek assistance from the irregular forces of the agrarian warlords, and up to 20,000 of these *agrarista* armed peasants (including women) fought against the *Cristeros*. The pattern of early 1927 was for the rebels to seize a small town and then be driven out by the superior government forces. The *Cristeros* attacks on trains could be profitable but cost public support as civilians were killed. The government now adopted a strategy of reconcentration—forcing peasants into strategic hamlets so that areas could be declared free-fire zones, though they were unsuccessful in containing the rebellion.

In January 1928, the rebels went on the offensive; combat was particularly intense in May. Between January and June 1928, the government admitted losing 3,218 troops while claiming that the rebels had suffered 6,176 killed. During the rainy season, the numbers of rebels and attacks declined. The rebels scored an important political victory on July 17, 1928, when President-elect Obregón was killed by a *Cristero* assassin. The result was a political crisis, and as President Calles began keeping loyal units near the capital, it weakened the forces facing the *Cristeros*. Seeking better coordination, the LNDLR named Enrique Gorostieta as first chief of the Liberating Army in October. Despite shortages of ammunition, some bands scored remarkable victories during the summer and fall. Gorostieta released a manifesto summarizing the objectives of the *Cristeros*, including a return to the 1857 Constitution and the creation of a *Cristero* National Guard to protect the Church. The rebels quickened the pace of attacks: in December 1928, there were at least 114 engagements reported. After President-elect Obregón's assassination, Emilio Portes Gil was appointed provisional president, taking office on December 1, 1928.

In the first two months of 1929, the government mounted an offensive against the rebels. As the rebels were being defeated, politics intervened to save them. Obregón had enjoyed the loyalty of the military, but President Gil was distrusted by many generals, who began plotting against him. On March 2, Gen. José Gonzalo Escobar rebelled against Gil, taking one-third of the Mexican Army with him (Intra-state War #707). As the government withdrew loyal units to fight Escobar, the *Cristeros* occupied their positions, expanding their control in the West and North. Escobar promised to revoke all laws limiting the freedom of worship, which enhanced his appeal among *Cristeros*. Although there was a vague agreement between Escobar and the LNDLR, there was no coordination between the two rebellions, for geographic distance separated them. Taking advantage of the situation, Gorostieta planned a *Cristeros* March offensive to capture Guadalajara. The rebels lost two battles and were forced to retreat, demoralized and low on supplies.

Having defeated Escobar (who was forced to flee to the United States in May), the government redeployed its best units to the *Cristero* front. Simultaneously, Gil began negotiating with Catholic bishops, trying to find an acceptable arrangement. On June 1, Gorostieta was killed. Though the rebellion had not been defeated—10,000 to 12,000 *Cristeros* remained in the field (killing 800 to 1,000 soldiers each month), with little hope of military victory, most *Cristeros* were ready to take almost any offer to settle the conflict.

Termination and Outcome: By 1929, US ambassador Dwight Morrow was able to craft an agreement acceptable to all the parties. On June 21, the government announced an end to the "strike" by the clergy, who in turn condemned further fighting against the government. Rebels began to surrender en masse, and on July 1, the LNDLR accepted the deal and ordered its followers to lay down their arms. The orders took some time to reach isolated bands, and the last skirmish was fought at Cerro Grande on July 17, 1829. About 14,000 rebels formally surrendered; the rest simply went home. Although the war is coded as ending with a compromise agreement, it was a lopsided one with the *Cristeros* and the Church gaining only amnesty and few actual changes in government policy. Following the war a wave of assassinations—almost surely government-sponsored—took the lives of 500 former *Cristero* leaders. Unsurprisingly, another rebellion broke out in 1934, although it did not reach the level of civil war.

Coding Decisions: The human costs of the war were significant for Mexico: in addition to 70,000 to 100,000 deaths,[160] Mexico lost another 450,000 citizens to external migration, mostly to California, and another 200,000 were internally displaced.[161] The most commonly cited fatality figures are 45,000 to 60,000 killed among the federal forces and *Agraristas* and 25,000 to 40,000 deaths among the *Cristeros*,[162] with civilian deaths in the tens of thousands.[163]

Sources: Bailey (1974); Butler (2004); Camín and Meyer (1993); Clodfelter (1992, 2008); Cumberland (1972); Gonzales (2002); Krauze (1997); Marley (1998); Meyer (2005); Munro (1942); Parkes (1966); Pernell (2001); Phillips and Axelrod (2005); Purnell (1999); Scheina (2003b); Schlarman (1950); Tomán (2006); Tuck (1982).

INTRA-STATE WAR #707
Escobar Rebellion of 1929

Participants: Mexico versus Escobar-led Rebels.
Dates: March 3, 1929, to May 4, 1929.
Battle-related Deaths: Mexico: Less than 1,000;[164] Escobar-led Rebels: More than 1,000 battle-deaths.[165]
Initiator: Escobar-led Rebels.
Outcome: Mexico wins.
War Type: Civil for control of the central government.
Total System Member Military Personnel: 70,000 (prewar, initial, peak, final).[166]
Theater Armed Forces: Armed Forces of Mexico: 74,000 (prewar); 56,000 (after initial defections); 64,000 (peak, final—which include the 8,000 *agraristas* the government mobilized against Escobar).[167] Escobar-led Rebels (Rebel Army): 18,000 (initial, peak); 1,000 (final).[168]

Antecedents: For the 1928 Mexican presidential elections, liberal (radical) President Plutarco Elias Calles had supported his predecessor, pragmatist Álvaro Obregón, who had served as president from December 1, 1920, to November 30, 1924. By doing so, Calles may have intended to alternate terms of office with Obregón to circumvent the 1917 Constitution's ban on reelection. The selection of Obregón angered a number of the Mexican generals who also had presidential aspirations. In preelection violence, a number of the generals were murdered. Obregón was duly elected, but before he could take office, he was killed by a *Cristero* assassin on July 17, 1928. Calles was in the midst of fighting a conservative challenge to his rule from the *Cristeros*, or supporters of the privileges of the Catholic Church (Intra-state War #701), which at that point was in its final year.

The murder of Obregón created another political crisis as people tried to determine if it was part of a larger conspiracy. Attempting to diffuse the situation, Calles convened a meeting of thirty top generals. Because Obregón had been scheduled to take office on December 1, 1928, an interim president would have to be appointed to serve until a new election could be scheduled, and Calles wanted the generals' support for the nomination of a civilian as president. Calles selected Emilio Portes Gil, a young lawyer and former member of congress. Calles then assumed the role of *Jefe Máximo* (or Mexico's most powerful *caudillo*), and the period of his continued dominant political power (1928–1934) has been called the *Máximato*.

Dissatisfied officers began planning a revolt almost as soon as Gil was sworn in as president (on December 1, 1928). One of the generals opposed to Gil was José Gonzálo Escobar, who had fought with Obregón in the Mexican Revolution. In preparation for the upcoming presidential election, Calles devoted his energies to the creation of the Partido Nacional Revolucionario (PNR), which was officially founded March 4, 1929, and its upcoming convention would be where the presidential candidate would be chosen. The generals' preferred candidate was Gilberto Valenzuela, who had been secretary of the interior but had resigned in protest to what he saw as Calles's attempts to impose his own preferences. Valenzuela declined to participate in the PNR (the predecessor of today's *Partido Revolucionario Institucional* [PRI]) convention and decided to run instead as an opposition candidate on a platform that opposed Calles's version of *agrarismo* (land reform) and that promised support for the army.

Meanwhile, the would-be putschists were far from discreet. They decided on a simultaneous rising of military zone commanders throughout the country. This meant that plans for rebellions were circulated widely, even within the government. For the upcoming election, the early favorite was *Obregonista* Aarón Saenz, but as Saenz had little support among the *agraristas*, Gil endorsed the then-ambassador to Brazil, Pascual Ortiz Rubio, the more radical candidate, for the PNR's nomination. Rubio was formally nominated on March 4, the day after the revolt began.

Narrative: On March 3, the government instructed Gen. Jesus M. Aguirre in Veracruz to send reinforcements to the capital just in case the nomination of Rubio sparked violence. This action had the effect of prematurely triggering the military revolt, which had been scheduled for March 9. General Aguirre instead sided with Escobar, seized the governor's palace, and secured the loyalty of the fleet in Veracruz harbor. In Sonora, presidential candidate Valenzuela already had drafted a program condemning the government for imposing its candidate on the people. Together with Sonoran governor Fausto Topete, General Escobar led a mutiny in the North, proclaiming Valenzuela's "Plan of Hermosillo," which called for the overthrow of the government and designated Escobar as supreme chief of the revolution.

President Gil immediately appointed Calles as minister of war, and he began rallying the army generals. Just over one-fourth of the Army rebelled, consisting of 17,000 men. The addition of the fleet gave the rebels about 18,000 total military personnel. The government retained the loyalty of the rest of the army (56,000 men) and the air force. Almost immediately, Gen. Saturnino Cedillo of San Luis Potosí organized a division of 5,000 *agraristas* to assist the government in the North, where it was badly outnumbered. The rebellion quickly spread, bringing virtually the entire Northwest into the rebels' hands. In other areas of the country, many officers who had planned to lead the revolt were caught out of position (many were in Mexico City on March 3) and arrested. Nonetheless, the rebels soon claimed control of a large, contiguous territory in the North and West of the country, with a disconnected area on the eastern coast (Veracruz).

The government struck first at Veracruz because its port might allow the rebels to purchase weapons. At Veracruz, Aguirre had about 3,500 rebel soldiers, against which the government deployed 8,000 soldiers and about 1,000 *agraristas*. Aguirre decided to withdraw with a handful of loyal followers, and the government assumed control of the port on March 6. Soon after, control of the navy also was restored to the government. Aguirre and his companions were tracked down and killed from March 19 to March 21. Further north, on March 4, Escobar advanced to Monterrey in Nuevo Leon, which was defended by 100 soldiers of loyalist general Juan Andreu Almazán. After a brief struggle, Escobar took the city. The government responded by ordering Almazán to coordinate a two-pronged offensive against Escobar. Perhaps sensing the trap, Escobar withdrew to Saltillo. By March 7, the rebels had been reduced from 18,000 to 13,500 though engaging in little combat.

The second major government offensive focused on the central northern states. The rebels retreated from Saltillo to Torreón, prompting a small engagement in which 70 rebels and 10 government soldiers were killed. A government attack in Durango also drove the rebels to retreat to Torreón. Declining to make a stand there, the rebels then retreated into Chihuahua, where reinforcements awaited them. Federal forces occupied Torreón on March 18 and used it as their base of operations for the next stage of the campaign. The rebels gathered about 8,000 at Jimenez, Chihuahua, finally determined to fight and hoping that the government's distance from its supply lines would impede its preparedness. Yet 9,000 government troops advanced and nearly encircled the rebels, triggering the decisive Battle of Jimenez from March 30 to April 3. The rebels lost nearly their entire force: 3,000 captured, 1,000 killed, and 2,000 dispersed. Government losses were only 161 dead. Escobar fled to mountainous Sonora with about 2,000 men, pursued by government forces.

Farther north, the government moved west against the 2,000 to 3,000 rebels in Sonora. Fighting was particularly severe around Naco, where the rebels were repulsed by loyal forces on April 8. Though aircraft were used to bomb rebel formations, the rebels put up a strong fight against government forces at Loz Azogues before being forced to retreat. More than 1,000 rebels surrendered to the government, rebel leaders fled to the United States, and by May 4, the last of the rebels had been defeated.

Termination and Outcome: The government won an unconditional military victory. While there were executions for disloyalty during the war (particularly in its first week), there do not appear to have been any reprisals taken after the government victory.

Sources: Clodfelter (1992, 2008); Dulles (1961); Gonzales (2002); Krauze (1997); Marley (1998); Purnell (1999); Scheina (2003b); Schlarman (1951); Tomán (2006).

INTRA-STATE WAR #712
Matanza War of 1932

Participants: El Salvador versus Leftists.
Dates: January 18, 1932, to January 29, 1932.
Battle-related Deaths: El Salvador: 100;[169] Leftists: 2,500.[170]
Initiator: Leftists.
Outcome: El Salvador wins.
War Type: Civil for central control.
Total System Member Military Personnel: Armed Forces of El Salvador: 132,000 (prewar, initial, peak, final).[171]
Theater Armed Forces: Armed Forces of El Salvador, plus National Guard and Police: [ ]. Leftists: 16,000 peasants (*campesinos*)[172] and 400 Communists (peak).[173]

Antecedents: After gaining independence from Spain, El Salvador, Costa Rica, Guatemala, Honduras, and Nicaragua remained united in the Central American Confederation. Conflicts between the conservative and liberal factions among the countries led to four wars (Non-state Wars #1510, #1528, #1540, and #1550, during which the Confederation dissolved). These conflicts over ideology and control of the region continued as the countries gradually became members of the interstate system (with El Salvador gaining system membership in 1875), and El Salvador went to war with former allies (Interstate Wars #60, #70, #88, and #91).

Subsequently El Salvador entered a relatively short period of stability in which the government was controlled by the Meléndez-Quiñónez dynasty representing the National Democratic Party (1913–1927). An affiliate of the dynasty, Pio Romero Basque, served as president from 1927 to 1931, and before his term expired, he planned for free elections in 1930. The government had faced opposition from peasants seeking a redistribution of land. One of the instrumental leaders of the movement was Agustín Farabundo Martí Rodríguez. Farabundo Martí had helped found the Communist Party of Central America and had worked with Nicaraguan revolutionary leader Augusto César Sandino before returning to El Salvador. Fearing that Martí would run in the upcoming presidential elections, the government exiled Martí in December 1930. In the election, Arturo Araujo of the Labor Party came to power on March 1, 1931, yet his government lasted only nine months, during which time Martí returned to El Salvador. Araujo was overthrown in a coup by military officers, led by Araujo's vice president and minister of war, Gen. Maximiliano Hernández Martínez, who subsequently was named acting president on December 4, 1931. The tyrannical government of acting president Martínez began a brutal suppression of the rural resistance. This policy, along with the great disparity of wealth in the country, led to the increasing opposition from the left, including the Communist Party of El Salvador. Along with Abel Cuenca and university students Alfonso Luna and Mario Zapata, Martí organized the resistance of leftists that initiated this war.

Narrative: The communists began organizing within the military and among the peasants for a revolt to take place on January 22, 1932. Martínez scheduled municipal and legislative elections for early January, allowing the Communist Party to participate. The elections were characterized by fraud and involved local violence, in which a number of communists were killed. In areas in which the Communist Party was strong, the elections were cancelled altogether. Realizing the futility of the electoral process, the communists continued developing plans for a revolution. Communists within the army, led by Inocente Rivas Hidalgo, the "Red Commandant" of the Red Army in the capital of San Salvador, were to spearhead the revolution. The largest contingent of rebels was the *campesinos*, or rural peasants, particularly in the western departments, among whom the communists had been organizing. In late January, the communist plans for the rebellion rapidly began to disintegrate as communists in Guatemala were prevented from sending aid to their compatriots in El Salvador. Martínez learned about the planned revolt and declared a state of siege on January 18, which led to a mass roundup of leftists that night, during which Martí and other leading communists were arrested. This precipitated a premature start of the revolt, as a group of 500 communist supporters attacked a police detail. Information about communists within the San Salvador Army was leaked to the local commandant, who proceeded to disarm the soldiers and confine them to the barracks. On January 19, a group of armed peasants began advancing against the barracks, and officers used machine-gun fire to disperse the crowd, killing as many as 50 rebels.

Realizing that the chances of a successful revolt had been lost, some of the Communist Party leaders tried to send messages to abort the uprising, but communications were poor, so a number of revolts did take place in areas beyond the capital on January 20, and attacks increased in number on January 22, particularly in the West, where rebels assaulted local military barracks and seized control of a dozen towns. The rebels suffered serious defeats in La Libertad, though a number of smaller towns were overrun by the rebels. In Sansonate, one of the fiercest of the successful assaults was made by 300 rebels from January 22 to January 23. The rebels advanced through the town of Juayúa, killing the commandant and several police officers. The next day, Juayúa was the target of government aerial bombing. Sonzacate became a major communist stronghold of about 5,000 rebels including "Red Julia." The westernmost department of Ahuachapán was also the site of rebel activity: on January 23, the garrison was attacked by approximately 1,400 rebels, who were turned back after suffering heavy losses.

Martínez appointed Gen. José Tomás Calderón to defeat the rebellion. On January 24, the government offensive began, and within days, most of the rebel-captured towns were occupied by government troops. On January 25, the government forces proceeded to Juayuá, where the rebels decided to take a stand. In hand-to-hand fighting, government forces slowly occupied the town. A machine-gun crew moved toward Tacuba in Ahuachapán. In fighting that lasted two and a half hours, the government was victorious against the poorly armed 5,000 rebels, who were slaughtered by machine-gun fire.

The United States had been concerned about the communist threat, and on January 25, three American warships and one Canadian warship were moved to the coast of El Salvador to offer assistance. However, General Calderón and President Martínez declined their offer. On January 29, a group of rebels attempted to seize the town of Huizúcar but were repulsed, which marks the end of sustained combat.

Termination and Outcome: The war ended in a complete military victory for the government. When a number of the rebels fled into Guatemala, many were captured, returned to El Salvador, and executed. On February 1, 1932, three of the rebellion's primary planners, Martí, Alfonso Luna, and Mario Zapata, were executed. Abel Cuenca survived, fled to Guatemala then on to Honduras, where he was imprisoned. Wanting to eliminate the leftist threat more generally, government troops conducted a series of massacres called *La Matanza* (the Slaughter), after which this war has been named. As it was difficult for the government to distinguish the combatants from peasants in general, the government established some arbitrary criteria: for instance, anyone carrying a machete was considered to be guilty and was shot. Troops also would announce that townspeople needed safe-conduct passes and then kill all of those who arrived to collect one. The slaughter was horrific, consuming somewhere between 9,000 and 40,000 peasants. As a result, the war that Clodfelter calls the "first communist-led insurrection in the Western Hemisphere" ended in disaster and the suppression of the leftist movement in El Salvador for many years.[174] However, the spirit of Farabundo Martí lived on in the 1980 creation of the leftist Farabundo Martí National Liberation Front (FMLM, or *Frente Farabundo Martí para la Liberación Nacional*). The FMLN was one of the main participants in the Salvadoran Civil War (Intra-state War #817 of 1979 to 1992). After peace accords were signed in 1992, the FMLN became a legal political party, and on March 15, 2009, the FMLN candidate, Mauricio Funes, won the presidency, taking office on June 1, 2009, and another FMLN member, Salvador Sánchez Cerén, assumed the presidency on June 1, 2014.

Coding Decisions: In terms of calculating battle-deaths, we are focusing upon the brief, eleven-day period of war and excluding the massacres that make up *La Matanza* (the Slaughter). Most sources, however, combine the deaths of the combatants and civilians who died as a result of this conflict, with their estimates of the number killed ranging from 10,000 to 40,000.[175] Several scholars have agreed with Anderson's judgment that 90 percent of the deaths were civilians and 10 percent were combatants.[176] Thus we are taking the midpoint of the overall fatality estimates (or 25,000) and using 10 percent of that (or 2,500) as our best guess about the deaths suffered by the leftists. Scholars have been more consistent in reporting the deaths suffered by the armed forces of El Salvador (including the army, the National Guard, and the police), generally concluding that 100 were killed.[177]

Sources: Anderson (1971); Anderson (1992); Ching and Tilley (1998); Clodfelter (1992); Montgomery (1982); Phillips and Axelrod (2005); Scheina (2003b); White (1973).

INTRA-STATE WAR #730

Costa Rica War of 1948 (aka War of National Liberation)

Participants: Costa Rica versus National Union Party (PUN), Army of National Liberation, and Caribbean Legion.
Dates: March 12, 1948, to April 17, 1948.
Battle-related Deaths: Costa Rica: 1,500; Army of National Liberation and Caribbean Legion: 100.[178]
Initiator: National Union Party.
Outcome: National Union Party wins.
War Type: Civil for control of the central government.
Total System Member Military Personnel: 1,000 (prewar, initial, peak, final).[179]
Theater Armed Forces: Armed Forces of Costa Rica: 1,930 (prewar, initial); 3,430 (peak, final—including the 330-man army, 1,600 police, and 1,500 *Vanguardista* militia).[180] Army of National Liberation and Caribbean Legion (Rebel Army): 450 (prewar, initial); 700 (peak, final).[181]

Antecedents: World War II (Inter-state War #139) precipitated unrest and a number of intra-state wars globally. Even Costa Rica, which had a history of being relatively free of violent internal conflict, was affected. Prior to the war, Costa Rican politics had been dominated by the National Republican Party (PRN), which generally promoted the interests of the conservative coffee growers. In 1940, Rafael Ángel Calderón Guardia, representing the PRN, assumed the presidency. The more progressive shift of the PRN was evidenced in 1942, when Calderón created an alliance with the Communist Party, led by Manuel Mora Valverde (paralleling an alliance between the United States and the Soviet Union). The same year, anti-German rioters attacked a warehouse owned by José María Hipólito "Pepe" Figueres Ferrer, a successful farmer. Figueres's denunciation of the government's failure to protect his business persuaded Calderón (who portrayed Figueres as a Nazi sympathizer) to deport Figueres to Mexico. Calderón's political program continued to evolve as Mora disbanded the Communist Party, creating the *Vanguardia Popular* in its place. In 1943, the PRN and the Vanguard joined to create the new Victory Bloc, which chose Teodoro Picado Michalski as its presidential candidate. Meanwhile, Figueres returned from exile, and in 1944 was instrumental in creating the Democratic Party (which became the Social Democratic Party in 1945), which supported the candidacy of former president León Cortés Castro. Picado won the election by a landslide. The Victory Bloc began to disintegrate as the PRN and the Vanguard increasingly went their own ways. Figueres gathered arms and men in *La Legion del Caribe* (or the Caribbean Legion) to support the Social Democratic Party. The legion was a regional group of reformers who wanted to overthrow dictatorships: many were leftists, including Fidel Castro and Ernesto "Che" Guevara.

In 1948, Calderón was eligible to run for the presidency again, and in this contest, he faced the opposition right-wing candidate, Otilio Ulate Blanco, the candidate of a new political party, *Partido Union Nacional* (PUN). The 1948 campaign was quite polarized, marked by violent incidents, and the results were expected to be close. The February 1948 electoral returns showed that Ulate had won the presidency by 10,000 votes. Citing claims of voting fraud, Congress (which was controlled by Calderón's party) declared on March 1, 1948, that the election was void, and President Picado announced that a new election would be held. While electoral negotiations were still underway, Picado declared a state of siege, and the country's tiny army was called out to maintain order. When *Calderonistas* announced their intention to designate Calderón as president for four years once Congress reconvened (scheduled for May 1), Figueres launched the war in support of Ulate and the PUN.

Narrative: Figueres began the war in possession of La Lucha, on the border with Panama. Pushing westward, he succeeded in establishing a viable defense perimeter using the mountains that roughly bisected the country. The war began on March 12, 1948, when the rebels seized the town of San Isidro del General, with its important airport. Two captured planes were used to ferry legion troops (including many Dominicans) from its base in Guatemala to Costa Rica. On March 14, Figueres blocked the Inter-American Highway across the mountains in the West, capturing Santa Maria on the way. Figueres's forces began to grow, receiving supplies of arms, fuel, and ammunition from his Caribbean Legion base in Guatemala.

Because the government's army was too small to play a decisive role, much of the fighting was done by local police and militias. Manuel Mora assembled a force of 1,500 urban workers (*vanguardistas*) who ended up engaging in the bulk of the fighting against the rebels. The government also received assistance from Nicaragua president Anastasio Somoza and Honduras president Tiburcio Carías Andino. The government launched repeated attacks on the rebel-held El Empalme and was driven back. The government then launched an amphibious operation at the rear of the rebel forces on March 20, which succeeded in advancing inland and taking part of San Isidro. The next day, a rebel counterattack smashed the government forces and secured the town.

Nicaragua offered to intervene on behalf of the government if it would distance itself from its communist supporters. The idea of intervention by right-wing Nicaragua was anathema to the *vanguardistas*, and the government formally rejected the offer. Nevertheless, Nicaraguan soldiers entered Costa Rica in large numbers. In the end, the Nicaraguans formally remained neutral, though volunteers may have assisted the government forces. By early April, the rebel force had increased to about 700 men, and Figueres prepared an offensive against the neighboring provinces of Cartago and Puerto Limón. Setting forth on April 10, his first column reached the provincial capital of Cartago on April 12. The government forces nearby attempted to counterattack, triggering the war's most deadly engagement. At the Battle of El Tejar on April 13, the government lost 200 killed, while the rebels suffered only 14 killed. Puerto Limón was seized by a small rebel airborne force on April 11. At this point, the rebels controlled most of the country.

Termination and Outcome: On April 12, the government decided to sue for peace. After personal negotiations between Figueres and Mora, a negotiated compromise between the two (known as the Pact of Ochomogo) was reached on April 15. On April 19, both sides signed the agreement, which called for Picado to surrender power to a provisional president, who would then hand power to Figueres. Ultimately, Figueres took the presidency as part of the *Junta Fundadora* (Founding Council), which stayed in power for eighteen months, during which its policies included abolishing the army.

Coding Decisions: This brief war has been referred to as the bloodiest event in Costa Rican twentieth-century history. A commonly cited fatality figure is 2,000 total deaths,[182] of which the government losses are reported as 1,500.[183] The rebels admitted losing 67, which many seem unreasonably low. Thus, we are estimating 100 rebel deaths.

Sources: Ameringer (1978, 1996); Arnold (1995); Bell (1971); Bird (1984); Cady and Prince (1966); Clodfelter (2002, 2008); Marley (1998); Phillips and Axelrod (2005); Scheina (2003b); Wilson (1998).

INTRA-STATE WAR #745
Cuban Revolution of 1958 to 1959

Participants: Cuba versus *Fidelistas* (supporters of Fidel Castro).
Dates: May 24, 1958, to January 2, 1959.
Battle-related Deaths: Cuba: 2,000; *Fidelistas* (aggregate): 1,000 (See Coding Decisions.)
Initiator: Cuba.
Outcome: *Fidelistas* win.
War Type: Civil for central control.
Total System Member Military Personnel: Armed Forces of Cuba: 19,000 (prewar, initial, peak, final).[184]
Theater Armed Forces: Armed Forces of Cuba: 19,000 (prewar, initial); 28,000 (peak). 26th of July Movement (Rebel Army): 450 (prewar, initial); 50,000 (peak, final).[185] Revolutionary Directorate (Rebel Army), participating until it was absorbed by the 26th of July Movement in late October; 800 (initial, peak).[186] Second National Front of Escambray (Rebel Army), participating from its split with the Revolutionary Directorate in July 1958: 300 (initial); 1,500 (peak).[187]

Antecedents: Fulgencio Batista y Zaldívar had participated in the "Revolt of the Sergeants" that overthrew the government of Gerardo Machado (and appointee Carlos Manuel de Céspedes y Quesada) in 1933. As head of the armed forces, Colonel Batista effectively controlled the five-man presidency until he was elected president in 1940. He served until 1944, after which he lived in the United States. Batista ran for reelection in 1952, and when it looked like he would lose, he launched a coup instead and created a corrupt and repressive regime with ties to large American multinational corporations. Resistance from the left emerged quickly, a segment of which was led by Fidel Alejandro Castro Ruz, who had been radicalized as a student and had participated in rebellions in the Dominican Republic (1947) and Colombia (1948). Castro created a group, referred to as "The Movement," which recruited members from among Cuba's poor. On July 26, 1953, 164 Movement members led by Castro attacked the Moncada Barracks in the southeastern city of Santiago de Cuba in the hopes of instigating a widespread uprising against Batista. The attempt failed, and both Fidel and his brother Raúl (a member of the Cuban Communist Party, *Partido Socialista Popular* [PSP]) were imprisoned for almost two years on the Isla de Pinos. While imprisoned, Castro renamed his group the "26th of July Movement" (or MR-26–7) in honor of the attempted uprising. After their release, Fidel and Raúl fled to Mexico, where they met Ernesto "Che" Guevara, and they began studying guerrilla tactics and planning their next revolution.

On December 2, 1956, a group of 83 men, led by Fidel, Raúl, and Guevara, landed their ship, the *Granma*, at Playa Las Coloradas (on the southeastern coast) in another attempt to spark a revolution. Unexpected delays in their arrival ruined their planned coordination with a local urban uprising, so the rebels began a trek toward the Sierra Maestra (mountains); only 17 members (including Fidel, Raúl, and Che) reached the mountains. In 1957, Castro began small attacks against government forces, which continued throughout the year. In March, Castro publicized the Sierra Maestra Manifesto (which outlined demands for a new civilian government) to the foreign press, making him an international celebrity. By June 1957, the *Fidelistas* had increased to almost 200 rebels. That month the government launched an ineffective operation against the rebels with 4,000 troops. By the end of summer, the *Fidelistas* had established a safe haven, or *foco*, where they could train the new recruits. The *Fidelistas* also benefitted from the growing urban opposition movement. The survivors of a small urban uprising fled to the hills, where they formed the Revolutionary Directorate (DR). Similarly the naval officers involved in a failed revolt fled to the Escambray mountains, where they created the Second National Front of Escambray (SFNE), which affiliated with the DR.

By early 1958, Castro's 26th of July Movement controlled six columns of 50 to 100 guerrillas each (or a total of 900 men and women) in the Sierra Maestra. In addition, Raúl managed operations in the Sierra Cristal with only 65 men. About 100 guerrillas were operating in the Sierra de los Organos (at the western end of the island) and another 100 in the centrally located Escambray. They were aided by the middle class, who had become increasingly angry with the Batista regime. Civilians organized themselves into the Civic Resistance Movement, which waged a propaganda war, raised money, and gathered intelligence for the rebellion. The government's inability to end the rebellion was leading to a loss of support among the elite business community and foreign interests as well. Their dissatisfaction prompted the United States to impose an arms embargo against the government on March 18, 1958, further demoralizing the Cuban military. At that point, Fidel decided that the time had come for a general strike to bring down the government, which he called for April 9, 1958. The strike's failure emboldened the government to launch an offensive against the rebels on May 24, 1958, which marks the start of the war.

Narrative: Although the guerrilla struggle had been raging for eighteen months, it was transformed into a civil war when the government decided to mount a massive anti-guerrilla offensive, Operation Verano, against the 26th of July Movement on May 24, 1958. Batista sent 10,000 to 15,000 troops against the rebels, and the navy and air force bombarded rebel positions. The rebels eluded capture and persistently ambushed the government forces, inflicting heavy casualties. The government did succeed in surrounding Castro's force on July 28 at Las Mercedes, but Castro requested a cease-fire and used the time to escape the trap. By the end of the offensive on August 7, the government had suffered 207 battle-deaths compared to the rebels' 27. Elsewhere in the country, SFNE defeated a minor government offensive in August, and soon the SFNE was the largest group in the Escambray region.

Meanwhile, representatives of the leading opposition groups had met in Caracas in July to develop more coordination among the rebel groups. The 26th of July Movement had had an ideological aversion to leadership institutionalization, both internally and in relation to other rebel organizations. However, MR 26–7 did shift from a broad political focus (which had included the civil resistance efforts) to an emphasis on military command structure, with Fidel Castro heading both the political and military efforts. The Pact of Caracas also unified the anti-Batista movement under Castro's leadership. Castro now prepared a rebel offensive to expand the revolution westward to the center of the country. He sent Che Guevera and Camilo Cinfuegos to the Escambray mountains, where they established a new front and attempted to exert control over the other rebel groups. About 200 of the 1,500 SFNE guerrillas defected to Guevera, but the rest remained separate. Che did succeed in subordinating the DR to the 26th of July Movement. A new structure for the urban resistance movement was created, the Base Revolutionary Cells (CRB), and urban guerrillas were inflicting damage but taking horrendous casualties (typically 50 percent fatalities) in the process. About fourteen operations took place in September and October, usually involving bands of 10 to 12 urban guerrillas that would target a police or army barracks.

By October, total rebel forces in the countryside numbered 7,000 in twenty columns and were able to mount raids against towns and cities. Correctly believing that Batista was isolated and his military ineffective, Castro launched a general offensive on November 17, pushing westward toward Havana. The urban guerrillas also increased their efforts, conducting thirty-two operations in November. The first serious fighting by the *Fidelistas* was at Guisa on November 30, where the government lost 200 casualties compared to only 8 rebel battle-deaths. By mid-December the rebels had occupied most of the East, with the exceptions of Santiago and Guantanamo (which were loosely besieged). Bombings were everyday occurrences in the cities; more than 100 bombs were detonated in Havana on the single evening of December 7. Guevera and Cienfuegos now shifted to the offense in the center. They struck the North and South, severing communications between the East and West halves of the country. The southern offensive was conducted by SFNE, which was now coordinating its operations with Castro's forces.

The United States finally had decided that Batista had to be removed from office, and it sent a secret envoy, William D. Pawley, to meet with Batista on December 9 to offer him a retirement in Florida. Batista refused, and the rebel momentum continued. Santa Clara stood between the rebels and the capital, and rebel columns (now totaling close to 50,000 rebels) converged on the city. On December 29, rebels entered the city, although they could not take it. Two days later, the eastern suburb of Yaguajay fell, prompting Batista to conclude that the war was lost. He left the country the following morning, and garrisons began surrendering or defecting to the rebels en masse. On January 2, 1959, the rebels—first the SFNE and then the 26th of July Movement—marched into Havana, ending the war.

Termination and Outcome: Military commanders tried to negotiate terms with the rebels, who insisted on an unconditional surrender. Though Castro initially appointed Manuel Urrutia as president and José Miró Cardona as prime minister, within weeks Castro assumed the office of prime minister. He created the same type of informal, egalitarian leadership style that had characterized the 26th of July Movement to transform quickly Cuba's social, economic, and political systems.[188] The new government vigorously prosecuted members of the former regime; as many as 1,000 Batista supporters and "counterrevolutionaries" were executed after the war's end.

Coding Decisions: In terms of coding the initiator of the war, though the overall conflict was begun by the rebels, the specific incident that raised the insurgency to war-level fatalities was the government's offensive of March 24, 1958, and thus the Cuban government is coded as the war initiator.

The estimates of total fatalities in this war vary widely, ranging from 10,000 to 20,000 total deaths, though the vast majority of these would have been civilians. After the rebels' victory, they published a list of 898 war dead, with "over half of these being combatants." At the lower end of the spectrum, Phillips and Axelrod provide figures of 100 rebels killed and 500 government losses. After considering these estimates of total fatalities, we follow Scheina in adopting a modest estimate of 3,000 total battle deaths, with the armed forces of Cuba sustaining 2,000 battle-deaths and the rebels suffering 1,000 deaths, though we cannot determine how many deaths each specific group sustained.

Sources: Arnold (1995); Bonachea and San Martín (1974); Cady and Prince (1966); Clodfelter (2002, 2008); Fermoselle (1987); Goldstone (1998); Mallin (2000); Marley (1998); Mydans and Mydans (1968); Perez (1993); Phillips and Axelrod (2005); Scheina (2003b); Selbin (1993); Shetterly (2007); Taylor and Hudson (1972); Wickham-Crowley (1990); Wood (1968).

INTRA-STATE WAR #766
Dominican Republic War of 1965 (aka Guerra de Abril)

Participants: Dominican Republic and United States versus Leftists (or Constitutionalists).
Dates: April 24, 1965, to September 6, 1965.
Battle-related Deaths: Dominican Republic (aka Leales or Junta): 825; United States: 44;[189] Leftists: 600.
Initiator: Leftists.
Outcome: Conflict continues at below war level.
War Type: Civil for control of the central government.
Total System Member Military Personnel: Armed Forces of Dominican Republic: 17,000 (prewar, initial, peak, final); Armed Forces of the United States: 2,660,000 (prewar, initial, peak, final).[190]
Theater Armed Forces: Armed Forces of the Dominican Republic (aka *Leales* or *Junta*): 14,650 (prewar); 13,900 (initial); 17,000 (peak); 17,000 (final).[191] United States (Pro-government State Intervener): 0 (prewar); 538 (initial); 20,463 (plus 10,059 sailors offshore—peak, final).[192] Leftists and Constitutionalists (Rebel Army): 2,350 (prewar); 3,100 (initial); 6,000 (peak, final).[193]

Antecedent: In 1861, the Dominican Republic (fearing Haitian aggression) briefly annexed itself to Spain. However, by 1863 Santo-Domingo again revolted against Spanish rule (Extra-state War #353), at the conclusion of which the Dominican Republic regained its autonomy. In the twentieth century, the United States began to expand and implement the Monroe Doctrine and the Roosevelt Corollary in the Western Hemisphere, and America became more involved in Dominican affairs. In response to domestic turmoil in the Dominican Republic, American marines occupied the country from 1916 to 1922, and the United States maintained its interest in the country thereafter. In 1930, Gen. Rafael Leonidas Trujillo Molina was elected to the presidency, and he established a repressive dictatorship, ruling for thirty years. For most of this period, Trujillo had the support of the United States. Even though the Organization of American States (OAS, created in 1948) established a policy of nonintervention among the members, the United States reserved the right to intervene, with the OAS or unilaterally, specifically in the face of challenges posed by communism. When Trujillo was involved in the attempted assassination of Venezuela president Rómulo Betancourt, the OAS voted to sever diplomatic ties and impose economic sanctions. Almost a year later, on May 30, 1961, Trujillo himself was assassinated. Following a period of military coups, elections were held, and the left-wing nationalist Juan Emilio Bosch Gaviño won power, taking office in February 1963. Just seven months into Bosch's rule, his refusal to suppress the communists precipitated a military coup that succeeded (with the acquiescence or support of the United States) in overthrowing him and installing a three-man military junta. Infighting among military officers produced a progression of juntas, which eventually installed a new civilian president, Donald Reid Cabral, on December 29, 1963.

Narrative: President Reid had the support of the United States, but antigovernment plots continued, hatched by leftist groups, including: left-wing supporters of Bosch; those who resented American interference; and elements of the military that feared another dictatorship. An uprising had been planned for April 26, 1965; however, when the government attempted to arrest four military officers, the plans were moved up. On April 24, 1965, between 1,000 and 1,500 Bosch supporters in the military led by Col. Francisco Caamaño Deñó rose up in rebellion and seized key installations and the army chief of staff, Gen. Marco Rivera Cuesta. In support of the military rising, the pro-Bosch leader of the Dominican Revolutionary Party (*Partido Revolucionario Dominicano* [PRD]), Jose Francisco Peña Gomez, called for a popular uprising, and thousands of people took to the streets. President Reid authorized Gen. Elías Wessin y Wessin, commander of the elite forces at the San Isidro military base (located east of the capital Santo Domingo), to suppress the revolt. Unsure of his level of support within the military, Wessin remained at the base. Fighting spread on April 25 as the rebels, calling themselves the Constitutionalists (now 3,000 to 3,200 strong) with 5,000 armed civilians immediately took control of most of the capital and called for the return of Bosch from exile. They seized the presidential palace, arresting Reid, and created an interim government with Jose Rafael Molina Urena as temporary president. Meanwhile, the majority of the Dominican armed forces supported the Reid government (adopting the name the *Leales*, or Loyalists), and the military units formed a junta (led by Air Force Commander Col. Jose Benoit). Benoit launched air strikes on the palace, with the approval of the American embassy. Assured of air force support, General Wessin began a tank advance on the capital on April 27, joined by military units from across the country (about 4,000 troops). In heavy fighting, the Loyalists forces recaptured control of segments of the capital (including the palace) but were turned back at the Battle of Duarte Bridge and decimated by rebel attacks.

In reports to Washington, American ambassador William Tapley Bennett mistakenly described the Constitutionalists as being led by communists and requested direct US military assistance to protect American citizens. On the same day (April 27), the United States landed some unarmed soldiers to assist in the evacuation of Americans. US president Lyndon B. Johnson initially authorized the landing of 500 marines for defensive purposes. As the embassy began to take heavier incoming fire from the Constitutionalists, another 1,166 American troops were deployed on April 29. American involvement soon escalated into an invasion as elements of the 82nd Airborne Division landed at the junta's San Isidro headquarters. Ultimately, the United States deployed more than 20,000 military personnel in Operation "Power Pack," and by April 30, their focus had shifted from protecting civilians to actively attempting to stymie the Constitutionalists. Advancing from San Isidro, the American forces attempted to enter the capital by the Duarte Bridge, where they came under heavy fire from the Constitutionalists, prompting American assaults on their positions from May 2 to May 3. The rebels began to retreat and agreed to mediation by the OAS.

On May 5, a truce, the Act of Santo Domingo, was signed by Colonel Caamaño (for the Constitutionalists), Colonel Benoit (for the Loyalist junta), and the OAS, calling for a provisional government to be formed. The peace was to be enforced by an Inter-American Peace Force (IAPF) composed of 2,000 Brazilian, Paraguayan, Honduran, Nicaraguan, and Costa Rican soldiers and police. The peace was short-lived, as rival "provisional governments" were sworn into power on May 7. Sensing an opportunity to win before the IAPF's Latin American contingents could act, the junta attacked the Constitutionalists on May 13. The cease-fire collapsed, and sporadic fighting between the two sides occurred throughout the rest of the month. The IAPF forces began arriving at the end of the month, and the United States began withdrawing some of its troops. However, remaining US troops engaged in heavy fighting against the Constitutionalists on June 15 and June 16, resulting in five American deaths and sixty-seven rebel deaths.

Termination and Outcome: Fighting in the streets of the capital continued until August, while negotiations made steady progress. The junta was discomfited to find that the OAS was seeking a mutually acceptable settlement rather than helping them win the war. A peace agreement (the Reconciliation and Institutional Act sponsored by the OAS) was signed on August 31, 1965. The terms of the agreement provided for a provisional government, an end to the fighting, reintegration of Constitutional military personnel into the armed forces, and elections to be held in 1966. A compromise interim government was created with Hector Garcia-Godoy serving as president. On September 6, General Wessin launched an attempted a coup against the new government, which was blocked by American troops. This action marks the end of this war. Both Wessin and Caamaño were given positions outside the country.

Coding Decisions: Though the war was over, armed conflict continued at below-war levels between the military and the Constitutionalists. The 1966 presidential election pitted two former presidents against one another: Juan Bosch of the Dominican Revolutionary Party, and Joaquin Balaguer representing the new Reformist Party. The election campaign in early 1966 was extraordinarily violent; perhaps 350 Bosch partisans were killed and Bosch essentially was confined to his home. Balaguer had the support of the military, the business community, and the United States and won the election handily.

IAPF was designed as a peacekeeping force and thus is not considered a war participant (although eleven of its members were wounded). The IAPF was disbanded in 1967.

Sources: Bercovitch and Fretter (2004); Bracey (1980); Cady and Prince (1966); Carey (1972); Ciment (2007g); Clodfelter (2002, 2008); Gleijeses (1978); Heinl and

Heinl (1978); Korb (1999); Lafeber (1993); Marley (1998); Mydans and Mydans (1968); Phillips and Axelrod (2005); Scheina (2003b); Taylor and Hudson (1972); Wood (1968).

INTRA-STATE WAR #770
First Guatemala War of 1966 to 1968

Participants: Guatemala and United States versus Leftists.
Dates: October 3, 1966, to March 30, 1968.
Battle-related Deaths: Leftists: 1,400; Guatemala: 1,000; United States: 28.[194] (See Coding Decisions.)
Initiator: Guatemala.
Outcome: Guatemala and United States win.
War Type: Civil for central control.
Total System Member Military Personnel: Armed Forces of Guatemala: 10,000 (prewar); 9,000 (initial); 11,000.[195] Armed Forces of the United States: 2,660,000 (prewar); 3,090,000 (initial); 3,550,000 (peak, final).[196]
Theater Armed Forces: Guatemala, including the Armed Forces of Guatemala and the *Policía Nacional*: 12,000 (initial); 22,000 (peak). United States: 33 (initial);[197] 1,000 (peak)[198] aided by aircraft from bases in Panama.[199] Leftists (*Fuerzas Armadas Rebeldes* [FAR], MR-13 *Alejandro de León, Frente Guerrillero Edgar Ibarra* [FGEI]): 125 (initial); 1,790 (peak). (See Coding Decisions.)

Antecedents: In 1944, Guatemala's October Revolution, led by Jacobo Árbenz Guzmán and Maj. Francisco Javier Arana created a democratic regime under President Juan José Arévalo Bermejo, representing the leftist *Partido Acción Revolucionaria* (Revolutionary Action Party [PAR]). Arévalo's government, which favored worker's rights, was met with growing opposition from American business interests, especially the United Fruit Company (UFCO). Arévalo's government began to unravel as its radical and moderate elements split. The radicals left the PAR to form the Communist Party (PGT) and later the Socialist Party (PS), whereas the moderates left PAR in 1947 to re-create the Popular Front Liberator (FPL). The government also was challenged in 1949 by a revolt, which was defeated through actions taken by Defense Minister Arbenz, who subsequently was elected president in 1950. Árbenz continued agrarian reform, including the appropriation of unused land (some belonging to the UFCO) to distribute to peasants. Members of American president Eisenhower's administration had economic ties to UFCO and were sympathetic to UFCO's arguments encouraging the US government to overthrow Árbenz. The arrival in Guatemala of a shipment of weapons from Czechoslovakia provided an excuse for the American government to invade Guatemala in 1954. The Guatemalan military did little to defend the government, and Arbenz resigned on June 27, 1954.

A military government was installed, which garnered the support of UFCO and the United States, which gave Guatemala millions of dollars in assistance in the hopes of making Guatemala into a "showcase for democracy." Gen. José Miguel Ramón Ydígoras Fuentes was elected president in 1958, and in 1960, he agreed to the American request to establish a base in Guatemala to serve as a training base for the Bay of Pigs invasion of Cuba. Both the failure of the invasion and Ydígoras's ties to the United States led to a revolt by the more liberal members of the military on November 13, 1960. The coup was defeated within days, but many of the rebels (some trained by the United States) fled to Honduras, El Salvador, or into the Zacapa Mountains. In 1961, rebels including Col. Alejandro de León, Luis Turcios Lima, and Marco Antonio Yon Sosa returned to Guatemala and created *Movimento Revolucionario 13 de Noviembre*, or Revolutionary Movement of November 13 (MR-13). MR-13, based in the eastern Sierra de las Minas, adopted the Cuban "*foco*" strategy (*foquismo*), whereby small groups of revolutionaries act with the local populace in armed attacks upon the government. MR-13 began its activities in July 1961 with attacks on army outposts and UFCO offices. The advent of MR-13 exacerbated the division within PGT between those who favored direct military action and those who promoted a peaceful road to socialism. As a compromise, in 1962, the PGT also formed an armed group, the *20 de Octubre* (20th of October Front), which began guerrilla attacks north of the capital and cooperated with MR-13. In December 1962, this collaboration was institutionalized by the creation of *Fuerzas Armadas Rebeldes*, Rebel Armed Forces Mejia (FAR), which included MR-13, *Movimiento 20 de Octubre*, and *Movimiento 12 de Abril* (which consisted of secondary and university students).[200] FAR grew rapidly from 1963 to 1966, with a number of cadres receiving training in Cuba. However, in 1964, Turcios Lima and Yon Sosa split over ideological issues. Trotskyite Yon Sosa left FAR but continued as the leader of MR-13 *Alejandro de León*, which opened a front in Izabal. Turcios Lima, whose views were more in line with those of Fidel Castro, established a second front in Zacapa called *Frente Guerrillero Edgar Ibarra* (FGEI). A third front, *Resistancia*, was established in the capital. In 1965, the PGT and FGEI created a new FAR that excluded MR-13.

Meanwhile, opposition to President Ydígoras continued within the military, and in March 1963, the officer corps, led by reactionary defense minister Col. Enrique Peralta Azurdia, seized power in a coup (in which the United States may have been complicit). By the mid-1960s, Guatemala was receiving more US military aid than any other Central American country.[201] Despite its support of the military government, the United States also applied pressure for a return to democratic rule. Consequently, in March 1966, Peralta conducted a relatively open presidential election that pitted Peralta's favorite, Col. Juan de Dios Aguilar (of the *Partido Instrucional Democráci*, [PID]), against a civilian lawyer, Julio César Méndez Montenegro (representing the center-left *Partido Revolucionario* (Revolutionary Party [PR]), and former defense minister Col. Miguel Angel Ponciano (of the *Movimiento de Liberacíon Nacional* [MLN]). Méndez's candidacy further divided the leftist groups. The FAR leadership was hesitant about participating in elections, while the PGT supported Méndez. The military vote was divided, and Méndez won a plurality of the votes. The election was then thrown to the congress, which chose Méndez as president. In the meantime, FAR continued its guerrilla activities with such success that it prompted a popular impression that it was close to seizing power.[202] Méndez became president on July 1, 1966, and he proclaimed a truce with PGT-FAR, which began a partial demobilization. Méndez also tried (unsuccessfully) to reach an agreement with the other leftist groups, though FGEI, with the support of Cuba, wanted to continue the guerrilla war. Méndez tried to chart a middle course of supporting the military while promoting moderate reforms encouraged by the US Alliance for Progress. In the end, most of the benefits went to the wealthy, and growing disenchantment in the country precipitated increased activity among the leftists.

Narrative: Méndez's capitulation to the military in the Pact of Conditions gave the army greater autonomy, especially in its counterinsurgency measures, which led to both a new anti-guerrilla campaign and to the increasing involvement of US Special Forces in Guatemala. In addition to providing military training, the United States was now permitted to station Green Beret Special Forces in Guatemala, and they played a significant role in the attacks against the guerrillas, using tactics similar to those used by the United States in Vietnam. The direct involvement of the United States in this conflict has led to this period being referred to as "a Cold War civil war" in Guatemala.[203] The campaign, including both overt and covert methods, was planned by American John P. Longan and was organized, financed, and run directly by the United States.[204] Within the Guatemalan military, "Operation Guatemala" was led by Col. Carlos Araña Osorio. July to October 1966 was set aside for training by the Green Berets. After that, the military forces would launch an enhanced counterinsurgency campaign with two major components: a military offensive, conducted by the Guatemalan army and air force (aided by the United States) against the rebel fronts or strongholds; and a government-sponsored, right-wing terrorist campaign that targeted leftists and guerrilla sympathizers (also involving the United States).[205]

The first strike of the counterinsurgency program was launched against FGEI, which was in disarray due to the death of its leader, Turcios Lima, in a car accident on October 2, 1966. FGEI then came under the leadership of César Montes. Immediately thereafter, forces from Guatemala and the United States began an intense campaign against the rebels in the Sierra de las Minas in the Zacapa and Izabel provinces. US involvement was substantial as American helicopters were used to hunt the guerrillas and US forces accompanied Guatemalan troops on their anti-guerrilla offensives. In an attempt to deprive the guerrillas of their popular support among the peasants, the offensive soon involved American bombings and napalm raids from US bases in Panama, which led to indiscriminate killing.

The second component of this overarching American strategy was reliance upon specific anti-terrorist organizations, both governmental and nongovernmental (sometimes referred to as paramilitary groups and irregular groups).[206] What developed was a terror campaign against leftists, "Operation Cleanup," which blurred the distinction between official actions and right-wing death squad terror. Within the Guatemalan army itself, the United States and Méndez established a counterterrorism unit, the Special Commando Unit of the Guatemalan Army (SCUGA), under the leadership of Col. Rafael Arriga Bosque (who would become defense minister in 1967). The regime expanded the network of military commissioners, who were usually former army personnel who now led paramilitary forces to protect the interests of the landowners. Governmental forces also included *Policía Militar*; the *Policía Nacional*; the *Policía Regional*; the *Policía Judicial*; and the *Policía de Hacienda*. US support fueled the growth of the national police force from 3,000 to 11,000 men. Colonel Araña also deputized and provided weapons directly to landowners and local vigilantes, who were given the right to consider themselves as representing the government. On the nongovernmental level, the political party MLN created hit squads, and individuals on the right formed their own paramilitary anti-Communist terrorist groups, including the *Mano Blanca* (White Hand), *Ojo por Ojo* (An Eye for an Eye), and *Ejército Secreto Anticomunists* (the Anticommunist Secret Army), many of which were composed of off-duty or former members of the army and the police. In 1967, the rightist paramilitary organizations launched an intensified series of attacks, referred to as the "White Terror" against the workers and peasants who lived in areas with active guerrillas. Evidence of the cooperation between the military and the paramilitary organizations in this system of terror can be seen in the fact that thousands of civilians who were picked up for questioning by the army or police would then disappear, supposedly into the hands of paramilitary organizations.

In Zacapa, Colonel Araña was vested heavily in both the military offensive and in the terrorist campaign, becoming known as the "Jackal of Zacapa" or "Butcher of Zacapa" for killing an estimated 15,000 persons between 1966 and 1970.[207] By October 1967, the counterinsurgency efforts were successful in virtually destroying Edgar Ibarra Front (FGEI). The military then concentrated on Yon Sosa's MR-13 *Alejandro de León*. On January 10, 1968, FGEI leader César Montes announced its separation from PGT, and FAR and Yon Sosa's MR-13 reunited. The rebels, who were not prepared for the army's offensive, made a number of strategic mistakes and suffered a temporary defeat in 1968, though 100 guerrillas shifted to continue their struggle in urban areas.

Termination and Outcome: The major guerrilla fronts in the rural areas were temporarily defeated; however, the conflict continued in urban areas into early 1968. Booth dates the significant decline in violence from the end of March 1968, thus March 31, 1968, is coded as the end date of the war.[208] The outcome is that conflict continues but at below-war levels. The growing power of the military would lead to the return of military rule, and war-level combat would resume in two years later (Intra-state War #781: Second Guatemala War of 1970 to 1971).

Coding Decisions: There are a number of elements that make the coding of this war complex, some of which are particular to this war, and others of which are common to all guerrilla wars, including: identifying the combatants (and distinguishing them from civilians); identifying the start and end dates of the war; identifying the initiator; and determining the battle-deaths of combatants (distinguishing them from civilian deaths). A difficulty in delineating combatants in guerrilla warfare comes from the overlap of the roles of combatant, support system, and noncombatant and especially from the overlap between civilians and combatants in areas in which civilians participate in peasant militias or urban raids. The distinction between combatants and civilians can be blurred intentionally by both the guerrilla organizations and the government. Wickham-Crowley characterizes the Guatemalan experience in 1966 and 1967 as "the most brutal regime of terror imposed upon a peasantry in all the time period under review" [1956–1970].[209] Booth notes, "The dissident belligerents . . . included both full-time guerrillas and irregular, part-time elements."[210] These "part-time elements" included peasant militias and student radical groups, which could be involved in combat or support roles. As measures of state military personnel include those engaged in combat support roles, guerrilla support personnel should be included in the number of guerrilla combatants as well. There are no exact figures of the numbers of these "part-time elements" involved in combat. In trying to quantify the relationship between the full-time and part-time guerrilla combatants, Jonas noted that one guerrilla column contained 59 percent peasants and 2 percent students.[211] It has been estimated that the active guerrillas peaked at 500 during this war.[212] If we assume that this ratio of guerrillas to "civilian combatants/support" (39 to 61 percent) was fairly consistent in all elements of the conflict, then 500 guerrillas would have been aided by 1,282 "civilian combatants," producing the rounded total of 1,790.

Conflict between the left and the right in Guatemala continued intermittently from 1954 onward. A number of authors consider the entire period as one conflict: for instance, Clodfelter has a single entry titled "Political Violence in Guatemala: 1954–1996." However, during this entire period, battle-related deaths among the combatants were low, even though large numbers of civilians were killed or massacred either by the government or by paramilitary organizations. These periods or activities of state-sponsored terrorism against civilians are not considered by COW coding rules as being part of the war. Thus, from the entire period of violence, we have identified periods of sustained combat in which combatant deaths exceeded a thousand per year. As evident in the history of this war, there was a link between the military actions undertaken by the government and its use of terror against the populace. In his study of political violence, Brockett identified three periods of heightened violence: 1967 to 1968, 1970 to 1972, and after 1980.[213] In the same vein, Jonas identified two separate periods of civil war: 1966 to 1968 and 1981 to 1983.[214] Jonas notes that some authors have never seen the conflict as a "real" civil war, but she (like COW) argues that they are wars and sees the dismissal of these conflicts as wars as reflective of differing perceptions of those in the capital and those in the conflict zones.[215] To these earlier wars we have added the more recent period of 1989 to 1990, thus coding four wars since 1966: Intra-state War #770 of 1966 to 1968; Intra-state War #781 of 1970 to 1971; Intra-state War #811 of 1978 to 1983; and Intra-state War #845.5 of 1989 to 1990. Armed conflict continued between these periods but was at below war-level fatality rates (of combatants).

In terms of identifying the initiator of this war, the leftists did begin the armed conflict in an attempt to overthrow the government. However, the activities that began the war (elevated the level of conflict to war level) were begun by the government's offensive; thus the government is coded as the initiator of the war.

Distinguishing the battle-deaths of the combatants is critical in determining the periods of war but is more difficult in this case because of the comingling of the war with practices designed to terrorize and punish the public at large (or at least those who opposed the government). The killing in Guatemala was horrific, with estimates of 200,000 civilians being killed or disappeared during the entire thirty-six-year period (1954–1990).[216] In terms of the specific period of this war, accurate fatality statistics (battle-death statistics) are not available. The estimates of civilians killed during the specific period of this war (October 3, 1966—March 30, 1968) range from 8,000[217] to 15,000.[218] A common figure reported is 8,000 deaths, with most of those being civilian deaths.[219] From the perspective of the Guatemalan government, the vast majority of these deaths would be considered battle-related deaths in that the mass murder of peasants was described by the government as legitimately eliminating FAR's collaborators or the "peasant infrastructure."[220] However, under COW coding rules, massacres of civilians are not considered as an integral component of a war: thus groups like *Mano Blanco* are not considered to be war participants and the deaths of civilians in terror activities are not considered as battle-deaths. Though the government's claims concerning the involvement of large segments of the populace in the rebellion are substantially exaggerated, there were individuals who assisted the guerrillas in combat as members of peasant militias and support personnel. As already described, we have estimated that there were 1,290 "part-time" combatants on the side of the leftists. The fatalities among the guerrillas themselves were quite high. Both of the major guerrilla armies virtually were destroyed by the government offensive, though 100 guerrillas moved from the countryside into the urban areas to continue the struggle. If the guerrillas peaked at 500 members, this would seem to imply that the guerrillas suffered 400 battle-deaths, or an 80 percent fatality rate. A similar number is provided by Paige, who mentions 300 guerrillas (or 60 percent) being killed in the government's offensive.[221] Because the government's offensive including bombing and the use of napalm against the rebel strongholds, fatality levels among support personnel could be equivalent to those of the guerrillas. If the lower number of guerrilla deaths is used, and if the lower of these percentages (60 percent) is applied to the "support personnel," that would mean that the leftists also suffered an additional loss of 1,074 (or a rounded total of 1,400 for the leftists). US forces suffered a fatality rate of 2.8 percent (28 out of 1,000 troops). Applying this same ratio to the total Guatemalan forces would yield a fatality estimate of 600 (which would be low, given their broader involvement). Thus we are estimating 1,000 government battle-deaths.

Sources: Anderson (1988); Ball, Kobrak, and Spirer (1999); Bercovitch and Fretter (2004); Booth (1980); Caballero Jurado and Thomas (1990); Clodfelter (2002); Crain (1975); Doyle and Osario (2014); Gambone (2001); Gross (1995); Handy (1994); Hodges (1977); Jonas (1991, 2000); Korb (1999); Lafeber (1993); May (2001); Paige (1983); Peralta and Beverly (1980); Scheina (2003b); Schlesinger and Kinzer (1982); Tallmer (2003); Wickham-Crowley (1987, 1992).

INTRA-STATE WAR #781

Second Guatemala War of 1970 to 1971

Participants: Guatemala versus Leftists.
Dates: November 13, 1970 to September 15, 1971.
Battle-related Deaths: Leftists: [ ]; Guatemala: [ ]; Total Combatant Deaths: 1,000. (See Coding Decisions.)
Initiator: Guatemala.
Outcome: Guatemala wins.
War Type: Civil for central control.
Total System Member Military Personnel: Armed Forces of Guatemala: 13,000 (prewar, initial, peak, final).[222]
Theater Armed Forces: Guatemala (includes the Armed Forces and the National Police): 24,000; Leftists (FAR and PGT): [ ].

Antecedents: The First Guatemala war (Intra-state War #330) was an offensive by the Guatemalan military to crush the leftist opposition movement, including: *Fuerzas Armadas Rebeldes*, or Rebel Armed Forces (FAR); *Movimento Revolucionario 13 de Noviembre*, or Revolutionary Movement of November 13 (MR-13); *Movimiento 20 de Octubre*; *Partido Guatemalteco del Trabajo* (PGT); *Movimiento 12 de Abril*; MR-13 *Alejandro de León*; and *Frente Guerrillero Edgar Ibarra* (FGEI). At this point, the government was under the leadership of President Julio César Méndez Montenegro (representing the center-left *Partido Revolucionario*, or Revolutionary Party [PR]). The Guatemalan military, led by Col. Carlos Araña Osorio (assisted by the United States), launched a combined military offensive and counterinsurgency terror campaign conducted by both government forces and independent right-wing armed groups. By 1968, both FGEI and MR-13 *Alejandro de León* were essentially defeated, though some of the rebels continued low-level urban conflict against the Guatemalan government after that point, primarily by kidnappings and assassinations. Subsequently there were significant changes within the rebel groups. FAR attempted to assemble the remnants of the defeated rebel groups in a new front in the jungles of northern Guatemala. Though the first effort in 1968 collapsed, a second effort was made in 1971 and 1972. The rebels also lost several of their influential leaders: in early 1969 César Montes lost his position as head of FGEI; and Yon Sosa was killed on May 18, 1970, by Mexican border police.

In 1970, the growing rebel urban attacks prompted increased support for the right-wing political party the *Movimiento de Liberacíon Nacional* (MLN). For the approaching May 1970 presidential election, the MLN chose Col. Carlos Araña Osorio (the architect of the counterinsurgency operation in 1966) as its candidate. Araña's conduct of the war and his associated terror campaign had earned him the name of the "Butcher of Zacapa," or the "Jackal of Zacapa," for the number of civilians killed during that campaign. The MLN was able to persuade the conservative *Partido Instrucional Democrácia* (PID) to support Araña as well. The more liberal political parties, however, split: the PR candidate was Mario Fuentes Pieruccini; and the *Democracia Cristiana Guatemaltea* backed Jorge Lucas Caballeros. Though the more liberal parties together received a majority of the votes, the MLN gained a 42.9 percent plurality. The election was sent to the congress, which was controlled by MLN and PID, ensuring Araña's selection.

Narrative: Araña assumed the presidency on July 1, 1970, and vowed to complete the guerrillas' demise. Using the recent killing of four police agents by the rebels as a pretext, Araña launched a new war against the guerrillas. Unlike the previous moderate administration, Araña was able to describe the conflict in more ideological terms, claiming that the violence was the result of "communist subversion" that has led to a virtual state of civil war.[223] On November 13, 1970, Araña declared desperate measures were necessary to save the country, including a state of siege, martial law, and a 9:00-p.m.-to-5:00 a.m. curfew throughout the country. He vowed to eliminate all the guerrillas, even "if it is necessary to turn the country into a cemetery."[224] Similar to the

1966-to-968 war, Araña's plans included both overt military action along with a covert reign of terror against segments of the population. The United States also continued to be virtually the sole supplier of military aid and weapons to Guatemala. However, in this war, US direct military participation was limited, with only twenty-five American military officers and seven former police officers working with the Guatemalan military (consequently the United States is not coded as a war participant).

As the rebels continued their small-scale attacks against government forces in urban areas, a new practice in the government's policy was that of mass arrests, with 4,000 people arrested in the first few months of the campaign. These were accompanied by a broader wave of terror, and thousands were abducted, tortured, and murdered, including key leaders of PGT, trade unionists, peasant opposition activists, university students, and journalists. Though the right-wing nongovernmental groups were still somewhat active, the institutionalization of the counterinsurgency efforts under Araña meant that terror was conducted mostly by government forces, and killings by irregular groups declined considerably.[225] It has been estimated that 1,000 civilians were murdered in just twelve weeks.[226]

In an attempt to rebound from the virtual destruction of FGEI and MR-13, FAR and the PGT reunited in 1971 in an effort to oppose the government. Shifting from the urban efforts, the rebels launched Penetración, by which they established a front in difficult terrain in the northernmost department of Petén. They also began efforts in the western part of the country as well. But here, as in the first war, the rebels adopted the *foco* strategy, meaning that the emphasis was on small guerrilla armies. The rebels had some initial successes in attacking government troops and installations, but their small numbers and remote locations made them easy targets for the military. While the focus of popular attention was on the government's urban actions, by January 1971, the army had been able (in the words of an American Defense Intelligence Agency Bulletin) to "quietly eliminate" 200 terrorists in the western department of San Marcos alone.[227] Though the guerrillas retaliated, their attacks were ineffective, and ultimately they were crushed.

Termination and Outcome: By early fall of 1971, the rebel groups mostly had disbanded, and diverse forms of opposition to the regime appeared. FAR and PGT continued to exist, and after a period of self-critique, they began to reorganize. Learning from their past mistakes, they shifted their bases to the western highlands, where they began to forge links with mass movements: 500,000 of the indigenous Mayan population would become active participants in the continuation of the conflict in the late 1970s and 1980s.

Coding Decisions: As with the earlier war, determining the number of battle-deaths suffered by the combatants is difficult. Most fatality statistics refer to persons killed or missing in the terror, not combatants. Estimates of the numbers killed between 1970 and 1973 range from 3,500 to 15,000 dead,[228] with perhaps 7,000 killed in 1970 and 1971 alone. As the vast majority of these would have been civilians, we are reporting 1,000 total combatant deaths.

Sources: Anderson (1988); Ball, Kobrak, and Spirer (1999); Bercovitch and Fretter (2004); Booth and Walker (1999); Brockett (2005); Caballero Jurado and Thomas (1990); Clodfelter (2002); Crow (1971); Doyle and Osario (2014); Gross (1995); Jonas (1991, 2000); Keesing's (1971–1972); Lafeber (1993); May (1999); Peralta and Beverly (1980); Scheina (2003b); Schlesinger and Kinzer (1982); Small and Singer (1982); Taylor and Hudson (1972).

INTRA-STATE WAR #811
Third Guatemala War of 1978 to 1983

Participants: Guatemala versus Leftists and Mayans.
Dates: May 29, 1978, to August 8, 1983.
Battle-related Deaths: Leftists and Mayans (Rebel Aggregate):17,500; Guatemala: 4,200. (See Coding Decisions.)
Initiator: Guatemala.
Outcome: Guatemala wins.
War Type: Civil for control of central government.
Total System Member Military Personnel: Armed Forces of Guatemala: 14,000 (prewar, initial); 40,000 (peak, final).[229]
Theater Armed Forces: Guatemala: 59,000 (peak composite): includes the Armed Forces of Guatemala; plus *Policia Nacional*: 10,000; Armed Civilian Patrols: 9,000 (estimate). Leftists (Rebel Aggregate): 32,000 (peak composite); consists of Guerrillas (composite): 8,000 peak;[230] consists of *Guatemalan Workers Party* (PGT, Rebel Army): a

few hundred guerrillas throughout the war;[231] 300 (peak—estimate). *Fuerzas Armadas Rebeldes* (FAR, Rebel Army): 500 (prewar); 500 (initial); 1,000 (peak); 500 (final). *Ejército Guerrillero de los Pobres*, Guerrilla Army of the Poor (EGP, Rebel Army): 1,200 (prewar); 1,200 (initial); 4,400 (peak); 1,500 (final).[232] *Organización del Pueblo en Armas*, Organization of the People in Arms (ORPA, Rebel Army): 1,000 (prewar); 1,000 (initial); 2,300 (peak); 1,500 (final).[233] Mayan Rebel support personnel: 24,000 (peak). (See Coding Decisions.)

Antecedents: Armed conflict against the government of Guatemala was conducted by rebel groups from 1954 to 1990 in what some people have referred to as a thirty-six-year civil war. Most of the fatalities during this period were caused not by war but by one-sided violence conducted by the government against its citizens. Though the levels of armed conflict waxed and waned, there were two prior periods when conflict between the rebels and the government reached war-level hostilities: from 1966 to 1968 (Intra-state War #770) and 1970 to 1971 (Intra-state War #781). The primary rebel forces in these wars were: the umbrella rebel group *Fuerzas Armadas Rebeldes* (FAR); the *Movimento Revolucionario 13 de Noviembre* (MR-13); and the *Movimiento 20 de Octubre* (the armed wing of the Communist Party in Guatemala, the *Partido Guatemalteco del Trabajo* [PGT]). Though these groups had disagreed over revolutionary tactics, in general they had utilized the *foco* concept of guerrilla war, with its reliance upon small groups of armed guerrillas with support from the *ladino* peasants. Military offensives and state-sponsored repression by the government and affiliated right-wing paramilitary organizations eventually reduced the guerrilla groups to minor irritants (coded as a government victory in the 1970–1971 war) but never entirely suppressed them.

Thereafter, the rebels determined to alter their tactics and to organize a rebel movement with the support of Guatemala's large indigenous population. In the early 1970s, the *Ejército Guerrillero de los Pobres*, Guerrilla Army of the Poor (EGP), and the *Organización del Pueblo en Armas*, Organization of the People in Arms (ORPA), were founded as peasant movements that embraced the concept of a long struggle. EGP and ORPA began their work with predominantly Mayan communities, while the remnants of FAR continued their work among the *ladino* peasants. Though all three groups worked in the remote areas of the country, they expanded their urban activities as well and were joined there by the PGT. Government repression continued during the presidency of Gen. Kjell Eugenio Laugerud García (1974–1978) but at lower fatality levels than under the previous administration. An earthquake on February 4, 1976 (which killed 27,000 people and left 1 million Guatemalans homeless), diverted the government's resources, allowing the rebels to reorganize and provide social services to villagers with the government's acquiescence. However, in August 1976, EGP launched new offensives (which lasted till February 1977), and the government forces resumed attacks on the EGP organizers in Quiché. Meanwhile, the Guatemalan government began losing its support, domestically and internationally, becoming alienated from the Catholic Church. The Indians (predominantly Mayans) shifted their support increasingly to the rebel organizations. In 1977, the American Carter administration cut off military aid because of chronic human rights abuses, though the American military advisory group (MAAG) remained in the country.

Narrative: The election of March 7, 1978, brought Gen. Fernando Romeo Lucas García to power, and even before he was inaugurated (on July 1, 1978), the government's position shifted to more direct confrontation with the opposition groups. Two key members of the government were Defense Minister Gen. Otto Spiegeler Noriega and Interior Minister Donalda Alvarez Ruiz, and between them, they controlled government's primary security personnel: the armed forces and the *Policia Nacional.* They continued the government's two-pronged general plan of repression against opposition groups in the urban areas, military advances against the rebels, and widespread repression against the peasants in the rural areas. Ultimately, the Lucas administration would encompass the "bloodiest years in recent Guatemalan history."[234] A feature was the emergence of a new death squad, the *Ejército Secreto Anti-Communista* (ESA), which was linked to the president, and thus there were no attempts to separate its brutal attacks from the military and national police.[235]

The key turning point in the conflict was a demonstration in the town of Panzós on May 29, 1978, by 1,000 to 1,500 Kekchi Indians; Army Special

Forces fired into the crowd, killing hundreds of Kekchis (who were then dumped into previously prepared mass graves). This attack served as a declaration of war against the guerrillas and the Kekchis (and marks the start of this war). It not only radicalized the formerly passive Indians, but it also fueled rebel attacks against military personnel. Soon thereafter, the EGP developed and displayed a capacity to successfully launch large-scale attacks, such as those against a military airfield in Escuíntla. On June 14, fourteen government soldiers were killed by an EGP bombing, prompting the government's all-out war on the guerrillas once Lucas was inaugurated.

The EGP stepped up its activities against the government, organizing the Mayans located northwest of the capital around Ixcan (in the department of Quiché). The government's armed forces, despite the use of helicopters and superior weapons, made few gains. Soon EGP became the largest of the rebel groups and spread its activities to Chimaltenengo, Alta Verapaz, and Baja Verapaz. Meanwhile, ORPA took to the mountains in the southwest of the country and along the southern coast, while the FAR operated in the northern jungles of Petén and the eastern highlands. Guerrilla attacks frequently would entail the capturing towns, during which the local police would be shot, and attacks against military personnel. From July to November 1980, EGP conducted thirty-two attacks on military personnel and outposts.[236] The rebel military offensive increased throughout 1980 and 1981, involving 6,000 to 8,000 rebel combatants. In contrast to the earlier wars, 90 percent of the guerrillas were Indians who had the active support and collaboration of 250,000 to 500,000 peasants. The guerrillas launched their largest offensive early in 1981, controlling much of the West and South. By summer the rebels claimed to have advanced to nineteen of Guatemala's twenty-two departments. The rebels began planning for an offensive against Guatemala City itself, but premature attacks on the Pan-American Highway triggered a brutal government response. After coming to power in 1981, the Reagan administration covertly funneled millions of dollars of military equipment to Guatemala and approved a covert CIA program for counterinsurgency planning, thereby enabling the Guatemalan government to launch a renewed offensive in July 1981 under the name *Operación Ceniza* (Operation Ashes), which lasted to March 1982.

Another new feature of the government's campaign was the creation of armed civilian patrols, by which the government began conscripting Chimaltenango peasants into civil defense militias (thereby forcing them to choose sides in the war). In response, thousands of peasants fled into the mountains. About the same time, the rebels finally were coming together. After pressure from Cuban leader Fidel Castro, on February 7, 1982, the EGP, ORPA, FAR, and the PGT announced the formation of an alliance called the *Unidad Revolucionaria Nacional Guatemalteca* (URNG), though it lacked a unified command until 1985.

On March 23, 1982, the newly elected government of Gen. Angel Aníbal Guevara Rodriguez was overthrown by a group of military officers disenchanted with the government's counterinsurgency strategy and who had the support of the business community and the United States. They handed leadership of a new junta to popular retired general Efrain Rios Montt, who then laid out a plan, Operation Victory '82, which was designed to end the war in six months by combining the total elimination of the armed subversion with economic and social development programs. Montt referred to the strategy as "beans and bullets" (or the two Fs—*fusiles and frijoles*, rifles and beans). The implementation of Operation Victory '82 began in earnest on July 8, 1982, and produced a reign of terror against the Mayan people: tens of thousands of Mayan civilians were massacred and subjected to indiscriminate aerial bombing. Throughout the summer, the government pushed the EGP back and created a new task force in the fall to tackle the ORPA. By October, the government had not only defeated the EGP and ORPA but was beginning to push into FAR territory in Petén. By November, both the government and the rebels were said to have lost 1,200 soldiers each, while 75,000 peasants (mostly Mayans) were killed between April and November.

The intensity of fighting subsided in 1983. Montt was deposed in a Catholic-endorsed coup by Defense Minister Gen. Oscar Gumberto Mejía Víctores on August 8, 1983. By then the military's counterinsurgency efforts had eradicated most of its opposition, and the new government offered the rebels a ninety-day amnesty; thus August 8, 1983, is used as the end date of the war.

Termination and Outcome: The outcome was a limited government victory. The government briefly suppressed the level of violence, but by 1984, EGP renewed its armed actions. War would return in

Intra-state War #845.5 of 1989 to 1990. In 2013, Montt was convicted of crimes against humanity during the 1982-to-1983 campaign.

Coding Decisions: At the beginning of the war, the EGP was larger than ORPA, and both were much larger than FAR, while PGT remained the smallest throughout the war. By the end of the war, ORPA had fared the best, with at least as many fighters left as the EGP, which took the bulk of the casualties. The total number of guerrillas peaked at between 6,000 and 12,000 in early 1982. As already noted, a distinctive feature of this war was the Mayans, who participated on both sides of the conflict. Up to 500,000 Indians were seen as collaborators and supporters of the rebels, while the government "recruited" up to 900,000 as members of the civil defense patrols. Both of these groups had segments who participated in the war as combatants, though most reports of this war are unable to distinguish the activities and fatalities of the two groups. Similarly, on the government side, it is unclear how many members of the civil defense patrols were active combatants. As an Americas Watch Report noted, the civil defense patrols played an important part in the last two years of the war. Their strength was about 900,000 in early 1984; however, most were not well armed. In the 1966-to-1968 war, information by Jonas produced a ratio of identified guerrillas to civilian combatants and support of 39 to 61 percent.[237] The involvement of the peasants in this war was much greater than then, thus as a best guess, we are estimating 25 percent guerrillas to 75 percent Mayan combatants and support personnel, or a peak of 8,000 guerrillas aided by 24,000 civilian combatants, producing a total of 32,000. The relationship between government forces and the Mayan war participants was the opposite as that of the rebels. For the government, the civilian patrols, though numerous, appear mostly to have been utilized to repress or terrorize the population rather than in combat operations. However, even a low estimate of 1 percent would mean that there could have been 9,000 civil defense war participants. This figure is in line with an observation that only 10,000 of the 700,000 men in civil defense patrols in 1990 were armed.[238]

Most efforts to examine the violence in Guatemala, such as the extensive investigations by the International Center for Human Rights Investigations (CIIDH), have focused upon the deaths that occurred as a result of state-sponsored terrorism. There are in the neighborhood of 200,000 civilian deaths and disappearances over the entire thirty-six-year period.[239] Of those, an estimated 100,000 to 150,000 civilians were killed or "disappeared in the 1981–1983 era."[240] The battle-deaths of combatants seem small by comparison. The army refused to release casualty reports to the truth commission (CHE), hence our estimates of battle-deaths rely on limited information. Torres-Rivas refers to an estimate from the Central American Institute for Documentation and Social Research (CADIS) that 4,200 security forces were killed by the rebels between 1980 and 1984.[241] Caballero Jurado and Thomas claim to cite official sources that indicate 2,500 losses among the military personnel, though the time frame is not specified, and they admit that guerrilla estimates are much higher.[242] We gathered battle-deaths for specific engagements, and using the usual 3:1 ratio of wounded to killed, we count 50 dead in 1978, 100 in 1979, 100 in 1980, 1,057 in 1981, 744 in 1982, and 428 in 1983. These figures—most of which are taken from rebel claims—total about 2,500, somewhat lower than the estimate of 4,200. However, as our time frame is slightly different from Torres-Rivas (using mid-1978 to mid-1983), the 4,200 figure seems plausible so we are retaining it here.

The rebels also lost heavily, but no reliable estimates of their losses are available. The army routinely underreported casualties on both sides throughout the war in order to deny its culpability. The rebels did not deny the army's estimate of 510 guerrilla deaths in 1983. Most authors describe rebel deaths being lower in 1983 than in 1981 or 1982. One source reports that losses were about equal for the government and the rebels throughout much of 1982, which would suggest in excess of 1,000 rebel battle-deaths that year given our estimates for the government. Using these estimates would give us a figure of 3,500, which would be lower than the government figure. Caballero Jurado and Thomas (claiming to cite official sources) indicate that the guerrilla war cost 20,000 lives, but again the time frame is not specified.[243] If we subtract their government deaths from that figure, it would seem to indicate that the rebels suffered 17,500 deaths, which seems excessive considering the peak number of guerrillas during this period. Differentiating rebel battle-deaths also is complicated by the fact (as already noted) that there were a considerable number of Mayans who were involved in the war on the side of the rebels as combatants (we estimated 24,000). However, it is likely that the deaths of the Mayan combatant support personnel would have been included in the overall fatalities of civilians. In the 1966-to-1968 war (Intra-state War #770), we calculated that the number of leftist battle-deaths was 60 percent of their peak numerical strength. If we applied the same percentage here to the peak total number of leftist combatants (32,000), that would mean that 19,200 leftists died in this war. This calculation makes the Caballero Jurado and Thomas figure seem more plausible, if the 17,500 figure includes the deaths of the Mayans who were active combatants. Thus we are reporting that here as our best guess, aware that it could be either an over- or underestimate.

Sources: Ball, Kobrak, and Spirer (1999); Brockett (2005); Brogan (1998); Caballero Jurado and Thomas (1990); Ciment (2007g); Clodfelter (2002, 2008); Corum (2004); Costello (2002); "Country Profile: Guatemala" (2002); DeRouen and Heo (2007); Digital National (1996); Doyle (2013); Doyle and Osario (2014); Frundt (1990); Hey (1995); Higgonet and Mersky (2009); Hunt (2002a, b); Jonas (1996); Lafeber (1993); Luciak (2001); Manz (1988); McCleary (1999); O'Kane (2006); Peralta and Beverly (1980); Research Directorate (1991); Sante (1996); Schirmer (1998); Schlesinger and Kinzer (1982); Torres-Rivas (1990).

INTRA-STATE WAR #815
Sandinista Rebellion of 1978 to 1979

Participants: Nicaragua versus Sandinistas.
Dates: September 9, 1978, to July 18, 1979.
Battle-related Deaths: Sandinistas: 2,000; Nicaragua: 1,000.
Initiator: Sandinistas.
Outcome: Sandinistas win.
War Type: Civil for control of the central government.
Total System Member Military Personnel: Armed Forces of Nicaragua: 6,000 (prewar, initial, peak, final).[244]
Theater Armed Forces: Nicaragua: Armed Forces and the National Guard: 7,500 (prewar, initial); 11,000 (peak); 10,000 (final).[245] Sandinista National Liberation Front (Rebel Army): 1,000 (prewar, initial); 5,000 (peak, final).[246]

Antecedents: The United States greatly expanded its influence in Nicaragua based on its understanding of the Monroe Doctrine, its economic interests in the region, and involvement in the Panama Canal. In 1909, the United States supported a successful revolution (Intra-state War #649), and the United States then stationed military forces in Nicaragua, where they remained in control until 1933. When the United States pulled its forces out of Nicaragua, it bequeathed the country a National Guard dedicated to internal stability. Within three years, its commander, Anastasio Somoza García, had crushed a leftist rebellion led by Augusto César Sandino (who was killed in 1934) and effectively seized power. Somoza created a repressive dictatorial government that still had American support as long as it did not include leftist elements. Somoza's rule continued until an assassin took his life in 1956, whereupon his sons assumed power. Luis Anastasio Somoza Debayle served as president from 1956 till 1963, and his brother, Anastasio Somoza Debayle, was the head of the National Guard and in effect dictator of Nicaragua from 1967 to 1979 (though he also served as president from 1967 to 1972 and 1974 to 1979). The thirty-six-year Somoza family repressive regime would be ended by a small group of revolutionaries during this war.

The leftist guerrillas who rose up against the government in the 1960s were organized in the National Liberation Front (FLN), created in 1961 by Carlos Fonseca, Silvio Mayorga, and Tomás Borge. Two years later they added the name "Sandinista," in honor of Sandino's rebellion, becoming the *Frente Sandinista de Liberación Nacional*, or Sandinista National Liberation Front (FSLN). By the 1970s they were conducting small-scale guerrilla operations. They received limited support from the Cuban and Costa Rican governments but for more than 15 years were kept in check by Somoza's secret police and the National Guard. In December 1974, a spectacular FSLN raid on the home of a wealthy government supporter killed several people and allowed the rebels to take hostages, which they exchanged for political prisoners. The next year, one of the political prisoners ransomed and flown to Cuba was Daniel Ortega, who would be instrumental in the FSLN and ultimately would become Nicaragua's president. The government responded to these incidents by declaring a state of siege and dramatically increasing repression. The National Guard particularly targeted the FSLN, and in 1976 Carlos Fonseca was apprehended and executed. To assist the Nicaraguan government in its efforts, the United States supplied military aid and trained Nicaraguan military officers at the School of the Americas in the Canal Zone.

Starting in 1977, fissures emerged within the FSLN, and three wings developed: the first group worked among the peasants in the North; the second focused upon working with factory workers; and the third, led by Daniel Ortega and his brother Humberto, favored creating alliances with all opposition groups, attacking the National Guard directly and creating a provisional government in Costa Rica. They were able to capitalize on this strategy in January 1978, when the conservative editor of the anti-Somoza newspaper *La Prensa*, Pedro Joaquín Chamorro, was assassinated (January 10, 1978). Another brazen attack showed the vulnerability of the Somoza regime. On August 22, some 25 Sandinistas disguised as National Guard took the entire Chamber of Deputies hostage—2,000 politicians and staff, including Somoza's son. Led by Edén Pastora (aka "Commander Zero"), they ransomed the hostages for $10 million (only $500,000 of which was ultimately paid), the release of more political prisoners, and safe passage out of the country. The strategies of the third FSLN front, the *Terceristas*, were attracting widespread support. On August 25, the Broad Opposition Front (or FAO, an amalgam of the *Terceristas*, democrats, and others opposed to Somoza) declared a national strike, paralyzing business in the country; Somoza sent the National Guard to break the strike. The National Guard killed 50, injured 200, and arrested hundreds more. Three days later, a popular uprising in Matagalpa was bombed by the air force. Though it was torn by its competing focus on human rights, the US administration of President Jimmy Carter maintained its support of Somoza, sending more military assistance.

Narrative: Somoza's refusal to capitulate to the FAO and its supporters triggered full-scale civil war. On September 9, 1978, Sandinista factions occupied the cities of Diriamba, Rivas, Chinandega, Estelí, Léon, and Massaya, and by September 15, the populace of fifteen towns had revolted. The government responded by aerial bombing and using its elite units to storm each city in turn, carrying out mass executions on the spot. In all, perhaps up to 6,000 Nicaraguans, mostly civilians, died by the time the last town was recaptured on September 22. Sandinista and government losses were low, probably between 100 and 600 rebel fighters killed, with the government reporting 52 soldiers killed, though the FSLN claimed that the National Guard lost 1,200 killed, and another 700 defected to the FSLN.[247] In the aftermath of the first wave of insurrection, the FSLN attracted support. Cuba, Costa Rica, and Panama served as a conduit for arms, while volunteers from Mexico, Venezuela, and Colombia joined the FSLN. By December, the organization's strength had grown to 2,500 armed guerrillas supported by thousands of young Nicaraguans (men and women).

The second round of the war began in January 1979, when the Sandinistas announced a new offensive. They were able to coordinate multiple, simultaneous attacks around the country on February 21, attacking National Guard units rather than seizing towns. On March 9, 1979, representatives from each of the three FSLN wings and tendencies met and reunited the FSLN in a new National Directorate that would coordinate the continuing war. By April, five separate FSLN fronts had been launched. By May 1979, the FSLN was 5,000 strong, compared to the government's National Guard of 13,000. On May 4, the Sandinistas attacked government forces in Managua and other cities, forcing many National Guard units to retreat. It took nearly a month of fighting to drive the rebels out of Managua. Meanwhile, the United States government had removed its monetary support from Somoza and tried to urge Somoza to depart, while also seeking an alternative to the FSLN. At the end of the month, the FSLN (moving from bases in Costa Rica) launched an operation it called its "final offensive." On May 28, Sandinistas attacked throughout the country at Léon, Estelí, Matagalpa, Puerto Caáas, Rivas, and Managua. The government was able to counterattack in the South, where Edén Pastora had been appointed commander of the FSLN Southern Front. In the North, the rebels were more successful, capturing Léon on June 5. Urban uprisings now became common, and on June 11, Somoza took the unusual step of ordering aerial bombing of pro-rebel districts in his own capital. The government reported that the rebels had suffered 900 to 1,000 casualties (killed and wounded) since May 28, while it claimed that it suffered only 200. However, the heavy civilian casualties from Somoza's aerial and land bombardment of densely populated neighborhoods prompted a number of countries to openly oppose his rule, and the Organization of American States (OAS) took the unprecedented step of recognizing a pro-rebel government in exile. The next day, Pastora reentered the country in the South, cutting off a government force of 1,000. In the North, government attempts to retake Léon were repelled, and the National Guard's last positions were overrun on June 18. By early July, the FSLN controlled twenty-six cities and towns and was able to repel poorly coordinated government counterattacks. Its major fear was American involvement. On July 10, the United States presented the FSLN with an ultimatum that carried an implied threat of military intervention. The statement called for the FSLN to broaden the five-man junta of two conservatives and three FSLN leaders by appointing more moderates, to call for a cease-fire, and to organize elections.

Interestingly, it was the two "moderates" on the junta—Violetta Chamorro (widow of the murdered *La Prensa* editor) and businessman Luis Alfonso Robelo Callejas—who vetoed the appointment of more moderates. Nevertheless, the FSLN issued a statement of policy on July 12 that promised that Nicaragua would remain a mixed economy with respect for private property rights. On July 15, the junta announced a cabinet stocked with moderates. Though Somoza secretly attempted to rally foreign support for his government, he finally agreed to an American plan that called for him to resign and transfer power to an interim president, who would then hand over power to the FSLN. He fled on July 18, and the National Guard disintegrated.

Termination and Outcome: The outcome of the war was an unconditional military victory by the rebels. In the last days of the revolt and for a short period thereafter, there were numerous summary executions by local FSLN commanders. The Sandinistas initially constructed the Government of National Reconciliation, which incorporated non-leftist factions as well as FSLN leaders.

Coding Decisions: Scholars report 10,000 to 60,000 total deaths in the war, most of whom were civilians. Clodfelter, Phillips, and Axelrod report 10,000 killed, 7,000 of whom were civilians, thus indicating that there were 3,000 total deaths among the combatants. The ratio of government to rebel losses (1:2) is agreed upon in most accounts of the war, meaning a best estimate of battle-deaths is 1,000 National Guard and 2,000 Sandinistas.

Sources: Anderson (1988); Brogan (1998); Clodfelter (2002, 2008); DeFronzo (1996); Grynspan (1991); Jung (1983); Kagan (1996); Keesing's (1979); Lafeber (1993); *New York Times* (1978–1979); Phillips and Axelrod (2005); Scheina (2003b); Selbin (1993).

INTRA-STATE WAR #817
El Salvador War of 1979 to 1992

Participants: El Salvador versus Salvadorian Democratic Front.
Dates: October 15, 1979, to February 1, 1992.
Battle-related Deaths: Salvadorian Democratic Front: 14,000; El Salvador: 10,000.
Initiator: Salvadorian Democratic Front.
Outcome: Compromise.
War Type: Civil for control of central government.
Total System Member Military Personnel: Armed Forces of El Salvador: 11,000 (prewar); 14,000 (initial); 60,000 (1992): 49,000.[248]
Theater Armed Forces: Salvadorian Democratic Front (Rebel Aggregate), consisting of *Popular Liberation Forces*, aka FPL-FM: less than 1,000 (prewar); less than 1,000 (initial); more than 3,000 (peak), 2,600 (final).[249] People's Revolutionary Army, aka ERP: less than 1,000 (prewar); less than 1,000 (initial); more than 4,000 (peak); 2,700 (final).[250] Communist Party—Armed Forces of Liberation, aka FAL: less than 1,000 (prewar); less than 1,000 (initial); 500 (final).[251] National Resistance, aka RN or FARN: less than 600 (prewar); less than 600 (initial); more than 900 (peak); 600 (final).[252] Workers' Revolutionary Party, aka PRTC: less than 1,000 (prewar); less than 1,000 (initial); more than 3,500 (peak); 250 (final).[253] *Farabundo Martí National Liberation Front*, aka FMLN, from October 10, 1980: 6,000 to 8,000 (initial); 20,000 (14,000 regulars and 6,000 militia, peak); 12,362 (including more than 6,000 militia, final).[254]

Antecedents: In 1931, El Salvador's government war overthrown by a military coup led by Gen. Maximiliano Hernández Martínez. Opposition to the regime developed, and one of the instrumental leaders was Agustín Farabundo Martí Rodríguez. Farabundo Martí had helped found the Communist Party of Central America and had worked with Nicaraguan revolutionary leader Augusto César Sandino before returning to El Salvador. Martí organized an unsuccessful revolt against the regime (Intra-state War #712), which led to the massacres of thousands of peasants. Since then, El Salvador has experienced some form of direct or indirect military rule intended to protect the interests of the country's wealthiest fourteen families. El Salvador had strong ties with the United States, and the Kennedy and Johnson administrations funneled millions of dollars to El Salvador under the Alliance for Progress. While a strictly pro forma democracy was constructed, opposition parties were not permitted until 1964. Even then, leftist parties were banned. By 1969, 300,000 Salvadorans, or 13 percent of the total population, had fled to neighboring Honduras seeking better lives. When Honduras began expelling the immigrants, El Salvador attacked, launching Inter-state War #175. Though El Salvador was seen as the victor, the military regime was undermined by the return of nearly 100,000 Salvadoran refugees from Honduras, with demands for agrarian reform and political change.

Some of the regime's opponents formed a militia called the Popular Liberation Forces–Farabundo Martí (FPL–FM) in 1970, named after the one of the founders of the Communist Party and the leader of the 1932 revolt. Two years later, another group, dominated by a hybrid of Maoism and left-wing Christianity, was formed—the People's Revolutionary Army (ERP). In 1975, the Armed Forces of National Resistance (FARN or RN) split from the ERP. The same year, the Revolutionary Party of Central American Workers (PRTC) was formed. The fifth guerrilla group was formed in 1979, when the remainder of the Communist Party decided on war and formed a militia called the Liberation Armed Forces (FAL).

In February 1977, Gen. Carlos Humberto Romero, the candidate of the National Conciliation Party (PCN), won the presidency in an election marred by fraud and voter intimidation. The overall government reaction to its challengers was to create a string of paramilitary fronts (or death squads) composed of members of the police and security forces, some of which were directed by Maj. Roberto D'Aubuisson. Leftist guerrillas, led by ERP, engaged in limited attacks against the government in 1978 and early 1979. There was a noticeable increase in violence after the successful Sandinista revolution in Nicaragua in July 1979 (Intra-state War #815). The United States began to fear that the spread of revolutionary fervor would produce a new domino effect in Central America. On October 15, the Revolutionary Government Junta (JRG), made up of civilians and reformist military officers, launched a coup overthrowing Romero (perhaps with American encouragement) and creating a military–civilian government.

Narrative: Leftist attacks against the new government mark the start of this war. On October 24, 1979, about 1,000 leftists stormed the Ministries of Labor and Economy, taking more than 300 people hostage and demanding the release of 500 political prisoners. The government reacted to the incident by intensifying its repression of demonstrations. In December, three rebel armies took the first steps toward unification, and then within a month, their political wings created the Revolutionary Coordination of the Masses (CRM). The deadliest year of the war was 1980, when political violence claimed about 1,000 lives each month. The civilians, who composed three-fifths of the government, realized that they had little control over the military, and all of them resigned on January 3, 1980. Almost immediately, the CRM issued a call for a general insurrection on January 12. Within three weeks, right-wing militias and the military fired on the largest protest march in the nation's history and then stormed the university. Death squads stepped up their activities, killing leftists and centrist reformers. Leftists responded in kind but also stepped up armed confrontations with army and National Guard forces.

In early March, the leader of the Christian Democratic Party, José Napoleon Duarte, joined the junta, which was now composed exclusively of his party and military officers. On March 24, D'Aubuisson ordered the assassination of Archbishop Oscar Romero, whose sermon the day before had called on troops to refuse to obey orders to kill. On March 30, Archbishop Romero's funeral was attacked, with many civilians killed. Romero's murder did not dampen American support for the government, and Congress approved new shipments of military supplies to strengthen the Salvadoran regime.

The leftist CRM was supplanted by the Democratic Revolutionary Front (FDR), which combined political parties, mass associations, and unions. On the military side, ERP, FARN, PRTC, and FPL–FM formed a Unified Revolutionary Directorate to coordinate their activities. Only FAL remained aloof. On May 1 and May 2, D'Aubuisson and wealthy businessmen sponsored a coup attempt against reformist officers; the junta moved sharply to the right. Cuba had pressed the rebels to unify, and the FMLN was formed on October 10, 1980. The country was divided into revolutionary fronts, which were assigned to preexisting organizations by the FMLN, which now controlled 6,500 to 7,000 guerrillas.

On January 10, 1981, the rebels launched a major offensive, striking forty-three targets across the nation. As a rebel victory looked possible, the United States increased its aid to the Salvadoran government. The offensive ended on January 15, after more than 1,500 had been killed, including at least 500 rebels and 97 government soldiers. The rebels regrouped in the North and East, where they began to defend operational zones from government incursions. In January 1982, a rebel operation at Ilopango Air Base destroyed a substantial portion of the government's airlift capacity. Rebels continued to sabotage infrastructure, destroying fifty-eight bridges between January 1 and July 31, 1982. Elections for a constituent assembly and provisional president took place in March 1982. The left boycotted them; the right-wing party Nationalist Republican Alliance (ARENA) nominated D'Aubuisson; and the Christian Democrats nominated Duarte. ARENA and the military's National Conciliation Party (PCN) won 60 percent of the seats, and Duarte was ousted as president, while D'Aubuisson became president of the assembly. On April 29, 1982, the legislative assembly chose Álvaro Alfredo Magaña Borja (of the moderate Democratic Action) as president. After a government offensive (Operation Torola) against FMLN (ERP) positions, the government focused on action in the North, allowing the rebels in the East to make gains. Alternating victories in battles in the last few months of 1982 brought the government's total battle-deaths for the year to about 1,200; the rebels suffered about twice that number, while civilian deaths decreased.

By the end of the year, both sides were stronger than they had been a year before, and by 1983, the guerrillas controlled a third of the nation's territory. Although they could seize towns in their areas of operation almost at will, they could not hold them. On the government side, the infighting among D'Aubuisson, Magaña, Minister of Defense Guillermo Garcia, and junior officers continued. In a November shake-up the conservative "professionals" gained control of the military command. The March 1984 election produced a return to civilian rule with the victory of Duarte, who promised protection of human rights. Duarte moved quickly to end ties with the death squads. In early October, Duarte called for peace talks with the FMLN, though little progress was made. Low-intensity conflict continued for the remainder of 1984 and throughout 1985, though by the end of 1986, rebel-controlled areas were reduced from their peak of one-third of the country to below one-tenth. The government also declared twelve free-fire zones in the areas controlled by the guerrillas, in which villages were burned and any group of people spotted in these areas by reconnaissance aircraft was to be fired upon.

The same pattern of small-unit actions by guerrillas continued in 1987. On August 7, President Duarte signed the Esquipulas II agreement, better known as the Arias Peace Plan, which committed El Salvador to negotiate a formal peace agreement with the FMLN. Additional talks were held later that year, and though the peace process had shown significant progress, the positions of the two sides were still far apart. Legislative and local elections took place in 1988; ARENA and other right-wing parties were able to form a majority coalition. September 1988 saw a resumption of intense fighting between the FMLN and government in rural areas. Both casualties and atrocities increased markedly. In February 1989, the FMLN proposed a peace plan by which it would participate in elections; the offer was rejected by the government. In the presidential elections on March 19, the victor was ARENA nominee Alfredo Cristiani, who took office on June 1, 1989. Even though the FMLN announced a unilateral cease-fire in September as a prelude for peace talks, the government was now less likely to compromise, and after two weeks, the rebels resumed fighting. An infusion of weapons from Nicaragua enabled the rebels to plan major offensive operations. On November 11, the FMLN initiated its second "Final Offensive," which consisted of simultaneous attacks on fifty cities and military posts around the country. The government was caught by surprise, and the rebels achieved a number of successes before withdrawing. The offensive claimed the lives of 476 government soldiers, 675 rebels, and more than 1,000 civilians.

The first months of 1990 were marked by diplomatic maneuvers, as the FMLN, Cristiani, and the United States all expressed support for a negotiated end to the war (a first for the United States, which had previously opposed negotiations). Meanwhile, Nicaragua's president was defeated by a conservative candidate, signaling an end to that country's support for the FMLN. After gestures of compromise on both sides, peace talks were set for May 3. Talks that year made progress on human rights, but negotiations on military reform stalled in August, leading to further fighting during the rest of the year. Peace talks resumed in January 1991, and a second round in April proved to be very successful. The Mexico Agreements were signed on April 27, to become effective once a cease-fire agreement was reached. The New York Act was signed on September 25, which included government commitments to reduce the size of the army and purge officers guilty of human rights abuses.

Negotiations continued through the end of the year, and on January 16, President Cristiani and the FMLN leadership signed the El Salvador Peace Agreement in Mexico City. It included a cease-fire that went into effect on February 1, 1992.

Termination and Outcome: The outcome of the war was a negotiated settlement that was very favorable to the government. In March 1993, the National Assembly passed a broad amnesty for political crimes and human rights abuses committed during the war, leading to an increase in killings by death squads.

Coding Decisions: In terms of war participants, we have provided data on the FMLN as well as its five member groups for the entire period of the war because scholars do not yet agree when the FMLN became a unified command capable of controlling the member organizations. We do not count the United States as a state war because its theater forces did not exceed the thousand-person baseline and its deaths (twenty-seven) did not reach the hundred-death criterion. In addition, we do not count the foreign non-state organizations that assisted the FSLN because there is no evidence that any one of them reached the hundred-combatant threshold.

During the war, an estimated 75,000 Salvadorans were killed, though two-thirds of these were civilians. Plausible estimates of total battle-deaths range from 14,000 to 33,000. We have accepted the official estimate of 10,000 government battle-deaths, which with the most plausible estimate of 14,000 rebel battle-deaths, produces a total of 24,000 combatants.[255]

Sources: Arnold (1995); Barry (1991); Bracamonte and Spencer (1995); Brogan (1998); Call (2002); Central Intelligence Agency (1982); Clodfelter (2002, 2008); De La Peña (1994); DeRouen and Heo (2007); Digital National Security (1994); "El Salvador 30 Day" (1979); "El Salvador Leftists Take Refuge" (1980); "El Salvador Officials Resign" (1980); "El Salvador Violence" (1979); Greentree (2008); Grenier (1991); Lafeber (1993); Laffin (1989, 1990, 1991); Landau (1993); "Leftists Free 276" (1979); "Leftists Revolution" (1979); Little (1994); Mason (2004); Montgomery (1982, 1995); *New York Times* (1979–1981); Phillips and Axelrod (2005); Scheina (2003b); Schooley (1987); Seligson and McElhinny (1996); "Soldiers Kill Leftists" (1979); Stanford Central America Action Network (1983); Villalobos (1987); "Violence Rips Salvador" (1979); Wood (2003).

INTRA-STATE WAR #828
Contra War of 1982 to 1988

Participants: Nicaragua versus Contras.
Dates: March 14, 1982, to March 23, 1988.
Battle-related Deaths: Contras: 25,250; Nicaragua: 7,150.
Initiator: Contras.
Outcome: Stalemate.
War Type: Civil for central control.
Total System Member Military Personnel: Armed Forces of Nicaragua: 41,000 (prewar, initial); 80,000 (peak); 74,000 (final).[256]
Theater Armed Forces: Contras: (Rebel Aggregate), consisting of FDN/RN (includes MILPAS): 500 (prewar—before 2,500 MILPAS integrated); 3,000 (initial); 12,000 (peak, final).[257] MISURA/KISAN: 3,000 (prewar); 4,000 (initial, peak); 500 (final).[258] UDN–FARN/UNO–FARN/FARN: a few dozen (prewar); 100 (initial); 400 (peak); several hundred (final).[259] FRS/ARDE/ "Poor ARDE": low hundreds (initial); 3,000 (peak); 80 (final). BOS: a handful (prewar); 100 (initial); a few hundred (final).[260] *Los Astros*/MISURASATA: 60 (prewar); 100 (initial, peak, final).[261]

Antecedents: In 1979, the Nicaraguan dictatorship led by President Anastasio Somoza Debayle was overthrown by a group of rebels calling themselves *Frente Sandinista de Liberación* (Sandinista National Liberation Front [FSLN], Intra-state War #815).

The Sandinistas established a new government, headed by a Council (or junta) of National Reconstruction, made up of five appointed members: three from FSLN (militants Daniel Ortega, Moises Hassan, and novelist Sergio Ramírez) and two opposition members (businessman Alfonso Robelo and Violeta Barrios de Chamorro). Upon assuming power, the council began to implement a platform that included land reform; improved public services; protection of democratic liberties; equality for women; and nationalization of property owned by the Somozas and their supporters. The Sandinista's reforms engendered opposition among: supporters of the former Samoza regime (*Somocistas*); the privileged elites; the Miskito Indians; and the Democratic Revolutionary Alliance. The counterrevolutionaries collectively were referred to as the contras (*contra-revolucionarios*), and they received significant assistance from the United States in their attempt to overthrow the Sandinista government (the administration of President Jimmy Carter expended $1 million in covert funds to bolster the contras).[262] In 1981, the new administration of President Ronald Reagan additionally approved CIA covert actions and an additional $19.5 million to aid the contras.[263]

By mid-1981, the Sandinistas were faced with four internal potential sources of counterrevolution. Many members of Somoza's National Guard had fled into neighboring countries, where these *Guardistas* began to organize in opposition to the Sandinistas. The most notable of these was the Fifteenth of September Legion, led by Enrique Bermudez Varela, whose 2,000 soldiers began launching raids from Honduras into Nicaragua, reportedly with assistance from the Honduran army, bringing the two countries close to war. The *Guardistas* united with Miami-based opponents of the Sandinistas to form the Nicaraguan Democratic Front (FDN). A second major resistance group was *Milicias Populares Anti-Somocistas* (MILPAS), a mass organization of peasants originally formed to fight Somoza, which now opposed the Sandinista's emphasis on Marxism and class war. The organization kept its acronym, simply substituting "Sandinista" for "Somoza" in its name *Milicias Populares Anti-Sandinistas*. In 1980, MILPAS loosely allied itself to the *Guardistas* in Honduras. The Sandinistas also faced dissidents in the South. Edén Pastora (aka "Commander Zero") had led the largely autonomous rebel Southern Front in the 1978-to-1979 civil war. As the new government was formed, the Sandinistas did not reward his contributions during the war, and in 1981, he resigned from the government and retreated to Costa Rica, preparing for armed rebellion with his Sandino Revolutionary Front (FRS). Another former Sandinista and Pastora ally, a low-level commander named Fernando "El Negro" Chamorro, and his cousin also formed a southern resistance group called UDN–FARN. The fourth source of opposition was the Miskito Indians in the eastern Zelaya Department who had historically resisted incorporation into Nicaragua. The Sandinista government both helped organize and alternatively provoked the Miskito, permitting the creation of a mass organization representing the Indians of Zelaya—Miskito, Suma, Rama, and Sandinistas Working Together (MISURASATA); however, the regime's hostility to American business interests devastated the local economy. The regime began to suspect MISURASATA leader Steadman Fagoth of being an American agent, and it attacked the organization's directorate, triggering a firefight in which the government and MISURASATA each lost four killed.

As the Sandinista movement began implementing socialist policies and established close relations with Cuba, foreign opposition increased as well: American aid flowed freely to the FDN, leading to its expansion and eventual absorption of most other groups in the North, including MILPAS leaders and units. The Nicaraguan government banned MISURASATA, leading to its split into MISURA, led by Steadman Fagoth and allied with FDN and MILPAS and much smaller organization under Brooklyn Rivera, *Los Astros*, which soon took the well-known name MISURASATA. By the beginning of 1982, the northern resistance groups in Honduras numbered about 500 FDN, 2,000 to 3,000 MILPAS, about 3,000 MISURA, and 60 MISURASATA. In the South, the FRS numbered in the low hundreds, and UDN–FARN was a small band. To this point, casualties in conflicts were relatively low. In October 1981, Nicaragua, wary of upcoming joint American–Honduran naval maneuvers, announced a general mobilization.

Narrative: With the influx of enhanced American aid, contra activities increased dramatically in early 1982. Starting on March 14, 1982, contra guerrillas launched 106 attacks on Nicaraguan targets along the Honduran border within 100 days, marking the start of the war.[264] The offensive included attacks against military patrols, assassinations of government officials, and sabotage of infrastructure. After April, the United States, Argentina, and Honduras assumed greater command. The first major encounter between the FDN/MILPAS forces and the Nicaraguan army occurred on March 18, 1982, resulting in eleven rebels and three government soldiers killed. Pastora's FRS entered the war in the South, though most engagements were small. The rebel groups continued to evolve, and in December, the FDN restructured and fully incorporated MILPAS into its leadership. Pastora formed the Democratic Revolutionary Alliance (ARDE) with other exiles, including Luis Alfonso Robelo Callejas, who became the political face of ARDE, while Pastora controlled the troops. Chamorro was expelled by Costa Rica, and he allied himself with the FDN.

The number of armed conflicts expanded significantly in 1983 as the size and capabilities of the forces on each side grew. The northern rebels struck first in an unsuccessful amphibious assault by 120 guerrillas (most of whom were killed). From February 15 to March 27, the FDN moved 2,000 contras into Nicaragua, hoping to be able to establish a bridge head there, and launched four unsuccessful attempts to take Jalapa between March and June. ARDE formally launched its offensive on April 15, fighting its first battle against government forces on May 1. The Sandinista government viewed former war hero Pastora as its greatest threat and deployed its best units to the South to confront him. Combat continued through the remainder of 1983, with both ARDE and FDN growing substantially. FDN had the use of American aircraft operating from CIA bases in Honduras, and starting in August 1983, the United States engaged in joint military exercises along both the Caribbean and Pacific coasts of Nicaragua, leading to a virtual perpetual US presence. FDN and ARDE established a pattern of coordinated attacks within Nicaragua.

The contras reached their peak strength in 1984, with a force of about 15,000 guerrillas—12,000 in the North and 3,000 in the South. The government also increased the size of its armed forces from 46,000 in 1983 to 67,000. The Sandinistas retained control of the cities—with the exception of San Juan del Norte, which was taken and held by ARDE for two days early in the year—but the contras took the mountains and swamps. Despite their increased capabilities, the contras suffered from political defeats throughout the year: Honduras closed contra camps in the West, and the government launched a massive relocation program that resettled nearly 200,000 people away from border regions, especially Miskitos in the Northeast, cutting rebel supply links. The CIA responded by ramping up its own activities, utilizing a force of "unilaterally controlled Latino assets" (UCLAs) recruited from El Salvador, Honduras, Chile, Argentina, Ecuador, and Bolivia. CIA commandos attacked Nicaraguan ports and mined Nicaragua's harbors, with ARDE publicly claiming credit for the operations. When commercial ships began to sink after hitting mines in Nicaraguan ports, the United States denied responsibility. The political uproar led the American Congress to reject requests for military aid to the contras, although covert aid continued through efforts led by Col. Oliver North that would later be known as the Iran–Contra scandal.

ARDE began to disintegrate in late May 1984, as Robelo (and US aid) allied himself to the FDN. Pastor's ARDE was nicknamed "poor ARDE." On May 30, a bomb exploded during a press conference being held by Pastora, severely injuring him. A few months later, the FDN and Robelo created a political umbrella, subsequently named the United Nicaraguan Opposition (UNO). The 1984 elections produced a major political victory for the Sandinistas, though the government was suffering financial difficulties. The FDN called 1985 the "year of the Final Offensive," and it began a campaign to seize cities using battalion-sized units, a strategy that resulted in much higher casualties and a string of military defeats and dispersed its forces into small units. Meanwhile, a small faction of MISURA (about 200 strong) reached a negotiated agreement with the government on May 17, while the bulk of MISURA continued the struggle. MISURA reorganized itself under the acronym KISAN (Indians of Nicaragua's Atlantic Coast), which joined the UNO with its 500 to 1,000 troops. Most of the attacks in the South were mounted by Pastora's forces, which numbered between 2,500 and 3,000. Pastora's ARDE succeeded in setting up base camps inside Nicaragua, but a government offensive drove it back into Costa Rica by the end of the year. According to one estimate, the government suffered 1,143 battle-deaths, while contra battle-deaths totaled 4,760 that year. By all accounts, 1985 was a terrible year for the rebels, and they remained on the defensive in 1986.

With the contras seemingly on the verge of defeat, the government mounted a cross-border offensive from March 22 to 26, 1986, hitting UNO bases in the North and capturing or destroying vital supplies. To rebuild the contras, the United States began a secret airlift of military equipment to UNO—including, for the first time, portable surface-to-air missiles. The operation was revealed publicly when one of the cargo planes was shot down and an American crew member captured. The subsequent scandal in the United States eventually led to complete termination of aid to the contras in February 1988. Meanwhile, Pastora's ARDE collapsed as Pastora resigned in May 1986 and sought asylum in Costa Rica. Most remaining rebels in the South merged to form the Southern Opposition Bloc (BOS), to be led by Alfredo César.

On February 15, 1987, the government of Costa Rica proposed a region-wide initiative, often referred to as the Arias Peace Plan. In August, the presidents of Costa Rica, El Salvador, Nicaragua, Guatemala, and Honduras signed the agreement, though implementation was slow. As it appeared that the war might end through negotiated settlement, the contras tried to improve their position by launching several offensives, which entailed high casualties but caused little change in the strategic balance. By the end of the year, the government had suffered another 1,613 killed, its worst losses for any year of the war. The rebels suffered 4,700 casualties. On March 10, 1988, just days before scheduled cease-fire negotiations, the Sandinistas launched their largest coordinated offensive against rebel forces around the country. The offensives pushed the rebels back but produced threats of American intervention, causing the government to pull back.

Termination and Outcome: The outcome of the war was a negotiated settlement in a cease-fire accord on March 23, 1988, which provided for disarmament of the rebels, reduction of the government army, and a promise of elections. The final peace accord was reached in February 1989, though a number of rebels refused to disarm before elections were held and continued sporadic attacks that mostly killed civilians. In February 1990, the promised elections were held, and the Sandinistas were defeated by Violeta Chamorro.

Coding Decisions: In terms of the war participants, although Cuba had up to 2,000 military advisors in Nicaragua, it did not actively participate in the war, and is thus not considered a war participant. The role of the United States is a bit more difficult to code, primarily because the role of the CIA was complex as both an enabler of actions by others but also an active combat participant itself. However, it does not appear that the US activities reached the level that would label it as a state war participant (a thousand combatants or a hundred battle deaths).

In terms of battle deaths, the most common estimates range from 20,000 to 30,000, with the higher number being the most common. Our own estimates from battles show a total of 32,500 battle-deaths; 25,250 suffered by the contras and 7,150 government losses.

Sources: Arnold (1995); Baracco (2004); Brogan (1998); Brown (2001a, b); Clodfelter (2002, 2008); Ford (1987); Gold (1987); Gunson and Thompson (1991); Hale (1996); Hannum (1996); Hartzell (2002); Honey (1994); Horton (1998); Kornbluh (1987); Lafeber (1993); Laffin (1989, 1990, 1991); Minahan (2002); Miranda and Ratliff (1993), Pardo-Maurer (1990); Prevost (1987); Phillips and Axelrod (2005); Scheina (2003b); Schooley (1987); Selbin (1993); Seligson and McElhinny (1996); Sklar (1988).

INTRA-STATE WAR #845.5
Fourth Guatemala War of 1987 to 1990

Participants: Guatemala versus Leftists.
Dates: September 1987 to September 1990.
Battle-related Deaths: Leftists: 6,000; Guatemala: 3,000. (See Coding Decisions.)
Initiator: Guatemala.
Outcome: Guatemala wins.
War Type: Civil for control of central government.
Total System Member Military Personnel: Armed Forces of Guatemala: 43,000 (prewar, initial, peak, final).[265]
Theater Armed Forces: Guatemala (Government Aggregate): 53,000. Armed Forces of Guatemala: 43,000 (prewar, initial, peak, final). Civil Defense Patrols: 10,000.[266] Leftists (Rebel Aggregate): 16,000. *Unidad Revolucionaria Nacional Guatemalteca* (URNG, Rebel Army): 4,000.[267] EGP alone; 3,500 (initial); 4,000 (peak); 1,500 (final).[268] Mayans: 12,000 (peak). (See Coding Decisions.)

Antecedents: Guatemala had confronted armed opposition by leftists since 1960. During three prior periods, the level of hostilities had reached war level: Intra-state War #770 in 1966; Intra-state War #781 in 1970; and Intra-state War #811 in 1978. The last war had ended as a government victory as Minister of Defense Gen. Oscar Humberto Mejia Victores came to power in a coup on August 8, 1983, and immediately offered the rebels an amnesty. However, even as Mejia tried to move Guatemala toward civilian rule, the last two years of his term (1984–1985) were marked by rising levels of violence. In the rural areas, people living outside of the areas controlled by the government created their own stable communities, particularly in the northern area of Quiché. Referring to them as the "population in resistance," the government considered these 20,000 to 25,000 people as guerrillas or subversives, and the army continued to pursue and attack them. The guerrilla groups were also still active: the largest group, Ejército Guerrillero de los Pobres (Guerrilla Army of the Poor, [EGP]), claimed to have killed 686 soldiers in 181 operations in 1984.[269] By 1985 EGP claimed to have 4,000 armed and 12,000 unarmed members. The other major leftist rebel groups were: *Organización del Pueblo en Armas* (Organization of the People in Arms [ORPA]); *Fuerzas Armadas Rebeldes* (Rebel Armed Forces [FAR]); and *Partido Guatemalteco del Trabajo* (Guatemalan Workers Party, Communist Party [PGT]). Between January and October 1985, more than 210 guerrilla actions were committed by EGP, FAR, and ORPA.[270] In 1982, the EGP, ORPA, FAR, and the PGT had formed an alliance called the *Unidad Revolucionaria Nacional Guatemalteca* (Guatemalan National Revolutionary Unit [URNG]). Each of the leftist groups had maintained its own armed forces until early in 1985, when they were united under the *Comandancia General* (General Command), after which URNG became the primary rebel group.

The URNG was banned from participating in the 1985 presidential election, leaving the Guatemalan Christian Democrats (DCG) as the major alternative to the military and Evangelical Protestant parties of the right. Thus, the election was contested along religious rather than political or class lines. The DCG nominated Marco Vinicio Cerezo Arévalo as its presidential candidate, who was pitted against Jorge Carpio Nicolle of the National Centre Union and a number of others. On December 8, Cerezo beat Jorge Carpio with 68.4 percent of the vote, and though civilian rule was restored, Cerezo agreed to appoint the military's choice for defense minister, thereby shielding the military from civilian control.

A brief period of relative calm ended as the right-wing death squads became active, with more than 1,600 political assassinations carried out in eighteen months. The leftist guerrillas also were active in eight of Guatemala's twenty-two departments. In 1986, the UNRG began attempts to negotiate with the government but put forth demands that were unacceptable to Cerezo, who insisted that the UNRG would first have to lay down its arms. Accordingly, the URNG renewed major operations on January 26, 1987. The government increased its military collaboration with the United States, receiving military aid and hundreds of millions of dollars as economic support funds. On August 7, President Cerezo signed the Arias Peace Plan, even though the Guatemalan Army maintained that there was no civil war in Guatemala, making peace negotiations unnecessary. Preliminary talks were held in Madrid in October, but they were accompanied by an increase in armed conflict as both sides sought to improve their military positions.

Narrative: The military mounted a "Year-End Offensive" (*Operacíon Fín de Año*) in September, which marks the start of this war. The offensive brought 20,000 government soldiers into contact with URNG units along the southern coast and in northern Quiché. One of the goals of the offensive was to eliminate the CPRs, which had never surrendered to government forces and who were now defended by the EGP. The largest of the CPRs, the settlements around Sumal, in the north-central department of Quiché, fell to the government in 1988, and thousands of peasants were killed or captured. Many refugees fled northward with the guerrillas to the more defensible areas near Amajchel.

An attempted coup against President Cerezo on May 11, 1988, reflected discontent in the military with Cerezo's inability to win the war. To retain office, Cerezo agreed to twenty-three of twenty-five demands made by military hard-liners, including refraining from dialogue with the URNG and ending efforts to establish a civilian police force. State-sponsored violence increased after the coup, frequently targeting religious, peace, and human rights groups, and Cerezo effectively was reduced to a mere figurehead as the coup plotters were pardoned. Another coup was foiled in May 1989 and again was followed by an increase in urban terror attacks. That year, government forces were dug in near Amajchel in the heart of EGP territory. They conducted raids on settlements in cooperation with local civil defense patrols. American–Guatemalan military cooperation expanded to include exercises by American National Guard units in the department of Chimaltenango, which coincidentally was a scene of considerable rebel activity. By 1989, the government claimed to have reduced the rebels to 800 fighters, an implausibly low estimate; the real figure was probably 1,500.

The rebels stepped up sabotage operations in October 1989 and by January claimed to be operating throughout 60 percent of the country. The army mounted more offensives in late 1989 and 1990, spending almost half of the country's budget on the war. The government prohibited publication of information relating to military operations, and the exact military events of these years are still not well understood by historians. By 1990 the UNRG admitted that war could not be militarily won, prompting renewed peace talks. Throughout the year, the CNR and UNRG also met for discussions, and URNG promised to avoid undermining CNR by disrupting the November elections. Military operations did not entirely end, but the level of violence fell below that of war level probably a month before the elections.

Termination and Outcome: The outcome was a limited victory by the government, as it retained power, while the URNG reduced its attacks. Similarly, the human rights violations and political violence slowed but did not disappear entirely. A peace treaty between the groups was not signed until December 29, 1996. A truth commission sponsored by the United Nations concluded that 200,000 Guatemalans had been killed, with 90 percent of the deaths attributable to the government forces.[271]

Coding Decisions: As with the previous Guatemalan civil wars, this war is difficult to code, both in terms of identifying the combatants and in calculating the battle-deaths. This is partly due to the role that the Mayans played as combatants and combatant support personnel on both sides of the war. On the government side, the Mayans served as members of the civil defense patrols that assisted the military in both the conduct of the war and in the state-sponsored repression of civilians. At this time, there were 600,000 to 700,000 members in the patrols; however, only 10,000 of these were armed.[272] Thus we code 10,000 as potential combatants. Similarly, though the Guatemalan government claimed that 500,000 Mayans supported the leftist rebels, that refers to more generic support, rather than active combat support. At the beginning of this war, EGP claimed to have 4,000 armed guerrillas and 12,000 unarmed members.[273] We assume that the 12,000 unarmed members are the Mayans who assisted in combat support and thus are using this number as the number of Mayan combat personnel on the rebel side. The Mayan percentage used here is thus just slightly larger than the 61 percent used earlier.

Coding battle-deaths is of course linked to being able to identify the combatants, but it is also more difficult in this case because the Guatemalan Army refused to release casualty reports to the truth commission (CHE) established after the war and because the deaths of the Mayan combatants were likely just included in the overall civilian fatality statistics. Hence, our estimates of battle-deaths must rely on limited information. Alejandría Revolucionaria (2006) aggregates rebel claims together, with a total of 11,800 "operations" producing 14,000 battle casualties inflicted on the army from 1986 to 1992. Using the typical conservative estimate of three wounded for every one killed, this would yield 3,500 government battle-deaths for the period. Our own summation of government battle-deaths produced a rounded total of 2,400, though our figure may be lower because it may not include the deaths suffered by the Mayan civil defense patrols. Thus a midpoint between these two estimates (3,000) is reported here. In terms of rebel battle-deaths, in the earlier wars, it was argued that the rebels suffered fatalities that were 60 percent of their peak combatant numbers (which would yield an estimated 9,600 battle-deaths. During a segment of this war, it was observed that the rebel deaths were twice those suffered by the government, which is reasonable given the government's superiority in weaponry. If this observed ratio were to be valid for the entire war, this would produce an estimate of 6,000 rebel deaths. Because combat in this war was less intense than in the previous war, we are reporting the lower number here as our best guess. We make no attempt to disaggregate government and rebel battle-deaths within these totals.

Sources: Americas Watch (1988); Ball, Kobrak, and Spirer (1999); Barber (1997); Booth and Walker (1999); Brogan (1998); Clodfelter (2008); DeRouen and Heo (2007); Digital National (1996); Gross (1995); Human Rights Watch (1989); Inter-Press Service (1990); Jonas (1991, 1996, 2000); Kempster (1987); Lafeber (1993); Laffin (1989, 1990, 1991); McQuerry (1988); Research Directorate (1991); Stoll (1993).

Notes

1. Calcott, 1964; Fowler, 2000a; Schlarman, 1951.
2. Correlates of War Project, 2010.
3. Calcott, 1964; Fowler, 2000a; Schlarman, 1951; DePalo, 1997.
4. Calcott, 1964; Fowler, 2000a; Schlarman, 1951.
5. Jaques, 2007, 816.
6. Correlates of War Project, 2010.
7. Archer, 2000, 325.
8. Scheina, 2003a, 158.
9. Fehrenbach, 1973, 372.
10. Ibid., 372.
11. Scheina, 2003; Clodfelter, 1991; Calcott, 1964.
12. Correlates of War Project, 2010.
13. Clodfelter, 1991.
14. Scheina, 2003; Axelrod, 2007, 112, claims there were 5,300 Texans at San Antonio in December 1835; DePalo, 1997; Santos, 1982; Clodfelter, 1992.
15. Scheina 2003a, 164.
16. Correlates of War Project, 2010.
17. DePalo, 1997, 72.
18. Correlates of War Project, 2010.
19. Costeloe, 1988, 342.
20. Ibid., 352, 353.
21. Ibid., 345.
22. Fisher and Fisher, 1970, 498.
23. Costeloe, 1988, 347; Fowler, 2007, 206.
24. Costeloe, 1988, 355.
25. Reed, 2001, 70.
26. Ibid., 100; Dumond, 1997, 106.
27. Clodfelter, 2002, 338.
28. Reed, 2001, 40.
29. Clodfelter, 2002, 338.
30. Dumond, 1997, 131.
31. Clodfelter, 2002, 338.
32. Scheina, 2003a, 370.
33. Reed, 2001, 123, 125.
34. Correlates of War Project, 2010.
35. Clodfelter, 1991.
36. DePalo, 1997; Appendix.
37. Dumond, 1997, 100.
38. Reed, 2001, 139.
39. Ibid., 114.
40. Ibid., 122, 122.
41. Clodfelter, 1992; 540; Dumond, 1997, 176, estimates the figure at 60,000.
42. Dumond, 1997.
43. Clodfelter, 1991; Reed, 1964; Rugely, 1996.
44. Reed, 2001, 141.
45. Correlates of War Project, 2010.
46. Broussard, 1979, 55, 56.
47. Ibid., 56.
48. Ibid., 56.
49. Fowler, 2012, 189.
50. Broussard, 1979, 55–56.
51. Correlates of War Project, 2010.
52. Bancroft, Howe, Nemos, Savage, and Peatfield, 1886; Marley, 1998; Meyer, Sherman, and Deeds, 1999.
53. Correlates of War Project, 2010.
54. Clodfelter, 2008; Correlates of War Project, 2010; Nofi, 1995.
55. Clodfelter, 2008; Reid, 1999; Dupuy and Dupuy, 1993; Nofi, 1995.
56. Clodfelter, 2008.
57. Clodfelter, 1998, 67.
58. Board of Commissioners, 2005, 302.
59. Clodfelter, 1998, 40.
60. Heard, 1864, 50.
61. Kessel and Wooster, 2005, 12.
62. BCI Eclipse, 2005.
63. Singer, 1972, 215.
64. Berghold, 2007, 142; Oehler, 1959, 235.
65. Clodfelter, 2007, 227.
66. Clodfelter, 2002, 290.
67. Keenan, 2003, 17.
68. Clodfelter, 1998, 43.
69. Small and Singer, 1982, 71.
70. Keenan, 2003, 82.
71. Clodfelter, 1998, 59.
72. Marley, 1998; Alec-Tweedie, 1906; Martin, 1914; Stevenson, 1899. For the volunteers, this includes the deaths on April 8, but deaths in other engagements are unknown.
73. Correlates of War Project, 2010.
74. Alec-Tweedie (1906) maintains that 200,000 were in arms at the end of hostilities and that 100,000 (presumably Republicans) were quartered in Mexico City alone. We suspect that the second estimate represents the organized Republican forces after their victory.
75. Correlates of War Project, 2010.
76. Heinl and Heinl, 1978, 242.
77. *The New York Times*, December 6, 1868.
78. *The New York Times*, June 26, 1869.
79. Leger, 1970, 216.
80. Hazard, 1873.
81. Sarkees, 2010b, 374.
82. Heinl and Heinl, 1978, 242.
83. Correlates of War Project, 2010.
84. Clodfelter, 1991.
85. Ibid.; Alec-Tweedie, 1906; Bancroft, Howe, Nemos, Savage, and Peatfield, 1888; Payno, 2010; Perry, 1978.
86. Correlates of War Project, 2010.
87. *Appleton's Annual*, 1886.
88. Ibid.; *Annual Register*, 1885.

89. Rodman, 1954; Clodfelter, 2008; *Appleton's Annual*, 1886; *Annual Register*, 1885; Correlates, 2009.
90. Paquin, 1983; Price-Mars, 1948; Jackson, 1999; Clodfelter, 2008.
91. Correlates of War Project, 2010.
92. Hu-DeHart, 1984, 142.
93. Spicer, 1980, 149.
94. This war is classified as a non-state war because, at that time, Mexico was considered an autonomous entity that did not become a system member until 1831.
95. Hu-DeHart, 1984, 144.
96. Clodfelter, 2002, 337.
97. Hu-DeHart, 1984, 143.
98. Wells and Joseph, 1996, 50.
99. Correlates of War Project, 2010.
100. Including 3,000 with General Bravo and 1,000 at Sombrerete; Dumond, 1997, 395.
101. Ibid., 382.
102. Ibid., 394.
103. Richard, 1999; Robins, 2005.
104. Wells and Joseph, 1996.
105. Correlates of War Project, 2010.
106. Woodward, 1993.
107. Teplitz, 1973.
108. Correlates of War Project, 2010.
109. Vanderwood, 1976; Correlates of War Project, 2009; Clodfelter, 1991.
110. Vanderwood, 1976; Meyer, 1967.
111. Correlates of War Project, 2009; Knight, 1986.
112. Atkin, 1969; McLynn, 2000.
113. Meyer, 1967; Camín and Meyer, 1993; Clodfelter, 2008; Scheina, 2003.
114. Camín and Meyer, 1993; Knight, 1986; Atkin, 1969.
115. Knight, 1986; Marley, 1998.
116. Boot, 2002, 155.
117. McCaa, 2003, 394.
118. Boot, 2002, 152–153.
119. McLynn, 2000, 240.
120. Singer, 1972, 45.
121. Krauze, 1997.
122. Gonzáles Navarro, 1970, cited in McCaa, 2003, 372.
123. McCaa, 2003, 396.
124. Ibid., 385.
125. Clodfelter, 2002, 422.
126. Correlates of War Project, 2010.
127. Fermoselle, 1987, 121.
128. Ibid., 123; Helg, 1995, 225.
129. Gerome, 1997, 14.
130. Clodfelter, 2002, 425.
131. Fermoselle, 1987, 123.
132. Helg, 1995, 225; Gerome, 1997, 21.
133. Correlates of War Project, 2010.
134. Clodfelter, 2008; McLynn, 2000; Correlates of War Project, 2009.
135. McLynn, 2000; Knight, 1986; Atkin, 1969; Clodfelter, 2008.
136. McLynn, 2000; Knight, 1986; Clodfelter, 2008, Boot, 2002, 188.
137. McLynn, 2000; Knight, 1986.
138. Knight, 1986.
139. Ibid.
140. Clodfelter, 2008; Scheina 2003a and b; Boot, 2002, 192.
141. Matthews, 2007; Clodfelter, 2008.
142. McLynn, 2000, 301.
143. Krauze, 1997; Koth, 2002; Clodfelter, 2008.
144. Correlates of War Project, 2010.
145. McLynn, 2000, 396.
146. Ibid., 396.
147. Gonzales, 2002, 193.
148. Correlates of War Project, 2010.
149. Ross, 1969.
150. Ibid.
151. O'Brien, 1999; Ross, 1969.
152. *Dallas Morning News*, 1924.
153. *The New York Times*, February 28, 1924.
154. Camín and Meyer, 1993; Clodfelter, 2008; Gonzales, 2002, 218; Purnell, 1999.
155. Camín and Meyer, 1993; Clodfelter, 2008.
156. Correlates of War Project, 2010.
157. Clodfelter, 2002, 426.
158. Ibid., 426.
159. Phillips and Axelrod, 2007, 749
160. Clodfelter, 2002, 427.
161. Krauze, 1997.
162. Phillips and Axelrod, 2007, 749.
163. Gonzales, 2002, 218.
164. Clodfelter, 2002, 428; Gonzales, 2002, 217.
165. Dulles, 1961; Krauze, 1997.
166. Correlates of War Project, 2010.
167. Carriedo, 2005; Correlates of War Project, 2009; Dulles, 1961; Schlarman, 1951; Purnell, 1999.
168. Nearly every estimate of rebel strength uses a figure of 30,000 (17,000 regulars and 13,000 irregulars), but this figure is actually an estimate of total rebels—both *Cristero* and pro-Escobar.
169. Clodfelter, 2002, 428
170. Montgomery, 1982, 52.
171. Correlates of War Project, 2010.
172. Clodfelter, 2002, 428.
173. Ching and Tilley, 1998, 142.
174. Clodfelter, 2002, 428.
175. See Anderson, 1992, 174–175.
176. Ibid., 176.
177. Ibid., 176.
178. Bird, 1984; Bercovitch and Jackson, 1997; Clodfelter, 2008.
179. Correlates of War Project, 2010.

180. Bird, 1984; Bercovitch and Jackson, 1997; Clodfelter, 2008.
181. Scheina, 2003b, 181.
182. Small and Singer, 1982, 228.
183. Phillips and Axelrod, 2005, 362; Clodfelter, 2002, 701.
184. Correlates of War Project, 2010.
185. Bonachea and San Martin, 1974; Perez, 1993, 93; Scheina, 2003b, 218, 225.
186. Bonachea and San Martin, 1974; Scheina, 2003b.
187. Ibid.; Shetterly, 2007.
188. Selbin, 1993, 46.
189. Atkins and Wilson, 1998.
190. Correlates of War Project, 2010.
191. Atkins and Wilson, 1998; Correlates of War Project, 2010; Gleijeses, 1978.
192. Atkins and Wilson, 1998; Gleijeses, 1978; Korb, 1999.
193. Atkins and Wilson, 1998; Clodfelter, 2008; Gleijeses, 1978.
194. Lafeber, 1993, 171.
195. Correlates of War Project, 2009.
196. Ibid.
197. Korb, 1999, 36.
198. Lafeber, 1993, 171.
199. Schlesingeer and Kinzer, 1982, 247.
200. Peralta and Beverly, 1980, 94.
201. Scheina, 2003b.
202. Peralta and Beverly, 1980, 96.
203. Jonas, 2000, 119.
204. Ibid., 21.
205. Crain, 1975, 191.
206. Peralta and Beverly, 1980, 110.
207. Jonas, 2000, 21; Anderson, 1988, 26.
208. Booth, 1980, 200.
209. Wickham-Crowley, 1992, 207.
210. Booth, 1980, 198.
211. Jonas, 1991, 67.
212. Gross, 1995, 103.
213. Brockett, 2005, 208, based on data from the CIIDH database.
214. Jonas, 1991, 2000.
215. Jonas, 2000, 36.
216. Ibid., 35.
217. Ibid., 21.
218. Anderson, 1988, 26.
219. May, 2001, 58; Jonas, 2000, 21.
220. Wickham-Crowley, 1992, 222.
221. Paige, 1983, 699–736.
222. Correlates of War Project, 2010.
223. Peralta and Beverly, 1980, 106.
224. Lafeber, 1993, 256.
225. Peralta and Beverly, 1980, 111; Jonas, 1991, 121.
226. Lafeber, 1993, 256.
227. Doyle and Osario, 2014.
228. Scheina, 2003b, 283; Schlesinger and Kinzer, 1982, 249.
229. Correlates of War Project, 2010.
230. Jonas, 2000, 23.
231. "Guatemalan Guerrillas," 1983 for the descriptive text.
232. Brown, 1984; Valentino, 2004.
233. Gross, 1995, 108.
234. May, 1999, 76.
235. Ibid., note 13, 88.
236. Gross, 1995, 101.
237. Jonas, 1991, 67.
238. Research Directorate, 1991, 5.
239. Jonas, 2000, 35.
240. Jonas, 1996, 145.
241. Torres-Rivas, 1990.
242. Caballero Jurado and Thomas, 1990, 11.
243. Ibid., 12.
244. Correlates of War Project, 2010.
245. Brogan, 1998; DeRouen and Heo, 2007.
246. Scheina, 2003a and b; Schulz, 1984; DeFronzo, 1996, 217.
247. Jung, 1983, 32.
248. Correlates of War Project, 2010.
249. Jurado and Thomas, 1990; Little, 1994; Prisk, 1988; Scheina, 2003b.
250. Jurado and Thomas, 1990; Prisk, 1988; Scheina, 2003b.
251. Jurado and Thomas, 1990; Prisk, 1988.
252. Jurado and Thomas, 1990; "Lessons of Nicaragua's," 1979; Little, 1994; Prisk, 1988.
253. Jurado and Thomas, 1990; Little, 1994; Prisk, 1988.
254. Bracamonte and Spencer, 1995; Call, 2002; Seligson and McElhinny, 1996.
255. Bracamonte and Spencer, 1995; Rosello, 1993.
256. Correlates of War Project, 2010.
257. Brown, 2001b; Clodfelter, 2008.
258. Ford, 1987; Minahan, 2002.
259. Ford, 1987; Honey, 1994; Prevost, 1987.
260. Ford, 1987; Hartzell, 2002.
261. Ford, 1987; Honey, 1994.
262. Kornbluh, 1987, 21.
263. Selbin, 1993, 115.
264. Kornbluh, 1987, 25.
265. Correlates of War Project, 2010.
266. Research Directorate, 1991, 5.
267. Gross, 1995, 102.
268. Laffin, 1989, 1991; Schirmer, 1998.
269. Gross, 1995, 102.
270. Manz, 1988, 64.
271. Ciment, 2007g, 440.
272. Americas Watch, 1988; Laffin, 1991; Research Directorate, 1991, 5.
273. Gross, 1995, 102.

CHAPTER FOUR

Intra-state Wars in South America

Below is the list of the intra-state wars that took place in South America. Each war will then be described individually with the pertinent basic data provided.

TABLE 4.1 List of Intra-state Wars in South America

(Continued)

TABLE 4.1 **List of Intra-state Wars in South America** (Continued)

Individual Descriptions of Intra-state Wars in South America

INTRA-STATE WAR #520.3

Cabanada War of 1832 to 1835 (aka War of the Cabanos)

Participants: Brazil versus Cabanos of Pernambuco.
Dates: April 1832 to May 29, 1835
Battle-related Deaths: Brazil: [ ]; Cabanos; [ ].
Initiator: Cabanos.
Outcome: Brazil wins.
War Type: Civil for local issues
Total System Member Military Personnel: Armed Forces of Brazil: 17,000 (prewar); 17,000 (initial); 17,000 (peak); 12,000 (final).[1]
Theater Armed Forces: Cabanos of Pernambuco (Rebel Army): "thousands" (peak), 500 (final).[2]

Antecedents: Beginning in the early sixteenth century, Portugal imposed its monarchical government over Brazil. A republican movement raised its first challenge to colonial control in 1788 and 1789, and it continued to grow, even though Rio de Janiero briefly became the capital of the Portuguese empire (1808–1820). When King John VI returned to Lisbon, he left his son, Dom Pedro, as a prince regent in Brazil. When the Lisbon government tried to recall the prince, Dom Pedro refused, and on September 7, 1822, he declared the independence of Brazil. During the first several decades of Brazil's independence, the central government had only loose control over the fragmented provinces. There was increasing opposition to the monarchy and to Dom Pedro I personally. Brazil's loss in an unpopular war against the Argentine provinces from 1826 to 1828 (Extra-state War #315) further damaged the emperor's support (leading to revolts in 1827, 1828, and 1830). Dom Pedro was forced to abdicate in 1831, leaving the throne to his five-year-old son under a regency. The abdication precipitated a number of major provincial rebellions revolving around racial issues and relative support or opposition to the emperor (though only five of these reached war level, Intra-state Wars #520.3, #525, #526, #531, and #532.8).

The Brazilian population was quite stratified, with two-thirds of the population being poor blacks and mulattos (of whom 25 percent were slaves). The term *cabanos* refers in general to the lower classes, or those who lived in the interior or outside of the major cities. Popular discontent in the northeastern province of Pernambuco reflected both the *cabanos'* opposition to the new government and their deteriorating economic conditions precipitated by the decline in the sugar trade. The ensuing Cabanda War was largely a royalist and reactionary revolt by the poor against the new regency. Those opposed to the regency, or Restorationists, launched an armed revolt just south of Recife in April or early May 1832 (authors disagree).

Narrative: The revolt initially was led by Torres Galindo and António Timóteo (who later was succeeded by Vicente Ferreira de Paula). This war was agrarian based, and the backbone of the rebel army consisted of fugitive slaves and free natives. The revolt began in Pernambuco, soon spread to the neighboring province of Alagoas, and quickly assumed the character of a guerrilla war. The war dragged on until May 29, 1835, when most rebel leaders surrendered to the government (which marks the end of the war). However, Vicente de Paula and 50 to 60 loyalists continued his resistance in the backwoods, and pacification was not considered to be complete until August 1835, when Vicente de Paula founded a small town and the fighting stopped.

Termination and Outcome: The outcome of the war was a government victory accompanied by a surrender by nearly all rebel forces, though some leaders of the revolt were at large until 1850.

Coding Decisions: We have been unable to locate detailed combatant fatality figures for this war. It has been reported that as many as 15,000 people died during the war either in battle, of disease, or of hunger, but it is unclear how many of these people were armed personnel.[3] However it seems likely that the combatant fatality figures reached war level.

Sources: Barman (1988); Bento (2002); Burns (1993); Chilcote (1972); Correia de Andrade (1972); Graham (1990); Levine (1992); Treece (2000); Williamson (2009).

INTRA-STATE WAR #525

Cabanos Revolt of 1835 to 1837 (aka Cabanagem, Cabanado do Pará, Paraense Civil War)

Participants: Brazil versus *Cabanos.*
Dates: January 6, 1835, to July 12, 1837.
Battle-related Deaths: Brazil—5,500; *Cabanos*—6,500.
Initiator: Cabanos.
Outcome: Brazil wins.
War Type: Civil for local issues.
Total System Member Military Personnel: Armed Forces of Brazil: 12,000 (prewar); 17,000 (peak, final).[4]
Theater Armed Forces: The Armed Forces of Brazil were assisted by the Ayres (Bararoa)-led Mercenaries, participating from December 25, 1835, strength estimates: 254 (initial and peak); 139 (final).[5] Mundurucu Indians, participating from May 27, 1836. *Cabanos* (Rebel Forces): peak combined rebel strength is estimated at 6,000, consisting of *Exaltados* (Rebel Aggregate—no common commander), strength estimates: 2,000 (as of August 1835). *Forças dos Brazileiros Reunidos,* aka United Brazilian Forces, participating from 1835, strength estimates: 1,000 (peak). *Magotes,* participated from September 1836.

Antecedents: This war should not be confused with the similarly titled Cabanada War (Intra-state War #520.3), which occurred earlier in the northeastern Pernambuco and Alagoas provinces. Both wars arose in opposition to Brazil's new regency government, and both featured the lower-class *cabanos,* but the rebels were different groups, separated by considerable distance, with completely different leaders and somewhat varying goals.

This revolt began in the northwestern Grão-Pará province as a reaction against the dominant Portuguese elite by nativist, largely white, radical liberals known as *Exaltados.* After independence (in 1822), the Brazilian government had difficulty in establishing control over the remote Grão-Pará, which was incorporated into the empire in 1823. The abdication of emperor Dom Pedro in 1831 (in favor of his young son under a regency) encouraged the nativists. However, in Grão-Pará the National Guard remained under the control of the Portuguese faction. Thus the nativists formed their own militia of *cabanos* from a variety of racial groups (including slaves). This racial component made the Cabanos Revolt more threatening to the elite. In 1833, the *Exaltado* militia clashed with supporters of the Portuguese elite (*caramurús*) in street battles in the provincial capital of Belém. The province was also rife with banditry by small groups called *magotes,* which remained incapable of waging war until consolidation and radicalization began in September 1836. In late 1834, a group of *Exaltados* plotted a revolution against the government, and though they were dispersed, the remaining group planned another assault on Belém for January 6, 1835. They wrote a manifesto listing many national and local grievances, including a claim that the president of Grão-Pará was a Freemason. While they refrained from calling for the overthrow of the regency governing the country, they declared it to be illegitimate. Their demands were for reforms, regional leadership, and a conditional de facto independence for Pará until the majority of Pedro II.

Narrative: The revolution began at the barracks in Belém on January 6, when the *Exaltados* shot the military commander and middle-ranking officers before killing the president of Grão-Pará. Felix Malcher, the political leader of the rebellion, assumed the presidency of Grão-Pará; and Francisco Vinagre was appointed as the chief military commander. In less than one month, the supporters of the two leaders came to blows. Malcher was killed, and Vinagre assumed the presidency. The Brazilian government responded by blockading Belém and attempting to retake the city in May 1835. The government expedition met with disaster, but Vinagre was persuaded to resign the presidency in favor of the government's new appointee. However, coexistence with the rebels soon proved impossible. On August 14, a force of 2,000 to 4,000 rebel red shirts (natives, mestizos, and blacks) stormed the city, restoring rebel control after nine days of fighting. Their leader, Eduardo Angelim, was proclaimed president of the state. By this time, the rebellion had spread into the countryside, where some rebel groups included escaped or former slaves. One of the most notable groups established itself at a fortress called Ecuipiranga, and by late 1836, it housed more than a thousand rebels under the banner of the *Forças dos Brazileiros Reunidos* (United Brazilian Forces), led by former members of the National Guard. At this point, most towns and villages in the Lower Amazon recognized Angelim as president, but the tide soon turned against the rebels.

The Brazilian regent, threatened by other revolts (such as the Farroupilha War, Intra-state War #526), appointed a new military commandant to end the rebellion. In February 1836, government commander Francisco José Soares Andréa prepared a force of about 2,500 soldiers and freed convicts to retake Belém. He began a propaganda campaign to unite whites against Indians and blacks in a race war. An assault by his forces retook Belém on May 13, 1836, and the rebels retreated into the interior. Two weeks later, Joaquim Fructuoso, a headman of the Mundurucu Indians, pledged the tribe's loyalty to the government and willingness to fight the rebels (becoming a war participant at this point).

Ecuipiranga now became the linchpin of the revolt, and *magotes* were forced to side with the rebels as the government tried to both fight a civil war and stamp out banditry. Government victories were marked by post-battle atrocities, including massacres of slaves and Indians who had joined the revolt. A government army of 500 soldiers with naval support began to advance up the Amazon, recapturing Santarém on October 3 and 4, 1836. Fighting continued through the end of the year as the government reduced the territory under rebel control.

In 1837, there were about 6,000 rebels: 1,000 at Ecuipiranga, 3,000 in the Lower Amazon, and another 4 rebel garrisons along the Curuá River. At the end of March, 1,000 rebels failed to retake Santarém. The government blockaded Ecuipiranga, and on June 20, the government mounted an assault with only three ships and 100 soldiers. They successfully destroyed some fortifications before withdrawing. On July 12, government reinforcements and Mundurucu Indians overran Ecuipiranga, suffering only eleven battle-deaths while the defenders suffered only five. Over the next few days, more than 500 rebels surrendered to the authorities. Ecuipiranga marked the end of conventional fighting by rebels and thus the end of the war.

Termination and Outcome: The outcome was a government military victory, though some rebels retreated westward to defensive strongholds. By the end of 1838, the government efforts emphasized the notion of a race war as it launched a campaign of indiscriminate violence against civilians. The promise of amnesty convinced nearly a thousand rebels to surrender on March 25, 1840, which ended most of the hostilities in this region.

Coding Decisions: In terms of the war participants, we have included on the government side the mercenaries led by Ayres (Bararoa), though it is not clear on whose authority he acted. The fatalities during this war were substantial, with up to 20 percent of the province's population dying due to disease or violence surrounding this war. Most accounts give a figure of 30,000 deaths for the rebellion but do not distinguish civilian and military fatalities. One contemporary estimate of battle deaths was 10,000 to 12,000 combatant deaths (killed in combat or died in prison). We have adopted the higher figure of 12,000 as it might include combatants who died of disease. Harris regards a claim that deaths were about equal on both sides to be "misjudged" but offers no alternative division (save the general sense that the rebels suffered more than the government). Thus we are dividing the 12,000 deaths into 6,500 rebel deaths (which include more than 1,500 who died in prison during the war) and 5,500 government deaths.

Sources: Barman (1988); Bento (2002); Bethell and de Carvalho (1989); Burns (1993); Chasteen (1994); Chilcote (1972); Clodfelter (2002); Comissão Executiva Central do Sesquicentenário sa Independência do Brasil (1972); Correia de Andrade (1972); Fausto (1999); Graham (1990); Harris (2010); Klein and Luna (2010); Levine (1992, 1999); Treece (2000); Williamson (2009); Worcester (1973).

INTRA-STATE WAR #526

Farroupilha War of 1835 to 1845 (aka War of the Farrapos, War of the Ragamuffins)

Participants: Brazil versus Farrapos.
Dates: September 19, 1835, to March 1, 1845.

Battle-related Deaths: Brazil—[ ]; Farrapos—[ ]; Total Combatant Deaths: 20,000. (See Coding Decisions.)
Initiator: Farrapos.
Outcome: Brazil wins.
War Type: Civil for local issues.
Total System Member Military Personnel: Brazilian Armed Forces: 12,000 (prewar); 12,000 (initial); 26,000 (peak); 23,000 (final).[6]
Theater Armed Forces: Farrapos (Rebel Army): 2,000 (initial); 2,500 (in 1838); 9,372 (peak); 1,200 (final).[7]

Antecedents: By the 1830s, Brazil was facing political divides, both within the central government and in relation to its provinces. The regency emerged as the *moderado*, or moderate group in government, which was confronted by opposition from the right by the *Caramurú* party that favored the return of Emperor Pedro I and from the left by the *Exaltados* (nativist, largely white, radical liberals) and the *cabanos* (or lower classes), who were opposed to the Portuguese elites, and continued domination of the government and society. Groups in the provinces opposed Brazil's increasing centralization, and this war is the third of the five rebellions whose severity reached war-level during the 1830s (see also Intra-state Wars #520, #525, #531, and #532.8). It erupted in Rio Grande do Sul, the southernmost province of Brazil, on the border with Uruguay, and it was the longest and deadliest of the period. The name *Farroupilha* (Farrapos, or ragamuffins, refers to the fringed leather worn by cowboys or *gauchos* of Rio Grande do Sul) was applied to the radicals of the province.

Tension between the people of Rio Grande do Sul and the central government derived from both the opposition to central control and the Portuguese elite and from specific provincial concerns, such as heavy taxes on locally produced beef products. Local cowboys (*gaúchos*) who served in the Brazilian cavalry resented their Portuguese officers. Local landowners, who were not necessarily loyal to the central government or the appointed provincial president, maintained their own armed forces, which were the backbone of the National Guard. In addition, instability in neighboring Uruguay provided the prospect of safe havens and assistance for potential rebels. These factors came together in 1835, initiating a decade-long war that encompassed three general phases: initially the provincial president was overthrown; the war evolved into a drive for provincial independence; then the rebels established the Rio Grande Republic with support from neighboring Uruguay (which was not yet a state system member).

Narrative: The war began on September 19, 1835, when a group of armed *gaúchos* and local units of the National Guard (under the command of Bento Gonçalves do Silva) attacked the provincial capital of Porto Alegre, which was defended by the forces of Brazil. The rebels were aided by Bento Manuel Ribeiro, a Brazilian military officer, who would switch sides several times during the war. Within two days, the rebels evicted provincial president Fernandez Braga and took control of Porto Alegre. Marciano Ribeiro was appointed provincial president. Meanwhile, the national government under the regency of Diogo Antônio Feijó, which was facing a more threatening rebellion in the North (Intra-state War #525), initially sought a negotiated settlement in Rio Grande do Sul by winning over some of the political elites, including Bento Manuel Ribeiro. The national government then appointed Araújo Ribeiro (a relative of Bento Manuel Ribeiro) as president of the province, triggering a rupture between those rebels who had merely sought autonomy within Brazil (primarily the elites) and those who now viewed autonomy as insufficient to secure their interests.

The second phase of the war began in mid-February 1836, when armed conflicts resumed. Regent Feijó confronted increasing demands by the *Caramurú* party in the legislature to take military action against the rebels, and provincial President Araújo Ribeiro also decided to crack down on the rebels. The fighting now pitted both government forces, including some former rebels like Bento Manuel Ribeiro, against the secessionists. *Farrapos* led by José de Almeida Corte Real defeated an army led by Bento Manuel. Rebel leader João Manuel de Lima e Silva crushed government forces at the southern city of Pelotas. However, on June 15, 1836, pro-government forces seized control of Porto Alegre and imprisoned former rebel president Marciano Ribeiro. Gonçalves then mounted an unsuccessful attack on Porto Alegre.

The rebels now gained outside assistance that enabled them to carry on the fight. Uruguay (once the province of Cisplatina) had won its independence from Brazil in 1828 as a result of the

Brazil–Argentine War of 1826 to 1828 (Extra-state War #315). Uruguay had two major factions, the *Blancos* and the *Colorados*, both of which made common cause with Brazil's *Farrapos*, providing arms, supplies, and places of refuge. After receiving assistance from Uruguay's forces, a *Farrapo* army led by Gen. Antônio de Sousa Neto reentered Brazil, winning a stunning victory over government troops at Seival on September 9 and 10, 1836. The next day, General Neto proclaimed Republic of the Rio Grande as an independent state (also called the Riograndense Republic, or the Piratini Republic) with Bento Gonçalves da Silva as its president.

Rebel successes were short-lived. Government troops led by Gen. Bento Manuel chased Gonçalves to the island of Fanfã and, blocking the *Farrapos* retreat, defeated the rebels from October 3 to 6, 1836. Nine hundred *Farrapos*, including Gonçalves and most of the *Farrapo* senior leadership, surrendered and were imprisoned. Government troops then embarked on a campaign of reprisals against the populace, which only served to increase volunteers for the *Farrapos*. João Manuel de Lima e Silva and General Neto decided to continue the war, establishing a capital in Piratini and reorganizing the army.

Five factors prevented the conflict from ending at that point. First, the *Farrapos* easily could rearm and reorganize in their Uruguayan sanctuary. Second, the government removed Araújo Ribeiro from power, appointing a loyal Royalist in his place, which caused Bento Manuel Ribeiro to rejoin the rebels on March 28, 1837. Third, the government's attention was focused on revolts elsewhere. Fourth, the imperial assembly was skeptical that the current regent could win the war, so they withheld funds, allowing the *Farrapos* to retake objectives with ease. Only in September 1837, after a change in regent, did the assembly release the funds needed to suppress the rebellion. Fourth, the key to winning battles was horses, and it was easier for the rebels than the government to secure and maintain large herds. Thus for most of the period from 1836 to 1840, the rebels had the upper hand. The *Farrapos* swiftly reentered Brazil and besieged Porto Alegre; General Neto overran the major government arsenal at Caçapava in 1837. On April 30, 1838, the *Farrapos* scored a major victory, capturing Rio Pardo.

Both sides frantically were increasing the sizes of their forces. The rebels found a useful ally in Italian adventurer Giuseppe Garibaldi, who helped them establish a small fleet, which won several engagements. In an attempt to broaden the base of the revolt, the *Farrapos* invaded northward into the province of Santa Catarina. The *Farrapos* then proclaimed the Juliana Republic (also known as the Santa Catarina Republic), which would be confederated with the Rio Grande Republic. Though the rebels reached a peak of 9,372 soldiers by this point, they were unable to dislodge loyalists from the provincial capital. Brazil moved to destroy the minuscule rebel fleet on November 15, 1839. Cut off from the sea, the rebels were forced to abandon Santa Catarina, and the government put a swift end to the Juliana Republic.

In 1840 the government achieved a series of military successes against the *Farrapos*. The rebel capital at Caçapava was seized, forcing Rio Grandense administrators to flee. A battle at Taquari was the largest of the war, with more than 10,000 combatants involved. Although the result was indecisive, the superior resources of the government were beginning to have an impact. The government won more victories, and by the end of the year, Bento Manuel Ribeiro decided to abandon the rebel cause. In 1842 most *Farrapos* were driven into Uruguay, but they no longer received assistance there. The Farrapos crossed back into Brazil and scored early successes: on April 15, 1843, they seized São Gabriel. However, a new government army of 11,000 began to defeat the rebels.

Termination and Outcome: By 1844, the Farrapos were willing to negotiate, but a sticking point was their insistence that enlisted slaves be given their freedom. In one of the most bizarre incidents in the war, known as the "Surprise of Porongos," the local government commander bribed a *Farrapo* general to commit his Afro-Brazilian forces to battle on November 14, 1844, unsupported by other units. Unsurprisingly, they were cut down, and this battle cost the lives of eighty Afro-Brazilians and twenty whites. At the end of the year, Piratini, the capital of the Republic of the Rio Grande, was occupied by government forces. Because Brazil anticipated war with Argentina (Inter-state War #19, the La Plata War, which began in July 1851), it offered the rebels fairly generous terms to surrender, and on March 1, 1845, a formal peace agreement was signed.

Coding Decisions: In terms of assessing the size of the *Farrapo* army, estimates of strength vary considerably, generally mentioning forces between 2,000 and 6,000. Scheina provides the oddly specific number of 9,372 men (6,903 cavalry, 2247 infantry, 222 artillerymen) on October 23, 1839. We take this to be an accurate estimate of the rebels' peak strength.

In terms of battle-related deaths, scholars differ in their conclusions as to whether this war or the War of the Cabanos was the deadliest during this period. Their competing conclusions probably are based on differing definitions of war deaths. The War of the Cabanos was deadliest if one includes the thousands of civilian deaths by both disease and government slaughters. This war is deadliest if one focuses upon combatant deaths caused during the much longer time period and the greater number of significant battles. That said, there is relatively little information on the number of combatant fatalities. Clodfelter says there were "tens of thousands" of battle deaths, and the lowest estimate consistent with this statement would be an estimate of 20,000 killed on both sides.

Sources: Barman (1988); Bento (2002); Bethell and de Carvalho (1989); Calogeras (1939); Chasteen (1994); Clodfelter (2002); Dawson (1903); Fausto (1999); Leitman (1972, 1977); "Revolução Farroupilha" (2010); Scheina (2003a); Williamson (2009).

INTRA-STATE WAR #531

Sabinada Rebellion of 1837 to 1838

Participants: Brazil versus Bahian Sabinada Rebels.
Dates: November 7, 1837, to March 16, 1838.
Battle-related Deaths: Bahian Sabinada: 1,200; Brazil: 600.[8]
Initiator: Bahian Sabinada.
Outcome: Brazil wins.
War Type: Civil for local issues.
Total System Member Military Personnel: Armed Forces of Brazil (Government Army), participating throughout war, strength estimates: 15,000 (prewar); 15,000 (initial); 19,000 (peak); 19,000 (final).[9]
Theater Armed Forces: Restoration Army (including elements of the imperial navy, the National Guard, local police, and private militias): 4,000 to 5,000 (peak).[10] Sabinada Rebels: 5,000 (peak); 4,247 (final).[11]

Antecedents: This war took place in Bahia province in northeastern Brazil. This is the fourth revolt that reached war status in the wake of the abdication of Emperor Pedro I in 1831 (see also Intra-state Wars #520.3, #525, and #526). Two of these, the Cabanos Revolt in the North and the Farroupilha War in the South, were still ongoing as 1837 began. The Sabinda Rebellion is related tangentially to the Farroupilha War in that the rebel leaders in Bahia were suspected of helping *Farrapo* leader Bento Gonçalves da Silva escape from a federal prison in Bahia.

Bahia had seen political instability before 1837: a military uprising in October 1832; federalist revolts in February 1832 and April 1833; and a slave rebellion (often termed the *Muslim uprising*) was defeated in 1835. A source of the uprisings was unhappiness with the current regency government in Rio de Janeiro and a desire for a more federal structure that would provide for greater local autonomy. The federalist movement began primarily among the urban professionals but soon won the support of the army and police as well as many free blacks and slaves. The name *Sabin da* refers to a founder of the rebel movement, a newspaper editor and physician, Dr. Sabino Alvares da Rocha Vieira. The war began in Salvador, the capital of the province of Bahai, at the time Brazil's second-largest city.

Narrative: The rebellion was initiated on November 7, 1837, by the Third Artillery Battalion (stationed at Fort São Pedro, in Salvador), which was soon joined by the Third Infantry Battalion and local police. Though the central government had the support of some senior officers, the National Guard, and the navy, the rebels soon had control of the capital and declared the independence of Bahia. Within four days, the rebel leaders, like *Exaltados* elsewhere, announced that the declaration would expire when future emperor Pedro II came of age. The rebels quickly seized all of the provincial arsenals and recruited free blacks, who eventually made up two-thirds of rebel forces. The government, aided by private militias of the local sugar barons, responded quickly by forming a Restoration Army to besiege the city by land and sea. The siege prevented the rebels from spreading the revolt to the countryside, a tactic that had enabled other revolts to endure. There was one outbreak in the interior at Barra, though it was defeated by local National Guard units. By January, the Restoration Army had increased to 4,000 men. Under siege, the rebels permitted women, children, and the elderly to leave the city in January 1838, and many of the Portuguese elites fled as well. Slaves were originally prohibited from leaving or enlisting, but on January 3, the rebel leadership created a new unit of slaves. Six weeks later, the rebel leadership declared emancipation for the one-third of slaves who were Brazilian born.

In mid-February 1838, the rebels mounted an attempt to break the siege. After the effort failed, a rebel schooner defected to the government, and discipline within rebel units broke down. Government forces went on the offensive, breaking the rebel lines on March 13. House-to-house fighting continued for three days before government control of the city was secured, ending the war.

Termination and Outcome: The government did accept some mass surrenders on March 13, but fighting continued until March 16, 1838. The outcome of the war was a complete government victory. The victory was accompanied by mass killings of civilians by the government, as well as deportations and imprisonment of 3,000 former rebels and supporters, each with a frightfully high death rate. The government's victory over proponents of liberal and republican ideals presaged a period of imperial consolidation that would endure for forty years.

Coding Decisions: There is disagreement and vagueness over the battle-related deaths. Kraay reported an estimate of 1,091 rebels and 40 government soldiers killed, though that figure seems to be only for the final assault.[12] Bethell and de Carvalho conclude that about 1,200 rebels and 600 loyalists were killed,[13] and those are the figures we have reported here. The real number of battle-deaths could be higher due to earlier engagements, deaths from disease, and reports that "black military leaders fought until the bitter end."[14]

Similarly, scholars also indicate varying estimates of the number of civilians massacred in this war, ranging from hundreds to a thousand.

Sources: Barman (1988); Bethell and de Carvalho (1989); Burns (1993); Clodfelter (2002); Comissão Executiva Central do Sesquicentenário sa Independência do Brasil (1972); Holub (1969); Kraay (1992); Treece (2000); Williamson (2009); Worcester (1973).

INTRA-STATE WAR #532.7
Balaiada Revolt of 1838 to 1841

Participants: Brazil versus Balaida Rebels.
Dates: December 13, 1838, to January 19, 1841.
Battle-related Deaths: Brazil: [ ]; Balaida Rebels: 5,000.[15]
Initiator: Balaida Rebels.
Outcome: Brazil wins.
War Type: Civil for local issues.
Total System Member Military Personnel: Armed Forces of Brazil: 15,000 (prewar, initial); 22,000 (peak, final).[16]
Theater Armed Forces: Armed Forces of Brazil: 1,000 (initial); 8,000 (peak).[17] United Rebel Army: 11,000 (August 1839),[18] consisting of *Balaios*, *Bem-te-vis*: 4,000 (initial); 2,000 (final).[19] Quilombolas: 3,000 (initial); 500 (final).[20]

Antecedents: This war took place in Brazil's northern provinces of Maranhão and Piauí. It was the last of five revolts that reached war status in the wake of the abdication of Emperor Pedro I in 1831 (see also Intra-state Wars #520.3, #525, #526, and #521). Though there were many commonalities in these uprisings, a significant difference was the leadership of the revolts. The earlier revolts had been led by regional elites or middle-class professionals, whereas the Balaiada war was fundamentally a peasant war. The economy of Maranhão was based primarily upon cotton plantations, and consequently it had a high proportion of slaves (about 55 percent of the population).[21] For the peasants and slaves, Brazil's independence from Portugal in 1822 had not produced the anticipated benefits or the removal of the Portuguese elites. An additional peasant complaint concerned the military draft, whereby the free peasants (if captured) had to serve seven years in the police, the army, or the militia. The installation of a new conservative provincial legislature and provincial president in 1836 and 1837 prompted stricter interpretations of laws and a corresponding increase in opposition.

War erupted when the interests of three groups—liberals, peasants, and slaves—coalesced in opposition to the conservative provincial administration. The liberals, called *bentevi* or *bem-te-vis* (hummingbirds) after the local liberal newspaper, feared losing their positions of influence. A peasant, Francisco dos Anjos Ferreira, nicknamed *Balaio* (basket maker—the origin of the name of this war), may have had two grievances: some claim he was motivated by vengeance, believing that local police had assaulted his daughter; others argue that *Balaio* was driven to action to free his son, who had been captured by military recruiters. After freeing his son in November 1838, *Balaio* announced that he would free all of the draftees, prompting others to act. At the same time, fugitive slaves began to form bands and organize themselves for resistance.

Narrative: The first action of the war was an assault on the prison of the village of Manga on December 13, 1838, by a band led by Raimundo Gomes. The band freed the prisoners, and the next day, Gomes demanded the dismissal of the provincial president and those who implemented the conscription policies. This became the rallying cry for the revolt, as peasants, some led by *Balaio*, flocked to join Gomes. As disorder spread in Eastern Maranhão, a former slave, Cosme Bento das Chagas, gathered 3,000 runaway slaves known as *quilombolas* at a former plantation. Violence escalated as the three rebel groups joined forces to lay siege to the liberal stronghold of Caxias (the second-largest city in the province) on May 24, 1839. The two liberal bands (*bem-te-vis*) of 2,000 peasant each, led by Raimundo Gomes and Balaio, were joined by a group of 3,000 runaway slaves led by Cosme. The government had only 1,000 soldiers there at the time under the leadership of João Paulo Dias. The rebels (swelling to a total of 11,000) took Caxias after a forty-six-day siege. There a provisional rebel government was established. The rebels then moved against the provincial capital São Luis and into the neighboring province of Piaui, but their advance was limited by the lack of support of the liberal elite in the capital.

The Brazilian government responded on December 2, 1839, by dispatching a talented military leader, Luís Alves de Lima e Silva (who would later become the baron, the count, marquis, and duke of Caxias) to quell the uprising in Maranhão. Arriving on February 4, 1840, Colonel Lima also was appointed as president of the province, giving him control over both elements of the national army and the provincial National Guard. He gathered an army of 8,000 and launched more than thirty small engagements per month. Meanwhile, the Rio de Janiero regency government was becoming increasingly unpopular, and there was a growing fear that Brazil would be torn apart before the young Pedro could assume the throne. On July 22, 1840, the legislature appealed to the fourteen-year-old future emperor to claim his majority early. He did so the following day (though the coronation wasn't until the following year). The first problem Pedro II tried to address was that of ending the conflicts in Brazil (including the ongoing Balaiada and Farroupilha wars). Colonel Lima once had served as Pedro's horsemanship and swordsmanship instructor, and the new emperor encouraged Lima to conclude the Balaiada war. Most of the fighting was over by mid-August, and many rebels surrendered during an amnesty period from August 22 to October 22, 1840. Raimundo Gomes himself surrendered on January 15, 1841. He was pardoned and sent on to São Paulo but died along the way.

Termination and Outcome: On January 19, 1841, Colonel Lima announced the pacification of Maran hão, which marks the end of the war and victory for the government. Cosme continued to resist the government until September 1842, when he was captured and hanged. In reward for this victory, Lima was promoted to brigadier, and Pedro II appointed him to the nobility, allowing him to choose his title. Lima selected the title of baron of Caxias to commemorate his recapture of the Maranhão city. The baron was soon dispatched by the emperor to conclude the Farroupilha war in the South (Intra-state War #526).

Coding Decisions: We have not located any fatality figures for the government during this war.

Sources: Academia de História Miltar Terrestre do Brazil (2010); Assunção (1999); Barman (1988); Bento (2002); Bethell and de Carvalho (1989); Burns (1993); Comissão Executiva Central do Sesquicentenário sa Independência do Brasil (1972); Correlates of War Project (2009); Fausto (1999); Gonçalves de Magalthhaes (1999); Treece (2000).

INTRA-STATE WAR #536

First Colombian War of 1840 to 1842 (aka War of the Supremes or War of the Convents)

Participants: Colombia versus Progressives.
Dates: July 15, 1840, to May 1842.
Battle-related Deaths: Colombia: [ ]; Progressives: [ ]; Total Combatant Deaths: 7,100.
Initiator: Progressives.
Outcome: Colombia wins.
War Type: Civil for central control.
Total System Member Military Personnel: Armed Forces of Colombia: 6,000 (prewar); 20,000 (initial); 25,000 (peak); 6,000 (final).[22]

Theater Armed Forces: Armed Forces of Colombia, aided by Ecuador (a non-state actor), participating from August to October 1840: more than 1,000 (peak).[23] Progressive *Caudillos* (Rebel Aggregate): 200 (initial)[24] aided by Royalists (Rebel Army), participated until Noguera was killed by Obando; 800 (peak).[25]

Antecedents: A rebellion against Spain led by Simón Bolívar achieved the independence of the Viceroyalty of New Granada in 1819. The new Gran Colombia/ Republic of Colombia (with Bolívar as its first president) consisted of what would become modern-day Colombia, Panama, Venezuela, Ecuador, and northwest Brazil. Gran Colombia was involved in a brief war with Peru (1828–1829, Non-state War #1512) over Bolívar's aim to unite the two. Venezuela and Ecuador withdrew from the republic in 1830. In 1839, President José Ignacio de Márquez and the congress attempted to enforce an 1821 order to close small monasteries and convents. The predictable reaction was a pro-clerical rebellion in the southwestern conservative province of Pasto, ostensibly led by Padre Francisco de la Villota, whereupon the provincial government of Antonio José Chavez reached a settlement halting the closures. The central government refused to accept this agreement, and an army of 2,000 government troops suppressed the revolt by several hundred Indians at the Battle of Buesaco on August 30, 1839, though fatalities were not at war level. The monasteries were closed the next month.

The moderate government then faced a new challenge, this time launched by the progressives who wanted to remove the president, led by the southern liberal caudillo José María Ramón Obando del Campo. Obando had had a military career before becoming vice president and acting president (1831–1832). Obando ran for the presidency in 1837 but was defeated by Márquez. Obando retired to his hacienda of Las Piedras near the southern city of Pasto, and he avoided involvement in the 1839 uprising. However, the government (seeking to discredit Obando for future political office) launched a prosecution of Obando for allegedly murdering revolutionary hero Antonio José de Sucre a decade before. Obando traveled to Popayán (the capital of the southwestern province of Cauca) to clear his name. However, given the political situation, on January 26, 1840, Obando led a force of 200 Afro-Colombian and Indian supporters in a brief revolt against the central government. Skirmishes began almost immediately, although government commander Gen. Pedro Alcántara Herrán convinced Obando to accept an amnesty for rebellion and submit to a trial for Sucre's murder.

Narrative: Since his political enemies had control of the judicial process, Obando continued to Pasto, where he formally pronounced his rebellion against the government in July 1840. He declared himself to be supreme director of the war in Pasto, general in chief of the Restoring Army, and protector of the religion of Christ crucified and called for the ousting of President Márquez and the creation of a more federal system of government. At the same time, a royalist rebellion was launched in Pasto by Andrés Nogueras with up to 800 men; he occasionally coordinated his activities with those of Obando. Following Obando's pronouncement, a string of local "liberal" *caudillos* initiated revolts, declared their provinces to be sovereign states, and also assumed the title of *jefes supremos* (supreme heads) of their provinces—hence the alternative naming of this war.

The revolt shifted to a national conflict over federalism, and soon twelve of the twenty provinces were controlled by rebels, four partially controlled by rebels, and only four in the hands of the central government. Márquez asked Ecuador president Juan José Flores for military assistance. Because Obando was calling for a revolution in Ecuador against Flores, Flores was willing to help, and he led Ecuadoran troops northward toward Pasto to assist in the suppression of Obando's revolt. The Colombian army under General Herrán occupied Pasto, and with the aid of the Ecuadorans and troops led by Gen. Tomás Cipriano de Mosquera, General Herrán defeated Obando at Huilquipamba on September 29, 1840. Obando fled northward, and President Flores returned to Ecuador.

Rebels in the North led by Manuel González, Juan José Reyes Patria, and Juan Gómez defeated the government army led by Col. Manuel María France and Maj. Alfonso Acevedo at La Polnia on September 29, 1840. The rebel success prompted rebels in Panama to join the war in November 1840. As Bogotá was relatively undefended, González led the rebel army toward the capital, but a government army led by colonels Juan José Neira and José Vargas Paris, aided by local citizens, defeated the rebels at the battles of Buenavista and Culebrera at the end of

October. Yet, it took General Herrán and the army's effective core of 5,000 soldiers another eighteen months to suppress the uprisings. González retreated northward, where he was defeated by a government army led by General Mosquera (which had returned from the south) on January 9, 1841. Meanwhile, in the West and South, government advances continued, and on July 11, 1841, Obando was defeated decisively in a bloody battle at La Chanca by government forces led by Col. Joaquín Barriga.

Termination and Outcome: Even though General Herrán was elected president, on May 2, 1841, he continued leading the government army until he defeated rebels led by Gen. Lorenzo Hernándes near Ocaña on September 9, 1841. General Mosquera then took command, and he continued to fight the rebels until May 1842, when the rebellious regions had been reintegrated into Colombia.

The defeat of the progressives led to a conservative restoration in which the Catholic Church regained its prerogatives, and to the conservative government's protection, and even to the expansion of slavery. Obando went into exile in Peru and then Chile. He returned in 1849 and was elected president in 1853.

Coding Decisions: Some authors include the earlier 1839 revolt as part of this war, though we see these as different conflicts. There is also some disagreement concerning the aims of this war—and thus its war type. Some describe it as a series of individualized proclamations of secession or autonomy by the *caudillos* and thus see it more as a civil war for local issues (autonomy and independence). Here the war is seen as a more overarching drive to replace the central government and overhaul the entire structure of the government into a more federal system.

In terms of battle-deaths, little specific information is available. Deaths due to disease were particularly high among government forces, which would lose nearly half the men from desertion and disease. For instance, in Pasto, the army lost only 200 dead in battle, but 746 died in its military hospital of wounds or disease. The execution of prisoners was also common. The most comprehensive number we have found was a total of 7,100, though there was no division among the parties involved.

Sources: Earle (2000); Henao (1938); Henao and Arrubla (1938); Jaques (2007); Mejia (1976); Richardson (1960); Safford and Palacios (2002); Scheina (2003a).

INTRA-STATE WAR #538

First Argentina War phase 2 of 1841 to 1842

Participants: Argentina versus Unitarios.
Dates: January 1, 1841, to December 6, 1842.
Battle-related Deaths: Unitarios: 4,000; Argentina: 1,800.
Initiator: Unitarios.
Outcome: Argentina wins.
War Type: Civil for central control.
Total System Member Military Personnel: 7,000 (initial).[26]
Theater Armed Forces: Armed Forces of Argentina: 10,000 (initial).[27] *Unitarios*: 3,500 under Lavalle (initial),[28] aided by Uruguay: 7,500 (peak).[29]

Antecedents: After gaining independence, the United Provinces of the Rio de la Plata (the future Argentina) were embroiled in a series of military conflicts over the makeup of its new government, with the *Unitarios* favoring a strong central government and the federalists favoring more autonomy for the provinces. Because the federalist ideal had dominated under the 1819 constitution, there was no head of state, but disputes over the desired degree of unity would continue to bedevil the provinces. The larger of these conflicts were non-state wars (#1503, #1513, #1518, and #1527) because Argentina was not a member of the interstate system until 1841.

In the 1829 war (Non-state War #1513), a coalition of federalists (including Juan Manuel de Rosas) overthrew the Unitarian governor of Buenos Aires, Juan Galo Lavalle, and Rosas was installed as governor. He served until 1832 and was reelected in 1835 as well as serving as head of the Federalist Party. A mass movement of his supporters was known as *La Mazorca*, represented by an ear of corn to symbolize the unity of the people. Rosas was given absolute power, which he used to suppress the liberal opposition, the *Unitarios*. The *Rosismo* movement promoted a totalitarian regime, required citizens to wear red (the color of the federalists), and launched a campaign of state terrorism (including executions) against Rosas's opponents. The governors of

Buenos Aires Province were given the power to manage the international relations of the United Provinces, and in this role, Rosas led Argentina (along with Chile) to declare war against the Bolivia–Peru Confederation of the Andes (Non-state War #1523 in 1837–1839).

Many of the *Unitarios*, including Lavalle, had fled to Uruguay, where they formed a coalition with Uruguay's Colorados, led by Frustuoso Rivera, and overthrew Uruguay's Blanco president, Manuel Oribe, who then fled to Buenos Aires on October 24, 1838, where he joined Rosas's army. The new Uruguayan government then declared war against Rosas specifically (not against Argentina) on February 24, 1839 (Non-state War #1527). Five of the northern provinces entered a coalition against Rosas, and their 2,000-man army advanced to join with Lavalle in Córdoba province. Meanwhile, Rosas had amassed an army of 10,000 and placed Oribe at its head. Oribe's troops pursued Lavalle as he marched westward. At Quebracho Herrado, a battle between Lavalle's 4,600 troops and Oribe's 6,500 federalists on November 28, 1840, was an overwhelming victory for Oribe, who lost few men compared to almost 2,000 *Unitarios* deaths. Lavalle withdrew to the North and attempted to reconnect with the coalition forces commanded by Col. Major Gregorio Aráoz de Lamadrid.

Narrative: The non-state war was still ongoing as of the end of 1840. However, on January 1, 1841, Argentina, with Rosas as president, became a member of the COW interstate system. Thus the conflict was transformed from a non-state war into this intra-state war (phase 2), which begins on that date.

Both Lavalle and Lamadrid retreated northward toward Tucumán province, with Lavalle trying to delay Oribe's advance. A secondary column led by Col. José María Vilela was surprised and decimated (400 rebels killed) during the night of January 19, 1841, by a smaller federalist cavalry force commanded by Gen. Ángel Pacheco. LaValle then moved on to Tucumán, where he and Lamadrid created a new plan: Lavalle would remain in Tucumán, where he would join forces with Tucumán's governor and await the arrival of Oribe, while Lamadrid with a new army would move toward the Cuyo region along Argentina's western border. Lavalle and Oribe met again at Famaillá on September 19, 1841, where the 2,400 federalists defeated the 1,400 *Unitarios*, with 600 rebels killed. Lavalle fled northward toward Bolivia with 200 men but was killed by federalist troops on October 9, 1841, thus ending the war in the Northeast.

In the West, La Rioja province had joined the northern coalition, and while waiting for Lamadrid to arrive, Unitarian Gen. Mariano Acha advanced from toward the city of San Juan, which he captured on August 13, 1841. A small federalist force led by Gen. Nazario Benavídez was soon joined by the main Federalist Army of the West under the command of José Félix Aldao. On August 16, Acha arrayed his 500 troops to await the federalist army and the Battle of Angaco. Benavídez and the cavalry charged first, and when they faltered, the infantry led by Aldao attacked. The Unitarian positions held, and the battle is one of the bloodiest of the war, costing 200 rebel and 1,000 federal deaths. Fortunes were reversed two days later, when Benavídez surprised Acha's force, and 150 *Unitarios* were killed, including Acha, who was executed.

In the wake of Acha's defeat, the main northern coalition army of 1,600 men commanded by Lamadrid arrived and met the federalist armies under generals Aldao and Pacheco with 3,000 troops at the Battle of Rodeo del Medio on September 24. The outnumbered rebels were defeated, suffering 400 deaths in the battle and subsequent slaughter, in comparison to 18 federalist deaths. Several hundred of the rebels tried to flee to the Andes, where more than 100 died. Resistance in the North was reignited later that year by Brigadier Gen. José María Paz y Haedo. By November 26, 1841, Paz felt that his army of 5,000 was ready to attack the 5,000-man federalist army, and the federalists were routed in the Battle of Caaguazú, suffering 1,350 casualties.

Paz carried on the struggle for another year before fleeing to Uruguay in 1842. There were several naval engagements between the federalists and the Unitarians aided by Uruguayans. Three of the Uruguayan ships were commanded by Italian patriot Giuseppe Garibaldi, who had fled to Uruguay after the defeat of the rebels in Brazil's Rio Grande do Sul (Intra-state War #526). In October 1842, Uruguay's President Rivera signed an alliance with the *Unitarios* and took command of a joint Unitarian–Uruguay army. Rivera crossed into Entre Ríos with a 7,500-strong army and confronted the 8,500-man federalist force led by Oribe. In the Battle of Arroyo Grande on December 6, 1842, Rivera was defeated, with 2,000 rebel deaths, while the federalists suffered 300 deaths. This battle ends the war.

Termination and Outcome: This war ended as a victory for the Rosas government. However, the conflict between Argentina and Uruguay continued. Rosas mounted a siege of the Uruguayan capital of Montevideo on February 16, 1843, thus beginning Extra-state War #327: Uruguay War of 1843 to 1851.

Coding Decisions: Small and Singer originally coded this as one long civil war from 1841 to 1851 because the civil war aspects became enmeshed with the war against Uruguay. Subsequently, COW divided this period into this intra-state war and an extra-state war (#327). It was classified as extra-state because Uruguay did not become a member of the interstate system until 1882.[30]

We have been unable to locate any comprehensive battle-death statistics for this war. Our summation of figures reported for individual battles, mostly from Marley, yields totals of 3,850 *Unitarios* deaths and 1,651 federalist deaths. As these figures do not include figures for all engagements of the war, nor do they include the deaths of soldiers who were subsequently killed, executed, or died from their wounds, we are reporting rounded figures of 4,000 and 1,800, respectively, here, though these may well be underestimates.

Sources: Acevedo (1934); Best (1960); Cady (1929); Crow (1971); Jaques (2007); Kirkpatrick (1931); Lynch (1992); Marley (1998); Munro (1942); Scheina (2003a); Williamson (2009).

INTRA-STATE WAR #548
First Venezuela War of 1848 to 1849

Participants: Venezuela versus Páez-led Rebels.
Dates: February 4, 1848, to August 15, 1849.
Battle-related Deaths: Venezuela: 1,500; Páez-led Rebels: 500. (See Coding Decisions.)
Initiator: Páez-led Rebels.
Outcome: Venezuela wins.
War Type: Civil for central control.
Total System Member Military Personnel: Not coded by COW at this time.
Theater Armed Forces: Armed Forces of Venezuela: 2,000 (prewar); 6,000 (initial); 10,000 (peak); 5,000 (final).[31] Figures include mobilized militia. Páez-led Rebels (Rebel Aggregate): 800 (initial); 3,000 (peak); 649 (final).[32]

Antecedents: After Venezuela gained its independence from Gran Colombia in 1830, the weakness of its central government contributed to the increasing power of its leading *caudillos*. Initially the dominant *caudillo* was José Antonio Páez Herrera, who had been instrumental in the drive for independence and served as president from 1830 to 1835. After a brief interregnum, Páez was succeeded as president in 1835 by José María Vargas, who resigned in 1836 and was succeeded by several caretaker governments before Páez was reelected to the presidency from 1839 to 1843. Páez then secured the election of fellow conservative Carlos Soublette as his successor from 1843 to 1847. By this time, those dissatisfied with Páez's continued influence formed the Liberal Party to oppose him. Minor liberal revolts occurred in June and September 1844.

As Soublette's term in office was ending, Páez supported fellow conservative José Tadeo Monágas for president. Monágas was elected and took office on March 1, 1847. Monágas soon abandoned his alliance with Páez and the Conservative Party and began appointing liberals to the government. Monágas reduced the size of the regular army to 2,500 in May, and new reserve militias were organized, numbering 22,000 by January 1848. Though Monágas supported legislation that rewarded liberals, his alliance with them disintegrated as it became clear that Monágas was trying to increase his own power relative to that of the oligarchs (who could command a bipartisan majority in Congress). Fear of the new militias kept Congress in check until early 1848, when the conservatives began discussing the possible impeachment of Monágas, and Congress established an armed guard for its protection. On January 24, 1848, Congress assembled in a convent, guarded by 30 young men. Outside, a detachment of the government militia gathered, as did a pro-Monágas mob. Hearing that a governmental minister had been detained by the Congress, the crowd and militia stormed the building, and 8 people were killed, at least half of them members of Congress. Monágas demanded—and received—extraordinary powers from a cowed Congress, using these to call up 10,000 militia.

Narrative: On February 4, 1848, Páez denounced the attack and began a rebellion against the government. His call to arms attracted at least 800 and as many as 3,000 men, mostly forces raised by *caudillos* of the West, including former rebel general Ezequiel

Zamora and former president Soublette. Páez soon had control over the northwestern coastal province of Coro. The government's army quickly increased in size to 6,000 men. As the government army approached, Zamora withdrew his 1,300 men, and Páez was forced to fight at Los Araguatos in the southwestern province of Aspure with a force of 500 untrained recruits, and the rebels were crushed. With only 12 men, Páez escaped Venezuela, finding refuge on several Caribbean islands. The rebels had more success at sea, when the commander of one of only two government warships, carrying 6,000 muskets and a considerable amount of money, defected to the rebels. The government then assembled a much stronger naval force and blockaded the rebel-held port of Maracaibo. Páez briefly joined the rebels at Maracaibo but soon retreated to St. Thomas from which he still tried to oversee the war. In early April, the conservatives of the West were defeated on land in the Battle of Taratara, and the remnants of the rebel forces fled to Maracaibo.

The most deadly battle of the war was fought in May 1848, when the government mounted an unsuccessful amphibious assault that cost it 1,000 soldiers. The outnumbered rebels retreated on May 30 to the fort at San Carlos Island, overlooking Maracaibo. The rebel navy, with 344 men, launched a series of inconsequential raids, until September 2, when they managed to outmaneuver the larger government navy and retake Maracaibo. Further indecisive naval engagements occupied the two sides for another few months. On December 23, 400 rebels left the island of San Carlos and proceeded to occupy the village of San Carlos on the mainland, where recruiting increased their numbers to 1,200. Yet they were surprised and defeated on December 31 by a much smaller government force. Monágas declared victory on January 20, 1849, but a small cadre of rebels remained in the Caribbean with Páez.

The conservatives once again proclaimed a revolt on June 21, unsuccessfully attempting to assassinate Monágas on June 24. On July 2, Páez landed at La Vela de Coro to take command of about 2,000 rebels. However, Páez was unable to link up with rebels in the *llanos* (eastern plains), who were defeated in a series of bloody engagements by July 22. By this point, Páez had only 750 to 800 men under his command as he tried to cross into the *llanos*. On August 12 or 13, his forces were surrounded by 4,000 to 5,000 government troops. He negotiated terms and surrendered on August 15, 1849.

Termination and Outcome: The outcome of the war was an unconditional government victory with a partial amnesty for the rebels. Páez was at first imprisoned in violation of the accord but then permitted to leave for exile in the United States. Monágas and his brother then dominated the country for over a decade. Páez returned to Venezuela in 1858 and in 1861 once again became president.

Coding Decisions: Battle-death statistics for this war are difficult to find. One estimate put casualties at up to 8,000. Given that one naval battle alone resulted in the deaths of 1,000 government soldiers, we take the 8,000 figure to be the best available. Given the usual ratio of 3 wounded to 1 killed, 8,000 casualties amounts to about 2,000 battle-deaths.

In terms of the start and end dates of this war, there was a period (December 31, 1848–June 21, 1849) during which no fighting apparently took place. COW codes periods of temporary interruptions when wars stop and restart (producing a second set of start and end dates). However there must be a truce, cease-fire, or armistice agreement that stops the fighting for more than thirty days and less than a year to ensure that all the parties to the war understand and agree that fighting has stopped, which was not true in this case.

Sources: Clodfelter (2002); Crichfield (1908); Irwin (2008); Lynch (1992); Marsland and Marsland (1954); Morón (1964); Páez (1862); Paul (1974); Phillips and Axelrod (2005); Scheina (2003a); Wise (1950).

INTRA-STATE WAR #555

First Chilean War of 1851 to 1852 (aka Chilean Civil War of 1851)

Participants: Chile versus Liberals.
Dates: September 5, 1851, to January 8, 1852.
Battle-related Deaths: Liberals: 2,500; Chile: 1,500.
Initiator: Liberals.
Outcome: Chile wins.
War Type: Civil for central control.
Total System Member Military Personnel: Armed Forces of Chile: 3,000 (prewar, initial, peak, final).[33]
Theater Armed Forces: Armed Forces of Chile: 2,266 (prewar); 3,239 (after initial defections and mobilizations); 6,000 (peak).[34] The peak figure includes: 150 Argentine mercenaries,

Bulnes's expeditionary force of 3,335, the 1,500 reinforcements raised in Talca, and at least 1,000 government soldiers besieging La Serena. Liberal Rebels: Aggregate of La Serena Rebels (2,000); Cruz-led Rebels (4,800); Copiapó Rebels (1,000): 7,800 (peak).[35]

Antecedents: After gaining independence in 1818 (through Extra-state War #302), Chile fought alongside Argentina to break up the confederation of Peru and Bolivia (Non-state War #1523 of 1837 to 1839). Chile was dominated politically by the rivalry between conservative landowners and liberal commercial interests who disagreed *inter alia* about the role of the Catholic Church. In 1850, the conservatives who were in power were split into factions over the presidential succession: President Manuel Bulnes Prieto had anointed the civilian Manuel Montt Torres as his successor, but he was distrusted as an unknown quantity by many conservatives, while being reviled as a reactionary by liberals. This split prompted some liberals to believe that they had a chance to win the presidency. However, the Chilean liberals were divided into three factions: conservative liberals who supported the reformist Manuel Vial; the radical *Sociedad de la Igualdad* (Society of Equality); and the anticlerical, pro-civil liberty, and to a lesser extent pro-federalist *Pipiolos* (the "youngs" upper-class liberals). What these factions shared was a common opposition to the imposition of Montt. On August 19, 1850, government supporters attacked a meeting of the *Sociedad de la Igualdad*, radicalizing the movement and swelling its membership. However, in November, the government disbanded the group and arrested its leaders.

From February to March 1851, the liberals united behind the candidacy of conservative war hero Gen. José María de la Cruz Prieto, a cousin of President Bulnes. Cruz's candidacy energized the opposition, and some of the younger liberals attempted an insurrection, bribing soldiers to create a 600-strong rebel army in Santiago, which unsuccessfully attempted to seize the barracks on Easter day, April 20, 1851. The next two months were dominated by the increasingly vituperative presidential campaign. On June 25 and 26, 1851, the government's machine delivered a predictable victory for Montt.

Narrative: Despite liberal charges of election fraud, Montt was proclaimed president-elect on August 31, but before he could take office, liberals in the northern cities of Valparaíso and La Serena rose in revolt on September 5 and 7, respectively. As Montt took office on September 18, 1851, the cities of Coquimbo in the North and Concepcion in the South then joined the revolt, and Cruz formally pronounced against the government from Concepcion on September 22. Liberals fled from Santiago, providing reinforcements to the contingent in La Serena. The government's immediate strategy was to: secure the central area of the country near the capital; rally its forces before more of them defected to Cruz; and then dispatch the army to confront the rebels. The rebels of La Serena moved south with a force of 1,000 toward Santiago. To oppose them, the government sent about 1,000 soldiers led by Col. Juan Vidaurre, and in the Battle of Petorca on October 14, the rebel force was defeated decisively, suffering seventy killed. Vidaurre then advanced and besieged La Serena. On October 28, in a liberal insurrection in Valparaiso, 600 rebels were defeated by 150 government regulars in mere hours, with a cost of forty deaths on both sides.

The northern revolt was limited in scope, but the southern one controlled much of the region. Of two regiments in Concepcion, one remained loyal, which constituted the government's only substantial forces in the South. On September 13, noted *pipiolo* Pedro Félix Vicuña persuaded prominent citizens to declare Concepción's independence, with the support of Cruz and his force of 4,000 infantry and cavalry. The rebels' strategy was to control the sea to maintain contact between the northern and southern sectors of the revolt. They captured two small commercial steamers, but British naval forces not only recaptured them but also blockaded the rebel-held port of Coquimbo.

Former president Bulnes personally commanded the army sent to suppress the rebellion in the South. His combination of militia, presidential guards, and loyalists numbered 3,335 infantry and cavalry, and on November 2, 1851, they advanced to meet the rebels. The southern rebels had 2,800 regulars and militia plus up to 2,000 Araucanian Indian volunteers. The two forces met near Chillán, east of Concepcion, and the rebels won a minor victory in the Battle of Monte de Urra on November 19, 1851. The government raised another 1,500 men at Talca, and Bulnes abandoned Chillán to march north and unite with these forces. Cruz pursued him with 3,411 men, and on December 8, the two forces met again in the Loncomilla Valley, about halfway between Santiago and Concepcion. The battle reduced the effective strength of both armies by two-thirds, killing 1,800 to 2,000 and wounding another 1,500. While both sides claimed victory, the government was in a better position to rebuild its forces. Bulnes received reinforcements and bribed a battalion of the rebels to defect to the government. Consequently, the two commanders opened negotiations, culminating in the Treaty of Purapel on December 14. Cruz agreed to surrender his forces and to recognize Montt as president. Although the rebels abandoned the blockaded port of Coquimbo, the treaty did not end the northern rebellion of La Serena. Moreover, an additional pro-Cruz rebellion had started in the northern city of Copiapó, with uprisings by miners in October and December 26. A government advance first took La Serena on December 31 and then defeated the Copiapó revolt on January 8, 1852; the next day, the Copiapó rebels surrendered.

Termination and Outcome: The outcome was a government victory with minor concessions as the negotiated settlement of Purapel put the country on the path to peace.

Coding Decisions: In terms of the onset of this war, some authors utilize the start date of April 20, 1851, thereby including the Easter rebellion. Because it seems distinct from the postelection uprisings, we consider it a separate (not war-level) event.

Concerning battle-related deaths, comprehensive estimates range from 2,000 to 4,000. Given the uncertainty surrounding Loncomilla and missing information for the siege at La Serena, we are reporting the most commonly cited total of 4,000 battle-deaths here.[36]

Sources: Bernstein (1965); Collier (2003); Collier and Sater (2004); Davis (1968); Hancock (1893); Mackenna (1862); Nunn (1976); Richardson (1960); Scheina (2003a); Williams, Bartlett, and Russell (1955).

INTRA-STATE WAR #557

First Peru War of 1853 to 1855 (aka Liberal Revolution)

Participants: Peru versus Liberals.
Dates: October 21, 1853, to January 7, 1855.
Battle-related Deaths: Peru: [ ]; Liberals: [ ]; Total Combatant Deaths: 4,000.[37]
Initiator: Liberals.
Outcome: Peru wins.
War Type: Civil for central control.
Total System Member Military Personnel: 11,000 (prewar, initial, peak, final).[38]
Theater Armed Forces: At its high point, the war involved a total of 20,000 men under arms.[39] Armed Forces of Peru: > 5,000 (peak). Liberating Army (Rebel Organization): greater than 3,500 (peak). Huarez Indians (Antigovernment Aggregate), participating from January 1854 to later that year: 2,000 (initial and peak.)[40]

Antecedents: Peru achieved its independence from Spain in 1824 through the military campaigns of José de San Martín and Simón Bolívar (Extra-state War #312). Later in 1825, Upper Peru declared its independence from Peru, naming itself Bolivia. Bolívar attempted to join both Peru and Bolivia to Gran Colombia against their wishes, leading to war in 1828 (Non-state War #1512), after which Peru was forced to evacuate disputed territory. The goal of reuniting Bolivia and Peru remained popular, prompting Bolivia's invasion of Peru in 1835 (Non-state War #1520), which was successful in producing the Bolivia–Peru Confederation, or the Confederation of the Andes. The confederation lasted for three years until it was dissolved as a result of a war against it by Argentina and Chile (Non-state war #1523). Peru then was included as a member of the COW interstate system as of 1839. The dream of Peru–Bolivia unity was still a political goal, however, prompting another war as Peru invaded Bolivia in 1841 (Extra-state War #325). Peru's defeat ended the plans for unity.

Peru experienced a period of stability under the presidency of Ramón Castilla y Marquesado (1845–1851). His successor, José Rufino Echenique, had an administration noted for graft. This issue, along with the treatment of blacks and Indians, led to widespread uprisings fueled by the liberals. One of Echenique's critics was Domingo Elías Carbajo, a wealthy landowner who had briefly served as president in 1844 and who unsuccessfully sought the presidency in 1851. Beginning in 1852, Elías wrote a series of articles charging Echenique with corruption, for which Elías was exiled to Ecuador.

Narrative: The war began on October 21, 1853, when a group of liberals under Elías rose in rebellion and advanced from their base in Ecuador to occupy the border town of Tumbes. They were defeated almost immediately. Elías returned to his land near the southern coastal town of Pisco, where he gathered his followers and proclaimed himself the political leader of the revolution. The next battle (over the town of Saraja) took place on January 7, 1854, between the rebels and government forces led by Minister of War Juan Crisóstomo Torrico, after which Elías was forced to withdraw to Chile. That same day, the town of Arequipa (located further south) revolted against the government. Castilla hesitated before joining the rebellion, but finally he boarded a ship sailing south to Arequipa. Arriving in mid-February, Castilla assumed leadership of the rebellion and its Army of Regeneration. While the government was able to gather an army triple the size of Castilla's by mobilizing local and police units, Torrico hesitated to advance on Arequipa as similar revolts broke out throughout the country. While some government soldiers were killed in rebel attacks and the rebels lost an engagement at Colca on April 18, the bulk of the government's army simply fell back toward the capital without a major fight. On April 14, Castilla was proclaimed provisional president. Leaving Elías in Arequipa, Castilla advanced northward to Cuzco, which he occupied after reaching an agreement with the city's leaders on May 1. He then spent forty days organizing his forces and ordering 4,000 rifles.

Meanwhile, other contenders entered the fray. In Arequipa, former president Manuel Ignacio de Vivanco Iturralde assembled an army, initially planning to join the rebels against Echenique, but instead, he broke his agreement with Castilla and moved southward to Islay province, where he aligned with Echenique. Castilla was thus boxed in-between the two governmental forces, yet his army continued to expand with the arrival of military leaders who had been exiled by Echenique, liberal partisans, and an increasing number of Indians who joined the rebels in appreciation of Castilla's July 5 decree abolishing the Indian tribute (tax). Castilla thereby harnessed an ongoing, low-level Indian rebellion to his cause. About 2,000 Indians fought against the government during 1854, but many were defeated and then conscripted into the government's own army; hundreds of these conscripts died in a ship sinking later that year.

Castilla, with his 3,500 men, decided to strike Echenique's army of 5,000 to gain control of the capital. The first engagements of the new campaign occurred on August 2, and by October 9, Castilla's forces were able to advance toward Lima. Shortly thereafter, the government dispatched a second army toward Arequipa under the command of General Moran. Elías's troops advanced to meet the government column at Alto del Conde, where the rebels were defeated and forced to retreat to Arequipa with 100 infantry and 80 cavalry on November 16. The citizens rallied to defend the city, which was attacked by the forces of both Vivanco and Moran on November 30 to December 1, 1854. On December 5, Castilla issued a proclamation abolishing slavery, apparently attempting to incite a slave rebellion. A four-day battle for Lima followed. At this point, the rebels outnumbered the government army, and the Battle of La Palma, fought from January 5 to 7, 1855, sealed the government's fate. Even though the rebel army suffered 1,000 deaths compared to the government's loss of only 500, Castilla was victorious, and Echenique and his forces fled while the "liberating army" marched into Lima.

Termination and Outcome: The outcome was a military victory by the rebels. Echenique was exiled following the war, though an amnesty law pardoned most of Echenique's followers. On July 14, 1855, Congress elected Castilla as Peru's new president.

Coding Decisions: In terms of deaths during this war, estimates of total deaths range from 4,000 to 5,000. Because it is known that civilians died in the fighting, we accept 4,000 as the highest plausible number of battle-deaths among combatants.

Sources: Basadre (1940); Basadre (1970); Marett (1969); Markham (1868, 1892); Munro (1942); Pike (1967); Reano (2002); Soto (1985); Stearns (2001); Thurner (1997).

INTRA-STATE WAR #557.3

Colombia's Barracks Rebellion of 1854 (aka Golpe de Cuartel)

Participants: Colombia versus Constitutionalists.
Dates: April 19, 1854, to December 4, 1854.
Battle-related Deaths: Colombia: 1,400; Constitutionalists: 600. (See Coding Decisions.)

Initiator: Constitutionalists.
Outcome: Constitutionalists win.
War Type: Civil for control of the central government.
Total System Member Military Personnel: 2,000 (prewar, initial, peak, final).[41]
Theater Armed Forces: Armed Forces of Colombia (includes the remaining Melo army and the National Guard): 10,000 (prewar and initial); 11,000 (peak); 4,600 (final).[42] *Constitutionalists* (rebel army): 200 (prewar); 4,600 (initial); 8,337 (peak, final).

Antecedents: In the First Colombia War of 1840 to 1842 (Intra-state War #536), the defeat of the progressives (led by southern *caudillo* and former acting president José María Ramón Obando del Campo) led to the presidency of Gen. Pedro Alcántara Herrán and a conservative restoration in which the Catholic Church regained many of its prerogatives. Obando went into exile in Peru and then Chile, where he remained until January 1, 1849, when then President Tomás Cipriano de Mosquera gave amnesty to all those who committed political crimes. Later that year, Obando's friend and fellow liberal, José Hilario López, assumed the presidency of New Granada (Colombia) and appointed Obando to political office until he was elected to the congress as a representative of the province of Bogotá.

At the time of the presidential election of 1853, the Liberal Party was divided in to three factions: the radicals; the Golgothas (the young, progressive liberals); and the older (more moderate) liberals called the Draconians because of their support for the death penalty. Draconians nominated Obando as their candidate, running against Tomás de Herrera (the Radical Party) and José de Obaldía (of the Golgothas). The Conservative Party abstained from the election. Obando won the election and was inaugurated on April 1, 1853, with Obaldía as vice president. One of Obando's first projects was to get approval for and implement the liberal Constitution of 1853, which *inter alia*, abolished slavery, expanded suffrage, and reduced the power of the Church. The constitution was too liberal for many Colombians, and Obando's support was fractured as both the conservatives and the Golgothas began planning coups. The Conservative and Radical Parties also alienated much of the professional military as both parties (for differing reasons) favored reducing the size of the army. On April 17, 1854, after just over a year in office, Obando was approached by liberal Gen. José María Melo (who, like Obando, had been active in the *Sociedad Democrática*), who asked him to suspend the government and create a provisional dictatorship. When Obando declined, he was overthrown in a bloodless coup and taken prisoner, as were other members of the government.

There was widespread support for the coup. However, as President Melo began implementing reforms, including forming "worker's battalions" to defend his new government instead of the army, he triggered opposition from both radical liberals and conservatives, who united under the label of *Constitutionalists.*

Narrative: On April 19, 1854, Col. Jose Maria Rojas Pinzon left Bogotá with 200 men to oppose Melo; the governor of Tequendama declared his opposition to Melo and called up the National Guard. The first recorded encounter between the Constitutionalists and the government was on April 21, although no casualties are reported. Most anti-Melo soldiers fled to the countryside, where they were organized under three generals (Rafael Mendoza, Joaquin Paris, and Roman Espina). The government army was about 2,000 regulars, plus 8,000 National Guardsmen. On June 10, Melo authorized an increase in the regular army to 8,000 men, resorting to conscription to fill the ranks. Many conscripts repeatedly mutinied when sent to the front line, weakening Melo's government. By August 17, the government claimed to have more than 11,000 soldiers, but it proved unable to win a series of battles in September that cost it hundreds of soldiers and further demoralized its forces. Both desertion and outright defection to the rebels increased dramatically that month, and by October 5, even Melo was claiming a strength of only more than 4,600, a clear decline from his army's peak strength. Moreover, disease took a heavy toll of both civilians and government soldiers fighting in the South.

The rebels decided that the time had come for an advance on Bogotá. Their forces almost doubled in a month, going from a combined strength of 4,600 (at the beginning of November) to 8,337 soldiers, so they were soon able to reorganize into two armies: the Division of the North (with 4,037) and the Division of the South (with 4,300). These armies advanced on Bogotá and Cali, taking both of them between December 2 and December 4. The fall of Bogotá marked the end of the war.

Termination and Outcome: The war ended with a complete rebel military victory. Melo fled to Costa Rica and then on to Nicaragua where he would assist the fight against Thomas Walker (Non-state War #1540: Filibuster War of 1856 to 1857). The presidency was vacant for more than two years until after an election in 1857, when conservative Mariano Ospina Rodríguez was chosen.

Coding Decisions: In terms of battle-related deaths, evidence is sketchy and fragmentary. A number of the sources refer to casualties, and using a standard 3:1 ratio of wounded to killed and the most conservative assumptions, there must have been at least 1,369 to 2,069 battle-deaths. Of course, none of the figures includes missing data or combatant deaths due to disease. Therefore, 2,000 is likely a conservative estimate of battle-deaths.

It is also evident from the table that in all the engagements where comparable data is available, government losses considerably exceeded those of the rebels. Given that government battle-deaths are about 70 percent of total identifiable battle-deaths, 1,400 is a reasonable estimate for the government's battle-deaths, and the best estimate for rebel battle-deaths is 600.[43]

Sources: Bushnell (1993); Henao and Arrubla (1938); Ortiz (2004); Picon (1972); Richardson (1960); Safford and Palacios (2002); Sanders (2004); Scheina (2003a).

INTRA-STATE WAR #557.8

Barquisimeto Rebellion of 1854

Participants: Venezuela versus Rodríguez-led Rebels.
Dates: July 12, 1854, to August 15, 1854.
Battle-related Deaths: Venezuela: minimal; Rodríguez-led Rebels: more than 1,000.[44]
Initiator: Rodríguez-led Rebels.
Outcome: Venezuela wins.
War Type: Civil war for central control.
Total System Member Military Personnel: COW does not code military personnel at this point.
Theater Armed Forces: Armed Forces of Venezuela: 10,000 (prewar); 7,000 (after initial defections); 7,000 (peak); 7,000 (final).[45] Rodríguez-led Rebels (Rebel Army): 3,000 (prewar); 3,000 (initial); 3,700 (peak); 1,000 (final).[46]

Antecedents: In 1849, the rebellion by former conservative president José Antonio Páez Herrera against his one-time ally, President José Tadeo Monagas, was defeated (Intra-state War #548). Monagas's victory was aided by the fact that he had begun to shift his political allegiance toward the Liberal Party. Páez went into exile in the United States, while Monagas remained in office until 1851. Monagas then created what came to be known as the *Monagato*, or the authoritarian Monagas Dynasty, when he supported his younger brother, Gen. José Gregorio Monagas, for the presidency. José Gregorio (who was inaugurated on February 5, 1851) was also a representative of the Liberal Party, and during his tenure, he signed an edict abolishing slavery on March 24, 1854.

However, the dictatorship of José Gregorio provoked a number of rebellions by both dissident liberals and conservatives in 1853, some favoring the return of Páez. Probably the most significant of these was a rebellion by 1,000 federalists in Cumaná that fell apart when an earthquake leveled the city and killed 200 of the rebels. All of the 1853 revolts were defeated by August, and the government responded to the opposition by increasing the size of its army to 10,000 men. The next summer saw unsuccessful revolts on June 15 and 28, 1854. By this time, plans for the next rebellion were already in motion, which united dissident liberals, Tadeista liberals, and conservatives as its core.

Narrative: On July 12, 1854, Juan Batista Rodríguez led 3,000 soldiers in revolt against Monagas near Barquisimeto, the capital of the northwest state of Lara. Rodríguez divided his forces into three battalions. The government moved quickly to respond to this major threat. On July 27, the battalion led by Rodríguez himself (now increased in size to 1,700 men) was destroyed in battle near Barquisimeto by 2,500 government soldiers. Three days later, another battalion of about 1,000 soldiers led by Antonio José Vásquez was also defeated. The third Portuguesa battalion dissolved itself and took to the hills to conduct a guerrilla war. Another uprising by 150 men was defeated on July 31, and the area of Barquisimeto was pacified by mid-August.

Termination and Outcome: The outcome of the war was a complete military victory by the government, with no amnesty for defeated rebels. Rodríguez and Vásquez were executed. José Gregorio remained in office until January 20, 1855, when José Tadeo Monagas would again assume the presidency.

Because he enjoyed serving as president, Monagas had a new constitution written that would allow him to run for a second consecutive term. Monagas won reelection, but the maneuver so angered the liberals and conservatives that they united in revolt against him (the Second Venezuela War of 1859 to 1863, Intra-state War #563, also known as the Federal War).

Coding Decisions: Because the degree of connectedness of this rebellion with the earlier Garcés revolt (on June 28, 1854) is unclear, we have not combined them and have coded this as a separate war, starting on July 12, 1854.

Sources: Marsland and Marsland (1954); Paul (1974); Scheina (2003a).

INTRA-STATE WAR #560

Second Peru War of 1856 to 1858

Participants: Peru versus Conservatives.
Dates: October 31, 1856, to March 7, 1858.
Battle-related Deaths: Peru: 1,000; Conservatives: 2,000. (See Coding Decisions.)
Initiator: Conservatives.
Outcome: Peru wins.
War Type: Civil for central control.
Total System Member Military Personnel: Armed Forces of Peru: 11,000 (prewar); 11,000 (initial); 12,000 (peak); 12,000 (final).[47]
Theater Armed Forces: Conservatives (*Arequipa Caudillo Colectivo*): 1,800 (peak); 600 (final).[48]

Antecedents: In 1855, a revolt by liberals, supported by Indians, had toppled the conservatives from power (Inter-state War #557). During this war, forces in the southern coastal Arequipa province led by Manuel Ignacio de Vivanco were allied with the conservative Peruvian government. As a consequence of his victory in this war, liberal Ramón Castilla y Marquesado was elected to the presidency for a second term on January 5, 1855. Thus empowered, the parliamentary liberals launched a program of reforms, including reducing the power of the Roman Catholic Church, ending the Indian tribute, and abolishing slavery. The measures aroused a new conservative movement, and the government was faced with minor rebellions in January and July 1855. As a new constitution was being prepared in 1856, opposition spread, with conservative revolts in March, April, June, August, and September 1856. The new constitution, presented in October 1845, was ultimately a compromise between the liberals and conservatives, yet even Castilla objected to some of its provisions, and conservatives soon launched a new revolt.

Narrative: The war began on October 31, 1856, when a group of young men of leading families in the city of Arequipa revolted. They were joined by the troops stationed in the area and soon had seized control of the city. The next day, they declared Vivanco (who was in Chile) as president. At that time, Peru's navy consisted of three ships; the *Apurímac*, the *Loa*, and the *Tumbez*. On November 16, 1856, the *Apurimac* stopped at the southern port of Arica. Here younger officers mutinied and seized the ship in the name of the revolt. The *Apurímac* then sailed north toward the province of Islay (in the Arequipa region), where it was joined by the *Loa* and the *Tumbez*. Vivanco arrived in December, and he boarded the *Apurímac* and sailed to several ports seeking support.

In April 1857, Vivanco and a number of troops sailed to Callao, the seaport west of the capital of Lima. They disembarked and confronted the local National Guard, which had been reinforced with 400 North American and European soldiers. The combined forces were able to repel the rebels, with numerous fatalities and more than 400 prisoners taken. Vivanco returned to the city of Arequipa. The rebels, still centered in Arequipa, became known as the *Caudillo Colectivo*, a loose association of *caudillos*. Meanwhile, Castilla commissioned an old steamboat, the *Santiago*, which he sailed to Arica, where he organized an army of 3,000 to march toward Arequipa. Negotiations were attempted on June 19 but were soon broken off. The rebels, amounting to 1,800 men (including 500 defecting National Guardsmen), attacked the government forces on June 29, 1857, routing them at the Battle of Yumina, in which government losses (killed, wounded, captured, or dispersed) amounted to 1,200. Three days later, government forces lost again at the Battle of Cerro Gordo. Castilla then began an eight-month siege of Arequipa. The rebels and *cholos* or half-castes in the city began digging trenches and setting up barricades. In early 1858, the rebel-controlled *Apurímac* (with future president Lizardo Montero Flores on board) captured Arica. This persuaded Castilla that the rebellion had to be defeated. On March 5, 1858, Castilla launched a decisive attack against Arequipa itself. Initially, two battalions under General San Roman attacked the area of the church with artillery, forcing the rebels to retreat to the San Pedro area. San Pedro had been fortified, and a fierce battle took place: a force of 600 *cholos* (paid by Vivanco) aided the defense, and 540 of them fell at the barricades. The rebels then fell back to the convent of Santa Rosa. After the initial assault was thrown back, a second attempt on March 7 succeeded. During this assault, Vivanco fled to Chile. The rebels abandoned Arica, and Montero surrendered the *Apurímac* at Callao.

Termination and Outcome: The outcome was an unconditional government military victory. Even though the conservatives were defeated, an element of their program was achieved when Castilla disbanded the liberal assembly, and a new, more workable, constitution was framed in 1860 (it endured until 1920). Castilla served as president until 1862, and Grand Marshal San Roman succeeded him. However, Castilla's opposition to subsequent governments led to his exile in Gibraltar and Chile before his death in 1867.

Coding Decisions: In terms of theater armed forces, most of the male population of Arequipa fought against the government by the end of the war, but specific numbers at any one point in time are scarce.[49] In terms of battle-deaths, the commonly cited figure is 3,000 total combatant deaths.[50] Some sources describe the rebels having experienced 2,000 battle-deaths, and if we accept that, it generates an estimate of 1,000 government battle-deaths.

Sources: Basadre (1940); Marett (1969); Markham (1868, 1892, 1968); Munro (1942); Pike (1967); Ripley and Dana (1861).

INTRA-STATE WAR #562.5

Constituent Revolution of 1859

Participants: Chile versus Constituents.
Dates: January 5, 1859, to May 12, 1859.
Battle-related Deaths: Chile: [ ]; Constituents: [ ]; Total Combatant Deaths: 2,000.
Initiator: Constituents.
Outcome: Chile wins.
War Type: Civil for central control.
Total System Member Military Personnel: Chile: 4,000 (prewar); 4,000 (initial); 4,000 (peak); 4,000 (final).[51]
Theater Armed Forces: Chilean Armed Forces: 2,695 (prewar); 2,695 (initial); 7,000 (peak); 7,000 (final).[52] Constituent Army (Rebel Army): 1,000 (initial); 2,700 (peak); 700 (final).[53] *Montoneras* (Rebel Aggregate): 200 (initial armed force at Talca); 2,000 (peak—may be an underestimate).[54]

Antecedents: After liberal opponents of Chile's conservative president Manuel Montt Torres were crushed in the First Chilean War of 1851 to 1852 (Intra-state War #555), Montt was able to complete his five-year term and have himself reelected to another term in 1856. However, his autocratic rule alienated both liberals and conservatives as well as anticlericals and Catholics. For the legislative elections of 1858, both traditional parties formed the Liberal–Conservative Fusion to oppose the president's new National Party. Agitation increased toward the end of the year, when liberals and radicals demanding constitutional reform proposed a meeting to form a reformist society, to be held on December 12, 1858. The government forbade the meeting, broke it up, and arrested 150 who attended. Fusionists responded by planning a revolution.

Narrative: The Fusionists planned simultaneous uprisings in five cities—San Felipe, Valparaíso, Concepción, Talca, and Copiapó—to take place on January 5, 1859, which marks the start of the war. The army remained loyal to the government, and all but the northern Copiapó revolt were quickly suppressed. In Copiapó (the capital of the Atacama Region), the militias supported the liberal rebels, and wealthy miner Pedro León Gallo was proclaimed leader of the revolution on January 6. He used his wealth to build a Constituent Army of 1,000. Government forces sent to the region were beset with illness. On January 27, the rebels took Vallenar after a day of combat, and the government abandoned the Atacama to Gallo.

Meanwhile, Talca (south of the capital) joined the revolt on January 19 with about 400 to 500 revolutionaries armed with only 200 rifles. A government force sent to retake the city found the defenders entrenched and hesitated to attack. Guerrilla bands called *montoneras* sprang up around the area; one of about 500 men was led by Juan Antonio Pando. Another, led by wealthy rancher Antonio Arce, failed to take Chillán but briefly occupied Parral on January 27 and Linares the next day. A force of 600 to 800 guerrillas under Alemparte Lastra took Talcahuano then attacked Concepción on February 2. The attack was a total failure, resulting in sixty total deaths, most suffered by the rebels. On February 10, Arce's band was destroyed by government forces, and Talca was abandoned by the guerrillas by the end of the month. Guerrillas were defeated at San Felipe and Valparaíso (north of the capital) on February 28, 1859. While the guerrilla war in the middle of the country was being crushed, Gallo moved south, toward the capital. After a 300-mile march through the Atacama Desert, his force of about 1,400 soldiers met and defeated a government force of 1,600 at the Battle of Los Loros on March 14, 1859. The government suffered sixty to eighty killed, while the rebels suffered about forty-five killed. The rebels followed their victory at Los Loros by taking La Serena and Coquimbo.

The government continued to build its army, which reached a peak strength of 7,000 in April, while four rebel bands united into an army of about 2,000 poorly armed men. Operating under the command of Nicolás Tirapegui, the rebels moved north to attack Chillán. On April 12, they were defeated outside the city by a force of 1,000 government soldiers, with the rebels losing twenty killed and most of their rifles and artillery. The remnants of Tirapegui's army were destroyed nine days later.

The government now had enough strength to simultaneously attack the guerrilla bands and the Constituent Army. It sent 3,000 men to oppose Gallo in La Serena. The Constituent Army had 2,700 men, but one-third was unarmed. On April 29, the government attacked Gallo's forces at the hill of Cerro Grande. The Constituent Army was defeated when it ran out of ammunition and quickly disintegrated. Gallo and at least 70 rebels fled to Argentina. The government also defeated the last of the organized *montoneras* at Pichidegua on May 2.

Termination and Outcome: The outcome of the war was an unconditional government victory. More than 2,000 were deported by the government, and 31 were executed. After the war, Montt shifted his position on succession, from the ultraconservative Antonio Varas to the more moderate José Joaquín Pérez, who emerged as a consensus candidate.

Coding Decisions: Collier and Sater suggest a figure of 4,000 for the 1851 and 1859 wars combined. This would imply fewer than 2,000 battle-deaths in 1859, given our estimates for the 1851 civil war. Scheina credits the claim in Hancock that 5,000 were killed, yet given the number of deaths reported in the various engagements, this is probably a gross overestimate. We consider the most likely estimate to be 2,000 battle-deaths.

Sources: Collier (2003); Collier and Sater (1996, 2004); Hancock (1893, 2014); Legion de los Andes (2011); Rector (2003); Scheina (2003a); Zeitlin (1984).

INTRA-STATE WAR #563

Second Venezuela War of 1859 to 1863 (aka Federal War and the Long War)

Participants: Venezuela versus Liberals.
Dates: February 20, 1859, to May 23, 1863.
Battle-related Deaths: Venezuela: [ ]; Liberals: [ ]; Total Combatant Deaths: 40,000.
Initiator: Liberals.
Outcome: Liberals win.
War Type: Civil for central control.
Total System Member Military Personnel: 10,000 (prewar, initial, peak, and final).[55]
Theater Armed Forces: Armed Forces of Venezuela, aka Constitutionalists: 3,500 (after initial mobilization and defections); 5,000 (peak); 3,000 (final).[56] Liberals–Federalist Army: 2,000 (prewar); 3,000 (initial); at least 5,400 (peak); at least 5,400 (final).[57] No estimate of battle-deaths is available.

Antecedents: During the eleven years of Venezuela's Monagas Dynasty or Liberal Oligarchy (1847–1858, under José Tadeo Monagas and his brother José Gregorio), two civil wars (Intra-state Wars #548 and #557.8) and several smaller rebellions broke out, calling for the return of former conservative president José Páez. In 1857, José Tadeo Monagas instituted a new constitution that allowed him to seek another successive term as president. The move alienated both liberals and conservatives, producing a revolution supported by both, launched on March 5, 1858, by the liberal governor of Carabobo, Julián Castro Contreras. As entire units of the national army deserted to the revolutionaries, Monagas resigned on March 15, and Castro became president on March 18. As Castro was given dictatorial power, Monagas and fellow exiled liberals Gen. Juan Crisóstomo Falcón y Zavarce and Gen. Ezequiel Zamora began plotting a revolution. They were joined in St. Thomas by other disaffected liberals, including journalist Antonio Leocadio Guzmán and his son, future president Antonio Guzmán Blanco. Reportedly, Antonio Leocadio Guzmán provided the justification for the revolt—that of federalism—and many of the former liberals now referred to themselves as federalists. Back in Venezuela, there was more or less constant revolt in the hills, conducted by a variety of *caudillos*, bandits, and outlaw groups, and some of them, including a band of thousands led by Marlin Espinosa, began referring to themselves as federalists or *monaguistas*.

Narrative: The war began on February 20, 1859, when forty federalist rebels took control of the town of Coro near the western coast, roughly halfway between Caracas and Maracaibo. Seizing the opportunity, Zamora landed and, two days later, proclaimed a provisional government in nearby La Vela de Coro. Coming from exile in Trinidad, former Monagas army official Gen. Antonio Sotillo landed in the East. Most of the conflict was fought using guerrilla tactics, with only a handful of major pitched battles. Zamora began a southward drive to the *llanos* (plains) with 3,000 barely trained soldiers, attacking San Felipe and then Barinas on April 16. When government troops threatened to retake the town, the federalists burned it, destroying the wealthy community before withdrawing. A similar attack and hurried retreat destroyed Guanare on May 12 and 13. By the summer, Zamora centered control over most rebel forces by absorbing Manuel Espinosa's men after Espinosa was executed.

Meanwhile, Gen. Juan Falcón returned to Venezuela in July to provide political leadership to the federalists, and he was named the supreme chief of the rebel movement in August. At the same time, political conflict in Caracas prevented the government from acting as President Castro was ousted on August 2, 1859, by some of the more conservative constitutionalists. The conservatives were internally divided, with one faction seeking the return former president José Antonio Páez to office, while others favored a civilian government, like that of Manuel Felipe de Tovar, who took office on September 29, 1859. The rebels continued to win minor engagements. The conflict also had involved attacks against civilians by both sides, and by October the war had cost the lives of 15,000 to 20,000 Venezuelans.

The first large-scale battle of the war was the Battle of Santa Inés on December 10, 1859, in which 2,500 rebels defeated 3,200 government soldiers, inflicting 800 casualties on the government while suffering only 200 themselves. The tide turned against the rebels when Zamora was shot on January 10, 1860, and many rebel troops deserted as a result of his death, even though Falcón soon assumed leadership of the rebellion. Falcón and Sotillo joined forces, creating a federalist army (now 7,000 strong). On February 10, 1860, the federalists met 5,000 government soldiers at the Battle of Coplé, the second major battle of the war. The constitutionalists inflicted a crushing defeat on the Federalist Army with the rebel losses (killed, wounded, or taken prisoner) of 2,200, compared to 500 government losses. The rebel defeats fractured the federalists: Falcón remained political leader but fled the country. Falcón invited Antonio Guzmán Blanco to assume control of the Federalist Army, and the rebels fought a number of inconclusive engagements through the beginning months of 1861.

In March 1861, former dictator Páez was invited to return from exile to command the constitutionalist armed forces, and the intensity of fighting rose somewhat. Páez seized power later that year, becoming president on August 29, 1861. By 1862, the rebels had regained their footing, partly due to assistance from Colombia, and generally won small victories throughout the year. In August of 1862, Guzmán was able to unite the rebels in the center of the country, and they won a victory at Quebrada Seca on October 21, with only five government troops surviving the battle. The rebels won another major victory at the Battle of Buchivcoa, destroying a 2,500-strong constitutionalist force. As additional *caudillos* joined the rebels, they now controlled the majority of the countryside and began to advance on multiple fronts. By early 1863, the government controlled only to the Federal District, which was ringed by rebel armies. By April 14, 1863, the rebels were approaching Caracas itself, and over the next four days, the rebels won a string of battles in the Federal District and then entered Caracas.

Termination and Outcome: The capture of Caracas did not end all fighting, though it now was apolitical banditry rather than any organized or effective resistance to the new government. On May 23, 1863, representatives of both sides signed the Treaty of Coche, which marks the end of the war. The outcome of the war was a de facto rebel military victory, implemented in the form of a de jure negotiated compromise. Paez stepped down, and a power-sharing assembly was created with an equal number of federalist and constitutionalist appointees. Recognizing the military situation, on June 17 the assembly appointed Falcón and Guzmán as president and vice president, respectively. A new constitution for the country was written and passed on March 28, 1864, which created a federal form of government, and the country was renamed the United States of Venezuela.

Coding Decisions: The costs of this war were horrific. Some scholars indicated that 150,000 to 200,000 Venezuelans (or 8 to 11 percent of the population) died as a result of this war. These numbers include not only combatant battle-deaths but also civilian deaths, due to savagery during the war, and accompanying diseases. Specific figures for combatant deaths are difficult to locate. Small and Singer originally coded this war as having 20,000 total battle-deaths. More recent research by Clodfelter, Rudolph, and Rudolph cite a total of 40,000 combatant deaths. That figure is reported here.[58]

Sources: Alvarado (1975); Clodfelter (2002); Fortoul (1976); Gilmore (1964); Jaques (2007); Memoria de la Direccion General de Estadistica (1873); Marsland and Marsland (1954); Morón (1964); Munro (1942); Paul (1974); Phillips and Axelrod (2005); Rudolph and Rudolph (1971); Scheina (2003a); Spindler (1987); Stearns (2001); Tarver and Frederick (2005); *The Times* (1860, January 30); Williams, Bartlett, and Miller (1955); Wise (1950, 1970).

INTRA-STATE WAR #565
Second Colombian War of 1860 to 1862 (aka Colombian Civil War)

Participants: Colombia versus Liberals.
Dates: February 22, 1860, to October 13, 1862.
Battle-related Deaths: Colombia: [ ]; Liberals: [ ]; Total Combatant Deaths: 2,500 to 4,000.
Initiator: Liberals.
Outcome: Liberals win.
War Type: Civil for central control.
Total System Member Military Personnel: 1,000 (prewar, initial, peak, final).[59]
Theater Armed Forces: Armed Forces of Colombia (aka Legitimists): 1,000 (prewar); 600 (after initial defections); 5,000 (peak, final). Confederationists (Rebel Army): 2,000 (initial); 20,000 (peak, final).[60]

Antecedents: Since the death of Simón Bolívar in 1830, Colombian politics was dominated by the rivalry between the liberals (who promoted local government and the separation of church and state) and the conservatives (who favored a strong central government and preservation of rights for the Roman Catholic Church). In 1842, a revolt by the liberals was defeated (Intra-state War #536). Yet in 1849, liberal Gen. José Hilario López was elected president, and the liberals ruled until the Barracks Rebellion of 1854 (Intra-state War #557.3) prepared the way for the election of conservative Mariano Ospina Rodríquez in 1857. The next year, a new constitution created the Granadine Confederation, and its extreme decentralization encouraged both the liberals and conservatives to resort to armed combat in states where they were repressed by the opposition. The fighting grew fierce in late 1859, and President Rodriguez responded by attempting to recentralize power by granting the government the ability to use force against the states and bringing local militias under central control.

One such provincial conflict that was decisive in the development of this war occurred in the state of Cauca (southwest of the capital), whose governor was former president Tomás Cipriano de Mosquera y Arboleda. Mosquera had converted to the liberal cause and was faced by a conservative uprising within Cauca. Initially, limited fighting occurred in Cartago, but the conflict soon spread to the entire Cauca Valley. In January 1860, the central government moved to confiscate the weapons controlled by Mosquera and to provide assistance to the conservative rebels.

Narrative: Mosquera responded by allying himself to his onetime opponent in the 1840-to-1842 war (Intra-state War #536), former liberal president José María Obando. The military engagement starting the war, the Battle of Derrumbado, was fought on February 22, 1860, between Mosquera and Obando's force of 2,000 men and 600 government soldiers. Obando subsequently led rebel forces up the Cauca Valley, taking all of its towns. After these successes, Mosquera proclaimed the independence of Cauca on May 8, 1860, and announced the existence of the revolutionary movement of dissident liberals calling themselves confederationists in opposition to the government, or legitimists. Within the month, the northern states of Bolívar, Magdalena, and Santander also declared independence from the Granadine Confederation. The states formed a loose confederation with Mosquera as their political leader and as military commander. They soon won control of much of the Magdalena River, which runs west of Bogotá, allowing them to quickly shift their forces as needed.

In the North, the rebels did not fare as well. In Santander, a government offensive soon took most of the state, and a large battle on August 18 cost 600 lives. The government then reentered the Cauca Valley but was beaten back at the battle of the Hacienda de la Concepcion, near Palmira, on August 20. Meanwhile, Mosquera led a combined rebel force of 3,000 in an invasion of the conservative-controlled province of Antioqua (west of Santander). On August 12, the rebels won a victory at the Battle of Las Guacas. However, they soon found themselves unable to progress against an entrenched foe, and a prolonged stalemate ensued. In late 1860, a new government army was assembled by Julio Arboleda, equipped with modern artillery from Europe. It was initially deployed to Santa Marta in Magdalena, where it was besieged by the forces from the states of Magdalena and Bolivar from November 19 to December 11. Arboleda withdrew and redeployed his force to the Panamanian isthmus, whence he was able to attack Cauca by sea, taking Tumaco and advancing as far as Pasto by March 1861. The rebels retreated to Popoyan, the capital of Cauca.

At Santa Barbara on March 25, 1861, a 5,000-man legitimist army defeated the 2,700-man confederationist army, with high rebel losses. The same month, Mosquera's rebels unsuccessfully assaulted the trenches of Manizales (in the nearby state of Caldas) on March 28. When this attack failed, Mosquera asked the government for peace; however, President Ospina rejected the offer. Combat continued, and the war was becoming increasingly sanguinary. A campaign in Boyaca (north of the capital) from February to April 1861 killed hundreds or thousands more. On April 25, a government force of 4,325 troops was defeated, losing 2,000 killed, wounded, or taken prisoner against losses of only 125 dead and 244 wounded on the confederationist side. After Obando was killed in a skirmish on April 29, Mosquera assumed full control of the rebellion. He reorganized his army and began a campaign against Cundinamarca, which proved to be pivotal. On July 17, Mosquera won a crushing victory outside Bogotá: more than 600 prisoners were taken, including President Ospina and several top commanders, who were immediately sentenced to death. Up to 30 soldiers were shot on July 19, but Mosquera commuted the rest of the sentences to imprisonment.

Mosquera began his term as provisional president on July 18, 1861. The war was not over as three major legitimist armies remained in the field: Arboleda's in Cauca; one under Leonardo Canal in Santander; and *Antioquenos* under the command of Braulio Henao. Arboleda's forces continued to advance, taking Popoyan on August 10. The confederationist government forces resumed their offensives, winning a series of decisive victories in early 1862: Arboleda's force was defeated at the Battle of Silvia on January 11, 1862, and Canal was defeated at Cucuta on January 19, though both were able to reconstitute their armies in the Southwest. During a raid into Ecuador in pursuit of pro-Mosequera guerrillas, Arboleda's forces attacked an Ecuadorian garrison on June 19, costing him the goodwill of that country's president, Garcia Moreno. Indeed, Moreno prepared to retaliate with a tiny force of 800, but Arboleda struck first with his 3,500 legitimists at Tulcan, inflicting heavy losses and capturing Moreno. The two concluded a treaty of alliance, and Moreno was freed to return to Quito. Mosquera finally moved against Antioquia in September 1862, with a combined force of 2,100 of his men and another 600 liberals from Santander. On September 17, this force defeated 3,500 legitimists in the second Battle of Santa Barbara.

Termination and Outcome: On October 13, Antioquia surrendered to Mosquera, ending the war as a rebel victory. Only Arboleda and Canal remained in the field. Arboleda was assassinated on November 12, and Canal signed a peace agreement on December 29.

Coding Decisions: This coding of this war differs from other accounts (including Small and Singer) in considering February 22, 1860, as the start date rather than May 8, 1860. The difference depends upon how one describes the armed conflict that took place in Cauca in early 1860. Some see it as merely a provincial conflict, whereas we accept the judgment of General Mosquera, who described the conflict there as being fomented by agents of the general government and thus part of the broader civil war.

In terms of battle-deaths, Small and Singer originally coded this war as having 2,500.[61] Though we have no record of battle-deaths in most engagements, even the very limited figures we have add up to more than the 2,000 killed. Given the sheer amount of missing data on major engagements and the likelihood that disease took a toll during the three years of warfare, the real toll was probably at least twice that. Jurado notes that one historian claimed 10,000 were killed by the end of 1860, but that figure likely included civilian deaths. We report a battle-death range of 2,500 to 4,000, though that may be an underestimate.

Sources: Berthe (1889); Clodfelter (2002); "Colombia" (1879); Henao and Arrubla (1938); Jurado (2003); Kirkpatrick (1939); Kohn (1999); Llano (1997); Munro (1942, 1960); Payne (1968); Phillips and Axelrod (2005); Richardson (1960); Safford and Palacios (2002); Scheina (2003a); "United States of Colombia" (1862, March 7); Williams (1945).

INTRA-STATE WAR #573

Third Buenos Aires War of 1861 to 1862

Participants: Argentina versus Buenos Aires and Liberals.
Dates: August 20, 1861, to March 21, 1862.
Battle-related Deaths: Argentina: [ ]; Buenos Aires and Liberals: [ ]; Total Combatant Deaths: 1,000.
Initiator: Buenos Aires.
Outcome: Buenos Aires wins.
War Type: Civil central control.
Total System Member Military Personnel: Armed Forces of Argentina: 5,000 (prewar, initial, peak, final).[62]
Theater Armed Forces: Argentina: 5,000 (prewar, initial); 22,000 (17,000 under Urquiza plus 5,000 regulars, peak); 1,600 (final).[63] *Porteño* Army (Rebel Army): 15,500 (prewar, initial); 16,000 (peak, final)[64] aided by *Santiago del Estero Liberals* (Rebel Army): 2,000 (initial, peak), Tucumán Liberals (Rebel Army): 2,000 (initial, peak, final).[65]

Antecedents: The first Buenos Aires war was a non-state war (#1503) between the independent entity of Buenos Aires and the United Provinces of Argentina in 1820. The relationship between the two entities remained contentious, contributing to the Argentine War for Unity of 1829 to 1831 (Non-state War #1513) and the Anti-Rosas War of 1839 to 1840 (Non-state War #1527), which was transformed into a civil war (Intra-state War #538) when Argentina became a member of the interstate system in 1841. After the overthrow of Argentine dictator Manuel Rosas in 1852 during the LaPlata War (Inter-state War #19), the new director, and later president, of the Argentine Confederation, Justo José de Urquiza, angered *porteños* (residents of the city and province of Buenos Aires) by forming a coalition with the federalist *caudillos* who previously had supported Rosas. When a constitutional convention produced a document that would weaken the power of Buenos Aires, the province revolted on September 11, 1852, and fighting at below-war levels took place between Buenos Aires and Argentina. In 1854, a truce between the two governments was signed, which postponed the resolution of the status of Buenos Aires. In May 1859, Argentine officials voted to incorporate Buenos Aires forcibly into the confederation. Buenos Aires, led by Bartolomé Mitre Martínez mobilized, and the outcome of the subsequent war (Extra-state War #351) was the defeat of the *porteños* at the Battle of Cepeda on October 23, 1859. Buenos Aires and the confederation then negotiated a Pact of Union. In July 1860, Urquiza and new president Santiago Derqui visited Buenos Aires and met with Mitre, but the conciliatory spirit did not last. On April 1, 1861, the national congress convened, but federalists opposed to the hegemony of Buenos Aires and refused to seat its representatives. President Derqui ordered Buenos Aires to hold new elections for its deputies, but on April 25, Mitre refused. Both sides now initiated preparations for war. On June 11, Urquiza was named Argentina's commander in chief, and Derqui gathered an infantry at Córdoba that was augmented by Urquiza's cavalry from Entre Ríos. On July 5, the national congress declared that Buenos Aires had violated the Pact of Union and authorized intervention to suppress the rebellion. A series of unsuccessful negotiations followed, resulting in an agreement to delay the war by five days, which expired on August 20, and marks the start of the war.

Narrative: Mitre gathered his Buenos Aires army of 12,000 to 16,000 soldiers and marched into the province of Santa Fe, located west and across the Paraná River from the Entre Rios capital of Paraná. The first major combat of the war was the decisive Battle of Pavón, fought there on September 17, 1861, between equally sized armies led by Mitre and Urquiza. The confederation's poorly trained militia could not withstand the advance of the *porteño* infantry, and Urquiza quickly withdrew, leaving 1,650 prisoners in *porteño* hands. As the *porteño* army advanced toward Paraná, supportive liberal uprisings broke out in other confederation provinces, including 2,000 liberals commanded by José Maria del Campo, who rebelled in the northern Santiago del Estero province. Although a government army of 4,000 men defeated Campo's forces in the Battle of Arroyo Manantial on October 4, it was unable to restore confederation control of the province and eventually withdrew to Catamarca, while Urquiza retreated back to Paraná. Meanwhile, Mitre's forces occupied Rosario (in Santa Fe) in early October, which contributed to the collapse of the confederation government as Derqui resigned the presidency on November 5. Liberal rebellions began to take control of other federalist provinces, supported by troops from Buenos Aires. Uruguayan Colorados commanded by Venancio Flores crossed the border to assist Mitre and the liberals, and on November 22, a *porteño* cavalry column surprised 1,300 confederation soldiers, killing 300, while suffering only 2 killed. By the end of November, Urquiza agreed to the dissolution of the Argentine Confederation, and on December 13, 1861, the confederation dissolved, leaving Mitre as the country's de facto leader.

The war continued, however, as Mitre and the liberals attempted to reunite Argentina under the leadership of Buenos Aires against the remaining federalist opposition. On December 17, in the Battle of Seibal, Tucumán liberals defeated 2,400 federalists, and on February 10, they defeated a federalist force at Monte Grande. Confederation Gen. Ángel Vicente "Chacho" Peñaloza withdrew and moved against Rioja, occupying it without a fight on March 4, when its 600-strong *porteño* garrison retreated. One week later, Peñaloza's forces were cornered and defeated by the *porteños*. On April 3, 300 confederation partisans were defeated at Chañaral Negro. Nine days later, Peñaloza attacked again, only to be defeated with heavy losses. He besieged San Luis, then defended by only 300 men against his 1,600-strong force. But on April 21, forces loyal to Mitre arrived and raised the siege (which marks the end of the war). Peñaloza fled, and in June he signed a formal truce with the government of Buenos Aires.

Termination and Outcome: The outcome of the war was a rebel victory, as Peñaloza acknowledged the domination of Buenos Aires in a formal agreement known as the Treaty of La Banderita. Mitre then formed a new national government, and the capital was moved to Buenos Aires. The treaty was ultimately a failure as Peñaloza would rebel against the new government less than a year later (Intra-state War #580).

Coding Decisions: We have been unable to locate specific fatality statistics for this war. However, on balance, we conclude that this conflict met the 1,000 battle-death criterion for a civil war classification.

Sources: Best (1960); Bunkley (1950); Clodfelter (2002); De la Fuente (2004); Jaques (2007); Jeffrey (1952); Katra (1996); Kohn (1999); Marley (1998); Phillips and Axelrod (2005); Rock (2002); Scheina (2003a); Scobie (1955); Williams, Bartlett, and Miller (1955).

INTRA-STATE WAR #578

Bolivian Perez Rebellion of 1862

Participants: Bolivia versus Rebels led by Gregorio Perez.
Dates: September 3, 1862, to October 16, 1862.
Battle-related Deaths: Bolivia: [ ]; Gregorio Perez Rebels: [ ]; Total Combatant Deaths: 1,500.
Initiator: Rebels led by Gregorio Perez.
Outcome: Bolivia wins.
War Type: Civil for central control.
Total System Member Military Personnel: Armed Forces of Bolivia: 2,000 (prewar), smaller than the rebel army (after initial defections).[66]
Theater Armed Forces: Perez-led Rebels (Rebel Army): 1,000 (after La Paz defections), larger than the government army (peak).[67]

Antecedents: Simon Bolívar was instrumental in winning the independence of Peru from Spain (in Extra-state War #312 in 1824 to 1825). On August 6, 1825, Upper Peru declared its independence from

Peru and adopted the name Bolivia in Bolívar's honor. Relations between Bolivia and Peru remained contentious. Bolívar wanted to join Peru and Bolivia to Gran Colombia (consisting of Venezuela, Colombia, and Ecuador), leading to a war between Peru and Gran Colombia in 1828 (Non-state War #1512). Bolivia, desirous of creating a confederation with Peru, went to war, defeating Peru in 1835 and creating the Bolivia–Peru Confederation (Non-state War #1520). The confederation was dissolved as the result of a war in 1837 (Non-state War #1523). Finally, Peru's attempt to conquer Bolivia in 1841 was defeated (Extra-state War #325).

The end of the wars with Peru did not mean internal peace for Bolivia, and it used to be said that Bolivia experienced more rebellions than years of independence. From 1848 to 1855, Bolivia was ruled by Manuel Isidoro Belzú, a general who was popular with the poor, particularly those denigrated as *cholos* (people of both Spanish and Indian ancestry). Belzú defeated three major revolts in his first year in office and then faced four more in a one-year period from 1853 to 1854 (though they did not reach war levels). In 1855, he pronounced the country ungovernable and stepped down from office in favor of his son-in-law—who was soon overthrown by yet another revolt. His successor lasted two years before being overthrown by José María Linares. Rebellions continued to wrack the country, and in January 1861, Gen. José María de Achá led a successful coup against Linares, who had made himself vulnerable by ordering a large reduction in the size of the army. Achá then was elected president by the congress—the closest thing to a democratic election up to that point in Bolivian history. Belzú supporters attempted their own countercoup on October 23, 1861. The uprising failed, and sixty of the captured conspirators were massacred to prevent a rumored jailbreak. A new revolt against Achá, on March 7, 1862, was crushed by the forces of Gen. Gregorio Pérez in just one month.

Narrative: Apparently sensing his opportunity, Pérez then gathered his supporters and attempted his own rebellion on August 18, 1862, taking command of the First and Second Battalions and an artillery regiment in the capital of La Paz before having himself declared president. He rapidly raised an army of 1,000. On August 24, government forces in Oruro (southeast of the capital) declared for Pérez and moved toward La Paz to unite their forces with his. The first combat occurred on or soon after September 3 in Oruro between a vanguard of 100 government soldiers and a rebel force. Achá proposed terms of reconciliation to the rebels, but was rebuffed. On September 7, Pérez moved south from La Paz, seeking the main government force.

On September 15, 1862, Achá convened a council of war. All of his commanders save one recommended withdrawal. However, a somewhat inebriated commander, Mariano Melgarejo, announced that he would attack the rebels forthwith. Achá attacked Pérez's combined forces on the Plain of San Juan, near Oruro. Pérez was defeated in combat that left more than 1,000 dead. Pérez fell back to La Paz, where his popularity enabled him to assemble a force for the defense of the city. Achá had hesitated to move north, but on September 26 his forces set out from Oruro. After negotiations failed, hostilities recommenced on October 15, when government forces shelled La Paz. The next day, Achá's forces attacked and advanced to the central plaza in eight hours of fierce house-to-house fighting. Battle-deaths were high on both sides; Pérez died in the fighting.

Termination and Outcome: The outcome was an unconditional government victory. Achá's government lasted two more years without major incident.

Coding Decisions: We have not located specific battle-death data for the participants in this war. More than 1,000 total combatant deaths occurred at San Juan,[68] and there were a significant number of deaths at La Paz, so this conflict clearly meets the war battle-death criterion. We code 1,500 total combatant deaths as a best guess.

Sources: Aranzaes (1918); Fagg (1963); Scheina (2003a).

INTRA-STATE WAR #580

Second Argentina War of 1863 (aka First *Montoneros* Revolt or Peñaloza Rebellion)

Participants: Argentina versus *Montoneros*.
Dates: March 31, 1863, to November 12, 1863.
Battle-related Deaths: Argentina: [ ]; *Montoneros*: [ ]; Total Combatant Deaths: 2,500.

Initiator: *Montoneros.*
Outcome: Argentina wins.
War Type: Civil for central control.
Total System Member Military Personnel: Armed Forces of Argentina: 12,000 (prewar, initial, peak, final).[69]
Theater Armed Forces: Confederationists, aka Federalists or *Montoneros* (Rebel Army): "a few thousand" (initial); 4,000 (peak).[70]

Antecedents: Argentina had faced a series of wars over control of the country and its structure (federation or unitary). In the most recent war, the Third Buenos Aires War of 1861 to 1862 (Intra-state War #573), Buenos Aires, led by Bartolomé Mitre, defeated the federalist Argentine Confederation and established a united Argentina under Buenos Aires control with Mitre recognized as president. During that war, federalist Gen. Ángel Vicente "Chacho" Peñaloza (a *caudillo* of La Rioja province who intermittently controlled the neighboring San Juan province as well) maintained sustained resistance to the new government but eventually signed a peace accord in which he promised to restrain remaining federalist forces in La Rioja. The agreement broke down over Peñaloza's inability to control other *caudillos* and *montoneros* (cavalry militias) of the interior provinces, who opposed the concentration of power in the central government, and an invasion of La Rioja by pro-Mitre liberals from Cordoba, incidents that convinced each signatory of the bad faith of the other. In March 1863, Peñaloza declared a rebellion against the government.

Narrative: Peñaloza's rebellion soon became widespread throughout the northwestern provinces. The first engagement of the war was fought on March 31, 1863, at Callecita in San Juan. An urban uprising in support of Peñaloza was suppressed in the first days of April. On April 2, the Battle of Punta de Agua resulted in a defeat for the rebels, who lost 200 killed out of a force of 800. Later that month, the rebels lost another 120 killed against a 700-strong force. Further engagements were fought at Villaprima on April 21, Chumbicha a day later, and Mal Paso on May 3. Peñaloza suffered defeats against troops led by Comandante Morillo at Santa Rosa on May 7 and again on May 20, when he was defeated by 620 men at Lomas Blancas in La Rioja.

A revolution in the neighboring state of Córdoba deposed its governor and requested Peñaloza's leadership. Peñaloza entered Córdoba with only 100 men but soon had an army of at least 3,500 with which to confront an approaching government force of 4,000. The two forces met in the Battle of Las Playas, where Peñaloza was badly defeated, losing 300 dead against only 14 dead on the government side. The rebels fell back toward La Rioja, and the next series of engagements was fought near the rivers along the frontier between La Rioja and Córdoba. About 200 confederationist guerrillas under Fructuoso Ontiveros were defeated in the Battle of San Francisco in San Luis province on August 21. Four days later, 150 rebels under Manuel Puebla were crushed at Rio Seco, suffering 100 killed.

Peñaloza was eventually able to mobilize about 2,000 men once more but continued to suffer a series of defeats. In October, Peñaloza led 1,000 men into San Juan, where he was defeated on August 30 by numerically inferior militia commanded by Pablo Irrazábal, each side losing about 70 killed. Another battle the next day sealed the rebels' fate. Peñaloza's forces were scattered, and on November 12, he was captured with only 50 followers at Olta in La Rioja. Irrazábal immediately ordered him executed, and his head was displayed on a pike.

Termination and Outcome: The outcome of the war was a complete government victory. The issue of the degree of governmental control was unresolved, and tensions between Buenos Aires and other provinces, especially in the interior, continued and would lead to war again in three years (Intra-state War #586: the Third Argentina War of 1866 to 1867).

Coding Decisions: In terms of battle-related deaths, we have determined that at least 790 rebels and 84 government soldiers were killed in the battles for which casualty estimates are available. However, there were many more battles, and government losses are seldom reported in the histories examined. Malamud reports that from June 1862 to June 1868, there were 117 insurgencies, resulting in 4,728 deaths. McLynn estimates that 5,000 were killed between the civil wars of 1863 and 1866 to 1867. The rough equality of fatality figures obtained by simply adding up the confirmed death tolls for each of these wars persuades us that the 5,000-fatality total could be divided in half and suggests that the best estimate currently possible is about 2,500 battle-deaths for each of the wars.

Sources: Best (1960); De la Fuente (2004); Kirkpatrick (1931); Malamud (2000); Marley (1998); McLynn (1980); Richmond (1989); Toyos (2006).

INTRA-STATE WAR #582.5

Constitutionalist Rebellion of 1865 to 1866 (aka Anti-Melgarejo Revolt)

Dates: January 24, 1865, to January 24, 1866.
Participants: Bolivia versus Constitutionalists.
Battle-related Deaths: Bolivia: [ ]; Constitutionalists: [ ]; Total Combatant Deaths: 1,720.[71]
Initiator: Constitutionalists.
Outcome: Bolivia wins.
War Type: Civil for central control.
Total System Member Military Personnel: Armed Forces of Bolivia: 2,000 (prewar, initial, peak, final).[72]
Theater Armed Forces: Armed Forces of Bolivia: 2,000 (prewar); 1,613 (after initial defections, peak, final). Constitutionalists (Rebel Aggregate including Belzú-led Rebels): 1,000 (June 1865); 2,000 (peak); 700 (final).[73]

Antecedents: During the previous Bolivian war (Intra-state War #578 of 1862), President José María de Achá defeated a rebellion by Gen. Gregorio Pérez. President Achá continued in office until he was overthrown in a coup by Gen. Mariano Melgarejo, who took Achá prisoner on December 28, 1864, and proclaimed himself president the following day. Historians are unusually united in their condemnation of Melgarejo, a brutal and ruthless dictator who ruled by decree for over six years. While many of his worst excesses occurred after this war, he was already known for his drunkenness, brutality, and venality. In an attempt to establish popular rule, the constitutionalists proclaimed a rebellion against the Melgarejo government in January 1865. There were numerous uprisings against Melgarejo that year, and as all adopted constitutionalism as a slogan, we consider these as part of one war conducted by the constitutionalist rebel aggregate, even though we have been unable to identify the initial leaders of the revolt.

Narrative: Vanguard forces of the two sides met at Tacaquira in the southern department of Chuquisaca on January 24, 1865, where the rebels won the small engagement. On February 3, the two sides fought a larger battle on the banks of the river Oscara. When the government received reinforcements, the ill-trained constitutionalist army fled. Also in early 1865, populist former president Manuel Belzú, who had resigned in 1855, returned to Bolivia. He promptly proclaimed a revolution against Melgarejo and defeated government forces in La Paz on March 22, aided by an enthusiastic populace. On March 27, Melgarejo's 1,613 soldiers attacked La Paz. The attack failed, with many rebel soldiers defecting to Belzú's forces. However, Melgarejo and a handful of followers were able to make their way to the national palace, where Belzú was preparing his victory speech. One account says that they forced their way in by killing the guards and that Melgarejo used his pistol to shoot Belzú dead. Others describe Melgarejo as proposing a meeting with Belzú, at which Melgarejo killed the unsuspecting Belzú. In any case, Belzú was killed, along with 200 to 564 combatants. After this victory, Melgarejo created an elite battalion with which he traversed the country defeating his opponents.

On May 25, 1865, another constitutionalist revolt broke out in La Paz, led by Alejo and Cirilo Barragán. One week later, on June 1, a constitutionalist rebellion was proclaimed in Oruro by a committee including Francisco Velasco, Donato Vásquez, and Ignacio León. After short, sharp fighting, the rebels captured the city's palace. Two days later, Velasco led a similar revolution in Chayanta. On June 8, the constitutionalists of La Paz sent 1,000 well-equipped troops commanded by Major Gen. Vásquez to the South, toward Oruro. Melgarejo's forces won a minor victory on July 1 and occupied Oruro two days later. However, Melgarejo was unable to restore control as additional areas declared for the rebellion. On July 10, the rebels of La Paz, Oruro, and Chayanta formed a popular committee to lead the revolution. They sent small contingents to raise rebellion in other towns, and soon Potosí, Sucre, Camargo, Cobija, Tarija, and Cochabamba had joined the revolution.

Melgarejo's counterattack began in earnest on August 8, when he recaptured Cochabamba, Sucre, and Potosí. The advances of the revolution were stalled as Gen. Ildefonso Sanjinés and Gen. Nicanor Flores competed for military leadership. Constitutionalist forces under Flores finally decided to attack Melgarejo, occupying a hill outside Potosí on

September 5. The rebels were exposed positions, and Melgarejo was able to defeat them in a battle costing more than 200 lives. Flores fled to Argentina. On October 25, Santa Cruz declared for the constitutionalists, but its forces were defeated in a small skirmish on November 22.

The northern rebels then decided on an offensive to be led by Gen. Casto Arguedas. His army lost about 300 men in a series of maneuvers and skirmishes over the next few weeks and eventually retreated to the town of Viacha. On January 24, 1866, the government cornered the rebels at the nearby hill of Letanias. In the ensuing fighting, another 654 combatants were killed before the rebels unconditionally surrendered.

Termination and Outcome: The government won an unconditional victory. Melgarejo took La Paz bloodlessly after he acquiesced to the proposals of foreign consuls that allowed its defenders to simply return home. Melgarejo's rule would not be challenged seriously again for nearly five years (Intra-state War #595).

Coding Decisions: In terms of battle-deaths, we estimate 1,720 total combatant deaths based upon a total of the various battles, though we still regard our total as being more likely to be an underestimate than an overestimate.[74]

Sources: Aranzaes (1918); Arguedas (1929); de Mesa, Gisbert and Gisbert (2001); Fagg (1963); Munro (1960); Scheina (2003a).

INTRA-STATE WAR #586

Third Argentina War of 1866 to 1867 (aka Second *Montoneros* Revolt or Revolution of the *Colorados*)

Participants: Argentina versus *Montoneros.*
Dates: November 9, 1866, to October 15, 1867.
Battle-related Deaths: Argentina: [ ]; *Montoneros:* [ ]; Total Combatant Deaths: 2,500.
Initiator: *Montoneros.*
Outcome: Argentina wins.
War Type: Civil for central control.
Total System Member Military Personnel: Armed Forces of Argentina: 15,000 (prewar); 15,000 (initial); 15,000 (peak); 15,000 (final).[75]
Theater Armed Forces: *Montoneros,* aka Federalists or *Colorados* (Rebel Army): 2,000 (initial); 7,500 (peak); 700 (final).[76]

Antecedents: The *montonero* (cavalry militias) leftists were opposed to the centralist constitution for Argentina that had been promoted by President Bartolomé Mitre. In 1863, the *montoneros* had launched an unsuccessful rebellion from La Rioja province (Intra-state War #580). Subsequently, Argentina had become involved in the divisive and costly inter-state war, the Lopez War with Brazil against Paraguay over events involving Uruguay (Inter-state War #49 of 1864 to 1870). During the war, Paraguay had seized the northern Argentine river port of Corrientes, which prompted Argentina's entry into the war. The allies (Argentina, Brazil, and the *Colorados* of Uruguay) were able to regain the port on May 25, 1865. However, as the war continued, the allies advanced into Paraguay, where they suffered their worst defeat at the Battle of Curupaití on September 22, 1866. The war, with the related Argentine practice of conscription, meant increased hardships for the *gauchos,* and the defeat at Curupaití fueled antiwar sentiments and precipitated this second *montonero* rebellion.

Narrative: On November 9, 1866, about 280 recruits in the province of Mendoza mutinied. While the Mitre's military was able to suppress this mutiny bloodily, similar ones involving attacks on government buildings occurred throughout Mendoza, Corrientes, Salta, Juguy, Cuyo, and central Cordoba. Almost immediately, Juan Saá (sometimes referred to as "Lanza Seca," the former governor of the province of San Luis, who had been deposed and had gone into exile in 1861 after the Argentine Confederation's defeat by Mitre in Intra-state War #573) crossed into Argentina from Chile with a force of about 2,000 soldiers, including two Chilean battalions. His primary commanders were his brother Felipe Saá and Col. Juan de Dios Videla, who soon occupied several cities in the western province of San Juan.

On December 10, 1866, Felipe Varela, a *caudillo* in the western province of La Rioja, also issued a proclamation calling for the overthrow of the Mitre regime. The revolt then spread to almost all of the other interior provinces—San Juan, San Luis, La Rioja, Catamarca, and Salta. On January 5, 1867, Varela defeated government forces at Guandacol, giving him control of La Rioja Province. Three days later, a force under Videla decisively defeated a government force of 1,200 under Col. Julio Campos. This victory, the Battle of Rinconada del Pocito, buoyed the rebel forces with new recruits, and by April 1867, Saá had 3,500 men, and Varela commanded 4,000. The *montonero* advance continued, with rebels defeating the governor of Cajamarca on March 4. The first major setback for the rebels came on March 19, when the government was able to retake La Rioja. A much more serious blow came on April 1, when Saá's entire force was defeated and dispersed by 4,000 government soldiers under the command of Gen. Wenceslao Paunero in the Battle of San Ignacio. Following their victory, government forces retook control of Mendoza and San Luis as many of Saá's troops fled into Chile. Government troops under Gen. Antonio Taboada vigorously pursued Varela's force, and near the city of La Rioja, on April 10, a mere 2,100 government troops defeated his 4,000-strong force in the Battle of Pozo de Vargas, inflicting 300 deaths. After these defeats, the rebellion withered: some rebels fled north to the province of Catamarca; others went to Chile.

Perhaps a total of 1,200 Varelistas remained in August; Varela crossed into Bolivia with 1,000 of them on August 4. After resting and reorganizing his forces, Varela recrossed the border on August 29, 1867, and immediately reengaged government forces, winning a victory at Rincón de Amaicha that day and another one a day later in the Molino Valley. However, Varela was unable to rally the forces that previously had supported him. After more than a month of cat-and-mouse maneuvering, he attacked the northern city of Salta on October 10. This marked the last major engagement of the war as Varela suffered 125 battle-deaths, while the government only lost 15. Varela once again crossed into Bolivia. This time, Bolivian authorities disarmed his force, ending the war.

Termination and Outcome: This was a clear and unconditional government military victory. After another unsuccessful invasion in 1869, Varela went into exile in Chile, where he died a year later.

Coding Decisions: In terms of war type, some authors have argued that this was a war over local issues, including opposition to conscription, anti-capitalism, and an assertion of provincial autonomy (such as Juan Saá's declaration that the aim of the revolt was the secession of Mendoza from Argentina and merger with Chile). However, McLynn convincingly responds that such analyses ignore the significant threat to the legitimacy of the regime posed *inter alia* by: the opposition to Mitre's policies; the rebels' support for former president Santiago Derqui; the call to overthrow the Mitre regime; the desire to return to the 1853 constitution; and the expectation by some of the leaders of the rebellion that former president Justo José de Urquiza would use the opportunity to stage a revolution. Thus we have coded the war as a civil for central control.

In terms of the participation of Chile and Bolivia, both countries provided only limited direct assistance to the rebels. The rebels did recruit troops from both countries. Saá was said to have incorporated two Chilean battalions in his forces, and Varela had one. Because of this integration, we treat the Chileans as part of the rebel army rather than as a non-state intervener.

Battle-related Deaths: The number of battle-deaths is difficult to estimate. McLynn reports that the 1863 rebellion (Intra-state War #580) and the 1866-to-1867 revolt together constituted four major battles, twelve minor engagements, and about 5,000 killed. If one simply adds up the confirmed death tolls in battles, it produces 750 battle-deaths, but fatalities are unrecorded for many of them. Doing the same for the 1863 revolt produces 874 battle-deaths. The rough equality in recorded casualties suggests that the best estimate currently possible is about 2,500 total combatant battle-deaths for each of the wars.

Sources: Best (1960); Clodfelter (2002); de la Fuente (2004); Jaques (2007); Katra (1996); Kirkpatrick (1931); Kolinski (1965); Malamud (2000); Marley (1998); McLynn (1980); Richmond (1989); Rock (1998).

INTRA-STATE WAR #587.8

Third Venezuela War of 1867 to 1868 (aka Blue Revolution or Conservative Revolution)

Participants: Venezuela versus Blue Coalition.
Dates: December 24, 1867, to August 14, 1868.
Battle-related Deaths: Venezuela: [ ]; Blue Coalition: [ ]; Total Combatant Deaths: 1,000.
Initiator: Blue Coalition.
Outcome: Blue Coalition wins.

War Type: Civil for central control.
Total System Member Military Personnel: Armed Forces of Venezuela: 10,000 (prewar); 6,000 (after initial defections); 5,000 (final).[77]
Theater Armed Forces: Blues (Rebel Army): 4,000 (prewar, initial, peak, final).[78]

Antecedents: During the mid-nineteenth century, Venezuela had been plagued by fighting between liberal and conservative factions and violent uprisings by regional *caudillos* (see Intra-state Wars #548, #557.8, and #563). At the end of the last war in 1863, the dictatorship of José Antonio Páez was ended, and the federalists (liberals) had come to power. Recognizing the military situation, on June 17, 1863, the assembly appointed two of the leaders of the revolution, generals Juan Crisóstomo Falcón and Antonio Guzmán Blanco, as president and vice president, respectively. A new constitution was written and passed on March 28, 1864, which created a federal form of government, and the country was renamed the United States of Venezuela. Falcón had little interest in actually governing (taking frequent vacations), and this coupled with the decentralized government structure led to a collapse of central authority and a corresponding rise in the power of the regional *caudillos* (warlords). Politically, the central political dimension was the divide between the Liberal (Federalist) and Conservative (Constitutionalist) Parties, but both were loose coalitions, and splinter movements and defection were common. A coalition of conservatives and disaffected liberals united in opposition to Falcón, and they soon assumed the name of the Blue Revolution to distinguish it from colors associated with existing parties (Liberal Party was gold, and Conservative Party was red).

Narrative: On December 12, 1867, Gen. Migual Antonio Rojas, president of the state of Aragua, issued a proclamation announcing the formation of the opposition re-conquerors, who would wear blue badges. The centrally located provinces of Carabobo and Guárico joined Aragua in revolt. On December 24, 1867, the government reported a victory near Caracas, which marks the start of the war. At the time, the government had perhaps 6,000 men in the field against approximately 4,000 Blue rebels. In March 1868, former president José Tadeo Monagas, who had switched from the Liberal Party to the Constitutionalists, assumed leadership of the Blue Revolution, although General Rojas also claimed that honor. The two forces appear to have coordinated their activities, with Rojas operating near the capital of Caracas and Monagas operating in the East near the coast. Negotiations for a compromise cabinet went nowhere when it became clear that Falcón was determined to secure reelection from Congress. A notable increase in violence followed the collapse of this peace attempt as the revolt spread westward while entailing near-daily skirmishes on the outskirts of Caracas. On April 25, 1868, Falcón resigned, and Congress elected Manuel Ezequiel Bruzual as interim president. This failed to satisfy the demands of the Blue rebels. On May 6, the government and rebels clashed at the Battle of Las Adjuntas, with total combined losses estimated at 200 to 400. A battle for possession of Mount Cavalry on May 10 produced another 200 casualties. New peace negotiations were opened, and a treaty of peace was arrived at between Bruzual and Rojas. It called for the forces of Rojas to become part of the government army, for Rojas to recognize Bruzual as president, for constitutional government, and for amnesty. The agreement collapsed when Monagas rejected it and turned his forces, then numbering about 4,000, toward the capital. From June 22 to June 25, a battle raged for Caracas between 3,300 rebels and 2,300 government soldiers. Reports at the time estimated about 1,000 killed and wounded in the battle, perhaps three-fourths of them being rebels (who suffered high casualties assaulting fortified buildings in the city). Later, Bruzual would claim that two-thirds of the defenders had perished. Monagas entered the city in triumph. Guillermo Tell Villegas was named provisional president on June 28, 1868, while Bruzual and his forces fell back to La Guayra, then to Puerto-Cabello, where he was mortally wounded and his forces decisively defeated after a ten-day battle on August 14, 1868, at a cost of 50 Blues and 40 of Bruzual's men. It also marked the end to effective resistance by opponents of Monagas, although some partisans under Gen. Pedro Manuel Rojas still held out in the West.

Termination and Outcome: The war ended with the rebel victory. Monagas was the power behind the presidency for a brief period, until his death on November 18, 1868. The conservative–liberal coalition chose José Tadeo Monagas's son, Gen. José Ruperto Monagas, to become the next president, and he assumed office on February 20, 1869. Opposition from the liberals under the leadership of

Antonio Guzman Blanco would lead to a new war within six months (Intra-state War #592.5).

Coding Decisions: Small and Singer originally had coded this war and the subsequent Yellow Revolution (Intra-state War #592.5) together as one war (Venezuela vs. conservatives) from January 11, 1868, to January 7, 1871, with a pause in fighting between August 14, 1868, and August 14, 1869. Following the adoption of our somewhat more detailed coding rules, we have decided to separate these into two distinct wars.[79]

In terms of battle-deaths, there is limited information available. Taking only the reports of casualties in a couple of the major conflicts, combined with the usual 3:1 ratio of wounded to killed, suggests that there were more than 515 battle-deaths. If we take the highest estimates and accept Bruzual's (implausible) boasts at face value, there were more than 1,762 battle-deaths. Thus a figure of 1,000 total combatant deaths seems reasonable.[80]

Sources: Gilmore (1964); "Historia de Venezuela Para Nostros" (2008, July 9); "Juan Cristosomo Falcon" (2010); Marsland and Marsland (1954); Morón (1964); *New York Times* (1868–1871); Papers Relating to the Foreign Relations of the United States (1865); Phillips and Axelrod (2005); Rondon Marquez (1944); Scheina (2003a); Spence (1878); Wise (1950, 1970).

INTRA-STATE WAR #592.5

Venezuelan Yellow Revolution of 1869 to 1872 (aka Revolution of April)

Participants: Venezuela versus Liberals.
Dates: August 18, 1869, to May 17, 1872.
Battle-related Deaths: Venezuela: [ ]; Liberals: [ ]; Total Combatant Deaths: 2,000.
Initiator: Liberals.
Outcome: Liberals win.
War Type: Civil for central control.
Total System Member Military Personnel: Armed Forces of Venezuela—Blues: 5,000 (prewar); 6,500 (initial—including temporary assistance by 1,500 armed citizens of Caracas); 6,500 (peak).[81]
Theater Armed Forces: Liberal Yellows (Rebel Army): 6,000 (initial—actually in April 1870); 18,000 (peak).[82]

Antecedents: During the previous Blue Revolution (Intra-state War #589.8), President Juan Crisóstomo Falcón had been removed from office and a liberal, Guillermo Tell Villegas, had been appointed provisional president. Villegas served less than eight months, until the conservative–liberal coalition that had won the revolution chose Gen. José Ruperto Monagas (the son of former president José Tadeo Monagas, one of the leaders of the revolt) to become the next president, and he assumed office on February 20, 1869. However, opposition from the liberals under the leadership of Antonio Guzman Blanco (who had served as Falcón's vice president) would lead to this war within six months.

Narrative: Monagas proceeded to establish a largely conservative government, and the conservative–liberal coalition that had selected him began to fracture. Liberals began to move into open opposition to the new government, adopting Antonio Guzmán Blanco as their electoral standard-bearer. Guzmán Blanco had left the country after Falcón's defeat but had returned despite the fact that anti-Falcón sentiments were commonplace. In an attempt to garner support, Guzmán held a ball for leading figures in the government and diplomatic circles on August 14, 1869. A mob (apparently paid by the conservatives) attacked the ball, while government soldiers looked on indifferently. As a result, on August 18, Guzmán Blanco fled briefly to Cuaçao, while the liberals organized themselves as the Regeneration and prepared their armed forces. They adopted the color yellow, the color of the flag of the Liberal Party, hence the name of the rebellion.

Meanwhile, the government used the occurrence of a barracks revolt in San Carlos (southwest of the capital) to target prominent liberals. This had the predictable effect of leading liberal generals José Ignacio Pulido, Joaquín Crespo, and Francisco Linares Alcántara to proclaim against the government. In response, by September 24, 1,500 armed citizens were assisting the government in Caracas. In October, the rebels defeated the government at the western city of Cuidad de Nutrias. Continuing their gains in the West, in January 1870, the liberals won control of Barquisimeto after a nine-day battle.

While in Cuaçao, Guzmán Blanco had assembled a fleet of fifty-two ships, and on February 14, 1870, he landed in the western port of La Vela de Coro with a small force. Here he was able to unite the various rebel forces into an army of 18,000 men and began a seventy-day campaign toward Caracas. As the Yellow army approached the capital, Monagas was replaced on April 16 by the appointment of liberal Guillermo Tell Villegas as provisional president. His tenure lasted only eleven days. On April 27, Guzmán Blanco and 6,000 of his Yellow forces entered the capital after three days of fighting against 1,600 Blues, and Guzmán Blanco assumed the presidency. Fighting did not stop, however, and the remainder of 1870 consisted of a series of Yellow assaults on Blue strongholds: in the Northwest Carora fell in April; La Mara finally fell on September 21; and more than 300 died in fighting over Irapa in the Northeast. By the end of the year, Blues had been defeated almost everywhere.

Guzmán Blanco also devoted himself to adopting a liberal political program: within two months he had established a system of public primary education, launched extensive economic reforms, and had begun efforts to control corruption. Guzmán Blanco's governance provoked dissent, and soon the Blues found themselves with useful allies in the military. In May of 1871, a revolt by mutinous troops broke out in Valencia. During July and August, Gen. Juan Arnajo raised a large Blue force, briefly seizing control of Trujillo. By the end of October, the Blues were able to storm San Fernando del Apure. Both sides moved to reinforce their positions during November and December, which set the stage for the decisive battle. On January 1, 1872, the seven-day Battle of Apure began. The battle ended in a crushing Yellow victory, as more than 2,000 Yellow troops cornered fleeing Blues, led by the inept general "El Chingo" Olivo. About 300 Blues drowned while attempting to escape the rout; more than 300 Blues were taken prisoner, and the rest were annihilated.[83] On January 28, Blues surrendered Ciudad-Bolivar to Yellow forces. Although it seemed that Blue forces had been defeated, liberal general Matias Salazar defected to the Blue side in early 1872 in what the Yellows called "the treason of Salazar." It took three months for Yellow forces to bring him to bay in the Battle of Tinaquillo. Salazar was captured on May 10 and executed by Yellow forces on May 17, which appears to have ended organized resistance.

Termination and Outcome: Despite the liberals' decisive military victory, they did not accord amnesty to the defeated Blues, having killed most of their leaders through war or execution. Elections were held in June 1872 but were clearly rigged to deliver the presidency to Guzmán Blanco.

Coding Decisions: Small and Singer originally had coded this war and the previous Blue Revolution (or Third Venezuelan War: Intra-state War #587.8) together as one war (Venezuela vs. conservatives) from January 11, 1868, to January 7, 1871, with a pause in fighting between August 14, 1868, and August 14, 1869. Following the adoption of our somewhat more detailed coding rules, we have decided to separate these into two distinct wars (Intra-state Wars #587.8 and #592.5).[84] Small and Singer initially reported the total fatalities for the combined war as 3,000 battle-deaths. As we allocated 1,000 combatant deaths to the first war, we are reporting 2,000 total combatant deaths for this war, which seems reasonable in terms of its longer duration.

Sources: Gilmore (1964); "Historia de Venezuela Para Nostros" (2008, July 9); "Juan Cristosomo Falcon" (2010); Marsland and Marsland (1954); *New York Times* (1868–1871); Papers Relating to the Foreign Relations of the United States (1865); Phillips and Axelrod (2005); Rondon Marquez (1944); Scheina (2003a); Spence (1878); Wise (1950, 1970).

INTRA-STATE WAR #593

Fourth Argentina War of 1870 to 1871 (aka First Entre Rios War)

Participants: Argentina versus Entre Rios Province.
Dates: May 20, 1870, to March 13, 1871.
Battle-related Deaths: Argentina: 200; Entre Rios Province—1,300.[85] (See Coding Decisions.)
Initiator: Argentina.
Outcome: Argentina wins.
War Type: Civil for local issues.
Total System Member Military Personnel: Armed Forces of Argentina: 15,000 (prewar, initial, peak); 9,000 (final).[86]
Theater Armed Forces: Armed Forces of Entre Rios—Jordánista faction (Rebel Army): 6,000 (prewar); 12,000 (initial, peak); 1,000 (final).[87]

Antecedents: State formation in Argentina had involved conflict over whether the structure of the government would be federal with more power to the provinces or more unitary with a dominant role being played by the government in Buenos Aires. The last two civil wars (Intra-state Wars #580 in 1863 and #586 from 1866 to 1867) had involved rebellions by the leftist *montoneros* in the western provinces against the national government led by President Bartolomé Mitre. Both of these revolts had been suppressed by the government. Mitre also has become involved in the Lopez War of 1864 to 1870 (Inter-state War #49, which pitted Brazil and Argentina against Paraguay). During these wars, former confederate leader and longtime Entre Rios governor Justo José de Urquiza remained loyal to the Unitarian governments of Buenos Aires notables under Mitre and his successor, Domingo Faustino Sarmiento. On April 11, 1870, a group of disgruntled federalists assassinated Urquiza, and three days later, former Confederation Gen. Ricardo López Jordán took control of Entre Rios Province. The central government refused to recognize the new provincial government, and both sides mobilized for war. Initially President Sarmiento posted the Army of Observation to Entre Rios, with 500 government troops disembarking at Gualeguaychú (in the southeast) on April 19. On April 24, Jordán proclaimed himself commander of an army in the defense of the autonomy of Entre Rios (with an army of about 6,000 men). Sarmiento responded by declaring war. The government was able to persuade some pro-Urquiza loyalists in the overall 15,000-strong Entre Rios army to oppose Jordán, but the latter soon built up his forces to 12,000 men.

Narrative: The war began as federal troops attacked Entre Rios at three points: at Gualeguaychú in the East, Paraná in the West, and from Corrientes in the North. The first substantial combat of the war was the Battle of Arroyo Sauce on May 20, 1870. López Jordán was able to muster 9,000 to 12,000 cavalry, but they were defeated by about 3,000 government soldiers, losing 200 killed. The government went on to capture Concepción de Uruguay, the capital of Jordán's government. However, Jordán was able to take 4,000 cavalry and move quickly down the coastline with Uruguay, recapturing the city on July 12. During the same month, the *Jordánistas* were alleged to have plundered the port of Encamacion and put 200 prisoners to death. On July 19, the government repulsed an attack on its positions at Gualeguaychú. Jordán then avoided combat, while he rebuilt his army and the government reoccupied its positions and advanced into major towns. A peace commission was established to settle the war, but it failed because the government was unwilling to accept the rebel demands, which included compensation and a full amnesty.

Combat resumed by September 7, when 3,500 rebels were defeated, losing 60 killed. Jordán regrouped his forces and struck again on October 12 at Santa Rosa Creek near Villaguay. Again his 9,000 cavalry were repulsed, this time by 4,000 government troops under the command of Gen. Ignacio Rivas. The government lost only 36 killed, while the rebels lost about three times as many (though another report describes a battle at Santa Rosa occurring on September 23, with 1,500 casualties on both sides, including heavy government losses). Only 600 troops remained with Jordán in the aftermath of Santa Rosa, but he was again able to reorganize his forces. On November 18, the rebels took Gualeguaychú, suffering 150 killed to 32 government deaths. Yet, an assault by 3,000 rebels failed to take Paraná on December 5. In January 1871, Jordán invaded Corrientes to the North, mounting a surprise attack on Corrientes provincial forces of 3,000 men, led by General Rivas, at Ñaembe Lagoon, on January 26. Rebel forces were once again routed, losing 600 dead to only 190 casualties on the government side. On February 14, Jordán's forces suffered another setback at Gená Creek. The final major action of the war was fought at Punta del Monte near Gualeguay on March 6. The rebels lost, suffering another 50 killed. After this defeat, Jordán fled into Brazil with 1,000 troops, who subsequently were disarmed by Brazilian authorities.

Termination and Outcome: The outcome of the war was an unconditional government victory. A decree issued by General Arredondo granted amnesty to the rebels, but the government subsequently narrowed the decree to exclude high-ranking officers, murderers, and the instigators of the revolt.

Coding Decisions: In terms of battle-deaths, simply adding up the battles for which data is available produces a total of 1,180 rebel and more than 100 government battle-deaths. However, government battle-deaths are unreported for most battles, and 200 government soldiers may have been executed by the rebels. We conservatively estimate 1,500 battle deaths.

Sources: Best (1960); Clodfelter (2002, 2008); Duarte (1988); Jaques (2007); Marley (1998); Newman (1881); Poggi (2004).

INTRA-STATE WAR #595

Bolivia–*Criollos* War of 1870 to 1871

Participants: Bolivia versus *Crillos.*
Dates: November 3, 1870, to January 19, 1871.
Battle-related Deaths: Bolivia: [ ]; *Crillos*: [ ]; Total Combatant Deaths: 1,500.
Initiator: *Crillos.*
Outcome: *Crillos* win.
War Type: Civil for central control.
Total System Member Military Personnel: Armed Forces of Bolivia: 2,000 (prewar); more than 2,800 (peak); final (2,000).[88]
Theater Armed Forces: Rendon-led Forces (Rebel Army): 1,200 (initial).[89] Morales-led Forces (Rebel Army), participated from November 23, 1870; 2,000 (initial); 2,271 (peak).[90]

Antecedents: In December 1864, Gen. Mariano Melgarejo overthrew President José María de Achá in a coup, and Melgarejo assumed the presidency on December 28. Almost immediately he faced challenges to his regime, including a revolt by the constitutionalists, including former President Manuel Belzú, which began on January 24, 1865 (Intra-state War #582.5). During the war, Belzú was killed (on March 23, 1865) reportedly by Melgarejo personally. Melgarejo then went on to defeat the remaining constitutionalist challengers. Melgarejo established an increasingly brutal and repressive regime: he expropriated Indian land to sell, triggering a rebellion that was crushed by the massacre of more than 2,000 Indians in 1869. He also concluded a highly unfavorable treaty with Chile in exchange for funding. It is said that his own generals decided to depose him once he ordered the Bolivian Army to march to the rescue of Napoleon III during the Franco-Prussian War. On July 27, 1870, Bolivian exiles attempted an insurrection in and around La Paz, to be led by civilian Cesáreo Machicado, but were handily defeated by its garrison. Over the course of the summer, the *criollos* (whites and *mestizo* native-born Bolivians of Spanish descent—as opposed to Indians and Indian-related *cholos*) of La Paz pledged financing for an anti-Melgarejo revolution and persuaded elements within the army to rebel.

Narrative: The first to rebel was Gen. José Manuel Rendón on October 20; he raised 1,200 men in the southwest department of Potosí. The nearby department of Sucre followed his lead on November 1, and it contributed a few armed men to the defense of Potosí. On November 3, the government mounted a campaign against Rendón's forces and other rebels in the South. The rebellion continued to spread, and Santa Cruz declared for the rebels on November 8. Melgarejo's greatest weakness was the uncertain loyalty of many of his units, which required him to be at or near the front. This meant that the government could confront no more than one serious threat at a time. Taking advantage of Melgarejo's absence, prominent *criollos* in La Paz paid Col. Hilarión Daza, commander of the elite Colorado Battalion, 10,000 pesos to join the rebellion on November 23. The rebels quickly seized the capital, although at least 9 men were lost. Col. Agustín Morales (a former supporter of Melgarejo) was named supreme leader of the rebellion, and he raised a force of 2,000 men.

On November 20, Melgarejo defeated a unit of rebels under Nicanor Flores, a prominent rebel in the 1865 war, on a hill outside the city of Potosí. Melgarejo learned of the revolt in La Paz, while his forces were in Oruro, though he decided to finish off the rebels in Potosí first. There he defeated Rendón on November 28, 1870, in a battle that cost more than 400 lives and forced Rendón to flee southward to Cotagaita, where he would organize a new front on December 13. Rather than pursue him, Melgarejo first allowed his troops to sack Potosí, then reoccupied Sucre without firing a shot, and finally turned north and marched against La Paz.

Near the capital, Morales had advanced southward to the small town of Sicasica (Sica Sica), hoping to give his new recruits some experience but then learned that Melgarejo's main force of 2,300 men and 500 officers was approaching. Morales pulled his forces back to La Paz and began constructing barricades and trenches on January 13, 1871. Two days later, Melgarejo's forces attacked the 2,271-strong rebel force. In the bitter fighting that followed, between 1,027 and 1,378 combatants were killed, including those killed by Indians during Melgarejo's retreat. Taking advantage of Melgarejo's focus on the capital, Col. Narciso Campero joined forces with Rendón, bringing with him arms purchased in Argentina. In Cochabamba, most of the government's division of 500 men defected to the rebels in December. Rendón returned to Potosi to defeat the garrison Melgarejo had left behind under Gen. Sebastián Agreda in the last battle of the war, a brief skirmish on January 19, which cost only 3 lives and resulted in Agreda's capture.

Termination and Outcome: The outcome of the war was an unconditional rebel victory. As Melgarejo abandoned much of his army at La Paz, Bolivian Indians harassed Melgarejo's guard of a few dozen soldiers during his withdrawal, killing all but five of them. Melgarejo himself reached exile in Peru, only to be murdered a few months later by the brother of one of his mistresses. Col. Agustín Morales became provisional president on January 21, 1871, and subsequently president from August to November 1872.

Coding Decisions: In terms of battle-related deaths, there are varying reports of fatality statistics: for instance, Scheina says that 1,087 were killed in the war; however, de Mesa, Gisbert, and Gisbert give a total of 1,378 battle-deaths in the Battle of La Paz alone. Given that there were other engagements, the total could range from 1,087 to even 2,000. Given the short duration of the war and the small size of the forces involved, we regard 1,500 as a reasonable estimate.

Sources: Aranzaes (1918); de Mesa, Gisbert and Gisbert (2001); Fagg (1963); Scheina (2003a); Schneider (2007).

INTRA-STATE WAR #597.5
Entre Rios War of 1873 (aka Second Entre Rios)

Participants: Argentina versus *Jordánistas.*
Dates: May 9, 1873, to December 31, 1873.
Battle-related Deaths: Argentina: 500; *Jordánistas:* 1,500.
Initiator: Argentina.
Outcome: Argentina wins.
War Type: Civil for local issues.
Total System Member Military Personnel: Armed Forces of Argentina (Government Army): 7,000 (prewar, initial, peak, final).[91]
Theater Armed Forces: *Jordánistas* (Rebel Army): 9,000 (initial, peak), 5,000 (final).[92]

Antecedents: In 1870, the governor of the Argentine province of Entre Rios, Justo José de Urquiza, was assassinated, opening the way for Gen. Ricardo López Jordán to become the new governor. López Jordán immediately led a revolt against the Argentine government of President Domingo Faustino Sarmiento, seeking autonomy or independence for Entre Rios. The revolt was crushed in 1871, and López Jordán retreated into Brazil with 1,000 to 1,500 followers, who were disarmed by the Brazilian government. In Jordán's absence, Emilio Duportal briefly served as the new governor of Entre Rios, followed by Leónidas Echagüe. In 1873 López Jordán returned to Entre Rios and again overthrew its government on May 1. By the end of the month, President Sarmiento proposed legislation that would offer a bounty of 100,000 pesos for the death of the Entre Rios governor. López Jordán returned the favor later that year by hiring two assassins to shoot Sarmiento, though they were unsuccessful. The central government quickly moved to crush the rebellion.

Narrative: Government troops moved into Entre Rios, and the first engagement of the war was fought at Gualeguaychú (located in southeast Entre Rios on the Gualeguaychú River). There, on May 9, 1873, forces under Col. Luis Maria Campos defeated a rebel force of 800 men. The two sides clashed again at Arroyo Ayuí on May 13. A rebel army of 1,800 suffered a serious defeat on June 26. On June 29, the two sides fought an engagement near Arroyo Lucas, north of Villaguay, and another engagement on August 30 resulted in the defeat of 2,100 rebel troops. Further engagements were fought at Gualeguaychú on October 17 and Arroyo Atencio on October 25.

The government suffered substantial casualties during a botched withdrawal of it garrison from La Paz, Entre Rios, on October 31. As 3,000 rebels approached, government forces were caught off guard, and half of the 500-man garrison was lost in action or drowned trying to escape. On December 9, the decisive battle of Don Gonzalo was fought as government troops attacked Jordán's main force of 6,500 men and a smaller force of 2,000 rebels nearby. The rebels lost 450 killed in battle, and another 300 drowned trying to retreat, while government battle-deaths were only 100. The final major clash occurred on December 22 between 300 government soldiers and 600 rebels. Despite their numerical inferiority, the government forces prevailed. While a few more skirmishes followed, on December 25, 1873, López Jordán fled into exile in Uruguay. Government forces controlled Entre Rios, more than 5,000 *Jordánistas* were disarmed, and hundreds were arrested.

Termination and Outcome: The war terminated with López Jordán's flight into Uruguay. The government's victory was complete. López Jordán attempted another takeover of Entre Rios in November 1876, though this time he was unable to garner mass support. His forces were quickly defeated, and many of those who surrendered were executed. López Jordán was captured on December 16, 1876, and was imprisoned for almost three years until he was able to escape and go into exile in Uruguay.

Coding Decisions: The limited data on the fatalities in the individual battle yield totals of more than 350 government battle-deaths and 1,165 rebel deaths. However, given the amount of missing data, battle-death estimates of 500 for the government and 1,500 for the rebels are reasonable.[93]

Sources: Best (1960); Clodfelter (2008); Duarte (1988); Marley (1998).

INTRA-STATE WAR #600

Fifth Argentina War of 1874 (aka Mitre's Rebellion)

Participants: Argentina versus Mitre-led Rebels.
Dates: September 24, 1874, to December 7, 1874.
Battle-related Deaths: Argentina: [ ]; Mitre-led Rebels: [ ]; Total Combatant Deaths: 1,000.
Initiator: Mitre-led Rebels.
Outcome: Argentina wins.
War Type: Civil for central control.
Total System Member Military Personnel: Armed Forces of Argentina: 7,000 (prewar); 7,000 (initial); 7,000 (peak); 7,000 (final).
Theater Armed Forces: Nationalists (Rebel Army), participating throughout war, strength estimates: 2500 (initial); 14,000 (peak); 4500 (final).

Antecedents: This war was sparked by a contested presidential election but took place in the context of the long-standing rivalry between the Argentine provinces and Buenos Aires. Autonomists drew support from most of the provinces of the former Argentine Confederation, while nationalists drew support from the province and city of Buenos Aires. Liberal Bartolomé Mitre had ruled Argentina from 1862 to 1868, when he lost the presidential election to Domingo Faustino Sarmiento. Although Sarmiento was one of the famous reformers in South American history, he had been an ineffective leader. Consequently, nationalist leader Mitre ran for the presidency again in 1874, but this time he lost to Nicolás Avellaneda (a minister in Sarmiento's government), who had the support of the military and the Autonomist Party. Mitre claimed that the election had been rigged, and before Avellaneda could assume office, Mitre pronounced against the government on September 24.

Narrative: On the same day as Mitre's *pronunciamiento*, Gen. Ignacio Rivas began an insurrection in southern Buenos Aires. The revolution spread as other rebels moved westward, including Gen. José Miguel Arredondo, who executed government officials in the province of San Luis before advancing to Mendoza, where the first major battle of the war was fought at Santa Rosa on October 29, 1874. Arredondo, leading 2,500 rebels, defeated a government force of 2,000 in an engagement that left 350 killed or wounded. To augment his forces, Mitre appealed to the Indians, some 1,500 of whom flocked to the rebels after the victory at Santa Rosa. Mitre then moved to the southern part of Buenos Aires to join his troops together with those under Rivas. On November 10, the two sides met again at the Battle of Gualicho Creek, and the government suffered 180 killed. However, it proved difficult for Mitre to hold his coalition together; on November 18, 600 Indians went over from his forces to the government. Encouraged by this development, the government pressed Mitre, resulting in the Battle of La Verde on November 26, in which Mitre led an army of 5,500 into battle, but suffered 260 casualties, and another 1,500 soldiers promptly deserted his side. On December 2, Mitre—now reduced to 2,500 men—surrendered himself and his field army. However, nationalists still controlled Santa Rosa, and from December 6 to December 7, the two sides fought the

Second Battle of Santa Rosa. The government suffered only 200 killed and wounded; the rebels under Arredondo suffered 120 to 300 killed. This marked the end of the brief civil war.

Termination and Outcome: The war ended in a military victory by the government. However, the government opted for a conciliatory policy toward the rebels, sparing Mitre's life and permitting the rebels a role in politics after the war.

Coding Decisions: In terms of battle-deaths, simply adding together the losses reported in battles generates a total of 264 to 374 government fatalities and 285 to 530 rebel battle-deaths, for a total estimate of between 549 and 904, but these estimates do not account for other battles or for deaths from disease.[94] Thus, we consider a total of 1,000 battle-deaths to be plausible.

Sources: Best (1960); Clodfelter (2002); Herring (1966); Jaques (2007); Jeffrey (1952); Katra (1996); Kohn (1999); Levene (1963); Marley (1998); Pennington (1910); Phillips and Axelrod (2005); Sanchez (1906).

INTRA-STATE WAR #605

Third Colombian War of 1876 to 1877

Participants: Colombia versus Conservatives.
Dates: July 12, 1876, to April 6, 1877.
Battle-related Deaths: Colombia: 2,430; Conservatives: 2,070.
Initiator: Conservatives.
Outcome: Colombia wins.
War Type: Civil for central control.
Total System Member Military Personnel: 3,000 (prewar, initial, peak); 2,000 final.[95]
Theater Armed Forces: Armed Forces of Colombia: 2,585 (prewar); 3,000 (initial); 24,000 (peak). These figures include the armies of loyal states. Conservative Forces (Rebel Army): 4,000 (initial); 16,000 (peak).

Antecedents: Politics in Colombia in the nineteenth century were dominated by the rivalry between liberals and conservatives. The liberals controlled the presidency from 1861 as a consequence of the Second Colombian War of 1860 to 1861 (Intra-state War #565). However the party suffered from factionalism, and under its lax rule, several regional states gained virtual independence. The trigger for conflict in 1875 was a bitterly fought presidential campaign between the radical liberal supporters of Aquileo Parra and independent liberal supporters of Rafael Núñez. Incumbent president Santiago Pérez supported Parra, but his cabinet contained a number of *Nuñistas* as well. In early February, a near-coup occurred when Pérez sacked his *Nuñista* minister of war and the commander of the National Guard (the Federal Army) for their refusal to sign a statement pledging neutrality in the elections. Later that month, violence between the factions broke out in Magdalena. The former minister of war, Gen. Santodomingo Vila, began to purchase arms in Panama and collaborated with the plotters of a state-level coup in Magdalena. The government sent several hundred troops to restore *Parrista* power in the state, enraging other provinces.

On July 18, 1875, the state of Bolívar declared war on the federal government, followed by Panama three days later. Rebellions spread in the coastal, pro-Núñez states. On August 7, Pérez declared a state of insurrection and ordered a military buildup and the imposition of martial law in Bogotá. Radical liberal forces increased to 10,000 men. The conflict consisted of scattered engagements between small units, and fatalities were low and frequently were of civilians (thus it is not coded as a war). The last rebels surrendered on October 11, 1875, in Panama. Parra assumed the presidency on April 1, 1876.

Narrative: On July 12, 1876, the conservatives in southwestern Cauca led by Gen. Francisco de Paula Madriñán mounted a revolt against the liberal government, ostensibly to protest the liberal program of secular education but also due to opposition to government railroad projects that would disproportionately benefit a few states. The conservatives captured the city of Palmira. While the conservatives had expected the *Nuñistas* to join them, the highly religious nature of the Cauca rebellion dissuaded most liberals from embracing the revolt. Government forces recaptured Palmira on July 26 with 500 soldiers in the battle of La Granja. Meanwhile, the conservative states of Tolima and Antioquia joined the rebellion, the former sending 2,000 men with modern weapons to assist the rebel cause.

Conservatives in Cundinamarca and Boyacá organized guerrilla units.

In Bogotá, the government was able to muster 3,000 volunteers, sending troops to the state of Panama and moving against the rebels in Cauca. The first major battle of the war was fought at Los Chancos (near the city of Buga) on August 31. After eight hours of fighting, the combined expeditionary forces of Tolima and Antioquia—some 4,000 rebels in all led by Gen. Joaquín M. Córdoba—were defeated by 3,000 government troops armed with at least one machine gun and modern rifles under the command of Gen. Julián Trujillo. About 458 rebels and 256 government soldiers died. The rebels fell back northward to Manizales, and many of the government's volunteers went home.

From Manizales, 7,000 rebels led by Gen. Marcelino Vélez mounted an offensive toward Bogotá, but were blocked at Garrapata by 5,000 government soldiers from November 20 to 22, 1876. The death toll was between 1,600 and 2,000, with at least 970 on the government side and 500 on the rebel side. The two sides were each unable to sustain the fight, and a sixteen-day truce was negotiated. However, General Vélez rejected peace overtures from the government, and the rebels once again retreated to Manizales.

There were still multiple rebel armies and guerrilla units in the field. Further south, on December 19, a conservative uprising captured the city of Cali, though the government quickly was able to raise a force of 2,000 men and women to retake the city on December 24, with 400 killed, mostly civilians. Meanwhile, in Santander (north of the capital) the two sides clashed at La Donjuana on January 27, 1877. The government had a modest numerical advantage (5,000 soldiers against 4,000 rebels), and government forces prevailed in another bloody battle—500 government battle-deaths against 250 rebel dead. Meanwhile, General Vélez fortified Manizales with 5,000 men, and government forces led by General Trujillo assaulted Manizales from April 3 to April 5, killing 250 rebels compared to 140 government deaths. The rebels' conventional army was destroyed, and the following day the main guerrilla leaders in Cundinamarca agreed to lay down their arms.

Termination and Outcome: The outcome of the war was a government victory, ratified by the April 6, 1877, cease-fire in San Antonio. Scattered resistance continued until the last conservative leaders surrendered in 1879; however, we find no evidence of sustained combat after the April 6 cease-fire. One of the victors in the war, Gen. Julián Trujillo, would become president of Colombia in 1878.

Coding Decisions: In terms of battle-related deaths, one source reports a figure of 80,000 killed through 1879, but this is considered implausible by other historians. Adding up the fatalities from only the four major battles yields a total of 3,880 combatant deaths, but losses due to fatal wounds, disease, and minor engagements (especially guerrilla fighting) make this figure an underestimate.[96] Thus we consider a figure of 4,500 total combatant deaths plausible. Of the 3,880 known deaths, 54 percent were sustained by the government, and 46 percent were sustained by the rebels: applying the same percentages to the 4,500 total produced estimates of 2,430 government deaths and 2,070 rebel deaths.

Sources: Bushnell (1993); Delpar (1971); Henao and Arrubla (1938); Jaques (2007); Mejia (1976); Mendoza (2008); Moreno (2001); Ocampo (2007); Olarte (1993); Palacios (2006); Park (1985); Posada-Carbo (1994); Richardson (1960); Sanders (2004); Scheina (2003a).

INTRA-STATE WAR #606

Ecuador's Veintemilla Revolt of 1876

Participants: Ecuador versus Liberals.
Dates: September 8, 1876, to December 26, 1876.
Battle-related Deaths: Ecuador: [ ]; Liberals: [ ]; Total Combatant Deaths: 1,000.
Initiator: Liberals.
Outcome: Liberals win.
War Type: Civil for central control.
Total System Member Military Personnel: Armed Forces of Ecuador, aka Constitutionalists: 1,000 (prewar, initial, peak, final).[97]
Theater Armed Forces: Liberal Forces (Rebel Army): [ ].

Antecedents: As with most of Ecuador's internal conflicts, this war pitted liberals against conservatives and, in this case, the leaders in Guayaquil against those in the capital city of Quito. After 1861, Ecuador was dominated by conservative president Gabriel García Moreno. His autocratic rule brought stability to Ecuador, though generating increasing animosity among the liberals. García Moreno founded the Conservative Party in 1869 as he began his second term as president. When he won election for a third time in 1875, the liberals had enough. Prior to his scheduled inauguration, García Moreno was assassinated on August 6. He was succeeded by two interim presidents before presidential elections were held. García Moreno did not have a designated successor, and the Conservative Party was divided, so the Liberal Party candidate, Antonio Borrero Cortázar, won, assuming the presidency on December 9, 1875. Borrero, who had served as vice president from 1863 to 1864, attempted to restore a more balanced government by trying to assuage both the conservatives and liberals. The strategy backfired, and Borrero was faced by opposition from both factions.

In May 1876, conservative military officers in Guayaquil began to conspire against the government, prompting Borrero to replace its commander with Col. Ignacio de Veintimilla. Soon Veintimilla began plotting his own revolt. On August 19, the minister of the interior ordered the closing of any papers that attacked Church dogma or encouraged dissent, and the liberals decided to revolt.

Narrative: While the conservatives clustered in the northern highlands around Quito, the liberals congregated along the southern coast around Guayaquil. It was here that the Radical Liberal Party was formed on September 8, 1876, when the liberals launched a revolt against President Borrero. The rebellion was to be led by Veintemilla, and that day he appeared at the Guayaquil barracks, where he was proclaimed as supreme chief and captain general of the armies of the republic. Veintemilla also received the support of the Guayaquil city council. Borrero remained in the northern capital, where surprisingly he received the support of the Conservative Party. Some of the liberals became disenchanted with Veintemilla when they realized that he was more of an opportunist than a true liberal, and Veintemilla began to be attacked in the liberal press. Veintemilla solicited arms from the United States, but it is unclear if anything came of these efforts.

No battles were recorded until December 14, 1876, on which there were two battles: the liberals won a victory at the Battle of Loma de los Molines; and liberal forces led by Gen. José Maria Urbina (or Urvina) defeated the main body of pro-government constitutionalist soldiers at the bloody Battle of the Pass of Galte. In this action, 1,000 were killed and 600 wounded. On December 26, 1876, Quito was occupied by Veintemilla's forces.

Termination and Outcome: The outcome of the war was a military victory by the rebels. Borrero was jailed, and Veintemilla governed as dictator for two years, until elections ratified his rule in 1878. In October 1877, 1,000 conservatives attacked Quito to oust the liberal government, but were defeated. Interestingly, Colombia sent a force of 3,000 men in this conflict to assist the government, but they arrived too late to participate in the brief affair.

Coding Decisions: Available information on this war is limited. Reports indicate that 1,000 soldiers were killed and 600 wounded in the final battle of the war.[98] Battle-deaths prior to that day are unknown, thus this figure may be an underestimate.

Sources: Gonzales (1987); Lauderbaugh (2012); Scheina (2003a); Spindler (1987).

INTRA-STATE WAR #608

Argentine Indians War of 1878 to 1879 (aka Conquest of the Desert)

Participants: Argentina versus Indians.
Dates: December 6, 1878, to July 8, 1879.
Battle-related Deaths: Indians: [ ]; Argentina: [ ]; Total Combatant Deaths: 1,700. (See Coding Decisions.)
Initiator: Argentina.
Outcome: Argentina wins.
War Type: Civil for local issues.
Total System Member Military Personnel: 10,000 (initial); 10,000 (peak); 8,000 (final).[99]
Theater Armed Forces: Armed Forces of Argentina: 1,000 (initial); 6,000 (peak).[100] Ranqueles Warriors: 4,000 (initial).[101]

Antecedents: The election of Nicolás Remigio Aurelio Avellaneda Silva as Argentina's president in 1874 had led to a revolt by the liberal and former president, Bartolomé Mitre (Intra-state War #600). The revolt's defeat allowed Avellaneda to continue the process of developing state institutions and infrastructure that would bring the country together, including Patagonia, which was inhabited by indigenous peoples including the Ranqueles tribes. The United Provinces of Argentina had gone to war with the Ranqueles tribes in 1833, primarily over control of the pampas grasslands (Non-state War #1518, so classified because Argentina does not become a member of the COW interstate system until 1841). Since then, the Indians had engaged in periodic attacks against settlements and the Argentine Army and thus were perceived as a threat to national unity. For instance, in 1872, a leader of the Mapuche Indians, Juan Calfucurá, had led 6,000 followers against towns in the Buenos Aires province and killed 300 *criollos*. Small expeditions against the Indians in 1875 and 1876, led by Minister of War Adolfo Alsina, had had some success in pushing the Indians further south. After Alsina's death (December 29, 1877), Avellaneda's new minister of war, Gen. Julio A. Roca, wanted to pursue a more aggressive strategy and developed a plan to occupy Patagonia and pacify the Indians.

Narrative: Roca decided to personally lead the offensive, and he immediately began planning what he expected to be a two-year campaign. During the first year, the government would stay on the offensive by cycling in new 1,000-man contingents every twenty days. By late 1878, this phase had begun, and on December 6, 1878, government troops clashed with an Indian party at Lihué Calel (in current La Pampa province), with 50 Indians killed. By the end of the month, more than twenty-six such expeditions had been conducted, resulting in 5,000 Indians captured or killed (with more than 400 in the latter category).

The following spring, the second phase of the Conquest of the Desert was launched: it entailed a five-pronged offensive by 6,000 soldiers, with the five separate divisions (including a large cavalry) advancing from different routes to surround and capture the Indians. General Roca departed from Buenos Aires on April 6, 1879, and, commanding the First Division, moved south against Indians, most of whom were armed only with spears. The Fourth Division, which was to prevent the Indians from fleeing into Chile, encountered problems with the cold and the mountainous terrain. They were successful in capturing Indians, but a number of them had smallpox, which then spread to the soldiers. In some areas, the Indians offered little resistance, while in others the Indians would charge the government troops to engage in hand-to-hand combat. Roca and the First Division reached the Rio Negro, and on May 25 (Independence Day), the troops celebrated their achievements, which included rescuing 480 Christians from captivity and capturing 14,000 Indians. The efforts to clear the Indians from the *pampas* continued, with hunger and disease causing many fatalities on both sides. Roca returned to Buenos Aires on July 8, 1879, claiming to have driven the Indians from 175,000 square miles of land.

Termination and Outcome: The outcome of the war was a government victory. Many of the captured Indians (especially their leaders) were confined on Martín García Island in the Río de la Plata on the border with Uruguay; others were forced into servitude. To encourage settlements in the newly occupied territory, the government distributed some land to soldiers who had taken part in the campaign.

Roca resigned his military career in October 1879 so that he could participate as a candidate in the presidential election, in which he defeated Dr. Carlos Tejedor, the governor of the province of Buenos Aires. However, before Roca could take office, the citizens of Buenos Aires took up arms against the central government in June 1880 (Intra-state War #610). Roca led the army that quickly defeated the revolt, and he went on to serve as president and launched another offensive against the southern Indians from 1882 to 1883, though this round of fighting does not appear to have reached war level.

Coding Decisions: As Carroll describes, portrayals of this conflict have shifted radically in recent years. Initially General Roca (who also served as Argentina's president from 1880 to 1886 and 1898 to 1904) was seen as a hero of the republic who made Argentina a modern nation by pacifying the frontiers, removing the threat posed by "vicious" Indians, and opening the South to European settlement. More recent interpretations have argued that Roca was instead a genocidal murderer who slaughtered Indians, stole their land, and gave it to his cronies. A third position seeks to give agency to indigenous rebels as patriots.

Our interpretation falls more along this third vein, in portraying the Indians not just merely as victims of genocide but also as persons resisting the advancement of Argentinian control. Though there was no doubt a genocidal policy was conducted against Indian civilians, we also have decided that the Ranqueles warriors engaged in sufficient direct combat for this conflict to be coded as a war.

Related to the ways in which this war is seen are the ways in which battle-deaths were reported or ignored. Argentina-as-heroic portrayals might emphasize the superiority of the government's weaponry in the army's ability to kill the "savage" warriors while suffering few deaths itself. Conversely, the genocide, the killing of noncombatants or the execution of prisoners rarely was discussed, and soldiers' hardships and deaths caused by hunger and disease were minimized. Consequently, we have been unable to locate government battle-death statistics for this war. In terms of the Indians, Rauch indicates that 400 Indians were killed in December 1868 and 1,313 killed the 1869, with more than 15,000 Indians captured (including noncombatants). Thus, we estimate 1,700 total combatant deaths, with the vast majority being borne by the Indians.

Sources: Carroll (2011); Hasbrouck (1935); Kirkpatrick (1931); Levene (1963); Perry (1972); Rauch (1999); Richardson (1960); Rock (2002); Scheina (2003a); Williamson (2009).

INTRA-STATE WAR #609

Revindication War of 1879

Participants: Venezuela versus *Revindacadores* (Liberals led by Guzmán Blanco).
Dates: January 3, 1879, to February 13, 1879.
Battle-related Deaths: Venezuela: [ ]; *Revindacadores*: [ ]; Total Combatant Deaths: 2,000.[102]
Initiator: Revindacadores.
Outcome: Revindacadores win.
War Type: Civil for central control.
Total System Member Military Personnel: 12,000 (prewar, initial, peak, final).[103]
Theater Armed Forces: Armed Forces of Venezuela: 12,000 (prewar); 3,000 (after initial defections); 300 (final).[104] *Revindacadores* (Rebel Army): 10,000 (initial); 10,000 (peak); 10,000 (final).[105]

Antecedents: During Venezuela's Yellow Revolution of 1868 to 1872 (Intra-state War #592.5), President José Ruperto Monagas had resigned, and after a brief interregnum, liberal Antonio Guzmán Blanco became president on April 27, 1870. Guzmán Blanco served for seven years, during which time he instituted a number of liberal reforms. His successor, fellow liberal Francisco de Paula Linares Alcántara, assumed office on February 22, 1877, though he served less than two years of his term. His death on November 30, 1878, precipitated a factional struggle among the liberals between supporters and opponents of Guzmán Blanco. Guzmán Blanco's absence in Europe as a representative of Venezuela enabled his opponents in Congress to control the situation and to appoint Linares Alcántara's half-brother, José Gregorio Valera, as provisional president on November 30. By December 12, statues of Guzmán Blanco were being torn down in Caracas. From Paris, Guzmán Blanco lobbied (by cable) a number of Venezuelan generals to begin a rebellion, including Gen. Gregorio Cedeño, who felt that he should have been chosen as president.

Narrative: On January 3, 1879, Guzmán Blanco wrote to President Valera, urging him to dismiss the current government and reunite the factions of the Liberal Party. The same day, Guzmán Blanco arranged for the delivery of 3,000 rifles to the revolutionary forces to start a revolution (which marks the start of the war). President Valera rejected Guzmán Blanco's suggestion, but his pleas were accepted by the generals. General Cedeño declared war on the interim government and proclaimed Guzmán Blanco (still in Paris) as supreme director of the revolution. The rebels called themselves *Revindicadores*—the Revindicators.

Cedeño was able to organize a revolutionary force of 10,000 divided into three armies, while interim President Valera had the allegiance of only 3,000 soldiers. It is not clear when the first engagement was fought, though it may have been later in January. By then, only 2,300 actual soldiers were available to Valera, the rest being "ghost soldiers" kept on the ration books by unscrupulous commanders or those who had defected to the rebels. The war was decided by one major engagement, the Battle of La Victoria on February 6, 1879. This bloody battle cost 2,000 lives, with even more being wounded. The government army largely was destroyed, with only 300 still available for military operations. On February 13, General Cedeño's forces captured Caracas.

Termination and Outcome: The outcome was a rebel military victory. On the news of the rebel victory, Guzmán Blanco left Paris, arriving in Caracas on February 25, 1879. He condemned those who had opposed him and listed their names in the press; most found it expedient to leave the country. There were no mass arrests or executions. Guzmán Blanco assumed the presidency on February 26, 1879.

Coding Decisions: The only battle-death information we have located is the report of approximately 2,000 deaths in the only major engagement of the war. As there may have been other armed conflicts, this figure may be an understatement.[106]

Sources: Güell y Mercader (1883); Wise (1950).

INTRA-STATE WAR #610

Fourth Buenos Aires War of 1880

Participants: Argentina versus Buenos Aires.
Dates: June 12, 1880, to June 22, 1880.
Battle-related Deaths: Buenos Aires: 825; Argentina: 550.[107]
Initiator: Buenos Aires.
Outcome: Argentina wins.
War Type: Civil for local issues (secession).
Total System Member Military Personnel: Armed Forces of Argentina (Government Army): 9,000 (prewar); 9,000 (initial); 9,000 (peak); 9,000 (final).[108]
Theater Armed Forces: *Porteños* (Rebel Army): 15,000 (peak, final). This total includes a foreign legion, which was largely composed of Italians.[109]

Antecedents: Conflict between the *porteños* of Buenos Aires and the provinces of Argentina had led to a series of wars over which would control Argentina and over the degree of control the government would have. In 1862, the victory of Buenos Aires in the Third Buenos Aires War of 1861 to 1862 (Intra-state War #573) led to Buenos Aires's domination of Argentina and the moving of the base of the national government to Buenos Aires.

Once again, the rivalry resurfaced during the campaign leading up to the 1880 presidential election, which pitted former minister of war Julio Roca against Carlos Tejedor, the governor of the Buenos Aires province. When Roca announced his candidacy in April 1879, Tejedor threatened civil war should anyone oppose his own run for office. Both sides prepared for armed action in the event of an unfavorable outcome in the election: in essence, two governments based in the city of Buenos Aires were arming against each other and trying to use displays of military force to intimidate the other. In February 1880, Argentine president Nicolás Avellaneda issued a decree to dissolve militias, and Tejedor threatened war. In March, 8,000 of Tejedor's supporters marched through the capital, protesting governmental policies.

In April, Roca, whose popularity had soared after his victory against the Ranqueles Indians in 1879 (Intra-state War #608), was elected as the incoming president. When the electoral college certified Roca's victory in June 1880, Tejedor declared the secession of the province of Buenos Aires, and President Avellaneda declared that Buenos Aires was in rebellion. As conflict erupted, Avellaneda moved governmental personnel from Buenos Aires to the nearby city of Belgrano.

Narrative: The *porteños* militia had dug trenches around the important center of Buenos Aires, and the first recorded skirmishes of the war took place on June 12 between small units. On June 17, *porteño* cavalry units were attacked while moving toward the main rebel army, which soon numbered more than 7,000 men. The cavalry succeeded in bolstering Buenos Aires on June 18, just before Roca's main assault on the city. While an initial probe failed to make progress, resulting in 50 killed on each side, the government forces attacked the bridges coming into the city from the south on June 19. The casualties were horrific as the government infantry attempting to cross the bridge was mowed down by the rebels. In the fighting, characterized as the bloodiest day in Buenos Aires history, the lives of at least 1,200 troops were lost, with many of their bodies thrown into the river below. Roca finally managed to seize a bridge into the city, and there were at least 300 additional killed or wounded in subsequent fighting. Running low on ammunition, the rebels under Tejedor asked for terms on June 22.

Termination and Outcome: A truce and negotiations followed, and Tejedor resigned his position as part of a peace deal on June 24 that required the rebels to disarm and stripped them of public office. Roca established his presidency and severed the city of Buenos Aires from the province of Buenos Aires, making the newly federalized city the nation's capital.

Coding Decisions: In terms of armed forces, the rebels may have raised an additional 10,000 volunteers in the provinces but were unable to arm them, and thus they are not included here.[110] The figures for the total combatant deaths tend to cluster in the 1,000 to 2,000 range. The most detailed discussion indicates that there were 1,300 fatalities plus an additional 300 casualties. Using the usual 3:1 rule of thumb for the ratio of wounded to killed results in an estimate of 75 additional deaths, for a total of 1,375.[111] Scholars also report that the majority of the fatalities were borne by the rebels, thus we are reporting estimates of 825 rebel deaths and 550 government fatalities.[112]

Sources: Akers (1912, 1930); Best (1960); Clodfelter (2002, 2008); Faríní (1970); Gorleri (2003); Kirkpatrick (1931); Langer (1968); Marley (1998); Palacio (1975); Richardson (1960); Rock (2002).

INTRA-STATE WAR #612

Fourth Colombian War of 1884 to 1885

Participants: Colombia versus Liberals.
Dates: September 24, 1884, to August 26, 1885.
Battle-related Deaths: Liberals: 820;[113] Colombia: 330.[114]
Initiator: Liberals.
Outcome: Colombia wins.
War Type: Civil for central control.
Total System Member Military Personnel: Armed Forces of Colombia: 3,000 (initial, peak, final).[115]
Theater Armed Forces: Armed Forces of Colombia (including forces of conservative *caudillos*): 8,000 (initial); 10,000 (peak).[116] Radical Liberals (Rebel Army): 3,000 (initial); 6,000 (peak); 1,000 (final).[117]

Antecedents: Liberals controlled the national government of Colombia after 1861. In the Third Colombian War of 1876 to 1877 (Intra-state War #605), the liberal government defeated the rebellion instigated by the conservatives in several of the provinces. The Liberal Party was fragmented into factions for the radical liberals and independent liberals; some independent liberals joined with conservatives in an attempt to end the monopoly on the national presidency enjoyed by the radicals. In 1880, Rafael Núñez won election as president as the standard-bearer of the independent liberals with the support of moderate conservatives (serving from April 8, 1880, to April 1882). Núñez ran for the presidency again in 1884, and the conservatives had endorsed Núñez outright. Núñez won, taking office on April 4, 1884. The new electoral configuration alienated many of the liberals as did evidence that Núñez was attempting to reduce the autonomy of the states. Thus, radical liberals and even some independent liberals began to resist the central government, leading to their open rebellion.

Narrative: The revolt began in Santander, where 3,000 liberal rebels under Gen. Solón Wilches faced off against an equal number of government soldiers over control of the state government. Fighting also broke out in Cundinamarca as early as September 24, with radical liberal Gen. Gaitan Obeso conducting a campaign against the government along the Magdalena River with a force that grew from just 8 to 10 men at the onset of his revolt to 2,000. Other revolts followed, and on December 18, Núñez declared direct federal rule in Santander, Boyacá, and Cundinamarca and sent troops to assist loyal state governments elsewhere in the country. Núñez turned to conservatives for support, reshuffling his cabinet and placing conservative Gen. Leonardo Canal in charge of the federal army. Many liberal officers then left the army, taking their men and supplies, but even so, within three months, federal forces had reached their peak strength of 8,000, while most rebel groups were limited to a few hundred. Thus, the campaigns in Boyacá and Santander consisted of many small actions rather than large battles. In Tolimá, the rebels were able to muster 3,000 men by the beginning of 1885.

The pattern of small engagements was broken in 1885, which saw the heaviest fighting of the war. In Cauca, the rebels numbered in the mere hundreds but still were able to engage the government in battle on January 23, 1885, near Cali. The rebels were defeated, though the government lost 64 killed or wounded. The first battle involving thousands of combatants on each side was fought at Santa Bárbara de Cartago from February 22 to 23, 1885, and resulted in a major government victory: rebel losses numbered 600, while the government lost 48 killed. On March 6, a battle at Cogotes cost the rebels 50 casualties, while the government lost 40 killed. On May 7, about 2,800 rebels unsuccessfully attempted to storm Cartagena, losing 300 dead against minor government losses. The two armies clashed again at La Humareda on June 17. In a costly victory, the rebels lost 300 killed, while the government lost 230 dead.

In Panama, the liberal garrison commanders supported the rebellion, and Col. Pedro Prestán burned Colon to keep the conservatives from gaining control of the city. Concerned about the canal, Britain, France, and the United States sent 2,000 troops to restore civil order. While these troops may have briefly clashed with rebels when they seized Panama City, they engaged in no substantial military action. Threats of force were sufficient to induce the rebels to surrender to government forces. The province was restored to national control on April 27, 1885.

On July 16, 1885, in Antioquia, 600 rebels were defeated by government forces, losing 40 dead. Five days later, the rebels abandoned their Magdalena River campaign, retreating to Barranquilla where they surrendered on July 31. Last to surrender were liberal forces in Boyacá and Santander, where about 1,000 rebels surrendered to the government in August, and the government declared the rebellion to be at an end on August 26, 1885.

Termination and Outcome: The outcome of the war was formal surrender by the rebels. Núñez was one of the critical figures in the Regeneration Movement that enacted a new constitution in 1886, which called for a strong government army, restricted the right to bear arms to the government, restored the power of the Roman Catholic Church, and took much of the independence from states. The constitution thus transformed what had been the United States of Colombia into a republic.

Coding Decisions: In terms of battle-related deaths, Mejia provides a figure of 3,000 total dead in ten months of fighting. When we simply add up the casualty figures for the specific engagements and apply the usual 3:1 ratio of wounded to killed, we calculate a figure of more than 1,153 battle-deaths. This is probably an underestimate as this does not include deaths from disease or minor engagements, but our best estimate is 830 fatalities for the liberals and 320 for the government.[118]

Sources: Delpar (1971); Henao and Arrubla (1938, 1984); Henderson (1985); Langley and Schoonover (1995); Mejia (1976); Munro (1942); Olarte (1993); Richardson (1960); Scheina (2003a); *The Times* (1885, August 1); Wicks (1980).

INTRA-STATE WAR #613

Peru's National Problem of 1885 (aka Huarez Revolt)

Participants: Peru versus Indians.
Dates: March 2, 1885, to May 11, 1885.
Battle-related Deaths: Indians: 2,000; Peru: 200.
Initiator: Indians.
Outcome: Peru wins.
War Type: Civil for local issues.
Total System Member Military Personnel: Armed Forces of Peru: 5,000 (prewar, initial, peak, final).[119]
Theater Armed Forces: Huarez Indians (Rebel Army): 8,000 (initial); 12,000 (peak); 6,000 (final).[120]

Antecedents: This war grew out of Peru's crushing defeat in the War of the Pacific (Inter-state War #64, 1879 to 1883) among Peru, Bolivia, and Chile. At the end of the war, Gen. Miguel Iglesias abandoned the Peruvian resistance to make peace with Chile, and consequently as Chile withdrew from Peru, it recognized Iglesias as the president of Peru. Peru then entered a period of political upheaval and guerrilla war against the Chilean-installed Iglesias regime, partially led by Gen. Andrés Avelina Cáceres. Cáceres formed an alliance between peasants and indigenous peoples to fight the "collaborationist" government but abandoned his allies during the struggle (which does not appear to have reached war level). However, it appears that their service against the Chileans left the Indians better armed and organized than before, and they continued their own resistance movement under the leadership of Pedro Pablo Atusparia. Indian opposition began over the issue of taxation, though it periodically broadened to include demands for the removal of Iglesista officials. On March 1, 1885, Indian leader Atusparia refused government orders to reinstate compulsory personal service and the head tax, and the first combat occurred the following day.

Narrative: On March 2, 1885, about 5,000 to 8,000 Indians armed with tools, machetes, and rifles gathered around the city of Huaraz (north of the capital of Lima), where government officials were meeting. A brief encounter between the garrison and a few Indians took place that day. The next afternoon, the Indians attacked, quickly defeating the government's Artisan Battalion and overrunning and sacking the town, with dozens of Indians and soldiers killed. Huaraz served as the clarion call, and armed Indian combatants gathered throughout the region. The next major target was Yungay, which a force of 4,000 to 8,000 rebels under the leadership of Atusparia and Manuel Mosquera captured on April 4, massacring both government soldiers and civilians. Many of the nearby towns surrendered without a fight, and soon the rebels controlled the Callejón de Huaylas valley. The rebels' primary goals were to remove the abusive Iglesista authorities, replace them with *Aceristas*, burn the tax records, and pillage the stores and property of government collaborators.

The uprising alarmed the government, and President Iglesias commissioned Col. José Iraola to crush the insurrection. Iraola's Northern Pacification Force departed, landing at the coastal town of Casma on April 12, 1885. Here Iraola heard the welcome news that the leader of the northern military resistance, José Mercedes Puga, had been killed by government troops, thus removing a major threat to the government. Iraola's march to Yanguay was difficult, engaging the Indians in five battles on the way. Once there, the government forces met and defeated 5,000 Indians, who retreated into the hills. On April 28, 1885, a rebel force of 10,000 to 12,000 Indians attacked the town. During the numerous assaults of the Battle of Yungay, the Indians suffered more than 1,000 fatalities against only 32 for the government forces. Atusparia was reportedly wounded, but second in command Pedro Cochachín (aka "Uchcu Pedro") continued the rebellion. Within days, the rebel army—now only 6,000 strong—was defeated again as a last-ditch assault on Huarez failed on May 11, marking the end of large-scale operations.

Termination and Outcome: The outcome of the war was an unconditional government military victory. A vicious campaign of repression followed, in which entire Indian villages were destroyed. This was massacre rather than war—not a single government soldier died in this punitive campaign. Uchcu Pedro was captured and shot in September. The government was overthrown by Cacáres on December 12, 1885, and Cacáres took office as president on June 5, 1866.

Coding Decisions: The final death toll for the rebels was in the thousands, with contemporary newspapers reporting 1,000 to 3,000 Indian deaths, but these figures may include civilians.[121] There were more than 1,000 Indian battle-deaths in the Battle of Yungay alone, so an overall total of 2,000 seems plausible.

Sources: Klaiber (1977); Klarén (2000); Mallon (1987); Thurner (1997).

INTRA-STATE WAR #616.5

Campos Mutiny of 1890 (aka Revolution of the Park)

Participants: Argentina versus Campos-led Rebels.
Dates: July 26, 1890, to July 29, 1890.
Battle-related Deaths: Argentina: [ ]; Campos-led Rebels: [ ]; Total Combatant Deaths: 1,000. (See Coding Decisions.)
Initiator: Campos-led Rebels.
Outcome: Argentina wins.
War Type: Civil for central control.
Total System Member Military Personnel: Armed Forces of Argentina: 5,000 (prewar, initial, peak, and final).[122]
Theater Armed Forces: Campos-led Rebels: 3,800 (1,300 soldiers and 2,500 militia).

Antecedents: In the ten years since Argentina had asserted its control over Buenos Aires (Intra-state War #610 of 1880), the government had begun a number of projects that would promote modernization, economic growth, and national cohesion (including building new railroads). Unfortunately for Argentina, such infrastructure projects required capital and expertise that Argentina did not have, and it increasingly relied on Great Britain and British businesses to provide these. Politically, since 1880 Argentina's government had been in the hands of the PAN (National Autonomist Party), the party formed by Julio Roca (the victor in the war), after Roca's presidential term ended in 1886, his brother-in-law, the PAN candidate Miguel Angel Juárez Celman, took office on October 12, 1886. Juárez Celman was unable to maintain Argentina's economic stability in the face of its foreign debt. A financial crisis erupted in 1889, when Baring Brothers of London failed to secure the funding for a project to rebuild Buenos Aires's water supply system. Argentina's government responded by beginning to sell off its assets to meet its foreign debts, and in Buenos Aires, unemployment grew, and wages fell by about 50 percent.

Opposition to Juárez Celman began in September 1889 among university students, who called their organization the Youth Civic Union. By the next year, the group had become a broad coalition, now called the Unión Cívica, headed by Leandro N. Alem and Aristóbalo de Valle, which included opposition politicians (including former liberal president Bartolomé Mitre), Catholic groups, and business interests. The Unión Cívica's first major protest on April 13, 1890, drew 30,000 demonstrators. The growing opposition precipitated a political crisis, and all of the government ministers resigned. In the meantime, the Unión Cívica had formed a revolutionary council, which began talks with disaffected military officers, some of whom were known as the Lodge of the 33 Officers. The opposition army was put under the command of Gen. Manuel Campos (an associate of Mitre), who met on July 17 with army and naval officers to discuss strategy for a revolt. The next day, Campos and other military leaders were arrested. Though the rebellion was thus delayed, on July 25, the leaders finally met and decided to go ahead the next day.

Narrative: The rebellion began on July 26, 1890. The Unión's manifesto claimed that revolution was necessary because it was impossible to secure political change by peaceful means. The rebels' plan was to launch simultaneous attacks; the army would occupy the Buenos Aires Artillery Park, and the navy would bombard the government center. General Campos even had been able to persuade the Tenth Infantry, which had guarded him, to join the revolt. The Revolutionary Army, aided by 2,500 local civilian militias, seized the park and the city's artillery. Government officials gathered at the railroad terminal, where they could coordinate troops raised from the provinces. At this point, Campos changed the plan and had the rebels stay in the park rather than advance toward the government position. There has been speculation that Campos's hesitation at this point was the result of a secret deal he had negotiated with Roca to stall the revolt and Leandro Alem's presidential aspirations in exchange for Roca's support in the removal of Juárez Celman. Whatever the reasoning, the rebels' delay allowed the government time to bring in reinforcements, and fierce fighting began. The rebels had stationed canons around the park, which they used against government positions, as did the rebel ships in the harbor. However, the effectiveness of the naval bombardment was limited by the lack of coordination with the troops in the park. The rebels also launched a cavalry attack that was driven back with heavy losses. Fighting continued through July 28. At a meeting that evening, the rebels' leaders were divided: some wanted to continue the fight, while others argued that the shortage of ammunition made continuing the war impossible. The later position prevailed, and the surrender was signed on July 29.

Termination and Outcome: Though the outcome of the war was a government victory, President Celman resigned on August 6, 1890, and was succeeded by the vice president, Carlos Pellegrini.

Coding Decisions: Though there is no definite enumeration and allocation of the fatalities of this war between the participants, the common conclusion is that 1,000 deaths occurred among the combatants.[123]

Sources: Clodfelter (2002); Levene (1963); Rock (1985); Snow (1965); Williamson (2009).

INTRA-STATE WAR #617

Second Chilean War of 1891 (aka Congressist War)

Participants: Chile versus Congressists
Dates: January 7, 1891, to August 29, 1891.
Battle-related Deaths: Chile: [ ]; Congressists: [ ]; Total Combatant Deaths: 5,500.
Initiator: Congressists.
Outcome: Congressists win.
War Type: Civil for central control.
Total System Member Military Personnel: Armed Forces of Chile: 9,000 (prewar, initial, peak, final).[124]
Theater Armed Forces: Armed Forces of Chile (aka *Gobiernistas*): 9,000 (prewar—5,037 on active duty plus reserves); about 8,600 (after initial defections and mobilization); 45,000 (peak).[125]

Congressists (Rebel Army): 400 (initial); 10,000 (peak); about 9,300 (final).[126]

Antecedents: During the 1880s, Chileans were divided fiercely over the conflicting roles of church and state. The liberals had occupied the presidency since 1871 and had implemented a number of reforms limiting clerical privilege, thereby angering Church leaders. On the other hand, Chile's finances, which had been depleted by the War of the Pacific (Inter-state War #64, 1879 to 1883), were further strained by some of the liberal infrastructure improvement programs. Some liberals, including those whose livelihoods were dependent upon exports, opposed the autocratic rule that characterized the recent governments. The growing polarization meant that elections became increasingly bloody affairs: 46 were killed and 160 wounded in the election of 1886, in which President José Manuel Balmaceda effectively was handed power by his liberal predecessor.

In 1890, when Balmaceda signaled support for his friend Enrique Salvador Sanfuentes Andonaegui as his successor by appointing him prime minister, Congress reacted with a vote of censure. Congress ended its session on October 17, 1890, without authorizing appropriations for 1891. Balmaceda continued to rule without congressional acquiescence, despite a Supreme Court ruling that the army and navy would cease to exist legally on January 1, 1891, due to the lack of an appropriations bill. Balmaceda ignored the ruling, and on January 1, Balmaceda announced that he would simply follow the 1890 budget until elections were held. Congress responded the same day by voting to remove Balmaceda from office and soon selected naval officer Jorge Montt as his replacement. As a condition of leading this revolt by Congress, Montt demanded written authorization for military action from Congress. Leading members of Congress provided him with this authority and he then sought sanctuary on his ships on January 6, 1891.

Narrative: The next day, Montt proclaimed a revolt against Balmaceda. The navy followed Montt's orders, while the army supported Balmaceda, who promptly declared martial law. To prevent its seizure by army troops in Valparaíso, Montt ordered the navy to sea. The two sides then began to marshal their forces and resources. While Montt commanded Chile's most powerful warships, he had only 120 to 200 men available for any landing. Fortunately for the Congressist rebels, the nitrate-rich North barely was garrisoned; a landing party of just sixty men took control of the entire province of Coquimbo without a shot being fired. The rebels briefly occupied some lightly defended ports, from which they were able to resupply the ships and extract revenue. On January 16, Montt declared a blockade of the country's major ports, and Balmaceda sought support from the British Navy to destroy them. The first casualties also occurred on January 16, when five rebel sailors were killed and eight wounded by government artillery near Valparaíso. A week later, government forces evicted the rebels from Coquimbo. During the remainder of the month, there were several other small engagements during which government soldiers defected to the rebels.

The rebels soon were able to assemble an army of 1,200 by consolidating their forces with northern militiamen. The rebels also gained popular support when government forces under Col. Eulogio Robles violently suppressed a demonstration by 2,000 workers in Iquique, allegedly executing 18 of the leaders. On February 15, 1891, Robles's force of 350 soldiers suffered a crushing defeat in the Battle of San Francisco (also known at the Battle of Cerro Dolores), which reportedly cost the lives of two-thirds of his soldiers, compared to rebel losses of 16 killed. Robles assembled a new army of 900 men (including 600 led by Col. José Soto) and marched to Huara, where he waited for the rebels to attack. The battle on February 17 was a government victory, with the rebels losing up to 240 killed.

Meanwhile, the rebels had already realized that Iquique was undefended and landed troops in the city on February 16. Outflanked, Robles and Soto turned south and attacked the city on February 18. The rebels retreated to the customs house, and their fleet bombarded the city the next day, causing significant civilian casualties. Soto negotiated a twenty-four-hour truce so that fires ravaging the city could be extinguished, but what remained of his forces melted away, leaving Soto with only 30 men. The arrival of government reinforcements of only 100 men convinced Soto that the recapture of the city was impossible, and he surrendered to the rebels, with many of his troops joining the rebel army. The loss of the port of Iquique completely cut off the nitrate-rich North from the rest of the country. The rebels concentrated their force at Iquique, assembling a land force of up to 3,000 soldiers by the end of the month. The government army sent additional reinforcements, but as Robles planned to march to meet them, the rebels dispatched 1,700 men to prevent his southward movement on March 5. On March 7, the rebels attacked, winning the Battle of Pozo Almonte, where Robles was killed. Only 500 government soldiers managed to escape the disaster. That night, the transport ship *Maipo* in Valparaiso went over to the rebels, arriving in Iquique on March 14 with 70 officers and 164 soldiers.

After Pozo Almonte, the 1,000 reinforcements sent by the government embarked on an epic march through Bolivia and Argentina, rejoining the war months later after having lost 200 men to disease and the elements. Meanwhile, the rebels moved south to take Antofagasta, which the government army evacuated in the face of the numerically superior rebel force. The rebels then captured Arica and Tacma, completing the rebels' conquest of the North. The only significant engagement that month was a naval combat in which two government torpedo boats, acquired from Argentina, sank the rebel ironclad Blanco Encalada, killing more than 182 rebels in the first successful use of automotive torpedoes.

By late summer, the Congressist army was prepared for its final offensive. On August 18, the rebel fleet appeared outside Valparaíso, and on August 20, the rebels landed 9,284 troops near Concón. The local commander threw his 6,335 soldiers against Concón the next day, but the terrain heavily favored the rebels, and the rebels were supported by naval gunfire. The unsuccessful attack cost the government 1,700 to 2,200 casualties, while the rebels suffered only 216 to 400 killed. The rebel army of 9,279 then attacked the 9,200 government troops at Valparaíso on August 28. At the Battle of Placilla, the government forces were defeated, losing 941 killed against rebel losses of 485 killed. On August 29, Balmaceda resigned and sought refuge with the Argentine legation. His successor ordered an end to resistance, and the rebels occupied Santiago on August 31 and installed a provisional government on September 4.

Termination and Outcome: The outcome of the war was an unconditional rebel victory. The majority of senior government officers were court-martialed and retired, jailed, or put under house arrest. Balmaceda remained in the Argentine legation, where he committed suicide on September 19.

Coding Decisions: Small and Singer originally coded this war as having 5,000 battle-related deaths.[127] Other estimates of deaths in this war range from "more than 6,000 killed"[128] to "at least 10,000 killed."[129] If one merely adds together minimum estimates of deaths in each battle, and assuming that the rebels missing were killed, it gives a total of more than 1,700 rebel battle-deaths and more than 2,100 government battle-deaths. In addition, disease and elements surely took their toll—a single government column (in admittedly difficult circumstances) lost 200 men in two months. Because these estimates are much closer to 6,000 than to 10,000, we use the estimate of 5,500, derived by subtracting up to 500 civilian deaths in Valparaíso from the 6,000 figure. Given at least 4,000 documented military fatalities and the presence of disease and missing data, this estimate is more likely to be an underestimate than an overestimate.

Sources: Akers (1930); Ashwell (1998); Bernstein (1965); Blakemore (1965); Clodfelter (2002, 2008); Collier and Sater (2004); Estado Mayor General del Ejercito (1980); Hancock (1893); Harbottle and Bruce (1971); Legion de los Andes (2011); Marley (1998); Nunn (1976); Phillips and Axelrod (2005); Richardson (1960); Scheina (2003a); Small and Singer (1982); Zeitlin (1984).

INTRA-STATE WAR #619

Venezuela's Legalist Revolution of 1892

Participants: Venezuela versus Legalists.
Dates: March 11, 1892, to October 6, 1892.
Battle-related Deaths: Venezuela: [ ]; Legalists: [ ]; Total Combatant Deaths: 4,000.
Initiator: Legalists.
Outcome: Legalists win.
War Type: Civil for control of the central government.
Total System Member Military Personnel: Armed Forces of Venezuela: 5,000 (initial, peak, final).[130]
Theater Armed Forces: Legalists (Rebel Army): 400 (initial); 9,000 to 10,000 (peak, final).[131]

Antecedents: At the end of the Revindication War of 1879 (Intra-state War #609), former president Antonio Guzmán Blanco had been returned to power, and he ruled Venezuela directly or indirectly until 1887. He was succeeded by a brief caretaker government under Gen. Hermógenes López (1887–1888) and then by two lawyers, Dr. Juan Rojas Paúl (1888–1890) and Dr. Raimundo Anducza Palacio, who both overturned a number of Guzmán Blanco's policies. Instead of leaving office at the end of his two-year term, Anducza Palacio (who assumed office on March 19, 1890) tried to have his rule extended by increasing the presidential term of office from two to four years, which would need congressional approval. This move was portrayed as illegal by former liberal president Joaquín Sinforiano de Jesús Crespo. When Anducza Palacio refused to step down in 1892 and dissolved the congress, he triggered a revolt by most of the country's *caudillos*. The revolutionaries called themselves legalists and followed the leadership of Crespo.

Narrative: Crespo launched the revolution on March 11, 1892, in the state of Guáico, southeast of the capital of Caracas. The revolt spread as the governors of the Venezuelan states and local *caudillos* took sides, supporting the government or the legalists. Anducza Palacio dispatched the government's "Iron Chancellor," Sebastian Casañas, with an army of 4,000 soldiers to subdue the rebels. Fighting began in the southwestern state of Tachira, whose governor (and future president) Cispriano Castro sided with the government. The commander of the Tachira frontier army, Gen. José Maria González, was attacked on March 20, 1892, at the town of Colón, by a legalist army led by former governor Espirtu Santo Morales. Castro led a small army to relieve González, and after twenty-six hours of fighting, Castro's forces were victorious, and the rebels scattered. The pro-government army of 400 soldiers under General González and Col. Juan Vicento Gómez (also a future president) then headed to nearby El Topõn, where on March 22 (or March 28), they engaged and defeated a much larger legalist force led by Gen. Elisco Araujo, who had been appointed as president of the Andes. The pro-government forces, later joined by Castro, forced Araujo to flee the state. This pattern repeated itself several times in the West, including engagements at Palmira, Trujillo, and the Battle of Táriba (fought from May 14–15), and Castro and Gómez finally entered the important city of Mérida at the head of a 3,000-man army. Castro then began to organize an expedition toward the capital.

Elsewhere in the country, rebels began winning small engagements and mobilizing larger forces. The rebel forces under Gen. Ramon Guerra numbered 2,500 at the beginning of May, while the total number of rebel forces overall numbered about 4,000. On June 10, rebels defeated a government force of 400. Anducza Palacio's term as president (which was supposed to have expired on February 20, 1892) ended on June 17, 1892, when an interim president, Guillermo Tell Villegas, was appointed. The war dramatically escalated that summer. On July 1, the Battle of La Cortada del Guayabo was fought between armies of about 5,000 men each. A battle on August 9 involved rebel forces of 9,000 and resulted in 600 killed or wounded. The war moved toward a conclusion in the fall, and after the government lost the Battle of Los Colorados on October 4, the government abandoned Caracas. Crespo at the head of an army of 10,000 rebels entered the capital on October 6, 1892. Most pro-government forces ceased fighting at that point, but a few retreated into the interior and continued the struggle.

Termination and Outcome: The war ended with a rebel military victory, and on October 7, the victorious rebels announced a partial amnesty for all those who fought against them up to that day. Crespo sent forces into the Cordillera, and there were some casualties, but the character of the expedition was largely punitive, with little combat. Crespo served two more terms as president, 1892 to 1894 and 1894 to 1898. Cispriano Castro went into exile in Colombia, where he spent the next seven years amassing a fortune and creating a personal army that he would use to secure himself Venezuela's presidency in 1899 (Intra-state War #633).

Coding Decisions: According to Venezuelan military historian Manuel Landaeta Rosales, 4,000 were killed and 66,000 "mutilated" during the war.[132]

Sources: Márquez (1973); McBeth (2001); Rourke (1969); Scheina (2003a).

INTRA-STATE WAR #620

Brazil Federalists War of 1893 to 1894 (aka War of the Maragatos or Federalist Riogransense Revolution)

Participants: Brazil versus Federalists of Rio Grande do Sul.
Dates: February 2, 1893, to August 31, 1894.

Battle-related Deaths: Brazil: [ ]; Federalists: [ ]; Total Combatant Deaths: 3,000.
Initiator: Federalists.
Outcome: Brazil wins.
War Type: Civil central control.
Total System Member Military Personnel: Armed Forces of Brazil: 38,000 (prewar, initial); 40,000 (peak); 32,000 (final).[133]
Theater Armed Forces: Federalists, aka *Maragatos* (Rebel Army): 5,000 (initial); 6,000 (peak); 2,000 (final).[134]

Antecedents: In 1889, Marshal Manuel Deodoro da Fonseca launched the coup that overthrew Brazil's Emperor Pedro II, and Deodoro was elected the country's first president in 1891. By November of that year, Deodoro had earned the enmity of the legislature, so he dissolved it on November 3, 1891, only to find his attempted coup d'état opposed by both branches of the military as well as civil society. Consequently, he stepped down in favor of his vice president, Marshal Floriano Peixoto, on November 23, 1891. Brazil's transition from empire to republic was turbulent, and three wars would break out within the next five years (Intra-state Wars #620, #621, and #632), with the first two occurring in 1893. The first involved the federalists who wanted greater autonomy from the centralist republican government.

In the southernmost state of Rio Grande do Sul, the Liberal Party had dominated over the Conservative Party during imperial times. The relatively new Republican Party of Rio Grande do Sul (PRR) was created, and conservatives often aligned with the PRR. After the provisional president appointed PRR member Júlio de Castilhos as secretary of state for Rio Grande do Sul, the latter used his power to remove liberals and to install PRR-aligned politicians and leaders of the National Guard, while creating a new military brigade. However, Castilhos was overthrown by a triumvirate of fellow PRR members. Out of office, Castilhos ultimately began to construct alliances with regional *gaucho caudillos*. He also allied with President Floriano, and with his tacit support, Castilhos overthrew the state government on June 17, 1892. Federalist commanders and politicians fled to Uruguay. The PRR relied upon the military brigade as a state army to prevent any attempt at counterrevolution, and as the brigade had only 1,265 troops, conscription was introduced to enlarge it. Over the next six months, at least 134 people, mostly federalists, were killed by the PRR, and perhaps as many as 10,000 federalists became refugees in Uruguay by February 1893. In Uruguay, the federalists, who were known as *Maragatos*, began to organize under the political leadership of Gaspar da Silveira Martins (a liberal who had served briefly as president of Rio Grande do Sol during the empire), while the military wing was under the command of Gumercindo Saraiva. The initial goal of the federalists was regional: the overthrow of the government of Rio Grande. However, the revolt would soon develop a national character due to the involvement of President Floriano.

Narrative: On February 2, 1893, the first armed federalist band crossed the border from Uruguay into Rio Grande do Sul. It was the vanguard of a 5,000-strong rebel army, albeit a poorly armed one, which included volunteers from Uruguay and Argentina, led by Saraiva. Saraiva's forces were soon joined by large armies under Joaquim Pedro Salgado and Col. João Nunes da Silva Tavares (who then assumed command of the rebels). The first engagement was fought on February 22; the rebels overwhelmed 250 government defenders at Dom Pedrito at the cost of only a few dead. Much of the government garrison then defected to the federalist rebels. The rebels soon laid siege to the small town of Santana do Livramento but were forced to retreat in March as reinforcements dispatched by Brazil's president arrived. The first major battle occurred on May 4, near the Inhanduí river, pitting the three major federalist generals and their 6,000 troops against 4,500 to 7,000 better-armed soldiers of Brazil and the PRR's military brigade. Tavares and Salgado were forced to retreat into Uruguay, while Saraiva continued to fight with only 1,100 men. As national troops and the military brigade (now jointly under the command of Brazil's war minister, Gen. Francisco Antõnio de Moura) pursued Saraiva's forces, the rebel leaders rebuilt and reorganized in Uruguay.

Federalist commander Salgado managed to collect 1,000 soldiers and reentered Brazil in August, linking up with Saraiva to win the Battle of Serro do Ouro, in which several hundred were killed. Meanwhile, opposition to President Floriano was spreading, leading to the naval war that began in September (Intra-state War #621). The federalists pushed toward Itaqui on the Uruguay river, where they hoped to find naval support for their own rebellion, but they were met with indifference on the part of local naval commanders. Also in September, Tavares reentered Brazil and captured Quarai on the southwestern border. In November, Tavares surprised a 1,000-strong government force in Bagé, on the banks of the Rio Negro. After a prompt surrender by government forces, Tavares ordered the execution of 300 prisoners, and they were dispatched by a single man during the night, using the *degola* (throat slitting) technique. Five months later, the government would retaliate by killing an equal number of captured prisoners in the same fashion.

At this point, the three most prominent rebel commanders went their separate ways. Saraiva pushed north, beginning a 750-mile march toward the state of Santa Catarina, hoping to link up with the naval rebels. Following victories in the battles of Tijucas and Lapa, he captured Curitiba, the capital of the state of Paraná, on January 20. The rebels now had parts of three states under their control, and Saraiva demanded the resignation of Floriano. For his part, Tavares besieged Bagé but was forced to evacuate his positions on January 8, 1894, when a government relief column arrived. Tavares retreated into Uruguay and gave up the fight, although other *gaucho* commanders continued the war in the Camphana area near the border. Meanwhile, Salgado had pushed east to meet up with the naval rebels. Unfortunately for his forces, the naval rebels were barely able to hold their capital in Santa Catarina. A joint naval-federalist attack on Rio Grande in April failed. With the defeat of the naval rebellion, on April 16, 1894, the government was now able to devote its energies and resources to combatting the federalists. Faced with the strong National Guard of the state of São Paulo and the bulk of the national army, Saraiva decided to retreat, and the rebels now were forced back largely into Rio Grande do Sul.

Saraiva's army, at 4,000 strong, was now the largest rebel force still in the field. Soon Salgado linked up with another force under Antônio Prestes Guimarães to fight the war's biggest battle, the Battle of Passo Fundo, on June 29, 1894. The federalists were defeated, suffering 400 casualties, while the government suffered only 240. On August 10, Gumercindo Saraiva was killed in a skirmish with government forces. As most of Saraiva's men were led into Argentina by his brother, Aparício Saraiva, sustained combat at war level ceased.

Termination and Outcome: The war ended in a rebel defeat, and by the end of the year, the government had stamped out most remaining resistance. Following negotiations among Brazil, Uruguay, and Argentina, the latter two agreed to intern the rebel forces on their soil. One last invasion of Rio Grande do Sul was defeated on April 22, 1895. An agreement with the rebels was signed August 23, 1895. A full amnesty followed two months later.

Coding Decisions: Detailed information concerning the battle-deaths in this war is limited. The war produced 10,000 to 12,000 combatant casualties. Using the standard rule of 3 wounded for every 1 killed, this translates into 2,500 to 3,000 combatant deaths. Taking into account that at least 600 prisoners were executed during the war, our best estimate is a total of 3,000 battle-deaths.[135]

Sources: Bello (1966); Chasteen (1995); Clodfelter (2002); Cortés (1974); Davis (1968); Love (1971); Marley (1998); McCann (2004); Schneider (1991); Topik (2000).

INTRA-STATE WAR #621

Brazil Naval War of 1893 to 1894

Participants: Brazil versus Naval Royalists.
Dates: September 6, 1893, to April 16, 1894.
Battle-related Deaths: Brazil: [ ]; Naval Royalists: [ ]; Total Combatant Deaths: 1,000.
Initiator: Naval Royalists.
Outcome: Brazil wins.
War Type: Civil for central control.
Total System Member Military Personnel: Armed Forces of Brazil: 38,000 (prewar); 30,000 (after initial defections); 40,000 (peak); 36,000 (final).[136]
Theater Armed Forces: Armed Forces of Brazil: 7,000 to 8,000.[137] Naval Rebels: 1,400 (initial); 5,000 (peak); 2,000 (final).[138]

Antecedents: After Marshal Manuel Deodoro da Fonseca launched the coup that overthrew Brazil's emperor Pedro II in 1889, he was elected the country's first president in 1891. By November of that year, Deodoro had earned the enmity of the legislature, so he dissolved it on November 3, 1891, only to find his attempted coup d'état opposed by both branches of the military. Seeing this resistance, he stepped down in favor of his vice president, Marshal Floriano Peixoto, on November 23, 1891. The losing vice presidential candidate in the 1891 election, Admiral Eduardo Wandenkolk, was one of a group military officers who demanded new elections and was subsequently forced to retire in 1892. Most of Brazil's states supported Deodoro's actions and therefore represented a political threat to Floriano. As he attempted to strengthen his position by undermining state governments, a number of states rebelled: minor revolts in Rio de Janeiro, Minas Gerais, Matto Grosso, São Paolo, Amazonas, and Maranhão were easily suppressed. However, in Rio Grande do Sul, full-scale civil war broke out on February 2, 1893 (see Intra-state War #620).

Because Floriano represented the army and relations between it and the navy were acrimonious, there was a danger of subversion by alienated naval officers. In addition, naval leaders were generally pro-monarchist, pro-federalist, and opposed to the new republic. It was therefore expected that a naval mutiny might occur. In April 1893, Adm. Custódio de Melo resigned his position as minister of the navy. Three months later, on July 6, 1893, Admiral Wandenkolk launched a revolt by commandeering a ship and sailing to Rio Grande to link up with the federalist rebels. Though Wandenkolk found little support and soon surrendered, his war actions paved the way for the upcoming rebellion.

Narrative: On September 5, 1893, Admiral de Mello went aboard the ship *Aquibadã* in the Rio de Janeiro harbor with his staff and a few deputies. The long-awaited naval mutiny occurred the next day, when de Mello raised the flag of revolt. Most of the navy in the Rio de Janeiro harbor (1,400 officers and sailors aboard fifteen warships)—but only one of the thirteen forts in the bay—joined the *Aquibadã* in rebellion. Mello ordered the city to be bombarded, but foreign warships united under the command of a French admiral to protect their commercial interests. They forbade the bombardment of the city and threatened to fire on Mello's much-smaller fleet if he disobeyed the order. The United States, anxious to keep the Europeans from interfering, sent several warships to assist President Floriano.

The rebels had expected the government to capitulate; however, instead Floriano transformed his presidency into a virtual dictatorship, arresting hundreds of political opponents, censoring the press, and cancelling legislative elections. No support for the rebellion was available from the now-quiescent states. Mello attempted to land forces several times, but each assault was repulsed easily by the army, which had remained loyal. There were almost daily battles between the fortifications of the harbor and Mello's ships, and several of the rebel ships were dispatched southward to link up with the Federalist Rebellion.

On October 7, Admiral Luís Saldanha da Gama, commander of one of the coastal forts, joined the rebellion. One week later, the naval rebels in the South captured Desterro (now Florianópolis) on Santa Catarina Island. There, the rebel Capt. Frederico Lorena established a provisional government (announced on October 24). A stalemate prevailed for nearly four months in the harbor, during which the rebel ships periodically would bombard the capital. Many of the larger rebel ships made their way south in an attempt to join the Federalist Rebellion in Rio Grande do Sul, including de Mello and the *Aquibadã* on December 1. The government utilized the time to reinforce its positions, and government forces sank three small rebel ships, while the rebels sank a troop transport, killing 500 soldiers. On February 9, 1894, the rebels attempted to take Niteroi with only 500 men but were driven back with significant losses. The government succeeded in assembling another navy, which entered the harbor on March 13; the remaining rebels there under Admiral da Gama sought asylum on Portuguese vessels and abandoned their ships.

The government fleet moved south to deal with Mello's forces. While Mello decided to sail into Argentine waters and surrender to the local authorities, the battleship *Aquibadã* determined to carry on the fight. It was soon torpedoed, beached, and abandoned. On April 16—the same day that Mello surrendered his ships—the government retook what was left of the *Aquibadã*. The naval rebellion was over.

Termination and Outcome: The outcome of the war was an unconditional military victory by the government. Nearly 2,000 rebels fled the country, either to Portugal or Argentina or to join the federalist rebels in Uruguay.

Coding Decisions: Williams states that the naval revolt resulted in the losses of thousands of lives. Yet there were few engagements of substance in the war, and those generally were fought with mere hundreds of soldiers. Given the strength of the two sides, a figure of 1,000 is more plausible, including the 500 government soldiers that drowned when their troop transport was rammed by the rebels.[139]

Sources: Bello (1966); Calogeras (1939); Clodfelter (2002, 2008); Davis (1968); Marley (1998); Martin and Lovett (1968); McCann (2004), Scheina (2003a); Schneider (1991); Smith (1970); Topik (2000); Williams (1945).

INTRA-STATE WAR #625

Third Peru War of 1894 to 1895 (aka Civilista Revolution or Revolution of 1895)

Participants: Peru versus National Coalition.
Dates: October 24, 1894, to March 19, 1895.
Battle-related Deaths: Peru: [ ]; National Coalition: [ ]; Total Combatant Deaths: 4,000.
Initiator: National Coalition.
Outcome: National Coalition wins.
War Type: Civil for central control.
Total System Member Military Personnel: Armed Forces of Peru: 6,000 (prewar); 4,000 (final).[140]
Theater Armed Forces: *Civilistas* (Rebel Army): 5,000 (peak); 5,000 (final).[141]

Antecedents: After Peru's defeat in the War of the Pacific (Inter-state War #64, 1879 to 1883), Chile recognized Gen. Miguel Iglesias as the president of Peru. Peru then entered a period of political upheaval and guerrilla war, partially led by Gen. Andrés Avelino Cáceres, who helped form an alliance between peasants and indigenous peoples to fight the collaborationist government. After Peru was victorious in a war with the Indians (Intra-state War #613) in 1885, General Cáceres marched his troops to the capital and demanded a presidential election. The lack of popular support for Iglesias became apparent as large numbers of the citizens of Lima began to support Cáceres. To spare Peru further bloodshed, Iglesias resigned on December 12, 1885. Elections were planned, and Cáceres, as the only candidate, easily won and took office on June 3, 1886.

Cacáres held the presidency for one term and then effectively passed control to a loyal ally, Morales Bermúdez. When Bermúdez died before the end of his term (on April 1, 1894), his civilian first vice president (an ally of José Nicolás de Piéroloa) was bypassed in favor of Justiniano Borgoño, a Cacáres loyalist representing the relatively liberal Constitutional Party, to serve as the caretaker president until new elections could be held. Piéroloa briefly had been president of Peru from 1879 to 1881 and had founded the Democrat Party in 1884. When Cacáres was again elected president, taking office on August 10, 1894, he was opposed by both aristocratic figures like Píerola and the reformist political parties. Píerola loyalists almost immediately began raising armed forces to oppose the government, and the Civilista Party (Civic Union) was persuaded to drop its former support of Cacáres and to enter into an alliance with its ideological rivals, the Democrat Party. The parties joined forces on March 30, 1894, in the National Coalition to oppose Cacáres to end the rule of military leaders in favor of civilians.

Narrative: When Cacáres assumed the presidency in August 1894, the National Coalition, in need of a leader, sought out Píerola, who had fled Peru in 1890 and was then in Chile. Píerola agreed to lead the opposition and embarked for Peru on October 19, 1894, arriving on the October 24. Píerola soon issued his revolutionary manifesto and began gathering an army of *montoneros* for the march on Lima. Revolts broke out throughout the South in the fall of 1894 as the rebels gathered strength for an assault on the central government. On March 16, 1895, Píerola ordered his 5,000 troops to attack Lima, held by 4,000 troops under Cacáres. Fighting raged from March 17 to 19, and more than 3,000 were killed before the diplomatic corps negotiated an armistice.

Termination and Outcome: Though the rebels had not technically won the war in that Cacáres's army was still intact, an armistice ended the war on terms highly favorable to the rebels. The terms of the agreement called for the government to step down (Cacáres agreed to leave Peru), while a provisional junta held elections. As in previous postwar elections, the results served to ratify the seizure of power, with Píerola assuming the presidency.

Coding Decisions: Regarding the deaths in this war, a total of about 10,000 to 11,000 Peruvians died. Of these, 2,000 to 3,000 died in the Battle of Lima, and 8,000 were killed prior to that point.[142] In focusing only upon combatant deaths, the figure of 4,000 combatant deaths seems plausible.

Sources: Akers (1912); Crichfield (1908); Gonzales (1987); Marett (1969); Pike (1967); Reano (2002).

INTRA-STATE WAR #626

Fifth Colombian War of 1895

Participants: Colombia versus Liberals.
Dates: January 22, 1895, to March 8, 1895.
Battle-related Deaths: Liberals: [ ]; Colombia: [ ]; Total Combatant Deaths: 1,125. (See Coding Decisions.)
Initiator: Liberals.
Outcome: Colombia wins.
War Type: Civil for central control.
Total System Member Military Personnel: Armed Forces of Colombia: 6,000 (prewar, initial); 12,000 (peak, final).[143]
Theater Armed Forces: War Liberals (Rebel Army): 2,000 (initial); 4,000 (peak, final).[144]

Antecedents: This war continued the pattern of earlier conflicts in Colombia that revolved around the feud between conservatives and liberals. In the civil war of 1884 to 1885 against President Rafael Núñez (Intra-state War #612: the Fourth Colombian War), the liberals were defeated, and the Liberal Party split into war and peace factions. As the reigning nationalist-conservative alliance showed signs of fracture in the 1892 presidential election, the war liberals got the upper hand in the Liberal Party and began planning for a revolt as early as 1893. There were a number of insurrections during this period, but in 1895, the fighting rose to the level of civil war against the government of President Miguel Antonio Caro (who used his previous title of vice president in deference to President Núñez, whose illness first brought Caro to power as acting president in 1892–1894).

Narrative: In response to the attacks that Vice President Caro had received during the election from both the traditional conservatives and the liberals, in 1893 Caro imposed new censorship laws on the opposition. As liberal newspapers were closed and liberal leaders put in jail or expelled from the country, the war liberals planned to take direct action. President Caro officially took office on September 18, 1894. The war began as an attempted coup d'état in which some 2,000 war liberals were to seize Caro on January 22, 1895. Preemptive arrests averted that plan. Nonetheless, war liberal forces rebelled throughout the country on the next day, leading to confused fighting in which some police and army units defected to the rebels. More than 2,000 rebels rose in the departments of Boyaca, Santander, and Tolima. Other insurrections broke out in other departments, but they were not coordinated or unified under a single command. Contrary to some war liberals' expectations, the dissident conservatives refused to join them in the field.

The initial military actions were relatively small engagements. In mid-February, fighting near El Posario de Cucuta resulted in 120 killed on both sides. Major rebel forces included 1,400 in the provinces of Sugamuxi and Tundama in Boyaca in the North and at least two other forces in the center, one of 300 and another stronger than 500. Some 2,000 rebels abandoned Cucuta (in the North) on February 18. The decisive battle of the war occurred on March 15, 1895, at Encisco, in the province of Santander in northeast Colombia. The rebels' largest remaining force—2,500 strong and bolstered by Venezuelan mercenaries—was defeated by 3,000 government soldiers. More than 1,005 were killed not counting those who died in the forests where cavalry couldn't penetrate to retrieve the bodies. The next day, the government surprised the rebels at Capitanejo, and the rebellion in Santander was defeated. In Panama, the war liberals continued to resist the government with assistance from foreign "adventurers" led by Catarino Garza. On March 8, 1895, the liberal forces were defeated and Garza killed, effectively ending the war.

Termination and Outcome: The outcome was a government victory. Caro became so disillusioned that he briefly resigned his position in March 1896, but he returned and completed his term in office, serving until 1898, when fellow National Party member Manuel Antonio Sanclemente was inaugurated.

Coding Decisions: Fatality estimates for this war are scarce, and even those that are reported are fairly divergent. For instance, Scheina reports both fewer numbers of troops engaged and fewer deaths in the major battle at Encisco (1,500 government troops and 500 total combatant deaths). In contrast, Peña reports 3,000 government soldiers and a total of 1,005 deaths, not counting the unrecoverable bodies. Peña also describes 120 battle-deaths in a string of engagements in February. We are reporting Peña's total figure of 1,125 here, which is probably an underestimate given the amount of missing data.

Sources: Bergquist (1978); Olarte (1993); Peña (1997), Scheina (2003a).

INTRA-STATE WAR #627

Ecuador Liberals War of 1895 (aka Alfarista Revolution)

Participants: Ecuador versus Liberal *Caudillos.*
Dates: February 12, 1895, to September 22, 1895.
Battle-related Deaths: Ecuador: [ ]; Liberal *Caudillos*: [ ]; Total Combatant Deaths: 1,000. (See Coding Decisions.)
Initiator: Liberal *Caudillos.*
Outcome: Liberal *Caudillos* win.
War Type: Civil for central control.
Total System Member Military Personnel: Armed Forces of Ecuador: 3,000 (initial); 2,000 (after initial defections); 2,350 (peak), 1,068 (final).[145]
Theater Armed Forces: Liberals (Rebel Army): 5,600 (peak).[146] Indians (allied to Liberals), participating from mid-August 1895: 10,000 (initial, peak).[147]

Antecedents: Since gaining independence, Ecuador has had a history of political instability with multiple constitutions and presidents unlikely to serve complete terms of office. The struggle between liberals and conservatives was compounded by the rivalry between the highland capital of Quito (generally controlled by conservatives) and the port city of Guayaquil (home of the liberals). The period of 1860 to 1895 generally has been described as the Era of Conservative rule, though in 1876, the Guayaquil radical liberals led by Col. Ignacio de Veintimilla defeated the conservative government in Quito (Intra-state War #606). However, Veintimilla, who remained in office until 1883, evolved into more of a populist dictator than a dedicated liberal. Subsequent presidents adopted a progressive program trying to bridge the divide between the liberals and conservatives, though not always successfully. In 1892, Luis Cordero Crespo was elected to the presidency over his conservative rival. In January 1895, a scandal erupted over Cordero's decision to let Chile use the Ecuadorian flag on a ship it was selling to Japan (which was then at war with China: Inter-state War #73). Protests against Cordero broke out across the country, leading soon to a revolution that many consider to be one of the most important in Ecuador's history since it launched the Radical Liberal Era that would last until 1944.

Narrative: On February 12, 1895, the liberals in Guayaquil began a general strike and issued a call for a nationwide revolution against the government. The campaign brought together a number of opposition groups, including the liberal bourgeoisie, professional revolutionaries, liberal *caudillos*, and the *montoneras* (armed paramilitary groups, frequently cavalry). Wealthy liberal Col. Carlos Concha Torres responded to the call and landed a force of sixty men at Esmereldas (on the northern coast, west of the capital) at the onset of the revolution. The first recorded combat occurred on February 18 at Hacienda Venecia (near Guayaquil), where deaths were said to be numerous on both sides.

During March and April, the revolt became more widespread. On April 10, 1895, Cordero was confronted in Quito with an angry mob demanding his resignation. The demonstration led to a bloody skirmish, and to avoid any further bloodshed, Cordero resigned on April 16, 1895, turning the office over to Vice President Vicente Lucio Salazar. The move served to divide the rebel movement, with some now supporting the new conservative government, while others continued to oppose it. After some confusion, the rebellion continued in the center of the county. On April 19, 1895, the competing forces met at Guaranda (inland between Guayaquil and Quito), and though their numbers were small—82 and 300 men—many were killed and wounded. On May 1, *montoneras* under the leadership of Dionisio J. Andrade fought the Battle de los Amarillos at the town of Chrone, southwest of the capital.

At this point, a dominant role in the revolution was taken on by José Eloy Alfaro Delgado. Eloy Alfaro was identified with anticlerical or radical liberalism, and his past involvement in opposition to the conservatives had led to his exile in Panama on several occasions. On May 5, Alfaro (his followers are sometimes referred to as *Alfaristas*) assumed command of the liberal forces in the field. Meanwhile, after a series of battles in May, liberal forces under Carlos Concha Torres finally succeeded in capturing the city of Esmereldas on June 6. In Guayaquil, a popular assembly declared Alfaro as supreme head of the republic, and Alfaro arrived in the city on June 19 to take control of the liberal forces there. Rebel forces elsewhere continued to score victories against government forces during the summer.

The government's failure to crush the uprising quickly proved to be its undoing. By the end of June, liberal forces numbered more than 4,000, while the government had begun the war with 3,360 soldiers, but its numbers soon declined as entire units defected to the rebels. As the government lost more battles, liberals gained more allies. Ten thousand Indians under commanders Sáez and Guamán offered their services to the revolution, although it is unclear whether all of them were combatants. Finally Alfaro led 3,000 rebels from Guayaquil against the government in Quito. Alfaro's forces defeated the 2,350 government troops on August 14 and 15 at the Battle of Cuenca. Alfaro then marched in triumph into Quito in August or September (sources disagree about the exact date). Limited fighting continued until the liberal victory at Caranqui on September 22.

Termination and Outcome: The war ended as a military victory by the liberal rebels. On October 9, 1895, the first Liberal Constituent Assembly met in Guayaquil, where Alfaro was appointed as acting president of Ecuador. Despite the conciliatory policy of Alfaro, his determination to preserve the new liberal government sparked opposition. After a hiatus of more than eight months, the struggle was renewed in 1896 by conservatives (Intra-state War #631.5).

Coding Decisions: We have been unable to locate total fatality statistics for this war. Merely adding together the fatality statistics we have for individual battles produces a total of 800 combatant deaths. Because information is missing for more than half of the battles and for many skirmishes, as well as for those who died from wounds or disease, we feel certain that this conflict meets the war-fatality criterion. However, as we don't feel able to make any more concrete conclusions, we are coding this as having 1,000 total combatant deaths.

Sources: Blanksten (1951); Clodfelter (2002); Garcia (1979); Mora (1994); Santovenia (1935); Spindler (1987); Vicuña (1984).

INTRA-STATE WAR #631.5

Ecuadorian Conservative Revolt of 1896

Participants: Ecuador versus Conservatives.
Dates: June 1, 1896, to August 28, 1896.
Battle-related Deaths: Ecuador: [ ]; Conservatives: [ ]; Total Combatant Deaths: 1,500.
Initiator: Conservatives.
Outcome: Ecuador wins.
War Type: Civil for central control.
Total System Member Military Personnel: Armed Forces of Ecuador: 3,000 (initial, peak, final).[148]
Theater Armed Forces: Conservatives: [ ].

Antecedents: The conservative government of Ecuador was overthrown in a revolution in 1895 by a coalition of liberals, including the liberal bourgeoisie, professional revolutionaries, liberal *caudillos*, and the *montoneras* aided by some of the indigenous population (Intra-state War #627). At the end of the war, the supreme liberal commander, José Eloy Alfaro Delgado, was selected as provisional president, and he began a full term as president on January 17, 1897. Alfaro's ascension began what became known as the Radical Liberal Era, which endured from 1895 to 1944. The conservatives did not accept this shift easily, and Alfaro's first year as president would experience a conservative counterrevolution.

Narrative: Once in office, Alfaro, who was avowedly anticlerical, began implementing the liberal agenda of stripping the Catholic Church of a number of its privileges: seizing land, closing monasteries, and secularizing public education. For the first time, representatives of Protestant churches were permitted in Ecuador, and the Catholic Church began to urge its followers to resist the "atheistic *Alfaristas*." Two foreign-born bishops, Pedro Schumacher and Arsenio Andrade, became particularly active in promoting political action. Conservative strength was centered in the vicinity of the capital of Quito, and the larger population in that area meant that the conservatives still controlled the legislature and could stall or block liberal legislation. Alfaro responded to the growing agitation by forcing the foreign-born clergy to leave the country. In June 1896, the conservatives launched a war that combined elements of both civil and religious conflict.

Conservatives in the Sierra revolted, taking control of a number of towns, and the government dispatched its own forces to regain control. The first battle took place at Huerta Redanda on June 1, 1896. On July 5, 1896, conservative forces led by Antonio Muñoz Vega captured Cuenca and held the city in the face of a government expedition led by President Alfaro until August 23. Vega then fled to Peru. In Quito, the civil/military chief prepared the town to resist the liberal government. There were excesses committed by the forces on each side, and in Quito, liberals stormed the archbishop's palace and burned the library. The final battle took place in the South at Cajanuma on August 28, 1896.

Termination and Outcome: The outcome was a victory for the government. Alfaro served as president until 1901 and then again from 1907 to 1911, during which time many of his reforms restricted the powers of the Church. Though Alfaro was relatively popular, opposition to his regime continued. On October 6, 1896, rebels came into Guayaquil and set fire to hundreds of houses. Ultimately, one-third of the city was destroyed. The assembly met in Guayaquil on October 9, 1896, where Alfaro was confirmed as president, but then it was forced to relocate to Quito due to the fire.

Coding Decisions: There is relatively little specific information available about this war. By adding up the fatalities reported in a number of the battles, we calculated that there were at least 1,500 battle deaths, though the true figure could be higher.

Sources: Linke (1960); Mora (1994).

INTRA-STATE WAR #632
Third Brazil War of 1896 to 1897 (aka Canudos Revolt)

Participants: Brazil versus Canudos *Conselhistas.*
Dates: October 1, 1896, to October 5, 1897.
Battle-related Deaths: Brazil: 5,000; *Conselhistas:* 10,000. (See Coding Decisions.)
Initiator: Brazil.
Outcome: Brazil wins.
War Type: Civil for local issues.
Total System Member Military Personnel: Brazilian Armed Forces: 36,000 (prewar, initial, peak, final).[149]
Theater Armed Forces: Brazilian Armed Forces and Bahai Army: 30 (initial); 8,526 (peak). *Conselhistas* (Rebel Army): 1,000 (prewar); 4,000 (initial); 10,000 (peak); less than 1,000 (final).[150]

Antecedents: In 1893, Antonio Maciel, known as the *Conselheiro*, and his followers (*Conselhistas*) created the religious colony Belo Monte at Canudos, 300 miles northwest Bahia's capital of Salvador. Their religion was a mixture of Catholicism, Indian traditions, and Portuguese mythology. Its fanaticism and aims of restoring God and the monarchy to Brazil drew a large following among the peasantry (*sertanejos*). By 1896, the flood of *Conselhistas* coming into Canudos had made the town into the largest urban area outside of the capital, with about 30,000 residents. Of these, at least 1,000 *jagunços* (armed men) served the *Conselheiro.* Bahia had been the site of an earlier revolt (Intra-state War #531 in 1837 to 1838) in which the rebels sought greater local autonomy from the central government. Thus, the government of Brazil saw the *Conselhistas* as a threat to the new republic.

The specific trigger for the war was a conflict between Canudos and the nearby town of Joazeiro during which the *Conselhistas* threatened to take prepaid but undelivered supplies by force. The town requested state assistance in dealing with the *Conselhistas.*

Narrative: The war began when the state government sent a detachment of thirty soldiers to quell the disturbance by intercepting a group of *Conselhistas.* Instead of calming the situation, the government force was attacked and wiped out by a group of *jagunços* who supported *Conselheiro.* The state, which had underestimated the seriousness of the conflict, then appealed to the national government for military assistance.

The remainder of the war largely consisted of four successive, increasingly large government expeditions against the *Conselhistas.* The first was a unit of 107 men sent to protect the town of Uauá from the threatened attack. On November 21, 1896, their offensive was halted by 500 *jagunços* who attacked the government force, suffering more than 150 killed against only 10 government dead. However, the government force retreated, burning the town behind them. The government followed up with a second expedition consisting of 543 soldiers. It reached Canudos after exhausting its supplies, forcing it to act precipitously to take the settlement for its food. The rebels first attacked along a narrow road leading to Canudos, suffering 115 battle-deaths against only 4 government dead. The following morning, government forces were attacked in their camp just over a mile from Canudos by what the government commander estimated to be 4,000 poorly armed rebels. The government lost 10 killed before retreating, against 300 rebel battle-deaths. Attacks continued until government forces retreated to the safety of Monte Santo the next day.

The third expedition was commanded by Moreira César, veteran of the recent suppression of the Federalist Rebellion (Intra-state War #620). He assembled a force of 1,281 soldiers and state police and set out from Salvador to Canudos. He opted to take an indirect route to Canudos, which took 27 days to reach Mount Favela, which overlooked the town. On March 2, 1897, César began the attack from positions about three miles from the settlement. The soldiers then charged into the mazelike alleys of the town. César was mortally wounded, and his second in command ordered a retreat at dusk. The government had lost 200 wounded and an unknown number of killed. Once word spread of César's death, government units disintegrated. The *sertanejos* attacked the next morning, and the remaining government forces were routed, abandoning their weapons. The rebels killed the wounded government soldiers and forced the government soldiers to retreat to the next outpost, Queimadas, without provisions. Many government soldiers also died of thirst or hunger along the way. News of the defeat prompted a violent reaction by the republicans against suspected monarchists in the country; one notable newspaper editor was lynched in Rio de Janeiro. The government was destabilized; for example, that year featured four successive ministers of war.

An army of 8,526 federal soldiers was assembled for the fourth and final expedition against Canudos. Malaria struck some units en route to the final assembly point. The first engagement was fought on June 25, 1897, at the Fazenda Cocorobó, five miles from Canudos. The *sertanejos* were dislodged from their dominating positions at the cost of 27 government battle deaths. A series of engagements followed until the forces arrived at Canudos on June 27. The bombardment of Canudos began late that day. By morning, Canudos was caught in a pincer movement by the two principal columns of the expeditionary force. The rebels attacked one column, forcing the other to come to its aid, leaving the soldiers surrounded by the *sertanejos*. Only about 5,000 soldiers remained. By July 5, their rations had run out, and desertion became a serious problem for the government. On July 13, supplies finally reached the besieged expedition, and five days later government forces broke out of the siege and seized a small portion of Canudos itself. The battle cost the government 1,014 casualties, or nearly a third of the remaining force of 3,349. The rebels suffered only 100 battle-deaths, but they were now besieged. The expedition requested another 5,000 men from the government. Hundreds of *sertanejos* and federal troops were killed each day.

The last rebel attack failed on July 24, and for the remainder of the war, they remained on the defensive. Conditions among government troops remained deplorable; the majority of evacuated wounded died en route. Reinforcements finally reached the expedition on August 15. In September, some rebels made an effort to surrender but were killed as soon as they disarmed. With the aid of the reinforcements, Canudos was finally encircled on September 24. Conselheiro had died of natural causes the day before, and only about 8,000 *sertanejos* and their families remained. However, a government attack on October 1 was repulsed with 587 government casualties and 400 *sertanejo* dead. From October 2 to 3, 1897, nearly 1,000 *sertanejos*, mostly women and children, surrendered to government forces. On October 5, the government razed what was left of Canudos, killing the remaining rebels and their families.

Termination and Outcome: The outcome of the war was a complete government victory.

Coding Decisions: Because the state of Bahai was fighting on behalf of the national government of Brazil, it is not coded as a separate war participant.

The death toll of this war was significant. The estimate of 5,000 government battle-deaths is frequently cited, and it is reasonable given the known presence of disease, deprivation, and dehydration among government soldiers.[151] As the town of Canudos was destroyed, some historians report rebel death figures of 30,000 fatalities, which assumes that no one fled from Canudos during the war and that all of the town's inhabitants were rebel soldiers. Though a few women were known to have fought with the rebels, the vast majority of females (who were the majority of the population) would have been civilians, not combatants. Schneider estimates 15,000 *sertanejo* casualties. Levine states that more than 15,000 died on both sides. If the government lost 5,000 combatants, then 10,000 rebel battle-deaths appears to be a reasonable figure.[152]

Sources: Akers (1930); Bello (1966); Clodfelter (2002, 2008); Cunha (1944); Davis (1968); Levine (1988, 1992); Madden (1993); Marley (1998); McCann (2004); Schneider (1991).

INTRA-STATE WAR #632.3
Revolución de Queipa of 1898

Participants: Venezuela versus José Hernández-led Rebels.
Dates: March 17, 1898, to July 14, 1898.
Battle-related Deaths: Venezuela: [ ]; José Hernández-led Rebels: [ ]; Total Combatant Deaths: 1,800.[153]
Initiator: Rebels.
Outcome: Venezuela wins.
Total System Member Military Personnel: Armed Forces of Venezuela: 4,000 (prewar); 4,000 (initial); 20,000 (peak); 20,000 (final).[154]
Theater Armed Forces: Armed Forces of Venezuela: 1,500 (initial); Nationalists or *Mochistas* (Rebel Army): 300 (initial); 16,000 (peak).[155]
War Type: Civil for control of the central government.

Antecedents: Gen. Joaquín Sinforiano de Jesús Crespo had been returned to Venezuela's presidency in 1892 as a result of the Legalist Revolution (Intra-state War #619). Crespo's regime had tolerated some political opposition, and Crespo indicated that he would allow a free election for his successor. Crespo's Liberal Party nominee was Ignacio Andrade, who as president of Miranda was the second-most powerful man in the country. Andrade faced a collection of contenders, one of whom was the nominee of the *Partido Liberal Nacionalista*, José Manuel "El Mocho" Hernández. Hernández had fought for the legalists in 1892 and had subsequently spent time in the United States. Returning to Venezuela, Hernández utilized the populist style of campaigning he had observed in America to garner widespread support. Nonetheless, Hernández lost the election on September 1. Charging voter intimidation and fraud, Hernández wanted to launch a rebellion immediately; however, he was under virtual house arrest. Finally with the help of his friends, Hernández was able to escape Caracas and flee westward to a supporter's *hacienda* of *La Queipa* near Valencia, whence Hernández launched his rebellion.

Narrative: Hernández and his ally Rámon Guerra declared their rebellion on March 2, 1898, after which both sides moved quickly. This civil war was fought between the government of Andrade and the nationalists or *Mochistas*, who demanded the resignations of Crespo and Andrade. The rebel army began with only 300 soldiers but quickly increased to a total of about 16,000 troops. The government's forces had a peak strength of about 20,000 soldiers, including loyal *caudillos*. About 100 skirmishes or battles were fought in the 105-day war.

On March 14, Hernández and his 300 soldiers marched southward to join up with troops under Luis Lima Loreto, creating a rebel army of 700. President Crespo personally took control of the 1,500 government soldiers. The first serious battle was Mata Carmelara in the state of Cojedes on April 16, where the government's army suffered heavy losses, including Crespo himself, who was killed in battle. Minister of War Antonio Fernández led the government troops in a battle on June 5, which resulted in a rebel defeat and a loss of 600 men.

The war ended when President Andrade (who had assumed office on February 28, 1898) approached Rámon Guerra and convinced him to switch sides, assuming the role of supreme commander of government forces against Hernández. Guerra defeated and captured Hernández at El Hacha (in Yaracuy) on June 12, 1898, and the last reported skirmish was July 14, 1898.

Termination and Outcome: The outcome of the war was a government military victory. Hernández was imprisoned by Andrade. In the shifting alliances that characterized nineteenth-century Venezuelan politics, Andrade would later release Hernández during the 1899 Liberal Restoration, a revolt provoked by Rámon Guerra (Intra-state War #633).

Coding Decisions: According to nineteenth-century Venezuelan military statistician Manuel Rosales, 1,216 died in combat, with 1,360 seriously wounded (about 20 percent of whom later perished of their wounds). An additional 218 soldiers died of disease, and 94 were drowned. In sum, about 1,800 soldiers died in this civil war. Unfortunately, the brief treatment of this war by Rosales does not specify whether these were the total battle-deaths of both sides or merely the government's fatalities. It would appear from his treatment of battles that the final total is intended to be comprehensive of both sides, but this is not explicitly stated.[156]

Sources: Jaques (2007); Márquez (1973); McBeth (2001); Rosales (1898); Rourke (1969); Scheina (2003a).

INTRA-STATE WAR #633

Fourth Venezuelan War of 1899 (aka Restorative Revolution)

Participants: Venezuela versus Castro-led Rebels.
Dates: May 24, 1899, to October 14, 1899.
Battle-related Deaths: Venezuela: [ ]; Castro-led Rebels: [ ]; Total Combatant Deaths: 3,000.[157]
Initiator: Castro-led Rebels.
Outcome: Castro-led Rebels win.
War Type: Civil for central control.
Total System Member Military Personnel: Armed Forces of Venezuela (Government Army): 4,000 (prewar, initial); 5,700 (peak); 5,500 (final).[158]
Theater Armed Forces: Castro-led Rebels, aka *La Restauracíon or Tachirenses* (Rebel Army): 60 (prewar); 300 (initial); 10,000 (peak, final).[159] Nationalists (Rebel Army): 400 (peak, probably also prewar, initial, final).[160]

Antecedents: Prior to the preceding war (Intra-state War #632.3: Revolución de Queipa of 1898), Venezuela had been controlled by the liberal dictatorship of Gen. Joaquín Sinforiano de Jesús Crespo (1894–1898). Crespo engineered the election of Gen. Ignacio Andrade as his successor, which led to the unsuccessful revolt by nationalist José Manuel "El Mocho" Hernandez and his imprisonment by Andrade. Hernandez's defeat was facilitated by the defection of his former ally, Rámon Guerra, to the government. Opposition to Andrade grew, both from the nationalists and within the liberals. Liberals were divided between those who supported Andrade, the *Andradistas*, and the *Crespistas*, or supporters of former president Crespo. The most serious threat to Andrade would come from Gen. José Cipriano Castro Ruiz. General Castro and his ally Juan Vicente Gómez had fought with the government of President Anducza Palacio against the legalists in 1892 (Intra-state War #619). After Crespo's victory, Castro went to exile in Colombia, where he amassed a fortune and built a private army.

Narrative: Objecting to Andrade's rule, Castro began what was referred to as the Revolution of Liberal Restoration. On May 23, 1899, Gen. Cipriano Castro and 57 followers crossed into the Venezuelan state of Táchira (in the Southwest) from exile in Colombia. They were known as *La Sesenta*, the 60, and demanded restoration of the country's old constitution. By the second day, they numbered 600 and "within a few weeks" numbered 6,000.[161] Local government forces were weak, but Castro mobilized to prepare for the inevitable expeditions that the government in Caracas would send against him. His *tachirenses* besieged San Cristobál, destroyed a relief column, and then turned around again to storm the city on May 28.

On June 10, Castro ambushed the main government force sent against him at the Battle of Zumbador Mountain. He soon won another victory near Yegüines Pass, defeating a column of 5,000 government troops, and then took Mérida, with only 700 soldiers opposing his advance. He evaded the larger government forces sent to track him down and descended on Nirgua, defeating its 800 defenders. Much of the garrison defected to the rebels. By the end of the summer, Castro had broken out of Táchira, and he worked out a loose alliance with nationalist rebels. He was still outnumbered but determined to fight a decisive defensive battle by luring government forces into a trap. The strategy worked, and at the Battle of Tocuyito (near Valencia) on September 12, a force of 4,000 to 4,600 government soldiers commanded by Gen. Diego Bautisti Ferrer suffered 2,000 casualties unsuccessfully assaulting his positions. Two days later, Andrade assumed personal command of the army, but Castro's forces and the nationalists mounted a coordinated offensive that took Barquisimeto. Other caudillos then began to defect from the government to the revolution, including 3,000 men under Leopoldo Baptista and 4,500 under Liciano Mendoza. Castro fought and won a total of 42 engagements in 153 days without a single defeat.

Despite an apparently superior military and territorial position, the government opened negotiations that offered the rebels a power-sharing deal. In the end, Andrade's distrust of his own generals killed the agreement. However, Castro honored a truce, beginning on October 14, which marks the end of the war.

Termination and Outcome: In the process of being deposed by coup d'état on October 20, 1899,

Andrade fled to exile in Curaçao. Castro entered Caracas on October 22 at the head of as many as 10,000 men (most of them last-minute volunteers and defectors). The outcome was a military victory by the rebels without any formal agreements. Castro created a despotic government that provoked a number of international conflicts and internal opposition, including a revolt led by Gen. Manuel Matos (Intra-state War #638 in 1901).

Sources: Clodfelter (2002, 2008); Contreras (1944); Ewell (1984); Gilmore (1964); Jaques (2007); McBeth (2001); Rourke (1969); Scheina (2003a); Yarrington (1997).

INTRA-STATE WAR #636

Sixth Colombian War of 1899 to 1902 (aka War of the 1,000 Days)

Participants: Colombia versus Liberals, Venezuela, and Ecuador.
Dates: October 17, 1899, to November 21, 1902.
Battle-related Deaths: Liberals: 53,000; Colombia: 47,000.
Initiator: Liberals.
Outcome: Colombia wins.
War Type: Civil for central control.
Total System Member Military Personnel: Armed Forces of Colombia: 1,000 (prewar); 9,000 (initial); 21,000 (peak).[162]
Theater Armed Forces: War Liberals (Rebel Army): 3,000 to 4,000 (initial); 8,000 (peak).[163] Ecuador (Pro-rebel State Intervener), participating March 27 to 30, 1900: [ ] (prewar); more than 1,000 (inferred from the presence of multiple battalions) (initial intervention, peak).[164] Venezuela (Pro-rebel State Intervener), participating before May 1900 and from early August to September 13, 1901, strength estimates: 1,000 (initial intervention); 1,400 (peak); a few hundred (final).[165]

Antecedents: This war represents the culmination of almost a century of battles between the liberals and conservatives in Colombia. After 1861, the liberals had dominated through the 1863 constitution. However, in the 1880s, the Nationalist Party, composed of independent (moderate) liberals and conservatives, gained power. Their period of dominance was called the Regeneration, and the 1886 constitution gave increased power to the president. The remnants of the Liberal Party, or radical liberals, were divided between "war" and "peace" liberals, and the war liberals revolted in 1895 (Intra-state War #626). While the war liberals were defeated, dissatisfied historical conservatives allied themselves politically with the peace liberals, forming a potent threat to the Regeneration.

It was the maneuvers of nationalists to retain power against this potent coalition that provided the *casus belli* for liberals. As the coalition gained power in the legislature in 1898, President Manuel Antonio Sanclemente seized full control of the government on November 3, 1898. Concluding that peaceful means had been exhausted, liberal leaders meeting on February 12, 1899, in the department of Santander entered into a war pact, and Rafael Uribe was pushed to the forefront of the war liberal faction. Sanclemente declared martial law on July 28, 1899, arresting Uribe. In the meantime, Venezuelan liberal Cipriano Castro had come to power in a revolt (Intra-state War #633), and he was willing to assist a similar revolution in Colombia. Thus, in the Colombian department of Santander, bordering Venezuela, Pablo E. Villar launched a revolution on October 17.

Narrative: The rebels in Santander secured control of the department over the next week. Another rebel force emerged in Cundinamarca, but it was soon defeated by government forces. After a few days, the political alignments solidified; the nationalist-conservative coalition generally supported the government on the war; peace liberals urged fellow liberals to renounce the revolt; thus, the war liberals were alone in rebellion.

The first phase of the war, lasting about six months, has been nicknamed "the Gentlemen's War," as conventional units fought and there were few reprisals or atrocities. In the liberals' next offensive, they quickly seized a navy and pushed north up the Magdalena River, overrunning garrisons and capturing weapons on the way. On October 24, the rebels encountered two government gunboats that essentially destroyed their flotilla and killed most of the rebels on board (204), including a number of leaders. A rebel attempt to regain control of Magdalena by storming Girardot in Tolima was defeated with heavy losses, and a subsequent army assault crushed the Tolima rebels on November 14. All in all, there would be more than 500 armed engagements during this war.

In Santander, the rebels lost at Piedecuesta, with more than 100 killed, but they seized the more strategic town of Cúcuta on November 1. Uribe attempted to besiege Bucaramanga, but his ill-disciplined troops charged the city on November 12, suffering more than 1,000 killed in a fruitless assault on an entrenched enemy with modern rifles. At this point, the main rebel force was only 3,000 strong, and fewer than half were equipped with modern firearms, so the rebels began to search for weapons from weakly defended government outposts. The rebels soon won their first major victory at Peralonso, where 5,600 government forces moved to block the rebel advance from December 15 to 16, 1899. An unexpected rebel charge by General Uribe across the river's bridge caught the government troops by surprise, and though the liberals suffered 750 casualties as opposed to 700 for the government, government morale broke first, and government units fled. The rebel victory at the Peralonso inspired foreign support and liberal uprisings in other departments. Venezuela sent 1,000 soldiers to assist the rebels along the Caribbean coast. In Cauca, the rebels were strengthened by Colombian exiles armed by the Ecuadoran liberal president Eloy Alfaro, but they were defeated near the border on January 23, 1900. On March 27, the rebels attacked the border town of Ipiales with the assistance of several Ecuadorean battalions but called off the attack three days later. Nicaragua's liberal president also armed liberal rebels and helped transport them to Panama, landing a group on March 31. The invaders won a minor victory on April 4, triggering a rush to reinforce the department by the nationalists. On June 8, the reinforcements were defeated by the Panama liberals; the rebels won another victory outside Panama City on July 21, but a frontal attack failed to take the city from July 24 to 26, 1900, resulting in more than 1,000 rebel battle-deaths and the outright surrender of the rebels.

Meanwhile in Santander, the most decisive battle of the war was fought at Palonegro, from May 11 to 16, 1900. By May 13, the 7,000 to 10,000 liberals outnumbered the government forces, and the battle became one of attrition. By May 25 the distribution of power changed with the arrival of government reinforcements, and 21,000 government troops now faced the rebels. The dispirited liberals withdrew by May 26, even though government forces suffered 1,000 deaths. What had been the liberals' strongest army was now down to 3,400 men. As the rebels retreated through the jungle, malnutrition and disease set in, and only 1,500 rebels remained when they turned to attack Bucaramanga on August 3, which reduced the rebel army to 1,000; this force was soon divided and defeated.

At the end of July, historical conservatives who favored diplomacy over war staged a coup against President Sanclamente in favor of conservative Vice President José Manuel Marroquín (who took office on July 31, 1900). Though he was prepared to offer amnesty to rebels who surrendered by September 1, 1900, the rebels again sought foreign assistance: Ecuador provided support to rebels along the border, and Venezuela provided the rudiments of a navy and 200 troops, which enabled the rebels to raise about 1,800 men and recapture the port of Riohacha. By mid-August 1900, more than 20,000 lives had been lost in just ten months of fighting. A guerrilla war dragged on from late 1900 to mid-1901, in Santander, Cundinamarca, and northern Tolima. Government troops were decimated by disease during counterguerrilla operations.

Venezuela's assistance to the rebels prompted Venezuelan conservatives, who had taken refuge in Colombia, to invade Venezuela in 1901 (Intra-state War #638). Nonetheless, Venezuela sent an additional 1,200 troops to Colombia in early September, bringing total Venezuelan strength to 1,400. On September 13, up to 3,000 liberals and Venezuelans were defeated by 1,500 government soldiers in the Battle of Carazúa. Colombia broke diplomatic relations with Venezuela in response to their intervention.

As Venezuela and Ecuador began to reduce their support, Nicaraguan assistance became critical, and Panama became the focus of the rebellion when Nicaragua landed (on September 16) another rebel force, which eventually occupied La Chorrera for several months. On December 24, 1901, Uribe once again returned to Colombia, and on March 12, his forces won the Battle of Gachalá but were defeated at El Amoladero on March 25. Rebels under Benjamín Herrera took control of the Pacific side of the isthmus with their warship *Almirante Padilla* and landed another group of 1,500 exiles on December 24, 1901. The rebels won a victory at Aguadulce on February 23, 1902, but 500 rebels were forced to surrender to government forces at Bocas del Toro. The government mounted a new offensive against the rebels in Panama on June 10, but a rebel stratagem succeeded in forcing them to retreat, and the 5,000 men of the government's expeditionary force surrendered on August 27 at Aguadulce.

In August 1902, the rebels under Uribe tried once again to mount a new campaign in Magdalena. On October 13, the dismal state of rebel forces led Uribe to open negotiations with the government. The Agreement of Neerlandia provided for a truce in the Caribbean region and the disarmament and safe return home of the rebels. On October 26, Herrera's forces in Panama also requested peace talks, which were held aboard the *U.S.S. Wisconsin*. The agreement was signed on November 21, effectively ending the war.

Termination and Outcome: The outcome of the war was a military victory by the government, and political power continued to be monopolized by conservatives. The agreement provided some concessions to the rebels, such as congressional elections and the freeing of political prisoners.

Coding Decisions: Fatality figures reported for this war vary somewhat: Demarest claims that 100,000 soldiers perished along with an equal number of civilians due to epidemics; while a number of scholars suggest that 100,000 died, not all are clear about whether this is just combatants or civilians as well.[166] Scheina suggests that between 25,000 and 40,000 soldiers died in combat, and if there were an equal number dying from disease (as Clodfelter suggests), that provides us with a range of 50,000 to 80,000 battle-deaths.[167] However, Bergquist says that throughout the war, epidemics killed more than battles, which then gets the total closer to 100,000 again. So we are reporting 100,000 total combatant deaths. Adding up the figures for the battles described in Scheina provides a rough estimate of 53 percent of the fatalities being suffered by the liberals and 47 percent by the government, thus producing estimates of 53,000 and 47,000 battle-deaths accordingly.

Sources: Bergquist (1978); Clodfelter (2002, 2008); Delpar (1971); Demarest (2001); Galbraith (1953); Henao and Arrubla (1938); Jaques (2007); Kohn (1999); Marley (1998); Phillips and Axelrod (2005); Scheina (2003a); Small and Singer (1982); Tomán (2006); Wood (1968).

INTRA-STATE WAR #638

Fifth Venezuelan War of 1901 to 1903 (aka Liberative Revolution)

Participants: Venezuela versus Matos-led Rebels.
Dates: December 19, 1901, to July 21, 1903.
Battle-related Deaths: Matos-led Rebels: [ ]; Venezuela: [ ]; Total Combatant Deaths: 12,000.[168]
Initiator: Matos-led Rebels.
Outcome: Venezuela wins.
War Type: Civil for central control.
Total System Member Military Personnel: Armed Forces of Venezuela: 4,000 (prewar, initial); 9,000 (peak); 9,000 (final).[169]
Theater Armed Forces: Matos-led Rebels (Rebel Army): 400 (prewar, initial); 14,000 (peak); 2,500 (final).[170]

Antecedents: Liberal Gen. Cipriano Castro seized power in October 1899 in the Restorative Revolution (Intra-state War #633). His subsequent efforts to centralize and professionalize the armed forces alienated regional *caudillos*, and he faced many small rebellions, including one that pitted nationalists under Gen. "El Mocho" Hernandez against the new government. On July 26, 1901, nationalist Rangel Garbiras invaded Venezuela with about 4,000 exiles from safe havens in Colombia, and Castro responded to Colombia's support for the rebels by arming and militarily supporting the liberal rebels in Colombia during that country's War of a 1,000 Days (Intra-state War #636), hoping to build a transnational liberal coalition.

Castro declined to meet the demands of Germany, Italy, and Britain for compensation for the losses that they suffered in earlier civil wars, and accordingly, the foreign powers worked together with Venezuela's domestic creditors to mount a revolution against Castro. In 1901, banker Manuel Antonio Matos created a political coalition of disaffected liberals, members of other parties, foreign creditors, and dissatisfied regional *caudillos*. He appointed two military commanders to lead the revolt—Domingo Monagas in the East and Luciano Mendoza in the West and Center—and, with financing from foreign-owned companies, bought a warship. Castro received news of the plot on November 21, 1901, and began making arrests.

Narrative: On December 19, 1901, Aragua's Governor Luciano Mendoza formally pronounced against the government at Villa de Cura. Six more uprisings occurred the following day. With their ship, the *Ban Righ*, and other steamships provided by the Orinoco Steamship Company, rebel leaders were able to distribute arms to the main centers of resistance.

Castro ordered his chief lieutenant, Juan Vicente Gómez, to attack Mendoza. The first engagement of the war was the Battle of San Mateo on December 21. The next day, Gómez defeated Mendoza at Villa de Cura but was unable to destroy his army. The government army continued to be victorious as it moved south and west of Caracas. By the end of February 1862, the only rebel victory of note had been the sinking of the government man-o-war *General Joaquín Crespo* by the *Ban Righ* (now called the *Libertador* and later renamed as the *Bolívar*) on February 7. Yet, external support for the rebels continued, and that summer, the French company that owned the telegraph lines began passing government communications to the rebels.

On March 18, the government mounted a new campaign against the rebels in the West, and Gómez won a significant victory on April 15. However, the eastern rebels had managed to outmaneuver government forces sent against them, so Gómez turned eastward and engaged them near Cumaná on May 4 and again in Carúpano, which they besieged and during which Gómez was wounded. In June, the rebels escaped the siege when they evacuated the city, and the German cruiser *Gazelle* prohibited any government assault on the undefended town.[171] Given a respite from Gómez, the rebels in the West recuperated and began defeating government forces; rebel *caudillos* soon controlled most of the country.

The rebels now mounted their own offensive toward Caracas, capturing Maiquetía in the North. Castro assumed personal command of the government army for a counteroffensive against Matos. The rebels forced a decisive battle at La Victoria in Aragua. The New York and Bermudez Company provided the rebels with ammunition and transportation. The rebel army was now united and 12,000 to 16,000 strong. The battle was joined on October 12, 1902. It lasted three weeks, ending with 3,000 killed or wounded and a humiliating rebel retreat. Matos left for Curaçao, appointing Nicolás Rolando and Juan Pablo Peñaloza to lead the rebel army while it reorganized.

The government continued its offensive, and Ciudad Bolívar was besieged. At this point, foreign powers again intervened, supplying ammunition to the rebels; Britain and Germany prepared a blockade of Venezuela over the debts. On December 7, a "peaceful blockade" was declared, and two days later, the allies seized much of the Venezuelan fleet. Unintentionally, the blockade proved disastrous for the rebels, as Castro garnered support in anticipation of an inter-state war to defend Venezuela's sovereignty. British and German vessels began to sink Venezuelan vessels and bombard Venezuelan ports. The rebels mounted no major operations until an agreement to end the blockade and arbitrate the claims was reached in February 1863.

Rolando was able to organize his forces around Peñaloza, and declining to wait for the disorganized western rebels, he immediately marched on Caracas in early April 1863. Three days of fighting forced Rolando to retreat. Gomez then turned against the western rebels, inflicting a series of defeats, culminating at Matalpo from June 2 to June 4. Fleeing to Curaçao, Matos announced on June 10 that the war was over and rebels should lay down their arms, though Rolando continued fighting. The government army reached the last rebel stronghold, Ciudad Bolívar, which Gomez attacked on July 19. After three days of fighting, the rebels surrendered on July 21. The final battle of the war cost the government 250 killed and 400 wounded, while the rebels suffered 800 killed or wounded.

Termination and Outcome: The outcome of the war was a complete military victory by the government. Most rebel leaders fled into exile. On December 19, 1908, while Castro was in Berlin for medical treatment, he was overthrown in a coup led by his vice president, Juan Gomez.

Sources: Clodfelter (2002); Contreras (1944); Ewell (1984); Gilmore (1964); Jaques (2007); McBeth (2001); Morón (1964); Rourke (1969); Scheina (2003a); Singh (1999); Yarrington (1997).

INTRA-STATE WAR #641

First Uruguay War of 1904 (aka Uruguayan Civil War or La Revolución de 1904)

Participants: Uruguay versus Blancos.
Dates: January 1, 1904, to September 10, 1904.
Battle-related Deaths: Uruguay: 900; Blancos: 700. (See Coding Decisions.)
Initiator: Blancos.
Outcome: Uruguay wins.
War Type: Civil for central control.

Total System Member Military Personnel: Armed Forces of Uruguay, aka *Colorados*: 4,000 (prewar); 10,000 (initial); 30,000 (peak, final).[172]
Theater Armed Forces: *Blancos* or Nationalists (Rebel Army): 9,000 (initial); 10,000 to 15,000 (peak); 10,000 to 15,000 (final).[173]

Antecedents: Uruguay was wracked by conflict between conservative *Blancos* (nationalists) and liberal *Colorados* for much of the nineteenth century—with conflicts frequently involving interventions by its neighbors Argentina and Brazil. A war from 1870 to 1872 (Non-state War #1554) pitted the *Blancos*, led by Timoteo Aparicio, against the government under the new president, *Colorados* general Lorenzo Batlle y Grau (who held office from 1868 to 1872). The war ended with a truce that effectively divided the country in two, with the *Blancos* dominant in the North and the *Colorados* controlling the Center and the South, including the capital, Montevideo. The ensuing *Blancos-Colorados* power-sharing deal was ratified on September 18, 1897, in the Covenant of the Cross that spelled out how governmental positions were to be distributed.

When José Batlle y Ordóñez (Lorenzo's son) was elected to a full-term as president, taking office on March 1, 1903, his awarding of positions was seen by the *Blancos* as violating the covenant. The leader of the *Blancos*, Gen. Aparicio Saravia, who had fought in the 1870 war, declared his intention to start a new war against the *Colorados* government on March 15, 1903, and soon raised an army of 15,000 men. War was averted by a new agreement, the Pact of Nico Pérez, on March 22, 1903. However, Saravia continued his military preparations as the pact broke down during the remainder of the year.

Narrative: On January 1, 1904, Saravia declared war, and on January 3, bridges presumably were dynamited by *Blancos* to prevent the advance of government troops. The *Colorados* government then launched an attack on Saravia's mobilizing *Blanco* forces. Both sides possessed large armies at the onset of the war—the rebels with 9,000 troops facing the government's 10,000 (which would soon grow to 30,000). The *Blancos* had a large cavalry that would aid in a mobile campaign but were short on weapons; only half the rebels were armed. Government forces won a victory at the city of Mansavillagra (north of the capital) but were unable to decisively defeat the rebellion. The rebels fled northward, pursued by government troops under Justin Muniz. Meanwhile, Saravia turned south toward Montevideo, and the rebels were able to surprise and defeat government troops on January 30 at Fray Marcos. The rebels were then able to arm their forces, reaching a peak strength of 15,000.

On March 2, the third major battle of the war was fought at Paso del Parque, where the larger rebel force was surprised by Muniz's 7,000 troops, losing 100 killed compared to the government's 70. By March 23, the rebel army of 9,000 faced government forces of 12,000 to 15,000 (though it claimed 36,000 soldiers). In the fourth major engagement of the war, the Battle of Tupambaé, from June 22 to 23, 1904, nearly the whole rebel force faced off against 6,500 government soldiers: nearly 20 percent of the troops on both sides were killed or wounded (estimated 1,000 rebel and 1,300 government casualties). The outcome was a stalemate, though the government still had large reserves (including 7,500 men and formations in the capital). After regrouping and acquiring artillery, Saravia decided on another battle. On September 1, 1904, the battle of Masoller, near the border with Brazil, resulted in a bloodbath even worse than Tupambaé. Saravia was severely wounded, and he retreated into Brazil, where he died on September 10. His death led to the dispersal of the rebel army, an armistice, and peace negotiations.

Termination and Outcome: An agreement was produced on September 23, which the *Blancos* accepted on October 3, and the legislature ratified it on October 15. The terms of the agreement included amnesty, disarmament of rebel forces, payment of $100,000 to rebel leaders, and promises of reform, though the peace left all political power in the government's hands. Batlle served his full term as president, 1903 to 1907, and a second term from 1911 to 1915. He is regarded as one of the great reformers in Uruguay's history.

Coding Decisions: Evidence on battle-deaths is sparse. Using the standard 1:3 ratio of killed to wounded on the Battle of Tupambaé's 1,000 rebel and 1,300 government casualties would mean 250 rebel and 325 government battle-deaths in this battle alone. Accepting the consensus that that Masoller was deadlier than Tupambaé produces total battle death estimates of 550 rebel and 720 government deaths. If we add the 100 rebel and

70 government deaths at Paso del Parque and adjust upward for the relatively small engagements of Mansavillagra and Fray Marcos, plus deaths due to disease, our best guess is rounded figures of 700 rebel and 900 government battle-deaths. The total of combatant deaths (more than 1,600 killed) is roughly consistent with historians' agreement that several thousand were killed or wounded.[174]

Sources: Acevedo (1934); Clodfelter (1992); Larrosa (2003); Munro (1960); Rodriguez Herrero (1934); Vanger (1963); Vives (1975).

INTRA-STATE WAR #656

Paraguay War of 1911 to 1912 (aka Radical Liberal Rebellion)

Participants: Paraguay and *Jaristas* versus Radical Liberals.
Dates: February 11, 1911, to March 17, 1911, and November 23, 1911, to May 11, 1912.
Battle-related Deaths: Paraguay: [ ]; Radicals: [ ]; Total Combatant Deaths: 4,000.
Initiator: Radical Liberals.
Outcome: Radicals Liberals win.
War Type: Civil for central control.
Total System Member Military Personnel: Armed Forces of Paraguay: 3,000 (prewar); 2,650 (initial, after initial defections); 3,650 (peak). These estimates include 600 to 700 armed police in the capital.[175]
Theater Armed Forces: Radical Liberal Juntas (Rebel Army): 1,800 (initial); 4,000 (peak, final).[176] *Jaristas* (allied with the government in phase two), participating from February 1912 to May 11, 1912: 1,600 to 2,000 (peak).[177]

Antecedents: Paraguay had been ruled by three long-term dictatorships from 1814 until 1870. Paraguay's loss in the Lopez War against Brazil and Argentina (Inter-state War #49) in 1870 began a period of internal conflict and short-term leaders, which ended with the domination of Paraguayan politics by the Colorado (Republican) Party after 1880. A Liberal Party was formed in opposition to Colorado rule, and it steadily gained some measure of elite support. By the opening years of the twentieth century, both parties were divided into factions, creating four major political groupings: Colorado *caballeristas*, Colorado *civilistas*, Cívico liberals, and radical liberals. The Colorado *caballeristas* included most of the country's military forces, led by Gen. Benardino Caballero; they attempted to monopolize political power after a 1902 coup. In early 1904, a revolt by the Cívico liberal Benigno Feirrera forced the Colorado government to sign the Pilcomayo Agreement, which provided for a new government that excluded the *caballeristas* and most radical liberals. Though the Cívico liberals emerged as the politically dominant force, their hold on power was tenuous, leading to a challenge by radical liberals on July 2, 1908; the government capitulated after two days of heavy fighting in the streets of Asunción, in which radical Col. Albino Jara played a key role. President Feirrera went into exile and radical liberal Manuel Gondra became acting president.

By early 1909, the Civícos had formed an alliance with the Colorados and began attacking the government from safe havens in Argentina and Brazil. The government moved quickly, crushing the southern rebel forces on September 14. The ambitious minister of war Colonel Jara, who led the successful counterattack, demanded more power. Though Gondra agreed to some of his demands, Jara saw this as insufficient and began to ally his faction of the radical liberals with the Civícos and *Colorados.* On January 17, 1911, Gondra ordered the police to arrest Jara; Jara reacted by leading a bloodless coup against Gondra using the 600 to 700 police in the capital. Jara became president that day, but his unwieldy coalition began to collapse almost immediately, and he turned to rule by decree. He formed his own political party, the Democratic Liberal Party (PLD), hoping to overturn both liberal and conservative policies.

Narrative: This war represents the attempts by the radical liberals to return to power. The period of early 1911 to mid-1912 includes two distinct periods in which the radical liberals were battling the government, and they are coded together in this war with a pause in the fighting coded in-between.

The first phase began on February 21, 1911, when the radical liberals revolted against Jara. North of the capital, the garrison of Concepción went over to the rebels, led by Gondra's former powerful interior minister, Adolfo Riquelme. Meanwhile, a separate force, possibly under the leadership of radical liberal Eduardo Schaerer, invaded the Misiones region of the Southeast. At their peak, the northern rebels numbered 1,000 to 2,000, while the southern rebels may have been as few as 800. However, the revolt represented a serious threat to Jara's government. Initially, about 2,000 government troops defeated 800 southern rebels near Yuty on March 7. By this time, the rebels of the North (with a flotilla that included some impressed Argentine ships) had advanced without opposition to within a few miles of the capital, Asunción. The army quickly was recalled from the South and began to push the rebels northward along the Paraguay River. The principal battle occurred on March 12, and the rebels were defeated in a final engagement near Bonete on March 17. The government admitted losing 100 soldiers and 4 officers killed; another report said that there were a total of 900 dead. This rebel defeat marks the end of the first phase of the war.

Though fighting stopped, opposition to the Jara regime did not end. When Jara broke with tradition and summarily executed twelve captured prisoners, Congress used the general revulsion among the elite to attempt to impeach him. Jara responded by arresting its leaders and forcing them to resign. Jara delegated extensive powers to his interior minister, Cipriano Ibañez. Jara's government was increasingly unstable, and Ibañez soon joined a plot that ousted Jara on July 5, replacing him with Liberato Marcial Rojas, who formed a cabinet similar in composition to that of Jara (*jarista* radical liberals, Cívico liberals, and *Colorados*). Rojas also was unsuccessful in holding his government together, and a coup attempt led to the arrest of Ibañez on July 15. With little power of his own, Rojas was unable to reconcile the competing demands of his coalition partners, and he ultimately would side with the *Colorados.*

The second phase of the radical revolt began on November 23. Eduardo Schaerer, one of the radicals defeated in the first phase, had formed a revolutionary junta with former president Gorda and José Montero. The rebels used Argentine territory to build and supply their forces. Argentina "impounded" a Paraguayan gunboat and turned it over to the rebels, who were able to use it to transport rebels advancing toward Asunción. Rebel victories mounted; they even briefly captured the capital. On December 13, the Cívicos formally left Rojas's government and entered into opposition. The remaining *Colorados* finally decided to dispense with Rojas altogether, overthrowing the government in a coup on February 27, 1912. Cívicos fled to the south, where they joined a new revolt led by Jara (who had returned to Paraguay on November 7, 1911).

Nonetheless, the radicals continued their revolt, with two columns led by Patricio Alejandro Escobar and Adolfo Chirife marching on the capital: one moved southward from Concepción; and the other northward from Villa Franca, with defectors from the government side swelling their ranks. From March 19 to March 21, 1912, the Battle of Ascunción was fought, ending in a defeat for the government, with more than 600 killed in the fighting. Radical Emiliano González Navero became the provisional president. The war, however, was not over. Though the radicals under Schaerer and his generals now controlled the capital, Jara was able to rally former government forces to his coalition. Jara then advanced northward in April with 1,600 to 2,000 troops, taking Villarica. On May 9, Jara met radical forces led by Chirife at the town of Paraguarí. Jara's forces then fell into a trap and were attacked by 4,000 radical liberal soldiers. The battle lasted two days and resulted in 900 combined battle-deaths, ending with the route of the *jaristas* and the mortal wounding of Jara himself.

Termination and Outcome: The war ended in victory by the radical liberals. Schaerer forced Navero out of the presidency on August 15, 1912, and enjoyed a brief period of uncontested rule.

Coding Decisions: Originally Small and Singer coded this as a war of Paraguay versus the liberals from July 1911 to May 1912. Additional information has now allowed us to include the first phase of the radical liberal revolt and more specifically to delineate the fighting in two distinct phases.

The coding of the participants is determined by their status at the time of the start of the war: thus the radical liberals are coded as fighting against the government of Paraguay. While the basic forces of the radical liberals were similar in phases one and two, the leadership differed somewhat between the juntas.

In terms of the battle-death figures for this war, the climactic battle of phase one killed at least 104 government soldiers and up to 900 rebels. The 1912 battle in Asunción killed 400 to 600. There was also an unsuccessful army expedition against the second revolt in which "three thousand men set out on this foray, seven hundred returned." The climactic battle of phase two killed about 900 combatants, of which the *jaristas* likely suffered 500 battle-deaths, and the radical liberals with 400 battle-deaths. Using this evidence, we estimate that the two phases of the war killed at least 2,500 combatants. If the unsuccessful expedition by the armed forces of Paraguay was characterized by the death (rather than the desertion or defection) of 2,300 soldiers, this total would rise to between 4,000 and 5,000. Given the knowledge that deaths due to disease and deaths in all other engagements are not reported, 4,000 is a reasonable estimate of total combatant deaths.[178]

Sources: Ferris (1919); "Fighting in Paraguay" (1912); Lewis (1993); "Paraguay Rebels Routed" (1912); "Paraguay Revolution" (1911); "Savage War Raging Among Paraguayans" (1911); "Severe Fighting in Paraguay" (1911); Warren (1949).

INTRA-STATE WAR #657.3

War of the Ecuadorian Generals of 1912 (aka Second Alfarista Revolution)

Participants: Ecuador versus *Alfaristas.*
Dates: January 11, 1912, to January 22, 1912.
Battle-related Deaths: Ecuador: [ ]; *Alfaristas*: [ ]; Total Combatant Deaths: 1,000
Initiator: *Alfaristas.*
Outcome: Ecuador wins.
War Type: Civil for central control.
Total System Member Military Personnel: Armed Forces of Ecuador (Government Army): 7,000 (prewar, initial, peak, final).[179]
Theater Armed Forces: *Alfaristas* (Rebel Army): [ ].

Antecedents: This war emerged from a divide within Ecuador's dominant Liberal Party, which had captured power in 1895 (Intra-state War #627). The war, also known as the *Alfarista* Revolution, had secured the presidency for José Eloy Alfaro Delgado, which began the Radical Liberal Era, which endured from 1895 to 1944. The conservatives did not accept this shift easily, and Alfaro's first year as president would experience an unsuccessful conservative counterrevolution (Intra-state War #631.5 in 1896). Disputes over leadership of the Liberal Party soon erupted between Alfaro and Gen. Leónidas Plaza and would last 20 years.

General Plaza succeeded Alfaro in office, serving until August 31, 1905. That year, a Plaza ally, Lizardo García, was elected to the presidency but would serve only a few months of his term before Alfaro launched a coup and seized the presidency in 1906. The 1911 presidential election pitted Emilio Estrada (Alfaro's chosen successor) against Alfaro's nephew, Flavio Alfaro, who had run despite his uncle's fear of nepotism charges. Estrada won the election, and when Eloy Alfaro refused to cede power, he was ousted from office. When Estrada died on December 22, 1911, the new government, led by provisional president Carlos Freire Zaldumbide, was dominated by allies of Plaza, prompting the *Alfaristas* to revolt.

Narrative: On December 28, 1911, risings by pro-Alfaro units preceded this brief war. On January 5, 1912, Eloy Alfaro (from his refuge in Panama) tried to convene a peace conference to stop the move to war. However, Flavio Alfaro (who was declared supreme commander for the rebels) and Pedro Montero (who was proclaimed chief for Guayas province) reached an agreement to abandon the peace negotiations and to gather their forces in Guayaquil for an advance on Quito. General Plaza took command of the government's army and advanced toward Guayaquil to meet the rebels.

There were three principal military engagements, all of them government victories. On January 11, the government stopped a combined rebel force advancing through the mountains at Huigra (east of Guayaquil), and about 400 died in this engagement. Government forces rapidly moved onto the coastal plain, where they once again defeated the rebels on January 14 at Naranjito, though the battle cost only 60 lives. Four days later, the decisive (and bloodiest) battle was fought at Yaguachi, near the outskirts of Guayaquil, entailing 400 to 600 deaths. Flavio Alfaro was injured during the battle and had to be taken into Guayaquil. Eloy Alfaro (age seventy), who had arrived in Guayaquil on January 12 at the request of Montero to serve as a mediator, was appointed as director general of war. The remaining rebels fell back to Guayaquil, which was taken by government forces on January 21 at the cost of only 10 killed on both sides. The commanders of the government forces offered amnesty, which the rebels accepted on January 22, ending the war.

Termination and Outcome: The outcome was a government military victory. Reneging on its commanders' promises, the government took the Alfaros and Montero into custody, along with between four and six other top rebels, and transported them to the capital. On January 28, a mob in Quito dragged the captives out of Garcia Moreno prison, and they were brutally killed and their bodies burned. Shortly thereafter, General Plaza assumed the presidency for the second time. He soon would be confronted by a revolt in Esmeraldas (Intra-state War #670).

Coding Decisions: The civil war coincided with epidemics in Guayaquil, one of the unhealthiest cities in the world at the time. Approximately 5,000 people were reported to have died in Guayaquil in 1912, which represents the deaths of civilians and postwar deaths from a yellow fever epidemic. Most authors cite a figure of 3,000 killed for this war, though the origins and meaning of the 3,000 figure are unclear—some authors claim it represents total deaths, while others describe it as the number of soldiers killed.[180] However, the fatalities suffered in the major battles only added up to about 1,000 deaths. Though this figure does not include deaths from disease or assassinations, it is reported here as a conservative estimate.

Sources: Clark (1998); Mora (1994); Pineo (1996); Schodt (1987); Spindler (1987); Vicuña (1984).

INTRA-STATE WAR #667

Ecuadorian Civil War of 1913 to 1916 (aka Conchista Rebellion or *Revolucíon de Concha*)

Participants: Ecuador versus *Conchistas.*
Dates: September 24, 1913, to September 14, 1916.
Battle-related Deaths: Ecuador: [ ]; *Conchistas:* [ ]; Total Combatant Deaths: 7,000.[181]
Initiator: *Conchistas.*
Outcome: Ecuador wins.
War Type: Civil for central control.
Total System Member Military Personnel: Armed Forces of Ecuador: 7,000 (prewar, initial); 8,000 (peak, final).[182]
Theater Armed Forces: *Conchistas* (Rebel Army): 400 (prewar, initial); 1,200 (peak); 400 (final).[183]

Antecedents: This war began in the aftermath of the War of the Generals (Intra-state War #657.3). With most of the leading *Alfarista* figures (supporters of former president Elroy Alfaro) dead, there was little organized opposition to the government led by Leónidas Plaza. The protracted absence of a constitutional government prompted Carlos Concha Torres, who had fought for Alfaro in 1895 and again in 1911 and 1912, to lead a new rebellion.

Narrative: On September 24, 1913, Concha led a force of about 150 men in an attack on a police station in the remote, heavily forested northern Ecuadorian province of Esmereldas. Three days later, he proclaimed a rebellion with the avowed goal of ousting the existing government and returning the country to constitutional government. By September 29, government troops aboard the destroyer *Libertador Bolivar* landed troops in Esmeraldas and dispersed rebels toward the south. From December 10 to December 12, Concha commanded a force of 700, part of which won a victory at the Battle of El Guayabo against 1,244 government troops, killing 312 government soldiers while suffering only 23 rebel deaths. After its defeat, the government soon abandoned the province to the rebels. In an attempt to weaken the rebels, the government had two ships, the *Libertador Bolivar* and the *Constitución,* bombard Esmeraldas for twelve days beginning on December 26, but they managed to attack civilians and burn the city rather than harm the rebels.

January 1914 was characterized by many small engagements. Meanwhile, liberal Carlos Alfaro raised a rebellion in Manabí in support of Concha. In February 1914, the government blockaded the province of Esmeraldas and sent 2,000 troops against Concha's forces, which now numbered more than 1,200. The government began with a bombardment of Esmeraldas, and on February 27, the government dispatched Col. Enrique Valdez Conca, nephew of the rebel leader, to take charge of military operations at Esmeraldas. The government forces generally were stationed in coastal cities (where disease took a steady toll) and then repeatedly embarked and disembarked along the coast in pursuit of the rebels. In early March, the government landed additional troops in Esmeraldas, and the rebels were forced to retreat. On April 12, both sides met nearby in the bloody Battle of Camarones, where the rebels were cornered and defeated, with more than 400 killed at Camarones and about 50 prisoners murdered afterward. Another bloody engagement followed on May 8 and May 9, the Battle of La Propecia, which resulted in another 200 government fatalities.

Thereafter there was a reduction in the intensity of the fighting as diseases such as tuberculosis, dysentery, typhus, beriberi, malaria, and yellow fever continued to take a deadly toll on the combatants: by May 1914, the government was losing six to eight men each day. The government responded by retreating into fortified areas and establishing hospitals. Meanwhile the rebels had opened fronts elsewhere: Carlos Andrade engaged in heavy fighting in the northern Imbabura and Carchi provinces, and in June Concha began operations in Manabi and Guyas. The war continued as a series of small-unit engagements, with larger ones at La Boca (fifty-seven rebels perished) and La Piedras (with a death toll of more than twenty-five).

In December 1914, the frequency of these engagements increased dramatically. The rebels took Las Piedras after a week of fighting, then attacked Tachina, where 159 were killed. More than sixty-one other engagements occurred in the next few months, but on February 24, 1915, the rebels were dealt a devastating setback when Concha himself was captured by government forces. The rebels selected Enrique Torres as their new leader and continued the struggle but at a lower intensity.

A resurgence of violence occurred in 1916. After several battles in the summer, the last serious engagements were government victories at El Piejo and Rio Verde, from September 11 to 14, 1916. A new president, Alfredo Baquerizo, assumed power on September 1 and decided on a policy of conciliation. On September 8, he declared amnesty for the rebels and opened negotiations that continued until September 13, when the government released Concha. By November 7, the last rebel force of 400 men had signed the armistice.

Termination and Outcome: The outcome of the war was a government victory.

Sources: Clodfelter (2002); Moreno (1939); Vicuña (1984); Ycaza (1980).

INTRA-STATE WAR #672.5
Contestado Rebellion of 1914 to 1915

Participants: Brazil versus *Fanaticos*.
Dates: August 1914 to December 1915.
Battle-related Deaths: Brazil: 1,000; *Fanaticos*: 6,000.[184]
Initiator: Brazil.
Outcome: Brazil wins.
War Type: Civil for local issues (autonomy).
Total System Member Military Personnel: Armed Forces of Brazil (Government Army): 25,000 (prewar); 25,000 (initial); 25,000 (peak); 25,000 (final).[185]
Theater Armed Forces: Armed Forces of Brazil: 9,000 (peak) including 7,000 soldiers of the national government, 1,000 of the forces of Paraná, and 1,000 local police and militia. *Fanaticos* (Rebel Army): 6,000 (initial); 10,000 (peak); 4,000 (final).[186]

Antecedents: At the beginning of the twentieth century, Brazil had established a republic, and infrastructure projects were bringing the country together. However, such changes to traditional ways of life were not always welcomed by traditionalists and religious leaders. One such opposition movement precipitated a war in the North in 1896, the Canudos Revolt (Intra-state War #632). A similar traditionalist movement emerged in the southern region called the *Contestado*, which was being claimed by the Brazilian states of Santa Catarina and Parná. Brazil had committed to building a railroad from São Paulo south to Santa Maria in the state of Rio Grande do Sul, which would run through the *Contestado*. The railroad engendered local opposition as it took peasant land and brought in foreign workers. One opposition group that sought return of the peasants' land was led by a religious leader known as José Maria, who had created a communal society in Santa Catarina that declared itself independent of government sovereignty. When they decided in October 1912 to relocate to Irani in Paraná, Paraná, seeing the movement as part of a landgrab by Santa Catarina, sent troops to stop José Maria's followers. In the ensuing battle, dozens were killed, including José Maria. José Maria's followers, now called *fanaticos* by their opponents and considered rebels by the governments of both Paraná and Brazil, decided to continue their opposition while awaiting José Maria's resurrection. Most of José Maria's followers now came under the leadership of a fifteen-year-old girl named Maria Rosa, who led a 6,000-strong group of rebels and is considered by some to be the Brazilian Joan of Arc.

The federal government sent 200 troops to deal with the opposition, and there was a clash with the rebels on December 29, 1913, but there were no casualties. The government dispatched several more expeditions to confront the *fanaticos*, and eventually the government soldiers simply declared victory and returned home. Meanwhile, the *fanaticos* were organizing for violent resistance, and in July and August their leaders ordered the people into redoubts. The rebels attacked land offices and burned government buildings, provoking a much more serious government response.

Narrative: The government then appointed Gen. Setembrino de Carvalho (one of the victors in the wars in Rio Grande do Sul—Intra-state Wars #620 and #621) to command a new offensive against the rebels. The first clear-cut combat operation of the war occurred in August 1914 as the rebels shifted from defensive to more offensive strategies. A group of 61 soldiers were ambushed, with perhaps 30 killed. On September 2, the rebels released a manifesto launching a holy war. By September, the rebels had assembled a force of 8,000 combatants out of perhaps 20,000 *fanaticos* in four main redoubts (Tamanduá, Santa Maria, Colônia Vieira, and Salseiro).[187] General Setembrino and the expeditionary force of 6,000 to 7,000 soldiers arrived in early September and constructed an airfield for three planes that accompanied the army. Setembrino divided his troops into four parts and adopted a strategy of encirclement, gradually surrounding areas of rebel activity from September to November.

The government then launched an offensive, capturing a redoubt and hundreds of prisoners with little combat on January 8, 1915. The war moved into a more intense phase with assaults by a number of government contingents. Among the rebels, an increasingly prominent role was being played by Deodata Manuel Ramos (known as Adeodata), who shifted the rebel center to Santa Maria. On February 8, Lt. Col. Estillac at the head of 600 government soldiers attacked 160 rebels at Santa Maria, suffering 40 deaths. Skirmishes continued, and on March 1, Brazil's first aviator, Capt. Ricardo Kirk, was killed. On March 28, a second government column of 1,085 men, led by Capt. Tertuliano Potyguara, began an advance on Santa Maria. From March 31 to April 4, battles for and around Santa Maria killed 242 rebels, including Maria Rosa. By April 2, government forces in the *Contestado* had lost more than 200 dead.

The armies under Estillac and Potyguara joined together for the final assault on Santa Maria, defended by starving rebels. In the final assault, on April 5, 1915, Santa Maria was overcome: 5,000 houses were destroyed, and 600 rebels (including women combatants) were killed. At this point, disease intervened. Typhoid fever struck government forces, and the government decided to declare victory and leave. Surviving rebels scattered.

Termination and Outcome: The outcome was a government military victory, with amnesty for at least some of the rebels. General Setembrino continued small mopping-up operations until the end of 1915, and Adeodata was arrested in August 1916.

Coding Decisions: In terms of the dates for this war, the start date reflects the new offensive that led to war-level fatalities. Similarly, the war ends with the destruction of Santa Maria and the ending of combat that produces war-level fatality rates.

In terms of fatality statistics, Tokarski reports that 5,000 perished from battle, hunger, or typhoid fever. Reports of disaggregated figures have a range of 800 to 1,000 for Brazil and from 5,000 to 8,000 for the rebels. Laps concludes that there were 1,000 government soldiers and 6,000 rebels killed, which are the figures reported here.

Estimates of the number of rebel combatants vary considerably from 8,000 to 20,000 rebels in September 1914. Diacon also uses the 20,000 figure, but the description makes it appear that this number included noncombatants. Levine reports that the strength of the rebels was only 10,000, which seems more plausible.

Sources: Calogeras (1939); Chilcote (1972); Diacon (1991); Hudson (1997); Laps (2003); McCann (2004); Tokarski (2002).

INTRA-STATE WAR #713

Aprista Revolt of 1932 (aka Trujillo Revolt)

Participants: Peru versus Aprista Rebels.
Dates: May 7, 1932, to July 17, 1932.
Battle-related Deaths: Aprista Rebels: 1,100; Peru: 110.
Initiator: Aprista Rebels.
Outcome: Peru wins.
War Type: Civil for central control.
Total System Member Military Personnel: Armed Forces of Peru: 11,000 (prewar, initial, peak, final).[188]
Theater Armed Forces: Aprista Rebels: 160 (initial).

Antecedents: After Peru's defeat in the War of the Pacific (Inter-state War #64, 1879 to 1883), Peru then entered a period of political upheaval encompassing two wars: Peru's war with the Indians (Intra-state War #613 in 1885) and the Civilista Revolution (Intra-state War #625 in 1894 to 1895). After that, the longest term of office was held by Augusto Bernardino Leguía y Salcedo, who had come to power through a coup in 1919 and served as president until 1930. Peru's borders with Chile and Colombia, which were unresolved after the War of the Pacific, finally were settled by 1922 Salomón-Lozano Treaty. Leguía's August 1930 transfer of the port city of Leticia to Colombia as part of the treaty fueled opposition, and on August 25, 1930, a military coup overthrew Leguía and brought Col. Luis Miguel Sánchez Cerro to power.

The overthrow of Leguía was good news for Victor Haya de la Torre. Haya de la Torre had become involved in the reform movement while a student as the National University in Lima and, consequently, had been exiled by Leguía in 1923. Residing in Mexico City, he founded the *Alianza Popular Revolucionaria Americana* (American Popular Revolutionary Alliance [APRA]) on May 7, 1924. APRA was one of the first serious reformist parties in South America, and it soon had supporters among Peru's working class and progressive intellectuals as well as in other countries throughout the region. In 1930, Haya de la Torre was studying in Bremen (Germany), but upon hearing of the end of Leguía's rule, he made plans for the APRA leadership to return to Lima, where an executive committee had been established led by Luis Enríquez.

The anticipated "democratic springtime" did not last long. Shortly after coming to power, Sánchez Cerro began cracking down on all political activity and forced the Peruvian Communist Party (PCP) underground. APRA soon became one of the leading groups in opposition to Sánchez Cerro, along with the moderate *Acción Republicana.* APRA (based in Turjillo) became more visible as it created its own political party, the Peruvian Aprista Party (PAP). After Sánchez Cerro had served only six months in office, naval officers informed him that he had lost their support, and Sánchez Cerro duly resigned. The navy then established caretaker governments pending presidential elections to be held in October 1931. All political parties, except the PCP, were allowed to participate in the election, including the new *Partido Unión Revolucionaria* with Sánchez Cerro as its candidate. Victor Haya de la Torre, as the candidate of PAP, began to attract a large following as he campaigned in the north coastal region with a message of anti-American economic imperialism.

There were four major candidates in the October election, with the highest numbers of votes going to Sánchez Cerro (150,000) and Haya de la Torre (106,000).[189] Haya de la Torre lost the presidency, though PAP was successful in electing 23 of the 145 delegates to the congress. PAP called for a general strike in December to protest what it considered to be voter fraud (claiming that 50,000 PAP votes had been nullified) and to disrupt Sánchez Cerro's inauguration on December 8, 1931. Sánchez Cerro responded by closing down APRA offices. On Christmas Eve, government soldiers raided an APRA party in an attempt to capture Haya de la Torre. By February 1932, the government crackdown included the arrest and exile of PAP's twenty-three congressional delegates. Haya de la Torre was captured on May 6, 1932, and he was put on trial, charged with plotting against the government. The government erroneously assumed that Haya de la Torre's capture would end the opposition.

Narrative: Despite the government's repression, *Aprista* leaders in Trujillo had begun planning a rebellion that would consist of coordinated civilian and military uprisings throughout the North. The revolt initially had been scheduled for December 1931 but had been postponed as the result of a security leak. In the revised timetable, the revolt was to be started on July 15, 1932, by an attack of a group of 150 rebels led by Manuel "Búfalo" Barreto against the O'Donovan army garrison in Trujillo. Coordinated attacks by rebels were to occur in Lima, Huaráz, and Chiclayo; Gen. Gustavo Jiménez (former commander of the Lima garrison who was in exile in Arica, Chile) would sail to Chimbote to assume military command of the rebellion. However, sentiment in favor of immediate action would start the war early.

On May 7, 1932, the day after Haya de la Torre's arrest, sailors with *Aprista* sympathies (who had been in contact with the *Apristas* in Panama) mutinied aboard the Peruvian cruiser *Colonel Bolognesi* in Callao harbor. They overpowered their officers, seized their ship, and then went on to seize the *Almirante Grau* and the *Teniente Rodríguez.* A sailor loyal to the government managed to escape and warn the military officials, who soon established a command post under the minister of the navy, Alfredo Benavides. A naval aide offered to try to negotiate with the rebels, but when his ship approached the *Colonel Bolognesi*, it was met with rifle shots, killing one of the party. The next day, the government warned the mutineers to surrender or face attack. Though the rebels on the *Almirante Grau* and the *Teniente Rodríguez* acceded, the *Colonel Bolognesi* refused. Government forces responded by using planes to drop bombs near the ship and by firing upon it from a submarine deck gun. The rebels surrendered, and 160 of them immediately were put on trial. Eight mutineers were condemned to death and executed, while another 15 received lengthy prison sentences. The following month, an *Apristas* uprising took place at Huaráz, and the government began augmenting its forces. Rumors that Haya de la Torre was being tortured further inflamed the sentiments toward rebellion. Barreto, unable to restrain his followers, prematurely launched the attack against the O'Donovan garrison on July 7, 1932. After a five-hour battle in which both sides sustained significant casualties, the garrison fell. However, the premature attack caused confusion elsewhere and prevented General Jiménez from sailing to take command. The rebels in Trujillo under the leadership of Victor Haya de la Torre's brother, Agustín Haya de la Torre, seized the weapons from O'Donovan and prepared to defend Trujillo with a force that now numbered more than 600 rebels, joined by much of the armed citizenry against the government army of 746 soldiers who had been dispatched from Lima. The *Almirante Grau* disembarked portions of the Seventh Infantry Regiment at Chimbote, whence they marched to Salaverry, which was captured from the *Apristas* on July 9. The government forces then marched on Trujillo but were driven back in stiff fighting that caused significant casualties on both sides. As it became clear to the *Apristas* that the anticipated revolts elsewhere had not occurred, some of the rebels proposed leaving the city to conduct a guerrilla campaign. However, the main rebel army determined to stay and fight. The next day, government forces led by Col. Manuel Ruíz Bravo surrounded Trujillo and used hydroplanes to bomb the city indiscriminately. In house-to-house fighting, the city fell on July 11, and Barreto was killed in the attack. Though Agustín Haya de la Torre was able to escape, many other rebel leaders were captured and shot. Fifty to 60 government military personnel from O'Donovan were killed in their cells by the rebels as they fled. Attempts to continue the rebellion outside of the city led to a few brief uprisings in the North, but all were quickly defeated, with the last town falling to government forces on July 17. During the next few weeks, up to 5,000 citizens (supposed rebels) were captured and executed along the walls of the Incan ruins at Chan-chan.

Termination and Outcome: The war or sustained combat ended at this point in a government victory. However, the executions fueled public opposition to Sánchez Cerro. Leading an uprising, General Jiménez was killed on March 14, 1933. On April 30, 1933, Sánchez Cerro was assassinated by an *Aprista*, Abelardo de Mendoza. APRA would remain outlawed for almost all of the next twenty-four years. Haya de la Torre was imprisoned for fifteen months, and then later from 1935 to 1945, and he sought asylum within the Colombian embassy in 1948 for five years. In 1956, his party was legalized, and in 1962, Haya de la Torre won the presidential election representing ARPA, but the military seized power before he could take office. In 1979, Haya de la Torre became president of the constitutional assembly and was instrumental in writing a new constitution for Peru.

Coding Decisions: This conflict raises a couple of interesting applications of coding rules. The scope of this conflict is portrayed differently in the historical literature. Clodfelter includes only the Trujillo Revolt as the war. Scheina devotes an entire chapter to the conflict between the Peruvian senior military versus the *Apristas*, for the entire period of 1930 to 1968, though he has separate sections dealing with the "1932 Fleet Mutiny" and the subsequent Trujillo "Massacre." We agree with Sheina in seeing both the mutiny and battle for Trujillo as part of the same overall conflict but focus upon the period of May to July 1932 as having war-level sustained combat.

A related question is whether this conflict did lead to war-level fatalities as information about battle-deaths is limited and somewhat contradictory. Most descriptions refer to 1,000 to 2,000 deaths or casualties, though sometimes this number refers only to those executed at the end of the war. The highest figure is reported by Rudolph, who refers to up to 5,000 deaths during the massacre.[190] Given the relatively low number of individuals killed in the specific battles, the question of whether this conflict should be coded as a war hinges upon both judgements about the missing data for some of the engagements and how one treats the executions of government and rebel personnel. Small and Singer argued that executions and massacres of combatants during the war should be included as battle-deaths because the extinction of the enemy is an integral part of the war. Similarly, they also include as part of the war the wave of killing that may take place in the immediate aftermath of a victory.[191] Thus we include the executions of at least 1,000 *Apristas* and report rounded totals of 1,100 rebel deaths and 110 government deaths to account for missing data.

Sources: Ciccarelli (1973); Clodfelter (2002); Klarén (1973); Marett (1969); Marley (1998); Masterson (1991); O'Brien (1999); Pike (1967); Rudolph (1992); Scheina (2003b); Stein (1980).

INTRA-STATE WAR #715

Paulista Rebellion of 1932 (aka Constitutionalist Revolution, the São Paulo Revolution of 1932)

Participants: Brazil versus *Paulistas*.
Dates: July 9, 1932, to October 4, 1932.
Battle-related Deaths: Brazil: 1,050; *Paulistas*: 2,200. (See Coding Decisions.)
Initiator: *Paulistas*.
Outcome: Brazil wins.
War Type: Civil for central control.
Total System Member Military Personnel: Armed Forces of Brazil: 71,000 (prewar); 47,000 (after initial defections); 100,000 (peak, final).[192]
Theater Armed Forces: *Paulistas* aka Constitutionalists (Rebel Army): 21,000 (initial); 70,000 (peak).

Antecedents: Brazilian politics often revolved around rivalry between and among the major states. The presidential election of March 1, 1930, pitted Júlio Prestes, supported by President Washington Luís (both of whom were *Paulistas* or from the state of São Paulo) against Getúlio Vargas (the governor of Rio Grande do Sul) with João Pessoa (the governor of Paraíba) as his running mate. Prestes won the presidency in an election Vargas saw as fraudulent, and Vargas's opposition to the government was heightened by the assassination of Pessoa on July 26, 1930. Vargas then participated in a coup that overthrew the government on October 24, 1930 (before Prestes could take office), and installed a military junta. Together, the states of Rio Grande do Sul, Paraíba, and Minas Gerais (referred to as the Liberal Alliance) backed Vargas, who was appointed interim president on November 3, 1930, thus effectively ending the near-monopoly on national rule by São Paulo.

Once in office, Vargas instituted policies to curb the relative autonomy of São Paulo and began to transform the military by relying on supportive junior officers. The older military professionals resisted the reforms, and military conspiracies against Vargas emerged at an alarming rate. One such conspiracy involved the São Paulo faction of the army, known as the *Paulistas*, led by Gen. Bertoldo Klinger. Klinger and his allies called themselves the constitutionalists because they wanted to overturn the government of the military revolt and return Brazil to a constitutional, elected government. Klinger's strategy was to first depose the national government's designated military governor of Mato Grosso and then to use the resources of the state and its presumed allies to bring 5,000 troops from Mato Grosso to aid in a rebellion against Vargas. The revolt was scheduled for July 14, 1932. Klinger's indiscreet recruiting for the conspiracy caused the government to relieve him of command on July 8, a decision that he accepted before leaving to take leadership of the revolt.

Narrative: On July 9, the planned revolt took place. Military units throughout São Paulo, including the Força Pública and all army garrisons, moved into blocking positions to prevent a government advance into the state. The strategy was then to simply wait for the anticipated insurrections in Mato Grosso, Rio Grande do Sul, and Minas Gerais to force the government out of office without the *Paulistas* having to put up a fight. However, their supposed allies never rebelled, leaving the *Paulistas* isolated. Klinger's unit remained in Mato Grosso, while the state forces of Rio Grande do Sul and Minas Gerais ended up joining the government's invasion of São Paulo.

The rebel army tried to advance toward Rio de Janiero but was stopped by loyalist troops, and the government successfully blockaded the province, preventing it from resupplying its forces. The government formed an expeditionary force to fight the *Paulistas*, and it utilized a three-pronged attack against the state. By mid-July, government forces advancing from the South captured the town of

Itararé, and the rebel troops began retreating toward the capital. Fighting continued with frequent air attacks, and the government army adopted a simple strategy of attrition and trench warfare, reminiscent of World War I. As the war continued, the government's expeditionary force, renamed the Army of the East, rose to 80,000 men. In August, the government declared its intent to write a provisional constitution for the country but offered no other concessions to the rebels, instead demanding their unconditional surrender. Klinger requested an armistice on September 29 but balked at unconditional surrender, delaying for better terms. He was overthrown by officers of the Força Pública, who refused to obey the orders of the rebel government and surrendered the state to federal forces on October 2, though fighting continued until October 4, 1932.

Termination and Outcome: The outcome of the war was a complete and unconditional victory by the government. Vargas avoided retribution and postwar executions because he wanted São Paulo peacefully reassimilated with the rest of the nation. He had a new constitution written and called for elections in 1934. Vargas ruled Brazil for nineteen years during the period of 1930 to 1954.

Coding Decisions: In terms of the size of the armed forces, the Paulistas had 180,000 to 200,000 volunteers but were unable to arm them all, so they are not included. Scholars have reported total casualties for the war of about 15,000, which include 1,050 government battle-deaths and 3,800 wounded. The remaining 10,150 casualties would have been borne by the rebels: assuming that the same ratio of deaths to casualties was experienced by the rebels (21.6 percent) produces an estimate of 2,200 rebel battle-deaths.[193]

Sources: Barclay (1971); Bello (1966); Bernstein (1965); Clodfelter (2008); Cortés (1976); Marley (1998); McCann (2004); Richardson (1960); Scheina (2003b); Williamson (2009); Young (1967).

INTRA-STATE WAR #727

Paraguay War of 1947

Participants: Paraguay versus Leftists.
Dates: March 7, 1947, to August 20, 1947.
Battle-related Deaths: Paraguay: 1,500; Leftists: 2,500. (See Coding Decisions.)
Initiator: Leftists.
Outcome: Paraguay wins.
War Type: Civil for central control.
Total System Member Military Personnel: Armed Forces of Paraguay: 9,000 (8,000 army and 1,000 navy prewar); 6,000 (after initial defections); 9,000 (peak, final).[194]
Theater Armed Forces: Revolutionary Army (Rebel Army): 3,000 (initial); 8,000 (peak); 1,200 (final).[195]

Antecedents: In 1940, Paraguay's President José Félix Estigarribia was killed in a plane crash, and on September 7, the cabinet chose War Minister General Higinio Morínigo as interim president, pending an election. Within months, Morínigo seized power: postponing the elections, banning political parties, sending liberals into exile, and suppressing uprisings by the left-nationalist Revolutionary Febrerista Party (PRF). The presidential election finally was held on February 15, 1943, though Morínigo was the only candidate. Morínigo retained his position with the strong support of the military, which received 45 percent of Paraguay's national income. The allied victory in World War II undermined the Axis-friendly Morínigo regime, and in 1946, Morínigo moved to partially liberalize his rule, permitting the existence of the traditional conservative *Colorado* Party and the PRF: the liberals and communists were not legalized but were permitted to operate openly. He formed a cabinet including military officers, *Colorados*, and PRF members, and he permitted PRF leader and former president Col. Rafael Franco to return from exile on August 3. Almost immediately, Franco (who had previously attained the presidency in a 1936 military coup) sought to maneuver Morínigo out of power. In December 1946 there was an attempted coup, and another on January 13, 1947, was foiled by an *autogolpe* by Morínigo, who declared a state of siege, narrowing his coalition to military loyalists and elements of the *Colorado* Party. Franco fled to Uruguay. Over the next two months, Franco united the PRF, liberals, and the communists in a coalition to oust Morínigo.

Narrative: On March 7, 1947, the initial coup attempt against Morínigo was launched: a raid on the police armory in Asunción was foiled by loyal police and cadets, with 25 rebels captured and only a handful of deaths. The government retained the loyalty of those in key positions around the capital (the chief of police, the chief of the cavalry, the mayor of Asunción, and other *Colorado* loyalists). The government also was able to rely on the paramilitary force of the conservative *Colorados*, the Red Standard (or Guión Rojo—the Red Dash), and to call upon the 60 officers and 400 cadets of the military school.

Undeterred by the failure of the coup attempt, the rebels expanded their efforts into a broader revolt. In the river city of Concepción, the Second Infantry Division joined the revolution on March 8. The rebels then issued a proclamation of revolution demanding democratic reforms and free elections. Four days later, the commander of the 3,000 troops in the Chaco declared for the revolution. The forces of the Chaco and Concepción almost immediately united in a revolutionary army, said to be 10,000 strong. The rebel leadership was so confident of victory that it refused a proposal to enlist 3,000 timber workers, fearing contamination of the military with communism. Eighty percent of active-duty officers eventually joined the rebels, forcing the government to rely on the armed forces of the Red Standard, which included many retired officers and combat veterans of the Chaco War. The *Colorados* also mobilized agrarian peasants to support the government. Government forces increased in April; by May they had more than 4,000 men under arms, and the army peaked at about 9,000. The slow pace of the rebel advance gave the government time to arm and train its new army with assistance from Argentina.

The rebels, having thoroughly infiltrated the Paraguayan Navy, settled on a strategy of naval assault. Navy Commander Sindulfo Gill mounted a naval revolt on April 26. The next day, army units sent to attack the Asunción Naval Yard went over to the rebels. After three days' fighting, however, the superior numbers of the government in Asunción won out, and the rebels were forced to flee to Argentina, where they were interned. Sixty-four people were killed and 175 wounded in the fighting, a majority of them civilians. Following their comrades to the North, the crews of the two Paraguayan gunboats in Buenos Aires went over to the rebellion on May 7. They sailed up the Plate River and entered Paraguayan waters on July 10. The air force, which had largely remained loyal, attacked one of the gunboats and forced it to beach; further air attacks prevented rebel movement upriver, and in fierce fighting from July 24 to July 29, the government retained possession of key forts.

The government's strategy was to contain the rebels and then march on Concepción from the East, making use of the railway between Horqueta and Concepción. In June, the rebels sent a column under Col. Alfred Ramos eastward to disrupt government movements. On June 11, Ramos and 400 men assaulted the town of Tacuatí, which was full of volunteers awaiting incorporation into the government army. The rebels inflicted numerous losses and destroyed valuable war materiel, but they failed to follow up the victory; Ramos's request for another 300 troops to exploit the victory was denied, and he eventually was forced to withdraw. Despite this setback, government forces pushed northward and reached Horqueta on July 17. The rebels decided to abandon Concepción and mount a last-ditch attack on Asunción by river using 2,500 to 3,000 soldiers and makeshift gunboats. On August 1, they took Puerto Milagro, but the hardest fighting occurred as rebels boarded and seized two government warships. The next day, the rebels occupied Puerto Ybapobó and then continued to San Pedro on August 3, where they were joined by a unit of cavalry. The air force continued to attack the rebel flotilla as it moved south, and the rebels disembarked about 2,700 troops at Arecutacuá, having advanced about four-fifths of the way to the capital. Unfortunately, they had lost many of their supplies during the advance, and the march on Asunción—just thirty miles to the south—was slow. The rebel army encountered increasingly stiff government resistance. The government hastily assembled defenses around the capital, relying on *Colorado* volunteers, police, 200 cadets, local university students, and Argentina-supplied arms. The rebels encountered the first defenses on August 12. Two days later, they mounted a nighttime assault that broke through in several places. They captured Cuatro Mojones just southeast of the capital but failed to complete the encirclement of the loyalists. Fighting raged in the outskirts and suburbs of Asunción from August 14 to August 18, but the rebels were demoralized and panicked when government forces from the North arrived to reinforce the capital on August 15. By August 17, rebel leaders still refused to surrender, leading to "massacres" of civilians in some areas. The rebel fleet surrendered on August 19; the next day, the rebel leadership fled to Argentina, while the rebel army surrendered.

Termination and Outcome: The war ended with an unconditional rebel surrender. Enlisted men were given amnesty, but thirty officers were executed.

In the aftermath of the war, *Colorado* dominance of the army made Morínigo's rule untenable; he was ousted from power by his wartime allies in 1948.

Coding Decisions: The strength estimates for the armed forces of Paraguay include the paramilitary force of the *Colorados*, the Red Standard (or *Guión Rojo*—the Red Dash). The strength of the latter is unclear, but a "grand march" of the Colorado Party on September 7, 1946, brought out only 5,000 *Colorados*, both men and women, thus it is likely that the actual number of Red Standard combatants was less than this.

In terms of battle-deaths, Clodfelter estimated 4,000 total deaths, of which 3,000 were suffered in the last weeks of the war. A rebel commander's memoir claims losses of 8,000 rebels, which presumably included those who surrendered. The rebels suffered 1,650 battle-deaths in the fighting around Asunción and almost certainly suffered more than 2,000 during the course of the war. The government probably suffered between 1,000 and 2,000 battle-deaths. Thus, our best estimate is 2,500 rebel and 1,500 government deaths.

Sources: Ashwell (1998); Cady and Prince (1966); Calvert (2001); Cardoza (1949); Clodfelter (2008); "General Rafael Franco Reported Leading Paraguay Rebels" (1947); Kolinski (1973); Lewis (2002); Nickson (1993); Phillips and Axelrod (2005); Scheina (2003b); Warren (1949).

INTRA-STATE WAR #731

Seventh Colombian *La Violencia* War of 1948 to 1953 (aka First Wave of *La Violencia*)

Participants: Colombia versus Liberals.
Dates: April 9, 1948, to September 12, 1953.
Battle-related Deaths: Liberals: 19,200; Colombia: 7,200; Conservative Guerrillas: 9,600; Communist Guerrillas: [ ] few. (See Coding Decisions.)
Initiator: Liberals.
Outcome: Colombia wins.
War Type: Civil for central control.
Total System Member Military Personnel: Armed Forces of Colombia: 17,000 (prewar, initial); 18,000 (peak, final).[196]
Theater Armed Forces: Armed Forces of Colombia: 29,000 (prewar, initial, includes 12,000 police); 49,400 (peak, final, includes 25,000 police and 5,000 irregulars).[197] Conservative Guerrillas (Pro-Government Aggregate): 12,000 (peak).[198] Liberal Guerrillas (Rebel Aggregate): 4,500 (initial—1950); 26,000 (peak); 20,000 (final).[199] Communist Guerrillas (Rebel Aggregate): 800 (peak).[200] Note that the communists spent much of their time fighting liberals as well as the government.

Antecedents: After the brutal War of 1,000 Days (Intra-state War #636, 1899 to 1902), Colombia experienced nearly fifty years of peace before civil war between liberals and conservatives once again ravaged the country. In the 1946 presidential election, the liberals split, putting forward two candidates: the official candidate of the Colombian Liberal Party, Gabriel Turbay, and the more radical liberal Jorge Eliecer Gaitán. This split enabled the candidate of the Conservative Party, Mariano Ospina Pérez, to capture the presidency by achieving a mere plurality of votes cast. However, the liberals won a majority in Congress, and Gaitán soon became the leader of a reunited Liberal Party. The first wave of violence began with attacks on liberals by conservatives in the departments north of Bogotá (Boyacá, Santander, and Santander del Norte), while liberal guerrillas began operating in the eastern plains (*llanos*), targeting police and conservative civilians.

By 1947 it became clear that the police, then part of the national executive, were arming conservatives. Liberals proposed a plan to "depoliticize" the police—by placing them under the control of the liberal-dominated congress. The minister of government called the plan an act of subversion and threatened violent repression, while liberal leaders began to call for armed revolt against conservative domination. Violence between the parties continued, and on March 1, 1948, Gaitán demanded that liberals leave all government positions. Tensions escalated as the 1949 presidential election approached as it was anticipated that Gaitán would win.

Narrative: On April 9, 1948, the popular Gaitán was assassinated. The murder sparked a long period of conflict known as *La Violencia*. The early days of *La Violencia* were dominated by the deaths of civilians at the hands of non-state actors, including the immediate capture and beating to death of Gaitán's alleged assassin. Bogotá was the site of riots known as the *Bogatazo*, which began as attacks against stores (frequently to seize weapons). Rioting and violence then spread across the countryside (now remembered as *nueve de abril*, Ninth of April). Yet, the initial violence also included elements of a war between the liberals and the government of Colombia as liberals attacked government installations and the army was brought in to confront them. In analyzing this conflict as a war, we focused upon the combat between the government forces (aided by conservative partisans) against the liberals and tried to omit activities and fatalities of noncombatants.

Liberals gained control of the radio stations and issued open calls for armed rebellion while urging President Ospina to resign. As the liberal partisans continued their attacks throughout the city, government troops with tanks intervened and dispersed the rebels. One hundred and nine public buildings were damaged, and anywhere from 549 to 10,000 people (including civilians) died. The army originally had been regarded as apolitical by liberals and conservatives. However, after *nueve de abril*, the Conservative Party began appointing its supporters to key military positions. The liberal governor of the department of Tolima sided with the rebels, allowing a revolutionary junta to be established in Ibagué headed by Germán Torres Barreto. The liberal militias then attacked the conservative armed groups, gaining control of many villages. The army was charged with restoring order, and within a short time, Tolima's villages were again under the control of the central government. Meanwhile, communist guerrillas also began striking railroads and refineries as well as government troop trains and airfields. Partisans on both sides redoubled their efforts to arm themselves, and the government filtered weapons to conservatives, sometimes using Catholic clergy as middlemen. The Conservative Party became divided between moderates like Ospina and extremists like party leader Laureano Gómez. For the November 27, 1949, presidential election, the Conservative Party nominated Gómez, while the liberals nominated Darío Enchandía. Having been the target of an attempted assassination, Enchandía withdrew from the campaign, and liberals moved to impeach Ospina. On November 9, Ospina declared a state of siege, suspended much of the constitution, and closed the legislature. The unopposed Gómez was elected president.

Gómez instituted a policy of persecution of all forms of opposition groups, including labor and peasant organizations as well as Protestants, liberals, and communists. In response, liberal militias retaliated by murdering large numbers of conservatives. By 1950, there were about 4,500 liberal guerrillas operating in the country. The army responded with large-scale sweeps that were too slow to catch most guerrillas but violent enough to depopulate the countryside. In 1951, the guerrillas of the eastern *llanos* mounted a major offensive but made little progress. By 1952, the number of liberal guerrillas had reached 26,000, and some units were capable of large-scale operations. A peace effort in April failed. Late in 1952, the army mounted a large-scale, but ultimately ineffective, counterinsurgency effort in the eastern *llanos*. Meanwhile, President Gómez had decided that Colombia should become involved in the Korean War (Inter-state War #151), and the commitment of troops ultimately led to the end of Gomez's presidency. Gomez dispatched popular Gen. Gustavo Rojas Pinilla to the Inter-American Defense Board in Washington, and when Rojas returned, he overthrew the Gómez regime with support from the moderate wings of both parties—on June 14, 1953. Military rule was established in Colombia for the first time since the nineteenth century. Four days later, liberal guerrillas on the *llanos* united under Guadelupe Salcedo.

Within days of the military coup, the government offered amnesty to the guerrillas who would renounce violence: liberal rebels began surrendering—six leaders on June 17 and another 4,000 guerrillas by July 4, 1953. By September 12, 10,000 guerrillas, most under Guadalupe Salcedo, laid down their arms, which marked the end of war-level violence and the end date of this war.

Termination and Outcome: The outcome of this war was a military victory for the government. Some violence continued, and the formation of new militia groups led to the next civil war two years later (Intra-state War #739).

Coding Decisions: Coding of this conflict has been quite complex, requiring the application of numerous specific coding rules, and COW's coding of the war and its subsequent phases have changed over time as more detailed information about fatalities has become available. In *Resort to Arms*, Small and Singer coded two separate wars in Colombia: #796 from April 9,

1948, to April 12, 1948, that pitted Colombia against the conservatives and #802 from April 1949 to the end of 1962, which was Colombia versus the liberals. Because evidence indicates that fighting continued in 1948 and 1949, we have continued the war until 1953 instead, with the next war starting in 1955 as fatality levels again reached war level.

The coding of the war type also is complicated as this war combined elements of civil and intercommunal conflict, which are so entangled with each other as to be inseparable given the available data. Accordingly, we treat the entirety of *La Violencia* as a single civil war for control of the central government, although the fighting itself was highly local in character. A major difficulty has been determining the battle-deaths for this war (deaths of combatants), and the timing of the fatalities is critical for coding the start and end dates of the distinct phases of this conflict. Much of our understanding and coding of the war has been determined by new research presented by Henderson and Oquist, which is instrumental in trying to separate the deaths of combatants from those of civilians. Though COW had at one point continued this war through 1958 because of the continuance of deaths during the period from 1953 to 1958, the deaths after 1953 were predominantly of civilians. The vast majority of the deaths overall were of unarmed civilians: of the 144,000 fatalities during this period, we estimate 36,000 total combatant deaths.

Sources: Cady and Prince (1966); Clodfelter (1992, 2008); Dubois (1959); Guevara (1985); Henderson (1985); Huntington (1962); Hylton (2006); Kende (1971); Kohn (1999); Loveman and Davies (1985a, b); Manwaring (2002); Maullin (1973); Mydans and Mydans (1968); Oquist (1980, 1998); Palacios (2006); Petras (1968); Phillips and Axelrod (2005); Ramsey (1970); Rummel (1972); Scheina (2003b); "Six Guerrilla Leaders in Colombia Surrender" (1953); Taylor and Hudson (1972); Wood (1968); Zackrison (1989).

INTRA-STATE WAR #737

Bolivian War of 1952 (aka Bolivian National Revolution)

Participants: Bolivia versus Leftists.
Dates: April 8, 1952, to April 11, 1952.
Battle-related Deaths: Bolivia: [ ]; Leftists: [ ]; Total Combatant Deaths: 1,000.
Initiator: Leftists.
Outcome: Leftists win.
War Type: Civil for central control.
Total System Member Military Personnel: Armed Forces of Bolivia: 9,000 (prewar, initial, peak, final).[201]
Theater Armed Forces: *Movimiento Nacionalista Revolucionario* (MNR Rebel Army): 4,000 (initial).

Antecedents: In the War of the Pacific (Inter-state War #64: 1879 to 1883), Bolivia had lost its territorial coastline to Chile. Bolivia's attempts to expand its territory in the Chaco region instead had brought it to war with Paraguay (Inter-state War #124 in 1932). The arbitration that ended the conflict awarded most of the territory to Paraguay. Bolivia's defeat left its civilian leadership severely weakened, and a coup in 1936 brought a military junta to power. Military and military-backed regimes ruled the country for the next generation. Many new political parties emerged, among them the *Movimiento Nacionalista Revolucionario* (MNR, or National Revolutionary Movement), which had started as a peasant–miner alliance led by the urban middle class. It then developed into a proto-fascist party that joined a 1943 coup against the elected pro-American regime of Gen. Enrique Peñaranda. The coup secured the presidency for fascist sympathizer Maj. Gualberto Villarroel. Villarroel and his MNR allies developed a pro-Axis foreign policy that caused problems in Bolivia's relations with the United States. A popular uprising against Villarroel's use of violence overthrew and killed the president in July 1946, leading to a return of the traditional elites to power, and six years of oligarchic rule known as the *Sexenio* followed. MNR's leader Víctor Paz Estenssoro, who had served as Villarroel's Minister of Finance, fled the country.

After 1946, the MNR moved to the left, echoing the radicalization of its miner members. A recession in 1949 hit the mining particularly hard, and the government responded to labor unrest with heavy-handed repression: that June, more than 300 workers were killed in one strike alone. The massacres both radicalized and legitimized the MNR, which had absorbed a number of disillusioned Marxists from other parties. On August 26, the MNR once again attempted to seize power, with the support of miners, workers, and peasants. The army remained loyal to the government, and by September 15, most rebel leaders had fled the country. A similar uprising took place in May 1950.

The MNR continued to increase its popular appeal and briefly shifted to electoral activity in 1951. MNR's Estenssoro apparently won the 1951 presidential election, but the military seized power before Estenssoro could assume office. Hernán Siles Zuazo, the MNR candidate for vice president, soon began planning a new rebellion.

Narrative: The rebellion originally was prepared for March 1952. However, a member of the ruling junta, Gen. Antonio Seleme, offered MNR the support of the 3,000-strong national police force for the rebellion in exchange for the presidency. The MNR took the deal, and the revolt was rescheduled for April 9. MNR members began gathering in La Paz on the evening of April 8. Then on the morning of April 9, the MNR forces (including the national police) seized government buildings in La Paz. At least 1,000 weapons were distributed to MNR members, bringing the total strength of the rebels to at least 4,000 (not including armed cadres outside of La Paz). Within the city, they were opposed by only 600 presidential guards, 240 men of the Second Engineer Battalion, and 400 military cadets. The regular army, which had been redeployed outside of the city on Seleme's request, mounted a counterattack in the afternoon and retook much of the city by nightfall. Fighting also occurred in Oruro, but elsewhere in the country, the cities were secured by the MNR without bloodshed. The next day, MNR reinforcement arrived from other regions of the country, while government forces declined: some soldiers defected to the rebels, many simply deserted, and air force personnel refused orders to bomb La Paz. The rebels attacked the capital and eliminated military resistance on April 11.

Termination and Outcome: The outcome of the war was an unconditional victory by the rebels. The army was disbanded. Because Seleme fled during the fighting, the presidency went to MNR party leader Estenssoro. The MNR stayed in power until 1964.

Coding Decisions: The primary difficulty in coding this conflict as a war stems from vague or contradictory fatality estimates. Scheina and Clodfelter mention that there were between 300 and 3,000 deaths. However, most of the historical descriptions of this conflict cite fatality figures in the 500 to 600 range, including the official death toll, published after the war, indicating that 552 had been killed and 787 wounded. The source of the high range of estimates appears to be Jorge de Solar, who was on the planning committee for the revolution and estimated 2,000 to 3,000 total "casualties."[202] Whitehead estimates 1,500 dead, which appears to be something of an average of high and low estimates. While the official death toll remains the best-documented and most reliable estimate of fatalities, there is sufficient uncertainty for us to conclude that there were approximately 1,000 total combatant deaths and thus include this case as a civil war.

Sources: Alexander (1958); Blasier (1971); Brill (1967); Cady and Prince (1966); Ciment (2007g); Clodfelter (2002); Dunkerley (1984); Goldstone (1998); Klein (1969); Kohn (1999); Malloy (1970); de Mesa, Gisbert, and Gisbert (2001); Morales (2003); Phillips and Axelrod (2005); Scheina (2003b); Selbin (1993); Taylor and Hudson (1972); Whitehead (1984); Wright (1965).

INTRA-STATE WAR #739

La Violencia Second Wave of 1955 to 1962

Participants: Colombia versus Liberal Guerrillas.
Dates: June 13, 1955, to December 31, 1962.
Battle-related Deaths: Colombia: [ ]; Liberal Guerrillas: [ ]; Conservative Guerrillas: [ ]; Total Combatant Deaths: 14,000. (See Coding Decisions.)
Initiator: Colombia.
Outcome: Conflict continues at below war level.
War Type: Civil for central control.
Total System Member Military Personnel: Armed Forces of Colombia: 12,000 (prewar); 15,000 (initial); 55,000 (peak); 55,000 (final).[203]
Theater Armed Forces: Liberal Guerrillas (Rebel Aggregate including the communists): 2,000 (initial, peak), 4,500 (final).[204] Conservative Guerrillas (Pro-Government Aggregate): [ ]. Communist Guerrillas (Rebel Aggregate): 2,000 (peak); 1,800 (final).[205]

Antecedents: This war occurred in the aftermath of the first phase of *La Violencia* 1948 to 1953 (Intra-state War #731). That war was terminated in September 1953 as a consequence of a military coup the preceding June, which temporarily provided the amnesty and security that the combatants needed to disarm. However, the remaining rebel groups, including the communists, continued to undermine the stability of the government.

The 1953 military coup had brought Gen. Gustavo Rojas Pinilla to power, and his desire to halt the violence initially had the support of both conservatives and liberals (though not of the communists or the supporters of deposed president Laureano Gómez). However, government actions led to increased opposition, uniting conservatives and liberals. A government massacre of students in Bogotá in June 1954 (killing eleven) ignited renewed violence by the conservative paramilitary groups known as *Pájaros* (the Birds). In March 1955, 500 liberal guerrillas increased activities in Villarrica. President Rojas, portraying communist activities as part of the global cold war, designated the eastern part of the Tolima department and the Sumpaz region of the capital as zones of military operations.

Narrative: In June 1955, the war began when Rojas personally orchestrated a June 13 large-scale army operation against the guerrillas in Tolima and Sumpaz. As six government battalions surrounded the area, a 2,000-man guerrilla force attacked the government forces near Villarrica but was soon driven back and dispersed. The offensive soon took on the character of an assault on *campesinos* (peasants), who fled into the mountains or into neighboring departments. The government mounted more than ten large sweeps that year alone. By extending the term of conscription, Colombia's military increased its effective strength to at least 36,000 soldiers. The liberal guerrillas grew as well, in some instances even creating their own military government structures, such as that of the Liberal National Revolutionary Movement of Southern Tolima. In February 1956, the army mounted a large-scale offensive in Tolima, succeeding in dispersing the larger units in the province but not in destroying them.

On July 10, 1956, when Rojas announced his candidacy for the 1958 presidential term, he triggered fears of dictatorship among both liberal and conservative leaders, who then began to discuss peace terms with each other. Meeting in Spain, former conservative president Laureano Gómez and liberal Alberto Lleras Camargo agreed on July 24, 1956, to the Pact of Benidorm, or the Civil or Civic Front, as the basis of the elite cooperation. However, large-scale violence began to increase, as did overall opposition to Rojas. To diffuse the situation, Rojas offered several concessions, yet the Civil Front further declared its opposition to military government in November 1956. On January 1, 1957, the former liberal guerrilla leader Guadalupe Salcedo was assassinated by police, and on March 20, 1957, the Civil Front issued the Pact of March, which explicitly opposed the reelection of Rojas. On May 8, the "assembly" convened by Rojas "reelected" him, but two days later, top military officers forced him to resign as they established a five-man junta with a cabinet of five liberals, five conservatives, and three officers. The first National Front candidate, liberal Alberto Lleras Camargo, was elected president May 4, 1958, though the junta continued to rule until he took office on August 7, 1958.

After Lleras took office, he announced that ending violence was his first priority, and by late 1958 a number of guerrillas began coming to terms with the government (thus, a number of scholars end the war at this point). Though violence continued, it began to decline: during the first half of 1958, there were at least 2,477 violent deaths, nearly all of which occurred in Tolima (1,074), Valle (690), or Caldas (566); during the second half of the year, there were only 1,203 deaths, mostly in the same three departments. By May 1959, the average number of deaths per day had been reduced from 15.2 to 4.[206] Most of the remaining active rebels were communists, who numbered about 655 in Cundinamarca, 217 in Tolima, and 40 elsewhere. In response to the continuing violence, President Lleras sought assistance from the United States, and the Eisenhower administration responded with covert military aid, which was increased under President Kennedy. In the early 1960s, Colombia began regaining control over some of the rebel-held areas.

Meanwhile, in the 1960s, students and workers, influenced by the Cuban Revolution (Intra-state War #745) and the writings of Che Cuevara, founded several new guerrilla organizations, the most important of which probably were the National Liberation Army (ELN) and *Frente Unido de Acción Revolucionaria* (FUAR) or United Front for Revolutionary Action), which received some direct support from Cuba. In 1961, the Colombian government began to regain control of the seventy-six communist-controlled republics, one of which was the Republic of

Marquetalia, which was the site of an assault from 1964 to 1965 and would become part of the revolutionary lore of the *Fuerzas Armadas Revolucionarias Colombinas* (FARC, or Revolutionary Armed Forces of Colombia). With American aid and military training, the government was able to organize rural self-defense leagues, and casualties dropped significantly. Even though by 1962 there were more than 160 guerrilla groups with 3,000 fighters, fatalities were reduced to about two-thirds of what they had been in 1958.[207]

Termination and Outcome: There is uncertainty about the end date of this war as unlike the first wave of *La Violencia*, this time there was no general surrender of forces, just a gradual decline in battle-deaths to below war level. Several scholars describe a decline in the level of hostilities happening by the end of 1962 as a result of the government's initiatives and American aid. Thus we code December 31, 1962, as the end of this war. The counterinsurgency efforts were successful in splintering the cohesion of the guerrilla groups but only in reducing the level of conflict. Thus the outcome of the war is coding as "conflict continues at below war level."

In 1966, the FARC was formed, and it continued low-level conflict through the 1970s and 1980s, which flared into war again in 1989 (Intra-state War #856).

Coding Decisions: Most reports of violent fatalities do not distinguish between civilians and combatants, though we have tried to determine the proportion of those killed who were actual combatants. We know that in general, *La Violencia* killed more civilians than military personnel, so battle-deaths as a proportion of total deaths must be lower than 50 percent. The raw numbers provided by Oquist indicate combatant fatalities at war level through 1962, after which the combatant deaths would be below war level. The total fatalities from mid-1955 to the end of 1962 are 29,422, which is similar to Clodfelter's mention of 20,000 fatalities between 1958 and 1962. If we assume that less than half of our total represents combatant deaths, it would mean about 14,000 total combatant deaths.

Sources: Clodfelter (2002); Dix (1987); Fluharty (1957); Henderson (1985); Loveman and Davies (1985a, b); Oquist (1980); Ramsey (1970); Rempe (2002); Sánchez and Meertens (2001); Scheina (2003b); Wolf (2002–2004a, b, c, d).

INTRA-STATE WAR #740

Argentine Military War of 1955 (aka Anti-Perón Revolts of 1955 or Liberating Revolution)

Participants: Argentina versus Army and Navy Rebels.
Dates: June 15, 1955, to September 19, 1955.
Battle-related Deaths: Argentina: [ ]; Army and Navy Rebels: [ ]; Total Combatant Deaths: 2,100. (See Coding Decisions.)
Initiator: Army and Navy Rebels.
Outcome: Army and Navy Rebels win.
War Type: Civil for central control.
Total System Member Military Personnel: Army of Argentina: 148,000 (prewar); 140,000 (after initial defections).[208]
Theater Armed Forces: Navy, Marines, and Rebel Army Units (Rebel Army): 8,000 (peak, final—4,000 in Cordoba and 4,000 naval personnel in Buenos Aires).[209]

Antecedents: Fascist Juan Perón was a populist president and dictator who had ruled Argentina since 1946. His policies created economic chaos, and he made enemies of the upper and middle classes, the Roman Catholic Church, other conservative groups, and the military. After a failed coup attempt in 1951, Perón declared the State of Internal Warfare, a law giving him broad powers, including the ability to promote, transfer, and retire members of the armed forces. At that point, the military began planning to overthrow Perón. When Perón's popular wife Eva died in 1952, much of his support began to evaporate. Issues came to a head in January 1955, when Perón announced a new deal with Standard Oil to develop Argentina's oil resources, which was widely unpopular. This issue, coupled with Perón's growing conflict with the Church, prompted a revolt in which the navy took the lead. The chief of staff of the marine corps, Adm. Samuel Toranzo Calderón, had been planning a rebellion that involved mostly naval personnel, though he had contacted civilian and army opponents of the regime as well. The timing crystalized after June 11, 1955, when a celebration of Corpus Christi Day turned into an antigovernment riot. On June 13 and June 14, Perón delivered fiery speeches against the Church, including the demand for the deportation of two bishops. The Vatican responded by excommunicating those responsible for the deportations.

Narrative: Meanwhile, Admiral Toranzo was indecisive. He scheduled the revolt for June 16, 1955, but by that day he had changed his mind and attempted to call it off. However, officers at the naval air base at Punta Indio did not get the message and went ahead as planned. The naval officers seized the naval academy and awaited the planned bombing of the *Casa Rosada*, the government house, an attempt to kill Perón, which finally started after noon. The plan also called for the marines and armed civilian allies to seize key buildings, for airborne army troops to secure the airport, and for the navy to push up the Rio de Plata. The Fourth Marine Battalion was able to capture navy headquarters and marched toward the *Casa Rosada*, but after a three-hour battle, they were turned back by army forces loyal to the government. The first phase of the revolt failed due to a combination of poor coordination, miscommunication, and bad weather. The attempt had cost about 360 killed, most of them civilians. The pilots fled to Uruguay, 106 officers including Toranzo were arrested. In the aftermath, numerous churches were sacked and burned by *Perónistas*. Subsequently, Perón reshuffled his cabinet, promulgated laws to undermine the power of the navy and marines, and began a *rapprochement* with the Church. The navy was undeterred and continued to plot against Perón.

The conflict between the pro- and anti-Perón factions continued. To diffuse the situation, on August 31, Perón offered to resign, a ploy that produced a general strike by his supporters, who demanded that he retract the offer. Perón then spoke to the crowd and issued a call for violence where the death of one *Perónist* would be met by the deaths of five opponents. This prompted the rebels in the navy to ramp up their planning for another revolt under the leadership of Adm. Isaac Rojas. The outstanding issue was whether the participation of the army was necessary. By September, elements of the army, under the leadership of retired general Eduardo Lonardi, were also planning for rebellion to begin in the interior provinces, where disenchanted officers commanded, instead of in Buenos Aires, which was controlled by army loyalists. The naval officers assented to Lonardi's plan as long as the revolt would begin before September 17, when an inspection of the navy might uncover the plot.

Assured of naval cooperation, Lonardi proposed to begin the rebellion from the western city of Córdoba, which was profoundly Catholic and anti-Perónist. On the morning of September 16, artillery cadets in Cordoba took control of the military academy after an eight-hour battle. Other uprisings secured Mendoza and San Juan for the revolution. The same day, Admiral Rojas proclaimed the revolt, and two ships were seized to institute a blockade around Buenos Aires and La Plata. The ships were attacked by loyalist air force units and sustained numerous casualties. Naval rebels at Rio Santiago faced stiff resistance from loyal army and air force units. By September 18, additional ships joined the rebellion, and Admiral Rojas established a blockade of the coast and threatened to bomb oil storage facilities south of Buenos Aires. Several air force units also defected to the rebellion. The same day, government forces pressed toward Cordoba, scheduling an all-out assault for September 19, which would have pitted 10,000 loyalists against 4,000 rebels. On the morning of September 19, a cruiser did bomb several oil storage tanks at Mar del Plata. Military steps were halted when, at 5:30 a.m. on September 19, Perón issued an ambiguous announcement of his resignation to his defense minister.

Termination and Outcome: Though Perón's offer was later revealed to be insincere, a military junta had been formed that accepted the resignation at face value, and later that day a truce was arranged between the remaining loyalist generals and the rebels. A formal agreement was negotiated the next day providing for the resignation of the rest of the government and the assumption of power by a military junta under General Lonardi. The agreement was signed by the government on September 21, and Lonardi assumed office on the September 23 with Admiral Rojas as provisional vice president. The new government was plagued by infighting and was overthrown by a new junta led by Gen. Pedro Aramburu in November. Peron fled to Paraguay and on to Panama, Venezuela, the Dominican Republic, and Spain but returned and reassumed the presidency in 1973.

Coding Decisions: There are no reliable estimates of overall battle-deaths. For the fighting in September, one report suggests 4,000 deaths, though Leitenberg suggests that half of these were civilians, leaving a total of 2,000 battle-deaths. Whitaker also claims that of the 360 deaths in June, 335 were civilians. Though some of the civilians could have acted as combatants, a conservative estimate of combatant deaths would be 2,100 (which we are reporting here). The real figure could easily be half or twice this number.

Sources: Alexander (1979); Brogan (1998); Cady and Prince (1966); Clodfelter (2002, 2008); Crassweller (1987); Leitenberg (2005); Page (1983); Phillips and Axelrod (2005); Rummel (1972); Scheina (2003b); Taylor and Hudson (1972); Whitaker (1956).

INTRA-STATE WAR #793

Chilean Coup of 1973

Participants: Chile versus Military Rebels.
Dates: September 11, 1973, to September 15, 1973.
Battle-related Deaths: Chile: 3,000; Military Rebels: 200. (See Coding Decisions.)
Initiator: Military Rebels.
Outcome: Military Rebels win.
War Type: Civil for central control.
Total System Member Military Personnel: 75,000 (prewar).[210]
Theater Armed Forces: The government of Chile was defended by *Grupo Amigos Personnes* (GAP, or Government Aggregate): 300 members; *Movimiento de Izquierda Revolucionaira* (MIR), Revolutionary Peasant Movement, worker and student paramilitary groups, and a few loyal military personnel: total number unknown. The military rebel armed forces included virtually all of Chile's military personnel (75,000) plus 35,000 *Carabineros*,[211] or 110,000.

Antecedents: In the 1958 presidential election, Jorge Alessandri Rodriguez, representing the Conservative Party, won 32.2 percent of the vote against 28.5 percent for Salvador Guillermo Allende Gossens of the leftist *Frente de Acción Popular* (FRAP, or Popular Action Front) and 20.5 percent for moderate Eduardo Nicanor Frei Montalva of the Christian Democratic Party of Chile (PDC). As no candidate had a majority, the selection of the president fell to Congress, which chose Alessandri. The 1964 presidential election pitted the PDC's Frei against Allende, again representing FRAP. Frei won the election with the backing of right-wing parties, garnering 55.6 percent of the vote to Allende's 38.6 percent.

In 1970, Allende ran again, this time as the representative of the *Unidad Popular*, which included most of the parties of the left. Allende was opposed by Radomiro Tomic, the leader of the more left-wing sector of the PDC, and former president Alessandri. On September 4, 1970, Allende won a plurality of the vote, 36.2 percent, narrowly defeating Alessandri, with 34.9 percent. The election then went to the congress, and the United States began clandestine efforts (known as Track I) to try to prevent Allende from taking office. With Tomic's support, Allende was nonetheless inaugurated on November 3, 1970, becoming the first freely elected Marxist president in Latin America. Allende's policies, called the Chilean Path to Socialism, which provided assistance to Chile's neediest citizens and began to restructure the economy, soon provoked opposition by industrial interests and conservative groups and nervousness on the part of the armed forces. Allende's government nationalized American-owned mining interests, further alienating the United States, which then increased its programs, known as Track II, to destabilize the regime and encourage a military coup. Meanwhile, Allende increased Chile's ties to the Soviet Union and Cuba (which provided training and weapons to the leftist groups).

On June 29, 1973, a coup attempt against Allende was launched by Col. Roberto Souper, who surrounded the presidential palace with his tank regiment in what came to be known as the *Tancazo* (or tank putsch). The attack was dispersed by Gen. Carlos Prats, commander in chief of the army. Though the putsch failed, it marked the start of a period of increasing opposition to the Allende government. Simultaneously, the flow of weapons increased dramatically to the paramilitary groups of the competing political factions, including the *Movimiento de Izquierda Revolucionaira* (MIR) on the left and the right-wing *Patria y Libertad.* Allende continued to express support for the military, and on August 9, he formed a new cabinet that included military officers in key positions. However, on August 22, the chamber of deputies passed a resolution that charged the Allende government with acting illegally, and then it encouraged military intervention. On August 24, Allende's minister of defense resigned and was replaced by Gen. Augusto José Ramón Pinochet Ugarte, who had become the general chief of staff of the army in 1972. Pinochet's role in the upcoming war has been a matter of some debate with Pinochet claiming that he was one of the primary planners of the revolt, while others have argued that he only joined the revolt a few days before it was launched. Planning for the rebellion began as early as March 1973 and included most of the top leaders of the military branches and the *Carabineros* (national police). The specific agreement to unite the military forces in a coup was signed on September 9 by the leaders of the navy, air force, and army (represented by General Pinochet). There is also disagreement about the extent of the role of the United States in the rebellion. However, at a minimum, the Central Intelligence Agency (CIA) had sought to instigate a coup, had relations with some of the plotters, had provided $40 million to opposition groups, and was aware of the activities of the plotters. The United States was also ready to assist the rebellion: it had naval vessels in the vicinity, had intelligence aircraft over the Andes, and may have landed navy seals into Chile.

Narrative: At 6:30 a.m. on September 11, 1973, American personnel were visited by one of the leaders of the revolt and were informed that the rebellion was taking place that morning. Delays pushed the timing back to 8:30, which meant that Allende was warned about the upcoming revolt, giving him time to assemble some of the members of his personal security force, *Grupo Amigos Personnes* (GAP), and to arrive at *La Moneda*, the presidential palace, by 7:30 a.m. Meanwhile, armed forces outside of the capital launched the revolt, seizing Valparaíso and gaining control of naval stations and towns where army troops were garrisoned. Allende was joined by a contingent of *Carabineros*, who fled at 9:00 a.m., when Allende heard the radio broadcast of the rebellion proclamation. The palace was soon surrounded by tanks, and the rebels threatened to bomb the palace unless Allende surrendered. Cuban embassy officials attempted to get a stockpile of weapons to MIR, and an armed contingent planned to go to fight alongside the president, an offer Allende declined. Allende decided not to surrender, and gunfire soon erupted between the GAP (aided by armed Allende supporters outside the palace) and the military. There was a brief attempt to negotiate the president's surrender, but at noon, the air force began to bomb *La Moneda*. Allende encouraged MIR to take up arms in the outskirts of the capital. By 2:00 p.m. the palace was captured by the rebels, and Allende was dead (by murder or suicide).

Fighting continued in some areas of the capital, and there were at least two gunfights between the military and the staff at the Cuban embassy. The leftists were disorganized and unable to mount a coordinated resistance. Sporadic fighting between the military and forces of MIR, aided by students and workers, continued in other cities including Linares, Concepción, Valvidivia, and Antofagasta for the next several days. In the South of the country, on September 12, workers, peasants, and activists of the Revolutionary Peasant Movement attacked a police checkpoint in the Valdivian Andes. There were also reports of combat between rebel and loyalist elements of the armed forces. By September 15, the resistance to the military had been crushed, ending the war.

Termination and Outcome: The military then established a military junta, of which General Pinochet was named president, and he soon consolidated his control. The military launched a campaign that involved torture and killing of the remaining leftists, killing thousands and causing 30,000 supporters of the former government to flee the country. Pinochet subsequently ruled Chile as a dictator for a decade and a half.

Coding Decisions: Coding of this conflict has been hampered by the highly politicized nature of the conflict and the corresponding differing portrayals of the fighting from the competing ideological perspectives: those on the right tend to portray the overthrow of Allende as merely a coup, with very little fighting and few deaths because of the lack of support for Allende, whereas those on the left highlight the activities of those who supported Allende in opposing the military takeover. These differing perspectives produce fatality figures that vary widely, ranging from 1,000 to 14,800 Chileans killed. It is unclear whether reports that discuss only civilian deaths are referring to noncombatants or whether that category includes the members of the armed paramilitary groups, specifically MIR, who were combatants. Official figures released in 1998 concluded that 2,095 Chileans were killed during the overthrow, with another 1,102 who disappeared.[212] Plausible figures for just the brief period of the rebellion would seem to be 200 rebel deaths and 3,000 deaths among those fighting for the Chilean government.

Sources: Alexander (1978); Angell (1984); Boorstein (1977); Ciment (2007g); Clodfelter (2002); Ensalaco (2000); Harmer (2011); Kornbluh (2014); Roxborough, O'Brien, and Roddick (1977); Scheina (2003b); Williamson (2009).

INTRA-STATE WAR #800

Argentine Leftists War of 1975 to 1976 (aka *Guerra Sucia* or the Dirty War)

Participants: Argentina versus *Montoneros* and *Ejército Revolucionario del Pueblo* (ERP).
Dates: February 22, 1975, to December 16, 1976.
Battle-related Deaths: *Montoneros*, ERP: 4,000; Argentina: 470.[213]
Initiator: *Montoneros*, ERP.
Outcome: Argentina wins.
War Type: Civil for central control.
Total System Member Military Personnel: Armed Forces of Argentina: 160,000 (initial, peak); 150,000 (final).[214]
Theater Armed Forces: Armed Forces of Argentina plus National Police: 179,000 (peak).[215] *Montoneros*: estimated 4,000 (1976). ERP: 600 to 2,000 (initial);[216] 6,000 (peak).[217]

Antecedents: In 1955, Argentina's populist president Juan Domingo Perón, who had ruled since 1946, was overthrown (Intra-state War #740). The election of right-wing president Héctor Cámpora in March 1973 paved the way for the return of Juan Perón in June 1973, and in elections in September, Juan Perón was elected president and his wife Isabel Martínez de Perón as vice president. As Perón solidified his position, he began to move to the right, favoring the military and implementing fascist-style statist policies (dividing his left-wing and right-wing supporters). Guerrilla warfare had continued throughout this period, conducted by two left-wing groups, the *Montoneros* and the Marxist ERP, the Revolutionary Army of the People. Perón soon repudiated the backing of the *Montoneros*, and with the support of the army and the trade unionists, he began to confront the leftists. Meanwhile, a right-wing paramilitary group called the Argentine Anti-Communist Alliance (AAA, or Triple A), led by a former police officer José López Rega, who had close ties to Martínez de Perón, also began attacks against the leftist groups.

On July 1, 1974, Juan Perón died, and the presidency passed to Martínez de Perón, who became a figurehead as the military gained increasing power and as she came under the influence of Rega. The leftists stepped up their activities, including the kidnapping of wealthy businessmen and attacking foreign businesses in addition to political and military figures. In November 1974, a state of emergency was declared, which gave the military the latitude to more actively pursue the leftists. There were two major prongs of the government's efforts: the military directly confronted the leftist armies (which is the war discussed here); and the government launched a broad antisubversive campaign that led to the arrests, disappearances, torture, and deaths of thousands of civilians (noncombatants) in which it was aided by the AAA. The government's shift from largely "legal" counterguerrilla tactics to the much more offensive and "illegal" terrorist activities constituted the basis of the Dirty War. It is difficult to disentangle the war activities from the terrorist activities, though we have attempted to do so here.

Narrative: Leftist attacks against government armed forces accelerated in February 1975, which marks the start of the war as combatant deaths reached war level that year. On February 22, 1975, *Montoneros* killed a number of police officers and within days had killed a US consular agent and at least one soldier. On March 5, a bomb placed at army headquarters killed one and injured twenty-eight. The two primary leftist groups, the *Montoneros* and ERP, pursued differing ideological and revolutionary strategies: the *Montoneros* (led by Mario Firmenich) conducted most of their activities in the urban areas of Buenos Aires, while ERP (commanded by Mario Roberto Santucho) focused upon the more disadvantaged countryside areas, especially in the northwest province of Tucumán. There the ERP attempted to create a semiautonomous liberated zone, and they conducted several attacks against the Fifty Infantry Brigade. Martínez de Perón authorized Operation Independence, which encouraged the military to take action against the rebels in Tucumán. The head of the army, Gen. Jorge Rafael Videla, initially deployed about 1,500 troops and 1,500 police officers to Tucumán in an offensive that would last over a year and lead to the creation of notorious concentration camps. During February 1976, both the *Montoneros* and the ERP sent additional troops to assist the guerrillas fighting in Tucumán, where it was estimated that 2,000 guerrillas were engaged in significant combat against 10,000 government soldiers. However, overall the military was unhappy with Martínez de Perón's direction of the conflict, and she was overthrown on March 24, 1976, by a military junta that was led by General Videla, who was installed as president two days later.

The new regime responded by doubling government efforts against the guerrillas, making 1976 the deadliest year in the conflict (in terms of both military engagements and civilian terror). The *Montoneros* (who had five columns operating in Buenos Aires alone) reportedly conducted eighty-seven military operations during the twenty-one months of the war. The government's enhanced campaign against subversives increasingly impacted the leftists' military endeavors as rebel sympathizers were arrested, taken to one of the 340 secret detention centers, and tortured, causing many to reveal significant information about rebel members and planned activities. The ERP was virtually destroyed by the government offensives, culminating on July 19, 1976, when ERP leader Mario Roberto Santucho was killed. The government then shifted its focus onto the *Montoneros,* and its enhanced offensive depleted them as well. At a meeting in October 1976, the *Montoneros* leadership acknowledged that their strategy of confronting the government militarily had not been successful. Their last major attack was against the ministry of defense on December 16, 1976. Many of the *Montoneros* leaders, including Firmenich, fled the country after Christmas.

Termination and Outcome: The *Montoneros* were defeated militarily in 1976, though some *Montonero* guerrilla activity did continue throughout the rule of the military junta, which ended in 1983. The military's repressive tactics not only led to the defeat of the rebels but also the deaths and disappearances of thousands of civilians.

Coding Decisions: The primary difficulty in coding this conflict as a war arises from the comingling of the military conflict between and among armed combatants with the killings, massacres, and disappearances of noncombatant leftist sympathizers. Much of the information about this period also has been distorted by the very political nature of this conflict. The total number of leftist rebels is a matter of conjecture, with estimates ranging from 2,000 to 40,000 armed fighters.

The number of battle-deaths in the war is also a matter of great disagreement. Attempts to count the deaths and disappearances during the war have ranged from 6,000 to 30,000 deaths and disappearances of left-wing militants, activists, and alleged sympathizers. The vast majority of these deaths were part of the terrorist Dirty War waged by the government and allied paramilitary groups against leftist sympathizers in the civilian population. The leftists claimed to have suffered 10,000 deaths in combat, with both the *Montoneros* and ERP claiming to have lost 5,000 comrades killed in the fighting.[218] These figures seem high, given the numbers reported killed in some of the major rebel actions. However, one could speculate that the rebel claims of 10,000 killed in fighting also could include sympathizers as well as combatants if one interprets the definition of *fighting* broadly. In that case, if the reported distribution of rebel members into 40 percent actual combatants and 60 percent supporters is accurate, that could calculate 4,000 rebel battle deaths, which we are reporting as our best guess.

The statistics for the governmental battle-deaths vary similarly. The guerrillas claimed to have caused the deaths of 6,000 military personnel, which seems high. Norden indicates a total of 472 deaths caused by guerrillas in 1975 and 1976, a rounded version of which is adopted here.

Sources: "Argentina Country at War" (1977); Arreche (2008); Clodfelter (2002); Goodsell (1976); Lewis (2002); Norden (1996); Phillips and Axelrod (2005); Scheina (2003b); Walsh (1977); Williamson (2009); Wright (2007).

INTRA-STATE WAR #827

Shining Path War of 1982 to 1992

Participants: Peru versus *Sendero Luminoso* (Shining Path).

Dates: November 28, 1982, to September 12, 1992.

Battle-related Deaths: Shining Path: 10,466; Peru: 2, 242.[219]

Initiator: Shining Path.
Outcome: Peru wins.
War Type: Civil for central control.
Total System Member Military Personnel: Armed Forces of Peru: 164,000 (prewar, initial); 167,000 (peak); 112,000 (final).[220]
Theater Armed Forces: Armed Forces of Peru (including National Police Forces): 160,500 (prewar); 160,500 (initial); 196,000 (peak); 196,000 (final).[221] *Sendero Luminoso* (Rebel Army): 500 (prewar); 1,500 (initial—1984 estimate); 8,000 (peak); 5,000 (final).[222]

Antecedents: The Aprista Revolt of 1932 (Intra-state War #713) had led to the defeat of the reformist *Alianza Popular Revolucionaria Americana* (American Popular Revolutionary Alliance [APRA]), founded by Victor Haya de la Torre. APRA was legalized in 1956, and in 1962, Haya de la Torre was elected president, though the military seized power before he could take office. In 1979 a new constitution required the transfer of power from the military government to civilian rule. In the May 1980 elections, former president Fernando Belaúnde Terry won, taking office on July 28, 1980. Belaúnde Terry faced growing opposition from the radical left. Communist insurgents had existed in Peru in the 1960s but repeatedly split into factions over the issue of armed struggle. In 1970, a university professor and Maoist, Ambimeal Guzmán, organized a new communist faction, the *Sendero Luminoso*, or Shining Path. The movement was initially concentrated in the small town of Ayacucho (southeast of Lima). By the end of the 1970s, Guzmán had gone underground, and Shining Path was steadily growing by mobilizing and recruiting the peasants and by assimilating defectors from other communist factions. On May 17, 1980, the Shining Path began a guerrilla insurgency, with the strategy of destroying the state through a policy of *batir el campo* (churning up the countryside). By early 1981, the rebels had conducted 1,342 low-fatality actions, and they moved to the second phase of their plan: to establish "liberated zones" in the Ayacucho region. In March 1982, Shining Path launched an attack against the town of Ayacucho and soon controlled virtually the whole department.

Narrative: The first substantial combat between Shining Path and the armed forces of the central government (in the form of the civil guard—regular military units were still confined to barracks) occurred when a column of twenty *Senderistas* engaged a government column near Cochabamba (north of the capital) on November 28, 1982: this event precipitated war-level combat. The next month, President Belaúnde declared martial law in the departments of Ayachuco and Apurímac and sent the military to retake the territory controlled by the *Senderistas*, with soldiers and marines entering Ayachuco on December 23.

In January 1983, the rebels began the third phase of their struggle, the plan to conquer military bases in highland regions across the country. The numbers of deaths that year were 63 security forces and 1,226 rebels. The new phase would eventually include 28,621 rebel actions against the government. Government troops retaliated indiscriminately, and the government created even more hostility in 1983, when it forcibly relocated some village residents to more defensible areas. Over the next six years, the rebels were able to steadily expand their operations as civil guard units pulled out of small villages and remained in larger towns for safety. Needing money to fund the rebellion, the Shining Path got involved in drug trafficking sometime in 1984 and 1985. The rebels intensified their attacks in mid-1985, as the presidential elections approached. Alan Gabriel Ludwig García Pérez became the first Aprista Party member to assume the presidency, taking office on July 18, 1985. As the government unsuccessfully sought a solution to the rebellion, it reportedly engaged in massacres of peasants and human rights violations, some of which were conducted by an Aprista paramilitary organization linked to the president.

The next year (1986), the *Senderistas* announced the fourth phase of their plan, the Plan to Develop Bases. The rebels carried out 63,052 armed actions over the next twenty-nine months. Despite heavy losses, the rebels were able to find enough recruits to replenish their ranks. The fifth, final, and most violent phase of the rebel campaign—the Great Plan to Develop Bases and to Serve the Conquest of Power—began in August 1989. By then, Shining Path operated around major cities, including launching attacks within Lima itself. Both the failures of the García regime and the successes of the Shining Path contributed to the election of an authoritarian government led by Alberto Fujimori, who was elected president in June 1990 on a platform that included promises to defeat the Shining Path. His military campaign faltered at first, but in his 1992 *autogolpe* (coup), Fujimori suspended the constitution, dissolved the legislature, and gave himself the power to deal with the insurgency.

He created a special antiterrorist organization separate from the army and established secret tribunals to try suspected terrorists. Top leaders of the Shining Path, including Guzmán, were captured in Lima by a police intelligence unit on September 12, 1992, and nearly 1,000 more were captured within weeks.

Termination and Outcome: The government won the war. Neither Guzmán nor his top aides were executed; they and thousands of others were imprisoned. Over the next year, Fujimori offered a limited amnesty to cooperative *Serendistas*, and many of the insurgents surrendered. Eventually the die-hard Maoists formed a splinter group, the *Sendero Rojo*, and continued actions against the government, despite the arrest of their leader in 1999.

Coding Decisions: Some accounts of this war include the Túpac Amaru Revolutionary Movement of Peru (MRTA) as a war participant. MRTA is excluded from this case because we consider the conflict between it and the government to be distinct from this war. Instead of working together against the government, *Sendero Luminoso* and MRTA occasionally battled each other during the conflict.

The coding of battle-related deaths for this war is complicated by the accompanying terror campaign launched by the government against civilians. The postwar truth and reconciliation commission estimated that 69,280 people died in the conflict from 1980 to 2000; about 80 percent were noncombatants. We have relied on figures of the combatants killed from 1983 to 1992 compiled by the Center for Studies and Development Promotion (DESCO). This records 12,708 total combatant deaths, with 2,242 experienced by the government and 10,466 for the Shining Path.

Sources: Brogan (1998); Burt (2007); Clodfelter (2008); DeRouen and Heo (2007); Laffin (1990); *The Military Balance* (1986–1993); Palmer (1995); Project Ploughshares (2000); Rochlin (2003); Scheina (2003b); Taylor (2006); Weinstein (2007); Williamson (2009).

INTRA-STATE WAR #849

Eighth Colombian War of 1988 to Present (aka Drug War)

Participants: Colombia and Right-Wing Militias versus Leftist Rebels and Drug Cartels.
Dates: August 23, 1988, to present.
Battle-related Deaths (as of December 31, 2011): Leftist Rebels and Drug Cartels: 20,778; Colombia: 10,181; Right-Wing Paramilitary Militias: 3,068.[223] (See Coding Decisions.)
Initiator: Leftist Rebels and Drug Cartels.
Outcome: War ongoing.
War Type: Civil for local issues.
Total System Member Military Personnel: 76,000 (prewar); 91,000 (initial); 209,000 (peak).[224]
Theater Armed Forces: Armed Forces of Colombia (including the National Police): 121,200 (prewar); 216,000 (initial); 321,000 (peak, present).[225] *Autodefensas Campesinas de Cordoba y Urabá* (AUC, Pro-government Militia), participating from April 18, 1997, to December 2006: 12,500 (peak, final).[226] Non-AUC Paramilitaries aka BACRIM or Neo-Paramilitaries (usually pro-government militia aggregate): 2,000 (initial, peak, present).[227] *Fuerzas Armadas Revolucionarias Colombianas* (FARC, Rebel Army): 6,000 (initial); 18,000 (peak); 9,000 (present).[228] *Ejercito de Liberacion Nacional* (ELN, Rebel Army): 2,500 (initial); 5,000 (peak); 2,500 (present).[229] *Ejército Popular de Liberacíon* (EPL, Rebel Army), participating until March 1991: 500 (initial); 3,000 (peak); 3,000 (final).[230] *Medellin Cartel* (Rebel Organization), participating until December 2, 1993. Hundreds of members were killed or imprisoned.[231]

Antecedents: During the late stages of *La Violencia* (Intra-state War #739), liberals and conservatives successfully brought violence against each other to relatively low levels. However, fighting against communist groups continued after 1962, albeit at sub-war levels. Over time, the government dismantled most of the autonomous zones controlled by communist groups, but the military efforts and the ban on communist political activity ensured the continuation of conflict. The instability in Colombia encouraged the growth of non-state actors who were capable of conducting warfare. By the 1980s, four major communist groups faced the government. The largest was FARC. Smaller groups included, from largest to smallest, the ELN, M-19, and the EPL.

While the government waged a desultory campaign against the leftist groups, drug cartels also began to rival the state's authority. The illegal drug export business had been growing since the 1960s, and by 1980 the value of drug exports was equal to the value of all the legal exports combined. The United States, which was conducting its own war on drugs, entered into an agreement with Colombia in 1979 to encourage the Colombian government to crack down on the drug czars. The United States provided Colombia with aid, advisors, and military equipment in exchange for an extradition treaty so that drug czars could be tried in the United States. The leftists and the drug cartels had a common short-term goal of weakening the Colombian government, and the parameters of the conflict changed in May 1982, as FARC and the drug lords developed a harmonious relationship in which FARC provided protection, and drug trafficking provided funds with which FARC was able to increase the size of its army and the deadliness of its attacks (some authors mark the start of this war as of this date).

In 1982, the liberal government of Julio César Turbay Ayala was replaced by the election of conservative president Belisario Betancur Cuartas. During Betancur's 1982-to-1986 term, the rate of combat deaths was 281 per year. Betancur had expressed a willingness to come to terms with the leftists, which led to the 1984 *La Uribe* Agreement, which produced a cease-fire that lasted from 1984 to 1987. Also in 1982, drug lord Pablo Escobar Gaviria of the Medellin cartel, who was popular with Colombia's poor, was elected as an alternate member of the chamber of representatives as part of the Colombian Liberal Party. However, several important developments during the Betancur administration contributed to the later escalation of violence. First, right-wing paramilitary groups formed death squads targeting suspected leftist rebels and their sympathizers. This meant that when the government opened a political space in 1986 for the newly formed leftist opposition political party, Unión Patriótica (UP), the death squads simply assassinated at least 500 candidates (and as many as 2,000 to 4,000 party members), blocking paths to peaceful reform. In 1987, the president of the UP, Jaime Pardo, was assassinated. Second, attempts to maintain a cease-fire constantly foundered as FARC and the Colombian military clashed. The new government of liberal president Virgilio Barco Vargas (1986–1990) continued trying to negotiate with the leftists but launched a major antidrug campaign. In response, at the end of 1987 Escobar declared war on the government.

Narrative: Up to 18,000 people were killed in political violence or massacres in 1988, which became known as the "year of the massacres." Escobar ordered a series of assassinations of government officials, and the government responded with curtailed civil liberties, the arrests of up to 10,000 individuals by the military and police, and seizures of drug cartels' property. The war began in August 1988, as the violence shifted from attacks against civilians to attacks against military personnel. Escobar offered bonuses for the killing if military officers, and his efforts drew in FARC and the other rebel movements. Deaths of both military personnel and rebels increased at that point to above war level (439 government and 540 rebels for 1988).

The pattern of violence continued in 1989. On August 19, 1989, the Medellín cartel had liberal presidential candidate Luis Carlos Galán assassinated for his strong antidrug position. Escobar and the other drug czars continued the terror, blowing up a civilian plane and several buildings and carrying out assassinations and kidnappings. FARC also escalated its use of violence against the government, while M-19 chose to disarm and accept amnesty in December 1989. Still, efforts to begin peace talks in 1990 foundered on the government's insistence on a unilateral cease-fire by the rebels. On December 9, 1990, the government bombed FARC headquarters in Casa Verde and then assaulted the rebel compound (defended by 700 rebels) with a 2,300-man force. At least 60 rebels and 19 soldiers were killed. By the end of 1990, the government had reportedly suffered 2,000 deaths among the security forces.

FARC and ELN responded by mounting a combined offensive throughout much of 1991. Almost 600 people were killed in rebel attacks in the first three months. During the year, there were sixty-seven ambushes perpetrated by the guerrilla factions: ELN attacked eight military bases, and FARC attacked fifteen. However, in March, most of the EPL made peace with the government. On June 19, Pablo Escobar surrendered once the government took extradition off the table. While he later escaped in July 1992 and was finally cornered and gunned down seventeen months later, his surrender marked the temporary decline of large-scale violence against the state by the Medellin cartel. All told, there were 210 urban attacks against police in 1991. Over time, the drug cartels began to fracture into smaller organizations that focused on more traditional criminal means of protecting their operations. Meanwhile, ideological differences (ELN refused to ally itself with the drug lords) soon ended the period of cooperation between ELN and FARC, though the two groups jointly participated in peace talks from August 1991 to May 1992. When peace talks broke down, the government declared renewed war on the rebels on November 9, 1992.

Meanwhile, Pablo Escobar had escaped from prison and resumed his violence against the security forces. The government began an intense manhunt, which steadily reduced the power of the Medellin cartel. The Cali cartel cooperated with various paramilitary death squads and the US Drug Enforcement Agency in efforts to dismantle the Medellin cartel. Escobar was cornered and killed on December 2, 1993, ending the Medellin cartel's threat to the state.

Fighting between the government and FARC and ELN continued. From 1993 to 1996, the government suffered 1,300 to 1,650 battle-deaths while inflicting 2,500 to 3,600 on the rebels. Despite these heavy losses, the rebels grew in strength. From 1994 to 1996, the ELN increased from about 2,800 guerrillas to a strength of 4,000 to 5,000. FARC had at least 7,000 guerrillas by 1995. Colombia lost significant military assistance from the United States after a scandal broke in 1995 that revealed that Colombian president Ernesto Samper took $6 million in campaign contributions from a drug cartel.

From 1994 to 1998, coca production increased by more than 600 percent, providing ample funding for the further expansion of FARC. In 1996, FARC began larger sustained attacks on government forces, and on August 30, it mounted twenty-two simultaneous attacks on government forces, capturing several outposts. The rebels won minor victories at Puerres in Nariño, Las Delicas, and La Carpa in 1996, Meta and Arauca in 1997, and El Billar in 1998. The rebels increasingly used light mortars, increasing their firepower and ability to sustain combat. The paramilitaries became a significant participant in the war with the formation of the *Autodefensas Campesinas de Cordoba y Urabá* (AUC) on April 18, 1997. The AUC involved 4,000 to 5,000 paramilitary fighters in an effort to defeat the leftist rebels. The organization quickly became infamous for its massacres of civilians, but it also engaged in combat with FARC and ELN forces, especially in the Northeast.

The rebels mounted another major offensive in August 1998. The deadliest battle, at Miraflores, resulted in 68 government battle-deaths and another 87 wounded. As the guerrillas became more powerful and successful, the new president, Andrés Pastrana, agreed to meet with FARC. A cease-fire was declared on November 7, and in February 1999, a temporary demilitarized zone (*Zona de Despeje*) was formed, giving FARC control of approximately one-third of the nation's territory. The cease-fire did not halt the fighting. FARC mounted a major military offensive in July, mobilizing between 12,000 and 15,000 guerrilla fighters. The offensive was a military failure, with the government claiming to have killed more than 200 rebels. From December 28 to December 29, FARC overran the headquarters of the AUC. The AUC took heavy losses, and the government sent troops to the area. The AUC responded over the next two weeks by massacring more than 100 civilian leftist sympathizers. The ELN also stepped up its violence in an attempt to win a demilitarized zone of its own. Fighting between the ELN and the armed forces was particularly intense at the end of the year; the government reported killing 30 ELN fighters from December 27 to December 29. In April 2000, the government also awarded the ELN its own safe haven in the North.

In mid-2000, the government, led by the conservative president Andrés Pastrana, adopted a new strategy in conjunction with the United States: called Plan Colombia, it called for negotiations to end the war; social, economic, and judicial reforms; increased military power; and the creation of a special counter narcotics brigade. Fighting continued during negotiations as neither side was willing to accept a unilateral ceasefire. FARC had used this period and the establishment of a "demilitarized" safe zone to increase its fighting capacity, up to about 17,000 guerrillas. Trainers from the Irish Republican Army were brought in to instruct FARC members on urban terrorist operations. Locally, Ecuador permitted FARC to use its territory for bases, as did Venezuela after the 1999 elections elevated a leftist to the presidency. By 2001, the government of Venezuela was actively arming FARC.

On February 20, 2002, the Colombian government ordered the armed forces to take back the demilitarized zones. FARC quickly withdrew, and the war settled into a series of tiny engagements. Later in 2002, Colombia's new president, Alvaro Uribe, renounced safe havens for guerrillas and increased the offensive against the guerrillas. As part of its Global War on Terror, the United States increased support to Colombia. The fighting took its toll on the ELN, which decreased from its peak strength of 4,000 to 5,000 to about 3,000 active fighters. The government also expanded its security zone around Bogotá, destroying some FARC units.

By 2004, FARC was increasingly assuming the role of a drug cartel, taking over some of the market from the collapsing Norte del Valle cartel: it concentrated on protecting its drug-producing areas while ceding other territory to the Colombian military. At the same time, the state increasingly came into conflict with the AUC, which demanded its own separate talks. In 1999, the government recorded killing only 26 members of paramilitary groups; by 2004, it was killing nearly 500 a year. The AUC was heavily involved in the drug trade, and some units allied with their former enemy, FARC.

The AUC's leadership had opened exploratory talks with the government in December 2002. In July 2003, the AUC agreed to demobilize by December 2005. Demobilization of the AUC reached a peak in 2006, which brought total collective demobilizations to 31,671. The exit of the AUC removed the largest paramilitary group from the war. Many former left-wing guerrillas also demobilized, but FARC and the ELN remain capable of inflicting civil war-scale casualties on the armed forces of the government. Since the mid-2000s, the government has scored some major successes against FARC, including a 2008 raid on a FARC headquarters in Ecuador and the 2010 killing of its senior military commander. Desertions have reduced the strength of FARC to less than 10,000. Both FARC and the ELN have expressed interest in peace talks, which began on October 17, 2012. In 2014, peace talks in Havana reached an agreement to end the cultivation and distribution of illegal drugs. FARC declared a unilateral cease-fire from May 20 to May 28.

Termination and Outcome: The war is ongoing.

Coding Decisions: In terms of battle-deaths and the dates of the war, we have relied on the data-collection efforts of *Centro do Recursos para el Análisis de Conflictos* (CERAC) in shaping our coding here. CERAC provides detailed fatality data, which attempts to separate out civilian from combatant fatalities and to allocate the combatant fatalities among the government, rebels, and paramilitary groups. In a previous version of our data, we had coded this war as starting on August 19, 1989, based on information that indicated a spike in battle-deaths at that time. However, the CERAC data has persuaded us that the spike occurred a year earlier, thus in this version of this data, we have changed the start date of this war to August 23, 1988. We are also using the CERAC data for our battle-death statistics: though they report slightly fewer deaths than those we found in other sources, they seem to be quite comprehensive, to have been gathered with great care, and to have fewer data anomalies.

Sources: Arnold (1995); Bagley (2005); CERAC (2008); Clodfelter (2002, 2008); "Colombia ELN Rebels Edge Toward Peace Process" (2012); "Colombia Tries Again to End Drug-Fed War" (2012); DeRouen and Heo (2007); Guáqueta (2003); Kaiser (2003); Keesing's (2014); Kline (1999); Manwaring (2002); McDermott (1999); Méndez (1992); *The Military Balance* (1987, 1990, 2002, 2003); Millett (2002); Ministerio de Defense Nacional (2012); Porch and Rasmussen (2008); Project Ploughshares (2008); Reno (2003); Restrepo, Spagat, and Vargas (2003, 2004); Ribetti (2002); Richani (2007); Richani (2002, 2005); Rochlin (2003); Ruiz (2001); Russell (2011); Safford and Palacios (2002); Scheina (2003b); Simons (2004); Skorupsky (2012); United States Institute of Peace (2004).

Notes

1. Correlates of War Project, 2009.
2. Levine, 1992.
3. Ibid.
4. Correlates of War Project, 2009.
5. Harris, 2010.
6. Correlates of War Project, 2009.
7. Calogeras, João Pandiá, 1939; Comissão Executiva Central do Sesquicentenário sa Independência do Brasil, 1972; Leitman, 1973; Scheina, 2003a.
8. Bethell and de Carvalho, 1989, 73; Clodfelter, 2002, 352.
9. Correlates of War Project, 2010.
10. Bethell and de Carvalho, 1989, 73.
11. Kraay, 1992.
12. Ibid., 520.
13. Bethell and de Carvalho, 1989, 73.
14. Kraay, 1992, 521.
15. Treece, 2000.

16. Correlates of War Project, 2009.
17. Bethell and de Carvalho, 1989, 75.
18. Ibid., 74.
19. Bento, 2002; Fausto, 1999.
20. Ibid.; Comissão Executiva Central do Sesquicentenário sa Independência do Brasil, 1972.
21. Assunção, 1999, 4.
22. Correlates of War Project, 2009.
23. Henao, 1938; Safford and Palacios, 2002.
24. Earle, 2000.
25. Ibid.
26. Correlates of War Project, 2009.
27. Scheina, 2003a, 119.
28. Kirkpatrick, 1931, 149.
29. Marley, 1998, 492.
30. Sarkees and Wayman, 2010, 216–217.
31. Páez, 1862; Irwin, 2008; Paul, 1974.
32. Paul, 1974; Clodfelter, 2001; Lynch, 1992.
33. Correlates of War Project, 2009.
34. Scheina, 2003a.
35. Ibid.
36. Scheina, 2003a, b; Hancock, 1893; Collier, 2003; Mackenna, 1862.
37. Basadre, 1970; Soto, 1985.
38. Correlates of War Project, 2009.
39. Basadre, 1970.
40. Thurner, 1997.
41. Correlates of War Project, 2009.
42. Picon, 1972; Ortiz, 2004; Scheina, 2003a; Sanders, 2004.
43. Ibid.
44. Paul, 1974.
45. Ibid.
46. Ibid.
47. Correlates of War Project, 2009.
48. Ripley and Dana, 1861; Markham, 1868; Basadre, 1970.
49. Marett, 1969.
50. Basadre, 1970; Ripley and Dana, 1861.
51. Correlates of War Project, 2009.
52. Estado Mayor General del Ejercito, 1980; Collier, 2003.
53. Collier, 2003; Scheina, 2003a; Hancock, 1893.
54. Legion de los Andes, 2011.
55. Correlates of War Project, 2009.
56. Gilmore, 1964; Wise, 1970; Scheina, 2003a.
57. Paul, 1974; Scheina, 2003a, b.
58. Small and Singer, 1982, 224; Clodfelter, 2002, 355; Rudolph and Rudolph, 1971.
59. Correlates of War Project, 2009.
60. Jurado, 2003; Payne, 1968.
61. Small and Singer, 1982, 224.
62. Correlates of War Project, 2009.
63. Ibid.; Jeffrey, 1952; Marley, 1998.
64. Jeffrey, 1952; Best, 1960.
65. Marley, 1998.
66. Correlates of War Project, 2009; Scheina, 2003a.
67. Scheina, 2003a.
68. Ibid.
69. Correlates of War Project, 2009.
70. Katra, 1996; Marley, 1998.
71. Scheina, 2003a, b; Aranzaes, 1918.
72. Correlates of War Project, 2009.
73. Arguedas, 1929; Aranzaes, 1918.
74. de Mesa, Gisbert, and Gisbert, 2001; Scheina, 2003a; Arguedas, 1929.
75. Correlates of War Project, 2009.
76. Clodfelter, 2001; Best, 1960; Rock, 1989.
77. Correlates of War Project, 2009; Papers Relating to the Foreign Relations of the United States, 1865.
78. Papers Relating to the Foreign Relations of the United States, 1865.
79. Small and Singer, 1982, 224.
80. Papers Relating to the Foreign Relations of the United States, 1865.
81. Correlates of War Project, 2009; *New York Times* (September 24, 1869).
82. Scheina, 2003a, b; "Historia de Venezuela Para Nostros" (July 9, 2008).
83. Spence, 1878.
84. Small and Singer, 1982, 224.
85. Best, 1960; Poggi, 2004; Marley, 1998.
86. Correlates of War Project, 2009.
87. Best, 1960; Poggi, 2004; Marley, 1998.
88. Correlates of War Project, 2009; Aranzaes, 1918.
89. Arguedas, 1929.
90. Aranzaes, 1918; de Mesa, Gisbert, and Gisbert, 2001.
91. Correlates of War Project, 2009.
92. Duarte, 1988; Marley, 1998; Best, 1960.
93. Ibid.
94. Best, 1960; Clodfelter, 2002; Marley, 1998; Sanchez, 1906.
95. Correlates of War Project, 2009.
96. Scheina, 2003a, 276.
97. Correlates of War Project, 2009.
98. Gonzales, 1987.
99. Correlates of War Project, 2009.
100. Scheina, 2003a, 369.
101. Hasbrouck, 1935, 203.
102. Wise, 1950; Güell y Mercader, 1883.
103. Correlates of War Project, 2009.
104. Ibid.; Güell y Mercader, 1883.
105. Güell y Mercader, 1883.
106. Wise, 1950; Güell y Mercader, 1883.
107. Best, 1960.
108. Correlates of War Project, 2009.
109. Akers, 1912; Best, 1960.
110. Ibid.

111. Best, 1960.
112. Clodfelter, 2002, 364; Kirkpatrick, 1931, 187.
113. Henao and Arrubla, 1984; Scheina, 2003a; Olarte, 1993.
114. Scheina, 2003a, b; Olarte, 1993; Henderson, 1985
115. Correlates of War Project, 2009.
116. Henao and Arrubla, 1984; Scheina, 2003a; Olarte, 1993.
117. Ibid.
118. Scheina, 2003a, 276–277; Olarte, 1993; Mejia, 1976.
119. Correlates of War Project, 2009.
120. Klaiber, 1977.
121. Ibid.; Klarén, 2000; Thurner, 1997, 427.
122. Correlates of War Project, 2009.
123. Clodfelter, 2002, 365.
124. Correlates of War Project, 2009.
125. Ibid.; Estado Mayor General del Ejercito, 1980; Hancock, 1893.
126. Hancock, 1893; Estado Mayor General del Ejercito, 1980; Nunn, 1976.
127. Small and Singer, 1982, 225.
128. Clodfelter, 2002, 365; Collier and Sater, 1996.
129. Richardson, 1960, 63; Zeitlin, 1984; Williams, Bartlett, and Miller, 1955; Munro, 1960.
130. Correlates of War Project, 2009.
131. Márquez, 1973; McBeth, 2001, 10.
132. Márquez, 1973.
133. Correlates of War Project, 2009.
134. Love, 1971; Bello, 1966.
135. Cortés, 1974; Love, 1971.
136. Correlates of War Project, 2009; Scheina, 2003a; Calogeras, 1939.
137. Topik, 2000, 126.
138. Bello, 1966.
139. Clodfelter, 2002, 365; Williams, 1945.
140. Correlates of War Project, 2009; Crichfield, 1908.
141. Akers, 1912; Crichfield, 1908.
142. Pike, 1967.
143. Correlates of War Project, 2009; Peña, 1997.
144. Scheina, 2003a; Peña, 1997.
145. Correlates of War Project, 2009; Clodfelter, 2001; Spindler, 1987; Garcia, 1979.
146. Spindler, 1987.
147. Ibid.
148. Correlates of War Project, 2009.
149. Ibid.
150. Levine, 1988, 1992; McCann, 2004; Schneider, 1991.
151. Marley, 1998, 593.
152. McCann, 2004; Schneider, 1991; Levine, 1992; Marley, 1998.
153. Rosales, 1898.
154. Correlates of War Project, 2009; Rosales, 1898.
155. McBeth, 2001, 13; Rosales, 1898.
156. Rosales, 1898.
157. Ewell, 1984.
158. Correlates of War Project, 2009; Gilmore, 1964; McBeth, 2001; Rourke, 1969.
159. Scheina, 2003a, b; McBeth, 2001.
160. Yarrington, 1997; Contreras, 1944.
161. Scheina, 2003a, 244.
162. Correlates of War Project, 2009; Clodfelter, 2002, 367; Bergquist, 1978.
163. Tomán, 2006; Demarest, 2001; Scheina, 2003a.
164. Tomán, 2006; Demarest, 2001.
165. Ibid.
166. Demarest, 2001, 1; Phillips and Axelrod, 2005, 1148; Small and Singer, 1982, 226; Clodfelter, 2002, 367; Kohn, 1999, 493.
167. Scheina, 2003a, 367.
168. Ewell, 1984; Yarrington, 1997.
169. Correlates of War Project, 2009; Gilmore, 1964.
170. Morón, 1964; Contreras, 1944; McBeth, 2001; Rourke, 1969.
171. McBeth, 2001, 72.
172. Correlates of War Project, 2009.
173. Vanger, 1963.
174. Ibid.; Vives, 1975.
175. Correlates of War Project, 2009; Ferris, 1919; Lewis, 1993; Warren, 1949.
176. Ferris, 1919; Lewis, 1993.
177. Ibid.; "Paraguay Rebels Routed" (May 12, 1912).
178. Warren, 1949; Lewis, 1993; "Savage War Raging Among Paraguayans" (December 26, 1911); "Fighting in Paraguay" (March 25, 1912); "Paraguay Rebels Routed" (May 12, 1912).
179. Correlates of War Project, 2009.
180. Schodt, 1987; Pineo, 1996; Clark, 1998; Mora, 1994.
181. Vicuña, 1984.
182. Correlates of War Project, 2009.
183. Ycaza, 1980; Vicuña, 1984.
184. Laps, 2003.
185. Correlates of War Project, 2009.
186. McCann, 2004; Levine, 1992.
187. Comissão Executiva Central do Sesquicentenário sa Independência do Brasil, 1972.
188. Correlates of War Project, 2009.
189. Klarén, 1973, 135–136.
190. Rudolph, 1992, 40.
191. Small and Singer, 1982, 215.
192. Correlates of War Project, 2009; McCann, 2004; Scheina, 2003b; Barclay, 1971.
193. McCann, 2004; Cortés, 1976; Barclay, 1971; Clodfelter, 2008.
194. Correlates of War Project, 2009.
195. Nickson, 1993; "General Rafael Franco Reported Leading Paraguay Rebels" (March 24, 1947); Warren, 1949; Ashwell, 1998; Clodfelter, 2008; Scheina, 2003b.

196. Correlates of War Project, 2009.
197. Ramsey, 1970.
198. Ibid.
199. Ibid.; Zackrison, 1989; Scheina, 2003a, b.
200. Henderson, 1985.
201. Correlates of War Project, 2009.
202. Brill, 1971.
203. Correlates of War Project, 2009; Ramsey, 1970.
204. Rempe, 2002.
205. Henderson, 1985; Rempe, 2002.
206. Loveman and Davies, 1985a, b, 242.
207. Ibid., 282.
208. Correlates of War Project, 2009.
209. Page, 1983; Clodfelter, 2002.
210. Correlates of War Project, 2009.
211. Alexander, 1978, 335.
212. Clodfelter, 2002, 719; Scheina, 2003b, 326.
213. Norden, 1996, 59.
214. Correlates of War Project, 2009.
215. Phillips and Axelrod, 2005, 118.
216. Marchak and Marchak, 1999.
217. Lewis, 2002, 124.
218. Arreche, 2008, 1.
219. Palmer, 1995.
220. Correlates of War Project, 2009.
221. *The Military Balance*, 1986–1993.
222. Weinstein, 2007; Laffin, 1990; Clodfelter, 2008; Palmer, 1995; Scheina, 2003b.
223. CERAC, 2008; Ribetti, 2002; Richani, 2007; Scheina, 2003b; Ministerio de Defense Nacional, 2012.
224. Correlates of War Project, 2009.
225. *The Military Balance*, 1987, 1990, 2003.
226. United States Institute of Peace, 2004.
227. Rochlin, 2003.
228. Scheina, 2003b; *The Military Balance*, 2002; "Colombia Tries Again to End Drug-fed War" (October 18, 2012).
229. Scheina, 2003b; Safford and Palacios, 2002; Guáqueta, 2003; "Colombia ELN Rebels Edge toward Peace Process" (November 12, 2012); "Colombia Tries Again to End Drug-fed War" (October 18, 2012).
230. Scheina, 2003b; Bagley, 2005.
231. Kline, 1999.

CHAPTER FIVE

Intra-state Wars in Europe

Below is the list of the intra-state wars that took place in Europe. Each war will then be described individually with the pertinent basic data provided.

TABLE 5.1 List of Intra-state Wars in Europe

(Continued)

TABLE 5.1 **List of Intra-state Wars in Europe** (Continued)

Individual Descriptions of Intra-state Wars in Europe

INTRA-STATE WAR #500

First Caucasus War of 1818 to 1822

Participants: Russia versus Chechnya, Dagestan, and Georgia.
Dates: June 10, 1818, to November 1822.
Battle-related Deaths: Chechnya, Dagestan, and Georgia: 6,000; Russia: 5,000. (See Coding Decisions.)
Initiator: Chechnya.
Outcome: Russia wins.
War Type: Civil for local issues.
Total System Member Military Personnel: Armed Forces of Russia: 700,000 (prewar); 600,000 (initial); 1,001,000 (peak, final).[1]
Theater Armed Forces: Russia: 61,800 (prewar);[2] 70,300 (peak—under Ermolov).[3] Chechnya: [ ]. Dagestan, participating from August 1818 to June 18, 1820: 1,000 (initial from Avaristan); 26,000 (peak—6,000—Avar Khan; and 20,000 in Kazi-Koumoukh). Georgia, participating from summer 1819: 20,000 (peak).

Antecedents: The Caucasus region was an area of contestation among Russia, the Ottoman Empire, and Persia. In 1801, Russia's Alexander I ratified an agreement whereby Georgia was incorporated into the Russian empire. In asserting sovereignty over Georgia, Russia also claimed the intervening territories, inhabited by Muslim tribes less willing to give their allegiance to a Christian sovereign. Tsar Alexander I had a desire for reform yet also a fear of disorder, and it was the latter perspective that dominated in Russia's dealing with the Caucasus. In Georgia, Alexander I extended imperial control by removing the remaining members of the Georgian royal family and installing Prince P. D. Tsitsianov as the commander in chief in Georgia. During 1804, the severity of Russian rule in Georgia led to growing opposition by tribes in Dagestan and by independent Muslim khans, against whom Tsitsianov sent several expeditions.

Seeing the region as primitive, the Russians' ultimate goal was Russification of all the Caucasian peoples. In Georgia, this policy centered upon the suppression of the Georgian Orthodox Church, which imperial officials worried might become a rallying point for opponents to Russian rule. Thus on June 30, 1811, Tsar Alexander issued an order revoking the independent status of the Georgian Orthodox Church. The peasants of Kakheti (in western Georgia) revolted and proclaimed young Prince Grigol as king, but the revolt was quickly and harshly suppressed. Most of Georgia now lay under direct imperial rule. In 1813, the Treaty of Gulistan that concluded the Russo-Persian War completed the transfer of Eastern Georgia, Dagestan, and Azerbaijan to Russia. A Russian policy, revived in 1815, that also aroused increasing resentment in the region was the creation of military colonies, which involved billeting soldiers with peasant families and requiring that all able-bodied men in the colonies in essence become soldiers. By 1825 approximately one-third of the army, or 200,000 men, were stationed in military colonies.

The Georgian city of Tiflis (known after 1936 as Tbilisi) became the Russian regional military headquarters, partly because of its central location. Between 1816 and 1827, the man who commanded the Russian forces and who functioned as the de facto governor general in North Caucasus and Transcaucasus was Gen. Lt. Aleksei P. Ermolov (or Yermolov). In 1816 he launched a devastating military campaign to solidify Russian control over the region. His brutality toward the native peoples prompted them to unite in revolt against Russia. Ermolov's plan involved not only the establishment of military colonies but also the construction of a series of new, larger forts that would serve as anchors for military operations in the Caucasus.

His plan was to start with the existing Russian fortress at Vladikavkaz and move eastward into Chechnya then south into Dagestan.

Narrative: In the summer of 1818, Ermolov planned to build a new military outpost that he called Groznaia (meaning terrible or menacing, which later became the city of Grozny in Chechnya). It was here that the conflict between Russia and the Caucasus increased in intensity to war level. The Chechens initially tried to stop the construction of the fort at Groznaia through negotiations. However, Ermolov saw Groznaia as the key link in his chain of forts and continued the fortification plan. When the Russians laid the foundations of the fort on June 10, 1818, the Chechens initiated hostilities. The Chechens began an escalating pattern of violence, starting with harassing tactics (firing on the workers and stripping the materials from the fort at night). In an attempt to ensnare the rebels, Ermolov ordered that a field canon be left outside the walls in plain view, and when the rebels returned to steal the gun, the fort's artillery opened fire, leaving more than 200 dead.[4] Consequently, the Chechens, under the leadership of Beybulat Taymi, appealed to Nur Muhammad Khan of Avaristan (in west-central Dagestan) for assistance in the rebellion at Groznaia. The Chechens and an Avaristan force of 1,000 launched an unsuccessful attack in August 1818 to try to prevent the completion of the fort. In retaliation, Ermolov launched a series of military punitive expeditions into Dagestan from 1818 to 1820, into Chechnya from 1819 to 1822, and into Georgia from 1819 to 1822. During these campaigns, Ermolov adopted a policy of cruelty toward the inhabitants, destroying towns and crops and taking captives who were sold into slavery.

After the defeat at Groznaia, local rulers in Dagestan decided to unite against the Russians. On October 25, 1818, Ermolov began a major campaign against Dagestan with two armies: the smaller force under Colonel Pestel advanced to Bashli, where his forces were surrounded by the allies and attacked, losing 12 officers and 500 men. Meanwhile, Ermolov attacked Paraoul and Djengoutai and later destroyed Bashli. Ermolov then returned to Georgia and successfully appealed to the tsar for an increase in troops. In the summer of 1819, the Russians returned to Dagestan, where the allied leaders gathered their forces to attack the Russians in both the North and the South. This time, Russian Colonel Pestel had been replaced by Major-General Madatoff, who was able to raise a large native cavalry to augment the infantry. This force was able to move quickly, and it attacked and defeated the rebels in a series of engagements, including against the Avar Khan's force of 6,000 in August 1819. Ermolov and Madatoff then joined forces in an attack against Akousha, and on December 19, a large battle was fought at Lavashee, and the Akoushintsi were defeated. In 1820, General Madatoff renewed the campaign in Dagestan. This time, on June 11, the Russians crossed into Kazi-Koumoukh and defeated the rebel army of 20,000 in fierce fighting. By June 19, 1820, the war against Dagestan was complete.

Meanwhile, starting in February 1819, the Russians returned to Chechnya and began a series of punitive expeditions. In line with his policy of repression, Ermolov ordered Russian troops to destroy the town of Dadi-Yourt. Though the ensuing combat on September 27 entailed serious losses on both sides, the Russians eventually slaughtered virtually all the inhabitants, with many of the women attacking the troops or killing themselves rather than be captured. This event was instrumental in shaping the Chechens' attitude toward Russia into the twentieth century. Between February 1819 and July 1821, Russian Commander Nikolai Vasil'evich Grekov carried out four punitive expeditions throughout greater Chechnya. One distinctive feature of his expeditions was that many of them involved tree removal to facilitate Russian troop movements. The construction of Fort Burnia (Burnaya) in June 1821 precipitated an all-Chechen gathering and a guerrilla campaign to fight the encroaching Russians. Beybulat conducted raids in the Kachkalyk range, and one of his rivals, Mullah Abd al-Qadir, led an uprising in the Argun and Shavdon river basins. Ermolov responded by marching through Chechnya, destroying villages and driving the Chechens into the mountains. Aimiakee was destroyed, and Akhmet, khan of Avaria who had taken the lead in the disturbances, was wounded. Mullah Abd al-Qadir was killed in battle on February 23, 1822.

Also in 1819, the Russians expanded their efforts in Georgia. In April, the tsar had agreed to Ermolov's request for the creation of a Georgian army corps with 26,000 men. The Russians also continued their attempts to solidify their control over the

Georgian church. Two of the leading bishops, Metropolitan Dositheus of Kutais and Metropolotan Euthemius of Gelati, had begun an organization to resist any further alterations to Georgian society. These bishops, hearing of the imposition of new Russian regulations on East Georgia, convinced the nobility of western Georgia to consider an armed revolt. The visit of the Russian exarch of Georgia, Theofilakt Rusanov, to western Georgia in the summer of 1819 sparked the uprising (and marks Georgia's entry into the war). Theofilakt had begun measures to replace the Georgian liturgy, and he wanted to see how his decrees were being implemented in the Imeretia area. He encountered stiff opposition from the clerics and local nobility, and he called upon the military to enforce his decrees. Because the Russians already were involved in the campaign to pacify Chechnya and Dagestan, the Georgian rebels hoped that a mere show of force would persuade the Russians to back down. This was initially the case, and on July 11, 1819, Russian Gen. I. A. Veliaminov advised Theofilakt that he was unable to send troops. Thus localized resistance to the exarch continued for more than a year, while the Russians were tied down in the North. However, the successful expedition of Madatov in the summer of 1820 freed up troops to be sent to Georgia. In 1820 the archbishops of Gelati and Kutaisi (Dositheus and Euthemius) both were arrested, and Archbishop Dositheus was stabbed in the process and died soon thereafter. Uprisings followed, with the insurgents desiring the restoration of the monarchy. The area around Ratcha (or Racha) was the scene of bitter fighting, but Racha was finally pacified in 1822.

Termination and Outcome: In November 1822, Grekov conducted another expedition in Chechnya, though its advance was halted by Beybulat, supported by a few Dagestani forces. Beybulat sought a meeting with Ermolov, which marks the end of the war. The meeting between Beybulat and Ermolov did not take place until January 1824, at which time the Russians put forward conditions that were seen as unacceptable by the Chechens.

In assessing the impact of this war, the focus is generally upon Ermolov and his successes in incorporating the Caucasus into Russia. Yet Russia's gains also entailed significant costs. Ermolov's ruthless methods aroused significant opposition among the tribes of Chechnya and Dagestan and thus set the stage for the Murid wars to confront Russia in the near future (Intra-state Wars #511, #523, and #530).

Coding Decisions: This war is coded as ending in 1822 and as a victory for Russia because the regions submitted to Russian control. The battle-death figures provided are rough estimates derived from adding the reported deaths in several engagements and based on the number of troops involved.

Sources: Baddeley (1908); Banac, Ackerman, and Szporluk (1981); Baumann (1993); Chapman (2001); Gammer (2006); Gvosdev (2000); King (2008); Lang (1962); LeDonne (1997, 2004); Pushkarev (1963); Raleigh (1996); Schaefer (2001); Seton-Watson (1967); Thompson (2000); Westwood (1993); Williams (1907); Wright, Goldenberg, Schofield (1996).

INTRA-STATE WAR #502
First Two Sicilies War of 1820 to 1821

Participants: Two Sicilies and Austria versus Liberals.
Dates: July 2, 1820, to March 23, 1821.
Battle-related Deaths: Two Sicilies: [ ]; Austria: [ ]; Liberals: [ ]; Total Combatant Deaths: 2,000.
Initiator: Liberals.
Outcome: Two Sicilies and Austria win.
War Type: Civil for central control.
Total System Member Military Personnel: Two Sicilies: 35,000 (prewar); 42,000 (initial); 49,000 (peak, final).[5] Austria: 242,000 (prewar); 258,000 (initial); 273,000 (peak, final).[6]
Theater Armed Forces: Two Sicilies: 10,000 (peak). Austria: 60,000 (peak); Liberals (rebel aggregate including sectors of the army, the *carbonari*, and Sicilian nationalists): 50,000 (peak).[7]

Antecedents: The kingdom of the Two Sicilies was formed by the unification of the kingdom of Sicily with the kingdom of Naples (which controlled most of southern Italy) in 1442. They were subsequently separated and reunited as control of the territories alternated among Spain, France, and the Holy Roman Empire. In 1799 Napoleon Bonaparte captured Naples (overthrowing the monarch, King Ferdinand III, of Sicily and Ferdinand IV of Naples) and installed his brother Joseph Bonaparte as king of Naples in 1806. Meanwhile Ferdinand fled to Sicily, where he was protected by Great Britain. In 1808 Napoleon recalled Joseph and appointed his brother-in-law Joachim Murat as King Joachim I of the Two Sicilies (though he controlled only Naples). King Joachim participated with Napoleon during the War of the Sixth Coalition (1812–1814). In 1815, as Napoleon escaped Elba, King Joachim realigned himself with the French leader and went to war against Austria, Tuscany, Sicily, and the United Kingdom. On May 23, 1815, the victorious Austrian army entered Naples and reinstalled Ferdinand on the throne. Murat fled to Corsica and was seized and executed when he tried to return to Calabria in October. The Congress of Vienna, which marked the end of the Napoleonic wars, confirmed Ferdinand as the King of Two Sicilies, a unitary state.

During King Ferdinand's stay in Sicily, the British had encouraged him to adopt a relatively liberal constitution. However in 1816, he adopted the new title of Ferdinand I, King of the Two Sicilies, which reduced Sicilian status as a separate kingdom; abolished the constitution; created new provincial militias (organized by the regular military generals); and established a more reactionary and centrally controlled government. Hostility to the government centered in the *carbonari*, which were largely middle- and upper-class secret organizations opposed to what they perceived as the tyranny of the government in Naples. The *carbonari* were rumored to have begun plotting a revolution, and the government tried to ban them in 1816. Yet their membership was widespread, and when the military leaders began to create the new provincial militias, many of the recruits came from the *carbonari*.

Narrative: A plan for a revolution was developed in a *carbonari* lodge in Salerno in 1817 and approved at a meeting of *carbonari* organizations in January 1818. Their goal was to create a democratic, federalist government under a constitutional monarchy, similar to the 1812 Spanish constitution. There was also opposition to the government within the military itself, as officers who had served Murat were displaced by the royalist forces that returned with King Ferdinand from Sicily. Several former Muratist generals were given the task of organizing the new militias, and they deliberately may have placed men connected to the *carbonari* in command positions. Encouraged by the initial success of the revolution in Spain in 1820, Lt. Michele Morelli announced a rebellion for a new constitution on July 2, 1820, in Nola (along the western coast). He immediately was joined by a Luigi Minichini (a priest), *carbonari* lodges, the military commander of Avellino, and a local regiment so that 1,000 rebels marched on Avellino. The government sent three armies, one led by Gen. Michele Carrascosa, to meet the insurgents; however, their advance was halted by the rebels, and as the revolution spread rapidly, the government troops returned to Naples. The announcement that Field Marshal Guglielmo Pepe (along with two regiments of cavalry and one of infantry) had joined the rebels prompted King Ferdinand to promise on July 6 that a constitution based on the Spanish 1812 model would be introduced, and he then withdrew from politics, citing health issues. The same day, a military junta was formed, but the *carbonarists* were persuaded to disperse. To that point the revolution had been virtually bloodless, and the liberal constitutionalist parliament did not support a continuation of the rebellion.

News of the revolt reached Sicily on July 6. In Sicily, there was significant opposition to the government over Sicily's loss of autonomy. Yet, there were differences in opinion among the provinces, with Palermo supporting independence, while other provinces supported constitutional reform. In the countryside, resistance to the government had led to growing ties between the *carbonari* and *maestranze* (guild workers), armed gangs of peasants, or bandits, angered by the increased taxation. Thus, in parts of Sicily, the peasant violence would merge with the armed struggle for local government. Demonstrations were held in Palermo on July 15, and though the governor tried to restore order, he ultimately had to flee the city. A new municipal junta in Palermo declared its independence from Naples, and the junta and Prince Villafranca encouraged armed action against groups opposing independence. The rebels also began to develop plans for military campaigns against the Sicilian provinces that had declared support for the central government, including Messina. In August, the provisional government in Naples sent an army under Gen. Florestano Pepe against Palermo. The rebels in Palermo sent a delegation to Naples to discuss Sicilian autonomy, but they were arrested unceremoniously. When the prince of Villafranca attempted to negotiate a peace with the government with General Pepe, the rebels in the countryside sacked his palace and countryside villas.

The government in Naples decided to suppress Palermo's move by force: Gen. Florestano Pepe was replaced by Gen. Pietro Colletta, and on September 26, a bombardment of Palermo from the sea was begun. As the Neapolitans landed their army of 7,000 troops, they were joined by armed Sicilian volunteers, many from Messina. Palermo finally was occupied on October 5, 1820, after suffering heavy damage during the months of insurrection. Also in October, Austria issued invitations for representatives of the European powers to meet in Troppau to discuss ways to suppress the revolution in Naples. The Troppau Protocol was signed on November 19, 1820, by Russia, Prussia, and Austria, and it authorized the use of force. Austria invited King Ferdinand to a subsequent conference at Layback in January 1821, supposedly to discuss revisions to the constitution. The king's announcement on December 7 of his decision to attend precipitated demonstrations in Naples led by the *carbonari*. At the January meeting, the king reneged on his promises and instead requested Austrian assistance to restore his position. Consequently, on February 4, 1821, the Neapolitan Parliament met and declared war against Austria. The Austrians invaded Naples in March 1821, and the king called on the Neapolitan army to welcome the Austrians. The Neapolitan army of 50,000 citizen–soldiers was paralyzed, but Gen. Guglielmo Pepe led a force of 12,000 to confront the 60,000- to 80,000-man Austrian army. Pepe attacked the Austrians near Rieti (in central Italy) on March 21, 1821. The liberals were crushed, and on March 23, the Austrian army entered Naples.

Termination and Outcome: The outcome of the war was a victory by the government of the king with the assistance of Austria. The Austrian troops remained in Naples to support Ferdinand for another six years. King Ferdinand restored order by purging the army and using terror against his opponents, many of whom fled the country, including Guglielmo Pepe. King Ferdinand died in 1825.

This war reflects the wave of liberalism that was sweeping Europe at that time, and a similar uprising in support of a liberal constitution took place in Sardinia (see Intra-state War #505: the Sardinian Revolt of 1821), which also was suppressed with the aid of Austria.

Coding Decisions: King Ferdinand is considered to represent the government in this war as he was in charge of the executive branch at the start of hostilities.

Sources: Berkeley (1932); Clodfelter (1992); Davis (2006); Emerson (1902); Hearder (2014); Hearder and Waley (1963); Jaques (2007); Kohn (1999); Langer (1952); Phillips and Axelrod (2005); Quatriglio (1997); Riall (1998); Richardson (1960); Shinn (1985); Smith (1968); Solmi (1970).

INTRA-STATE WAR #502.1
Ali Pasha Rebellion of 1820 to 1822

Participants: Ottoman Empire versus Ali Pasha Loyalists.
Dates: July 1820 to January 24, 1822.
Battle-related Deaths: Ottoman Empire versus Ali Pasha Loyalists.
Initiator: Ottoman Empire.
Outcome: Ottoman Empire wins.
War Type: Civil for local issues (provincial leadership).
Total System Member Military Personnel: Armed Forces of the Ottoman Empire: 161,000 (prewar, initial); 200,000 (peak, final).[8]
Theater Armed Forces: Armed Forces of the Ottoman Empire: 20,000 (initial). Ali Pasha Loyalists: 25,000 (prewar); 10,000 (initial, peak); 100 (final).[9] Suliots (Rebel Army), participating from December 12, 1820, to November 1821: 900 (initial); 3,500 (peak).[10]

Antecedents: Ali Pasha was an Albanian Ottoman soldier who seized power in the Ottoman Pashalik of Yannina in 1788. Ali Pasha's capital was Ioannina (now in northwestern Greece), and he took advantage of the weak Ottoman government to expand his empire within an empire gradually. His growing power posed a threat to the Ottoman state, but the government hesitated to act against him both because of his power and because of his advanced age (he was eighty in 1820). However, at the beginning of February 1820, when Ali Pasha attempted to have his chief political opponent Ismael Pasho assassinated in Constantinople, the Ottoman Sultan

Mahmud II determined to act against him. A forty-day ultimatum to surrender was sent to Ali Pasha, and when it expired, he was declared a rebel, and Ismael Pasho was named his successor. Ali immediately began to issue promises of rewards to his Greek and Albanian subjects, hoping to induce them to join his rebellion against the Sublime Porte.

Ali Pasha had twenty-five fortresses and at least 25,000 men under his command; he assigned 15,000 of them to guard the pass of Metzovo, dispatching other armies to other regions. The government massed its own army of 20,000 under Ismael Pasho and the governors of neighboring provinces. Both sides appealed to the Greeks and as early as June, the government had gained the seeming adherence of some Greek *armatoloi* (soldiers).

Narrative: It is not clear when actual combat first occurred, but July seems likely. As the government's expedition advanced, it faced guerrilla resistance from some Ali loyalists. The first battle was an affair of outposts at Krionero, which Ali's forces lost. Rather than attempting to seize well-defended Metzovo, government forces occupied alternative passes and only then approached Metzovo, whose commander promptly defected and dispersed his force of 15,000. Thus when more intense combat began, Ali Pasha had no more than 10,000 men, and the way was already open to his fortresses at Ioannina. As Ismael Pasho's forces approached, Ali destroyed his capital so that it could not be used for cover by the invaders. The siege of the fortresses of Ioannina began on August 19. The garrison was 6,000 to 8,000 strong and well supplied. By the end of September, the besiegers were running low on provisions, but in October, the government forces finally moved their artillery into position and began the bombardment of the castle of Litharitza. Some 1,500 of Ali's men deserted. Previssa, held by one of Ali's sons, was also besieged, although his son quickly defected to the government, received a pashalik, and turned over the city and his army. Ali Pasha had placed another one of his sons in command of Albania; he too defected with the promise of a pashalik. His sister remained loyal, however, and was alleged to have spread contaminated clothing throughout the land, causing an outbreak of plague. The number of casualties during these months is unknown, but several sacks of ears were sent back to Constantinople, indicating that they were substantial.

Ali Pasha resolved on a sortie, and against expectations, the attack succeeded at a high cost on both sides, driving the Turkish army from its positions and causing it to flee to Dgelova, a few miles away. The government mobilized the nearby Suliots against Ali (he had taken their lands earlier in his rule), but they soon became disaffected, and they secretly began corresponding with Ali, and a plan was developed in which they would defect to Ali in return for their lands. On December 12, 900 Suliots fought their way out of the besieging forces and made for their lands. Ismael's army soon was reinforced by an additional 15,000 men. After one of his supply caravans, guarded by 500 men, was plundered by the Suliots (now numbering 3,500), Ismael diverted 5,000 men to crush the Suliot insurrection. Ali warned the Suliots of the government's movements, and when the Turks attacked the prepared Suliots, they were thrown back "with great slaughter."[11] Ali Pasha now made a proposal for common action with the Suliots: his forces would sally forth and then push the government forces into a Suliot ambush. However, Ismael received a copy of the battle plan. On February 7, 1821, Ali Pasha's forces attempted to spring the trap but were beaten back, losing 500 killed in the process.

A second government army of 24,000 men led by Kurschid Pasha arrived at Ioannina on March 2, 1821. Kurschid Pasha took control of the Ottoman forces and began unsuccessful negotiations with Ali Pasha, who recommenced hostilities by bombarding the Imperial Army. On March 25, 1821, the Greek War of Independence (Intra-state War #504) began in the Morea, diverting at least some government troops from Ioannina (by May, 10,000 were left under Kurschid's command). On June 8, an assault on Litharitza was thrown back, with about 300 government battle-deaths. Despite the two sides observing a truce during Ramadan, at the beginning of the Ottoman holiday of Bairam, Ali had his forces bombard the government-controlled mosque, killing 200 government soldiers and 60 officers. On August 6, the Suliots attacked a supply convoy but were thrown back. Further negotiations were unsuccessful, so the government forces turned to subterfuge to defeat Ali Pasha. Toward the end of October, the Albanian defenders of Litharitza were persuaded to defect to the government, leaving only 600 men inside loyal to Ali Pasha. The Suliots also abandoned the fight. As an epidemic broke in the garrison, those who remained loyal soon surrendered. Ali Pasha was forced to retreat into his citadel with only a handful of faithful soldiers. On January 24, 1822, Ali Pasha capitulated to the government under a promise of amnesty from Kurschid Pasha.

Termination and Outcome: The outcome of the war was a government victory, with a possible amnesty. On February 5, the government had Ali Pasha killed, along with virtually his entire family. Interestingly, Ismael Pasho had been deposed in November 1821 and was executed at around the same time as his mortal enemy.

Coding Decisions: It is clear that many more than 1,000 were killed in 1821, but the battle-deaths for 1820 and 1822 are unknown. Given the length of the siege and the number of soldiers engaged, it is likely that deaths due to disease were at least as high as deaths due to combat. We cautiously assign a figure of 2,000 battle-deaths to this war, but the real toll is likely to be substantially higher.[12]

Sources: Aksan (2007); Davenport (1837); De Beauchamp (1823); Finlay (1861).

INTRA-STATE WAR #503
Sardinian Revolt of 1821

Participants: Sardinia (Piedmont) and Austria versus Liberals in Piedmont.
Dates: March 10, 1821, to May 8, 1821.
Battle-related Deaths: Austria: [ ]; Sardinia: [ ]; Liberals: [ ]; Total Combatant Deaths: 1,000.
Initiator: Liberals (in Military and *Carbonari*).
Outcome: Sardinia and Austria win.
War Type: Civil for central control.
Total System Member Military Personnel: Sardinia: 41,000 (prewar, initial, peak, final). Austria, participating on April 7, 1821: 258,000 (prewar); 273,000 (initial, peak, final).[13]
Theater Armed Forces: Sardinia: 7,000 (peak).[14] Austria (Pro-government Intervener): 2,000. Liberals: 300 (initial); 15,000 (peak).[15]

Antecedents: Piedmont (on the west coast of contemporary Italy, bordering France) was the primary component of the kingdom of Sardinia. Piedmont was annexed by France in 1801, and the king at the time, Charles Emmanuel IV, was forced to retreat to the island of Sardinia, which was the only part of the kingdom not conquered by France. In 1802 Charles Emmanuel abdicated in favor of his younger brother, who was crowned Victor Emmanuelle I. The king ruled Sardinia until the end of the Napoleonic wars, when the Congress of Vienna restored the kingdom's independence. When Victor Emmanuel returned to Piedmont, he was accompanied by the heirs to the throne, his younger brother Charles Felix, and a distant cousin Charles Albert. Victor Emmanuel reestablished the absolute monarchy and abolished all of the freedoms granted under the Napoleonic codes. These measures angered the liberals, who had been encouraged by the movements toward reform throughout Europe and the desire to rid Sardinia of foreign control. Liberal ideas spread through the universities, the military, and in secret societies or *carbonaria*, which were widespread groups of middle- and upper-class individuals opposed to authoritarian government.

On January 11, 1821, four students at the University of Turin demonstrated for liberal reforms: one was arrested and imprisoned, prompting antigovernment demonstrations by 300 students the next day, which were dispersed by government troops in an attack that left at least eleven students dead. Liberal ideals even reached the twenty-three-year-old Prince Charles Albert, who had been educated in Paris during the reign of Napoleon Bonaparte, where he had developed sympathy with liberal and anti-Austrian positions. The liberal Constitution of 1812 adopted by Spain precipitated not only Spain's attempt to limit the absolute monarchy of Ferdinand VII (Intra-state War #505) but also spread to the kingdom of Two Sicilies, where it fueled a liberal uprising in 1820 (Intra-state War #502). Both the promise of reform represented by the Constitution of 1812 and the experience in Two Sicilies served to precipitate this war in Sardinia as well.

Narrative: In his conversations with friends, a number of whom were *carbonari*, Charles Albert expressed sentiments in favor of action to promote liberal reform in Sardinia, as long as it did not threaten the king. Thus, he was considered to be part of a conspiracy developing among members of the military and *carbonari*. Toward the end of the liberal revolt in Two Sicilies (Intra-state War #502), a liberal army of 10,000 men led by Gen. Guglielmo Pepe marched to confront the 60,000 to 80,000 men of an Austrian army that was acting on behalf of King Ferdinand. Liberals within the Sardinian military felt that they had to act in support of Pepe and began planning a revolt under the leadership of Count Santorre di Santarosa. On March 2, 1821, some of the conspirators' plans were captured by the police, prompting Santarosa to act. On March 6, he visited Charles Albert and told him of the plans for a revolt on March 8 and that the rebels were awaiting Charles Albert's approval. Charles Albert agreed but then changed his mind the next day. Charles Albert continued to vacillate as the rebels developed an alternate plan for March 10. Though Charles Albert may have tried to stop the plans again, the rebellion went ahead.

On March 10, the cry for revolution in support of a constitution was raised at the citadel in Alessandria (southeast of Turin) by *carbonari* and military officers, and they created a committee of government. The rebels in Turin dispersed to neighboring garrisons to gather troops to move toward Turin. Santarosa and a few of his colleagues continued to Alessandria, where 300 cavalry officers joined them. As the rebels advanced toward Alessandria's citadel, additional garrisons mutinied and joined them, while the regiments that remained loyal withdrew under the leadership of the governor. In Alessandria, Santarosa took charge of the city and the rebel National Guard units, while fellow conspirator Marquis of San Marzano marched with 400 cavalry and a contingent of National Guardsmen toward Casale. The next day, a group of 200 to 1,200 liberals in Turin surrounded the citadel and its 6,000 defenders. Though several were killed, the citadel proclaimed for the revolution. The rebels hoped to be joined by 60,000 soldiers, 20,000 volunteers from Piedmont, and another 70,000 from elsewhere so that they (under the leadership of the king or Charles Albert) could attack the Austrians as they retreated from Naples.[16] Instead, Charles Albert went to support the king and queen, and on March 12, he proceeded to the citadel in an attempt to negotiate on their behalf. The rebels demanded the Spanish constitution, which Charles Albert promised to try to get. Meanwhile, the Holy Alliance of Austria, Prussia, and Russia had been meeting at Laibach (Ljubljana), where they agreed to mobilize their forces to suppress liberal movements. Thus faced with unpleasant options of a rebellion (it was reported that 30,00 rebels were approaching Turin) or foreign intervention, the king decided to abdicate in favor of Charles Felix and asked Charles Albert to serve as regent pending Charles Felix's arrival. Thus Charles Albert was in essence facing a revolt of which he had initially been a part. Though he realized that the liberals had no chance of winning (at least half the army remained loyal), Charles Albert granted the Spanish constitution to prevent further bloodshed, and he signed the oath to the constitution on March 15.

Opposing such reforms, Charles Felix repudiated the concessions made by Charles Albert. He ordered Charles Albert to leave Turin and appealed to Austria for assistance. Charles Albert vacillated: he appointed Santarosa as minister of war then moved with loyalist troops toward Novara on March 21 and then on to meet the Austrians in Milan before going into exile. The same day, the Austrians crushed the liberals in Two Sicilies, and the Austrian army entered Naples on March 23. Santarosa, as minister of war, ignored the actions of Charles Felix and began preparations for war with Austria and loyalist troops. The 15,000 rebel troops were dispersed, mainly at Genoa, Turin, and Alessandria, with smaller bands elsewhere. Santarosa issued a call for support as the rebel army marched toward Novara.

Termination and Outcome: Austria came to the aid of Charles Felix as he opposed the liberal constitutionalists. At Novara, on April 7, 1821, a government army of 7,000 aided by 2,000 Austrian troops, commanded by Count Ferdinand Bubna, crushed the liberal army of 5,000.[17] A military tribunal was established that on April 19, 1821, condemned 91 rebels to death and 53 to perpetual imprisonment. Charles Felix entered Turin on October 18, 1821, and reestablished tyrannical rule. Santarosa fled to Paris and London before volunteering to fight in the Greek war of independence, where he was killed in 1824. Charles Albert was exiled as Charles Felix tried to have him removed from the line of succession. Charles Albert was able to redeem himself by fighting with the French under Louis XVIII against Spain and was then allowed to return to Piedmont.

Coding Decisions: This war is coded as an internationalized civil war due to the intervention of Austria on the side of the government of Sardinia. There is lack of agreement about the level of battle-deaths in this conflict. Richardson included this war but coded it as a "<3?," indicating that he wasn't sure if it resulted in 1,000 fatalities.[18] There were limited numbers of deaths reported in the early engagements and subsequent executions, and so the fatalities mostly are linked to the battle at Navaro, which is portrayed as either a battle in which the 5,000 rebels were defeated or crushed[19] or as a battle in which only a few rebels fought to the bitter end, while most fled. Even if only 20 percent of the rebels fought to the end, that would mean that there were close to 1,000 liberal battle-deaths, and we assume that there also would have been some government and Austrian deaths as well. Thus, we include this war with an estimate of 1,000 total combatant deaths.

Sources: Berkeley (1932); Clodfelter (2002); Emerson (1902); Hearder and Waley (1963); Jaques (2007); Phillips and Axelrod (2005); Richardson (1960); Smyth (1828); Solmi (1970).

INTRA-STATE WAR #504

Greek Independence War of 1821 to 1828 (aka Greek Revolution)

Participants: Ottoman Empire versus Greek rebels, United Kingdom, France, and Russia.
Dates: March 25, 1821, to April 25, 1828.
Battle-related Deaths: Ottoman Empire: 50,000; Greeks: 15,000 (see Coding Decisions); United Kingdom: 75;[20] Russia: 59; [21] France: 43.[22]
Initiator: Greek rebels.
Outcome: Transformed into Inter-state War #4.
War Type: Civil for local issues (secession).
Total System Member Military Personnel: Armed Forces of the Ottoman Empire: 161,000 (prewar); 181,000 (initial); 206,000 (peak); 129,000 (final).[23] Armed Forces of United Kingdom, participating on October 20, 1827: 149,000 (prewar); 155,000 (initial, peak, final). Armed Forces of France, participating on October 20, 1827: 237,000 (prewar); 247,000 (initial, peak, final). Armed Forces of Russia, participating on October 20, 1827: 578,000 (prewar); 675,000 (initial, peak, final).
Theater Armed Forces: Greeks (Rebel Aggregate): 16,600 (initial); 25,000 (peak, final). Greek Allies: 22 ships from the United Kingdom (Pro-rebel State Intervener), participating on October 20, 1827: [ ]. France (Pro-rebel State Intervener), participating on October 20, 1827: [ ]. Russia (Pro-rebel State Intervener), participating on October 20, 1827: [ ].

Antecedents: As reform movements swept Western Europe in the early 1820s, the growing weakness of the government of the Ottoman Empire prompted several rebellions against its authority, including that of Ali Pasha in western Yannin (Intra-state War #502.1 in 1820 to 1822). The Pashlik of Yanin was located north of Greece, which at that time was limited to the *sarea* around the Peloponnese peninsula, and Ali Pasha's efforts against the Ottomans encouraged similar efforts in Greece. In Greece, while most landed elites saw themselves as leaders of the *Rum millet*, the Orthodox subjects of the empire, a growing number of urban elites, subscribed to Greek nationalism, or the idea that Greeks were a separate people from the Ottomans. Ottoman Sultan Mahmud II reacted to the centrifugal tendencies in the provinces by trying to create a more centralized state. This approach generated resentment among local elites, whether they were nationalists or not.

The *Filiki Etairia* was a Greek nationalist organization located in Russia, which gained the support of Alexandros Ypsilantis, a Greek with military experience. The group's goal was to create a general uprising in every city with a substantial Greek presence—even Constantinople itself—to create independent states or a federation in the region. The date of the uprising was set for March 25 O.S. (Old Style date format, or April 6 in the Gregorian calendar). However, before then, Greeks began slaughtering Muslim inhabitants. On March 6 Ypsilantis and his Etairists entered the Danubian principality of Moldavia in the hope of gaining Russian and Serbian intervention. On March 7, Ypsilantis (prematurely) proclaimed that all of Greece was in arms and called for volunteers to rescue her. Using conscription, Ypsilantis brought his strength up to 2,000 by March 13, when he began his march to Bucharest, where he hoped to gain additional support. He was able to rally Serbs, Montenegrins, Bulgarians, and Moldavaians to his cause and soon had 4,500 men, including the "sacred band" of about 700 Greek students. He crossed into Wallachia on March 25, having yet to fire a shot.

Narrative: Although the war traditionally is assigned a start date of March 25 O.S. (a date retained for commemorative purposes when the Greeks switched to the Gregorian calendar) or April 6 on the Gregorian calendar, combat actually occurred before then as a band of 300 men led by a *Filiki Etairia* member named Soliotes engaged a force of 60 Albanian reinforcements at Bersova, killing 20 of them. However, most of the early fatalities were the results of massacres of Muslim populations by Greeks. On April 2, Kalaviyta was attacked by 600 Greek insurgents and taken when the Ottoman forces surrendered on April 7, while the Greeks then burned the town of Patras. On April 15, 300 to 1,000 Ottoman soldiers detached from the siege of Ioannina (see Intra-state War #502.1) and attempted to lift the siege of the castle of Patras. They were opposed by 6,000 armed Greeks, but when the latter fled, the Turks then massacred the Greek inhabitants and burned 700 houses. In all 10,000 to 15,000 Turks were massacred in the first month of the rebellion. Reciprocal massacres of Greeks also became common, and up to 50,000 people (mostly civilians killed in these massacres) died in the first year of the rebellion alone.

In May, the Cretans joined the rebellion, and in the Dardanelles, a naval action on June 8 killed 300 to 400 Turkish sailors. The rebellion spread northward across the Gulf of Corinth; the city of Athens was captured by the Greeks, although the Ottomans fortified the Acropolis and held out through the end of the year. In Wallachia 2,000 of Vladimirescu's *panduri* fought a successful battle against 3,000 Ottoman troops from May 28 to May 29. But, having evidence that Vladimirescu planned to join the Turks, Ypsilantis had him seized and executed. Ypsilantis now had sole control over the revolution in the Danubian provinces. On June 6, the Ottomans advanced on Tirgoviste, and Ypsilantis had to retreat. The rebels suffered defeats on June 19 and June 29, which ended the rebellion in the Danubian provinces.

In the second half of 1821, Kolokotronis assumed leadership of the Greek movement. He besieged Tripolis with 10,000 men, forcing its 9,000-strong garrison to capitulate in October. By the end of 1821, the rebellion had won many successes. A Greek government was formed with Alexandros Mavrokordatos as the first president. However, the movement was in danger of fragmenting: local leaders had little confidence in the *Filiki Etairia*, which sought centralized authority, and the government had little real control over many military units.

Early in 1822, the government's defeat of Ali Pasha allowed it to divert more resources to the suppression of the Greek rebellion. Off the coast of Asia Minor, the island of Chios rose against the Ottomans in March, but the Ottomans quickly massacred or enslaved its Greek population. From June 18 to June 19, the Greeks won a naval battle off the coast of Chios, steering fireships into the Ottoman flagship, killing 2,106. The Greeks also secured the surrender of the Ottoman garrison at the Acropolis in Athens. The sultan ordered invasions of continental Greece from the East (led by Mahmud Dramali Pasha) and West (under Omer Vrioni). On July 16, some 5,600 Ottoman troops attacked the 3,000-strong Greek force at Petta. The Greeks suffered 400 battle-deaths in their defeat. While an Ottoman advance was delayed for some time by logistical difficulties, 8,000 government troops were able to besiege the remnants of the Greek army under Mavrokordatos (just 2,500 men) at Mesolonghi on November 6. On January 6, 1823, the Ottomans unsuccessfully attempted to storm Mesolonghi, costing the government 200 killed against only 4 rebels killed.

The 1822 Ottoman offensive in the East also failed. Mahmud Dramali Pasha led 20,000 men into Greek-held territory. The government met with early success, occupying Corinth without a fight in July. Dramali besieged the fortress of Larissa, but without adequate provisions, Dramali could not afford a long siege. The Ottomans gained possession on August 1, after the retreat of the Greek garrison. Dramali resolved on a retreat to Corinth, where they were attacked by the Greeks as they attempted to force passage through the passes. Dramali died in December, and perhaps 17,000 Ottoman soldiers perished in the campaign in the East out of the initial force of 23,000.

As 1823 began, the Greeks were ascendant in the struggle, having managed to defeat two Ottoman invasions. The government repeated the 1822 strategy of two main invasions in 1823 but was not appreciably more successful. Internally, the Greeks had divided themselves further. There were two rival governments by the end of 1823. Whereas the Orthodox church had been a source of coordination in earlier years, rivalry now emerged between the primates and military figures. The division was also sectional, with the Morea (Peloponnese Peninsula) loosely allied together and opposed to figures from continental Greece (where most of the fighting was happening) and the three Nautical Islands of Hydra, Spetses, and Psara. By 1824, the Sultan was strengthened by the end of his war against Persia (Extra-state War #309) and could therefore devote more resources to reconquering Greece. The Ottomans called upon the province of Egypt to supply soldiers and ships for a seaborne invasion of Greece from the south. This stratagem caught the Greeks off guard and produced a few early successes for the empire. In the spring, the government forces were able to largely put down the rising in Crete, giving the Egyptians a major base for operations. The next assault was directed at the Nautical Islands. The Greeks managed to delay their capture by attacking the Turko-Egyptian fleets; nevertheless, Psara fell with its 4,000 defenders.

The Egyptians were able to move a substantial army to Crete for use against the Morea in 1825. On February 24, 1825, Ibrahim Ali landed his Egyptian forces in the Morea, and by April 2, he had concentrated more than 11,000 soldiers at Methoni. About 7,000 Greek soldiers were sent against him, with disastrous results. In May the fortifications of Navarino capitulated to Ibrahim; he made this sheltered port his base of operations. Egyptian strength quickly increased to 24,000, producing further victories. Finally, Ibrahim Ali turned his main force to meet the 10,000 Greeks led by Kolokotrones near Tripolitsa on July 6. Kolokotrones was defeated, and his forces dispersed. By 1826, Ibrahim controlled most of Morea and was in position to coordinate with Ottoman troops to his north. However, foreign powers—Russia, Britain, and France—had taken an interest in the conflict, partly prodded by their populations, who were moved by the sacrifices of the philhellenes like Lord Byron, who fought—and mostly died—in the struggle.

In April 1826, a protocol regarding the conflict was reached between Great Britain and Russia, calling for mediation of the conflict and explicitly mentioning the possibility of a Russo-Turkish war. The Turks accepted the offer of mediation and Russia's terms, which postponed European intervention for a time. By April 1826, Mesolonghi had been reduced to near starvation, and the Greeks attempted to cut a way out through the siege lines and allow the noncombatants to escape. They attacked on April 22 and April 23, but only 1,500 managed to escape. The Ottomans then stormed the fort and massacred most of the town's inhabitants. The rest of 1826 was largely a guerrilla war of Greek bands against Ibrahim's forces. His losses were appalling—of the 24,000 Egyptians sent to Greece, only 8,000 remained alive, and 1,500 of these were sick or wounded. Yet, the Ottoman forces in the West were able to march eastward, capturing Athens and besieging the Acropolis.

As 1827 opened, the Greeks largely were confined to a few fortresses, with perhaps 25,000 Greeks still fighting. The Greek government mounted a major operation to relive the siege of the Acropolis, mustering 18,000 soldiers in all, though the Ottoman government had 30,000 men in Attica with which to oppose them. On July 6, Russia, France, and Britain reached the Treaty of London, which demanded an autonomous Greece under Ottoman suzerainty. It called for an armistice and authorized the three allied powers to forcibly separate the combatants if either side refused the armistice. The Greek government accepted the armistice; the Porte refused. The Allies then undertook to prevent Ibrahim from receiving reinforcements and supplies. By October 17, the fleets of Russia, France, and Britain were at Navarino, essentially blockading both Egypt's fleet and the Ottoman fleet proper. On October 20, when the Egyptians fired on an Allied vessel sent to negotiate, the Allied ships opened fire on the entire Ottoman–Egyptian fleet. The resulting battle killed anywhere from 2,000 to 8,000 Turks and Egyptians, 43 French, 75 British, and 59 Russians. When the Greek insurgents received the news of the Battle of Navarino Bay, there was a hurried attempt to extend the boundaries of the rebellion. However, poor finances kept the Greeks from mounting major operations until May, by which time the Russo-Turkish War of 1828 to 1829 (Inter-state War #4) had broken out.

Termination and Outcome: The outcome of the war was a transition from civil war to inter-state war (Inter-state War #4) as Russia took on the bulk of the fighting against the Ottoman Empire. Most of the Ottoman forces in the North also had withdrawn to fight the Russians, enabling the Greeks to advance against little opposition. On September 25, 1829, the remaining Turkish forces capitulated to the Greeks. The Greeks later were granted full independence but had their territory reduced.

Coding Decisions: Due to the large number of people killed in this war, and the intermingling of the deaths of combatants and deaths of civilians in massacres, the estimates of fatalities vary widely. Richardson coded the Greek War of Independence of 1821 to 1829 as a "4," meaning about 10,000 deaths.[24] Phillips and Axelrod report 15,000 Greeks and 6,000 Ottomans killed from 1821 to 1832.[25] Cummins records 25,000 Greeks and 20,000 Ottomans killed, along with 105,000 civilian deaths.[26] Our summation of the battle-deaths from individual battles adds up to 44,000 to 50,000 for the Ottoman Empire. Given the amount of missing data and the huge toll that disease took on those forces where totals are known, an estimate of 50,000 seems reasonable.[27] Similarly, our total of Greek battle deaths is 15,000.[28]

Sources: Albrecht-Carrié (1958); Anderson (1952); Bodart (1916); Brewer (2001); Clodfelter (2002, 2008); Crawley (1930); Cummins (2009); Dakin (1972); Dakin (1973); Elliadi (1933); Finlay (1861); Goldstone (1998); McCarthy (1997); McCarty (1995); Miller (1913); Palmer (1992); Papageorgiou (1985); Phillips (1897); Phillips and Axelrod (2005); Richardson (1960); Sonyel (1998); Tappe (1973); Treptow (1996); Woodhouse (1952).

INTRA-STATE WAR #505
Spanish Royalists War of 1821 to 1823

Participants: Spain versus Royalists.
Dates: December 4, 1821, to April 6, 1823.
Battle-related Deaths: Spain: [ ]; Royalists: [ ]; Total Combatant Deaths: 1,500.
Initiator: Royalists.
Outcome: Transformed into Inter-state War #1.
War Type: Civil for central control.
Total System Member Military Personnel: 146,000 (prewar); 165,000 (initial); 165,000 (peak); 114,000 (final).
Theater Armed Forces: Royalists: [ ].

Antecedents: In 1808, Napoleon Bonaparte invaded Spain, overthrew its Bourbon monarch, Ferdinand VII, and installed his brother, Joseph Bonaparte, as the new king. Soon a general insurgency erupted as the Spanish resisted French rule. The resistance was organized by a supreme central junta, which functioned as a Spanish government until 1810 in preparation for the creation of the Cortes that would include representatives from throughout the Spanish empire. The Cortes met for the first time in the city of Cádiz on September 24, 1810. The Cortes established three branches of government, the most important of which was the legislative. Conservatives saw the Cortes as temporary pending Ferdinand's return, while liberals saw it as a means of governmental reform. The liberal interpretation dominated, and in March 1812, the Cádiz Cortes created the first modern Spanish constitution, the Constitution of 1812, which created a limited monarchy and guaranteed popular liberties. This constitution became a model as reform movements spread throughout Europe. When Ferdinand VII was restored to the throne by Napoleon on December 11, 1813, he refused to recognize the constitution, arguing for an absolute monarchy. This position was unpopular both within Spain and in the Spanish colonies, a number of which moved toward independence. In Spain, opposition to Ferdinand emerged both among the liberals (frequently organized in Masonic lodges) and within the military. The military was resistant to plans for further campaigns in the Americas, though the government was recruiting for an expected new war to be fought against New Granada, the Second Bolivar Expedition of 1821 to 1822 (Extra-state War #808). On January 1, 1820, Maj. Rafael del Riego declared a revolution in the name of the Constitution of 1812. He and a band of followers seized the officers at the military headquarters at Arcos and then tried to incite soldiers who had gathered in Cadiz for an expedition to the Americas. Riego was joined by 5,000 soldiers, but as this was insufficient for a major assault, they escaped into the countryside. Riego's bold move had widespread consequences: soldiers and citizens throughout the country began declaring themselves in favor of the constitution. The growing opposition and defections of senior military officers finally persuaded Ferdinand VII to change his position, and he announced (on March 7, 1820) to uphold the 1812 Constitution. A provisional junta took charge until a new Cortes could be elected. This began a three-year period called *el Trienio Liberal* (or Liberal Triennium). Initially the new, moderate Cortes attempted to reconcile constitutional liberties with the monarchy, earning the moderates the enmity of both the radical liberals and the conservatives. In August 1820, Riego, now a general, arrived in the capital and succeeded in inciting radical opposition (some linked to the Masons or the related *Comuneros*) to the government. The government created a new liberal national militia to defend the constitution and to reduce the size of the army, which was splintering into liberal and royalist factions. The militant royalists from their headquarters in Bayonne were in secret communication with the king, who continued to back royalist plots to overthrow the new government, which further reduced his popularity so that whenever he appeared in public, he was met by threatening mobs.

Narrative: The next year, emboldened by the split between the moderate and radical liberals, and by the stationing of French troops on the border (to contain the yellow fever epidemic), the king decided to confront his opponents, hoping thereby to gain international support for his restoration. When addressing the Cortes on March 1, 1821, the king complained about his lack of executive power; he then dismissed the government's ministers and selected a new government from among the moderates in the Cortes (the Bardaxi ministry), who were more acceptable to him. This initiative had contradictory results: it fueled demonstrations by the radicals in the provinces against this perceived unconstitutional act, and it prompted royalist disturbances in Valencia, Corunna, Seville, and Barcelona. Low-level armed conflict broke out in the countryside between radicals and supporters of the king. One such incident, at Salvatierra in the North, pitted radical Juan Martín Díez, known as *El Empecinado* (a guerrilla leader in the 1808 fight against the French) against a soldier–priest, Jerónimo Merino, known as *El Cura Merino*, who was the leader of the royalists and absolutists in the North. The new ministers began to confront the radicals, dismissing Riego from his position as governor of Aragon. In response, the radicals staged a pro-Riego demonstration in Madrid on September 18, 1821, which led to a riot known as the battle of Las Platerías.

On September 24, 1821, the Cortes convened an extraordinary autumn session in an attempt to reassert its control. It censured the king's ministers and called for new elections for the Cortes, hoping to ensure the installation of a more radical government. The king agreed to appoint new ministers, but they were still unacceptable to the radicals. The elections for the Cortes were held on December 3, 1821, and the victory of the radicals prompted increased levels of conflict between the king and the Cortes. The royalist supporters of the king gathered troops to March against Seville, while General Velasco gathered 6,000 men to support the radicals. On December 4 the king was forced to return from Escorial to Madrid, and radicals who amassed to show their displeasure were fired upon by royalist troops. Throughout the next few weeks, soldiers in the army were forced to decide on which side their allegiance lay, and elements fought on both sides. The Cortes dissolved on February 14, 1822. The king chose as his chief minister Martinez de la Rosa, and the king's cabinet once again attempted to govern without the support of the majority in the Cortes. Cities including Valencia and Seville were on the side of the radical Cortes and soon faced royalist insurrections. On May 30, 1822, royalist revolts at Aranjuez and Valencia were defeated by the militia. On June 21, 1822, the royalists had their first major victory when the Apostolic Army of the Faith commanded by "the Trappist" (Antonio Marañon) seized the city of Seo de Urgel, where it established a royalist stronghold and established a regency in the name of the king.

Ferdinand's palace was the focus of the vast conspiracy against the government, and the king contacted Louis XVIII to gain French funding and support for the reestablishment of an absolute monarchy. Civil war raged as radicals moved against friends and supporters of the king throughout the country, while bands of armed men resisted government troops and called upon Spaniards to liberate their captive king. Cruelty against civilians was practiced by both sides. On June 30, demonstrations against the king took place outside the palace in the capital. The following events, often referred to as "the July Days," reflected the frustrations of the royal guard with the attacks upon the king. On July 1, the king sent some of his royal guards to Prado. Returning on the night of July 6, the four rebel royal battalions fought a pitched battle against the national militia in the Plaza Mayor. On July 7, the king, unwilling to openly support the rebels, stood by as the guard was defeated by the militia, with most of the rebels being killed as they attempted to flee. The king, however, was now forbidden to leave Madrid. The remaining royalist guards retreated to the countryside (particularly to the north and the mountains of Catalonia), where they participated in more widespread conflict. Ferdinand's recent behavior undermined his support, and many royalists shifted their hopes toward his brother, Don Carlos. Even though constant fighting continued, it had become clear that the royalists could not win without additional arms and assistance. As the royalist military status faltered, its headquarters at Seo de Urgel was abandoned, with many royalists fleeing into France in November 1822. Meanwhile, in October 1822, the Congress of Verona with representatives from France, Russia, Prussia, Austria, and the United Kingdom, met to decide Spain's fate. The treaty, signed on November 22, provided a commission for France to support the royalist rebellion. On January 6, 1823, notes from Russia, Prussia, France, and Austria ordered Spain to change its constitution or face punishment.

Termination and Outcome: What had begun as an intra-state civil war ended on April 6, 1823. The next day, French troops crossed the border and took over the bulk of the fighting from the Royalists against the constitutional government of Spain. Thus the civil war is coded as being transformed into Inter-state War #1 between France and Spain.

Coding Decisions: Most historical accounts of this war combine the intra-state and inter-state components into a single war encompassing the period of 1820 to 1823, though Richardson only includes the 1823 inter-state war. During this period, the most important branch of government was the legislative, which controlled the institutions of government, thus it, instead of the king (a constitutional and restricted monarch at this point), is coded as Spain's government. Small and Singer report total deaths of 7,000 combatants and civilians during this war.[29]

Sources: Campos y Serrano (1961); Carr (1982); Clarke (1906); Clodfelter (2002); Emerson (1902); Gambra (1972); Holt (1967); Hume (1900); Menendez Pidal (1968); Oliveira (1946); Phillips and Axelrod (2005); Richardson (1960); Smith (1965); Urlanis (1960); Vaudoncourt (1824); Williams (1907); Wright (1965).

INTRA-STATE WAR #507.5
Greater Chechnya Revolt of 1825 to 1826

Participants: Russia versus Chechnya.
Dates: January 1825 to 1826.
Battle-related Deaths: Russia: [ ]; Chechnya: [ ]; Total Combatant Deaths: 1,000.
Initiator: Chechnya.
Outcome: Russia wins.
War Type: Civil for local issues.
Total System Member Military Personnel: Russian Armed Forces: 1,032,000 (prewar); 574,000 (initial, peak); 570,000 (final).[30]
Theater Armed Forces: *Russian Armed Forces*: [ ]. Chechnya and Dagestani Volunteers: 2,000 (initial); 4,000 (peak).

Antecedents: In 1816, Russia forces under the command of Gen. Lt. Aleksei P. Ermolov (or Yermolov) launched a military campaign to solidify Russian control over the North Caucasus and Transcaucasus region. His plan to build a series of forts from Russia into Chechnya and Dagestan prompted the people of Chechnya, Dagestan, and Georgia to unite in revolt against Russia in 1818 (Intra-state War #500), which began as Chechens led by Beybulat Taymi, and launch attacks against the Russians with the assistance of troops from Dagestan. Ermolov then began a major campaign that lasted for four years, during which many Chechen villages were destroyed and the Chechens were driven into the mountains. The last offensive in Chechnya in November 1822 was halted by Beybulat, who then sought a meeting with Ermolov. Instead Beybulat was able to meet with one of Ermolov's commanders, Maj. Gen. N. V. Grekov, who treated Beybulat with contempt, reigniting the Chechen's commitment to confronting the Russians. The meeting between Beybulat and Ermolov finally took place in January 1824, and instead of negotiating, the Russians put forward conditions that were seen as unacceptable by the Chechens.

Later in January an all-Chechen gathering took place at Mayurtup, hosted by Mullah Muhammad, Beybulat, and Avko of Germemchuk. The Chechens again decided to unite in an armed struggle against the Russians to be led by Beybulat. Initially Grekov ignored the reports of the rebellion as fatalities were low. However, in January and March 1825, Grekov conducted expeditions in Chechnya, but the rebels evaded him. A second all-Chechen gathering convened on June 25, 1825, at which Shaikh Muhammad of Kudatli was appointed imam and issued a call for troops to support the revolt. This reveals the extent to which Islam was becoming institutionalized among the Chechens and would play an increasingly important role in a series of wars against Russia.

Narrative: The war began on June 25, 1825, when Beybulat and 2,000 armed followers threatened the town of Gerzel Aul but withdrew as Grekov's army arrived on June 27. The fact that Beybulat departed before the Russians arrived was seen by the people as a sign that the imam and his party were protected by God. Joined by Dagestani volunteers, Beybulat's forces stormed the Fort of Amir-Hajji-Yurt on July 20 and July 21, killing 98 of its 181 defenders. The success of the attack contributed to the spreading of the revolt, and by the end of the month, Beybulat's followers had increased to 4,000. As they launched attacks throughout the countryside, Grekov's forces were becoming encircled, so they retired to Groznaia. Once the Russians had left, Beybulat turned his forces to besiege the Russian fort at Gerzel Aul. The fort was relieved only on July 27, when Russian troops under Grekov and his superior, Gen. Vasily Ivanovich Lisanevich, arrived. A meeting between the Russians and 318 regional elders erupted in violence when Lisanevich ordered the elders to give up their daggers. Both Grekov and the Lisanevich were killed, as was the entire Chechen delegation. Hearing news of his comrades' deaths, Ermolov gathered an army and advanced into Chechnya. Meanwhile the Chechens attacked a series of Russian forts and even attacked Groznaia on September 10, 1825. Beybulat almost captured Ermolov in an ambush on December 7. In January 1826, Ermolov began the final campaign, in which he engaged the Chechens in a few skirmishes while burning villages and destroying crops.

Termination and Outcome: Ermolov returned to Tiflis in triumph, and the war is considered a Russian victory. Russia was involved in a lengthy struggle to extend imperial control throughout the Caucasus. One of the by-products of Russia's punitive measures during the first war in the region (Intra-state War #500) and this one was that Russia's co-opting of tribal elites produced a shift in the types of groups opposing Russia from the regional secular governing structures to an emerging religious organization, the fundamentalist *Naqshbandi* (Sufi) religious movement, referred to as the Murids by the Russians. The Murids would go to war with Russia in 1830, 1834, and 1836 (Intra-state Wars #511, #523, and #530). Ermolov would soon participate in the Russo-Persian War of 1826 to 1828 (Extra-state War #316).

Coding Decisions: There are few fatality statistics presented for this war. Since the ones mentioned above total over 400 fatalities, our best guess is at least 1,000 total combatant deaths for this war.

Sources: Gammer, 2006; Zelkina (2000).

INTRA-STATE WAR #510

Miguelite War of 1828 to 1834 (aka War of the Two Brothers)

Participants: Portugal versus Constitutionalists and United Kingdom.
Dates: May 1, 1828, to May 26, 1834.
Battle-related Deaths: Portugal: 12,000; Constitutionalists: 8,000; United Kingdom: 100.
Initiator: Constitutionalists.
Outcome: Constitutionalists and United Kingdom win.
War Type: Civil for central control.
Total System Member Military Personnel: Armed Forces of Portugal: 26,000 (prewar); 42,000 (initial); 54,000 (peak, final). Armed Forces of United Kingdom: 155,000 (prewar, initial, peak); 137,000 (final).
Theater Armed Forces: Armed Forces of Portugal including Miguelite Recruits: 23,000 (initial); 80,000 (peak); 40,000 (final).[31] Constitutionalists: [ ] (initial); 7,500 (1832); 26,000 (peak, final).[32] Armed Forces of United Kingdom (Pro-rebel Intervener), participating from April 1831: 1,000 (peak). (See Coding Decisions.)

Antecedents: King John VI had fled to Brazil, establishing his capital there in 1807, while leaving a regency behind in Portugal. Encouraged by the liberal movement in Spain and the Spanish Constitution of 1812, the liberals in Portugal had risen against the regency in Portugal in 1820 but agreed to have King John return to Portugal in 1821 as a constitutional monarch. His second son, Dom Miguel, could not accept restrictions on the power of the monarchy and led an unsuccessful rebellion from 1823 to 1824, after which he left for Vienna. When King John died in 1826, the crown passed to King John's eldest son, Dom Pedro, who preferred to remain as emperor of Brazil and established a charter that outlined a regency for his seven-year-old daughter (Queen Maria II), with Dom Miguel serving as regent and intended husband. Dom Miguel returned and accepted the charter in late

February 1828. However, again seeking to restore the absolute power of the monarchy, Dom Miguel seized power, denouncing the charter and dissolving the legislature in April. Most of the military switched its support from Queen Maria to Dom Miguel, occasionally encouraged by funds provided by the former queen.

Narrative: By the beginning of May, uprisings broke out, led by those who felt betrayed by Dom Miguel. A pro-chartist revolutionary junta (the constitutionalists) was formed in Oporto (Porto) and began a march southward toward Lisbon. Dom Miguel's army advanced from Lisbon, and the two met in the middle at Coimbra in June. In several engagements, the constitutionalists were driven back north, pursued by the Miguelites. Dom Miguel's forces occupied the city on July 3, 1828, and the liberals fled to England, Spain, and Terceira in the Azores. On July 11, 1828, Dom Miguel was proclaimed as king of Portugal by a compliant Cortes.

As the king established a repressive regime (thousands of his opponents would be imprisoned), the constitutionalists began to act. Dom Pedro sought to bring Queen Maria (age nine) to Brazil, though she was diverted to Britain instead. Liberals gathered at Terceira in the Azores, the only part of Portugal not controlled by Dom Miguel. Liberals who had fled to Britain were forced to leave, with some under the leadership of Marshal João Carlos de Saldanha moved to France. The constitutionalists in the Azores raised a rebellion in support of Dom Pedro and the queen and against Dom Miguel's usurpation. Reinforced by volunteers from Brazil, Britain, and France, the constitutionalists repelled a Miguelite naval attack on August 12, 1829. At Terceira, the constitutionalists, led by the Duke of Palmela, established a regency sanctioned by Dom Pedro in 1830. In April 1831, Pedro abdicated his Brazilian throne and, with the assistance of the British, headed to the Azores (arriving on March 3, 1832). Meanwhile, the constitutionalists were able to purchase a navy in England, while the French seized some of the Miguelite fleet in July 1831. Dom Pedro, now known as the Duke of Bragança, established a government in the name of his daughter and assembled a constitutionalist expedition from the Azores to reconquer the Portugal with British assistance.

On July 9, 1832, Dom Pedro and an expedition of 7,500, including British and French volunteers, was transported by the constitutionalist navy under the command of British Adm. George Sartorius to Oporto. The rebels were able to occupy the city as the Miguelites withdrew, but the government attacked the next day and was repelled by Sartorious's ships. The constitutionalists were soon besieged by 23,000 Miguelites. The siege lasted eleven months, during which an attack on July 23 by 10,000 Miguelites soldiers was repelled by liberal forces with 1,000 total fatalities. A second assault on September 29 was also repelled, with each side suffering 2,000 casualties. During the siege, the liberal army increased its strength to 17,800, while the government forces increased to 30,000 before dwindling to 24,000 by the time the siege was broken in June 1833. The rebels within the city still received some supplies from Britain but suffered from starvation and disease. In January 1833, Marshal Saldanha arrived in Oporto. The supporters of Queen Maria in Britain and France had persuaded the governments to provide a small fleet to the constitutionalists in Oporto. Sir Charles Napier sailed to Oporto, where he took command of the liberal fleet. Ruling out a direct attack on Lisbon, the Duke of Terceira utilized the fleet to transport 2,500 men, landing at Algarve (south Portugal) on June 24, 1833. On its return voyage, on July 5, 1833, the liberal navy defeated a much larger Miguelite fleet off Cape St. Vincent.

On land, the constitutionalist forces grew as they captured towns (including Almada on July 23 against a much larger government army) while advancing on Lisbon. Terceira took Lisbon as government troops fled, and Dom Pedro arrived on July 26. The constitutionalists were making advances on other fronts as well. On July 25 an attack against the liberals at Oporto by a government army of 12,000, led by French Gen. Louis Bourmont, was repulsed by the liberals commanded by Saldanha, who then succeeded in capturing the city. Saldanha then moved his army to join the liberals in Lisbon, and on August 9, Dom Miguel also withdrew his army and retreated toward Lisbon. Government forces retreating from Lisbon and Oporto gathered at Coimbra, uniting in a 40,000-strong army. Meanwhile the constitutionalists fortified their positions in Lisbon. Dom Miguel ordered two attacks against Lisbon, on September 5 and September 14, 1833, leading to 2,000 government and 1,000 rebel casualties. The constitutionalists, led by Saldanha, then went on the offensive and by October 10 had driven the Miguelites to

Santarem, where a relative stalemate ensued. In early 1834, Spain also intervened on the side of the constitutionalists (though not at levels to be considered a war participant). Dom Miguel had given refuge to the pretender to the Spanish throne, Don Carlos (see Intra-state War #522: the First Carlist War of 1834 to 1840). In the final battle of the war at Asseiceira on May 16, 1834, constitutionalist led by Terceira and aided by Spanish troops defeated the Miguelites, who suffered significant casualties.

Termination and Outcome: Don Miguel fled his capital and surrendered on May 26, 1834, ending the war as a constitutionalist victory. Dom Pedro died on September 1834, and the fifteen-year-old Maria assumed the throne. Don Miguel was banished, and Spain's Don Carlos fled to England.

Coding Decisions: We have coded the United Kingdom as a participant in this war, though British involvement was a matter of great contestation. Foreign Affairs Secretary Lord Palmerston espoused Britain's policy of nonintervention while favoring the removal of Don Miguel. Palmerston's chance for "nonintervention intervention" came in April 1831, when Don Pedro abdicated and headed to the Azores. Palmerston allowed Pedro to acquire ships, "volunteers," weapons, and a British naval commander.[33] In 1833, the naval fleet under Captain Napier has been described as being sent by Britain.[34] Though we have not located specific figures for Britain's troop strength or fatalities suffered, we think on balance that it would be sufficient for them to be considered a war participant. Though Richardson codes this war as a "4?," meaning about 10,000 fatalities, we follow Clodfelter, Phillips, and Axelrod in coding 20,000 total combatant fatalities, with the majority being suffered by the Miguelites.

Sources: Anderson (2000); Bollaert (1870); Clodfelter (1992); Jaques (2007); Livermore (1966); Phillips and Axelrod (2005); Richardson (1960); White (1909).

INTRA-STATE WAR #511
First Murid War of 1830 to 1832 (aka Great Gazavat)

Participants: Russia versus the Murid Forces of Ghazi Muhammad.
Dates: February 24, 1830, to October 17, 1832.
Battle-related Deaths: Russia: 3,000; Murids: 2,000. (See Coding Decisions.)
Initiator: Murids.
Outcome: Russia wins.
War Type: Civil for local issues.
Total System Member Military Personnel: Armed Forces of Russia: 803,000 (prewar); 826,000 initial); 875,000 (peak, final).[35]
Theater Armed Forces: Armed Forces of Russia: 6,000 (initial); 60,000 (peak); 10,000(final).[36] Murids: 8,000 (initial); 13,000 (peak); 60 (final).[37]

Antecedents: Russia was involved in a lengthy struggle to extend imperial control throughout the Caucasus (Intra-state Wars #500 and #507.5). One of the by-products of Russia's punitive measures during the first war in the region and its co-opting of tribal elites was a shift in the types of groups opposing Russia from the traditional governing structures to an emerging religious organization. This was the first of three wars involving resistance to Russian rule by a fundamentalist *Naqshbandi* (Sufi) religious movement, referred to as the Murids by the Russians (from the word *murid*, meaning disciple). The *Naqshbandis* traced their religious heritage to a fourteenth-century mystic, Baha al-Din Naqshbandi, who emphasized following the practices of the Prophet Muhammad. Sufi teachings focused on the application of religious law, or *shari'a*, as a means of resisting foreign encroachment.[38] Only once the *shari'a* had been reestablished would Muslims become virtuous and strong enough to be able to wage *jihad*—holy war—to liberate themselves from foreign threat or occupation.[39] The first *gazavat* against the Russians in the Caucasus occurred in the eighteenth century, led by a Chechen named Ushurum.

As Russia extended its control throughout most of Dagestan after 1824, the *Naqshbandi* order shifted its base of operations to the independent communities in the mountainous regions that remained outside Russian control. The influence of the *Naqshbandi* grew as Russia's military presence in the region declined during the wars with Persia in 1826 (Extra-state War #316) and the Ottoman Empire (Inter-state War #4). The village of Gimrah became one of the most important *Naqshbandi* centers, particularly by being linked to the activities of Mullah

Muhammed, also known as Ghazi Muhammed al-Daghestani. Ghazi Muhammad launched the next holy war (frequently referred to as the Great Gazavat). Muridism arose as Ghazi Muhammed transformed the *Naqshbandi* into a religious-political movement that dominated the North Caucasus for more than 30 years.[40]

Ghazi Muhammed had been born in the village of Gimrah but at the age of ten was sent to study Arabic and the Koran in Karanay. In 1825 he was so impressed with teachings of *Naqshbandi* sheikh Jamal al-Din that he joined the order and brought along a close friend, Shamil, who later became one of the most famous Dagestani imams. In 1827, Ghazi Muhammed returned to Gimrah, where he established himself as a sheikh and began to gather followers or *murids.* As Ghazi Muhammed's popularity spread, he urged the people to declare *gazavat,* or holy war, initially against the local secular leadership and later the Russians. Ghazi Muhammed was increasingly accepted as the supreme religious authority in the region and was confirmed as imam of Dagestan in 1829.

To further consolidate Russian power in the Caucasus, Tsar Nicolas I proposed a major military offensive under the leadership of General Velyaminov. Up until that point, Ghazi Muhammed had been preaching a passive attitude toward the Russians, but he decided that force had to be used to implement *shari'a* as a means to unite the mountaineers to resist the Russian encroachment. In early 1830 he summoned *Naqshbandi* mullahs to a gathering at Gimrah, and the *gazavat* was declared, and this time the Dagestanis (not the Chechens) would take the lead.

Narrative: The *gazavat* began as a challenge to the existing religious authorities. Ghazi Muhammad also militarily defeated some of his opposition, but by February 1830, he had won most of the local leaders to his side. One exception was Pahu Bike (or Pachu Bike), the regent of Avaristan. Ghazi Muhammed appealed to her to break Avaristan's relations with the Russians, and when she refused, Ghazi Muhammad's forces entered Avaristan and laid siege to Khunzakh (which marks the start of the war). The legend reports that Pahu Bike called on her warriors to resist the Murids, and when they hesitated, she seized a sword and urged them to arm their wives instead. The warriors, thusly shamed, followed her into battle.[41] There the Murid force of 8,000, under the leadership of Sheikh Shamil, was defeated, and on February 24, 1830, they retreated to Gimrah. The level of support for Ghazi Muhammed increased at the end of February 1830, when Dagestan and Chechnya were struck by a severe earthquake, which the people saw as God's punishment for their failure to follow the *shari'a.*[42] Consequently, many of the Chechen resistance leaders pledged their support to Ghazi Muhammed. Once the Russians began to understand Ghazi Muhammed's plans, they made several attempts to assassinate him, and their failure further increased Ghazi Muhammed's reputation.

In March 1830, the Russian forces, now under the command of Gen. (Count) I. F. Paskevich, began an offensive to bring the region under its control. Initially, Count Paskevich decided to implement his one-blow approach, whereby he ordered Maj. Gen. Grigorii Vladimirovish Rosen to enter the Dagestan mountains and to attack in all directions. The Russian plan was based on the indiscriminate destruction of villages, and in May 1830 they attacked Kazanischa, Erpeli, and Karanay. Ghazi Muhammad again went on the offensive, and between May and December 1830, several large Murid forces descended into the southwestern Alazan Valley and clashed with the Russians. The result of Baron Rosen's campaign was that the Russians alienated all of Dagestan. During the winter of 1830 and 1831, the Russians launched a series of punitive expeditions, destroying thirty Chechen villages, which further increased Chechen support for the Murids.

At the beginning of March 1831, Ghazi Muhammed moved his base of operation to Aghach Qala, which the Russians tried to storm unsuccessfully on April 19 and May 1. After the imam moved to Alti Bunyun, the Russians attacked his new position unsuccessfully on May 16. In the meantime, rebellion broke out in the kingdom of Poland (Intra-state War #51), and the tsar ordered some of the units from the Caucasus to be sent northward. Ghazi Muhammad took advantage of these events to go on the offensive, and he initiated a series of successful attacks, capturing Tarku at the beginning of June and besieging the fortress of Burnaia, until Russian reinforcements arrived, leading to several days of severe fighting. Meanwhile Murid forces under the command of Abdallah al-Ashilti were able to mobilize the Chechens and Ghumuqs, and on June 7, 1831, they began to surround Vnezapnaina. On June

26 the Murids besieged the fortress, and they were aided by the arrival of the imam on June 29. On July 10, a Russian relief column arrived, and the Murids retreated. The Russians decided to pursue the Murid force but were ambushed in a forest near Aktash Aukh on July 13, with a loss of 400 men.[43] The imam advanced into Dagestan and southward toward the Caspian Sea and the fort at Derbend, which was besieged from August 31 until a Russian relief column arrived on September 8, 1831. On October 15, 1831, the Russians launched another major offensive, which secured only limited gains, while the imam threatened Groznaia. By 1831, Ghazi Muhammed had reached the height of his power, controlling most of Chechnya and Daghestan.

Consequently, the new commander in chief in the Caucasus, Lt. Gen. Baron Grigorii Vladimirovich Rosen (who had served under Paskiewicz), was ordered by the tsar to launch a new offensive to destroy the Murid threat. In December 1831, the imam established a base at Aghach Qal'a with a force of about 600.[44] Though an initial Russian attack was repelled on December 6, a second attack on December 13 was successful. Most of the defenders were killed, though the imam and a few others escaped. Ghazi Muhammed regrouped and attacked Nasran for three days in March 1832, though the Russians were able to repel the attacks. On April 8, Ghazi Muhammed moved on toward Groznaia, where he threatened the Russian fort, and Hamza Bek led a campaign in Chartalah in July and August.

Termination and Outcome: Much of Chechnya yielded to Russian demands, and due to his declining support, the imam moved back to Dagestan. Ghazi Muhammed tried in July of 1832 to negotiate with the Russians and offered a truce if the Russians would allow the people of Dagestan to uphold the *shari'a.* The Russians refused and in August 1832 launched a two-pronged attack against the Murids, which together destroyed more than 100 villages. The two Russian armies united into a force of 15,000 to 20,000, and they crisscrossed Chechnya. Ghazi Muhammad came to aid the Chechens, and on August 31, he ambushed a Russian contingent, causing 155 casualties. This was Ghazi Muhammad's last success against the Russians. Realizing he could not stop the Russian advance, Ghazi Muhammed retreated to Gimrah on September 10, where he attempted to both fortify his position and negotiate with the Russians. Velyaminov insisted on the complete disarmament of the Murids. The Russians continued their advance, and the imam's warriors began to desert him. On October 29 a force under Field Commander Franz Klüge-von-Klegenau stormed the Murid fortress at Gimrah, killing the imam and virtually all his remaining 60 supporters there, which ended the rebellion at that point. The Russians decided to try to persuade the Dagestanis that further resistance was futile by displaying the body of Ghazi Muhammed. This tactic backfired when the body did not begin to decompose. The people of Gimrah became convinced that Ghazi Mohammed had been a messenger of God, and religious fervor was revived. Sheikh Shamil escaped the Russian attack on Gimrah and would go on to lead Murid revolts in 1834 (Intra-state War #523) and in 1836 (Intra-state War #530).

Coding Decisions: This war is coded as starting with the Murid attack on Khunzakh because the Avarian khanate was seen as the local representative of Russian rule. Others have argued that the war didn't officially begin until Ghazi Muhammed issued a direct call for a ghazavat against the Russians in late 1830.[45] Battle-death statistics for most of the engagements have not been reported. Clodfelter reports 3,000 Russian casualties during the war, which seems like a plausible fatality figure given the deaths reported in several of the major battles. Our summation of Murid deaths is 1,040, but because figures for a majority of engagements are missing, we are reporting an estimate of 2,000 here, though that may be an underestimate. The largest numbers of deaths were of civilians killed in the Russian destruction of villages.

Sources: Baddeley (1908); Baumann (1993); Clodfelter (2002); Gammer (1992, 2006); King (2008); Mackie (1856); Schaefer (2011); Stone (2006); Zelkina, 2000.

INTRA-STATE WAR #512

First Albanian Revolt of 1830 to 1832 (aka Albanian and Bosnian Revolts, Great Bosnian Uprising)

Participants: Ottoman Empire versus Albanians and Bosnians.

Dates: June 1830 to July 5, 1832.
Battle-related Deaths: Albanians and Bosnians: 10,000; Ottoman Empire: 5,000.
Initiator: Albanians.
Outcome: Ottoman Empire wins.
War Type: Civil for local issues.
Total System Member Military Personnel: Armed Forces of the Ottoman Empire: 129,000 (prewar, initial, peak, final).[46]
Theater Armed Forces: Armed Forces of the Ottoman Empire: 10,000 (initial); 16,000 (peak).[47] Albanians led by Scodra Pasha, participating through December 1831: 30,000 (prewar, initial); 40,000 (peak, final).[48] Southern Albanians, participating through 1830: [ ] (prewar, initial, peak, final). Bosnians, participating from March 29, 1831, to August 10, 1831, and October 1831 to July 5, 1832: 4,000 (initial); 25,000 (peak); 10,000 (final).[49]

Antecedents: The Ottoman state was substantially weakened by the Greek War of Independence (Intra-state War #504) and subsequent Russo-Turkish War of 1828 to 1829 (Inter-state War #4). Its strongest military contingent was the Albanian army commanded by Mustafa Reshit Pasha Bushati of Scodra (Shkodër), who was also known as Scodra Pasha. In 1829, Scodra Pasha (the leader of northern Albania), the *beys* (local government leaders) of southern Albania, and the Bosnian leader Husein Gradaščević, who had supported the Ottomans in the war with Russia, were angered that the Treaty of Adrianople, which ended the Russo-Turkish War (signed on September 14, 1829), had given sovereignty to Serbia, along with Bosnian territory. Scodra Pasha immediately rebelled against the peace settlement, but his forces had dispersed without real combat. In 1830, he encouraged the *beys* (local government leaders) of southern Albania to join him in revolt, and Ottoman Sultan Mahmud II decided to end their disobedience.

Narrative: In June 1830, the Ottoman government dispatched an expedition against them led by Grand Vizier Reschid Pasha, which had the effect of uniting the three most powerful *beys* against the Ottoman Empire. Reschid Pasha declared an amnesty and then invited the Albanian chiefs to parley. About 500 men, chiefs, and their followers turned up. He promised to meet their demands (higher pay and an end to administrative and military reforms) and invited them to a banquet. When the rebel force appeared at the feast on August 26, 1830, they were met by 1,000 Ottoman regulars, who ambushed and killed most of them. Two of the three southern rebel leaders (Veli Bey and Asrln Bey) were killed in the Monastir massacre, but one remained—Selictar Poda—who occupied much of Ioannina. Reschid Pasha sent 16,000 soldiers against him, causing him to flee, and thus Southern Albania had been conquered.

However, Scodra Pasha also had intrigued with Bulgarian and Bosnian rebels to overthrow the government and halt the reforms. In December 1830 and January 1831, Bosnian official Husein Gradaščević (known as Husein Kapetan) hosted meetings with Bosnians opposed to the reforms. After being chosen to head the movement, Husein Kapetan issued a call for volunteers and assembled a force of 4,000 men for a march toward the unofficial Bosnian capital of Travnik on March 29, 1831. In the nearby town of Pirot, the Bosnian rebels defeated the Ottoman 2,000-man army on April 7. Bosnians then flocked to the rebel cause. Leaving a portion of his army in Bosnia for defense, Husein Kapetan led an army of 25,000 Bosnians into Kosovo, seizing Peć and Pristina, where he established his headquarters. His goal was to meet up with the Albanian army of 40,000, and then the two would advance in July to confront the Ottoman army led by the Grand Vizier.

In the meantime, however, the Albanians were already successfully engaging the Ottomans. Scodra Pasha's army met Reschid Pasha's army at the decisive Battle of Perlepe (Prelepeh), and the Albanians seemed poised to win until more than half of Scodra Pasha's force of 40,000 defected, ensuring the Ottoman victory. After their defeat, Scodra Pasha's forces retreated to Scodra, where they were besieged in the fortress of Rosapha (Rozafat) by Reschid Pasha. The Bosnians marched further into Kosovo, and Reschid Pasha led a division against them. The two armies met on July 18, 1831, at Shtimje, where the Ottomans were defeated as Albanian troops deserted to the Bosnian rebels. Reschid Pasha was badly wounded in the battle. But instead of relieving the siege of Scodra, the Bosnians paused for negotiations. When Reschid Pasha agreed to meet their demands (no reforms in Bosnia and the elevation of their leader to the vizier of Bosnia), they turned back on August 10, 1831, leaving Scodra Pasha to his fate. Scodra surrendered at the end of 1831. Many of Scodra Pasha's followers were executed, although he was permitted to live in Constantinople as an official.

The Bosnian agreement led to a brief lull in the fighting. However, the settlement soon came apart as the Bosnians began fighting the Ottomans in the Bosnian region of Herzegovina. The *bey* of Stolac, Ali Rizvanobegović, had opposed the Bosnian conflict against the Ottoman Empire. When Husein Kapetan had defeated the Ottoman garrison at Travnik on March 29, 1831, the Ottoman official Namik-paša had fled to Stolac for refuge. Thus in the fall of 1831, the returning Husein Kapetan decided to confront the Ottomans in Herzegovina. In October, the Bosnians secured a major victory when a contingent led by Ahmed-beg Resulbegović seized control of Trebinje from his loyalist cousin. At this point, Reschid Pasha again offered to negotiate with Husein Kapetan, offering him an appointment as the vizier of an autonomous Bosnia in November. Yet the next month he attacked Bosnian units at Novi Pazar. During the winter of 1831 and 1832, Husein Kapetan won a number of victories so that he controlled virtually all of Herzegovina, except Stolac.

Reschid Pasha launched an offensive against Bosnia in February 1832. The Ottomans divided their army in two prongs, both heading toward Sarajevo. The armies met near Sarajevo at the end of May. The rebels were commanded by Husein Kapetan, while the Ottomans were led by the newly appointed vizier of Bosnia, Kara Mahmud Hamdi-paša. In several engagements, the Bosnian rebels were forced to retreat. The final battle took place at June 4 at Stup. Though Husein Kapetan had initial successes, his army was attacked from behind by a small force from Stolac led by Ali Rizvanobegović. Husein Kapetan finally decided against further resistance and retreated. The Ottomans entered Sarajevo on July 5, 1832.

Termination and Outcome: The outcome was an unconditional government victory. In 1832, the government conducted a repression campaign in Bosnia, led by Ömer Pasha, which destroyed 200 villages, killed 6,000 Bosnians, and conscripted or deported another 20,000. Husein Kapetan fled into Austrian territory.

To reward the loyalty of Ali Rizvanobegović, the Ottoman government separated Herzegovina from Bosnia and named him the first vizier of Herzegovina, with the title of Ali-paša. Though Ali-paša hoped to make the position permanent, he was executed by Ömer Pasha in 1851, at which time Herzegovina was reincorporated with Bosnia as Bosnia-Herzegovina.

Coding Decisions: Because there was a negotiated settlement between Bosnia and the Ottoman Empire that lasted for two months, it is coded as a temporary interruption in the war.

Sources: Aksan (2007); Giaffo (2000); Hehn (1984); Pollo and Puto (1981); Ranke (1853); Richardson (1960); Slade (1837); Tozer (1869); Urquhart (1838); Vickers (1999).

INTRA-STATE WAR #513
First French Insurrection of 1830 (aka July Revolution or *Trois Glorieuses*)

Participants: France versus Liberals.
Dates: July 27, 1830, to July 29, 1830.
Battle-related Deaths: Liberals: 1,800; France: 400.[50]
Initiator: Liberals.
Outcome: Liberals win.
War Type: Civil for central control.
Total System Member Military Personnel: Armed Forces of France: 265,000 (prewar); 269,000 (initial, peak, final).[51]
Theater Armed Forces: Armed Forces of France (including 1,400 police): 11,400 (initial, peak, final).[52] Liberals: 4,054 (initial, peak, final).[53]

Antecedents: After the defeat of Napoleon Bonaparte, the French monarchy under Louis XVIII was restored. When he died in 1824, his younger brother assumed the throne as Charles X. His desire to restore the absolute monarchy was resented by the middle classes and the liberals, many of whom hoped for a government led by Napoleon II. The elections of 1827 created a chamber of deputies, with half its seats held by liberals who supported François-René de Chateaubriand. Chateaubriand was originally a royalist who had served Charles X as minister of foreign affairs but gradually had moved toward the liberal opposition, though he also still was able to garner the votes of independents and moderate monarchists. In August 1829, Charles appointed his reactionary favorite Jules de Polignac to form a new government. Resistance in the chamber of deputies prompted 221 deputies to sign an address that expressed opposition to the government in March 1830. Charles chose to dismiss them. New elections led to an even greater preponderance of liberals in the chamber, leading to greater resistance. On July 26, 1830, Charles and Polignac published the July Ordinances, which further restricted the electorate. A revolt promptly broke out in Paris.

Narrative: By July 27, 1830, the liberals created barricades that blocked the streets of Paris. That afternoon, divisions of military soldiers and of the royal guard were dispersed throughout the capital. That evening, armed civilians attacked the soldiers. Fighting continued throughout the night, as members of the guard defected to the liberals. The next day negotiations were attempted but rejected by Charles on the advice of Polignac. By July 28, the liberal rebels were organized, better armed, and had established more than 4,000 barricades. They had been able to loot arms shops and make bullets and had been joined by former soldiers from Napoleon's army and the banned National Guard. Thus full-scale military clashes occurred, and Charles fled the city. On July 29, the Hôtel de Ville was seized and became the site of the provisional government. The government issued an order for the soldiers to withdraw, thus ending the war.

Termination and Outcome: The war resulted in a liberal victory. On August 2, Charles X and his son abdicated and fled to Britain. The provisional government chose a distant cousin, Louis-Philippe, as king (crowned on August 9, 1830). The monarchy would be overthrown in 1848 (Intra-state War #552).

Coding Decisions: This armed conflict is coded as a civil war through the application of one of the specific coding rules. The general requirement for a conflict to be a war is that it has two sides that are initially organized for armed conflict (which is not true for the rebels in this case.) However, an alternate coding rule specifies that a conflict can be a war if "the weaker side, although initially unprepared, is able to inflict upon the stronger opponents at least 5 percent of the number of fatalities it sustains."[54] This latter rule is applicable here.

Sources: Beach (1971); Bertier de Sauvigny (1955); Bodart (1916); Clodfelter (2002); Gemie (1999); Kohn (1999); Leys (1955); Phillips and Axelrod (2005); Tombs (1996).

INTRA-STATE WAR #515
Belgian Independence War of 1830

Participants: Netherlands versus Belgians.
Dates: August 25, 1830, to December 19, 1830.
Battle-related Deaths: Belgians: 600; Netherlands: 500.
Initiator: Belgians.
Outcome: Belgians win.
War Type: Civil for local issues.
Total System Member Military Personnel: Armed Forces of the Netherlands: 29,000 (prewar); 30,000 (initial, peak, final).[55]
Theater Armed Forces: Armed Forces of the Netherlands: 9,000 (initial, peak).[56] Belgians: 6,000 (initial, peak, final).[57]

Antecedents: The kingdom of Holland was established by Napoleon Bonaparte and survived from 1806 to 1810 as a puppet kingdom governed by his brother, Louis Bonaparte. Louis Bonaparte was forced to abdicate on July 1, 1810, at which point the emperor incorporated the Netherlands into the French empire until 1813, when Napoleon was defeated. At that point, a member of the former ruling house, William Frederick, proclaimed himself as the prince of the Netherlands. Two years later, the major powers at the Congress of Vienna agreed that the Belgian provinces (formerly the Austrian Netherlands) should be united with the kingdom of the Netherlands (partially in compensation to the Netherlands for the British seizure and retention of Ceylon). The new United Kingdom of the Netherlands would be ruled by William Frederick as William I of the house of Orange. The union would not last long. The people of the southern Belgian provinces were predominantly Catholic, with half speaking French (Walloons).

The Flemings (who speak variations on Dutch) were predominantly Protestant. Discontent with the regime grew among liberals, influenced by the growing movement for reform spreading throughout Europe, who saw King William as despotic; the working class, unhappy with high levels of unemployment; and the Walloons, who claimed mistreatment by the Flemings. The Belgians also were specifically influenced by the workers' revolution that took place in France in July 1830 (Intra-state War #513).

Narrative: The specific precipitant for the war was a play at the theater in Brussels that was set in the context of a popular, nationalistic uprising. The crowd left the theater on August 25, 1830, shouting nationalist slogans, which prompted the seizures of government buildings, the raising of a Belgian flag, and growing demands for independence. King William relied on his two sons to resolve the crisis. Prince William tried to negotiate a settlement that included a separation of the North and South, but his father rejected the terms. Prince Frederick led a force of 9,000 Dutch troops against Brussels, where they engaged in bloody fighting from September 23 to September 26. Unable to take control of Brussels, Prince Frederick and his army retreated to the fortresses of Maastricht, Venlo, and Antwerp. On September 26, proposals for a new provisional government under Charles Latour Rogier were drawn up, and the Declaration of Independence was proclaimed on October 4, 1830. Sporadic fighting continued: the Dutch force that remained at Antwerp bombarded the rebels in the city for several days at the end of October. The great powers meeting in London secured a cease-fire agreement on November 4, 1830, that generally ended the fighting, except for a small campaign that took place around Maastricht. The major powers meeting in London recognized Belgian independence on December 20, 1830.

Termination and Outcome: On June 4, 1831, the Belgian congress chose Prince Leopold of Saxe-Coburg as king. King William was not satisfied with the situation and invaded Belgium from August 2 to 12, 1831. He defeated the small Belgian force but was stopped by the French army (fighting did not reach war level). William I recognized the independence of Belgium only in April 1839.

Coding Decisions: Though limited fighting continued around Maastricht until a separate armistice was reached on January 20, 1831, Belgium's status had changed before then. With the great power recognition of Belgium on December 20, 1830, Belgium is considered to have become a state system member as of that date, thus it could no longer be engaged in intra-state fighting against the Netherlands. Thus this war is coded as ending on December 19, 1830.

Sources: Clodfelter (1992); Langer (1952); Phillips and Axelrod (2005); Richardson (1960).

INTRA-STATE WAR #517
First Polish War of 1831

Participants: Russia versus Polish nationalists.
Dates: February 7, 1831, to October 18, 1831.
Battle-related Deaths: Polish Nationalists: 20,000; Russia: 15,000.[58]
Initiator: Russia.
Outcome: Russia wins.
War Type: Civil for local issues.
Total System Member Military Personnel: Armed Forces of Russia: 826,000 (prewar); 851,000 (initial, peak, final).[59]
Theater Armed Forces: Armed Forces of Russia: 127,000 (initial); 250,000(peak); 70,000 (final).[60] Polish Nationalists: 53,000 (initial); 190,000 (peak).[61]

Antecedents: In the aftermath of the Napoleonic Wars, Russia entered a period of consolidation, or "Fortress Empire," in which it tried to solidify its hegemony over its peripheral regions through repressive measures.[62] In this vein, Russia had already engaged in two intra-state wars in the Caucasus (#500 and #507.5). Russian focus now shifted to the West to address issues in Poland. During the Napoleonic wars, the Duchy of Warsaw had fought on the side of the French. Consequently the Congress of Vienna divided Poland up among the victorious allies. The Duchy of Warsaw was enlarged and transformed into a Polish kingdom united with Russia. Russian Grand Duke Constantine (the brother of Czar Alexander I) was the de facto viceroy of the kingdom and served as commander in chief of the Polish Army and the Lithuanian Corps (a force of 69,000 troops in 1823). Upon the death of Czar Alexander in 1825, Constantine renounced his claims to the throne and retained his position in Poland under Czar Nicholas I. In general, the Poles resented Russian rule, and in December 1828, the secret Patriotic Society was formed within the Polish military, which began planning actions in pursuit of

Polish independence, including plans to assassinate Czar Nicholas. Their planning accelerated in the late summer and early fall of 1830, partially prompted by the success of the French rebellion in Paris (Intra-state War #513) and by Czar Nicholas's plan to utilize the Polish troops if necessary to suppress the French liberals. Czar Nicholas learned of the activities of the organization and ordered Grand Duke Constantine to begin court-martial processes against the conspirators.

The society then decided to start the revolution on the evening of November 29, 1830, and junior Polish army officers occupied public buildings. A number of difficulties hindered the revolt, including the unwillingness of anyone to take command. The grand duke, perceiving Polish actions as purely a Polish affair, did not intervene. The next day, the Polish Administrative Council became involved, dividing the Poles into two camps: the council that favored negotiations with the czar and the radicals favoring open revolution. Upon hearing of the events in Warsaw, Czar Nicholas responded on December 17, rejecting negotiations and demanding unconditional surrender. The *Sejm* (parliament) assembled, appointed Prince Michael Radziwill as the new commander in-chief, and voted on January 25, 1831 in favor of a revolution against the czar.

Narrative: Czar Nicholas ordered Field-Marshal Dybiez to form an army to crush the insurrection. The Russian army of 127,000 men crossed into Poland on February 5 and 6, 1831. Dybiez planned to use his numerically superior army to defeat the rebels across a wide front and divided the army into eleven columns. The rebels managed to assemble an army of 53,000. Though hampered by snow, the Russians advanced quickly, catching the rebels by surprise. The Russians won a few skirmishes, though the Poles did manage to win an engagement on February 14 against a division of Russian cavalry. The Russian army continued to advance toward Warsaw, and on February 17, two battles were fought. Though offering strong resistance, the two Polish divisions finally were compelled to retreat. The Polish command decided to concentrate all of its divisions on the Grochow plain outside the capital. The battle began on February 20 but then paused as the armies awaited reinforcements. The battle resumed on February 24, and though neither side achieved a decisive victory, the Polish forces were forced to retreat in heavy fighting. Fatalities were severe, with the Russians losing 10,000, while the Poles lost 7,000. The Russians established winter camps to allow their troops to arrest, which also enabled the rebels to rebuild their army.

The Russians planned to resume their offensive on April 4; however, the Polish nationalists decided to act first: on the night of March 30 to March 31, the rebels surprised the Russian Sixth corps and were able to break the Russian line. The Russians dispersed after losing about 13,000 soldiers. The Russians decided to retreat and regroup. The Poles were unable or unwilling to capitalize on their victory. The Russians resumed their offensive, winning the battle of Ostroleka from May 24 to May 26. On June 10, Dybiez died, leading to some confusion within the Russian army. The nationalists, led by Commander-in-Chief Skrzynecki, decided to launch two offensives, both of which failed. Field Marshal Ivan Paskevich arrived to take command of the Russian forces and switched strategies to move toward Warsaw from the north. Errors and hesitancy on the part of Skrzynecki led to his recall and replacement by General Dembinski. Dembinski ordered Polish forces to fall back toward Warsaw. After restoring his army to 80,000 men, Paskevich approached Warsaw on August 18. He attempted unsuccessfully to negotiate terms with the Poles. On September 6, the Russians attacked. After horrific losses, the Polish army abandoned Warsaw on September 8. The remaining 33,000 Polish troops retreated north (other units brought the total Polish army to 70,000 at this point).

Termination and Outcome: The Polish government was still unwilling to capitulate, and isolated combat continued into October. Many of the soldiers fled to Prussia or France, where they surrendered. Many of the deaths were due to disease. As a result of the war, the Polish constitution was suspended, and Poland became more integrated into the Russian empire. At least 80,000 Poles were captured and sent to Siberia.[63]

Coding Decisions: A number of sources refer to this war as the November Insurrection and begin it on November 29, 1830; our start date of February 5, 1831, represents the date when Russian troops crossed the border into Poland and armed conflict began. Similarly, though the Polish nationalists announced their intention to revolt, armed combat began after the Russian troops crossed into Poland, thus Russia is coded as initiating the war.

Sources: Brzozowski (1833); Clodfelter (2002); Curtiss (1965); Gnorowski (1839); Górka (1942); Grunwald (1955); Hordynsky (1832); LeDonne (2004); Leslie (1956); Morfill (1972); Phillips and Axelrod (2005); Puzyrewsky (1893); Rapport (2009); Reddaway (1941); Schiemann (1913); Stone (2006).

INTRA-STATE WAR #522
First Carlist War of 1834 to 1840

Participants: Spain, United Kingdom, France, and Portugal versus Carlists.
Dates: July 10, 1834, to June 2, 1840.
Battle-related Deaths: Spain: 65,000; Carlists: 60,000; France: 3,000; United Kingdom: 2,500; Portugal: 50.[64]
Initiator: Carlists.
Outcome: Spain, United Kingdom, France, and Portugal win.
War Type: Civil for central control.
Total System Member Military Personnel: Armed Forces of Spain: 60,000 (prewar); 110,000 (initial, peak); 79,000 (final). Armed Forces of France: 299,000 (prewar); 267,000 (initial); 446,000 (peak, final). Armed Forces of United Kingdom: 144,000 (prewar); 137,000 (initial); 168,000 (peak, final). Armed Forces of Portugal: 54,000 (prewar, initial, peak); 31,000 (final).[65]
Theater Armed Forces: Spanish Loyalists: 25,000 (initial);[66] 100,000 (peak); 80,000 (final).[67] United Kingdom (British Legion and Mercenaries), participating from July 10, 1835: 9,600 (initial);[68] 10,000 (peak).[69] France (French Foreign Legion), participating from July 10, 1835, to January 17, 1839: 6,432 (initial).[70] Portugal, participating from October 15, 1835, to February 15, 1836: [ ]. Carlists: 8,000 (prewar); 35,000 (initial, peak); 4,000 (final).[71]

Antecedents: Conflict between the liberal government and the royalists broke out in Spain in 1821 (Intra-state War #505). King Ferdinand VII appealed to the Holy Alliance for assistance, and France intervened, restoring the king to the throne in 1823 (Inter-state war #1). To avenge himself against his opponents, the king then launched a wave of killings that alienated many of his former supporters. Just before King Ferdinand died in September 1833, he set aside Salic law and named his two-year-old daughter Isabella as his heir instead of his brother Don Carlos. Young Isabella II succeeded to the Spanish throne, though her mother, Queen Maria Cristina, served as regent. Don Carlos claimed that he was the rightful heir and was supported by conservatives and traditionalists (mostly in the Basque and Navarre region), referred to as Carlists, while the supporters of the queen and Maria Cristina (mostly liberal and urban) were called Cristinos. Don Carlos declared his revolution on November 4, 1833, and immediately began gathering an army in the North under the leadership of Tomas Zumalacarregui. By the beginning of 1834, the Carlists had only 1,000 men and thus conducted only small-scale attacks (below war level) in the North, while Don Carlos went to England seeking assistance. Don Carlos returned to Spain via Paris, where he received funds from French legitimists, arriving at Elizondo in Navarre on July 9, 1834. Meanwhile, on April 22, 1834, Maria Cristina formed the Quadruple Alliance with Portugal, France, and Britain to gain assistance in the conflict. Britain sent 9,600 men of the British Legion, and France supplied 6,432 men of the French Legion in July 1835.

Narrative: By the time of Don Carlos's return, Zumalacarregui had amassed an army of 35,000 troops, and the rebels immediately went on the offensive, ambushing and slaughtering Cristino troops. Maria Cristina was faced with financial difficulties, a lack of leadership within her army, and the growing radical movement in the Chamber of Deputies, who tended to downplay the threat posed by the rebellion. On January 17, 1835, an army garrison in Madrid mutinied, and the government forces were unable to respond. This finally persuaded the government of the seriousness of the situation. In April 1835, command of government forces was handed to General Valdés. Valdés was beaten by Zumalacarregui in their first engagement on April 21. The ferocity of the fighting was such that the two generals finally signed an agreement providing that the lives of prisoners should be spared. Don Carlos then decided to attack Bilbao. On June 10, 1835, the artillery attack began. On June 14, two battalions of the Carlist infantry rashly marched against the garrison of 4,000 regulars, and most of the rebels were slaughtered. The next day, Zumalacarregui was wounded and died on June 23, though the Carlists continued to besiege the city.

Though Valdés was ready to retreat from Bilbao, Col. Baldomero Espartero argued that the city had to be relieved, and his leadership turned the tide of the war. In July 1835 the siege at Bilbao was raised by government forces, handing the Carlists their first major defeat. The arrival of the English and French Legions and the Portuguese auxiliary strengthened government forces and led to a Cristino victory at Terapegui in April 1836. In May, the Carlists attacked the allied headquarters at St. Sebastian, but their siege was broken by the bombardment by British ships and the arrival of the British reinforcements. The Carlists again besieged Bilbao in November 1836 but were defeated by the arrival of Espartero and his army of 18,000.

In 1837, the Cristino government was weakened by factional fighting in the Cortes between the moderates and the radicals, prompting Don Carlos to take advantage of the situation by launching an offensive with 20,000 troops against government forces (of 12,000) at Huesca, handing the government costly defeats on May 24 and June 2. The rebels then marched toward Madrid but were turned back by the arrival of Espartero with 20,000 reinforcements in September. The Carlists fled east back to their base at Morella. By 1838, government forces totaled 100,000 against 32,000 Carlists. That year, government forces launched several unsuccessful attacks against Morella. By 1839, the Carlists had lost hope. English Adm. John Hay attempted to negotiate a settlement between the Carlists and Cristinos, though neither side found the terms acceptable. Don Carlos made one last attempt to rally his forces, which was unsuccessful, persuading the rebels to accept terms. The Treaty of Vergara was signed on August 31, 1839, and the same day Don Carlos fled to France.

Termination and Outcome: Some Carlist resistance remained. The rebel stronghold at Morella finally was captured by the government forces on May 23, 1840. A small contingent of Carlists engaged in fighting as they escaped into France on June 2, 1840, ending the war. The Carlist cause would lead to another war in 1847 (Intra-state War #546).

Coding Decisions: This war is coded as an internationalized civil war due to the involvement of troops from the governments of the United Kingdom, France, and Portugal. The fatalities in this war were horrific due to the ferocity of combat, the slaughter of prisoners, and the spread of disease. In all, there were 140,000 combatant battle-deaths. The numbers of battle-deaths suffered by the British and French legions are estimates as their levels of desertions were high.

Sources: Bollaert (1870); Carr (1982); Clarke (1906); Clodfelter (1992); Harbottle and Bruce (1971); Holt (1967); Hume (1900); Phillips and Axelrod (2005); Urlanis (1960).

INTRA-STATE WAR #523
Second Murid War of 1834

Participants: Russia versus Murid Forces led by Hamza Bek, Sheik Shamil, and Tasho Hajji.
Dates: August 20, 1834, to October 27, 1834.
Battle-related Deaths: Russia: [ ]; Murids: [ ] Total Combatant Deaths: 1,000.
Initiator: Murids.
Outcome: Conflict continues at below-war level.
War Type: Civil for local issues.
Total System Member Military Personnel: Armed Forces of Russia: 900,000 (prewar); 784,000 (initial, peak, final).[72]
Theater Armed Forces: Armed Forces of Russia: 54,000 (prewar). Murids 15,000 (initial).[73]

Antecedents: In contrast to earlier wars against encroaching Russian domination in the Caucuses (Intra-state War #500 in 1818 and #507.5), the First Murid War (Intra-state War #511 in 1830) represented a different type of conflict, in which an armed religious group, the *Naqshbandi*, or Murids (disciples or warriors), engaged in a *gavazat* (*jihad* or holy war) to oppose Russian domination to live under *shari'a*. This First Murid War ended in 1832 with the Russian storming of the Murid stronghold at Gimrah and the killing of the Murid leader Ghazi Muhammad. This Second Murid war marks the continuation of the Murid opposition to Russian rule by two of Ghazi Muhammad's deputies, Hamza Bek (who became the second imam) and Sheikh Shamil (who would become the third imam). In 1833, Shamil had been injured during the attack on Gimrah and was too weak to assume leadership of the Murids. Thus Hamza Bek became the new, or second, Murid imam. Hamza Bek came from Hutsal in Avaria (or Avaristan), and as a teenager, he lived for a few years at the residence of the khan, where the khan's widow, Pakhu Bike, served as regent. Hamza Bek had led one of the contingents against the Russians at Chartalah in 1830. Having gone to fetch reinforcements, Hamza Bek was not in Gimrah at the time of the Murid defeat by the Russians. Learning of the death of Ghazi Muhammed, Hamza Bek made a decisive claim over the imamate in early 1833, which was supported by the mother of Ghazi Muhammad. Sheikh Shamil, after recovering from his wounds, also gave his support to, and became a close ally of, Hamza Bek.

Even so, the new imam was not in a strong position and began trying to gain support in the North Caucasian communities while also trying to negotiate a truce with the Russians. The talks collapsed, the Russians attempted to assassinate Hamza Bek and to foster a coalition against him among the Dagestani secular rulers who did not accept the imam's authority, and ultimately declared war on him. In October 1833, Hamza Bek and the Murids responded to this opposition militarily. That month, he had his first major victory over the people of Girgil, yet the conflict only reached war level in 1834, when Hamza Bek confronted Avaria (or Avaristitan).

Narrative: One of the major obstacles to Hamza Bek's leadership was the khanate of Avaria, which was subservient to, and in the pay of, the Russian government.[74] In the spring of 1834, Hamza Bek returned to his native village of Hutsal, not far from Khunzakh, the capital of Avaria, where he began agitating against the Avar rulers and their acceptance of Russian sovereignty and urging the people to revolt against them. At the beginning of August 1834, Hamza Bek gathered an army of 15,000 Murids and laid siege to Khunzakh, which marks the start of the war. On August 25, during negotiations to resolve the standoff, Hamza Bek ordered the deaths of two khans, sons of the regent Pakhu Bike. Hamza Bek then stormed Khunzakh, overwhelming the defenders. He ordered the killing of Pakhu Bike, after which Hamza assumed the position of the Avar khan. Conflict continued, and Hamza Bek suffered a defeat when he attacked nearby Tsoudakhar. Meanwhile, the Russians, under General Lanskoi, attacked and destroyed the village of Gimrah.

Hamza Bek's actions in Avaria earned him the disapproval of many Muslims, including Sheikh Shamil. Two brothers, Osman and Hajji Murad, disturbed by the murders of the khans, organized a conspiracy to kill Hamza Bek, On Friday, September 19, 1834, Hamza Bek, along with twelve disciples, entered the mosque for prayers, where he was attacked by the conspirators and killed. In the ensuing struggle, several of the conspirators and a number of the Murids also died. The remaining Murids retreated to the fortress, which was then set afire by Hajji Murad and his supporters, leading to the deaths of 70 of the 100 Murids.[75] This conflict within the Murids served to reinforce the authority of the traditional secular elites upon whom the Russian empire had depended.

Hajji Murad was elected as the new Avar ruler. He then accepted Russian citizenship and appealed to the Russian army for assistance. Russian Baron Grigorii Vladimirovish Rosen (the commander in chief of the Separate Caucasian Corps) sent a significant number of troops to Avaria. Many of the *jama'ats* (village confederations) affirmed their loyalty to the Russian tsar, while others supported the Murids. At this point, Shamil emerged as a candidate to lead the Murids. Shamil was related to the ruling house of Kazi-Kumuk, a powerful khanate in Dagestan. Shamil's reputation had been burnished when miraculously he had escaped Gimrah in 1832 by vaulting over ranks of Russian soldiers. At the age of thirty-seven, Shamil was chosen as the third imam. Shamil initially sought accommodation with Russia as long as *shari'a* could be practiced, but the Russians refused, and military conflict resumed. Most of the military operations were small-scale raids, and the support of the local population was crucial.

A Murid leader in Chechnya, Tasho Hajji, emerged as a challenger to Shamil, and he launched raids against the Russians as well. The Russians responded with punitive expeditions during which they destroyed villages and seized livestock and prisoners. The results were disastrous, with hundreds of settlements and thousands of people, mostly civilians, being massacred.[76] Ultimately the severity of the Russian attacks forced Tasho Hajji to align himself with Shamil.

Yet Chechnya played a secondary role in the struggle, while Avaristan remained the base of Russian support. The Russians again advanced toward Gimrah and initially captured the village fairly easily. However, Shamil then arrived with the Murids and retook the village from the superior Russian force, which experienced serious losses.[77] Upon hearing of the Russian defeat, Gen. Kluke von Klugenau set out with a second army toward Avaria. Destroying inhospitable villages along the way, the Russians entered into Khunzakh and established Aslan Khan as khan under Russian protection (though Hajji Murad remained as de facto ruler).[78]

Termination and Outcome: This phase of the war ended when the imam's guerrilla forces merely withdrew into the forest. Attacks continued at below-war levels. Shamil would resume his guerrilla war against the Russians two years later (see Intra-state War #530).

Coding Decisions: This war (similar to the First Murid War) is coded as starting with the Murid attack on Avaria because the khanate was seen as the secular government sanctioned and supported by the Russian central government. This war is a brief one, a time in which hostilities briefly flared to war level before declining again. Though specifics about battle-deaths are available only in a few instances, the number of troops involved and the number of engagements persuades us that there were at least 1,000 combatant deaths during this period. Battle deaths apparently did not reach war-level thresholds again until 1836 and the Third Murid War.

Sources: Baddeley (1908); Baumann (1993): Gammer (1992, 2006); King (2008); Mackie (1856); Schaefer (2011); Stone (2006); Zelkina (2000).

INTRA-STATE WAR #528
First Bosnian War of 1836

Participants: Ottoman Empire versus Bosnians.
Dates: 1836
Battle-related Deaths: Ottoman Empire: [ ]; Bosnians: [ ]; Total Combatant Deaths: 1,000.
Initiator: Bosnians.
Outcome: Ottoman Empire wins.
War Type: Civil for local issues (hereditary privileges, autonomy).
Total System Member Military Personnel: Armed Forces of the Ottoman Empire: 129,000 (prewar, initial, peak, and final).[79]
Theater Armed Forces: Total Combatants: 40,000. *Bosnian Kapetans:* 6,000 (initial, peak, final).[80]

Antecedents: Bosnia had been an independent country until the late fifteenth century, when it was conquered by the Ottoman Empire. The Ottomans created the *Kapetanate*, a system by which Bosnia was governed by forty-eight feudal lords (or *beys*) called *kapetans*, who ruled on behalf of the sultan. In 1835, the Ottoman government's reforms abolished the position of *kapetan* and replaced it with appointed officials. Although many *kapetans* were appointed to the new positions, some of those who were not rebelled.

Narrative: A few *kapetans* in western Bosnia rose against the government in the summer of 1836, led by Ali Fidaah Pasha. He assembled 6,000 troops and was successful in attacks against the local governments into the autumn. At that point, the Ottoman government sent 800 regulars from Anatolia plus a large Albanian detachment to subdue the rebellion. The rebels were ambushed and defeated in a gorge but reconcentrated and made a stand near Schebze. After a bloody battle that spilled over into the town itself, the rebels were again defeated. The rebels retreated to Bielina, where they were besieged by government forces. After a bombardment destroyed most of the town, the rebels surrendered on the condition that their lives were to be spared. It is unclear whether this promise was kept.

Termination and Outcome: The outcome of the war was a military victory by the government with a promise of limited amnesty. The government proceeded with the abolition of the *kapetan* system; the following year, another rising occurred, which was also suppressed. As it involved different *kapetans*, we treat it as a separate conflict (and find no evidence that 1,000 were killed). It was only in March 1850 when the Ottomans defeated the last of the Bosnian *beys*.

Coding Decisions: In terms of battle-deaths, Degenhardt reports that 3,000 were killed, but this figure probably includes civilian deaths as whole towns were destroyed. Richardson codes this war as a "3," which means 1,000 battle-deaths, which is the figure we are reporting here.[81]

Sources: *The Annual Register* (1837); Degenhardt (1987); Malcolm (1994); Palmer (1992); Richardson (1960); Von Sax (1913).

INTRA-STATE WAR #530
Third Murid War of 1836 to 1852

Participants: Russia versus Shamil-led Murids
Dates: July 6, 1836, to April 24, 1852.
Battle-related Deaths: Russia: 20,000; Murids: [ ].
Initiator: Russia.
Outcome: Stalemate.
War Type: Civil for local issues.
Total System Member Military Personnel: Armed Forces of Russia: 668,000 (prewar); 1,020,000 (initial, peak); 756,000 (final).[82]
Theater Armed Forces: Armed Forces of Russia: 2,500 (prewar); 30,000 (initial); 200,000 (peak).[83] Murids: 20,000 (peak).

Antecedents: Opposition to Russian rule in the Caucasus increasingly was expressed by the fundamentalist *Naqshbandi* (Sufi) religious movement and its Murids (or warriors). The first Murid imam Ghazi Muhammed had begun the call for *gazavat*, a *jihad* or holy war against both those who did not follow *shari'a* and the foreign invaders in 1830 (Intra-state War #511). After the deaths of Ghazi Muhammed and the second imam, Hamza Bek (Intra-state War #523), Sheik Shamil was chosen as the third imam, and he would continue the fight against the Russians from his base in Dagestan for another twenty-five years.

After a brief war in 1834 (Intra-state War #523), hostilities between the Russians and the Murids declined to below-war-level intensity as the Russians were preoccupied by problems in the western Caucasus (though Gammer argues that Shamil and Russian Gen. Franz Klüge-von-Klugenau had an agreement not to fight during this period).[84] Instead, in 1835 and 1836, Shamil had to confront the challenge of the claim to the imamate posed by Tasho Hajji in Chechnya. Initially, Shamil attempted to consolidate his support by uniting several hundred smaller political units into an overarching ruling structure. Meanwhile, Tasho Hajji continued raids against the Russian positions in Chechnya.

Narrative: The war began in the pattern of the two previous wars as low-level engagements, and in July 1836, Shamil's base at Gimrah was attacked three times, forcing him to move to Ashilta, which also was attacked twice after his arrival. Russian offensives, especially the destruction of Tasho Hajji's stronghold near Zandak on September 4, 1836, were sufficient to persuade Tasho Hajji to accept Shamil's authority. Shamil then urged the Chechens who lived in exposed areas to retreat into the forest and develop secure food supplies, while Shamil established his headquarters at the well-fortified village of Akhulgo, deep in the mountains of Dagestan. As the war spread, it would ultimately involve the entire populations of Chechnya, Ingushetia, and Dagestan.

In February 1837, Baron Grigorii Vladimirovish Rosen (the commander in chief in the Caucasus) and the Russians decided to launch a major offensive against Shamil in Dagestan and ordered Gen. Franz Klüge-von-Klugenau to prepare a battle plan. When Klugenau instead suggested negotiations with Shamil, he was given a medical leave and the assignment given to others. General Fesi's forces began with a string of successes, including building a fortress at Chunsach and driving Ali Bey, one of Shamil's Murids, out of the fortress at Akhulgo. He then marched with an army of eight battalions of regular troops and 12,000 local militia to relieve Russian forces being attacked by Shamil near Tiletli.[85] Shamil clearly was outnumbered by the united Russian forces, which also had artillery, which the Murids lacked. Though the initial Russian assault on the village failed, the Russians were finally able to succeed in capturing half of the town despite suffering serious losses. The Russians could not remain in their position for long due to a lack of provisions, yet they did not want to retreat, giving the appearance of a Murid victory. Thus General Fesi decided to negotiate with Shamil: the Russians required that Shamil take an oath of fealty to the tsar in exchange for which he would be allowed to keep possession of his territories. Though Shamil had no intention of being bound by the pledge, the Russians withdrew. General Fesi was rewarded for subduing Dagestan, while Shamil's reputation soared for facing down a superior force.

The Russians attempted only a few small expeditions in 1838, while Shamil augmented his army and rebuilt forts that had been destroyed by the Russians the previous year, including Akhulgo, where he stationed 15,000 of the best warriors. Under the new leadership of Evgenii Golovin, the Russian forces began a new campaign to subjugate Dagestan and Chechnya. At this point Shamil began to pursue a new tactic by seeking the support of the Ottoman sultan and the pasha of Egypt, Muhammed Ali. In May 1839, Lt. Gen. Ivan Grabbe led a force of 8,500 Russian troops against the Murids with the aim of capturing Shamil. After several defeats with heavy losses, Shamil's forces retreated to Akhulgo, which had been fortified strongly. By the time Grabbe's forces arrived, about 6,000 Murids faced 7,000 Russian troops. On June 12, 1839, the attack on Akhulgo began with Russian artillery, which destroyed many of the fortifications but had no impact on the underground defenses. The Russians attacked the fort unsuccessfully four times. The Russians then besieged the fortress for eighty days, and disease began to ravage both sides. Shamil sent his young son out to try to arrange a settlement, but the Russians demanded his complete surrender. The Russians attacked again on August 21; they overran the fortifications, and slaughtered most of the Murid force. The Russians suffered an additional 500 battle-deaths, while virtually the entire Murid army was destroyed. Only Shamil and a few followers escaped the carnage. Grabbe returned to Temir-Chan-Schura in triumph. The Russians now believed that they successfully had broken the back of the rebellion and expected no further uprisings as they consolidated their role in Chechnya as well.

The Russians then launched punitive expeditions into Chechnya. The harshness of these expeditions prompted the Chechens and Dagestanis to prepare for another offensive in 1840. The Murids went on the offensive, not only in the eastern Caucasus but in the West as well. In 1840, raiding parties of up to 12,000 warriors pillaged Georgia, and the Cherkes tribes attacked the Russian forts along the Black Sea. Shamil took refuge in Chechnya and began to rebuild his support in both Chechnya and Dagestan. Shamil decided to abandon the practice of defending a fortified village against a major attack, and he now concentrated on developing mobile guerrilla forces to ambush Russians. The Russians stuck with their strategy of trying to crush the resistance with major offensives. They therefore mounted successive expeditions into Chechnya during the early 1840s, with armies on both sides numbering in the tens of thousands but with greater losses each time and no conclusive victories. Thus, General Grabbe and his superior, Governor-General Golowin, were recalled, and the tsar banned any large-scale Russian offensives for the next two years.

This ban benefited Shamil, who launched two major offensives in September and November 1843 in which he conquered most of the Russian-controlled territories in Dagestan. In response, Tsar Nicholas sent a significant number of reinforcements to the Caucasus in the hope that a full-scale offensive in 1844 would redeem their losses, though no progress was made. In 1844, Count Mikhail Semyonovich Vorontsov took command, and he developed a plan to defeat the Muslim resistance by resettlement of the local population and clearing the forests. It took years, but this patient counterinsurgency plan chipped away at Shamil's support. Meanwhile, Vorontsov was ordered to undertake a major offensive at Dargo in the summer of 1845, throughout which the 18,000 Russians were attacked by Shamil's forces. The Russians ultimately captured and abandoned Dargo, and by the time their mission was over, they had lost more than 3,700 men.

Given his failure to capture Shamil, in 1846 Vorontsov shifted his focus back to Chechnya. To allow for more maneuverability, the Russians continued cutting down the Chechen forests. That same year, Shamil was successful in gathering a contingent of 20,000 horsemen that was able to ride quickly through the Russian line and destroy Cossack colonies. However, in 1847, Shamil's fortunes began to wane as the Russian counterinsurgency efforts began to succeed. Daring raids were conducted by one of Shamil's confederates, Hadji Mourád, against Shourá (the capital of Dagestan) in 1850 and Bouinakh in 1851, though they ultimately failed to have an impact on the Russians or the populace, and Hadji Mourád surrendered. Although Shamil continued his fight against the Russians, as the number of his Murids declined, so did the intensity of the conflict.

Termination and Outcome: As Russia's attention was shifting to the upcoming Crimean War (Inter-state War #22), the war against the Murids gradually slipped into a stalemate. In 1852 Hadji Mourád escaped from Russian captivity with a small group of supporters. On April 23, they were surrounded by a large party of militia. Though outnumbered 100 to 1, furious fighting by the Murids kept the militia at bay until the next day, when all the Murids were killed. Shamil continued his opposition to the Russians, though battles were rare after that point. In 1859, when Prince Baryatinski led 40,000 troops against Shamil, the imam had only 500 Murids fighting with him. Most of the Murids were slain, though Shamil was captured and sent to exile in Russia. The capture of Shamil did not end the uprisings against Russian rule in Chechnya and Dagestan. In the early 1860s, the Russians sent large armies to the regions to subdue the uprisings, but relatively little direct military combat took place as the rebels withdrew into the forests.[86]

Coding Decisions: As the level of fatalities fell below war level in 1852, we are coding the end of the last battle between the Russians and Hadji Mourád as the end of the war (April 24, 1852).

The number of fatalities during this long war was substantial. The Chechen population alone suffered approximately 50,000 fatalities (including civilians) during the years 1830 through 1860.[87] Aside from comments about Murid fatalities in a few conflicts, no total battle-death figures are available. Limited information about Russian battle-deaths suggests that more than 20,000 Russians soldiers were killed.[88]

Sources: Baddeley (1908); Baumann (1993); Clodfelter (2002); Gammer (1992, 2006); King (2008); Mackie (1856); Schaefer (2011); Stone (2006).

INTRA-STATE WAR #539

Nish Uprising of 1841 (aka Bulgarian Revolt of 1841)

Participants: Ottoman Empire versus Nish villagers.
Dates: April 6, 1841, to April 27, 1841.
Battle-related Deaths: Ottoman Empire: [ ]; Nish villagers, Bulgarians, and *Haiduks* (brigands): [ ]; Total Combatant Deaths: 1,000. (See Coding Decisions.)
Initiator: Nish villagers.
Outcome: Ottoman Empire wins.
War Type: Civil for local issues (taxes, military presence).
Total System Member Military Personnel: Armed Forces of the Ottoman Empire: 137,000 (prewar); 145,000 (initial, peak, final).[89]
Theater Armed Forces: Armed Forces of the Ottoman Empire and Albanian irregulars: 2,000 (initial); 16,000 (peak). Nish villagers, Bulgarians, and *Haiduks* (brigands): hundreds (initial); 15,000 (peak, final).[90]

Antecedents: The Ottoman Empire promulgated a series of reforms in a period known as the *Tanzimat* (1839–1876), which were designed to modernize and centralize Ottoman power and revenue. Initially introduced in the Edict of Gülhane of 1839, the reforms included a reorganization of the financial system, including the introduction of paper bank notes and a new system of taxation with salaried tax collectors, along with a new system of forced military conscription. These reforms were partially a response to the growing incursions by the great powers into the region (as evidenced in the Greek War of Independence: Intra-state War #506, 1821 to 1828). Toward the end of 1840, Sabri Mustafa Pasha, the governor of Nish (Niš, now southern Serbia) began to implement plans for the new tax. When the Bulgarians claimed that the tax was too high, the central government quartered troops on them until arrears were paid off. The abuses of the soldiers appear to have triggered this rebellion. In 1841, two Bulgarian leaders, Miloïe and Gavra, visited Serbia seeking military assistance for a revolt. In the end all they received were some arms and gunpowder, with which they resolved to revolt anyway. In one last attempt at peaceful resolution, they sent delegates to the Sultan to plead their case; these were arrested en route and nearly executed.

Narrative: On April 6, 1841, several hundred people rebelled in one village; the word quickly spread to neighboring villages, and hundreds more were recruited. The rebels overpowered the garrisons in their villages, forcing Sabri Mustafa Pasha to call upon the services of 2,000 Albanian irregulars to suppress the revolt. The rebels entrenched themselves in the defile of Kotna Bogaz, having been reinforced by rebels fleeing the pashalik of Vidin. The Albanians began to plunder and burn villages in an effort to stamp out the insurgency, but this appears only to have increased rebel recruitment. Thousands of refugees fled into Serbia, while others fled into the mountains. Some 2,000 cavalry pursued the rebels into the mountains but were virtually wiped out by the rebels. One account, probably exaggerated, states that only 30 escaped the rebels. In any case, it is clear that substantial casualties were suffered by the cavalry.

Wishing to put a stop to the pillaging of villages, the rebels assembled an army and began more conventional operations. They drove government forces out of Corvingrad and Derbend and then took the fort of Ak-Palanka (garrisoned by 6,000 Albanians) by surprise. Miloïe then besieged Nish with a peasant army of 10,000. Some 6,000 Albanians marched to relieve the siege. The two forces met at the village of Leskovats. The government was victorious, killing at least 300 rebels. The rebels retreated, and some of their leaders, including Miloïe, were cut off and surrounded. While Miloïe committed suicide, the rest managed to cut their way through to escape. In only three weeks, the rebels had been militarily defeated.

Termination and Outcome: The Ottoman government now responded to the rebellion with a policy of conciliation. Sabri Mustafa Pasha was dismissed, and a delegation was sent to Sophia to hear the rebels' demands—and to bribe as many of their leaders as possible. The policy was successful; without major policy change, the government dissolved the rebellion. The outcome of the war was a government military victory with a promise of amnesty for the defeated insurgents and the promise of some cosmetic concessions (which were, in any case, ignored). Most rebels took advantage of the amnesty. About 600 to 1,500 crossed into Wallachia, and later attempted to renew the rebellion, but were defeated by Wallachian troops.

Coding Decisions: While the accounts of thousands of government fatalities sound exaggerated, it is likely that the government and rebels lost at least 1,000 killed, given the number of battles, sizes of the forces involved, and descriptions of the combat.[91]

Sources: Aksan (2007); Pinson (1975); Ranke (1853); Spencer (1851).

INTRA-STATE WAR #540

Second Bosnian War of 1841

Participants: Ottoman Empire versus Bosnians.
Dates: 1841.
Battle-related Deaths: Ottoman Empire: [ ]; Bosnians: [ ]; Total Combatant Deaths: 1,000.
Initiator: Bosnians.
Outcome: Ottoman Empire wins.
War Type: Civil for local issues.
Total System Member Military Personnel: Armed Forces of Ottoman Empire: 137,000 (prewar); 145,000 (initial, peak, final).[92]
Theater Armed Forces: Bosnians rebels: 16,000 (peak).

Antecedents: In the First Bosnian war (Intra-state War #528), the Bosnian Kapetanate (or local administrators) revolted against the Ottomans when their positions were abolished in Ottoman reforms in 1836 and 1837. Wider unrest among Bosnian Muslims followed the *Tanzimat* reforms, launched in the Gülhane Decree, which offered equality to Christians and Jews.

Narrative: The Second Bosnian war was precipitated in Travnik, where the governor was driven out of the city in 1840. The following year, the Ottomans sent an army to suppress the rebellion.

Termination and Outcome: The outcome was an Ottoman victory. Opposition continued, leading to another Ottoman expedition, led by Omer Lutfi Pasha, that defeated the Bosnian *beys* at Lake Jezero in March 1850.

Coding Decisions: Richardson codes this war as a "3?," which means approximately 1,000 battle deaths, which is reported here.

Sources: Palmer (1992); Richardson (1960); Von Sax (1913).

INTRA-STATE WAR #546

Second Carlist War of 1847 to 1849

Participants: Spain versus Carlists.
Dates: May 17, 1847, to April 30, 1849.
Battle-related Deaths: Carlists: 7,000; Spain: 3,000.
Initiator: Carlists.
Outcome: Spain wins.
War Type: Civil for central control.
Total System Member Military Personnel: Armed Forces of Spain: 121,000 (prewar, initial, peak); 118,000 (final).[93]
Theater Armed Forces: Armed Forces of Spain: 40,000 (initial); 50,000 (peak). Carlists: 4,000 (initial); 10,000 (peak).

Antecedents: Just before Spain's King Ferdinand VII died in September 1833, he set aside Salic law and named his two-year-old daughter Isabella as his heir instead of his brother Don Carlos. Young Isabella II succeeded to the Spanish throne, though her mother, Queen Maria Cristina, served as regent. Don Carlos claimed that he was the rightful heir and was supported by conservatives and traditionalists (mostly in the Basque and Navarre region), referred to as Carlists; while the supporters of the Queen and Maria Cristina (mostly liberal and urban) were called Cristinos. The First Carlist War (Intra-state War #523) in 1835 had involved Don Carlos and his Carlist or royalist followers trying to seize the throne of Spain from Regent Maria Cristina, who was supported by the United Kingdom, France, and Portugal. The Carlists were defeated, and Don Carlos went into exile.

Don Carlos, who had been proposed as a husband for Queen Isabella by King Ferdinand, tried unsuccessfully to arrange a marriage between Queen Isabella and his eldest son, Don Carlos II. The Cortes was persuaded to declare the thirteen-year-old Isabella of age, which it did in 1843, and Queen Isabella II acceded to the throne. In 1845, Don Carlos renounced his claim to the Spanish throne in favor of his eldest son, Don Carlos II (also known as Carlos VI and count of Montemolin). Gaining the throne for Don Carlos II now became the goal of the royalist Carlists.

Narrative: The Carlists began their revolt with a series of guerrilla attacks to seize money from the government in 1846. No major fighting took place until the next year. The intensity of the attacks increased after May 17, 1847, when a Carlist leader, a priest called Tristany, was captured and executed. The government, which was distracted by the conflict between its moderate and liberal factions, had difficulty confronting the rebels. When Marqués del Duero took command of the government forces, he made little headway against the Carlists, who were primarily located in the northeast province of Catalonia, even though the government had 40,000 troops at its disposal compared to 4,000 for the rebels.

During the fall of 1847, Isabella decided to confront the divisions within the government. She recalled Ramón Maria de Narváez to resume his position as prime minister, and he was given a free hand to restore order within the government within the royal palace and within the military. On March 23, 1848, Narváez dissolved parliament and began to govern under martial law. On the military front, General Pavia had assumed command of the army in January 1848 and issued an appeal for the citizens to join the conflict. The Carlists issued a similar appeal, and Gen. Ramón Cabrera returned to Catalonia from France, and General Alzáa took command of the Carlist forces in the Basque provinces. The Carlists' attempt to rally their supporters from the last Carlist war in the mountains failed, and Alzáa was captured and shot on July 3, 1848. Cabrera held out for eight months in northeast Spain, where his army increased from 4,000 to about 10,000 and engaged in several major engagements with 50,000 government troops. In April 1849, Don Carlos II attempted to return to Spain from France, but was detained by the French, and so never joined the war. Without him, the war ended with a Carlist defeat as Cabrera fled to England.

Termination and Outcome: This war ended in a government victory. The Carlist cause endured and would lead to a third war in 1872 (Intra-state War #597).

Coding Decisions: The most commonly reported fatality statistic is 10,000 deaths. Because most of the fighting took place in more remote areas, it is likely that the deaths are predominantly combatants, though Phillips and Axelrod indicate that the figure includes a large number of civilians. Small and Singer reported 3,000 battle-deaths suffered by Spain, which are retained here.[94]

Sources: Bollaert (1870); Clarke (1906); Godechot (1971); Holt (1967); Phillips and Axelrod (2005); Smith (1965).

INTRA-STATE WAR #547
Second Two Sicilies War of 1848 to 1849

Participants: Two Sicilies versus Liberals.
Dates: January 12, 1848, to January 29, 1848, and August 15, 1848, to May 15, 1849.
Battle-related Deaths: Two Sicilies: 1,500; Liberals: [ ].
Initiator: Liberals.
Outcome: Two Sicilies win.
War Type: Civil for central control.
Total System Member Military Personnel: Armed Forces of Two Sicilies: 47,000 (prewar); 49,000 (initial, peak); 46,000 (final).[95]

Theater Armed Forces: Armed Forces of Two Sicilies: 5,000 (initial); 25,000 (peak). Liberals: 25,000 (peak).

Antecedents: During 1848, another series of reform revolutions that involved liberal opposition to monarchical rule rose throughout most of Europe and parts of Latin America (in what some call the Spring of Nations). Within Europe, major rebellions occurred in the Italian states, France, and the Austrian empire (and the kingdom of Hungary). Though tens of thousands of workers and reformers were killed, in most cases the conflicts produced few enduring changes. Because there is little concrete evidence of coordination among the rebelling groups, and because the rebellions occurred in dispersed locations, in different circumstances, with different goals, and against different states, they are considered as five separate wars here. A number of the rebellions included little actual armed combat and thus are not included here. The first of the wars that erupted in 1848 occurred in January in the kingdom of Two Sicilies (which encompassed the island of Sicily and the southern half of the Italian peninsula).

During the earlier (1820) reform war in the kingdom of Two Sicilies (Intra-state War #502), the liberals had revolted against King Ferdinand II, seeking reforms and a constitutional monarchy like those in the Spanish Constitution of 1812. The king secured the assistance of an Austrian army to defeat the liberals in 1821, after which he dismissed the parliament and established a repressive regime, targeting the liberals and the *carbonari*, the members of a secret organization favoring reform. Such measures reduced the numbers of the king's supporters: Ferdinand had the support of the army and government officials but had lost the majority of the elites and the Church. In Sicily in particular, the increase in the number of large landowners also contributed to the development of the *squadre* (an early *mafia*), both of which posed economic challenges to the king's authority. The growing economic problems contributed to working-class unhappiness with the government, and demonstrations inspired by the liberals broke out in Sicily in September 1847.

Narrative: The revolt began at Palermo in Sicily on January 12, 1848, which happened to be King Ferdinand's birthday. Armed citizens, including the *squadre*, gathered and began to attack the government's garrison. The government forces bombarded the city, and by the end of the day, 36 people had been killed. Violence spread throughout the island, and within days the only government forces were those left in the garrison at Messina. The rebels formed a provisional government led by Ruggero Sèttimo. The king responded by sending ships with 5,000 troops toward Messina. News of the revolt spread to the mainland. Liberal leader Carlo Poerio was released from prison, and he organized a gathering of 25,000 liberals and peasants in front of the palace on January 27. The rebels in Sicily had demanded a new constitution, while some of the intelligentsia in Naples also hoped that the rebellion would lead to Italian unification. The king, unable to get Austrian assistance at this point, promised on January 29, 1848, to grant a constitution (which was published on February 10) modeled on France's 1830 charter. Fighting ceased, but news of the king's capitulation prompted demonstrations in Rome and the creation of a new constitution by King Charles Albert of Piedmont on March 4.

Back in Sicily, on April 13, 1848, Ruggero Sèttimo declared the independence of Sicily, and Sèttimo served as head of state of Sicily's liberal regime for more than a year. In August, King Ferdinand dispatched an army of 20,000 under the command of Gen. Carlo Filangieri to Sicily to rescue the Royal Garrison at Messina. An accompanying naval fleet heavily shelled the Sicilian city of Messina from September 1 to September 6, despite the fact that the city had surrendered on September 3, which earned Ferdinand the nickname "Re Bomba" or King Bomb. By September 6, more than two-thirds of the city was in ruins. However, conflict in the lowlands continued, and on March 13, 1849, the king ordered the army to subdue the riots and dissolve the parliament.

The government army advanced, conquering the island and destroying the revolutionary movement by May 15, 1849.

Termination and Outcome: The outcome was a victory by the government of King Ferdinand. Ferdinand continued his repressive policies, arresting dissidents and prompting many to go into exile. Similar conflicts in 1848 in Milan (Intra-state War #551) and Sardinia (Inter-state War #10), and in 1849 in the Papal States (involving Two Sicilies—Inter-state War #16) all contributed to the movement toward Italian unification (Inter-state War #28).

Coding Decisions: After the initial outbreak of the war, King Ferdinand accepted the constitution, and this agreement marks an end to the fighting. Though some riots took place, armed combat did not resume until the invasion of Sicily, so this period is coded as a temporary interruption or pause in the war.

Sources: Davis (2006); Godechot (1971); King (1899); Langer (1952); Orsi (1914); Rapport (2009); Stearns (2001).

INTRA-STATE WAR #549

Second French Insurrection of 1848

Participants: France versus Republicans.
Dates: February 22, 1848, to February 24, 1848, and April 26, 1848, to June 26, 1848.
Battle-related Deaths: Republicans: 1,500; France: 1,100.[96]
Initiator: Republicans.
Outcome: France wins.
War Type: Civil for central control.
Total System Member Military Personnel: Armed Forces of France: 394,000 (prewar); 387,000 (initial, peak, final).[97]
Theater Armed Forces: Armed Forces of France: 119,900 (initial—regular troops, municipals, and National Guard); 40,000 (final).[98] Republicans: 50,000 (peak, final).[99]

Antecedents: This is the second of the wars that broke out in Europe during the Spring of Nations of 1848, a series of reform revolutions that involved liberal opposition to monarchical rule. In the first war, beginning in January (Intra-state War #547 in Two Sicilies), King Ferdinand was forced to accept a liberal constitution. News about the king's capitulation spread to France, where republicans had been working for political reform. King Louis Philippe had been installed as a result of the liberal revolution of 1830 (Intra-state War #513), yet by 1848, there was a general feeling that his government had failed to solve the country's problems, a feeling that was shared by both moderate republicans and radicals. The republicans scheduled a demonstration against the regime for February 22, 1848.

Narrative: Despite attempts to derail the demonstration, the radical republicans insisted that it be held. On February 22, the crowds gathered and became emboldened as they marched toward the Chamber of Deputies to demand reform. Violence erupted, and fighting soon spread throughout the city as the insurgents armed themselves with makeshift weapons and stolen guns. That night barricades were built throughout the city, and attacks were launched against the municipals (police). The next day, though the king resisted concessions, he did remove First Minister Françoise Pierre Guillaume Guizot from office. As a celebratory crowd marched toward Guizot's lodgings, 200 soldiers blocked the boulevard, and in the ensuing melee, five people were killed. On February 24 the government dispatched troops throughout the city, while many National Guard units joined the revolutionaries. The rebels soon occupied the Tuileries Palace. King Louis Philippe finely abdicated on February 24 in favor of his ten-year-old grandson and fled to Britain. A provisional government was established, and the moderate republicans were willing to cease the rebellion at this point; however, the radicals continued to oppose what they felt were insufficient reforms.

In the elections on April 23, the vast majority of the deputies chosen were moderates: the results destroyed the radicals' hopes for democratic and peaceful reform. The radicals demonstrated against the election results on April 26, and the National Guard charged the crowd, provoking a full-scale insurrection in some of the provinces. In Paris, on May 15, most of the recognized leftist leaders were arrested, leading to the conflict of the June Days. On June 22, 800 protesters marched through Paris, and protests gathered adherents so that the Paris military garrison was put on a state of alert. On June 23, about 8,000 workers joined the protests, and by the end of the day, almost all of eastern Paris was held by the insurgents (whose numbers have been estimated at between 40,000 and 50,000) who confronted 25,000 regular troops and 15,000 mobile guard. The barricades were attacked by the National Guard, and its superior weapons ensured that it would prevail. Many of the insurgents were killed as fighting continued to June 26.

Termination and Outcome: The message of the government victory in this war was that revolutionary traditions could be defeated, a message that motivated conservative groups in some of the other revolutions during this period.

Coding Decisions: After the king abdicated on February 24 and moderates agreed to the creation of the provisional government, there was a pause in the fighting, which has been coded as an interruption in the war.

Sources: Bodart (1916); Cayley (1856); Clodfelter (2002); Godechot (1971); Phillips and Axelrod (2005); Rapport (2009); Robertson (1952).

INTRA-STATE WAR #550
Viennese Revolt of 1848

Participants: Austria versus Liberal Viennese.
Dates: March 13, 1848, to March 15, 1848, and October 6, 1848, to October 31, 1848.
Battle-related Deaths: Liberal Viennese: 3,000; Austria: 241.[100]
Initiator: Liberal Viennese.
Outcome: Austria wins.
War Type: Civil for central control.
Total System Member Military Personnel: Armed Forces of Austria: 317,000 (prewar); 409,000 (initial, peak, final).[101]
Theater Armed Forces: Armed Forces of Austria: 10,000 (initial, peak). Liberal Viennese: [].

Antecedents: This is the third of the wars that broke out in Europe during the Spring of Nations of 1848, a series of reform revolutions that involved liberal opposition to monarchical rule. News of Two Sicilies King Ferdinand acceding to a constitution (Intra-state War #547) and of the abdication of French King Louis Philippe (Intra-state War #549) reached Vienna and Austrian chancellor and foreign minister Prince Klemens von Metternich on February 29, 1848. Austria's Hapsburg Empire was a particular target of liberal condemnation because of its repressive measures internally and its suppression of liberal movements in Italy (Intra-state Wars #502 and #503). Metternich soon also heard of the increasing demands of the Hungarian Diet for greater autonomy. The Austrian *Staatskonferenz* (that served as the regent for Emperor Ferdinand) began discussing possible concessions, though Metternich advocated resisting liberal reform. Meanwhile, the news of the initial successes of liberal movements also reached Viennese university students, who were energized to press for liberal reforms in Austria as well.

Narrative: On the morning of March 13, university students (numbering 4,000) joined by local workers gathered to hear speakers urging action to ensure liberal reforms, including the speech delivered by Lajos Kossuth in the Hungarian Diet demanding parliamentary government for Hungary. The liberals then began marching toward the Estates (which was in session) to present a petition to the government. When denied entry, the protestors attempted to break down the doors. The government then ordered its soldiers to disperse the crowd. The liberals, now armed with makeshift weapons, were fired upon by the troops. Violence spread throughout the city, directed against both Emperor Ferdinand I and Metternich. At least thirty Viennese were killed. As a concession to the liberals, the emperor demanded the resignation of Metternich (who fled to London). Two days later, the promise of a constitution was announced, and the jubilation with which that announcement was received served to dampen armed conflict for a time. The attention of the government also was devoted to a revolt in Milan (Intra-state War #551); uprisings in Kraków (April 25–26) and Prague (June 11–18); and the start of the war with Hungary in September (Intra-state War #554).

Over the summer, the tide was turning back toward the conservatives, who tried to stop the liberalization process. In early October, the rebellion was revived, and the liberals returned to the barricades. A 10,000-man army returned from Prague and marched into Vienna, and by the end of the month, the rebellion had been quashed.

Termination and Outcome: Though the war ended in a government victory, ultimately Emperor Ferdinand I succumbed to liberal pressures and abdicated in favor of his nephew Franz Joseph on December 2, 1848.

Coding Decisions: Small and Singer originally coded one war of the Austrians against liberals throughout the Austrian empire. It is coded here as three separate wars. Because the revolt in Vienna had a different goal than the others (for central control), it is coded individually. Because the uprisings in Milan and Hungary are in disparate locations, and there seems to be no real coordination between the rebels in the two cases, they are also coded here as separate wars. The uprisings in Kraków and Prague appear to have involved relatively little armed conflict and thus are not coded as wars.

Sources: Bodart (1916); Cayley (1856); Clodfelter (2002); Droz (1957); Godechot (1971); Macartney (1968); Maurice (1887); Phillips and Axelrod (2005); Rapport (2009); Sorokin (1937).

INTRA-STATE WAR #551
Milan Five Day Revolt of 1848

Participants: Austria versus Milan Liberals.
Dates: March 18, 1848, to March 23, 1848.
Battle-related Deaths: Austria: 600; Milan liberals: 430.[102]
Initiator: Milan Liberals.
Outcome: Transformed into Inter-state War #10.
War Type: Civil for local issues.
Total System Member Military Personnel: Armed Forces of Austria: 317,000 (prewar); 409,000 (initial, peak, final).[103]
Theater Armed Forces: Armed Forces of Austria: 12,000 (initial, peak).[104] Milan Liberals: 15,000 (initial).[105]

Antecedents: This is the fourth of the wars that broke out in Europe during the Spring of Nations of 1848, a series of reform revolutions that involved liberal opposition to monarchical rule. The Treaty of Utrecht in 1713 had confirmed Austrian control over Lombardy and its capital, Milan. Under Napoleon's occupation after 1796, Milan was the capital of the Cisalpine Republic and later the kingdom of Italy. After the defeat of Napoleon, Lombardy (including Milan) was returned to Austrian control. Further south, the kingdom of Two Sicilies was ruled by the Austrian-supported King Ferdinand II. Liberals in both Milan and Two Sicilies chafed against the monarchical regimes. The first violent conflict arose when young nobles in Milan decided to hurt Austria economically and organized a boycott of tobacco and demonstrations, starting on January 1, 1848. The Austrian viceroy of Lombardy and Venetia, Archduke Joseph of Austria, ordered Austrian soldiers, under the command of Gen. Joseph Radetzky, to disperse the crowd. A scuffle ensued in which six civilians were killed and fifty wounded.[106] News of liberals in Two Sicilies revolting against King Ferdinand on January 12, the king's acceding to liberal demands for a constitution on January 29 (Intra-state War #547), and the abdication of French King Louis Philippe of France on February 24 (Intra-state War #549) prompted increasing unrest among the liberals in Milan. Martial law was declared on February 25.

Meanwhile in Austria, Chancellor and Foreign Minister Prince Klemens von Metternich had become concerned with the events in Milan and, on February 21, had sent Count Joseph von Hübner as an emissary, arriving in Milan on March 5. The situation deteriorated as liberals were encouraged by the news of Metternich's fall on March 15, and Radetzky prepared his army for combat.

Narrative: On March 18, a gathering of 15,000 Milanese liberals marched against the Austrian barracks. They gathered weapons and built barricades throughout the city. Radetzky and his well-armed troops spread out and engaged in fierce urban fighting. The liberals established a provisional government and arrested Hübner on March 21. The Austrian barracks fell, and after fighting on March 22, the soldiers began to withdraw from the city. In the meantime, the Milanese liberals appealed to the king of the nearby kingdom of Sardinia for assistance.

Termination and Outcome: The king of Sardinia was Charles Albert, who desired to lead the movement to unite Italy and eliminate Austrian influence. On March 23, he declared war on Austria and took over the bulk of the fighting from the Milanese.

Coding Decisions: This intra-state war ends as the fighting is transformed into Inter-state War #10, which would bring together Sardinia, Tuscany, and Modena in their fight against Austria, which ended in Austrian victory in 1849.

Sources: Clodfelter (2002); Macartney (1968); Phillips and Axelrod (2005); Rapport (2009).

INTRA-STATE WAR #554
Hungarian War of 1848 to 1849

Participants: Austria and Russia versus Hungary.
Dates: September 11, 1848, to August 11, 1849.
Battle-related Deaths: Austria: 45,100; Hungary: 45,000; Russia: 14,500. (See Coding Decisions.)
Initiator: Austria-sponsored Croatia.
Outcome: Austria and Russia win.

War Type: Civil for local issues.
Total System Member Military Personnel: Armed Forces of Austria: 317,000 (prewar); 409,000 (initial, peak); 408,000 (final).[107] Armed Forces of Russia: 803,000 (prewar); 526,000 (initial); 699,000 (peak, final).[108]
Theater Armed Forces: Armed Forces of Austria (including Croatian Army): 18,000 (prewar in Hungary); 53,000 (initial—Croatian attack); 170,000 (peak).[109] Armed Forces of Russia, participating from June 17, 1849: 190,000 (initial); 360,000 (peak).[110] Armed Forces of Hungary: 152,000 (peak); 22,000 (final).[111]

Antecedents: This is the fourth of the wars that broke out in Europe during the Spring of Nations of 1848, a series of reform revolutions that involved liberal opposition to monarchical rule. After a period of Ottoman rule, the kingdom of Hungary had come under the rule of the Austrian Hapsburgs, though Hungary maintained its own parliament (diet) and viceroy of Hungary. In 1825, Hungary had entered the Reform Period, in which liberals sought more protections for individual liberties. In the 1847 election, the moderate and radical liberals united in a platform called the Ten Points (of expanded liberties), and they won control of the diet. Though conservatives considered dissolving the diet, news of the 1848 liberal uprisings in Two Sicilies and France (Intra-state Wars #547 and #549) spread to Hungary by March 1, 1848. At a meeting of the Lower House of the Diet on March 3, Louis Kossuth pronounced a rousing attack on the Hapsburg regime and called for a democratic constitution. On March 14, Archduke Stephen, the viceroy of Hungary, heard news of Austrian Chancellor Metternich's fall (Intra-state War #550). He called a meeting of the Upper House of the Diet that agreed that Hungary should demand a separate government. A delegation of 150 Hungarians, including Kossuth, boarded ships to cruise to Vienna. On March 17, Austria gave Hungary its own government, though still under Austrian auspices, with Stephen as the plenipotentiary to the emperor. Back in Budapest, radicals issued a new set of demands, the Twelve Points, which were approved by the diet as the April Laws, which created a democratic government.

Meanwhile, Austria was confronted by an uprising in Milan (Intra-state War #551) that evolved into the Austro-Sardinian War of 1848 to 1849 (Inter-state War #10). Thus Austria had limited resources to deal with Hungary's growing independence movement. Instead, Austria encouraged Croatia, which was a dependency of Hungary, to launch its own revolt against Hungarian control. Croatia declared its separation from Hungary on April 19, 1848.

Narrative: A Croatian army led by Count Josip Jelačić invaded Hungary on September 11, 1848. Hungary issued a call for volunteers, and the two armies met near Lake Velence on September 29, but Jelačić, realizing the superiority of the opposing forces, used a cease-fire to move his troops toward Vienna. On October 1, Emperor Ferdinand dissolved the Hungarian Diet and reappointed Jelačić the commander of all troops in Hungary. Given the revival of the liberal uprising in Vienna on October 6 (Intra-state War #550), Jelačić moved his troops to join the Austrian forces at the capital. The Hungarian army, heeding a call for assistance from the Viennese, sent troops under the command of General Móga into Austria, where they were defeated by an army led by Jelačić on October 30.

On December 2, 1848, Emperor Ferdinand I abdicated in favor of his nephew, Franz Joseph. Austrian forces went on the offensive, entering into Hungary and defeating Hungarian troops at Parndorf on December 16. The Hungarian government fled to Debrecen, and Austrian forces captured Budapest on January 5, 1849. The Hungarian army regrouped and unsuccessfully tried to recapture the capital on February 26 and February 27. They were able to defeat Austrian forces in several engagements, forcing the Austrians to leave Hungary in the early spring. The Austrians then appealed to Russia for assistance. In June 1849, the Russians intervened on the side of the Austrians, and the Hungarians were defeated in a string of engagements. On August 9, 1849, the Austrian forces defeated the Hungarian army at the Battle of Temesván. Two days later, 22,000 Hungarians surrendered.

Termination and Outcome: The war was a victory for Austria and Russia. Hungary was stripped of its power.

Coding Decisions: This war was by far the deadliest of the 1848 Spring of Nations wars. The battle-death figures for Austria include 16,600 killed or wounded (which using the 3:1 ratio of casualties to deaths is

4,125 deaths) plus 41,000 who died from disease rounds to 45,100. Russian battle-deaths include 903 killed and 13,554 dead of disease, which rounds to 14,500. Estimates for Hungarians deaths are in the range of 45,000.[112]

Sources: Albrecht-Carrié (1958); Bodart (1916); Clodfelter (2002); Curtiss (1965); Headley (1852); Macartney (1968); Phillips and Axelrod (2005); Rapport (2009).

INTRA-STATE WAR #554.3

Third Bosnian War of 1850 to 1851 (aka Great Bosnian Uprising, Ömer Pasha's Campaign of 1850 to 1851)

Participants: Ottoman Empire versus Bosnian and Montenegrin *Beys.*
Dates: August 1850 to April 1851.
Battle-related Deaths: Ottoman Empire: [ ]; Bosnians and Montenegrins *Bey:* [ ]; Total Combatant Deaths: 4,000
Initiator: Ottoman Empire.
Outcome: Ottoman Empire wins.
War Type: Civil for local issues (autonomy).
Total System Member Military Personnel: Armed Forces of the Ottoman Empire: 140,000 (prewar); 145,000 (initial); 150,000 (peak, final).[113]
Theater Armed Forces: Armed Forces of the Ottoman Empire: 10,000 (initial). Bosnian and Montenegrins Beys: 6,000 (initial); 25,000 (peak).[114]

Antecedents: The Ottoman Empire continued to attempt to impose administrative reforms in Bosnia. The Ottomans created the *Kapetanate*, a system by which Bosnia was governed by forty-eight feudal lords (or *beys*) called *kapetans*, who ruled on behalf of the sultan. In 1835, the Ottoman government's reforms abolished the position of *kapetan* and replaced it with appointed officials. Many *kapetans* were appointed to the new positions, some of those who had not rebelled in 1836 (Intra-state War #528). Such reform measures continued in the *Tanzimat* era, beginning in 1839, and the *kapetans* who had not been appointed to the new administrative positions were seemingly always ready to revolt to oppose reforms.

In 1849, a revolt of disaffected Bosnian Muslim notables broke out, led by Ali Kieditch. The rebellion's fortunes peaked in the spring of 1850, as the government was distracted by a rising in neighboring Bulgaria. The rebels asked for and received some assistance from Montenegrins. Later that year, the Ottomans turned their attention to the rebellion in Bosnia and appointed Ömer Pasha as the *Müşir* of the Rumeli third army and governor of Bosnia, with the assignment to restore order in Bosnia and Montenegro. A campaign led by Ömer Pasha entered Sarajevo in May 1850 against little resistance.

Narrative: Major combat first occurred in August 1850. While the exact number of rebels is unknown, Ömer Pasha had 8,000 regulars and 2,000 Albanian irregulars. In November, a major engagement occurred at Brlosci, where 6,000 rebels besieged 1,200 Ottoman soldiers under Ibrahim Pasha for nine days. The rebel forces were said to have reached 25,000 by the end of the siege, but they were defeated by just 2,000 Ottoman troops under Ömer Pasha. Ibrahim had suffered 200 killed or wounded in the siege.

The Posavena *beys* then rose up under the leadership of Mahmud Pasha Tuzla. Tens of thousands participated on both sides in the subsequent battle for Tuzla. Ömer Pasha won and massacred the defeated rebels. His campaign then turned to Herzegovina. In quick succession, the government forces took Mostar, Buna, and Stolac. Ömer Pasha then turned to Jajce, Banja Luka, Prijedor, and Bihac. On March 20, 1851, Ömer Pasha executed Ali-paša Rizvanbegovi , the vizier of Herzegovina, who was attempting to create a personal power base. The Pashaluk of Herzegovina was then incorporated into that of Bosnia, creating the new entity of Bosnia-Herzegovina. In April 1851, the insurrection was renewed in the Krajina but quickly put down.

Termination and Outcome: By June 12, 1851, most rebels had been captured. The outcome of the war was a complete military victory by the government. Eight hundred prisoners were detained, and several rebel leaders were executed.

Coding Decisions: Between 5,000 and 6,000 were killed, but this total doubtless includes some civilians. Therefore, our estimate is of 4,000 battle-deaths.[115]

Sources: Aksan (2007); Arbuthnot (1862); Glenny (1999); Hadžiselimović (2001); Jelavich (1983).

INTRA-STATE WAR #556

First Turco-Montenegrin War of 1852 to 1853 (aka Herzegovina Uprising)

Participants: Ottoman Empire versus Montenegro and Herzegovina
Dates: September 1852 to March 9, 1853.
Battle-related Deaths: Ottoman Empire: 4,500;[116] Montenegro and Herzegovina: 2,000. (See Coding Decisions.)
Initiator: Montenegro.
Outcome: Negotiated settlement.
War Type: Civil for local issues (autonomy).
Total System Member Military Personnel: Armed Forces of the Ottoman Empire: 150,000 (prewar, initial); 160,000 (peak, final).[117]
Theater Armed Forces: Armed Forces of the Ottoman Empire: 20,000 (initial); 30,000 (peak, final).[118] Montenegro: 6,000 (initial); 20,000 (peak, final).[119] Herzegovina: [ ].

Antecedents: This revolt is tied to the Bosnian revolt of 1850 to 1851 (Intra-state War #554.3), during which Montenegrins assisted Bosnian *beys* who were rebelling against the Ottoman Sultan and, in the process, overran much of Herzegovina. After a campaign by Ottoman Gen. Ömer Pasha, the rebels withdrew, and the Porte looked for a pretext to reestablish its control over Montenegro. The rulers of Montenegro traditionally had been both secular rulers and Greek Orthodox priests. In 1851, Montenegro declared itself to be a secular principality when Prince Danilo II declined the religious duties and separated the offices of prince and bishop. Thereby, he created a hereditary monarchy (now referring to himself as Danilo I), which violated his authority as a vassal of the Ottomans. The sultan ordered Gen. Ömer Pasha to invade Montenegro to restore Ottoman control; however, before he could cross into Montenegro, the Montenegrins acted first.

Narrative: Herzegovina, led by Luka Vukalović, also again rebelled against the Ottoman measures of taxation by refusing to pay a debt to the Ottomans, and Montenegro once again sent its support to Herzegovina. Beginning in September 1852, Montenegrin troops took part in combat against Ottoman forces in Herzegovina, and Montenegro declared war against the Ottoman Empire. Ömer Pasha proceeded against Montenegro with an army of 20,000. Ömer Pasha based his army in Albania, near the Montenegrin border, and recruited additional Albanians to augment his forces. The Montenegrins initially scored several victories. Late in October, Montenegrins ambushed an Ottoman column at Duga, killing twenty-one. Ömer Pasha attempted to foment revolt within Montenegro by promising Piperi tribes land and freedom from taxation. Montenegro responded by asserting a claim to Ẑabljak, and an army led by Danilo's uncle, George Petrović, seized the city in November. Montenegro soon withdrew the troops as the Ottomans recaptured Ẑabljak and blockaded all of Montenegro's ports. Danilo appealed to Austria and Russia for assistance.

Then in December, Ömer Pasha began his bloody three-month campaign against Montenegro, and a *firman* (Ottoman decree) to that effect was duly issued on December 15, 1852. Ömer Pasha had 30,000 troops for the expedition against Montenegro; the latter had 20,000. The Ottomans planned a four-pronged attack on the tiny principality. Combat operations against Montenegro began on January 8, 1853. The Ottomans then advanced on two fronts, one toward Grahovo and another toward Ostrog. The main Ottoman army occupied the Zeta valley near Ostrog after two weeks of combat. On January 20, the Montenegrins attacked the Ottoman camp, defeating them. The Ottomans then turned toward the capital of Cetinje.

Russia and Austria now intervened diplomatically, presenting the Porte with a note demanding the immediate cessation of offensive operations in Montenegro. Unprepared to defy both nations at once, the government complied, and from mid-February Ömer Pasha suspended his operations. On March 3, a peace agreement was reached between Montenegro and the Ottoman Empire. It provided for the territorial status quo ante and made reference to an earlier Ottoman *firman*, which had acknowledged that Montenegro was not part of Ottoman suzerainty. A final battle occurred after the peace agreement, possibly before it had been received by the combatants. On March 9, a battle resulted in 100 government battle-deaths.

Termination and Outcome: The outcome of the war was a negotiated settlement. The Ottomans withdrew from Montenegro in 1853; however, Montenegro's status was not resolved, leading to another war in 1858 (Intra-state War #562).

Coding Decisions: One source cites an estimate of 4,500 Ottoman losses, while another reports about 8,000 total combat deaths (both for the three-month war with Montenegro).[120] We estimate 6,500 total combatant battle-deaths to include rebel deaths and deaths in the conflict in Herzegovina, which thus estimates 2,000 deaths suffered by Montenegro and Herzegovina.

Sources: Aličić (1981); Andrijasevic (2006); Arbuthnot (1862); Bouthoul and Carrère (1978); Clodfelter (1992); Djordjevic and Fischer-Galati (1981); Frilley and Wlahovitj (1876); Gopcevic (1877); Jaques (2007); Kohn (1999); Miller (1972); Palmer (1992); Phillips and Axelrod (2005); Reid (2000); Richardson (1960); Roberts (2007); Williams (1904).

INTRA-STATE WAR #557.1
Epirus Revolt of 1854 (aka Epirotic Revolt)

Participants: Ottoman Empire versus Greek Nationalists in Epirus.
Dates: January 30, 1854, to May 2, 1854.
Battle-related Deaths: Ottoman Empire: [ ]; Greek Nationalists: [ ].
Initiator: Greek Nationalists.
Outcome: Ottoman Empire wins.
War Type: Civil for local interests (secession).
Total System Member Military Personnel: Armed Forces of Ottoman Empire: 160,000 (prewar, initial, peak, final).[121]
Theater Armed Forces: Armed Forces of Ottoman Empire: 4,600 (initial); 15,500 (peak). Greek Nationalists: [ ].

Antecedents: Greece had obtained its independence from the Ottoman Empire on January 1, 1828 (Intra-state War #504). However, it controlled only a small territory. The Greeks who remained in areas still under Ottoman control had sought independence from the Ottoman Empire and formed a number of secret societies to promote the *megále idea* of uniting all Greeks in a single state. Their efforts were frequently aided by the "Russian Party," while Britain and France favored maintaining Ottoman territorial integrity.

After the outbreak of the Crimean War (Inter-state War #22), which pitted the Ottoman Empire, France, Sardinia, and the United Kingdom against Russian expansionism, the Greek government tacitly or overtly encouraged Greek nationalists within the Ottoman Empire to revolt. Two of these revolts reached war level, one in Epirus (on the western coast) and one in Macedonia (north of Greece).

Narrative: On January 30, 1854, Spyridon Karaïskákes (son of the chief famous in Greece's war of independence) gave a speech urging Greeks to take action. Thereafter, he led 2,500 Greek irregulars in a successful attack on Ottoman forces in Arta (the Epirus capital). A second band of 300, led by Greek Gen. Theódoros Grívas, also began attacks in the region. The war spread to other communities in Epirus and into nearby Thessaly, where the Greeks created an army 3,000 strong. A number of Greek army officers resigned to join the rebellion.

An Ottoman army of 4,600 was able to recapture Arta. In early March, Grívas advanced north, and seized Metsovo, but was forced to retreat in the face of Ottoman attacks. On March 19, the Ottoman government warned Greece to withdraw its support of the nationalist efforts. When the Greek response was unsatisfactory, diplomatic relations between the two countries were broken. British and French ships blockaded Greek ports, cutting the flow of weapons to the rebels. The Ottomans sent additional reinforcements into the region. On April 13, a 6,000-strong Ottoman army supported by British and French artillery attacked the rebel headquarters at Petra; after fierce fighting, the Greeks were forced to retreat. The Ottomans then moved north into Ioannina, where an Ottoman army of 15,500 was pushed back, suffering heavy losses.

After heavy fighting, the city of Peta fell to Ottoman forces under Osman Pashaon April 26, 1854. Vicious fighting also took place on May 2, which ended the revolt as the nationalists retreated into Greece.

Termination and Outcome: The war ended as an Ottoman victory. The war was followed by a period of repression in which towns in Epirus were destroyed.

Coding Decisions: There was virtually a simultaneous war in Macedonia (Intra-state War #557.2). Though both involved Greek nationalists fighting against the Ottoman Empire, they occurred at disparate locations, and there is no evidence of collaboration between the rebel forces, so they are coded as separate wars.

Sources: Miller (1936); Reid (2000).

INTRA-STATE WAR #557.2

Greek Nationalists of Macedonia War of 1854 (aka Macedonia-Ottoman War)

Participants: Ottoman Empire versus Greek Nationalists in Macedonia.
Dates: February 1854.
Battle-related Deaths: Ottoman Empire: [ ]; Greek Nationalists: [ ].
Initiator: Greek Nationalists.
Outcome: Ottoman Empire wins.
War Type: Civil for local interests (secession).
Total System Member Military Personnel: Armed Forces of Ottoman Empire: 160,000 (prewar, initial, peak, final).[122]
Theater Armed Forces: Armed Forces of Ottoman Empire: [ ] (peak).[123] Greek Nationalists: 3,000 (initial); 18,000 (peak).[124]

Antecedents: Greece had obtained its independence from the Ottoman Empire on January 1, 1828 (Intra-state War #504). However, it controlled only a small territory. The Greeks who remained in areas still under Ottoman control had sought independence from the Ottoman Empire and formed a number of secret societies to promote the *megáli idéa* of uniting all Greeks in a single state. Their efforts were frequently aided by the "Russian Party," while Britain and France favored maintaining Ottoman territorial integrity.

After the outbreak of the Crimean War (Inter-state War #22), which pitted the Ottoman Empire, France, Sardinia, and the United Kingdom against Russian expansionism, the Greek government tacitly or overtly encouraged Greek nationalists within the Ottoman Empire to revolt. Two of these revolts reached war level, one in Epirus (on the western coast) and one in Macedonia (north of Greece).

Narrative: Greek nationalists had begun an uprising against Ottoman rule in January 1854 in Epirus (Intra-state War #557.1). In February, Greek nationalists began threatening the Ottoman garrison at Thessalonika in Macedonia. Though the nationalists were attacked and dispersed, Greek British subjects supported the movement with money and weapons. Theódoros Ziákas led the movement in Macedonia. He and a small band initially appeared in February at Grevená, but the presence of a Turkist and Albanian force persuaded Ziákas of the need for a larger army. He gathered forces into a large army and occupied a number of villages by April 4, 1854. On May 22, Ziákas led a column of 2,000 against an Ottoman cavalry, killing 250 of the 350 men.

The Ottoman victory against the uprising in Epirus on May 2 enabled it to shift resources to Macedonia, including a division led by Osman Pasha. He joined a division of 12,000 troops commanded by Abdî Pasha and 800 Albanian irregulars. Fighting occurred against the Greek rebels toward the end of May. However, intervention by the British, French, and Austrians prevented the Greeks from being crushed, and Ziákas was allowed to return to Greece. Various other bands of Greeks continued the fight near Mount Olympus, but they were defeated by an Ottoman army of 7,000 in bloody engagements.

Termination and Outcome: The war ended in an Ottoman victory.

This war does not include other rebellions against Greek authority in other regions. For instance, during the period of this war, fighting between the Greeks and Ottomans in the region of Chalkidiké (along the south central coast) was led by Tsámes Karatásos, who attacked 100 Ottomans on April 16, 1854. However by April 29 more than 3,000 Ottoman reinforcements arrived, driving the Greeks from the region by mid-June. However, agitation by Greek nationalists meant increases in the size of Greece would continue.

Coding Decisions: Much of the fighting also involved the slaughter of large numbers of noncombatants.

There was virtually a simultaneous war in Epirus (Intra-state War #557.1). Both involved Greek nationalists fighting against the Ottoman Empire; however, they occurred at disparate locations, and there is no evidence of collaboration between the rebel forces, so they are coded as separate wars.

Sources: Miller (1936); Reid (2000).

INTRA-STATE WAR #562

Second Turco-Montenegrin War of 1858

Participants: Ottoman Empire versus Montenegro.
Dates: May 4, 1858, to May 14, 1858.
Battle-related Deaths: Ottoman Empire: 3,000;[125] Montenegrins: 400.[126]
Initiator: Ottoman Empire.
Outcome: Montenegro wins.
War Type: Civil for local issues.
Total System Member Military Personnel: Armed Forces of the Ottoman Empire: 160,000 (prewar, initial, peak, final).[127]
Theater Armed Forces: Armed Forces of the Ottoman Empire: 7,000 (prewar, initial); 8,000 (peak);[128] Montenegrins: 7,500 (initial, peak, final).

Antecedents: Both Montenegro and Herzegovina sought independence from the Ottoman Empire, fighting together in the First Turco-Montenegrin war (Intra-state War #556 in 1852). Though Montenegro's ultimate status had not been determined by the war, it had gained limited autonomy from the Ottoman Empire as a result of the pressure applied by Austria and Russia. Nonetheless, in 1856, at the Paris Peace Conference, Ali Pasha (ruler of the Ottoman Empire) asserted that Montenegro was a part of the empire, and Montenegro's Prince Danilo I responded on May 31 with a demand that the great powers both recognize Montenegro's independence and expand its borders with territory from Albania and Herzegovina. As a compromise, the next year the great powers promoted a settlement by which Montenegro would gain additional territory in exchange for recognizing Ottoman sovereignty—an offer that Danilo considered accepting despite popular opposition. Of the great powers, Russia claimed to recognize Montenegro's independence, but only France's Napoleon III pledged to support Montenegro's independence and provided financial support.

Hostilities began in 1857, when Herzegovinian chieftain Luka Vukalovic resumed attacks against the Ottomans and the rebels won a victory at Orahovica in December. Beginning in January 1858, Montenegro lent support to the rebels, sending 4,000 soldiers to aid the 5,000 Herzegovinians. Montenegro's actions were denounced by Austria, and under diplomatic pressure, Montenegro withdrew its troops in the early spring of 1858.

Narrative: As diplomatic talks foundered, Ottoman commander Hussein Pasha stationed an army of 7,000 men along Montenegro's northern border, while the Montenegrins organized an army commanded by Prince Danilo's brother, Mirko Petrovich. The war began on May 4, 1858, as Ottoman troops crossed into Montenegro and captured several villages, including Grahovo, near to where the Montenegrin force was stationed and 50 kilometers east of Dubrovnik. Here, the armies clashed in two battles, on May 11 and May 13 through 14, 1858. The armies were fairly evenly matched, with the Turks having about 8,000 men (including some from Bosnia), while Montenegro had about 7,500. In the first engagement, the Ottomans generally were successful as they attacked the Montenegrin position. However, in the second battle, the Montenegrins went on the offensive, surrounding the Ottoman troops and slaughtering thousands. The Ottomans suffered at least 2,500 killed, while Montenegrin losses amounted to a maximum of 400 killed.

Termination and Outcome: The battle at Grahovo was considered a major Montenegrin victory, and Mirko became a national hero. The Ottomans withdrew from Montenegrin territory, and the Montenegrins captured a significant amount of Ottoman artillery. Yet, Danilo declined to have Montenegrin troops go on the offensive. Though the Ottoman Empire wanted to launch a full-scale war against Montenegro, it was dissuaded by the great powers, especially France and Russia. An international commission was formed to demarcate the borders between Montenegro and the Ottoman Empire, and the commission gave some of the disputed territory to Montenegro. Prince Danilo was assassinated in 1860, and Mirko's son, Nicholas Petrovich, became Montenegro's ruler, Nicholas I.

Coding Decisions: Some sources report as many as 6,000 Ottoman fatalities in the war, though the figure of 3,000 is more commonly cited, thus we report it here. Though the Montenegrins won the battle and were victorious in forcing Turkish withdrawal, Montenegro's independence was not recognized, and the two parties would go to war again in 1862 (Intra-state War #575).

Sources: Andrijasevic (2006); Armour (2006); Clodfelter (1992); Djordjevic and Fischer-Galati (1981); Frilley and Wlahovitj (1876); Gopcevic (1877); Jaques (2007); Miller (1972); Richardson (1960); Roberts (2007); Stevenson (1971); Williams (1904).

INTRA-STATE WAR #575

Third Turco-Montenegrin War of 1861 to 1862 (aka Second Attack of Ömer Pasha)

Participants: Turkey versus Montenegro and Herzegovinians.
Dates: September 16, 1861, to August 31, 1862.
Battle-related Deaths: Ottoman Empire: 5,000;[129] Montenegro: 2,000;[130] Herzegovinians [ ].
Initiator: Ottoman Empire.
Outcome: Compromise.
War Type: Civil for local issues (secession).
Total System Member Military Personnel: Armed Forces of the Ottoman Empire: 160,000 (prewar, initial, peak); 159,000 (final).[131]
Theater Armed Forces: Armed Forces of the Ottoman Empire: 50,000 (peak). Montenegro: 20,000 (initial, peak, final).[132] Herzegovinians: [ ].

Antecedents: As with the two preceding wars (Intra-state Wars #556 and #562), this war involved Montenegro's desire for independence from the Ottoman Empire and the Ottoman's desire to reassert control. In the Second Turco-Montenegrin War of 1858 (see Intra-state War #562), Montenegro had secured border expansion (Ottoman forces had been forced to withdraw, partially due to Great Power pressure), but Montenegro did not get recognition of its sovereignty by the Ottoman Empire. When Montenegrin King Danilo I was assassinated in 1860, the Ottoman Empire took advantage of the ensuing disorder to try to reassert its control.

As in 1858 (see Intra-state War #562), an insurrection against the Ottomans broke out in Herzegovina in 1861, led by Luka Vukalovic, and Montenegro at first covertly aided the insurgents. Vukalovic made Suttorina his capital and attempted to raise fellow Christians in revolt across the Bosnian frontier. Preparations for Ottoman military operations against the rebels in Herzegovina began on September 3, 1861.

Narrative: The first combat occurred on September 16, 1861. Montenegrins fought on the side of the rebellion against Ömer Pasha, who had been appointed by the Ottoman sultan to pacify Herzegovina. A battle on October 26 killed several hundred rebels and almost 100 Turks. On November 21, the government won a decisive victory at Piva, reducing the insurgents to small areas of the province. In an effort to save the rebellion, Montenegro mobilized and threatened to intervene more actively in the struggle. Ömer Pasha responded by blockading Montenegro during the winter and invading it during the spring. More than sixty engagements were fought in this bitterly contested struggle as the rebels were steadily pushed inland. More died of hunger than of the war itself. Ömer Pasha's 50,000 troops may have suffered more than 20,000 lost, while Montenegrin losses may have been as low as 2,000 battle-deaths. Even though Ottoman losses outnumbered rebel losses, the Montenegrins could not afford them, having less than one-third as many troops as Ömer Pasha. Montenegrins led by Regent Mirko Petrovich defended the monastery at Ostrog for some time but were forced to retreat toward the capital. Cornered at Rijeka Crnojevica, they were decimated by the Ottomans on August 23. The way to the capital of Cetinje lay open, but the diplomatic intervention of Russia and Austria-Hungary exerted pressure on the government to settle for a compromise.

Termination and Outcome: The Convention of Scutari was reached on August 31, 1862. It ended the war by leaving the territory and internal administration of Montenegro intact but imposing severe conditions requiring Montenegro to destroy border fortifications, to refrain from importing arms, to refuse travelers without Turkish passports, and to use only Ottoman mediation in any border disputes that might arise. Mirko Petrovich (the father of Prince Nicholas I) was to be banished. The negotiated agreement represented a defeat for Montenegro, which found itself in a worse position than the status quo ante. Montenegro's status would again become an issue in 1875 (Intra-state War #601).

Coding Decisions: In terms of battle-deaths, Clodfelter suggests that 3,500 were killed. However, Langer estimates 2,000 rebels killed and more than 20,000 government losses. Using the typical 3:1 ratio of wounded to killed, this would imply at least 5,000 government battle-deaths.

Sources: Arbuthnot (1862); Clessold (1966); Clodfelter (2008); Frilley and Wlahovitj (1876); Jacques (2007); Kohn (1999); Langer (1931); Miller (1936); Murray (1910); Phillips and Axelrod (2005); Rastoder (2003); Reid (2000); Richardson (1960); Stearns (2001); Stevenson (1971); Williams (1904).

INTRA-STATE WAR #579

Second Polish War of 1863 to 1864

Participants: Russia versus Polish nationalists.
Dates: January 22, 1863, to April 19, 1864.
Battle-related Deaths: Russia: 5,000; Polish Nationalists: 6,500. (See Coding Decisions.)
Initiator: Poles.
Outcome: Russia wins.
War Type: Civil for local issues.
Total System Member Military Personnel: Armed Forces of Russia: 682,000 (prewar); 812,000 (initial); 812,000 (peak, final).[133]
Theater Armed Forces: Armed Forces of Russia: 80,000 (initial, peak).[134] Polish Nationalists: 10,000 (initial).[135]

Antecedents: The once-independent entity of Poland had been partitioned among Russia, Austria, and Prussia, with Russia gaining the largest portion. Though Poland initially had a degree of independence within the empire, it was lost as a result of the First Polish rebellion (Intra-state War #517). After coming to the Russian throne in 1856, Tsar Alexander II adopted some conciliatory policies toward the Poles, yet he was firmly committed to integrating Poland even more firmly into Russia. His limited reforms failed to dampen the Polish desire for independence. Opposition to Russian rule was one of the few things upon which the Polish conservatives (the Whites) and radicals (the Reds) could agree. Poles began to use public demonstrations and events such as funerals to highlight Polish culture. In February 1861, two such demonstrations were dispersed by the military, causing five deaths, which served to heighten tensions further. The issue over which conflict would arise was the Russian measure to conscript Poles into the Russian military.

Narrative: Marquis Alexander Wielopolski, Russia's local administrator in Poland, tried to force Polish youth into the army with a new decree on January 15, 1863, and this led to open rebellion in January 1863. On January 22, the National Committee of the Reds declared that a state of insurrection had begun, a resolution that was soon endorsed by the Whites as well. The Polish nationalists conducted guerrilla warfare against the numerically superior Russian forces for more than a year. The Polish independence movement was unable to garner sufficient international support, and the rebellion was ultimately suppressed.

Termination and Outcome: The outcome of the war was a Russian victory. Poland lost all elements of self-government, and Russia implemented a strict policy of Russification.

Coding Decisions: Battle-death estimates for Russia have ranges from 5,000 to 10,000 as disease took as many lives as battles. Polish deaths were likely between 5,000 and 8,000.[136] We consider the lower Russian figure and the midpoint of the Polish estimates to be plausible.

Sources: Clodfelter (2002); Edwards (1865); Florinsky (1953); Leslie (1963); Phillips and Axelrod (2005); Reddaway (1941).

INTRA-STATE WAR #580.5

Bandit War of 1863

Participants: Italy versus Bandits.
Dates: May 1863 to December 31, 1863.
Battle-related Deaths: Italy: [ ]; Bandits: [ ]; Total Combatant Deaths: 9,000. (See Coding Decisions.)
Initiator: Italy.
Outcome: Conflict continues at below-war level.
War Type: Civil for local issues.
Total System Member Military Personnel: Armed Forces of Italy: 185,000 (prewar); 275,000 (initial, peak, final).[137]
Theater Armed Forces: Armed Forces of Italy: 2,000 (initial); 120,000 (peak, final).[138] Bandits: 80,702 (peak).[139]

Antecedents: The process of Italian unification had encountered resistance both from the exiting kingdoms within Italian territory and from foreign powers that maintained possessions in Italy, leading to a series of wars. Gradually the former separate kingdoms were integrated into the kingdom of Sardinia, and at the conclusion of the war against the Kingdom of Two Sicilies (Intra-state War #37), Sardinia controlled the territory of virtually all Italy so that on May 17, 1861, Victor Emmanuel II was crowned king of the united Italy.

Italy's last acquisition proved problematic. During the war, banditry had played an increasing role in Sicily where the most power group was the mafia, while Naples had to deal with a secret society known as the *Camorra*. In 1862 the Italian government heard reports that monarchist opponents of the regime were utilizing the bandits and draft evaders in attempts to destabilize the regime. Thus the government launched an unpopular campaign to round up the draft evaders. This enforcement of the conscription laws also earned the government the enmity of local governments, especially in Sicily, where groups of bandits and draft evaders were organizing in hopes of being able to seize control from the government.

Narrative: In May 1863, the government launched a new program whereby the military was empowered to pursue draft evaders, bandits, and the citizens who supported them. In July the efforts began in earnest as 2,000 troops were sent to Caltanissetta and then to Palermo as the military established a forty-kilometer cordon around the brigands. Violence soon became indiscriminate, with some towns almost razed. Ultimately, almost half of Italy's military force would be involved in the offensive that year.

Termination and Outcome: The major government offensive was in 1863, though conflict between the government and brigands continued at lower levels until 1865.

Coding Decisions: The number of those who died in the government's anti-brigand campaign is controversial. Estimates range from 5,000 to 150,000, though the higher number no doubt includes civilians. Government figures indicate that it killed 3,450 brigands that year, though the number of soldiers who died is not reported.[140] Moreover, it is likely that more brigands and soldiers died from malaria than fighting. So if we double the minimum number of brigand deaths, 9,000 seems a plausible estimate of total combatant deaths.

Sources: Duggan (2008); Riall (1998); Smith (1958).

INTRA-STATE WAR #583
First Cretan War of 1866 to 1868

Participants: Ottoman Empire versus Cretans.
Dates: August 28, 1866, to December 30, 1868.
Battle-related Deaths: Ottoman Empire: [ ]; Cretans: [ ]; Total Combatant Deaths: 30,000.
Initiator: Cretans.
Outcome: Ottoman Empire wins.
War Type: Civil for local issues (*enosis*).
Total System Member Military Personnel: Armed Forces of the Ottoman Empire: 160,000 (prewar, initial, peak); 133,000 (final).[141]
Theater Armed Forces: Armed Forces of the Ottoman Empire (including 7,000 Egyptian forces and 5,000 Muslim volunteers): 18,000 (initial); 45,000 (peak).[142] Greek Cretans: many fewer than 30,000 (initial); 50,000 (peak); less than 5,000 (final).[143] Greek Volunteers: 200 (initial); 1,000 (peak, final).[144]

Antecedents: Crete, which is the southernmost island of Greece, had long suffered under Ottoman attempts to suppress Christianity. During the Greek War of Independence of 1821 to 1828 (Intra-state War #504), the Greeks of Crete had revolted but then were suppressed. In 1858, the Porte had promised to institute several reforms, the most important of which would have given Christianity equal standing with Islam. By 1866, however, this had not been done, and an annual fair was transformed into a traditional assembly to petition the government for a redress of grievances. On May 29, the Ottoman government ordered the 3,000-member Cretan Assembly to disperse. When it refused, the governor of the province called the Muslims into the cities, causing the Greeks to flee into the hills. Resentment over the forced displacement magnified Muslim–Christian intercommunal tensions. About 12,000 Christians fled the island. The government called for Egyptian reinforcements to put down the as-yet unconsummated "rebellion," and 6,000 to 8,000 Egyptians landed in Crete on July 26. The governor distributed rifles and ammunition among Muslim Cretans. The Cretans now openly advocated *enosis*, or union with Greece.

Narrative: The first combat between the Crete rebels and Turkish troops occurred on August 28, followed by a minor clash at Selinos. Soon, hostilities broke out across the island. Egyptian forces were surrounded and cut off from supplies at Apokorona and forced to surrender their position. Meanwhile, the Turks at Selinos were driven into the fortress of Kandanos. The new Ottoman governor, Mustafa Kiritli (Na îlî) Pasha, made plans for action to relieve Kandanos. Some 5,000 Muslim volunteers were armed to assist the government forces. A force of 10,000 was sent to relieve Kandanos. On its return, it was ambushed at Kakopetra, losing 120 killed and 800 wounded. Meanwhile the first shipment of supplies and volunteers from Greece arrived for the insurgents. Mustafa Kiritli (Na îlî) Pasha then assembled 13,000 troops for offensive actions against the rebel strongholds. On October 24, they attacked about 1,000 rebels and 200 Greek volunteers at Vafé. The rebels repulsed the first attack, causing heavy Ottoman casualties, though the Cretans were finally routed, although they suffered only 30 killed. A month later at Arkadi, nearly 23,000 Ottoman regulars and irregular volunteers defeated about 150 defenders and massacred 500 of the 600 civilians who had sought refuge there. The battle had cost the Ottomans 1,500 killed or wounded.

When the government renewed its offensive, winter was approaching, and hundreds of Egyptian soldiers died of cold and an epidemic of pneumonia. Nevertheless, the government was grinding down the rebellion. By January 1867, nearly 1,140 Greek volunteers accepted the government's offer of transportation back to Greece. British and Russian ships also transported some civilian refugees to Greece. That same month, 600 rebels ambushed the expeditionary force as it passed through the defile of Krapi, inflicting heavy losses on the government troops. By February 6, when the force was reassembled, it numbered only 6,000 men out of the 17,850 who had set out against the rebels. The overall government strength on the island had dropped from its peak of 30,000 to perhaps 20,000. Later that month, the rebels won a significant engagement at Yerakari, splitting a Turkish column of 10,000 in two and forcing one part to retreat. Desultory combat continued until the arrival of Ömer Pasha, who set out late in April to conquer the rebel stronghold of Sphakia with 15,000 men. His forces, along with others sent against the rebels, were ambushed in the narrow passes of the island and forced to retreat, destroying villages as they went. In May, Ömer Pasha and 18,000 troops successfully attacked the eastern rebel headquarters at Lasithi, dispersing its 5,000 defenders. Turco-Egyptian casualties in this summer campaign were as high as 20,000 to 25,000, with many more succumbing to sunstroke or disease than to combat. A peak force of 45,000 slowly had been whittled down to 20,000 at the end of the campaign. In mid-September, the rebels were offered amnesty and a six-week armistice. On October 3, the Egyptians withdrew from the island. At about the same time, most of the Greek volunteers also went home. The inability of Ömer Pasha to definitively defeat the rebellion forced him to leave Crete in disgrace in November 1867.

Low-intensity fighting continued from the winter of 1867 through the summer of 1868 as government troops were dying as well from disease. Turkish forces were reduced to a total of less than 17,000 men. A final contingent of 1,000 Greek volunteers under Petropoulakis landed on December 14 but were defeated, losing 300. Although 5,000 rebels remained in the eastern districts, the threat of war with the Ottoman Empire caused Greece to cut off further support to the rebels. By December 30, Petropoulakis surrendered with about 600 to 1,000 Cretans and Greeks under his command; he was permitted to leave the island. This appears to have marked the end of major combat operations.

Termination and Outcome: The outcome of the war was a government victory with a limited amnesty. The war was followed by a peace conference on January 9, 1869. In February, a peace plan was approved that provided for amnesty and administrative reforms to give Greeks more political power in the province. Most rebels accepted the agreement. The rebels had been defeated, but not crushed, and war would return in 1896 (Intra-state War #631).

Coding Decisions: We have found no complete fatality statistics for this war, though scholars generally talk about tens of thousands. One report estimates that the government lost more than 30,000 soldier but that not all of them died. Still, when one includes the unknown number of rebel fatalities, this may be the best estimate of total combatant deaths.[145]

Sources: Clodfelter (2008); Dontas (1966); Florinsky (1953); Gerolymatos (2002); Miller (1913, 1927); Phillips and Axelrod (2005); Reid (2000); Stillman (1966); Williams (1907).

INTRA-STATE WAR #591

Spanish Liberals War of 1868 (aka Glorious Revolution, *La Gloriosa*)

Participants: Spain versus Liberals.
Dates: September 18, 1868, to September 29, 1868.
Battle-related Deaths: Spain: 800; Liberals: 800.[146]
Initiator: Liberals.
Outcome: Liberals win.
War Type: Civil for central control.
Total System Member Military Personnel: Armed Forces of Spain: 109,000 (prewar); 98,000 (initial, peak, final).[147]
Theater Armed Forces: Loyalist Armed Forces of Spain: 10,000 (initial).[148] Liberals: [ ].

Antecedents: Queen Isabella II had inherited the Spanish throne in 1833 from her father, Ferdinand VII, despite the opposition of her uncle, Don Carlos, and the Carlists in the two Carlist wars (Intra-state Wars #522 and #546). Isabella was declared of age in 1843, assuming the throne from the regency of her mother, Maria Christina. At the age of sixteen, Isabella was forced by the Moderate (conservative) Party to marry her cousin, Francisco de Asis de Borbón. Her rule became increasingly autocratic, and her refusal to appoint progressives to lead the government prompted liberal exiles, under the leadership of Juan Prim, to develop plans for a revolution in 1866 and 1867. Isabella's vacillations between liberal and conservative positions had made her unpopular with the people, the government, and the military; and opposition to her crossed party lines. Some of her ministers tried to oust her in July 1868, and though the coup attempt failed, opposition to her reign continued.

Narrative: When Isabella went to France to negotiate an alliance with Napoleon III, a revolutionary proclamation was issued, and rebels within the navy led by Admiral Juan Bautista mutinied in Cádiz on September 18, 1868. The proclamation also triggered popular uprisings in Madrid. The queen returned to Spain to find that much of the army had joined the rebellion, following the return to Spain of exiled Gen. Francisco Serrano. Meanwhile, cities like Santander joined the rebellion, though it was recaptured by the loyalist forces. Serrano gathered a rebel army and marched toward Cordóba. The main engagement of the war was the battle of Alcolea, near Cordóba on September 28, 1868, where the loyalist elements of the Spanish Royal Army were defeated by the rebels in ending the war.

Termination and Outcome: This brief war was a victory for the liberal rebels. Isabella was deposed and she fled back to France.

Coding Decisions: Self-explanatory from cited sources.

Sources: Bollaert (1870); Carr (1982); Clarke (1906); Phillips and Axelrod (2005); Sorokin (1937).

INTRA-STATE WAR #596

Paris Commune War of 1871

Participants: France versus Communards.
Dates: March 18, 1871, to May 29, 1871.
Battle-related Deaths: Communards: 20,000; France: 879.[149]
Initiator: Communards.
Outcome: France wins.
War Type: Civil for central control.
Total System Member Military Personnel: Armed Forces of France: 452,000 (prewar); 1 million (initial, peak, final).[150]
Theater Armed Forces: Armed Forces of France: 25,000 (initial); 130,000 (peak).[151] Armed Forces of the Communards (National Guard): 27,000 (initial); 50,000 (peak); 20,000 (final).

Antecedents: During the reform movements that swept Europe, France had overthrown conservative regimes in 1830 and 1848 (Intra-state Wars #513 and #549) in search of more democratic government. France's defeat in the Franco-Prussian War (Inter-state War #58, which ended on February 26, 1871) led to the end of the reign of Emperor

Napoleon III and the creation of the Third French Republic. Germans had besieged Paris from September 1870 to January 1871, and the citizens were armed and angry about the French defeat. The largest armed force in Paris was the National Guard, numbering about 300,000 (on paper) organized by the neighborhoods. On January 22, members of the National Guard and Parisian radical groups presented demands to the French government that there be the creation of a commune and that the military should be placed under civilian control. Elections in February led to a royalist-dominated government led by Adolphe Thiers. The decision by Thiers to try to disarm the popular National Guard prompted demonstrations that led to this war.

Narrative: At the end of the Franco-Prussian War, the National Guard had placed its cannons in city parks to keep them away from the regular military. On March 18 two brigades of soldiers went to the park in Montmarte to seize the 170 cannons located there. In the confrontation with the National Guard a guardsman was shot, thus starting this war. National Guard units from all over the city hurried to the site, while the army proceeded to seize cannons at other strategic locations. By the end of the day, citizens had erected barriers throughout the city. Thiers ordered the evacuation of the regular army units to Versailles, where they would regroup, while National Guard units began seizing the abandoned assets of the army. The leading liberals organized an independent republican French government called the Commune of Paris, and on March 26, the commune had elections. The commune held its first meeting on March 28, choosing radical Louis Blanqui as its honorary president.

The Communards' troops first occupied the streets of Paris. The Communards then organized an offensive against the government military at Versailles on April 2, but it was repulsed. A second advance on the morning of April 3 came under heavy fire and was similarly unsuccessful. National Guard soldiers captured by the government were summarily executed. The French government sent an army against a Communard-controlled fort at Issy, which it captured later that month. In May the government's army began moving systematically toward Paris and by May 19 had reached the outskirts of the city. The final offensive was launched on May 21. Street battles took place at barricades throughout the city as citizens rushed to support the National Guard. The National Guard and citizens were no match for the army, and citizens captured with weapons immediately were shot. On May 27, the army attacked the National Guard's last position in the cemetery of Père-Lachaise, defended by 200 men who were quickly overwhelmed and the survivors were shot. All resistance finally ceased on May 28.

Termination and Outcome: The Communards were defeated, and many fled into exile. The conservative government led by Thiers continued till 1873.

Coding Decisions: The number of Communards killed during the war consistently has been contested, with conservatives tending to report smaller numbers (6,600) and others reporting 10,000 to 20,000. We follow Tombs in seeing 20,000 as plausible.

Sources: Bodart (1916); Clodfelter (1992); Perre (1962); Phillips and Axelrod (2005); Richardson (1960); Sorokin (1937); Tombs (1998); Urlanis (1960).

INTRA-STATE WAR #597
Third Carlist War of 1872 to 1876

Participants: Spain versus Carlists.
Dates: April 21, 1872, to February 28, 1876.
Battle-related Deaths: Carlists: 43,000; Spain: 7,000. (See Coding Decisions.)
Initiator: Carlists.
Outcome: Spain wins.
War Type: Civil for central control.
Total System Member Military Personnel: Armed Forces of Spain: 97,000 (prewar, initial); 111,000 (peak); 104,000 (final).[152]
Theater Armed Forces: Carlist Armed Forces: 4,000 (initial); 100,000 (peak); 10,000 (final).[153]

Antecedents: After Queen Isabella II of Spain was overthrown by the military in the Spanish Liberals War in 1868 (Intra-state War #591), a period of consolidation took place in which the government planned to write a new constitution. However, the government was divided, with radicals preferring a unitary republic, while the federalists preferred more power for the provinces. The Cortes decided to keep the monarchy and chose the second son of King Victor Emmanuel II of Italy, Duke Amadeus, as

King Amadeo I. The Carlists, who had supported claims to the throne by the family of Don Carlos (Queen Isabella's uncle) in two earlier rebellions (Intra-state Wars #523 and #546), rose again in revolt, this time in support of Don Carlos III (the grandson of Don Carlos and later Carlos VII, the Duke of Madrid).

Narrative: The leaders of the Carlists, including Don Carlos, met on April 20, 1872, and developed plans for a rebellion to begin the next day. The Carlists gathered in Navarre, carrying out attacks there, while other parties carried out attacks across Catalonia. Their plans were similar to those in the earlier wars: to primarily engage in guerrilla tactics in the North and East, away from the major urban areas. Don Carlos arrived from France on May 2 and took command of his forces at Orokieta. Two days later a government army of 1,000 commanded by General Morienes attacked, forcing Don Carlos to retreat into France. The battle at Orokieta cost the Carlos 50 dead and 700 taken prisoner, which decimated their forces in the Basque region for the rest of the year. A number of the Carlists in Biscay also decided to surrender to General Cerrado. However in other regions, the Carlists engaged in savage fighting.

In 1872, Don Carlos's brother, Alfonso, arrived to take command of the 6,000-man Carlist army. The army was reorganized, and a successful offensive on December 18, 1872, led to a significant increase in Carlist recruits, with the rebels numbering 50,000 by early 1873. Meanwhile, conflicts within the Spanish government persuaded King Amadeo to resign on February 11, 1873. The first Spanish republic was then created, which lasted only a year, and on November 1874, Alfonso XII, the son of Isabella, was proclaimed king. During this period the Carlist forces continued their attacks, handing the Republican Army a defeat on May 5. Don Carlos reentered Spain that August, and the Carlists established their capital at Estella.

The year 1874 marked the peak of Carlist successes: their numbers had increased to 100,000, and they decided to take their fight against the city of Balbao. An army of 12,000 Carlists besieged the city until May 2, 1874, when a government relief force of 27,000 men forced the Carlists to retreat. Government forces then continued their advance and unsuccessfully attacked Estella on several occasions, suffering severe casualties. In the East the Carlist forces led by Alfonso captured Cuenca near Madrid before being forced to retreat.

After Alfonso XII assumed the throne, a number of Carlists switched their support to the government. Carlist attacks did continue, but the government forces continued to advance toward their positions. The final battle was fought at Estella, which was attacked on February 17, 1876. A number of Carlists fled, and the war ended on February 28.

Termination and Outcome: The war was a victory for the government. Don Carlos III fled to France.

Coding Decisions: Though Richardson codes this war a "4?," which represents about 10,000 deaths, the most commonly reported figure in terms of battle-deaths is the total of 50,000, without mentioning the relative losses of each side. Small and Singer coded 7,000 battle-deaths for Spain, which would mean about 43,000 Carlist deaths.[154]

Sources: Clarke (1906); Clodfelter (2002); Harbottle and Bruce (1971); Holt (1967); Latimer (1898); Phillips and Axelrod (2005); Richardson (1960); Sorokin (1937).

INTRA-STATE WAR #598

Catonalist Uprising of 1873 to 1875 (aka Cantonal Revolution)

Participants: Spain versus Rebel Cantons.
Dates: July 19, 1873, to January 1875.
Battle-related Deaths: Spain: [ ]; Rebel Cantons: [ ]; Total Combatant Deaths: 2,000.
Initiator: Spain.
Outcome: Spain wins.
War Type: Civil for local issues (secession).
Total System Member Military Personnel: Armed Forces of Spain: 97,000 (prewar); 100,000 (initial); 111,000 (peak, final).[155]
Theater Armed Forces: Armed Forces of Spain: 3,000 (initial);[156] Cantons: [ ].

Antecedents: After Queen Isabella II of Spain was overthrown by the military in the Spanish Liberals War in 1868 (Intra-state War #591), a period of consolidation took place in which the government planned to write a new constitution. The Cortes maintained the monarchy and chose the second son of King Victor Emmanuel II of Italy, Duke Amadeus, who assumed office on November 16, 1870, as King Amadeo I. During his reign, the government was confronted in 1872 by the Third Carlist War (Intra-state War #597). The Carlists had supported claims to the throne by the family of Don Carlos (Queen Isabella's uncle) in two earlier wars (Intra-state Wars #522 and #546) and were now supporting the claims by Don Carlos's grandson, Don Carlos III. In addition to the war, conflicts within the Spanish government persuaded King Amadeo to resign on February 11, 1873.

The first Spanish Republic was then created. However, the republicans were divided, with radicals preferring a unitary republic, while the federalists preferred more power for the provinces or cantons. The republic endured for less than two years, during which time it had four presidents. Elections for the Cortes in May 1873 produced a majority for the federalists, though voter turnout was low. The government continued discussing a new constitution, but the slow pace of reform led to popular unrest. On June 30, 1873, the city of Seville declared itself to be a social republic. Federalist deputies left the Cortes, and a revolutionary strike was called by leaders of the First International. Though the federalists had envisioned a government of joined autonomous states, what was emerging were the creation of independent cantons instead. The movement spread, with cities led by leftist social revolutionaries such as Valencia, Granada, and Cartagena declaring themselves to be independent. In many of the cities, like Cartagena, after the declaration of independence was announced, government troops would in essence mutiny by refusing to obey orders to go to fight in the Carlist War, and in Cartagena, naval officers seized four ships to be put under the control of the canton.

Narrative: The war began when the Spanish government decided to send troops to reassert its control. After the resignation of his predecessor, Nicolás Salmerón was chosen by the Cortes as the president of the executive power, taking office on July 18, 1873. He immediately met with General Pavia, who was sent with a force of 3,000 men to defeat the Cantonalist rebellion. The cities did not create a united front, and though they individually engaged in heavy fighting, the government was able to conquer them one by one. After two days of fighting, the canton of Seville fell to the government. In August, the government troops were successful in defeating Cadiz and Granada. However, when Salmerón learned that the generals would execute any rebels captured with weapons, he resigned on September 7, 1873. He was succeeded by Emilio Castelar. Castelar moved away from republicanism and more to the right, thus he was soon able to regain much of the trust of the army and able to recruit more generals to help defeat the cantons. Cartagena was the most difficult, and capturing the canton required a long siege and a naval blockade.

Termination and Outcome: The war ended when Cartagena fell in January 1875, and the government had won a victory.

Coding Decisions: Clodfelter admits that fatality statistics are hard to find, though he concludes that several thousand died (2,500 from Cartagena were sent into exile).[157] Thus we are coding 2,000 total combatant deaths as plausible.

Sources: Carr (1966); Clodfelter (2002); Latimer (1898).

INTRA-STATE WAR #601

Bosnia and Bulgaria Revolt of 1875 to 1876 (aka Balkan Crisis of 1875 to 1876)

Participants: Ottoman Empire versus Bosnia-Herzegovina and Bulgaria.
Dates: June 30, 1875, to June 29, 1876.
Battle-related Deaths: Ottoman Empire: 10,000; Bosnia-Herzegovina: 12,000; Bulgaria: 1,000. (See Coding Decisions.)
Initiator: Bosnia-Herzegovina.
Outcome: Transformed into Extra-state War #373 and Inter-state War #61.
War Type: Civil for local issues (taxation and annexation to Serbia and Montenegro).
Total System Member Military Personnel: Armed Forces of the Ottoman Empire: 144,000 (prewar); 151,000 (initial); 411,000 (peak, final).[158]
Theater Armed Forces: Armed Forces of the Ottoman Empire: 3,600 (prewar); 30,000 (initial).[159] Rebel Aggregate consisting of Bosnia-Herzegovinian Rebels: 10,000 (initial); 15,000 (peak); 5,400 (final).[160] Montenegrin Volunteers (External Non-state Intervener), participating from August 1875: 250 (initial, peak, final).[161] Dalmatian Krivoshijans (External

Non-state Intervener), participating from August 1875: [ ]. Bulgarian Rebels, participating from May 2, 1876, to the beginning of June 1876: 3,000 (initial, peak, final).[162]

Antecedents: The Balkan provinces of the Ottoman Empire were restive under Ottoman rule, and wars seeking independence had broken out in Greece (#506), Albania (#512), Bosnia (#528, #540, and #554.3), Bulgaria (#539), Montenegro (#556, #562, and #575), Epirus (#557.1), Macedonia (#557.2), and Crete (#583). Though Herzegovina had received autonomy within the Ottoman Empire in 1832, it had lasted only into 1851, when Herzegovina was reintegrated back into Bosnia as Bosnia-Herzegovina (Intra-state War #554.3). Peasant rebellions became more common in Bosnia-Herzegovina in the 1870s, and by 1873 small peasant rebellions against taxation were endemic. Two events encouraged potential rebels to believe that outside help might be forthcoming. First, a diplomatic affray between Montenegro and the Ottoman Empire led Orthodox Serbs to believe that Montenegro would side with them in the event of war. Second, a sympathetic visit of the Austro-Hungarian emperor to Dalmatia convinced many Catholics of his willingness to support them. Perhaps these events explain why a small Christian peasant revolt escalated in 1875 into a civil war, which then spread into an extra-state war of the Ottoman Empire, Serbia, and Montenegro (#373) in which the brutality of the Ottoman forces enflamed international interest and led to the intervention of Russia, resulting in the Second Russo-Turkish War (Inter-state War #61), all within two years.

Narrative: The rebellion broke out in Nevesinje (in the Herzegovina region of Bosnia-Herzegovina), where attacks by armed rebels, some calling themselves the Nevesinje Rifles, led to uprisings throughout Bosnia-Herzegovina. The rebels' initial goal was tax reform, but slowly more peasants demanded union with Montenegro. Government offers of reduced taxation were rejected by the rebels, thus on July 17, two battalions of Ottoman soldiers and a squadron of cavalry were dispatched from Sarajevo to Herzegovina, where government forces consisted of eight battalions. Because of the small size of the force, it was repeatedly defeated by insurgents. Krivoshijans from Austria-Hungary poured across the border into Herzegovina, and Montenegrin volunteers under Peko Pavlovich also crossed the frontier to fight the Ottomans.

By the middle of August, the government had deployed 30,000 troops against the insurgents. On August 15 a new revolt broke out at Kozaratz in Northwest Bosnia. While the bulk of Turkish forces were engaged in Herzegovina, the Bosnian revolt extended rapidly eastward. In late November, the government gathered 3,000 troops to relieve its besieged garrisons near the Herzegovinian border. At the pass of Muratovitza, local rebel leader Lazar Socitza inflicted a defeat on the Ottoman army, in which the government lost 760 killed and 900 wounded, most of whom later died of their wounds, while the rebels lost only 57 killed and 96 seriously wounded. Following this battle, the insurgents overran much of Herzegovina, capturing even blockhouses and strongpoints so long as they didn't face artillery. The Ottoman garrisons were besieged, and isolated units in the mountains lost men due to exposure. The war assumed a clear pattern over the winter. The Ottoman government attempted to resupply its fortresses in rebel-held areas of Herzegovina, and the rebels would use the opportunities to attack the supply columns. By the end of December, the number of insurgents in Herzegovina reached 10,000, while the number of government effectives had fallen from the 30,000 sent to Herzegovina since August to just over half that number.

Another offer of amnesty, reforms, and an armistice was made on February 22, 1876 (based on the great power mediation effort called the Andrassy Note) and was similarly spurned by the rebels. Nevertheless, there was a lull in fighting from mid-December through March, as winter weather made campaigning difficult for both sides. The rebels began to attract more outside support. From early 1876, Russia began funding the insurgents. During the spring of 1876, Serbia, under considerable domestic pressure for war with Turkey, recalled its previously dismissed hawkish premier to power and prepared to aid the insurgents. Both the Serbian and Montenegrin governments moved toward open war with the Ottoman Empire.

In April, the war resumed, with the rebels mounting a series of attacks on Ottoman forces around Nevesinje, but the rebellion was beginning to slacken. However, on May 2 (April 21 O.S.), a new revolt broke out in Bulgaria. The rebels, who directed at least some of their attacks on Muslim civilians, were quickly crushed by government forces. Perhaps 15,000 Christians were killed in the bloody campaign that followed the suppression of the revolt. Muslim losses were much smaller—a low estimate accepted by local Turkish leaders at the time was 500 killed, the majority of them combatants slain in battle. Ottoman actions led the rebels to appeal to Serbia for assistance.

Termination and Outcome: On June 30, Serbia, followed quickly by Montenegro, declared war on the Ottoman Empire. This transformed the war into Extra-state War #373 of Serbia and Montenegro against the Ottoman Empire, as the former (who were autonomous entities, though not yet members of the interstate system) took over the bulk of the fighting from the Bosnian and Bulgarian rebels. Over the next few years, Russia also would declare war on the Ottoman Empire, leading to an Inter-state War #61. The Treaty of Berlin at the end of that war recognized Montenegro's independence and gave some autonomy to Bulgaria. Bosnia-Herzegovina was annexed to Austria-Hungary rather than Serbia or Montenegro. Serbian desire to gain the provinces for itself proved to be one of the causes of World War I.

Coding Decisions: Disentangling the battle-related deaths for this war from the other wars is difficult. Several sources combine all Ottoman deaths for the period ending in September 1876 into a total of 20,000.[163] If we subtract 10,000 suffered against Montenegro, it suggests 10,000 Ottoman deaths for this war. We estimate 12,000 for Bosnia and Herzegovina, which may be an underestimate. The fatalities in Bulgaria were horrific, with numbers ranging from 3,000 to 100,000. The most plausible estimates are in the 12,000-to-15,000 range. However, the vast majority of the fatalities in Bulgaria were suffered by civilians, with 1,000 being burned to death in one church alone.[164]

Thus we are using 1,000 as a reasonable estimate for Bulgarian battle-deaths.[165]

Sources: Allen and Muratoff (1953); Castellan (1992); Clodfelter (2002); Dumas and Vedel-Peterson (1923); Finkel (2005); Florinsky (1953); Gerolymates (2002); Gewehr (1967); Glenny (1999); Harris (1936); Hentea (2007); Hösch (1972); Hozier (1878); Jelavich (1983); Langer (1931); *London Times* (1875–1987); MacGahan (1876); MacKenzie (1967); Miller (1936); Palmer (1992); Petrovich (1976); Phillips and Axelrod (2005); Quataert (2000); Reid (2000); Richardson (1960); Schafer (1995); Schevill (1966); Seton-Watson (1952); Stavrianos (1958, 2000); Von Sax (1913); Von Sternegg (1866–1889); Stillman (1901); Sumner (1937); Sumner (1962); Williams (1907).

INTRA-STATE WAR #631

Second Cretan War of 1896 to 1897

Participants: Ottoman Empire versus Cretan Muslims.
Dates: March 10, 1896, to February 14, 1897.
Battle-related Deaths: Ottoman Empire: [ ]; Cretan Muslims: [ ]; Total Combatant Deaths: 1,000. (See Coding Decisions.)
Initiator: Cretan Muslims.
Outcome: Transformed into Inter-state War #76.
War Type: Civil for local issues (autonomy, independence, and annexation).
Total System Member Military Personnel: Armed Forces of the Ottoman Empire: 231,000 (prewar); 231,000 (initial); 436,000 (peak, final).[166]
Theater Armed Forces: Armed Forces of the Ottoman Empire: 1,600 (initial); 25,000 (peak, final).[167] Cretan Muslims (Pro-government Aggregate): [ ]. Greek Volunteers (Pro-rebel Aggregate): [ ]. Cretan Christians (Rebel Army): 2,000 (prewar, initial, peak, final).[168]

Antecedents: Greek Orthodox Cretans repeatedly rebelled against the Ottoman Empire. Major risings occurred: during the Greek War of Independence (Intra-state War #504), in 1841, from 1866 to 1867 (Intra-state War #583), and in 1889 (when 3,000 people were killed, mostly civilians, in a conflict that involved up to 20,000 combatants). The expectation of future conflict made it all too easy for intercommunal tensions to escalate to open rebellion; Muslims had targeted Christians on the island as early as 1894 in an outbreak of intercommunal violence, in which the government seemed to favor the Muslims over the Christians. In September 1894, the Christians formed a committee called the *Epitropi*, which advocated either independence for a Christian-ruled Crete or union with Christian-ruled Greece. They also convoked an assembly that addressed a petition to the sultan for the restoration of the Organic Statute of 1868 (which had been abrogated in 1889). The sultan granted some of the petition's demands, including appointing a Christian governor, Alexander Karateodori Pasha, but did not reinstate the island's autonomy.

Bands of insurgents began gathering in the summer of 1895, and minor attacks against Ottoman officials began. On November 7, small bands of armed insurgents gathered at Apokorona, preparing for a spring uprising. In December, an attack by Turkish troops was repulsed, and reinforcements were sent to the island. On March 8, 1896, Governor Karateodori was replaced by Turhan Pasha, a Muslim. Christians in general were outraged; the new governor ordered the *Epitropi* to disband.

Narrative: When the *Epitropi* refused to disband, the government sent a battalion of troops to arrest the fifteen leaders of the organization. About 1,500 rebels flocked to the defense of the *Epitropi*, attacking the Turks, who were repulsed. This action was followed in mid-April by the Battle of Selia, in which the rebels defeated two government battalions. On May 18, the rebels invested Vamos, garrisoned by 1,600 Ottoman troops, with 1,800 armed troops commanded by the *Epitropi*; from May 31 to June 2 some 9,000 Ottoman soldiers and the Vamos garrison battled the rebels.

On May 24, a street battle broke out in Canae between Muslims and Christians. Within a week, dozens were dead, mostly Christians. This triggered escalation on both sides. The Ottomans sought to reinforce their garrison of fifteen battalions with an additional sixteen and prepared eight more to sail if they should be needed. About 10,000 troops landed from May 29 to June 4. The size of the rebel forces also expanded. Arms and volunteers began to flow from Greece to the rebellion, and combat continued with the Christians holding their own against the government forces.

In June, the great powers demanded that the Ottoman Empire implement reforms in Crete to include autonomy and a Christian governor for the island. The Ottoman government finally issued such a proclamation on July 31, and the Christian rebels accepted the offer. However, a series of Muslim revolts occurred over the next few months, including a large-scale Muslim attack in Canae in November and attacks on Christians and some massacres in early 1897. By February, the Christian insurgents had given up on the peace process, and on February 4, a group raised the Greek flag and proclaimed union with Greece (*enosis*). As fighting resumed, the Greek government decided to intervene and sent two ships to Canae. When the Ottomans moved to reinforce their forces, the Greek government sent torpedo boats to interdict them. On February 13, the Greek government sent an expedition of 1,500 men to Crete with orders to unite it with Greece.

Termination and Outcome: The Greek marines landed on February 15, quickly assuming the bulk of the fighting against Ottoman forces. Because this action triggered war between Greece and the Ottoman Empire, the war was transformed from a civil war into an inter-state war (#76, the Greco-Turkish War of 1897). Though Greece lost that war militarily, at the end of the war Crete was given near independence, and it would eventually unite with Greece.

Coding Decisions. No source provides an estimate of the battle-deaths in this war. Bouthoul estimates 2,000 battle-deaths for this conflict and the inter-state war that followed combined, while Richardson codes the same period as a "3.3," which is closer to 3,000. Because the inter-state war portion is coded as incurring 2,000 fatalities, a total of 1,000 battle deaths for this war is plausible as the narrative indicates that it is possible that 1,000 died from combat or disease.

Sources: Bickford-Smith (1898); Bouthoul (1978); Clodfelter (1992); Dakin (1966); Ekinci (2006); Palmer (1992); Părvanova (1989); Perris (1897); Phillips and Axelrod (2005); Richardson (1960); Tatsios (1984); Williams (1907).

INTRA-STATE WAR #640

Ilinden War of 1902 to 1903 (aka IMRO Revolts or Macedonian Struggle)

Participants: Ottoman Empire versus IMRO Rebels.
Dates: October 11, 1902, to November 1903.
Battle-related Deaths: Ottoman Empire: 4,500.[169]
IMRO Rebels (probably includes Bulgarians and Serbians): 1,500.[170]

Initiator: IMRO Rebels.
Outcome: Ottoman Empire wins.
War Type: Civil for local issues (independence or union with Bulgaria).
Total System Member Military Personnel: Armed Forces of the Ottoman Empire: 275,000 (prewar); 266,000 (initial, peak, final).[171]
Theater Armed Forces: Armed Forces of the Ottoman Empire: 80,000 (prewar); 175,000 (initial); 300,000 (peak).[172] IMRO: 5,000 (prewar); 4,000 to 5,000 (initial); 25,000 (peak, final).[173] Supreme Command and Bulgarian Volunteers (Pro-rebel Non-state Intervener): 2,000 to 3,000 (peak).[174] Serbian Volunteers (Pro-rebel Non-state Intervener): 200 to 800 (initial, peak).[175]

Antecedents: After the Second Russo-Turkish War in 1878 (Inter-state War #61), which the Ottoman Empire lost, the great powers met at the Congress of Berlin to decide upon the disposition of Ottoman territory. Greater Bulgaria was divided into three parts: Bulgaria became a principality under Ottoman control, eastern Rumelia became an autonomous province, and Macedonia remained as part of the Ottoman Empire. Bulgaria resented the loss of Macedonia, and Serbia had designs on Macedonian territory as well, leading to the Serbian-Bulgarian war of 1885 (Extra-state War #391). After the Bulgarian victory over Serbia, Bulgaria united with eastern Rumelia in 1885. Bulgaria (still part of the Ottoman Empire), Serbia, and Greece were all interested in expanding their control into Macedonia.

The Macedonians also had goals of their own. In 1893, the Internal Macedonia Revolutionary Organization (IMRO) was founded with the goal of gaining autonomy for Macedonia. It remained a minor player until the twentieth century. Initially, the Greeks, Serbs, and Bulgarians tried to win the support of the Macedonians through propaganda campaigns. IMRO countered with its own vision of an independent Macedonia and tried to encourage the Ottomans to fulfill its treaty obligations to provide self-government to its European provinces. One means to prompt Ottoman action was through a terror campaign that would make the region unsafe for foreign investment. It entrusted the revolutionary program to its paramilitary wing, composed of armed units known as *chetas*. The first of these units was led by a former major in the Bulgarian army. The *chetas* attacked the Ottomans as well as the Greek and Serbian movements.

The relationship between IMRO and the Bulgarians was complicated. The Bulgarian supreme command had been established by Macedonians living in Bulgaria who wanted to see the union of Macedonia and Bulgaria, thus at times the groups worked at cross-purposes, while at others they collaborated. The Turks began to take action against IMRO in 1901, as the organization was attempting to import arms for a rebellion. Conflict also erupted between IMRO and the supremists, who were trying to goad the IMRO into action. The first firefights occurred in 1902, and by May 1902, the government, expecting an insurrection, reinforced its troops in the territory to 80,000.

Narrative: Conflict at war level begins before the rebellion is formally declared. In October, a premature uprising was launched in Macedonia by the supremists, but many villages failed to participate. In a major battle at the defile of Kresna, fought on October 11, the supremists ambushed Turkish forces; in three days of fighting, the government lost 350 to 500 men. The Turks, blaming IMRO (though they had tried to prevent the rebellion),[176] responded by burning villages and killing peasants. The insurrection was crushed, and the supremists and Bulgarian volunteers returned to Bulgaria by the end of the year. During the beginning of 1903, the violence spread, though most of it was attacks by civilians against one another. A number of towns appealed to the Ottomans for more protection. By the end of March, there were 2,700 insurgents in various bands around the province. The Turks took armed action against the bands, inflicting a significant number of casualties—704 battle-deaths in thirty-nine engagements from March through July. In June, a rebel attack on the Turkish forces inflicted 220 battle-deaths at the cost of only 14 rebel battle-deaths. Bulgarian volunteers began crossing the frontier in large numbers, and the rebels' numbers grew despite their heavy losses.

On August 2, 1903, IMRO launched a revolt, which took its name from the day the revolt was launched, St. Elijah's Day (Ilinden). On paper, IMRO could call upon 1,600 armed combatants and 32,000 armed and drilled levies. The government, on the other hand, had 300,000 troops in Macedonia, although some 50,000 were deployed in the Albanian regions. The only major battle, on August 2, was the

IMRO capture at Krushevo. The revolt was concentrated in western Macedonia, where IMRO ordered the villagers to take to the mountains. At about this point, between 200 and 800 Serbian volunteers, led by Serbian officers, intervened in the conflict on behalf of the rebels (to little effect).

The campaign consisted largely of guerrilla warfare, fighting in terrain that favored the defense and those who knew the territory. Over the next three months, the insurgents suffered 750 battle-deaths in at least 150 engagements, most of them minor. While they inflicted heavy losses on the government forces sent against them, they failed to maintain either defensive positions or the loyalty of the villagers, leading to the collapse of the insurrection.

However, the Turks sent 351,000 troops to try to put down 27,000 resistance fighters.

Termination and Outcome: By November, an informal truce prevailed. The government had been victorious everywhere, and the insurrection had been quelled. Indeed, the government massacred up to 4,700 people after the war. The relative shares of Greece, Serbia, and Bulgaria in the partition of the territory would become a key issue in the Second Balkan War.

The Turks won the war and then retaliated by destroying 200 villages.

Coding Decisions: The destruction of the war left 70,836 people homeless and 8,816 civilians killed. In terms of battle-deaths, at least 1,000 died before the outbreak of the Illinden revolt itself and another 4,694 during the Illinden phase of the war, for a total of at least 5,694. We estimate 6,000, which is likely to be accurate to the nearest thousand.[177]

Sources: Anastasoff (1977); Castellan (1992); Clodfelter (1992); Dakin (1966); Georgieva and Konechni (1998); Gerolymatos (2002); Glenny (1999); Hupchick (2002); Karpat (1972); Kazemi and Waterbury (1991); Palmer (1992).

INTRA-STATE WAR #643
Bloody Sunday War of 1905 to 1906

Participants: Russia versus Workers and Peasants.
Dates: January 22, 1905, to January 1, 1906.
Battle-related Deaths: Russia: 2,300; Workers and Peasants: 3,000. (See Coding Decisions.)
Initiator: Russia.
Outcome: Russia wins.
War Type: Civil for central control.
Total System Member Military Personnel: Armed Forces of Russia: 1,160,000 (prewar); 2,365,000 (initial, peak); 1,236,000 (final).[178]
Theater Armed Forces: Workers and Peasants: [ ].

Antecedents: Popular discontent over the lack of food and reforms confronted Russia's Romanov dynasty at the start of the twentieth century, and consequently there was a growth of political parties and independent organizations dedicated to promoting social reforms and overthrowing the monarchy. In response, Tsar Nicholas II resisted any restrictions on the power of the monarchy, while the Marxists and social democrats were educating the workers about class struggle. Consequently the number of worker strikes increased significantly in 1904. Popular unrest was heightened in response to Russia's participation (and ultimate defeat) in the Russo-Japanese War in 1904 and 1905 (Inter-state War #85). Russia already had participated in two wars in an attempt to maintain a dominant position in Asia: the Boxer Rebellion in 1900 (Inter-state War #82) and The Sino-Russian War of 1900 (Inter-state War #83), and the government had felt that domestic tension could be reduced by rallying the country for war once again. Instead, the hardships caused by the war intensified worker discontent. One of the pro-worker organizations was created by Father Georgii Gapon, a leftist priest. He assembled factory workers in St. Petersburg into groups that served the functions of a trade union, a mutual aid society, and a revolutionary organization. Gapon led worker strikes in December 1904 that enjoyed some success, which soon encompassed 111,000 workers in a general strike throughout St. Petersburg. Gapon then developed a plan for workers to present their concerns and demands directly to the tsar. Gapon gave notice of the proposed march to the palace to the government, giving it time to prepare, organizing 2,300 Cossacks to monitor the demonstration.

Narrative: On January 22, 1905, approximately 200,000 workers led by Father Gapon marched to the Winter Palace in St. Petersburg to present a petition listing grievances and asking for Tsar Nicholas's assistance. They were attacked by government soldiers in what became known as the Bloody Sunday massacre in which at least 100 demonstrators were killed. The massacre precipitated riots and clashes between armed workers and government soldiers in many parts of the country, though for the most part the crowds offered no resistance. Marxists and social democrats spread their information and promoted political activism widely in Poland, the Baltic states, Georgia, and the Caucasus, and even the armed forces were affected. A number of strikes and conflicts occurred on May Day. Even some units of the army and navy rebelled, the most well-known of which occurred in June, when sailors on the battleship *Potemkin* mutinied. About 2,000 people died in the ensuing violence in Odessa.

As peace with Japan was declared in August, the number of strikes declined significantly.

Yet activities of the Marxists in Poland led to strikes and demonstrations that had to be suppressed by force, and at least 250,000 Russian troops were stationed there. During late October, a general strike gripped all of Russia, and a radical Soviet counsel of workers' deputies was formed under the leadership of Leon Trotsky. The government was now under increasing attack by both the workers and peasants and by the middle class as well. Thus, the tsar, yielding to the advice of his prime minister, Count Sergei Witte, offered concessions in the form of the October manifesto, which granted freedoms of speech and an elected state duma. Though the manifesto had some appeal to the middle class, it had negligible influence on the mood of the workers and peasants. In October and November, a pro-tsarist organization, the League of the Russian People (the Black Hundreds) conducted pogroms in which 4,000 Jews were butchered.

Because most of the army had remained loyal, the tsar was able to send military units to the villages in rebellion, and thousands of people were executed or forced into exile. On December 16, the tsar approved the roundup of 200 members of the St. Petersburg Soviet, which incited a violent insurrection by 1,600 armed workers in which 100 soldiers were killed.

The rebellion was suppressed by January 1906, though revolutionary sentiment would flare again in 1919 (Intra-state War #677).

Termination and Outcome: The revolution failed as the upper and middle classes deserted the revolutionary cause, and the workers were not in a position to coordinate their individual rebellions.

Coding Decisions: Determining the fatality rates for this war are complicated in terms of separating out deaths of civilians and workers massacred by the government from those who were engaged in actual armed combat. Clodfelter estimates that 3,611 government officials were killed or wounded, while 1,500 tsarist soldiers had died. About 15,000 rebels and noncombatants were killed, and between 1905 and 1910, 4,449 revolutionaries were executed.[179] If we apply the usual 3:1 ratio of wounded to deaths, the 3,611 government casualties would mean 800 deaths: added to the deaths of 1,500 soldiers produces a Russian total of 2,300 battle-deaths. Of the 15,000 combatant and civilian deaths, the overwhelming number were of massacred civilians. If we estimate that 20 percent of the deaths were of armed combatants, that yields 3,000 rebel deaths.

Sources: Ascher (2004); Clodfelter (2002); DeFronzo (1996); Goldstone (1998); Harcave (1964); Kochan (1966); Moorehead (1958); Phillips and Axelrod (2005).

INTRA-STATE WAR #645
Romanian Peasant Revolt of 1907 (aka Great Peasant Revolt)

Participants: Romania versus Peasants.
Dates: March 16, 1907, to April 30, 1907.
Battle-related Deaths: Romania: [ ]; Peasants: [ ]; Total Combatant Deaths: 5,000. (See Coding Decisions.)
Initiator: Peasants.
Outcome: Romania wins.
War Type: Civil for central control.
Total System Member Military Personnel: Armed Forces of Romania: 70,000 (prewar); 69,000 (initial, peak, final).
Theater Armed Forces: Armed Forces of Romania (with new recruits): 140,000 (peak).

Antecedents: Between the end of the Crimean War in 1856 (Inter-state War #22) and the Congress of Berlin in 1878 at the end of the Second Russo-Turkish War (Inter-state War #61), Romania gradually gained its independence (incorporating the provinces of Moldavia and Wallachia) from the Ottoman Empire. However, independence did not solve all of Romania's problems, the primary ones being government corruption and the system of landownership. The government had created a pattern of large landholders who would lease the land from the government and then sublet it to farmers for more for two to three times what they paid. The result was that the majority of peasants did not have enough land to be economically independent. A severe drought in 1887 had led to two months of clashes between the peasants and local authorities in early 1888. The harsh conditions under which the majority of peasants lived had not changed much, and a drought in 1904 brought many to the brink of starvation. The government contributed to unrest by imposing taxes, which in some parts of the country could amount to 80 percent of a peasant's production.[180] Other complaints centered on absentee landlords and the practices of Jewish moneylenders.

Narrative: In the small village of Flămînzi, a group of peasants gathered on February 21, 1907, to draw up petitions for lower rents. Initially their demonstrations were peaceful, though they soon began attacking the houses of the landlords. Armed conflict began on March 16, 1807, when the peasants clashed with the army. The revolt spread across Moldavia and then into Wallachia, where the fighting became more severe as village intellectuals had prompted the peasant to revolutionary action. The government also blamed the recent war in Russia (Intra-state War #643) as being instrumental in encouraging peasant revolt.

The war reached its greatest intensity between March 25 and March 28. The government at the time was led by the conservatives, and their inability to acknowledge, or deal with, the peasant uprising prompted King Carol I to form a new government (on March 25) with the Liberal Party. The new government declared a state of emergency and a general mobilization of the army, which had 140,000 soldiers commanded by Gen. Alexandru Averescu by the end of the month. Violence included reservists who refused to join the active army. The government then launched a ruthless suppression campaign, including using artillery to bombard villages, killing a total of 11,000 peasants.

Termination and Outcome: Though the peasants were defeated, the government did begin to consider limited land reform. However, most of its provisions benefitted the more well-off peasants and had limited impact on the majority.

Coding Decisions: Hitchens refers to 11,000 lives lost during this war.[181] However, a large percentage of these would have been civilians killed in the riots or the bombardments. Richardson codes this war as a "3?," which represents about 1,000 battle-deaths and seems low given the large number of troops involved and the national scope of the revolt.[182] Even if we assume that the major of deaths were civilians, that would produce a figure of 5,000 total combatant deaths, which we are coding here.

Sources: Clodfelter (2002); Hitchens (1994); Iorio (1979); Richardson (1960); Stavrianos (1958).

INTRA-STATE WAR #650
Second Albanian Revolt of 1910 to 1912

Participants: Ottoman Empire versus Albanian Nationalists.
Dates: March 1910 to October 16, 1912.
Battle-related Deaths: Ottoman Empire: 5,000; Albanian Nationalists: [ ].
Initiator: Albanian Nationalists.
Outcome: Transformed into Inter-state War #100.
War Type: Civil for local issues (autonomy, independence).
Total System Member Military Personnel: Armed Forces of the Ottoman Empire: 312,000 (prewar); 324,000 (initial); 336,000 (peak); 241,000 (final).[183]
Theater Armed Forces: Armed Forces of the Ottoman Empire: 40,000 (initial); 60,000 (peak). Muslim Albanians (Pro-Government Army), participating from April to June 10, 1911: 3,000 (initial, peak, final).[184] Muslim Tribal Rebels (Rebel Army): 7,000 (initial); 45,000 (peak, final).[185] Malissori (Rebel Army), participating from June 1910 to July 1910 and again from March 27, 1911, to August 3, 1911, and finally from May 1912: 8,000 (peak, final).[186] Mirdites (Rebel Army), participating from June 5, 1911, until perhaps late June or

July, 1911, and from May 1912: 10,000 (initial); 10,000 (peak, final).[187]

Antecedents: After the loss of Bulgaria and Bosnia-Herzegovina in 1908, the Ottoman Empire (contrary to its earlier commitments) sought to "Turkify" its remaining European territory populated by Albanians, revoking many of Albania's special privileges and suppressing schools and newspapers. The new Young Turk government began to implement a new system of taxation and conscription. In 1909, a revolt broke out in northern Albania against the new measures, led by Isa Boletini (though it did not reach war level). By mid-June, the government had destroyed about 100 fortified houses and imposed taxation and conscription. In August, it won a major battle against Isa Boletini's forces, and by late September, the revolt largely was suppressed.

Narrative: In 1910, Isa Boletini assembled a broader coalition of conservative *beys* in the area of Kosovo and nationalists elsewhere in the country. The *beys* took an oath to unite in their efforts to oppose the Ottoman regime and began coordinated actions. Some 5,000 Albanians under Idris Sefer then cut the rail line at the Kachanik Pass, which stalled the initial government counterattack; 2,000 more under Isa Boletini attacked Prizren and Firzovik. In March 1910, the government sent a military expedition to subdue the Kosovar rebels. There was resistance in both the North and South of the province and the Ottomans had about 40,000 troops in the region, eventually growing to 60,000. By early April the rebels had increased to 10,000 soldiers around Prizren. The only set-piece battles of the campaign were fought at the passes of Kachanik and Crnoljeva from April 23 to April 29. After tough fighting, the government took both passes, inflicting 500 battle-deaths on Idris Sefer's force and an unknown number of Isa Boletini's force.

By June 11, the government claimed to have crushed the rebellion in northern Albania and Kosovo, and the government set about punishing the rebels. For example, the Kosovo military tribunal executed 41, sentenced 325 to hard labor, and imprisoned or exiled another 250. The government seized rebel weapons, but arms continued to be smuggled into Albania via Montenegro, Austro-Hungarian Dalmatia, Greek Corfu, and Serbia. A number of the Albanian bands fled into Montenegro, whence they proposed a settlement, which was not accepted by the Ottomans. The Ottomans continued their advance into Albania, imposing new restrictions as they came.

Operations now shifted to the vicinity of Scodra on the coast, where the Catholic Malissori had taken up arms. After a number of severe firefights, the expedition reached Scodra in July. About 2,500 to 3,000 Malissori fled rather than disarm. A large number of Albanians fled into Montenegro where they continued planning for the rebellion, encouraged by Nicholas I of Montenegro, and the Albanian National Committee was founded. On about March 27, 1911, the Malissori revolted again, aided by the exiles returning from Montenegro. The rebellion was launched prematurely, and only the Malissori rose with about 8,000 troops in all. This allowed the governor of the province to declare a holy war and urge Muslim Albanians to fight the Christian tribe; some 3,000 heeded the pasha's call. On May 11, the government commander proclaimed martial law and commenced offensive operations against the rebel stronghold of Decic. About a month of intense fighting followed. The rebels succeeded in defeating the Albanian Muslims in battle on June 10; afterward the Albanians dispersed back to their homes. But by the end of June, the rebels were surrounded and isolated, fleeing into Montenegro. The government proclaimed the end of the rebellion on June 12 and offered the rebels amnesty if they would return and disarm; the offer was rejected. Finally, on August 3, 1911, a peace agreement was signed with the Malissori, providing for amnesty, reduced taxes, economic and educational reforms, a right to bear arms, and a spatial limitation on military service to Albania itself. Meanwhile, the war continued as, on June 5, the Catholic Mirdite tribe rebelled with about 10,000 insurgents. They proclaimed autonomy and attacked Lezhë, storming its citadel. A punitive force set out to subdue them but was repulsed with heavy losses. The government then promised the Mirdites autonomy, and a peace agreement was reached. By this point, the Albanian revolt had cost the government 8,000 casualties.

The next phase of the war was preceded by a Montenegrin propaganda campaign among the Malissori. But the initial uprising was in Kosovo, where Muslim tribes again revolted on April 23, 1912. By May 20, the insurrection had become general, with the Mirdites joining the uprising after some of their men were conscripted in violation of the earlier accord with the government. The Malissori joined after the Mirdites. On June 18, in the battle of Hasi (near Prizren), the government suffered a defeat, losing 300 killed; the rebels hanged the captured commander of the Turkish force. On June 22, some ethnic Albanian government troops mutinied, effectively deserting to the insurgents. In succession, a battalion, then the gendarmerie, and then the First Division all defected to the rebels. By mid-July, the combined armies of the rebels were rumored to be 50,000 strong. About 20,000 rebels occupied Skopje. Negotiations followed, and a cease-fire was reached, but it collapsed in September, when the rebels struck a government battalion near Nonhelin, inflicting heavy casualties.

Termination and Outcome: On October 8, Montenegro (not a member of the state system) declared war on the Ottoman Empire. Some rebels continued to fight the Turks, and the Malissori assisted the Montenegrin advance. But the bulk of the Muslim Albanian tribes responded to Montenegro's declaration of a holy war by rushing to oppose Montenegro. It was too late. On October 17, Serbia and Bulgaria declared war, and Serbia advanced into Kosovo. Although Muslim resistance leaders like Isa Boletini sided with the government, they were overwhelmed by Serbian forces. By November, even the Malissori had ceased their cooperation with Montenegro, disgusted by the behavior and territorial demands of their erstwhile allies. The war therefore became subsumed in the First Balkan War on October 17.

Coding Decisions: This war is coded as continuing during the entire period of 1910 to 1912: though the fighting in this war waxed and waned, and participants individually reached agreements with the Ottoman government and ended and restarted their individual participation, there was no overarching agreement that stopped the Albanian campaign entirely.

The government suffered 8,000 casualties in the second phase of the revolt, or 2,000 battle-deaths if the conventional 3:1 ratio of killed to wounded holds. On the basis of this evidence, the omission of the other two phases or any reliable totals of rebel fatalities, we guess that 5,000 died in the revolt, which could be too high or too low by several thousand.[188]

Sources: Clodfelter (2002); Gawrych (2006); Glenny (1999); Jelavich and Jelavich (1977); Pearson (2004); Phillips and Axelrod (2005); Stavrianos (2000); Swire (1929); Tallon (2012); Treadway (1983).

INTRA-STATE WAR #677
Russian Civil War of 1917 to 1920

Participants: Russia versus Anti-Bolsheviks, Estonia, Finland, France, Greece, Japan, Latvia, Lithuania, Poland, Romania, Serbia, United Kingdom, and the United States.

Dates: December 9, 1917, to November 20, 1920.

Battle-related Deaths: Russia: 702,000; Anti-Bolsheviks: 325,000; Czechoslovakia: 3,200; Japan: 1,500; United Kingdom: 350; Greece: 300; United States: 275; Austria-Hungary and Finland: 50; France: 50.[189]

Initiator: Anti-Bolsheviks.

Outcome: Russia wins.

War Type: Civil for central control.

Total System Member Military Personnel: Armed Forces of Russia: 10,900,000 (prewar); 5,500,000 (peak, final).[190]

Theater Armed Forces: Armed Forces of Russia: 50,000 to 60,000 effectives (initial—February 1918); 500,000 (1920).[191] White Russian Armies (Rebel Aggregate): 3,500 (initial);[192] 500,000 (peak);[193] 318,000 (1920).[194] Austria-Hungary and Czech Legion, participating from August 3, 1918, to October 27, 1918: 50,000 (initial, final). Czechoslovakia, participating from October 28, 1918, to February 7, 1920: 50,000 (initial); 61,000 (peak, final). China, participating from August 3, 1918: 2,300 (peak). France, participating from April 18, 1918, to September 30, 1919: 13,600 (peak).[195] Greece, participating from June 23, 1918, to April 8, 1919: 40,000 (peak).[196] Italy, participating from August 3, 1918, to January 1920: 2,500 (initial), 3000 (peak).[197] Japan, participating from August 3, 1918, to October 15, 1920: 28,000 (initial); 74,000 (peak).[198] Lithuania, participating during 1919: 6,500 (peak).[199] Poland, participating from its independence on November 3, 1918, to the onset of its inter-state war with Russia on February 14, 1919: 32,000 (peak).[200] Romania, participating from December 1918: 33,000 (peak).[201] Serbia, participating from April 18, 1918: 4,000 (peak).[202] United Kingdom, participating from June 23, 1918, to March 1920: 44,600 (peak—includes 3,900 Canadians).[203] United States, participating from June 23, 1918, to April 20, 1920: 5,800 (initial); 13,200 (peak).[204]

Antecedents: Vladimir Ilyich Ulyanov was born on April 22, 1870, in the Russian city of Simbirsk. As a teenager Vladimir was influenced by the political activities of his older brother Aleksandr, who had become involved in a plot to assassinate Tsar Alexander III and was arrested and executed. Vladimir was expelled from the university for his own political activities, and he joined a revolutionary circle through which he became acquainted with the works of Karl Marx. He soon rose to leadership in a social democratic revolutionary organization. After serving three years in exile in Siberia, Vladimir settled in western Europe, where he adopted the nom de guerre of Lenin. In a meeting of the Social Democratic Party in London in 1902, Lenin championed the section of the party called the Bolsheviks, who emphasized the need for strong central control in opposition to the Mensheviks. Lenin urged the Bolsheviks to take a greater role in the growing anti-tsar opposition movement that was the root of the Bloody Sunday uprising in St. Petersburg in 1905 and 1906 (Intra-state War #643).

World War I (Inter-state War #106) broke out in 1914, and Lenin was discouraged by the fact that the German social democrats supported the German war effort. Lenin ultimately saw World War I as an imperialist war that would lead to the crash of European capitalism, and he wanted to return to Russia to spread revolutionary unrest that would pull Russia out of the war. Before Lenin arrived, Russia experienced the first of the three revolutions it would face in 1917. In the February Revolution, popular demonstrations against the costs of the war forced Tsar Nicholas to abdicate in March 1917. A provisional government was created that included the liberals, the conservatives, and the progressives. It became clear however that the actual power was exercised less by the government and more by the Petrograd Soviet (workers' council). In April the two groups were divided over Russia's role in the war, with the Petrograd Soviet in favor of ending Russia's participation in the war as soon as possible. The same month, Lenin, with the assistance of Germany, was able to return to Russia. The moderate socialists, including the Mensheviks, were persuaded to join the liberals and the government in support of the war effort. The Bolsheviks, whose major support was among the factory workers, were becoming increasingly popular among those who wanted to withdraw from the war, including many disenchanted soldiers. In June, Russia launched a new military offensive under the provisional government of Alexander Kerensky, and as news of Russian defeats spread, supporters began to push the Bolsheviks to seize power. Particularly vociferous were the Latvian Rifles Regiments (*strelki*), who backed the Bolsheviks in the northern Baltics. They promised Lenin 40,000 *strelki* in the event of a Kerensky counterattack if the former should seize power in the capital city of Petrograd.

In October 1917, Bolshevik Leon Trotsky, leader of the Military-Revolutionary Committee of the Petrograd Soviet, began taking control over the garrisons in the city (although only 300 soldiers of the 100,000 in and around Petrograd initially would rally to the cause). With the arrival of 3,000 Baltic sailors, Petrograd was taken. Prime Minister Alexander Kerensky decided to suppress the Bolsheviks, and loyal Cossack units advanced as far as Pulkovo Hills. These forces were routed on November 13 by a combination of Bolshevik workers' militias, the 3,300 Bolshevik troops in Petrograd, and the Latvians' threat to Kerensky's rear forcing his forces to retreat. Opposition to the new government began almost immediately; Kuban, Terek, and Don Cossacks (who eventually reached a combined strength of 75,000 troops) rebelled. So too did 4,800 Finnish home guards, the Ukrainian rada (which eventually mustered up to 12,500 troops), a volunteer army of several thousand in south Russia, and Mustafa Chokaev's Union of Muslims in Kokhand. Against these forces the Bolsheviks could muster 3,300 soldiers, various workers' militias in Petrograd and provincial capitals, and 30,000 Latvian *strelki*. The Bolsheviks decided that their primary goal was to remove Russia from World War I, and they began negotiations with Germany for what eventually became the Treaty of Brest Litovsk on December 9, signing an armistice six days later.

Narrative: The first combat between the rebellious Cossacks and Red forces began on December 9 in

Rostov-on-Don; this was followed by combat between the White Volunteer Army led by Lavr Kornilov and newly formed echelons of the Reds. What would become the Red Army grew quickly, and when Cossacks returning from the German front were deployed against the Red Guards, most of them defected or deserted, giving the latter a numerical advantage on the southern front. Meanwhile, about 10,000 Bolshevik troops advanced into the Ukraine against scant opposition. In December, Grigory Semyonov led a revolt in Transbaikal; however, Semyonov was soon defeated and forced to seek refuge in Manchuria, where his troops were rearmed and reorganized by the Chinese, his Buryat Mongols reentering Transbaikal in January. By the end of the year, the Reds had blunted the various rebellions against them but lacked the troops to reoccupy all of Russia (particularly as most of the prewar armed forces self-demobilized after the armistice). On January 28, they decreed the formation of the Red Army, which was created over the next two months by amalgamating Red Guards and some surviving units of the old Imperial Army in the Northwest. Still, by February 18, there were only 50,000 to 60,000 Soviet fighters capable of effective combat (bolstered, of course, by the Latvians, who were not incorporated into the Red Army or repatriated until 1920).

The fighting can be divided into three major geographic regions: the South, the East, and the Northwest. In the East, the Reds handily defeated Kokhand's Union of Muslims by February 17; more than 14,000 were killed in the indiscriminate violence. In the South, the Volunteer Army and Cossack Whites launched their first Kuban campaign early in 1918 but were forced back in great disorder by the end of March. Meanwhile, Alexander Dutov led a Cossack revolt in Orenburg (followed by a semi-coordinated revolt of the Bashkirs of Orenburg), and the Central Powers resumed their advance with support from a Polish corps recruited from Russian Poles. On March 3, Russia agreed to the Treaty of Brest-Litovsk, ending its participation in World War I. Although fighting stopped in the North, the Central Powers continued to advance in the South, deposing Soviets as they went. Moreover, on March 6 and March 7, another revolt in the East broke out, led by Ataman Gamov in Blagoveshchtik. After a hard-fought battle from March 9 to March 11, his force of 800 officers, 700 Cossacks, and 50 Japanese militiamen was dispersed by local Red Army forces.

After the Treaty of Brest Litovsk, Russia's former allies, primarily Britain, France, and the United States, feared both a possible German-Soviet *rapprochement* and the spread of Marxism. Thus, they began to intervene in the war on the side of the Whites. The British moved first. On March 6, 150 British marines landed in Murmansk to secure the Allies' war supplies that had been shipped there from a potential German attack out of Finland. More troops, including 600 French and a Serbian unit, debarked on April 18. The buildup continued into the summer, but the Allies did not fight the Bolsheviks yet. They disarmed the 1,000-strong Red Army garrison; another 3,000 Bolsheviks retreated southward, burning bridges as they went. In early June, the British deployed 300 troops to Enzeli, which were reinforced by a like amount on June 15, forming a joint British-White Russian brigade with 1,200 Cossacks under Lazar Bicherakov. The first clear fighting between the Allies and Bolsheviks occurred during the Archangel landings of July 30 and August 1. Meanwhile, Finland invaded East Karelia on April 9; the invasion force quickly increased to 25,000 (and would suffer 2,000 battle-deaths before being driven back across the border later that year). The Bolsheviks also faced war with Estonia and Latvia, each seeking to consolidate its independence (Inter-state Wars #107 and #108).

While the Allies—who also deployed forces to Vladivostok, Odessa, and the Transcaspian area (which had revolted on June 17)—never posed much of a direct threat to the Red government, they provided aid and breathing room for White armies to gather. The Volunteer Army, now under the leadership of Anton Denikin, grew from 3,400 in February to 11,500 two months later and 20,000 by July 15 (with the defection of significant numbers of Red Army troops). A second Kuban offensive was mounted by the rebels, clearing the North Caucasus of the Red Army. Confused fighting broke out in Transcaucasia, with Georgians, Azerbaijanis, and Armenians variously allying with White, Red, Ottoman, German, British, French, and Greek forces. And in Siberia, a failed attempt to disarm the 50,000-strong Czech Legion, originally created to fight Austria-Hungary, instead brought it into open revolt against the Bolsheviks on May 23. A provisional government of western Siberia was formed, which soon morphed into a provisional government of Siberia and eventually into a provisional Russian government. A separate rebel government called KOMUCH was formed with the assistance of the Czech Legion on June 8; it eventually would raise more than 35,000 troops to fight the Bolshevik government.

In the second half of 1918, Allied intervention forces continued to build up. In Murmansk, a provisional government of North Russia was formed, led by Evgenii Miller. The Red forces also received some help, as Hungarian prisoners of war in Siberia, encouraged by Hungarian communist Bela Kun, joined the war on the government side. Moreover, as Whites occupied more territory, they encountered national and peasant resistance themselves. Indeed, both sides had to deal with constant peasant uprisings. In August, 50,000 workers and peasants just west of the Urals rebelled against the Bolsheviks, were defeated in battle, and continued to be pursued by CHEKA detachments.

In September, Denikin created the Armed Forces of South Russia (AFSR), which formally merged the Volunteer Army, the Don Army, the Crimean-Azov Army, the North Caucasus Army, the Army of Turkestan, and the Molodaya Army—altogether perhaps 70,000 troops, increasing to 90,000 by November. In October, a new threat emerged to the government in the Northwest, as the Northwest White Army was formed under Nikolai Iudenich—it soon mustered 6,000 Whites. The next month, control of White forces in the East formally passed to Alexander Kolchak in Omsk, Siberia, although it would take some time before all White forces adhered to the would-be government.

Over the following year, according to Lincoln, the Reds and Whites each put about 500,000 soldiers on the front lines in a more intense phase of the war. But the government forces were far better coordinated than their White rivals, allowing them to deal with the White armies piecemeal. Overall Red Army strength increased from 500,000 at the end of 1918 to 2 million at the end of 1919. Allied intervention peaked that year. In Siberia alone, there were 55,000 Czechs, 12,000 Poles, 4,000 Serbs, 4,000 Romanians, 2,000 Italians, 5,600 British and Canadians, 760 French, 28,000 Japanese (soon to increase to 70,000), and 7,500 Americans in March 1919; British strength in the Caucasus peaked at two divisions with 40,000 troops. In Odessa, the French, Greek, Romanian, and Polish volunteers added up to 80,000. In Murmansk, 600 Whites were protected by 6,330 British, 590 French, 1,520 Italians, 1,070 Serbs, and 2,980 Finnish Whites. At Archangel, 1,700 Whites were defended by 3,121 British, 1,400 French, and 4,200 Americans, and in the Baltics, the British navy attacked Soviet ships at sea, while a foreign army of West Russia made up of German *freikorps* units fought the Bolsheviks on land.

The Bolsheviks faced three major campaigns in 1919. In March, Kolchak began to advance in Siberia. The government mobilized 101,400 troops against the 136,000 rebels in the region (some 100,000 of them at least nominally led by Kolchak). The rebels began to experience setbacks in May, and soon the offensive was defeated. The long eastward retreat began. In the south, the AFSR attacked several months after Kolchak, just as his offensive was beginning to stall. At the same time, Iudenich stirred in the Northwest, mounting his first attacks. The Red Army was able to muster 140,000 against Denikin's forces, which with their allies numbered up to 153,000 (though only 45,000 to 50,000 were frontline troops). By October, Denikin had been contained. Iuedenich tried another advance on Moscow but was soon forced to flee into Estonia, where his forces were interned.

By early 1920, the Whites were nearly a spent force. Denikin's forces had been pushed back to Crimea, while Red cavalry units defeated the Cossacks. Kolchak's government was in shambles as troops rushed to Vladivostok for evacuation. Moreover, the Allies were withdrawing their forces. Still, more hard fighting remained, and the government was distracted by yet another inter-state war, this time with Poland. Moreover, peasant and ethnic minority resistance to the government increased as it advanced. Formerly anti-White rebellions became anti-Red ones as the government tried to centralize control and collect grain and taxes.

In Siberia, fighting continued against the forces of Semynov, who had largely taken up the mantle of White resistance once Kolchak's government had been crushed and the latter executed. Japan continued to aid Semynov; when the Red Army attacked his "capital" of Chita on

April 10, more than 200 Japanese were wounded in the first day of fighting. In August, Semynov fell back to Dauria; even in October, he still commanded 18,000 to 20,000 troops. But in November, Semyonov and other Transbaikal White forces fell back, entering China on August 24. Meanwhile in Crimea, the government mounted a final offensive, deploying 130,000 Red Army soldiers against the 34,000 remaining Whites there, led by Pyotr Wrangel. During October and November, Wrangel was defeated. On November 17, Sebastapol fell to the Red Army; the Whites were evacuated by Allied ships.

In August in Dagestan, Naqshbandi sheiks and White generals formed the anti-Bolshevik Sharia Army of the Mountain Peoples led by Said Bey (a grandson of Shamil), estimated by the government to number 9,690 fighters at its peak, including some 600 White officers. Soon after the onset of the revolt, the rebels numbered 3,000 and began attacking government regiments. The First Model Revolutionary Discipline Rifle Regiment suffered the most, losing 700 killed (400 of them massacred after being disarmed) to the rebels from November 9 to November 30; in all, the government lost 5,000 troops in Dagestan before suppressing the revolt on May 21, 1921. Nearly all of the rebels eventually were hunted down and killed.

Termination and Outcome: The fighting subsided after November 1920. A White army under Baron von Unger-Sternberg fled into Mongolia where it was embroiled in Extra-state War #466.

Coding Decisions: Though some researchers divide the Russian Civil War into several different wars based on geographic location, we consider this to be one civil war because there was cooperation among the various White armies. We exclude groups that did not cooperate with the Whites, such as many peasant movements (but see Intra-state War #686), various ethnic minorities, Makhno's anarchist forces, rival factions in the Ukraine (see Intra-state War #681), most forces in Turkestan, the Basmachi (see Intra-state War #691), and so on.

As the countries formerly under Russian control got their independence, they engaged in wars against Russia, and because they gained membership in the interstate system, these wars are coded as inter-state wars: Finland and Estonia versus Russia (#107); Latvia, Estonia, and Germany versus Russia (#108); and the Russo-Polish War (#109). The Russian Civil War also precipitated conflicts within Finland, Ukraine, and Hungary, which are coded as separate intra-state wars (#680, #681, and #683).

Note that Afghanistan sent only 400 troops to intervene against the Bolshevik government in October 1919 and hence is not included as a participant even though it remained until 1922. Likewise, the Ottoman Empire attacked the Baku Soviet in September 1918, but in the absence of any troop estimates, we do not include it as an intervener in the war.[205] The greatest sufferers in the war were the Russian citizens, and as many as 9 million may have died during the war.

Sources: Adelman (1980); Baerlein (1971); Bisher (2005); Bradley (1968); Brinkley (1966); Brovkin (1994); Broxup (1992); Clodfelter (2002); Cornell (2001); Dupuy and Dupuy (1970); Ezergailis (1983); Fedyshyn (1971); Figes (1996); Goldstone (1998); Heflin (1970); Hudson (2004); Kenez (1977); Liebman (1970); Lincoln (1989); Luckett (1971); Olcott (1981); Moore (2002); Onacewicz (1985); Page and Ezergailis (1977); Park (1957); Phillips and Axelrod (2005); Ritter (1990); Silverlight (1970); Smith (1958); Stephen (1994); Stewart (1933); Tschebotarioff (1961); Ulam (1965); Urlanis (1960); Wade (2000, 2001); Yanaga (1949).

INTRA-STATE WAR #680
Finnish Civil War of 1918

Participants: Finland and Germany versus Finnish Communists and Russia.
Dates: January 28, 1918, to May 16, 1918.
Battle-related Deaths: Finnish Communists: 17,500; Finland: 5,300; Germany: 950; Russia: 400.[206]
Initiator: Finnish Communists.
Outcome: Finland and Germany win.
War Type: Civil for central control.
Total System Member Military Personnel: Armed Forces of Finland: [ ]. Armed Forces of Germany: 5,380,000 (prewar); 8,000,000 (initial, peak, final).[207] Armed Forces of Russia: 9,050,000 (prewar); [ ] (initial, peak, final).[208]
Theater Armed Forces: Armed Forces of Finland (White Finland): 80,000 (initial, peak, final). Finnish Communists (Red Finland): 140,000

(initial, peak, final).[209] Armed Forces of Germany (Pro-government Intervener), participating from March 3, 1918: 12,000 (initial, peak, final).[210] Armed Forces of Russia (Pro-rebel Intervener): 10,000 (initial, peak, final).[211] Swedish and Polish Volunteers (Pro-government Interveners): 2,700 (peak).

Antecedents: Finland had been under Russian control since 1809. During World War I (Inter-state War #106) Russia and its allies were fighting a war against Germany and its allies. In the midst of the war, the government of Russia was overthrown in 1917 in a series of two revolutions during which power was ultimately assumed by the Bolshevik government. The first of the 1917 Russian revolutions (the February Revolution) precipitated a collapse in Russian control and conflict within the duchy of Finland between the social democrats and the conservatives. Though the social democrats (supported by Lenin) initially increased their power in the parliament, the conservatives controlled the senate. In the October 1917 elections, the social democrats lost their majority in parliament, and a new conservative government led by Pehr Evind Svinhufvud took office in November. November also brought the Bolsheviks to power in Russia. As one of the reasons for the rebellion was the enormous costs Russia was bearing in the world war, the new government led by Lenin decided to make peace with the Germans and withdraw from the war. An armistice between Russia and Germany was signed on December 6, 1917, and negotiations for what would become the Treaty of Brest Litovsk, in which Russia would surrender control of a significant amount of territory in eastern Europe as the price for peace, were begun on December 22, 1917. The duchy of Finland declared its independence on December 6, 1917 (which was approved by Lenin on December 31). The conservative Finnish government (referred to as White Finland) was determined not to share power with the socialists (or Red Finland), and Finland soon was divided along ideological lines. Germany already had begun returning the Finnish Jägers (fighting units) to Finland and supplying weapons to support the conservative regime and its civil guards (White guards), and the social democrats expanded their Red guards as well.

Narrative: In January 1918, the Finnish government took steps to legalize their White guards by changing their name to the Finnish White Army on January 25. The Red guards responded by launching a mobilization effort on January 26. Conflict began on January 28 as both sides scrambled to secure strategic positions and weapons being sent by train from Russia. The White guard controlled the northern part of the country, while the Red guards established their bases along the southern coast. The Red guard was numerically superior, being able to mobilize 140,000 troops, and it was assisted by 10,000 Bolshevik troops that had remained in the country. The White guard forces numbered at most 80,000, though Germany also sent 12,000 troops to their assistance.

The Red guard initially was successful, seizing Helsinki on January 28 and continuing advances through early March. The Red success prompted the Finnish government to request direct intervention by German troops, a proposal that was approved by Germany on February 21, and a military expedition was sent. The Whites also had professional military leadership, including Carl Gustaf von Mannerheim and the services of the Finnish Jägers, military units that had been trained in Germany. The Whites, led by Mannerheim, defeated the Reds at the decisive battle at Tampere on April 6 even though up to 50 percent of the troops in the assaulting units were killed. Meanwhile, a German naval squadron landed along the southeast coast, and the German troops advanced toward Helsinki, destroyed the remaining socialist strongholds and capturing the city on April 14. The Red guards retreated eastward, and their last major stronghold fell on May 5. Fighting continued until the Whites defeated Russian troops at Ino, and Mannerheim celebrated the White victory with a parade on May 16.

Termination and Outcome: The war ended in a complete government victory, and what followed has been called the White Terror, during which Red prisoners were executed or starved and thousands of civilians were massacred. A formal peace treaty with Russia was signed on October 14, 1920.

Coding Decisions: Because Finland's declaration of independence was recognized by some, though not all, of the great powers, Finland is coded as centering the COW interstate system on December 6, 1917.

Thus this war, which takes place within Finnish territory, is coded as an intra-state war.

Sources: Clodfelter (2002); Gerrard (2000); Kohn (1999); Langer (1952); Siaroff (1999); Singleton (1989); U.S. Library of Congress (2008); Wuorinen (1965).

INTRA-STATE WAR #681

Western Ukrainian War of 1918 to 1919 (aka Ukrainian-Polish War in Galicia)

Participants: Ukraine and Western Ukraine versus Ukrainian Poles and Poland.
Dates: December 1, 1918, to February 13, 1919.
Battle-related Deaths: Ukraine Poles and Poland: 1,000; Ukrainians and Western Ukrainians: 1,500. (See Coding Decisions.)
Initiator: Poles.
Outcome: Transformed into Inter-state War #109.
War Type: Regional Internal.
Total System Member Military Personnel: Armed Forces of Poland: [ ] (initial); 300,000 (peak, final).[212]
Theater Armed Forces: Armed Forces of Poland; 1,400 (initial).[213] Armed Forces of Ukraine: [ ]. Armed Forces of Western Ukrainian Galacian Army (UHA): [ ]. Armed Forces of Ukrainian Poles: 4,660 (initial).[214]

Antecedents: For Russia (now under the leadership of the Bolsheviks) to withdraw from World War I (Inter-state War #106), Russia and Germany signed the Treaty of Brest Litovsk on March 3, 1918, under which Russia lost a significant amount of territory in eastern Europe to Germany (including most of the Ukraine). However, Germany's loss in the war (on September 11, 1918) led to the nullification of the treaty (the abandonment of territorial claims was formalized in the Treaty of Rapallo on April 16, 1922). During 1919, Germany withdrew from the lands it had gained through Brest-Litovsk, a process that created contested claims of sovereignty in the affected areas, including the Ukraine. The Ukraine had competing Red (pro-Russian) and White (anti-Bolshevik) factions, and some of the conflict between these two occurred in the context of the Russian Civil War of 1917 to 1921 (Intra-state War #677). In January 1919, Ukraine tried to establish an independent Ukrainian Soviet Socialist Republic; however by June 1919, Ukraine signed a treaty with Moscow affirming Ukraine's status as affiliated with the Russian Soviet Federative Socialist Republic (SFSR).

Western Ukraine (eastern Galicia) declared its independence from the Austro-Hungarian empire on November 1, 1918, several days before Poland received its independence as part of the end of World War I. The region also was inhabited by a significant number of Poles (39 percent), who responded to the declaration by forming their own army and launching a rebellion in the city of Lviv (Lvov). On November 1, the Polish uprising began in Lviv, with the capture of the train station on November 2. The forces of the Ukranian Galician Army (UHA) were too small to confront the Poles, so the Poles increased their area of control. On November 9, the Galicians brought in armed troops that made attacks in the northern parts of the city. A stalemate ensued as each side brought in reinforcements. The Gonta Detachment from central Ukraine arrived in Galicia but faced a larger contingent of Poles (4,600), including 1,390 reinforcements from Poland. On November 21, the Polish captured a railroad station from the Ukrainians. The battle lines soon stabilized with the Poles occupying the western portion of the city, from which a rail line brought supplies from Poland.

Narrative: On December 1, 1918, an agreement was made to unite western Ukraine with the Ukrainian People's Republic; at that point, the Ukrainian army was fighting a war within Ukraine's borders, so the intra-state war begins at that point, with the Ukrainian army aided by the UHA fighting the Ukrainian Poles aided by forces of Poland (which had become an independent member of the inter-state system on November 3, 1918). The UHA consisted of units like the Sich Riflemen, former members of the Austrian-Hungarian military, and peasant militias. The senior leadership came from the Ukrainian army. In December the Ukrainian Pole-Polish army defeated the Ukrainian Shock Brigade, which was posted south of Lviv. The loss of these troops meant that the subsequent Ukraine/UHA attacks on Lviv at the end of the month did not succeed. Also that month, Polish troops invaded the Ukraine in Volhynia. On January 1, the Polish troops launched an offensive, clearing the Ukrainians from along the railroad lines. Meanwhile, the Ukrainians attacked Lviv again from the south, though it was halted on January 13 at the fortified Polish positions. Further attacks by both sides produced marginal gains during the remainder of January and early February.

Termination and Outcome: Fighting continued until the war was subsumed into the Russo-Polish War (Inter-state War #109) on February 14, 1919. Poland won that war, and western Ukraine was incorporated into Poland, though that status would change again in World War II.

Coding Decisions: This war is coded as a regional war because the fighting is between a regional subunit of Soviet Russia, the Ukraine, and the Poles within the Ukraine. Most sources that discuss this war refer to it as continuing from November 1, 1918, until July 17, 1919, which is partway through the Russo-Polish War that endured until October 18, 1920. Fatality figures for that entire period are generally in the range of 10,000 Poles and 15,000 Ukrainians. As the fatality level was lower in the initial period represented by this war, our best estimate would then be 1,000 for the united Poles and 1,500 for the united Ukrainians.

Sources: Brecke (1999); Clodfelter (2002); Hupchick and Cox (2001); Kubijovyč (1963); Prazmowska (2004); Sullivant (1962).

INTRA-STATE WAR #682
Spartacist Rising of 1919 (aka German Revolution)

Participants: Socialists versus German *Freikorps*.
Dates: January 6, 1919, to May 3, 1919.
Battle-related Deaths: Socialists: [ ]; German *Freikorps*: [ ]; Total Combatant Deaths: 3,000. (See Coding Decisions.)
Initiator: Socialists.
Outcome: German *Freikorps* wins.
War Type: Inter-communal.
Theater Armed Forces: Socialists: German *Freikorps* (aided by the Berlin Auxiliary): 3,000 (initial); 30,000 (peak, final).[215]

Antecedents: Following Germany's defeat in World War I (Inter-state war #106) on November 11, 1918, there was a fear among Germany's ruling elite that Germany faced the possibility of a Bolshevik uprising. In Bavaria, Kurt Eisner, an independent social democrat, called for regime change, and an insurrection on November 8 overthrew the monarchy and established a Bavarian republic. The reform movement spread to all the regional capitals. Kaiser Wilhelm II was soon on his way to exile, and a moderate government under Chancellor Friedrich Ebert was established. Seeing the reforms as insufficient, the leftists, including Karl Liebknecht, the head of the Spartacus League (later the German Communist Party) issued a call for the creation of a socialist republic, using the new revolutionary government in Russia as a model. The new German government had to organize the retreat of the German army from positions held during the war. While the army was being restructured, paramilitary units called the *Freikorps* (Free Corps) emerged to maintain order. Internal turmoil continued in January 1919 as the country prepared for elections for an assembly that would write a new constitution. The *Freikorps*, consisting of ex-military officers and mercenaries, became involved in a number of German cities to suppress popular demonstrations brutally. In December 1918, Ebert sent a message to the *Freikorps*, asking for their help in what he anticipated would be an imminent revolt by the socialists. To prevent socialists from coming to power, cities also removed socialists from their positions. For instance in Berlin, the ruling council fired the police chief of Berlin, Emil Eichorn, who was a socialist who had been accused of arming striking workers. His dismissal became the precipitant for an uprising led by the radical Spartacus League.

Narrative: The newly formed Communist Party (KPD) met in Berlin and called for mass demonstrations in support of Eichorn on January 5, 1919. Large crowds gathered, listened to inspiring speeches by Liebknecht and others, and dispersed peacefully. However that evening, a meeting of the KPD leadership (30 to 50 men) decided upon the need for a revolution. The leader of the People's Naval Division announced the support within his troops and others throughout Berlin for action to overthrow the Ebert regime. On January 6, the armed groups of revolutionaries began seizing government buildings and newspaper offices throughout Berlin, though they failed in an attack on the War Ministry. They also urged workers to seize the large factories. That day, 200,000 workers, some armed, gathered around the Tiergarten, awaiting orders that did not come. Finally on January 8, the leadership issued the call for the workers to take up arms against government institutions. They hoped to be able to establish a new government before the *Freikorps* could intervene. Three hundred sailors were sent to seize the War Ministry but were peacefully turned away. Meanwhile, the government also issued a call for citizens to defend it, and tens of thousands arrived to protect the Reich Chancellery.

Meanwhile, the government also had decided to take action and ordered Defense Minister Gustav Noske to gather forces to suppress the rebellion. Noske left town to gather retired or unemployed military officers for the *Freikorps*, while an auxiliary unit was formed to protect the government. On January 8, the government launched its counteroffensive. The Berlin garrison stormed and retook most of the government buildings, printing offices, and railroad stations, causing a number of casualties. Any captives carrying arms were shot. On the night of January 11, 200 rebels lost control of the police headquarters to government onslaught. The same day, Noske returned to the capital with 3,000 *Freikorps* troops. Ebert ordered them to attack the rebels, and they quickly stormed the barricades in fighting that cost 100 rebel and 17 *Freikorps* deaths. The anti-Spartacus efforts continued as the *Freikorps* was determined to eliminate the leftist threat through brutal terrorism of the population. On January 15, Rosa Luxemburg and Karl Liebknecht were captured in a friend's apartment and later killed.

Uprisings continued: the KPD launched another general strike in Berlin in March; as workers attempted to seize power in a number of cities, including Dusseldorf, Stuttgart, and Nuremburg, the pattern of using the *Freikorps* to suppress the revolts remained the same. In mid-April a leftist insurgency took over Munich, and on May 3, 1919, the *Freikorps* liberated the city, killing 600 workers.

Termination and Outcome: In March 1920, the *Freikorps* was involved in a plot to overthrow the Weimar Republic and, as a result, was dissolved.

Coding Decisions: There is little specific evidence of the battle-deaths in this war, and the figures that are presented are done from specific ideological perspectives. Reports of rebel fatalities in Berlin in January range from 200 to 1,200. Clodfelter reports rebel deaths of 200 in Berlin in January, 1,500 rebel deaths in Berlin in March, and 600 more in Munich, for a total of 2,300, which must be low given the number of uprisings elsewhere and the disagreement about the January deaths.[216] *Freikorps* deaths are reported only in a few instances (totaling 85), which again seems low in terms of the numbers of other engagements. Thus a total combatant death figure of 3,000 would be a conservative estimate.

Sources: Clodfelter (2002); Hamilton (1998); Phillips and Axelrod (2005); Waldman (1958).

INTRA-STATE WAR #683

Hungary's Red and White Terror War of 1919 to 1920 (aka Hungarian War)

Participants: Hungary versus Anti-Communists.
Dates: March 25, 1919, to February 15, 1920.
Battle-related Deaths: Hungary: 1,000; Anti-Communists: 500.
Initiator: Anti-Communists.
Outcome: Anti-Communists win.
War Type: Civil for central control.
Total System Member Military Personnel: Armed Forces of Hungary: [ ] (prewar); 27,000 (initial, peak, final).[217]
Theater Armed Forces: Anti-Communists (including National Army): 25,000 (peak).[218]

Antecedents: The dual monarchy of Austria-Hungary dissolved in the aftermath of its defeat in World War I (Inter-state War #106). Prime Minister Count Michael Karolyi proclaimed Hungarian independence on November 16, 1918. Karolyi faced harsh demands by the victorious Allies and resigned in protest. In effect, he surrendered the government to communist leader Bèla Kun. Kun declared the creation of the Hungarian Soviet Republic on March 21, 1919, and on March 25 created the Hungarian Red Army and the Red Militia, which he utilized on the domestic front to force nationalization of Hungary's estates. Kun's policies provoked a counterrevolution against him in March 1919. The communist government's effort to establish itself was further complicated when it was invaded from April to August 1919 by Romania and Czechoslovakia (Inter-state War #112).

Narrative: Bèla Kun's policy to nationalize private farms and convert them into collective farms alienated both the landed elite and the peasantry. Attacks by peasants against Red Militia units that were enforcing measures to collectivize farms initiated a growing counterrevolutionary movement. On April 3, 1919, counterrevolutionaries attacked the headquarters of the Communist Party, and the Red Army killed three of the rebels. In response, Tibor Szamuely, the people's commissar for military affairs, became the architect of counterinsurgency efforts referred to as the Red Terror. He organized mobile "flying" squads that would go into villages to suppress any resistance to the implementation of government policies, and his personal guards were known as Lenin's boys.

There were several foci of counterrevolutionary activities. In April, rebels overran Beregszás and Munkács near the Ukraine border, which became bases for their activities, though the government dispatched a special regiment that reoccupied the two cities. The growing counterrevolutionary movement led the government to declare martial law on May 4, 1919. On May 30, 1919, a counterrevolutionary government was formed in Szeged in the South. Its National Army was organized by former rear admiral Miklós Horthy, and its ideology, the Szeged Idea, was akin to fascism.

The Hungarian Soviet government fell on August 1, 1919, when Romanian forces captured Budapest (see Inter-state War #112). Kun fled the country. A counterrevolutionary regime was installed with István Friedrich as prime minister. Conflict continued as Horthy's National Army began a campaign against the officials of the former Kun government, referred to as the White Terror. On November 16, 1919, Horthy entered the capital at the head of the National Army, which now numbered 25,000. The White Terror continued under the new government of national concentration created on November 25, 1919, led by Christian social leader Károli Huszár, and would not end until the following February.

Termination and Outcome: The war ended as a victory by the anti-communists.

Coding Decisions: The communists were in power in Hungary at the start of the war and thus are referred to as the government for the entire war in terms of calculating battle-deaths. Scholars report 300 to 600 anti-communist deaths suffered during the Red Terror and 5,000 (communist—Hungarian government) lives lost during the White Terror.[219] As the latter number largely entailed the killing of noncombatants, we are reporting conservative estimates of 1,000 government battle-deaths and 500 anti-communist battle-deaths.

Sources: Adám (1993); Balogh (1971); Clodfelter (2002); Crampton (1997); Heflin (1970); Hentea (2007); Hupchick and Cox (2001); Goldstone (1998); Hoensch (1996); Jasci (1969); Kohn (1999); Phillips and Axelrod (2005); Volgyes (1971).

INTRA-STATE WAR #686

Green Rebellion of 1920 to 1921 (aka Tambov Rebellion or Antonov's Mutiny)

Participants: Soviet Russian Republic versus Peasants in Tambov.
Dates: August 19, 1920, to June 3, 1921.
Battle-related Deaths: Peasants in Tambov: 7,500; Soviet Russian Republic: 1,700. (See Coding Decisions.)
Initiator: Peasants in Tambov.
Outcome: Soviet Russian Republic.
War Type: Civil for local issues.
Total System Member Military Personnel: Armed Forces of Soviet Russia: 1,550,000 (prewar); 3,050,000 (initial); 5,500,000 (peak, final).[220]
Theater Armed Forces: Armed Forces of Soviet Russia: 20,000 (initial); 50,000 (peak).[221] Peasants in Tambov: 4,500 (initial); 40,000 (peak).[222]

Antecedents: Even after enduring a three-year civil war (Intra-state War #677), the new Soviet Union still had to face more rebellions over local issues in the years thereafter. One of the major rebellions was the Peasant War of 1918 to 1922, which is a collection of peasant revolts that arose throughout Soviet Russia. The individual conflicts (Russia faced 118 separate uprisings in February 1920 alone) varied in duration and intensity: some of the conflicts were short, punitive measures, while others entailed significant armed combat with Soviet forces.[223] The most widespread of these began in Tambov Province (southeast of Moscow) and was led by radical Aleksandr Antonov, who had been one of the leaders of the storming of the Winter Palace.

Narrative: Russian peasants who feared that their dreams of land ownership would be dashed by the new Soviet regime resisted the Bolshevik food requisitioning measures. In August 1920, the harvest was just coming in when the Russian food-levy brigades arrived. Peasants in two villages attacked the brigades, killing 7 soldiers. In reprisal, 20,000 Russian troops attacked but were driven off by Antonov's followers. Leon Trotsky's new Soviet army began to pour reinforcements into the garrison at Tambov. On May 6, 1921, the major Soviet offensive was launched by 50,000 troops, leading to thousands of deaths on both sides. By June 3, Antonov's main force had been broken. Peasant revolts did continue in other regions till 1922.

Termination and Outcome: The outcome was a victory for the government as Antonov's forces were dispersed. However, in April 1921, a new policy of a tax on grain rather than appropriation was launched, and in October 1921, Lenin admitted that the policy toward the peasants had hindered production and was the cause of the economic crisis. To that extent, the peasants had scored a victory.[224] Antonov was tracked down and shot in 1922.

Coding Decisions: Determining battle-deaths is complicated by the nature of the war, which included the use of artillery and poison gas. Overall, it is estimated that 240,000 people died through 1922, though this number includes civilian deaths and the fighting outside the scope of this war. The battle-death numbers reported are from Clodfelter.[225]

Sources: Clodfelter (2002); Conquest (1987); Read (1996); Ross (1923).

INTRA-STATE WAR #688

Italian Fascist War of 1920 to 1922

Participants: Blackshirts versus Leftists
Dates: October 1920 to October 1, 1922.
Battle-related Deaths: Leftists: 3,000; Blackshirts: 300.[226]
Initiator: Blackshirts.
Outcome: Blackshirts win.
War Type: Inter-communal.
Theater Armed Forces: Leftists: [ ]. Blackshirts: 200,000 (peak, final).

Antecedents: The aftermath of World War I (Interstate War #106) saw the emergence of leftist socialist movements encouraged by the victory of the Bolsheviks in Russia and right-wing organizations unhappy with the outcomes of the war. In March 1919, Benito Mussolini founded the Italian Fascist movement, with its voluntary militia referred to as the Blackshirts. The Blackshirts primarily were former soldiers angered by the growing power of socialism and the economic dislocations in postwar Italy.

Narrative: In 1920, Italian socialists engineered a number of strikes and seizures of factories and land in the countryside. The Blackshirts became "agents of capitalism" as they intervened to protect the landlords and factory owners by attacking the leftists. Over the course of two years, the fascists and leftists engaged in a series of attacks and riots. The fascists ultimately destroyed most of the leftist strongholds, while government forces did not intervene.

Termination and Outcome: The war ended as a victory by the Blackshirts. Encouraged by their successes, Mussolini undertook his march on Rome in October 1922, at the end of which Mussolini became the Italian prime minister on October 28.

Coding Decisions: Because neither side in the war is the government of the system member, nor a regional subunit, the war is coded as an intercommunal conflict.

Sources: Clodfelter (2002); Goldstone (1998); Phillips and Axelrod (2005).

INTRA-STATE WAR #690

Kronstadt Rebellion of 1921

Participants: Soviet Russia versus Sailors.
Dates: March 7, 1921, to March 18, 1921.
Battle-related Deaths: Soviet Russia: 1,900; Sailors: 2,700.[227]
Initiator: Sailors.
Outcome: Soviet Russia wins.

War Type: Civil for local issues.
Total System Member Military Personnel: Armed Forces of Soviet Russia: 3,050,000 (prewar); 5,500,000 (initial, peak, final).[228]
Theater Armed Forces: Armed Forces of Soviet Russia: 45,000 (peak).[229] Sailors: 10,000 (initial); 27,000 (peak).[230]

Antecedents: The giant Russian naval base at Kronstadt near St. Petersburg was one of the major Russian naval facilities. The sailors at the base had played pivotal roles in the Russian civil wars in 1905 and 1917 (Intra-state Wars #643 and #677) and thus for many had come to symbolize the glory of the revolution. By 1921, however, many of these revolutionary sailors had come to the conclusion that the new Soviet government had betrayed their ideals. Conversely, the Bolshevik government had grown to resent the independence of the sailors. Leon Trotsky, the people's commissar of military and naval affairs, had already reasserted government control over the army and began to propose a similar administration for the navy. Thus the navy became aligned with others who had become disenchanted with the government, including a number of workers in Petrograd (the former Saint Petersburg).

In February 1921, workers in Petrograd demonstrated against the government, which suppressed the disturbances. Naval officers presented information about the uprisings at a meeting held without official approval on February 28, at which a resolution was passed demanding government reforms. The naval officers sent a delegation to the Petrograd Soviet to explain their position, and when they were arrested, the Kronstadt sailors rebelled.

Narrative: On March 1, 1921, the sailors met to hear the government's position. The next day, the sailors formed a provisional government, and the Soviets responded with an ultimatum to surrender. Instead, 10,000 sailors rebelled, though the number of revolutionaries soon reached 27,000 as seamen, allied soldiers, and civilians flocked to support the sailors. A force of 45,000 Bolshevik troops commanded by Leon Trotsky and Marshal Mikhail Tukhachevsky were sent by Lenin to suppress the revolt. The first Soviet attack on Kronstadt on March 7, 1921, was repulsed, but the Soviets soon succeeded in taking Kronstadt on March 18, 1921.

Termination and Outcome: The outcome was a government. The harsh measures imposed on the remaining rebels (executions and imprisonment) earned Trotsky condemnation within the Communist Party.

Coding Decisions: The sailor battle-deaths include 600 who died in combat and the 2,103 mutineers who were executed in the immediate aftermath of the war.

Sources: Clodfelter (2002): Phillips and Axelrod (2005); Saunders (1958).

INTRA-STATE WAR #693
Agrarian Rising of 1923

Participants: Bulgaria versus Agrarian League.
Dates: September 23, 1923, to September 28, 1923.
Battle-related Deaths: Bulgaria: [ ]; Agrarian League: [ ]; Total Combatant Deaths: 3,000.
Initiator: Agrarian League.
Outcome: Bulgaria wins.
War Type: Civil for central control.
Total System Member Military Personnel: 20,000 (prewar, initial, peak, final).[231]
Theater Armed Forces: Agrarian League, aided by Communists and Yugoslavia: [ ].

Antecedents: Bulgaria's participation on the side of the losing central powers of World War I (Inter-state War #106) led to significant fatalities and losses of territory to the new state of Yugoslavia. A flood of refugees aggravated Bulgaria's economic situation. One of Bulgaria's major political parties was the Bulgarian Agrarian National Union (BANU), and its leader, Alexander Stamboliysky, was asked to serve as prime minister in a coalition government in 1919. Elections in 1920 gave the agrarians a large majority, and Stamboliysky headed the new, democratically elected government. BANU had campaigned in favor of agrarian revolution and reform, and Stamboliysky wanted to create a government that would be responsive to the 80 percent of Bulgaria's people who were peasants. Stamboliysky also formed a paramilitary organization known as the Orange Guards, which both protected him and implemented agrarian reforms. Some of Stamboliysky's policies garnered him the support of the Communist International, which met in 1922, and it urged the Communist Party in Bulgaria to support BANU as well.

Narrative: Stamboliysky's policies also earned him the enmity of some of the middle class and the military. A military coup ousted Stamboliysky on June 8, 1923, and the Communist Party refused to come to his aid. Stamboliysky attempted to launch a counter-revolt but was captured and killed on June 14. The Soviets again encouraged the Bulgarian communists to cooperate with the agrarians, and they did so when the agrarians launched a rebellion against the government on September 23. Troops from the agrarians and the communists, aided by Yugoslavia, began uprisings in several parts of Bulgaria, yet they were defeated by the government in five days, with the rebels sustaining heavy losses.

Termination and Outcome: The war ended as a government victory.

Coding Decisions: Clodfelter suggests that several thousand people were killed in the revolt, mostly agrarians. Thus we are coding a guess of 3,000 total combat fatalities in the absence of additional information.

Sources: Clodfelter (1992); Crampton (1987).

INTRA-STATE WAR #717
Spain–Miners War of 1934

Participants: Spain versus Asturian Miners
Dates: October 4, 1934, to October 18, 1934.
Battle-related Deaths: Asturian Miners: 1,051; Spain: 284.[232]
Initiator: Asturian Miners.
Outcome: Spain wins.
War Type: Civil for local issues.
Total System Member Military Personnel: Armed Forces of Spain: 146,000 (prewar); 138,000 (initial, peak, final).[233]
Theater Armed Forces: Armed Forces of Spain: 1,700 (initial); 26,000 (peak, final).[234] Asturian Miners: 70,000 (peak).[235]

Antecedents: This war is a prelude piece to the Spanish Civil War of 1936 to 1939 (Intra-state War #718). After the Spanish monarchy was deposed 1931, Spanish politics under the Second Spanish Republic was dominated by a bitter rivalry between left and right. In 1933, liberal president Alcalá Zamora dissolved the Cortes and called for new elections, which were won by the right. The party with a plurality was the conservative, Catholic, Spanish Confederation of the Autonomous Right (*Confederación Española de Derechas Autónomas*—CEDA), and Zamora refused to appoint CEDA's leader, José Maria Gil-Robles, as prime minister. Instead he appointed Alejandro Lerroux, the leader of the more moderate Radical Republican Party (*Partido Republicano Radical*) as prime minister. Lerroux (who took office on December 16, 1933) worked with CEDA, and CEDA's participation in the government prompted a rebellion by leftist and anarchists in the northwestern province of Asturias.

Narrative: In March 1934, the new government announced a new antistrike policy whereby the civil guard would be used to disperse demonstrations and strikes. Leftist newspapers also were targeted. The socialists in Asturias began discussing plans for a revolt against the government. The socialists launched a number of strikes in early 1934, during which some protesters were killed. These events increasingly radicalized the young miners in Asturias. The socialists began gathering weapons and were able to forge cooperative bonds with some of the anarchist groups. The socialists developed a detailed plan for the rebellion, which called for the miners to quickly seize the coalfields. The rebellion was launched on October 4, 1934, primarily in Asturias (planned uprisings elsewhere did not materialize). The miners gained control of the coalfield, and 1,200 of them marched toward Oviedo (capital of Asturias), where 1,700 government troops defended the city. Three days of street fighting ensued. The rebels also seized the port of Gijón.

The conservative government in Madrid dispatched troops under Gen. Francisco Franco to subdue the revolt. The revolts were squelched quickly, except for that in Asturias. Here, 70,000 miners had seized key positions. In heavy fighting, the miners were defeated within days amid reports of torture by Franco's troops of the 30,000 who had surrendered.

Termination and Outcome: The outcome was a government victory. After the war, about

30,000 rebels were captured and tortured. These events set the stage for the next war, the Spanish Civil War of 1936 to 1939 (Intra-state War #718).

Sources: Clodfelter (1992); Oliviera (1946); Phillips and Axelrod (2005); Preston (1993, 1994); Thomas (1961).

INTRA-STATE WAR #718
Spanish Civil War of 1936 to 1939

Participants: Spain (aided by International Brigades) versus Fascists (aided by Germany, Italy, and Portugal).
Dates: July 18, 1936, to March 29, 1939.
Battle-related Deaths: Spain: 175,000; Soviet Union: 158; Fascists: 110,000; Portugal: 8,000; Italy: 9,800; Germany: 300; International Brigades: 6,100.[236] (See Coding Decisions.)
Initiator: Fascists.
Outcome: Fascists win.
War Type: Civil for central control.
Total System Member Military Personnel: Armed Forces of Spain: 141,000 (prewar); 475,000 (initial); 550,000 (peak); 539,000 (final).[237] Armed Forces of the Soviet Union: 1,300,000 (prewar, initial); 1,789,000 (peak, final).[238] Armed Forces of Germany: 461,000 (prewar); 586,000 (initial); 2,750,000 (peak, final).[239] Armed Forces of Italy: 1,380,000 (prewar); 343,000 (initial); 581,000 (peak, final).[240] Armed Forces of Portugal: 37,000 (prewar); 36,000 (initial); 40,000 (peak, final).[241]
Theater Armed Forces: Armed Forces of Spain: 98,900 (initial).[242] Armed Forces of the Soviet Union (Pro-government Intervener), participating from September 14, 1936*:* 700 (initial); 2,000 (peak).[243] International Brigades (Pro-government Intervener), participating from August 13, 1936, to November 1938: 16,000 (initial); 59,400 (peak).[244] Fascists (Rebels—includes Militarized Police and Civil Guard): 91,500 (initial); 600,000 (1938).[245] Armed Forces of Germany (State Pro-rebel Intervener), participating from July 22, 1936: 700 (initial); 16,000 (peak).[246] Armed Forces of Italy (State Pro-rebel Intervener), participating from October 30, 1936: 3,000 (initial); 80,000 (peak).[247] Armed Forces of Portugal: 20,000 (peak).[248]

Antecedents: The election of 1933 had shifted Spain's government from liberal to conservative, and the inclusion of the conservative, Catholic, Spanish Confederation of the Autonomous Right (*Confederación Española de Derechas Autónomas*—CEDA) in the government of Prime Minister Alejandro Lerroux, of the more moderate Radical Republican Party (Partido Republicano Radical), prompted a rebellion by leftist and anarchists in the northwestern province of Asturias (Intra-state War #717). The government in Madrid dispatched troops under Gen. Francisco Franco to subdue the revolt of 70,000 miners. In heavy fighting, the miners were defeated within days amid reports of torture by Franco's troops.

Violence between the left and the right continued: CEDA and its leader, José-Maria Gil-Robles, adopted policies similar to the German Nazi Party and demanded an increased role in the government. The Lerroux government collapsed, and legislative elections were held in early 1936. The leftist Popular Front (a coalition of left-wing parties including the socialists, republicans, and communists) won the elections, and Manuel Azaña became prime minister, though he was replaced by Santiago Casares Quiroga in May. The right (including CEDA, the monarchists, sectors of the military, and the Falange Party) began plotting a revolution. The Falange Party had been formed in 1933 by José Antonio Primo de Rivera (son of the CEDA leader). As the government became aware of the activities of the plotters, Primo de Rivera was jailed, and a number of generals were removed. General Franco (who was serving as the military commander of the Canary Islands) was assigned to Morocco. The conspiracy was being organized by Gen. Emilio Mola, and it was expected to be a swift coup on July 17 that would begin in Spanish Morocco.

Narrative: A revolt by army officers in Melilla in Spanish Morocco on July 17, 1936, led to revolts at garrisons around Spain. Instead of a coup, the rebels (or nationalists) became involved in a three-year war. On July 18, Franco left for Africa, where he took control of the Moroccan forces. Germany provided Franco with planes, with which he was able to ferry his army to Seville to join up with General Mola's army, which secured most of northwestern Spain. Republicans controlled the area around Madrid as well as almost all of southern and eastern Spain and parts of the Basque country in the North. During the first phase of the war, policies of repression and terrorism were conducted against civilians by both sides. Since Franco's Moroccan army was the key component of the nationalist strength, he was able to take control of the nationalist armies in October. Franco was convinced of the need to make Spain into a one-party state, and so he united the traditionalists (monarchists) with the Falange. Though there was opposition within the two groups, the majority went along with Franco's goal to create a mass party as necessary for the war. The other key element that proved to be necessary for success was that of foreign assistance and the degree to which it enabled the Falange to build a combat force.

In fall 1936, the nationalists were saved by the arrival of planes and weapons from Germany. The main supplier of troops to the nationalists was Italy, which increased its commitment to 40,000 troops. In contrast, the western democracies established a policy of nonintervention and thus refused republican requests for arms and assistance. The war became more of a war of attrition and slow advances. Beginning in February 1937, the nationalists launched a new offensive, and the rebels soon threatened Madrid. The loyalists fortified the city with the help of foreign volunteers. Originally recruited by the Comintern, the International Brigades (of volunteers from France, Germany, Austria, Italy, the United States, Great Britain, Yugoslavia, Switzerland, Poland, Czechoslovakia, Canada, Hungary, Norway, Denmark, Sweden, Cuba, Mexico, and others) came to Spain to stop the spread of fascism. It was these volunteers that saved Madrid in spring 1937, though the city would be besieged.

Meanwhile, the rebels made gains in the North. The carpet-bombing campaign of the German Luftwaffe enabled the nationalists to capture Guernica on April 29, 1937. They also seized the coastal city Santander on August 26, 1937. The rebels then advanced toward Asturias, the last remaining republican stronghold along the coast. After weeks of heavy fighting, it fell on October 21. In the East, government forces (aided by Soviet tanks) launched an offensive against Teruel. Though initially successful, a nationalist soon recaptured the town in February 1938, with each side suffering severe casualties. In the fall of 1938, the republicans decided to disband the International Brigades in the vain hope that the nationalists might similarly send the German and Italian troops home. Instead the nationalists launched major offensives. Republican forces crumbled, and the nationalists seized the republican capital of Barcelona on January 26, 1939, and Madrid fell on March 28, 1939.

Termination and Outcome: The war ended as a rebel victory, and Franco was named chief of the Spanish state. His autocratic rule would last for four decades. The policies of repression caused huge numbers of civilian deaths by both sides, with estimates ranging from 144,000 to 200,000 (generally equally allocated to the nationalists and republicans).[249]

Coding Decisions: The number of people killed during this war has been a matter of significant disagreement, with a commonly cited figure being 1 million killed, though that apparently included civilian deaths during battle and the repression. More recent scholarship has yielded somewhat lower figures. Thomas concluded that there were 110,000 nationalist deaths and 175,000 for the republicans, though he later lowered these to 90,000 for the nationalists and 110,000 for the republicans.[250] He also added an additional 200,000 deaths due to disease but was not specific about whether this was just for combatants or civilians as well. Because COW includes the deaths of combatants due to disease during the war, we are citing Thomas's earlier figures here in the hope that it would then include some of the deaths from disease.

Sources: Carr (1982); Clodfelter (2002); Coverdale (1975); Payne (1970, 1987); Phillips and Axelrod (2005); Thomas (1961); Urlanis (1971); Whealey (1989).

INTRA-STATE WAR #720

Greek Civil War of 1944 to 1945

Participants: Greece and United Kingdom versus Communists.

Dates: December 3, 1944, to January 11, 1945.

Battle-related Deaths: Communists: 1,000; Greece: 500; United Kingdom: 237.[251] (See Coding Decisions.)
Initiator: Communists.
Outcome: Greece aided by United Kingdom wins.
War Type: Civil for central control.
Total System Member Military Personnel: Armed Forces of Greece: [ ] (prewar, initial); 117,000 (peak, final).[252] Armed Forces of United Kingdom: 4,145,000 (prewar); 4,900,000 (initial); 5,090,000 (peak, final).[253]
Theater Armed Forces: Armed Forces of Greece: 8,500 (peak).[254] Armed Forces of United Kingdom: 13,000 (peak).[255] Communists (ELAS): 15,000 (prewar); 25,000 (initial).[256] EDES and EKKA (Pro-government Militias): 20,000 (divided evenly, 1944).

Antecedents: During World War II (Inter-state War #139), communists in Greece had been prominent in the resistance against the Germans. In September 1944, the British liberated Greece from the Nazis and restored the prewar Greek government. Though the Communist National Liberation Front (EAM) party was included in the government, a faction of its military wing, the Greek People's Liberation Army (ELAS), was controlled by the Communist Party of Greece (KKE) and resisted cooperating with the British-backed government. The ELAS retreated into the mountains, where it received supplies from Yugoslavia and Albania. Terrorist attacks erupted against EAM–KKE and by EAM–KKE against government collaborators. In May 1944, representatives from all the political and military groups met in Lebanon, which produced a national contract and government (with Georgios Papandreou as prime minister) in which EAM was included. As Germany continued retreating from Greece, ELAS began taking control over the countryside. The first British troops arrived in Athens on October 12, 1944, and the Greek government returned from Egypt to Athens on October 18. Greek army units began arriving in November.

Almost immediately, criticism of the Greek government arose for its monarchist connections and its absence from Greece. Critics also were divided over how the government should deal with those who had collaborated with the Nazis. On December 1, the government decreed that all militia groups would be disarmed.

Narrative: Clashes involving the ELAS against government and British troops began on December 3, 1944. The *Dekemvriana* (or December events) began as 200,000 demonstrators took to the streets (prompted by EAM). When they arrived at the Tomb of the Unknown Soldier, they were fired upon from the police station, and fifty civilians were killed. The British ordered ELAS to leave the capital and committed British troops to the conflict. A period of thirty-seven days of full-scale fighting in Athens ensued that pitted the EAM–ELAS fighters against British and Greek troops. The ELAS, whose strength had been underestimated by the British, initially went on the offensive, pushing the British forces outside the capital. ELAS was joined by 10,000 local reservists. On December 18, ELAS seized a Royal Air Force (RAF) building, capturing several hundred British officers. ELAS also attacked EDES (the Republican Liberal Union), which had been established in Epirus with British assistance. ELAS defeated EDES forces until they were evacuated by the British at the end of the month.

Meanwhile, the British had been receiving reinforcements and, in cooperation with the Greek army, launched an offensive to drive the rebels from Athens. Ultimately, the British gained the upper hand, surrounding ELAS forces. On January 5, ELAS had evacuated the capital. On January 11, ELAS requested an armistice, while 5,000 rebels fled to Yugoslavia.

Termination and Outcome: The war ended as a defeat for the EAM. In February 1945, the Treaty of Varkiza was signed, which called for the demobilizing of the armed militias. Between 1945 and 1946, a reign of White Terror was conducted by right-wing gangs against remaining ELAS members. Fighting resumed on March 30, 1946, as communist rebels, supported by the neighboring Marxist-Leninist states (Yugoslavia, Bulgaria, and Albania), began a general revolt against the Greek government.

Coding Decisions: Because the agreement stopped the fighting for just over a year, when the fighting resumes, it is coded as a new war (Intra-state War #724). Shrader contends that the number of deaths in this war will probably never be known. Richardson codes this war as a "4," which represents about 10,000 fatalities. Clodfelter reports 237 British fatalities and casualty figures of 4,000 for ELAS and 2,000 for Greece. Using the 3:1 ratio of wounded to deaths, that would mean about 1,000 ELAS fatalities and 500 battle-deaths for Greece. Civilian casualties were also heavy.

Sources: Cady and Prince (1966); Clodfelter (1992); Heflin (1970); O'Ballance (1966a); Phillips and Axelrod (2005); Richardson (1960); Shrader (1999); Taylor and Hudson (1972); Wood (1968); Wright (1965).

INTRA-STATE WAR #721

Polish Ukrainians War of 1945 to 1947

Participants: Poland and the Soviet Union versus Ukrainian Partisan Army (UPA).
Dates: May 8, 1945, to November 18, 1947.
Battle-related Deaths: Poland: 8,100; UPA: 8,700; Soviet Union: 5,000. (See Coding Decisions.)
Initiator: UPA.
Outcome: Poland, aided by the Soviet Union, wins.
War Type: Civil for local issues.
Total System Member Military Personnel: Armed Forces of Poland: [ ] (prewar); 197,000 (initial, peak); 168,000 (final).[257] Armed Forces of the Soviet Union: 6,100,000 (prewar); 12,500 (initial, peak); 3,600,000 (final).[258]
Theater Armed Forces: Armed Forces of Poland: 30,000 (final).[259] Armed Forces of the Soviet Union (Pro-government Intervener): [ ]. UPA in Poland: 40,000 (initial); 15,000 (final).[260]

Antecedents: Though the Ukraine had been part of the Soviet Union, many Ukrainians sought their own state. During World War I (Inter-state War #106), the status of the Ukraine had been contested as the result of the Treaty of Brest-Litovsk, which Germany had demanded as the price Russia had to pay to withdraw from the war; it was later nullified by Germany's loss in the war. In 1918 and 1919, western Ukraine, which had been under the control of Austria-Hungary, sought to unite with Ukraine (Intra-state War #681). As part of the Peace of Riga, signed on March 18, 1921, which ended the Polish-Soviet War of 1919 to 1920 (Inter-state war #109), western Ukraine was given to Poland. During the course of World War II (Inter-state War #139), western Ukraine and Ukraine were again united under German control. In 1941, the organization of Ukrainian Nationalists (OUN) declared an independent Ukrainian state, and the OUN was suppressed by the Nazis. OUN created the Ukrainian Partisan Army (UPA), which fought for autonomy or independence against the Germans, Soviets, and Poles, though those conflicts were subsumed within that war. Ukrainians lived in areas that had been taken over by Poland, and in 1944, the Soviets launched Operation Vistula, whereby it asked Polish authorities to relocate Ukrainians from Poland into the Soviet Union, a process that led to brutality against the Ukrainians, while the Soviet Union was to deport Poles living in the Ukraine to Poland. OUN also engaged in efforts to eliminate Poles from the area by massacres.[261] As the Soviet Union and Poland engaged in this mutual transfer of populations in 1945 and 1946, they agreed that the Ukrainian activists needed to be eliminated. Soviet troops also remained in Poland so that the UPA fought against both the Polish and Soviet troops in Poland, oftentimes to protect ethnic Ukrainians from being deported. At the end of World War II, when the fighting continued, it marked the start of two separate Ukrainian wars aimed at gaining Ukrainian independence, this one, fought in Poland (which involved both Polish and Soviet troops) and another fought in the Soviet Union (Intra-state War #722).

Narrative: The war began on March 8, 1945, as the Ukrainian Partisan Army (UPA) continued its fight against its incorporation into Poland. The UPA would attack Polish forces attempting to register Ukrainians for deportation. Ukrainians also formed self-defense militias to protect themselves from attacks by Polish citizens. In April 1947, the Polish government launched Operation Wisla to eliminate the Ukrainian problem, which had both military and civilian components. A Polish force of 30,000 troops surrounded and killed a large contingent of the UPA partisans in fierce fighting. On the civilian front, the 150,000 members of the Lemko population that had harbored the Ukrainians were uprooted and dispersed. Overall, by 1947, at least 322,868 Ukrainians and 797,907 Poles had been moved.[262] Fighting continued, and on September 8, the Polish army engaged 15,000 Ukrainians in repeated engagements in the South. The Polish government forces gradually defeated the UPA by November 1947.

Termination and Outcome: The outcome was a victory by the Polish government, aided by the Soviet Union.

Coding Decisions: Coding the battle-deaths for this war is made more complicated by the politicized nature of this conflict and the widely divergent ways in which it is interpreted. We utilize Clodfelter's report of Poland's 32,400 casualties, which using the 3:1 ratio of casualties to deaths means 8,100 Polish deaths. He also reports 8,700 UPA and Ukrainian deaths in Poland during this period. The question of Soviet deaths is less clear. Clodfelter reports 40,000 deaths against the Ukrainians between 1945 and 1957, but presumably that figure includes not only this war but the one in the Ukraine itself as well as actions in Slovakia. As there have been reports of 25,000 Soviet deaths within the Ukraine, we are reporting an estimate of 5,000 deaths in this portion of the conflict.

Sources: Clodfelter (2002); Marples (2007); The *New York Times* Index (1947); Subtelny (1988).

INTRA-STATE WAR #722
Ukrainian Partisans War of 1945 to 1947

Participants: Soviet Union versus Ukrainian Partisan Army (UPA).
Dates: May 8, 1945, to December 31, 1947.
Battle-related Deaths: Soviet Union: 25,000; UPA: 56,600.[263]
Initiator: UPA.
Outcome: Soviet Union wins.
War Type: Civil for local issues.
Total System Member Military Personnel: Armed Forces of the Soviet Union: 6,100,000 (prewar); 12,500,000 (initial, peak); 2,700,000 (final).[264]
Theater Armed Forces: Armed Forces of the Soviet Union: 500,000 (peak).[265] Ukrainian Partisan Army (UPA): 6,000 (initial); 90,000 (peak).[266]

Antecedents: During World War I (Inter-state War #106), the status of the Ukraine had been contested as the result of the Treaty of Brest-Litovsk, which Germany had demanded as the price Russia had to pay to withdraw from the war and later was nullified by Germany's loss in the war. In 1918 and 1919, western Ukraine, which had been under the control of Austria-Hungary, sought to unite with Ukraine (Intra-state War #681). As part of the Peace of Riga, signed on March 18, 1921, which ended the Polish-Soviet War of 1919 to 1920 (Inter-state War #109), western Ukraine was given to Poland. During the course of World War II (Inter-state War #139), western Ukraine and Ukraine were again united under German control. In 1941, the organization of Ukrainian Nationalists (OUN) declared an independent Ukrainian state, and the OUN was suppressed by the Nazis. OUN created the Ukrainian Partisan Army (UPA), which fought for autonomy or independence against the Germans, Soviets, and Poles, though those conflicts were subsumed within that war. Toward the end of World War II, Poland and the Soviet Union engaged in a program of mutual forced migration, whereby Ukrainians living in Polish territory were forced to move to the Ukraine, while Poles living in the Ukraine were deported to Poland. Both Poland and the Soviet Union agreed that the Ukrainian activists needed to be eliminated. At the end of World War II, when the fighting continued, it marked the start of two separate Ukrainian wars aimed at gaining Ukrainian independence: one, fought in Poland (Intra-state War #721, which involved both Polish and Soviet troops), and this one, fought in the Soviet Union.

Narrative: In 1944, the Soviet Union had recovered most of the pre-1939 Ukraine, and in July it controlled western Ukraine as well, thus creating a united Ukraine. However, the UPA became the major obstacle to Soviet control, and in the last few months of World War II, the Soviet Union engaged in a brutal campaign of repression against the Ukrainian nationalists, reportedly killing 91,615 Ukrainian guerrillas.[267]

The end of World War II marks the start of this separate war, in which the UPA fought against the Soviet army and the NKVD (the Soviet secret police) within the Ukraine. As a result of the 1944 Soviet offensive, the UPA was depleted in May 1945, with only 6,000 active guerrillas. By 1946, as relations with the Soviet Union were becoming less friendly, the United States and Britain started funneling aid to the UPA. The terror campaign launched by the NKVD in the Ukraine also prompted a flood of volunteers to the UPA. Thus in 1946, UPA had 90,000 men engaged in a guerrilla war that involved at least 1,945 clashes that year. After that, the Soviet superior numbers and the forced deportations took a toll on the rebels, and the fighting was mostly over by the end of 1947.

Termination and Outcome: During the war, 30,000 Soviet civilians were also killed. Though most of the fighting ended in 1947, limited attacks continued until 1954. In 1947, the Soviet Union, Poland, and Czechoslovakia signed an agreement for joint operations against the UPA in border areas.

Coding Decisions: There are varying reports concerning the numbers of people killed in this war. Part of the difficulty in coding battle-deaths is due to the terror campaign waged by the Soviets against the populace in general.

Sources: Clodfelter (2002); Marples (1992, 2007); Rieber (2003); Wilson (2000); Yekelchyk (2007).

INTRA-STATE WAR #723

Forest Brethren War of 1945 to 1949 (aka Baltic Partisans War)

Participants: Soviet Union versus Baltic Partisans.
Dates: May 8, 1945, to December 31, 1949.
Battle-related Deaths: Baltic Partisans: 30,000; Soviet Union: 20,000. (See Coding Decisions.)
Initiator: Baltic Partisans.
Outcome: Soviet Union wins.
War Type: Civil for local issues.
Total System Member Military Personnel: Armed Forces of the Soviet Union: 6,100,000 (prewar); 12,500,000 (initial, peak); 5,000,000 (final).[268]
Theater Armed Forces: Armed Forces of the Soviet Union: 110,000 (peak).[269] Baltic Partisans (Rebel aggregate), consisting of Lithuanian Partisans: 17,524 (initial); 30,000 (peak); 916 (final).[270] Latvian Partisans: 15,000 (peak).[271] Estonian partisans: 10,000 (peak).[272]

Antecedents: In 1939, the Molotov–Ribbentrop nonaggression pact between Germany and the Soviet Union divided northern Europe into spheres of influence, and on the basis of the pact, after World War II broke out, the Soviet Union annexed Estonia, Latvia, and Lithuania. Germany then conquered the Baltics as it invaded the Soviet Union in 1941. Throughout the region, local guerrilla forces emerged during World War II to oppose first the Germans and then the return of the Soviets. In the Baltic states (Estonia, Latvia, and Lithuania), the partisans were known as the Forest Brethren or Forest Brothers. High levels of armed conflict including pitched battles between the partisans and the Soviet forces occurred in late 1944 and early 1945. The Soviets also launched a significant number of punitive expeditions and deported thousands to the gulag. The conflicts during this period were subsumed into World War II. This new war represents the continuation of the conflict between the Soviet Union and partisans in the Baltic states after World War II had ended.

Narrative: The fierce fighting that characterized the last year of World War II in the Baltics continued between the Soviet army and the Forest Brethren for the first two and a half years, and then conflict at lesser intensity lasted through 1949 (though continuing in Estonia till 1951). The goal of the Brethren was to persuade the Soviet Union to give up its dominant role so that the countries could attain independence, whereas the Soviet goal was to eliminate resistance to its administration through armed conflict or repressive measures. During the summer of 1945, the Soviet NKVD (internal forces) engaged in several major battles within the Baltic countries. Great Britain, the United States, and Sweden supplied the partisans with some intelligence, but those efforts were compromised by the Philby intelligence breach. From the end of 1946 to 1947, the Soviet tactics changed, with more emphasis placed on intimidation of the populace. The Forest Brethren responded by breaking into smaller groups, relying more upon guerrilla warfare. In July 1949, the government launched a new offensive in which smaller mobile units were to seek out and destroy the partisan bunkers. The effort was successful, and by the end of 1949, most of the active partisan units had been destroyed.

Termination and Outcome: The Soviets had crushed the partisans, though suffering heavy losses themselves. In addition to the combatants, partisan supporters were also the targets of Soviet repression, and between 1945 and 1949, at least 290,000 people were deported to the gulag.[273]

Coding Decisions: Although conflict between the Baltic partisans and the Soviet Union began in July 1944, the period of then until May 7, 1945, is subsumed into World War II. Thus this war cannot start until after World War II is ended. Battle-death statistics for this war vary widely, with partisan fatalities reported as between 20,000 and 50,000, while Soviet deaths appear between 20,000 and 80,000.[274] Based on Jankauskienė's estimate of 15,787 Lithuanian partisan deaths between 1945 and 1949, we are coding an estimate of 30,000 total fatalities for the Baltic partisans.[275] We follow Clodfelter in judging that a figure of 20,000 is plausible for Soviet battle-deaths.[276]

Gediminas and Jankauskienė have argued that the war in Lithuania should not be combined with the wars in Latvia and Estonia. However, the Soviet Union considered its operations in the region to be part of one offensive (not separate ones). Furthermore, there is evidence of some coordination among the partisans in the different entities, thus the actions of the partisans are coded as being one war. Gediminas also argues that this war should not be coded as an intra-state war at all, preferring the category of an extra-state war.

Sources: Clodfelter (2002); Gediminas (2012); Jankauskienė (2014); Kaszeta (1988); Kuodytė and Tracevskis (2006); Misiunas and Taagepera (1983); Nahaylo and Swobodo (1990); Raun (1987); Stašaitis (2000).

INTRA-STATE WAR #724

Greek Civil War—Round Three—of 1946 to 1949

Participants: Greece and United Kingdom versus Communists.
Dates: February 12, 1946, to October 16, 1949.
Battle-related Deaths: Communists: 50,000; Greece: 17,970.[277]
Initiator: Communists.
Outcome: Greece wins.
War Type: Civil for central control.
Total System Member Military Personnel: Armed Forces of Greece: [ ] (prewar, initial); 223,000 (peak, final).[278] Armed Forces of United Kingdom: 4,145,000 (prewar); 4,900,000 (initial); 5,090,000 (peak); 770,000 (final).[279]
Theater Armed Forces: Armed Forces of Greece: 90,000 (initial); 304,500 (peak).[280] Armed Forces of United Kingdom: 40,000 (peak).[281] Communists: 16,000 (initial); 50,000 (peak); 1,800 (final).[282]

Antecedents: During the initial phase of this war in 1944 and 1945 (Intra-state War #720), the communists in Greece, the Communist National Liberation Front (EAM) and its military wing, the Greek People's Liberation Army (ELAS), had launched an attack on the Greek government aided by the United Kingdom. ELAS was defeated, and a relative peace lasted for more than a year. The ELAS retreated into the mountains, where it received supplies from Yugoslavia and Albania. EAM was soon dominated by the KKE (the Communist Party).

Narrative: Fighting resumed in February 1946. The ELAS had reorganized and rebuilt its forces, supported by the neighboring Marxist-Leninist states (Yugoslavia, Bulgaria, and Albania). February 12 marked the formation of the DSE (Democratic Army of Greece), which united many of the leftist armies, and it proclaimed a rebellion against the Greek monarchy, though attacks were sporadic at first. The general election on March 31, 1946, produced a victory for the right, and conflict escalated between left-wing and right-wing organizations. The rebels, now organized into DSE, had an army of 16,000, while the Greek army now numbered 90,000. By early 1947, Britain announced that it would no longer be able to support the Greek government, so the United States stepped in with substantial aid to the government. The government went on the offensive against the DES (conducting twenty-one operations between March and September 1948). The rebels became demoralized by the split between the Soviet Union and Yugoslavia in 1948, but the KKE finally had to choose sides and chose to support the Soviet Union in 1949, prompting Yugoslavia to close its borders. Gradually the rebels were defeated in October, and many of them fled to Albania.

Termination and Outcome: The war ended as a government victory. Subsequently 100,000 ELAS fighters and sympathizers were imprisoned.

Approximately 700,000 Greeks became refugees, most of whom had been deported, and another 100,000 were killed as a result of terrorism efforts.

Coding Decisions: Richardson codes this portion of the civil war as a "4.65," which is in the neighborhood of 40,000 to 50,000 fatalities. The most commonly cited figure for the total deaths in this war is 158,000: with government losses of 17,970 killed or missing and 50,000 rebel deaths, that means that about 40,000 civilians were killed in the terror attacks surrounding the war.[283]

Sources: Cady and Prince (1966); Clodfelter (2002); Close (1995); Close and Veremis (1993); Forster (1958); Heflin (1970); Iatrides and Wrigley (1995); Phillips and Axelrod (2005); Richardson (1960); Smith (1993); Taylor and Hudson (1972); Wood (1968); Wright (1965).

INTRA-STATE WAR #856

Romania War of 1989

Participants: Romania versus Anti-Ceaucescu Rebels.
Dates: December 18, 1989, to December 26, 1989.
Battle-related Deaths: Anti-Ceaucescu Rebels: [ ]; Romania: [ ] Total Combatant Deaths: 1,100.[284]
Initiator: Anti-Ceaucescu Rebels.
Outcome: Anti-Ceaucescu Rebels win.
War Type: Civil for central control.
Total System Member Military Personnel: Armed Forces of Romania: 220,000 (prewar); 207,000 (initial, peak, final).[285]
Theater Armed Forces: Anti-Ceaucescu Rebels: [ ].

Antecedents: Communist president Nicolae Ceausescu had misruled this impoverished nation since 1974. The 1989 movement toward democracy that spread throughout eastern Europe arrived in Romania as well, and only in Romania did the collapse of the communist regime lead to war. The conflict began in Timisoara, where a Calvinist pastor was being removed from his position by the government because of his criticism of the regime.

Narrative: This precipitated large antigovernment demonstrations on December 16 and December 17, at which government forces opened fire on the protestors. The war began the following day. The government arranged a pro-government demonstration in Bucharest, which was attacked by protestors. This led to the defection of major segments of the armed forces either in support of the protestors or to a position of neutrality. Ceausescu fled on December 22, while the dissident officers seized power. The state Securitate and loyal army units then launched counterrevolutionary attacks against the protestors and the forces of the new government. Ceausescu was captured and executed, and the fighting soon stopped.

Termination and Outcome: The rebels were victorious in overthrowing the government.

Coding Decisions: Battle-death figures for this war vary widely, with initial reports claiming 80,000 deaths.

Sources: Clodfelter (1992); Hall (2000).

INTRA-STATE WAR #861.8

Georgia–South Ossetia War of 1991 to 1992

Participants: Georgia versus South Ossetia.
Dates: January 5, 1991, to June 10, 1992.
Battle-related Deaths: Georgia: [ ]; South Ossetia: [ ]; Total Combatant Deaths: 2,000.
Initiator: Georgia.
Outcome: Compromise.
War Type: Civil for local issues.
Total System Member Military Personnel: Armed Forces of Georgia: [ ] (prewar, initial); 25,000 (peak, final).[286]
Theater Armed Forces: South Ossetia: [ ].

Antecedents: In the 1980s, there was a growing emphasis on nationalism and autonomy as the Soviet Union began to falter. This led to conflicts over language, culture, and education between Georgia and the oblast of South Ossetia within its borders. As Georgia moved toward seeking independence from the Soviet Union, South Ossetia began to consider independence from Georgia for itself. On September 20, 1990, South Ossetia declared its independence from Georgia and asked the Soviet Union to recognize it as a separate part of the Soviet

Union. Georgia responded by sending its troops to South Ossetia, arriving in Tskhinvali on January 5, 1991.

Narrative: As fighting broke out, Tskhinvali became divided with Georgians in the East and Ossetians controlling the West. Twenty days of fighting ensued, and the Georgians ended up besieging the city while attacking and burning neighboring villages. As civil war broke out in the Georgian capital of Tbilisi (where Zviad Gamsakhurdia was ousted from power on December 26, 1991, in Intra-state War #871), conflict in South Ossetia declined somewhat but was revived again in the spring of 1992. Attacks were conducted against civilians, Tskhinvali was bombarded, and it was suffering from shortages of food.

Termination and Outcome: The war ended with a negotiated settlement. Georgia finally withdrew its forces from South Ossetia to deal with the growing unrest in Abkhazia (Intra-state War #877). On June 10, 1992, Georgian president Eduard Shevardnadze met with Russian president Boris Yeltsin to discuss ways to resolve the crisis. The result was the Sochi Agreement, which provided for a withdrawal of troops and a peace-keeping force. The war also created 60,000 displaced persons. The status of South Ossetia would become an issue in the Russo-Georgian War in 2008.

Coding Decisions: Death estimates for this war range from 1,000 to 4,000.

Sources: König (2014); Zürcher (2007).

INTRA-STATE WAR #864
Croatian Independence War of 1991 to 1992

Participants: Yugoslavia and Serbia versus Croatia.
Dates: May 2, 1991, to January 2, 1992.
Battle-related Deaths: Yugoslavia and Serbia: [ ]; Croatia: [ ].
Initiator: Yugoslavia.
Outcome: Negotiated settlement.
War Type: Civil for local issues (independence).
Total System Member Military Personnel: Armed Forces of Yugoslavia: 180,000 (prewar); 169,000 (initial, peak); 137,000 (final).[287]
Theater Armed Forces: Armed Forces of Croatia: 70,000 (peak). Serbian militia (Pro-government Actor); 12,000 (peak).[288]

Antecedents: After World War II, Croatia had become a component of the communist-ruled Yugoslav federation. Croatia was an amalgam of Serbian and Croatian peoples, and tensions between the two gradually escalated. In the 1970s, the reform movement led Yugoslavia to give greater autonomy to its federal units, which were increasingly seeking independence. By 1989, the conflict between Yugoslavia and its constituent republics was worsening. Both Slovenia and Croatia held free elections in April 1990, with Croatia electing Franjo Tudjman as president. Tudjman began removing Serbs from government positions and provoking disputes with the Yugoslav government. Croatia also began importing arms and building its own military in preparation for independence. Meanwhile, the Serbs living in the Krajina region of Croatia also sought greater autonomy within Croatia, and on December 21, 1990, Krajina declared its autonomy within Croatia. Though Yugoslavia wanted to keep Croatia within the federation, Croatia continued with its plans for independence.

Narrative: The war between Croatia and Yugoslavia began with a cross-border skirmish in which Croatian police were killed on May 2, 1991. On May 19, 1991, Croatia held a referendum whereby citizens could vote for independence. The Serb population boycotted the vote, which then delivered over 90 percent support for independence. Croatia's plans for independence had to be modified by the declaration of independence by the nearby republic of Slovenia on June 25, 1991. Not wanting to be left behind, Croatia declared its independence the next day. While Slovenia achieved independence with little fighting, Yugoslavia, led by Slobodan Milosevic, was determined to protect the Serbs and thus was committed to fight for Croatia. The Yugoslav government launched an invasion of Croatia on August 24, 1991. The next month, Dubrovnik was shelled. Soon the Yugoslav army controlled one-third of Croatia. The Serbians also created a militia that fought alongside Yugoslavia's army (the JNA). The most severe fighting took place at Vukovar, which was bombed by the JNA for two months and virtually destroyed. The JNA captured Vukovar in November 1991. Croatian forces were able to recapture some territory in December. Pressure from the European Union persuaded Yugoslavia to implement a cease-fire on January 2, 1992. Croatia's independence was recognized two weeks later.

Termination and Outcome: The outcome was a negotiated settlement, facilitated by the European Union. Croatia won the war to the extent that it achieved independence from Yugoslavia. The United Nations created a force (UNPORFOR) that was supposed to facilitate the return of Croatians to their homes but instead merely solidified the lines of conflict. The Serbs living in Croatia set up an independent republic in Krajina in December 1991, which basically reduced the size of the new Croatia by one-third. Croatia would go to war with Krajina in 1995 (Intra-state War #891).

Coding Decisions: Approximately 10,000 people died in this war, though we have not located battle-death statistics.

Sources: Bartlett (2002); Bassouni (1992); Brogan (1998); Ciment (2007g); Clodfelter (2002); Uppsala Universitet (1995b).

INTRA-STATE WAR #871
Georgia War of 1991 to 1992

Participants: Georgia versus Reform Movement.
Dates: December 26, 1991, to March 1992.
Battle-related Deaths: Georgia: [ ]; Reform: [ ]; Total Combatant Deaths: 5,000.
Initiator: Reform.
Outcome: Reform wins.
War Type: Civil for central control.
Total System Member Military Personnel: Armed Forces of Georgia: [ ] (prewar, initial); 25,000 (peak, final).[289]
Theater Armed Forces: Reform Movement (National Guard): 500 (initial).[290]

Antecedents: In 1991, President Mikhail Gorbachev's attempts to restructure the Soviet Union were faltering. The three Baltic republics declared independence in the spring. In March 1991, Georgia voted to secede from the Soviet Union, and in May, Zviad Gamsakhurdia was elected as its president. In an attempt to assuage internal unrest, Gorbachev negotiated a new treaty of union that would give more autonomy to the remaining Soviet republics. However, before the treaty could be implemented, Gorbachev was overthrown. Ultimately the leaders of ten of the Soviet republics decided to dissolve the Soviet Union in favor of a loose association called the Commonwealth of Independent States. Georgia was not invited to join the commonwealth due to internal unrest. Civil war broke out in late December 1991, when authoritarian president Zviad Gamsakhurdia opposed a reform movement.

Narrative: Opposition to Gamsakhurdia autocratic rule developed fairly quickly. Abkhazia and South Ossetia began agitating for independence. Pro-democracy protestors and the National Guard rioted against his leadership, while others, like Eduard Shevardnadze (a former Soviet foreign minister), urged that Georgia remain tied to the Soviet Union. Georgia became independent after the collapse of the Soviet Union on December 26, 1991, and civil war broke out immediately as the National Guard leader Tengiz Kitovani allied with former prime minister Tengiz Sigua led 500 National Guardsmen against the president. Gamsakhurdia headed to his bunker and declared a state of emergency. Kitovani and Sigua released Jaba Ioseliani from prison. Ioseliani was the leader of the Mekhedrioni (a paramilitary group) that was used to suppress Gamsakhurdia supporters in the capital. After a short siege, on January 6, 1992, Gamsakhurdia fled the country. Military rule was established, yet the fighting continued. Gamsakhurdia returned to his base of support in the West among the Mingrelians, where a full-scale Zviadist uprising soon began that lasted until fall 1993. Kitovani, Sigua, and Ioseliani formed a troika that ruled the country, though Shevardnadze was invited to serve as head of state. The level of fighting surged again when Gamsakhurdia returned to western Georgia in September 1993. The Zviadists were defeated by a joint National Guard–Mekhedrioni army.

Termination and Outcome: On December 31, 1993, Gamsakhurdia was found shot dead. The war was a victory for the anti-Gamsakhurdia reform rebels who seized power.

Coding Decisions: Some sources combine this war together with the uprisings in South Ossetia and Abkhazia into one Georgian civil war. However, they are not combined here because this war is for central control, whereas the other conflicts are for local issues, and because Abhkazia and South Ossetia are geographically separate. The conflict in South Ossetia does not appear to attain war level, though the war in Abkhazia appears as Intra-state War #877.

Sources: Bercovitch and Fretter (2004); Ciment (2007g); Kaufman (2001); Zürcher (2007).

INTRA-STATE WAR #872

Nagorno-Karabakh War of 1991 to 1993

Participants: Azerbaijan versus Nagorno-Karabakh and Armenia.
Dates: December 26, 1991, to February 5, 1993.
Battle-Related Deaths: Azerbaijan: 4,000; Nagorno-Karabakh and Armenia: 3,000.[291]
Initiator: Nagorno-Karabakh.
Outcome: Transformed into Inter-state War #216.
War Type: Civil for local issues.
Total System Member Military Personnel: Azerbaijan: 5,000 (initial, includes militias); 45,000 (peak, final). Armenia: 21,000 (peak, final).[292]
Theater Armed Forces: Nagorno-Karabakh: 7,000 (initial); 10,000 (peak, final). Armenia: 1,000 (initial); 13,000 (peak, final).[293]

Antecedents: Nagorno-Karabakh is an area that is inhabited by people who are Christian generally and ethnically Armenian. It was incorporated into the Russian empire in the early nineteenth century along with Armenia and Muslim Azerbaijan. Until 1920, Nagorno-Karabakh was considered a part of Armenia, but in 1921, Russia gave the region to Azerbaijan. From the 1950s onward, the Armenians living in Nagorno-Karabakh petitioned Moscow to be annexed to Armenia. On February 20, 1988 Nagorno-Karabakh voted to unify with Armenia. Attacks against the Armenian population in Nagorno-Karabakh prompted the Soviet Union to intervene, yet on March 21, 1988, the Soviet Union again rejected Nagorno-Karabakh's desire for secession. On June 15, Armenia's government also appealed to the Soviet government to approve an annexation of Nagorno-Karabakh by Armenia; on July 12, Nagorno-Karabakh passed a resolution of secession from Azerbaijan. These moves were denounced by both Azerbaijan and Moscow. Intercommunal violence continued involving the Armenians living in Azerbaijan and the Azeris living in Armenia. The intensity of conflict increased in January 1990, or "Black January," as Azeris attacked Armenians living in the Azerbaijan capital of Baku. The Soviet Union dispatched troops and seized control of the city. The unwillingness of the Soviet Union to protect Armenia's interests prompted the creation of a number of Armenian militias, the largest of which was the Armenian National Army with 5,000 soldiers. In September 1990, Armenia declared its intention to seek its independence; as the Soviet Union began to disintegrate in 1991, Armenia declared its independence on September 21, 1991. Azerbaijan became independent on December 26, 1991, after the Soviet Union's demise. As Soviet troops withdrew, they left military supplies, mostly for Azerbaijan, and both Armenia and Azerbaijan began expanding their armed forces and seeking foreign military assistance. Former Soviet soldiers joined both armies, as did international volunteers.

Narrative: With the independence of Azerbaijan, Nagorno-Karabakh declared its independence as the Republic of Nagorno-Karabakh, and the conflict assumed the character of an intra-state war of Nagorno-Karabakh against Azerbaijan. The army of Azerbaijan occupied former Soviet bases around the Nagorno-Karabakh capital of Stepanakert and began shelling the city. The forces of Nagorno-Karabakh (with the assistance of Armenia) then went on the offensive and captured Khojaly in February 1992 and the last Azeri stronghold in the region (Shusha) on May 8. Most importantly, on May 18, Nagorno-Karabakh captured Lachin, which created a land link, the "Lachin Corridor" between Nagorno-Karabakh and Armenia. In June 1992, the tide turned when Azerbaijan forces, under new president Aabulfaz Elchibey, launched a major offensive at Mardakert, in North Nagorno-Karabakh.

Termination and Outcome: Armenia then came to the aid of Nagorno-Karabakh, taking over the bulk of the fighting against Azerbaijan in a major offensive on February 6, 1993. This marks the end of this civil war and the beginning of Inter-state War #216. That war became virtually a stalemate, and a ceasefire was signed on May 12, 1994, which ended the war but left the ultimate status of Nagorno-Karabakh unresolved.

Coding Decisions: During the war, a significant number of those killed were civilians. It has been difficult to separate combatant from civilian fatalities, especially during the first year when both sides relied on armed militias (which are barely distinguished from civilians) as Azerbaijan was in the process of creating a national army. Most sources also do not divide the fatality estimates (which range from 25,000 to 40,000) by year or by the two different wars. The figures reported here are based on Zürcher, modified to align with the delineation of this war from the subsequent inter-state war.

Sources: Bercovitch and Fretter (2004); Brogan (1998); Clodfelter (2002); Croissant (1998); Kaufman (2001); Uppsala Universitet Conflict Data Project (1997); Zürcher (2007).

INTRA-STATE WAR #873

Dniestrian Independence War of 1991 to 1992

Participants: Moldova versus Dniestria.
Dates: December 26, 1991, to July 2, 1992.
Battle-related Deaths: Moldova: [ ]; Dniestria: [ ]; Total Combatant Deaths: 1,000.[294]
Initiator: Moldova.
Outcome: Compromise.
War Type: Civil for local issues.
Total System Member Military Personnel: Armed Forces of Moldova: [ ] (prewar, initial); 9,000 (peak, final).[295]
Theater Armed Forces: Dniestria: [ ].

Antecedents: When the Soviet Union annexed Moldova from Romania in 1940, the region now known as Transdniestria was detached from the Ukraine and given to Moldova. As the Soviet Union began to lose control in 1990, the residents of Transdniestria signaled a desire to secede from Moldova and either become independent or join Russia.

Narrative: Moldova rejected the Dniestrian requests for secession and sent its army out to assert control over the region. The major battle took place on June 19, 1992, at Bendery, where a daylong bombardment destroyed much of the city. The Dniestrians received assistance from the Russian Fourteenth Army, which was still stationed in the region and ensured success. The Dniestrians drove the Moldovans back, and in a series of engagements, Moldova had lost control of the region by July 1992. An accord, signed on July 21, 1992, gave Dniestria semiautonomous status within Moldova. In effect, Transdniestria is essentially an unrecognized but independent entity, supported by the presence of Russian troops.

Termination and Outcome: The result was a compromise, in that Dniestria got partial autonomy but not full independence.

Coding Decisions: The war is coded as starting on the day that Moldova gets its independence and becomes a member of the interstate system: December 26, 1991.

Sources: Bercovitch and Fretter (2004); Kaufman (1997); Kaufman (2001); King (2000); Minahan (2002).

INTRA-STATE WAR #877

Abkhazia Revolt of 1992 to 1994

Participants: Georgia versus Abkhazia.
Dates: August 18, 1992, to July 27, 1993, and September 27, 1993, to April 14, 1994.
Battle-related Deaths: Georgia: 5,000; Abkhazia: 3,000.[296]
Initiator: Georgia.
Outcome: Abkhazia wins (partially).
War Type: Civil for local issues (secession).
Total System Member Military Personnel: Armed Forces of Georgia: 25,000 (prewar); 7,000 (initial, peak, final).[297]
Theater Armed Forces: Armed Forces of Georgia: 6,000 (initial).[298] Armed Forces of Abkhazia: [ ]. North Caucasus Volunteers (Pre-rebel Intervener), participating from September 1992: 1,000 (initial).[299]

Antecedents: As Georgia became independent of the Soviet Union in December 1991, its government faced three civil challenges: independence movements in South Ossetia and Abkhazia and a reform movement that ultimately succeeded in overthrowing the central government (Intra-state War #867). Both South Ossetia and Abkhazia sought independence from Georgia, leading to two civil wars (Intra-state War #861.8 and this one).

In 1988, communists in Georgia and Abkhazia began organizing a campaign to secure independence for Georgia from the Soviet Union. A mass demonstration on April 9, 1989, was dispersed by Soviet troops using toxic gas, killing nineteen, leading to the incident being called the Tbilisi massacre. Georgian president Zviad Gamsakhurdia declared Georgia's independence in April 1991. Tensions between Georgia and Abkhazia prompted continued efforts to secure Abkhazia's independence from Georgia, including discussions with the Russian government.

Narrative: In 1992, in response to the Abkhazian reinstatement of the 1925 Abkhaz constitution, with its emphasis on Abkhazia's status as a sovereign republic, Georgia sent National Guard troops into Abkhazia on August 18. About 5,000 Georgian troops engaged the Abkhazian forces at Sukhumi, while another 1,000 landed at Gagra to seal the border with Russia. At first the government troops were successful, leading Georgian president Eduard Shevardnadze to declare that control had been restored. However, volunteers from North Caucuses assisted a new Abkhaz offensive. A Russian-sponsored cease-fire stopped the fighting from July to September 1993 (which is coded as a break in the fighting). Abkhazia then launched a major offensive that reoccupied all of Abkhazia by the end of September. The war continued until a cease-fire agreement in April 1994, which included the stationing of Russian peacekeepers and semiautonomy for Abkhazia.

Termination and Outcome: This was one of the bloodiest of the wars to result from the breakup of the Soviet Union, displacing more than 250,000 people (moving Georgians out of Abkhazia) and causing 10,000 to 30,000 deaths. The status of Abkhazia would become an issue in the Russo-Georgian War in 2008.

Coding Decisions: The war is coded as ending with an Abkhazia victory because Abkhazia defeated Georgia militarily. However, it was not a complete victory in that Abkhazia did not attain complete independence.

Sources: Bercovitch and Fretter (2004); Ciment (2007g); Demetriou (2002); Kaufman (2001); Petersen (2008); Toft (2003).

INTRA-STATE WAR #878
Bosnian-Serb Rebellion of 1992 to 1995

Participants: Bosnia, Croatia, and the United States versus Bosnian Serbs and Croatia.
Dates: June 6, 1992, to December 31, 1994, and March 20, 1995, to December 14, 1995.
Battle-related Deaths: Bosnia: 28,027; Bosnian Serbs: 14,237; Croatia: 6,689; United States: 0.[300]
Initiator: Bosnian Serbs.
Outcome: Bosnia, Croatia, and the United States win.
War Type: Civil for local issues (secession).
Total System Member Military Personnel: Armed Forces of Bosnia: [ ] (prewar); 60,000 (initial); 100,000 (peak, final).[301] Armed Forces of United States: 2,110,000 (prewar); 1,920,000 (initial, peak); 1,620,000 (final).[302] Armed Forces of Croatia: [ ] (prewar); 103,000 (initial, peak); 60,000 (final).[303]
Theater Armed Forces: Armed Forces of Bosnia: 9,000. Armed Forces of Croatia: 3,700. Armed Forces of United States: 22,000. Bosnian Serbs: [ ].

Antecedents: The Yugoslav federation was being torn apart by the desires for independence of its component parts. Slovenia and Croatia already had received their independence. The EC recognized the independence of Bosnia-Herzegovina on April 7, 1992 (making Bosnia a COW system member on that date). It also marked the beginning of an inter-state war (#215) involving the Yugoslav Army (the JNA) against Bosnia and Croatia.

Narrative: Under international pressure, most of the JNA forces withdrew from Bosnia by June 5, 1992, ending the inter-state war. The fighting then continued as this internationalized civil pitting of the Bosnian Muslim government against the Bosnian Serbs, who wanted to secede. Croatia also intervened, at one point assisting the Bosnians and at another time assisting the Serbs. In December 1994, Jimmy Carter was instrumental in persuading the parties to adopt a cease-fire, which lasted about three months (which is coded as a break in the war from December 31, 1994, to March 20, 1995). However, fighting resumed. In an attempt to end the conflict, the North Atlantic Treaty Organization (NATO) began Operation Deliberate Force, a bombing campaign against the Bosnian Serbs conducted primarily by the United States (Britain and Belgium also participated but not at levels that make them war participants). Fighting continued until the Dayton Peace Agreement, signed December 14, 1995.

Termination and Outcome: The war resulted in the defeat of the rebel goal of secession.

Coding Decisions: This war involved ethnic cleansing against civilians, which led to the deaths of more than 300,000 people, though the actual number of fatalities will probably never be known.

Sources: Clodfelter (2002); Hellenic Resources Network (2006); Human Rights Watch (2000a, b); Mosley (2000); NATO (2002); Tabeau and Bijak (2005); Williams (1907).

INTRA-STATE WAR #888
First Chechnya War of 1994 to 1996

Participants: Russia versus Chechnya.
Dates: December 11, 1994, to August 31, 1996.
Battle-related Deaths: Chechnya: 6,000; Russia: 4,000.[304]
Initiator: Chechnya.
Outcome: Chechnya wins.
War Type: Civil for local issues.
Total System Member Military Personnel: Armed Forces of Russia: 1,500,000 (prewar); 1,400,000 (initial, peak); 1,300,000 (final).[305]
Theater Armed Forces: Armed Forces of Russia: 40,000 (initial); 58,000 (peak).[306] Armed Forces of Chechnya: 1,500.[307]

Antecedents: Just prior to the fall of the Soviet Union, the Chechens declared their independence, which precipitated a brief conflict in 1991. Chechnya was at that time merely an autonomous region in the republic of Chechen-Ingush. In October, Dzhokhar Dudayev was elected president of Chechnya, and in November 1991, Dudayev declared Chechnya an independent state (thereby Chechen-Ingush was dissolved—as the Ingush decided to remain in the Russian Federation). Initially Russia's president Boris Yeltsin dismissed Chechnya's declaration; however, in 1994, he decided to take a more proactive stance against Chechnya and helped to create the Chechen Interim Council (IC) to oppose Chechen president Dzhokhar Dudayev. In September 1994, an armed conflict broke out between Dudayev's forces and those of the IC, which was defeated.

Narrative: In November 1994, Yeltsin issued an ultimatum, and when Dudayev's forces refused to capitulate, Russia attacked in December 1994. Approximately 40,000 Russian troops crossed into Chechnya and attacked the capital Groznyy. After weeks of heavy fighting, the Russians captured the city in February 1995. For the next eighteen months, an intense guerrilla war was fought in the Caucasus mountains. Dudayev was killed, and the Chechens were now led by Aslan Maskhadov. In August 1996, the Chechens recaptured Grozny. At this point, the Russians agreed to a negotiated settlement, by which Russia granted Chechnya autonomy but not formal independence and withdrew its troops by January 1997.

Termination and Outcome: In addition to the combatants, 60,000 Chechen civilians were killed during the war.

Coding Decisions: Chechnya is coded as the war participant (rather than Chechen fighters) because it was a geopolitical unit with a government and sovereignty.

Sources: Ayers (2001); Blank and Tilford (1995); Ciment (2007g); Clodfelter (2002); Perovic (2006); Project Ploughshares (2000).

INTRA-STATE WAR #891
Croatia–Krajina War of 1995

Participants: Croatia versus Krajinian Serbs.
Dates: May 1995 to November 1995.
Battle-related Deaths: Croatia: [ ]; Krajinian Serbs: [ ]; Total Combatant Deaths: 1,000.
Initiator: Krajinian Serbs.
Outcome: Croatia wins.

War Type: Civil for local issues.
Total System Member Military Personnel: Armed Forces of Croatia: 70,000 (prewar); 60,000 (initial, peak, final).[308]
Theater Armed Forces: Armed Forces of Croatia: 130,000. Serb Army of Krajinia: 30,000.

Antecedents: As a consequence of the War of Croatian Independence in 1991 and 1992 (Intra-state War #864), Croatia attained its independence from Serb-controlled Yugoslavia. However, Croatia itself contained several Serb dominated areas, including western Slovenia and Krajina. During the war, the Serbs of Krajina declared a Serb-Republic of Krajina (RSK), which was rejected by Croatia, and the area was patrolled by United Nations forces after 1992. The position of Krajina began to decline economically as it was dependent upon the now-smaller Yugoslavia. Yugoslav president Milošević was angered at the RSK's refusal to mediate the enduring conflict. In January 1993 clashes began to erupt between the Croatian army and Krajina Serb forces.

Narrative: In May 1995, the war started when Croatia sent forces to regain control over western Slavonia. Then in August, it launched Operation Storm against Krajina. The Croatians were able to gain control of Krajina in heavy fighting in which Krajina was supported by Yugoslavia. The Croatian victory led to an agreement of understanding that concluded the war, and it included provisions for the return of United Nations forces and then complete Croatian control by 1998.

Termination and Outcome: Croatian Gen. Ante Gotovina was charged with and then acquitted of crimes against humanity for actions taken against the Serb community in the wake of the war.

Sources: Amnesty International (2004); Bercovitch and Fretter (2004); Ciment (2007g); Gagnon (2004); Keesing's (1993, 1994); Ramet (2005).

INTRA-STATE WAR #900

Kosovo Independence War of 1998 to 1999

Participants: Yugoslavia versus Kosovo.
Dates: February 28, 1998, to March 23, 1999.
Battle-related Deaths: Kosovo: 800; Yugoslavia: 400.
Initiator: Yugoslavia.
Outcome: Transformed into Inter-state War #221.
War Type: Civil for local issues.
Total System Member Military Personnel: Armed Forces of Yugoslavia: 115,000 (prewar); 105,000 (initial, peak, final).[309]
Theater Armed Forces: Kosovo Liberation Army (KLA): [ ].

Antecedents: Kosovo was an area of Yugoslavia that was heavily populated by ethnic Albanians. It had been relatively autonomous within Yugoslavia until Yugoslavia revoked that status in 1990. In 1992, a vote within Kosovo expressed a desire for independence from Yugoslavia and perhaps unity with Albania. When Yugoslavia (Serbia) resisted the Kosovar demands, a number of Kosovars created the Kosovo Liberation Army (KLA) to fight for independence. In 1996 and 1997, the conflict involved only brief exchanges of gunfire.

Narrative: On February 28, 1998, the Yugoslav and Serbian government launched a major assault against the KLA stronghold in the Drenicia valley, which marks the beginning of the war. In March 1998, the KLA counterattacked, gaining control over a third of Kosovo by July. In August, a Yugoslav offensive retook most of the territory, during which thousands of Kosovar civilians were killed in a program of ethnic cleansing. As a result, NATO began bombing Kosovo and Serbia in an attempt to drive the Serb forces from the area.

Termination and Outcome: At this stage NATO took over the bulk of the fighting against Yugoslavia, this intra-state war ended, and the fighting continued as a new war, an inter-state war (#221).

Coding Decisions: Many reports focus on the total number of people killed during this war, with numbers ranging from 3,000 to 10,000 for this phase (most of whom were civilians).

Sources: BBC News (1999a, b, c); CNN (1998, 1999); Congressional Research Service (1998, 2000); Daalder and O'Hanlo (2000); Deployment Health Clinical Center (2006); Duke, Ehrhart, and Karadi (2000); FAS Intelligence Resource Program (2005); Haglund and Sens (2000); Human Rights Watch (2000a, b, 2001c); Independent International Commission on Kosovo

(2000); Jane's Defense (1999); Jones (2000); Judah (2000); Kostakos (2000); Lampe (2000); Loeb (1999); Makino (1998); Mennecke (2004); Møller (2000); NATO (1999); Project Ploughshares (2005a); Waller, Drezov, and Gökay (2001); Youngs, Oakes, and Bowers (1999).

INTRA-STATE WAR #915

Second Chechen War of 1999 to 2003

Participants: Russia versus Chechen Rebels (International Mujahideen).
Dates: August 7, 1999, to October 3, 2003.
Battle-related Deaths: Chechen rebels: 15,000; Russia: 5,000.[310]
Initiator: Chechen Rebels.
Outcome: Russia wins.
War Type: Civil for local issues.
Total System Member Military Personnel: Armed Forces of Russia: 1,000,000 (prewar); 900,000 (initial); 1,004,000 (peak); 961,000 (final).[311]
Theater Armed Forces: Armed Forces of Russia: 100,000 (peak). Chechen Rebels (International Mujahideen): 2,000 (initial).

Antecedents: Chechnya and Russia went to war in December 1994 over Chechnya's desire for independence (Intra-state War #890). The Russians were unable to defeat the Chechens during the two-year war, and as a result, Chechnya was granted limited autonomy. The second Chechen war concerned Russia's attempt to regain control over Chechnya; however, it began in August 1999, with Chechen rebels attacking into the Russian province of Dagestan.

Narrative: Border disputes between Chechnya and Dagestan prompted an attack into Dagestan by an international brigade of Chechen *mujahideen*. Russian troops in Dagestan were able to stop the rebel advances and push them back into Chechnya. In response, Russia's new president, Vladimir Putin, adopted a hard line against Chechnya and, on August 7, 1999, began a bombing campaign against the Chechen capital of Grozny. Military advisers had advised against a land campaign because of the greater likelihood of significant casualties. The air raids precipitated a flood of refugees from Chechnya into Ingushetia.

In October 1999, Putin ramped up the war by voiding the authority of Chechnya's president and launching a land offensive to contain the rebels, producing an even larger flood of refugees. Even though the rebels tried to recruit followers by declaring a holy war, Russia continued to make advances. By the end of 1999, the Russians surrounded the Chechen capital of Grozny. Much of the city was destroyed in the ensuing battles. In 2000, Russia continued its shelling and missile attacks. In May 2000, Putin reestablished control over Chechnya, and Russia established a new Chechen government, which was overwhelmingly elected in October 2003.

Termination and Outcome: The war ended at this point, though low-level guerrilla attacks continued after this date. During the war, somewhere between 25,000 and 55,000 civilians were killed.

Coding Decisions: In contrast to the first Chechen war (in which Chechnya was listed as a major war participant), in this war the primary combatants are a number of armed non-state groups.

Sources: Bercovitch and Fretter (2004); Ciment (2007g); Project Ploughshares (2004); Thomas (2001).

INTRA-STATE WAR #993

Ukraine Separatists War of 2014 and ongoing

Participants: Ukraine versus Separatists.
Dates: April 19, 2014, to ongoing.
Battle-related Deaths: Ukraine: 890 (to November 30, 2014);[312] Separatists: [ ].
Initiator: Ukraine separatists.
Outcome: None yet.
War Type: Civil for local issues (secession).
Total System Member Military Personnel: Armed Forces of Ukraine: [ ].
Theater Armed Forces: Ukraine Separatists: [ ]. Armed Forces of Russia (Pro-rebel Intervener): [ ].

Antecedents: On November 21, 2013, a wave of protests and civil unrest was launched in Ukraine by those seeking closer ties with Europe (also referred to as Euromaidan for the square in which the demonstration took place). The government violently dispersed protestors on November 30, which precipitated the resignation of President Viktor Yanukovych on February 21, 2014, and the release from prison of former prime minister Yulia Tymoshenko, one of the leaders of the 2004 Orange Revolution. Ukraine's move closer to the West triggered opposition within Russia, and Russia began moving special forces into the Crimean peninsula (the base of Russia's Black Sea Fleet), which Russia then seized and annexed in March. Though there was opposition to the Russian moves, pro-Russian demonstrations began to happen in the Donbass region of the Ukraine.

Narrative: Conflict between pro-Ukraine and pro-Russian groups in the Donbas region escalated into civil war on April 19, 2014. Ukrainian separatists who wish to join their territory to Russia have been engaged in low-level combat with Ukrainian government forces. The separatists have been aided by Russia, though whether this is only through the supplying of weapons or through the direct involvement of Russian troops in combat is still a matter of debate.

Termination and Outcome: War is still ongoing.

Coding Decisions: Though much of the data is still incomplete, the figures provided by the Ukraine Defense Ministry indicate that there are likely to have been sufficient battle-deaths within 2014 to code this dispute as a war.

Sources: *Chicago Tribune* (2014); Keesing's Record of World Events (2014); Ukraine Defense Ministry (2014).

Notes

1. Correlates of War Project, 2009.
2. Ledonne, 2004, 196.
3. Baddeley, 1908, 126.
4. Ibid., 108.
5. Correlates of War Project, 2009.
6. Ibid.
7. Clodfelter, 2002, 194.
8. Correlates of War Project, 2009.
9. Davenport, 1837.
10. Ibid.; Finlay, 1861.
11. Davenport, 1837, 402.
12. Ibid.
13. Correlates of War Project, 2009.
14. Clodfelter, 2002, 194.
15. Stillman, 1898, 40.
16. Berkeley, 1932, 60.
17. Clodfelter, 2002, 194.
18. Richardson, 1960, 74.
19. Clodfelter, 2002, 194; Jaques, 2007, 740.
20. Bodart, 1916.
21. Ibid.
22. Ibid.
23. Correlates of War Project, 2009.
24. Richardson, 1960, 52.
25. Phillips and Axelrod, 2005, 544.
26. Cummins, 2009, 50.
27. Dakin, 1973; Clodfelter, 2008.
28. Brewer, 2001; Papageorgiou, 1985; Clodfelter, 2008.
29. Small and Singer, 1982, 223.
30. Correlates of War Project, 2009.
31. White, 1909, 146.
32. Phillips and Axelrod, 2005, 754.
33. Livermore, 1966, 273,
34. Jaques, 2007, 199.
35. Correlates of War Project, 2009.
36. Baddeley, 1908, 152; Zelkina, 2000, 157.
37. Mackie, 1856, 155.
38. King, 2008, 69.
39. Gammer, 2006, 19.
40. Zelkina, 2000, 135.
41. Mackie, 1856, 150.
42. Zelkina, 2000, 150.
43. Gammer, 2006, 47.
44. Gammer, 1992, 56.
45. See Zelkina, 2000, 153.
46. Correlates of War Project, 2009.
47. Aksan, 2007, 359.
48. Miller, 1936; Ranke, 1853.
49. Ranke, 1853.
50. Clodfelter, 2002, 196.
51. Correlates of War Project, 2009.
52. Gemie, 1999, 25.
53. Clodfelter, 2002, 196.
54. Small and Singer, 1982, 215.
55. Correlates of War Project, 2009.
56. Clodfelter, 2002, 195.
57. Ibid., 195.
58. Ibid., 217.
59. Correlates of War Project, 2009.
60. Reddaway, 1941, 300; Clodfelter, 2002, 217.
61. Ibid.
62. LeDonne, 2004, 212.
63. Rapport, 2009, 16.

64. Clodfelter, 2002, 197; Small and Singer, 1982.
65. Correlates of War Project, 2009.
66. Hume, 1900, 314.
67. Clodfelter, 2002, 197.
68. Ibid., 197.
69. Hume, 1900, 326.
70. Clodfelter, 2002 197.
71. Phillips and Axelrod, 2005, 282; Clodfelter, 2002, 197.
72. Correlates of War Project, 2009.
73. Zelkina, 2000, 164.
74. Baddeley, 1908, 285.
75. Mackie, 1856, 160; Baddeley 1908, 288.
76. Gammer, 2006, 51–52.
77. Mackie, 1856, 195.
78. Ibid., 195.
79. Correlates of War Project, 2009.
80. *The Annual Register*, 1837.
81. Richardson, 1960, 78.
82. Correlates of War Project, 2009.
83. Gammer, 1992, 207; Schaefer, 2011, 78.
84. Gammer, 1992.
85. Mackie, 1856, 197.
86. Gammer, 2006, 70–72.
87. Schaefer, 2011, 78.
88. Clodfelter, 2002, 241.
89. Correlates of War Project, 2009.
90. Ranke, 1853; Spencer, 1851.
91. Ranke, 1853.
92. Correlates of War Project, 2009.
93. Ibid.
94. Clodfelter, 2002, 198; Phillips and Axelrod, 2005, 282; Small and Singer, 1982, 223.
95. Correlates of War Project, 2009.
96. Clodfelter, 2002, 196.
97. Correlates of War Project, 2009.
98. Rapport, 2009, 67, 217.
99. Ibid., 217.
100. Clodfelter, 2002, 199.
101. Correlates of War Project, 2009.
102. Clodfelter, 2002, 199.
103. Correlates of War Project, 2009.
104. Clodfelter, 2002, 199.
105. Rapport, 2009, 60
106. Ibid., 60.
107. Correlates of War Project, 2009.
108. Ibid., 2009.
109. Macartney, 1968, 379.
110. Clodfelter, 2002, 217.
111. Ibid., 217.
112. Ibid., 217–18.
113. Correlates of War Project, 2009.
114. Hadžiselimović, 2001.
115. Aksan, 2007; Jelavich, 1983.
116. Williams, 1904, 210.
117. Correlates of War Project, 2009.
118. Reid, 2000, 229.
119. Miller, 1972, 439; Andrijasevic, 2006.
120. Frilley and Wlahovitj, 1876; Richardson, 1960, 58.
121. Correlates of War Project, 2009.
122. Ibid., 2009.
123. Reid, 2000, 249–252.
124. Ibid., 249–252.
125. Miller, 1972, 447; Williams, 1904, 210; Andrijasevic, 2006.
126. Frilley and Wlahovitj, 1876.
127. Correlates of War, 2010
128. Miller, 1972, 445; Roberts, 2007, 226.
129. Langer, 1931.
130. Ibid.
131. Correlates of War Project, 2009.
132. Andrijasevic, 2006.
133. Correlates of War Project, 2009.
134. Florinsky, 1953, 914.
135. Ibid., 914.
136. Clodfelter, 2002, 218.
137. Correlates of War Project, 2009.
138. Duggan, 2008, 225; Smith, 1958, 75.
139. Smith, 1958, 73.
140. Ibid., 73.
141. Correlates of War Project, 2009.
142. Reid, 2000, 215.
143. Stillman, 1966; Clodfelter, 2008.
144. Dontas, 1966; Reid, 2000, 215.
145. Miller, 1927; Stillman, 1966.
146. Clarke, 1906, 305.
147. Correlates of War Project, 2009.
148. Clarke, 1906.
149. Tombs, 1998, 389; Clodfelter, 2002, 212.
150. Correlates of War Project, 2009.
151. Tombs, 1998, 389.
152. Correlates of War Project, 2009.
153. Clodfelter, 2002, 212.
154. Ibid.; Small and Singer, 1982, 225.
155. Correlates of War Project, 2009.
156. Carr, 1966, 334.
157. Clodfelter, 2002, 213.
158. Correlates of War Project, 2009.
159. Reid, 2000, 310.
160. Sumner, 1962; Djordjevic and Fischer-Galati, 1981; MacKenzie, 1967; Miller, 1913.
161. Stillman, 1901.
162. Stavrianos, 2000; Brockett, 1887; Glenny, 1999.
163. Gopčević, 1877; Brockett, 1887.
164. Gewehr, 1967, 36.
165. Gopčević, 1877; Brockett, 1887; MacGahan, 1876; Jelavich, 1983, 347.
166. Correlates of War Project, 2009.

167. Ekinci, 2006, 18.
168 Tatsios, 1984.
169. Dakin, 1966: Kazemi, 1991.
170. Kazemi, 1991.
171. Correlates of War Project, 2009.
172. Gerolymatos, 2002, 193.
173. Dakin, 1966.
174. Ibid.
175. Kazemi, 1991.
176. Glenny, 1999, 201.
177. Dakin, 1966; Kazemi, 1991.
178. Correlates of War Project, 2009.
179. Clodfelter, 2002, 382.
180. Hitchins, 1994, 176.
181. Ibid., 178.
182. Richardson, 1960, 100.
183. Correlates of War Project, 2009.
184. Swire, 1929.
185. Gawrych, 2006.
186. Pearson, 2004.
187. Treadway, 1983.
188. Swire, 1929.
189. Clodfelter, 2002, 385–86.
190. Correlates of War Project, 2009.
191. Benvenuti, 1997; Clodfelter, 2002.
192. Lincoln, 1989.
193. Clodfelter, 2002, 384.
194. Lincoln, 1989; Clodfelter, 2002.
195. Moore, 2002; Schmid, 1985.
196. Schmid, 1985; Clodfelter, 2002.
197. Bisher, 2005; Schmid, 1985; Clodfelter, 2002.
198. Hudson, 2004; Clodfelter 2002.
199. Arens and Ezergailis, 1997; Schmid, 1985.
200. Raun, 1987; Schmid, 1985.
201. Hudson, 2004; Schmid, 1985.
201. Moore, 2002; Hudson, 2004.
203. Schmid, 1985; Clodfelter, 2002.
204. Clodfelter, 2002, 384–85.
205. O'Ballance, 1993; Swietochowski, 1985.
206. Wuorinen, 1965, 222; Clodfelter, 2002, 386.
207. Correlates of War Project, 2009.
208. Ibid.
209. Library of Congress, 2008, 2.
210. Wuorinen, 1965, 222.
211. Clodfelter, 2002, 386.
212 Correlates of War Project, 2009.
213. Kubijovyč, 1963, 782.
214. Ibid., 782.
215. Clodfelter, 2002, 370.
216. Ibid., 370.
217. Correlates of War Project, 2009.
218. Hoensch, 1996, 100.
219. Ibid., 99.
220. Correlates of War Project, 2009.
221. Read, 1996, 271.
222. Ibid., 267; Conquest, 1987, 51.
223. Read, 1996, 266.
224. Ross, 1923, 340.
225. Clodfelter, 2002, 388.
226. Ibid., 371.
227. Phillips and Axelrod, 2005, 678.
228. Correlates of War Project, 2009.
229. Phillips and Axelrod, 2005, 678.
230. Ibid., 678.
231. Correlates of War Project, 2009.
232. Clodfelter, 2002, 372.
233. Correlates of War Project, 2009.
234. Preston, 1993, 129.
235. Phillips and Axelrod, 2005, 136.
236. Clodfelter, 2002; Urlanis, 1960, 98.
237. Correlates of War Project, 2009.
238. Ibid.
239. Ibid.
240. Ibid.
241. Ibid.
242. Clodfelter, 2002, 373.
243. Whealey, 1989, 23.
244. Ibid., 24.
245. Clodfelter, 2002, 373, 377.
246. Whealey, 1989, 8, 24.
247. Carr, 1982, 681.
248. Clodfelter, 2002, 380.
249. Payne, 1987, 217.
250. Thomas, 1961, 632; Clodfelter, 2002, 381.
251. Clodfelter, 2002, 598.
252. Correlates of War Project, 2009.
253. Ibid., 2009.
254. Shrader, 1999, 42.
255. Ibid., 42.
256. Ibid., 42.
257. Correlates of War Project, 2009.
258. Ibid., 2009.
259. Subtelny, 1988, 490.
260. Clodfelter, 2002, 597.
261. Marples, 2007, 205.
262. Ibid., 220.
263. Ibid., 1992, 69.
264. Correlates of War Project, 2009.
265. Marples, 2007, 177.
266. Magocsi, 1996, 648; Wilson, 2002, 133.
267. Yekelchyk, 2007, 146.
268. Correlates of War Project, 2009.
269. Misiunas and Taagepera, 1983, 277
270. Stašaitis, 2000, 122; Jankauskienė, 2014, 255.
271. Misiunas and Taagepera, 1983, 81.
272. Ibid., 81.
273. Ibid., 1983, 96.
274. Ibid., 1983, 84.

275. Jankauskienė, 2014, 274–75.
276. Clodfelter, 2002, 597.
277. Ibid., 598.
278. Correlates of War Project, 2009.
279. Ibid., 2009.
280. Close and Veremis, 1993, 118.
281. Phillips and Axelrod, 2005, 544.
282. Close and Veremis, 1993, 108, 123.
283. Clodfelter, 2002, 598.
284. Hall, 2000, 1069.
285. Correlates of War Project, 2009.
286. Ibid.
287. Ibid.
288. Bassouni, 1992, 2.
289. Correlates of War Project, 2009.
290. Zürcher, 2007, 127.
291. Ibid., 180.
292. Ibid., 179; Correlates of War, 2010.
293. Zürcher, 2007, 174–79.
294. Minahan, 2002, 536; Kaufman, 2001, 129.
295. Correlates of War Project, 2009.
296. Demetriou, 2002, 872.
297. Correlates of War Project, 2009.
298. Petersen, 2008, 191.
299. Ibid., 191.
300. Tabeau and Bijak, 2005,199.
301. Correlates of War Project, 2009.
302. Ibid.
303. Ibid.
304. Clodfelter, 2002, 606.
305. Correlates of War Project, 2009.
306. Ciment, 2007g, 872; Clodfelter, 2002, 606.
307. Clodfelter, 2002, 606.
308. Correlates of War Project, 2009.
309. Ibid.
310. Project Ploughshares, 2000, 4.
311. Correlates of War Project, 2009.
312. Ukraine Defense Ministry, 2014.

CHAPTER SIX

Intra-state Wars in the Middle East and North Africa

Below is the list of the intra-state wars that took place in the Middle East and North Africa. Each war will then be described individually with the pertinent basic data provided.

TABLE 6.1 List of Intra-state Wars in the Middle East and North Africa

(Continued)

TABLE 6.1 List of Intra-state Wars in the Middle East and North Africa (Continued)

War #	War Title	Page #
689	Simko Rebellion of 1921 to 1922	357
697.6	Shaikh Said's Rebellion of 1925	358
707.3	Ikhwan Revolt of 1929 to 1930	359
708	Ararat Revolt of 1930	360
718.5	Dersim Revolt of 1937 to 1938	361
728	Sanaa Revolt of 1948	362
743	First Lebanese War of 1958	364
747	Mosul Revolt of 1959	366
752	First Iraqi Kurds War of 1961 to 1963	366
753	Algerian Revolution of 1962	368
755	North Yemen War of 1962 to 1970	369
758	First South Sudan War of 1963 to 1972	372
765	Second Iraqi Kurds War of 1965 to 1966	373
777	Third Iraqi Kurds War of 1968 to 1970	374
780	Black September War of 1970	375
797	Fourth Iraqi Kurds War of 1974 to 1975	377
801	Second Lebanese War of 1975 to 1976	378
815.5	Iranian Islamic Revolution of 1978 to 1979	382
816	Anti-Khomeini Coalition War of 1979 to 1983	384
826.5	Hama Uprising of 1982	386
833	Fourth Lebanese War of 1983 to 1984	387
834	Second South Sudan War of 1983 to 2002	390
840	Fifth Iraqi Kurds War of 1985 to 1988	394
842	South Yemen War of 1986	395
850	Fifth Lebanese War of 1989 to 1990	397
862	Iraqi–Shiite Rebellion of 1991	398
862.1	Sixth Iraqi Kurds Rebellion of 1991	399
865	Turkey–PKK War of 1991 to 1999	399
866	SPLM/A Division (Dinka–Nuer) War of 1991 to 1992	401
875	Algeria's Islamic Front War of 1992 to 2002	402
885	South Yemeni Secessionist Revolt of 1994	404
887	First Iraqi Kurds Internecine War of 1994 to 1995	407
893	Seventh Iraqi Kurds War of 1996	408
897.5	Second Iraqi Kurds Internecine War of 1997	409
927	Darfur Rebellion of 2003 to 2006	409
935	First Al-Houthi Rebellion of 2004 to 2005	411
941	Second Al-Houthi Rebellion of 2007 to 2008	412
971	Iraqi–Sunni Revolt of 2010 to present	413
976	Libyan Civil War of 2011	414
978	Sudan Revolutionary Front Rebellion of 2011 to present	415
982	Syrian Arab Spring War of 2011 to present	417
991	South Sudan War of 2013 to present	418
991.5	ISIS–al Nusra Front War of 2014	419
992	Third Al-Houthi Rebellion of 2014 to present	420
996	IS–YPG War of 2014 to present	420
997	Rada'a War of 2014 to present	421

Individual Descriptions of Intra-state Wars in the Middle East and North Africa

INTRA-STATE WAR #504.3
Sidon–Damascus War of 1821 to 1822

Participants: Sidon versus Damascus and Aleppo.
Dates: May 21, 1821, to June 1822.
Battle-related Deaths: Sidon: at least 40; Damascus: at least 1,200; Total Combatant Deaths: at least 1,240.[1]
Initiator: Sidon.
Outcome: Becomes civil conflict.
War Type: Regional.
Theater Armed Forces: Armed Forces of Sidon—16,000 (initial).[2]

Antecedents: From the late eighteenth century, the provinces of Sidon and Damascus competed for control of what is now Lebanon. Wars fought in 1775 and around the turn of the century pitted the two against each other. Both wars brought victory to Damascus but did nothing to end the feud. In 1821, Darwish Pasha assumed the governorship of Damascus. When the Greek War of Independence broke out (see Intra-state War #504), all of the Christians in Damascus were fined as a punitive measure. Sometime after May, the Emir Bashir fled taxation, ending up under the protection of Abdullah Pasha of the province of Sidon. He called on a number of local warlords, including Shaykh Bashir Jumblatt, to join him.

Abdullah Pasha sent a message to the emir that a conspiracy in Constantinople secretly had relieved him of his governorship and annexed Sidon to Damascus to take effect once Darwish Pasha had returned from his pilgrimage to Mecca. He claimed that Mustafa Pasha of Aleppo and Bahram Pasha of Adana had been ordered to assist Darwish Pasha. He requested the emir's support and received it.

Narrative: The first violence was an internal rebellion against Darwish Pasha's temporary replacement (regent), Faydi Pasha. His attempts to "pillage" the land (i.e., tax it) led to rebellions. A larger rebellion broke out when he attempted to give rulership over the Rashayya Emir Mansur, a Yazbaki and traditional rival of the Jumblatt family. Emir Bashir and Shaykh Bashir Jumblatt intervened on the side of the previous emir of Rashayya, Jumblati Emir Efendi. The Damascene forces sent against the provincial rebels were defeated after several days of combat on May 21, 1821.

On the first day of the Islamic year 1237 (about September 28, 1821), Abdullah Pasha met with Emir Bashir and decided to take Damascus by force before other governors could reinforce Darwish Pasha. This would demonstrate his power to the Porte and present it with a fait accompli, while it was busy dealing with the Greek insurrection. He assembled about 4,000 of his own troops plus 12,000 from various shaykhs and emirs loyal to him. They marched on Damascus.

Darwish Pasha massed his troops, including Yazbaki refugees, from the fighting in Rashayya. The two forces met at al-Mazze in the Golan Heights at the end of May 1822; the result was a route of the Damascene forces. About 1,200 Damascenes were killed, many from drowning while trying to flee the battle. Only 40 or so Sidonese were killed. Abdullah Pasha refrained from entering Damascus, content to besiege it and seek political support from Mustafa Pasha for Darwish Pasha's removal from power.

Termination and Outcome: The war transformed into civil conflict in June 1822, when the Sultan issued a decree proclaiming Abdullah Pasha to be a rebel and ordering Mustafa Pasha, leader of the province of Aleppo, to come to the assistance of Darwish Pasha. At this point, Darwish Pasha and Mustafa Pasha became authorized to defeat an insurrection against Ottoman authority.

Mustafa Pasha declared that he was going to help Darwish Pasha and ordered the siege lifted. Abdullah Pasha and his allies arranged to seek the protection of the province of Egypt, with its influential governor Mehmet Ali Pasha, until such time as an imperial pardon could be negotiated.

Not content to wait while his enemies regrouped, Darwish Pasha set out to consolidate his control over the disputed areas. Emir Efendi was removed from power, and loyal emirs were appointed. Then he moved against Sidon, besieging Abdullah Pasha and his 2,000 defenders in the fortress capital of Acre by the end of July 1822. Mustafa Pasha of Aleppo and Bahram Pasha of Adana joined the siege. After five months, the siege had been unsuccessful, and Darwish Pasha was removed from his post; the governorship of Sidon (which had presumably been transferred to Darwish Pasha at some point) was given to Mustafa Pasha of Aleppo.

Four months later, Abdullah Pasha secured his pardon and restoration of the governorship of Sidon. Ustafa Pasha was ordered to return to Aleppo, an order that he obeyed. The conflict was over. In the aftermath of the conflict, Abdullah Pasha imposed punitive taxes on Shaykh Bashir Jumblatt, who had taken both sides in the conflict. Although the Shaykh paid the taxes, he feared further reprisals until communications between the governors of Damascus and Sidon reassured him. Taking about 1,000 men in arms, he returned home. After a further tax was demanded, he decamped to the Hawran in the province of Damascus.

In 1825, Shaykh Bashir raised an unsuccessful revolt at al-Mukhtara with about 12,000 men. Abdullah Pasha and Emir Bashir opposed his revolt and mobilized many tribal leaders against him. Three battles were fought. In the first battle at al-Samqaniyye, only a few men were killed on each side, but the emir's forces proved victorious, and some of Jumblatt's allies abandoned him the next day. The second fight occurred at Baq'lin, where 1,500 defenders held off a nighttime raid by Jumblatt's forces. The final battle was fought near al-Samqaniyye and included the full forces of each side. Casualties were low: 15 of Emir Bashir's troops and at least 51 of Jumblatt's. Shaykh Jumblatt was tracked down, captured, and eventually executed.

Coding Decisions: Note that the dates provided in Mishāqa, Philipp, and Farah conflict. These dates represent our best estimates, given the uncertainty of the sources.

Sources: Mishāqa (1988); Philipp (2001), Farah (2000).[3]

INTRA-STATE WAR #507
Egypt–Mehdi War of 1824

Participants: Egypt versus Mehdi Army.
Dates: March 23, 1824, to April 14, 1824.
Battle-related Deaths: Total Combatant Deaths: 4,000.[4]
Initiator: Mehdi Army.
Outcome: Egypt wins.
War Type: Regional Internal.
Theater Armed Forces: Armed Forces of Egypt: perhaps 8,000 (initial, peak); Mehdi Army: 600 (initial), 15,000 (peak—assumes half of Seyh Ahmed's followers were noncombatants).[5]

Antecedents: Mehmet Ali, the vali or governor of Egypt, attempted from the beginning of the nineteenth century to create a modern army loyal to him. He massacred the traditional warlords (the Mamlukes) in 1811 and 1812 using Albanian troops. Then in 1815 he turned on the Albanians, attempting to enforce discipline among them. When they rioted, he retreated from his plans. In 1818, he was able to get rid of them by sending them to fight the Wahabbis in Arabia (see Extra-State War #301).

Fighting with the Wahabbis sputtered on for seven years, providing ample opportunity to deploy potentially disloyal troops. He then attempted to build an army by enslaving the Sudanese. However, expeditions to the Sudan (see Extra-State War #307) suffered high casualties (especially from disease) and produced meager numbers of slaves. Finally, he turned to conscription of the peasantry to form his new army, the *nizami*.

His first order in 1822 was for the conscription of 4,000 peasants from Upper Egypt to replace his disgruntled and war-weary Turkish soldiers in the fighting in Sudan. His new forces numbered 8,000 in July 1823, with 30,000 more conscripts on the way. However, his efforts to conscript the peasantry led to frequent peasant rebellions in the early to mid-1820s. Most of these were suppressed violently and quickly, but the 1824 one proved far more dangerous than the others.

Narrative: Late in March, a charismatic leader named Seyh Ahmed mobilized 600 followers and began attacking government officials and storehouses near the Egyptian province of Asyut. He proclaimed himself to be the Mahdi, and his forces quickly swelled to

20,000 to 30,000 men and women (including noncombatants). The rebellion spread to nearly all of Qina province. Up to 700 soldiers defected to the rebels. Isna and Qina were both besieged by the rebels, as was Qus, an important center of commerce. The rebels mounted an offensive against Farshut, a center of cloth making and sugar refining.

Mehmet Ali ordered the suppression of the rising by force. The first recorded combat of the war took place on March 23, when Osman Bey defeated some 3,500 of the rebels' infantry and cavalry under Shaykh Radwan; his own forces were similar in number. In all, seven battles were fought between units of the *nizami* and the rebels during March and early April (as described in a report dated April 14). But by the middle of April, the back of the rebellion was broken, and Seyh Ahmed fled into the desert.

Termination and Outcome: The outcome of the war was unconditional victory for the Egyptian provincial government and its *nizami*. Many rebels were hanged in front of their villages, while disloyal units were decimated and forty-five officers were shot in front of their men. The victory allowed the expansion of the *nizami* through conscription, which eventually made Mehmet Ali more powerful than the empire he supposedly served.

Coding Decisions: In what just may have been the deadliest terrorist attack in history, the powder magazine inside the Citadel exploded on March 22, 1824. At least 4,000 people were killed. The new army was quickly able to isolate the powder magazine and restore order. Contemporary rumors held the Albanians (or even remaining Mamlukes) responsible for the blast, but the proof was circumstantial at best. We do not code this as a war in itself, for the evidence that it was a deliberate blast by domestic opponents is too weak, and in any case no one knows how many soldiers died in the explosion.

Sources: Fahmy (1997, 1998, 2002); Lawson (1981).

INTRA-STATE WAR #508
Janissary Revolt of 1826 (aka Auspicious Occasion)

Participants: Ottoman Empire versus Constantinople Janissaries.
Dates: June 14, 1826, to June 15, 1826.
Battle-related Deaths: Ottoman Empire: few; Constantinople Janissaries: 4,320; Total Combatant Deaths: slightly more than 4,320.[6]
Initiator: Constantinople Janissaries.
Outcome: Ottoman Empire wins.
War Type: Civil for central control.
Total System Member Military Personnel: Armed Forces of the Ottoman Empire: 182,000 (prewar, initial, peak, final). Figures exclude the Constantinople Janissaries themselves.[7]
Theater Armed Forces: Armed Forces of the Ottoman Empire: more than 20,000 (initial, peak); Constantinople Janissaries: 8,000 (prewar, initial, peak).[8]

Antecedents: The Janissaries were originally an elite infantry corps, but by the end of the eighteenth century, they were more effective at deposing sultans than winning battles. Refusing to accept military drill or to use new weapons, they strongly opposed the creation of a modern, new army that would degrade their social status as warriors in favor of mass formations trained with standardized drills to use muskets with bayonets. They deposed or killed no fewer than six sultans in order to protect their power and privileges.

In 1825, Sultan Mahmud II formed a new army, which everyone knew would trigger a revolt by the Janissaries. He simply tried to build it quickly enough to overcome the janissary threat. Once the new army was ready, he first ensured that he had the loyalty of the religious establishment, and then—in May 1826—issued orders for the Janissaries to adopt the same Egyptian (Western) training techniques.

Narrative: On June 14, the Janissaries in Constantinople assembled in the piazza of Etmeidan, rebelled, and marched on the palace. The sultan was ready for them and had assembled his 20,000-strong new army and other loyalist forces, including a few loyal Janissary units. The Janissaries were first met with cannon fire in the narrow streets leading to the palace and fell back to the Etmeidan, which they defended with musket fire. Finally, they retreated to their barracks. Rather than risk hand-to-hand fighting, the sultan simply had his artillery set the barracks ablaze. Those who tried to escape the flames were shot down. The Constantinople Janissaries were utterly destroyed by the next morning.

Termination and Outcome: The outcome of the war was an unconditional government victory. There was no amnesty. Indeed, the government immediately dispatched messengers to other provinces, and the janissaries in the provinces were massacred before they even heard the news of the revolt.

Coding Decisions: We do not count the massacres of Janissaries elsewhere in the empire as battle-deaths as there was no effective resistance: unlike the Janissaries of Constantinople, they were not organized or prepared for violent resistance. Similarly, we do not count the thousands of Janissaries captured in Constantinople who were executed over the following months but only the 320 immediate executions.

Sources: Brewer (2001); Creasy (1961); Wheatcroft (1993).[9]

INTRA-STATE WAR #516

Egyptian Taka Expedition of 1831

Participants: Egypt versus Hadendowa.
Date: 1831.
Battle-related Deaths: Egypt: 1500; Total Combatant Deaths: perhaps 2,000. (See Coding Decisions.)[10]
Initiator: Egypt.
Outcome: Hadendowa win.
War Type: Regional Internal.
Theater Armed Forces: Armed Forces of Egypt—100,000 (prewar, initial, peak); 98,500 (final).[11]

Antecedents: As part of Egypt's policy of dominating the tribes of the Sudan, Khurshid Pasha led 6,000 men into Taka, a region on the southeastern frontier of the Egyptian province, toward the end of 1831. His goal was to obtain the submission of the Hadendowa tribe and a tribute of cattle or slaves. His objective was Sabderat, twenty miles east of (present-day) Kasala, but it appears he never reached it. He made contact with the Hadendowa some distance from Goz Regeb. When the tribe refused his demands and withdrew into the nearby forests, he decided to pursue them.

Narrative: During three days of fighting, Khurshid first lost most of his cavalry, then his artillery, and finally much of his infantry force. On the third day, he had only 500 still under his command, the rest being dead or dispersed. He collected about 2,000 men at his camp and made a successful stand against the attacking Hadendowa.

He began a withdrawal, collecting the remnants of units along the way, but 1,500 soldiers died from combat or thirst. The Hadendowa sustained serious casualties as well, as he used grapeshot against them to great effect on the final day of the battle.

Termination and Outcome: The outcome of the war was a complete victory for the Hadendowa. The Hadendowa remained unsubdued. Another expedition against them was mounted in 1840, which failed to subdue them but captured some of their chiefs.

Coding Decisions: More than 1,500 died; rounding to the nearest thousand, 2,000 is probably a reasonable estimate, although the real toll could be lower or higher.

Sources: Hill (1970); McGregor (2006).[12]

INTRA-STATE WAR #518

First Syrian War of 1831 to 1832

Participants: Ottoman Empire versus Egypt and Emir Bashir-led Rebels.
Dates: October 1, 1831, to December 27, 1832.
Battle-related Deaths: Ottoman Empire: 10,000;[13] Egypt: 6000;[14] Total Combatant Deaths: more than 16,000. (See Coding Decisions.)
Initiator: Egypt.
Outcome: Negotiated settlement.
War Type: Civil for local issues (autonomy, territory).
Total System Member Military Personnel: Armed Forces of the Ottoman Empire: 129,000 (prewar, initial, peak, final).[15]
Theater Armed Forces: Armed Forces of the Ottoman Empire: 6,000 (initial); 44,000 to 53,000 (peak); Egypt: 30,000 (initial, peak) but overall strength was about 100,000 (prewar, initial); 125,000 (peak, final), excluding naval personnel;[16] Emir Bashir–led Rebels: 5,000 (initial, peak).[17]

Antecedents: During the Greek War of Independence (Intra-state War #504), the Ottoman Empire convinced Mehmet Ali's Egypt to join the fighting with the promise of territorial expansion for Egypt in Crete and Morea (later, Crete and Syria). When the Porte failed to deliver on its promises—possibly because of Egypt's lack of support during the Russo–Turkish War of 1828 to 1829—Mehmet Ali resolved to expand by force. He had to delay his initial invasion because a cholera epidemic in 1831 killed 2,000 of his sailors and 5,000 of his troops, but by October he was ready to move. A minor dispute with the Pasha of Acre (over whether Egyptian peasants fleeing conscription were being sheltered by Acre) provided a pretext for invasion.

Narrative: On October 1, 30,000 Egyptian troops crossed the border into the *pashalik* of Acre. They took Gaza, Jaffa, and Haifa in short order—the latter without firing a shot. Ottoman orders for a truce between Egypt and Acre were ignored by Mehmet Ali. On November 11, his forces besieged Acre itself, which had only 3,000 defenders at the time (although it received reinforcements that increased its strength to 6,000). Major forces were detached under Mehmet's son Ibrahim Ali to conquer the rest of the Syrian provinces, while the siege dragged on.

After the invasion, Emir Bashir joined the Egyptian rebellion with his warriors. On February 13, 1832, the governor of Aleppo sided with the government and Acre against the rebels. On March 25, the Ottoman government formally declared Bashir to be a rebel and ordered him to be deposed. At the end of April, the government also declared war against Mehmet Ali, ordering him to be deposed as well. The government appointed Reschid Pasha to stop him. The first clash between Ottoman regulars and Ibrahim's troops occurred just outside of Tripoli.

On May 27, 1832, Acre fell to an Egyptian assault. In the final assault, the rebels lost 512 killed in addition to the 4,000 they had lost during the siege. Acre's losses for the period of the siege amounted to 5,400 killed—only 600 survived out of a garrison of 6,000. The government refused to concede the provinces of Syria to Mehmet and appointed Reschid Pasha to stop him. The first clash between Ottoman regulars and Ibrahim's troops occurred just outside of Tripoli. On June 16, Damascus fell to the rebels without a fight.

The rebels took Aleppo on July 8; its population had been reduced from 200,000 to just 75,000. The next day at Homs, 15,000 Egyptians defeated 20,000 government troops. The rebels lost 500 killed or wounded, while the government lost 2,000 killed or wounded and another 3,000 captured. Then on July 29, a force of 14,000 Egyptians defeated 17,000 of the Pasha of Aleppo's troops at Beylan. The rebels lost only 102 battle-deaths and 162 wounded, while the pro-government forces suffered about 1,000 battle-deaths, plus 1,500 captured.

There was a pause for negotiations (which the sultan used to raise an army) until late October. The government refused to concede Syria, so Mehmet ordered Ibrahim to move into Asia Minor. It took just one day to disperse the troops guarding the passes, leaving Anatolia open. The terrain slowed Ibrahim's movement, and it was only on December 21 that the next major battle occurred. Ibrahim, together with Bashir, had 15,000 to 22,000 men, while Reschid had many more—44,000 to 53,000. These armies met at Konia, and the rebels were victorious, killing or wounding 3,000 government soldiers and taking up to 10,000 prisoners against only 262 dead and 530 wounded rebels.

Government troops fell back to Eskisehir, and negotiations resumed. The sultan finally agreed to meet most of the Egyptian demands, ending active hostilities.

Termination and Outcome: The outcome of the war was a pro-rebel negotiated settlement. Actual negotiations dragged on until May 1833 and resulted in the Peace of Kütahia. Egypt received the Hijaz, Crete, and (through Ibrahim) Acre, Damascus, Tripoli, and Aleppo. None of the parties was fully satisfied as Egypt didn't receive the autonomy that would allow it to negotiate with foreign powers, and the terms of the agreement were subject to yearly renewal by the sultan. Seeing an opportunity to expand his influence, the tsar of Russia had meanwhile dispatched 15,000 troops to the Bosphorous to protect the Ottoman government from the rebels. Russia eventually gained concessions from the Ottoman Empire, which provoked a backlash from other powers.

Coding Decisions: Using the usual 3:1 ratio of wounded to killed to transform casualty figures into battle-deaths, the historical record suggests a minimum of 5,601 rebel battle-deaths and 9,600 government battle-deaths (both figures being exclusive of any deaths due to disease aside from the siege of Acre). On this basis we assign 6,000 battle-deaths to the rebels and 10,000 to the government, a figure of 16,000 total battle-deaths.

Sources: Bodart (1908); Fahmy (1997); Farah (2000); Kuhnke (1990); McGregor (2006); Mishāqa (1988); Stavrianos (2000); Wilkinson (1843).[18]

INTRA-STATE WAR #521

Palestinian Anti-conscription Revolt of 1834

Participants: Egypt versus Palestinians and Bedouins.
Dates: May 19, 1834, to August 1834.
Battle-related Deaths: Total Combatant Deaths: 4,000. (See Coding Decisions.)[19]
Initiator: Palestinians.
Outcome: Egypt wins.
War Type: Regional Internal.
Theater Armed Forces: Armed Forces of Egypt: 6,000 (peak).

Antecedents: In 1834, Egypt determined to defend its newly won provinces (see Intra-state War #518) by making conquest pay in both economic and military terms. It instituted unpopular taxes, some of which had heretofore only applied to Christians; monopolized profitable industries; and adopted a policy of conscription in Syria to bolster its armies. The latter was especially feared because conscription was nearly a death sentence. The terms were for life, and poor sanitation and other conditions of campaigning made death by disease highly probable.

On May 19, 1834, Ibrahim Pasha, the military governor of the Syria provinces, met with the notables of Nablus and Jerusalem. The notables begged permission to go to their districts to see the decrees of conscription enforced, but as soon as they left, rumors of trouble began.

Narrative: The revolt began when peasants near Nablus refused to provide conscripts, unsuccessfully attempting to storm the city. Perhaps simultaneously in Salt, both the peasantry and the Bedouins engaged in serious fighting against the Egyptians. Near Sair, the peasants, reinforced by Bedouins of Taamrah, defeated an Egyptian force sent to pacify them, killing about twenty-five Egyptian soldiers; in Hebron the Egyptians were driven out.

The rebellion spread to Jerusalem and to the Bedouins of the Dead Sea area. Jerusalem was besieged by some 2,000 peasants based in Birah, and the Egyptians were forced to withdraw into the citadel. The Egyptians won several engagements against the peasants, but could not pursue them, and so requested cavalry reinforcements. Meanwhile, Jewish and Christian families were attacked by the peasants. A relief force of Egyptian cavalry sent on May 24 was ambushed at Bab-al-Wad and defeated before it could lift the siege, suffering 59 killed.

A pause in hostilities followed as the Egyptians massed men and water for an offensive against the rebels. About 3,000 soldiers under Ibrahim Pasha met the rebels in the second week of June at Bab-al-Wad. This time, the peasants were completely routed, suffering about 700 battle-deaths. But on his march to Jerusalem, Ibrahim lost almost an entire regiment to guerrilla attacks by the peasant rebels. Jerusalem was easily retaken as the rebels abandoned it on Ibrahim's approach.

After retaking Jerusalem, Ibrahim attacked the 2,000 peasants of Nablus, led by Nasir Mansur. In a brief battle, 500 peasant casualties were left on the battlefield. Soon, similar victories were recorded at Bayt Jala, Bethlehem, and Liftah. Meanwhile, an Egyptian regiment was harassed and forced to offer battle in narrow defile between the sea and the plain of Esdraelon. Only 300 of the 1,200 men escaped the trap, bereft of supplies and even uniforms.

By late June, the Egyptians had suffered thousands of casualties. On June 23, Emir Bashir was ordered to assist the Egyptians in quelling the revolt. By the end of June, most of Palestine was in the hands of the rebels. The government controlled Gaza, Jerusalem, Jaffa, and Acre, but the peasants controlled the countryside. Tiberais and Safad fell, and Haifa was besieged.

At the beginning of July, reinforcements were dispatched from Egypt to aid Ibrahim. Mehmet Ali himself arrived on July 1 or July 2, along with a squadron of ships. Ibrahim somehow pacified the areas of Jerusalem and Hebron without further use of force, perhaps with promises of immunity from conscription.

The revolt continued in the Nablus area, and the government sent forces to quell the insurgents. The forces met at the battles of Zayta and Dayr-al-Ghusun. The first battle cost the rebels 80 or 90 casualties left behind, while the second, fought on July 15, resulted in 300 peasant casualties left behind in the flight of the peasant army. Nablus was occupied without further opposition.

Emir Bashir led a few thousand Lebanese to the northern border of Palestine and succeeded in pacifying Safad without a struggle. Rebellion flared up again in Hebron, and on August 14, the town was stormed by Ibrahim at the cost of 260 Egyptian casualties. About 700 prisoners were taken; 400 were enslaved and 300 conscripted. He soon pacified Tiberias and Shaghur as well.

By late August, most of Palestine was pacified. A group of peasant rebels had taken refuge in the fortress of Karak, but Ibrahim pursued them with a force of 6,000 soldiers. On the way, they occupied Ghor, where 50 government soldiers died of thirst before water could be brought up. Around August 22, they reached Karak. Unable to mount a siege due to lack of water and fodder, the government forces decided to storm Karak immediately. The initial assault failed, though government losses were small. That night, the peasants left the fortress.

Ibrahim continued to pursue this last peasant force, which was led by the Hebron insurrectionaries. In two engagements, the peasants fled; in the second of these, they suffered 200 killed. The shaykh of Karak was put to death, and the town burned. Ibrahim then left to pursue the remaining rebel leaders, led by Ahmad al-Qasim. They were soon captured and put to death, ending the rebellion.

Termination and Outcome: The outcome of the war was an unconditional victory for Egypt. Notables were executed, and peasants were conscripted.

Coding Decisions: We estimate, on the basis of limited information, that the Egyptians and peasant rebels each lost 2,000, to the nearest thousand. This provides a total estimate of 4,000 battle-deaths, which could be several thousand too low or too high.

Sources: Farah (2000); Kimmerling and Migdal (2003); Polk (1963); Rustum (1938).[20]

INTRA-STATE WAR #532
Druze Rebellion of 1837 to 1838

Participants: Egypt and Christians versus Druzes.
Dates: 1837 to August 22, 1838.
Battle-related Deaths: Egypt: up to 15,000; Druzes: many more than 1,000; Total Combatant Deaths: 17,000. (See Coding Decisions.)[21]
Initiator: Druzes.
Outcome: Negotiated settlement.
War Type: Regional Internal.
Theater Armed Forces: Armed Forces of Egypt: 157,000 (total strength),[22] 450 (initial in-theater); Christians, participating from April 12, 1838: 0 (prewar); 4,000 (initial); 7,000 to 8,000 (peak);[23] Druzes—1,600 (initial).[24]

Antecedents: In late 1837, the Egyptian occupiers of the Syrian provinces attempted to enforce previously decreed conscription on the Druzes of the Hawran region in what is today Lebanon. They also attempted to collect new taxes in the region.

Narrative: These policies triggered armed combat in the Hawran late in 1837, which soon spread to the rocky terrain of al-Laja. In January 1838, the Egyptian government sent 450 Bedouin cavalry against the rebels. They were slaughtered at night in the mountains, with only a few escaping. The second expedition against the Druze rebels consisted of 6,000 regulars, including artillery. In March, this force also was ambushed and defeated, suffering heavy losses. Egypt responded by pouring in reinforcements, and both the number of Druze and the number of Egyptians increased dramatically (though the former was never more than one-fourth of the latter in number).

As a large force of Egyptians moved into al-Leja, they conducted a successful offensive against the Druze. However, in the middle of the Leja, the Egyptians were ambushed, and most perished from the attack of the reassembled Druze warriors. A new force was assembled in Damascus to fight the rebels, but this largely Kurdish force also was defeated when they were ambushed, pursued, and destroyed in narrow defiles. In short, there were "too many encounters to chronicle in detail" in which government forces were defeated by the Druzes.[25] The chief government success during this phase of the conflict was the poisoning of wells, which caused many Druze to die of thirst and to evacuate the Leja.

The Druze then attacked Rashayya, nearly wiping out the battalion of Egyptian troops guarding the town. Suffering severe casualties among their best troops, the Egyptians were then forced to turn to local Christians under Egyptian ally Emir Bashir, who were rearmed and assembled into a force about 7,000 to 8,000 strong. The order for their mobilization was given on April 12, 1838, and at least 4,000 of these warriors were sent against the Druze rebels.

As the Christians assembled at Hasbayya, they came under attack from Druze rivals from Rashayya. They fell back to the citadel until reinforcements arrived.

By this time, the Egyptian forces engaged were up to 20,000. Meanwhile, the Egyptians defeated a force of 1,000 Druze at Wad Bakka, killing all or nearly all of them. As the Egyptians approached Rashayya, the Druze fled to Jin'am, where they suffered a decisive defeat by the Egyptians (joined by their Christian allies after the battle had been won).

Termination and Outcome: Rather than fight the war to its bloody conclusion, both sides decided to negotiate. While the date of the last combat is unknown, the war was declared to be over on August 22, 1838. A few terms favored the Druzes, who were exempted from labor and military conscription as well as the new taxes. However, they were compelled to disarm. A general pardon was declared, although the Christian leaders killed two Druze leaders just afterward. The Christians were rewarded for their service with 16,000 rifles and the freedom to keep them and hand them down.

Coding Decisions: The battle-death estimate is little more than an informed guess, assuming that the Egyptians did lose in the neighborhood of 15,000 battle-deaths and that the rebels suffered at least a few thousand battle-deaths themselves. The real toll could be much lower or somewhat higher.

Sources: Abraham (1981); Aksan (2007); Bournoutian (2003); Farah (2000); Mishāqa (1988).[26]

INTRA-STATE WAR #533
Second Syrian War of 1839 (aka Battle of Nazeb)

Participants: Ottoman Empire versus Egypt.
Dates: June 10, 1839, to June 28, 1839.
Battle-related Deaths: Ottoman Empire: 1,500; Egypt: 500; Total Combatant Deaths: 2,000. (See Coding Decisions.)[27]
Initiator: Ottoman Empire.
Outcome: Rebels win.
War Type: Civil for local issues (territory).
Total System Member Military Personnel: Armed Forces of the Ottoman Empire: 278,000 (prewar, initial, peak).
Theater Armed Forces: Armed Forces of the Ottoman Empire: more than 33,000; Egypt: 43,000 (of 182,000 total).[28]

Antecedents: Ongoing disputes over how much tribute Egypt owed the Ottoman Empire and over possession of the town of Urfa in Anatolia poisoned already fragile Egyptian–Ottoman relations during the years following Egypt's victory in the First Syrian War (see Intra-state War #518). Despite an agreement on these issues, tensions rose between Egyptian governor Mehmet Ali and the government. Seeing that the Egyptian military forces of Mehmet Ali, led by his son Ibrahim, had suffered severe setbacks in Syria (see Intra-state War #532), the sultan decided to try to recover the provinces. By the end of the Druze Rebellion of 1837 to 1838, at least 50,000 Ottoman troops were concentrated in Urfa; Mehmet Ali responded with a buildup of his own.

In February 1839, the sultan ordered full-scale mobilization along the frontier. Three months of mutual mobilizations followed, during which the Ottomans were plagued by desertions by their Kurdish troops and the Egyptians were plagued by hunger and disease. In late May, the Ottomans crossed the frontier into Egyptian territory and began to construct fortifications.

Narrative: On June 10, Ibrahim led his entire army forward. The Ottoman commander, fearing that Ibrahim would retreat to Aleppo, resolved on an attack. Some days of maneuvering followed, and by June 24, Ibrahim was deployed between the Ottoman forces and their supplies. About 43,000 Egyptians advanced on 33,000 Turks near Nazeb. In the subsequent battle, many Turkish troops deserted or fled, providing an easy victory to Ibrahim. The latter began to advance, taking Antep, Maras, and Urfa by June 28 before being ordered to halt by his father; the European powers were threatening intervention.

Termination and Outcome: Militarily, the short war was a victory for the rebels, who maintained their own territory and advanced into government territory. The Ottomans' largest army was shattered and unable to offer serious resistance to further rebel advances. On July 5, the government opened negotiations, offering hereditary control of Egypt (but not Syria, which Mehmet demanded). To make matters worse, the Ottoman fleet sent against Egypt promptly defected on July 7. It would take a new rebellion and active intervention by foreign powers to defeat Mehmet Ali.

Coding Decisions: Estimates of deaths in the battle vary widely from a total of 1,500 killed or wounded to 4,000 killed on the government side alone. Our estimate is 2,000 killed—500 on the rebel side and the remainder on the government side. This may be an overestimate.

Sources: Aksan (2007); Bodart (1908); Farah (2000).[29]

INTRA-STATE WAR #535
Lebanon Insurgency of 1840

Participants: Egypt, Sidon, and Bashir-led Forces versus Lebanese Maronites and Shiites (Aggregate).
Dates: May 27, 1840, to July 31, 1840.
Battle-related Deaths: Total Combatant Deaths: 1,000. (See Coding Decisions.)[30]
Initiator: Lebanese Maronites.
Outcome: Egypt and Bashir-led Forces win.
War Type: Regional Internal.
Theater Armed Forces: Armed Forces of Egypt—12,000 of 207,000 total troops (initial); 24,000 of 207,000 total troops (peak).[31] Bashir-led Forces: 20,000 (peak).[32] Sidon, participating from July 1840: 20,000 (initial, peak).[33] Lebanese Maronites and Shiites: 10,000 (peak—Maronites only).[34]

Antecedents: Egypt occupied what is now Lebanon during the time of this insurrection. The Egyptians had previously armed the Christians of Lebanon with 8,000 weapons to put a stop to a serious Druze uprising (see Intra-state War #532). An order to Egyptian ally Emir Bashir to disarm the Christians, plus visible preparations to conscript them, led to a revolt against both Bashir and the Egyptians.

Narrative: On May 27, 1840, a small Druze revolt was launched by the Abu Nakad chiefs of Dayr al-Qamar. Many Maronites responded to the call to revolt, although none of the other Druze chiefs joined the rebellion. The rebellion thus quickly became a Maronite one against Egyptian rule, centered in Beirut.

The first phase of the rebellion consisted of little more than harassment of Egyptian lines of communication by the rebels. The government successfully dissuaded most Druze from joining the rebellion. But by late May, the Maronite rebels were beginning to attack Egyptian units on the roads and isolated barracks. In June, they threatened Beirut itself, winning many small engagements with the Egyptian forces, generally inflicting many more casualties than they suffered.

On June 22, several thousand Egyptians arrived aboard ships that had earlier defected from the Ottoman navy to the province of Egypt's navy. On July 12, some 7,000 mountaineers attacked the Egyptian garrison at Tripoli. The next day Dayr al-Qamar fell to Egyptian troops, while in Beirut the combined Egyptian forces, perhaps 12,000 to 15,000 in all, moved against the insurgents around the city. Their advance was rapid, wiping out 200 Shi'a rebels. In all, the offensive involved 12,000 Egyptian troops under Ibrahim Pasha, 12,000 more sent as reinforcements, 20,000 under the governor of Sidon, and an equal number led by Bashir. About 4,000 rebels surrendered under promise of amnesty, but most of the rebels fled into the Hawran.

That day (July 13), Bashir claimed that the rebellion was over, although some historians date the end of the rebellion as late in July. At a minimum, there appears to have been another battle at Zahle, which was attacked by 5,000 Egyptian troops. There were also ambushes of military supply convoys.

Termination and Outcome: By the end of July, the rebellion had been crushed. The outcome was a military victory by the Egyptians and Bashir. Some fifty-seven leaders of the rebellion (a majority of whom were commoners, illustrating the peasant nature of the revolt) were exiled. However, many rebels were still in the field against the government, refraining from active operations due to lack of supplies. These anti-Egyptian insurgents would be mobilized by the allied powers during the Third Syrian War (Intra-state War #537).

Coding Decisions: While we were unable to uncover quantitative estimates of deaths, considering the size of the forces involved and the toll that disease inevitably took, we suspect that at least 1,000 were killed.

Sources: Farah (2000); Harik (1968); Polk (1963); Ufford (2007).[35]

INTRA-STATE WAR #537

Third Syrian War of 1840 to 1841 (aka Allied Intervention in Syria)

Participants: Ottoman Empire, United Kingdom, and Bashir Qasim-led Insurgents versus Egypt and Emir Bashir-led Rebels.

Dates: September 9, 1840, to January 17, 1841.

Battle-related Deaths: Total Combatant Deaths: at least 15,000. (See Coding Decisions.)[36]

Initiator: Ottoman Empire.

Outcome: Ottoman Empire wins.

War Type: Civil for local issues (territory).

Total System Member Military Personnel: Armed Forces of the Ottoman Empire: 137,000 (prewar, initial, peak, final); United Kingdom: 168,000 (prewar, initial, peak, final).[37]

Theater Armed Forces: Armed Forces of the Ottoman Empire: more than 5,300 (initial); Bashir Qasim-led Insurgents: 5,000 (initial); 22,000 (peak).[38] Armed Forces of the United Kingdom: more than 1,500 (initial and peak).[39] Egyptian Army: 40,000 to 80,000 of 207,000 total (initial, peak).[40] Emir Bashir-led Rebels, participating until October 12, 1840: [ ].[41]

Antecedents: By 1840, all of the great powers except France had found it to their advantage to favor the Ottoman Empire over rebellious Egypt. This led to the London Convention of July 15, 1840, in which the United Kingdom, Austria, Prussia, and Russia agreed that Syria was to be returned to the Ottoman Empire's control, aside from the pashalik of Acre. Signed just as the Egyptians were defeating another rebellion (see Intra-state War #535), it gave the Ottoman Empire an incentive to initiate hostilities with Egypt.

Mehmet Ali of Egypt refused the terms laid down by the convention, and under British leadership, the allies of the convention prepared for military intervention. The British secured a token force from Austria and pressured the Ottoman Empire to at least send a few of its remaining ships to assist in the fighting. The Ottomans sent 8,000 muskets to arm the Syrian rebels against Egypt (mostly Maronite Christians); a strategy of shore landings to mobilize the population against Egypt was decided upon. This strategy would make the most of British naval power, given the local numeric superiority of Egyptian forces (some 40,000 to 80,000 in the Syrian provinces alone).

Narrative: On September 9, British ships began to bombard Beirut. For three days, they blasted away at its fortifications, killing about 1,000 people. Much of the fleet then moved on to bombard and capture Haifa (September 18), Tyre (September 24), and Sidon (September 25). Lebanese insurgents under Bashir Qasim, officially sanctioned by the Ottoman government, kept Egyptian troops busy in the interior. Ibrahim Ali, the leader of Egyptian troops in the Syrian provinces, was able to assault their mountain strongholds but not to hold them.

Meanwhile on September 10, allied troops—5,300 Ottomans, 1,500 British, and 200 Austrians—were landed at the village of Juniyah, about ten miles north of Beirut. By nightfall, 200 guerrilla fighters had been armed for combat against Egypt (eventually 20,000 would be armed). Ibrahim Ali and Emir Bashir (Egypt's local ally in the Lebanon, not to be confused with his nephew and eventual successor Bashir Qasim) quickly reinforced the passes leading from Juniyah to the interior. Over the next month, disease took its toll on the camp at Juniyah—one Ottoman unit of 1,500 was halved in strength by October.

It was essential to break out from Juniyah. On October 3, Bashir Qasim led 3,000 armed Maronites and a battalion of Ottoman infantry against one of the passes. His soldiers drove the Egyptians from their positions, killing 60 and taking 300 prisoners (many of whom were stripped of possessions and left to die of exposure).

On October 9, the allies assaulted the 2,000 to 3,000 defenders of Beirut with a force of about 3,000 to 4,000 allied troops, mostly Ottomans. The allies lost 40 to 50 men in this victory, and the Egyptians even fewer. Hundreds of prisoners were taken (including some Albanians, who seem to have been persuaded by their Ottoman countrymen to desert the Egyptians), and over the following days, the total number of Egyptian prisoners held by the allies reached 8,000. Three days later, Emir Bashir led his household into exile, depriving Egypt of its only local ally. Bashir Qasim was appointed to his position but lacked real authority; the mountaineers sometimes fought against each other and sometimes attacked the retreating forces of Egypt.

As Egyptians began to stream out of Syria, the allies tackled Acre, the largest remaining fortress of the Egyptians. The allies resolved to bombard the fort into submission before landing troops, so 3,000 Ottoman, 1,500 British, and 200 Austrian troops were embarked with the fleet. On November 3, the fleet attacked the 5,000 Egyptian defenders. The arsenal in the fortress was hit and detonated, inflicting massive casualties on the Egyptian defenders. The Egyptians surrendered, suffering 2,000 killed or wounded and another 1,200 captured. Allied losses were minor, at about 100 killed or wounded.

The interior of Syria was as yet untaken. Ibrahim had a force of 12,000 in Damascus, which would rapidly grow to up to 50,000. But by mid-November, Mehmet Ali had agreed to the allied terms, and negotiations between him and the Porte were opened. Meanwhile, attacks on the retreating Egyptians continued. On November 27, the sultan rejected the stipulations of the Convention of London and demanded unconditional surrender by Egypt. On December 11, this was agreed to by Mehmet Ali and accepted by the Porte on December 27.

The surrender did not end combat operations as the Ottomans and their local allies attempted to prevent the Egyptians from leaving Syria with their army intact. Ibrahim continued his counterinsurgency operations to clear his line of retreat. On December 30, Ibrahim's forces left Damascus for Egypt, along with 12,000 women and 15,000 children. The government dispatched its soldiers on the coast to harry Ibrahim's retreat. During the long march, his forces were harassed by Ottoman soldiers, Bedouins, and Syrian mountaineers. Nearly 10,000 were lost to desertion or death by January 6, 1841.

On January 14, the Ottoman army prepared to attack Gaza, the port from which the Egyptians were scheduled to leave Syria. British ships provided transportation. Although the attack was called off, Egyptian patrols encountered the Ottoman forces and were pursued, costing Egypt some 50 killed or captured. By the time the evacuation was complete, Ibrahim's army had shrunk from 60,000 to 30,000, including at least 5,500 killed against only 100 Ottoman combat deaths for the same period (deaths due to disease being unknown).

Termination and Outcome: The last offensive movement by the Ottomans was halted on January 17. Formally, the outcome of the war was an unconditional surrender by the rebels. The government then forgave Mehmet Ali and assigned to him hereditary possession of Egypt, subject to a tribute requirement and limit on his standing army. Practically, it was a tacit negotiated agreement in which each party gained something—the Ottomans regained Syria and Egypt's loyalty (it would send 8,000 troops to assist the Ottoman Empire during the Crimean War), while Mehmet Ali gained hereditary possession of Egypt. The specifics of the tribute and succession processes were later renegotiated in Egypt's favor. In Lebanon, the war left a large number of armed Christians and Druzes, led by a weak pro-Christian Emir, Bashir III (Bashir Qasim).

Coding Decisions: Clodfelter estimates at least 10,000 battle-deaths, but this figure appears to exclude at least 5,500 battle-deaths suffered by Ibrahim's army as it retreated from Damascus. Note that Austria contributed some ships and 200 soldiers to the allied campaign. We exclude it as a war participant because it failed to commit 1,000 personnel to the operation and suffered only trivial losses.[42]

Sources: Bodart (1908); Bournoutian (2003); Farah (2000); Joachmus (1883); Ufford (2007).[43]

INTRA-STATE WAR #541.2
First Maronite–Druze War of 1841

Participants: Maronites versus Druzes.
Dates: October 13, 1841, to November 19, 1841.
Battle-related Deaths: Maronites: 390; Druzes: 973; Total Combatant Deaths: 1,363. (See Coding Decisions.)[44]
Initiator: Druzes.
Outcome: Druzes win.
War Type: Intercommunal.
Theater Armed Forces: Maronites: 6,000 (peak); Druzes: 500 (initial); 6,000 (peak).[45]

Antecedents: Bashir III (Bashir Qasim) had taken power through the Allied Intervention in Syria (see Intra-state War #537). His leadership was strongly pro-Christian, and he had armed and led Christian insurgents during the war against Egyptian rule. In early 1841, Druze chiefs who had been exiled by Egypt returned and demanded their property and privileges back. This was consistent with the policy of the Ottoman government, but Bashir refused and encouraged the residents of Dayr al-Qamar to throw off their feudal lords.

Attempts to reintroduce taxation to Lebanon also were met with resistance, although the Druze tended to agree to government proposals, while the Maronites rejected them. The Druze demanded a

Druze (or at least Muslim) coruler to represent their interests. In general, the Druze insisted on solutions to the fiscal problems of an autonomous Lebanon that would restore or uphold their feudal privileges. The Maronite patriarch simply told his followers to ignore their Druze feudal lords and form militias. Both sides—the patriarch and the Druze feudal lords—began to mobilize for war.

Narrative: There were violent incidents through the summer and fall of 1841, but the first clear combat was on October 13, when a dispute between a Druze notable and a Maronite shopkeeper led to a Druze raid on Dayr al-Qamar. The Maronite patriarch declared a holy war, and two days later a Maronite ambush killed thirty-two Druzes. Relatively few Maronites answered the call for a holy war as the Maronite notables were concerned about losing their feudal privileges. By contrast, many Druze notables already had small armies with which they could fight.

Each side ravaged villages held by the coreligionists of the other. Then 800 to 1,000 Druzes under Sa'id Junblat countered the Maronite offensive into Druze areas. Joining with other Druze forces, he laid siege to a Maronite monastery. Meanwhile, the siege of Dayr al-Qamar came to a close on November 4. Bashir III was escorted out of the city. About a week later, the government sent five battalions to Zakr to separate and disarm the combatants. Within a week, order had been restored.

Termination and Outcome: The official close of hostilities was November 19. The outcome of the war was a win for the Druzes, who kept and even expanded their territory while gaining the expulsion of Bashir III. However, in April 1842, the government ordered the Druze chiefs to make restitution to the Maronite victims of the war. When the Druze chiefs refused, some were arrested, and the rest rebelled. The civil conflict lasted through December 1842 and eventually led to the surrender of most of the Druze rebels and an imperial decree effectively partitioning Lebanon into Druze and Christian areas of administration.

Coding Decisions: More than 3,000 lives were lost, but massacres were common, so battle-deaths must have been much lower; in recognition of this, we chose the lowest reasonable estimate of fatalities.

Source: Farah (2000).

INTRA-STATE WAR #542

Karbala Revolt of 1842 to 1843

Participants: Ottoman Empire versus Karbala Gangs (Aggregate) and Arab Tribal Rebels.
Dates: December 19, 1842, to January 13, 1843.
Battle-related Deaths: Ottoman Empire: 400;[46] Total Combatant Deaths: 4000. (See Coding Decisions.)[47]
Initiator: Ottoman Empire.
Outcome: Ottoman Empire wins.
War Type: Civil for local issues (autonomy and quartering of troops).
Total System Member Military Personnel: Armed Forces of the Ottoman Empire: 153,000 (prewar, initial); 162,000 (peak, final).
Theater Armed Forces: Armed Forces of the Ottoman Empire: more than 3,000 (initial); Karbala Gangs/Lutis: about 2,500 (initial).[48] Arab Tribal Rebels, participating from January 1, 1842: 5,000 (initial); 8,000 (peak).[49]

Antecedents: In the summer of 1842, a new governor, Najib Pasha, was appointed for the province of Iraq. Because of perceived insults by the government of Karbala, Najib ordered the autonomous Shiite town to quarter a military garrison. When the government of Karbala refused, Najib prepared a punitive expedition against the city. The expedition was duly assembled and departed on November 18.

Narrative: On December 19, the expedition reached the outskirt of Karbala, and fighting began. After a minor skirmish on December 22, government forces held back and shelled the city, though skirmishes occurred almost daily. But the government forces were poorly supplied and began to suffer from famine. By the end of December, only 40 townspeople had been killed, but the Ottomans had suffered about 1,000 casualties. The rebels, misled by a rumor of Persian intervention on their behalf, continued to resist.

While Persia did not intervene, the residents did gain the support of 5,000 Arab tribesmen, a force that quickly increased to 8,000 by January 12, following a fierce battle between the Karbala gangs leading the revolt and government forces. The next day, the Ottoman forces stormed the city, losing 200 men (at least 50 killed) in the assault. At this point, 3,000 Arab tribesmen, together with 200

Karbala rebels, attempted to break out of the city. They were pursued by 3,000 Ottoman troops with cavalry support, and their losses were extremely high. As sniper fire continued in the town, the Ottomans began to massacre civilians (about 450 of them before the Ottoman commander put a stop to the massacre).

Termination and Outcome: The outcome of the war was an unconditional government victory. The governor eliminated the autonomy that Karbala's Shiites had enjoyed. The leaders of the revolt fled but were later pardoned.

Coding Decisions: Up to 5,000 died, 3,000 of them within the city. Subtracting 450 known civilian deaths gives a maximum of 4,500 battle-deaths, and 4,000 is probably nearer the truth. Note that the Ottoman government claimed that 150 Persians were killed in the fighting, but no evidence exists that Persia itself participated in the war.[50] Rather, some of the gangs had Baluchi members from Persia.[51]

Sources: Cole and Momen (1986); Lorimer (1970).

INTRA-STATE WAR #543
Second Maronite–Druze War of 1845

Participants: Maronites versus Druzes.
Dates: April 30, 1845, to May 31, 1845.
Battle-related Deaths: Maronites: 700; Druzes: 350; Total Combatant Deaths: 1,050. (See Coding Decisions.)[52]
Initiator: Maronites.
Outcome: Negotiated settlement.
War Type: Intercommunal.
Theater Armed Forces: Maronites: 11,000 (initial, peak).[53]

Antecedents: In 1843, the Ottoman Empire had divided leadership over Lebanon between a Druze lieutenant governor and a Christian one, each responsible for the area under his control. This left Maronites and other Christians in the Druze zone unable to vindicate their rights against the Druze and vice versa. Strong pressure existed for each chief to expand his zone of control.

By 1845, preparations for war were underway in both camps. The Druze settled their most salient intracommunal feuds, while the Maronites gradually were united under the Shihabs (the family of former Emir Bashir II, who had been deposed after he sided with Egypt in the 1830s). Arms were shipped in from abroad, especially France. The Maronites had a force of 11,000 fighters prepared. The government had only 4,000 soldiers in all of Mount Lebanon, just 50 soldiers in the disputed town of Dayr al-Qamar, and 350 at B'abda and Hadath. A series of assassinations preceded the war, which altogether killed some 35 people. The assassins went unpunished due to the failure of the dual administration, which now held little real power.

Narrative: On April 30, armed Maronites entered the Shuf (Chouf) and sacked thirteen Druze villages. Within days, they entered the mixed districts and began to attack the Druze residing there. The first military combat appears to have occurred at 'Abayh; the battle was won by the Druzes. In general the Druzes followed their feudal leaders, whereas the Maronite peasants failed to achieve united leadership after the first few days. Battles generally involved small units, and the bulk of the casualties were inflicted upon already defeated foes.

By May 8, the Maronite offensive had stalled, and they had been driven out of all Druze-governed areas except for Dayr al-Qamar and the area around 'Abayh. On May 9, about 5,000 Maronites and Greek Catholics attacked a force of 800 Druzes, virtually annihilating it. The next day, a Druze counterattack on 'Abayh and 'Ayn Ksûr wiped out many Maronites, especially after the battle proper was over.

On May 16, the Maronites of Christian-ruled Mount Lebanon launched a general attack on the Druze within their territory. Despite initial successes, they were driven back the next day. A tenuous de facto truce prevailed, while peace negotiations, led by the Ottoman government, took place. At first the Maronite leaders resisted the forgive-and-forget clause of the proposed agreement, but when the government threatened to repress them if they didn't sign, they agreed to a peace accord.

Termination and Outcome: On May 31, leaders from both sides signed the government-created peace accord that essentially restored the status quo ante. Both sides committed themselves to rely on Ottoman troops for protection against each other. The agreement did nothing to resolve the dispute over governance of mixed-group territories.

Coding Decisions: The number of those killed is estimated variously at 1,500 to 3,000. Of course, these figures include civilians, but military losses were quite severe, especially around 'Abayh. We estimate that battle-deaths were at least 1,000. As Druze military losses were double those of the Maronites, we tentatively peg their battle-deaths at 700 and 350, respectively.

Sources: Abraham (1981); Farah (2000).[54]

INTRA-STATE WAR #554.5

Aleppo Revolt of 1850

Participants: Ottoman Empire versus Aleppo Rebels.
Dates: October 17, 1850, to November 10, 1850.
Battle-related Deaths: Total Combatant Deaths: 1,000. (See Coding Decisions.)[55]
Initiator: Aleppo Rebels.
Outcome: Ottoman Empire wins.
War Type: Civil for local issues (conscription, taxation).
Total System Member Military Personnel: Armed Forces of the Ottoman Empire: 145,000 (prewar, initial, peak, final).[56]
Theater Armed Forces: Armed Forces of the Ottoman Empire: 2,500 (peak). Aleppo Rebels: thousands (initial); 3,000 to 5,000 (peak).[57]

Antecedents: In 1850, the government introduced conscription into the Arab territories to meet a manpower shortage that made it all but impossible to maintain order throughout the provinces. The conscription edict, together with changes in how taxes were collected, prompted a rebellion in Aleppo.

Narrative: The rebellion began on October 17, 1850. It began as a simple anti-conscription demonstration but quickly transformed into an attack on Christians in the city. Up to eighteen Christians were murdered by the rioters. Thousands also attacked the local government residence. The titular leader of the rebels was Abdullah Bey Babilsi, who commanded many thousands of armed fighters. On the second day, he brought the rioting to a halt by agreeing to present the rioters' demands to the provincial governor.

The provincial government initially agreed to the rebels' demands to calm the situation but sent reinforcements into the town on November 2. The government then attempted to impose disarmament. On November 2, Abdullah Bey was removed from his position, causing a divide among the rebels. One faction sided with the government, while another followed his cousin's leadership into revolt.

The government now had 2,500 soldiers facing the 3,000 to 5,000 armed rebels. On November 5, the government began to shell the center of the rebellion. House-to-house fighting followed, and the government prevailed by November 10.

Termination and Outcome: The Aleppo rebellion ended with an unconditional government military victory on November 10. About 600 rebels were arrested and 200 exiled to Crete, the rest being conscripted. The impetus to revolt appears to have spread outside of Aleppo to the mountain people in Leja, Turkomans, and Bedouin. The resulting insurrections took two years to either crush or end with peace negotiations.

Coding Decisions: Estimates of fatalities range from 1,000 to 5,000. Accepting that civilians are included in these totals, we tentatively assign a figure of 1,000 battle-deaths to the revolt.

Sources: Aksan (2007); Ma'oz (1968); Masters (1990).

INTRA-STATE WAR #557.9

Libyan Insurrection of 1855 to 1856

Participants: Ottoman Empire versus Libyan Rebels.
Dates: June 1855 to January 1856.
Battle-related Deaths: Ottoman Empire: at least 1,400; Total Combatant Deaths: more than 1,400.[58]
Initiator: Libyan Rebels.
Outcome: Ottoman Empire wins.
War Type: Civil for local issues (secession).
Total System Member Military Personnel: Armed Forces of the Ottoman Empire: 160,000 (prewar, initial, peak, final).[59]
Theater Armed Forces: Armed Forces of the Ottoman Empire: 3,000 (initial); 12,000 (peak, final). Libyan Rebels: 14,000 (initial, peak); 4,000 (final).[60]

Antecedents: In 1835, the Ottoman Empire had reestablished its control over autonomous Libya.

Rebellions broke out within a few years but were defeated. One of the rebel leaders, tribal leader Ghuma bin Khalifa, was imprisoned in Trabzon in Anatolia. In 1855, he escaped his exile (with possible assistance from Russian or French agents) and returned to Libya to raise a new rebellion against the Ottomans.

Narrative: The first operation by Ghuma's resistance forces was an attack on the citadel of Yafran in June 1855. He had perhaps 14,000 rebels at his command, while the Ottomans had only 3,000 available troops to fight the insurgency. They sent half of their forces to relieve the siege of Yafran. However, Ghuma's forces ambushed them and killed 1,400 of them; only 100 prisoners were spared. The insurrection quickly gained control over most of the province of Tripoli, excepting the major cities.

The Ottoman Empire sent 1,800 troops from Anatolia as reinforcements. Drought caused a temporary lull in operations, but Ghuma moved against Ghariyan in September and then against Tripoli. The new Ottoman governor proclaimed an amnesty for all except Ghuma, and his forces soon dwindled to 4,000 men. In January 1856, the Ottomans, now 12,000 strong, attacked Ghuma's "capital," the citadel at Yafran. Ghuma's forces were defeated, and he was forced to retreat into the mountains and then into Tunisia.

Termination and Outcome: While Ghuma continued to attempt revolts in the spring of 1856, and in 1857, the main revolt was ended with a government military victory with promise of partial amnesty. Ghuma bin Khalifa was eventually killed in action in 1858.

Coding Decisions: Self-explanatory from cited sources.

Source: Martin (1990).

INTRA-STATE WAR #566
Third Maronite–Druze War of 1860

Participants: Maronites versus Druzes.
Dates: May 26, 1860, to July 12, 1860.
Battle-related Deaths: Maronites: 2,000; Druzes: 1,000; Total Combatant Deaths: 3,000. (See Coding Decisions.)[61]
Initiator: Maronites.
Outcome: Negotiated settlement.
War Type: Intercommunal.
Theater Armed Forces: Maronites: 50,000 (peak—may be an overestimate). Druzes: 12,000 (peak).[62]

Antecedents: Previous intercommunal wars (Intra-state Wars #542.3 and 543) had failed to settle the volatile issue of the control of mixed-faith districts and villages. By 1857, arms were being imported into Lebanon in significant quantities. Security began to collapse in 1858, as a peasant uprising in Kisrawan challenged the power of the shaykhs. Meanwhile, an insurrection in Hercegovina caused the Porte to withdraw 80 percent of its regulars from Syria. Continued European interference in the affairs of Lebanon increased the resentment of Druzes and the Ottoman government, making escalation more likely. The Maronites began to work with Catholic and Orthodox Greeks to form committees that would drill volunteers and distribute arms in the event of war. Presumably, the Druze took similar precautions.

On August 30, 1859, an incident between Druze and Christian youth at Beit Meri led to a reciprocal cycle of violence in the village. At least eighteen Druzes and eleven Christians were killed. As the risk of full-scale war increased, both sides prepared for conflict, and civilians began to emigrate. Looting followed, and a series of killings went unpunished, further aggravating the situation of insecurity. Violence began to escalate in early 1860. Further violent incidents occurred in March, April, and May but were scattered and random rather than systematic. Violence largely took place on major roads.

Narrative: On May 26 and May 27, Maronite bands first attacked Druze villages in the Metn district next to Kisrawan. On May 29, the attacks escalated, and a Druze killed a Maronite in retaliation for the earlier raids. The first clear battle was fought on May 30 and May 31 between 250 to 300 Kisrawani Christians and 1,800 to 2,000 Druzes on the road to Beit Meri. In Baabda and the Metn, a band of Christian militia was hit by the Druze; 600 of the former were killed in the rout.

On May 31, fighting also broke out near Zahleh, where the Druze ambushed a relief column of Christians approaching the town. In the nearby village of Dahr al-Baidar, 400 armed villagers drove off 200 Druze warriors but suffered defeat when they pursued the Druze to the village of Ain Dara. Three days later, the second battle of Ain Dara pitted 3,000 Christians against 600 Druzes. Total fatalities in the two battles were low—perhaps 7 in the first engagement and 30 in the second. Nevertheless, the Druze obtained local superiority and drove the Christians back into Zahleh.

Fighting also occurred around Dayr al-Qamar, a perennial zone of conflict between Druzes and Maronites. From June 2 to June 3, heavy fighting for the city cost up to 100 Druze and 25 Christian battle-deaths. After the city fell, many of its defenders and other Christians were slaughtered by the victorious Druze. Similar engagements were fought elsewhere, with Druze victories typically being followed by massacres of Christians.

By early June, indiscriminate massacre was becoming the rule rather than the exception. Given that the Druze were prevailing everywhere, this essentially transformed the conflict into a series of brief battles followed by Druze massacres of Christians in general, not just Christian fighters.

After a particularly bloody massacre at Hasbaiya, a Druze army marched on Rashaiya. When combined with local Druzes, the army was 5,000 strong. From June 10 to June 11, it overran the Christian defenses and killed half of the Christian population. Between them, the massacres of Hasbaiya, Rashaiya, and surrounding villages claimed 1,800 lives. The Druze now swept through the Bekaa Valley. By June 12, most Christian leaders had decided to end the war but were no longer in a position to do more than attempt to defend themselves and their districts.

The only major Christian stronghold to withstand the Druze offensive was Zahleh, with about 4,000 defenders. On June 14, the Zahleh Christian forces attacked the Druze at the mixed village at Qabb Elias but were routed. Most fell back to Zahleh, which was attacked and taken by at least 3,000 Druzes, Bedouins, and Shiites on June 18. Anywhere from 40 to 900 Christians were killed; the Druze lost between 100 and 1,500 killed.

Meanwhile, the Druze also had enjoyed success in the Shahhar in some of the war's most intense fighting. Near Sidon, nearly 400 Christians were killed, most of them in fighting outside the city. Despite the collapse of organized Christian resistance, the Druze kept up their attacks, burning and sacking villages. Dayr al-Qamal, which had surrendered early in the war, was sacked by the Druzes, who committed the largest massacre of the war on June 20 and June 21 against their largely unarmed Christian population. Perhaps 2,000 were slaughtered. Under threats from the Ottoman government, several Druze leaders proclaimed an end to hostilities in the mountains, which at least had the effect of reducing the bloodshed.

Termination and Outcome: By July 5, peace negotiations were opened on the insistence of the government and the consuls of the European powers. The Druze insisted on a *mada ma mada* (let bygones be bygones) clause in which neither side would make claims on the other. Some Maronite leaders rejected this clause, and peace negotiations dragged on for some time, but on July 12 both sides' leaders signed the agreement, which formally ended the war.

During the peace negotiations, intercommunal rioting broke out in Damascus, where for eight days and nights Muslims terrorized and massacred the Christian inhabitants. As both sides were essentially unarmed, this is not treated as part of the intercommunal war. After the war, France landed a "rescue" expedition that ended up conducting punitive actions against the Druze. The government also arrested hundreds of Druzes and executed ringleaders of the Damascus riots.

Coding Decisions: Estimates of those killed vary widely (from 3,600 to 10,000). As many died of hunger or exposure after the initial violence as were killed during the fighting. Given that Christian losses in the field were larger than Druze losses, we cautiously estimate 1,000 Druze battle-deaths and 2,000 Christian battle-deaths. The rest were massacred civilians or people who died of hunger and exposure after the war. Authors disagree about which side initiated full-scale hostilities, but the weight of the evidence supports the idea that the Maronite Christians determined to expel the Druzes from the mixed districts. The Ottoman government moved into a blocking position at Hazmiyi.

Sources: Farah (2000); Fawaz (1994).[63]

INTRA-STATE WAR #581

Sahil Revolt of 1864 to 1865 (aka Tunisian Revolt of 1864)

Participants: Tunisia versus Ghadam-led Rebels and Sahil Peasants (Aggregate).
Dates: March 1864 to February 1865.

Battle-related Deaths: Total Combatant Deaths: 2,000. (See Coding Decisions.)[64]
Initiator: Ghadam-led Rebels.
Outcome: Tunisia wins.
War Type: Civil for local issues (taxes and centralism—but see Coding Decisions).
Total System Member Military Personnel: Armed Forces of Tunisia: 20,000 (prewar, initial, peak, final).[65]
Theater Armed Forces: Armed Forces of Tunisia: 5,000 (initial, peak). Ghadam-led Rebels, participating through October 15, 1864: 4,000 (peak).[66] Sahil Peasants: 90,000 (peak—almost certainly an exaggeration).[67]

Antecedents: In 1861, the government of Tunisia adopted an unpopular, "modern" centralizing constitution. The Tunisian Bey's efforts to double taxes in 1864 sparked a rebellion against the constitution led by Ali Bin Ghadam. An insurrection was already underway in the neighboring French colony of Algeria, and the Tunisian rebels—though virulently anti-French—prepared their insurrection in such a manner as to give the least pretext for foreign intervention.

Narrative: The revolt began in March around Kairouan and Le Kef. Already the Algerian revolt had spread across the border, with another 1,300 or more killed or wounded in intertribal warfare on the Libyan frontier. The rebels, former conscripts, were heavily armed. Beja was besieged, and the rebels captured Matar. The government controlled that capital, while the rebels controlled most other regions of Tunisia. France, Britain, and Italy all landed troops to protect their nationals, but the rebels kept their distance from the capital.

The government sent an expedition to quash the rebels, but soon its 5,000 men had dwindled to mere hundreds due to battle, disease, and desertion (at least 500 defected to the rebels). At least 300 government troops were killed in one battle. Sfax was sacked on April 30, and the rebels there pronounced the deposition of the Bey, hoisting an Ottoman flag. Nevertheless, the Ottoman Empire supplied money to the government with which to pay its troops.

On May 1, the government abolished the constitution that had stirred the rebels and lowered taxes to their previous level. That day, 160 soldiers deserted the government army; the next day, another 930 deserted. In July, negotiations were opened with the rebels, and an agreement was reached for implementation of *sharia* law and an amnesty. However, the rebellion flared up again in August, and on August 29 the government mounted a two-month offensive against the rebels.

The rebels were now limited to an area around Susa, and at the end of September they were defeated outside the city. In early October, 3,000 Tunisian troops engaged thousands of rebels—an exaggerated official report says 90,000 of them. Although the rebels certainly outnumbered the government forces, the government's artillery won the day, and 200 rebels were killed. A new rising in Djerba was then put down. By October 15, the main rebellion had been militarily crushed by government commander Ahmad Zarraiq. However, Sahelian peasants remained in revolt and were not defeated until the government conducted a series of brutal sweeps in the winter.

Termination and Outcome: The rebellion lasted about a year. The government won a clear military victory and subsequently fined rebels. A new rebellion emerged in September 1866; famine, cholera, and typhus killed many, as they had in the 1864 revolt.

Coding Decisions: Given the size of the forces engaged and the prevalence of disease among them, we are confident that more than 1,000 died. Marsans-Sakly describes 450 government losses and 1,500 rebels "executed military style," but this likely covers only one of the campaigns in the war. Given this, we conclude that an estimate of 2,000 is more likely to be too low than too high. Although the rebels claimed to depose the government and sought an Ottoman replacement, the initial impeti for revolt were local issues, and so we do not code this as a war for control of the central government.

Sources: Broadley (1882); Ling (1967); Marsans-Sakly (2003); Papers Relating to Foreign Affairs (1865); Perkins (1986); Womble (1997).

INTRA-STATE WAR #610.5
Mahdist Rebellion phase 1 of 1881 to 1882

Participants: Egypt versus Mahdists.
Dates: August 12, 1881, to September 14, 1882.

Battle-related Deaths: Armed Forces of Egypt: more than 3,000; Mahdists: more than 6,000; Total Combatant Deaths: about 10,000. (See Coding Decisions.)
Initiator: Mahdists.
Outcome: Became extra-state.
War Type: Civil for local issues (independence and religion).
Total System Member Military Personnel: Armed Forces of Egypt: 15,000 (prewar, initial).[68]
Theater Armed Forces: Armed Forces of Egypt: 200 (initial); 15,500 to 18,000 (peak). Mahdists: 30,000 (peak).[69]

Antecedents: Egypt had incorporated the Sudan after bitter fighting earlier in the nineteenth century. However, Egypt largely exploited the Sudan's people and resources for the benefit of Egyptian projects. Frontier revolts were common (see Intra-state War #516). A Sudanese cleric, Muhammad Ahmad, preached a more fundamentalist version of Islam and soon found himself declared a rebel. He proclaimed himself the Mahdi in August 1881 and openly defied Egyptian rule.

Narrative: The first engagement of the war took place on August 12, 1881, when two companies (about 200 men) that had been sent after the Mahdi were attacked by perhaps 100 rebels and defeated, losing at least 120 killed. The government responded to the defeat by sending a larger force against the rebels. In December 1881, about 1,400 to 1,500 government troops were sent against the Mahdists, but elements of the expedition were ambushed at Ghedeer on December 9 and lost nearly 400 men.

A third expedition was prepared in April 1882. Meanwhile, the rebels had besieged Sennar and killed most of its garrison of 100 men. On April 15, the government suffered hundreds more casualties, with most of a 50-person force being killed and a further 200 lost elsewhere. The government made some progress in May, winning an engagement on April 6 and inflicting heavy losses on the Mahdists. On April 24, the government gained another victory near Sennar, the rebels losing 800. Yet another victory followed on June 3. However, on June 7, the government's main force of 3,500 to 6,000 was ambushed and almost annihilated.

On August 8, 1882, the garrison of Shatt was put to the sword by the rebels, the government suffering 200 killed. On June 28, an attack on Ouem was repulsed, the rebels losing more than 3,000. Following this, the Mahdi besieged El Obeid, the capital of Kordofan. On September 8, the city's 12,000 defenders were attacked by some 30,000 rebels in a failed attempt to storm the city. Thousands of rebels—some say 10,000—were killed; the government suffered less than 300 killed or wounded. A long, ultimately successful siege followed.

Termination and Outcome: Meanwhile, a coup attempt in Cairo had led to British intervention. As of September 15, 1882, Egypt ceased being an independent member of the state system. Hence, the war became an extra-state one. The Egyptians and British suffered further defeats before eventually winning an overwhelming victory over the Mahdi's forces.

Coding Decisions: While no comprehensive figures for this period exist, the events in the narrative imply perhaps 3,000 government battle-deaths and more than double that number of rebel losses. Given missing data and the inevitable toll that disease must have taken, we estimate 10,000 battle-deaths in all, which is likely a conservative estimate.

Sources: McGregor (2006); Royle (1900); Warner (1973); Wingate (1891).

INTRA-STATE WAR #616

First Yemeni Imamate Rebellion of 1890 to 1892 (aka al-Mansur's Revolt)

Participants: Ottoman Empire versus Muhammad al-Mansur-led Rebels.
Dates: 1890 to September 1892.
Battle-related Deaths: Total Combatant Deaths: 5,000. (See Coding Decisions.)[70]
Initiator: Muhammad al-Mansur-led Rebels.
Outcome: Ottoman Empire wins.
War Type: Civil for local issues (taxation and autonomy).
Total System Member Military Personnel: Armed Forces of the Ottoman Empire: 236,000 (prewar); 247,000 (peak); 241,000 (final).[71]
Theater Armed Forces: Armed Forces of the Ottoman Empire: 40,000 (peak). Zaidi Imam Muhammad al-Mansur-led Rebels: perhaps 75,000.[72]

Antecedents: The Ottoman Empire reconquered Yemen in the mid-nineteenth century, establishing control by late 1872. However, ordinary Ottoman procedures of taxation led to repeated revolts. In 1888, sustained rebellion occurred throughout Yemen, which the Ottomans put down with some difficulty. In April 1890, the government sent 2,990 reinforcements to Yemen as a preventive measure. But by July 1890, Ottoman rule was so unpopular that the various candidates for leadership of the local imamate agreed on a consensus candidate, Muhammad al-Mansur. In violation of the agreement his predecessor had made with the Turks, he fled Sanaa, ending up at Jabal al-Ahnum.

Narrative: Once at Jabal al-Ahnum, al-Mansur called for a general revolt of the Yemeni tribes against Ottoman rule. The first major battle may have been in the Sharafayn mountains in mid-1890, where an Ottoman force led by Mehmed Arif was defeated and Arif killed. On August 12, the Ottoman commander of Hodeida sent an expedition to storm the surrounding region, which was at least partially successful. Around the same time, another campaign dislodged the rebels from their defenses near Sanaa.

Early in 1891, Mansur ordered the tribes to lay siege to Sanaa. The siege would not be lifted until October. One tribal leader, Nasr Mabhut, captured several places in the vicinity of Haggah and then pretended to submit to the Ottomans. When government forces arrived to take control of Gabal Zafir from his forces, he ambushed and "massacred about a thousand of them."[73]

The fighting intensified during the summer of 1891. Ottoman strength in Yemen fell below 16,000 due to a cholera epidemic that had been raging for two years. Meanwhile, the Mansur-led rebellion reached its peak strength of anywhere from 50,000 to 100,000 men. In June, Hajjah fell to the imam's forces, and a battle at Shahil resulted in the rout of 1,000 Ottoman troops, 80 of them being killed. Additional revolts broke out in Iyal Surayh, Hamdan, and other places. About 400 Turkish troops sent to collect taxes from the Beni Mervan tribe in Asir were ambushed and nearly annihilated. Skirmishes between Ottoman reinforcements and the Arab rebels resulted in some 200 rebel deaths. August saw heavy fighting along the Sanaa-Hodeida road, and the rebels took Menakha between Sanaa and Hodeida. Nasr Mabhut led 12,000 rebels in an attempt to storm Sanaa, being repulsed with heavy losses.

On September 5, the insurgents managed to defeat government forces sent against them, inflicting some killed and wounded. Up to 70,000 rebels now surrounded Sanaa. But in October, about 30,000 Turkish reinforcements arrived, lifting the siege of the city. Unfortunately, the large influx of military personnel in Hodeida, the primary staging area for the reinforcements, led to an outbreak of cholera in the barracks and hospital that claimed 30 to 40 lives a day by mid-October. Peace talks foundered.

In mid-November, the government mounted an offensive out of Sanaa, pursuing the rebels who had besieged the city. Several thousand rebels were killed in this campaign, but an epidemic in Sanaa slowed the military operation, and the rebels regrouped. The siege was resumed briefly by the rebels, but troops from Hodeida lifted it within a month.

By the end of January 1892, the government had 40,000 troops in Yemen and had reconquered much of the Yemen, with the notable exception of Dhofir, which was still besieged by the rebels. The imam ordered his troops to attack Sanaa again in February. In May, the government launched another offensive against the rebels. Hajjah surrendered soon after the start of the offensive, and one by one the rebel strongholds fell. The last to hold out was Saade, about 130 miles north of Sanaa, but it fell after a bloody battle.

Termination and Outcome: By September, the Ottoman governor could report that the rebellion had been crushed. The rebels' military commander and twenty chiefs were killed. The outcome of the war was a complete military victory by the government, with promises of a general pardon. Low-level resistance resumed within a few years, and the Ottomans proved unable to stabilize the country.

Coding Decisions: Recorded losses exceed 3,000, but given the endemic cholera and the size of the forces involved, we suspect that 5,000 is nearer to the truth. The real toll could be much higher.

Sources: *Appleton's Annual Cyclopaedia and Register of Important Events of the Year 1883* (1886); Baldry (1976); Bang (1996); Dresch (2000); Farah (2002); Harris (1936); Ingrams and Ingrams (1993).

INTRA-STATE WAR #630

Druze Rebellion of 1895 to 1896

Participants: Ottoman Empire versus Druzes.
Dates: October 15, 1895, to March 1896, and June 1896 to October 1896.
Battle-related Deaths: Armed Forces of the Ottoman Empire: 6,000; Druzes: 4,000; Total Combatant Deaths: 10,000. (See Coding Decisions.)[74]
Initiator: Ottoman Empire.
Outcome: Ottoman Empire wins.
War Type: Civil for local issues (conscription).
Total System Member Military Personnel: Armed Forces of the Ottoman Empire: 231,000 (prewar, initial); 261,000 (peak, final).[75]
Theater Armed Forces: Armed Forces of the Ottoman Empire: 30,000 (early in the war, peak). Druzes: 9,500 (peak).[76]

Antecedents: In 1895, the Ottoman Empire decided to reintroduce conscription for the Druzes. That August, bonfires symbolizing rebellion were lit, and the Druzes refused to allow any such conscription. Some accounts argue that a dispute between Muslims and Druzes was the real reason for the campaign against the Druzes that followed, with the government taking the opportunity to intervene against the Druzes.

Narrative: The war began on October 15, 1895, as the government mounted an offensive against the Druze. The government forces outnumbered the Druzes by a ratio of 5:2. Small engagements followed in which the government lost 45 killed. By December 1895, government forces in the theater of operations numbered 30,000. The government forces suffered casualties from lack of food, exposure to the cold, and disease (which claimed the lives of one-sixth of the government expeditionary force), but by January 1896 it appeared that the uprising had been crushed as a general surrender of Druzes took place. Ottoman casualties had outnumbered those of the Druzes.

A peace agreement was reached in February that called for the surrender of Druze rifles, conscription, registration of land, and payment of taxes. But at least 2,000 Druzes were still defying the government in Jebal al-Duruz, although they may have ceased operations in March.

The agreement ultimately failed—in early June, a group of Druze, under the titular leadership of Shibli al-Atrash's niece, rebelled in the Hawran against what it claimed were violations of the agreement by the Ottomans and general mistreatment by the authorities. Fifty gendarmes were sent to arrest the Druze leaders, but all of them were killed by the rebels. The government followed up with between one and two battalions of regular infantry, accompanied by 100 mounted infantry. These forces, too, were ambushed, and all were killed or captured by the Druzes.

On June 16, Ottoman forces were ambushed at ‘Urman. Four battalions were cut to pieces; the government lost 600 killed against only 200 rebels killed. By July 8, another 2,000 Druzes had joined the insurgency, besieging Suwaida with a total of 9,000 to 10,000 troops. The Ottomans responded to the defeat by invading with twenty-nine battalions (about 25,000 to 30,000 troops), lifting the siege of Suwaida on July 11. The battle for Suwaida cost the rebels 1,200 to 2,000 casualties and the government 600 casualties.

The Druze forces retreated, opting to wage guerrilla war against the Ottomans. Further engagements took place that July, with both sides suffering heavy casualties. Many government soldiers were felled by disease. A government effort to negotiate another submission of the Druzes failed on July 29, but by the end of the month, the Druzes had been heavily defeated at Qanawat and driven from Jebal al-Duruz to the inhospitable Laja. The Jebal was reduced to less than a quarter of its prewar population.

The Druzes were now fighting for their continued existence. Government terms included handing over Druzes responsible for the initial attacks on government forces, surrendering 2,600 rifles and otherwise submitting to all government orders and regulations. The Druze mounted several minor attacks in August. By September 3, some Druzes surrendered to the government. However, the government began to arrest many of those who submitted, prompting continued resistance by some 6,000 rebels.

In October, the government mounted a new campaign against the Druze rebels. Many were killed in this offensive, including civilians, but the back of the revolt was broken.

Termination and Outcome: The outcome of the war was a military victory by the government without any promise of amnesty. There is no evidence of combat after the October offensive, but many

Druzes continued to hold out until March 11, 1897, when the government issued a partial amnesty for remaining refugees and fighters who had not yet submitted to the government. As late as the harvest season in 1897, there were still an estimated 8,000 Druze guerrillas, joined by some Sunnis and Bedouins. The central government then relieved the local government of its tax and conscription obligations. A general amnesty was not proclaimed until 1900.

Coding Decisions: While no direct estimate of battle-deaths is available, the government lost one-sixth of its force of 30,000 to disease during the first phase of the revolt. Battles alone killed at least 800, not including several instances in which authors describe heavy losses. In addition, one battle was fought near Basr al-Harir, which killed 500 government soldiers. We are unsure if this is the same battle as that of ‘Urman. Even less information is available on rebel battle-deaths, aside from the fact that they were catastrophic in the second phase of the war. On the basis of this limited information, we estimate 6,000 government battle-deaths and 4,000 rebel battle-deaths, for a total of 10,000 battle-deaths. The real toll could be somewhat lower or higher.

Sources: Firro (1992); Parsons (2000); Salih (1977); Schilcher (1991); Zürcher (1999).[77]

INTRA-STATE WAR #630.2
Second Zeitun Uprising of 1895 to 1896

Participants: Ottoman Empire versus Hunchaks.
Dates: October 24, 1895, to February 2, 1896.
Battle-related Deaths: Armed Forces of the Ottoman Empire: at least 4,400; Hunchaks: at least 125; Total Combatant Deaths: perhaps 5,000. (See Coding Decisions.)[78]
Initiator: Ottoman Empire.
Outcome: Negotiated settlement.
War Type: Civil for local issues (self-defense).
Total System Member Military Personnel: Armed Forces of the Ottoman Empire: 231,000 (prewar, initial); 261,000 (peak, final).
Theater Armed Forces: Armed Forces of the Ottoman Empire: 40,000 (initial, peak). Hunchaks: 1,500 (initial—a low estimate); 8,000 (peak—probably an overestimate by the Ottoman government).[79]

Antecedents: The Ottoman government distrusted the loyalty of its Armenian population. In 1895, a series of massacres occurred at strategically sited, majority-Armenian towns. By late 1895, both explicit warnings from a departing Ottoman official and military preparations by the government convinced the Armenian citizens of Zeitun that such a massacre was imminent. When government forces began to burn villages near Zeitun on October 24, locals led by the Hunchak Party began to retaliate.

Narrative: The government proclaimed a state of rebellion in Zeitun, and the Fifth Army Corps stationed at Maras was ordered to proceed against the rebels. Meanwhile, the rebels stormed the citadel, killing 97 soldiers of the garrison and taking the remaining 465 prisoners. This provided the rebels with some arms for the coming fight.

The rebels advanced outside of Zeitun and attempted to spread the rebellion, occupying outlying villages and defending these positions against strong government assaults. The government had more than 40,000 troops in the field against the rebels. Estimates of rebel numbers ranged from 1,500 to 8,000. Eventually in November, the government began to penetrate the Armenian defense perimeter. Possibly in response, the rebels massacred their prisoners, killing about 400 men from the garrison.

By December, the rebels had been checked by government forces and compelled to retreat to Zeitun. The government had lost thousands of men in combat and thousands more to exposure and disease. By January 1896, the rebellion and ongoing massacres of Armenians in Anatolia had attracted the notice of the great powers, who offered their services as mediators in the conflict. Both sides quickly accepted the offer.

Termination and Outcome: The outcome of the war was a negotiated settlement. A peace accord was worked out over a period of ten days of negotiations. Its key terms were for a Christian to rule over Zeitun, amnesty for the insurgents, and for the leaders of the revolt to emigrate. It also contained concessions to the rebels on other issues, such as taxation. The plan went into effect on February 12, ending the war. The government delayed implementation but eventually appointed a Christian ruler for Zeitun, following whose arrival the rebels surrendered their weapons. Four rebel leaders emigrated.

Coding Decisions: The Ottomans suffered thousands of deaths in combat or from wounds and thousands more from exposure to the cold during the winter months. In addition, 400 Ottoman prisoners were killed by the rebels. The rebels admitted only 125 battle-deaths, but given epidemics of disease it is likely that the toll was higher.

Sources: Bağçeci (2008); Dadrian (2004); McCarty (1995).

INTRA-STATE WAR #632.6

Second Yemeni Imamate Rebellion of 1898 to 1899

Participants: Ottoman Empire versus Imam Muhammad al-Mansur Loyalists.
Dates: April 1898 to June 1899.
Battle-related Deaths: Armed Forces of the Ottoman Empire: 6,000; Muhammad al-Mansur Loyalists: 4000; Total Combatant Deaths: 10,000. (See Coding Decisions.)
Initiator: Imam Muhammad al-Mansur Loyalists.
Outcome: Stalemate.
War Type: Civil for local issues (secession).
Total System Member Military Personnel: Armed Forces of the Ottoman Empire: 176,000 (prewar, peak); 218,000 (peak, final).[80]
Theater Armed Forces: Imam Muhammad al-Mansur Loyalists: 40,000 (peak).[81]

Antecedents: The Zaidi Imam al-Mansur continued to oppose Ottoman rule in Yemen after the war of 1890 to 1892 (see Intra-state War #616). He opposed virtually every aspect of Turkish rule and secretly assisted a number of abortive uprisings against the government, which responded by burning villages. In 1897, the sultan appointed a more conciliatory administration and opened peace talks. However, the sultan was unwilling to accept the terms laid out by the imam. In 1898, the violence again reached the level of civil war.

Narrative: The rebels first targeted Menakha, between Sanaa and the port of Hodeida. In or near April 1898, the rebels annihilated a battalion of the Ottoman army. Two months later at al-Quful (Kophal), the government lost 150 soldiers in another engagement. The government then launched an expedition to pacify the Kahra tribe in August. The campaign killed more than 214 rebels; government losses are unknown.

There followed a series of fierce combats over Shahil. From October through June, combat raged in that district. The First Battle of Shahil cost the government either 100 or 700 battle-deaths.[82] For its part, the government claimed that it had won a great victory, losing only 8 men killed and that the rebels suffered 2,500 deaths. By November the rebels were rumored to have 40,000 men. In the next two battles, the government lost 400 and 200 killed, respectively. Two entire battalions deserted to the rebels. On November 30, the fourth and bloodiest battle of Shahil took place, pitting 36 Ottoman battalions against 40,000 men loyal to the imam; the result was a government defeat that cost it 2,000 to 2,500 killed and the rebels 1,000 killed. Government forces temporarily retreated from Shahil.

By December 2, the rebels largely had been confined to Kolof and mountainous areas north of Sanaa. Over the next week or so, Turkish forces ejected the rebels from most of their Shahil strongholds, losing about 2,000 men and inflicting severe losses on the rebels. But in January or February 1899, the fighting resumed, the Ottomans losing 160 killed to the rebels' 75. In the Battle of Bani Madikha on March 9, the rebels won a victory while killing 100 government soldiers. They quickly retook the places they had lost to the recent government offensive.

The tribes in the area of Lohya joined the rebellion, and an engagement near Lohya in May wounded more than 150 government soldiers, likely killing at least 50. In June, the seventh and last major battle in the Shahil cost the government 2,000 deaths; the rebels may have lost as few as 250 killed. The government victory drove the insurgents from Shahil.

Termination and Outcome: The outcome of the war was largely a stalemate, but this amounted to a government victory of sorts. The government succeeded in driving the rebels from the lowlands, but was unable to make progress against the highlands. Combat continued, but at a sub-war level. In August, insurgents under Mahomed-al-Din rose; in an incident in September they succeeded in capturing seventy Ottoman troops.

By February 1900, there was a lull in the fighting; a minor revolt broke out when the Ottomans tried to collect taxes in November 1900, killing dozens or even hundreds of government troops. In 1901, the government dispatched 3,300 replacements to Yemen, just enough to replace losses due to disease (but the period of time over which losses were suffered is unclear). In 1902, the violence again reached the level of civil war (see Intra-state War #639).

Coding Decisions: Simply adding the known fatalities on the government side gives an estimate of more than 5,660 killed. Moreover, sickness took a heavy toll on the permanent garrison. While rebel losses are often missing, adding up the data from battles reveals about 1,500 to 4,000 known fatalities. On the basis of this limited information, we code government battle-deaths as 6,000 and rebel battle-deaths as 4,000. The real tolls may well be higher as some data on rebel fatalities and all data on disease deaths are missing.

Sources: Baldry (1976); Farah (2002); Ingrams and Ingrams (1993).

INTRA-STATE WAR #639
Third Yemeni Imamate Rebellion of 1902 to 1906

Participants: Ottoman Empire versus Zaidi Imamate and Zaraniq Tribe.
Dates: March 1902 to August 1902, and October 1902 to June 1906.
Battle-related Deaths: Ottoman Empire: 30,000; Total Combatant Deaths: 45,000. (See Coding Decisions.)[83]
Initiator: Ottoman Empire (but see Coding Decisions).
Outcome: Stalemate.
War Type: Civil for local issues (taxation, *sharia* law, and independence).
Total System Member Military Personnel: Armed Forces of the Ottoman Empire: 388,000 (prewar, initial); 610,000 (peak, final).[84]
Theater Armed Forces: Armed Forces of the Ottoman Empire: 76,000 (peak). Zaidi Imamate (led by al-Mansur and Yahya): 60,000 (peak).[85] Zaraniq Tribe: 2,000 (prewar); 5,000 to 6,000 (initial, peak).[86]

Antecedents: In 1901, the Zaraniq tribe began to resist Ottoman demands for taxes. At the time, only 2,000 rebels took the field, and the Ottomans easily maintained their control. However, the Zaidi Imam al-Mansur saw an opportunity and renewed major operations against the Ottomans in 1902.

Narrative: The first battle of the war was a government attack on Kafilet Idar in March, which was repulsed with 400 government soldiers killed or wounded. The imam was said to have lost about 300 men. By early April, there was fighting between Zaidis loyal to the imam and government forces at Abb (Ibb). The rebels took the town and then ambushed government forces sent to recapture it. The government lost at least 250 to 300 men, but some accounts say 360 troops or even an entire battalion of 400 was annihilated.

The rebellion spread to different areas of the provinces; Sayyid of Marawa worked with the imam, though the two operated in separate geographic regions. On May 7, the government sent 3,300 reinforcements, but these were barely sufficient to replace losses due to climate and disease (though when said losses were incurred is unclear). To add to the misery, cholera began to break out. An epidemic in Lahaiyah killed 200 over a period of four months, probably civilians.

In August, a two-month armistice between the imam and the government was concluded. But in November, there was a general rising of Arabs in Asir against the Turks. At Miol, perhaps in October, cholera struck the Turkish forces, sickening 400 and killing 250. A battle in December cost the government 204 killed. In January 1903, Rijal al-Ma rejoined the rebellion, and Turkish forces were defeated by antitax rebels in the Ghanad and Zakran districts of Asir. Operations appear to have slackened for the next five months.

In mid-June 1903, a battle near Bhowan killed 200 Arab rebels and 14 Turkish troops. A report in September 1903 claimed that the government annually lost 3,000 troops due to combat or disease in the province. At a minimum, this probably referred to 1902 totals, but it also reflected high ongoing losses at the time of the report. In October 1903, the insurrection in Asir killed the governor of the province, its military commander, and a large number (200 or more) of Turkish troops. These losses were compounded by hunger and fatigue. The situation produced a series of mutinies among the Ottoman forces.

From October to November, the government mounted a punitive expedition of three battalions under Mahmoud Bey against the tribes in Mansooria and Zaraniq territory who continued to refuse to pay taxes. The rebellions were crushed but not without heavy losses.

The imam continued to rebel, but the Zaraniq and many other tribes had been defeated. Fighting in December cost the lives of 254 government soldiers.

The fighting was reduced greatly or eliminated for nearly a year, possibly due to the death of Imam al-Masnur, but then his son Yahya resumed the war with a vengeance. On November 8, 1904, the government garrison of 400 at Hafash was attacked and completely destroyed. Many tribes, including the Zaraniq, now used the opportunity afforded by a change in the province's leadership to defy the government.

This was a prelude to seven months of fighting from Sanaa to Menakha between December and July 1905. The rebels besieged Sanaa on December 12, and soon starvation and disease ran rampant in the city. By May, the government had suffered 6,000 to 7,000 deaths in Sanaa and another 1,000 in fighting near Menakha. Sanaa fell to the rebels on March 5, but the fighting around the city continued. A series of other towns and garrisons also fell to the rebels, and the government dispatched yet more reinforcements to Yemen.

In June, the government assembled a relief expedition of thirty-seven battalions in Hodeida. It brought total strength in Yemen to 76,000 soldiers, facing some 20,000 to 40,000 (rumor had it at 100,000) rebels. By mid-August, the government was on the offensive. It killed about 1,000 rebels near Abha in Asir while suffering only trivial casualties of its own. In the South, the government forces slowly moved toward Sanaa, retaking towns and forts as they advanced. The setbacks disheartened the rebels, and Sanaa was recaptured on August 30 without a fight. Some local tribes now submitted to the government.

In an attempt to capture Imam Yahya, the government sent a series of expeditions against his positions; all were defeated, the last one suffering very high casualties in the mountainous terrain. The imamate forces pursued the fleeing government soldiers and forced them to abandon Sanaa. Another series of mutinies broke out among the underfed and unpaid government troops, virtually paralyzing the government army. After regrouping, the government launched an offensive, but it soon stalled, and more serious mutinies broke out, one of which cost 300 killed and wounded to suppress.

From February through April 1906, there was a lull in the fighting, although small skirmishes continued to be fought. In May, the government mounted a series of operations against the rebels. Another mutiny followed in June, which was suppressed at the cost of 100 killed or wounded.

Termination and Outcome: We take June 1906 as being the end of sustained armed conflict between the imamate and the Ottoman Empire. While the Ottomans continued to suffer heavy casualties throughout 1906 and early 1907, these appear to have been from disease rather than fighting. Certainly, the imam was inactive for some time, attempting to keep his rival, the Kasimi, in check. The outcome of the war was a stalemate, although it amounted to a de facto government victory because the government completely suppressed the insurrection in Asir and wound up controlling most of the disputed territory outside of the mountains in Yemen.

Coding Decisions: Government losses amounted to about 3,000 battle-deaths per year in 1902 and probably 1903. The government lost 400 men in a single battle in 1904 (it is possible that overall battle-deaths dipped below 1,000 in 1904, which would make this two wars—given the prevalence of disease; however, we think it is somewhat more plausible that 1,000 combatants died as a result of the conflict in 1904). Government losses amounted to at least 30,000 in 1905: at least 6,000 killed at Sanaa, 9,000 dead of disease, and another 15,000 killed, wounded, missing, or captured in other battles. The government suffered another 5,000 killed of disease or combat in the first six months of 1906. Our estimate of government battle-deaths is therefore 26,400 to 41,400. We settle on a conservative estimate of 30,000. No comparable figures for rebel battle-deaths are available, but they lost heavily as well, and we note this by estimating total battle-deaths at 45,000. The real toll could be lower or higher than this. The initiator of the war could be either side; in the presence of limited data on prior engagements, we code the Ottoman Empire as the initiator based on the fact that it was the attacker in the first major battle.

Sources: Baldry (1976); Bang (1996); Farah (2002); Ingrams and Ingrams (1993).[87]

INTRA-STATE WAR #641.5
Saudi Revolt of 1904

Participants: Ottoman Empire and Muhamad Ibn Rashid versus Abdul Aziz bin Abdul Rahim bin al Saud.
Dates: May 8, 1904, to September 27, 1904.
Battle-related Deaths: Armed Forces of the Ottoman Empire: 1,500; Muhamad Ibn Rashid: 300 to 500; Abdul Aziz bin Abdul Rahim bin al Saud: 200 to 1,000; Total Combatant Deaths: 2,500. (See Coding Decisions.)[88]
Initiator: Ottoman Empire.
Outcome: Negotiated settlement.
War Type: Civil for local issues (control of province).
Total System Member Military Personnel: Armed Forces of the Ottoman Empire: 239,000 (prewar, initial, peak, final).
Theater Armed Forces: Armed Forces of the Ottoman Empire: 4,000 (initial, peak); 2,000 (final). Muhamad Ibn Rashid: [ ]. Abdul Aziz bin Abdul Rahim bin al Saud, aka Ibn Saud: 5,000 (prewar, initial); 10,500 (peak—may be an overestimate).[89]

Antecedents: This war began as an intercommunal struggle between Ibn Saud's forces and those of Ibn Rashid. The two dynasties were longtime rivals, and Rashid had defeated Ibn Saud's family back in 1891 and did it again in 1901, driving them into British-protected Kuwait. Rashid then allied himself to the Ottomans. In 1902, Ibn Saud began raids into the Nejd, and by 1904 the violence had escalated to full-scale battles between tribes allied to one or the other.

On February 7, 1904, Saud defeated a tribal ally of Rashid's at Faizet-us-Sir, killing up to 350 men. On March 22, Ibn Saud's men inflicted a major defeat on Rashid's men near Qassim. Saud claimed that he had killed 370 of Rashid's men while losing only two of his own. By April 13, Saud controlled 5,000 men. At this point, Turkish intervention was still uncertain as the governor of the province disliked Rashid. But when Saud captured Boreidah in mid-April, the government deployed troops against him and sent arms to Rashid, authorizing him to fight the Saudi forces.

Narrative: On May 8, 4,000 government troops were deployed against Ibn Saud's forces. They were to bear the brunt of the fighting against Saud. One force of 2,000 troops was "considerably reduced by disease and desertion before it reached the scene of action."[90]

The opening battle was fought between Saud's forces and both Ottoman and Rashid's forces at Bukairiyah on July 15. The Ottoman commander, a dozen officers, and many Ottoman soldiers were killed. The losses of Rashid's men were lower because they drove the Ottoman troops ahead of them and even fired into the retreating Ottomans, inflicting 100 fatalities and wounding 90. One estimate of the casualties of Bukairiyah holds that 1,000 to 1,500 Ottoman regulars were killed, 300 to 500 of Rashid's men were killed, and 1,000 of Saud's men were killed. Another holds these figures to be exaggerated (and include deaths due to disease and heat) and argues that Saud lost only 200 killed in the battle.

In August, a 700-strong force of Ottoman soldiers was besieged in Shanajnah. More than half of them died during the siege. On September 27, Saud attacked and defeated a combined force of Rashid's men and Ottoman soldiers at al-Russ, inflicting dozens of battle-deaths on the Ottoman forces. By October 1904, the British were reporting that the Ottoman force had been cut in half by combat and disease, with only 2,000 Ottoman troops remaining in the province.

Termination and Outcome: The outcome of the war was a negotiated settlement. In October, Ibn Saud sent a letter of submission to the Porte, arguing that he had killed only 210 government troops (certainly an underestimate). A new expedition was dispatched in November but encountered no resistance as Saud ordered his forces to cease hostilities. It did, however, suffer severe losses due to disease. Of the 2,000 who were sent to fight Ibn Saud, only 700 remained by February 18, 1905.

That same month, the government appointed him to the military command of the southern Nejd area in return for his allowing Ottoman garrisons to evacuate and Ottoman forces to reoccupy Qassim. Ibn Saud resumed combat operations against Rashid (but not government troops) late in 1905, defeating and killing him in April 1906. The Turks withdrew their forces in late October 1906, having lost 3,500 men to combat, disease, and desertion since the outbreak of the 1904 rebellion.

Coding Decisions: Estimates of battle-deaths range from 2,000 to 3,000. The Ottoman estimate assumes that 500 of the 2,000 Ottoman losses were desertions and is consistent with the higher-end combat death figures.

Sources: Al Rasheed (1991); Anscombe (1997); Burdett (1998); Lorimer (1970); Tuson and Burdett (1992); Vassiliev (1998).

INTRA-STATE WAR #646

Hafiziyya Uprising of 1907 to 1908 (aka Overthrow of Abd el-Aziz)

Participants: Morocco and France versus Mulai el-Hafid–led Forces and Bu Himara–led Forces.
Dates: August 16, 1907, to August 21, 1908.
Battle-related Deaths: Total Combatant Deaths: about 1,000. (See Coding Decisions.)[91]
Initiator: Mulai el-Hafid–led Forces.
Outcome: Mulai el-Hafid–led Forces win.
War Type: Civil for central control.
Total System Member Military Personnel: Armed Forces of Morocco: 6,000 (prewar); 7,000 (initial, peak); 100 (final).[92]
Theater Armed Forces: Armed Forces of Morocco: 7,000 (initial, peak); 100 (final).[93] France, participating from September 11, 1907, but see Narrative: 5,000 (prewar); 6,000 (initial).[94] Mulai el-Hafid–led forces: 3,000 (initial); 36,000 (peak).[95]

Antecedents: Sultan Abdul Aziz came to power as a constitutional reformer, but his program undermined the power of many traditional chiefs, generating resentment. Pretender to the throne Bu Himara had established a parallel government in northeastern Morocco in 1903, which the sultan was unable to subdue. Moreover, some of the Westernizing reforms were unpopular with the conservative populace.

In March 1907, a French doctor was murdered in Marrakesh. The French responded by occupying Oujda on March 29. Following the deaths of more French nationals in July, France bombarded Casablanca. When the French finally landed troops in response to antiforeign riots, the stage was set for a new rebellion against the sultan.

Narrative: On August 16, 1907, Mulai el-Hafid mobilized the tribes of the Chaouia against the government and French. Most of the cities in the South proclaimed for Hafid, who quickly controlled Marrakesh and much of the South. Abdul Aziz controlled most of the North and Fez. There were thus three claimants to the throne: Bu Himara, Hafid, and Abdul Aziz. The French initially declared their neutrality as to the civil conflict but were soon drawn into fighting in the country. The war essentially became split into two wars—an anti-French insurgency that occupied the bulk of the French forces and an antigovernment rebellion in which the French occasionally intervened when attacked.

In September, Hafid formed a 3,000-strong rebel army under Muhammad Wuld Mawley al-Rashid. The French landed troops in the Chaouia, but locals offered resistance, and on September 11, the French attacked a rebel camp in response. On September 26, al-Rashid arrived with his forces and mobilized the locals against France. Combat between France and Rashid in the Chaouia dragged on into October.

Meanwhile, the government mobilized 4,500 men to pacify the Chaouia and asked France for passage to fight the rebels. Soon, the expedition numbered 7,000, but it was attacked by the rebels on November 24 and routed. The French aided the government against the rebels at Essaouria; by this time, Rashid's forces had swollen to 10,000. The government suffered from massive defections.

On November 23, the Beni Snassen tribe rose against the French; although the latter won a major victory at Wadi Kiss on November 29, the tribal revolt was not put down until January 12. While the Beni Snassen were not affiliated with Hafid, they generally had been sympathetic to his causes, especially his willingness to fight the French. The French had deployed 8,000 troops against the Beni Snassen.

In December, resistance to the government reached Fez, where it was led by notables under al-Kattani. On December 15, a peasant revolt seized Fez with the aid of Kattani's followers. A similar revolt occurred at Meknes a few days later, but both were suppressed within days. Kattani and his 2,000 followers then turned to Hafid, allying with him; the Fez *ulema* joined the cause of Hafid on January 3, 1908, and Hafid was proclaimed sultan. The government retreated to Rabat.

In the winter of 1907 and 1908, Bu Himara mounted an offensive against the government of Abdul Aziz. At Mar Chica, his forces surrounded 800 government troops, who managed to hold out into 1908. On January 28, the government forces retreated into Spanish-controlled territory. Spain deployed 700 men to "assist" the government, but these ultimately served as defenders for Bu Himara's positions and a deterrent to a government assault on him. Spain does not appear to have participated in combat operations against either side in the rebellion.

From January to March 1908, the bulk of Hafid's forces remained locked in combat with the 14,000 or so troops of France. On January 21, the rebels inflicted a defeat on more than 2,000 French soldiers at Wadi M'Koun. Five weeks later, the rebels ambushed government troops at R'Fakha Ridge, inflicting 12 killed and 25 wounded. But on March 15, the French slaughtered Rashid's forces in a virtual massacre at Bou Nouala. Hafid then moved north to Fez to escape the French pressure.

Meanwhile in the spring an anti-French force of 4,000 under Mawlay Ahmed Hasan al-Saba had assembled in the upper Guir valley. From April 16 to May 14, the French attacked this force. On May 13, the French inflicted a crushing defeat on 6,000 insurgents at Bou Denib. As more tribes joined the opposition to France, the Guir valley insurgents increased to 20,000. Overall rebel strength may have peaked that summer at 36,000—some 12,000 of whom were defectors or new recruits, the rest being tribal levies.

By mid-1908, Hafid and Bu Himara had come to blows, but the government could not capitalize on the hostilities. On July 12, 4,000 government soldiers marched on Marrakesh in the last organized government offensive of the war. On August 19 at the battle of Bou Ajiba, Aziz's forces were defeated utterly; the bulk of his forces went over to the enemy at the first shot. He was left with only 100 followers, and two days later, Aziz abdicated at Casablanca.

Termination and Outcome: On August 21, the sultan fled to the protection of the French. The outcome of the war was a complete military victory by the rebels. No reprisals were reported. The fighting between France and the anti-French insurgents continued. On September 1, in a battle near Bou Denib, the insurgents lost at least 170 killed. On September 7, the French took on the largest insurgent force and defeated it at Djorf (also near Bou Denib), inflicting more than 300 battle-deaths. The French struck again at Wadi Kiss on November 29, inflicting 300 battle-deaths on a group of 4,000 anti-French insurgents. As for Bu Himara, the Hafid-allied Beni Urrighali tribe inflicted a major defeat on his forces in early September, securing Hafid's claim to the throne.

Coding Decisions: While there were many more battle-deaths in the French war against the anti-French insurgents, the actual battle-deaths in the civil war probably did not amount to many more than 1,000, given the events in the Narrative. The various rebel factions claimed to have inflicted hundreds of battle-deaths on the French.

Sources: Ashmond-Bartlett (1910); Bazaz (2002); Burke (1972); Clodfelter (2008); Dunn (1977); El-Khattabi (1998); Jacques (2006); Pennell (2000).[96]

INTRA-STATE WAR #647

Iranian Constitution War of 1908 to 1909 (aka Lesser Despotism, Constitutional Revolution)

Participants: Iran, Russia, and Shahsevan versus Constitutionalists, Bakhtiyaris, and Transcaucasians (Aggregate).

Dates: June 23, 1908, to July 17, 1909.

Battle-related Deaths: Total Combatant Deaths: 1,500. (See Coding Decisions.)[97]

Initiator: Iran.

Outcome: Constitutionalists win.

War Type: Civil for control of central government.

Total System Member Military Personnel: Armed Forces of Iran: 30,000 (prewar, initial, peak). Armed Forces of Russia: 1,381,000 (prewar); 1,434,000 (initial, peak, final).[98]

Theater Armed Forces: Armed Forces of Iran: up to 30,000. Armed Forces of Russia (initially favored the rebels when it intervened on April 22, 1909, but was generally regarded as pro-government, fighting an engagement with rebel forces on June 23: 4,000 (initial); 6,300 (peak, final). Shahsevan, aka Qarahdaghi Forces, participating from July 8, 1908: 500 (initial, peak).[99] Constitutionalists, aka Nationalists or Mujahidin: 7,000 (prewar); 2,000 in Tehran (initial); 6,000 (peak).[100] Bakhtiyaris, participating from January 1, 1909: 4,000 (peak, final).[101] Transcaucasians (from Russia), participating from fall 1908: 750 (initial); 1,150 (peak); 350 (final).[102]

Antecedents: By 1905, the pro-Western (despite occasional tensions with the British) and pro-Russian government of Iran had antagonized key sectors of the populace: nationalists who resented foreign influence, liberal intellectuals who sought constitutional governance, merchants and businesses who were ruined by free trade with the West, consumers angered by foreign-owned monopolies, and urban dwellers frustrated with high inflation. The key demands of the revolutionaries were enforcement of *sharia* law and the establishment of a House of Justice, which would simultaneously reduce foreign influence and the authority of the shah (technically padishah), Muffazar al-Din Shah. To this, the intellectuals added a demand for a Constituent National Assembly (Majlis). The popular revolution, largely bloodless, led to the convening of a Majlis in August 1906, charged with formulating a constitution.

The Majlis was weighted heavily in favor of Tehran and against ethnic minorities, who organized their own societies to press their views; these societies quickly proliferated until it seemed that there was one for every group one could think of, whether it was represented in the Majlis or not. In the Majlis itself, there were three primary factions. Royalists were outnumbered and unpopular; the central factions vying for control of policy were the liberals (associated with the intelligentsia) and moderates (associated with the landed classes). Working together, liberals and moderates agreed on a strong parliament, gaining a set of fundamental laws with the dying shah's signature.

In 1907, the new monarch, Muhammad ʿAli Shah, began to backtrack on the reforms, instructing his deputies to ignore the Majlis and trying to exacerbate intercommunal tensions to divide and rule. For its part, the Majlis—now writing the second phase of the constitution, the supplementary fundamental laws—gave the legislature extensive powers, including control over the appointment of executive branch officials. Even the shah had to take his oath of office before the legislature. With the addition of a bill of rights, the constitution resembled that of Belgium, save for sections on religious life and provincial administrations (the latter was to be important in determining the outcome of the war).

The shah rejected the proposed constitution and submitted his own ideas for extensive royal and executive authority. In response, strikes occurred in the main cities (the core of the constitutionalist movement), and the shah agreed to accept the new constitution early in 1908. However, he was able to exploit the differences between liberals and moderates on key issues (extension of the franchise and representation for religious minorities) as well as the activity of radicals outside the legislature who sought a shift to secular governance. Worried by the intentions of liberals and radicals, conservative clergy moved toward a tactical alliance with the shah. He also was able to exploit popular resentment at the austerity budget passed by the Majlis; the resentment was especially strong among the poor.

A march on the Majlis by the shah's supporters was met by 7,000 armed volunteers from the Society of Azerbaijanis and the Society of College Graduates; it was apparent that the Majlis had the ability to defend itself. The situation became perilous when the Shah succeeded in mobilizing armed supporters to counter those of the Majlis. He was able to use loans to pay the Cossack brigade in Tehran—Persian cavalry under "former" Russian officers whose pensions and reinstatement were contingent upon acting in accordance with the wishes of the Russian government. Whether through money or Russian policy, he retained the loyalty of the Cossacks. He also was able to win the loyalty of two tribes—the Shahsevan in Azerbaijan and the Bakhtiyaris; the latter marched into Tehran to support the shah. A tense standoff developed between the armed supporters of each side.

Narrative: The war began on June 23, when the shah instructed the Cossack brigade to disperse the armed volunteers of the Majlis. In the subsequent battle, 23 Cossacks were killed and 46 wounded. Other government forces suffered 120 killed or wounded, and pro-Majlis forces suffered between 270 and 300 killed (this last estimate may be inflated—one source gives a total of 250 killed on both sides). Tribal units occupied other strategic positions, and the city's poor looted the Majlis and the headquarters of those societies that had supported it. The shah declared martial law, banned all societies and public meetings, and dissolved the Majlis.

In the provinces, a number of prominent clergy immediately declared their support for the constitution. In the cities, armed supporters of the Majlis calling themselves constitutionalists formed military units to protect the constitution. However, for four months the only real resistance to the central government was in Tabriz (in Iranian Azerbaijan).

In Tabriz, the remnants of the provincial administration declared themselves the provisional government of Azerbaijan. Their military forces were led by Sattar Khan and Baqir Khan, and at first they only controlled one or two of the city's thirty quarters. They allied themselves to other small armed groups in the city, facing off against royalists and a group of Shahsevan from Qaradagh under Rahim Khan Chalabianlu.

In their first victory, the constitutionalist forces succeeded in expelling their opponents from most of Tabriz in July. However, they then found themselves loosely besieged by the 500 Shahsevan under Rahim Khan and a much larger force of Azerbaijani tribesmen, many of them Kurds. Interestingly, the rebels continued to send telegrams to Tehran professing their loyalty to the shah (who many believed was being kept in the dark about events) and reaffirming their opposition to any separation from the Iranian state. Both sides claimed to be fighting for Islam.

Over the next few months, the royalist forces besieging Tabriz grew; one source contends that they grew to more than 30,000, although this is probably an exaggeration. The city's *mujahid* defenders, on the other hand, had a peak strength of about 4,000 fighters (including an undetermined number of women), although one source claims that some estimates put their numbers "as high as 10,000."[103] Inspired by the continued resistance of Tabriz, constitutionalists in other areas of the country began to plot takeovers of major cities. While Russia threatened to intervene against the constitutionalists, Britain opposed the move, and the Ottoman Empire sent token expeditions to the border to signal its opposition to Russia.

Hostilities ceased for a brief period between August 7 and September 6, but no agreement could be reached. Fighting resumed, and the constitutionalists gained a victory at the bridge over the Aji Chay on October 9 and drove the royalists out of their last footholds in Tabriz three days later. Characteristically, they also sent telegrams professing their loyalty to the shah. In response to the setback, the government dispatched 400 Cossacks—its best troops—to Tabriz. There was no immediate relief for the royalists as the rebels were able to expand their influence to several neighboring communities, preserving supply lines into the city.

In a worrisome development for the government, the Tabriz rebels were able to win support from liberal and socialist Russians. From across the border, Transcaucasian volunteers came to assist the rebels—eventually, 800 proceeded to Tabriz, and 350 entered the neighboring province of Gilan. Both Azerbaijani Muslims and Armenian Christian irregulars (Dashnaks) assisted the rebels. Subsequent Russian efforts to stem the flow of arms and men to the rebellion were only partially successful. The volunteers were particularly important for their knowledge of explosives manufacture—they assisted in the construction of one of the first known parcel bombs on October 28, which killed a prominent royalist supporter.

As the bulk of the government's army was besieging Tabriz, it left itself weak throughout the rest of the county. Open demonstrations were now held by constitutionalists in many cities, including Isfahan (in the country's center), Lar (in the South), and Rasht (on the Caspian Sea in Gilan). Martial law was declared in Isfahan, triggering a revolt on January 1, 1909. Although they were ideologically conservative, the Bakhtiyari tribes supported the rebellion to weaken the central government. By January 5 the rebels controlled the city and had about 1,000 troops at their disposal. The Bakhtiyari chiefs who occupied Isfahan immediately arranged elections for a local constitutionalist administration.

The war now began to shift away from Tabriz. Two things occurred on February 8. First, the government forces finally completed the siege of Tabriz, preventing the rebels (and the inhabitants of Tabriz) from receiving food or supplies. Second, an anti-landlord rebellion broke out in Rasht, where a royalist commander (formerly a participant in the siege of Tabriz) defected to the rebels and marched on the nearby town of Langarud with 2,000 men.

At about the same time, constitutionalists seized control of Lar. The government now faced rebellion in Azerbaijan in the Northwest, Isfahan in the center, and Lar in the South. Despite the difficulty of communication between these widely separated centers of revolt, the rebels succeeded in coordinating their movements against the government.

Despite these difficulties, the government made some progress in its campaigns against the rebels. First, a handful of Russian troops moved into some major Iranian cities to protect legations. Second, the siege of Tabriz left its volunteer defenders without adequate food and provisions. Their strategy was now to attempt raids on neighboring communities for supplies, but the government was able to repel these sorties. The first such action occurred on February 22 near the Julfa road, which the government had blocked on February 11. On March 5, the government began to reoccupy most of the towns that were captured by the rebels in January, advancing into the outer quarters of Tabriz itself before being thrown back. The number of constitutionalists in Tabriz dwindled to about 500. The first deaths due to starvation were reported on March 30.

Interestingly, the constitutionalists of Tabriz were probably saved by Russia, despite their frantic attempts to avoid Russian intervention (including an offer to surrender to the shah). After royalist commanders failed to honor an Anglo-Russian-Iranian agreement to permit food into the city and to evacuate foreigners, a force of about 4,000 Russian troops crossed the border on April 22. Advancing without opposition, they reached Tabriz on April 29, preventing the final collapse of its defenders. Although the Russian forces were ordered to remain neutral in Iran's civil war, their mere presence in Tabriz and the surrounding area and the reopening of roads leading into the city effectively broke the government's siege. Hostile to the revolutionary cause, the Russians disarmed the city's remaining defenders. The 800 Transcaucasian volunteers in Tabriz either surrendered or filtered back north to Russia.

Although a local cease-fire took effect around Tabriz, the civil war continued. By the time the Tabriz rebellion was ended, other cities had joined the constitutionalist cause: Turbat-i-Haydari on March 14, the Persian Gulf ports of Bandar-i-ʿAbbas and Bushire on about March 17, Hamadan and Shiraz on March 25, and Masshad on April 7. At Rasht, where the constitutionalists had been reinforced by Armenian Dashnaks, the rebels began an advance on Tehran. By May 5, their expeditionary force of perhaps 600 had taken the city of Qazwin about halfway between Rasht and Tehran, despite pauses in their advance to allow for Isfahan's Bakhtiyari rebels to organize and launch an offensive from south of the capital. The disorganization of the latter prevented any offensive from Isfahan for more than a month after the fall of Qazwin.

Rebels continued to pledge loyalty to the Shah, even as they advanced on Tehran to compel him to honor his promises to the Iranian people. On May 10, acting on the "advice" of an Anglo-Russian note and the pressure of the rebel offensives, the shah announced that the constitution would be restored without any changes and that former rebels would be granted amnesty and permitted to engage in electoral activity. The rebels rejected the promise, believing that the shah would renege on it as soon as the rebellion was ended. The rebels also issued their own demands, including the dismissal of prominent royalists from power, the disarmament of the shah's irregular forces, and the evacuation of foreign troops. They continued their advance on Tehran, while both Russia and Britain began to deploy troops to protect their citizens or exert political influence. Total Russian strength in the North would reach 6,300 men, while British forces were never large (perhaps 100 men at any given time) and seldom overstayed their welcome.

The government dispatched Cossacks to contain the northern rebels, while it sent larger forces to defeat the Bakhtiyaris (now 3,000–4,000 strong) in the South. About 5,750 troops remained to defend Tehran, including 750 Cossacks in or near the capital (of a total force of 1,300 to 1,350). The shah began to implement the provisions of the constitution, although he had reservations that delayed the process until June 17.

Perhaps the reservations of the shah were overcome by the news that on June 16, the Bakhtiyaris had finally organized a column of 800 to advance northward from Isfahan. By June 23, they reached Qum, only eighty miles south of Tehran and were soon reinforced to a strength of 2,000. That same day, a dispute between the Russian forces and constitutionalists at Masshad led to open fighting, with the constitutionalists suffering 130 casualties. On June 30, Russia assembled an expeditionary force at Baku, threatening to intervene. The rebels ignored the threat and continued to advance.

On July 4, skirmishing between the Cossacks and Bakhtiyaris began at Shahabad, only sixteen miles from Tehran. Russia responded to developments by deploying another 1,800 to 2,000 troops, occupying Rasht and Qazwin by July 11. This brought its in-country strength up from about 4,400 to about 6,300. A brief cease-fire for negotiations expired on July 7, and the next day the two groups of rebels—the constitutionalists of Rasht and the Bakhtiyaris of Isfahan—made contact with each other west of Tehran. On July 11, elements of the united rebel forces faced government troops at the village of Badamak in a skirmish that produced few casualties on either side.

A battle for Tehran followed. On the night of July 12, at least 300 rebels slipped through a gap in the royalist lines and entered Tehran itself. They reinforced their positions early in the morning, and a fierce struggle for the city ensued. By noon, the rebels controlled the northern half of the city, and government forces began defecting or surrendering en masse. Nevertheless, royalist forces—the Cossack brigade, in particular—were able to stabilize the situation, and fighting continued to rage the next day. By now, 2,500 constitutionalists were in Tehran. On July 15, the rebels captured the southern gates of the city, but the Cossacks continued to resist in the center until the following day, when the shah and 500 of his men sought refuge in the Russian Legation, marking the final victory of the constitutionalists. Between the two sides, the Battle of Tehran resulted in about 500 casualties.

Termination and Outcome: The rebels won a complete military victory. The Cossack brigade had been negotiating with rebel leaders, and an agreement was reached that permitted the brigade to continue to serve under the new constitutional regime, albeit without its Russian officers. The constitutionalists maintained the monarchy, elevating Muhammad Ali's young son to the position of shah. Ministerial posts were distributed to leaders of the revolt. A special tribunal was set up to try top royalists, five of whom were executed.

Coding Decisions: "Many thousands died during the long siege" of Tabriz.[104] If even half of these were soldiers, that would imply a minimum of 1,000 battle-deaths in the Tabriz sector. Other recorded engagements produced about 500 battle-deaths, given the usual ratio of 3 wounded for every 1 killed. This generates an estimate of 1,500 battle-deaths, although the real toll may have been much larger or smaller.

Sources: Afary (1996); Arbrahamian (1982); Atabaki (1993); Bayat (1991); Browne (1995); Burrell (1997); Fathi (1979); Garthwaite (1983); Swietochowski (1985); Tapper (1997); Yapp (1987).[105]

INTRA-STATE WAR #647.5
Asir-Yemen Revolt of 1909 to 1911

Participants: Ottoman Empire and Grand Sherif–led Bedouins versus Zaraniq Tribe, Sayyid Muhammad al-Idrisi, and Imam Yayha Muhammad Hamid al-Din.

Dates: February 18, 1909, to February 1910 and October 1910 to September 28, 1911.

Battle-related Deaths: Grand Sherif–led Bedouins: one battalion "wiped out;"[106] Total Combatant Deaths: 10,000. (See Coding Decisions.)

Initiator: Ottoman Empire.

Outcome: Stalemate.

War Type: Civil for local issues (secession, local rulership, and *sharia* law).

Total System Member Military Personnel: Armed Forces of the Ottoman Empire: 312,000 (prewar, initial); 336,000 (peak); 241,000 (final).[107]

Theater Armed Forces: Grand Sherif–led Bedouins, participating from April 16, 1911: 5,000 (initial, peak).[108] Zaraniq Tribe, participating to February 1910: 10,000 (initial, peak).[109] Sayyid Muhammad al-Idrisi, participating through January 1910 and again from October 1910 to the end of the war: 20,000 (initial); 43,000 to 58,000 (peak).[110] Imam Yayha Muhammad Hamid al-Din, participating from January 2, 1911, to May 1911: 60,000 (peak).[111]

Antecedents: Imam Yahya in eastern Yemen had been in rebellion against the Turks since 1904 (see Intra-state War #642), although he was relatively quiet until 1910. The Zaraniq tribe in the Tehama also repeatedly had rebelled against Ottoman control. This revolt once more reached the level of civil war in 1909 as the Turks mounted expeditions to suppress the rebels, fearful of British or Italian encroachments on their sovereignty over the area.

Narrative: The war began on February 18, 1909, when the government sent an expedition of 800 men against the 10,000 or so warriors of the Zaraniq tribe. On February 23, an ambush near Beit-el-Fakih killed about 30 government soldiers. About three days later, a second engagement cost the Turks 30 battle-deaths. But on March 7, the government won a victory against the Zaraniq at Husayniyah, killing 80 of them while claiming to have suffered only 3 deaths of its own.

The government now demanded taxes, disarmament, submission, hostages, and the deforestation of rebellion-prone areas. The Zaraniq kept fighting. On March 18, the Zaraniq were defeated again, this time losing more than 100 men against small Turkish losses. Neighboring tribes now allied to the Zaraniq, which saved them from defeat. The results of the expedition had been inconclusive.

Soon, a larger and more serious insurrection broke out in Tehama, headed by Sayyid Muhammad al-Idrisi. The Idrisi Imam's revolt began in the summer of 1909 as a revolt against a local Shaykh rather than one against the government. However, in August the government decided to support the deposed and defeated Bani Pasha against the Idrisi. The rebels responded by attacking government-held towns, beginning with Loheia on August 23.

The government mounted another expedition into Tehama, and from November to February, operations were slow and protracted, resulting in serious losses on the Turkish side. The Ottomans had 4,000 troops in Asir fighting the Idrisi (and possibly the Zaraniq tribe as well), but the force lost a third of its strength due to illness.

The government appears to have concluded a peace agreement, the treaty of al-Hafar (Hafa'ir), with the Idrisi rebels late in 1909 or early in 1910. Idris's terms were the control of Asir and northern Tehama in return for the collection of taxes and implementation of *sharia* law. The treaty was ratified by the Turkish government in January 1910. No more combat between Idris and the government is recorded until October of that year.

In February 1910, the government struck the Zaraniq rebels again, this time inflicting more than 750 killed or wounded. The Turkish commander refused to grant amnesty to the Zaraniq until they disarmed; it is unclear whether this offer was accepted. There appears to have been a pause in combat operations following the defeat of the Zaraniq, however, during which the Treaty of al-Hafar held.

In September 1910, tribes loyal to the Imam Yahya began harassing the Turks at places like Dhamar, Ta'izz, Yarim, Anis, and Haijah. In October, Idris proclaimed independence. He claimed that the Ottomans were violating the treaty of al-Hafar by refusing to accept the results of *sharia* law, although it has also been noted that the new military governor for the region was opposed to the treaty.

In November, forces loyal to Idris laid siege to Abha, and a battle was fought there in December, with the rebels suffering 280 battle-deaths. Meanwhile, Imam Yahya had decided that the time was propitious for a full-scale rebellion in the East. He launched his revolt on January 2, 1911. His forces soon clashed with government troops at Ta'izz, where he lost 63 killed and 113 wounded against 56 government troops killed. The government now faced loosely coordinated rebellions from both the Idrisi Imam and Imam Yahya. On January 9 or January 12, Imam Yahya besieged Sanaa.

While it is unclear how many men Yahya initially commanded, his force quickly grew to about 60,000. The Idrisi forces numbered 25,000 to 30,000, plus 18,000 to 28,000 fighters in allied tribes (which we count as Idrisi forces given their coordination). The government began to rush reinforcements to Yemen and Asir, but disease took its usual toll of the forces sent. In Hodeida, 200 to 300 new recruits died of cholera before they could march on the Yemeni rebels.

Fighting around Abha was costly for both sides, and the siege stretched into the spring, as did the siege of Sanaa. On March 25, 1911, the government asked the grand sherif of Mecca for assistance in Asir; he mobilized about 5,000 men and marched on Abha on April 16. In May, the Sharifian forces engaged the rebels near El Goz. The Sharifians lost 31 killed, including 20 of sunstroke, while the rebels suffered about 150 battle-deaths.

Meanwhile, the government had mounted an expedition out of Hodeida to relieve Sanaa. It first cleared the rebels from near the gates of Hodeida on January 13, killing more than 500 of them against "trifling" government losses—according to the official government account. A combat at Menakha, between Hodeida and Sanaa, killed 61 government troops and 130 rebels. The government also inflicted a serious defeat on the imamate's forces near Nebi Shaib on April 2 (the government claiming that it killed more than 1,000 rebels, which was probably exaggerated). It succeeded in lifting the siege on April 4.

While the government enjoyed military successes against the imam, it repeatedly suffered high casualties due to thirst and disease. In late April, the government lost 100 men in a combat at Suk-el-Jamaa, plus more fatalities from thirst. Cholera broke out at Kanaoos, with 50 soldiers dying per day for a total death toll of more than 500. Operations against Yahya ceased after April 1911, as peace negotiations continued.

Meanwhile in Asir, the sequence of events is somewhat unclear, but the following is an approximation, even if some events are out of order. The rebels suffered a defeat; rebel losses amounted to between 500 and 1,500. The rebels were able to turn the tables at Jazan, surprising the government's advance guard, killing 1,100 government troops and wounding another 500. But on June 19, the government sent a force to raise the siege of Abha. They were surprised near Teecan and severely defeated, losing 1,000 to 1,600 killed and 400 wounded, but rebel losses were almost as high at 1,000 killed. The expedition persevered, raising the siege on July 16, but 800 Ottoman regulars had died of disease.

Termination and Outcome: The outcome of the war was a stalemate, with the government and rebels unable to defeat each other, while combat fell below the threshold required for civil war. The relief of Abha practically put an end to the insurrection in Asir. The rebels withdrew into the mountains, and many tribes submitted to the government. Meanwhile, the weather turned wet, practically halting campaigning by the government. On September 29, war broke out with Italy. The Italians had been covertly supplying the rebels with arms since at least 1910 and now supplied Idris overtly. They also shelled Turkish coastal forts; Hodeidah was shelled on October 2.

On October 9, Imam Yahya signed a peace agreement known as the Treaty of Da'an. It provided for autonomy in Upper Yemen under his control. He now became a loyal government ally, declaring a *jihad* against Italy. Idrisi forces, backed by Italy, began a campaign against the imamate.

The next significant combat between the government and rebels does not appear to have occurred until February 1912, when Idrisi rebels began to attack coastal forts with the support of the Italian navy. Further operations by the rebels continued through March and April, including a siege of Lohaiya. In June, he seized the Farasan Islands with the aid of an Italian naval blockade. Idris had been weakened by defections from his coalition but still commanded 46,000 troops and claimed to be able to raise 200,000 in the event of emergency. His revolt continued until the eve of World War I; during that conflict, he signed a treaty with the British promising to fight the Ottomans.

Coding Decisions: Simply adding up the fatalities from the Narrative gives a total of about 9,000. Given missing data, we expect 10,000 to be closer to the truth.

Sources: Baldry (1976, 1985); Bang (1996, 1997); Burdett (1998); Dresch (2000); Farah (2002); Gavin (1963); Ingrams and Ingrams (1993).

INTRA-STATE WAR #650.8
Hawran Druze Rebellion of 1910

Participants: Ottoman Empire versus Druzes and Druze-allied Bedouins.
Dates: September 11, 1910, to November 8, 1910.
Battle-related Deaths: Ottoman Empire: 38 to 100; Druzes: 1,000; Total Combatant Deaths: more than 1,000. (See Coding Decisions.)[112]
Initiator: Ottoman Empire.
Outcome: Ottoman Empire wins.
War Type: Civil for local issues (disarmament).
Total System Member Military Personnel: Armed Forces of the Ottoman Empire: 324,000 (prewar, initial, peak, final).
Theater Armed Forces: Armed Forces of the Ottoman Empire: 21,000 (prewar, initial). Druzes: 8,000 (initial).[113] Druze-allied Bedouins: 3,000 (initial).[114]

Antecedents: This conflict had its origins in conflict between the Druze and their neighbors in the Hawran. For example, in May 1909, there had been a clash between the Druze and the village of Basr al-Harir, and Ottoman troops had aided the villagers. In this instance, the government took the side of Bedouins who had clashed with the Druze and ordered the Druze to disarm. They responded that they could not disarm in the face of a Bedouin threat. On August 2, the government threatened to send a military expedition against the Druzes. Skirmishes continued between Bedouins and some Muslims on one hand and the Druzes on the other, with 40 Bedouins and a few Muslims killed. The government mobilized 21,000 men under Sami Pasha.

Peace efforts continued into September, and the Druzes sent a letter offering to disarm if some foreign power would protect them from the Bedouin. The Ottomans took this to be a thinly disguised declaration of autonomy and moved against the Druze. On September 11, the Druze lit their beacon fires. They do not appear to have entertained the hope of winning, as Destani notes: "[T]he Druzes fear that that the Turks will accept only of unconditional submission, and therefore that they will be compelled to fight, though they seem to understand clearly that they cannot oppose effectual resistance" (241).

Narrative: On September 18 or 19, government forces advanced on Druze positions. On

September 21, the Druze leader, Yahya Atrash, attempted to negotiate with the government but was arrested. The government adopted a village-by-village strategy, and at the first village on October 1 and October 2, nearly 100 government personnel were killed against 150 (rebels' claim) or 500 (government's claim) rebels. It was the Druzes who were compelled to retreat.

The second battle took place on October 12, pitting government forces against some 8,000 Druzes and 3,000 Bedouins to whom they had allied themselves. The government claimed to have suffered only 38 battle-deaths in other battles combined and claimed to have inflicted another 500 rebel battle-deaths. In any case, the outcome of the battle was a clear government victory. It was then able to use its artillery to shell the mountain villages into submission. Up to 2,000 Druze were killed and another 2,000 wounded; hundreds of prisoners were sent back to Acre and Damascus.

Termination and Outcome: The outcome of the war was an unconditional government victory over the Druzes. Druzes began surrendering after the first battle, and by November 8 the insurrection was over, with 4,000 rifles having been handed in. In the end, the government may have collected 10,000 weapons in all. Conscription was imposed, and more than 1,000 Druze were enrolled on the spot. In March 1911, many Druze leaders were executed.

Coding Decisions: Sources vary on the number killed. On the high end, Rogan estimates 2,000 rebels and Druze civilians killed and another 2,000 wounded. Destani has reports that add up to more than 1,000 battle-deaths, mostly rebels. Finally, Winstone estimates only 93 government killed or wounded and 400 to 500 Druze killed or wounded. We consider it sufficiently probable that 1,000 combatants died to include this struggle as a civil war.

Sources: Destani (2006); Rogan (1999); Winstone (1982).

INTRA-STATE WAR #684.5

Gilan Marxist Rebellion of 1920 to 1921

Participants: Iran and the United Kingdom versus Russia, Jangalis, and Mazandaran Rebels.

Dates: June 17, 1920, to November 23, 1921.

Battle-related Deaths: Total Combatant Deaths: at least 1,500.

Initiator: Jangalis.

Outcome: Iran wins.

War Type: Civil for central control.

Total System Member Military Personnel: Armed Forces of Iran: 40,000 (prewar, peak); 37,000 (final). Armed Forces of the United Kingdom: 596,000 (prewar, initial, peak); 448,000 (final). Armed Forces of the Russian Soviet Federated Socialist Republic: 3,050,000 (prewar, initial); 5,500,000 (peak, final).[115]

Theater Armed Forces: Armed Forces of Iran: 10,000 (initial). Armed Forces of the United Kingdom, participating until May 25, 1921: 1,000 (prewar, initial, peak).[116] Jangalis: 4,000 (peak).[117] Mazandaran Rebels, participating until September 24, 1921: 2,500 (peak); 500 (final).[118] Russian Soviet Federated Socialist Republic, participating until September 8, 1921: 1,500 (initial); 4,000 (peak).

Antecedents: In 1916, a group of revolutionaries inside the Social Democratic Party of Iran split to form a communist party called ʿAdalat (Justice). Traveling across the border, they formed an army of Iranian expatriates to fight for the Bolsheviks in the Russian civil war. In Iran itself, they formed local parties throughout the North. By 1920, they had mobilized 30,000 volunteers and stood ready to spread the revolution to Iran. Calling themselves the Perarmiia, they usually are referred to as the Persian Red Army.

Meanwhile in 1917, the nationalist Jangalis of Gilan province in Iran rebelled against increasing British influence in the country under the leadership of Kuchik Khan. After the British engaged their forces, they were forced to reach a peace agreement with the occupying forces. As the British withdrew, the government attempted to reassert its authority using British assistance and 20,000 troops to disperse the Jangalis in the summer of 1919. For the rest of the year, the Jangalis reorganized themselves (increasing from 200 to 500 by fall) and sought foreign sponsorship to counter Britain's support of the Iranian government. In January 1920, Kuchik Khan reached a peace agreement with the government. However, he dragged out its implementation while watching the Soviet Russians evict Britain from the Caspian region.

On April 27, 1920, Bolsheviks in Tabriz (who had received assistance from Soviet Russia) seized power in Iranian Azerbaijan. The nest day, the Caspian port of Baku was taken by the Soviet Red Army, driving some of the White Army to seek refuge in Iran. Three weeks later, on May 18, Soviet Russia used this pretext to bombard and then occupy the Iranian Caspian port of Enzeli (Anzali). ʿAdalat leaders entered Iran and held a party congress where they formed the Iranian Communist Party (ICP). They quickly divided into national-revolutionary and purely communist factions; the former wanted to work with traditional leaders such as Kuchik Khan (who by now had added leftist elements to his program), while the latter wanted to liberate peasants from local landed elites.

Taking matters into his own hands, Kuchik Khan—who had been forewarned of the landing by Russia—used the chaos created by the Soviet occupation to seize Tabriz, install his longtime Kurdish subordinate Qualu Qurban in Resht, enter the occupied port of Enzeli, and even briefly take Qazvin, within striking distance of Tehran. The Soviet Russians met with him on May 20 and declared him to be the head of the Persian Soviet Republic—an entity that is also referred to as the Soviet Socialist Republic of Iran (SSRI) or Soviet Republic of Gilan. The ICP was included within the government, backed by 2,000 (soon only 800) troops from Russia. In Mazdaran (adjacent to Gilan), forces led by Ihsanullah Khan (Kuchik's radical second in command) and Saed-ed-Dowleh (a longtime Kuchik lieutenant) attempted to spread the Revolution eastward.

Narrative: The first clash between the SSRI and forces loyal to the government occurred on June 17, when the rebels stormed the Cossack quarters in Resht, resulting in several casualties. Some 800 Cossacks were disarmed, and 36 officers were arrested (although all were soon released). Shortly afterward, the rebels attacked Manjanil, where they made little progress against government forces reinforced with British regulars.

The chief threat to the rebellion was disunity stemming from fundamental disagreements over land reform and other purely communist measures. By early July, the SSRI had 800 *Kronstadt* sailors (Russian soldiers) under the command of Abukov and Mdivani, about 750 Persian Bolsheviks (the Persarmii from Baku, now part of the Azerbaijan SSR), 1,700 Jangalis, and 3,000 other Iranian communists who were reported to be in Northern Iran the previous month. The exact figures are open to question because Soviet Russia conducted a number of other landings around this time. These landings—unauthorized by Kuchik Khan—sowed dissension between his forces and those of the ICP.

When 2,000 ʿAdalatists arrived to bolster the SSRI, Kuchik Khan took it upon himself to disarm them. On July 9, Kuchik Khan left Resht; the government attempted to capitalize on the split by encouraging him to defect, but he demanded an end to Qajar rule, abruptly terminating the negotiations. In Resht, Jangalis began moving munitions into forest areas, while the ICP began plans for a coup. The SSRI finally took government-held Manjil in late July; using this victory to rally communists, the ICP took control of the SSRI in Resht on July 31, arresting Kuchik Khan's officials at the cost of only 2 wounded. Ehsanullah Khan sided with the SSRI, retaining command of his force of 350 Jangalis.

Taking advantage of the chaos, the government counterattacked at Manjil with a motley force including tribal (Shahsevan and Bakhtiyar) irregulars. Altogether, the government employed 10,000 troops to retake the town in a campaign lasting from August 10 to August 18. The government's primary constraint was finance; each push forward required a foreign loan. Britain assisted the Manjil campaign both financially and militarily, by supplying air support to the government.

The Cossack forces took Resht on August 23 but attempted to continue to Enzeli, where withering fire from Soviet warships mauled the division; by August 26, the SSRI was back in Resht, and the Cossacks had retreated to Manjil. On September 1, they once again moved against Resht. The campaign was little but a series of skirmishes, notable only for the intervention of Soviet Russia's aircraft, which bombed and strafed the Cossacks; this provoked the British to send forces against the seaport and airfield at Enzali. On September 22, the Cossacks once again took Resht. By this point, the armed forces of the SSRI were reduced to about 900, although they were reinforced by 300 more Azerbaijanis on September 25.

While the SSRI was weak, Soviet Russia's intervention enabled it to defeat larger forces. In October, the SSRI defeated a large force of Cossacks with the assistance of two warships, four seaplanes, and two other Russian aircraft. Just 700 Armenians under Mdivani forced the Cossacks to evacuate Resht on September 24. The British again intervened, deploying their army at Imamzâdeh Hâshem on the road to Resht. By November 7, the British advanced on Resht but either could not or would not take it. British aircraft severely damaged the port facilities in Enzali during the next two months, making reinforcement all but impossible.

In the meantime, the SSRI adopted a more nationalist program calling for the overthrow of the shah and the expulsion of Britain. It also considerably increased in strength. While Ihsanullah Khan's regular forces were limited to only a few hundred Kurds (he was not permitted to command other SSRI forces), his father-in-law raised a force of 1,900 for internal security (and confiscation of food from non-supporters). During January 1921, the Soviets increased their strength in Iran from about 1,500 to 4,000 soldiers. For his part, Kuchik Khan recruited 1,600 Jangalis and 400 deserters from the SSRI and plotted with an underground nationalist committee in Tehran to overthrow the government and proclaim a republic.

On or around February 1, the Russians attacked a British outpost near Naglobar, suffering twelve killed in the engagement. Over the next few weeks, the Soviets negotiated a Friendship Treaty with Iran, which provided for withdrawal of the British, mutual nonsupport for each other's revolutionaries, and amnesty for the Gilan Marxists. The British, hoping to salvage their position, backed a coup by Reza Khan that ousted the nationalist cabinet. Nevertheless, the treaty was signed on February 26.

It was followed a few weeks later by the Anglo-Soviet Trade Agreement, in which both states promised to refrain from actions hostile to the interests of the other. Both the British and Soviets were now committed to withdrawing their forces. As the British began to withdraw, the government deployed its 6,000 Cossacks to replace them. The Russians and the SSRI reached an agreement for communist revolution in Iran without active Russian participation.

On February 21, the Persian Red Army under the SSRI had about 7,000 men, including a core of 400 Russian regulars and many from the Caucasus. In addition, its forces—even the independent ones of Ihsanullah Khan and Qualu Qorban—were supplied by Russia. On April 18, a cease-fire was signed between the Soviets and the government of Iran. Soviet Russia promised to withdraw all of its forces—both the Russians and the various Caucasian contingents—by May 18. The process took considerably longer, and Russia repeatedly conducted new landings after having "withdrawn" its forces.

At first, the rebels were able to hold their own without direct foreign intervention. By May 21, Kuchik Khan had once again allied himself to Qualu Qurran and Ihsanullah Khan, giving the Iranian communists about 4,000 men. On June 1, an engagement between the Iranian communists and the government resulted in the death of 15 rebels and 2 government soldiers. By July, the rebels had assembled a loose coalition: Qualu Qorban in Resht and Anzali with 900 men; Lahijan and Tonokabon under Ihsanullah Khan with 2,000 men; and the forested areas under Kuchik Khan with 3,000 men. A few foreigners remained in the rebel forces (about 200 Caucasians and 60 Russians), but the SSRI was now a largely indigenous force.

In Mazandaran, the rebels had achieved little in a year of operations. There was little support from the local populace, and attempts to ally with local warlords failed. But in June, the rebels managed to cobble together a coalition of local notables whose interests had been threatened by the February coup. About 1,200 locals joined and were soon augmented by more than 1,000 of Kuchik Khan's Jangalis. Assisting the Mazandaranis, Ihsanullah attacked toward Qazvim, the first serious attempt by the rebels to open the road to Tehran.

On June 29, a dispute between forces loyal to Ihsanullah and Quola Qurban led to fighting that claimed the lives of 8 of Ihsanullah's men. Ihsanullah then retreated from the strategic city of Khorramabad on July 9, leaving the Mazandaranis exposed. On July 26, the rebels lost 38 killed in another defeat. Their most powerful leader, Saed od-Doleh, promptly defected to the government, taking most of Ihsanullah's forces with him. This essentially ended rebel activity in Mazandaran. In all, the government claimed that it had killed 300 rebels during its campaign in the province.

Ihsanullah's Mazandaran foray had been disastrous. His men were reduced to 200 by mid-August, before a modest recovery enabled him to field 500 men in a successful attack on the coastal town of Langeroud in Gilan. The government lost only 13 killed, however, and it drove his forces from the city in less than three days, inflicting 200 casualties and taking 150 prisoners on August 25.

The Soviets evacuated Ihsanullah Khan on September 1, but he refused to give up the struggle. In a replay of the previous battle, he assembled 300 of his own men and 200 provided by Kuchik Khan. Once again, he attacked Langeroud—and once again he was defeated and lost 200 killed or wounded. He tried again on September 24 but was driven back again.

Infighting between Iranian communist leaders and nationalists like Kuchik Khan produced the Molla Sara Incident on September 28, when Kuchik clashed with leaders of the SSRI and then marched on Resht. On October 1 and October 2, his forces won a bloody battle for the city that cost between 200 and 600 lives and resulted in the deaths of many SSRI leaders (either during the battle or afterward). Unsurprisingly, Kuchik Khan's purge exacerbated tensions within the rebel movement. On October 10, Qualu Qurban defected to the government with 500 men; fighting broke out between his forces and those of Kuchik Khan five days later.

Taking advantage of the situation, the government attacked Resht from October 13 to October 15. The fighting resulted in heavy casualties on both sides, and Kuchik's forces were pushed out of the city. After a forty-eight-hour truce for negotiations expired, the government renewed operations against the Jangalis. Perhaps the deadliest battle of the war was fought on October 20; one source claimed 680 government battle-deaths and at least as many rebel fatalities.

While this figure seems high, other authors acknowledge that the battle was unusually bloody for the war and that Kuchick Khan lost most of his men by the end of the month. Unable to withstand such fighting, most of Kuchik Khan's force disintegrated, leaving him with only 300 men by November 12. He decided to revert to guerrilla warfare in the jungle, and the government suffered a considerable number of casualties in skirmishes as it attempted to corner him. The unrelenting pressure destroyed his remaining forces; by November 23 he was left with only 6 men and lived as a fugitive.

Termination and Aftermath: Kuchik Khan was captured and handed over to Qualu Qurban, who executed him on December 10. However, there was no retaliation against his followers, who were either enrolled in the Iranian army or disarmed and released. Ihsanullah Khan was pardoned and allowed to live the life of a private citizen.

Coding Decisions: Self-explanatory from cited sources.

Sources: Arfa (1964); Burrell (1997); Lenczowski (1968); Sabahi (1990).[119]

INTRA-STATE WAR #689
Simko Rebellion of 1921 to 1922

Participants: Iran versus Shikak Kurds.
Dates: March 1921 to September 30, 1922.
Battle-related Deaths: Iran: more than 1,065;[120] Total Combatant Deaths: 2,000. (See Coding Decisions.)[121]
Initiator: Shikak Kurds.
Outcome: Iran wins.
War Type: Civil for local issues (independence).
Total System Member Military Personnel: Armed Forces of Iran: 37,000 (prewar); 33,000 (final).[122]
Theater Armed Forces: Armed Forces of Iran: 8,000 (peak). Shikak Kurds: 1,500 (prewar, initial); 10,000 (peak); 1,000 (final).[123]

Antecedents: World War I had weakened Iran, which tried to remain neutral but ended up being contested by the various combatants, who sponsored tribal revolts, new militias, and coups. Accordingly, the central government was unable to maintain order far from the capital. By 1919, a Kurdish leader named Isma'il Agha Shikak—but known as Simko—was the strongest power in the far Northwest, reinforced by several hundred former Ottoman soldiers (mostly Kurds). In mid-1919, he seized Dilman, looted Khoy, and besieged Urmiyeh, massacring some ethnic Azeris. The government sent an expedition against him, which inflicted a heavy defeat on his forces.

Simko reached a negotiated agreement with the government and agreed to disarm in February 1920. However, by April 1920, Simko had rearmed and throughout the rest of 1920, he reestablished his authority and began to tax local towns. He was now supported by the Ottomans' successors, the Turkish nationalists under Gen. Kazim Karabakir in Anatolia. In January 1921, he formed alliances with other tribes in the area, greatly increasing his forces. By February, he had 1,000 cavalry, 500 infantry, and possibly some Turkish regulars as well. After he seized another town, the government dispatched its Cossacks against his forces.

Narrative: The first recorded combat between the forces under Simko and those of the government occurred in March at Qizilja, when Simko—fighting under a Turkish flag—defeated a force of 600 Cossacks, killing 350 of them. His forces quickly swelled to 4,000 after this victory. At this point the government—distracted by other rebellions in Gilan, Luristan, Khamseh, and other provinces—could do little to stop him and focused its efforts elsewhere, resulting in a pause in the fighting for about five months. However, the other rebels do not appear to have coordinated their activities with Simko—even within his own tribe, Simko was only one of several factional leaders. Simko attempted to win more Kurdish tribes to his side. While the timing is unclear, he was able to attract the support of the Kurdish Dohbukri (1,700 troops), Mamash (700 troops), and Mangur (500 troops) tribes.

The fighting resumed in October when Simko's forces attacked and overran government forces at Mahabad (also referred to as Saojbulah, Sawj Bulaq, or Sauj Bulagh) on October 7, killing 200 gendarmes and wounding 150. Simko then attacked government irregulars under Qaradagh leader Amir Arshad, inflicting another 200 fatalities. At about this time, Simko seems to have run afoul of the government of Turkey and an armed clash occurred between the two.

In November, the suppression of the most serious revolts in the North enabled the government to turn its full attention to Simko, now estimated to have 6,000 to 7,000 troops. A skirmish in mid-November cost the government 40 killed or wounded. A battle at Qara Tappa on December 19 resulted in defeat for the government, which suffered 66 battle-deaths against severe casualties among the rebels.

Although several more engagements were fought, major combat operations appear to have halted for another few months. With 5,000 of his own men and 2,900 from other tribes, Simko was stronger than ever in March. Within two months, government soldiers were beginning to take casualties from an epidemic of typhus that broke out among its units facing Simko.

Major combat resumed on May 22, when Simko mounted a surprise attack on Bukan, south of Mahabad. The government suffered 200 battle-deaths including Qalu Qurban, the leader of 900 irregulars who had been sent to oppose Simko. By June, however, it appeared that the government had contained Simko. Turkey sent troops to its border to prevent Simko from retreating into its territory, but then a series of other revolts broke out among Jangalis, Kuhgilis, and Lurs. Once again the government was forced to postpone its full-scale offensive against Simko.

On July 23, the government finally mounted an offensive using 8,000 troops. Among them was a battalion of Armenian volunteers, formed from Armenian refugees who had little love for Kurds. They faced 10,000 men under Simko. The next day, an engagement resulted in nearly 80 government killed or wounded but succeeded in dispersing many of Simko's troops. On August 22 the government reported a major victory over Simko (probably the Battle of Salmas, fought on August 9), claiming to have inflicted 200 battle-deaths and suffered just 7. Whatever the truth of the report, it is clear that Simko suffered a decisive defeat. Simko was reduced to less than 1,000 men. He fought his last engagement on August 16, and at the end of the month he retreated into Turkey.

Most of the rebellious Kurds surrendered to the government in September and October, although a small force under Iskandar Khan resisted and fought a skirmish on September 15, suffering 10 battle-deaths against 12 by the government. Simko's forces, harried by both the Turks and the Iranians, were reduced to 200 men by the end of the month, ending his ability to engage in significant combat.

Termination and Outcome: The war ended with a complete military victory by the government. It immediately turned its attention to other tribal revolts, suppressing them one by one, only to see new ones emerge. This pattern continued until 1927. Indeed, Simko himself eluded capture and raised a new revolt in 1926, although it was quickly suppressed. We have found no evidence of reprisals against the former rebels.

Coding Decisions: With a minimum of 1,065 deaths on the government side, more than 260 on the rebel side in the last month alone, and an epidemic of typhus (a disease with a 20 to 60 percent mortality rate) in government camps, our estimate of 2,000 battle-deaths is conservative.

Sources: Arfa (1964); Bayat (2003); Burrell (1997); Cronin (1997); McDowall (1996); Van Bruinessen (1983); Yildiz (2004).

INTRA-STATE WAR #697.6
Shaikh Said's Rebellion of 1925

Participants: Turkey versus Zaza Kurds.
Dates: February 8, 1925, to September 16, 1925.

Battle-related Deaths: Turkey: somewhat more than 2,000; Zaza Kurds: less than 3,000; Total Combatant Deaths: about 5,000.[124]
Initiator: Zaza Kurds.
Outcome: Turkey wins.
War Type: Civil for local issues (religion and independence).
Total System Member Military Personnel: Armed Forces of Turkey: 129,000 (prewar, initial, peak, final).
Theater Armed Forces: Armed Forces of Turkey: 50,000 (peak). Zaza Kurds: 15,000 (initial, peak).[125]

Antecedents: The Kurds had been promised a referendum on an independent state in the Treaty of Sevres (1920). Even after Kemal Atatürk became the de facto leader of Turkey, there was still talk of Kurdish autonomy after the government had to suppress the Koçgiri Rebellion of 1920 to 1921, killing 500 rebel Alevi Kurds in the process. However, this option fell from favor, and the Treaty of Lausanne (1923) made no mention of it.

Without autonomy, Kurdish political aspirations rested on representation in the national assembly. In May 1923, some Kurdish deputies who had failed to be reelected in that year's elections formed a revolutionary party named Azadi. The party set to work constructing the basis for revolution among the Zaza-speaking Kurdish tribes. It also received the backing of local religious leader Sheikh Said. In 1924, a premature rising by Azadi officers gave the government warning of the impending revolution.

Narrative: On February 8, 1925, some of Said's men exchanged shots with gendarmes attempting to arrest some of his supporters. Similar incidents soon occurred all around the region, once again prematurely initiating the uprising before the Kurds could unite. As it was, some tribes refused to join the rebellion, and some actively fought against it. The Sasunah and Takutan tribes refused to join the revolt and were attacked by the Zaza-speaking tribes commanded by Said; 400 of their fighters were killed by the estimated 15,000 fighters the rebels could muster at the onset of the revolt. The government initially had only 25,000 soldiers in the area, and only 12,000 of those had rifles.

The rebels attacked and besieged the city of Diyarbakir on February 29, but the government was able to mobilize more than 50,000 troops for the campaign and soon relieved the siege. By the end of March, the rebels were incapable of such large-scale military actions, as government troop strength and its air dominance took their toll on the rebellion. On April 8, the Kurdish leadership decided on a strategy of guerrilla warfare.

Sheikh Said was captured with many other leaders of the rebellion by April 27. This momentarily stopped the fighting, but in May the revolt flared up again under the leadership of Sayyid Abdullah. Most of the combat took place in July and August. During this phase of the rebellion, the government suffered about 200 battle-deaths.

Termination and Outcome: On September 16, Sayyid Abdullah crossed the frontier and sought refuge in British Iraq. This marked the end of the revolt, the outcome of which was an unconditional government military victory. Sheikh Said and dozens of his followers were executed in June 1925; further executions followed, totaling 660 people in the end. About 7,500 were arrested. According to some authors, thousands of peasants were massacred after the end of the war. Minor clashes between Kurds and Turks continued into early 1927.

Coding Decisions: Self-explanatory from cited sources.

Sources: Durham (2000); Howard (2001); Olson (1989, 2000); Van Bruinessen (1992); White (2000).

INTRA-STATE WAR #707.3

Ikhwan Revolt of 1929 to 1930

Participants: Saudi Arabia versus Ikhwan.
Dates: March 30, 1929, to January 10, 1930.
Battle-related Deaths: Total Combatant Deaths: 2000.[126]
Initiator: Saudi Arabia.
Outcome: Saudi Arabia wins.
War Type: Civil for central control.
Total System Member Military Personnel: Armed Forces of Saudi Arabia: 15,000 (prewar); 28,000 (initial and peak).[127]
Theater Armed Forces: Armed Forces of Saudi Arabia: 15,000 (prewar); 28,000 (initial, peak).[128] Ikhwan: 8,000 to 20,000 (initial, peak), 6,500 (final).[129]

Antecedents: The Ikhwan were religious warriors committed to Wahabbi Islam, who were used to great effect by Ibn Saud in his consolidation of power. But by 1926, they were becoming an impediment to the state-building enterprise. Although they had won the Hijaz for Ibn Saud, they were not to rule it or share in its wealth. Finally, they were opposed to the close relations developed between Ibn Saud and the British.

In October 1926, a meeting of Ikhwan leaders demanded the repeal of new taxes, a holy war against tribes in Iraq and Transjordan that grazed their herds in Ikhwan territory, and the imposition of the Wahabbi faith on Hasa's Shiites. A compromise settlement was reached with the aid of the clergy. In November 1927, a second revolt broke out, taking the form of cross-border raids into British-controlled Iraq. By early 1928, at least 12,000 Ikhwan had gathered to wage a holy war against tribes in Iraq but ultimately called off the enterprise. When talks between Saudi Arabia and Iraq failed later that year, the Ikhwan blamed the failure on Ibn Saud.

In December 1928, Ibn Saud summoned the leaders of the Ikhwan, the clergy, and other Bedouin leaders to a meeting in which his authority was confirmed. He thereby isolated the most rebellious factions. In 1929, after continued raiding and local crime, Ibn Saud led an expedition of 15,000 warriors against the Ikhwan, increasing his forces by adding friendly tribes along the way.

Narrative: The first and largest battle of the war was fought at Sabila on March 30. Ibn Saud had about 28,000 men against anywhere from 8,000 to 20,000 rebels. The government victory left 500 rebels dead and another 500 wounded; government losses were about 200 killed and 200 wounded. After the battle, part of the Ikhwan surrendered, but in May 1929, a botched negotiation with one of the rebel chiefs led to bloodshed, and the revolt flared up again. Ibn Saud requested British assistance and was provided with arms and ammunition.

Minor engagements were fought from July to August, when Britain agreed to sell four aircraft to Ibn Saud and to provide pilots and maintenance personnel for them. On September, another major battle occurred. The government captured and massacred a rebel force, killing more than 100 rebels. In late October, the government-aligned Awazim tribe attacked the rebellious Muteih and Ajman, killing about 700 of them. In November, most Ikhwan either deserted the rebellion or fled into Kuwait. The remaining Ikhwan were crushed in December.

Termination and Outcome: On January 10, 1930, the last Ikhwan leaders and about 6,500 Ikhwan (including their families) crossed into Iraq and surrendered to the British. The outcome of the war was an unconditional government victory without promises of amnesty. However, Ibn Saud agreed with the British government to spare the lives of the rebels on January 26. Instead, the remaining leaders of the revolt were imprisoned until 1934.

Coding Decisions: Self-explanatory from cited sources.

Sources: Clodfelter (2008); Darlow and Bray (2012); Habib (1978); *Saudi Arabia: Secret Intelligence Records, 1926–1939* (2003); Silverfarb (1982); Vassiliev (1998).[130]

INTRA-STATE WAR #708

Ararat Revolt of 1930 (aka Ağri Rebellion)

Participants: Turkey versus Kurmancî-speaking Kurds.
Dates: April 1930 to November 14, 1930.
Battle-related Deaths: Total Combatant Deaths; 4,000. (See Coding Decisions.)[131]
Initiator: Turkey.
Outcome: Turkey wins.
War Type: Civil for local issues (independence).
Total System Member Military Personnel: Armed Forces of Turkey: 149,000 (prewar, initial, peak, final).[132]
Theater Armed Forces: Armed Forces of Turkey: 10,000 to 15,000 (initial); 66,000 (peak). Kurmancî-speaking Kurds: 5,000 (initial); 5,000 to 8,000 (probable peak—but some sources estimate as high as 12,000); 1,500 (final).[133]

Antecedents: Like the Sheikh Said rebellion before it, this war was precipitated by a Kurdish nationalist movement, the Khoybun (Xoybûn). The movement formed in 1927 under the leadership of Ihsan Nuri Başa. It was a propitious moment for the formation of such a movement, for there had been isolated Kurdish revolts in many areas, including Dersim and Mount Ararat. The government mobilized about 10,000 soldiers against the rebellions in its own territory, losing a battle at Zilan Plain in September. In late October, 4,000 rebels took Bayazid, only to be driven out by perhaps 40,000 Turkish soldiers. The government and rebel fought another battle again in December.

Another battle was fought in March 1928. In its attempt to prevent a full-scale war, the government resorted to a conciliatory policy. In May of that year, the government offered amnesty to the insurgents, and violence temporarily subsided as most guerrillas aside from the Jelali tribe around Mount Ararat surrendered. However, Ihsan Nuri's forces refused an offer of amnesty in September because it didn't take Kurdish nationalist aspirations into account. By February 1929, the rebel army was 5,000 strong, and it was able to engage and destroy a battalion of government troops.

Further efforts at negotiation proved fruitless, and the government decided on a military solution to the Ararat Revolt. Note that while the government claimed that the rebels were backed by 1,500 Muslim refugees from Russia and volunteers and arms from Persia (Iran), neither of these claims has been substantiated. For their part, the Kurds alleged that Russian and Persian (Iranian) troops aided the government during the final stages of the uprising.

Narrative: Numerous engagements were fought in April of 1930. The rebels suffered heavily in the initial engagements but also won successes. A battle in late April resulted in numerous casualties for the government and the capture of five Turkish officers, who were subsequently executed by the rebels. In May or June, the rebels inflicted 100 battle-deaths on the government forces and succeeded in downing three aircraft.

On June 11, the government launched its military offensive, sending 10,000 to 15,000 troops against the largely Kurmanci-speaking Kurds in rebellion (in all, 66,000 troops would be mobilized to fight the rebels). On June 12, the first battle was fought, involving 15,000 combatants and resulting in heavy casualties.

In July, a Kurdish offensive backed by 5,000 well-armed troops failed. On July 5 and July 6, a major battle resulted in at least 1,500 killed and at least 3,000 rebel casualties. By the end of the month, the government had encircled the rebels on Mount Ararat. According to some figures, which are likely exaggerated, the battles of July cost the government as many as 2,800 killed, 4,000 wounded, and 1,700 captured; the rebels may have suffered as many as 900 killed, 2,400 wounded, and 240 missing. Certainly, government losses were higher than rebel losses.

On August 22, the government launched three successive attacks on the rebels' positions at Ararat, all of which were defeated. By the end of August, the Kurds were down to 3,000 fighters. The Turks bombed and shelled indiscriminately, killing more than 3,000 noncombatants before the end of the month. In early September a final battle crushed the Kurdish resistance, with more than 1,500 Kurds taken prisoner by the government. The Kurds were driven from Mount Ararat from September 7 to September 10.

On September 15, the government declared the rebellion to have been crushed. A punitive campaign against civilians in the area followed this victory. Scattered fighting probably continued but was censored by the Turkish press.

Termination and Outcome: A British telegram reported that military operations were completed as of November 15 but that ongoing "operations" similar to the Armenian massacres were being carried out against the Kurds of Dersim. The outcome of the war was an unconditional government victory; many Kurds were killed even after the end of combat. On November 20, eleven rebels were sentenced to death.

Coding Decisions: Estimates of battle-deaths are unreliable, but a total of 4,000 is most consistent with the evidence, plus or minus a couple of thousand.

Sources: Meiselas (1997); Olson (1996, 2000); Van Bruinessen (1992); White (2000); Yildiz (2004).

INTRA-STATE WAR #718.5

Dersim Revolt of 1937 to 1938 (aka Seyh Riza Rebellion)

Participants: Turkey versus Dersim Kurds.
Dates: May 8, 1937, to June 1938.
Battle-related Deaths: Turkey: 200;[134] Total Combatant Deaths: 1,200. (See Coding Decisions.)[135]
Initiator: Dersim Kurds.
Outcome: Turkey wins.
War Type: Civil for local issues (identity).
Total System Member Military Personnel: Armed Forces of Turkey: 211,000 (prewar, initial, peak, final).
Theater Armed Forces: Armed Forces of Turkey: 25,000 (initial); 50,000 (peak). Dersim Kurds: 4,200 (initial), 5,000 (peak).[136]

Antecedents: While Turkey had experienced a number of major Kurdish revolts since World War I, the inhabitants of Dersim (today known as Tunceli) had not participated in them actively. The Alevi Kurds of the area were Zaza-speaking and had been separated from the earlier revolts by geography, language, or religion. Nevertheless, Kurds of Dersim were targeted by the government in retaliation for the 1930 Ararat Revolt (see Intra-state War #708). As the government moved to assimilate the Kurds, it began preparation for armed conflict in Dersim as early as 1935. When a delegation was sent to protest a new assimilation law in 1937, its members were arrested and executed.

Narrative: In retaliation for the executions, the Kurds ambushed a police convoy and took some prisoners. A rebellion led by Sayyid (Sayh) Reza broke out across Dersim. Military operations against the rebels began in May; on May 8, the first battle was fought, resulting in 69 government soldiers or gendarmes killed. The Kurds had some initial success, with Kurdish snipers inflicting serious losses on the government forces. The rebels had more than 1,500 insurgents at this point, but the government had 25,000 in the area.

In June, a number of rebel bands surrendered to the government. However, the government hanged many of those who surrendered, and active resistance resumed in July. Turkish casualties were running higher than rebel losses at this point, with most losses being suffered by the gendarme and serious losses of materiel being suffered by the Turkish air force. By late August, Sayyid Reza had been captured. He was executed along with 10 other rebels in November.

Military operations appear to have paused from the beginning of September 1937 until the government mounted a second offensive in February 1938, with up to 50,000 soldiers, aimed at disarming the villagers and permanently destroying Kurdish identity in Dersim. Stirrings of revolt in early 1938 led the government to commit 50,000 troops to its pacification campaigns that year. The main tool was the massacre of a village's male inhabitants followed by the deportation of the women and children. Perhaps 10,000 Dersimis perished in the campaign, most of them probably civilians.

Termination and Outcome: By summer 1938, armed resistance to the Turks had ended. A report on September 8 described the military operations as complete and claimed that the government had seized 12,000 arms. The outcome of the war was a complete government victory, followed by continued massacres and deportations in an attempt at ethnocide, or the extermination of Kurdish identity. The province would remain a closed military-ruled district until the 1940s.

Coding Decisions: "Hundreds" of government troops were killed, according to the sources cited. The government maintained that it killed "thousands" of "bandits." Given that most of those killed by the government were civilians, we estimate 200 government battle-deaths and at least 1,000 rebel battle-deaths. The real toll could be several thousand higher or a few hundred lower.

Sources: Aras (2010); Durham (2000); Gavin (1963); Jwaideh (1960); Kieser (2003); Olson (2000); Şïmşïr (1991).

INTRA-STATE WAR #728
Sanaa Revolt of 1948 (aka Yemeni Imamate)

Participants: Yemen (Pro-Waziri Forces) versus Pro-Ahmed Forces.
Dates: February 25, 1948, to March 20, 1948.
Battle-related Deaths: Total Combatant Deaths: 2,000. (See Coding Decisions.)[137]
Initiator: Pro-Ahmed Forces.
Outcome: Pro-Ahmed Forces win.
War Type: Civil for central control.
Total System Member Military Personnel: Armed Forces of Yemen (Pro-Waziri): 14,000 (prewar); 16,800 (initial, peak).[138]
Theater Armed Forces: Armed Forces of Yemen (Pro-Waziri): 14,000 (prewar); 16,800 (initial); 16,800 (peak).[139] Pro-Ahmed Forces: 30,000 (peak, final—see Coding Decisions).[140]

Antecedents: The Zaydi (a branch of Shiism) Imams nominally ruled Yemen from about 897. Their base of support was the tribes in the mountains of the country. This rule continued and expanded through armed rebellions in the last decade of the Ottoman Empire, and when Yemen gained independence in 1918, the Imam Yahya ruled the country. Opposition to the monarchy existed from other tribes, from non-Zaydis, and from reformists. In particular, many were critical of Yahya's apparent disinterest in economic growth. He maintained a strictly isolationist course, preventing trade and even many diplomatic missions from other countries. He was especially hostile toward the United Kingdom, which ruled Aden (now South Yemen) as a colony and with whom he had territorial disputes.

The Free Yemen Movement (FYM) largely was composed of pro-modernization reformists. They criticized the collection of the *zakat* as contrary to *sharia*, in that it was collected from the poor and went to support the wealthy. Safely based in Aden, they couched nearly all of their reforms in the language of Islam and *jihad* but largely limited themselves to printed propaganda—a serious limitation in a country in which the majority was illiterate. Their propaganda simply didn't penetrate most tribes.

In 1946, Yahya's health problems led a group of FYM officers to prepare for a succession. They opposed the idea of allowing Yahya's son Ahmed to rule the country. They allied themselves with ʿAbd Allah al-Wazir, whose family was somewhat stricter in their Zaydi beliefs. Together, they drew up the Sacred National Pact, a list of policies heavily influenced by *sharia* and constitutionalism. They sought the support of Saudi Arabia, which initially favored their plan (although it insisted that nothing should be attempted while Yahya lived) but later backed away from al-Wazir. In late 1947, al-Wazir began to suspect that Yahya was planning a preemptive move. He arranged for Yahya to be assassinated, whereupon the FYM would seize power in the capital of Sanaa.

The date of the assassination was to be January 14, 1948. In a series of blunders, the assassination was not carried out, but the FYM in Sanaa—unaware that the attempt had not occurred—duly published news of Yahya's death and the formation of a new government under al-Wazir. Embarrassed, al-Wazir reaffirmed his loyalty to Yahya, disclaimed any knowledge of the affair, and endorsed Ahmed as Yahya's successor. Yahya attempted to investigate, while calling his son Ahmed to Sanaa (which Ahmed declined for some reason). The would-be rebels were forced hastily to assemble another plot before Yahya could gain support from the clergy for a crackdown.

On February 17, 1948, Yahya was assassinated by a tribal sheikh affiliated with al-Wazir. Immediately, al-Wazir seized the palace and informed the clergy, military leaders, and other notables that Yahya had died of a heart attack and demanded that they endorse him as imam. He was quickly acclaimed a constitutional successor to Yahya, and the 2,800 soldiers of the Sanaa garrison spread out to secure the capital. There was no combat, although two emirs were killed by a pro-FYM Iraqi officer, and the 3,000-strong palace guard stationed outside Sanaa refrained from supporting the new regime.

Ahmed learned of the event as soon as it happened and had the local telegraph office shut down. Unaware that the plot had succeeded in Sanaa, his would-be assassins failed to act, and he was able to move with loyal troops to the northern town of Hajjah, surrounded by the northern Zaydis, who had supported Yahya. Meanwhile, the FYM in Aden moved to reinforce Sanaa with their own forces and tribal allies of al-Wazir (three tribes with about 14,000 warriors in all), while the British allowed them to drop leaflets encouraging citizens to remain calm and deployed a naval force to salute the new government.

Although the new government controlled Sanaa, it was militarily inferior to its opponents. Ahmed controlled most of the tribal warriors, including several thousand Hashid warriors provided by Prince Hassan and several thousand Bakil tribesmen. The military remained neutral at first, uncertain of its orders.

Narrative: On February 25, Ahmed declared himself the rightful imam and called for the overthrow of al-Wazir. Fighting broke out in the provinces and on the outskirts of Sanaa. Lower-ranking members of the military began to rally to his side. The support of most of the 18,000-man armed forces proved critical for Ahmed. Outside of Sanaa, the coup appears to have been wildly unpopular, particularly the tactic of assassinating the imam. Moreover, the FYM had little influence beyond urban elites. Arab countries condemned al-Wazir's actions.

On February 29, most of the Sanaa garrison went over to Ahmed. By the end of the first week in March, the Zaydi tribes led by Ahmed had besieged Sanaa. At this point, Ahmed controlled a majority of the 15,000 to 20,000 tribal militiamen, nearly all of the 18,000-man army, and the 3,000 men of the palace guard. On the other hand, the government controlled few troops, and its tribal irregulars hastened to return home and make peace with Ahmed.

On March 13, the rebels took Sanaa. A few days later, the nearby mountain of Jubul Nuqum, the last outpost of the pro-Waziri forces, fell to Ahmed's army.

Termination and Outcome: The outcome of the war was a complete and unconditional victory by the rebels. As imam, Ahmed immediately had al-Wazir and thirty of his followers executed; the new government continued to search for FYM members, and further executions followed.

Coding Decisions: There were 5,000 deaths in Sanaa, but the majority was civilians. Hence, our imprecise estimate is 2,000 battle-deaths. Pro-Ahmed force estimates are derived from the size of the armed forces, plus half the militia, plus the palace guard. The real total may have been somewhat higher or lower. Note that as a full week passed between the coup and Ahmed's response, we code the Waziri faction as being in control of the institutions of governance and the capital city at the onset of the war.

Sources: Al-Abdin (1979); Bidwell (1983); Douglas (1987); O'Ballance (1971).[141]

INTRA-STATE WAR #743
First Lebanese War of 1958

Participants: Lebanon, United States, Lebanese Gendarmerie, Syrian Socialist National Party, Moghabghab-led Loyalists, Kata'ib, and Tashnaq versus Syria (United Arab Republic) and United National Front (Aggregate).
Dates: May 9, 1958, to August 4, 1958.
Battle-related Deaths: United States: 1;[142] Tasnaq: 100;[143] Syria (United Arab Republic): at least 1,000;[144] Total Combatant Deaths: 2,500. (See Coding Decisions.)[145]
Initiator: Lebanon (but see Coding Decisions).
Outcome: Stalemate.
War Type: Civil for control of central government.
Total System Member Military Personnel: Armed Forces of Lebanon: 8,000 (prewar, initial, peak, final) but remained "neutral" during war; Armed Forces of the United States of America: 2,411,000 (prewar, initial, peak, final).[146] Armed Forces of the United Arab Republic: 169,000 (prewar, initial, peak, final).
Theater Armed Forces: Armed Forces of the United States of America, participating from July 15, 1958): 14,000 (initial, peak, final).[147] Lebanese Gendarmerie: 2,000 (initial), 2100 (July 1958—probably peak).[148] Syrian Socialist National Party, aka PPS, participating from about May 13, 1958: 3,000 (initial, peak).[149] Moghabghab-led loyalists: 100 or more (peak: 500 combined for all non-PPS paramilitaries).[150] Kata'ib, aka Lebanese Phalange, participating from late May 1958 but at a low level: 100 or more (peak: 500 for non-PPS paramilitaries);[151] *Tashnaq* (participated from late May)—hundreds (peak—500 for non-PPS paramilitaries).[152] United National Front: 2,000 (initial); 8,000 (peak—excludes Syrian "volunteers"); 7,000 (final). Syria (United Arab Republic): up to 3,000 "volunteers" (peak).[153]

Antecedents: In 1956, the Lebanese government adopted the Eisenhower Doctrine, turning to the West for support. The government had antagonized Egypt by refusing to break relations with the United States and Britain during the Suez Crisis. The next year, parliamentary elections were manipulated to give incumbent president Camille Chamoun a majority and hence another term in office in 1958. Chamoun proposed to amend the country's constitution to allow himself reelection. The opposition—a coalition of dissatisfied Maronites and pan-Arab Muslims—attacked the regime in the press, through provocations, and through political assassinations. In February of 1958, Egypt and Syria reached an agreement to form a pan-Arab republic. A month later, Lebanon refused to become a member of the newly formed United Arab Republic. Chamoun's government began firing civil servants unhappy with his policies.

Religious leaders, disenchanted with the favoritism practiced in the administration, were inclined to adopt Egypt's call for a united Arab people, despite the secularism of the pan-Arab movement. Domestically, the president instituted an electoral reform that reduced the amount of pro-Nasser leaders in government. In turn, religious leaders formed the United National Front comprised of Muslims under Salam, Yafi, and Marouf Saad of Sidon. Jumblat's Druze party, Adanan Hakim's Najjadah party Ali Bazzi's National Call Organization, and several Maronite leaders combined their efforts in this group as well.

Large-scale violence erupted after Nassib Al Matni, an editor for the newspaper *Al Telegraph,* was murdered on May 8, 1958. The opposition portrayed the assassination of the independent Maronite journalist as the work of Chamoun because Matni opposed his pro-Western policies.

Narrative: Following the murder of Matni, protesters in Tripoli collided with internal security forces on May 9 and May 10, resulting in at least ten killed and sixty injured. The insurrection quickly assumed a confessional character, with largely Muslim rebels fighting largely Christian loyalists. The army itself remained "neutral" during the war, leaving the defense of Chamoun's government to the gendarmerie, pro-government militias, and—eventually—the United States. On May 12 and May 13, violence erupted as Kamal Jumblat led an assault on the presidential grounds at Beit al Dine, checked over three days' fighting by the intervention of the army garrison, armed members of the Syrian Socialist National Party (PPS), and small loyalist militias. Just weeks later, the resistance had managed to gain control of coastal areas, other cities in the southern region, the Akkar, the Bekaa, and the Chouf (where Chamoun relied on a private army of armed Christians and a few Druzes led by Naim Moghabghab). In all, these constituted more than two-thirds of Lebanon's territory. The rebels called for President Chamoun to resign his position in government immediately.

The rebels were supported by massive infiltration of arms and fighters (up to 3,000 Syrian "volunteers") from the UAR, while the government issued an emergency request for arms and other support to the United States. Forced to rely on the gendarmerie, Chamoun solicited support from the Syrian PPS and the Kata'ib. A cabinet decree following a bombing on May 26 authorized the formation of civilian militias to defend the government. On June 11, the United Nations Security Council voted to dispatch unarmed observers to monitor intervention by the UAR.

Fighting was heavy in Tripoli, where the army was persuaded to commit armored cars, tanks, and heavy artillery to the defense of the city. Close to 170 insurgents and civilians were killed, and the government security and loyalist forces probably suffered about as many fatalities themselves. From June 14 to June 15, heavy fighting raged in Beirut. Only in the Chouf did the rebels attempt to form their own government; Kamal Jumblat declared autonomy for the region, leading to heavy fighting throughout the month of June and into early July. On June 13 and again on July 2, the army intervened against the rebels with tanks, artillery, armored transports, and air cover.

On June 30, Chamoun announced that he would not seek a second term as president. The legislature announced that it would select his successor in July. However, the conflict continued. On July 14, a pan-Arabist coup toppled the government of Iraq. The next day, American marines began landing in Lebanon. Within days, 14,000 American troops were in the country to support the Chamoun regime against pan-Arabism. In late July, Gen. Fuad Shihab of the Lebanese army was elected in a landslide vote, forty-eight to eight, by the Lebanese Chamber of Deputies.

The rebels refrained from engaging United States forces, which were concentrated in Beirut and did not take part in any offensive operations; the civil war continued in other areas of the country, albeit at a much lower intensity. The opposition in Tripoli ordered a cease-fire on August 4. Fighting elsewhere died down after the election of Shihab, who was acceptable to the leaders of factions on both sides of the war.

Termination and Outcome: The outcome of the war was a stalemate—essentially the outcome of informal and tacit bargaining by the various leaders on all sides—with neither side managing to seize or retain the presidency, which went to a neutral party. Battle-deaths dropped below the civil war threshold in early August. Only isolated reprisals occurred on either side, with kidnappings and assassinations continuing into 1959. Shihab formally replaced Chamoun on September 23. The new president appointed Rashid Karami, the main voice in the rebellion, to be prime minister. Further, Shihab created a diverse cabinet to quell religious tensions: three Muslims, four Christians, and one Druze. The United States removed the last of its troops in October as the newly formed government signaled a period of uneasy peace for Lebanon.

Coding Decisions: According to Harris, various sources report death tolls in the range of 1,000 to 4,000. Most of the army remained neutral during most of the fighting, but units occasionally acted to keep roads clear and intervened against the rebels in multiple instances, especially in Tripoli. Halaf states that the PPS "assumed the brunt of the heavy fighting" on behalf of the government (125). But given the participation of the gendarmerie on the government's side and that this was a contest for control of the central government, we code the war as civil and not intercommunal.

Sources: Arnold (1995); Brogan (1998); Goria (1985); Halaf (2002); Khalidi (1979); Korbani (1991); Winslow (2003).[154]

INTRA-STATE WAR #747

Mosul Revolt of 1959

Participants: Iraq, Kurds (Aggregate), and Communists (Aggregate) versus Second Division—Pro-Western Faction.
Dates: March 7, 1959, to March 10, 1959.
Battle-related Deaths: Total Combatant Deaths: 1,200. (See Coding Decisions.)[155]
Initiator: Second Division—Pro-Western Faction.
Outcome: Iraq wins.
War Type: Civil for central control.
Total System Member Military Personnel: Armed Forces of Iraq: 57,000 (prewar); 54,000 (initial, peak, final—excludes rebels).[156]
Theater Armed Forces: Armed Forces of Iraq: 12,000 (initial); perhaps half of the Second Division, or 7,500 troops (peak). Second Division—Pro-Western Faction: 3,000 (initial); about half of the Second Division, or 7,500 troops (peak).[157]

Antecedents: In 1958, the pro-Western government of Iraq was overthrown by a group called the Free Officers. The new government began carrying out purges of the military and other institutions. In reaction, and in anticipation of further purges, a conspiracy to overthrow the new government was hatched by a group of officers with disparate agendas—pro-Western views, pan-Arab views, and traditionalist views. On March 6, 1959, a huge peace rally by leftists was scheduled to take place. The conspirators planned their revolt for the next day.

Narrative: The rally took place without violence, but violence began the next day, with nationalists and communists fighting each other in the streets. On March 8, 'Abd al-Wahhab Shawwaf, the commander of the Mosul garrison, announced his revolt, naming a number of other disaffected Free Officers as supporters. Fighting broke out between military units loyal to rival commanders and within units. Shawwaf commanded the Fifth Brigade of the Second Division, and some other brigades helped the revolutionary cause, but Kurdish soldiers in the Fifth Brigade mutinied against their Arab officers. The coup attempt was crushed by March 10. Shawwaf himself was killed in the fighting.

Termination and Outcome: The fighting ended on March 10. The government won an unconditional military victory. Massacres followed this victory. The remaining rebel leaders were tried and executed. During and after the brief war, the government had armed Kurds under Barzani; three years later, those arms would be turned against the government of Iraq.

Coding Decisions: Conservative landowners mobilized the Shammar tribe in favor of the rebellion, but the tribe, located outside the city, mobilized too late to participate in the fighting, as the coup attempt was crushed by March 10. Estimates of total deaths range from 200 to 2,500, but the best single estimate is 2,426, the majority of them extrajudicial executions (only some of which would qualify as battle-deaths). We estimate 1,200 battle-deaths, but the real toll could be considerably higher or lower.

Sources: Al-Marashi and Salama (2008); Arms Control and Disarmament Agency (1969); Farouk-Sluglett and Sluglett (2001); *New York Times* (1959, March 10).[158]

INTRA-STATE WAR #752

First Iraqi Kurds War of 1961 to 1963

Participants: Iraq, Syria, and Jash (Aggregate) versus Barzani-led Kurdish Tribes and the Kurdish Democratic Party.
Dates: September 11, 1961, to December 1963.
Battle-related Deaths: Armed Forces of Iraq: 4,000; Total Combatant Deaths: 8,000. (See Coding Decisions.)[159]
Initiator: Barzani-led Kurdish Tribes.
Outcome: Stalemate.
War Type: Civil for local issues (autonomy and independence).

Total System Member Military Personnel: Armed Forces of Iraq (excluding the Jash): 80,000 (prewar); 77,000 (after initial defections); 80,000 (peak); 77,000 (final).[160] Armed Forces of Syria—52,000 (prewar, initial); 75,000 (peak, final).[161]

Theater Armed Forces: Armed Forces of Iraq: 32,000 (peak—estimated by taking 40 percent of total strength). Armed Forces of Syria, participating from July 1963: 5,000 (initial, peak, final).[162] Jash, aka Pro-government Kurdish Tribes: 10,000 (initial, peak); 3,000 (final).[163] Barzani-led Kurdish Tribes: 600 (prewar); 5,000 to 7,000 (initial); 10,000 to 20,000 (peak).[164] Kurdish Democratic Party, participating from December 1961: less than 3,000 (initial: 3,000 in summer 1962); 15,000 (peak).[165]

Antecedents: The Kurds and the Iraqi government coexisted reasonably well in the aftermath of the revolution of 1958, although the tribes lost the representation they had enjoyed in parliament. Rebellions in 1959 were crushed with the assistance of Kurds under Mulla Mustafa Barzani, who then became the dominant leader in Iraqi Kurdistan. Worried about this increase in power, the government began to assist anti-Barzani tribes in their intercommunal feuds with Barzani. Moreover, an agrarian reform law began to be implemented in Kurdish areas—a direct threat to the power and income of landowning Kurdish elites.

In February 1961, the Kurdish Democratic Party (KDP), a revolutionary Kurdish party, successfully carried out a political assassination. In June, the government turned back a Kurdish delegation asking for suspension of some reforms in Kurdistan, including a tax on the area's major crop, tobacco. Some Kurdish tribes began openly to defy the government by refusing to pay the tax or follow the provisions of the agrarian reform law. Intertribal conflict increased, and in August Barzani attacked rival tribes, inflicting heavy casualties and consolidating his influence in the area.

Narrative: On September 11, an army column was attacked by Kurdish insurgents. The government responded by indiscriminately bombing the area. This prompted Barzani to come out openly against the government. The Iraqi armed forces had initial success due to the 7,000 or so rebels' poor coordination, and the rebels retreated into the mountains.

In December, Barzani struck the army's camps and communications, and the KDP (banned by the government as of September 24) joined the rebellion and began building an army of *peshmerga.* Kurdish soldiers (3,000 of them by the end of the year) began to defect to the rebels. Meanwhile the government had mobilized anti-Barzani tribes derisively called Jash by the rebels. Their numbers declined throughout the conflict as more and more tribes sided with Barzani and the KDP or opted for neutrality. But in the first year of the conflict, they bore the brunt of the fighting against Barzani.

By the beginning of 1962, thousands of Kurdish fighters had been killed or wounded. Government air raids had killed up to 3,000 people (a Kurdish claim). The area under rebel control expanded southward, where the KDP set up its forces (practically independent of Barzani at this stage of the war). In the northern area under rebel control, Barzani and his rival Talibani fought the government throughout the winter.

The government offered amnesty in March, but the rebels rejected it, and Barzani launched an offensive in the Mosul and Sulaymaniya provinces. The KDP mounted its first major attack on the army in April 1962. Kurdish forces won some victories in the mountains and occupied virtually all of the high ground around Mosul, lacking only the heavy weapons necessary to capture the city. About 40 percent of Iraq's combat troops were now deployed against the Kurds. By August, the rebels numbered from 10,000 to 20,000.

By October, the rebels were able to attack the country's oil infrastructure, but the government finally retook Penjwin, using human shields to discourage rebel resistance. The KDP was becoming increasingly dominant in the revolt, and many government soldiers had defected to the rebels. Entire units had to be transferred to prevent their largely Kurdish soldiers from defecting.

On February 8, 1963, Arab nationalists mounted a coup against the government. The KDP proclaimed its support for the coup in what appears to have been an unwritten agreement not to launch an offensive, while the coup plotters moved units to Baghdad in return for some vague promises about autonomy. Whatever promises had been made, they were soon forgotten, and the war resumed on June 10. In the first four days of fighting, the rebels claimed to have killed 38 Jash and 435 government troops (some of whom also may have been Jash fighters). From June 25 to June 27, they claimed to have killed another 400, including more than 100 Jash.

Syria entered the war by the end of June, sending a brigade of 5,000 soldiers to fight the Kurds. Brutal fighting continued until the new Baathist government was itself overthrown on November 18, 1963. The new government asked for negotiation and a cease-fire, promising constitutional reform to protect Kurdish rights within Iraq.

Termination and Outcome: Fighting continued into December, but otherwise there was little combat until 1965. The cease-fire negotiations dragged out until an agreement was signed on February 12, 1964, with the government agreeing to permit decentralization (but not autonomy), to disband the Jash (who numbered no more than 3,000 by the end of the war), and to grant amnesty. These concessions were insufficient for the rebels, and bargaining continued throughout 1964. Meanwhile, Barzani essentially took over the KDP, enrolling his own fighters in the *peshmerga* and eventually ousting the central committee, which retained just 300 loyalists. Eventually this split led to fighting between the KDP–Politburo under Talibani and the KDP–Barzani faction.

Coding Decisions: Saddam Hussein later admitted that Iraq lost 10,000 soldiers from 1961 to 1975. We estimate that 2,000 government soldiers died in the 1965-to-1966 war and that 1,640 died in the 1974-to-1975 war. This leaves an estimate of 6,360 for the 1961-to-1963 and 1969-to-1970 wars combined, or about 160 per month. Applied to this war, that implies just over 4,000 government battle-deaths. Rebel, Syrian, and Jash deaths remain unknown, and we estimate that they probably at least equaled government deaths when combined. We therefore estimate 8,000 battle-deaths for this war, but the real toll could be half or double this figure.

Sources: Arms Control and Disarmament Agency (1969); Farouk-Sluglett and Sluglett (2001); Jawad (1981); *Keesing's Record of World Events* (January 1962, December 1963, July 1964); Pelletiere (1984); Rubin (2007); Yildiz (2004).[166]

INTRA-STATE WAR #753
Algerian Revolution of 1962

Participants: Algeria (Internal Faction) versus National Liberation Army and External Faction.
Dates: July 25, 1962, to December 4, 1962.
Battle-related Deaths: Total Combatant Deaths: 2,000. (See Coding Decisions.)[167]
Initiator: External Faction.
Outcome: National Liberation Army wins.
War Type: Civil for central control.
Total System Member Military Personnel: Armed Forces of Algeria (Internal Faction only): 6,000 (prewar); perhaps 2,000 to 3,000 (after initial defections, peak).[168]
Theater Armed Forces: Armed Forces of Algeria (Internal Faction only): 6,000 (prewar); perhaps 2,000 to 3,000 (after initial defections, peak).[169] National Liberation Army, aka ALN: 45,000 (prewar, initial, peak, and final).[170] Pro-External Faction Wilayas: 0 (prewar), perhaps 3,000 to 4,000 (after initial defections).[171]

Antecedents: During the Algerian war of independence, divisions had developed between the "internal" guerrilla armies called Wilayas and the "external" army, the National Liberation Army (ALN), which largely ceased offensive operations after serious defeats in the "battle of the frontiers" earlier in the war. The result was factionalism in the insurgents' party, the National Liberation Front (FLN), to which all were ostensibly loyal.

When the French handed over the reins of a new "provisional government" to Ben Khedda of the internal faction on July 3, 1962, the leaders of the 45,000-strong ALN were determined not to be sidelined. On July 22, Ahmed Ben Bella of the FLN's political bureau declared that it, not the provisional government, was assuming the duties of government.

Narrative: On July 25, clashes in Constantine between factions within Wilaya 2 killed twenty-five and left thirty wounded. That same day, Wilaya 3 declared itself unwilling to follow the political bureau. An internal struggle broke out in Wilaya 2, and Wilayas 1, 5, and 6 joined the political bureau. On July 28, Ben Khedda announced that he accepted the composition of the political bureau.

By August 28, Wilayas 1, 2, 5, and 6 supported the political bureau, while Wilayas 3 and 4 remained opposed. From August to September, the ALN advanced through Wilaya 4 on its way to the capital, losing several hundred soldiers killed. Clashes in Boghari and El Asnam left more than 1,000 dead. The Battle of Aumale may have killed 3,000 people, although this is likely an exaggeration.

Ben Bella arrived in Algiers on September 4. Heavy clashes continued over the next few days, while demonstrators demanded a halt to the fighting. By September 9, only Wilaya 3 was not under the control of the political bureau. Guerrilla resistance continued.

Termination and Outcome: By December 4, Ben Bella could announce that the insurgent bands had been smashed. The outcome of the war was an unconditional victory by the rebels. During and after the war, mass killings of Muslims who had sided with the French occurred, as did killings of French settlers.

Coding Decisions: More than 3,000 were killed in the fighting, but many were civilians. We therefore estimate 2,000 battle-deaths.

Sources: Arslan (1964); "Insurgents Crushed, Ben Bella Reports" (1962); Ottaway and Ottaway (1970); Stora (2001).[172]

INTRA-STATE WAR #755

North Yemen War of 1962 to 1970 (aka Yemen Arab Republic)

Participants: Yemen Arab Republic, Egypt, and Popular Resistance Force versus Royalists and Third Force/YRF.
Dates: October 6, 1962, to March 28, 1970.
Battle-related Deaths: Egypt: 26,000; Total Combatant Deaths: 53,500. (See Coding Decisions.)[173]
Initiator: Royalists.
Outcome: Yemen Arab Republic wins.
War Type: Civil for central control.
Total System Member Military Personnel: Armed Forces of the Yemen Arab Republic: 2,000 (prewar); 6,500 (initial); 14,000 (peak); 13,000 (final).[174] Armed Forces of Egypt: 220,000 (prewar, initial); 255,000 (peak, final).[175]
Theater Armed Forces: Popular Resistance Force, participating from December 1967: 10,000 (initial); 40,000 (peak, final).[176] Armed Forces of Egypt, participating until December 1967: 3,000 (prewar); 5,500 (initial—extrapolated from 8,000 by October 23); 70,000 (peak).[177] Royalists—9,600 (initial); 55,000 (peak).[178]

Antecedents: In 1948, Saif-al-Islam Ahmad bin Yahya (known as Imam Ahmad bin Yahya) won a brief civil war against tribal and constitutionalist opponents. He continued the absolutist style of monarchal, nominally theocratic rule of his father Imam Yahya. During the last years of his life, he allied Yemen to the United Arab Republic (Egypt and Syria), even joining the state in a pro forma manner and accepting Egyptian and Soviet technical advisors.

However, his son Muhammad al-Badr plotted against him with the aid of Egypt's Nasser, who was convinced that the imam would not accept republicanism or secularism. Eventually, al-Badr confessed the plot, leading his father to move toward Saudi Arabia and the United Kingdom, Egypt's rivals in the region. For its part, Egypt stepped up its support for the antimonarchist Free Yemeni Movement (FYM), which had played an instrumental role in the 1948 war.

When Ahmed bin Yahya died on September 19, 1962, his estranged son assumed power with the consent of the clergy. He appointed the Nasserite socialist Col. Abdullah Sallal to head the armed forces. However, Republican elements in the government opposed the continuation of the monarchy. Sallal sided with them, and on September 26—just a week after Badr had taken power—the military revolted, shelling the palace in an unsuccessful attempt to kill the imam.

Almost immediately, Zaydi tribes north of Sanaa revolted in opposition to the coup. Because they thought Badr was dead, they proclaimed his uncle Sayf al-Islam al-Hasan as imam. However, once Badr arrived in the North, Hasan pledged allegiance to him. Badr decided on a quick counteroffensive as his tribal allies were fragmented and their long-term allegiance uncertain. In addition, the armed forces of Yemen largely had disintegrated or gone over to the rebel side, while the tribes of the Hashid and Bakil confederations could raise between 30,000 and 80,000 fighters.

Egypt quickly moved to defend the regime. Within days of the coup, 3,000 Egyptian soldiers were in North Yemen. Within a month, that figure had risen to 8,000 men with tanks, modern aircraft, and artillery. The Egyptian force outnumbered and outclassed the ragtag government army, which was thrown together after the coup from about 2,000 soldiers and 4,000 to 5,000 republican volunteers.

Narrative: The first reported combat of the war was an engagement between 100 royalist rebels entering the country from Saudi Arabia and soldiers of the army, fought on October 6. The country quickly became the battleground for a proxy war between the monarchies and republics of the region. Saudi Arabia provided extensive support and bases for the rebels. Jordan contributed about 60 officers to organize the royalist armies. The British also supplied limited support from Aden in the South.

A royalist attempt to quickly recapture Sanaa was foiled by the republican seizure of Sada, a town at a critical crossroad between the northwest mountains and Sanaa, on October 16. The focus of the fighting moved eastward to the area around Marib, where the government and rebels fought for the rest of the month. The royalists claimed victory and moved toward Sanaa against fierce resistance by the government. On November 9 the two sides fought a particularly bloody battle, and the rebels advanced to within twelve miles of Sanaa. The rebels were able to besiege both Sada in the North and Sanaa itself.

The government forces sent to fight the rebels were largely untrained and poorly led, suffering terrible casualties against the (temporarily) better-organized royalists. Progressively, the Egyptians took over more of the fighting. Egyptian paratroopers retook Marib but found themselves besieged by royalists; repeated attempts to relieve the paratroopers were beaten back, and the city fell to the rebels. Following a week-long battle in the Northwest, the rebels overran the fortress of Washha on December 9.

The Egyptians responded to the rebel victories by conducting napalm attacks against rebel positions and villages. The rebels were forced to lift their sieges and retreat eastward to Marib and Harib. By 1963, Egypt had 15,000 troops in Yemen. Having bought breathing space for the government, they organized their forces for a spring offensive against the rebels. In March 1963, they recaptured Marib and Harib, driving royalists into the mountains and desert. Royalist losses were light because of their willingness to retreat into the mountains.

For the rest of 1963, the rebels largely limited themselves to guerrilla attacks against the Egyptian and Yemeni forces. Egypt retaliated with airpower (including the use of napalm and CN) and escalated its commitment, increasing its forces to 22,000 by September. The rebels were reinforced by small numbers of fighters from the shaykh of the Beihan state in the neighboring British protectorate of Aden (where the British themselves were facing a major rebellion). Perhaps 50 French and British mercenaries also aided the royalists.

In the spring of 1964, the Royalists organized a major counteroffensive against Egypt, retaking most of the towns they had lost the year before. Egypt increased its forces to 36,000 by June, launching a new offensive on June 12. As the offensive began to bog down and suffer from royalist ambushes, further deployments brought Egyptian strength to more than 50,000 over the next month. The Egyptians inflicted a series of major defeats on the rebels, causing thousands of rebel casualties. Indeed, the Egyptians captured a number of strongholds that had been held by the rebels since the war began, gaining control of the mountains between the major cities of the center.

The two sides met to work out a peace accord in October; a cease-fire began on November 8. The extended war, combined with the fact that the government was still dominated by Zaydi officials, led a group of Sharis (adherents of a Sunni school) who proclaimed themselves as a political Third Force favoring compromise and the withdrawal of Egyptian forces. Notwithstanding their efforts, the royalists ended the cease-fire in December, despite their weak military position. The Egyptians responded with a three-month offensive that ultimately failed with high casualties, despite the small-scale use of mustard agents (possibly left over from stockpiles left by the British after World War II). They conducted further strikes using both mustard and phosgene in March and April of 1965.

At the beginning of that year, the government controlled less than 6,000 soldiers and perhaps 6,000 to 8,000 auxiliaries, the Egyptians had nearly 50,000 soldiers in the country, and the royalist armies had up to 14,000 men divided into seven armies. They could sometimes win the loyalty of Hashid or Bakil tribes, which could field 30,000 and 80,000 men, respectively. By the middle of the year, nearly 100,000 Yemenis were dead, and Egypt had suffered between 5,000 and 15,000 battle-deaths since the onset of the war.

The government and the Third Force grew further apart during the spring and summer, and some government units defected to the rebels. During the summer, the rebels launched another counteroffensive, retaking many objectives they had lost a year before. Many Egyptian garrisons were isolated, and Egypt began peace talks with Saudi Arabia that culminated in the Jeddah Agreement. The agreement called for a provisional government drawn from both sides and national elections a year later. Egypt was to withdraw its forces—then more than 70,000—from the country.

As it turned out, the Jeddah Agreement was a political success for Egypt, buying them time to withdraw their isolated garrisons and concentrate their forces in the cities. They withdrew some of their soldiers but maintained control of the major cities, keeping about 20,000 soldiers in the country. Renewed rebel pressure led them to withdraw from more towns in 1966 but also triggered a buildup to about 60,000 men by November.

In essence, the country was divided into two parts: an urban area controlled by the republic (in name) and the remaining two-thirds of the country controlled by the royalists. By this point, those loyal to the Third Force had joined the rebels in the struggle against the Egyptians. They intended the formation of a large guerrilla force under the name YRF. Interestingly, the primary cleavage was no longer the form of government but rather the foreign relations of the country. For its part, Egypt began the sustained use of chemical weapons in January 1967 and continued attacks through May.

Under both domestic and international pressure (in particular, rising tensions with Israel), Egypt began to withdraw once more. Its presence was reduced to 30,000 by the beginning of May, and it withdrew another 10,000 that month. By the time it lost the Six-Day War in June, Egypt had only 15,000 soldiers left in Yemen. After the war, Nasser agreed to withdraw his forces completely in return for financial assistance from Saudi Arabia.

On November 5, 1967, a coup by more conservative nationalist officers overthrew the republican government. Almost immediately, the rebels launched a new offensive, nearly taking Sanaa. The rebels' military position was at its peak; they claimed to control 5,000 regulars and 50,000 tribal warriors (in addition to the 300 or so mercenaries fighting for the royalist cause). The Yemeni army, by contrast, had fewer than 7,000 soldiers, and the Egyptians were completing their withdrawal in December.

The government hurriedly created its own militia, the PRF, which accounted for more than 10,000 men. It managed to beat back much of the rebel offensive by February 1968, with assistance from the Soviet Union (which sent aircraft), Syria (which sent pilots for the thirty Mig-19s), and the newly formed People's Republic of Yemen (known as South Yemen, which lent the government the services of 600 fighters). In March, the Saudis cut off aid to encourage the royalists to reach agreement with the new government. However, the siege of Sanaa dragged on through the year as the rebels continued periodically to shell and raid the city from the surrounding mountains.

After the failure of the offensive, the rebels lost much of their tribal support. Some tribes went over to the government, which had 10,000 regular soldiers by the middle of the year. Fighting continued in the Jawf through May. Infighting between the Third Force and the government was ended by a new government formed in September containing seven Shaifis and nine Zaydis. In the royalist camp, Imam Badr was deposed by two of his cousins but returned in October. Although the royalist regulars kept fighting throughout the year, the mercenaries went home once the money stopped flowing. In December, the rebels suffered a double blow. First, they lost Hajjah to the government. Second, royalist general Kassem Munnassar, who had been leading the siege of Sanaa, defected to the government.

By the beginning of 1969, the government had pushed the royalists back and reduced their ability to fight more than occasional skirmishes. An attempted coup on January 27 gave the rebels some respite from government attacks because it was carried out by its best general, who successfully had defended Sanaa the year before. However, the government continued a liberalization process meant to include former rebels, and fighting largely ceased until it seized Sada on September 3. The rebels struck back in January 1970, taking Sada the following month. Negotiations followed, which ended the war on March 28, 1970.

Termination and Outcome: The war ended with a Saudi-mediated formal agreement that amounted to a government victory. The government remained a republic, although most royalists were allowed to participate (the imam and his family were exiled). Political power remained firmly in the hands of the majority republicans, so the agreement was closer to an amnesty rather than a power-sharing arrangement.

Coding Decisions: Combined battle-deaths include 25,000 to 30,000 between the government and rebels; the rest were Egyptians. It is possible that Egypt assumed the bulk of the fighting on behalf of the government for some years in the war, which could justify splitting this case into two intra-state wars and an extra-state war. However, because the information available is too vague to make a firm determination that Egypt assumed the bulk of the fighting, we retain a single unified case rather than splitting it. Bercovitch and Fretter allege that 1,000 Saudis were killed during the war, yet we find no evidence that the Saudis ever deployed more than a handful of technicians and hence do not include Saudi Arabia as a war participant. On the government side, the Soviet Union deployed 500 advisors from 1963 to perhaps 1967, and the Yemen People's Republic deployed 400 to 600 from 1968, but neither met the threshold for inclusion as a state war participant.[179]

Sources: Arnold (1995); Bercovitch and Fretter (2004); Brogan (1998); Clodfelter (2008); Correlates of War Project (2009); DeRouen and Heo (2007); Dresch (2000); McGregor (2006); O'Ballance (1971); "1000 Die in Fierce Battle..." (1962); "Paratroopers in Sheba's City" (1962); Pollack (2004); "Rebel Chief Defects" (1969); Schmidt (1968); Shoham (1998); "Travelers Thrown Into Sanaa Battle" (1968); "Yemen Rebels, Royalists" (1962); "Yemen Rebel Surrender Forecast" (1962); "World News Briefs" (1969).[180]

INTRA-STATE WAR #758

First South Sudan War of 1963 to 1972 (aka Anya Nya Rebellion)

Participants: Sudan and Egypt versus Anya Nya (aggregate for the first few years).

Dates: September 9, 1963 to February 27, 1972.

Battle-related Deaths: Total Combatant Deaths: 100,000 maximum. (See Coding Decisions.)[181]

Initiator: Anya Nya.

Outcome: Negotiated settlement.

War Type: Civil for local issues (secession).

Total System Member Military Personnel: Armed Forces of Sudan: 17,000 (prewar, initial); 35,000 (peak, final). Armed Forces of Egypt: 135,000 (prewar, initial); 390,000 (peak, final).

Theater Armed Forces: Armed Forces of Sudan: 12,000 (initial); 16,000 (peak, final). Armed Forces of Egypt, participating from 1970 at the latest: 10,000 (peak).[182] Anya Nya, aka SSLM (aggregate at first, but a single organization after a few years): 1,300 (prewar, initial); 10,000 to 15,000 (peak, final).[183]

Antecedents: Southern Sudan historically was subordinate to the North. Upon the country's independence, fears of Northern domination were rekindled. Disturbances occurred even before independence in 1955 but only assumed alarming proportions in late 1962, when the Southern Anya Nya movement was formed to resist Northern hegemony. The movement incorporated some 500 mutineers left over from the 1955 disturbances, plus 800 more who had been released from prison in 1961. Between them they had a mere 200 firearms; the rest were armed with spears, machetes, and bows.

Narrative: On September 9, 1963, Anya Nya attacked a police post in Pachalla, killing several police and holding the town for about a week. A second police post was overrun on September 19, the same day that the rebel commanders formed the joint Land Freedom Army to better coordinate operations. By 1964, Anya Nya controlled most of the countryside. In January of that year, 120 insurgents mounted an attack on Wau, but 60 of them were captured and later executed. Anya Nya conducted only minor operations from then until September.

That month, local governments in the South openly began supporting the rebels, providing them with important political support and a source of new recruits (but not weapons). By the end of the year, Anya Nya had 5,000 fighters, many armed with weapons obtained from retreating Simba guerrillas from the Congo. Within another year, they had obtained some 6,000 firearms this way.

On July 8, 1965, the relative calm was broken by North–South riots in Juba, which claimed 1,018 lives. By this point, Anya Nya had doubled again to 10,000 fighters, although it possessed only 2,000 firearms. Against them were deployed 12,000 government troops in the South. The war was low intensity; the vast majority of deaths were due to disease (sometimes brought on by malnutrition or outright starvation).

Between 1965 and 1969, a string of coalition governments ruled; on multiple occasions, amnesties were offered and conferences held, but all proved fruitless. In 1966 there were many rebel attacks, but 1967 and 1968 were relatively calm. A provisional government was established by Southern politicians in 1967, but Anya Nya remained largely independent of it. In May 1969, a government commander reported that there had been no major operations for quite some time. But the war was far from over. During this time, Anya Nya had secured training and possibly arms from Israel.

Meanwhile, the government had changed yet again. On May 25, a military coup was mounted by Col. Gaffar Mohammed al-Nimieri. On June 9, the new government made another peace proposal, but when it went nowhere, the government stepped up operations against Anya Nya. By the end of the year, 1,000 Soviet advisors were present in the Sudan; Soviet and Egyptian pilots may have flown combat missions for the government. By 1971, both Soviet advisors and Egyptian troops reportedly were serving in Sudanese combat units. Egypt, in particular, had deployed 10,000 troops to the Sudan, which were serving in the field.

The violence escalated in 1970, but the rebels managed to unify their political and military wings under the leadership of Joseph Lagu. Prior to this, negotiations always had been complicated by the absence of a united political front that could speak for the rebels. In 1971, an attempted left-wing coup against the government was foiled with Egyptian assistance. Relations with the Soviet Union deteriorated.

By this point, Anya Nya was able to defend territory against government attacks. In September 1970, 3,000 government troops attacked Morta. The rebels resisted, shooting down a fighter and two helicopters (one of whose pilots was Soviet). Two months of fighting followed. After some resistance, the rebels simply retreated into the forests and then retook the town with reinforcements. Another battle took place in December at Pachola, when the rebels took 450 government troops by surprise, killing up to 157 of them.

In 1971, fighting continued, with the government indiscriminately bombing villages in rebel-held areas. About 16,000 troops now faced the 10,000 rebels, but the government was unable to crush the rebellion. A large-scale offensive at the end of the year, aided by two battalions of Egyptian commandos, simply caused the rebels to retreat into neighboring countries, especially Uganda. By 1972, the government was again prepared for peace talks, and the rebels now had a unified command with which to negotiate.

Termination and Outcome: The outcome of the war was a negotiated settlement. The negotiators were able to resolve many issues, providing a clear form of autonomy for the South, but on February 19, the talks stalled over security issues. The two sides eventually agreed on the integration of 6,000 Anya Nya (now SSLM) soldiers into the government army to be stationed in the South. The Addis Ababa peace accord, along with its accompanying cease-fire, was signed on February 27, 1972. It held until 1983.

Coding Decisions: Some 500,000 people were killed in the war, but at most 20 percent of these (100,000) were combatant deaths. Given the size of the forces involved, the real toll was probably considerably smaller. The evidence for Soviet participation in the war is limited, while that for Egyptian participation is relatively strong; hence the former is excluded from the list of participants, and the latter is included.

Sources: Arnold (1995); Assefa (1987); Clayton (1999); Collins (1975, 2008); Edgerton (2002); Jendia (2002); O'Ballance (2000); Ruay (1994).[184]

INTRA-STATE WAR #765

Second Iraqi Kurds War of 1965 to 1966

Participants: Iraq and Jash versus KDP (Barzani) and KDP (Talibani–Ahmad).
Dates: April 3, 1965, to June 21, 1966.
Battle-related Deaths: Armed Forces of Iraq: 2,000;[185] Total Combatant Deaths: 3,000. (See Coding Decisions.)[186]
Initiator: Iraq.
Outcome: Negotiated settlement.
War Type: Civil for local issues (autonomy).
Total System Member Military Personnel: Armed Forces of Iraq: 90,000 (prewar, initial, peak, final).[187]
Theater Armed Forces: Armed Forces of Iraq: 30,000 (peak); Jash: 3,000 (initial).[188] Kurdish Democratic Party (Barzani): 11,000 (peak).[189] Kurdish Democratic Party (Talibani–Ahmad), participating from early in the war: 4,000 (prewar, initial).[190]

Antecedents: After the First Kurdish–Iraqi Civil War (Intra-state War #752), the Kurdish Democratic Party (KDP) split into two factions, one led by Mulla Mustafa Barzani and the other—driven into exile in Iran—by Jalal Talibani and Ibrahim Ahmad. Moreover, after negotiations with the government stalled in 1964, Barzani unilaterally declared a Kurdish autonomous zone on October 4. Both the division of the rebels and the open defiance of Barzani convinced the government to mount a new offensive against the Kurds in 1965.

Narrative: The offensive began on April 3, directed against Barzani. However, the Talibani–Ahmad faction soon joined the defense of the Kurdish zone, with its 4,000 fighters. The offensive stalled in September. The government mounted a second offensive late in 1965, but it also stalled quickly. Finally, in the spring of 1966, the third major offensive of the war was mounted by government forces. On about May 23, a climactic battle took place in the Hondrin–Zozik valley, where at least 2,000 government troops were cut off and virtually annihilated (casualty estimates vary by author) by 1,700 of Barzani's *peshmerga*. Another source has 30,000 government troops (probably the entire force deployed against the Kurds) against 3,500 *peshmerga*. Negotiations between Barzani and the government resumed in June.

Termination and Outcome: On June 29, the government agreed to a list of rebel demands in an agreement called the 29 June Declaration—decentralization, national rights, and linguistic and cultural rights. The fighting between the Kurd and the government was halted by the negotiated settlement, but fighting continued between Kurdish factions, a problem that would eventually escalate into full-scale intercommunal wars decades later. The cease-fire between the government and Barzani lasted for more than two years before breaking down again in 1969.

Coding Decisions: Estimates for the decisive battle of the war in the Hondrin–Zozik valley range from hundreds of government troops killed to 2,000 government bodies being counted on the battlefield by the rebels. We take the latter as being closer to the truth and estimate 2,000 government battle-deaths for the war. Rebel losses were probably lower, so we estimate 3,000 total battle-deaths. The real toll could be several thousand lower or higher.

Sources: Jawad (1981); O'Ballance (1996a, b); Pollack (2004).[191]

INTRA-STATE WAR #777
Third Iraqi Kurds War of 1968 to 1970

Participants: Iraq, Jash, and Kurdish Democratic Party (Talibani–Ahmed) versus Kurdish Democratic Party (Barzani).
Dates: December 1968 to March 11, 1970.
Battle-related Deaths: Armed Forces of Iraq: perhaps 2,000; Total Combatant Deaths: 3,000. (See Coding Decisions.)[192]
Initiator: Kurdish Democratic Party (Barzani).
Outcome: Negotiated settlement.
War Type: Civil for local issues (autonomy).
Total System Member Military Personnel: Armed Forces of Iraq: 90,000 (prewar, initial); 95,000 (peak, final).[193]
Theater Armed Forces: Jash: 2,000 (initial, peak).[194] Kurdish Democratic Party (Talibani–Ahmad): 10,000 (initial).[195] Kurdish Democratic Party (Barzani): 20,000 (initial); 21,000 (peak).[196]

Antecedents: In October 1968, clashes broke out between the two rival factions of the KDP, a revolutionary Kurdish party. Government forces aided the weaker faction (KDP–Talibani–Ahmad) against the stronger (KDP–Barzani). During the war, Iraq's rival Iran provided assistance to the *peshmergas* of Barzani, including artillery support.

Narrative: By December, government support for the Talibani–Ahmad faction had grown, and the Barzani faction began attacking government officials and soldiers. The government retaliated with a major offensive on January 3, 1969. Later, the pan-Arab nationalist Baath Party overthrew the government and strengthened the offensive against the Kurds. On March 1, 1969, the rebels mounted a counteroffensive that killed or wounded 1,000 government troops at a cost of 150 rebels killed.

The fighting paused in June as war with Iran seemed imminent; negotiations resumed. However, the negotiations failed, and in August, a new government offensive against the Kurds was mounted. The government forces mostly were defeated by October, but scattered fighting (costing the rebels about 100 killed) continued until March.

Termination and Outcome: On March 11, 1970, an agreement was reached calling for Kurdish autonomy to be phased in over a four-year period. Kurdish governors were appointed for the Kurdish provinces, the Jash was disbanded, and the *peshmerga* were to be integrated into a frontier guard. The status of oil-rich Kirkuk was to be determined by a census of its inhabitants. The outcome of the war was thus a negotiated agreement that in some ways amounted to a rebel victory as the autonomous status of Kurdistan was acknowledged by the government for the first time. In the end, the government failed to live up to its commitments, and about four years later the two sides returned to war.

Coding Decisions: Saddam Hussein later admitted that Iraq lost 10,000 soldiers from 1961 to 1975. We estimate that 2,000 government soldiers died in the war from 1965 to 1966[197] and that 1,640 died in the war from 1974 to 1975.[198] This leaves an estimate of 6,360 for the 1961-to-1963 and 1969-to-1970 wars combined, or about 160 per month. Applied to this war, that implies somewhat more than 2,000 government battle-deaths. Rebel battle-deaths were much lower, according to rebel claims. We estimate that losses between the rebels, the Jash, and the KDP–Talibani–Ahmad faction were at least 1,000 and certainly could be higher. Thus we estimate 3,000 battle-deaths. The true figure could be higher or lower than this estimate.

Sources: Jawad (1981); McDowall (1996); O'Ballance (1996a, b); Pollack (2004); Rezun (1992).[199]

INTRA-STATE WAR #780
Black September War of 1970 (aka Jordanian Civil War)

Participants: Jordan versus Syria and Palestinians (Aggregate).
Dates: September 13, 1970, to September 24, 1970.
Battle-related Deaths: Armed Forces of Jordan: 750; Armed Forces of Syria: 100; Palestinians: 900; Total Combatant Deaths: 1,750. (See Coding Decisions.)[200]
Initiator: Jordan.
Outcome: Stalemate.
War Type: Civil for central control.
Total System Member Military Personnel: Armed Forces of Jordan: 70,000 (prewar, initial, peak, final). Armed Forces of Syria: 110,000 (prewar, initial, peak, final).[201]
Theater Armed Forces: Armed Forces of Syria, participating from September 20 to September 23, 1970: 16,000 (initial, peak).[202] Palestinians: 20,000 (prewar, initial, peak).[203]

Antecedents: In 1967, Israel defeated Jordan in the Six Day War and occupied the West Bank of the Jordan River. Palestinian refugees flooded across the river to unoccupied Jordan. Already resentful of Jordanian rule, the Palestinians accused the Jordanian government of essentially surrendering their land without a fight because the army was designed to repress instead of defend the West Bank. Given that more than half of the population of the East Bank was now Palestinian, Jordan adopted a conciliatory attitude toward them, attempting to integrate them into the polity.

Seeking to both exploit the grievances of the Palestinians and keep their regional rivals from doing the same, Arab states began sponsoring Palestinian militias with money and promises to win back the lost land. There were already two: the Palestine Liberation Organization (PLO) was backed by Syria, while Fatah was backed by Saudi Arabia. In addition to numerous state-sponsored groups, an independent Popular Front for the Liberation of Palestine (PFLP) was organized.

The PFLP soon fragmented into three groups: the PFLP, the People's Democratic Liberation Front of Palestine (PDFLP), and later the PFLP–General Command. Surprisingly, many other Palestinian groups managed to unite, notwithstanding the rivalries among their sponsors. During 1968, Fatah and most other major groups joined the PLO. Its ranks swelled after Fatah helped the Jordanian army defeat an Israeli incursion on March 21. Palestinian militias now formed in the cities, including Amman, and the PLO moved most of its bases further inland to avoid Israeli artillery.

Banned left-wing parties coalesced around the Palestinian cause, hoping to use them to overthrow the monarchy. The regime reacted quickly; when the small Palestinian militia al-Nasr clashed with police in Amman, the regime made an example by attacking it, capturing its leader, and sentencing him to death. Palestinian organizations agreed to respect the authority of the Jordanian government. In February 1969, Fatah leader Yasser Arafat assumed leadership of the PLO and worked directly with King Hussein to reduce tensions.

Ultimately, the peace failed because smaller Palestinian groups—or factions of larger ones—continued to engage in confrontations with Jordanian security forces. Palestinian anger was fueled in part by Hussein's peace overtures to Israel, which were widely interpreted as willingness to sell out the interests of Palestinians (both residents of the West Bank and refugees from land annexed by Israel during its war for independence) for the interests of the monarchy. Both the PLO and Jordanian government feared that the other would use these incidents as a pretext to strike first.

On June 9, 1970, Palestinians clashed with Hussein's supporters in Amman. When Hussein went to investigate, he was fired on and one of his bodyguards killed. Several units of elite Bedouin fighters immediately moved against the two Palestinian refugee camps near Amman: al-Wahadat and al-Husseini. Fighting continued for three days, until the PFLP seized foreigners as hostages and demanded the shelling stop. The government complied, but Fatah refused to reciprocate unless Hussein undertook changes in the army command and dismissed his most prominent advisers. Hussein agreed, temporarily ending hostilities and securing the release of the hostages. Nearly 200 people had been killed in the three days of conflict.

As with the other agreements, this one quickly broke down. The PFLP and its splinter organizations continued to call for the overthrow of King Hussein. Another attempt on the king's life occurred on September 1. Five days later, the PFLP hijacked three international aircraft and forced them to land in Jordan, embarrassing the Hussein government. On September 9, they hijacked a fourth aircraft, and three days later they destroyed the planes and released most hostages, keeping fifty-four. The hijackings had the effect of forcing Arafat's hand—he could either side with the PFLP or against it. He chose the former, endorsing the hijackers' demands.

Narrative: Arafat's move temporarily united the Palestinian groups, so it is difficult to pinpoint the operations of any one group in the subsequent civil war. Throughout the rest of this summary, we use the term *Palestinians* to refer to the various militias. Where a particular organization is involved (usually the PLO), we specify its name.

Skirmishes broke out on September 13, when King Hussein demanded that Palestinian militias disarm. Clashes were reported in Irbid, Zaarqa, and Maan; the Palestinians lost 105 fighters in three days. On September 15, Palestinian fighters gained control of Irbid in the North and proclaimed a new people's government. Hussein responded by declaring martial law and constructing a cabinet dominated by military officers. Beginning on September 17, Jordanian forces once again bombarded al-Wahadat and al-Husseini, while Jordanian army units attacked Palestinian guerrillas in Irbid.

The government had anticipated a two-day campaign, but the Palestinians managed to resist long enough to trigger foreign intervention on their behalf. Libya provided financial assistance, while Egypt sent Palestinian commandos to assist the rebels. The most threatening intervention came from Syria, which committed a reinforced division to assist the rebels, including a Palestinian Liberation Army (PLA) armored brigade.

On September 20, more than 16,000 Syrian soldiers and 200 Syrian tanks crossed into Jordan. The government rushed its best armored brigade to block them and requested Western intervention. Israel moved troops to the Syrian border at the behest of the United States, which wanted to warn Syria against intervention. When Jordan failed to condemn the Israeli move, Libya and Egypt suspended aid to the government. While Syria hesitated to commit its air force, the Jordanian air force ambushed the vulnerable armored columns. Within three days, the Syrians had lost 75 tanks and suffered 100 killed; they withdrew from Jordan on September 23.

Meanwhile, combat continued in Amman, where the government had leveled and occupied the refugee camps but still had to contend with pockets of resistance around the city. On September 24, the Arab League dispatched a team to help resolve the issue. Three days later, a cease-fire was announced between the adversaries.

Termination and Outcome: The cease-fire ended the war but did not resolve the underlying conflict or the factors that had caused previous agreements to collapse. Both sides were to withdraw from cities, and all prisoners were to be released. Jordan essentially had destroyed the Palestinians' ability to challenge the army and now feared a drawn-out guerrilla war, while the Palestinians retained their battered state within a state. When it became clear that Jordanian sentiment was anti-Palestinian, the PLO made further concessions on October 13, affirming King Hussein's supremacy and restricting the activity of Palestinian forces in Jordan.

The peace was fragile, and in March 1971, government forces drove the Palestinians out of Irbid. The government also ordered the PLO to move its forces away from Amman; Palestinian groups outraged by the demand (and the acquiescence of the PLO) launched guerrilla attacks against government forces from the forested area around Ajlun. On July

13, the Jordanians moved against the Palestinians in the Ajlun area, including the PLO. After five days' fighting, more than 2,000 were captured (and subsequently permitted to leave), and the rest fled the country through Syria. Some 70 actually surrendered to Israel. The Palestinians had ceased to exist as a fighting force in Jordan.

Coding Decisions: We add together the government's estimate of its own battle-deaths, the Palestinians' estimate of their battle-deaths, and our estimate of Syrian battle-deaths to arrive at the total of 1,750.

Sources: Abu-Odeh (1999); Clodfelter (2008); Dunér (1985); Mobley (2009); O'Ballance (1974); Salibi (1993); Tillema (1991).[204]

INTRA-STATE WAR #797

Fourth Iraqi Kurds War of 1974 to 1975

Participants: Iraq and Jash versus Kurdish Democratic Party (Barzani), Iran, and Iranian Kurds.
Dates: March 12, 1974, to April 1, 1975.
Battle-related Deaths: Iraq: 2,500; Kurdish Democratic Party (Barzani): 2,000; Total Combatant Deaths: 4,500. (See Coding Decisions.)[205]
Initiator: Kurdish Democratic Party (Barzani).
Outcome: Iraq wins.
War Type: Civil for local issues (autonomy).
Total System Member Military Personnel: Armed Forces of Iraq: 110,000 (prewar, initial); 155,000 (peak, final). Armed Forces of Iran: 310,000 (prewar, initial); 355,000 (peak, final).[206]
Theater Armed Forces: Jash: several thousand.[207] Kurdish Democratic Party (Barzani): 105,000 (initial, peak).[208] Armed Forces of Iran, participating from January 1975 to March 6, 1975: two regiments in-country, plus two battalions of artillery across the border (initial).[209] Iranian Kurds, participating from summer 1974 to March 6, 1975: [ ].

Antecedents: The government was slow to implement the peace plan that had ended the Third Iraqi–Kurdish War (Intra-state War #777), and sporadic clashes broke out in 1971 and again in 1972. Moreover, it attempted to Arabize some strategic areas that Kurds saw as part of Kurdistan. Iran, the United States, and Israel all provided Kurdish leader Barzani with aid, raising the suspicions of the Iraqi government. Finally, the government passed an autonomy bill as promised by the 1970 accords, on March 11, 1974. However, the bill failed to include all of the terms of the settlement, and Barzani's Kurdish Democratic Party rejected the law.

Narrative: The first clashes between the Kurds and the army occurred on March 12 and March 13. On March 25, the KDP under Barzani mounted a new insurrection. Barzani controlled 40,000 *peshmergas* and another 60,000 tribal militia members. In addition, 5,000 police defected to the rebels at the start of the war.

The government launched a major offensive against the rebels on April 6. Barzani attempted to defend Kurdish territory in conventional fighting, and his forces were mauled badly. That summer, Iran began allowing its Kurds to cross the border and fight with the KDP. Some 500 rebels under Shaikh Uthman Ahmad defected to the government.

By the winter, the KDP and its Iranian Kurd allies had been forced into the mountains, and perhaps the only thing that saved the rebels from total destruction was the intervention by Iran, which escalated to dressing Iranian regulars as Kurds and ordering them into action against Iraq. Iranian heavy artillery also pounded Iraqi positions. Military operation reached a standstill in late 1974 and early 1975 as the Iranian (and secret American) assistance to the rebels proved just sufficient to keep them in action against the Iraqi government but insufficient to allow them to defeat it.

On March 6, 1975, Iran and Iraq reached the Algiers Accord, by which a border dispute was settled in favor of Iran, and in return the Iranians promised to cut off aid to the rebels. Within hours of the accord, Iran withdrew its forces and artillery from Iraq. Government forces surged forward and surrounded the rebels before offering them a truce, as mandated by the accords, to either surrender or withdraw into Iran.

Termination and Outcome: On March 21, Barzani ordered his forces to withdraw into Iran. At the expiration of the truce on April 1, there was no effective resistance to the government remaining. The outcome of the war was a government win with a promise of amnesty (which expired on May 20). The government created a security zone between its Kurdish areas and Iran, razing some 500 villages. At least 600,000 people were deported to resettlement camps. Many residents were forced out of majority-Kurdish cities and replaced by Arab settlers, and provincial lines were redrawn to prevent a Kurdish-majority province.

Coding Decisions: The government admitted to losing 1,640 killed and 7,903 wounded, but the Red Cross estimated that the government lost 7,000 killed. Other estimates are 10,000 to 16,000 government casualties, which given the traditional 3:1 ratio of wounded to killed would imply 2,500 to 4,000 killed. The government claimed that 7,600 rebels were killed or wounded. Given the traditional 3:1 ratio of wounded to killed, this implies about 1,900 rebel battle-deaths. The Kurds claim that only 2,000 Kurds were lost, which is entirely consistent with the government's claim. We therefore estimate 2,500 government battle-deaths and 2,000 rebel battle-deaths, for a total of 4,500 battle-deaths. These figures may be a little high but are more likely to be underestimates as they exclude Jash and Iranian battle-deaths.

Sources: Arnold (1995); Ghareeb (1981); McDowall (1996); O'Ballance (1996a, b).[210]

INTRA-STATE WAR #801
Second Lebanese War of 1975 to 1976

Participants: Phalange, Tigers, Zgharta Liberation Army, Order of Maronite Monks, Guardians of the Cedars, Al Tanzim, Lebanese Forces, Christian Lebanese Army Forces (Aggregate), and Syria versus Lebanese National Movement, Fateh, Democratic Front for the Liberation of Palestine, Popular Front for the Liberation of Palestine, Arab Liberation Front, Popular Struggle Front, Popular Resistance, Popular Front for the Liberation of Palestine (General Committee), Lebanese Arab Army, Palestinian Liberation Army, and Sa'iqa.
Dates: April 13, 1975, to April 16, 1975, and May 25, 1975, to November 14, 1976.
Battle-related Deaths: Total Combatant Deaths: 15,000. (See Coding Decisions.)[211]
Initiator: Phalange (but see Coding Decisions).
Outcome: Negotiated settlement.
War Type: Intercommunal.
Total System Member Military Personnel: Armed Forces of Syria: 230,000 (prewar, initial); 240,000 (peak, final).
Theater Armed Forces:

Side A: Phalange militia, aka Kataeb Party, participating to January 31, 1976, when it merged into Lebanese Forces: 8,000 (initial); 10,000 (peak).[212] Tigers, aka National Liberal Party militia, participating to January 31, 1976, when it merged into Lebanese Forces: 4,000 (initial).[213] Order of Maronite Monks, participating to January 31, 1976, when it merged into Lebanese Forces: 200 (initial, peak).[214] Guardians of the Cedars, participating from soon after the onset of war to January 31, 1976, when it merged into Lebanese Forces: 750 (peak).[215] Al Tanzim, participating from soon after the onset of war to January 31, 1976, when it merged into Lebanese Forces: at least 200 (peak).[216] Lebanese Forces, aka Lebanese Front, participating from January 31, 1976: 12,950 (initial).[217] Zgharta Liberation Army, aka Marada Brigade: 1,000 (initial); 7,000 (peak).[218] Christian Lebanese Army Units, participating from March 1976: 10,000 (initial, peak).[219] Armed Forces of Syria, participating from April 9, 1976: 3,000 to 4,000 (initial); 25,000 (peak); 25,000 (final). No estimate of battle-deaths is available.[220]

Side B: Lebanese National Movement: 19,500 (initial).[221] Fateh, aka Fatah, participating from January 17, 1976: 6,000 (prewar); 7,000 (initial).[222] Democratic Front for the Liberation of Palestine, participating from January 17, 1976: 2,500 (prewar).[223] Popular Front for the Liberation of Palestine: 2,000 (initial).[224] Arab Liberation Front: 2,500 (initial).[225] Popular Struggle Front: 200 (initial).[226] Popular Resistance, participating by October 1975: 2,200 (initial).[227] Popular Front for the Liberation of Palestine–General Committee: 2,000 (initial).[228] Lebanese Arab Army, participating from January 1976: 2,000 (initial).[229] Palestine Liberation Army, aka PLA, participating on Side B from January 19, 1979, but switched sides in April 1976: 8,000 (initial).[230] Sa'iqa, participating on Side B until March 15, 1976, when it switched sides: 4,000 (initial); 7,000 (peak—many of these may have been Syrian regulars).[231]

Antecedents: Intercommunal relations between Christians and Muslims deteriorated after the 1958 civil war (see Intra-state War #743). In addition, the country became more urbanized, and the capital of Beirut eventually grew to encompass 40 percent of the country's population. This trend further polarized the religious groups as Christians accumulated most of the wealth in the cities and Muslims generally continued life in the impoverished countryside. Syria also continued to lay claim to Lebanon in the name of "a Greater Syria." Finally, the new flood of Palestinians into Lebanon after the Jordanian Civil War (Intra-state War #780) strained the delicate relationship between Christians and Muslims. Most settled in specific regions: in Tripoli, directly south of Beirut, in the South by Tyre and Sidon, and in the Bekaa Valley's Baalbek. Palestinians, primarily used as inexpensive labor, were viewed as allies of Muslim Lebanese, which left Christians (even further) in the minority demographically.

In terms of government, Maronite Christians continued to hold power. Other parties, like those representing Shiites and the Druze, openly protested their inferior representation in the Lebanese government. For example, Shiites—in the South under Imam Musa Sadr as well as largely poor areas of Beirut—displayed opposition to both the Christian government and Israel. Musa Sadr mobilized many of these people in his militia, Amal. The proliferation of other militias followed. Radical Palestinian commandos also targeted the status-quo-oriented government with guerrilla attacks beginning in 1973.

In general, Palestinian armed groups became convinced that the Lebanese state was planning to eliminate their movement. The Lebanese establishment became convinced that the Palestinians were interested in turning Lebanon into a pawn against Israel, threatening the country's sovereignty. Fighting between the Lebanese military and Palestinian groups continued, with occasional cease-fire agreements. By early 1974, Muslim ministers began to resign from the government, which became seen as a Maronite creature.

From October 1, 1974, Israeli incursions into south Lebanon became routine. Usually, no resistance was offered by the Lebanese army. The left and the Palestinians demanded that the government fight the Israelis, while the establishment and most rightists considered a policy of confrontation to be self-destructive. The cross-border violence intensified in December and January, with a weeklong, pitched battle between Israeli and Palestinian units in the village of Kafr Shuba.

A political crisis predated the outbreak of large-scale hostilities between right Christian and left Muslim groups. In February, a fishermen's strike in heavily Palestinian Sidon turned violent, and the army attempted to crush it over the next two weeks. In all, six soldiers and ten civilians—some of whom may have been engaged in armed resistance—were killed. Protests broke out by leftist and pro-Palestinian groups across Lebanon. The army was condemned for its intervention; in response, the rightist Maronite parties proclaimed March 5 as Army Day. A wide array of Muslim leaders demanded reform of the military's Maronite-dominated command to render the army less partial in civil disputes. The Maronite parties refused.

Narrative: On April 13, 1975, an assassination attempt was made against Maronite politician Pierre Gemayel, whose son Bashir led the Phalange militia. Four people, including one of his bodyguards, were killed in the attack. Phalangists immediately retaliated against Palestinians, believing them to be responsible for the attack. They ambushed a busload of Palestinians and their Lebanese Arab allies, killing twenty-seven and wounding nineteen. As news spread, fighting also spread across the country, pitting Palestinians and armed members of the Lebanese National Movement (an association of Druze and Muslim parties led by Kamal Jumblatt) against Phalangists and the Tiger militia of the ruling National Liberal Party.

The three main Maronite Christian militias had a strength of 13,000 armed fighters. The Lebanese National Movement was composed of some fifteen groups, including the Progressive Socialist Party (PSP, 5,000 armed fighters), the two Baath Parties (1,500 in the pro-Iraq faction and 2,000 in the pro-Syrian one), the Lebanese Communist Party (5,000), the Syrian Social Nationalist Party (5,000), the Organization of Communist Action (100), al-Murabitan (200), the Movement of 24 October (500), and possibly the Arab Labor Socialist Party (200) and Association of Working People (200). In sum, the Lebanese National Movement could muster more than 19,000 armed fighters. Those Palestinian factions that joined the initial fighting were about 10,700 strong, leading to an intercommunal balance of about 13,000 Maronites against about 30,000 leftists, Palestinians, Druze, and Muslims. After three days of fighting, a truce was reached on April 16, but mistrust was high. Between 250 and 350 people had been killed.

The peace was short-lived. The country's Muslim prime minister was pushing economic reforms that would have cost the Maronite elite; he also was demanding political reform. After political pressure by Kataeb and other Maronite parties, the Muslim prime minister was forced to resign, blaming Kataeb and the Phalange for the bus massacre and for starting the war. He demanded citizenship for Palestinians and other Muslim noncitizens in Lebanon.

In a surprise move on May 25, the Christian president announced the formation of a military cabinet. Reaction to the announcement was swift; violence again erupted across Lebanon, pitting the Kataeb and its allies against the Lebanese National Movement and its allies. A few days later, the military government collapsed, and Rashid Karami spent the next month trying to form a government, succeeding on June 30.

There was a lull in the fighting after the government's formation, but combat resumed around August 24, with fierce battles in the suburbs of Zaleh (where a new Shiite militia, Amal, had made itself public and joined the Lebanese National Movement in July) and in Tripoli (where the Zgharta Liberation Army massacred a dozen Muslims on a bus en route to Beirut). This intensified the Muslim resistance, and the next day Christian leaders in Tripoli asked the army to intervene. The army succeeded in imposing a cease-fire in the North, but combat in Beirut continued.

Further peace attempts failed when the Phalange was discovered to be importing arms with the assistance of the army and president. The Phalange advanced out of Christian areas and into Muslim and Druze ones. In December fierce battles broke out in the largely Christian hotel district of Beirut. When five Maronites were murdered, Kataeb militiamen shot 100 Muslim civilians (an event known as Black Saturday). Meanwhile a battle raged for control of the hotels and other high-rise buildings. Eventually, most of the Phalange retreated into Christian-affiliated areas, but the left Muslim forces took much higher casualties in the hotel battles. By the end of 1975, perhaps 6,650 lives had been lost in the struggle.

January 1976 marked a new phase in the conflict as Christians became better organized and both sides attempted to secure their enclaves by eliminating surrounded centers of potential resistance. On January 4, the Phalange and Tigers blockaded the Palestinian at Tal Zaatar and Dubaya. The sieges lasted until January 14. Meanwhile Palestinian–LNM forces besieged the Christian towns of Damour and Jiye. On January 17, the Maronite militias occupied and destroyed the Muslim slums of Karantia and Maslakh, slaughtering 1,500 Palestinians and Lebanese Arabs in the process. This event triggered active participation by moderate Palestinian groups Fatah (with at least 7,000 armed militia) and Democratic Front for the Liberation of Palestine (with 2,500). On the same day, Damour and Jiye fell, leading to a massacre of 300 to 400 Christians. Syria permitted two brigades of the Palestinian Liberation Army to cross the border and assist the LNM–Palestinian alliance at Zahle.

Prime Minister Karami resigned on January 18. Three days later, a Syrian-sponsored cease-fire went into effect. Perhaps in response to the growing success of the LNM–Palestinian alliance, the Phalange, Tigers, Guardians of the Cedars, and al-Tanzim formed a unified military command under the name Lebanese Forces, led by Bashir Gemayel of the Phalange. Only the Zgharta Liberation Army and some Lebanese army units remained outside the unified command as of January 31.

Syria's indirect intervention tilted the balance of forces toward the LNM–Palestinian alliance. Moreover, the creation of the Lebanese Arab Army added twenty-five garrisons and camps—about 2,000 soldiers—with their equipment to the LNM–Palestinian alliance. Over the next few months, this coalition took the offensive, seizing downtown Beirut, shelling the presidential palace (forcing the president to flee), and overrunning Christian enclaves. On February 14, the president issued a plan for constitutional reform with support from Syria, but it was rejected as too status-quo oriented by the Muslim and left groups.

The army virtually collapsed after mutinies on March 10, disintegrating within weeks. About half of its 19,000 soldiers simply went home, while most of the remaining Christians affiliated themselves with Maronite Christian militias, although no single commander held sway over all of them. The remaining Muslims in the army formed the Lebanese Arab Army (LAA).

On March 13, the LAA spearheaded a new general offensive by the LNM–Palestinian alliance. This brought about the closest thing to a civil war experienced in 1975 and 1976 as Christian units of the Lebanese armed forces assumed the primary role in combat at strategically located Fayadiyah and surrounding towns. They were opposed by PSP elements of the LNM and by the LAA. The fighting lasted from March until May and claimed about 1,000 lives. Only the disconnect between the president and the actual army commanders on the ground kept this from being a civil war within the broader intercommunal war.

By early April, the alliance controlled two-thirds of Lebanon, although it was unable to take the port areas supplying the Christian fighters in Beirut. Syria quickly was becoming concerned that having averted the destruction of pan-Arab forces and the partition of Lebanon, it might now be facing a radicalized Lebanese state if the LNM–Palestinian alliance won a decisive victory. PLA units were moved across the border to undermine the alliance between the LNM and Palestinians but were unsuccessful.

The government of Syria then ordered the PLA, its client, to fight for the Maronites and against the LNM. Other pro-Syrian groups began to desert the LNM. The response of the LNM was to proclaim a joint command, incorporating the PLO and LNM. This grouping was known as the LNM (Joint Forces). Negotiations between the LF and LNM (Joint Forces) were attempted but had made little progress when Syria, which had first intervened against the LAA on April 9, intervened massively on May 31.

During the first week of June, 12,000 Syrian troops entered Lebanon, encountering stiff resistance from the LNM–Palestinian alliance. Some PLA and Sa'iqa forces began to defect from Syrian control when faced with the task of fighting fellow Palestinians. On June 22, the Lebanese Front mounted a new offensive against several slums in Beirut and the Palestinian refugee camps of Jisr al-Basha and Tall al-Za'tar. Both fell and were totally destroyed; the battle for the latter was especially fierce, with 4,000 killed and 12,000 wounded (after the fall of the camp, up to 3,000 Palestinian civilians were massacred by the victors).

Nearly everywhere, the LNM–Palestinian alliance was now in retreat as the Syrians, their Lebanese allies, and the Maronite factions pressed their advantage. Fighting became especially pronounced around Mount Lebanon, where the LNM was holding positions in the Christian heartland and peremptorily refused a Syrian order to relinquish them. The Battle of the Mountain that followed began as a stalemate, but on September 27, Syria directly attacked the LNM–Palestinian positions, capturing them within a day of heavy fighting.

Flush with victory and committed to a quick victory to keep the Arab League from interfering, the Syrians mounted a major offensive on September 29. Over the next week or so, 13,000 more Syrian troops entered Lebanon to drive the LNM–Palestinian alliance away from the Christian areas of Lebanon. Fighting was especially intense around Bhamdoun, where the Syrians suffered hundreds of battle-deaths.

On October 25 and October 26, the Arab League resolved that Lebanese and Palestinian fighters should return to their prewar positions, while an Arab Deterrent Force would enforce a cease-fire. By November 14, when the Arab Deterrent Force (dominated by Syria, which contributed 25,000 of the 30,000 troops) was activated, resistance had ceased throughout the country.

Termination and Outcome: The outcome of the war was a settlement largely imposed from outside Lebanon. While the PLO participated in the negotiations, none of the domestic factions were directly represented at the Arab League's summit. The result of the war was a substantial weakening of the Palestinians and LNM, although the government promised to pursue constitutional reform. Between the militias, the Maronites emerged victorious by way of Syrian intervention.

Coding Decisions: Estimates of total deaths range from 20,000 to 65,000. Considering that more historians use the lower figure and that at least half of those killed were civilians, we conclude that there were about 15,000 battle-deaths, but the real toll could have been many thousands more or less. Note that Palestinians may have been responsible for the assassination attempt that sparked the intercommunal war, but the first organized actor to use force was the Phalange.

Sources: Arnold (1995); Brogan (1998); El Khazen (2000); Hiro (1993); Jureidini, McLaurin, and Price (1979); Khalidi (1979); O'Ballance (1998); Petran (1987); Sirriah (1989); Winslow (2003); Weinberger (1986).[232]

INTRA-STATE WAR #815.5

Iranian Islamic Revolution of 1978 to 1979 (aka Overthrow of the Shah)

Participants: Iran versus Mujahideen e-Kalk, Fedayeen Kalk, and Pro-Khomeini Rebels.
Dates: November 16, 1978, to February 12, 1979.
Battle-related Deaths: Armed Forces of Iran: perhaps 500; Fedayeen Kalk: less than 22; Total Combatant Deaths: 1,000. (See Coding Decisions.)[233]
Initiator: Mujahideen e-Kalk.
Outcome: Pro-Khomeini Rebels win.
War Type: Civil for central control.
Total System Member Military Personnel: Armed Forces of Iran: 415,000 (prewar, initial, peak); 30,000 (final).[234]
Theater Armed Forces: Armed Forces of Iran: 30,000 (final). Mujahideen e-Kalk: several hundred (prewar); 2,000 (peak, final).[235] Fedayeen Kalk: several hundred (prewar); 5,000 (peak, final).[236] Pro-Khomeini Rebels: there is no published estimate of how many soldiers Khomeini controlled, but the army largely held together until the end, with desertion being far more common than defection. The rebels must have controlled at least 20,000 soldiers, and references to a "small fraction" or "significant fraction" suggest that they may have had as many as 80,000 (20 percent) by the end.[237]

Antecedents: After deposing nationalist prime minister Mossadeq in 1953, Shah Mohammed Reza Pahlavi built his power while undermining institutions that might check his influence. From the 1960s, he ruled Iran as an absolute dictator, attempting to preserve support through a combination of terror by his secret police (SAVAK) and an educational and land reform program called the White Revolution. While incomes increased dramatically, the White Revolution alienated the clergy because of its secular education and the fact that the clergy owned much of the land that was redistributed. During the early 1970s, several resistance groups existed, including the Marxist Fedayeen Kalk and the Mujahideen e-Kalk, who combined Islamic fundamentalism with the leftist nationalism of the National Front (the late Mossadeq's party). Foregoing a formal association with either group, Ayatollah Ruholla Khomeini led underground Muslim societies and neighborhood associations, building mass support for his fundamentalist ideas.

The spark for the violence was a belated government attempt to discredit Khomeini. The attempt backfired as Khomeini's followers rioted in the city of Qom on January 9, resulting in 10 to 100 deaths among the rioters. Exactly forty days later—the traditional Islamic day to mourn the dead—huge demonstrations erupted in Tabriz. The police were unable to repress the demonstrations, and military units were deployed. Although the shah's opponents were divided, the Mujahideen e-Kalk and those loyal to Khomeini were able to coordinate ever-larger demonstrations.

Throughout the summer, the shah tried a variety of tactics to conciliate the opposition, but violence intensified. On June 18, Khomeini called for the shah's overthrow. Although violence mounted in the streets, there was still little if any armed conflict. When a fire in a crowded theater killed 377, many if not most Iranians attributed the arson to SAVAK. In August, the shah attempted to end the disturbances by reshuffling his cabinet and dismissing a number of Bahai officers from the armed forces.

Whatever progress the shah may have made among the moderate opposition was destroyed by the Black Friday massacre on September 8, in which hundreds of protesters were massacred when they demonstrated in defiance of martial law. It was this event that seems to have united the opposition. About a week later, a large earthquake struck Tabas, claiming tens of thousands of lives. The opposition blamed the government for the death toll, arguing that the government failed to take protective measures after an earlier quake.

There was surprisingly little violence from the opposition. On September 5, the Fedayeen bombed a police station (with no casualties reported), but this was essentially the same type of terrorist attack that the Fedayeen had been carrying out for years (from 1977 to 1979, the Fedayeeen lost only twenty-two killed—including those executed). In mid-September, a group wearing military uniforms as disguises ambushed a regular army patrol in Tabriz, killing six. However, these incidents were the exception rather than the rule. In October, the only reported casualties on the government side were about a dozen "hooligans" who had been hired by the government to disrupt protests. It was only in November that sustained armed conflict began to occur.

Narrative: On November 16, three soldiers were killed in Isfahan; a separate incident killed another soldier at about the same time. Three days later, two police were killed. On November 24, a grenade attack inflicted seven battle-deaths on the government; around the same time, a group of ten officials and soldiers were killed in a separate attack. Two more police were killed around the end of the month, and a group of soldiers formed the Revolutionary and Liberation Army, urging other soldiers to defect to them. Given the available data, the November 16 attack best marks the beginning of sustained combat.

The civil war that followed was a different kind of war, characterized by huge masses of urban demonstrators, a small portion of them armed with often makeshift weapons, facing police or military units. That combat occurred in the midst of hundreds of thousands or even millions of demonstrators does not change the fact that armed forces were killing each other.

It was in late November or early December that mass protests adopted a new tactic—persuading or compelling soldiers to distribute arms to the crowd, which were then given to militants. The government's losses mounted in December as armed rebels engaged in guerrilla attacks across the country. The military and police suffered at least 103 killed that month.

Another problem faced by the government was the defection of soldiers to the Revolutionary and Liberation Army. By December 7, some thirty-two garrisons with 5,434 troops had gone over to the rebels. By January 1979, the defections and desertions had reached 1,000 a day, although the vast majority of these were the latter. In general, the army still held together, but the locus of combat now moved from the streets to military bases, where loyalists battled rebels.

By 1979, forces loyal to Khomeini led the revolution. The Fedayeen and Mujahideen had attracted less support, while the National Front remained a largely political organization. It became clear to both sides that the shah would be deposed, but the rebels feared that a coup would replace him with a hostile military junta. Khomeini began reaching out to senior officers. When the shah finally left on January 16, a regency council was formed, and a constitutional government took office led by National Front member Shahpur Bakhtiar. His concessions failed to mollify any of the radical factions (the National Front expelled him), and revolutionaries began to take over government-held towns, installing their own municipal governments. The 12,000 Homafaran (a corps of air force technicians) defected to Khomeini en masse.

Khomeini formed an alternative government under Mehdi Bazargan and proclaimed the existing one to have no authority. This appears to have triggered large-scale combat between units loyal to Khomeini and units loyal to Bakhtiar. The imperial guards, a 30,000-strong unit that had remained loyal to the government, were called upon to put down demonstrations by military personnel and reestablish control over units in and around Tehran. On February 8 and February 9 combat throughout the country claimed at least 394 lives. On February 10, they were repulsed by a combination of mutinous air force personnel and armed leftists in a battle that left 417 dead. The next day, the army declared its neutrality, and Bakhtiar fled the country. The takeover was complete when the shah's palace and barracks of the imperial guards fell on February 12; between 22 and 28 soldiers were killed.

Termination and Outcome: The end of this particular war brought no peace because the new Khomeini regime was almost immediately attacked by some of its partners in revolution (#816). However, the government side had been defeated and never reappeared in the new war. The new regime immediately began executing high-level generals and officials from the old regime, especially the leadership of the imperial guards. In the year following the revolution, at least 582 people were executed.

Coding Decisions: We have made an effort to estimate deaths among those who actively participated in armed struggle on both sides and to exclude the deaths of unarmed civilians. On the government side, about 158 were killed by January 31, 1979. The fighting in February claimed at least 833 lives. Rebel fatalities are not known, but the current government of Iran claims that 744 to 895 were martyred in Tehran, where the vast majority of actual fighting took place. Of course, many of these were civilians. On the basis of this incomplete information, we estimate 1,000 battle-deaths, about evenly split between the government and its armed opponents.

Sources: Arjomand (1988); Arnold (1995); Bashiriyeh (1984); Brogan (1998); Clodfelter (2008); Daneshvar (1996); Parsa (1989).[238]

INTRA-STATE WAR #816
Anti-Khomeini Coalition War of 1979 to 1983

Participants: Iran versus Mujahideen e-Kalk, Fedayeen Kalk, and the Kurdish Democratic Party of Iran.
Dates: February 14, 1979, to December 1983.
Battle-related Deaths: Iran: 3,000; Mujahideen e-Kalk: 1,000; Kurdish Democratic Party of Iran: 4,000; Total Combatant Deaths: about 10,000. (See Coding Decisions.)[239]
Initiator: Iran.
Outcome: Iran wins.
War Type: Civil for control of central government (but see Coding Decisions).
Total System Member Military Personnel: Armed Forces of Iran: 207,500 (initial—this figure is the earliest available but refers to June 1979); 305,000 (peak); 240,000 (final).[240]
Theater Armed Forces: Armed Forces of Iran: 6,000 to 10,000 (initial). Mujahideen e-Kalk, participating from June 20, 1981: 2,000 (prewar); 10,000 (initial, peak).[241] Fedayeen Kalk (multiple factions existed, all of which used the same name; our data describes only the factions fighting the government): 5,000 (prewar, initial, peak).[242] Kurdish Democratic Party of Iran (KDPI), participating until November 1979 and again from May 1980: 10,000 (prewar, initial); 25,500 (peak—8,500 regulars and 17,000 part-time guerrillas).[243]

Antecedents: During the Islamic Revolution, forces loyal to Ayatollah Ruhollah Khomeini came to dominate the resistance. While other rebel movements such as the leftist, secular Fedayeen Kalk were prepared to cooperate against the shah and the Iranian military, they had no intention of allowing themselves to be governed by Khomeini. The Kurdish Democratic Party of Iran, a group demanding regional autonomy, already was engaged in sporadic fighting against the Iranian army as early as January. When parts of it were absorbed by Khomeini during his victory, they simply kept fighting many of the same soldiers for autonomy.

The Fedayeen Kalk and Mujahideen e-Kalk had played key roles defending Khomeini loyalists from the attack of the imperial guard. At the end of the Islamic Revolution, they were in possession of the former government's arsenal and the Tehran arms factory, leaving them well armed and well organized in the capital. They had handed out more than 300,000 weapons in the last days of the civil war. However, instead of being used as the nucleus of a new revolutionary army, they found themselves sidelined as Khomeini ordered the reconstitution of the old regime's armed forces. While the officer corps was decimated by postwar purges, the new regime was able to hold together much of the army, rendering the leftist Fedayeen Kalk and Mujahideen e-Kalk unnecessary. The new provisional government condemned the Fedayeen and raided its offices, causing some factions to opt for immediate armed struggle.

Narrative: The first fighting occurred between pro-government Mujahideen units and the Fedayeen from February 14 to February 18. Khomeini called for Iranians to return the weapons that had been handed out during the last days of the rebellion, but 200,000 remained unaccounted for in Tehran and more than 1 million nationwide. Factions began to take sides. On February 18, the PLO provided 800 fighters for the government's newly formed Pasdaran forces, only 6,000 strong at the time. By the middle of February, the government and loyalist Mujahideen (about one-third of them), the Pasdaran, and units of the army were engaged in hostilities with the Fedayeen.

After being forced out of its positions in Tehran, the Fedayeen resorted to guerrilla warfare against the government. They quickly reached an alliance with the Kurds, supporting their struggle beginning in March. That month, the government reported 200 dead from fighting in Kurdish areas. A major battle near Bona resulted in more than 100 killed. A second round of fighting began on April 20, with the KDPI reporting that 500 were killed in government attacks by April 23. The government resorted to arming pro-government Kurdish tribes in rural areas, especially the Mangur and Zarza. Fighting between the urban KDPI and these tribes broke out in July, but the KDP eventually won the intercommunal battles by allying itself with other rural tribes and organizations, including the Shakak tribe.

The fighting intensified in August, when the KDPI besieged Paveh for three days before government air strikes forced it to retreat. Two government aircraft were shot down, and the rebels beheaded 18 prisoners. On the same day, the government executed 110 Kurds. The KDPI allied itself with one of Iraq's major Kurdish forces, the PUK. It was even able to draw some support from the Barzanis, who formed the backbone of the Iraqi KDP. Mahabad was besieged by the government on August 29, falling after five days of fighting that saw many government soldiers defect to the rebels. By this point, the government estimated that the KDPI had 50,000 fighters in the hills of Kurdistan.

After another heavy bout of fighting in October, the government reached a cease-fire with the KDPI. From November to April, the cease-fire largely held, with only minor skirmishes being reported. Meanwhile, the Fedayeen splintered into several factions, some of which renounced violence against the government by other factions. The seizure of the American embassy and the failure of the April 1980 rescue attempt prompted many on the left to support the government as the best strategy for checking American imperialism.

The fighting between the KDPI and the government resumed in April and intensified in May. The KDPI admitted to losing 1,500 fighters in Sanandaj, while diplomats reported heavy civilian casualties from government air strikes. By the end of May, the KDPI suffered 2,500 battle-deaths against only 500 for the government. In another blow, the Iraqi KDP turned against the KDPI, reaching an agreement with the government to fight the KDPI in return for support against its own government. Some Iranian Kurds with closer ties to Barzani than the KDPI joined the struggle, effectively supporting the Iranian government.

The intensity of the fighting decreased during the summer, as a string of government victories prompted several ranking members of the KDPI to agree to the government's demand for disarmament. When the KDPI expelled them and set up a headquarters in Mahabad, a government offensive took the city. By August, the KDPI was reduced to operating as an underground group and could no longer hold cities against government attacks.

Iraq invaded Iran on September 22, 1980. The invasion fundamentally changed the dynamics of the civil war. During the early months of the war, some 30,000 government soldiers were tied down in actions against the KDPI. By the middle of January, Iraqi forces had reached the positions of the KDPI and now could support it directly. With its front secured, the KDPI was able to recruit additional fighters, bringing its strength to between 7,000 and 10,000 regulars, along with 14,000 to 20,000 part-time guerrillas. A spring offensive retook most of the cities the government had occupied, and a lull in hostilities began as government forces focused their efforts on the Iraqi invasion.

Although fighting subsided on the Kurdish front, the government faced a new challenge in Tehran. Fundamentalists had clashed with Prime Minister Bani Sadr since he was elected, and when they attempted to remove him, the Mujahideen e-Kalk took his side. On June 20, 1981, the MEK openly attacked Khomeini and called for his ouster. Small units of MEK fighters launched insurrections in sixteen cities, and a force of 10,000 marched against the government in Tehran. The first day of fighting killed about 150 people. By August 20, the group claimed to have killed 500 Islamic revolutionary guards.

In its most spectacular actions, the MEK threatened to destroy the country's leadership. On June 28, a bomb planted in the ruling party's headquarters killed the chief justice (one member of the triumvirate that had replaced Bani Sadr), along with four cabinet ministers, twenty-seven members of the legislature, and forty other party functionaries or assistant ministers. On August 20, a bomb planted in the premier's office killed the country's president and premier (the other two members of the triumvirate).

The government's response was extreme. Anyone who participated in antigovernment demonstrations was subject to execution—about 3,300 were executed between June and September. Even children were executed. With the suppression of open opposition, the MEK was limited to bombings and a campaign of assassination against government officials.

Bani Sadr fled the country and formed the National Resistance Council, which was joined by the MEK, KDPI, and Fedayeen Kalk. Fighting continued but at a lower intensity. Occasionally, the MEK would put up a fight—an engagement was fought on September 27—but it was largely reduced to urban guerrilla warfare and terrorism. In late October, they claimed to have reached the 1,000-assassination mark but also had been decimated by executions.

The government launched an offensive against the KDPI in September, with limited success. Although bombings and assassinations continued, there was little real fighting between September 1981 and April 1982, when the government mounted a major offensive against the KDPI. Within three days, 100 Kurds had been killed. After a temporary lull that encouraged the KDPI to overextend itself, the government attack resumed in May, and the KDPI nearly was destroyed. An attempt to organize a counteroffensive in June failed; the organization was no longer able to maintain a cohesive front. Iraqi forces could not save them, for Saddam Hussein had ordered them withdrawn in an unsuccessful gambit for peace. Indeed, Iran now invaded Iraq. The government continued to press the KDPI with an offensive near Urumiyeh from September to November.

After the winter, the government resumed offensive operations in the middle of March 1983. Fighting continued throughout the year, but by the end of 1983, the KDPI was no longer capable of independent military operations in Iran. Its subsequent activities fell below the level of civil war. The other rebel organizations also were largely defeated that year. By September, between 3,000 and 6,000 members or supporters of the MEK had been executed by the government. For their part, the rebels claimed to have killed 2,000 government officials by November. There is no evidence of active combat in 1984.

Termination and Outcome: The government defeated the rebels with a combination of military force and massive repression. The KDPI, the Fedayeen, and the MEK all had been destroyed or forced to flee into Iraq. There was no amnesty, and executions continued into 1985. Iraq subsequently rebuilt the MEK and KDPI and used them against Iran in 1987 and 1988; they succeeded in killing thousands of Iranian soldiers. However, we do not consider these battles to be part of a civil war because the bulk of the fighting clearly was being done by Iraq rather than the rebels.

Coding Decisions: The government lost more than 500 soldiers against the MEK in the first two months of its rebellion and thousands against the Kurds (although lower estimates exist). Casualties against the Fedayeen are unknown but are unlikely to be larger than those against the MEK. A conservative estimate of government battle-deaths is 3,000. The most precise estimate of MEK deaths is 7,746 (including executions) through September 1983, with 85 percent being executions, 90 percent of which were MEK. If true, this would limit MEK battle-deaths to about 1,000. This is our best estimate. We have no estimate for the Fedayeen Kalk, but it would be surprising if their battle-deaths were much lower than 1,000. KDPI battle-death estimates range from 4,000 to 27,000. We find 4,000 to be the most plausible estimate, given that its source is the rebels themselves and that it distinguishes between military and civilian fatalities. This provides us with our estimate of 10,000 battle-deaths, which easily could be an underestimate.

Iraq surely deployed some troops in Iranian Kurdistan during its war with Iran, but it does not appear to have been intervening for the rebels in any meaningful sense but rather prosecuting its separate inter-state war against Iran. The Iraqi Kurdish factions (KDP and PUK) as well as the armed political party Komala also participated in the fighting, although we have no information about how many combatants were on Iranian soil at any one time. In general, the KDP sided with Iran, the PUK sided with the KDPI, and Komala was allied to the KDPI. The PLO provided 800 fighters for the government's newly formed Pasdaran forces, but because it is unclear whether these troops were Palestinians or PLO-trained Iranians, and because they were absorbed into the Pasdaran, we do not list them as separate actors.

The KDPI was fighting for autonomy, while its allies were fighting to control the central government. Because the latter was a precondition for the former, we code this as a war for control of the central government.

Sources: Abrahamian (1989); Bakhash (1984); Brogan (1998); Cordesman and Wagner (1990a, b); Coyle (1993); Hiro (1985); McDowall (1996); O'Ballance (1997); Rose (1984); Stempel (1981).[244]

INTRA-STATE WAR #826.5
Hama Uprising of 1982 (aka Muslim Brotherhood Rebellion)

Participants: Syria versus Muslim Brotherhood.
Dates: February 3, 1982, to February 28, 1982.
Battle-related Deaths: Syria: 1,000;[245] Muslim Brotherhood: 2,000; Total Combatant Deaths: 3,000. (See Coding Decisions.)[246]
Initiator: Muslim Brotherhood.
Outcome: Syria wins.
War Type: Civil for central control.

Total System Member Military Personnel: Armed Forces of Syria: 300,000 (prewar, initial, peak, final).[247]
Theater Armed Forces: Armed Forces of Syria: 300 (initial); 12,000 (peak). Muslim Brotherhood: 400 (prewar, initial); 2,400 (peak).[248]

Antecedents: The Muslim Brotherhood had long opposed the ʿAlawi (a branch of Shiism) regime in Syria. From June 16, 1979 (when an attack killed 60 unarmed army cadets), to the end of 1981, the Muslim Brotherhood killed perhaps 300 people, while the government executed more than 1,000. The largest action by the Muslim Brotherhood was a car bombing of a military headquarters in Damascus in November 1981; the attack killed more than 150 people. The government followed a general strategy of occupying cities where the Muslim Brotherhood was strong, then searching for weapons in an attempt to disarm them.

Narrative: On February 2, 1982, a force of 300 government troops entered the city of Hama to disarm the Muslim Brotherhood. In response, the Muslim Brotherhood—about 400 strong in Hama—ambushed them and killed about 100 government and party representatives in the city. Either sympathy with the rebels or fear of the government's indiscriminate attacks on Hama (artillery bombarded the city, while whole families were taken out and shot by the army) caused about 2,000 citizens to join the fight against the government. In addition, parts of the Twenty-first and Forty-seventh Brigades refused to fire on the rebels, although the rest of the army remained loyal.

A small war followed as the government stormed rebel positions, suffering high casualties in the process. The government committed 12,000 soldiers to the struggle. By February 5, the rebels had been reduced to less than 1,000 fighters. Nevertheless, fighting continued until February 28, when the last pockets of resistance were eliminated.

Termination and Outcome: The outcome was an unconditional government victory. The government conducted mass executions of suspected opponents, although the disloyal elements of the Twenty-first and Forty-seventh Brigades were merely expelled from the armed forces. The Muslim Brotherhood in Syria was all but destroyed by the operation and did not mount any more major attacks.

Coding Decisions: No estimate of rebel battle-deaths is available, but only a handful of Muslim Brotherhood made it out alive. Given this, we conclude that an estimate of 2,000 battle-deaths is reasonable, although the real total could be lower. The most credible range of total fatalities is 5,000 to 25,000 total deaths, but these figures include both civilian deaths and mass executions. Because all the authors agree that most of those killed were civilians, we simply add our estimates for government and rebel battle-deaths together to arrive at our estimate of 3,000 battle-deaths.

Sources: Abd-Allah (1983); Clodfelter (2008); DeAtkine (2009); Middle East Watch (1991); Van Dam (1996).[249]

INTRA-STATE WAR #833

Fourth Lebanese War of 1983 to 1984

Participants: Lebanon, Lebanese Forces, United States, and France versus Amal, Progressive Socialist Party, Palestinians (Aggregate), Iran, Hezbollah, and Syria.
Dates: April 18, 1983, to February 29, 1984.
Battle-related Deaths: United States: 264; France: 74; Total Combatant Deaths: 1,000. (See Coding Decisions.)[250]
Initiator: Hezbollah and Progressive Socialist Party.
Outcome: Negotiated settlement.
War Type: Civil for central control.
Total System Member Military Personnel: Armed Forces of Lebanon: 27,500 (prewar, initial, peak—figures include internal security personnel).[251] Armed Forces of the United States: 2,201,000 (prewar, initial); 2,222,000 (peak, final). Armed Forces of France: 578,000 (prewar, initial, peak); 571,000 (final). Armed Forces of Iran: 240,000 (prewar, initial); 335,000 (peak, final). Armed Forces of Syria: 400,000 (prewar, initial); 402,000 (peak, final).[252]
Theater Armed Forces: Lebanese Forces, aka Phalange, participating throughout war, but only cooperated with the government from July 1983: 10,000 (prewar, initial, peak); 6,000 (final).[253] United States, participating until February 26, 1984: 1,600 (prewar, initial, peak—about 400 were stationed offshore).[254] France, participating from September 22, 1983: 2,000

(prewar, initial, peak).[255] Amal, participating from July 1983: 2,000 (prewar, initial); 4,000 (peak, final).[256] Progressive Socialist Party, aka Druze Rebels, participating from May 5 at the latest: 800 (prewar); more than 4,000 (peak).[257] Palestinians (participation dates unclear): 2,000 (peak).[258] Hezbollah (includes Islamic Amal): 180 (prewar).[259] Iran, participating sporadically during the war, assisting Hezbollah against the Lebanese armed forces: 1,500 (prewar, initial, peak, final).[260] Syria (participation dates unclear): 40,000 (peak).[261]

Antecedents: This phase of Lebanon's long period of conflict from 1975 to 1989 followed the Israeli invasion of Lebanon and its subsequent war against Syria and the PLO (see Inter-state War #205). The invasion temporarily eliminated the PLO as an organized military force in Lebanon and greatly strengthened the position of Maronite Christian-affiliated actors against Muslim- and Druze-affiliated ones. The war caused the collapse of the National Salvation Committee, which had brought together leaders of the major militias for dialogue.

After the new Maronite Christian president was assassinated, his militia forces took revenge by massacring inhabitants of two Palestinian refugee camps. His successor and brother Amin Gemayel was also a member of the Lebanese Forces (LF, or Phalange) militia, which had carried out the attacks. Soon LF forces were fighting Druze forces in the Chouf and Muslims in the South. Gemayel's orders to disarm were ignored by the LF, which feared for its security once Israel withdrew from Beirut. The Lebanese army moved in to fill the security vacuum created by the withdrawal, and a search for "illegal" Palestinians and arms turned up a few hundred detainees and $138 million worth of weapons. The government further demolished the homes of some "illegal" Shiites, earning the enmity of the Shiite community. The control of the army gradually was extended to the LF-dominated East Beirut, and illegal ports were closed down to redirect revenue to the state.

By all appearances, the state was resuming control of the country and the radicals of both sides had been defeated or outmaneuvered. However, an anti-Gemayel coalition began to emerge. In the north, 800 Iranian revolutionary guards had entered the country during the war with Israel; they subsequently were reinforced by 700 more Pasdaran. They trained and armed Shiite revolutionaries, splitting with Amal to form the Islamic Amal Movement, which eventually became part of Hezbollah.

On November 22, 1982, the Pasdaran attacked and overran an army barracks near Baalbek. And while the Pasdaran stayed out of fighting in south Lebanon, their Lebanese affiliates began to attack remaining Israeli troops in the region. Meanwhile, the United States openly aligned with the Lebanese army, seeking to build its capabilities and conducting joint patrols using the American component of the Multinational Force (MNF). Armed conflict remained at a low level until mid-1983, although sporadic attacks on the MNF occurred in the first months of 1983.

Narrative: On April 18, 1983, a suicide bomber attacked the American embassy. Among the sixty-five killed were seven CIA officers, several soldiers, and a marine. This attack most clearly demarcates the previous period from the subsequent civil war as it marked a clear escalation of the level of violence. Responsibility was claimed by a pro-Iranian Shiite group, the small Islamic Jihad Organization.

On May 7, the American marines of the MNF were ordered to protect the US embassy. Joint patrols with the Lebanese armed forces continued. Iranian-affiliated groups continued to attack the MNF and government forces throughout the year, particularly after the government finalized a peace treaty with Israel on May 17. Government security forces fired upon Shiite demonstrators on May 17 and again on July 9. By July, Amal had joined the fighting against the government in the Shiite neighborhoods of Beirut.

By this time, the government had come into conflict with the largely Druze militia of Walid Jumblatt's Progressive Socialist Party. On May 5, Druze forces shelled the international airport, claiming to be targeting the Lebanese army. Full-scale hostilities erupted on July 14, when PSP militiamen ambushed a government patrol, killing fourteen government soldiers at a cost of two Druze killed. Afterward, shelling of the airport resumed, killing thirty, mostly civilians, in the first few days. Sporadic artillery duels continued through the summer, with government accusing Syria of joining in the shelling. On September 1, Jumblatt declared that the "Druze are now in a state of war" against the government.[262]

Beginning in mid-August, a general strike took place in West Beirut. This marked the onset of two weeks of combat between Amal and the Lebanese army. At the end of August, Amal's attacks against the MNF triggered a military assault by the Lebanese army, backed by the artillery and helicopter gunships of the MNF. In four days, at least 79 were killed and 326 wounded. One source places government fatalities at 40 and Amal battle-deaths at "many more."[263]

By July, there was active cooperation between the Maronite Christian Lebanese Forces militia and the Lebanese army. A joint operation against Druze fighters was undertaken near Aley in early September, and the government allowed the LF into areas it had captured. The Lebanese government insisted that it was fighting Syrians and Palestinians, while the Druze denied any direct military support from other groups or states. Israel sometimes actively cooperated with the LF, providing transport and artillery support, while at other times it forcibly evicted them from their positions. Also in early September, American warships began shelling Druze positions in response to casualties suffered by the MNF.

On September 3, Israel withdrew its forces from the Shouf. Almost immediately, conflict broke out between the army and the LF on one side and 4,000 PSP and 2,000 Palestinians, backed by Syrian armor and artillery fire, on the other. Druze fighters overran Bhamdoun on September 6 and killed about 1,500 Christians, destroying 62 villages. Fighting between the Syrian-armed Druze and the government led to a major battle for control of Souk al-Garb; the army succeeded in beating back the Druze attack with American and French air support, although it was unable to take fortified Druze positions nearby. The Druze laid siege to the town and to Deir el-Kamar. After a French UN soldier was killed by a Druze attack on September 22, French warplanes joined air strikes on Druze and Syrian gun emplacements.

On September 16, Islamic Amal occupied the Baalbek barracks in the Bekaa Valley. This was made possible by extensive support from the Iranian Pasdaran. In response to this and other incidents of direct Pasdaran support for Hezbollah-affiliated forces in the Bekaa, the government eventually broke diplomatic relations with Iran on November 23.

Despite foreign support, the Lebanese army was beginning to crack. Its poorly equipped units had taken at least 163 killed and 958 wounded. More than 800 Druzes defected to the PSP. Furthermore, the army's units were disproportionately Shiite, and these personnel routinely refused to fight Amal. On October 1, Jumblatt declared a zone of local autonomy for his Druze forces. In early November, the commander of the Israeli-trained Shiite brigade of the Lebanese armed forces announced his intention to defect to Amal.

On October 23, two truck bombs struck the American and French MNF forces. The attacks killed 241 US marines and 59 French soldiers. The Shiite extremist group the Islamic Jihad Organization claimed credit for both attacks; the MNF responded with air strikes against the positions of Iran-affiliated groups such as Islamic Amal and by continuing strikes against the Druze.

The net effect of the truck bombings was to undermine the staying power of Lebanon's allies. On December 8, the United States redeployed offshore 300 marines. On December 15, the sieges of Souk al-Garb and Deir el-Kamar were lifted by the Druze, permitting thousands of Christian civilians and hundreds of LF fighters to exit the towns. The French began to evacuate some of their positions in Beirut, and fighting between the Lebanese army and Amal broke out over possession of these positions on December 24. Jumblatt's Druze militia joined the battle against the Lebanese army, which was forced to withdraw after five days of fighting.

Peace initiatives were frequent but also unsuccessful. After unproductive talks in January 1983, Jumblatt declared them to be a waste of time on February 1. A few days later, a joint offensive by Amal and the PSP hit the Lebanese army in West Beirut. The offensive led to the heaviest fighting in Beirut since the 1975-to-1976 intercommunal war (see Intra-state War #801). After a call for Muslims to defect from the army, government forces began to disintegrate. The Druze Fourth Brigade in Aley was rendered incapable of combat by a mutiny and bloodletting, allowing Jumblatt's militia to take control of the area. And when Shiites on the Sixth Brigade deserted or remained in their barracks, the army was defeated in a two-day battle for West Beirut that left 300 to 600 dead (mostly civilians) and at least 800 wounded.

American warships fired on Druze positions in the hills, but this failed to save government forces from defeat. On February 13, the Druze managed to drive out the Lebanese army and LF units from a series of towns in the Chouf, and Amal drove them out of the southern approaches to Beirut over the next two days. Much of the capital had fallen to the rebels. On February 14, the United States announced that it would fully withdraw its remaining marines from Lebanon within thirty days. Over the next weeks, the rebels also took Souk al-Garb and shelled the presidential palace at Baabda. The American marines reembarked on February 26, handing over control of Beirut's airport to mutinous Shiite units of the Lebanese armed forces.

Termination and Outcome: The outcome of the war was a negotiated settlement that amounted to a limited rebel victory. On February 29, Gemayel visited Syria and reached an agreement with its leader to abrogate the treaty with Israel and meet several other rebel demands. The rebels did not succeed in assuming the presidency, but they captured and held West Beirut and all but destroyed the Lebanese army. The fighting had not ended, but the civil war had. Future fighting would be intercommunal until some semblance of control was reestablished over some Lebanese army units.

In the wake of the rebel victory, a general ceasefire settled over Beirut, which was largely observed and subsequently formalized on March 12. As MNF forces evacuated their positions, Amal assumed control of them, eventually handing over formal authority to the Lebanese army's Sixth Brigade, which consisted mainly of Shiites with a Shiite commander.

Coding Decisions: On the basis of the limited information available, we conclude that many of the dead were civilians. Based on the number of battles and their intensity (see Narrative), we are nonetheless confident that at least 1,000 battle-deaths were suffered by the various participants in the war.

Sources: Chebabi (2006); Hallenbeck (1991); Hiro (1993); O'Ballance (1998); Ranstorp (1997); Russell (1985).[264]

INTRA-STATE WAR #834

Second South Sudan War of 1983 to 2002

Participants: Sudan, Libya, Murahileen, Mundari Tribe (Aggregate), Eritrean People's Liberation Front, Sudan People's Liberation Army (Nasir), Western Bank Nile Front, Lord's Resistance Army, South Sudan Defense Force, and South Sudan Unity Movement versus Anya Nya II, 105th Battalion in Bor, Sudan People's Liberation Army (Garang), Uganda, Darfur Militias (Aggregate), Sudan Alliance Forces, and Beja Congress Force.

Dates: May 17, 1983, to September 10, 1991, and March 9, 1992, to October 15, 2002.

Battle-related Deaths: Total Combatant Deaths: 100,000. (See Coding Decisions.)[265]

Initiator: 105th Battalion at Bor and Anya Nya II.

Outcome: Negotiated settlement.

War Type: Civil for central control (but see Coding Decisions).

Total System Member Military Personnel: Armed Forces of Sudan: 86,000 (prewar); 65,000 (after initial defections); 117,000 (peak, final); Armed Forces of Libya: 68,000 (prewar, initial); 91,000 (peak); 76,000 (final). Armed Forces of Uganda: 13,000 (prewar initial); 70,000 (peak); 55,000 (final).[266]

Theater Armed Forces:

Pro-government: Armed Forces of Sudan: 20,000 in Juba alone (1992). Libyans, participating from March 5, 1986, to April 1987—the force still existed in Sudan after this date but seems to have limited itself to fighting the government of Chad and local militias, not the SPLA: 2,000 (peak).[267] Murahileen/PDF, participating from 1984: 150,000 (peak).[268] Mundari Tribal Militia, participating in the mid-1980s but largely defected to the SPLM in 1988: 10,000 (peak).[269] Eritrean People's Liberation Front, participating from October 1989 to early 1990: one brigade (initial, peak).[270] Sudan People's Liberation Army (Nasir)/ Sudan People's Liberation Army—United/South Sudan Independence Movement, clearly cooperated with the government from 1992 to 1997, when the South Sudan Defense Force was formed from its pro-government remnants: more than 2,000 (peak).[271] Western Bank Nile Front, participating from August 1995 to 2000: 2,000 (peak, final).[272] Lord's Resistance Army, participating from 2000: 4,500 in Sudan (peak).[273] South Sudan Defense Force/UDSF, participating from 1997: [ ]. South Sudan Unity Movement/ Army, participating from 1998: [ ].

Pro-Rebel: Anya Nya II, participating from the beginning of the war, turned to the government by 1984, ceased fighting the rebels in late 1985, and eventually was absorbed in large part by the

SPLA: [ ].[274] 105th Battalion in Bor, participating to July 1983, when most of its members joined the SPLA: 1,000 (initial, peak); 500 to 600 (final).[275] Sudan People's Liberation Army (Garang Faction), aka SPLA–Torit or SPLA Mainsream, participating from July 1983: 500 to 600 (initial); 55,000 (peak—1991 estimate that takes into account the subsequent creation of the New Sudan Brigade in the North, which may have numbered up to 2,000); 25,000 (final).[276] Uganda, participating in 1986 on the government side but was then overthrown and replaced by a pro-rebel regime, participating on the rebel side from 1987 to January 1990 and again from September 1995 to an unknown date after April 22, 1997, but before 2000: 14,000 (peak).[277] Darfur Militias, participating from November 1990 to late 1991, when the SPLA was driven from Darfur, making coordination between the two implausible: [ ]. Sudan Alliance Forces/NDF, participating from June 1995: 500 (initial, peak).[278] Beja Congress Force, participating from 1995: 500 (initial); more than 500 (peak).[279]

Antecedents: At the conclusion of the First South Sudan War (Intra-state War #758) there were some Anya Nya rebels who refused to join the Addis Ababa Accord of 1972, naming themselves Anya Nya II. Despite this fact, and despite incidents of mutiny by former Anya Nya soldiers integrated into government forces, the peace agreement held until 1982, when the government decided to abrogate its terms.

In September 1982, the government ordered southern garrisons—the guarantors of the peace agreement—to move into the North, where they would be surrounded by loyal troops. Garrisons at Bor, Pachalla, and Pibor refused. More Bor troops refused orders from the central government in February, and over the next two months a series of mutinies occurred in Bor. On May 16, 1983, the garrisons of Pibor and Bor mutinied again, but this time the government moved to quash the rebellion militarily.

Narrative: On May 17, the rebels of Bor ambushed government troops and inflicted a defeat on them. Over the next few days, however, the government defeated the mutineers at the cost of 70 killed. The mutineers fled into the bush, some to join Anya Nya II and some to organize a new resistance movement under former Anya Nya rebel John Garang in July. This new organization was called the Sudanese People's Liberation Movement/Army (SPLM/SPLA) and advocated the overthrow of the central government, as opposed to the secessionist Anya Nya II.

By July 1983, about 3,000 soldiers had defected to the rebels. By September, fighting broke out between the SPLM and Anya Nya II over leadership of the rebellion. The Ethiopian army aided the SPLM against Anya Nya II, and by 1984, Anya Nya II—nearly eliminated as a fighting force—turned to the government for support against the SPLM, accepting arms to continue its intercommunal struggle. On September 8, 1983, the government began to implement *sharia* law, which was anathema to most Christian and animist Southerners. In December, two weeks of battle in Nasir led to inflated claims of casualties by both sides, the government claiming that 400 rebels had been killed.

The SPLM had grown rapidly from its original strength of 500 to 600 deserters to an army of 2,000 at the end of 1983. It grew further in 1984 (as many as 15,000 fighters) and 1985 (20,000). Ethiopia began to support the rebels with arms, sanctuaries, artillery support, and air support. Libya initially shipped arms to the rebels in April 1985 but supported the government thereafter. East Germany and Bulgaria provided training for the rebels, and by January 1986 so did Cuba.

In mid-1985, a major SPLA offensive against Anya Nya II (now a pro-government militia) failed with heavy losses. In late 1985, a truce was reached between the two groups. Over the next few years, Anya Nya II fighters deserted to the SPLM en masse, until agreements made from 1987 to 1989 finally incorporated the remnants of the organization into the SPLM. In 1988, a reported 10,000 members of the Mundari pro-government militia also deserted to the SPLA.

The infighting did not preclude conflict between government troops and rebel forces, and the government suffered heavy losses in 1984 and 1985. In 1986, a coup overthrew the government, and the new government did nothing to enforce *sharia*—but also declined to repeal it. A Ugandan rebel group called UNLA fled into Sudan, where they received support from the government in return for defending towns from the SPLA. In May 1987, 14,000 Ugandan troops entered Sudan, fighting together with the SPLA against UNLA and Sudanese government forces. Relations between Sudan and Uganda deteriorated further over the next few years, and the two states fought a number of border skirmishes in 1989. That year, the Ugandans began to withdraw troops and substitute advisors to the SPLA.

Meanwhile, Libya was supporting the government, with Libya deploying about 800 advisors to the Sudan on March 5, 1986. In May of that year, the Libyans not only coordinated an offensive against the SPLM but also flew air support for the government offensive. By February 1987, about 2,000 "Libyans" were in Sudan. Libya claimed that half were native Sudanese and the other half were mostly Chadian volunteers from its Islamic brigades. From April 17 to April 24, the Chadian army entered Sudan's Darfur province and all but destroyed the Libyan and Chadian forces operating there. Another incursion in November killed 200 of the "Libyan" force. A failed counterattack killed 44 of the "Libyans." By January 1988, more than 3,000 had been killed in just one year of fighting in the peripheral front of Darfur.

Also in 1987, the rebels focused on weakening government garrisons, even if this meant disrupting food supplies to civilians. Starvation claimed many lives—virtually all civilians—in Malakal. The government carried out massacres of the Dinka and Nuer tribes, considered loyal to the SPLA. The SPLA captured Kurmak and Gizen in the Arab North, potentially threatening Khartoum itself. "Libyan" troops recaptured the towns later in the year, just after the SPLA evacuated them.

In 1988, violence spread to Khartoum, as nearly 1 million refugees flooded the city. On January 25, the SPLA captured Kapoeta and made as if to defend it. Once the government prepared an expedition to retake the city, the SPLA withdrew and attacked garrisons elsewhere that had been weakened by the government's concentration against Kapoeta. By the end of 1988, the SPLA was at least 21,000 strong and may have numbered more.

In 1989, the rebels inflicted a series of defeats on government forces, taking and holding sixteen garrison towns. The government turned to recruiting and arming units from neutral tribes in the South to provide it with a better counterinsurgency capability. Former Anya Nya leader Joseph Lagu gave the government his support for mobilizing the south against the SPLA. On June 30, a coup by an Islamic fundamentalist overthrew the government, ending what had been tentative peace feelers by both sides. More talks were held later in the year, but the rebels' demand for the repeal of *sharia* was unacceptable to the new government. The SPLA nearly doubled in size, reaching a strength of perhaps 50,000 fighters.

Despite these successes, the rebels lost a key regional ally when the government of Ethiopia began to lose its civil war. Ethiopia was providing the SPLA with artillery support, but in 1989 an entire EPLF brigade, with assistance from the Sudanese government, mounted an offensive on Sudanese territory against the SPLA. The EPLF redeployed to Ethiopia in early 1990, but conflict continued even after the EPLF (as a member of the successful EPDRF) won its civil war, as it sought to evict SPLA units from Ethiopian soil in 1991. Once the government of Ethiopia collapsed, the SPLM changed its demands to include a referendum on secession in the South, moving away from a strictly revolutionary line.

During 1990, the war was marked by government attempts to relieve its beleaguered garrisons in the South, which often gave the rebels opportunities to ambush government columns. By this point in the war, the government was also arming northern nomadic tribes and setting them loose on tribes it considered disloyal. The Dinka were particularly hard-hit by this strategy, which was eventually responsible for the Darfur genocide (see Intra-state Wars #866 and 927). The rebels lost another regional ally as Uganda largely stayed out of Sudan after 1990 except for the occasional hit-and-run operation against Ugandan insurgents.

On August 28, 1991, the SPLM split into two factions, largely along tribal lines. The SPLM–Garang faction continued its largely revolutionary orientation, while three of thirteen commanders formed the SPLM–Nasir faction, which called for independence for the South. The SPLM Nasir already may have approached the government at this stage for its support. In any case, the two sides engaged each other in an intercommunal war (see Intra-state War #866), and thousands of Dinka, viewed as associated with the SPLM–Garang, were killed by SPLM–Nasir fighters from the Nuer and Shilluk tribes. The remnants of Anya Nya II also sided with the Nasir faction against Garang. The period of that war is coded as a break in this war from September 11, 1991, to March 8, 1992.

By early 1992, the rebels reported combat with Iranian troops, alleging that 8,000 Iranians were fighting in the South. In truth, the Iranian presence was limited to a relatively small number of advisors who trained government military units. The war resumed on March 9, as the government mounted a major offensive that succeeded in taking many rebel strongholds and relieving sieges of southern garrisons. By the time that the offensive ended in mid-July, the government had suffered perhaps 3,000 killed in the fighting. SPLM–Nasir reached an agreement with the government in 1992 and formed the SPLM–United faction on March 27, 1993, absorbing other anti-SPLM–Garang groups in the South. Meanwhile, the Organization of African Unity (OAU) conducted peace talks between May 1992 and May 1993.

On August 5, 1993, the government mounted a major offensive against SPLM–Garang. Renewed fighting broke out between the SPLM factions. In addition, the SPLM–United witnessed an intercommunal struggle between the Lou Nuer and Jikany Nuer. By February 1994, the SPLM–United was disintegrating as the government mounted another offensive against SPLM–Garang. A faction opposed to coordination with the government broke off as the SSIM/SSIA.

From 1995 to 1997, the SPLM–Garang faction and an alliance of anti-Khartoum groups called the National Democratic Front (NDF) won some successes against government forces. On June 1995, the NDF had founded a northern resistance army called the Sudanese allied forces, consisting of about 500 combatants. The SPLM–Garang had 30,000 fighters.

After a rebel offensive in September 1997, the government claimed that 7,000 Ugandan and Tanzanian soldiers fought on behalf of the rebels; both governments denied involvement. But on October 25, Ugandan army units supported an SPLA–Garang attack on government positions in Parajok and Magure. In return, the SPLA–Garang repeatedly clashed with Ugandan rebel groups operating in the South, ambushing a group of 4,000 insurgents and their families, killing 2,000 and capturing more than 1,000. Eritrean forces also operated in the Sudan that year, supporting the NDF in the North.

The front line stabilized somewhat in 1998, as the SPLM–Garang tried and failed to take Wau and Torat. Meanwhile, splits in the SPLM–United had produced twelve different small groups by 1997. The intra-Nuer struggle continued until 1999 or 2000, when the Nuer united to form the SSLM, opposed to the government but not allied with any other rebel groups.

In April 1997, the SSIM reached a peace accord with the government, as did several other former factions of the SPLM–United. The rebels were integrated into a pro-government militia called the SSDF, but in January 1998 its leader defected back to the SPLM–Garang, with a handful of troops in tow. The government encouraged a breakaway faction of the SSDF, the SSUM, and then used it to attack the SSDF, forcing the latter into open rebellion once more. In 1999, more than 1,000 SSUM troops defected to SPLA–Garang, while another group defected to the SSDF. The government simply could not rely on its southern militias (probably because it kept violating its agreements with them—agreements that had called for autonomy for the South).

In January 2000, yet another rebel group, the SSLM, formed in the Upper Nile. The fighting continued, with an unsuccessful advance by the SPLA–Garang into Darfur in 2001, but efforts to reach a peace agreement finally bore fruit in 2002. On July 20, a peace agreement between the government and the SPLM–Garang was signed, providing for *sharia* law in the North but self-determination for the South.

Nevertheless, fighting continued as each side sought to improve its position at the peace talks. In September, the SPLM seized Torit, which brought the Ugandan Lord's Resistance Army (LRA) into the war. On March 26, Sudanese army troops had clashed with LRA forces in the South. More than twenty-four government troops were killed. But soon the government had reached an accommodation with the LRA and in October, the LRA aided government forces retaking Torit from the SPLM–Garang.

Termination and Outcome: On October 15, 2002, the SPLM–Garang and the government signed a cease-fire for the South. The cease-fire essentially ended the conflict between the two factions, even though now-independent conflicts with rebel groups in western Upper Nile and Darfur (see Intra-state War #927) escalated. The outcome of the war was a negotiated settlement, although it would be three years (2005) before the terms of that settlement were finalized. Six years after the settlement, South Sudan gained independence through a referendum provided for in the 2005 Comprehensive Peace Agreement. Given the SPLM's revolutionary ambitions, secession was not the complete rebel victory it might have seemed, and territorial disputes between Sudan and South Sudan continued to pose the danger of escalation.

Coding Decisions: About 2 million died in the civil war, but the vast majority was civilians felled by famine and disease. We estimate 100,000 battle-deaths, but the real battle-death toll easily could be half or double this figure. Ethiopia militarily aided the rebels from September 1983 to October 1989 and again from October 1995 to May 12, 1998, but with too few troops to qualify as a war participant.[280] Similarly, Eritrea fought sporadically, definitely operating in Sudan during October 1995 and April 1997, but there is no evidence that it met the 1,000 troop and 100 battle-death threshold.[281] Note that the South Sudan Liberation Movement is excluded for lack of coordination with either side, Iran is excluded for lack of personnel in the war zone, and about a dozen domestic groups are excluded due to lack of evidence of participation in combat. For a more comprehensive review of the plague of initials in Sudan, see Johnson (2003). Some of the rebels were secessionists, but the main rebel forces were revolutionary, and we thus code this case as a civil war for control of the central government.

Sources: Anderson (1999); Barltrop (2011); Burr and Collins (2003); De Waal (2004); Glickson (2005); Human Rights Watch (2003); Hutchinson (2001); Jendia (2002); Johnson (2003); Johnson and Prunier (1993); Lacey (2002); Laffin (1989, 1990, 1991); O'Ballance (2000); Ofransky (2000); Petterson (2003); Prunier (2005); Rolandson (2005); Say (2005).[282]

INTRA-STATE WAR #840
Fifth Iraqi Kurds War of 1985 to 1988

Participants: Iraq and Jash versus Kurdish Democratic Party, Patriotic Union of Kurdestan, Iraqi Communist Party, Socialist Party of Kurdistan–Iraq, and Iran.
Dates: January 1985 to August 28, 1988.
Battle-related Deaths: Total Combatant Deaths: more than 4,000. (See Coding Decisions.)
Initiator: Iraq.
Outcome: Iraq wins.
War Type: Civil for local issues (autonomy).
Total System Member Military Personnel: Armed Forces of Iraq: 788,000 (prewar, initial); 1 million (peak, final). Armed Forces of Iran: 345,000 (prewar, initial); 654,000 (peak, final).[283]
Theater Armed Forces: Jash: 20,000 (prewar—1983 estimate); 150,000 to 250,000 (peak).[284] Kurdish Democratic Party: 6,000 (initial); 10,000 (peak).[285] Patriotic Union of Kurdistan: 5,000 (initial); 10,000 (peak).[286] Iraqi Communist Party: more than 1,000 (initial).[287] Socialist Party of Kurdistan-Iraq: less than 1,000 (initial); 1,500 (peak).[288] No in-theater estimates for Iraq or Iran are available.

Antecedents: By 1975, Iraq had destroyed the military capacity of the main Kurdish parties, leaving them with few alternatives but negotiation or low-intensity conflict. Moreover, Iran ceased supporting the Iraqi Kurds in any meaningful way. The split between the largest two Kurdish rebel groups, the Patriotic Union of Kurdistan (PUK) and Kurdish Democratic Party (KDP), widened, and internecine violence was common.

In 1980, Iraq invaded Iran. While fighting was initially confined to Iranian territory, Syria used the opportunity to back the PUK against Iraq, while Iran harnessed the KDP in Iran, fighting against Iran's own Kurdish rebels (the KDPI). The rebellion achieved little; Saddam Hussein's government actually was able to reduce its troops in Kurdistan, instead relying on Jash (pro-government Kurds) to defend itself in the Kurdish regions.

In 1983, the war with Iran moved onto Iraqi territory; in July, Iran opened a second front by conducting a joint operation with the KDP to seize the border town of Hajj Umran. The government retaliated by executing 8,000 Barzani males. The PUK was hard-hit by the Iranian offensive, being forced to move its headquarters closer to Iraqi troops. It therefore reached out to the Iraqi government, and a PUK–government cease-fire was signed in December. At least 3,000 PUK supporters promptly defected to the KDP, which was in an alliance with smaller rebel groups the Iraqi Communist Party (ICP) and the Socialist Party of Kurdistan–Iraq (SPKI). In March 1984, the peace talks broke down entirely, but the cease-fire remained in place.

Narrative: Assured of American support, the Iraqi government decided that it no longer wished to grant enough Kurdish demands to end the conflict. The cease-fire collapsed, and the PUK returned to conflict with the government in January 1985. Having lost Syrian sponsorship due to its cease-fire with the Iraqi government, PUK now sought to align itself with the KDP and Iran but initially found itself in conflict with both them and the government.

Most of the conflict took the form of guerrilla warfare. Hundreds of small guerrilla units roamed the countryside, while the government controlled the cities and could send patrols to any area at will. The government mounted a major offensive against the PUK in autumn of 1985, razing 199 villages and killing hundreds of civilians. Hundreds more, including children, were arrested.

Kurdish operations expanded in 1986. The KDP captured Manjish in May and then besieged Dohuk. The PUK waged fierce battles around Sulaymaniya. In October, the PUK shelled the oil refineries of Kirkuk. By 1987 the Kurdish groups controlled most of the countryside. The reasons for this success appear to have included the extension of the draft to Kurds, which caused many Kurds to defect to the rebels, including an entire battalion of 400 men with their weapons. Another reason is that the government withdrew some units to deal with repeated Iranian offensives. Finally, the PUK and KDP reached an accommodation in 1986, and Iran subsequently gave significant aid to the former.

By May 1987, all major anti-regime forces were allied to one another under the umbrella of the Kurdistan Front. The month before, Kurdish forces—in concert with Iranian formations—had seized the heights around Sulaymaniya, inflicting heavy casualties on government forces. Rawanduz, Shaqlawa, and Atrush quickly fell to the combined Iranian–Kurdish forces. The government resorted to chemical attacks on Kurdish villages and razed 500 villages from April to September. The Iranians responded by distributing gas masks to the rebel *peshmerga*, which limited rebel casualties but did nothing for civilians.

By February 1988, the Iranians and Kurds had mounted another joint offensive, seizing more of Kurdistan and killing or wounding 600 Iraqi troops. The Iraqi government responded to the new threat with a series of genocidal operations against the Kurds, collectively known as Operation Anfal. In February, the government attacked the Jafati valley, indiscriminately targeting villages with airpower and artillery. After three weeks of fighting, the government retook the area; its prisoners "disappeared." By this point in the conflict, 12 towns and 3,000 villages had been destroyed by the government.

On March 15, PUK and Iranian forces captured Halabja, inflicting heavy losses on government troops. The following day, the government countered with chemical attacks that killed 5,000 civilians. The government followed up with an assault on Qara Dagh, a mountainous area already encircled by government forces. Civilians generally were killed if they surrendered; sometimes women and children were spared. In mid-April, the government repeated the genocidal strategy in Garmiyan. Even—or perhaps especially—after a cease-fire between Iran and Iraq came into effect on August 20, the government continued its extermination of the Kurds. The final Anfal was mounted on August 25.

Termination and Outcome: There was no resistance to speak of by the end of August 26, but the final Anfal continued for two more days anyway, ending on August 28. Kurdish resistance had simply collapsed. Perhaps 150,000 to 200,000 were killed in the Anfal series of operations. The government announced an amnesty on September 6, 1988, which marked the end of the genocide, although the fighting had ended on August 26. The outcome was an unconditional government victory. Guerrilla fighting resumed at a low level by 1989 and continued until the next full-scale Kurdish rebellion (Intra-state War #862).

Coding Decisions: The number of battle-deaths is unknown but was surely larger than 4,000 based on the forces involved and the intensity of the fighting described in the descriptive text of the sources. While in-theater troop estimates and casualties are unavailable for both Iraq and Iran, we are confident based on the historical record that more than 1,000 Iranian soldiers participated in the civil war.

Sources: Arnold (1995); McDowall (1996); Middle East Watch (1993); Van Bruinessen (1986); Yildiz (2004).[289]

INTRA-STATE WAR #842
South Yemen War of 1986

Participants: Yemen People's Republic versus Hard-line Politburo Faction.
Dates: January 13, 1986, to February 1, 1986.
Battle-related Deaths: Total Combatant Deaths: 4,000. (See Coding Decisions.)[290]
Initiator: Yemen People's Republic.
Outcome: Hard-line Politburo Faction wins.

War Type: Civil for central control.

Total System Member Military Personnel: Armed Forces of Yemen People's Republic: 34,000 (prewar); 30,000 (initial, peak—including Hassani's tribal supporters).[291]

Theater Armed Forces: Armed Forces of Yemen People's Republic: 30,000 (peak).[292] Hard-line Politburo Faction: 30,000 (peak—based solely on the fact that virtually all of the 30,500-strong army went over to the rebels).[293]

Antecedents: Throughout the 1970s, the People's Democratic Republic of Yemen (South Yemen) was ruled by a triumvirate. One of the men was Ali Nasser Mohammed al-Hassani, who is referred to as Nasser, Mohammed, and Hassani in different accounts (we use the last of these). The other two members were Abdel Fatah Ismail and Salim Rubai Ali. The uneasy balance of power among the three was disrupted in June 1978, when the relatively moderate Marxist Rubai was ousted from power and executed. The coup triggered fighting between the Marxist factions in South Yemen, which was almost immediately followed by a war with North Yemen. In the aftermath, Hassani and Ismail were left to rule the country in an uneasy alliance.

In 1980, Hassani turned on Ismail and deposed him in a coup. Ismail fled to the Soviet Union. Five years later, the two reconciled under pressure from anti-Hassani politburo members. Ismail was permitted to return and serve on the politburo, and a new triumvirate was formed. Essentially, by late 1985 the hard-line majority had limited the authority of Hassani, who relied on his tribal support to maintain some level of authority. It appeared that a coup against Hassani might be imminent.

Hassani found a creative way out of the arrangement. On January 13, 1986, the politburo was summoned for a 10 a.m. meeting. Hassani did not attend, retiring to his tribal stronghold in the mountains—but his bodyguards did. Once all were seated and waiting for Hassani, his bodyguards opened fire. The other members' bodyguards then rushed to the room, and the subsequent gunfight claimed twenty lives, including those of Ismail and the vice president. Simultaneously, Hassani loyalists killed large numbers of his political opponents throughout South Yemen.

Narrative: A few politburo members survived by diving out the window and fleeing to their supporters. We code these as rebels because Hassani was the chief executive and began the war in control of the capital. Of course, it was Hassani who had stepped outside the law in his preemptive coup. Early media accounts at the time were spectacularly wrong about almost every aspect of the conflict, reporting the government line that there had been a coup attempt against Hassani. Soviet advisors fled in panic, having been taken completely by surprise (and perhaps due to their association with the now-deceased Ismail). Throughout the conflict, the 12,000 Soviet advisors refused to take sides or arm either side.

Hassani won the loyalty of the navy (1,000 men) and air force (2,500), which he used to bomb and shell opposition forces in Aden. Hassani's tribal allies marched on the capital, engaging both the army and the tribal allies of his opponents. In the confused situation, he also controlled much of the army, but on January 15 units began going over to the politburo survivors. The air force largely was neutralized by the next day.

For ten days, Hassani's tribal faction fought the militias of the hard-liners (other tribes) in the capital of Aden. Both sides made attempts to reduce civilian casualties, but the urban fighting was inherently deadly for the residents. The battle largely was decided by the defection of the army's only tank regiment to the rebel side. It appears that most of the army defected after Hassani began to massacre perceived opponents in the military—essentially any unit that attempted to avoid taking sides. By January 22, Aden was firmly in the hands of the politburo. Hassani's forces (about 30,000 strong) retreated northward from Aden, destroying the Soviet embassy on the way. The country's armed forces, now largely reunited, pursued him. On February 1, the last pro-Hassani stronghold fell, ending the war.

Termination and Outcome: The rebels won the war militarily and unconditionally. Hassani and key supporters took refuge in Marxist Ethiopia, while most of his army crossed into North Yemen. The Soviet Union supported the new regime once it was clear that it would prevail. The new government conducted a series of executions and demanded the extradition of Hassani and 47 of his supporters. By the time a year had passed, however, the government released 2,900 political prisoners and invited the exiles in North Yemen to return.

Coding Decisions: Estimates range from 2,000 to 17,000 total deaths. Initial reports suggested that as many as 12,000 died, but later reports suggested a lower toll. The new government reported that 4,230 party members died in the war. When the initial mass killings are taken into account, a figure of 4,000 battle-deaths is reasonable.

Sources: Arnold (1995); Brogan (1998); Dresch (2000); *Keesing's Record of World Events* (May 1986); Kifner (1986).[294]

INTRA-STATE WAR #850

Fifth Lebanese War of 1989 to 1990 (aka War of Liberation)

Participants: Lebanon versus Lebanese Forces, Lebanese Armed Forces (Lahoud Faction), Progressive Socialist Party, and Syria.
Dates: February 14, 1989, to October 13, 1990.
Battle-related Deaths: Syria: perhaps 400;[295] Total Combatant Deaths: 2,000. (See Coding Decisions.)[296]
Initiator: Lebanon.
Outcome: Lebanese Forces, Lebanese Armed Forces (Lahoud Faction), and Syria win.
War Type: Civil for central control.
Total System Member Military Personnel: Armed Forces of Lebanon (Aoun Faction only): 16,000 (prewar, initial, peak); 8,000 (final).[297] Armed Forces of Syria: 400,000 (prewar, initial); 408,000 (peak, final).[298]
Theater Armed Forces: Armed Forces of Lebanon (Aoun Faction): 16,000 (prewar, initial, peak); 8,000 (final). Lebanese Forces, aka Phalange, participating from February 12 to 16, 1989, and again from January 30, 1990: 6,000 (prewar, initial); 12,000 (peak).[299] Lebanese Armed Forces (Lahoud Faction): 10,000 (peak, final).[300] Progressive Socialist Party (PSP) militia, aka Druze Militia: 5,000 (prewar, initial, peak, final).[301] Syria, participating from August 10 to 13, 1989, and on October 13, 1990: 30,000 (prewar, initial); 42,000 (peak, final).[302]

Antecedents: As President Amin Gemayel approached the end of his term, a dispute over succession paralyzed the government. When no candidate could be agreed upon before the expiry of his term, Gemayel appointed a caretaker government led by Michel Aoun, the formal head of the Lebanese armed forces (though he controlled only its Christian brigades). Almost immediately after the government was convened, its Muslim officers resigned.

When parliament's Chamber of Deputies met and elected a new president, Aoun refused to recognize his legitimacy. Lebanon had two competing governments—the pro-Christian Aoun government (which controlled the presidential palace and other key institutions of governance) and the pro-Syria, pro-Muslim Salim al-Hoss government, which also was supported by the factionalized Christian Phalange militia, the Lebanese Forces (LF).

Narrative: Aoun moved quickly to secure control of East Beirut. In addition, he set out to deprive militias of their sources of customs revenue by returning ports to state control. On February 14, he launched an assault on the LF. He quickly succeeded in establishing control over its port; the LF lost eighty killed in the two days' fighting and withdrew from the city.

Next, he turned against the Muslim and Druze militias that held ports near Beirut, soon declaring a war of liberation against their Syrian backers. After he declared a blockade of their ports, shelling between the PSP and government broke out in Beirut and lasted for six months, costing 850 lives and wounding another 3,000 (about 90 percent of them civilians). From August 10 to August 13, a battle for the strategic ridge of Souk al-Gharb broke out between the PSP and Syrians on one side and Aoun's forces on the other. More than 100 were killed in the artillery barrage, but after initial successes, the Syrians and Druze were driven back. After a United Nations Security Council resolution calling for a cease-fire on August 15, the scale of fighting was reduced dramatically.

During this lull in the fighting, the deputies met under Saudi auspices to hammer out a peace accord. The Ta'if Agreement was immediately repudiated by the PSP, Hezbollah, and Amal. Aoun first rejected the agreement but later relented, only to reject its terms again. The deputies again elected a new president, who was promptly assassinated. Their next choice was Hirawi, who dismissed Aoun from his military position; Aoun refused to recognize the legitimacy of the new government.

On January 30, 1990, Aoun declared the compulsory induction of LF personnel into the army. The LF preemptively attacked the army, and the first eighteen days of fighting cost 615 lives and 2,128 wounded. At least half of these were military casualties. In late May, a temporary truce was reached between the army and the LF. Aoun had lost half of his strength—of his 16,000 men, 2,000 had been captured by the LF or fled to the Syrians, and only 8,000 remained. In June, the LF accepted the Ta'if Agreement.

In August, the parliament met again and adopted the reforms stipulated in the Ta'if Agreement, which would increase Muslim power in the government at the expense of Christians. All factions except Aoun supported the session. Aoun's isolation was increased by changes in international relations that followed Saddam Hussein's August 3 invasion of Kuwait. The Syrians gained a free hand in Lebanon in return for their participation in the anti-Iraq coalition. On September 26, the LF handed over the LF–Lebanese armed forces to the Ta'if government. On October 9, the Ta'if government formally requested Syrian intervention to evict Aoun from the presidential palace.

Syria intervened in support of the brigades of the Lebanese army that were loyal to its alternative government, but it also permitted the LF/Phalange and much smaller Syrian Socialist National Party to take part in the offensive. The Syrian intervention led to unprecedentedly intense combat. In the battle for the Suq al-Gharb ridge on October 13, 400 Syrians were killed. Aoun's losses were about 300 killed in battle, and he surrendered his forces the same day—perhaps 100 of whom were massacred by the victorious Syrians. One incident alone resulted in 73 executions. Aoun fled to the safety of the French embassy, and the Ta'if government took control of Beirut.

Termination and Outcome: The outcome was an unconditional victory for the rebels, and many government troops were killed after surrendering. The amnesty law passed in August 1991 applied to all, even war criminals, except for the perpetrators of political assassinations. Syria would dominate Lebanon for the next generation.

Coding Decisions: Several thousand were killed in 1989, although it seems clear that the vast majority were civilians (see the Narrative). Up to 4,400 were killed in 1990. We consider the figure of 2,000 battle-deaths to be most plausible, although the real total could be half or double that amount.

Sources: El Khazen (2004); Harris (1997, 2012); O'Ballance (1998); Van Dam (1996).[303]

INTRA-STATE WAR #862
Iraqi–Shiite Rebellion of 1991

Participants: Iraq versus Shiites (Aggregate) and Supreme Assembly of the Islamic Revolution in Iraq.
Dates: March 2, 1991, to March 31, 1991.
Battle-related Deaths: Total Combatant Deaths: perhaps 1,000. (See Coding Decisions.)[304]
Initiator: Shiites.
Outcome: Iraq wins.
War Type: Civil for central control.
Total System Member Military Personnel: Armed Forces of Iraq: 475,000 (prewar, initial, peak, final).[305]
Theater Armed Forces: Shiites: hundreds (initial), tens of thousands (peak).[306] Supreme Assembly of the Islamic Revolution in Iraq (SAIRI), participating from March 7: 20,000 (initial, peak).[307]

Antecedents: Just before Iraq's defeat in the Gulf War of 1991, the United States urged the Iraqi people to overthrow the government of Saddam Hussein. Expecting American support and having seen Saddam's armed forces handily defeated by the American-led coalition, uncoordinated Shiite and Kurdish groups (see also Intra-state War #862.1) rebelled against the state just after the war.

Narrative: The rebellion began as a Shiite revolt by hundreds of deserters at Nasiriyah on March 2. The uprising quickly spread, and many towns fell to the tens of thousands of rebels. In Karbala, the rebels hanged or decapitated 75 military officers and Baathist officials. On March 7, the Supreme Assembly of the Islamic Revolution in Iraq (SAIRI) committed its 20,000 fighters to the fray.

Just two days later, the government mounted a counteroffensive, leading to bloody fighting between the two sides. By March 14, the Iraqi army counterattacked at Karbala, which was defended by some 2,000 to 3,000 insurgents. Shortly after Karbala, the Battle of Najaf resulted in 1,400 civilian deaths. The rebellion in the south was over by March 18, when Iran proclaimed a day of mourning for those who had fallen (30,000, it alleged). The war ended after the Republican Guard moved north and captured Kirkuk at the end of March.

Termination and Outcome: The outcome of the war was an unconditional victory against the Shiites and SAIRI. Shiite resistance to the government ended, but executions continued after the war.

Coding Decisions: There were 5,000 battle-deaths in the Shiite and Kurdish uprisings of 1991. Given the known government losses in the Kurdish rebellion (Intra-state War #862.1), it is unlikely that this war claimed more than 1,000 combatants.

Sources: Hiro (2001a); Laffin (1994).[308]

INTRA-STATE WAR #862.1
Sixth Iraqi Kurds Rebellion of 1991

Participants: Iraq and Jash versus Kurdish Democratic Party, Patriotic Union of Kurdistan, and Jash Defectors.
Dates: March 4, 1991, to October 20, 1991.
Battle-related Deaths: Total Combatant Deaths: 4,000. (See Coding Decisions.)[309]
Initiator: Kurdish Democratic Party.
Outcome: Stalemate.
War Type: Civil for local issues (autonomy).
Total System Member Military Personnel: Armed Forces of Iraq: 475,000 (prewar, initial, peak, final).
Theater Armed Forces: Jash: 100,000 (initial, peak), up to 50,000 (final).[310] Kurdish Democratic Party: 15,000 (initial).[311] Patriotic Union of Kurdistan: 4,000 (initial).[312] Jash Defectors, participating from March 14: 50,000 (initial); 50,000 or more (peak).[313]

Antecedents: Just before Iraq's defeat in the Gulf War of 1991, the United States urged the Iraqi people to overthrow the government of Saddam Hussein. Expecting American support and having seen Saddam's armed forces handily defeated by the American-led coalition, Shiite and Kurdish groups rebelled against the state just after the war.

Narrative: On March 4, the KDP attacked and took Ranya. Ten days later, a slight majority of pro-government *fursan* (Jash) troops in the North—a force some 100,000 strong—switched sides to join the rebels. The defectors demanded the surrender of local army garrisons, some of which did so while others held out. Some 900 Mukhbarat (secret police) were killed in a single day of fighting in Sulaymaniyah, most of them executed by the rebels.

The government defeated a Shiite rising to the south by March 18, and on March 28, the government mounted a counteroffensive toward Kirkuk. By April 6, the government had regained most or all cities from the rebels. Refugees fled into neighboring countries, and on April 16, the United States announced the creation of a safe haven along the border with Turkey, effectively preventing Iraqi military operations in this zone. Fighting decreased dramatically toward the end of April but continued at civil war levels.

On July 18, the Kurds captured Sulaymaniyah in a battle that cost 250 battle-deaths and 600 wounded; 2,500 government troops were taken prisoner. On the whole, fighting in July cost the government 5,000 casualties. Another bout in September and October led to similar losses among the government forces. On October 6, the government bombarded rebel-held Sulaymaniyah, killing hundreds.

Termination and Outcome: On October 20, the government ended military operations against the Kurds, withdrawing its military forces from most of the area and placing it under an economic blockade. The outcome of the war was a stalemate—the Kurds gained a measure of autonomy due to foreign intervention but had clearly been unable to defend Kurdistan from the government forces. Executions continued after the war.

Coding Decisions: There were 5,000 battle-deaths in the Shiite and Kurdish uprisings of 1991 (see also Intra-state War #862). Given the sustained nature of the fighting in this revolt and the high reported government losses in the Narrative, we conclude that about 4,000 of those must have been suffered in this revolt; the real toll could be higher.

Sources: Laffin (1994); Yildiz (2004).[314]

INTRA-STATE WAR #865
Turkey–PKK War of 1991 to 1999

Participants: Turkey versus Kurdistan Workers Party.
Dates: July 10, 1991, to November 27, 1999.

Battle-related Deaths: Armed Forces of Turkey: 4,819; Kurdistan Workers Party: 23,238; Total Combatant Deaths: about 28,000. (See Coding Decisions.)[315]
Initiator: Turkey.
Outcome: Turkey wins.
War Type: Civil for local issues (independence).
Total System Member Military Personnel: Armed Forces of Turkey (including both Village Guard and National Police, both of which were used against the rebels): 804,000 (prewar, initial); 820,000 (peak); 789,000 (final).[316]
Theater Armed Forces: Armed Forces of Turkey: 300,000 (peak). Kurdistan Workers Party (PKK), aka AGRK: 10,000 (prewar, initial, peak); 5,000 (final).[317]

Antecedents: Contemporaneously with a bloody crackdown on Kurds in the late 1970s, the PKK was formed as a revolutionary movement to seek Kurdish independence. In 1984, it launched an armed rising against Turkey, but the state responded with effective enough violence to keep the insurgency suppressed below civil-war levels. Gradually, the PKK gained more recruits and its tactics became more effective. In 1990, several pro-Kurdish members of parliament broke off to found the People's Labor Party (HEP). On July 9, 1991, the tortured body of the HEP chairman was found.

Narrative: The next day, his funeral turned violent. Tens of thousands of demonstrators gathered, and the government responded with force. Police fired on the crowds, killing 12 and wounding 122. Over the next few months, clashes between the PKK and security forces became more intense as the PKK attempted to create a popular uprising against the government.

The PKK's tactics relied on the fact that the government troops were reluctant to fight at night. It would set up checkpoints and shoot police, village guardsmen, or other state security personnel. It also assassinated civilians perceived as state functionaries or sympathizers, such as teachers. It would retreat into mountains and forests, where government troops were loath to pursue. It also pursued an urban insurgency strategy, with elaborate networks of safe houses. Finally, they would target isolated military posts, picking off isolated soldiers on guard duty or traveling to or from the post. These tactics had some success as the government forces withdrew from many isolated outposts during the period from 1992 to 1993.

The PKK suffered heavy casualties and a high desertion rate in this period. Whereas the government claimed to have killed 356 PKK fighters in 1991, the figure for 1992 was 1,055, that for 1993 was 1,699, and that for 1994 was 4,114. However, the existence of safe havens in the Syrian-controlled Bekaa valley (until mid-1992) and in the de facto autonomous Kurdish no-fly zone in Iraq allowed the organization to keep recruiting, forming new units, and arming and training them. Moreover, the organization's willingness to recruit women increased its strength by approximately 50 percent (i.e., one-third of all fighters were women by 1993). The PKK had approximately 10,000 fighters at this point, although 2,000 of these were in Iraq at the time.

At the end of September 1992, the rebels staged a major attack on a Turkish border outpost. The government replied by sending troops to the border, killing 100 PKK members. On October 2, about 5,000 Iraqi KDP or PUK Kurdish fighters attacked the PKK in Iraq, while Turkish jets bombed the rebels. Turkish ground troops entered Iraq in mid-October. The PKK was forced to make peace with the Iraqi KDP and PUK on October 30 and temporarily lost its bases in Iraq. The PKK and the Iraqi Kurds each lost about 160 fighters in the conflict; Turkish government losses were minor.

In early 1993, the rebel declared a series of unilateral cease-fires, hoping to negotiate with the Turkish president. When he unexpectedly died of a heart attack, the group's local members saw no point in continuing the cease-fire and attacked a bus full of unarmed soldiers, killing thirty-three of them. The government responded by undertaking offensive operations against the rebels, rolling back what progress the PKK had made.

Villages were hit hard by the government's new strategy: whereas 1,100 villages had been forcibly evacuated from 1990 to 1993, another 1,000 settlements were evacuated in 1994. By 1994, the government had 300,000 security forces deployed in southeastern Turkey. Villagers were conscripted forcibly into the village guards to fight the rebels; these increased from 18,000 in 1990 to 63,000 in 1994. Death squads targeted suspected rebel sympathizers and pro-Kurdish politicians. In general, the rebels were either destroyed or forced to retreat in 1994.

By 1995, the PKK was in decline. In March, the government sent 35,000 troops across the border into Iraq in what practically would become an annual ritual. It claimed to have killed 552 "terrorists" and to have lost only 11 personnel of its own. While it also captured some supplies, the rebels were able to avoid the brunt of the offensive and simply return to their bases afterward. The PKK and Iraqi KDP also clashed again before agreeing to a cease-fire in December. By 1996, the PKK was reduced to 5,000 to 6,000 fighters.

The PKK's bases in Iraq and support from the Syrian and Iranian governments allowed it to continue the struggle even against the ever-increasing power of the state. In 1997, Turkey launched another major operation in northern Iraq. In May, 30,000 Turkish soldiers entered Iraq. This time, they stayed for a month and fought an extra-state war, claiming to have killed 2,500 of the PKK at the cost of only 100 government soldiers killed.

Turkey also put pressure on Syria to refrain from helping the rebels, and in 1998 PKK leader Abdullah Ocalan was forced to leave Syria. While he was able briefly to find refuge in Italy, he shuttled from country to country in a vain search for asylum. On February 15, 1999, he was captured by Turkish authorities. He called on the PKK to cease fire, but when a delegation of PKK tried to surrender to the government under a flag of truce, it was fired upon. The Turkish general staff issued a statement rejecting a rebel surrender:

> The terrorist delegation planning a symbolic surrender to the Turkish state is . . . part of [Ocalan's] propaganda. . . . The terrorist organization has always used such tactics to gain time and then redouble its attacks. For this reason, the Turkish armed forces are determined to continue the battle until the last terrorist has been neutralized.[318]

Beginning in August 1999, up to 500 PKK members died during the retreat from Turkey that accompanied the unilateral cease-fire. The last combat reported for the war occurred on November 27.

Termination and Outcome: The war ended with a government victory without concessions. Indeed, Ocalan was sentenced to death (though this was later commuted to life in prison). After years of the cease-fire passed without substantive change, the PKK eventually restarted operations under new command but was unable to raise the level of violence to civil war. In May 2013, the government conducted peace talks with the group, and a new cease-fire and withdrawal from Turkey (this time unhindered by the Turkish military) was proclaimed.

Coding Decisions: By subtracting the totals before 1991 in the Turkish Ministry of Foreign Affairs from the totals of government forces killed in Nachmani, we arrive at the subtotals of 3,455 soldiers, 216 police, and 1,148 village guards killed, for an overall total of 4,819 government battle-deaths. A similar technique using the estimate of rebels killed in Clodfelter yields 22,738 rebel battle-deaths. Taking into account the additional 500 battle-deaths suffered by the rebels by war's end, we estimate 23,238 rebel battle-deaths. Total battle-deaths are therefore about 28,000, a figure that includes some from January 1 to July 9, 1991, and excludes government fatalities after Ocalan's capture.

Sources: *Agence France-Presse* (1999); Anatolia News Agency (1999); BBC News (2013); Clodfelter (2008); Kirişci and Winrow (1997); Minorities at Risk Project (2013); Nachmani (2003); Turkish Ministry of Foreign Affairs (1995).[319]

INTRA-STATE WAR #866
SPLM/A Division (Dinka-Nuer) War of 1991 to 1992

Participants: Sudan People's Liberation Army (Garang) versus Sudan People's Liberation Army (Nasir) and Anya Nya II.
Dates: September 11, 1991, to March 8, 1992.
Battle-related Deaths: Total Combatant Deaths: up to 1,200. (See Coding Decisions.)[320]
Initiator: Sudanese People's Liberation Army (Nasir).
Outcome: Conflict continues at below-war level.
War Type: Intercommunal.
Theater Armed Forces: Sudan People's Liberation Army (Garang): 55,000 (prewar total strength—not all were in the same theater of operations).[321] Sudan People's Liberation Army (Nasir): more than 2,000 (peak).[322] Anya Nya II: several hundred (prewar).[323]

Antecedents: This war takes place in the midst of the war between Sudan and the SPLA (Intra-state War #836). The Sudan People's Liberation Army/

Movement (SPLA/SPLM) recruited heavily from the Dinka population in southern Sudan. In "the mother of all drafts," some 10,000 young men were conscripted from Dinka areas around Bor in 1991. Soon after, the SPLA in Sudan lost a key regional ally when the government of Ethiopia began to lose its civil war. Indeed, even after the government fell, the victorious EPDRF waged war against the SPLA in Ethiopia, leading to heavy SPLA casualties and its withdrawal several months later. The catastrophe triggered a coup attempt by Nuer and Shilluk officers in the Dinka-dominated SPLA.

On August 28, 1991, the Dinka-dominated SPLM split into two factions, largely along tribal lines. The SPLM–Garang (or SPLM–Torit or SPLM–Mainstream) faction, led by John Garang, continued its largely revolutionary orientation, while three of thirteen commanders formed the Neur aligned SPLM–Nasir faction, led by Rick Machar, which called for independence for the South. The Neur aligned SPLM–Nasir may already have approached the government at this stage for its support. It was encouraged by the government to attack SPLA–Garang.

Narrative: The first skirmish within the SPLA was fought at Waat on September 11, 1991. In late September, SPLA–Nasir and SPLA–Garang fought a battle around Ayod. The SPLA–Garang was forced to retreat, and Dinka civilians were massacred by the Nuer of the Nasir faction. SPLA–Garang reinforcements from Bor drive northward against the Nasir forces, destroying many of their supplies at Kongor.

In October, the Nasir–Nuer forces mounted a counteroffensive into Dinka territory. By this point, the largely Nuer and Shilluk forces of SPLM–Nasir were joined by thousands of Nuer tribal warriors. They attacked ethnic Dinkas, killing hundreds of civilians in the Bor Massacre. The civilians ostensibly were targeted because they were believed to have benefited from cattle raids carried out by the Dinka and SPLM–Garang. The primary victims were women, children, and the elderly as the young men had been drafted a few months earlier.

The SPLA–Garang struck back, inflicting heavy casualties on the Nuer warriors and retaking Bor. The Nuer retreated back to Ayod. The SPLM–Garang retaliated by leveling Nuer villages, but thousands of Dinka, viewed as associated with the SPLM–Garang, were killed by SPLM–Nasir fighters from the Nuer and Shilluk tribes. The remnants of Anya Nya II also sided with the Nasir faction against Garang. On November 27, the two sides signed a truce, but each side accused the other of violating it. Two days later, Garang's troops retook Gemeiza from the Nasir faction.

Fighting resumed at a low level in February 1992 but declined as SPLA-Garang faced a renewed government offensive in March 1992.

Termination and Outcome: The two factions suspended their operations during OAU peace negotiations in May 1992. Low-level fighting resumed September 26 as another coup attempt against Garang was supported by troops from SPLA–Nasir. In November, a group of SPLA–Nasir called the Blockbusters attacked SPLA–Garang positions. Many lives were lost on the Garang side, according to SPLM–Nasir leader Lam Akol. By year's end, the SPLM–Nasir controlled Upper Nile, and SPLM–Garang controlled most of Equatoria and the Bahr el Ghazal.

In March 1993, Garang's forces raided a meeting of SPLA–Nasir leaders (who were setting up a new organization called SPLA–United), killing sixty of them. These actions simply drove the SPLA–United into the government's arms.

Coding Decisions: Thousands were killed, but the majority of them were women, children, and the elderly. On the basis of this limited evidence, it is possible that the intercommunal war threshold of about 1,200 battle-deaths was met.

Sources: Akol (2003); Collins (2008); de Waal (2004); Guarak (2011); Jok and Hutchinson (1999); Lesch (1998).[324]

INTRA-STATE WAR #875

Algeria's Islamic Front War of 1992 to 2002

Participants: Algeria versus Armed Islamic Movement, Armed Islamic Group, Movement for the Islamic State, Islamic Salvation Army, and Salafi Group for Preaching and Combat.

Dates: February 8, 1992, to 2002.

Battle-related Deaths: Armed Forces of Algeria: perhaps 5,000; Combined Rebel Groups: 15,200; Total Combatant Deaths: about 20,000. (See Coding Decisions.)[325]

Initiator: Armed Islamic Movement.
Outcome: Conflict continued at below-war level.
War Type: Civil for central control.
Total System Member Military Personnel: Armed Forces of Algeria: 126,000 (prewar, initial); 624,000 (peak—includes 500,000 militia and communal guards).[326]
Theater Armed Forces: Armed Forces of Algeria: more than 200,000. Armed Islamic Movement, participating to 1994, when it was largely suppressed: 2,000 (initial).[327] All Rebel Forces combined: 40,000 (peak); 1,000 to 10,000 (final).

Antecedents: At the end of 1991, the democratizing, but still authoritarian, Algerian regime held national elections. When the Islamic FIS won the elections, a coup was mounted in January 1992, and the elections were cancelled. The FIS initially chose to resist the decree through peaceful means. However, other groups like the GIS called for a holy war against the government. Sporadic violence broke out, several soldiers were killed, and the leader of the FIS was arrested.

Narrative: On February 8, 1992, simultaneous riots and clashes broke out in Algiers and twenty other towns across the country. This marked the beginning of large-scale resistance to the regime. The next day, the FIS was banned and a state of emergency declared. In just three days of violence, anywhere from 40 to more than 500 were killed. Islamic guerrilla groups began to emerge, and on February 10, 10 police were killed in a suburb of Algiers.

The first organization to emerge clearly in rebellion was the Armed Islamic Movement (MIA), led by Abdelkader Chebouti, which quickly grew to 2,000 fighters. Guerrilla resistance to the government continued throughout the year. The official death toll for 1992 was somewhat fewer than 600 soldiers and police killed against an unknown number of rebels killed.

The years 1993 and 1994 saw the proliferation of armed groups. By March, the Armed Islamic Group (GIA) was active in the resistance; the two factions would clash later in the year. The Movement for the Islamic State (MEI), formed in 1991 as a nonviolent organization emphasizing civil disobedience, also joined the rebellion in 1993; later, the SIS would be formed as well. In July 1994, FIS formed the Islamic Salvation Army (AIS) to resist the government, while the MIA largely was suppressed by the end of the year.

By 1993, the guerrillas began emphasizing urban operations over actions in the hills; the former simply produced more results. As a consequence, the number of urban fighters increased. From 2,000 guerrillas in 1992, the total rebel forces increased to 22,000 in 1993 and peaked at 40,000 in 1994. The hard core of each group was considerably smaller than these numbers would seem to indicate—in 1995, the GIA had a hard core of 2,000 to 3,000 fighters, the AIS had 4,000, while the MEI and MIA had been reduced to small groups incapable of large-scale operations.

The government promulgated a limited amnesty for those who had not committed major crimes in 1995, and perhaps 6,000 took advantage of it. Also in 1995, the 10,000 rural police were transformed into a government militia. By 1997, it was 200,000 strong. It was clear that the government was winning the war. It won a major victory against the GIA at Ain Defla in late 1995, killing at least 650 rebels. Already in 1996, total guerrilla strength had declined to about 10,000. Deaths had declined from 500 a week to 500 a month. In October 1997, the AIS declared a unilateral truce (which was formalized two years later).

Since the reverses of 1995 and after, the rebels switched tactics from ambushing government forces to targeting civilians. Whereas about three-quarters of those killed by the rebels in 1992 and half of those killed by them in 1993 were government forces, these figures dropped to about one-sixth by 1997 and one-tenth in 1998. Increasingly, the war became little more than reciprocal massacres of civilians, interrupted by the occasional armed skirmish.

In 1998, the Salafi Group for Preaching and Combat (GSPC) was formed from GIA members repelled by the shift in tactics. Whereas the GIA focused its attacks on civilians, the smaller GSPC focused on attacking security forces. The government permitted elections in which the FIS and other Islamic parties were banned, and a new president came to power. In June 1999, he promulgated a new amnesty for fighters who surrendered and negotiated what amounted to the end of the AIS. However, the number of submissions under the new law was less than 400, and combat with other groups continued.

The GSPC's entry into the war increased the proportion of casualties that were security forces. About

2,700 people were killed in 2000 (479 of them government security forces), and another 3,000 died in 2001. In December 2000, 25 percent of the casualties were state security or military personnel. Though the evidence is ambiguous without disaggregation into civilian deaths and battle-deaths, we conclude that the war continued through these years.

Termination and Outcome: The war ended sometime near the end of 2002, falling just below the threshold of civil war. That year, 1,562 people were killed, including 278 members of the security forces and 651 rebels—a total of 929 battle-deaths. The outcome of the war was a stalemate, with casualty levels falling below the war threshold, while the political contest remained unresolved. As a practical matter, a stalemate in a civil war for control of the central government amounts to a government victory as it retains power.

In 2005, the government issued another amnesty, again exempting both those guilty of major crimes against civilians and the FIS. Perhaps 250 to 300 people surrendered; the remainder of those amnestied was already in prison. In 2007, the government estimated that 1,000 "terrorists" were still active. Battle-deaths continued at sub-war levels: 412 in 2005, 419 in 2006, and 520 in 2007.

Coding Decisions: The government claims to have killed 15,200 "terrorists." As rebel losses were consistently higher than government losses after 1992, we estimate that the government lost about 5,000 security forces, for a total of about 20,000 battle-deaths. Considering that the government may have included some civilians in its body counts, this could be an overestimate.

Sources: DeRouen and Heo (2007); *Financial Times* (2001); Hafez (2003); Joffé (2008); *Keesing's Record of World Events* (January 2001); Laffin (1996); Martinez (2000); Tlemcani (1986); Volpi (2003); Werenfels (2007).[328]

INTRA-STATE WAR #885
South Yemeni Secessionist Revolt of 1994

Participants: Yemen, Hashid Militia, Hassani-led Forces, and "Afghanis" versus South Yemen.
Dates: February 21, 1994, to July 7, 1994.
Battle-related Deaths: Combined Pro-government Forces: about 1,226; South Yemen: more than 1,226; Total Combatant Deaths: 3,000. (See Coding Decisions.)[329]
Initiator: Yemen.
Outcome: Yemen wins.
War Type: Civil for local issues (secession).
Total System Member Military Personnel: Armed Forces of Yemen: 69,000 (prewar); 40,000 (initial). The Northern (government) portion of the army had 20,000 regulars and 40,000 reservists.[330]
Theater Armed Forces: Armed Forces of Yemen: [ ]. Hashid Militia: up to 100,000 (peak—total strength). Hassani-led Forces: 40,000 (peak). "Afghanis": 3,000 (initial, peak). South Yemen: 47,500 (prewar, initial—excludes 45,000 reservists but includes up to 20,000 tribal militia).[331]

Antecedents: To understand the conflict, it is useful to examine the preunification politics of each state. In the North, the regime ruled using a single-party system (the General People's Congress [GPC]) maintained by familial ties and patronage. President Ali Abdullah Saleh (sometimes spelled Salih) had no fewer than ten of his relatives, including four of his brothers, elevated to senior officer status. About half of the top political posts and more than two-thirds of public officials were chosen from the president's clan, part of the Hashid tribal confederation. Saleh used oil revenues essentially to bribe the leaders of potential opposing forces. Since the civil war of 1962 to 1970, the government also had become a somewhat Islamic regime as a concession to supporters of an imamate. It generally allowed fundamentalist groups to operate and even sponsored them as long as they did not challenge the central government.

In the South, there was a single communist party (the Yemeni Socialist Party [YSP]) that ruled through force rather than co-option. President Ali Salim al-Bid's (often referred to as Beihd or Bayd) support was primarily urban and secular, and there was constant tension with the country's tribes. While both countries were poor, the South was poorer, suffering from the loss of Soviet assistance toward the end of the Cold War.

In 1990, a unification agreement was signed by both leaders. The North hoped to gain access to the oil and ports of the South, while the South sought to protect itself from the internal and external enemies it had made as a communist state. Of course, other factors also drove unification—many attempts had been made since the beginning of the 1970s, only to fall apart.

The institutional structure of the new state evolved quickly. It began as a loose federation with a provisional government and many parallel institutions that would have to be merged. Northern leader Saleh became president and southern leader al-Bid became vice president. A multiparty system was immediately permitted, and more than forty parties emerged, including former rebels in both countries.

In a shock to both sides, the economy plunged in the aftermath of the Persian Gulf War of 1990 to 1991, when Saudi Arabia and the United States responded to Yemen's pro-Iraq stance by cutting aid and expelling the guest workers who had provided valuable remittances. The economic crisis led to strikes, which sparked riots. Political assassinations and fundamentalist terrorism became more common, with the YSP becoming the most frequent target.

Rivalry quickly emerged between the former ruling parties of each state. The YSP found it more difficult to secure allies than the GRC, which quickly allied itself with a large northern Islamic fundamentalist party, the Yemen Reform Grouping (YRG), that advocated *sharia* law. The YSP found some support in the Bakil tribes of the North, longtime rivals with the Hashids favored by Saleh. The GPC also favored keeping traditional tribal structures in place, while the YSP proposed economic and democratic reforms that would have the effect of undermining tribal autonomy.

Nonetheless, elections went ahead as scheduled in April 1993. They probably were manipulated to ensure the dominance of the large parties—the GPC, YRG, and YSP. However, the large population imbalance (9 million in the North vs. 2.4 million in the South) ensured that the GPC and YRG dominated the new legislature. GPC leader Saleh formed a unity government, granting the YSP significant portfolios, including the ministry of defense.

The unity government did not allay the fears of the YSP, which had come to suspect that the GPC intended to follow the same tactics of patronage in the South as it had in the North, effectively absorbing the outnumbered South into the political system of the North.

Several moves contributed to the insecurity of the YSP. First, northern leaders such as Saleh refused to unify the armed forces, which would have the effect of placing all of them under the control of the YSP defense minister. Second, the government seemed incapable of responding to political assassinations and terrorist attacks against the YSP. In all, 150 of its members were assassinated, and repeated attempts were made on the lives of al-Bid and his son. Instead of cracking down on terrorism, the Interior Ministry (held by the GPC) allowed 3,000 "Afghans" (largely Arab fundamentalists who had opposed the Soviets in Afghanistan) to train in the mountains of the South. Third, Saleh quietly had moved northern units into southern cities in greater strength than allowed by the unification agreement. Finally, Saleh established an alliance with former southern rebel Ali Nasser Mohammed al-Hassani (see Intra-state War #842), who controlled 40,000 followers. Perhaps in response to these issues, al-Bid overlooked or encouraged the formation of militias in the South.

In August 1993, al-Bid left the national capital of Sanaa for the former southern capital of Aden. That October, he presented the government with a list of eighteen demands, including a new institution to provide equal representation for both North and South (despite the far larger population of the North), anti-assassination and antiterrorist measures, merger of the military forces, and a new form of presidency. Shortly after, the YSP defense minister demanded the removal of troops from urban areas, a measure that would have allayed the South's fears about its cities and allowed it to transfer some of its own elite units (isolated in the North) back to the South. Al-Bid also demanded the expulsion of the "Afghans" and removal of the relatives of leaders from military commands.

Both Saleh and al-Bid began to order troop movements along the former border. The first military clash between forces loyal to each side occurred on November 9, when northern troops attempted to enter a southern border town and were opposed by armed civilians, perhaps one of the militias permitted by al-Bid. Five people were killed (one later account said that all five were northern troops), but the violence was quickly contained by the YSP defense minister. It may have been a test of strength by one or both sides; in any case, it showed a reluctance in the South to escalate to war. Both sides resumed military redeployments near the border.

In an effort to prevent the new state from disintegrating, a group of Yemeni notables proposed an accord that met most of the YSP's demands on January 18. The parties in the North were determined to prevent the South's secession and acceded to the accord, while the YSP insisted that the 16,000 northern troops deployed in the South be removed before the agreement could be implemented. In a classic security dilemma, the South wanted the ability to secede if Saleh did not honor the terms of the agreement. They did not trust in paper institutions because the key forces of the North were personally loyal to Saleh, not the established chain of command. The North was satisfied with the 1993 status quo, which left the YSP marginalized, and determined not to allow the South to develop a capacity to secede.

The two sides were to sign the accord in January, but another clash and fears for personal safety of the party leaders prevented it from being signed until February 20. Even after Saleh had signed the accord, al-Bid declined to return to Sanaa with him, instead flying to Riyadh. In response to what Saleh claimed was a bid for external support to the South, the North initiated limited hostilities the next day.

Narrative: Fighting broke out at a number of places along the border as northern troops tried to push the South out of key positions. The main strategy of northern forces appeared to be clearing a path for movement into the southern region of Abyan, which contained a string of southern cities—Zinjibar, Mudiyya, and Lawdar—that would cut the South in two if taken. Intermittent fighting across the country lasted for about a week before a cease-fire sponsored by Oman and Jordan took effect. Most troops returned to their barracks, but northern troops in the province of al-Bayda (bordering Abyan) refused to vacate their positions.

In April, southern units in the North were besieged. At the end of the month about 400 were killed or wounded at ʿAmran (near Sanaa) as northern forces routed a brigade of southern troops and thereby secured the capital of Sanaa. The southern troops retreated to the mountains and found shelter with the Bakil tribes. Still, the South took no offensive military action, simply maintaining its positions against northern assaults. By the end of the month, the North had succeeded in neutralizing the elite southern forces in the North and establishing a strong position against the South, keeping its forces near southern cities intact and holding most of the border with Abyan.

On May 4, the North launched a large-scale offensive against the South, with four columns advancing into the South and planning to unite at Aden, encircling the southern capital. While the Southerners were able to hold against some columns, the North was able to push quickly into Abyan then turn east to cut off the Hadramawt region from the rest of Yemen. While the South was able to establish a perimeter around Aden and nearby cities and even launch a few successful counterattacks, it was unable to block forces in the East driving toward the city of Ataq on the road to Hadramawt. Only after the fall of Ataq did its units have some success in holding back their opponents, but on May 21 the North broke through and cut the South in two.

International observers and the South repeatedly called for a cease-fire, and the North repeatedly agreed to mediation, only to continue its advance without pause. On May 20, Saleh declared the South to be independent and sought international recognition, perhaps hoping that longtime ally Saudi Arabia would assist it in its struggle. A brief cease-fire was followed by an all-out offensive by northern forces, which seized the oil fields on Hadramawt and a number of cities surrounding Aden, including Lahij just to its North. The South temporarily prevented an advance on Aden by launching a strong counterattack at ʿAnad, north of Lahij, thereby threatening to cut off and encircle one of the northern spearheads.

Aware of the danger, the government of the North agreed to a cease-fire, which it used to withdraw troops from exposed positions and prepare a new offensive. On June 10, it besieged and began shelling Aden. During another brief cease-fire on June 23, it reinforced northern soldiers around Aden with Hashid tribal militia. The South walked out of peace talks, claiming that the North simply wished to buy time for new offensives.

The final battle for Aden began that day, with the North pushing into three of Aden's suburbs. After another week of fighting, the North also succeeded in retaking ʿAnad, securing its lines of communication and supply. Aden's airport fell at about the same time. Fighting continued in Hadramawt, with the government capturing its largest city on July 5. Over the next two days, northern forces repeatedly broke southern lines of defense in Aden, taking the rest of the city by July 7 and causing al-Bid and other southern leaders to flee the country.

Termination and Outcome: Over the next three days, the government peacefully occupied the rest of the South, with rebel units fleeing the country to Saudi Arabia. The outcome of the war was an unconditional government victory. There are no reports of executions following the government's victory. The government almost immediately announced an amnesty and freed its prisoners but refused to grant amnesty to sixteen top YSP officials, including al-Bid. The Islamic fundamentalist party YRG was rewarded for its loyalty with four additional cabinet posts, while the YSP was excluded from the government (but not banned).

Coding Decisions: Observers estimated 7,000 killed, but this figure is probably too high (and includes civilians). The government admitted losing 613 killed, but its real losses were probably double that (about 1,226). The rebels lost more.[332] Simple addition produces a total of more than 2,452 battle-deaths, and 3,000 is probably the most reasonable estimate, plus or minus a thousand.

Sources: Cooper (1994); "Five Killed in Clash Between (1993); Ghalib (1994); Ghattas (1994); *Keesing's Record of World Events* (July 2004); Kostiner (1996); "Troops in Bloodbath" (1994); "*Yemen Times* Publishes Maps" (n.d.); "Yemen Troops Defy Orders" (1994); "Yemeni Leaders Sign Deal" (1994); "Yemeni Socialists Expel Former Leader" (1994).[333]

INTRA-STATE WAR #887
First Iraqi Kurds Internecine War of 1994 to 1995

Participants: Patriotic Union of Kurdistan versus Kurdish Democratic Party and Islamic Movement of Kurdistan.
Dates: May 1, 1994, to April 1995, and July 1995 to August 11, 1995.
Battle-related Deaths: Total Combatant Deaths: 1,500. (See Coding Decisions.)[334]
Initiator: Islamic Movement of Kurdistan.
Outcome: Stalemate.
War Type: Intercommunal.
Theater Armed Forces: Patriotic Union of Kurdistan: 12,000 (prewar, initial, peak, final). Kurdish Democratic Party: 25,000 (prewar, initial, peak, final). Islamic Movement of Kurdistan: [ ].[335]

Antecedents: As a de facto autonomous Kurdish area emerged in 1991 and 1992, the main contenders for power over the area were the Patriotic Union of Kurdistan (PUK) and the Kurdish Democratic Party (KDP). While they formed a coalition government in 1992, the PUK drifted toward Turkey while the KDP pursued negotiations with the Iraqi government. The institutions of the joint government became more polarized as each party sought an advantage over its rival.

In addition, an Islamic party called the Islamic Movement of Kurdistan (IMK) clashed with PUK troops and was badly mauled by them in December 1993; more than 200 were killed in the intercommunal fighting. The PUK agreed to accept KDP mediation, but the KDP was on friendly terms with the IMK and KDP–PUK tensions escalated further over the incidents.

Narrative: On May 1, 1994, a land dispute sparked conflict between the two parties' militias. The IMK, supported by Iran, sided with the KDP and took Halabja, Panjwin, and Khurmal from the PUK. Efforts to control the violence were made by each party's leadership, but local incidents continued to escalate, and there were more than 600 civilian and military casualties by June. Both sides began executing prisoners. Fighting raged in Qala Diza (the site of the initial land dispute), Rawanduz, and Shaqlawa. By the time hostilities paused in August, up to 1,000 had been killed in the fighting and 70,000 civilians had fled their homes.

In December, fighting erupted again, killing 500 people. The PUK took Erbil during the fighting. The United States managed to broker a cease-fire in April 1995, by which time the death toll may have been as high as 3,000. Open warfare resumed in July, and hundreds were killed by the end of the month. By this point, the KDP had received significant supplies of heavy weapons from the government of Iraq.

Termination and Outcome: The outcome of the war was effectively a stalemate. The United States sponsored another round of talks from August 9 to August 11. The talks concluded with an immediate cease-fire between the factions and an agreement to work on a comprehensive peace treaty based on the following principles: demilitarization of Erbil, submitting customs revenues to a neutral commission, and reconvening the regional parliament once Erbil was demilitarized. Further peace talks in September proved unproductive, and in 1996 the two parties fought again, leading to a civil war when the Iraqi government intervened at the behest of the KDP (see Intra-state War #893).

Coding Decisions: The total death toll may have been as high as 3,000 plus hundreds, but given that this figure includes civilians and is high compared to other estimates, we think it more realistic to place battle-deaths at 1,500. The real total could be somewhat lower or higher.

Sources: Gunter (1996); McDowall (1996); Yildiz (2004).[336]

INTRA-STATE WAR #893
Seventh Iraqi Kurds War of 1996

Participants: Iraq and Kurdish Democratic Party versus Patriotic Union of Kurdistan and Iraqi National Congress.
Dates: August 31, 1996, to October 23, 1996.
Battle-related Deaths: Iraqi National Congress: up to 200;[337] Total Combatant Deaths: up to 1,000. (See Coding Decisions.)
Initiator: Iraq and Kurdish Democratic Party.
Outcome: Stalemate.
War Type: Civil for local issues (control of Kurdish no-fly zone).
Total System Member Military Personnel: Armed Forces of Iraq: 450,000 (prewar, initial, peak, final).[338]
Theater Armed Forces: Armed Forces of Iraq: 12,000 (initial, peak). Kurdistan Democratic Party: 30,000 (initial, peak).[339] Patriotic Union of Kurdistan: 12,000 (initial, peak).[340] Iraqi National Congress: a few hundred (initial).[341]

Antecedents: This war was an intercommunal conflict transformed into a civil one. The Patriotic Union of Kurdistan (PUK)—allied with the Iraqi National Congress (INC)—and Kurdish Democratic Party (KDP) had been at odds over government of the de facto Kurdish autonomous region in northern Iraq as it was born in the aftermath of the Sixth Iraqi–Kurdish War (Intra-state War #862.1). A tenuous peace was established on August 11, 1995 (see Intra-state War #877). However, the PUK continued to accuse the KDP of withholding revenues from oil and customs duties from it, and fighting broke out again in the spring of 1996. After Iranian forces intervened on the side of PUK, the latter was able to seize key objectives.

On August 9, PUK forces bombarded a town near Erbil, killing 9 and wounding 30. The fighting escalated, and by August 18 PUK and KDP forces engaged each other constantly. On August 23, Barzani of the KDP announced that an offensive by 1,000 PUK fighters had been crushed, with 400 PUK killed or captured. The United States rushed to secure a cease-fire between the rivals, which came into effect on August 28.

Narrative: On August 31, about 12,000 Iraqi soldiers entered the PUK's area of operations in northern Iraq. Fighting together with the KDP, they attacked the "capital" of Erbil, taking it by the next day after a battle that cost 150 to 180 lives, almost all of them combatants. A nearby INC base at Salahuddin was overrun, and hundreds of prisoners were executed by the Iraqi government. The United States responded to the Iraqi incursion by firing cruise missiles and conducting air strikes against Iraq. Although the Iraqi army handed over control of Erbil to the KDP, it continued to operate elsewhere, massing up to 200 tanks against Sulaymaniyah, which fell to the KDP without resistance two days later. However, as Iraqi forces withdrew, Iranian forces once again aided the PUK, which regained much of the lost territory over the next six weeks.

Termination and Outcome: On October 23, a US-mediated cease-fire came into effect between the PUK and KDP, ending the conflict. Because Iraq was not a party to the cease-fire agreement, the war was a stalemate, with neither side able to defeat the other at an acceptable cost. PUK and the KDP would resume fighting the next year (see Intra-state War #897.5).

Coding Decisions: This war combined elements of intercommunal and civil wars. However, acting on the basis that Iraq took over the bulk of the fighting for the PUK, as well as on the principle of exclusivity, we have coded this case as a civil war.

Sources: Freij (1997); Katzman (2000); Minorities at Risk Project (2010a).[342]

INTRA-STATE WAR #897.5

Second Iraqi Kurds Internecine War of 1997

Participants: Patriotic Union of Kurdistan versus Kurdish Democratic Party.
Dates: October 13, 1997, to November 25, 1997.
Battle-related Deaths: Total Combatant Deaths: 1,200. (See Coding Decisions.)[343]
Initiator: Patriotic Union of Kurdistan.
Outcome: Stalemate.
War Type: Intercommunal.
Theater Armed Forces: Patriotic Union of Kurdistan: 27,000 (prewar, initial, peak, final).[344] Kurdistan Democratic Party: 30,000 (prewar, initial, peak, final).[345]

Antecedents: The rival Patriotic Union of Kurdistan (PUK) and Kurdistan Democratic Party (KDP) sporadically fought for control of the de facto Kurdish autonomous area. The PUK's alliance with Turkey's PKK rebels was also an issue, with the KDP condemning the "foreign" influence in the autonomous zone. In September 1997, KDP–PKK clashes intensified.

Narrative: Taking advantage of the KDP's distraction, the PUK mounted Operation Vengeance Storm (*Gardaluli Tula*) on October 13, 1997. The PUK gained ground at first, but the KDP was able to turn the tide with assistance from the anti-PKK Turkish air force. The front lines eventually stabilized near the prewar armistice line. On November 24, the KDP declared a unilateral cease-fire.

Termination and Outcome: Notwithstanding an alleged KDP attack on the PUK the next day, the latter agreed to reciprocate the cease-fire, ending the war. The outcome of the war was a stalemate. Negotiations sponsored by the United States eventually would lead to an agreement about a year later, providing for a joint administration and the expulsion of the PKK.

Coding Decisions: While most sources list 1,200 killed in the fighting, some estimates (e.g., Tahiri, 2007) are much lower, such as 200 casualties on both sides. On the principle of inclusion, we nonetheless include this as a war.

Sources: Minorities at Risk Project (2010a); Stansfield (2003).

INTRA-STATE WAR #927

Darfur Rebellion of 2003 to 2006

Participants: Sudan, Chad, and Janjaweed versus Darfur Liberation Front, Sudanese Liberation Army (AW), Sudanese Liberation Army (G-19), and Justice and Equality Movement.
Dates: February 26, 2003, to October 14, 2006.
Battle-related Deaths: Total Combatant Deaths: 10,000. (See Coding Decisions.)[346]
Initiator: Darfur Liberation Front.
Outcome: Fighting continues at below-war level.
War Type: Civil for local issues (resource allocation—but see Coding Decisions).
Total System Member Military Personnel: Armed Forces of Sudan: 104,000 (prewar, initial); 105,000 (peak, final). Armed Forces of Chad: 30,000 (prewar, initial, peak, final).[347]
Theater Armed Forces: Armed Forces of Sudan: 40,000 (peak). Armed Forces of Chad, participating on the government side until July 2003 and occasionally intervening on the rebel side later that year: 500 to 2,000 (initial, peak).[348] Janjaweed, participating throughout the war but were increasingly incorporated into the army and police as the war dragged on: 15,000 (prewar).[349] Darfur Liberation Force/Sudanese Liberation Army/Sudanese Liberation Army (MM), participating on the rebel side until sometime between February and April 2006 and on the government side thereafter: at least 330 (initial), at least 10,000 (peak—2004–2005 estimate); a few hundred (final).[350] Sudanese Liberation Army (AW), participating from 2005—there was no obvious moment when it became formally independent of SLA–MM, but the two fought each other that year: [ ].[351] Sudanese Liberation Army (G-19), participating from March 2006: 5,000 (peak, final).[352] Justice and Equality Movement, participating from March 5, 2003: 100 (initial); 3,000 to 4,000 (peak); 3,000 to 4,000 (final).[353]

Antecedents: While tension between nomadic Arabs and sedentary non-Arabs existed before the 1990s, it became more dangerous when the second South Sudan war spilled over into Darfur in the 1990s. Light arms became common, and militias were formed on both sides of the divide. Among these was the Darfur Liberation Front (DLF), a largely

Zaghawa-dominated organization that also incorporated some of the Fur. It attacked a police station in Gulu in June 2002. In October 2002, the *janjaweed*—government-backed Arab militias—raided Darfur with three units of 5,000 men each. Meanwhile, peace negotiations between the government of the Sudan and southern insurgents took place, excluding Darfur. For some groups, rebellion may have become a means to win a seat at the negotiating table. The DLF received support from Eritrea; some of it funneled through the SPLA rebels in the South.

Narrative: On February 26, 2003, some 330 DLF fighters seized Gulu. On March 5, the revolutionary Justice and Equality Movement (JEM) entered the war. The DLF soon renamed itself the Sudan Liberation Army (SLA). Two weeks later, another engagement at Gulu killed 195 government soldiers. In early March a cease-fire was agreed to, but it collapsed on March 18, when JEM continued fighting against the government.

On April 25, the rebels attacked Nyala and El-Fashir; at the latter, only thirty government soldiers were killed in battle, but the rebels also destroyed military aircraft. In general, the fact that many Zaghawa members of the SLA had had combat experience in Chad's civil conflicts made the SLA the more effective fighting force. However, the emphasis on Zaghawa fighters came at the expense of Fur cadres, who nearly formed a separate command under Abdel Wahid to defend their territory when Zaghawas withdrew.

In late May, the rebels scored one of their biggest successes when a government battalion was destroyed by the SLA at Kutum, resulting in the deaths of 500 soldiers. The government responded by arming the *janjaweed.* In mid-July, a second battle at Tine (Tinay) killed 250 government soldiers. Some Chadian Zaghawas, including some Chad army personnel, aided the rebels in this battle.

The government now launched a major offensive using the *janjaweed.* The *janjaweed* attacked and burned villages but engaged in little combat with the rebels. Their objectives were to loot the villages and then force the population to relocate to displaced persons camps, where they could be controlled, similar to a strategic hamlet program but much cheaper and more brutal. The actions of the *janjaweed* made Chad's previous modest support for the government impossible, and by August, there were unconfirmed reports that Chadian troops were protecting refugees and rebels from the *janjaweed.*

On August 1, the rebels took Kutum, killing a substantial portion of its garrison. But in late August, the SLA suffered a severe reverse north of Kutum, suffering heavy losses. In September, it signed a cease-fire with the government. The JEM began to take a larger role in the fighting, and on December 27, it ambushed a *janjaweed* column, inflicting severe losses. The cease-fire between the SLA and government broke down.

At the beginning of January 2004, the government mounted a major offensive using 25,000—soon reinforced to 40,000—regulars. Abdel Wahid was surrounded and requested reinforcements from the SLA leadership, which failed even to respond to the request. Abdel Wahid was evacuated by air with Eritrean and SPLA support. The JEM defended Tine from a government attack, killing more than 1,000 government troops and militia fighters. By February 12, the rebels numbered 27,000.

By May, the death rate among IDPs was up to 4,000 per week. The government proclaimed a cease-fire, but both the JEM and the SLA rejected it. The rebels launched hit-and-run attacks against government columns and downed two helicopters. After an attempted coup in Chad, the government began to support the Darfur rebels. Clashes between the *janjaweed* and rebels increased in September.

The government of Sudan launched a new offensive in January 2005. Hundreds of civilians died in the subsequent fighting. The SLA began to fragment along tribal lines. The Zaghawa wing of the movement (SLA–MM) began to attack both the JEM and the Fur wing of the movement (SLM–AW). This internal fighting substantially weakened the rebel front in 2005.

In February 2006, violence escalated dramatically, but much of it was between rebel factions. In March, a dispute over control of Korma led the SLA–MM to conduct a joint operation with *janjaweed* and government troops to expel the SLA–AW. More than seventy were killed by the SLA–MM, which acquired the nickname *Janjaweed 2* from locals. Some nineteen commanders of the SLA rejected both the SLA–MM and SLA–AW and formed the G-19, which quickly attracted most SLA fighters. Following intensive mediation efforts by the African Union, the SLA–MM signed a draft peace agreement, eventually known as the Darfur Peace Agreement (DPA) with the government on May 5, 2006. The two became effective allies after that point.

Not all of the parties signed the accord, and the JEM, G-19, and SLA–AW created a military alliance known as the National Redemption Front (NRF), which won some successes against government forces in September at Um Sidr and on October 7, 2006, at Karihari. At Um Sidr, the NRF defeated several thousand government troops and captured vehicles and arms. Government forces also suffered heavy losses at Karihari. The NRF also succeeded in pushing the SLA–MM, now widely despised by the population, out of North Darfur. After its victories, the NRF numbered up to 10,000 fighters. As for the SLA–MM, it became more marginalized even by the government, which no longer saw it as capable of delivering stability in Darfur.

Termination and Outcome: After its losses in the west, Sudan signed a peace agreement with rebels in the east on October 14, 2006, which marks the end of the war. Fighting continued, and the outcome of the war was that casualties fell below the threshold for war without a resolution on the ground. Yet, the government of Sudan had effectively won, reducing the insurgents to a minor threat. Atrocities continued after the war.

Coding Decisions: Up to 10,000 people died of gunfire. On the other hand, up to 35,000 died violent deaths. The majority of these were civilians. Our estimate of battle-deaths is 10,000, but the real toll could be much lower or somewhat higher. The JEM fought for control of the central government (power sharing), but as the war began over local issues (resource allocation), we code it as being one over local issues. The armed forces of the African Union and the National Movement for Reform and Development are excluded because they did not participate in combat operations against one side or the other during the civil war period.

Sources: Burr and Collins (2008); Keesing's Contemporary Archives; Prunier (2005); "SUDAN: Special Report II" (2004); Tanner and Tubiana (2007).[354]

INTRA-STATE WAR #935

First Al-Houthi Rebellion of 2004 to 2005 (aka First Yemeni Cleric)

Participants: Yemen versus Houthi Rebels.
Dates: June 20, 2004, to April 8, 2005.
Battle-related Deaths: Total Combatant Deaths: 1,000. (See Coding Decisions.)[355]
Initiator: Yemen.
Outcome: Yemen wins.
War Type: Civil for central control (see Coding Decisions).
Total System Member Military Personnel: Armed Forces of Yemen: 66,000 (prewar, initial, peak, final).[356]
Theater Armed Forces: Armed Forces of Yemen: 2,000 (initial—August 5, 2004). *Shabab al-Moumineen* aka al-Houthi Rebels: 200 (initial); 3,000 (peak).[357]

Antecedents: In 1992, a fundamentalist Shiite organization called the Believing Youth (*Shabab al-Moumineen*) was founded in the Saada Governate of Yemen. It appealed to Zaidis and quickly grew, alarming the authorities. The United States invasion of Iraq in 2003 further radicalized the movement. Although not a member himself, Hussein al-Houthi shared the movement's anti-American and anti-Israel focus. When his supporters began to chant "Death to America" and "Death to Israel" in Sanaa's grand mosque after Friday prayers, the government moved against al-Houthi, arresting 800 of his supporters. Seeking assurances that he was not attempting to revive the Zaidi imamate and take over Yemen, the government invited al-Houthi to a meeting, but he declined to attend.

Narrative: On June 20, 2004, the government sent eighteen military vehicles in an unsuccessful attempt to arrest al-Houthi. Clashes immediately broke out, lasting for two days. Al-Houthi's followers may have numbered only 200 at the time but soon grew as more *Shabab al-Moumineen* members joined his movement. The fighting was centered in Saada Governate, where the rebels retreated to mountain redoubts, inflicting heavy losses on attacking government troops. In the first week of the war, between 53 (government estimate) and 200 (rebel estimate) people, mostly combatants, were killed. By July 16, the government claimed that 300 rebels had been killed.

On August 5, the government launched a new offensive with 2,000 troops. The next day, the last al-Houthi stronghold fell to government forces, but guerrilla war continued, and the rebels retreated to Jabal Salman. On August 19, military sources claimed that the conflict had claimed 900 lives. On August 23, the military announced that it had captured the rebels' new base in Jabal Salman. The following day, a rebel ambush killed 11 government soldiers. Further fighting followed, and on September 9 and September 10, thousands of government troops stormed a cave complex housing al-Houthi, who was killed. The government declared victory, and fighting was ended for a period of six months.

After al-Houthi was killed, his father, Badr al-Din al-Houthi, became the leader of the *Shabab al-Moumineen.* He negotiated with the government, but the talks ultimately failed. On March 19, skirmishes between government forces and the *Shabab al-Moumineen* broke out, and eight days later the rebels mounted an offensive against police and security forces in the area. The government responded with its own operation, and a single day of fighting killed 10 police and up to 40 rebels. Skirmishing continued through April 12, claiming a total of 170 lives since the war restarted.

Termination and Outcome: On April 12, the government announced that its troops had taken control of the al-Houthi strongholds and that most fighting had ended on April 6 (which appears to be incorrect). The outcome of the war was an unconditional government victory; the rebellion was temporarily suppressed, and some 800 were arrested. Minor terrorist attacks persisted. While trials began in August, on September 26 the jailed rebels were amnestied by the government. In late November, further clashes claimed at least 23 lives. The insurgency continued to simmer well below the war threshold until 2007.

Coding Decisions: Note that the rebels deliberately made no demands (aside from the release of captured members once the war was underway), but the government interpreted the movement as revolutionary, so we treat the war as one over control of the central government. While battle-death figures are contested, some estimates of more than 1,000 are plausible. We estimate 1,000 in light of the uncertainty involved.

Sources: Burrowes (2010); Freeman (2009); Integrated Regional Information Networks (2008); Salmoni, Loidolt, and Wells (2010).[358]

INTRA-STATE WAR #941

Second Al-Houthi Rebellion of 2007 to 2008 (aka Second Yemeni Clerics)

Participants: Yemen and Anti-Houthi Tribal Levies versus Houthi Rebels.

Dates: January 29, 2007, to July 16, 2008.

Battle-related Deaths: Armed Forces of Yemen: 1,700 to 2,000;[359] Houthi Rebels: hundreds in 2007 alone;[360] Total Combatant Deaths: about 3,000.[361]

Initiator: Houthi rebels.

Outcome: Stalemate.

War Type: Civil for central control (see Coding Decisions).

Total System Member Military Personnel: Armed Forces of Yemen: 67,000 (prewar, initial, peak); 66,700 (final).[362]

Theater Armed Forces: Anti-Houthi Tribal Levies, participated from April 2007: hundreds (initial); 20,000 (peak—may be overestimate).[363] *Shabab al-Moumineen* aka al-Houthi rebels: 10,000 (peak—2009 estimate).[364]

Antecedents: The al-Houthi insurrection (see Intra-state War #935) continued to simmer at low levels, with periodic outbursts of violence, from 2005 to 2007, when violence again crossed the threshold of civil war. The rebels threatened a Jewish village for selling alcohol, leading to the exodus of forty-five refugees. The regime responded with military checkpoints to protect Jewish villages.

Narrative: The conflict increased in intensity beginning on January 27, 2007, when the group, now led by Abd al-Malik al-Houthi, attacked army checkpoints in Sadaa, inflicting 6 battle-deaths while suffering 7. Other attacks followed in February; the government admitted to losing 90 killed since the beginning of the war, while perhaps 100 rebels had perished in the fighting. Another spike in the fighting occurred during mid-March, leading to the flight of 2,500 refugees. In April, the government estimated 157 soldiers and 315 rebels had been killed.

By this time, the government had mobilized tribal levies against the rebels, and in May the government mounted a huge offensive involving heavy use of armor, air, and artillery. Thousands may have been killed, although a security source estimated 450 government battle-deaths and 600 Houthi deaths since the beginning of the war. The government put out peace feelers; the rebels responded with a list of short-term demands: amnesty, approval for the formation of a political party, and reconstruction and compensation. On June 16, both sides agreed to a cease-fire, but it partially unraveled as a split emerged in the Houthi movement, and attacks on government forces resumed by June 23.

Thereafter, violence decreased dramatically, although more fighting broke out in October at Ghamr. On January 10, 2008, Houthi forces attacked army camps in Jabal Marran, setting off another round of skirmishes. A new implementation plan for the cease-fire was signed on February 1, but deadly skirmishes resumed in April. The government charged the rebels with failing to withdraw from fortified positions they had agreed to evacuate; the rebels responded that the government had to withdraw to pre-2004 positions first.

Fighting intensified in May as rebels moved into Bani Hushaysh and government forces mounted an offensive to drive them out. The Seventeenth Military Division was besieged by rebels. The Houthi rebels advanced toward Sanaa, being halted just twelve miles from the capital. Heavy fighting resumed toward the end of June, and the government attempted to relieve the Seventeenth Military Division. The government declared the end of the fighting on July 16, although isolated incidents continued in 2008.

Termination and Outcome: The government declared a unilateral cease-fire on July 17. The rebels largely honored the cease-fire, ending the war. The outcome of the war was a stalemate. In July 2009, seven Houthis were sentenced to death for their involvement in the hostilities in Bani Hushaysh.

Renewed fighting broke out in August 2009 and has continued sporadically ever since (see Intra-state War #978).

Coding Decisions: Note that the rebels deliberately made no demands until the war was underway, but the government interpreted the movement as revolutionary. Al-Qaeda in the Arabian peninsula is excluded due to lack of coordination with either side.

Sources: Project Ploughshares (2014d); Salmoni, Loidolt, and Wells (2010).[365]

INTRA-STATE WAR #971
Iraqi–Sunni Revolt of 2010 to present

Participants: Iraq and the United States versus Iraqi Sunnis (Aggregate).
Dates: September 1, 2010, to present.
Battle-related Deaths: United States: 66 to date;[366] Total Combatant Deaths: 13,000 to date. (See Coding Decisions.)[367]
Initiator: Iraqi Sunnis.
Outcome: War continues.
War Type: Civil for central control.
Total System Member Military Personnel: Armed Forces of Iraq: 660,000 (initial); 802,000 (peak to date). Armed Forces of the United States of America: 1,563,996 (prewar, initial, peak to date).[368]
Theater Armed Forces: Armed Forces of the United States of America, participating to December 31, 2011 and again later: 49,775 (prewar, initial, peak to date).[369] Sunni Insurgents: at least 6,000 to 10,000 (2013—counts only 3,000 to 5,000 ISIS/ISIL in Iraq and an equal number of its insurgent allies).[370]

Antecedents: After the United States–led invasion of Iraq in 2003, an insurgency developed that became a full-blown extra-state war, with the United States and its allies doing the bulk of the fighting against the insurgents. However, the United States ended combat operations in Iraq on August 31, 2010, transforming the ongoing war into a civil one. The United States remained active in an advisory capacity as part of Operation New Dawn. US troops, which had once numbered 176,000, were reduced to 49,775 by the transformation and continued to decline afterward.

Narrative: The primary issue under contention after the transformation of the war was the centralizing policy of the Shiite-supported al-Maliki government, which bypassed parliamentary controls on its behavior to coup proof the security forces. Various insurgent groups demanded decentralization or the overthrow of the government. Violence increased notably in 2013, and again in 2014, as ISIS entered the war against the government. By 2014, the regular armed forces were down to a strength of 177,600. ISIS attacks had revealed many formations to be paper tigers unable actually to fight. By the end of summer 2014, several divisions had been lost to relentless ISIS attacks. The United States then mounted air strikes to degrade the capability of ISIS; other states soon joined the campaign.

Termination and Outcome: The war is ongoing as of 2015.

Coding Decisions: Iraqi ministries reported totals of 1,350 government battle-deaths from September to November 2010 and 1,883 government-battle-deaths from 2011 to 2012. As of 2013, then, government battle-deaths stood at 3,233 plus what was likely several hundred from the month of December 2010. Rebel battle-deaths for September 2010 to December 2012 stood at 1,040. Total battle-deaths as of the beginning of 2013 were therefore about 4,500. While 2013 battle-deaths are unclear, those for 2014 numbered at least 5,000. Interpolating 2013 figures, we estimate at least 13,000 battle-deaths as of the beginning of 2015. Because it is not clear that 1,000 US troops have been involved in combat operations in Iraq since summer 2014, we do not include a second period of war participation for the United States; other coalition members are excluded for the same reason.

Source: *The Military Balance* (2011, 2015).

INTRA-STATE WAR #976
Libyan Civil War of 2011

Participants: Libya versus United States, United Kingdom, Canada, France, Italy, Spain, and National Liberation Army (Aggregate).
Dates: February 18, 2011, to October 20, 2011.
Battle-related Deaths: Armed Forces of Libya: about 4,500;[371] National Liberation Army: up to 4,500;[372] All Interveners: 0; Total Combatant Deaths: up to 9,000. (See Coding Decisions.)[373]
Initiator: National Liberation Army.
Outcome: National Liberation Army wins.
War Type: Civil for central control.
Total System Member Military Personnel: Armed Forces of Libya: 76,000 (prewar); less than 75,000 (peak after initial defections).[374]
Theater Armed Forces: Armed Forces of Libya: 20,000 (July 2011). National Liberation Army, aka Free Libyan Army: at least 3,000 (after initial defections); 17,000 (July 2011); more than 17,000 (peak).[375] Armed Forces of the United States of America, participating independently from March 19 to March 31 and as part of NATO thereafter: 8,507 (final).[376] Armed Forces of the United Kingdom, participating independently from March 19 to March 31 and as part of NATO thereafter: 3,500 (final).[377] Armed Forces of Canada, participating independently from March 19 to March 31 and as part of NATO thereafter: 2,561 (final).[378] Armed Forces of France, participating independently from March 19 to March 31 and as part of NATO thereafter: 4,200 (final).[379] Armed Forces of Italy, participating as part of NATO from March 31: 4,800 (final). Armed Forces of Spain, participating as part of NATO from March 31: 1,200.[380]

Antecedents: When nonviolent protests succeeded in toppling the regimes of Tunisia and Egypt, the protests spread to other dictatorships in North Africa and the Middle East. On February 15, 2011, mass protests broke out in Libya, with the largest ones in Benghazi in the East. The regime repressed the protest in Benghazi with violence, killing one, but the protests grew over the next few days. Leader Muammar Qadhafi deployed his own irregulars against the demonstrators, which led to a heavy death toll among protesters and other unarmed civilians.

Narrative: On February 18, rebels began a three-day assault on the military barracks of Katiba. By February 20, armed protesters and military defectors took over Katiba, gaining control of Benghazi. The rebels now included 1,000 military defectors and 2,000 former police who switched sides. Benghazi was bombed from the air, but the rebellion grew as government soldiers in and around Benghazi defected to the rebels. On February 24, the coastal city of Misrata fell to the rebels. The rebels were still disorganized, but in late February a national transition council (NTC) emerged and began to assert command authority over the rebels, declaring itself the sole political representative of the Libyan people on March 5.

The rebels lost ground in the first half of March, and loyalist forces seemed poised to retake Benghazi.

However, the conflict was internationalized on March 19, two days after the United Nations Security Council voted to authorize a no-fly zone and military action to protect civilians. Qadhafi's forces were halted by fierce aerial attacks outside Benghazi, while other attacks targeted the country's air defense system. There were four simultaneous operations: Odyssey Dawn (United States), Harmattan (France), ELLAMY (British) and Mobile (Canada). On March 31, these countries handed over responsibility for the operation to NATO.

A period of stalemate followed as the rebels were not strong enough to overcome Qadhafi, but airpower prevented large-scale offensives by his forces. Desertion and defection were common, and by the end of May the government army may have been reduced to only 20 percent of its nominal prewar strength. Mercenaries and tribal levies augmented government forces. The rebels used the time to train their ragtag army (thought to number about 17,000 in July, as opposed to 20,000 loyal government troops) and then advanced against Qadhafi's loyal troops in August. On August 21, the capital of Tripoli fell to the rebels without much resistance.

Qadhafi urged his supporters to fight on and continued the war from his hometown of Sirte. Sabha and Bani Walid also held out against the rebels. The war continued for two more months. On October 13, the rebels captured portions of Sirte, but the next day Qadhafi supporters in Tripoli engaged the rebels in firefights.

Termination and Outcome: On October 20, Sirte finally fell, eliminating organized resistance to the NTC. Qadhafi was killed the same day, and small-scale massacres of the defeated by the victors appear to have taken place. The outcome of the war was a military victory by the rebels. Later, revenge attacks against communities and tribes that had supported Qadhafi took place. No amnesty was promulgated, and as of 2012, thousands of former government fighters or other supporters were still being held by the victorious rebels. At least a dozen of them were killed while in detention.

Coding Decisions: Some 4,700 rebels and their civilian supporters were killed; government losses were similar or somewhat lower. About 2,100 are still missing. We estimate 4,500 rebels and 4,500 government soldiers killed in the fighting, for a total of 9,000. This is probably an overestimate. NATO took part in the fighting as an organization from March 31; while those states that contributed 1,000 or more personnel are included as war participants, the following states contributed more than 100 but less than 1,000 personnel to Operation Unified Protector and are therefore excluded as participants: Belgium (157), Bulgaria (160), possibly Greece (unknown), Netherlands (500), Norway (130), Romania (207), Sweden (a non-NATO member—122), and Turkey (unknown). Overall NATO forces committed to the campaign numbered at least 27,000.[381]

Sources: Amnesty International (2012); "The Day the Katiba Fell" (2011); Johnston (2012); "Timeline: Libya's Civil War" (2011).

INTRA-STATE WAR #978

Sudan Revolutionary Front Rebellion of 2011 to present

Participants: Sudan versus Sudanese People's Liberation Movement–North, Justice and Equality Movement, Sudanese Liberation Army al-Nur, Sudanese Liberation Army Minnawi, and Beja Congress Forces.

Dates: June 5, 2011, to present.

Battle-related Deaths: Total Combatant Deaths: 3,500 to date (see Coding Decisions).

Initiator: Sudan.

Outcome: Ongoing as of 2015.

War Type: Civil for central control.

Total System Member Military Personnel: Armed Forces of Sudan (including Popular Defense Forces): 126,800 (initial); 264,300 (peak as of 2013).[382]

Theater Armed Forces: Armed Forces of Sudan: 40,000 to 70,000 (initial); 70,000 to 100,000 (peak to date). Sudan People's Liberation Movement–North: as many as 30,000 (initial); 30,000 (peak to date).[383] Justice and Equality Movement (displayed coordination with the SPLM–N from November 11, 2011: 2,000 to 5,000 (initial).[384] Sudanese Liberation Army al-Nur, aka SLA–AW (displayed coordination with the SPLM–N from September 8, 2011: 1,000 to 2,000 (initial).[385] Sudanese Liberation Army Minnawi, aka SLA–MM (displayed coordination with the SPLM–N from August 7, 2011: 2,000 to 3,000 (initial).[386] Beja Congress

Forces (displayed coordination with the SPLM–N from November 16, 2011: [ ].

Antecedents: The settlement to the second South Sudan war provided for an independent state in the South Sudan. The main rebel force, the SPLM, was supposed to withdraw most of its forces from the North, but it left some northern SPLM members behind. These members formed the SPLM–North (SPLM–N) and insisted on political reforms provided for by the 2005 Comprehensive Peace Agreement (CPA). The government insisted on their removal or disarmament before reform could proceed and built up its military forces in violation of the CPA.

On May 21, the government of Sudan occupied the disputed territory of Abyei, forcibly evicting the SPLM from the area. On June 1, 2011, the government of Sudan began to forcibly disarm the SPLM members of the jointly integrated units set up by the CPA. For the SPLM–N, this was practically a declaration of war.

Narrative: On June 5, the first shots were fired when SPLA jointly integrated forces members in Um Durein refused to be disarmed. Government soldiers were forced to withdraw, under attack by both the SPLM–N and local civilians. Later that day, Popular Defense Forces militia attacked SPLA members in Tolodi. The fighting expanded the next day but remained limited to South Kordofan province. South Sudan became independent on July 9, 2011. Sudan accused the South of supporting the SPLM–N, which was probably true. Fighting continued in South Kordofan, with the government deploying 40,000 to 70,000 soldiers, police, and militia members against the rebels there.

The first year of the war saw a government offensive drive the SPLM–N away from Kadugli and cut the road to South Sudan. Battles occurred at Tess, al-Hamra, and al-Ihemir.

On August 7, the SPLM–N and the Darfur rebel group SLA–MM inked an agreement to cooperate against the government. On September 2 the war spread to Blue Nile province as well, where most of the rest of the SPLM–N was located. The government banned the SPLM–N as a political party, and fighting escalated. The government began bombing the rebels, and although the rebels initially controlled the garrisons of Dindiro, Kurmuk, and Baw, the latter fell to government forces soon after. The government mounted an offensive against remaining Blue Nile rebel positions using at least 15,000 to 20,000 troops, later increased to 30,000. Dindiro and Kurmuk fell by November.

On November 11, the main forces in opposition to the government signed an alliance creating the Sudan Revolutionary Front, which included the SPLM–N, SLA–MM, SLA–AW, JEM, and (as of November 16) the Beja Congress Forces. That month, the Sudanese government, in cooperation with militias from South Kordofan and South Sudan, captured Troji on the road from Jaw, South Sudan.

Although some fighting had taken place elsewhere in Sudan, notably the Blue Nile province, most of the fighting was concentrated in South Kordofan. The SPLM–N tried to take Jaw in February but only succeeded after mounting a joint operation with the JEM and the South Sudanese SPLA. Later that month, the rebels recaptured Troji. Fierce fighting took place around the garrison town of Tolodi from February through April, and a government effort to capture Angolo to the east of Troji failed on May 20.

In March, the Sudanese government began bombing positions inside South Sudan's Unity state. Fighting between the two states broke out in the West in Panakuach and Teshwin, and another round broke out later in the month, when JEM, Misseriya tribal militia, and South Sudanese forces pressed northward into Sudan. South Sudan pulled its forces back to its own borders on April 20, and the Misseriya went on to join the SPLM–N. The rainy season inhibited fighting until November.

As of 2013, the rebels in the Nuba mountains were attempting to control roads, especially the ones leading into South Sudan. In the Blue Nile province, the rebels were limited to guerrilla warfare and unable to hold territory. The rebels captured the city of Abu Karshola and claimed that 411 government soldiers were killed in an unsuccessful bid to reclaim it on May 15. Casualties continued to be reported throughout the year. In the first five months of 2014, the government admitted suffering 163 battle-deaths, while it claimed to have inflicted 110 battle-deaths on the rebels in one June engagement alone.

Termination and Outcome: The war appears to be ongoing as of 2015, although we cannot be certain due to the lack of battle-death estimates.

Coding Decisions: There are no reliable casualty figures for the rebellion as a whole. Nevertheless, we find it plausible based on the narrative and size of the engaged forces that total battle-deaths (including those due to disease) exceed the 3,500 necessary for this conflict to qualify as a civil war for the dates listed.

Sources: Amin (2014); "Attack on Abu Karshola" (2013); "Bashir Gives Rare Toll" (2014); "Beja Congress Joins Sudan" (2012); Gramizzi and Tubiana (2013); International Crisis Group (2013); "Sudan Revolutionary Front" (2013).

INTRA-STATE WAR #982

Syrian Arab Spring War of 2011 to present

Participants: Syria, Shabbiha Militias (Aggregate), and Hezbollah versus Syrian Rebel Groups (Aggregate).

Dates: June 7, 2011, to present.

Battle-related Deaths: Armed Forces of Syria: up to 45,385; Shabbiha Militias: up to 17,311; Hezbollah: 640; All Rebel Forces: up to 38,325; Total Combatant Deaths: up to 101,661. (See Coding Decisions.)[387]

Initiator: Syria.

Outcome: Ongoing as of 2015.

War Type: Civil for central control.

Total System Member Military Personnel: Armed Forces of Syria: 295,000 (prewar); somewhat less than 295,000 (initial, peak to date).[388]

Theater Armed Forces: Hezbollah: perhaps 4,000 (peak).[389] Armed Rebels/Free Syrian Army/ Islamic Rebels: 7,000 (initial—early autumn); 70,000 (peak to 2015).[390]

Antecedents: In 2011, the Arab Spring swept through the Middle East and North Africa. Regimes in Tunisia and Egypt were toppled by mass demonstrations. On March 18, 2011, demonstrations broke out in Darra, calling on Syrian dictator Bashar Assad to reform the Syrian political and economic systems. When the government brutally suppressed the initial demonstrations, new ones broke out throughout the country. Ordered to fire on demonstrators, some elements of the army deserted.

Narrative: The first clear effective resistance of the war was reported on June 7, 2011, when the government announced that 120 government security forces were killed battling "gangs" in Jisr al-Shughour. The government mounted a military operation to retake the town. On July 29, the Free Syrian Army, a loosely organized association of defectors and armed civilians, announced its existence. A Syrian national council to better coordinate the rebellion was announced on August 25 and established on September 15. It courted foreign support and was soon accepted by a number of nations as the representative body of the Syrian people.

In the fall of 2011, the war escalated. The Free Syrian Army rose from an initial strength of 7,000 to 10,000 in early autumn to a claimed strength of 15,000 in November, the majority of which were in Syria; some were also in Jordan, Lebanon, or Turkey. The government laid minefields near the border to deter the rebels from using foreign sanctuaries. By the end of 2011, some cities such as Homs had been placed under military siege, and the government conceded that 2,000 security forces and army personnel had been killed in the war.

The pattern established during the Homs operation provided the model for much of the urban fighting in 2012. The area was first closed off with checkpoints then bombarded and bombed, and then government troops moved in for house-to-house searches and executions. Often the pro-government *Shabbiha* militias, drawn heavily from Alawis, took part in the last phases of these operations, becoming notorious for their brutality.

In general, the opposition gained control of much of the countryside in 2012, while the government retained control of most urban centers. The rebels attempted to counter government air supremacy with raids on air bases and were sometimes supplied with antiaircraft weapons from captured stocks or countries like Libya, Iraq, Lebanon and Turkey. In the summer, the rebels mounted major operations in Damascus and Aleppo, but both offensives stalled, revealing the limitations of rebel capabilities.

Government forces suffered 20 to 30 killed per day throughout most of 2012. Government strength fell considerably due to casualties, but more serious were losses due to defection or desertions. When the government mobilized reserves, only half reported for duty. While the government army was theoretically 220,000 strong, its effective strength was probably half that by autumn. And the loyalty of even these units was uncertain; the government probably had no more than 50,000 actual soldiers whose reliability could be trusted.

A dramatic shift in the conflict occurred in the late spring of 2013. Lebanese group Hezbollah, long sponsored by the Syrian regime, intervened on the side of the government inside Syria. While the intervention was announced on May 25, Hezbollah troops already had been entering Syria before that date. With the aid of Hezbollah forces, Syria was able to retake most border towns from the rebels, winning a major victory in street fighting in Qusair.

Fragmentation on the rebel side continued, as Free Syrian Army and Islamist rebels both clashed with Kurdish rebels in the East and had difficulty coordinating their operations. The formation and rebellion of ISIS, which fought both the government and other rebels, created a new civil conflict and intercommunal wars with the Kurds and al-Nusra Front (see Intra-state Wars #979 and #981). By 2015, the Syrian government controlled all of the major cities and most of the population.

Termination and Outcome: The war is ongoing as of 2015.

Coding Decisions: All battle-death estimates are as of as of February 5, 2015. ISIS is excluded due to lack of coordination with other groups; in any event, there was a tacit truce between ISIS and the government in 2013 and much of 2014 as the government focused on defeating more moderate groups and ISIS focused on expanding its territory at the expense of other insurgent groups.[391] Of course, eventually the rebellion of ISIS created a new civil conflict. However, disentangling its battle-deaths against Syria and the latter's battle-deaths inflicted by ISIS have proven to be impractical or impossible at present, so we have not yet coded the ISIS–Syria conflict as a separate civil war.

Sources: Giglio (2013); "A Key Battle Cheers" (2013); Lesch (2012); MacQueen (2013); *The Military Balance* (2013); Phillips (2012); "Syria: What Really Happened" (2011); "Syria's Homs Under" (2011).

INTRA-STATE WAR #991
South Sudan War of 2013 to present

Participants: South Sudan, Uganda, South Sudanese Liberation Movement/Army, Sudanese People's Liberation Army–North, and the Justice and Equality Movement versus Sudanese People's Liberation Army in Opposition and Nuer White Army.

Dates: December 15, 2013, to present.

Battle-related Deaths: Total Combatant Deaths: perhaps 5,000 or more to date. (See Coding Decisions.)[392]

Initiator: South Sudan.

Outcome: War is ongoing as of 2015.

War Type: Civil for central control.

Total System Member Military Personnel: Armed Forces of South Sudan: 210,000 (prewar); 185,000 (after initial defections, peak to date). Armed Forces of Uganda: 45,000 (prewar, initial, peak to date).[393]

Theater Armed Forces: Armed Forces of Uganda, participating from December 20, 2013: 1,600 (initial—includes ground forces in South Sudan only).[394] Nuer White Army Militia: 25,000 (initial).[395] Sudanese People's Liberation Movement in Opposition: 10,000 to 25,000 (after initial defections).[396]

Antecedents: Even while it was at war with the Sudanese government, the Sudanese People's Liberation Movement was fractured along ethnic lines, Dinka versus Nuer (see Intra-state War #866). Once independence was gained, factionalism remained problematic. A contest for power between President Salva Kiir and Vice President Riek Machar ensued. In 2012, the assassination of a prominent pro-Machar Dinka journalist—quite possibly by state security forces—inflamed tensions between the factions. The next year, after Machar announced his intention to seek leadership of the Kiir-controlled SPLM, he was relieved of his position as vice president by executive decree; a purge followed. A protest rally by purged elements of the SPLM took place in the capital of Juba on December 14, 2013.

Narrative: The next day, the government preemptively moved selectively to disarm Nuer elements of the presidential guard, leading to scattered fighting in Juba. The rapidity with which events moved suggests planning by one side or the other—within days, the fighting killed hundreds. About 5,000 eventually would die in Juba alone. Violence between the two factions spread to the states of Upper Nile (where the SPLA Seventh Division split along ethnic lines), Unity (where the same happened to the

Fourth Division, commanded by a Nuer), and Jonglei (where the Eighth Division defected to the rebels) as Nuer in the SPLA responded to news of massacres of Nuer civilians in Juba.

Machar formed the Sudan People's Liberation Movement in Opposition (SPLM–IO) and mobilized his Nuer White Army militia, while on December 20, Ugandan (UPDF) forces intervened on the side of the government. UPDF firepower in Juba and then Jonglei and the Upper Nile ultimately prevented these states from falling entirely into rebel hands. The government was able to recapture all three provincial capitals, although significant stockpiles of weapons and ammunition fell into rebel hands. On December 22, the SSLM/A militia, which had been scheduled for integration into the SPLA, joined the government side in the war. On December 27, the Justice and Equality Movement, a rebel group in Sudan, intervened on behalf of the government in Unity state.

Fighting spread to Equatoria in January 2014, and UPDF reinforcements were deployed to halt a rebel advance on Juba. By January 20, elements of the Sudanese rebel group SPLM–N were reported to be aiding the government. Three days later a cease-fire agreement was reached, which would later be extended and modified. However, it failed to stop the fighting, which continues in 2015.

Termination and Outcome: The war is ongoing as of 2015.

Coding Decisions: Up to 50,000 have been killed, most of them civilians. We estimate perhaps 5,000 battle-deaths given the sizes of the forces engaged and the intensity of the fighting in the first months of the war, which could be a considerable underestimate of the true toll.

Sources: Juba-Based Observer (2014); Martell (2014); Small Arms Survey Sudan (2014).

INTRA-STATE WAR #991.5
ISIS–al Nusra Front War of 2014

Participants: Islamic State versus Jabhat al-Nusra.
Dates: January 2014 to November 2014.
Battle-related Deaths: Total Combatant Deaths: 5,000. (See Coding Decisions.)[397]
Initiator: Islamic State.
Outcome: Negotiated settlement.
War Type: Intercommunal.
Theater Armed Forces: Islamic State: 6,000 to 7,000 (initial—total strength); 30,000 (peak—total strength).[398] Jabhat al-Nusra: 7,000 to 8,000 (initial, peak to date).[399]

Antecedents: In 2013, the Islamic State of Iraq entered the Syria's Arab Spring War (see Intra-state War #982). It changed its name to Islamic State in Iraq and the Levant (ISIL) and announced that it had authority over and was absorbing the al Qaeda-backed Jabhat al-Nusra. The leaders of al-Nusra, dominated by Syrian fighters whose first priority was the overthrow of the Assad government, responded that they had not been consulted and refused to accept the authority of ISIL. Al Qaeda's leadership backed up al-Nusra, ordering ISIL to remain in Iraq and threatening to abolish it. ISIL refused to accept al Qaeda's decision.

Narrative: The fighting started near the beginning of January 2014. ISIL attacked al-Nusra positions in the provinces of Raqqa, Idlib, and Aleppo. Al-Nusra temporarily allied with other groups to push ISIL back; both sides suffered substantial losses and ISIL had to retreat from areas around the Deir al-Zor (Deir Ezzur) oil fields. On February 2, al Qaeda's leader expelled ISIL from the organization. This escalated the violence as ISIL sought to increase the territory under its control at al-Nusra's expense.

In March, ISIL mounted another offensive to take Deir al-Zor, suffering heavy casualties in village-to-village fighting. By the middle of the month, some 3,000 had been killed in the fighting. In two days of fighting in late May, al-Nusra killed more than 90 ISIL fighters. That summer, ISIL claimed a global caliphate and leadership of global *jihad*, changing its name to Islamic State (IS). Sporadic fighting continued through the year. While IS had to retreat from some areas of the country, its relative influence generally expanded while that of al-Nusra declined.

When the United States and coalition partners mounted airstrikes on IS, al-Nusra condemned the strikes; early in November, the two groups agreed to work together against the Western-backed Kurdish and moderate forces in the civil war. The United States began striking al-Nusra targets in addition to IS ones.

Termination and Outcome: Although a year has not yet passed, the war appears to have ended with the November agreement to ally against the West. The durability of this agreement has yet to be tested.

Coding Decisions: Some 3,000 were killed in the infighting, the most intense among Syrian rebel groups, through March 28, 2014. By late June, the dead were estimated at 7,000, a figure that includes some civilians killed in cross fire and some deaths from other rebel infighting. Because battle-deaths were probably more than 3,000 but less than 7,000, we estimate 5,000. This figure could be either an overestimate or underestimate.

Sources: Hadid and Mroue (2014); Hubbard (2014); "ISIL Says It Faces War" (2014); "ISIS, Islamist Rebels Clash" (2014); "Nusra Front Kills 90" (2014); Terrill (2014).

INTRA-STATE WAR #992

Third Al-Houthi Rebellion of 2014 to present

Participants: Yemen and Salafist Tribes versus Houthi Rebels.
Dates: February 28, 2014, to present.
Battle-related Deaths: Armed Forces of Yemen: 600; Houthi Rebels: up to 4,000; Total Combatant Deaths: up to 4,600. (See Coding Decisions.)[400]
Initiator: Houthi Rebels.
Outcome: War is ongoing as of 2015.
War Type: Civil for central control.
Total System Member Military Personnel: Armed Forces of Yemen: 66,700 (prewar, initial, peak to date).[401]
Theater Armed Forces: Unknown.

Antecedents: Throughout the period of their revolts (e.g., Intra-state Wars #935 and #941), the Houthi rebels grew stronger over time, while government strength was undermined by reshuffling of commanders and the attrition of years of fighting with al Qaeda, the Houthis, and southern secessionists. The Arab Spring gave Yemen a new president, and eventually a national dialogue conference (NDC) was created to reconcile opposing forces. But on January 21, 2014, a Houthi representative in the NDC was assassinated; the Houthis withdrew from the NDC. Fierce fighting between the Houthis and rival Salafist tribes broke out later that month. When the government announced a plan for federalism that would marginalize the Houthis in a majority-Sunni province, the Houthis denounced it.

Narrative: On February 28, clashes broke out between Houthis and government forces allied to the Salafis over control of Hizm, the capital of the province of Al-Jawf in the North, killing at least 24. What had been an intercommunal struggle between Houthis and Salafists was thus transformed into a civil war. Fighting increased in intensity, and by July the Houthis were nearing the capital of Sanaa. It finally fell on September 21 after a fight that caused 500 casualties; the government offered to meet previous Houthi demands, but the war continued as the Houthis refused to agree to security-related provisions. The government eventually fled Sanaa and continued to resist Houthi advances with a parallel army of loyal units previously held back from fighting the Houthis.

Termination and Outcome: The war is ongoing as of 2015.

Coding Decisions: Some Houthi deaths were no doubt due to intercommunal fighting both before and during the war, so 4,000 is probably an overestimate of their battle-deaths in the civil war. Note that although the fighting between al Qaeda in the Arabian peninsula (AQAP) and the Yemen army produced up to 800 to 900 battle-deaths in 2014, it is excluded from this case because there was no coordination with the Houthi rebels. Similarly, the battle-deaths fall just below the level needed for the AQAP rebellion to be included as its own civil war. However, we do code the conflict that broke out in Rada'a between the Houthis and AQAP as Intra-state War #982.

Sources: Abaad Studies & Research Center (2015); *The Military Balance* (2015); "NDC Extends Hadi's Term" (2014); "One Step Forward" (2014); "Sanaa Falls to Rebels" (2014); "24 Killed in Yemen Clashes" (2014); "Warnings of War" (2014).

INTRA-STATE WAR #996

IS–YPG War of 2014 to present (aka Kobane War)

Participants: Islamic State versus People's Protection Units and Kurdistan Worker's Party.
Dates: July 2014 to present.

Battle-related Deaths: Islamic State: more than 600; People's Protection Units: up to 537; Total Combatant Deaths: perhaps 1,200. (See Coding Decisions.)[402]
Initiator: Islamic State.
Outcome: War is ongoing.
War Type: Intercommunal.
Theater Armed Forces: Islamic State: 1,000 (initial—Kobane area only); 20,000 to 31,500 total (peak to date—includes forces in both Iraq and Syria).[403] People's Protection Units, aka YPG: 30,000 total (initial).[404] Kurdistan Worker's Party, participating from about July 16, 2014: 800 (initial).[405]

Antecedents: During Syria's Arab Spring War (Intra-state War #982), the Kurds of Syria mobilized to defend three majority-Kurdish cantons in the North, collectively referred to as Rojava by the Kurds. People's Protection Units (YPG) were created for the war. When the Islamic State (IS) began its rebellion in Syria (as ISIL), it came into conflict with other rebel groups, including the Kurds.

Narrative: Early in July 2014, IS increased its pressure on Rojava, aiming at the city of Kobane. Within a week, the Kurds claimed to have killed 100 IS troops and destroyed four tanks. However, IS forces advanced, and Syrian Kurdish leaders asked for help from the Kurdish rebels in Turkey, the Kurdistan Worker's Party (PKK). At least 800 PKK crossed the border to help the YPG hold Kobane.

IS tried again beginning on September 16, this time advancing into Kobane itself before being stopped by the YPG, PKK, and—beginning on September 23—American-led (including Bahrain, Jordan, Qatar, Saudi Arabia, and the United Arab Emirates) air strikes. By November 15, IS had lost about 600 fighters in and around Kobane, compared with 370 on the Kurdish side. The battle for Kobane continued into 2015. Although most reports focus on Kobane, it should be noted that fighting also took place between the YPG and IS on other fronts throughout 2014 and into 2015.

Termination and Outcome: The war is ongoing as of 2015.

Coding Decisions: We do not have evidence that enough personnel participated in the American strikes on IS in Rojava to code the United States of America as a war participant. A YPG source claimed to have killed 5,000 IS while suffering only 537 killed itself (throughout the year against all foes). The IS figure is implausible, but this may be an accurate count of YPG fatalities. The IS estimate of 600 is taken from November 15 and hence is too low, probably by hundreds. Our estimate of 1,200 battle-deaths takes these factors into account and may well be an underestimate.

Sources: "ISIS Attack on Northern Syria Continues" (2014); "Islamic State Faces War of Attrition" (2014); "Kurds Enter Northern Syria" (2014); Soguel (2014); "US-led Coalition Hits Jihadist Positions" (2014).

INTRA-STATE WAR #997
Rada'a War of 2014 to present

Participants: Houthis versus Al Qaeda in the Arabian Peninsula and Tribal Allies.
Dates: September 16, 2014, to present.
Battle-related Deaths: Houthis: 1,000; Al Qaeda in the Arabian Peninsula: 300 to 400; Total Combatant Deaths: about 1,200. (See Coding Decisions.)[406]
Initiator: Houthis.
Outcome: War is ongoing.
War Type: Intercommunal.
Theater Armed Forces: Al Qaeda in the Arabian Peninsula: 1,000 (prewar, initial, peak to date).[407]

Antecedents: Just before and during the fall of Sana'a to the Houthi rebels (see Intra-state War #992), the rebels sought to expand their influence into areas held by al Qaeda in the Arabian Peninsula (AQAP). What was already a low-level conflict between the non-state actors greatly intensified when the Houthis advanced into central Yemen.

Narrative: According to AQAP, the fighting for Rada'a, a district in the Al Baida governorate, began on September 16, 2014. AQAP claimed that some 1,500 to 2,000 Houthis were killed in the subsequent fighting, although independent estimates put Houthi casualties in and around Rada'a at 1,000. By October 29, the Houthis had taken much of Rada'a, but AQAP attacks on Houthi positions continued into 2015.

Termination and Outcome: The war is ongoing.

Coding Decisions: AQAP suffered only 400 to 500 battle-deaths in 2014 against the Houthis and the government. We have no disaggregated AQAP battle-death data, but Aboluhom implies that 300 to 400 were suffered against the Houthis.

Sources: Abaad Studies & Research Center (2015); Aboluhom (2015); Al-Moshki (2014).

Notes

1. Mishāqa, 1988.
2. Ibid.
3. Other sources used to code this war include Hitti, 1962; Polk, 1963; Richardson, 1960.
4. Fahmy, 1997.
5. Fahmy, 2002.
6. Creasy, 1961; Wheatcroft, 1993.
7. Correlates of War Project, 2010; Wheatcroft, 1993.
8. Wheatcroft, 1993; Creasy, 1961.
9. Other sources used to code this war include Atamian, 1955; Clodfelter, 2002 Deans, 1854; Dumont, 1963; Eversley, 1924; Mathieu, 1856; Palmer, 1992; Phillips and Axelrod, 2005; Richardson, 1960.
10. McGregor, 2006.
11. Polo, 1833.
12. Other sources used to code this war include Hill, 1970; Holt and Daly, 2000; Mowafi, 1981; Oliver and Atmore, 1994.
13. Bodart, 1908; Fahmy, 1997; McGregor, 2006.
14. Fahmy, 1997; Bodart, 1908; Wilkinson, 1843.
15. Correlates of War Project, 2010.
16. Polo, 1833; Scheidel, 2001.
17. Mishāqa, 1988; Polk, 1963.
18. Other sources used to code this war include Cattaui and Cattaui, 1950; Clodfelter, 1992; Dodwell, 1931; Farah, 2000; Florinshy, 1953; Hitti, 1962; Jaques, 2007; Phillips and Axelrod, 2005; Polites, 1931; Polk, 1963; Rood, 2002; Sabry, 1930; Sicker, 1999; Williams, 1907.
19. Rustum, 1938.
20. Other sources used to code this war include Farah, 2000; Hitti, 1962; Nazzal and Nazzal, 1997; Richardson, 1960a.
21. Farah, 2000; Mishāqa, 1988.
22. Scheidel, 2001.
23. Farah, 2000; Abraham, 1981.
24. Mishāqa, 1988.
25. Ibid., 185.
26. Other sources used to code this war include Clodfelter, 2002; Kisirwani, 1980.
27. Eversley, 1924; Bouron, 1952; Bodart, 1908.
28. Scheidel, 2001.
29. Other sources used to code this war include Clodfelter, 2002; Farah, 2000; Jaques, 2007; Phillips and Axelrod, 2005; Polk, 1963.
30. Halaf, 2002.
31. Scheidel, 2001.
32. Halaf, 2002.
33. Ibid.
34. Ibid.
35. Other sources used to code this war include Cbe, 1993; Farah, 2000; Farah, 1967; Hitti, 1962; Moosa, 1986; Polk, 1963; Richardson, 1960.
36. Clodfelter, 2008; Joachmus, 1883.
37. Correlates of War Project, 2010.
38. Aksan, 2007; Ufford, 2007; Polk, 1963.
39. Ufford, 2007.
40. Scheidel, 2001; Ufford, 2007.
41. Ufford, 2007.
42. Farah, 2000; Bodart and Kellog, 1916.
43. Other sources used to code this war include Anderson, 1952; Cattaui and Cattaui, 1950; Clodfelter, 2002; Dodwell, 1931; Farah, 1967; Jaques, 2007; Jochmus, 1883; Jordan, 1923; von Moltke, 1935; Phillips and Axelrod, 2005; Polites, 1931; Sabry, 1930; Temperly, 1964.
44. Winslow, 2003; Farah, 2000
45. Abraham, 1981; Farah, 2000.
46. Lorimer, 1970.
47. Lorimer, 1970; Cole and Momen, 1986.
48. Cole and Momen, 1986.
49. Ibid.
50. Lorimer, 1970.
51. Cole and Momen, 1986.
52. Farah, 2000.
53. Ibid.
54. Other sources used to code this war include Cbe, 1993; Churchill, 1862; Farah, 2000; Firro, 1992; Hitti, 1962; Richardson, 1960; Trabuolsi, 2007.
55. Ma'oz, 1968; Masters, 1990.
56. Correlates of War Project, 2010.
57. Ma'oz, 1968; Aksan, 2007.
58. Martin, 1990.
59. Correlates of War Project, 2010.
60. Martin, 1990.
61. Farah, 2000; Fawaz, 1994.
62. Fawaz, 1994.
63. Other sources used to code this war include Clodfelter, 2002; Dau, 1984; Farah, 2000; Hitti, 1962; Makdisi, 2000; Moosa, 1986; Palmer, 1992; Richardson, 1960.

64. Marsans-Sakly, 2003.
65. Correlates of War Project, 2010.
66. Broadley, 1882.
67. Marsans-Sakly, 2003.
68. Correlates of War Project. 2010.
69. Warner, 1973.
70. Baldry, 1976; Harris, 1893.
71. Correlates of War Project, 2010.
72. Ingrams and Ingrams, 1993, 332.
73. Baldry, 1976, 169.
74. Bouron, 1952.
75. Correlates of War Project, 2010.
76. Schilcher, 1991.
77. Other sources used to code this war include Betts, 1988; Firro, 1992.
78. McCarty, 1995; Dadrian, 2004; Bağçeci, 2008.
79. Dadrian, 2004; McCarty, 1995.
80. Correlates of War Project, 2010.
81. Ingrams and Ingrams, 1993, 469–71.
82. Ibid., 437–42—the figure is barely legible.
83. Ibid., 388, 489.
84. Correlates of War Project, 2010.
85. Burdett, 1996.
86. Farah, 2002; Ingrams and Ingrams, 1993, 396–411.
87. Other sources used to code this war include Baldry, 1976; Dresch, 2000; Farah, 2002; Kuneralp, 1987.
88. Anscombe, 1997; Vassiliev, 1998; Tuson and Burdett, 1992.
89. Burdett, 1998; Tuson and Burdett, 1992.
90. Lorimer, 1970.
91. Estimated from narrative.
92. Correlates of War Project, 2010; Ashmond-Bartlett, 1910.
93. Ashmond-Bartlett, 1910.
94. Ibid.
95. Ibid.; Pennell, 2000.
96. Other sources used to code this war include Burke, 1972; Chandler, 1975; Clodfelter, 2002; Cooke, 1972; Dunn, 1981; Freeman-Grenville, 1973; Harris, 1893; Mercer, 1976; Phillips and Axelrod, 2005; "Recent Disturbances in Morocco," 1907; Richardson, 1960; Usborne, 1936.
97. Mafinezam and Mehrabi, 2008; Burrell, 1997; Browne, 1995.
98. Correlates of War Project, 2009.
99. Afary, 1996.
100. Browne, 1995; Afary, 1996; Bayat, 1991; Garthwaite, 1983; Yapp, 1987.
101. Cordesman and Wagner, 1990.
102. Bayat, 1991; Afary, 1996.
103. Atabaki, 1993.
104. Mafinezam and Mehrabi, 2008.
105. Other sources used to code this war include Browne, 1966; Clodfelter, 1992; Lenczowski, 1987; Wilbur, 1963.
106. Ingrams and Ingrams, 1993, 602.
107. Correlates of War Project, 2010.
108. Burdett, 1996.
109. Ingrams and Ingrams, 1993, 540–43.
110. Ibid., 617–21.
111. Farah, 2002.
112. Rogan, 1999; Destani, 2006; Winstone, 1982.
113. Destani, 2006.
114. Ibid.
115. Correlates of War Project, 2009.
116. Sabahi, 1990.
117. Burrell, 1997, vol. 6.
118. Ibid.
119. Other sources used to code this war include Chaqueri, 1995; Lenczowski, 1987.
120. McDowall, 1996; Burrell, 1997, vol. 6; Arfa, 1964.
121. Ibid.
122. Correlates of War Project, 2009.
123. Burrell, 1997, vol. 6; McDowall, 1996; Van Bruinessen, 1983.
124. Olson, 1989.
125. Ibid.
126. Mullenbach, 2013a, b.
127. Darlow and Bray, 2012; Habib, 1978.
128. Ibid.
129. Ibid.
130. Other sources used to code this war include Aburish, 1995; Clodfelter, 1992; Lacey, 1981; Lenczowski, 1987.
131. Şïmşïr, 1991; Olson, 1996.
132. Correlates of War Project, 2010.
133. Yildiz, 2004; Şïmşïr, 1991.
134. Yavuz, 2007.
135. Ibid.; Aras, 2010.
136. Watts, 2000.
137. O'Ballance, 1971.
138. Douglas, 1987.
139. Ibid.
140. Douglas, 1987; Correlates of War Project, 2009; O'Ballance, 1971.
141. Other sources used to code this war include Burrowes, 1987; Cady and Prince, 1966; Ingrams, 1963; O'Ballance, 1971.
142. Clodfelter, 1991.
143. Gambill, 2009.
144. Clodfelter, 1991.
145. Harris, 1997.
146. Hiro, 1993; Kerr, 1972; Correlates of War Project, 2009.
147. Haddad, 1971.
148. Al-Aiban, 1996; Attié, 2004.
149. Halaf, 2002.

150. Al-Aiban, 1996
151. Halaf, 2002; Al-Aiban, 1996.
152. Halaf, 2002.
153. Al-Aiban, 1996; Goria, 1985; Haddad, 1971; Hiro, 1993; Clodfelter, 1991.
154. Other sources used to code this war include Agwani, 1965; Cady and Prince, 1966; Clodfelter, 2002; Lenczowski, 1987; Nantet, 1963; Phillips and Axelrod, 2005; Rabinovich, 1985.
155. McDowall, 1996; Dann, 1969.
156. Correlates of War Project, 2010; *New York Times* (March 10, 1959), 1, 7; *New York Times* (March 11, 1959), 1, 34.
157. *New York Times* (March 10, 1959), 1, 7; *New York Times* (March 11, 1959), 1, 34.
158. Other sources used to code this war include Ciment, 2007g; Lenczowski, 1987; O'Ballance, 1989; Taylor and Hudson, 1972.
159. The Implications of the Iran–Iraq Agreement, 1975; Arms Control and Disarmament Agency, 1969; Clodfelter, 2008.
160. Correlates of War Project, 2010; Yildiz, 2004; Arms Control and Disarmament Agency, 1969; O'Ballance, 1996a, b.
161. Correlates of War Project, 2010.
162. Bercovitch and Fretter, 2004.
163. Yildiz, 2004; O'Ballance, 1996.
164. Pollack, 2004; Pelletiere, 1984; Burdett, 2005.
165. O'Ballance, 1996.
166. Other sources used to code this war include Bercovitch and Fretter, 2004; Ciment, 2007g; Clodfelter, 2002.
167. Tlemcani, 1968; Arslan, 1964.
168. Ottaway and Ottaway, 1970; *Keesing's Record of World Events*, 1962.
169. Ottaway and Ottaway, 1970; *Keesing's Record of World Events*, 1962.
170. Stora, 2001.
171. Ottaway and Ottaway, 1970; Ciment, 1997.
172. Other sources used to code this war include Cady and Prince, 1966; Ciment, 2007g; Clodfelter, 2002; Horne, 1977; *Keesing's Record of World Events*, 1962; Ottaway and Ottaway, 1970; Stearns, 2001; Stone, 1997.
173. Arnold, 1995; Pollack, 2004; Clodfelter, 2008; Correlates of War, 2009.
174. O'Ballance, 1971; Edmons, 1972; Dresch, 2000.
175. Correlates of War, 2009.
176. O'Ballance, 1971.
177. Pollack, 2004; Clodfelter, 2008; Arnold, 1995; McGregor, 2006.
178. Schmidt, 1972; O'Ballance, 1971.
179. Schmidt, 1968; Clodfelter, 2008.
180. Other sources used to code this war include Burrowes, 1987; Cady and Prince, 1966; Clodfelter, 2002; *Keesing's Record of World Events*, 1963; Mydans and Mydans, 1968; O'Ballance, 1971; Phillips and Axelrod, 2005; Taylor and Hudson, 1972; Wenner, 1991; Wood, 1968.
181. Clayton, 1999; Cummins, 2010.
182. Edgerton, 2002.
183. Clayton, 1999; Assefa, 1987.
184. Other sources used to code this war include Clodfelter, 2002; Cordesman (1993a, b); Edgerton, 2002; Eprik, 1972; Johnson, 2003; Meredith, 2005; Taylor and Hudson, 1972; Wood, 1968.
185. Arms Control and Disarmament Agency, 1969.
186. Jawad, 1981; Pollack, 2004; Arms Control and Disarmament Agency, 1969.
187. Correlates of War Project, 2010.
188. O'Ballance, 1996.
189. Jawad, 1981; McDowall, 1996.
190. Jawad, 1981.
191. Other sources used to code this war include Bercovitch and Fretter, 2004; Clodfelter, 2002; *Keesing's Record of World Events* 1964–1966.
192. The Implications of the Iran–Iraq Agreement, 1975; Arms Control and Disarmament Agency, 1969; Clodfelter, 2008; O'Ballance, 1996.
193. Correlates of War Project, 2010.
194. O'Ballance, 1996.
195. Ghareeb, 1981.
196. O'Ballance, 1996; Ghareeb, 1981.
197. Arms Control and Disarmament Agency, 1969.
198. Clodfelter, 2008.
199. Other sources used to code this war include Bercovitch and Fretter, 2004; Brogan, 1998; *Keesing's Record of Word Events*, 1970; Tripp, 2000.
200. O'Ballance, 1974; Mobley, 2009.
201. Correlates of War Project, 2010.
202. Tillema, 1991.
203. Clodfelter, 2008.
204. Other sources used to code this war include Cleveland, 1994; Clodfelter, 2002; Higham, 1972; Lenczowski, 1987; Snow, 1972.
205. Ghareeb, 1981.
206. Correlates of War Project, 2010.
207. Ghareeb, 1981.
208. O'Ballance, 1996.
209. Ghareeb, 1981; Catudal, 1976.
210. Other sources used to code this war include Brogan, 1998; Clodfelter, 2002.
211. Weinberger, 1986; O'Ballance, 1998; Winslow, 2003.
212. Sirriah, 1989; El Khazen, 2000; O'Ballance, 1998.
213. El Khazen, 2000.
214. Library of Congress (Federal Research Division), 1989.

215. Hiro, 1993; Jureidini and Price 1979.
216. Ibid.
217. Sirriah, 1989; O'Ballance, 1998; El Khazen, 2000.
218. El Khazen, 2000; O'Ballance, 1998.
219. O'Ballance, 1998; Weinberger, 1986.
220. O'Ballance, 1998; Ma'oz, 1995; Hiro, 1993.
221. Hiro, 1993; El Khazen, 2000.
222. Ibid.
223. Ibid.
224. El Khazen, 2000
225. Ibid.
226. Ibid.
227. Ibid.
228. Ibid.
229. Library of Congress (Federal Research Division), 1989.
230. Ma'oz, 1995; Abraham, 1996.
231. El Khazen, 2000; O'Ballance, 1997; Ma'oz, 1995.
232. Other sources used to code this war include Ciment, 2007g; Clodfelter, 2002; Goldschmidt, 1991; Haley and Snider, 1979; Lenczowski, 1987; Meo, 1977; Phillips and Axelrod, 2005; Rabinovich, 1985; Salibi, 1976.
233. Parsa, 1989; Daneshvar, 1996; Clodfelter, 2008; Kurzman, 2004.
234. Correlates of War Project, 2009; Milani, 1994; Daneshvar, 1996.
235. O'Ballance, 1997; Arnold, 1995
236. O'Ballance, 1997; Parsa, 1989; Arnold, 1995.
237. Parsa, 1989; Arjomand, 1988.
238. Other sources used to code this war include Ciment, 2007g; Clodfelter, 2002; Hiro, 1996; Lenczowski, 1987; Phillips and Axelrod, 2005.
239. Stempel, 1981; Coyle, 1993; Hicks, Sharifpour, and Hicks, 2007; Hiro, 1985; Parsa, 1989; Bakhash, 1984; Cordesman and Wagner, 1990a, b.
240. Correlates of War Project, 2009; Stempel, 1981; Coyle, 1993; Hicks et al., 2007; Hiro, 1985.
241. O'Ballance, 1997; Hiro, 1985; Parsa, 1989; Bakhash, 1984.
242. O'Ballance, 1997.
243. Parsa, 1989; Cordesman and Wagner, 1990a, b; Hicks et al., 2007.
244. Other sources used to code this war include Brogan, 1998; Clodfelter, 2002; Lenczowski, 1987; Phillips and Axelrod, 2005.
245. Clodfelter, 2008.
246. Degenhardt, 1987; Van Dam, 1996.
247. Correlates of War Project, 2010.
248. Middle East Watch, 1991.
249. Other sources used to code this war include Cleveland, 1994; Clodfelter, 2002; Hiro (2003); *Keesing's Record of World Events*, 1982; Stearns, 2001.
250. Cimbala and Forester, 2010.
251. Correlates of War Project, 2010; Hallenbeck, 1991; *The Military Balance*, 1983.
252. Correlates of War Project, 2010.
253. *The Military Balance*, 1983; *The Military Balance*, 1984.
254. Hallenbeck, 1991.
255. Ibid.
256. Russell, 1985; *The Military Balance*, 1983; Hiro, 1993.
257. Hallenbeck, 1991; *The Military Balance*, 1983; Hiro, 1993.
258. Hiro, 1993.
259. Chebabi, 2006.
260. Ibid.; Ranstorp, 1997.
261. Arnold, 1995.
262. O'Ballance, 1998, 128.
263. Hiro, 1993, 101.
264. Other sources used to code this war include Ciment, 2007g; Clodfelter, 2002; Phillips and Axelrod, 2005; Rabinovich, 1985.
265. Chelala, 2002.
266. Correlates of War Project, 2010.
267. Prunier, 2005.
268. Burr and Collins, 2003.
269. Johnson and Prunier, 1993.
270. de Waal, 2004.
271. Akol, 2003.
272. Prunier, 2004; Human Rights Watch, 2003; Burr and Collins, 2003.
273. Human Rights Watch, 2003.
274. Johnson and Prunier, 1993.
275. Jendia, 2002; Anderson, 1999.
276. O'Ballance, 2000; Anderson, 1999; *The Military Balance*, 1991; *The Military Balance*, 1998–2002.
277. Ofransky, 2000; O'Ballance, 2000; Arnold, 1995; de Waal, 2004.
278. Burr and Collins, 2003; O'Ballance, 2000.
279. O'Ballance, 2000.
280. Johnson and Prunier, 1993; de Waal, 2004.
281. de Waal, 2004; Arnold, 1995.
282. Other sources used to code this war include Brogan, 1998; Cheeseboro, 2001; Clodfelter, 2002; Collins, 1999; Cordesman, 1993a, b; Cutter, 2007; Hutchinson, 2001; Johnson, 2004; Project Ploughshares, 2004.
283. Correlates of War Project, 2010
284. Yildiz, 2004; McDowall, 1996.
285. Van Bruinessen, 1986; McDowall, 1996.
286. Ibid.
287. Van Bruinessen, 1986.
288. Ibid.; *The Military Balance*, 1988.
289. Other sources used to code this war include Bercovitch and Fretter, 2004; Brogan, 1998; Ciment, 2007g; Cleveland, 1994; Leezenberg, 2004; Phillips and Axelrod, 2005; Project Ploughshares, 2005a, b.

290. *New York Times* (December 7, 1986); *Keesing's Record of World Events*, 1986; Cordesman, 1993a, b.
291. Correlates of War Project, 2009; Dresch, 2000.
292. Dresch, 2000.
293. Correlates of War Project, 2009; Kifner, 1986.
294. Other sources used to code this war include Clodfelter, 2002; *Congressional Quarterly*, 1994; Cordesman, 1993a, b; Ismael and Ismael, 1986; Phillips and Axelrod, 2005.
295. Preston, 2004.
296. Laffin, 1991.
297. Harris, 1997; Zahar, 2002.
298. Correlates of War Project, 2009.
299. O'Ballance, 1998; *The Military Balance*, 1989, 1990; Winslow, 2003.
300. *The Military Balance*, 1989, 1990.
301. Ibid.
302. Ibid.
303. Other sources used to code this war include Brogan, 1998; Ciment, 2007g; Clodfelter, 2002; *Congressional Quarterly*, 1994; Phillips and Axelrod, 2005.
304. DaPonte, 1993.
305. Correlates of War Project, 2010.
306. Hiro, 2001a.
307. Ibid.
308. Other sources used to code this war include Brogan, 1998; Cleveland, 1994; Clodfelter, 2002; Kohn, 1999; Phillips and Axelrod, 2005; Project Ploughshares, 2004.
309. DaPonte, 1993.
310. Hiro, 2001a.
311. *The Military Balance*, 1991.
312. Ibid., 1991.
313. Hiro, 2001a; Yildiz, 2004.
314. Other sources used to code this war include Brogan, 1998; Cleveland, 1994; Clodfelter, 2002; Kohn, 1999; Phillips and Axelrod, 2005; Project Ploughshares, 2004.
315. Nachmani, 2003; Clodfelter, 2008; Turkish Ministry of Foreign Affairs, 1995; BBC News, 2013.
316. Correlates of War Project, 2010; Nachmani, 2003.
317. O'Ballance, 1996; *The Military Balance*, 1999.
318. *Agence France-Presse*, 1999.
319. Other sources used to code this war include Brogan, 1998; Clodfelter, 2002; *Keesing's Record of World Events*, 1990–1993; Kutschera, 1994; McKiernan, 1999; O'Ballance, 1996; Project Ploughshares, 2000; Yavuz, 2001.
320. Collins, 2008; Guarak, 2011.
321. *The Military Balance*, 1992
322. Akol, 2003.
323. Hutchinson, 2001.
324. Clodfelter, 2002; Collins, 1999; Cordesman, 1993a, b; Cutter, 2007; Hutchinson, 2001; Johnson, 2004.
325. Joffé, 2008.
326. Correlates of War Project, 2010; Martinez, 2005.
327. Martinez, 2000
328. Other sources used to code this war include Brogan, 1998; Ciment, 2007g; Clodfelter, 2002; Meredith, 2005; Mortimer, 1996; Project Ploughshares, 2004.
329. Gunter, 1996; McDowall, 1996; Yildiz, 2004.
330. *The Military Balance*, 1994, 1995.
331. Other sources used to code this war include Brogan, 1998; Gunter, 1996; Kohn, 1999; Project Ploughshares 2004; Tripp, 2000.
332. *Keesing's Record of Word Events*, 2004; *The Military Balance*, 1994; Kostiner, 1996.
333. Correlates of War Project, 2009; *The Military Balance*, 1994.
334. *The Military Balance*, 1994; Kostiner, 1996; Cooper, 1994.
335. Kostiner, 1996; Cooper, 1994.
336. Other sources used to code this war include Bercovitch and Fretter, 2004; *Congressional Quarterly*, 1994; *Keesing's Record of World Events*, 1994.
337. Katzman, 2000.
338. Correlates of War Project, 2010.
339. Cushman, 1996.
340. Ibid.
341. Katzman, 2000.
342. Other sources used to code this war include Brogan, 1998; Project Ploughshares, 2000.
343. Project Ploughshares, 2005a, b.
344. *The Military Balance*, 1997.
345. Ibid.
346. Lederer, 2008; Guha-Sapir and Degomme, 2005.
347. Correlates of War Project, 2010.
348. Prunier, 2005; "SUDAN: Special Report II," 2004.
349. Prunier, 2005.
350. Ibid.; Tanner and Tubiana, 2007.
351. Tanner and Tubiana, 2007.
352. Ibid.
353. Ibid.
354. Other sources used to code this war include BBC News, 2004; Cutter, 2007; Johnson, 2004; *Keesing's Record of World Events*, 2006; Project Ploughshares, 2008; Timberg, 2006.
355. Burrowes, 2010.
356. Correlates of War Project, 2010.
357. Integrated Regional Information Networks, 2008; Yadav, 2013.
358. Other sources used to code this war include BBC News, 2005; *Keesing's Record of World Events*, 2004–2005; Project Ploughshares, 2008.

359. Project Ploughshares, 2014.
360. Ibid.
361. Project Ploughshares, 2014d; Salmoni, Loidolt, and Wells, 2010.
362. Correlates of War Project, 2010; *The Military Balance*, 2009.
363. Salmoni et al., 2010; *The Military Balance*, 2008.
364. Arrabyee, 2009.
365. Other sources used to code this war include *Al Jazeera*, 2007; Project Ploughshares, 2008.
366. US Department of Defense, 2013.
367. Iraq Body Count, 2013; Iraq Body Count, 2010; "2010 Iraq Death Toll Tops 2009," 2011; Iraq Body Count, 2015.
368. *The Military Balance*, 2010–2015.
369. *The Military Balance*, 2011.
370. Terrill, 2014.
371. Black, 2013; Westwood, 2011.
372. Ibid.
373. Black, 2013.
374. *The Military Balance*, 2012.
375. Westwood, 2011; Johnston, 2012.
376. Vira and Cordesman, 2011; Mackowski, 2012.
377. Ibid.
378. Ibid.
379. Ibid.
380. Ibid.
381. Ibid.
382. *The Military Balance*, 1912, 1913.
383. International Crisis Group, 2013.
384. Ibid.; *The Military Balance*, 2012.
385. *The Military Balance*, 2012.
386. Ibid.
387. Syrian Observatory on Human Rights, 2015.
388. *The Military Balance*, 2013, 2014.
389. "Hezbollah Braces," 2013.
390. "Syria: What Really Happened," 2011; Lesch, 2012.
391. Terrill, 2014.
392. Martell, 2014.
393. *The Military Balance*, 2014–2015.
394. Juba-Based Observer, 2014.
395. "South Sudan: 'White Army' Militia," 2013.
396. "South Sudan's Army Advances," 2014. The higher estimate is simply the difference in government force size between 2014 and 2015 from *The Military Balance*, 2014–2015.
397. Terrill, 2014; "ISIL Says It Faces War," 2014.
398. "Who's Who Among Syria's Rebel Groups," 2014; Terrill, 2014.
399. "Who's Who Among Syria's Rebel Groups," 2014.
400. Abaad Studies & Research Center, 2015.
401. *The Military Balance*, 2014–2015.
402. "YPG Releases Balance-Sheet," 2014; "Islamic State Faces War of Attrition," 2014.
403. "ISIS Attack on Northern Syria Continues," 2014; "CIA Says IS Numbers Underestimated," 2014.
404. "Kurdish People's Protection Unit YPG," 2015.
405. "Kurds Enter Northern Syria," 2014.
406. Abaad Studies & Research Center, 2015, Aboluhom, 2015.
407. Freeman, Henderson, and Oliver, 2014.

CHAPTER SEVEN

Intra-state Wars in Asia and Oceania

Below is the list of the intra-state wars that took place in Asia outside the Middle East and in Oceania. Each war will then individually be described with the pertinent basic data provided.

TABLE 7.1 List of Intra-state Wars in Asia and Oceania

War #	War Title	Page #
567	Taiping Rebellion phase 2 of 1860 to 1866	432
568	Second Nien Revolt of 1860 to 1868	437
570	Miao Rebellion phase 2 of 1860 to 1872	440
571	Panthay Rebellion phase 2 of 1860 to 1874	444
576	Tungan Rebellion of 1862 to 1873	447
582	Xinjiang Muslim Revolt of 1864 to 1866	450
582.3	Kanto Insurrection of 1864 to 1865	452
585	Yellow Cliff Revolt of 1866	454
586.5	Kashgar–Khotan War of 1867	454
588	Meiji Restoration War of 1868 to 1869	455
592.7	First Kashgarian–Tungan War of 1870	457
596.7	Second Kashgarian–Tungan War of 1871 to 1872	457
603	Defeat of Xinjiang Muslims of 1876 to 1878	458
607	Satsuma Rebellion of 1877	459
618	Zaili–Jinden Revolt of 1891	460
623	Tonghak Rebellion phase 1 of 1894	462
628	First Gansu Muslim Revolt of 1895 to 1896	463
657	First Nationalist Revolution of 1911	464
665	Second Nationalist Revolution of 1913	466
672	China Pai Ling (White Wolf) War of 1914	466
674	Anti-monarchy War of 1915 to 1916	467
675	Russian Turkestan Revolt of 1916 to 1917	468
676	First Yunnan–Sichuan War of 1917	469
676.5	Southern China Revolt of 1917 to 1918	470
684	Second Yunnan–Sichuan War of 1920	471
685	Zhili–Anfu War of 1920	472
687	Basmachi Rebellion of 1920 to 1924	473
692	First Zhili–Fengtien War of 1922	474
697	First Afghan Anti-reform War of 1924 to 1925	475
697.3	Second Zhili–Fengtien War of 1924	476

(Continued)

TABLE 7.1 List of Intra-state Wars in Asia and Oceania (Continued)

TABLE 7.1 List of Intra-state Wars in Asia and Oceania (Continued)

Individual Descriptions of Intra-state Wars in Asia and Oceania

INTRA-STATE WAR #567
Taiping Rebellion phase 2 of 1860 to 1866

Participants: China, United Kingdom, Hunan, Anhui, and Chu versus Taipings.
Dates: October 25, 1860, to February 9, 1866.
Battle-related Deaths: Total Combatant Deaths: 250,000 (See Coding Decisions.)[1]
Initiator: Taipings.
Outcome: China wins.
War Type: Civil for central control.
Total System Member Military Personnel: Armed forces of China: 1 million (initial, peak, final).[2]
Theater Armed Forces: United Kingdom, participating from February 21, 1862, to December 4, 1863: 650 (initial), 2,500 (peak).[3] Hunan, Anhui, and Chu Armies (all under Hunnanese command): 230,000 to 240,000 (peak), perhaps 50,000 (final).[4] Taipings: 1 million (peak in pre-civil war period), more than 1 million (peak).[5]

Antecedents: In the 1840s, China was ripe for rebellion. Government fiscal policy triggered antitax protests and revolts. Then China was defeated by small numbers of foreign troops in the Opium War. The result was a nationalist reaction that was able to draw upon large numbers of disgruntled peasants. In 1844, a would-be bureaucrat named Hong Xiuqan converted to a version of Christianity in which he was adopted as the younger brother of Jesus Christ and sent on a mission to destroy idolatry. He soon converted his cousins Feng Yunshan and Hong Rengan, who in turn assembled a congregation of 2,000.

Discrimination against ethnic Hakkas like Hong's followers grew his congregation and caused it to turn toward self-defense. Entire Hakka clans joined. Among the most powerful factions was that of Yang Xiuqing, a former charcoal burner. By 1850, there were at least 10,000 followers—perhaps as many as 30,000—at Jintian. Weapons were made in secret, institutional structure was planned, and converts submitted to the segregation of men from their families. Armed conflict began in 1850 as Non-state War #1534 as the government attacked the congregation toward the end of the year, only to be defeated, its commander beheaded by the rebels.

Hong Xiuqan proclaimed the Taiping Tianguo, or Heavenly Kingdom of Transcendent Peace. Yang Xiuqing was acknowledged as third in the hierarchy and associated with the Holy Spirit. Though outnumbered by local Green Standard (Chinese natives, as opposed to Manchu forces) units by more than 10:1, the rebels were left unmolested for nearly a year. In 1851, the rebels broke through the lines of the Green Standards surrounding them and made for Yongan. On September 25, some 40,000 Taipings (only half of them combatants) captured Yongan.

Flush with success but running low on gunpowder, the Taipings broke out of another siege using swords and headed for Guilin, which they unsuccessfully attempted to storm, taking 10,000 casualties. They turned north, toward the headwaters of the Xiang River. Meanwhile, local notable Jiang Zhongyuan had raised a force of auxiliaries with which to combat the provincial rebellion in Hunan. On June 10, 1852, the Taipings were defeated severely by Jiang's forces at Soyi Ford, losing 20 percent of their force, including Feng Yunshan.

Despite the defeat, the rebels advanced northward, issuing a nationalist proclamation for the Chinese to rise up against the Manchus. At Changsha, some 6,000 Hunan militia held back the force of 40,000 Taipings. When a local shipowner joined the rebellion, the rebels were able to amass a fleet of 26,000 vessels with which they headed east along the Yangtze. The rebels took Wuhan, then abandoned it in the face of an imminent government attack. In 1853 the Taipings took Jinjiang, Anqing, and then Nanjing (where more than 30,000 died), which they established as their capital. By this point, the rebel army had swollen to 340,000, partly through conscription.

Including civilian auxiliaries, their forces may have numbered more than half a million.

The rebels now made a strategic error and split their forces into three: a western expedition to capture towns and forts along the Yangtze, a northern expedition against Beijing, and a defensive force to hold Nanjing. Two huge government military camps to the North and South of Nanjing were left untouched. The western expedition failed to recapture Wuhan, although it did recapture Jinjiang and Anqing. The northern expedition had more success at first, gaining anti-Manchu adherents—including support from the Nien rebels (see Intra-state War #568)—as it took each town, until its numbers reached 100,000 at Kaifeng. However, it was delayed in crossing the Yellow River, and when its vanguard threatened Tianjin in June 1853, the government concentrated its forces against the Taipings.

The northern expedition first anticipated reinforcements, which failed to arrive. It then began a long retreat, harried by winter and government troops. The expedition was utterly destroyed, its leaders executed by the government. It suffered between 20,000 and 30,000 battle-deaths. The rebels now were forced to attempt to consolidate their positions in the Yangtze provinces, control of which alternated over the next several years. Wuhan was retaken, lost, retaken, and lost once more. Hunan and Hubei were unsuccessfully attacked by rebel forces.

In 1854, the rebels took Jiangxi, aside from its capital of Nanchang. By 1855, they had also taken much of Anhui and Jiangsu, although the military camps near Nanjing remained. In the spring of 1856, these finally fell to the Taipings. They consolidated their hold on Luzhou, Jinjiang, Suzhou, Anqing, and the territory in between, a quadrilateral that gave them theoretical revenues far greater than those of the Beijing government. Their strength had reached a peak of perhaps 1 million troops. Some 70,000 government troops mounted a desultory siege of Nanjing, but it was sufficiently porous that it caused the rebels little inconvenience.

Then when Yang Xiuqing emerged as a threat to Hong Xiuquan's power, the latter recalled troops that had been sent away by Yang; when forces led by Wei Changhui reentered the city, a complex bloodbath began. Wei proceeded to kill Yang, his family, and 20,000 of his followers. He then turned on rival prince Shi Dakai and executed his family. Finally, he attempted to storm Hong's palace but was stopped short of his goal by the guards. He, his family, and his followers were killed, and Shi Dakai, who had escaped death, was appointed as second in command by Hong.

After a few months, a new western expedition was organized by Shi. The rebels invested the major part of their forces in this endeavor, which was personally led by Shi. While the rebels were able to raise substantial forces from the Triads in the South, their efforts to conquer Hunan and Hubei failed, and they increasingly were hemmed in by pro-government forces as they moved southwest and remained cut off from other Taiping forces for the rest of the war, occasionally cooperating with local Miao rebels (see Intra-state War #570) to attack government forces. Meanwhile, resistance to the rebels in Hunan, now led by Zeng Guofan, increased. He defeated multiple attacks on his headquarters in the capital of Changsha, where he commanded some 10,000 followers. Moreover, imperial forces retook the northern and southern camps near Nanjing.

The rebels reorganized their forces into four armies. In 1858, one of these, led by Li Xiucheng, succeeded in destroying the northern camp, defeating a relief force from the southern camp. The Taiping rebels allied with the Nien rebels in Anhui, allowing Li's forces to retake the strategically vital South of the province. The other Taiping armies were less successful, and Zhen Guofan's forces destroyed Taiping naval power along the middle Yangtze.

In 1859, Hong Rengan arrived in Taiping, was promoted to second in command, and began a series of reforms aimed at reversing the tide of the war. Meanwhile, the Taipings suffered serious setbacks. The two great camps were restored by imperialist forces; Anqing was threatened by the Hunanese forces, while Luzhou was exposed due to a falling-out between the Taipings and their Nien allies. Hong Rengan planned a complex series of operations to restore the situation; the first of these, the capture of Hangzhou and diversion of imperial troops from the southern camp, was successful. The southern camp was retaken by Li's forces. In July 1860, Li's troops took Songjiang near Shanghai. But when he attempted to take Shanghai, his efforts were rebuffed by Chinese, French, and British troops, supported by British artillery. Though Britain was at war with China, it also viewed the Taiping movement as a threat to its commercial interests in the region.

From late 1860 to 1861, the western theatre of war dominated. In the summer of 1860, Zeng Guofan began his campaign against Anqing, a strategic city vital for the riverine supply of any march on Nanjing. The garrison of 20,000 (along with 5,000 women and 10,000 children) was soon surrounded by 10,000 of Zeng's troops. The rebels planned a great envelopment of the Hunan army besieging Anqing while also linking up with Shi Dakai (who had long since been cut off from other Taiping forces) and capturing Wuchang.

Narrative: On October 25, 1860, the Second Opium War (or Arrow War) between China and the British and French ended. Among other concessions, both Britain and France were given the right to station ambassadors in Beijing. This integrated China into the modern state system and transformed what had heretofore been a non-state war into a civil war under our definition. On the ground, of course, operations continued as they always had.

While Li marched southwest, Chen Yuchang took 100,000 troops northwest of the Yangtze (briefly allying himself with a Nien general along the way), turning south toward Anqing in November. Finding his path blocked by 20,000 imperial cavalry, he holed up at Tongcheng for winter quarters, defending the city from imperial attacks throughout the winter. At the beginning of March 1861 he turned to the west, outflanking the imperial forces and moving toward the cities of Wuchang, Hankow, and Hanyang on the Yangtze, the fall of which would compel Zeng to lift the siege on Anqing. He took Huangzhou on March 17, slaughtering its entire garrison of 2,000. But the British warned him against continuing to Hankow, and he heeded their threats, sending a messenger to Nanjing and pausing for months at Huangzhou. The imperials began furiously to build defenses and reinforce the cities threatened by Chen's forces.

Meanwhile, Li's forces had approached Zeng's headquarters at Qimen, crossing the Sheep's Pen and entering the valley on December 1, 1860. The next day, Bao Chao led a force of the Hunan army against Li, defeating him after two days of fighting. The rebels left behind 4,000 killed and wounded. Li took his personal army to relieve Anqing, while other Taiping forces continued to harass Zeng at Qimen, fighting significant engagements in February and March 1861. By April, Zeng was himself surrounded in Qimen. But disastrously for the rebels, Li did not proceed at once to link up with Chen's forces. Instead, he claimed to be unable to ford the Gan river and turned south into Jiangxi, where he expected to find hundreds of thousands of new recruits. His army moved slowly, having to take imperial-controlled towns by siege as it went. He paused at Ruizhou, where he attracted 300,000 followers armed with farm implements.

Chen did not wait for the tardy Li. He took 30,000 of his best troops to relive the siege of Anqing, whose defenders had been kept supplied by foreign merchants—whom Zeng's forces did not dare to attack—and corrupt officials in Zeng's own army. The Hunan army units took to their fortifications, and after three days of hard fighting failed to take them, Chen simply built a new ring of fortifications around them. On May 1, Hong Rengan arrived at Tongcheng with 20,000 troops—half the size of the Hunan army at the time. Five days later, they attacked the imperial cavalry that still stood between Tongcheng and Anqing, only to be defeated.

Li finally arrived at the rendezvous point in Wuchang in June—two months late. Unable to communicate with Chen, he waited until the end of June and began to lead his forces back east and into Zhejiang, evading Bao Chao's forces along the way. Chen withdrew most of his men from the Anqing siege and attacked the imperial cavalry in concert with Hong's forces. The rebels' plan had been betrayed by a spy, and they marched into an ambush. Chen was forced to retreat north to Tongcheng, cut off from the 12,000 troops he had left at Anqing and Jixian Pass. The stockades at Jixian Pass immediately were attacked and surrendered to Bao Chao in early June. All but one of the 4,000 defenders were butchered then by their captors. On July 7, the 8,000 men in the stockades outside Anqing surrendered to Zeng himself; they, too, were slaughtered after being disarmed.

The British withdrew their naval protection for foreign ships supplying Anqing, and the town began to run out of food. The rebels under Chen now mounted a counterattack, retaking Jixian Pass on August 24. A seven-day battle followed, and on September 3, Chen retreated north, abandoning Anqing to its fate. Most of the garrison succeeded in escaping the city, but the civilians (possibly only the male ones) were put to the sword. Chen was trapped in northern Anhui with what remained of his army.

The rebels decided on a new offensive into Zhejiang in the East, China's third-most populous province. After a two-month siege, the capital of Hangzhou fell to Li's forces at the end of December. The rebels honored their promises of safe treatment, which probably hastened the surrender of the city. The rebels mounted a simultaneous campaign to capture the treaty port of Ningbo, despite British warnings, and stormed it with 60,000 troops on December 9. Again, the rebels refrained from massacre. Li now counted more than a million soldiers under his command.

In 1862, the Taipings continued to attack eastward, setting their sights on Shanghai, despite the risk of European (especially British) intervention. By this point, offensive operations against the Taipings largely were limited to Zeng's Hunan army in the West. In need of men, Zeng authorized the recruitment of a militia from Anhui province under Li Hongzhang, subordinate to Zeng.

The rebel campaign for Shanghai started on January 11. Within weeks, 2,000 to 3,000 rebels had captured Wusong, just ten miles north of Shanghai. Cold weather delayed the rebel advance until February, only to find Songjiang newly defended by a well-armed and trained Chinese militia assembled by American filibusterer Frederick Townshend Ward. Ward's militia drove off an attack by 20,000 Taipings on February 3, killing 2,000 rebels and taking another 700 prisoner (who were sent to Shanghai to be executed). Ward took the offensive, dubbing his forces the Ever-Victorious Army (EVA) to attract more Chinese recruits. On February 13, local British and French commanders agreed to defend a 30-mile radius around Shanghai jointly using both their own troops (650 British and 900 French) and those of Ward. Their first joint action was on February 21, capturing the village of High Bridge.

On March 24, some 25,000 soldiers of the Hunan army began to advance on Nanjing from the west. In April, Zeng also sent aid to Shanghai—9,000 soldiers and support personnel from the subordinate Anhui army—on British steamships that the rebels dared not attack. On May 6, the British began to bombard Ningbo in concert with an imperialist attack on the port. The city fell easily, and a massacre of the rebel garrison followed. Qingpu fell to the combined forces on May 13, with some 3,500 men of the EVA storming the town after a concentrated British-French artillery bombardment. An assault on South Bridge led to French casualties, and the French retaliated by storming Zhelin and massacring 3,000 people, civilians and rebels alike, before burning the town.

The rebels responded by threatening Songjiang, causing Ward to withdraw 2,000 men from Qingpu, which subsequently was stormed by the rebels after a siege and unsuccessful rescue attempt by Ward. A number of imprisoned European officers were killed by the rebels along with the rest of the garrison. The allies pulled their ships back to Shanghai for the defense of the city, giving up the villages they had won from the rebels. Ward's EVA continued the fight.

Meanwhile in the West, Chen's forces had been trapped in Luzhou, unable to play their part in a joint Nien–Taiping offensive to the north. Chen finally broke out with 4,000 men on May 13, heading north to meet imperial defector Miao Peilin. Unbeknownst to Chen, Miao had been defeated on April 25 and agreed to return to the imperial side; instead of joining Chen, he had him imprisoned. Chen was executed in June.

The Shanghai campaign had caused Li Xiucheng to rush reinforcements to the East, leaving the West relatively undefended. Zeng's march eastward was easy as rebel garrisons bereft of reinforcements retreated before him. By late May, the 20,000-strong Hunan army was on the outskirts of Nanjing. A siege commenced. Late that summer, cholera struck. About 10,000 of Zeng's men were sickened; throwing in all Hunanese reinforcements brought the total number of effectives up to 30,000—but with no reserves (the remaining Hunanese troops under Bao Chao were entangled in fighting in southern Anhui, where the rebels had mounted a new offensive). The war against the Muslims in Shaanxi (see Intra-state War #576) siphoned off the 20,000 imperial cavalry with which Zeng had hoped to reinforce his siege.

Li now reversed course and sent troops from the Shanghai fighting to lift the siege of Nanjing and destroy the Hunan army. With 120,000 troops under his immediate command, Li approached Nanjing from the south in late September. On October 13, he assaulted the main Hunan camp at Yuhuatai, a strategic hill south of the city gate. Another 100,000 troops from Zhejiang arrived to press the attack, but casualties were lopsided: in one day of fighting in November, the entrenched defenders killed several thousand rebels while suffering only 100 killed and perhaps 200 wounded. After forty-five days of attack, Li called off the counteroffensive on November 26. His supply lines had been choked off by Hunanese naval power, and he withdrew into Nanjing for the winter, sending some units back to Zhejiang and Jiangsu to deal with disturbances there.

In Li's absence, the EVA was able to clear the rebels from most of the thirty-mile radius around Shanghai. Its command shifted after Ward was killed, and its up to 3,000 Chinese soldiers ended up under the command of the Briton Charles Gordon in March 1863. In coordinated operations with units of the Anhui army, the EVA won a string of victories and approached Suzhou, a strategic point from which to mount any attack on Nanjing from the east. At his point, American Henry Burgevine recruited about 70 mercenaries, including officers discharged from the EVA, and joined the Taipings, stealing an EVA gunboat and proceeding to train Taiping units in Suzhou.

After a number of initial successes, the Taiping troops in Suzhou were forced to fall back due to pressure from the EVA and the Anhui army. There they were attacked by Gordon's forces in October. Burgevine and many of his officers took the opportunity to defect to the EVA; he was expelled from China. By November, the situation at Suzhou was a bloody stalemate, but on December 4 some of the Taiping commanders mounted a coup inside the city and opened its gates to Gordon and the imperials on condition of mercy. The surrendering Taiping officers were killed anyway, and the town was sacked. Outraged, Gordon resigned his commission, and the EVA ceased to exist as a foreign-commanded group. Formal military cooperation with the British was sundered by the incident.

The rebels sent an army under Li Xiucheng to break through Hunan forces in northern Anhui, but it was repulsed by the defenders of a number of fortified towns and soon reduced to starvation. When the expedition finally returned in June, it was 100,000 fewer than when it had departed. Meanwhile, Shi Dakai finally surrendered what remained of his forces in Sichuan that summer.

Although the rebels made some progress in Jiangsu in mid-1863, both sides were hampered by the devastation of the war, which made supply next to impossible; Bao Chao gave up on a planned march through Anhui when he was unable to find food or forage. The rebels' small stone fort at Yuhuatai fell to the Hunan Army on June 13, with as many as 6,000 defenders being massacred. On June 30, an amphibious assault carried the forts protecting Nanjing on the northern bank of the Yangtze at the cost of more than 2,000 Hunanese sailors; predictably, the defenders were put to the sword. Bao Chao was sent to seal the northern entrance to the city, but failed when disease broke out in his ranks and threats to southern Anhui and Jiangxi from Taiping armies attacking from Zhejiang forced him to lead his forces away from the city.

Li led another expedition out of Nanjing, this time to recapture Suzhou and rescue Hangzhou. Zeng took the opportunity to expand his siege, taking control of the southwest roads and all but one eastern gate to the city. By December, the rebels controlled only the eastern Taiping Gate and the northern Shence Gate; the rest of the city was surrounded. Nanjing had only 10,000 defenders, along with 20,000 civilians. Li's return after being defeated at Suzhou bolstered the defenses but also meant more mouths to feed. In February 1864, the Fortress of Heaven fell to Zeng's forces, completing the encirclement of the city.

The Taipings spent the spring of 1864 unsuccessfully attempting to recruit new armies with which to relieve Nanjing. The Hunan army also recruited, with considerably more success: it increased to 120,000, not counting the Anhui army or forces under Hunan general Zuo Zongtang in Zhejiang. Meanwhile, one of Zeng's supporters managed to order the machinery for an entire modern weapons factory from an American company, which was shipped to Shanghai to make modern guns, cartridges, and cannons.

On March 31, Hangzhou fell to Zuo Zongtang, with assistance from a French-Chinese force operating out of Ningbo. Some rebels fled to Huzhou, while others moved westward into Jiangxi. The rebels had lost their last major eastern city. On July 4, the Fortress of Earth in Nanjing fell to the besieging forces; the last major rebel fortification around the capital was now in government hands. From the vantage point offered by the Fortress of Earth, Zeng's forces began to bombard the city. On July 19, a giant mine was detonated under the walls of Nanjing, and Hunanese troops rushed in. A predictable massacre of perhaps 7,000 to 10,000 rebels and many civilians followed (Zeng claimed to have killed 100,000) along with the abduction of most of the young women of the city. Three days later, Li—the last great general of the rebellion—was captured and later executed. In August, Zeng began to demobilize his Hunan army.

While the most intense phase of the war was largely over, some 200,000 to 300,000 Taiping troops remained at large in Jianxi, Hubei in the West (which had been cut off from the rest of the Taiping forces since the fall of Anqing), and at Houzhou. The Taiping remnants in Houzhou were the most dangerous; the city fell in August, and the retreating Taipings were finally surrounded and killed in the spring of 1865. On October 15, 1864, some 10,000 to 12,000 Taiping troops took Zhangzhou, Fujian, and continued to fight until they were ejected from the city on May 15, 1865. In June, these forces retreated into Guangdong, where they maintained themselves by recruiting local Hakka until February 7, 1866, when they were defeated in battle. Some 10,000 were killed and another 50,000 taken prisoner (the fate of the prisoners is unknown).

Termination and Outcome: North of the Yangtze, the remaining Taiping forces joined the ongoing Nien rebellion, creating composite units and giving it new impetus. At this point, the Taiping rebellion ended as no unified Taiping forces remained in the field. The outcome of the war was a military victory by the government; surviving Taipings usually were executed.

Coding Decisions: Although there were contacts and even periodic alliances between the Taipings and the Nien rebels, we regard the movements as sufficiently uncoordinated to count their rebellions as different civil wars. The French fought against the Taipings at sub-participant strength (about 900 troops) from February 21, 1862, to about December 4, 1863; thus we do not include France as a participant.[6] Note also that the EVA was formally a part of the armed forces of China. The death toll from the war was astounding. While earlier impressionistic estimates ranged from 20 million to 30 million dead, one recent estimate calculated 70 million dead from all war-related causes, although some of these missing people simply might have left the combat zones rather than died. Given the government's policy of massacring its prisoners, the periodic bouts of disease and starvation that afflicted both armies, the fact that some 600 cities changed hands during the war, and finally that some 10 million troops were involved in the war at one point or another, battle-deaths must have been extraordinarily high. We estimate that up to 1 million soldiers died during the entire period of the rebellion. During its civil war phase, perhaps 250,000 died. The real toll could be lower or higher.

Sources: Elleman (2001); Feuerwerker (1975); Gray (1990); Michael (1966); Platt (2012); Scalapino and Yu (1985); Uhalley (1966).[7]

INTRA-STATE WAR #568

Second Nien Revolt of 1860 to 1868 (aka Nien Rebellion Second Phase)

Participants: China versus Nien Society.
Dates: October 25, 1860, to August 16, 1868.
Battle-related Deaths: Total Combatant Deaths: 75,000. (See Coding Decisions.)[8]
Initiator: Nien Society.
Outcome: China wins.
War Type: Civil for central control.
Total System Member Military Personnel: Armed forces of China: 1 million (prewar, initial, peak, final).[9]
Theater Armed Forces: Nien Society: 20,000 (initial); 80,000 (peak).[10]

Antecedents: The Nien were a secret society, possibly influenced by the Buddhist White Lotus Society, in the Huai Valley. Among other criminal endeavors, they relied on salt smuggling for revenues and recruitment. As the plight of peasants grew worse in the early and mid-nineteenth century, mobilizing them became easier. Beginning with a series of floods and famines between 1851 and 1853, the Nien were able to mobilize bands (*nien*) and recruit followers against the corrupt central government. Attempts to arrest Nien leaders failed, with some Nien offering armed resistance but most simply disappearing before an arrest could be made.

Little is known about the very early stages of the revolt. In 1851, there was a Nien rebellion in Honan's Nan-yang prefecture. Local officials covered up the revolt, while they could, and when an expedition finally was sent to arrest the leaders of the Nien, the expedition's leader himself was captured. In early 1853, the rebels formally proclaimed war against the central government, eighteen of their leaders rallying to the banner of Chang Lo-hsing. In February, the Taipings (see Intra-state War #567) captured Anking, the capital of Anhwei province.

Nien in the northern parts of the province raised at least thirty bands in the ensuing power vacuum. The Nien concentrated on provincial border areas, taking advantage of the lack of coordination between the authorities of different provinces.

The initial revolt was brief; the several thousand Nien soldiers melted away as local government forces approached Chang Lo-Hsing's headquarters at Chi-ho. After the brief battle, Chang and other leaders surrendered and were given control of a local militia corps, which soon disbanded. Other Nien continued to try to unite, and late in the year, some fifty-eight bands merged together and began impressing peasants into service. By early 1854, they had 6,000 men and women, but soon the force was destroyed by local leader Yüan Chia-san. The Nien commanders were killed and their troops virtually annihilated.

By early 1855, Non-state War #1539 began between the Ham and the Nien. Chang Lo-hsing was back in the rebel camp for good. From spring, the Nien intensified their military operations. During the autumn, five big bands of Nien cooperated to invade Honan. By the beginning of 1856, the Nien north of the Huai River united around Chang, who led an alliance of five banners: Yellow, White, Red, Blue, and Black. These banners could consist of up to 20,000 men and women each. The Nien fortified the villages of the plains north of the Huai with earth walls that could take government forces months to break through. Large anti-Nien forces easily could exhaust their food supplies during such a siege and be compelled to retreat. When a joint provincial attack took Chih-ho in 1856, it was forced to abandon the rebel "capital" by less than 4,000 Nien. When government forces retreated, as the Honan army did at the end of the year, they did so through denuded territory filled with hostile Nien, with disastrous consequences.

From 1856 to 1859, the Nien focused on securing this base area by overcoming villages hostile to them and absorbing neutral or friendly ones. The government authorized the creation of local corps for defense, but these usually joined the Nien instead of fighting them. Thus the rebels established a secure base area for offensive operations into Shandong province. Meanwhile, the government besieged the major cities captured by the Nien (Fen-yang, Huai-yüan, then Lin-huai-kan, and Ting-yüan) but made little effort to enter Nien territory after the defeat of Yüan Chia-san in 1857 at the Battle of Sui-hsi-k'ou. By 1858, Chang led a force of 100,000 Nien. The following year, the government succeeded in retaking Fen-yang and Huai-yüan, but the Nien-controlled area between the Sha and Hui was well fortified against assault.

Although the Nien eventually numbered several hundred thousand, the core of their fighting force from 1860 on was 20,000 cavalry. The Nien raided Shandong and Honan every year from 1859 on, resupplying themselves with food, salt, horses, and other necessities. They seldom held ground outside their base areas for very long, preferring to plunder and then retreat into their defenses with the booty.

Narrative: The Nien rebellion continued into 1860, with the central government shifting to a passive containment strategy in January. But later in the year, the government appointed Mongolian prince Seng-ko-lin-ch'in to deal with "banditry" on the Shandong-Anhwei border. His expeditionary army contained 2,000 Manchu infantry, 5,000 Green Standard infantry from Chihli, and 4,000 men from the Shensi–Gansu armies. On October 25, the government signed conventions allowing Britain and France to station ambassadors in the country, thus integrating the state of China into the global state system. This transformed the war from a non-state one into a civil one.

Until 1865, the bulk of the fighting against the Nien rebels was done by the imperial army, with regional forces playing only a minor role in the rebellion. Seng-ko-lin-ch'in played the lead role on the government side, at first suffering catastrophic defeat against the Nien but then enjoying greater success against them from 1861 to 1863. In 1861, the Taipings sent an army to assist Chang Lo-hsing, but the union of the two forces was brief; the Nien soon retreated into Anhui to protect its own base. The Taipings and Nien remained allies in name, and from January 14 to April 1, 1862, a Nien force aided the siege of Yingzhou by Taiping forces.

At the beginning of 1863, the government forces captured hundreds of earth-wall communities, culminating in the capture of Chang Lo-hsing and the fall of Chih-ho. But just a month later, the rebellion was renewed under Miao P'ei-lin, who had switched sides several times during the war. The earth-wall communities subdued by the government immediately joined the rebellion. A new campaign subdued the rebels late in the year, but the rebellion soon flared up anew under the leadership of Chang Tsung-yü.

In 1864 the Nien were reinforced by Taiping remnants under Lai Wen-kuang. After defeats at Lo-shan and Teng-chou, Seng-ko-lin-ch'in was reduced from 4,000 to 5,000 cavalry to only 2,000 remaining. The Nien inflicted a particularly decisive defeat on his forces in August, killing a dozen of his top commanders. Then, on May 8, 1865, Seng-ko-lin-ch'in himself was killed and his force of 20,000 soldiers utterly defeated (most of them being lost) at the hands of the Nien at the bloody battle of Kao-chuang-chi in Shandong.

The death of Seng-ko-lin-ch'in seemed to alarm the government, which placed the elite Metropolitan Field Force between the rebels and Peking. On May 27, Tseng Kuo-fan was appointed commander of all units in Shandong, Honan, and Chihli. His plan was to encircle the rebels using rivers, steadily limiting the area of operations for the Nien. The government marshaled its resources, which had heretofore been focused on the Taipings, against the Nien. Peasants were wooed with a combination of threats, land reclamation, and assistance.

Through late 1865 and 1866, the Nien continued to win the engagements but were increasingly hemmed in by government troops. In late 1866, the Nien were split in two, with the 30,000 or so western Nien concentrating on the North China Plain and the 50,000 or so eastern Nien breaking out to move on Peking. Early in 1867, the eastern Nien threatened to advance on the capital, crossing the Grand Canal and defeating imperial forces sent against them. Li Hung-chang replaced Tseng at about the same time and continued his basic strategy.

On January 11, 1867, the rebels won a victory at Lo-chia-chi in Hupeh. They followed it up by battling 26,000 of the government's best troops at Yung-lung-ho (Yin-lung-ho) on February 19. The battle first favored the Nien, but government reinforcements mounted a pincer attack that cost the Nien up to 10,000 killed and 4,000 captured (according to government accounts). On March 23, 1867, the Nien inflicted about 3,000 killed on government forces in Hupeh. Meanwhile at Shih-tzu-p'o in Shensi, 30,000 rebels in the West inflicted a decisive defeat on the 14,000 government troops, killing 2,000 of them on January 23.

In June, the eastern Nien moved on Hsüchow and then broke through the Grand Canal line in Shandong, attempting to link up with Nien in the province. That July, reinforcements poured into Shandong, as the government attempted to encircle and trap the rebels on the Shandong peninsula. Both the Yellow river and Grand Canal were fortified by government forces, and steamers shelled rebel positions near the river. Government forces dug and manned a 100-mile trench against the Nien, but on August 28, 30,000 rebels passed through government lines and out of the trap. Li was reprimanded and demoted for the failure.

Nevertheless, the eastern rebels found themselves unable to recross the Grand Canal. Although they could move at will within much of the surrounded area, the government cordon began to shrink, and in December, the government won a major victory at Weihsien, killing 3,000 to 4,000 rebels. In subsequent months, the government captured nearly 30,000 rebels, critically weakening the eastern Nien. Still, the eastern rebellion was revived in late January 1868.

Meanwhile in the western theater, the government forces had been pushed back to the Shansi–Chihli border in 1867. Tso Tsung-t'ang was placed in charge of the defense line, but it was breached, and the rebels managed an uncoordinated pincer attack on the capital. Chang Tsung-yü led his Nien into Chihli and reached the Marco Polo Bridge near the capital in February 1868. The eastern Nien in Shandong penetrated to within a few miles of Paoting in the South during this same period.

After a month of fighting, the government managed to force the Nien to retreat back into the countryside toward Shansi, Honan, and Shandong. While the bands continued to roam more or less freely within their zone of control, the government succeeded in hemming them in and preventing them from returning to their base areas. From July 1868, the government won a string of victories against the Nien. The end of the rebellion came suddenly on August 16, when Chang Tsung-yü drowned while retreating with some of the last Nien forces. The government declared the rebellion to be over on August 27.

Termination and Outcome: The outcome of the war was a complete government victory, without promises of amnesty for the defeated. Nien commanders were commonly executed if captured. Nevertheless, the war does not appear to have been followed by any systematic mass killing. Government forces that fought the Nien were soon redirected to deal with the country's Moslem rebellions.

Coding Decisions: Although there were contacts and even periodic alliances between the Taipings and the Nien rebels, we regard the movements as sufficiently uncoordinated to count their rebellions as different civil wars. Bouthoul and Carrère estimate 8,000 dead from 1861 to 1867, but this is an implausibly low number given the reported battles. Similarly, Phillips and Axelrod's estimate of 4 million military and civilian dead is almost certainly too high. Perhaps the most reasonable estimate is 100,000 battle-deaths, with 75,000 occurring during the civil war period.

Sources: Chiang (1954); Chu (1966); Elleman (2001); Teng (1961); Wright (1962).[11]

INTRA-STATE WAR #570
Miao Rebellion phase 2 of 1860 to 1872 (aka Guizhou Revolt phase 2)

Participants: China, Hunan, and Sichuan versus Southeastern Miao Rebels (Aggregate), Red Signals, Yellow Signals, White Signals, Blue Signals, and Guizhou Hui Rebels (Aggregate).
Dates: October 25, 1860, to November 1872.
Battle-related Deaths: Total Combatant Deaths: 100,000. (See Coding Decisions.)[12]
Initiator: Southeastern Miao Rebels.
Outcome: China wins.
War Type: Civil for local issues (taxation and discrimination).
Total System Member Military Personnel: Armed Forces of China: 1 million (prewar, initial, peak, final).[13]
Theater Armed Forces: Hunan Army, participating from June 1866: unknown; Sichuan Army, participating from April 1865 to autumn 1867 and again from April 1868: unknown; Southeastern Miao Rebels, participating to May 28, 1872: more than 100,000 (peak), a few thousand (final). Red Signals, participating from 1861 to 1865: unknown. White Signals, participating to July 31, 1868: less than 100,000 (initial, peak). Yellow Signals, participating to July 31, 1868: 100,000 (initial, peak). Blue Signals, participating from 1864 to 1866: unknown. Guizhou Hui Rebels: unknown.[14]

Antecedents: Guizhou was a poorly governed frontier province dominated by subsistence farming on mountainous terrain. When government taxes effectively were raised due to the outflow of silver during the opium trade, peasants were faced with impossible demands. Folk religions banned by the government also bound many of the Miao and Han together. Meanwhile, government troops were diverted to deal with other rebellions in the early 1850s. A tax revolt by the Lang League was suppressed in late 1853, its leaders executed.

Armed conflict began as Non-state War #1537 as Yang Yuanbao of Dushan led more than 2,000 peasants in revolt against the government on March 25, 1854. This is traditionally regarded as the onset of the Miao revolt (something of a misnomer since more Han Chinese rebelled than did Miao). His revolt was suppressed in two months by a local militia led by Han Chao, but another revolt led by the Han shaman Yang Longxi followed on September 27. Some 1,000 rebels took the departmental seat of Tongzi; Yang's antitax forces increased by thousands—perhaps even tens of thousands—afterward. In late October, Wang San "Zhaba" led a rebellion that eventually merged with that of Yang Longxi after an unsuccessful siege of Qianxi. Tu Lingheng led 1,000 men into revolt on December 17, seizing Xincheng before being killed and dispersed (respectively) after three days' fighting.

Yang's rebellion began to peter out during the winter. By early 1855 about 1,000 troops under Han Chao relieved the sieges of towns under threat and retook Tongzi. Although Yang Longxi had perhaps 20,000 followers at his peak, he avoided direct clashes with the government forces. Han Chao spread an offer of amnesty to all but the ringleaders of the rebellion, and by February, Yang's forces (combined with those of Wang) numbered only 2,000. The government harried his forces and killed Yang himself on April 22. The last remnants of his force were dispersed on June 2, although elements would turn to banditry and rebellion again over the next year.

Yang Longxi's revolt inspired others, and the ethnic Bouyei in Zhenning and Langdai departments rebelled in April and May 1855. The Bouyei rebels mounted attacks in the second half of the year, and in the autumn, one of their base areas was overrun by Yunnan troops under Guizhou's new commander in chief, Xiaoshun. Some 500 rebels were reported killed in this battle. The government largely suppressed the Bouyei rising, but further small-scale rebellions would recur over the following years. On the government side, the Green

Standard army virtually ceased to exist in Guizhou due to deaths, desertions, and transfers. Fighting against the rebels was taken over by locally recruited militia and troops from other provinces.

Around April 30, the Miao of southeastern Guizhou, led by Gao He and Jiu Song, rebelled at Taigong. An ill-advised and unsuccessful extermination policy by the local gentry swelled the ranks of the rebels. Rebels led by Luo Guangming and others took many towns through sieges that lasted as long as a year, thinning the ranks of the defenders through starvation. They would hold some of these towns for a decade. Miao throughout the province—often demobilized militia who had fought the Taipings—began to take up arms. Some of these rebellions were led by Han Chinese. On October 24, Danjiang fell to Luo's forces after a three-month siege that killed several hundred soldiers and thousands of civilians. More towns fell, including Bazhai on December 10, where the Miao rebels embarked on a massacre of Han civilians. They would control the town for sixteen years.

In northeastern Guizhou, several thousand tax resisters following the Red Signal rebelled and on November 11 captured the prefectural capital of Tongren. By January 1856, they may have mobilized 10,000 men. The Red Signals soon pushed into Hunan and southern Sichuan. Their cross-border plundering triggered a military response from Hunan that reversed the rebels' fortunes. Though soon defeated and scattered, the remnants of the Red Signals were subsequently joined by White, Yellow, and Blue Signals in rebellion. A string of towns fell to them over the next few years as the Signal armies (principally composed of Han Chinese) ranged over eastern and central Guizhou.

During the first seven months of 1856, government forces steadily gained against the rebels. On February 17, the government reported a major victory, claiming (with gross exaggeration) to have killed 4,000 to 5,000 rebels and captured 6,000 to 7,000 more at Datang. On March 25 at Luzhou, the government claimed more realistic figures of 300 killed and 67 captured in its victory. Another battle near Taigong killed 500 to 600 rebels and 200 government forces under Han Chao. By the end of April, the Bouyei had been defeated again. Government forces began to massacre even loyal Miao (a process that may have begun earlier in the war).

In July the Sparks from the Lamp rebellion broke out in Guizhou. Led by Han sectarians, the insurrection involved up to 10,000 rebels. While the government initially was able to check the insurgents, it soon found itself pressed on other fronts. In the southeast, the towns of Shengbing and Kaili fell to the rebels after more than a year of siege warfare. Much of the population of the latter had died of starvation. On August 23, Guzhou fell after a similar siege, with similar catastrophic consequences for civilians. A week later, Duyun fell; Qingjiang and Taigong (where the Miao had used cannon to destroy the city gate) soon followed. But as the rebels approached Guiyang, the government counterattacked, taking back Duyun. And in December, the remnants of the Red Signals were all but wiped out.

In 1857, the rebels continued to besiege administrative seats but were unable to take any important ones. Fighting was most intense in the Southeast, but in late October one Jiang Yingfang rebelled with 3,000 followers in Tianzhu. The fighting against Jiang's forces lasted well into 1858. In northern Guizhou, rebels established a base at Bikongshan, which lasted until 1859, when a government commander promised the rebels amnesty (a promise he failed to keep, executing all of them). Such incidents made it more difficult for the government to induce rebels to surrender.

In January 1858, thousands of White Signals (inspired by the Sparks from the Lamps rebellion) led by He Kuanyi rebelled in northeastern Guizhou. Exaggerated reports put their strength at 100,000 as they gained control over local militia units and incorporated them into the rebellion. In the Southeast, the rebels took Maha—the last of the administrative towns encircling the Miao area of settlement—on March 3, concluding a two-year siege. The Miao of the Southeast then assumed a defensive posture, occasionally raiding beyond their area of control but not mounting serious expeditions to expand it. For its part, the government largely ignored the area, while it dealt with other zones of rebellion.

March also marked the beginning of the Yellow Signal revolt, which involved at least three independent groups, two of which were quickly suppressed. The largest of the three groups is reported to have numbered 11,000. By 1860, this band—led by He Desheng—is said to have numbered 100,000. The Yellow and White Signals often collaborated on military operations and shared the same spiritual leader, Liu Yishun of the Sparks from the Lamp sect. They established base areas on isolated plateaus that had sources of water and arable land for crops. These bases were extremely hard to take because they usually had sheer cliffs on at least three sides. The Yellow and White Signals could seize towns as well but rarely held them for long. Their war was concentrated in central and northeastern Guizhou.

In 1856, the Muslim Hui of neighboring Yunnan had revolted (see Intra-state War #571); in December 1858, Muslims in Guizhou also rebelled, taking the Han village of Shatuo and killing most of its residents in what would become a pattern in the Han-Hui conflict. Han, Miao, and Hui bands generally cooperated with each other throughout the Miao rebellion, but leadership was highly fragmented and frequently turned over, with more than eighty major rebel leaders emerging during the Guizhou revolt. Because the rebels were generally poorly armed, they preferred to fight in the rain, conditions under which the government's firearms were less likely to function.

At the beginning of 1859, mutineers captured Weng'an with aid from the Yellow Signals. It was soon retaken by government forces, although it fell again in September. In May, more than twenty clashes in Longquan killed more than 6,000 rebels, according to the official reports. But government forces were spread thin, and when rebels in one place were defeated, new rebellions emerged elsewhere. On the whole, the Miao rebellion was a guerrilla war.

In 1860, the rebels mounted a loosely coordinated campaign against the provincial capital, Guiyang. The Miao, White Signals, and Yellow Signals conducted joint operations near the capital. In May 1860, some 10,000 Taiping rebels entered the province from neighboring Guangxi. While there were some contacts between the Guizhou rebels and the Taipings, there was no coordination between them. By early July, the rebels and Taipings were within fifteen miles of Guiyang's walls. Government forces led by Tian Xingshu counterattacked and drove the rebels from their positions near the capital. He was made commander in chief of provincial forces (a post that changed hands ten times over the course of the revolt). At about the same time as the rebels were approaching Guiyang, Miao under Tao Xinchun in the Northwest set up a base area at Zhugongjing on the border with Yunnan. These rebels cooperated with local "cudgel bandits" to take a number of government-controlled towns in the Northwest.

Narrative: On October 25, 1860, the Second Opium War (or Arrow War) between China and the British and French ended. Among other concessions, both Britain and France were given the right to station ambassadors in Beijing. This integrated China into the modern state system and transformed what had heretofore been a non-state war into a civil war under our definition. On the ground, of course, operations continued, but little information is available on the revolt between the second half of 1860 and 1863. It is known that the Red Signals mounted a new revolt in 1861 that lasted until 1865.

In autumn 1863, two groups of rebels began to approach Guiyang. A number of administrative seats were captured in October and November by the Yellow Signals, and several government militias went over to the rebel side. In December, the rebels got within two miles of the provincial capital but were driven back as government reinforcements poured in. With the failure of the rebel offensive, an uneasy equilibrium existed between government and rebel forces in the province.

Early in 1864, the rebels again approached the capital and were again beaten back by government forces. A provincial force of 3,000 government "braves" largely cleared the rebels from the approaches to Guiyang. Later that year, a group called the Blue Signals joined the rebellion in Renhuai district, participating in the revolt until 1866. The stalemate between the provincial forces and the rebels continued until April 1865, when the government moved to reinforce the province in response to rebel raids into Sichuan province.

Some 6,500 Sichuanese troops under Liu Yuezhao moved south into Guizhou, fighting the rebels in the border area—and suffering terribly from disease. Operations slowed during the months of summer; indeed, outbreaks of disease routinely caused provincial forces sent into Guizhou to withdraw during the summer months. It was common for outside units to suffer 60 to 70 percent illness rates and 30 to 40 percent fatality rates during the summers. Rebel troops also fell ill; in the summer of 1865, more than 10,000 Miao in the Dading prefecture alone were said to have died of disease.

When Liu's campaign resumed in the fall, it had considerable success, forcing rebel leader Song Yushan to surrender about 200 rebel stockades. In the spring of 1866, Suiyang fell to Liu's forces after two months of siege warfare. Some 4,000 rebels and 6,000 civilians surrendered. Liu's campaign to pacify the rebels near Sichuan lasted until autumn 1867, by which time rebel activity on the border had been reduced greatly. Meanwhile, some 18,000 to 19,000 Hunanese troops were sent into Guizhou in June of 1866 to pacify the eastern part of the province.

The reinforcements allowed the government to pursue a strategy of taking and holding territory against the insurgents. However, their performance was disappointing. In nearly a year of combat, no major rebel base areas fell, and little territory was secured. In March 1867, government forces finally moved against Tao Xinchun at Zhugongjing. The bloody assault lasted two months until Zhugongjing fell. Rebel activity in the Northwest declined afterward.

In January 1868, Hunan reinforced its depleted forces in Guizhou with 10,000 new troops. They joined an ongoing assault on the White and Yellow Signal base of Jingzhuyuan, which fell by the end of the month. While many rebels were killed or captured, others escaped to continue resistance. In early April, Sichuan sent in 6,900 men, many armed with modern rifles. These forces collaborated with the Hunanese in an assault on the White Signal base of Biandaoshui, which succeeded in May; some 6,000 to 7,000 rebels surrendered, and 1,000 rebels died in the combat. By the end of July, Hunan–Sichuan troops had overrun five major and several minor White and Yellow Signal bases, killing or capturing all remaining leaders of importance. Northeastern Guizhou was now pacified, limiting serious resistance to the south of the province.

The fighting was far from over. By May 1868, the government had captured a number of towns protecting rebel-held Taigong. In the fall of 1868, Sichuan troops moved southward, recapturing Weng'an, Pingyue, Maha, and Huangping. An English citizen named William Mesny joined the Sichuan army, helping it procure copious quantities of foreign arms. The Hunan–Sichuan armies suffered two major defeats in 1869 as they moved into the South: an ambush in April cost the government hundreds of casualties, and a second ambush in August 1869 resulted in hundreds of government soldiers killed and the loss of Duyun.

In general, the Miao put up more resistance than the Han Chinese Signal armies had done, slowing government progress. As they captured more foreign-made weapons, their sniping took a heavy toll (e.g., 40 to 50 troops per day from the Sichuan army). But Guizhou provincial troops became more effective, contributing to the war-winning offensives of the government. In 1870, the government resumed its offensive against the Miao, killing, capturing, or otherwise bringing thousands under government authority. However, supply problems and concomitant starvation forced the Sichuan army to withdraw to its supply depot, allowing the rebels to recapture Huangping. Sichuan disbanded this army and sent 5,900 new troops under a new commander, which reached the province in December.

Meanwhile, the Hunan army had taken Taigong on November 12, killing or capturing 10,000 rebels. The Hunanese pressed their offensive, killing many Miao and capturing many more. By summer 1871, Bazhai, Danjiang, and Kaili had been retaken. Only a few thousand Miao rebels remained in the field. They were tracked down and their leaders captured and executed by the government. In the Southwest, mixed Han–Miao units were mopped up by government forces, with their last major leader being captured in December 1871. Gao He was the final major commander in the Southeast to be caught, being captured near Leigongshan on May 28, 1872. One report claimed that 100,000 Miao rebels had surrendered in the Southeast and were suffering from starvation.

All that remained were the Hui rebels, but on May 31, 1872, Xingyi fell to government forces, with 2,400 Hui defenders slain. The town of Xincheng remained in rebel hands, and an August assault by government forces failed to carry it.

Termination and Outcome: Negotiations ensued, and around November the Hui leader surrendered (only to be executed by the government). At least some Hui appear to have been massacred following this surrender. The outcome of the war was a government military victory with a limited promise of amnesty to ordinary insurgents. Sporadic rebellions in 1873 were quickly snuffed out by government forces. In December 1873, provincial leaders claimed that all of Guizhou had been pacified.

Coding Decisions: A figure of 4.9 million dead is almost certainly an overestimate, but total deaths in the millions cannot be discounted. Farwell estimates 1.5 million total casualties, including civilians. Deaths from disease and deprivation were unusually high in the generally unhealthy, poorly productive province of Guizhou. For example, in July 1868 some 30 to 40 percent of the Sichuan army in

Guizhou died of illness, a rate typical of the outside armies operating in the province. More than 50 percent were dead for the period of April to August. "Similar reports were made by most other government military commanders."[15] The rebels also suffered from disease and deprivation, losing 10,000 to starvation and an epidemic in August 1865 in Dading prefecture alone.

If we assume a figure of 1.5 million dead and that at least 10 percent of these were military fatalities, we arrive at a minimum of 150,000 battle-deaths, with perhaps 50,000 in the pre-civil war phase and 100,000 during the civil war phase. This estimate is little better than an educated guess, however. The real toll could be somewhat lower or much higher.

Sources: Jenks (1994); Teng (1971).[16]

INTRA-STATE WAR #571

Panthay Rebellion phase 2 of 1860 to 1874 (aka Du Wenxiu Rebellion)

Participants: China versus Pingnan Sultanate, Ma Rulong–led Forces, and Eastern Hui Rebels (Aggregate).

Dates: October 25, 1860, to May 4, 1874.

Battle-related Deaths: Total Combatant Deaths: 75,000. (See Coding Decisions.)[17]

Initiator: Pingnan Sultanate.

Outcome: China wins

War Type: Civil for local issues (independence—but see Coding Decisions).

Total System Member Military Personnel: Armed forces of China: 1 million (prewar, initial, peak, final).[18]

Theater Armed Forces: Pingnan Sultanate: 20,000 to 30,000 (initial 1860); 250,000 to 350,000 (peak).[19] Ma Rulong–led Forces participating on the rebel side to March 1, 1862, and on the government side thereafter: 10,000 (initial 1860); 15,000 (peak).[20] Eastern Hui Rebels, participating to August 1864: [ ].[21]

Antecedents: Tensions between Muslim Hui and the Han Chinese were high in the Yunnan of the 1840s and 1850s. There were a number of massacres of Hui, some of which went unpunished by the central government. Indeed, it appears that the central government's ability to protect the Hui from Han militias and mobs all but disappeared in the early 1850s, and Han bands attempted to exterminate Muslims from the province. Massacres were concentrated near mines, although Atwill (2005) states that "what fueled them was not so much economic rivalry as ethnic resentment" (87).

In early 1855, a Hui named Ma Rulong organized Hui miners into a self-defense force, but they found themselves unable to both mine and protect themselves at the same time. When they abandoned the mine of Shiyang to 1,000 bandits from Xizhuang, the latter began a two-year rampage that looted and exterminated Hui villages and drove the Hui from the mines. By February 1856, more than 8,000 had been killed. In the absence of higher authority (which was busy dealing with the neighboring Miao rebellion—see Intra-state War #570), the anti-Hui governor of Yunnan, Shuxing'a, treated a minor skirmish near the capital of Kunming as a major threat. This conflict began as Non-state War #1541 on May 19, 1856. Orders were issued to form militias and kill Hui. From May 19 to May 21, at least 8,000 more Hui were exterminated. The local government's apparent endorsement of anti-Hui massacres led to a series of them in outlying areas, killing thousands more.

The violence escalated in the aftermath of the Kunming massacre, and organized resistance began in the East. In the first months after Kunming, fighting was most intense in this theater, where the richest mines were located. The communications hub of Yanglin was seized by the rebels. Non-Hui indigenous Yi also took the opportunity to revolt—June Li Wenxue had established himself at the head of thousands of Yi (eventually 10,000 or more) in the Ailao mountains of the Southwest.

In August, a group of rebels seized the walled city of Yaozhou and held it until October 26 against a siege by provincial forces. Meanwhile, more Hui self-defense militias were formed under leaders such as Ma Jinbao, Lan Pinggui, and Du Wenxiu (who seized the more important western city of Dali, while the government forces were busy besieging Yaozhou). Tens of thousands of Han and Hui perished at Dali, and Du Wenxiu went on to establish an independent sultanate (the Pingnan state) with Dali as its capital. Intercommunal fighting between Han and Hui militias broke out across Yunnan.

Until 1857, many Hui placed their hopes in intervention by Beijing. But when the central government interpreted the violence as a Hui revolt, the Hui finally mobilized in open rebellion against the central government. In March, under pressure from the central government, the provincial government mounted a campaign against Hui insurgents. Du Wenxiu led the rebellion in West Yunnan around Dali (with assistance from Li Wenxue), while Ma Rulong led it in Guangyi in the Southwest and Ma Liansheng led rebels in the East. Xu Yuanji, a follower of prominent Muslim Ma Dexin, also led a force southeast of Kunming.

Government troops soon retook a series of rebel-held towns and cities throughout the province but failed to retake the major cities held by the rebels in the West and South. On June 13, Ma Rulong led his own forces as well as those loyal to Ma Dexin to besiege the provincial capital. On July 21, thousands of rebels attacked the outlying areas of the depleted capital, razing its suburbs and slaughtering the civilian population; the governor committed suicide. At about the same time, a government expedition against Dali was turned back by rebel harassment and supply problems.

A truce seems to have been worked out late in 1857, and Ma Dexin was given a title by the new Yunnan governor. Still, the main rebel commanders remained in revolt. Ma Rulong spent much of 1858 at the head of 5,000 troops, attempting to unite the Hui of the South with the non-Han indigenous Yi of the region. Reports of non-Hui participation in the revolt soon emerged, and eventually all major non-Han ethnic groups in the region participated in the revolt.

The government launched or condoned new waves of massacres by Han militias in early 1859, effectively ending any truces. An effort by one Han militia to take Dali was repulsed bloodily in the spring. Ma Rulong's influence continued to expand. He took a series of towns that year—Tonghai, Kunyang, Anning, Lufeng, and Guangtong—but was unable to seize the prefectural seat of Lin'an (or any major city, for that matter).

In late February 1860, the government mounted a new offensive against the rebels in Dali. By early March, at least 2,000 rebels had been slain, and government forces continued to push west. Du Wenxiu called on the influential Ma Dexin for assistance and recalled its best forces from an offensive in the Southwest. Soon, the rebels had retaken a few towns and on September 9, they defeated the imperial troops and killed the imperial commander. Meanwhile, Ma Rulong led his 10,000 rebels on an offensive to relive the pressure on Dali. On June 11, they seized Chuxiong, killing all but one of its Han officials.

The rebels now reached a strange agreement to split Yunnan between the forces of Ma Rulong and those of Du Wenxiu until the Qing forces were expelled, at which time a unified expedition was to be formed to dethrone the Qing dynasty. In the autumn, Ma Rulong mounted an offensive against Kunming itself. And in September, Du Wenxiu's forces took Binchuan to the west of Dali, killing many of the Qing troops there. By mid-October, he had taken Northwest Yunnan's three major cities of Jinchuan, Heqing, and Lijiang.

Narrative: On October 25, 1860, the Second Opium War (or Arrow War) between China and a British-French alliance ended. Among other concessions, both Britain and France were given the right to station ambassadors in Beijing. This integrated China into the modern state system and transformed what had heretofore been a non-state war into a civil war under our definition.

As the rebels besieged Kunming, the provincial government opened negotiations with Ma Rulong and Ma Dexin. These talks started no later than January 1861 but were ultimately unsuccessful, collapsing within two months. A government ambush succeeded in killing Xu Yuanji. However, the Dali rebels made important gains in the Southwest. The government followed up its success against Xu Yuanji with an offensive against Ma Dexin at Chengjiang. Ma Rulong led his forces to cut off government supply lines, then defeated the government forces as they retreated. Once again, Ma Dexin forged agreement among the rebels of the South, and in December, Ma Rulong's multiethnic forces commenced a third siege of Kunming.

The government again commenced negotiations with the rebels, which concluded on March 1, 1862, with the occupation of the city by the rebel forces. In return, Ma Rulong and Ma Dexin agreed to formally surrender, taking up imperial titles and issuing them to their troops. Fighting in and around Kunming died down, and early in 1863 Ma Rulong agreed to lead an expedition against a renegade Han commander who had resisted the authority of the government. In his absence, eastern Hui leaders Ma Rong and Ma Liansheng took Kunming in March, killing the governor general. However facile his earlier surrender may have been, Ma Rulong now clearly aligned himself with government forces, storming the city on March 19. After five or six days of fighting, the eastern Hui leaders fled the city and

Ma Rulong captured Ma Dexin, forcing him to relinquish his seals and keeping him under virtual house arrest.

The new governor general appointed by the central government was a pragmatist committed to restraining Han militias and using Hui to pacify the Hui/Yi uprising. In 1864, Ma Rulong mounted a campaign against Ma Rong, capturing him in August and bringing him to Kunming for execution. Meanwhile, the power of the Pingnan state continued to increase as it brought border tribes and other non-Han under its control. Many of Ma Rulong's former supporters went over to the Dali government, which united most of the rebels for the first time in the war. Sporadic negotiations between Ma Rulong and Du Wenxiu proved unproductive.

In 1866, the government charged Ma Rulong with defeating the Hui in Yunnan, while provincial judge Cen Yuying was tasked with subduing the rebels on the border with Guizhou, where the Hui were in revolt. The latter led 5,000 troops against the border rebels and then moved into Guizhou to fight the Miao and Hui of that province.

Early in 1867, Ma Rulong led Qing forces against Dali. In the spring, the Pingnan rebels responded with a major offensive against Kunming, by now the only major city still in government hands. The Dali rebels, numbering in the tens of thousands, carried all before them. Government troops also died from the plague in large numbers. By fall, Kunming—and most of the imperial forces in the province—were surrounded, leaving the Dali rebels in control of Yunnan. Many Hui under Ma Rulong defected to the rebels; among these were the government's garrison in Dayao, which surrendered the city and joined the eastward march of the rebels. By the end of the year, Ma Rulong had lost much of his influence on both sides.

The government effectively replaced Ma Rulong and the strategy of using Hui to fight Hui with Cen Yuying, whose campaign against the Miao had been very successful. In early 1868, Cen was directed to lift the siege of Kunming, whose outlying towns had already fallen to the rebels. In the city, starvation loomed, disease took a frightful toll on the residents, and Hui kept defecting to the rebels. The rebels eventually mobilized some 200,000 to 250,000 soldiers for the campaign. Ma Rulong had only 15,000 troops, and their loyalty was questionable.

Cen's forces—about 10,000 strong—mounted a counterattack on the rebels around Kunming. A three-pronged attack succeeded in restoring supply routes to Kunming on May 18. On November 19, Cen entered Kunming. The war now became one of capturing and recapturing towns, as each side sought to improve its strategic position. But Du's forces were being spread thin from responding to the attacks, preventing another coordinated assault on Kunming. Rebel losses to disease were high.

By 1869, most of central Yunnan was in government hands, and imperial forces were pushing westward. The increasing government support made possible by the end of the Taiping Rebellion began to be felt that year, as the government retook the rebels' valuable salt wells and then proceeded to reoccupy much territory between Kunming and Dali: Gungtong, Chuxiong, Na'nan, Midu, Dingyuan, Lufeng, Xinxing, and Binchuan all fell in the second half of the year. Cen made use of 60,000 of his 80,000 troops in the campaign.

The government advance then slowed; the last years of the rebellion were characterized by fighting over major cities and prolonged sieges rather than fast-moving campaigns such as Cen's in 1869. Yazhou fell in the spring of 1870, followed quickly by a number of other important towns. By June 1871, some thirty-two cities had shifted to government control. Zahozhou—the last administrative seat other than Dali—fell in spring 1872. Beginning on June 12, the government assaulted Dali itself with the assistance of Han fifth columnists. Six months of combat followed.

On December 26, 1872, Du Wenxiu surrendered. The government disarmed the rebels, but three days later, government forces began a systematic massacre of the residents of Dali, who managed to put up some resistance to the slaughter. Some 4,000 of the 10,000 Muslims killed were women, children, and the elderly. Remaining pockets of rebellion resisted the government out of sheer self-defense. From March to June 1873, the government retook the walled towns of Shunning, Yunzhou, and Tengyue.

Termination and Outcome: Ma Dexin was assassinated in April 1874. The last rebel outpost did not fall to government forces until May 4; although some non-Han rebels remained in the field after that, the level of violence clearly dropped below that of a civil war. The war ended with a complete government military victory. Given the previous massacres of Hui, it is likely that some sort of revenge was taken upon the Hui even after hostilities ceased.

Many Hui fled into what are now northern Burma, Laos, and Thailand. In 1875, a new minor rebellion broke out among the Yi of the Southwest.

Coding Decisions: The rebels also sought eventually to depose the government, but we treat this as primarily a secessionist rebellion. The revolt claimed 300,000 lives, but many of these were doubtless civilians. Still, given the mortality of military forces due to disease and the frequent battles of the rebellion, we estimate 100,000 battle-deaths in all, with perhaps 75,000 of these occurring in the civil war period.

Sources: Atwill (1997, 2005); Dillon (1999).[22]

INTRA-STATE WAR #576

Tungan Rebellion of 1862 to 1873 (aka New Teachings Rebellion or Shaanxi-Gansu Revolt)

Participants: China versus Muslim Rebels in Shaanxi and Gansu (Aggregate).
Dates: June 9, 1862, to November 12, 1873.
Battle-related Deaths: Total Combatant Deaths: 200,000. (See Coding Decisions.)[23]
Initiator: Muslim Rebels in Shaanxi and Gansu.
Outcome: China wins.
War Type: Civil for local issues (intercommunal fighting).
Total System Member Military Personnel: Armed Forces of China: 1 million (initial, peak, final).[24]
Theater Armed Forces: Armed Forces of China: 4,550 (initial); more than 120,000 (peak). Muslim Rebels in Shaanxi and Gansu: 100,000 (initial); 200,000 (peak).[25]

Antecedents: A number of incidents between ethnic Hui (Tungan) Moslems and Han Chinese led to tensions in Shaanxi. The rise of the reformist New Teachings sect among Muslims aroused suspicion of fanaticism among non-Muslims. In April 1862, Taipings invaded the province and swept away government forces outside of the provincial capital of Xi'an. The government responded by authorizing the formation of local corps. The Han gentry organized such corps, but these frequently accused Hui being in league with the rebels, culminating in a series of massacres of Hui.

Narrative: The conflict escalated when Mei Chin'tang took 2,000 local corps members and began to massacre the Hui. Muslim bands retaliated, and the governor of Shaanxi tried to negotiate a peace in June, but his emissary was kidnapped and killed by a Muslim leader on June 9, transforming the intercommunal struggle into a Hui rebellion against the government. Beginning on June 21, the rebels besieged T'ung-chou for eight days, then turned west, and attacked the suburbs of Xi'an (defended by 10,000 or so government troops), surrounding the city in short order. On July 5, the central government issued an ultimatum to the rebels, demanding the surrender of Hui and promising good treatment for all but the top conspirators.

When the rebels ignored the ultimatum, imperial troops were ordered into Shaanxi under Ch'en-ming, who assembled 4,550 troops before pressing on against the Hui rebels. In late August, he was defeated; only 1,200 of 3,000 government troops engaged survived the battle. More imperial troops under Sheng-pao entered the province and marched to Xi'an, lifting the siege. But a Muslim offensive isolated both T'ung-chou and Ch'ao-i. An offensive to relive T'ung-chou failed short of the city; Sheng-pao claimed that more than 100,000 rebels were in the field. The imperial court responded by sending To-lung-a to replace Sheng-pao as commander and suppress the rebellion.

Meanwhile, rebellion had spread to neighboring Gansu, where hundreds of rebels attacked Pai-chi-chen on September 11. Some 10,000 Muslims attacked eastern Gansu; local Muslims joined their ranks. A rebel leader named Ma Chao-yüan succeeded in uniting many of the rebel groups, claiming that the Chinese were planning to annihilate all Muslims. They attacked Ling-chou, but were driven back by a relatively small force of government troops. The Gansu government sought negotiated peace with the rebels of the province, which quickly paid dividends in the form of rebel surrenders and the execution of many rebel commanders.

On January 17, 1863, To-lung-a arrested Sheng-pao and began his own offensive against the center of the rebellion, leading to more than a month of continuous battle. His supplies dwindling, To-lung-a then attempted to negotiate peace with the rebels while he resupplied for war. Upon receiving supplies, he refused the surrender of Muslim units, arguing that it was insincere: "You know, as I know, that you are not sincerely surrendering. I will not be tricked by you. Go back and ready to fight out a life-or-death decision. Wait until you are really beaten . . . then come again to talk peace" (Chu, 41–42).

To-lung-a resumed his offensive, capturing the forts of Ch'iang Pai-chen and Wang-ke-ts'un on March 19. But more forts blocked his advance, and plague struck his army.

On May 18, a force of seven battalions from Xi'an succeeded in restoring the food supply to the capital and cleared much of the area surrounding it. More forts began to fall to To-lung-a; by June, East Shaanxi virtually was pacified. However, the city of Feng-hsiang was besieged by rebels. In September, the government sent 3,000 soldiers to lift the siege. After doing so on November 23, he opened negotiations with the rebels, who despite their defeat retained the ability to inflict severe losses on his forces.

In Gansu, the rebels took Ku-yüan on February 18. After a few dozen Hui were massacred in P'ing-Liang, tens of thousands of Muslims mobilized to besiege the city. The city finally fell on September 24, followed by Ti-tao on October 8. Meanwhile, the government's conciliatory policy and dissolution of local defense forces in the district of Ningxia allowed rebel Ma Hua-long and others to build up his forces. Late in the year, the Muslims took the cities of Ninxia and Ling-chou. In the former city alone, 100,000 Han Chinese were butchered by the rebels. The massacre marked a new level of escalation in the Gansu rebellion. The rebels then assaulted the Tartar city on December 12, killing many government soldiers. Hso-chou was besieged in January 1864; it would finally fall to the rebels on October 31.

In January, To-lung-a accepted the results of the peace negotiations in Shaanxi: the Hui were to surrender their prisoners and ringleaders, but would be allowed to move back to their homes, from whence they had been expelled by Han militia. Lei Cheng-kuan was appointed to lead forces into neighboring Gansu to suppress the Muslim rebellion there. The peace agreement soon broke down when former rebels refused to fight "bandits" that had invaded from Sichuan. To-lung-a ordered the offensive resumed, and the rebels began to retreat into Gansu.

At this point, a second Taiping advance, in combination with the Sichuan bandits, forced To-lung-a to divert his resources to face the more immediate threat. He attacked Chouh-chih, which fell on March 31, but was himself mortally wounded in the fighting, and the bulk of his forces subsequently were dispersed or demobilized. Tu-hsing-a was appointed to command the remnants.

In Gansu, government troops retook P'ing-liang on June 2 and June 3, and a pro-government army of 4,000 Muslims recaptured Ku-yüan—which the rebels would retake later in the year after its unsupplied and starving garrison dispersed to gather food. The government strategy was to secure the highway from P'ing-liang to the provincial capital of Lanchow, splitting the rebels north and south of the line, allowing government forces to turn against each in succession. By the end of the summer, the road was secured, and government forces—numbering 31,600 in the province—turned southward. In September, several centers of rebel activity in the South were taken before the government forces were checked at Lien-hua-ch'eng, which finally fell in November. The rebels besieged Ch'in-chou in the Southeast, but a government counteroffensive drove them from their positions and captured several rebel strongholds in December.

Meanwhile, Tu-hsing-a's first task was to rescue Ningxia. In July, he was ordered to move against the rebels; on the way, he absorbed 2,000 reinforcements sent from the province of Zhili. He kicked off his offensive on August 6, taking Pao-feng on August 16 and lifting the siege of P'ing-lo. By January 1865 he was at the gates of Ningxia, where the offensive stalled. The rebels destroyed dikes, flooding the area and depriving the government of supplies; both conditions contributed to an outbreak of disease in the government camp. On July 2, the siege of the Tartar city was finally lifted, but Ningxia itself held out for another five months. Starvation took hold in the city.

In Gansu proper, the rebellion spread to the western side of the Yellow river in January 1865, taking Su-chou and many other towns while suffering appalling losses due to combat and massacres of Muslim civilians. North of the P'ing-liang-Lanchow highway, Ku-yüan was retaken on February 26, and the government mounted an offensive in the North using friendly Muslims to fight the rebels. The government forces were short of supplies—in May some 6,000 to 7,000 Shaanxi troops deserted en masse and returned to Shaanxi, pillaging as they went. An-ting and Lanchow were exposed by the mass desertion, and the rebels briefly besieged the former before reinforcements drove them off. Peasants in Gansu suffered heavily, and loyal Muslims starved from government exactions, while the rebels managed to keep themselves fed. At about the same time as the mass desertion, a new governor was appointed over Gansu and Shaanxi—Yang Yüeh-pin, who had previously fought against the Taipings. He marched to Lanchow with 5,000 reinforcements from Hunan.

The government's campaign in northern Gansu ran into problems. Pursuing rebels led by Ma Hua-lung—leader of the New Teachings movement—government forces attacked the stronghold of Chin Chi-pao, south of Ningxia. The rebels destroyed wells and cut government supply lines before routing the starving and dehydrated government forces on July 29. Yang was unable to stockpile enough grain for a counterattack. Mutinous forces rampaged through October before the government regained control. During the winter, starvation swept through Gansu. Entire families drowned themselves in the Yellow river rather than face death by starvation. The highway to Lanchow was soon blocked by rebels and bandits that interdicted food shipments into the province and blockaded Lanchow in particular.

The long siege of Ningxia drew to a close on January 10, 1866, when ten Muslim leaders agreed to surrender the city. On January 23, the city was officially given up by the rebels, who surrendered twenty-six cannon, more than 1,000 rifles, and 10,000 swords and spears. Government soldiers clashed with each other during the surrender, as their commanders disagreed about whether the Muslims were sufficiently honoring its terms. Mu-t'u-shan was appointed overall commander of the district by the government and pursued a policy of seeking peace with the Muslims. Even Ma Hua-lung was spared so that he might convince other rebel leaders to surrender.

In February, Yang was forced to withdraw many of his troops from Lanchow, lest they starve to death. With the aid of remnants of other government forces, he planned to attack nearby rebel strongholds and lift the blockade of Lanchow. But while he was away trying to restore order to a group of previously mutinous soldiers, five battalions of imperial troops (1,500 to 2,500 men) at Lanchow revolted and looted the military supply bureau, killing more than 100 imperial soldiers and officials. On May 17, four more battalions stationed at Lung-chou deserted, allowing the rebels to take the city. Everywhere in eastern Gansu, the rebels were advancing due to the government's supply crisis. More government troops deserted, and while nine battalions were recovered at P'ing-liang, others filtered over the border into Shaanxi.

While order was restored in Lanchow on June 16, Yang's career was over. In September, he was replaced by Tso Ts'ung-t'ang, who had wiped out the last of the Taiping armies earlier in the year. As government forces collapsed in early 1867, rebels poured into Shaanxi from Gansu, getting as far as San-yüan north of Xi'an. Meanwhile, the Nien rebels (see Intra-state War #568) invaded Shaanxi from the East. On January 23, government forces in Shaanxi were routed by the Nien, but on February 3 the Nien suffered a defeat outside of Xi'an that secured the provincial capital for the government.

Tso's first priority was food. He brought more than 20,000 of the Hunan army into Shaanxi, intending to establish military colonies and restore agriculture to supply his troops. When Tso arrived, he found that the province was threatened by not only Muslim rebels but also the Nien, with whom they sometimes cooperated. Deserters from Gansu also were raiding, as were native bandits in groups up to thousands in strength. Indeed, Tso estimated that only 60 percent of the "bandits" in the province were Muslim, the remaining 40 percent being mutineers. Although he fought many indecisive skirmishes against both, he resolved to destroy the Nien before moving against the main Muslim strongholds. Indeed, when the Nien crossed the Yellow river, he pursued them into the neighboring province of Shanxi, leaving Mu-t'u-shan in charge of Gansu and Liu Tien in charge of Shaanxi.

Liu proceeded to clear most Muslim rebels from Shaanxi itself in 1868 but refrained from advancing into Gansu. In Gansu, Mu-t'u-shan had advanced in 1867 by negotiating surrenders with Muslim forces. He succeeded in securing Lanchow that year, only to find that government forces in Gansu amounted to 140 battalions (70,000 soldiers on paper) with little in the way of supply or payment. Little progress was made against the rebels in Gansu in 1868.

Tso returned to Shaanxi, where approximately 50,000 soldiers were engaged in guarding the frontiers with Gansu, in November 1868. By this time, the majority of people in the two provinces had died. With the Taiping and Nien rebellions stamped out, the government now was able to release substantial funds for Tso's forthcoming campaign in Shaanxi-Gansu. Tso estimated Muslim rebel strength at 200,000 and intimated to the imperial court that Ma Hua-lung was the mastermind behind the otherwise poorly coordinated revolts.

Tso launched a three-pronged attack on the rebels. First, one prong secured the surrender of 170,000 non-Muslim bandits and refugees in Shaanxi itself, securing the supply lines for the other prongs. A second prong sought to clear the road to Lanchow. A third prong attacked the eighteen Muslim battalions at Tung-chih-yüan, limiting their movement, repulsing their attempt to enter Shaanxi, and finally taking the city on April 4, 1869. Within a week, some 20,000 to 30,000 Muslims were annihilated—frequently during the war, all of the adult males would be slaughtered when cities were retaken. The remainder fled toward Chin-chi-pao. Mutinies slowed down the government's offensive, but soon government forces were bearing down on Chin-chi-pao.

As government forces approached in September, Ma Hua-lung claimed to be negotiating the surrender of the Shaanxi Moslems. He was warned to keep Gansu Muslims out of the conflict, but in the end both sides were reinforced substantially and a battle began, which turned into a sixteen-month campaign to conquer Chin-chi-pao, with its more than 500 forts. In the end, the government besieged the main fort and took it through slow starvation. Ma Hua-lung surrendered for the second time on January 6, 1871. On March 2, Ma, his son, and eighty other high-ranking Muslim rebels were executed.

After the death of Ma, no other leaders could concentrate the majority of Muslims behind them, making the government campaign a series of local battles against uncoordinated rebel forces. Despite government pressure to finish his campaign, Tso paused to allow his troops to plant and harvest crops in order to supply his next campaign. On September 18, he began an attack on Hu-chou, where the rebels were led by Ma Chan-ao. In November, Tso sent twelve battalions to besiege Su-chou in response to the Russian occupation of Ili.

Ma Chan-ao surrendered on February 25, 1872. On September 12, Tso mounted a campaign to relieve Hsining. After difficult battles resulted in government victories, the rebel siege was lifted on November 19, although it took until April 1873 to fully pacify the area. He then focused on Su-chou and finally retook it. On October 24, some 7,000 surrendered rebels were executed. Su-chou itself fell on November 12.

Termination and Outcome: The fall of Su-chou marked the end of hostilities in Shaanxi and Gansu. The outcome of the war was an unconditional victory for the government. Surviving Muslims from Shaanxi, Chin-chi-pao, and Su-chou were not permitted to return but were resettled in isolated areas of Kansu deemed suitable for farming, with implements and seed provided by the government. There is no evidence of postwar massacres. In areas under Tso's rule, the New Teachings were prohibited, although they were permitted elsewhere in the country.

Coding Decisions: Millions of people died in the civil war, mostly due to starvation and its attendant diseases. Supposedly, the population of Kansu was reduced from 15 million to 1 million, with 90 percent of Han Chinese and two-thirds of Muslims perishing. Of 700,000 to 800,000 Muslims who fled Shaanxi into Kansu, only 60,000 or so survived. Given the large size of the contending armies, and the fact that the resources of Kansu were insufficient to supply them, it is likely that hundreds of thousands of combatants died during the war. We estimate 200,000 battle-deaths; the real toll may have been higher.

Sources: Chu (1966); Elleman (2001); Fields (1978).[26]

INTRA-STATE WAR #582

Xinjiang Muslim Revolt of 1864 to 1866 (aka Turkestan Muslim Revolt)

Participants: China versus Xinjiang Muslims (Aggregate).

Dates: June 4, 1864, to April 11, 1866.

Battle-related Deaths: Total Combatant Deaths: 10,000. (See Coding Decisions.)[27]

Initiator: Xinjiang Muslims.

Outcome: Xinjiang Muslims win.

War Type: Civil for local issues (independence).

Total System Member Military Personnel: Armed Forces of China: 1 million (prewar, initial, peak, final).[28]

Theater Armed Forces: Armed Forces of China: 2,100 (initial), at least 12,000 (peak). Xinjiang Muslims: 75,000 (estimated peak).[29]

Antecedents: By 1864, the Chinese treasury was in dire straits and unable to support Xinjiang with its usual subsidies. As a result, local taxes increased dramatically. Moreover, China faced Muslim revolts in Yunnan in the Southwest and the provinces of Kansu and Shaanxi in the Northwest. Rumors and mutual tensions ran high. When a rumor spread that the Chinese were about to massacre the Muslim population of Kucha, the latter, led by Hui (also known as Tungans), revolted.

Narrative: The rebellion began on June 4, 1864, when a group of Hui began looting and pillaging in Kucha. Many non-Muslims were slain; local Turkic Muslims (the majority of Muslims throughout Xinjiang) quickly joined the uprising. When the 300 local troops were ordered to quell the riot, they were defeated by the rebels. The rebels—a mix of Hui, Kasgharis, Khoqandis, and Turkic Kuchean Muslims—proclaimed Rāshidīn Khwāja as their Khān Khwāja, or priest king. The rebels then sent expeditions to raise the revolt in other cities. On June 15, some 2,100 government soldiers were sent from Urumchi against the rebels; the result was a major rebel victory, and the surviving soldiers quickly retreated back to Urumchi.

Revolts broke out in other cities following the same general pattern—rumors of massacre spread among the Hui traders and refugees, a Hui-initiated revolt occurred, the local Turkic Muslims joined the rebellion, and the massacre of government officials commenced. Yarkand rebelled on June 23 (killing 2,000 Qing soldiers, their families, and 7,000 other Chinese civilians), Kashgar three days later (in response to an actual massacre of Hui rather than a mere rumor), and Ush Turfan and Aqsu in July. The Kashgar rebels were unable to unify or defeat the Manchu garrison and requested assistance from the state of Khokand in the West, which sent Gen. Yaqub Beg to assist the Kashgaris.

In Urumchi, the Hui were in the majority, but the government had two fortresses with 10,000 troops. Revolt broke out on June 26. The Urumchi rebels proclaimed a Kingdom of Islam with Tuo Ming as their king. They laid siege to the local Manchu fort and sent others to spread the revolt. Manas (also known as Sulai) fell on July 17; its Manchu fort would fall more than two months later. The Urumchi rebels called on the Kucheans for aid, and the latter sent 5,000 troops, taking the Manchu fort at Urumchi on October 3. In the East, Qur Qarausu fell and Hami revolted on September 29, Changji fell on October 6, Barkul rebelled on October 19, and Qutubi fell on October 20. In the North, Ili rebelled on November 10.

The Kuchean expeditions to the east and west resulted in several battles. In the East, Turfan was besieged and the towns around Urumchi looted. In the West, the rebels met a severe check at the battle of Yaqa Ariq, where nearly 2,800 rebels were killed by government forces from Aqsa. A rebel counterattack succeeded in taking Aqsa on July 17; imperial officials in the city killed themselves. The Kucheans then advanced to Ush Turfan, taking it on July 23. The Kuchean rebels then prepared to march on Kashgar. On October 12, the rebels set forth from Ush Turfan with 3,200 troops but were defeated.

The rebellion spread during the winter. At the beginning of 1865, the Kucheans sent 7,000 troops against Yarkand. The garrison surrendered, and non-Muslims were forced to convert, but the Chinese fort held out. By March 1865, the Urumchi regime took Jimsa and Gucheng. Khotan in the Southwest also had rebelled; up to 20,000 Muslims assaulted its Manchu fort, storming it and killing perhaps 2,700 ethnic Hans and Manchus. At Ili, the rebels finally succeeded in taking the nearby fort of Bayandai on February 8, slaughtering 20,000 residents. Turfan fell to the Kuchean Muslims in March; although promised safe passage to China, its garrison was slaughtered after the fort was surrendered.

Yaqub Beg approached Kashgar, then in the control of the Qirgiz, early in 1865. He and his few dozen followers were admitted into the city, from where they commenced organizing a rebellion to drive the Qirgiz out. A series of battles between forces loyal to Yuqub Beg and the Qirgiz followed. Then his forces laid siege to the Qing fort at Yanghissar, which fell on April 11. In the summer, he focused on defeating an expedition sent against him from Kucha in a major battle at Khan Ariq in which he routed up to 72,000 Kuchean troops (probably an overestimate) with only 2,000 troops of his own. This battle ultimately led to the fall of the Kuchean regime. Then he turned to the fortress at Kashgar, still held by government forces. It fell at the beginning of September; in spite of a safe conduct agreement, about 3,000 of its Chinese troops were massacred.

The fortress at Yarkand still held out against Yaqub Beg's forces. At Kashgaria, he absorbed some 7,000 Khoqandian soldiers fleeing a change of government in his native land. In so doing, he essentially declared himself independent of the Khoqand khanate. By the spring of 1866, he had solidified his personal rule over Kashgar. Elsewhere, the fortress at Ili held out until March 8, 1866. About 12,000 Manchus and Han Chinese were massacred by victorious ethnic Taranchis (Turkic Muslims). On April 11, 1866, Tarbaghatai finally fell to the rebels, although it was then abandoned to the Mongols.

Termination and Outcome: By this point, the primary emphasis of combat had shifted from Muslim-versus-government confrontations to Muslim-versus-Muslim battles for supremacy of the area. One example of this was Yaqub Beg's conquest of Khotan (see Intra-state War #586.5) in early 1867; another was his campaign against Kucha from May to June of that year. Between the fall of Tarbaghatai and 1876 only Xu Xuegong's 5,000 or so Chinese militia continued resistance to the rebels—and it is unlikely that this guerrilla action generated enough battle-deaths to qualify as war. The war thus ended with the fall of Tarbaghatai, a complete rebel victory. Most Chinese troops had been killed, subdued, or swept away in Xinjiang, leaving the rebels to squabble among themselves over the future of any Muslim state.

Coding Decisions: No source estimates the battle-deaths in Turkestan (Xinjiang), but given the history of battles and sieges, the number of battle-deaths cannot have been much lower than 10,000 and might be considerably higher.

Sources: Chu (1966); Kim (2004); Tsing (1961).[30]

INTRA-STATE WAR #582.3

Kanto Insurrection of 1864 of 1865 (aka Mito Civil War)

Participants: Japan versus Mito Rebels.
Dates: July 10, 1864, to January 23, 1865.
Battle-related Deaths: Mito Rebels: up to 1,300; Total Combatant Deaths: 2,000. (See Coding Decisions).[31]
Initiator: Mito Rebels.
Outcome: Japan wins.
War Type: Civil for central control.
Total System Member Military Personnel: Armed Forces of Japan ("new army" forces only: perhaps 3,000 (initial); at least 13,000 (peak).[32]
Theater Armed Forces: Armed Forces of Japan: 2,500 (initial); about 12,000 (peak). Mito Rebels: 200 to 300 (initial); 2,000 (peak); 823 (final).[33]

Antecedents: In the early 1860s the Tokugawa shogun's government, the *bakufu*, ruled Japan but was under pressure from various groups to reform the nation's institutions. Other daimyos were excluded from any role in decision making until 1862. Foreign intervention had highlighted the weakness of the *bakufu* and also prompted many factions to seek greater influence over the *bakufu*. Proposed military and political reforms stalled in late 1862 and early 1863, when the *bakufu* largely lost its role of primacy after its leader was detained in Kyoto; while some authority was assumed by the imperial court, a political vacuum was created, and major daimyo began to mobilize forces to influence national policy.

A political crisis over whether to expel foreigners developed, and the *bakufu* was charged by the court with implementing such a policy. However, elements of the *bakufu* were reluctant to do so because of the fear of foreign invasion. Chōshū daimyo began to fire on foreign ships without the authorization of the *bakufu*, which was seen as a sign of rebellion. In 1863, a coup ousted pro-Chōshū elements from the government. Days later, it became clear that Chōshū was preparing for civil war, although the government refrained from taking provocative action, and the crisis temporarily abated.

By early 1864, disorder was becoming rampant in Kanto, as bands of marauders and ronin formed with the public objective of expelling the foreigners. Pacification of the Kanto was discussed by the government in February. The government cracked down in the region and deployed military forces while raising civilian militias. Months later, the government abandoned a planned expedition against Chōshū to focus on external threats and the situation in Kanto. The *bakufu* was able to reassert its authority over the most important daimyo.

However, new problems arose in the Kanto. In early 1864, Fujita Kohiro of Mito formed a band of antiforeign samurai and other warriors, commanded by Tamaru Inanoeman. The nominally loyal—but unauthorized—force of about 130 men occupied Mt. Tsukuba in May. By the end of the month, they numbered several hundred at Ohira. They began to extort weapons and supplies from the countryside, then returned to Mt. Tsukuba.

Narrative: On July 10, some 200 to 300 of the rebels demanded payment from the town of Tochigi; when payment was refused, they overcame the town's defenders and sacked it. Three days later, the *bakufu* mobilized daimyos to prevent any union between the Kanto rebels and Chōshū. A force of 700 Mito loyalists was sent to pacify Mt. Tsukuba on July 20; it would soon unite with thousands of troops from nearby vassals, forming a 2,500-strong force against the rebels. The first major battle of the war was fought on August 8 and saw the insurgents routed, but two days later the rebels mounted a surprise counterattack and forced the government forces to withdraw.

After the insurgent victory at Tsukuba, recruits poured in. Some 300 rebels unsuccessfully invaded Mito. Hundreds of Mito fighters disobeyed orders, although they did not yet join the rebels. Meanwhile, Chōshū had marshaled forces in Kyoto itself, and the *bakufu* found itself short of support, finally mustering just 600 of its traditional, elite troops (its newly mobilized forces having been deployed to Kanto and Kyoto). An attempt by Chōshū forces to seize Kyoto was defeated on August 20 with heavy loss of life and destruction of parts of the city, but after this victory the *bakufu* found it easier to sway heretofore neutral daimyo to send troops to suppress the Kanto insurrection.

On August 31, Matsudaira Yorinori was ordered by the *bakufu* to assume leadership of Mito and pacify its rebels. He gathered up to 3,000 followers but was refused access to Mito castle, whose leader Ichikawa feared that Yorinori was too sympathetic to the Mito rebels. By September 11, the two Mito factions faced off against each other, and Yorinori engaged Ichikawa's forces in battle, supported by units of the Tsukuba rebels. He captured Nakaminato by September 17, but in fighting from September 25 to September 27, his forces were defeated outside of Mito by a combination of the castle's few hundred defenders and 1,400 elite government troops.

Yorinori's rebels retreated to Nakaminato, joined by Fujita and Tamaru (their combined forces numbering altogether about 2,000 men, mostly armed peasants), where they soon were surrounded by government loyalists. The *bakufu* had at least 5,000 troops of its own deployed against the rebels, along with Ichikawa's forces (numbering in the high hundreds) and another 6,000 who had been ordered to assist the *bakufu.* The war ground on during October, with scores dying daily of battle, execution, and suicide. On October 16, Yorinori surrendered and was sentenced to commit suicide. Some of his retainers also committed suicide, while twenty of his followers were beheaded as common criminals. At this point, the rebels still hoped for a settlement, but the *bakufu* had no interest in compromise.

A ferocious battle on November 9 cost the government forces—some 7,200 strong in the area—80 killed and 200 wounded or missing, against only 6 killed on the (2,000-strong) rebel side. Government forces were routed again in battles on November 16 and November 17. But the rebels were encircled, and by late November the government pacification force numbered 11,500 troops. Secret negotiations resulted in the surrender of 1,100 rebels when the government attacked again on November 22. The remainder of the rebels broke out of the encirclement to the northwest and then headed for Kyoto, naïvely hoping to plead their cause before the emperor. During December, they slowly made their way toward Kyoto, eluding their pursuers. The government mobilized at least 10,000 men to block the advance of 700 to 1,000 remaining rebels. Stymied by these forces, the rebels turned to mediation, but their efforts were for naught, and a few days before the Japanese New Year—on or about January 23, 1865—they capitulated on a promise of mercy. Some 823 men were interned by government forces.

Termination and Outcome: The outcome of the war was a military victory by the government with a promise of mercy for the rebels if they surrendered. This promise certainly was not honored. The rebels surrendered, but 24 were executed on February 4, and over the next few days another 328 were slaughtered. Most of the rest were banished. Another 100 to 200 of the previously surrendered group of rebels died in captivity. The Mito clan essentially was destroyed as a major power during the war. During the war, the *bakufu's* focus on the Kanto insurrection over Kyoto's priorities of punishing Chōshū and closing ports to foreigners led to a growing divide between the *bakufu* government in Edo and the imperial court in Kyoto, eventually culminating in the Boshin War of 1868 (Intra-state War #588).

Coding Decisions: Some 1,300 rebels died, but this figure may include 353 executed during the months following the war as well as scores of suicides. Given that most engagements were rebel victories, government losses in combat were probably at least as great as those of the rebels. Clement reports a rebel claim to have killed thousands of their opponents, but the veracity of this claim is open to doubt. We conservatively estimate 2,000 total battle-deaths. These figures exclude those of the Chōshū rebellion of August 20; although the gathered Chōshū forces had expressed support for the Mito insurrection, there is no evidence of coordination between the two rebel groups.

Sources: Clement (1891); Koschmann (1987); Tutman (1980).

INTRA-STATE WAR #585

Yellow Cliff Revolt of 1866

Participants: China versus Zhang Jizhong–led Rebels.
Dates: October 1866.
Battle-related Deaths: Total Combatant Deaths: 2,000. (See Coding Decisions.)[34]
Initiator: Zhang Jizhong–led Rebels.
Outcome: China wins.
War Type: Civil for local issues (autonomy).
Total System Member Military Personnel: Armed Forces of China: 1 million (prewar, initial, peak, final).[35]
Theater Armed Forces: Armed Forces of China: 12,000 (initial, peak, final).[36] Zhang Jizhong–led Forces: 800 (ten days before war).[37]

Antecedents: Zhang Jizhong, once a follower of heterodox religious figure Zhou Xingyuan, was forced to flee to the northeastern province of Shandong during the Taiping rebellion. He migrated again within the province due to the Nien threat in 1861. There he led his own heterodox religious community on the top of a mountain called Yellow Cliff. Refugees flocked to the safety of the community, which Zhang fortified in 1862 and 1863.

In October 1866, when the threat from the Nien was high, the government uncovered a conspiracy to raise a rebellion in Yidu county, 100 miles to the northeast. The ringleader accused Zhang of fomenting the rebellion and claimed that five leaders of the would-be revolt were to be found at Yellow Cliff. The violence began when a governmental investigative party was driven off by Yellow Cliff residents, losing two killed. The government issued a five-day ultimatum to Zhang, but he refused to surrender. The government learned that arms were being imported through salt smugglers, that a red flag had been raised on Yellow Cliff, and that several hundred Yellow Cliff soldiers or bandits had raided nearby villages, killing several people. The 800-man Yellow Cliff militia deserted the rebels, leaving their former headquarters near the mountain.

Narrative: About 12,000 government troops and local auxiliaries approached Yellow Cliff, and the first few days of fighting favored the rebels, who held the high ground. After several days of intense fighting, the government offered a cease-fire and a lenient policy for any who surrendered. The rebels dragged out the process, and when a captured spy revealed that the Nien were sending forces to Yellow Cliff, the government commander decided to immediately seize it before they could arrive. Thousands were killed in the ensuing battle, with many falling off the cliffs to their deaths.

Termination and Outcome: The outcome of the war was a complete government victory. Not 1 of the 10,000 inhabitants surrendered. Only 400 women and children and a handful of captives (for interrogation) were spared. Zhang and 200 of his associates committed suicide by gunpowder explosion. After the destruction of Yellow Cliff, other disciples of Zhou Xingyuan continued to spread his teachings clandestinely.

Coding Decisions: Thousands were killed in battle, and most of the 10,000 people in Yellow Cliff were slaughtered. We estimate 2,000 battle-deaths; given the indiscriminate massacre that merged with the battle, the real figure might be lower or higher.

Sources: Perry and Chang (1980).[38]

INTRA-STATE WAR #586.5

Kashgar–Khotan War of 1867 (aka Yakub Beg's Conquest of Khotan)

Participants: Armed Forces of Kashgar versus Khotanese.
Dates: January 1867 to February 1867.

Battle-related Deaths: Khotanese: up to 2,000;[39] Total Combatant Deaths: up to 2,000.[40]
Initiator: Armed Forces of Kashgar.
Outcome: Armed Forces of Kashgar Win.
War Type: Intercommunal.
Theater Armed Forces: Armed Forces of Kashgar: more than 7,000 (initial).[41] Khotanese: 10,000 (peak).[42]

Antecedents: During the Muslim revolt in Xinjiang (see Intra-state War #582), different Muslim forces contended for control of Xinjiang. In 1866, Yaqub Beg of Khokand attempted to expand his Kashgar-centered state to encompass other towns. Khotan, held by Muslims independent of Beg, was one obstacle to his expansion. He decided to take the town through subterfuge. On December 16, Yaqub Beg led his forces into Yarkand and beyond to Piyalma. There the leader of Khotan, Habib Allah, sent one of his sons and an army to discern Yakub Beg's intentions. The latter swore an oath on the Quran and invited Habib Allah to a feast—where he promptly was arrested and soon executed. Yakub Beg used Habib Allah's seals to send a message to Khotan that both armies would march into the city side by side.

Narrative: On the appointed day (sometime in January or February of 1867), Yakub Beg led his army into the open gates of the city. When Khotan's citizens realized the deception, they attacked his army with clubs. Some 2,000 were killed by Yakub Beg's forces.

Termination and Outcome: The outcome was a complete victory for Yakub Beg's Kashgarian forces. Khotanese leaders were executed, and Yakub Beg would retain control of Khotan for years to come.

Coding Decisions: Self-explanatory from cited sources.

Source: Kim (2004).

INTRA-STATE WAR #588
Meiji Restoration War of 1868 to 1869 (aka Boshin War)

Participants: Japan versus Tokugawa Bakufu and Northeastern League/Republic of Ezo.
Dates: January 27, 1868, to June 27, 1869.
Battle-Related Deaths: Armed forces of Japan: 3,556; Tokugawa Bafuku: 300 to 400 (including component armies such as that of Aizu);[43] Northeastern League/Republic of Ezo: 4,300 to 4,400;[44] Total Combatant Deaths: about 9,000. (See Coding Decisions.)[45]
Initiator: Japan.
Outcome: Japan wins.
War Type: Civil for central control (but see Coding Decisions).
Total System Member Military Personnel: Armed Forces of Japan: perhaps 115,000 (peak).
Theater Armed Forces: Armed Forces of Japan: 30,000 (peak). Tokugawa Bakufu: 13,000 (initial, peak).[46] Northeastern League/Republic of Ezo: at least 10,000 (peak, estimated by doubling forces within Echigo).[47]

Antecedents: In 1864, Chōshū forces attacked Kyoto, leading the imperial court to mandate punitive expeditions against them. But in 1866, the Tokugawa *bakufu* (shogun government) failed to defeat Chōshū's more modern forces in a sub-war civil conflict known as the Summer War. The conflict revealed that the *bakufu* could no longer command obedience from the regions, thereby rendering it vulnerable to challenges. Advisors to the emperor pressed for the abolition of the *bakufu* altogether. In autumn 1867, the *bakufu* planned to recentralize power using French loans and military advisors. Dissident daimyos—Chōshū and its ally Satsuma in particular—moved forces toward the imperial seat of Kyoto. Others responded in kind, and by the end of November there were 22,000 to 24,000 troops facing each other in and around Kyoto. Imports of foreign weapons, especially rifles, skyrocketed. Meanwhile, Britain had established a close working relationship with the Chōshū–Satsuma alliance.

On January 3, 1868, the emperor ordered *bakufu*-aligned (Tokugawa, Aizu, and Kuwana) troops to withdraw from Kyoto. Two days later, these forces fell back to Osaka, where they began to establish a line of defenses to guard against surprise attack. The court also ordered Tokugawa to surrender vast swathes of territory, which the Osaka forces countered with a proposal for proportional land contributions from all daimyo. Negotiations continued through the end of December, but tensions mounted with an attack on the Satsuma and Sadohara mansions in Edo, which killed several Satsuma men and captured 150 more. The next day, orders for general mobilization were issued from Edo. A note condemning Satsuma was dispatched to the imperial court in Kyoto. On January 23, Tokugawa forces began to advance toward Kyoto.

Narrative: On January 27, 1868, Chōshū–Satsuma forces seized control of Kyoto, and the emperor abolished the office of shogun. Fighting began almost immediately. The *bakufu* had about 13,000 troops, including its allies. Of these, some 5,500 were to advance on Kyoto, 3,000 were to advance on Fushimi and Toba, and about 4,500 were reserved for the defenses in the South and along the Yodo river. An alliance of Satsuma, Chōshū, Tosa, Hizen, Echizen, and other regions formed an imperial army to defend the government in Kyoto. The rebels were halted on the lower Toba on January 27 after a brief battle with 900 Satsuma men, and the forces headed for Fushimi were routed that night by about 1,400 from Satsuma, Chōshū, and Tosa. The next day's fighting was bloody but inconclusive, but on January 29 the *bakufu* forces were driven back, and on January 30 some 3,500 Kyoto troops completed the defeat of the remaining 3,050 to 4,300 rebels deployed for battle.

The Battle of Toba–Fushimi cost the government about 100 killed—Satsuma lost 61 killed and 124 wounded, and Chōshū suffered 35 killed and 106 wounded. The rebels lost more—Aizu suffered between 92 and 138 killed and 116 to 185 wounded, Kuwana lost 25 killed, and the *bakufu's* own forces suffered about 163 killed and 300 to 500 wounded. Including other marginal combatants, battle-deaths may have numbered as many as 500, with 1,000 to 1,300 wounded. The battle ended the Tokugawa threat to Kyoto, but it did not end the war. The rebels fell back to Edo, and the Tokugawa leader prepared to capitulate, but forces remained in the field on the Tokugawa side. Relatively little fighting occurred as the imperial forces fanned out across Japan (a brief combat at Kōshū Katsunuma on March 29 cost the rebels about 180 men), and Edo was surrounded by the summer. Nonetheless, many daimyo in Northeast Japan, including Aizu, held out against the new regime.

Before it could deal with the Northeast, the government had to deal with 3,000 to 4,000 pro-Tokugawa guerrillas who harassed the government advance. Finally, they were defeated in battle near Ueno on July 4, losing 300 troops. But even after Edo surrendered, several thousand troops left by sea, along with the Tokugawa navy, to join the Northeastern League, consisting of twenty-six domains but dominated by the Tokugawa ally Aizu. The league itself disclaimed any intention of restoring the *bakufu* but disputed the legitimacy of the Chōshū–Satsuma-dominated imperial army. The government then planned a campaign against Aizu's eastern flank, which it easily carried out in seven weeks during the autumn.

On Aizu's western flank, resistance was most serious in Echigo. From the seizure of the port of Naoetsu on June 7, it took until September 26 for the government to seize Murakami Castle. The offensive stalled in front of Nagaoka Castle on July 8. Of the following seven engagements, six were won by the rebels, including a major victory at Enoki Pass. Government forces were compelled to make a hasty withdrawal across the swollen Shinano river, losing many men to drowning in the process.

Reinforcements were brought in from elsewhere on the front, and at the peak of the campaign in Echigo, about 30,000 government troops were deployed against no more than 5,000 rebels (including some 600 from Aizu, 2,000 from Yonezawa, and others from Shonai and the refugees from Tokugawa). Using its superiority in numbers—and the absence of effective coordination between the Tokugawa fleet and the Northeastern League—the government mounted a surprise landing at Niigata (the rebels' major port for weapons imports) on September 11, the same day the rebels mounted their own surprise attack on the imperial headquarters at Nagaoka Castle. In about two more weeks of fighting, Echigo was secured by the government, which now surrounded Aizu on three sides.

Government forces now attacked Aizu itself. What followed was fighting and destruction on such a scale that to some in Aizu today *the war* refers to the Boshin War rather than World War II. Still, it took only one month to subdue Aizu as the loss of Wakamatsu Castle on November 6, with losses of 3,000 samurai, undermined its strategic position. Aizu and several other domains then submitted. Resistance continued in what is now Hokkaido, where an independent Republic of Ezo was formed, seeking autonomy. The Tokugawa navy joined the republic and its leader Enomoto Takeaki was elected as the first president of Ezo.

In 1869, the government built up its forces for an invasion of Hokkaido; the government's aggregate forces eventually exceeded 100,000 men—one source estimating 120,000 and another fewer than 115,000. Still, it was not until June 27 that the commanding fortress of Hakodate was captured by imperial troops, ending resistance to the Meiji restoration.

Termination and Outcome: The outcome of the war was an unconditional military victory for the government. The rebels capitulated on June 27. Surprisingly, there was no wave of postwar executions, and even Enomoto Takeaki was released and given a royal appointment after a few years. In the long run, the war fueled a new rivalry between Chōshū and Satsuma for political and economic supremacy in the new Meiji regime.

Coding Decisions: The rebels demanded autonomy after the drive to replace the central government failed, but we nonetheless consider the primary issue to have been control over the central government. Although Sheldon cites an estimate of 10,000 battle-deaths, more precise figures are given by Tsuzuki: 3,556 government killed and 4,707 rebel dead. Allowing for incomplete data and fatalities due to disease, we consider the most plausible estimate to be about 9,000.

Sources: Jansen (1995); McClain (2002); Murdoch (1964); Olitho (1979); Sheldon (1974); Tsuzuki (2000); Tutman (1980); Wert (2013).[48]

INTRA-STATE WAR #592.7
First Kashgarian–Tungan War of 1870

Participants: Armed Forces of Kashgaria versus Urumchi Tungans.
Dates: January 1870 to November 1870.
Battle-related Deaths: Total Combatant Deaths: 1,000. (See Coding Decisions.)[49]
Initiator: Urumchi Tungans.
Outcome: Armed Forces of Kashgaria win.
War Type: Intercommunal.
Theater Armed Forces: Armed Forces of Kashgaria: 20,000 (peak).[50] Urumchi Tungans: 20,000 (peak).[51]

Antecedents: During and after the Muslim revolt in Xinjiang (see Intra-state War #582), different Muslim forces contended for control of Xinjiang. Among these were Hui (Tungan) forces as well as Turkic Muslims led by Yaqub Beg in Kashgar. In late 1868, forces from Urumchi raided the Kashgarian territory around Kurla but were suppressed by Yaqub Beg's forces.

Narrative: In early 1870, some 20,000 Tungans seized Kurla. Yaqub Beg ordered the forces of Ishaq Khawja and Hakim Khan to defeat the Tungans. The Tungans won the initial Battle of Qara Yighach and occupied Kucha, but fearing a counterattack they retreated into Urumchi just over a week later, looting as they went. On March 11, Yakub Beg left Kashgar with an army of 20,000 to subdue the Tungans. In late March, he easily took Toqsun from the Tungans. Two Kashgarian victories—the Battles of Yamish and Yar—followed.

Yaqub Beg then besieged Tungan-held Turfan. During the siege his forces captured Lukchin, east of Turfan, cutting off any relief expedition. Turfan held out for more than half a year but surrendered in November. Yaqub's 16,000-strong force then moved to Daqiyanus, where the Tungans attempted a night attack but only reached the Kashgarian encampments at dawn, when they were routed. Yaqub pursued the fleeing Tungans to Urumchi, which he surrounded.

Termination and Outcome: Late in November, Urumchi surrendered to the forces of Yaqub Beg. The outcome of the war was a complete victory for Kashgarian forces. No executions in Urumchi were reported; indeed, the leader of Urumchi survived to lead another Tungan revolt against Yakub Beg just over a year later.

Coding Decisions: No estimate of battle-deaths is available, but given the size of forces engaged over multiple battles, we are confident that at least 1,000 perished in the fighting.

Source: Kim (2004).

INTRA-STATE WAR #596.7
Second Kashgarian–Tungan War of 1871 to 1872

Participants: Armed Forces of Kashgaria versus Urumchi Tungans and Xu Xuegong–led Guerrillas.

Dates: December 1871 to August 1872.
Battle-related Deaths: Total Combatant Deaths: 1,000. (See Coding Decisions.)[52]
Initiator: Urumchi Tungans.
Outcome: Armed Forces of Kashgar win.
War Type: Intercommunal.
Theater Armed Forces: Armed Forces of Kashgar: 20,000 (prewar); up to 40,000 (peak).[53] Urumchi Tungans: 16,000 (peak).[54] Xu Xuegong–led Guerrillas: 4,000 (peak).[55]

Antecedents: During and after the Muslim revolt in Xinjiang (see Intra-state War #582), different Muslim forces contended for control of Xinjiang. Among these were Hui (Tungan) forces as well as Turkic Muslims led by Yaqub Beg in Kashgar. In 1871, Yakub Beg defeated the Tungans and occupied their capital of Urumchi (see Intra-state War #592.7), but in 1872 the Kashgarian army was sent in pursuit of Chinese guerrilla Xu Xuegong. In their absence, the Tungans of Urumchi seized control of the city, reappointing their former leader Dāūd Khalīfa to lead them once more. Sometime between November 22 and December 21, the Kashgarians returned to find the city held against them.

Narrative: There is little detail available, but Kashgarian leader Yaqub Beg's offensive against Urumchi involved "intense battles" that culminated in the storming of Urumchi.[56] Dāūd Khalīfa fled to Manas, where he raised a force of 16,000 Tungans and allied himself with Xu Xuegong's 4,000 Chinese guerrillas. Together, they besieged Yaqub Beg's forces in Urumchi. Throughout the winter and spring, Kashgarian forces lost control of the surrounding area but succeeded in holding Urumchi itself.

In the spring of 1872, Yaqub Beg sent an additional 7,000 men to raise the siege of Urumchi. Finding the fort of Dabanchin held against them, they attacked it for forty bloody days. The fort fell on June 8, its commander dying in battle. The Kashgarians pushed on to Urumchi, where the Tungan forces surrendered on June 11, having suffered many casualties. One report claims that 15,000 Tungans died in and around Urumchi. Dāūd Khalīfa once again fled to Manas but seems to have been unable to raise a sizeable force there. Two months after the fall of Urumchi, the Kashgarians resumed their advance, taking Gumadi and Manas (where one report estimates 2,000 Tungans were killed).

Termination and Outcome: The outcome of the war was a complete military victory for the Kashgarian forces. Dāūd Khalīfa died soon after the defeat. Kashgarian territorial gains were substantial.

Coding Decisions: No estimate of battle-deaths is available, but given the size of forces engaged and the qualitative intensity of the fighting, we are confident that at least 1,000 perished.

Source: Kim (2004).

INTRA-STATE WAR #603

Defeat of Xinjiang Muslims of 1876 to 1878

Participants: China versus Xinjiang Muslims.
Dates: April 1876 to January 2, 1878.
Battle-related Deaths: Total Combatant Deaths: 4,000. (See Coding Decisions.)[57]
Initiator: China.
Outcome: China wins.
War Type: Civil for local issues (independence).
Total System Member Military Personnel: Armed Forces of China: 1 million (prewar, initial, peak, final).[58]
Theater Armed Forces: Armed Forces of China: 30,000 to 40,000 (initial); 90,000 (peak). Xinjiang Muslims: 40,000 (prewar); 45,000 (initial, peak).[59]

Antecedents: While China was debilitated by other revolts, Muslim rebels seized control of Xinjiang (see Intra-state War #582), eventually creating a state centered on Kashgar and ruled by Yaqub Beg. In 1875, the Chinese government approved the recovery of Xinjiang, and in 1876 it borrowed the money necessary to fund the reconquest. The leader of the expedition, Zuo Zongtang (Tso Ts'ung-t'ang), had established himself first against the Taipings, then against the Nien, and finally against the Muslim Hui of Shaanxi and Gansu. Russian merchants supplied (at exorbitant prices) the grain needed for the expedition into Xinjiang. Some 25,000 of Yakub Beg's troops concentrated at his advance headquarters of Toqsun, which he fortified in 1875.

Narrative: Although some towns in eastern Xinjiang were reoccupied in 1875, Zuo's 30,000 to 40,000 troops (which eventually grew to perhaps 90,000) were readied, and the campaign proper began in April 1876. Not wishing to engage Yaqub's forces before it was necessary, Zuo planned a northerly route for his expedition. His troops had reached Fukang by the end of July 1876. Government general Liu Jintang's forces took Huangdian for its water supply and then moved against Gumadi, which he reached on August 12. Gumadi fell after a five-day battle; approximately 5,000 to 6,000 Muslims died in the assault. The government shortly won another victory at the minor battle of Qidaowan.

Seven days later, Urumchi fell to the Qing forces almost without a fight. Northern Manas had fallen to another government column, aided by a force of guerrillas under Xu Xuegong, the day before. Southern Manas held out, and Tungan (Hui) reinforcements arrived. Yaqub Beg made no attempt to support them, and they finally capitulated on November 6. The northern part of Xinjiang, known as Zungharia, was now in Zuo's hands (with the notable exception of Ili, which had been occupied by Russian troops and which Zuo left for the diplomats). Zuo rested his army during the winter.

Meanwhile, Yakub Beg moved his headquarters back to Kurla and assembled 30,000 troops in the East to face the expected government assault. On April 14, 1877, Liu Jintang sent nineteen battalions (about 10,000 troops) from Urumchi to Yakub Beg's forward position at Dabanchin. They attacked the fort on April 16 and took it on April 20, killing about 2,000 of its defenders, while the rest fled westward. On April 25, Liu reached Toqsun, which the rebels had evacuated. Meanwhile, other government forces closed in on Turfan. Chiqtim, Pichan, and Lukchin were taken, and after a minor skirmish Turfan fell on April 26. Yaqub Beg sent an order to his troops not to fire on the Qing, while he sought a diplomatic solution. The Chinese government, which had been willing to negotiate in 1876, was no longer willing to do so given its clear military superiority.

On or around May 22, Yaqub Beg died (of stroke, disease, or suicide) at Kurla. His highly personalistic regime began to fall apart. A succession struggle resulted in an intercommunal struggle between Yaqub Beg's sons and his generals. The government forces allowed the fighting to weaken the rebels before advancing. Qarashahr fell on October 7; Kurla fell two days later. Bugur was next, followed by Kucha (October 17), Qizil (October 20), Bai (October 21), Aqsu (October 23), and Ush Turfan (October 28). Some 3,000 to 4,000 rebels crossed the border into Russia, fleeing the Qing advance. Resistance collapsed, with Kashgar falling on December 18, Yarkand on December 21, and finally Khotan on January 2, 1878.

Termination and Outcome: The outcome of the war was a complete military victory for the government. Many of Yakub Beg's commanders were tortured and executed. Some 370 rebels were executed immediately, although more executions followed over time. Xinjiang was formally transformed into a province of China on November 18, 1884.

Coding Decisions: Thousands perished, but it is not clear that all of them were soldiers. Still, the rebels alone must have lost at least 3,000 troops. Government losses were much smaller. We estimate a total of 4,000 battle-deaths; the real toll could be somewhat lower or much higher.

Sources: Elleman (2001); Kim (2004); Lattimore (1950); Saray (2003).[60]

INTRA-STATE WAR #607
Satsuma Rebellion of 1877 (aka Seinan War)

Participants: Japan versus Satsumas.
Dates: January 29, 1877, to September 24, 1877.
Battle-related Deaths: Armed Forces of Japan: 6,399 (including 32 missing); Satsumas: about 7,000; Total Combatant Deaths: about 13,400. (See Coding Decisions.)[61]
Initiator: Japan.
Outcome: Japan wins.
War Type: Civil for central control (inferred from the rebel march on Tokyo).
Total System Member Military Personnel: Armed Forces of Japan: 38,000 (prewar, initial); 65,000 (peak, final).[62]
Theater Armed Forces: Armed Forces of Japan: 65,000 (peak).[63] Satsumas: 30,000 to 40,000 (prewar expectation); more than 16,000 (initial); 42,000 (peak); 21,000 (final).[64]

Antecedents: The samurai class had been instrumental in the overthrow of the Tokugawa shogunate (see Intra-state War #588). In particular, the major domains of Satsuma and Chōshū had backed the Meiji restoration. However, Chōshū gained considerably more influence than Satsuma, and further Meiji reforms threatened the very existence of Satsuma as a semiautonomous domain. By 1871, the samurai were the main element of the feudal system that remained. The government pensioned them off, eventually compelling them to accept lump sums as payment. While the government was thus trying to eliminate the samurai, Satsuma's leader Saigō Takamori in Kagoshima was wooing them with thousands of positions. Concerned that Saigō might be preparing a revolt, the government attempted to confiscate his armaments.

Narrative: On January 29, 1877, government naval forces attempting to seize the arsenals of Kagoshima were resisted by some of Saigō's followers. Although he was likely surprised by the initial resistance of his men, Saigō mobilized his forces for a march on Tokyo to demand an explanation from the government. The rebels numbered more than 16,000 when they set out on February 7, and samurai and other volunteers poured in. The first battle, fought on February 20, was a rebel victory near Kumamato. Upon reaching Kumamato on February 22, the rebels were joined by more than 5,000 additional volunteers, reaching their peak strength of 42,000. The rebel army then besieged the remainder of the government garrison.

The government did not formally authorize a punitive expedition until February 20; it then mobilized the 18,000-strong national police against the rebels, sending thousands into combat. From March 8 to March 20, the Battle of Tawarazaka was fought between 9,000 rebels and 11,000 government troops. The former lost 1,200 killed and 2,100 wounded, while the latter suffered 1,766 killed and 2,399 wounded. The rebel advance had been checked, and by April 5 the government had mobilized another 10,000 troops, eventually deploying 65,000 against the Satsumas. The rebels lost another 500 killed at the Battle of Mifune on April 20. Meanwhile the rebels withdrew from Kagoshima and turned south.

The government offered amnesty to any insurgents who surrendered, and at least 300 rebels took up the offer. But many of the rebels remained in the field against the government, a substantial proportion of them turning to large-scale guerrilla activity. By June, government columns were being ambushed. At the Battle of Miyaka-no-jô on July 24, the government lost 300 men and the rebels many more. By August 15, the government's campaign had been so successful that fewer than 10,000 rebels remained in arms.

The rebel collapse was swift; the last rebel victory was a minor skirmish on September 3 near Kagoshima, which won the rebels about 400 more samurai followers. Including these reinforcements, the rebellion was reduced to 500 men. On September 10, a government bombardment killed nearly 200 rebels. By September 24, the situation was hopeless, and Saigō led his men in a reckless charge at government forces. About 100 rebels were killed in the attack; the government lost only 38 men. Saigō was killed in the battle, his second in command committed suicide, and 210 rebels finally were captured by government forces, ending the war.

Termination and Outcome: The government won an unconditional military victory. After the war, some 42,740 persons were accused of collaboration with the rebels. Of these, the majority were pardoned and discharged from military service, but 2,842 were sentenced to prison or fined, and 20 were condemned to death—an overall result that was considered merciful by observers.

Coding Decisions: Due to lack of data, our battle-death figures may omit those who died of wounds after the end of hostilities.

Sources: Mounsey (1979); Vlastos (1995).[65]

INTRA-STATE WAR #618

Zaili-Jinden Revolt of 1891 (aka Jindandao Incident)

Participants: China versus Jindan Sect, Lin Yushan-led Zailis, and Wushengmen Sect.
Dates: November 11, 1891, to December 16, 1891.
Battle-related Deaths: Armed Forces of China: at least 300;[66] All rebels combined: up to 10,000; Total Combatant Deaths: about 10,000. (See Coding Decisions)[67]
Initiator: Jindan Sect.
Outcome: China wins.
War Type: Civil for central control (but see Coding Decisions).

Total System Member Military Personnel: Armed Forces of China: 1 million (prewar, initial, peak, final).[68]

Theater Armed Forces: Armed Forces of China: 10,000 (initial, peak); Jindan Sect: 2,000 (initial), more than 15,000 (peak).[69] Lin Yushan-led Zailis: [ ].[70] Wushengmen Sect: 4,000 (peak).[71] Overall, there were tens of thousands of rebels (peak).[72]

Antecedents: Security was weak in the district of Rehe (Jehol), with brigands a constant menace. Moreover, Han Chinese in Rehe resented some of the privileges accorded to the Mongols (due to state policy) and Catholics (due to the threat of foreign intervention). Secret societies were popular means of resistance and mutual support. The Jindans, led in Rehe by Yang Yuechun, were often known as the learning-to-do-good sect because their religion prescribed vegetarianism and doing good deeds. However, they also transmitted slogans secretly such as "defeat the Qing dynasty and sweep away the barbarians" and "kill Mongols to clear away accumulated resentment."[73]

The Zailis were a syncretic religious movement with a legacy that stretched back to the White Lotus Society. One report suggests that they were a majority in Zhili province. They, too, congregated to perform meritorious deeds. Prominent Zaili Lin Yushan was involved in a dispute with Christians over grain that had resulted in the death of a Han Chinese man. Fearful of retaliation, Christians began casting cannon in the courtyard of their church. The government observed this but said nothing, fearful of provoking foreign intervention. Yang Yuechun began organizing the Jindan for a revolt sometime in the summer of 1891, accumulating supplies through "banditry." Such tensions and incidents rose in the months preceding the revolt. The grain harvest was poor. Moreover, famine struck southern Zhili, driving hungry Han refugees into Rehe, where corrupt officials withheld relief.

Narrative: Later, Yang Yuechun would claim that he had discovered orders from the local Mongolian prince to exterminate the Han in the province and retake Mongol lands. For whatever reason, he led 2,000 members of the Jindan sect into revolt on November 11, raiding the prince's offices and targeting Mongols more generally. He took for himself the title of "the Grand Priest of the Dynasty-founding Estate." Taking advantage of the Jindan revolt, Lin Yushan led Zailis in attacks on Christians. Following the revolt of the Jindans and Zailis, one Li Guozhen led the Wushengmen sect into rebellion in the northern part of the district, targeting Mongols. Within days, the number of rebels was in the tens of thousands.

Before the government even could take measures to suppress the rebellion, about 10,000 Mongols were killed by the rebels; many more would die over the course of the revolt. Christian casualties were much lower. On November 11, 1,000 to 2,000 Zaili and Jindan rebels harassed the countryside around Zhaoyang, taking it three days later. Two days later, the rebels took Shanshijiazi, massacring some 300 Christians. A similar massacre took place two days later at Pingquan. Government troops were poorly armed and had difficulty fighting the rebels; one garrison was entirely exterminated by the rebels.

The central government dispatched 10,000 well-armed disciplined army troops from southern Zhili and Fengtian to suppress the rebellion. Traveling by rail and making use of the telegraph, they advanced rapidly, meeting their first rebels on November 20. Only a dozen rebels were killed that day, but a series of bloody and one-sided battles followed. At Taohuatu, 2,000 rebels were defeated and 700 of them killed, but only 200 weapons were recovered. At Laoyaigou on November 23, more than 140 rebels perished. Five days later at Wuguanyingzi, 500 rebels fell in battle and another 300 were executed or committed suicide. On December 5 at Maojiawopu, 2,000 insurgents who had entrenched and fortified themselves over several days, and who possessed considerable artillery power, were destroyed by government forces, losing 1,300 killed in a matter of hours.

One band of rebels after another was crushed by government forces, each taking heavy casualties. By mid-December, the only remaining large-scale resistance was among the Wushengmen of the North, augmented by Zaili and Jindan rebels who had fled from other areas.

Li Guozhen had taken the city of Wudancheng on December 2 and now fortified his new headquarters against assault. On December 15, 500 of his troops were killed in a major government assault. Several engagements with his forces in the countryside then transpired, and the next day, Li Guozhen was captured, ending the last organized resistance to the government.

Termination and Outcome: The outcome of the war was a complete military victory by the government. Yang Yuechen was found hiding in a cave with relatives on December 27. In the short run, the government proscribed the rebellious sects, and surviving rebel leaders were executed after interrogation. Arrests of the sectarians continued into 1893. As a longer-term response to the rebellion, the government promulgated reforms that favored Han residents of the area.

Coding Decisions: Because the rebels proclaimed a new dynasty, we code this as a war for control of the central government. However, local issues—ethnic discrimination and food supply—clearly triggered the revolt. Official reports counted 20,000 unclaimed corpses in need of burial, but the real death toll was probably much higher. As for an estimate of battle-deaths, 10,000 is a conservative figure.

Sources: Borjigin (2004); McCaffrey (2011); Sheck (1980).

INTRA-STATE WAR #623

Tonghak Rebellion phase 1 of 1894 (aka First Tonghak Rebellion or Peasant War of 1894—phase 1)

Participants: Korea and China versus Tonghak Society.
Dates: March 23, 1894, to June 10, 1894.
Battle-related Deaths: Armed Forces of Korea: 500; Tonghaks: 500; Total Combatant Deaths: 1,000. (See Coding Decisions.)[74]
Initiator: Tonghak Society.
Outcome: Negotiated settlement.
War Type: Civil for local issues (taxation and corruption).
Total System Member Military Personnel: Armed Forces of Korea: 5,000 (prewar, initial); 10,000 to 11,000 (peak).[75] Armed Forces of China: 1 million (prewar, initial, peak, final).[76]
Theater Armed Forces: Armed Forces of Korea: 10,000 to 11,000. Armed Forces of China, participating from June 8, 1894: 1,500 (initial, peak, final).[77] Tonghak Society: 3,000 (initial); 20,000 to 30,000 (peak).[78]

Antecedents: The Tonghak Society was a religious movement focused on a renewal of Confucian teachings and the rejection of Western ones, especially Christianity. The Korean government outlawed the movement, driving its activities underground. The Tonghak Society was popular among peasants who protested the practices of feudalism. By 1893, tens of thousands of Tonghaks were involved in sporadic protests and violent confrontations with landowners. They also protested Japanese and Western influence in Korea.

In February 1894, peasants in Kobu County of Chŏlla province rebelled against local corruption and abuses, especially onerous taxes and fines levied by the local government. Three Tonghaks—Chŏn Pongjun, Son Hwajung, and Kim Kaenam—soon took control of the peasant movement (Chŏn becoming its chief general), drawing in the Tonghak Society. They demanded the dismissal of corrupt officials at both the local and national level as well as a policy to remedy the country's fiscal problems. The government sent an inspector to investigate, but he sided with the local government against the Tonghaks. The rebellion grew, and by March 22, some 3,000 peasants were in arms.

Narrative: The first engagement of the war was a minor skirmish in Kobu County on March 23, but there was little real fighting until the battle of Hwangt'ohyŏn on April 7. The government suffered up to 1,000 casualties in the battle from at least 6,000 to 7,000 rebels. The second major battle of the war was fought at Changsŏng on April 23; the government lost about 300 killed. A minor skirmish at Chŏngu on April 27 revealed that rebel forces had now grown to 20,000 to 30,000. Government forces, too, were growing as it mobilized a civilian militia of 5,000 to 6,000 to augment its regular forces (though many simply deserted to the rebels). It scored a military success on May 3, when an ambush killed several hundred rebels.

Nevertheless, the government was unable to overcome the poorly armed but more numerous insurgents, who controlled all of Chŏlla province by early June. But on June 1, the government called on China to help it suppress the rebellion. China responded promptly with 1,500 soldiers and two warships; the first soldiers landing on June 8, just a week after the government's request. However, Japan also sent soldiers (against Seoul's request to refrain from entering the war), and China responded by reinforcing its troops.

Termination and Outcome: On the approach of Chinese troops, the Tonghaks dispersed, and because both sides now feared a foreign takeover, on June 10 they negotiated the Peace of Chŏnju, providing for amnesty, the partial disarmament of the rebels, and the formation of peasant directorates for local rule. So ended the period of the First Tonghak Rebellion. The government then requested the withdrawal of all foreign troops, but on July 23 Japan responded by storming the royal palace, overthrowing the government and replacing it with a Japanese puppet. Thus purged by the Japanese, the new Korean puppet government ordered China only to withdraw its forces. This directly resulted in the onset of the Sino-Japanese War of 1894 (Inter-state War #73) on July 23, 1894. During the inter-state war, the Tonghaks remobilized and began to attack the Japanese, who "had to fight a rear-guard action in Korea" as the "rebellion became specifically anti-Japanese."[79] The former rebels declared a war to rid Korea of Japanese influence on September 14, seizing arms and mobilizing a larger army than that of the First Tonghak Rebellion. A week later, the Japanese-controlled government adopted a policy of carnage toward the rebels. The Tonghaks responded by resuming their revolt with tens of thousands of peasants. However, the bulk of the fighting against the Tonghak rebels was done by a relatively small number of Japanese troops (a combined force of 2,000 Japanese and Koreans); even "government" units were placed under Japanese command. In this extra-state conflict, the rebels were crushed by the Japanese, suffering thousands of casualties. The Japanese then executed whatever Tonghaks they could find. Guerrilla fighting continued into 1895 and 1896.

Coding Decisions: Adding the known casualties gives a total of about 450 government battle-deaths and several hundred rebel battle-deaths, but we regard it as likely that the rebels suffered significant casualties in their victories of April 7 and April 23 and that government forces ambushing rebels on May 3 also suffered some loss, suggesting that there were about 1,000 battle-deaths, about evenly split between the sides. Note that Japan is not a participant in this war despite sending troops (the first arriving in Seoul on June 10), ostensibly in support for the government, for these were sent against the government's explicit requests and in any event did not engage the Tonghaks during the period of the First Tonghak Rebellion.

Sources: Jae-gen (1994); Kallendar (2013); Kim (1967, 2012); Lee (1984); Paine (2003); Suh (1994).[80]

INTRA-STATE WAR #628
First Gansu Muslim Revolt of 1895 to 1896

Participants: China versus Gansu Muslims (Aggregate).
Dates: April 2, 1895, to April 1896.
Battle-related Deaths: Total Combatant Deaths: 10,000. (See Coding Decisions.)[81]
Initiator: Gansu Muslims.
Outcome: China wins.
War Type: Civil for local issues (intercommunal conflict).
Total System Member Military Personnel: Armed Forces of China: 1 million (prewar, initial, peak, final).[82]
Theater Armed Forces: Gansu Muslims: thousands.[83]

Antecedents: In the spring of 1895, riots broke out between Han and Hui in Xunhua, Gansu. The government sent soldiers to quell the unrest. Entering Xunhua, the government's commander executed eleven prominent Muslim leaders. This led to open revolt on April 2.

Narrative: Muslim Salars besieged Xunhua; casualties from fighting between the rebels and government were high on both sides. Across the district, Muslims armed themselves and launched preemptive attacks on government garrisons. In response, the government mobilized reinforcements. The Muslim revolt was led by Han Wenxiu. The Salar Muslims soon found themselves outmatched by government forces, suffering heavy casualties in ambushes.

Seeking broader support, the Muslim rebels approached Hezhou, where Ma Yonglin led a Hui rebellion. On June 12, Xunhua was relieved by government forces, but Hezhou was besieged by Muslim rebels. The Hezhou Muslims then spread the revolt to Didao, and Siwashan fort was attacked, causing 600 Han casualties. On June 29, the walled city at Didao was besieged by the rebels. Small Chinese forts and stockades fell to the rebels, who killed thousands of the defenders. The revolt spread as Muslims feared they would be targeted in revenge for the Xunhua rebellion.

By September 1, the rebels were bombarding the walls of Xining. A major battle a few days later proved to be sanguinary but indecisive. Battles continued throughout the month. A related rebellion broke out in Ninxia, with 10,000 Muslims marching to the support of the Gansu revolt until they were intercepted and disarmed by government forces.

The tide of the war turned in late autumn. Beginning on November 17, the government won a decisive victory at the Battle of Niuxinshan (Ocheart Mountain), killing thousands of Hui defenders in a week of fighting. On December 3, government forces broke through to relive the siege of Hezhou. Captured rebel leaders were held for trial, and on December 25 the government executed more than 100 of them at Hezhou. The fighting in and around Hezhou had cost tens of thousands of lives.

The government now enlisted the help of Tibetans against the rebels around Xining. The government offensive stalled on January 2, 1896, possibly because of bribery. Negotiations broke down when the Hui reneged on a promise to surrender if their lives were spared. As late as mid-February, Xining Muslims still dominated some areas but quickly lost ground. The revolt had previously spread to Toba, and in late April, these rebels finally were induced to surrender unconditionally, ending the war.

Termination and Outcome: The war was an unconditional military victory by the government, with a formal surrender by the last rebels. Rebel leaders were executed, while common soldiers merely were disarmed. Fearing Han revenge, some 20,000 Hui fled towards Russia; of these, only 2,000 survived.

Coding Decisions: Tens of thousands were killed in the uprising. While Lipman asserts that the government responded to the outbreak of the revolt by trying to exterminate the Hui, it is also clear that many thousands died in battle. A reasonable estimate of battle-deaths would be 10,000.

Source: Lipman (1981, 1997).[84]

INTRA-STATE WAR #657
First Nationalist Revolution of 1911 (aka Xinhai Revolution)

Participants: China versus Republicans.
Dates: October 11, 1911, to December 18, 1911.
Battle-related Deaths: Total Combatant Deaths: more than 6,000. Government battle-deaths outnumbered those of the rebels.[85]
Initiator: Republicans.
Outcome: Negotiated settlement.
War Type: Civil for central control (but see Coding Decisions).
Total System Member Military Personnel: Armed Forces of China: 1,003,000 (prewar); 994,500 (after initial defections); 994,500 (peak); 325,000 (final).[86]
Theater Armed Forces: Republicans: 2,000 (prewar); 8,500 (after initial defections); 800,000 (peak); 800,000 (final).[87]

Antecedents: The implementation of centralizing and Westernizing reforms in early twentieth-century China produced discontent among the anti-Western public, jealous provincial governors, and radicals seeking a republic. For example, a plan to nationalize the railways and turn the concessions over to foreign bankers to pay debts stemming from the Boxer Uprising generated strong resistance among provincial elites and nationalists alike. Secret revolutionary societies gained many adherents in the military, despite efforts to purge them.

Unrest was particularly intense in Sichuan, where provincial elites had been generating enormous revenue for the railway project while actually building little. When the government offered lower compensation for Sichuan than elsewhere and turned aside attempts at peaceful persuasion, Sichuanese elites and commoners of the *Paoge*, or Gowned Brotherhood, protested in 1911. When the protests were repressed, rioting occurred, and when the rioting was suppressed, rebellion broke out, with more than 100,000 *Paoge* members surrounding the provincial capital of Chengdu and attacking it on September 18 and September 19.

As most of Sichuan's troops were deployed in Tibet, the central government ordered troops from Wuchang, capital of Hubei province, to deal with the rebels. On October 5, they departed, leaving

Wuchang itself weakened. On October 10, a revolution broke out at Wuchang, led by 2,000 troops of the Hubei New Army.

Narrative: The next day, the rebels faced the Eighth Transportation and Supply Battalion (about 2,000 strong), the governor general's personal bodyguard, and a few additional loyalist troops. The rebels suffered a few score casualties, while government losses were heavier. The rebels took control of the city and proclaimed the independence of Hubei, the deposition of the Qing Dynasty, and the establishment of a republic.

In further fighting, government battle-deaths climbed to 400. Hundreds of Manchus were massacred. About 6,500 troops in Wuchang defected to the rebels. Five days later, the sister cities of Hanyang and Hankow were taken by the republicans. The government counterattacked heavily at Hankow in late October, inflicting more than 2,000 casualties on up to 40,000 revolutionaries and burning the city, killing thousands of civilians. But soon more cities joined the revolt. Government forces suffered enormous casualties at Jingzhou, and soon modern army units across China were taking control of provinces, declaring independence, and pledging loyalty to the republic. In Shaanxi, a massacre following a battle on October 24 killed up to 10,000 Manchus.

By November, only six provinces remained completely loyal to the government. In Fujian, several hundred government troops were killed from November 7 to November 11. The navy defected to the rebels on November 11. In Guangdong, some 10,000 rebels fought the government over Huizhou from November 3 to November 7, before government forces capitulated and joined the rebels. At the same time, the government executed 400 suspected revolutionaries in Nanjing, but soon a rebel army of 30,000 faced the 20,000 government defenders of the city. On December 3, the rebels broke through and commenced a general massacre of Manchus.

Combat seems to have been the most intense in Hubei. Fighting around Wuchang killed thousands of rebels beginning on November 9. On November 16 and November 17, a second battle for Hankow left 667 rebels killed or wounded, but hundreds of government soldiers were mowed down by rebel machine guns each day of the fighting. Most of the government wounded were then left on the field to die. At Hanyang, 2,830 soldiers (or perhaps rebels alone) were killed in a week of intense fighting from November 20 to November 27. And at Jingzhou from November 19 to December 13, the government suffered heavy losses.

The government's military commander, Yuan Shikai, became its first constitutional premier on November 13. The rebels proceeded to organize their own government in Hankow on November 30, electing one Tan Renfeng as president of the parliament. On December 4, a three-day cease-fire began. The government sought peace by implementing constitutional rule and negotiating with the rebels. An agreement that would allow the emperor to keep his wealth and called for the equality of nationalities (a protection for the ruling Manchu minority) broke down, and Qing resistance hardened. The rebels had perhaps 200,000 troops against 325,000 who remained loyal to the government.

In early December, cease-fires repeatedly broke down as Yuan Shikai attacked the revolutionaries, especially in northern provinces. However, other nations were pressuring both sides to make peace. Peace talks were held in Shanghai beginning on December 18. From this point forward, the cease-fire held.

Termination and Outcome: On December 20, an agreement in principle was reached for a republic. On December 28, a government ministerial conference agreed that the national assembly should be convened to decide the fate of the Qing dynasty. A meeting of close relatives of the empress dowager confirmed Yuan's authority to reach such an agreement.

Just at this moment, however, the rebels formed a provisional government in Nanjing that elected Sun Yat-sen as president, which would deny Yuan Shikai the position. Sun Yat-sen took up his position on January 1, 1912, and almost immediately decided on an expedition against the provinces of the North. But peace talks continued, and on February 3, due to pressure from her own armed forces, the empress dowager empowered Yuan to negotiate the end of the dynasty. The emperor abdicated on February 11, and Yuan Shikai became president of the new Republic of China on February 15.

The outcome of the war was formally a negotiated agreement and contained elements of a compromise settlement, such as Yuan becoming president and Li Yuanhong (leader of the Wuchang Uprising) becoming vice president.

Coding Decisions: Although the war was fought primarily as a revolution, the fact that the rebels declared independence muddies the waters. On balance, we conclude that control of the central government was the more contested issue.

Sources: Bowei and Guoping (1991); Ch'en (1972); Chien-Nung (1956); Dingle (1912); Dutt (1968); Elleman (2001); Esherick (1976); Hsüeh (1961); Rhoads (2000); Williams (2013).[88]

INTRA-STATE WAR #665

Second Nationalist Revolution of 1913 (aka Summer Revolution of 1913)

Participants: China versus Republicans.
Dates: July 12, 1913, to September 1, 1913.
Battle-related Deaths: Total Combatant Deaths: 5,000. (See Coding Decisions.)[89]
Initiator: China.
Outcome: China wins.
War Type: Civil for local issues (independence—but see Coding Decisions).
Total System Member Military Personnel: Armed Forces of China: 450,000 (prewar); 250,000 (after initial defections); 250,000 (peak).[90]
Theater Armed Forces: Republicans: 200,000 (peak).[91]

Antecedents: The Chinese Nationalist Party (KMT) was established in 1912 by the revolutionaries of Hubei, their wartime allies (see Intra-state War #657), and several smaller parties. Its strength lay in the South, with the members of the former provisional government at Nanjing. When its leader was assassinated in 1913, the party contemplated rebellion against President Yuan Shikai, who had taken out loans from foreign powers to consolidate his rule. Just prior to the revolt, Yuan began to purge KMT members from the government and military. The spark for rebellion was the importation of 7,000 foreign rifles by nationalist commander Li Liejun in Jiujiang (Kiukiang) in Jiangxi province. Yuan ordered him replaced, but Li refused. Two armies were dispatched: one against Jiujiang and one against Nanjing in Jiangsu.

Narrative: The first clashes occurred on July 12, 1913. From July 12 to July 25, the Battle of Hukow in the North raged, with the government eventually defeating Li Liejun's forces. Meanwhile, KMT-affiliated leaders in seven provinces declared independence, forming a loosely coordinated rebel army of several hundred thousand soldiers. However, the rebels quickly were defeated in each of these provinces. On July 22, the government claimed victory over the rebels at Suzhou. On August 18, the rebels lost the Battle of Nanchang in Jiangsi province. By the end of August, the government had defeated the rebels across the nation, with some provinces having withdrawn their declarations of independence to avoid being defeated militarily. Yuan's troops entered and sacked Nanjing, the last center of resistance, on September 1.

Termination and Outcome: The outcome of the war was an unconditional government military victory. Rebellious officials were replaced, and the purge of the KMT was completed. Yuan now had uncontested dominance over China.

Coding Decisions: About 10,000 people died; of these, 5,000 were battle-deaths. Behaviorally, the rebels acted to defend their "independent" provinces, and the government refrained from attacking those that retracted their declarations of independence. Therefore, even though the war usually is portrayed as a contest for control over the central government, we code it as being over local issues.

Sources: Ch'en (1972); Chien-Nung (1956).[92]

INTRA-STATE WAR #672

China Pai Ling (White Wolf) War of 1914 (aka Bai Lang Rebellion)

Participants: China versus Bai Lang-led Rebels.
Dates: March 1914 to August 7, 1914.
Battle-related Deaths: Total Combatant Deaths: 1,000. (See Coding Decisions.)[93]
Initiator: Bai Lang-led Rebels.
Outcome: China wins.
War Type: Civil for local issues (peasant revolt).
Total System Member Military Personnel: Armed forces of China: 460,000 (prewar, initial, peak, final).[94]

Theater Armed Forces: Armed Forces of China: 200,000 (initial). Bai Lang-led Rebels: 10,000 (prewar); 10,000 (initial); 20,000 (peak); a few dozen (final).[95]

Antecedents: In 1911, Bai Lang (Pai Lang, called Pai Ling or White Wolf by the government) led peasants in revolt against the government. In October 1912, some "bandit" leaders were promised amnesty and positions in return for laying down their arms—but when they were subsequently executed anyway, several hundred peasants rallied to Bai Lang. In the winter of 1912, he defeated several regiments of government troops, temporarily allying himself to pro-Manchu royalists resisting the government of Yuan Shikai. The government suffered heavy losses, but the rebellion did not rise to the level of a civil war.

By 1913, Bai Lang had 5,000 troops armed with modern weapons. His strength grew throughout the year, and he allied himself to the KMT in its summer revolution against Yuan Shikai (see Intra-state War #665), leading a campaign that lasted until October and resulted in the sack of Zaoyang in northern Hubei. His forces did not surrender with the KMT but instead maintained resistance to the government, raiding cities in Henan and Anhui. In early 1914, the government mounted a campaign to destroy Bai Lang using 100,000 troops. Bai Lang's 10,000 insurgents (among whom were 500 deserters from the government army) managed to evade government forces again and again, avoiding combat. By March, he began a long march westward into Shaanxi and Gansu provinces to link up with Hui (Muslim) insurgents; he was now being pursued by 200,000 government soldiers.

Narrative: Although the march through Shaanxi proceeded smoothly, Bai Lang's forces ran into heavy resistance in Gansu, where the governor and Muslim population were against him. At the battle of Tianshui, about 200 were killed. After capturing Old Taozhu, his forces massacred between 8,000 and 16,000 Muslims. By May, however, his forces were stymied by local resistance; he was defeated in battle on June 2 at Fuqian, Gansu. After a typhoid epidemic killed many rebels and many more of his troops were killed trying to ford a river, others began to desert; he was forced to retreat back toward his home base in western Henan. Upon reaching the Henan area, most of his core group of soldiers simply went home. On August 7, Bai Lang was cornered with a few dozen followers and mortally wounded. This was the last recorded combat of the war.

Termination and Outcome: The outcome of the war was a complete government victory. There were reprisals after the war. Those leaders captured by the government were executed after interrogation. Many of his followers were conscripted into the army to prevent them from reforming their "bandit" units. But within weeks, 1,000 of Bai Lang's followers had raised a new revolt under his former lieutenant Song Laonian; instead of fighting they retreated into northern Shaanxi. There, Son's forces joined the provincial army led by ex-bandit Chen Shufan.

Coding Decisions: An estimate of 5,000 killed is probably too low, given the Old Taozhu massacre, but the overwhelming majority of deaths were civilians. We estimate that the rebellion cost at least 1,000 combatants their lives through battle, disease, and drowning. Given the size of the forces engaged, the real toll may have been much higher.

Sources: Billingsley (1988); Friedman (1974); Kim (2004); Lipman (1981, 1997), Perry (1983).[96]

INTRA-STATE WAR #674
Anti-monarchy War of 1915 to 1916 (aka Third Revolution)

Participants: China versus National Protection Army.
Dates: December 25, 1915, to June 15, 1916.
Battle-related Deaths: Armed Forces of China: 2,000 in Sichuan alone. National Protection Army: 1,200 to 2,000; Total Combatant Deaths: 4,000. (See Coding Decisions.)[97]
Initiator: National Protection Army.
Outcome: National Protection Army wins.
War Type: Civil for central control (but see Coding Decisions).
Total System Member Military Personnel: Armed Forces of China: 500,000 (prewar); 494,000 (after initial defection); 494,000 (peak).[98]
Theater Armed Forces: Armed Forces of China: 30,000 (initial). National Protection Army: 6,000 (initial).

Antecedents: Yuan Shikai, president of the Republic of China, moved to turn the republic (in name only) into an empire with himself as founder of the royal dynasty. On December 11, 1915, the parliament "elected" him as emperor, and the next day he proclaimed the empire. This move provoked opposition from many quarters, but it was in Yunnan that the rebellion began. Military commanders seemed to fear the prospect of a Yuan able to rule without their support.

Narrative: On December 25, some 6,000 troops in Yunnan declared Yunnanese independence and proclaimed the Yuan monarchy to be illegitimate; fighting soon began as Yunnanese troops invaded Sichuan. About 30,000 government soldiers were mobilized to stop them between January and March. The rebels adopted the name National Protection Army (Ho-kuo-chün). On January 6, about 20,000 troops rebelled in Guangdong. The Guizhou army followed Yunnan into rebellion on January 27, 1916, and attacked Hunan. After heavy fighting, Sichuan's provincial government joined the revolt on February 1.

Japan refused to recognize the monarchy and treated both sides as belligerents, aiding the rebel cause. Jianxi rebelled on March 15, and six days later Feng Guozhang in Nanjing—one of the government's top commanders and part of the Beiyang army that Yuan relied on for support—declared his neutrality. The South was now united against the loyalist provinces of the North—and advancing. As Yuan's army crumbled, he abdicated on March 22. However, the rebels refused to stand down until he abandoned the presidency. Informal truces existed over much of the front, but hostilities continued. On June 6, Yuan died; nine days later, the new president, Li Yuanhong, declared the war to be at an end.

Termination and Outcome: The outcome of the war was a military victory by the rebels, but the price of victory was accepting a weak president who was dominated by northern political figure Duan Qirui. The new president announced the reinstatement of the constitution of 1912 and restoration of the republic. The rebels rescinded their declarations of independence, but the government of the North was unable to exert effective control over the former rebels in the South. Moreover, the ruling Beiyang group had been split, with Duan heading up the Anhui Clique and Feng becoming leader of the Zhili Clique. In 1917, the two would form dueling governments that set the stage for yet another civil war in China.

Coding Decisions: According to Sutton, Yunnanese casualties to April 1916 numbered between 1,200 and 1,600, but 2,000 were treated for wounds; this suggests that the casualty estimates refer to those killed rather than the total of killed and wounded. Some 2,000 northern (government) dead were reported in Sichuan, which is where most of the combat took place. We estimate 4,000 dead more or less evenly divided between the rebels and government. Yunnan declared independence but fought the war by first invading Sichuan and then advancing; accordingly, we code this war as a contest for control over the central government.

Sources: Chen (1999); Chien-Nung (1956); Dreyer (1995); McCord (1993); Sutton (1980).

INTRA-STATE WAR #675

Russian Turkestan Revolt of 1916 to 1917 (aka Anti-conscription Revolts)

Participants: Russia versus Kazakh, Kirghiz, Turkestan (Tashkent), and Uzbek Rebels.
Dates: July 4, 1916, to February 27, 1917.
Battle-related Deaths: Armed Forces of Russia: more than 97. Total Combatant Deaths: 2,000. (See Coding Decisions.)[99]
Initiator: Turkestan Rebels.
Outcome: Russia wins.
War Type: Civil for local issues (conscription).
Total System Member Military Personnel: Armed Forces of Russia: 10,900,000 (prewar, initial, peak); 9,500,000 (final).[100]
Theater Armed Forces: Kazakh Rebels: 30,000 (initial); 50,000 (peak).[101] Kirghiz Rebels, participating from August 6 to 31, 1916: unknown. Turkestan (Taskent) Rebels, participating to mid-October 1916: 5,000 (initial); 8,000 (peak).[102] Uzbek Rebels, participating to July 25, 1916: unknown.

Antecedents: In the midst of World War I, Russia decided to expand conscription to non-Slav peoples in the empire. On June 25, 1916, the government declared a labor draft of Turkestanis. Attempts actually to enforce the decree beginning on July 2 triggered revolts across Turkestan.

Narrative: The first overt acts against the government occurred in Khojand on July 4, where peasant mobs threw stones at the conscription office. Russian troops fired on the demonstrators, killing two. Waves of demonstrations—at least 131 open ones—swept through Russian Turkestan. Turkestani rebels formed a guerrilla force of about 5,000 to 8,000 near Tashkent; they were suppressed only in mid-October. They killed at least 2,325 civilians (another 1,384 Russians were missing) and 79 Russian and Turkestani officials. A revolt broke out at Djizak, where Uzbeks massacred 113 Russians, only to be suppressed by military force, followed by many executions. About 1,000 Uzbeks, mostly civilians, were killed in the fighting. By July 25 the area was calm. On August 6, the Kirghiz joined the rebellion, mostly targeting civilians. From August 13 to August 21, the Kirghiz besieged Tokmak, suffering 300 killed before retreating. In all, the Kirghiz rebels would kill about 2,200 mostly Russian civilians and only 80 government soldiers. The response of the government was brutal, killing perhaps 4,500 to 6,500 Kirghiz, mostly civilians.

Kazakhs also rebelled; the first were some 30,000 led by men such as Tokash Bokin in the northern Kazakh areas, who were suppressed with thousands of battle-deaths by mid-October. However, the largest and best-organized rebel forces were the Kazakhs from the Inner Horde area, commanded by Amangeldy Imanov. By October, they had reached a strength of 50,000 rebels, armed with crude but effective weapons manufactured by local workshops. But after defeat in a battle at Turgai, they reverted to guerrilla tactics and by November 30 only some 6,000 remained in the field. By mid-January 1917, Imanov's rebels were down to 2,000, and the government withdrew its forces on February 27, having crushed the rising.

Termination and Outcome: The government proclaimed a "truce," but the outcome of the war was a complete government victory. Kazakhs were resettled en masse to less-hospitable areas and given group fines and punishments. Some 347 Kazakhs were sentenced to death, although only 51 were executed before the Bolsheviks overthrew the government.

Coding Decisions: No estimate of rebel battle-deaths is available, but thousands were killed. Government losses may have been as low as 97 soldiers killed. We estimate 2,000 battle-deaths, a figure that is more likely to be an underestimate than an overestimate.

Sources: Olcott (1995); Pierce (1960); Rywkin (1990); Sanborn (2003); Wheeler (1964); Zenkovsky (1960).[103]

INTRA-STATE WAR #676
First Yunnan–Sichuan War of 1917

Participants: Yunnan and Guizhou versus Sichuan Military.
Dates: April 18, 1917, to August 2, 1917.
Battle-related Deaths: Total Combatant Deaths: at least 3,000. (See Coding Decisions.)[104]
Initiator: Sichuan Military.
Outcome: Sichuan Military wins.
War Type: Regional.
Theater Armed Forces: Armed Forces of Sichuan: 25,000 (peak).[105] Armed Forces of Yunnan and Guizhou: at least 10,000 (peak).

Antecedents: In addition to the divide between North and South, the emergence of warlordism after the Antimonarchy War (see Intra-state War #674), led to small-scale struggles between smaller warlords for possession of certain contested provinces. These struggles had the potential to alter the balance of power between the larger warlords—or even North and South—and therefore sometimes escalated to war. In 1917, pro-Northern general Liu Ts'un-hou was appointed to replace Tai K'an as the highest military authority in Sichuan. Tai K'an remained governor of the province, but when Liu sought to eject him from the capital of Chengdu, war broke out.

Narrative: On April 18, 1917, fighting broke out in Chengdu. More than 200 soldiers and 3,000 civilians died in the first three days of the war. Tai received support from Yunnanese and Guizhou units, which were also nominally part of the national army but really controlled by the respective warlords of each of the provinces. Together, they maintained Tai in power.

On July 1, the Manchu dynasty briefly was restored to power; Tai denounced it while Liu supported it. On or about July 6, Liu attacked the capital. On July 12, a cease-fire was agreed upon, and the remaining 2,000 Guizhou troops evacuated Chengdu. However, they were ambushed, and about 500 of them were killed. In Beijing, the two-week Manchu restoration came to an end.

Lo P'ei-chin, the military commander of Yunnan–Guizhou forces, immediately dispatched 10,000 reinforcements to Tai, which arrived too late to prevent Tai's death. They faced off against about 25,000 Sichuanese troops. Attacked on three fronts, the Sichuanese suffered 2,000 wounded on the Chengdu front alone. But then the Sichuanese mounted a counterattack, and almost 1,000 of Lo's men drowned or otherwise died during the ensuing rout.

Termination and Outcome: On August 2, a truce was signed; it later broke down when the Sichuan conflict became merged into the North–South War (see Intra-state War #676.5). Lo was dismissed as commander in chief by the Yunnan governor in September. The war effectively had been won by Sichuanese forces under Liu. Yunnan completed its withdrawal from the province in November.

Coding Decisions: Incomplete records add up to about 2,500 battle-deaths. The toll was likely higher than this—at least 3,000.

Sources: Sutton (1980).

INTRA-STATE WAR #676.5
Southern China Revolt of 1917 to 1918 (aka North–South War or Fourth Revolution)

Participants: China versus Constitution Protection Army.
Dates: August 16, 1917, to November 17, 1918.
Battle-related Deaths: Total Combatant Deaths: 1,500. (See Coding Decisions.)[106]
Initiator: China.
Outcome: Stalemate.
War Type: Civil for central control.
Total System Member Military Personnel: Armed Forces of China: 900,000 (prewar); less than 800,000 (peak).[107]
Theater Armed Forces: Armed Forces of China: more than 150,000 (peak). Constitution Protection Army: more than 200,000 (peak).[108]

Antecedents: After the Antimonarchy War (see Intra-state War #674), the rebels rescinded their declarations of independence. However, warlords emerged from the struggle—as did a split between North and South. In April 1917, fighting between warlords in Sichuan broke out; intervention by Yunnan and Guizhou escalated the conflict to an intercommunal war (Intra-state War #674.5); by August, the pro-Southern provinces largely had been defeated by the pro-Northern general Liu Ts'un-hou.

In June 1917, there was a brief dispute over whether the constitution of 1914 or that of 1912 should be used; when the navy defected to the southern politicians, the de facto northern leader, Premier Duan Qirui, conceded the point and assented to the restoration of the 1912 document. However, the parliament, being dominated by Southerners, would have little real influence. When it initially refused to declare war on the Central Powers, Duan threatened it with the Citizens' Corps, an act that eventually prompted a vote of no-confidence and his dismissal by President Li Yuanhong.

Duan pulled out of the capital, leaving it defenseless, and on July 1 monarchist general Zhang Xun announced the restoration of the Manchu dynasty. After pausing to allow the monarchists to dominate the capital, Duan moved in and quickly expelled them. He was reappointed to the government, and Li Yuanhong resigned the presidency. After being assured that his loyalists would remain in power in the Yangtze provinces, warlord Feng Guozhang agreed to take up the presidency. The government was thus a coalition of northern warlords.

The parliament was dismissed and a new northern parliament was organized, dominated by Anhui and Fujian militarists, the An-Fu coalition. Duan then attempted to install his own generals in the southern provinces, which eventually led to the formation of an alternate government in Canton and the effective independence of the South. He installed Fu liang-tso as the new military ruler in Hunan, but the old one mobilized his forces. Determined to reunite China, Duan ordered an expedition prepared against Hunan, which was not allied to any of the northern warlords and offered a gateway to the rebellious southern provinces.

Narrative: On August 16, two Hunanese militarists declared independence, and immediately fighting broke out between the northern militarists (the government) and Hunan's old military commander (Tan Yankai). Meanwhile, the newly organized Canton "government" in the South refused to recognize the parliament of the North. On September 3, Sun Yat-sen was selected as grand marshal of the military regime in Canton, although real power was in the hands of subordinate marshals Liu Jung-t'ing of Guangdong and Ch'en Pi-kuang, the naval chief. Military commanders in Guangdong and Guangxi, affiliated with the nationalist KMT, sent troops northward to aid Hunan in mid-October.

On November 14, the government's commanders in Hunan announced a cease-fire and circulated a telegram—supported by other members of Feng Guozhang's Zhili Clique—demanding that the war be stopped. The rebels ignored them and advanced; Fu was soon forced out of Hunan. On November 16, fighting stopped when Duan announced his resignation.

However, a new front in the North–South War was soon opened in Sichuan, which Yunna and Guizhou troops (calling themselves the National Pacification Army—a name that would subsequently be reused by other armies in other Chinese wars) invaded on December 1. The Yunnanese drove into the northern-controlled province, and Guizhou troops ejected northern forces from Chongqing (Chungking) on December 3 and December 4. Within three months, Sichuanese warlord Liu Ts'un-hou was forced to flee the capital of Chengdu. The Sichuan army was divided: the Third Division did most of the fighting, while the Second Division remained neutral; one brigade of the First Division even went over to the rebels.

Meanwhile, Hubei declared its independence and allied with the South in early December. Duan was appointed military leader of the new army, well equipped by the Japanese, being readied for combat in Europe, and augmenting northern military power. The government attacked Hubei in mid-January 1918, but southern forces were not dispatched to aid the province until January 27, by which time Hubei largely had been defeated by government forces. At the beginning of the year, the government mounted a new campaign against Hunan. Consisting of 150,000 troops led by Wu P'ei-fu, it conquered much of the province by April. By the end of the month, the South had all but conquered Sichuan but had lost Hubei and Hunan. Several mixed bodies of troops were sent by the North to aid Liu Ts'un-hou, who was still holding on in Sichuan.

Duan returned to the premiership on March 23; fighting continued, but under pressure from the Zhili Clique, negotiations resumed, and a cease-fire was reached between Wu and the rebels on June 15 (against government orders). It is not clear whether this cease-fire—which excluded Shaanxi—was honored on all fronts, however, and it was only on November 17 that an armistice was signed.

Termination and Outcome: The war ended with an armistice, not a negotiated settlement per se. A peace conference in 1919 ultimately failed to resolve the North–South split. The outcome of the war is best characterized as a stalemate. In 1920, the Sichuanese revolted against Yunnan's occupation, leading to severe fighting (see Intra-state War #684). Meanwhile, the split between the Anhui Clique led by Duan and the Zhili Clique led by Feng prevented the North from uniting in the future and all but assured a new round of warfare over possession the capital.

Coding Decisions: Although Ch'i estimates just 1,000 to 2,000 killed or wounded in Hunan—about 250 to 500 battle-deaths, assuming the usual rule of thumb of three wounded to one killed held—this omits the fighting in Sichuan as well as smaller encounters in Hubei and Shaanxi. It also omits disease, which must have affected the very large armies involved. Accordingly, we estimate 1,500 battle-deaths in the war, which Bouthoul and Carrère list as the deaths in the Yunnan Rebellion of the same time period.

Sources: Bouthoul and Carrère (1978); Ch'i (1976); Chien-Nung (1956); Gray (1990); McCord (1993, 2014); Sutton (1980); Wou (1978).[109]

INTRA-STATE WAR #684
Second Yunnan–Sichuan War of 1920

Participants: Sichuan versus Yunnan–Guizhou Forces.

Dates: May 23, 1920, to December 1920.
Battle-related Deaths: Total Combatant Deaths: 2,000. (See Coding Decisions.)[110]
Initiator: Sichuan.
Outcome: Sichuan wins.
War Type: Regional.
Theater Armed Forces: Sichuan: 100,000 (peak).[111] Yunnan–Guizhou Forces: more than 200,000 (peak).[112]

Antecedents: The North–South War (Intra-state War #675) left Yunnan and its ally Guizhou in control of Sichuan. Early in 1920, the governor of Sichuan, Hsiung Ko-wu, began negotiations for the withdrawal of this "guest army." At the time, Yunnan–Guizhou had 20,000 to 30,000 of its more than 200,000 troops deployed in Sichuan, and they had become deeply unpopular. About six months of negotiations failed, and Hsiung decided to take military action.

Narrative: On May 23, Hsiung used Sichuan's armed forces to attack Yunnanese and pro-Yunnanese positions, defeating many units. Yunnan, backed by Guizhou, counterattacked and regained the ground it had lost, at the cost of 1,200. As the war dragged on, Yunnan–Guizhou troops began to fall back. Outside Chengdu, 10,000 Yunnanese troops took to the hills, and 45,000 Sichuanese were unable to dislodge them. Then in October, the Yunnanese laid siege to the provincial capital. By mid-October, Hsiung had allied himself with his old enemy from the previous Yunnan–Sichuan and North–South Wars, Liu Ts'un-hou. A united Sichuan army now pushed out its unwanted "guests"—by December, the Yunnan–Guizhou units had fled in defeat.

Termination and Outcome: The outcome of the war was a military victory by the Sichuanese forces. Some internal fighting between Sichuan factions occurred over the next year, but Sichuan would not be occupied again until 1924.

Coding Decisions: About 4,000 were killed, although it is likely that half were civilians. We therefore estimate 2,000 battle-deaths.

Sources: Adshead (1990); Ch'i (1976); Kapp (1970); Sutton (1980).

INTRA-STATE WAR #685
Zhili–Anfu War of 1920 (aka First Warlord)

Participants: An-Fu Faction versus Zhili and Fengtien Factions.
Dates: July 14, 1920, to July 23, 1920.
Battle-related Deaths: Total Combatant Deaths: 1,000. (See Coding Decisions.)[113]
Initiator: Zhili Faction.
Outcome: Zhili and Fengtien Factions win.
War Type: Intercommunal.
Theater Armed Forces: 120,000 troops were mobilized by all sides.[114] Armed Forces of China (Fengtien Faction): 70,000 (initial, peak).[115]

Antecedents: When Duan Qirui (leader of the Anhui-Fujian—An-Fu—faction or clique) was premier of China and Feng Guozhang (leader of the Zhili Clique) was president, friction between them was constant. The two disagreed over policy in central China and the attitude to be adopted toward the South. A power struggle emerged between the two, but on the expiry of Feng's term as president, he agreed to step down if Duan would also resign. On October 10, 1918, both men resigned. Xu Shichang, viewed as a harmless civilian figurehead, became president. Duan stayed on, however, as director of the War Participation Bureau, through which he contracted loans from the Japanese to build his forces. Feng died in December 1919 and "leadership" of the loosely allied Zhili Clique was taken over by general Cao Kun and his subordinate Wei Peifu.

Duan continued to lose power, but his military forces still dominated the capital. In 1920, when pressure from the Zhili Clique and its ally Zhang Zuolin's Fengtien Clique compelled Xu to dismiss one of Duan's allies from government, Duan responded by declaring his units the National Pacification Army and forced Xu to dismiss generals Cao Kun and Wu Peifu. Both sides mobilized for war. On May 14, Wu Peifu's army began moving northward by rail. On May 25, Wu handed control of Hnegyang in Hunan over to southern military forces to prevent an An-Fu threat to his rear; the Southerners then pushed out the An-Fu forces. Zhang Zuolin's forces in Manchuria also marched on Beijing. On June 6, Duan sent three divisions to Tianjin to confront the combined armies.

Narrative: Fighting at Tianjin began on July 14 and lasted for five days, with only two days of serious combat. The result was a decisive victory for the Zhili–Fengtien forces. On July 23, they occupied Beijing.

Termination and Outcome: The next day, Duan resigned his positions and was allowed to go into seclusion. The outcome of the war was a complete military victory by the Zhili and Fengtien factions. Zhang Zuolin disbanded Duan's forces and took their Japanese-supplied equipment north to his troops. He also ensured that 30,000 of his soldiers remained in Beijing as "police" under the command of one of his loyalists.

Coding Decisions: Notably, neither faction actually seized the formal, legitimating institutions of government, despite their victory; this was an inter-communal war fought extralegally by factions of the country's armed forces rather than a revolution. A high estimate of casualties is 3,600, which—given the usual 3:1 ratio of wounded to killed—amounts to only 900 battle-deaths. But given the uncertainty inherent in this measurement technique, we include this conflict as a war because it is entirely possible that 1,000 were killed—because medical services were nonexistent, even superficial wounds often led to death in the warlord period.

Sources: Ch'i (1976); Gao (2009); Gray (1990); Wou (1978).[116]

INTRA-STATE WAR #687

Basmachi Rebellion of 1920 to 1924

Participants: Soviet Russia versus Basmachi.
Dates: September 1920 to February 4, 1924.
Battle-related Deaths: Total Combatant Deaths: perhaps 3,500. (See Coding Decisions and Narrative.)
Initiator: Soviet Russia.
Outcome: Soviet Russia wins.
War Type: Civil for local issues (independence and *sharia* law).
Total System Member Military Personnel: Armed Forces of Soviet Russia: 3,050,000 (prewar, initial); 5,500,000 (peak); 562,000 (final).[117]
Theater Armed Forces: Armed Forces of Soviet Russia: 120,000 to 160,000 (initial).[118] Basmachi: 6,000 (prewar); 6,000 (initial); 25,000 (peak); 3,500 to 4,000 (final).[119]

Antecedents: On February 17, 1918, Soviet Red Guards crushed the self-proclaimed Kokand Autonomous Government, killing perhaps 14,000 people in Kokand. In response, Turkestanis began attacking Russian settlements and Red Army detachments. Soviet takeovers in Khiva and Bokhara led to guerrilla resistance there as well. By the end of 1918, the largest of these Basmachi forces numbered 4,000 fighters; total Basmachi strength grew to 20,000 by the end of the following year. In July 1919, the government deployed the Fifth Army against the Basmachi rebels, having decisively defeated Siberian rebels under Kolchak (see Intra-state War #677). By September, local Red forces had recaptured the cities of Osh and Dzhelalabad; in the first half of 1920, the Fifth Army regulars inflicted a string of successive defeats on the Basmachi forces, forcing the latter to give up control of cities and resort to guerrilla war. But in the summer, many Muslims in Soviet forces defected to the rebels, bringing their strength to at least 6,000 again. The First Uzbek Cavalry Brigade was disarmed by Soviet authorities to prevent its wholesale defection.

Narrative: According to Rywkin, fighting became particularly fierce from September 1920 to September 1921, when there were 120,000 to 160,000 government troops deployed against the Basmachi. The government temporarily quashed the revolt, but on November 10, 1921, the former leader of the Young Turk government in Turkey made his way into eastern Bokhara. Enver Pasha was able to unify the Basmachi under his nominal leadership, calling for *jihad* against the Red Army. He gathered more than 20,000 fighters under his direct command and allied with thousands of others, often using Turkish officers. By spring 1922, he had recaptured eastern Bokhara and much of western Bokhara. The various resistance forces in Khiva, Bokhara, and the Fergana Valley coordinated their activities with Enver Pasha, and he shifted to a conventional war strategy despite his lack of artillery. On June 15, the government decisively defeated Enver Pasha's offensive at the Battle of Kafrun. In July 1922, a campaign against Enver Pasha smashed his personal forces; he was killed on August 8.

However, the Basmachi revolt continued, especially in the Fergana. The Soviet government responded with a combination of policy concessions, especially on *sharia* law and limited tribal autonomy, coupled with amnesty for leaders who surrendered and a military campaign including air support. By late 1922, the major Basmachi leaders in Fergana had been neutralized, their troops generally disbanded and given land. However, there were still many smaller Basmachi forces, and resistance was still fierce. In the first nine months of 1923, the Basmachi in Fergana "lost over 3,500 men."[120] But by the end of this period, armed resistance had become sporadic and largely ineffective. In Bukhara, two out of the three major Basmachi commanders retreated into Afghanistan in June; sole holdout Ibrahim Beg continued the fight with only 2,000 men. The last major battle took place after an Uzbek rising swelled the ranks of the Basmachi under Dzhunaid Khan, allowing them to take Khiva and hold it until January 29, 1924; some 300 Basmachi died in the siege.

Termination and Outcome: On February 4, Dzhunaid Khan retreated from the Khiva area with only 1,500 to 2,000 men. While it took some time for Soviet forces to run him down, the war was effectively over. The outcome of the war was a complete military victory by the government, with limited promises of amnesty. By and large, those promises were not honored for very long; most former rebel leaders were later killed.

Coding Decisions: It is unclear whether the fighting of 1919 and 1920 was sufficient to qualify as civil war, but the arrival of Enver Pasha certainly revitalized the Basmachi resistance and increased the intensity of fighting to civil-war levels. Battle-death figures are little better than guesses based on qualitative information about the intensity of fighting and the occasional statistic about some limited period of time during the war. This uncertainty is reflected in our decision to code the case at about 1,000 battle-deaths per year, just at the civil-war threshold. This is more likely to be an underestimate than an overestimate.

Sources: "Dzhunaid-Khan" (1965); Gankovsy (1996); Olcott (1981); Park (1957); Rezun (1992); Ritter (1990); Rywkin (1990).[121]

INTRA-STATE WAR #692
First Zhili–Fengtien War of 1922 (aka Second Chinese Warlord)

Participants: China (Fengtien Faction) versus Zhili Faction.

Dates: April 28, 1922, to April 4, 1922.

Battle-related Deaths: Armed Forces of China (Fengtien Faction/Government): 2,500; Armed Forces of China (Zhili Faction): 2,500; Total Combatant Deaths: 5,000. (See Coding Decisions.)[122]

Initiator: China (Fengtien Faction).

Outcome: Zhili Faction wins.

War Type: Civil for central control.

Total System Member Military Personnel: Armed Forces of China: 1,566,000 (but factionalized—prewar, initial, peak).

Theater Armed Forces: Armed Forces of China (Fengtien Faction): more than 100,000 (peak). Armed Forces of China (Zhili Faction): more than 100,000 (peak).

Antecedents: Zhili and Fengtien forces took control of Beijing in 1920 (see Intra-state War #685) but left its formal government administration undisturbed aside from forcing Duan Qirui from his office in the War Ministry. But soon Zhang Zuolin of the Fengtien faction insisted on a new finance minister, Liang Shiyi, who borrowed more money from Japan to fund government operations. On December 24, 1921, Zhang proclaimed Liang as premier. In 1922, when Liang insisted on further concessions to the Japanese during debt negotiations, the reaction was hostile throughout the country. Wu Peifu of the Zhili Clique demanded that Liang resign.

Convinced that Zhili was preparing to seize power, Zhang struck a deal with the KMT in the South, who agreed to invade Jiangsi. He also attempted to ally with the remnants of the An-Fu Clique. Liang then insisted that President Xu Shichang should order Zhang Zuolin's troops to Beijing to protect the government. With this formal order, Zhang's forces became the guardian of the Fengtien-dominated central government. Nevertheless, on April 25 a communiqué from the Zhili Clique denounced Zhang as a "rebel."

Narrative: Fighting began on April 28 and lasted until May 4. Zhang invaded Shandong but was repulsed in the Battle of Chaochou. Casualties were high; at least 100,000 soldiers from each side were involved in the fighting, although the total strength of each side (particularly the Zhili Clique) was higher. Fighting spread to the entire border between the factions. The Christian general Feng Yuxiang of the Zhili faction played an important role in the defeat of Zhang's Fengtien forces, who were driven beyond the Great Wall after a week of combat. Zhang's allies failed to come to his aid. Some 25,000 Fengtien troops surrendered, and another 60,000 left the field without fighting. Zhang retreated as Zhili forces maneuvered to cut off his line of supply.

Termination and Outcome: The outcome of the war was a military victory by the rebels. Wu Peifu posted Fen Yuxiang and his troops to Beijing, reinstated the Constitution of 1912 and recalled the 1913 parliament, which resolved to reunite the Northern and Southern governments. Zhang Zuolin was permitted to withdraw from Beijing and subsequently declared his base of Manchuria to be independent. In June, the president and premier resigned, leaving the government in Zhili-supported hands.

Coding Decisions: Because the Fengtien faction controlled the recognized capital at the onset of hostilities, we code it as the government and the case as a civil war rather than an intercommunal war. There were 10,000 to 30,000 casualties, distributed evenly between the two sides. Using the typical 3:1 ratio of wounded to killed in battle, this translates into 2,500 to 7,500 battle-deaths. We estimate 5,000 battle-deaths, although the toll could be half or half again as great as that number.

Sources: Ch'en (1979); Ch'i (1976); Chi (1969), Elleman (2001); Gray (1990); Pye (1971).[123]

INTRA-STATE WAR #697

First Afghan Anti-reform War of 1924 to 1925 (aka Khost Rebellion)

Participants: Afghanistan versus Khost Rebels.
Dates: March 15, 1924, to March 1925.
Battle-related Deaths: Armed Forces of Afghanistan: at least 671; Khost Rebels (Mangal and Other Tribes): at least 300; Total Combatant Deaths: at least 1,100.[124]
Initiator: Khost Rebels (Mangal Tribe).
Outcome: Afghanistan wins.
War Type: Civil for central control.
Total System Member Military Personnel: Armed Forces of Afghanistan: 65,000 (prewar, initial, peak, final).[125]
Theater Armed Forces: Khost Rebels (Mangals and Other Southern Tribes): 6,000 (initial—Mangal Tribe only); 5,000 (final).[126]

Antecedents: After winning a power struggle with his brother, Ahmanullah Khan claimed the throne of Afghanistan. He introduced some Western-style centralizing and secularizing reforms, including peacetime conscription, which provoked opposition from most tribes and the clerical establishment. In 1923, he promulgated the Nizamnama, an administrative code that granted women more freedom and allowed the government to regulate other issues seen as family problems heretofore handled by religious authorities. The new rules sparked protests by the clergy. Numerous anti-conscription protests also broke out late in the year.

Narrative: In mid-March 1924, the Mangal tribe around Khost demonstrated against the Nizamnama. The leader of the disturbances was Mullah Abdullah, also known as Mullah-i-Lang. The rebellion was small at first but soon grew in extent and numbers. An effort to replace the local governor failed when he was unable to get out of Khost and the newly appointed governor was unable to get in. The government sent raw recruits to deal with the uprising, and the rebels won some minor victories, ambushing a government regiment on April 22 and inflicting severe casualties while only suffering twenty rebel battle-deaths.

Further inconclusive combats occurred on about April 27 (60 rebels killed or wounded against 7 government killed and 26 wounded) and about a month later (when the government claimed to have killed 117 rebels and wounded 365 more against only 17 government battle-deaths and 27 wounded—figures that were generally regarded as unreliable by foreign observers). By June, the government claimed 94 government casualties against 564 rebel casualties, figures that observers regarded as wholly fictitious.

In response to the increasingly serious rebellion, the government summoned a *loya jirga*, which recommended the rollback of reforms that limited the power of the clergy. The government duly withdrew some of the reforms and opened negotiations with the rebels in early June. But by June 20, the talks broke down, and hostilities resumed four days later.

The government's army was officially 10,000 strong (some sources say 30,000), but most of the troops were seen as unfit for service or sympathetic to the rebels. By this time, the rebel Mangal tribe had been joined by the Zadran and (possibly) Ghilzais as well. Soon the Ahmedzais joined the revolt. A major battle on July 13 cost the government 250 troops lost. A small government force was wiped out at Bedak on August 2, and a larger force was soon decimated by the rebels.

Following these defeats, the government formally declared war on the Mangal tribe on August 11. The declaration further polarized the situation, and some 4,000 Suleman Khels joined the rebellion a few days later. Heavy fighting took place from August 23 to August 26, and four days later some 1,500 men under Mir Zamer Khan joined the government side. These forces engaged the rebels in a major battle from September 16 to September 17, killing 400 to 500 rebels at the cost of only 100 of Mir Zamer Khan's men killed. The Ahmedzais withdrew from the rebellion.

From September 18 to September 21, the government forces fought a combined force of 3,000 Suleman Khel, Zadran, and Mangal warriors. Forty rebels were killed or wounded as opposed to only 11 on the government side. The tide had turned in favor of the government, and this time when it called for tribal levies, about 4,600 responded.

Notwithstanding the government's advantage in men and materiel, the rebels still gained the occasional success, cutting up two government battalions near Kulangar on August 25. Several government detachments were wiped out from mid-September through October. On November 9 and November 10, a raid by 500 to 600 personal followers of Mullah Abdullah inflicted between 50 and 65 government casualties.

In December, the rebels asked for a truce and pardon. Peace negotiations followed, but ultimately failed, and by February the government had mounted a new campaign to crush the remnants of the rebellion. By March, the rebellion had been completely crushed, with the government taking some 5,000 prisoners.

Termination and Outcome: The outcome of the war was an unconditional government military victory. The government executed 75 people, 54 of whom had been prominent persons in the revolt. Among those executed were Mullah Abdullah and his son-in-law Mullah Abdul Rashid. Despite its victory, the government refrained from promoting further reforms for several years.

Coding Decisions: Self-explanatory from cited sources.

Sources: Adamec (1974, 1997); Burdett (2002); Gregorian (1969); Stewart (1973).[127]

INTRA-STATE WAR #697.3
Second Zhili–Fengtien War of 1924

Participants: China (Zhili Faction) versus Fengtien and An-Fu Forces.
Dates: September 3, 1924, to November 3, 1924.
Battle-related Deaths: Total Combatant Deaths: 8,000. (See Coding Decisions.)[128]
Initiator: China (Zhili Faction).
Outcome: Fengtien forces win.
War Type: Civil for central control.
Total System Member Military Personnel: Armed Forces of China (Factionalized): 1,700,000 (prewar, initial, peak, final).
Theater Armed Forces: Armed Forces of China (Zhili Faction): 130,000 mobilized (initial); more than 200,000 mobilized (peak); more than 140,000 (final).[129] Fengtien Forces: 170,000 (initial); 250,000 (peak); 250,000 (final). These estimates include "large numbers" of Japanese and Russian cavalry that fought with the Fengtien First Division.[130] An-Fu Forces in Zhejiang, participating through October 12, 1924: 50,000 to 74,000 (initial); 50,000 to 74,000 (peak).[131]

Antecedents: After the first Zhili–Fengtien War (Intra-state War #692), the Zhili faction appointed its supporters to the government of China. Soon splits within the Zhili Clique emerged. Feng Yuxiang was dissatisfied with his transfer to a post with only nominal power, albeit one in Beijing, where his troops provided security for the government. Similarly, Cao Kun had maneuvered to prevent Wu Peifu from occupying the capital.

Disputes between Cao and Feng over the funding of Feng's troops intensified on June 13, 1923, when the latter seized the revenue-generating Octroi, weakening the power of President Li Yuanhong. The move backfired when Cao Kun had himself elected to the presidency on October 25 by simply bribing enough parliamentarians, outraging the remnants of the Fengtien and An-Fu Cliques as well as the KMT in the South.

Wu Peifu remained loyal to the Zhili Clique but increasingly worried about fighting a two-front war against the Fengtien faction in the North and its potential allies in the South. In March 1923, he acted preemptively against Fujian; Zhili troops successfully ousted its An-Fu Clique warlord. The An-Fu troops retreated into neighboring Zhejiang, where they were incorporated into its armed forces. This and other small campaigns weakened the Zhili Clique, which was having trouble paying its large armies.

This security dilemma intensified in the spring of 1924, when Lu Yunxiang, the warlord of Zhejiang and an adherent of the defeated An-Fu Clique, supported Zhang Zuolin's Fengtien faction. Wu made plans to remove Lu from power, charging his subordinate Ji Xieyuan of Jiangsu with the task. On August 25, Ji's force of 60,000 to 100,000 troops (including troops from other Zhili-controlled provinces and the Sixth and Nineteenth National Army Divisions) deployed against Zhejiang (which had 50,000 to 74,000 troops) prepared for a two-pronged campaign toward Shanghai and Suzhou. War was formally declared on September 1.

Narrative: At 10 a.m. on September 3, Ji's forces began to bombard Zhejiang positions. Lu declared war on the central government of Cao Kun. The next day, Jiangsu forces suffered heavy casualties, attacking positions covered by machine guns. Although a quick war had been expected, a costly stalemate developed. On September 5, Zhang Zuolin announced that his Fengtien forces would support Zhejiang, and the conflict escalated. On the same day, the KMT announced that it would also fight the Zhili Clique. Two days later, the government issued a punitive mandate against Lu, relieving him of his position, and a Jiangsu attack was repulsed by Lu's forces, costing Ji 400 men.

Fierce fighting broke out in the North between the Fengtien and Zhili forces beginning on September 15. President Cao Kun and the Zhili-backed premier declared Zhang to be a rebel three days later. The Beijing government was able to mobilize more than 200,000 troops for the war effort, against perhaps 160,000 Fengtien troops. The Fengtien appeared to have foreign assistance, with "large numbers" of Soviet and Japanese cavalry. One US military intelligence report claimed that advance units of the Fengtien were "all Russians and Japanese in Chinese uniform."[132]

In the Battle of Chaoyang from September 25 to September 29, the Zhili and government forces lost 2,000 men, 800 of them captured. October 8 saw some of the bloodiest fighting of the warlord period, costing the Fengtien up to 4,000 to 5,000 killed. But by October 24, the government forces had suffered 10,000 casualties of their own.

Meanwhile, the slow campaign in Zhejiang ground on. A battle on September 27 cost Zhejiang 1,700 wounded and 2,000 missing, and three days later Zhejiang forces reported killing 400 of Ji's forces. On October 13, the An-Fu leaders fled the province to Japan, but elements of the Zhejiang military continued to hold out until the end of October. Altogether the Zhejiang campaign had resulted in 6,000 to 13,000 casualties. Note that while some classify the Jiangsu–Zhejiang war as separate from the fighting in the North, we consider them to be the same war due to the (at least tacit) prewar alliance between An-Fu and Fengtien.

Desertion was a serious problem; during the fighting more than 70,000 soldiers went over to Fengtien. On October 22, allegedly in response to a bribe offered by Zhang using Japanese money, Feng Yuxiang withdrew his 35,000 troops from the front and marched to Beijing, linking up with 5,000 garrison troops under Sun Yo and mounting a coup against the Zhili Clique the next day. Feng named a new cabinet—although the foreign powers refused to recognize it—and Cao was forced to dismiss Wu Peifu. Morale collapsed across the front, and

Fengtien forces drove south and west. Wu mounted an expedition to retake the capital but failed as the Japanese deployed an additional 500 troops to guard the railways and deny their usage to Zhili forces. Wu ended up retreating with only a few thousand troops.

Termination and Outcome: Hostilities ceased when Wu Peifu fled on November 3 (his forces were disarmed the next day), although there was no formal agreement to end the war. The outcome of the war was an unconditional rebel victory. No postwar reprisals were reported. On November 24, Duan Qirui of the old An-Fu coalition, now harmless, assumed power as provisional president and was recognized as the de facto government by foreign powers. Zhili-affiliated commanders were ousted from their positions. Their forces were absorbed by the Fengtien, which swelled to 340,000 troops.

Low-level violence resumed over the winter as Zhang tried to roll back the gains that Jiangsu had made during the war. Feng's forces also fell out with the Fengtien and formed their own *Guominjun*, or National People's Army. In a gesture toward reunification of the country, Sun Yat-sen of the KMT was invited to Beijing, where he died in 1925.

Coding Decisions: There were 6,000 to 13,000 casualties in Zhejiang and another 15,000 to 20,000 in Zhili–Fengtien fighting in the North. Given the usual ratio of three wounded for every one killed, this means 5,250 to 8,250 battle-deaths. Given reported Fengtien losses of 4,000 to 5,000 battle-deaths in a single battle, we estimate that the higher figure is closer to the truth.

Sources: Ch'en (1979); Ch'i (1976); Chi (1969); Gao (2009); Pye (1971); Waldron (1995); Woodhead (1969a, b); McCormack (1977).

INTRA-STATE WAR #697.8

Labrang War of 1925 to 1926 (aka Golok Tibetan–Gansu Muslim)

Participants: Golok Tibetans versus Gansu Muslims.
Dates: June 15, 1925, to 1926.
Battle-related Deaths: Total Combatant Deaths: 1,000, more of them Golok Tibetans than Gansu Muslims. (See Coding Decisions.)[133]
Initiator: Golok Tibetans.
Outcome: Gansu Muslims win.
War Type: Intercommunal.
Theater Armed Forces: Golok Tibetans: up to 40,000 (peak).[134]

Antecedents: Labrang was a Golok Tibetan monastery in the border areas of Gansu, a western province with large Hui and smaller Tibetan minorities. Since 1918, authority over Labrang had been in dispute between ethnic Tibetans and Hui leader Ma Qi, the military governor of Xining. A series of bloody clashes occurred over the next seven years. In 1925, negotiations between Goloks, Hui, and local Chinese units failed. Having lost control of Labrang, ethnic Tibetan leaders brought in allies from outside the province, even going to Beijing to seek Fengtien support.

Narrative: In mid-June 1925, as many as 40,000 Tibetan troops drove the Hui under Ma Qi from Labrang with heavy losses. About 3,000 Hui troops were sent to counterattack the Tibetans, both sides suffering casualties. A series of engagements followed in which the Muslims were victorious due to the possession of machine guns and modern rifles against the muskets and swords of the Tibetans. In 1926, Muslim forces retook the monastery, mowing down fleeing monks with machine guns. Muslim casualties "were in the thousands," while Tibetan losses were higher.[135]

Termination and Outcome: The war ended with a military victory by the forces of Ma Qi. A general massacre of the Tibetans took place following their first defeats, but it is not clear that the massacres continued after the end of the war.

Coding Decisions: On the basis of limited evidence, we find it plausible that this conflict killed more than 1,000 combatants, although the possibility that most of those killed were noncombatants cannot be ruled out.

Sources: Lipman (1981); Nietupski (1999).

INTRA-STATE WAR #698

Anti-Fengtien War of 1925 to 1926 (aka Third Chinese Warlord)

Participants: Guominjun and Guo Songling–led Forces versus Fengtien Army, Armed Forces under Wu Peifu, and Red Spear Society.

Dates: November 23, 1925, to April 21, 1926.
Battle-related Deaths: Total Combatant Deaths: 5,000. (See Coding Decisions.)[136]
Initiator: Guominjun and Guo Songling–led Forces.
Outcome: Transformed into Intra-state War #700.
War Type: Intercommunal.
Theater Armed Forces: Guominjun, aka National People's Army: 215,000 (prewar—March 15); 380,000 (initial).[137] Armed Forces under Guo Songling, participating to December 23, 1925: 70,000 (initial); 70,000 (peak).[138] Fengtien Army: 350,000 (prewar); 350,000 (initial).[139] Armed Forces under Wu Peifu, participating from about January 1, 1926: unknown. Red Spear Society, participating from January 1926: more than 463,000 (peak, final—but estimated from Henan only in 1927).[140]

Antecedents: After the Second Zhili-Fengtien War (Intra-state War #697.3), Beijing fell under the control of Feng Yuxiang, who had defected from the Zhili to the Fengtien faction during the conflict. But soon Feng fell out with the Fengtien and formed the *Guominjun*, or National People's Army. A low-level armed conflict began. Feng aligned himself with the Soviet Union, while Zhang Zuolin aligned himself with Japan and, in January 1925, brought White Russian units into the conflict. With White Russian help, Zhang's forces advanced against those of Ji Xieyuan (who commanded Jiangsu in the war) and Sun Chuanfang (who became leader of Zhejiang once it was conquered by Jiangsu) to roll back the gains they had made at the now-powerless An-Fu faction's expense during the war. Fengtien units advanced to Shanghai.

Feng, Ji, and Sun now aligned against the Fengtien. Feng also allied himself to Hu Ching-Yi of Henan, who may have had as many as 250,000 troops, and Sun Yo (30,000 troops), who had helped him carry out his 1924 coup, making them the Second and Third Guominjun armies, respectively. The weak government of Duan Qirui was unable to restrain either side as Duan had no army loyal to him despite the existence of 1.7 million troops officially in the national armed forces.

On October 17, 1925, Sun pushed northward against Fengtien forces, taking Jiangsu and Anhui provinces as he marched on Shandong. Feng had counted on Sun drawing troops from the North so that he could strike at their exposed flank, but the Fengtien had enough troops to both move south and protect their flanks, surrounding Feng's core positions. Feng refrained from entering the conflict, and on November 12, an agreement inked by the Guominjun and Fengtien ended the conflict in the South as Sun was satisfied with his territorial gains. Zhang withdrew his forces to the North.

Narrative: On November 23, Fengtien general Guo Songling defected to the Guominjun, and both armies attacked Fengtien positions. Guo's forces shredded the Fengtien units sent against him. However, when his forces approached the Fengtien headquarters at Mukden, Japan announced that it would not permit an attack on Mukden and aided Zhang in reorganizing his troops. Guo's men began to desert due to low morale, poor supply, and cold weather; in the climactic Battle of Xinmintun (Hsinmintun) near Mukden on December 23, his forces were crushed by the Fengtien. Guo himself was captured and executed a day later.

Meanwhile, Feng had attacked the positions of Li Ching-lin, who had declined to break with the Fengtien forces. The Battle of Tientsin (Tianjin) began on December 9 and lasted for two weeks. More than 4,000 casualties reached hospitals, and it is estimated that another 4,000 to 5,000 casualties didn't reach hospitals. An American doctor observed that the wounded received unusually poor care, noting that mortality must have been high. On December 23, Feng finally forced Li to withdraw from Tientsin.

But once he heard news of the defeat at Xinmintun, Feng concluded that the overall cause was lost; he resigned his position on January 1, 1926, and left the country. His subordinates in the Guominjun fought on, and Feng's ally Song Zheyuan was defeated in a brief, bloody campaign in Jehol, losing half his force. Seeking to deal with the Guominjun threat further south, Zhang reached an alliance with his old foes the Zhili Clique, effectively headed by Wu Peifu. Once Wu entered the war, he invaded the Guominjun-controlled province of Henan. The Red Spear Society aided Wu's relatively weak forces, defeating the Henan forces of the Guominjun. But in Hunan, one of Wu's generals—Tang Shengzhi (T'ang Sheng-chih), commander of the largest of the four divisions in the Hunan army—switched sides to the Guominjun.

In February, Fengtien under Zhang and Li attacked the Guominjun in Zhili province. Lu Chung-lin held out with 100,000 troops until March 21, when he evacuated Tientsin. On April 16, he was forced to evacuate Beijing, retreating with 90,000 troops to Nankow Pass, where he was besieged by 450,000 opponents until August 16, when he was forced to retreat to Shaanxi. By the summer, up to 400 Soviet soldiers fought on Lu's side at Nankow Pass, although the exact timing of the Soviet intervention is unclear. Also in April, Guominjun forces in Shaanxi suffered a string of defeats.

In Beijing, the victorious forces of Zhang and Wu created the Committee of Public Safety to oversee the government, appointing their generals to positions in the organization. This marked the establishment of a central government that also participated in the war, transforming the struggle from intercommunal to civil. While the government was not officially recognized by other powers, they carried on business with it anyway, emphasizing that "they recognized a state, China, with its capital at Peking, but did not at the moment recognize any head of state or any government of China."[141] Duan was forced to resign, and as his cabinet refused to continue to govern, the committee assumed power by April 21.

Termination and Outcome: The outcome of the intercommunal phase of this struggle was clearly favorable to the Fengtien and their allies in the Zhili Clique. However, the fighting did not stop once control of the capital and its institutions of governance were determined. The Guominjun and its regional allies continued to resist the forces of the new government. Moreover, the existence of these hostilities invited intervention by the southern KMT. In particular, sometime in April, Wu counterattacked Tang's forces in Hunan, driving the latter into the arms of the waiting KMT.

Coding Decisions: As neither side effectively controlled the central government at the start of the war, it is classified as intercommunal, even though the government of Duan Qirui—which controlled no troops of its own—had been playing the Guominjun off against the Fengtien. Casualties were in the tens of thousands. Perhaps 5,000 died, but this is little better than a conservative guess using the common 3:1 ratio of wounded to killed; the real toll could be somewhat lower or considerably higher.

Sources: Chi (1969); "Chinese Position," (1926); Correlates of War Project (2010); Dreyer (1995); Gao (2009); Sheridan (1966); Waldron (1995).[142]

INTRA-STATE WAR #700

Chinese Northern Expedition of 1926 to 1928

Participants: China (Fengtien and Zhili Factions) and Yen Xishan–led Forces versus Guomindang and Guominjun.

Dates: April 22, 1926, to June 8, 1928.

Battle-related Deaths: Armed forces of China (Zhili Faction): Sun Chuanfang alone suffered 10,000 to 20,000 casualties (perhaps 2,500 to 5,000 battle-deaths);[143] Yen Xishan–led Forces: 4,300;[144] Guomindang: more than 33,840 casualties (more than 8,460 battle-deaths);[145] Total Combatant Deaths: 65,000. (See Coding Decisions.)[146]

Initiator: Guomindang and Guominjun.

Outcome: Guomindang and Guominjun win.

War Type: Civil for central control.

Total System Member Military Personnel: Armed Forces of China (Factionalized): 1,700,000 (prewar, initial, peak, final).

Theater Armed Forces: Armed Forces of China (Fengtien Faction, aka Ankuochün): 200,000 (final).[147] Armed Forces of China (Zhili Faction), participating to June 3, 1928: 550,000 (peak).[148] Yen Xishan–led Forces, participated through summer 1926 on the government side and from September 1927 on the rebel side: unknown. Guominjun: 275,000 (initial); 300,000 (final).[149] Guomindang (GMD) aka Kuomintang (KMT): 100,000 (initial).

Antecedents: The South had established its effective independence from the North in the North–South War of 1917 to 1918. Since then, infighting was common in both the North and South, although it seldom rose to full-scale war in the latter. The Guangxi Clique controlled Guangdong and Guangxi, while the Yunnan Clique controlled Yunnan and Guizhou. The Nationalist Party founded by Sun Yat-sen, and the Guomindang (usually referred to as the Kuomintang [KMT]) eventually gained control of the Guanxi Clique (its rule was sometimes referred to as the New Guangxi Clique) and spread its influence to Yunnan, causing rifts among the Yunnan Clique.

The KMT turned to the Soviet Union in its efforts to unify and strengthen itself for a Northern Expedition against the warlords of the North. It allied itself with (essentially absorbed) the small Chinese Communist Party (CCP). In 1925, Sun Yat-sen died, producing a succession crisis within the KMT. On May 30, an international incident in Shanghai led to widespread nationalist protests. Zhang Zuolin moved to arrest some of the protesters, earning the enmity of the nationalist movement. Tang Jiyao of Yunnan invaded Guangdong in an attempt to seize the movement's "capital" at Guangzhou (Canton). The so-called Yunnan-Guangxi War followed, and Tang was driven back (little information is available about this conflict, especially an answer to the question of whether it actually reached war-level violence).

In the end, Chiang Kai-shek (Jiang Jieshi) and left-leaning Wang Jingwei shared power in the Canton government. Seeing the disunity and military exhaustion of the northern warlords, they resolved to begin the Northern Expedition at the first opportunity, despite the fact that the KMT's 100,000 soldiers were outnumbered heavily by the most powerful northern warlords.

Narrative: Meanwhile, after the Anti-Fengtien War was "won" by the Fengtien (but see Intra-state War #698), resistance to Zhang Zuolin's rule continued. In particular, the Guominjun established by Feng Yuxiang continued to fight against the armies loyal to Zhang and Wu Peifu (of the Zhili Clique) at Nankow Pass and at Xian (where the Guominjun was besieged from April 17 to November 28). Casualties must have been high given the size of the forces involved. Feng was pro-Soviet, and by the summer some 400 Soviet soldiers with artillery were fighting with his forces at Nankow. Also in April, Tang Shengzhi's forces in Hunan (which had rebelled against Wu's control in February) were driven out of the capital by Wu's forces.

On May 18, Guominjun forces clashed with those of Yen Xishan in Shaanxi. Full-scale fighting broke out in June, and 1,500 to 2,000 casualties reached hospitals. After more fighting in July, Guominjun units in the province retreated into Gansu, aside from those besieged in Xian; two of Feng's generals (Han Fuju and Shih Yu-san) defected to Yen (i.e., the government side). Fighting between Feng and Yen's forces continued into August.

On June 2, Tang officially allied himself to the KMT, which had planned a route for the Northern Expedition running through Hunan. His forces became the KMT's Eighth Army and were reinforced by the KMT's Fourth and Seventh Armies. On June 6, Chiang was appointed commander in chief of the KMT and decided to attack Wu first, ignore his Zhili Clique ally Sun Chuanfang, and appease Zhang until they could defeat him. The Northern Expedition officially started on July 9, although KMT forces had been ordered into Hunan as early as the first week of May. Changsha fell to Tang and the KMT just two days later.

Preoccupied with fighting at Nankow, Wu did little to hinder the KMT, which rapidly advanced despite suffering epidemics of cholera. Despite his Zhili Clique connections, Sun did nothing to halt the KMT advance. In the North, the Guominjun finally fell back from the Nankow Pass in August, making their way toward Shaanxi to reorganize. Feng rejoined his army, which succeeded in lifting the siege of Xian (where up to 500 were dying each day) on November 28. The eight-month siege had cost 15,000 to 35,000 lives.

By the time that Wu had finished taking Nankow, the KMT had advanced to within striking distance of the three cities of Wuhan in Hubei. Wu rushed reinforcements to the scene, and 100,000 troops on each side faced each other across lines of trenches. A single counterattack by Wu's forces resulted in more than 1,000 of them being killed and more than 2,000 being wounded. Despite Wu's efforts, the three cities fell to the KMT in September. That month the Guominchun also received a KMT commission, although it was not absorbed into the KMT structure. The alliance between Chiang and Feng was now formal rather than merely tacit.

Chiang now attacked the remaining forces of the Zhili Clique. The KMT invaded Jiangxi, Jiangsu, and Zhejiang, meeting stiff resistance from Sun's forces in some of the most intense combat of the war. From September to November, Sun lost 100,000 men. Feng regrouped in Kansu and Shaanxi; the Fiengten encouraged Muslims to revolt against him in the former. Yen Xishan was formally a government ally but now stood back and allowed the

Guominjun to reorganize. In December, Zhang formally united the Northern warlord forces into the Ankuochün with himself as commander in chief; while this did not increase his actual control over these units, it did enable him to draw a far larger share of funds from the central government. By December, the 264,000-strong KMT faced up to 1 million opponents.

As 1927 opened, the Guominjun stood ready to invade Henan, while the KMT remained bogged down in its operations against Sun. Splits in the KMT began to widen. In particular, Chiang's military command clashed with the now-Wuhan-based government of the South run by KMT leftists on both his role in the movement and on that of the communists. When Shanghai and Nanjing fell in March, the breach became open when Chiang declared Nanjing to be the new capital of the country, despite the existence of the KMT capital at Wuhan. Meanwhile, the Guominjun invaded Henan, making progress against Fengtien troops.

On April 12, Chiang's faction of the KMT turned against the communists in a massive purge that killed thousands and provoked an uproar in the Wuhan faction of the KMT. Soon, however, the Wuhan faction carried out its own purges of suspected communists. The CCP claims that in the following year, up to 300,000 were killed in anticommunist purges. Chiang had now broken definitively with the Soviet Union; in the controversy, Feng sided with Chiang's faction over the Wuhan faction and expelled the Soviets at the beginning of summer.

The KMT and Guominjun cooperated in an operation against the Ankuchün in May, fighting them in Henan from May 7 to May 28 and emerging victorious. The KMT's Wuhan faction suffered more than 10,000 wounded with missing limbs; Feng's troops suffered only 400 casualties. On May 25, Japanese troops were deployed to Shandong to defend Japanese lives and property. The KMT largely appeased the Japanese at this stage of the war.

Negotiations between the KMT and Zhang failed, and on June 18, the latter declared himself head of state as *generalissimo*. Most northern troops had now withdrawn across the Yellow river, but in July, Sun mounted a counteroffensive against the KMT, retaking Xuzhou in northwestern Jiangsu. He then turned against Feng's forces, leading to bitter fighting in September that cost Sun more than 50,000. The Guominjun emerged victorious and went on to recapture Xuzhou on December 16. Sun's forces had been crushed effectively.

Meanwhile, KMT forces under He Yingqin fought their way north and linked up with Feng's forces. They gained an ally on June 3, when Yen Xishan went over to the KMT. His forces clashed with those of the government in September; the latter declared the former to be a rebel on October 3. Combat between Yen's forces and those of the government continued until spring of 1928, when the KMT's advance made the theater irrelevant.

By January 1928, the KMT had some 700,000 troops against only 500,000 for the government. In February, the KMT was reorganized into four collective armies—one representing the old KMT, one for the Guominjun, one for Yen Xishan's forces, and one for Guangxi rebels under Li Zongren. In March, the Wuhan and Nanjing factions of the KMT were reconciled. The path was clear for resumption of the Northern Expedition.

Chiang advanced into the North China Plain, but on May 3 fighting between Chiang's forces and some 5,000 Japanese troops broke out at Jinan. By May 11, the KMT had been driven from Jinan. The Chinese claimed that 3,000 Chinese had been killed; Japanese deaths were much lower. Chiang then left the city alone and resumed his armies' march towards Beijing by an alternate route.

The central government of Zhang Zuolin still had 500,000 soldiers in the Ankuochün and counterattacked at Manch'eng at the end of May, leading to a battle that claimed 4,300 lives and wounded another 15,000. On June 3, Sun defected to the KMT. The next day, Zhang Zuolin was killed by a Japanese bomb while riding a train from Beijing to Manchuria. On June 8, Yen Xishan's units reached Beijing. Zhang Xueliang, who succeeded Zhang Zuolin two weeks after the bombing, immediately initiated negotiations to end the war.

Termination and Outcome: The outcome of the war was a military victory by the KMT. The negotiations with Manchuria eventually produced an agreement without further conflict or massacres. On December 29, Zhang Xueliang assumed a position in the KMT government and the KMT's nationalist flag flew over Mukden. Demobilization of the huge KMT would soon spark another revolt, as Feng fell out with Chiang's government.

Coding Decisions: Note that 400 Soviet troops supported the Guominjun to about June 22, 1927, but as there is no evidence that 100 battle-deaths were suffered or that 1,000 were ever deployed, we do not include them as participants in this war.[150] Bouthoul and Carrère's estimate of 65,000 battle-deaths is probably a conservative one. The real toll may have been higher.

Sources: Barnouin and Yu (2006); Ch'i (1976); Clodfelter (2008); Clubb (1972) Dreyer (1995); Lary (1985); McCormack (1977); Pye (1971); Sheridan (1966); van de Ven (2003); Waldron (1995), Wortzel (1999); Yu-Chang (1964).[151]

INTRA-STATE WAR #702
First KMT–CCP War of 1927 (aka Nanchang, Autumn Harvest, and Canton Uprisings)

Participants: Guomindang versus Chinese Communist Party.
Dates: August 1, 1927, to December 13, 1927.
Battle-related Deaths: Total Combatant Deaths: 2,000 (see Narrative and Coding Decisions).
Initiator: Chinese Communist Party.
Outcome: Guomindang wins.
War Type: Intercommunal.
Theater Armed Forces: Guomindang (aka Kuomintang [KMT])—356,000 (initial, peak).[152] Chinese Communist Party: 20,000 to 30,000 (initial, peak).[153]

Antecedents: As the commander in chief of the revolutionary KMT, Chiang Kai-shek mounted a purge of communists in April 1927. Elements of the CCP were still present in the KMT, however, several months later. The Soviet Union urged them to stage an urban insurrection, which was planned to occur in several places simultaneously. However, the CCP had strength only where its loyalists still commanded KMT armies.

Narrative: On August 1, 1927 some 20,000 to 30,000 troops of the KMT led by communists rebelled. The rebellion was centered in Nanchang, southeast of Wuhan, and primarily involved the Fourth Army (sometimes called the Second Front Army) of the KMT. In Nanchang, the communists greatly outnumbered their opponent, who could probably muster only two or three regiments (roughly 3,000 to 6,000 troops). After a brief but intense battle in which the communists inflicted 800 casualties on the garrison forces, some of these were disarmed, while others retreated northward.

However, the KMT leadership reacted quickly, and expected support from other units did not materialize. Under pressure, the communists began to leave Nanchang two days later, withdrawing entirely by August 5. The CCP lost 1,000 killed or wounded in the fighting and had to leave behind 7,000 troops that deserted or fell ill. They made for the province of Guangdong, losing one-third of their force to desertion, disease, and battle as they marched south. They suffered heavy casualties at the battles of Juichin and Hui Ch'ang, and left many of the seriously wounded under the care of British missionaries at Tingchou in western Fujian. On September 24, they took Chaozhou and Shantou (Swatow) in eastern Guangdong.

The communists next mounted a series of revolts in Henan, Jiangxi, and Guangdong—the Autumn Harvest Uprising—but were unable to mobilize mass support. Up to 800 communists were killed in the fighting. By October, most CCP forces had retreated into the Jinggangshan revolutionary base area in the Jinggang mountains and resorted to guerrilla warfare against the KMT.

On December 11, the communists mounted another urban uprising, this time in Guangzhou (Canton). Some of the troops from the Nanchang uprising took part. About sixty hours of fighting followed, killing 200 to 300 combatants. Guangzhou was regained by the KMT in the afternoon of December 13.

Termination and Outcome: The outcome of the war was an unconditional military victory by the KMT. After the KMT retook Guangzhou, they massacred up to 6,000 radicals over the next five days, including women and children The communist attempts at mass revolution in both the cities and the countryside had been crushed, and the CCP was reduced to pinprick guerrilla attacks. It would be unable to pose a serious threat to the KMT for many years, although casualties once again reached war levels in 1931.

Coding Decisions: Based on limited information from the sources used to write the Narrative, we find it likely that about 2,000 combatants died from fighting, disease, and the immediate postwar wave of executions. This could be an overestimate but is just as likely to be an underestimate.

Sources: Adelman (1980); Clodfelter (2008); Dirlik (1997); Guillermaz (1962); Wilbur (1983); Wortzel (1999).

INTRA-STATE WAR #702.5
Second Gansu Muslim Revolt of 1928 to 1929

Participants: China versus Gansu Muslims.
Dates: June 8, 1928, to May 20, 1929.
Battle-related Deaths: Total Combatant Deaths: 20,000. (See Coding Decisions.)[154]
Initiator: Gansu Muslims.
Outcome: Absorbed by Intra-state War #707.5.
War Type: Civil for local issues (control of Gansu).
Total System Member Military Personnel: Armed Forces of China: 1,720,000 (but still factionalized—peak).[155]
Theater Armed Forces: Gansu Muslims: 25,000 (initial); 40,000 to 50,000 (peak).[156]

Antecedents: In late 1925, a dispute over the governorship of Gansu led to heavy fighting. Feng Yuxiang's 195,000-strong Guominjun, then in rebellion against the government, used the opportunity to seize control of the province from its 15,000 irregulars and 10,000 Muslims under Ma Fuxiang. In May 1926, a general rebellion against Guominjun control broke out. Its leaders were first Chang Chao-Chia and Han Yu-lu and then K'ung Fan-chin and other Gansu warlords.

The conflict ended late in 1926 when the Guominjun pulled most of their troops from the province so that they could concentrate in Shaanxi for the relief of Xian and then an invasion of Henan (see Intra-state Wars #698 and #700).

In 1927, when Feng Yuxiang was in rebellion against the central government of Zhang Zuolin, the latter encouraged the Muslims (ethnic Hui) in Gansu to fight against Feng's Guominjun. Ma Tingxiang of Linagzhou received weapons from the Fengtien. The revolt, led by Ma Tingxiang and Ma Zhongying (who had about 10,000 men under his command), caused serious loss of life, particularly at the siege of Hezhou in the spring of 1928, which lasted eight months. Many of the Guominjun sent to relieve the city died of thirst en route. Ninghepu also was besieged by the Muslims, with fully one-half of its population being killed or starving to death.

Narrative: On June 8, the KMT, with which Feng had allied himself, took control of the central government. The Gansu Muslim rebellion against Feng was now a civil war rather than an intercommunal conflict (possibly an intercommunal war). By November, Ma Zhongying had 25,000 Muslim troops under his command, linking up with a Sichuanese army already in South Gansu. Meanwhile, the government mobilized ethnic Tibetans against the Muslim rebels. The Tibetans defeated Ma Tingxiang, who suffered heavy losses. Feng succeeded in raising the siege of Hezhou, but the rebellion was spreading to the north. In January 1929, a new round of fighting broke out. Four months later, Ningxia fell to the forces of Ma Zhongying. Over the past year, at least 200,000 and up to 500,000 in Gansu had died from battle, disease, or famine.

Termination and Outcome: The civil war ended when on May 20 Feng rebelled against the new central government of the KMT. Ma Zhongying allied himself to the KMT government, thereby transforming the rebellion into just another front in the Central Plains War (Intra-state War #707.5). Feng eventually would lose that war, and Ma Zhongying would participate in a failed invasion of Xinjiang, losing his government post in the process.

Coding Decisions: Between 200,000 and 500,000 were killed, died of disease, or starved to death. However, battle-deaths were likely much lower, given the small size of the armies actually engaged in combat. A figure of 20,000 is reasonable but little better than an educated guess.

Sources: Lipman (1981, 1984); MacNair (1931); Maillart (1937); Sheridan (1966); Toynbee (1929).

INTRA-STATE WAR #705
Second Afghan Anti-reform War of 1928 to 1929

Participants: Afghanistan, Ahmanullah Tribal Loyalists, Ghulum Nabi Khan-led Forces, and Nadir Khan-led Tribal Levies versus

Habibullah- or Bacha-i-Saqao–led Tajiks, Shinwari Rebels, Khugiani Rebels, and Army of Islam.

Dates: November 10, 1928, to October 13, 1929.

Battle-related Deaths: Armed Forces of Afghanistan: few (it saw little combat); Habibullah- or Bacha-i-Saqao–led Tajiks: perhaps 3,750 (see Coding Decisions);[157] Total Combatant Deaths: 7,500. (See Coding Decisions.)[158]

Initiator: Shinwari Rebels.

Outcome: Afghanistan (Nadir Khan) wins.

War Type: Civil for central control.

Total System Member Military Personnel: Armed Forces of Afghanistan—60,000 (prewar, initial, peak—largely disintegrated early in the war but elements continued to participate to January 17, 1929).[159]

Theater Armed Forces: Ahmanullah Tribal Loyalists, participating from November 1928 to late April 1929, when they either dissolved or were incorporated into Nadir Khan's forces: more than 9,000 (initial); 15,000 (peak).[160] Ghulum Nabi Khan-led Forces, participated from January 1929 to June 1929: 850 to 1,000 (initial).[161] Tribal Levies of Nadir Khan: 12,000 (peak); 12,000 (final).[162] Habibullah- or Bacha-i-Saqao–led Tajiks (Rebel Army): 3,000 (initial).[163] Shinwari Rebels, participating throughout the war but ceased to support the rebels by February 1929: 20,000 (initial); 20,000 (peak).[164] Khugiani Rebels, participating from early in the war but may have been internally divided, dropping out of the conflict in February 1929; some Khugianis subsequently fought against Bacha-i-Saqao in the East: 20,000 (initial); 20,000 (peak).[165] Ibrahim Beg–led Forces, aka Basmachi or Army of Islam, participating from April 1929: 1,000 (initial).[166]

Antecedents: Following the initial defeat of his reform plans, King Ahmanullah resolved on a second round of reforms. On August 16, 1928, he called a *loya jirga* to explain and promulgate his modernizing, centralizing, and secularizing reforms. Despite holding five sessions and gaining some support for his military reforms and taxes, he was unable to secure even modest support for his social reforms. The *loya jirga* concluded in September. When Ahmanullah arrested two politico-religious opponents for gathering signatures against his program that month, resistance moved outside the boundaries of the law. There was an uptick in banditry, and on October 2, there were violent antigovernment demonstrations in Kabul; Ahmanullah repressed them with force.

Narrative: On November 10, government tax collectors and military recruiters arrived in Shinwari (Pashtun) territory and were met with armed resistance. A government attempt to exploit tribal rivalries failed, and soon the rebels had cut the road from Jalalabad to Dakka and then captured Jalalabad itself, destroying the royal palace there. The Shinwaris soon were joined by at least segments of the Khugiani tribe and others. Tribal levies of Laghmans supported government forces around Jalalabad as the government feared that regulars would desert or defect. The Afghan army more or less disintegrated, leaving the capital vulnerable. Shinwaris in the army were arrested after they attempted to join their co-ethnics in rebellion. The government employed the services of Russian airmen to bomb rebel positions.

In November, a Tajik named Habibullah Kalakani, more commonly known as Bacha-i-Saqao, entered the war against the government. His forces attacked Kabul on December 14. After eleven days of fierce fighting, the attack was repulsed with the aid of Mangal and Jaji tribal levies, and Bacha-i-Saqao retreated into Kohistan, while Ahmanullah once again tried the tactic of rolling back reforms to preserve his power. However, the rebellions of both the Shinwaris and Bacha-i-Saqao continued, and the government forces were unable to make further progress.

On January 14, 1929, a second attack by Bacha-i-Saqao took Kabul with help from defecting army units; Ahmanullah abdicated. With support from traditionalist clergy, Bacha-i-Saqao declared himself monarch, taking the title Amir Habibullah Ghazi. His forces executed many of Ahmanullah's officials and suspected followers. Ahmanullah, from his base in Kandahar, rescinded his abdication and raised an army of 15,000 men. In northern Afghanistan, Ghulam Nabi Charki (also known as Ghulam Nabi Khan) entered Afghanistan with 850 to 1,000 mercenaries disguised as Afghanis to oppose the Bacha-i-Saqao, who had supported Ibrahim Beg's Army of Islam (Basmachi rebels) against the Soviet Union. But in the South, Ahmanullah's forces performed poorly in a combat near Ghazni, and in late April, he crossed the frontier into India.

By that point, the mantle of resistance to Bacha-i-Saqao had been taken over largely by Nadir Khan in the South. Beginning in March, he united southern tribes against the rule of Bacha-i-Saqao. On March 19, he called for a *loya jirga* of all tribes to determine the legitimacy of Bacha-i-Saqao. The latter responded by arresting Nadir Khan's family members and putting a price on his head. Nadir Khan reacted by forming a resistance based in the Khost region.

Meanwhile, Ghulum Nabi Khan's forces, either allied to or incorporating Hazaras, continued to resist the new government of Bacha-i-Saqao. In April, the latter asked Basmachi rebel Ibrahim Beg for assistance against Ghulum Nabi Khan. Beg raised a force of 1,000 Turkmen with which to fight the Hazaras, and Ghulum's forces briefly were pushed back into Soviet territory. From April to June, Ghulum's forces reentered the country and captured Mazar-i-Sharif and Tashkurglan, moving on Kabul before international pressure led the Soviets to withdraw their support.

The Shinwari tribe remained in rebellion, having never accepted Bacha-i-Saqao's authority. The latter also had trouble winning loyalty from other tribes, failing to cement his alliance with the Ghilzais to balance the powerful Durranis. Nonetheless, he was able to exploit tribal tensions within Nadir Khan's alliance; his forces even advanced and seized Gardez. But by June, the Ghilzai and their allies rallied behind Nadir Khan, and the tide of the war turned against Bacha-i-Saqao. By September 26, Nadir Khan's tribal levies numbered 6,800; their number rapidly climbed as success appeared more likely.

Four offensives by the rebels failed, but on September 25 the fifth rebel offensive made headway, defeating Bacha-i-Saqao's troops on October 6. Three days later, a Waziri tribal force entered Kabul and besieged its citadel, which fell on October 13. By this point, Nadir Khan's tribal forces numbered 12,000, mostly Waziris. Because he could not pay them, Kabul was plundered by his victorious forces.

Termination and Outcome: The outcome of the war was a complete victory for what had once been the government side in the conflict. On October 15, Nadir Khan entered Kabul. Bacha-i-Saqao was captured, and on November 1 he was executed along with his brother and at least seven of his closest aides. Nadir Khan was selected as the new amir, a result that Ahmanullah contested on the grounds that Nadir Khan had been fighting in Ahmanullah's name.

Coding Decisions: Bacha-i-Saqao lost 15,000 men, and given the usual 3:1 ratio of wounded to killed, this suggests 3,750 battle-deaths. Government losses are thought to have been similar to rebel losses, suggesting a total of 7,500 battle-deaths.

Sources: Burdett (2002); Gankovsy (1996); Goodson (2001); Gregorian (1969); Ritter (1990); Yunas (2002).[167]

INTRA-STATE WAR #707.5
Central Plains War of 1929 to 1930 (aka Intra-Kuomintang)

Participants: China versus Guominjun, Yan Xishan–led Troops, Guangxi Clique, and Reorganizationists.

Dates: March 31, 1929, to June 29, 1929, and September 17, 1929, to October 13, 1930.

Battle-related Deaths: Armed Forces of China: 37,500;[168] Combined Rebel Forces: 62,500; Total Combatant Deaths: 100,000. (See Coding Decisions.)[169]

Initiator: China.

Outcome: China wins.

War Type: Civil for central control.

Total System Member Military Personnel: Armed Forces of China: 1,620,000 (prewar), about 420,000 (after initial defections and declarations of neutrality); 862,600 (peak).[170]

Theater Armed Forces: Armed Forces of China: 150,000 (initial). Guomiinjun, participating from May 20 to June 29, 1929, and from the third week of September 1929 to the end of November 1929, and from March 1930: 230,000 (prewar); 120,000 to 200,000 (after initial defections).[171] Yan Xishan–led Troops, participating from December 21, 1929, on the government side and then from early March 1930 on the rebel side: 200,000 (prewar); 200,000 (initial).[172] Guangxi Clique, participating to June 27, 1929, and again from the third week of September 1929: 220,000

(prewar); 60,000 (after initial defections).[173]
Reorganizationists, participating from September 17, 1929: 20,000 to 27,000 (after initial defection).[174]

Antecedents: Due to the victory of the KMT's Northern Expedition (Intra-state War #700), China largely was reunified. However, the leadership of the KMT remained deeply factionalized, with left-wing reorganizationists seeking to supplant the leadership of Chiang Kai-shek. Moreover, because the victory had involved absorbing warlord armies into the KMT instead of disbanding them, the KMT was bloated with extra troops. There were probably about 2 million soldiers in 1929. The demobilization issue gave the KMT leadership under Chiang the opportunity to curb the power of regional warlords.

Another issue in contention was the status of branch political councils, which had offered autonomy to many warlords: Feng Yuxiang's Guominjun in Gansu, Shaanxi, and Henan; Yan Xishan's forces in Shanxi; Zhang Xueliang in Manchuria; and the Guangxi Clique of warlords at Wuhan. In late 1928, the government announced that these branch political councils would be abolished in March 1929.

In January 1929, a National Reorganization and Demobilization Conference convened in the new capital of Nanjing. While the conferees agreed on a reduction to 800,000 troops, the establishment of a unified command structure, and a limitation of 41 percent of revenue to be spent on the military, the specifics pitted Chiang against the regional warlords. Chiang wanted deeper cuts in warlord armies than in his own Nanjing troops (numbering 240,000). Facing these threats, a number of warlords determined to resist Chiang's centralizing policies.

A crisis over the governorship of Hunan and its tax revenues led Guangxi forces to evict the province's chairman forcibly on February 21. Chiang seized the opportunity presented. He bribed Feng and Yan to remain neutral with promises of Shandong and funds, and then he threatened the provinces controlled by the Guangxi Clique, using 150,000 soldiers (against only 60,000 Wuhan soldiers). Negotiations were held, and members of the Guangxi Clique began to defect to the government. Others agreed to defect once actual fighting broke out. On March 26, a punitive mandate was issued against the Guangxi Clique.

Narrative: The government's offensive began on March 31. Government forces moved forward against light resistance, capturing Wuhan on April 20. The government then invaded Guangxi itself; this campaign, which included a number of battles, was successfully concluded on June 27. In the interim, Feng had received neither funds nor Shandong, and began to mobilize for war on April 25. On May 20, he allied himself to the Guangxi Clique in the Safeguard the Party and Save the Nation Army. Three days later, two of his top commanders defected to the government with 100,000 troops. Some units that remained loyal to Feng suffered casualties withdrawing westward. Feng's forces were pushed out of Shandong and Henan.

Yan Xishan (200,000 troops) then persuaded both sides to end the war by threatening to enter it, and combat ceased on June 29. The government then turned its attention to an inter-state war that had developed between China and the Soviet Union over the Manchurian railway. Once the inter-state war was over, fighting resumed in the third week of September. Zhang Fakui rebelled on September 17, allied himself to the Guangxi Clique, and seized Guangzhou (Canton). This marked the beginning of the reorganizationist rebellion, led by Wang Jungwei.

On October 3, general Shih Yu-san rebelled with between 20,000 and 27,000 troops near Nanjing. While his forces hesitated to storm the capital, the government was able to bring in reinforcements to protect it. In Henan, Feng resumed hostilities against the government on October 10, allying himself with Zhang Fakui. In the Battle of Lo Hokow on November 12, fighting was so severe that the majority of government wounded suffered from sword cuts. At the end of November, the war with the Guominjun was once again suspended as Feng evacuated Henan. On December 4, a string of mutinies mounted by the reorganizationists occurred, causing a shift in alignments. On December 21, Yan and Zhang Xueliang joined forces with the government against the reorganizationists.

The war entered a new and deadlier phase in 1930. On February 10, Yan and Feng allied. In early March, both Feng and Yan turned on the government, allying themselves with Wang. Feng reentered Henan. The result would be a series of bloody battles across the Central Plains. On April 23, the order for a general attack was given by the rebels, who numbered perhaps 700,000 combined against only

300,000 loyalists under Chiang. Serious fighting began in early May, and over the next five months, the intensity of the war was higher than that of most of China's rebellions.

Yan's forces advanced into Shandong, where he prepared to set up a new national government with the reorganizationists, but his underfunded forces soon were defeated, and he fled to Manchuria. The Guominjun fought a bloody battle of attrition in Henan. Hundreds of thousands of casualties were suffered in the summer—90,000 on the government side and 150,000 on the rebel side, according to Chiang. The intervention of hitherto neutral Zhang Xueliang on the government side with 414,000 troops beginning on September 19 led to the defeat of the Guominjun. Little real fighting occurred after this date, but Feng's armies continued to defend positions as they fell back.

Termination and Outcome: The government army, larger than those of the rebels, was able to win the war with substantial aid from Zhang Xueliang's forces. On October 13, the government announced the successful conclusion of the war. The result of the war was a military victory by the government. Chiang offered a general political amnesty for the rebels and offered to pay warlords to surrender their forces. Feng was exiled and the Guominjun broken into smaller units that were absorbed into the KMT. Yan was permitted autonomy in Shanxi province.

The war had three obvious consequences: it weakened noncore elements of the KMT that had revolted; it caused Zhang Xueliang to station his troops outside of Manchuria, inviting outside aggression in the region; and it allowed the nascent Red Army of the Chinese Communist Party a breathing space in which to grow into the next serious challenger to the central government.

Coding Decisions: There were perhaps 300,000 casualties. Medical care was poor, and government data for June through October 1930 show a ratio of 30,000 killed to 60,000 wounded. Using this 2:1 ratio of wounded to killed rather than the usual 3:1 rule of thumb, we estimate 100,000 battle-deaths, a figure in agreement with Gillin. The ratio of government-to-rebel casualties was 3:5 during the summer of 1930. We extrapolate this ratio to estimate government and combined rebel battle-deaths as 37,500 and 62,500, respectively.

Sources: Christopher (1950); Dreyer (1995); Eastman et al. (1991); Gillin (1967); Lary (1985); MacNair (1931); Sheridan (1966); van de Ven (2003); Woodhead (1931, 1969a, b).[175]

INTRA-STATE WAR #709
Campaign against Ibrahim Beg of 1930 to 1931

Participants: Afghanistan versus Army of Islam.
Dates: October 1930 to March 1931.
Battle-related Deaths: Afghanistan: more than 700;[176] Total Combatant Deaths: more than 1,000. (See Coding Decisions.)[177]
Initiator: Afghanistan.
Outcome: Afghanistan wins.
War Type: Civil for local issues (secession—but see Coding Decisions).
Total System Member Military Personnel: Armed Forces of Afghanistan: 60,000 (prewar, initial, peak, final).[178]
Theater Armed Forces: Army of Islam: 2,450 (prewar, initial).[179]

Antecedents: In the aftermath of its Second Antireform War (see Intra-state War #705), the new government of Nadir Khan faced many challenges. The Shinwaris, Ghilzais, and Zadrans refused to accept Nadir Khan as king, with fighting breaking out in February 1930. In Kohistan, fighting with supporters of former king Ahmanullah killed many before the rebellion was crushed in mid-April.

Meanwhile, the Soviet Basmachi rebel Ibrahim Beg continued to maintain a private Army of Islam of 2,150 ethnic Uzbeks and 300 ethnic Tajiks, apparently all Afghanis. In June 1930, the Soviets intervened in Afghanistan against Ibrahim Beg's forces. Under heavy pressure from the Soviet Union to disarm Beg or face invasion, the government moved to arrest him. Beg resisted, proclaiming independence for the Uzbeks and Tajiks and also the illegitimacy of the government of Nadir Khan. From July to August, the government also had to contend with a rebellion in Koh-i-Daman, which killed hundreds. The Koh-i-Daman fighting revealed the regular army to be useless; the government had to rely on tribal levies to suppress the revolt.

Narrative: Combat between Beg's units and those of the government first was reported in mid-October. There were two major engagements of the war. The first was the Battle of Khanabad, which cost the government forces 700 killed. Soon after, the government was again checked at Aliabad, a battle that cost at least 280 Afghani lives. Toward the end of the year, the government mounted a successful counteroffensive against Ibrahim Beg's forces, which lasted until March 1931. Most of the fighting was done by tribal levies; when regulars were used against Beg, they suffered heavy losses. Unable to trap and defeat Ibrahim Beg's forces in the countryside, the government made a peace offer on March 22, offering general amnesty to the rebels and incorporation into the army. While Beg declined the proposal, he also decided to leave Afghanistan to raise a new revolt in the Soviet Union.

Termination and Outcome: The outcome of the war was a government military victory. In late March or early April 1931, Beg retreated into the Soviet Union. He launched a rebellion there on April 8 with 400 to 800 horsemen, half of them armed. It was soon defeated, and he surrendered to Soviet authorities on June 23; he was later executed. It is not clear what became of his Afghani soldiers in Afghanistan.

Coding Decisions: While Ibrahim Beg proclaimed the government to be illegitimate, he made no moves to depose it, and so we classify the war as one based on local issues. At least 980, and probably many more, died in the war as data on rebel fatalities are unavailable. One source implausibly claims 2,000 to 2,500 Afghan dead against 70 "émigrés" from the Soviet Union.

Sources: Burdett (2002); Gankovsy (1993, 1996); Goodson (2001); Ritter (1985).

INTRA-STATE WAR #710

Chinese Civil War phase 1 of 1930 to 1936 (aka Encirclement Campaigns and Long March)

Participants: China versus Chinese Workers' and Peasants' Red Army.
Dates: November 5, 1930, to December 25, 1936.
Battle-related Deaths: Total Combatant Deaths: 400,000. (See Coding Decisions.)[180]
Initiator: China.
Outcome: Negotiated settlement.
War Type: Civil for central control.
Total System Member Military Personnel: Armed Forces of China: 1,700,000 (prewar, initial, peak, final).[181]
Theater Armed Forces: Armed Forces of China: 100,000 (initial); 800,000 (peak). Chinese Workers' and Peasants' Red Army: 65,000 (prewar, initial); 200,000 (peak); somewhat higher than 60,000 (final).[182]

Antecedents: The Nanchang uprising and events over the subsequent year (see Intra-state War# 702) began the military struggle between the Guomindang (Kuomintang [KMT]) and Chinese Communist Party (CCP). For some time, casualties dropped below the threshold for civil war, particularly when the KMT government was distracted with the Central Plains War (Intra-state War #706). However, at the end of 1930 the government once again was able to fight the CCP, which had grown in the interim.

Narrative: The central government's First Encirclement and Suppression Campaign began on November 5, using regional armies, especially the 100,000 troops of Jiangxi province. The government advanced deep into the CCP's base areas, but then its leading units were cut off and destroyed by the CCP's Chinese Workers' and Peasants' Red Army. By the end of the campaign on January 3, 1931, the rebels had destroyed an entire division and captured (and executed) the deputy commander of the operation. The government lost 20,000 killed or captured; Red Army casualties were no more than 3,000 killed, wounded, and missing. The government regrouped and launched a second campaign in the same area in April using 120,000 to 150,000 troops—mostly central government forces—against only 30,000 Red Army soldiers. This, too, was a failure (the government losing 30,000 casualties and captured), and the CCP's Jiangxi Soviet base area tripled in size.

Beginning in July, the government mobilized 200,000 for the third encirclement operation, some 130,000 of which actually were employed in the campaign. The Red Army mobilized 55,000. The campaign kicked off in September, and the communists once again succeeded in defending their Jinggangshan base area, inflicting 20,000 casualties on the government forces. Moreover, an effort to overrun the Eyuwan Soviet in the Dabie Shan was foiled by the Red Army's victory in the nighttime Battle of Dongshao. The campaign ultimately ended when Japan invaded Mukden in Manchuria, leading the government to suspend its offensive.

With the Japanese apparently stabilized in Manchuria and stymied in Shanghai, Chiang once more turned to the communist threat in 1932. The KMT mobilized almost 600,000 soldiers for its fourth campaign (July 1932 to April 1933), which sought to destroy the Jiangxi, Eyuwan, and Central Soviets. The government initially had success against the Eyuwan Soviet, forcing the CCP's Fourth Front Army to withdraw from its base area. Moreover, anti-Mao elements were ascendant in the CCP, which attempted to mount an offensive outside the mountains. It was defeated, but the government was unable to take the Jinggangshan base area. The campaign was called off at about the same time as Japan invaded Manchuria.

The fifth encirclement campaign (October 1933 to October 1934) followed the Tangu Truce with Japan, used 800,000 troops, and involved building fortified lines to prevent Red Army movement out of the Jiangxi Soviet. Facing complete annihilation, the CCP (now possessing a total of 200,000 troops across the country) decided to abandon Jinggangshan. About 100,000 Red Army troops in the Jiangxi Soviet began what was to become known as the Long March, but most failed to escape the Soviet, consumed by rearguard actions, feint attacks, desertion, and heavy losses during the breakout. The Red Army lost 30,000 killed or wounded crossing the Xiang River.

For the next year, the retreating communists fought battle after battle, taking and abandoning some sixty-two towns and cities along the way. Nearly a million men were mobilized by the KMT. By June 1935, just 20,000 Red Army survivors were in Xinjiang, with hundreds dying of exposure every day. Then in July, the marchers joined up with 50,000 who had retreated from the overrun Eyuwan Soviet. Half of the combined force—some 35,000 marchers—went to establish a base area in the West in Tibet. The other half soon was reduced when 22,000 revolted, opting to join their comrades in the West. The remaining 13,000 communists under Mao would continue their march, with pneumonia taking a heavy toll. In mid-October, after a month of hard fighting against Muslim troops loyal to the central government, the 7,000 survivors of the Long March joined what had been a minor Soviet in the northwestern province of Shaanxi.

The central government deployed 60,000 troops to attack the 20,000 troops of the Shaanxi Soviet, but they suffered high losses from guerrilla attacks and were recalled. Meanwhile, the attempt to establish a Tibetan base area failed, with the remnants of the effort making their way to Shaanxi. A sixth encirclement campaign, although not bearing the name, was planned from Chiang's forward base in Xian. About 300,000 troops were massed for the attack, but the date for the offensive kept being pushed back, and most of 1936 passed with only desultory fighting

In December 1936, Chiang flew to Xian to goad his generals into action. Instead, he found himself under arrest by Zhang Xueliang, who had ruled Manchuria prior to the Japanese conquest. Chiang's wife represented him in negotiations with communist Zhou Enlai. Chiang agreed on December 24 and was released the next day; he flew back to Nanjing and immediately began implementation of the agreement.

Termination and Outcome: Fighting stopped, although negotiations lasted until September 1937. The outcome of the war was a verbal agreement followed by a formal negotiated settlement in July 1937. The Red Army was reorganized into the New Fourth Army and the Eighth Route Army, theoretically integrated into the KMT. The government extended some support to these armies, particularly in the beginning. However, after 1938, the Red Army rarely engaged the Japanese in pitched battles, leading to suspicions that it was husbanding its resources for another civil war. These suspicions, and the expectation of future conflict, led directly to the KMT–CCP Clashes of 1939 to 1941 (Intra-state War #719).

Coding Decisions: Our estimate of battle-deaths is conservative, but higher totals are implausible due to the number of troops engaged and the tendency to conflate civilian with military fatalities.

Sources: Clodfelter (2008); Gao (2009); Lew and Leung (2013); Morwood (1980); Worthing (2007); Wortzel (1999); Yuk-fun (2012).[183]

INTRA-STATE WAR #711
Xinjiang Muslim Revolt of 1931 to 1934

Participants: Xinjiang and Soviet Union versus Ma Zhongying–led Hui, Kumulliks, Ma Zhancang–led Forces, Temūr-led Forces, Khotanlik Amīrs.
Dates: April 4, 1931, to September 1934.
Battle-related Deaths: Total Combatant Deaths: 10,000.[184]
Initiator: Kumulliks.
Outcome: Xinjiang wins.
War Type: Regional.
Total System Member Military Personnel: Soviet Union: 940,000 (prewar, initial, peak, final).
Theater Armed Forces: Armed Forces of Xinjiang: thousands (initial); 5,000 (peak). These numbers include the White Russians, who were effectively conscripted to fight on the provincial government's behalf.[185] Armed Forces of the Soviet Union, participating from early January, 1934: 7,000 (initial); 7000 (peak).[186] Ma Zhongying–led Hui, participating from June 28, 1931: 500 (initial); more than 10,000 (peak). Ma Shih-ming here is treated as a subordinate to Ma Zhongying.[187] Kumulliks: 1,000 (initial).[188] Ma Zhancang–led Forces, participating from late 1932: 300 (initial).[189] Temūr-led Forces, participating from late 1932: 4,700 (peak).[190] Khotanlik Amīrs, participating from late 1932: more than 10,000 (peak).[191]

Antecedents: When Jin Shuren (Chin Shu-jen) assumed the governorship of Xinjiang (Sinkiang) in 1928, he aligned himself with the Soviet Union, which was economically dominant in Xinjiang. When he annexed the khanate of Kumul in 1930, he ruled corruptly, confiscating lands of Turkic Muslims (today known as Uyghurs) and "redistributing" them to Han Chinese refuges for the fighting in Gansu. Turkic Muslims blamed the Han Chinese for the expropriations, and local notables in Kumul planned a revolt.

Narrative: On April 4 (or February 20, according to Pahta, 1990), 1931, an attempt by a provincial official to marry a Kumullik led to violence in which dozens of his bodyguards were killed. The Kumilliks then killed the hundred or so Han immigrants in the area and seized two small forts, killing their garrisons and seizing weapons. They overran the Muslim portion of Kumul (Hami) easily, but the Han Chinese retreated into the old fortified city, and a temporary stalemate ensued.

Neighboring Kirgiz joined the revolt, and the provincial government decided to respond with a military expedition. An initial force of 300 was slaughtered by the rebels, who thereby gained weapons such as machine guns. But in late April the government lifted the siege of Old Kumul and began to massacre Muslims in retaliation. The insurgents looked to Kansu's Muslims for help in their struggle, and Ma Zhongying responded with about 500 Hui cavalry, fighting his first battle against provincial forces on June 28. On July 3, he mounted his first attack on Old Kumul, suffering heavy losses from machine guns.

Ma then left 1,000 insurgents to besiege the garrison of 2,000, while his cavalry attacked and seized Barkul, capturing 2,000 rifles. His forces grew rapidly. About 1,000 provincial reinforcements were sent, but they were ambushed and killed "almost to a man" (Forbes, 59). The siege of Old Kumul continued, with forty-three separate Muslim attacks on its garrison being repulsed from July 3 and October 16.

On October 1, 1931, Jin signed a secret treaty with the Soviet Union, which was not disclosed to the government in Nanjing (Sino-Soviet relations had been broken for some time). Jin also sent 250 White Russian "volunteers" (who were threatened with deportation to the Soviet Union if they failed to obey Jin's orders) to relieve the siege of Old Kumul. They were met by Ma's forces in a brief engagement that wounded Ma and killed one of the Russians. Most of Ma's forces then retreated to Northwest Gansu, while provincial forces spearheaded by the Russians relieved the city on November 1. Mass executions and the devastation of Kumul followed, driving even heretofore neutral Uyghurs into rebellion.

In early 1932, the government—probably discovering the treaty between the Soviet Union and Jin—anointed Ma's forces as the Thirty-sixth Division of the National Army of China. In May, Ma Zhongying sent a lieutenant, Ma Shih-ming, to take command of the remaining Kansu Hui forces in Xinjiang. The latter established a base in the mountains near Turfan that contained many refugees from the earlier fighting and closely cooperated with the remaining Uyghur insurgents. In the fall, the Hui-led Turfan garrison went over to Ma Shih-ming; its commander wired the provincial government for reinforcements and then ambushed them, killing all of them. Another detachment of 100 suffered the same fate.

Local Muslim forces then massed at Turfan for an attack on the capital of Urumchi, while a series of uncoordinated secessionist risings broke out in the South of the province. The provincial government counterattacked and retook Turfan after a sanguinary two-day battle, but Ma Shih-ming simply transferred his headquarters to Kara Shahr. In the midwinter, Ma resumed his advance on Urumchi. The government responded by mobilizing 1,500 White Russians under one Colonel Pappengut. On February 21, 1933, Ma's forces reached the capital, focusing their attack on its West Gate, where days of hand-to-hand combat ensued. At least 2,000 were killed in the battle, but the real toll may have been as high as 6,000. Ma Shih-ming was forced to retreat.

In Kara Shahr, the Uyghurs were led by Ma Zhancang (Ma Chan-ts'ang), who allied with the Muslims of Kucha to attack Aksu. In February, the rebellion spread south of the Tarim Basin to Surghak (near Keriya) and Kara Kash (near Khotan). The provincial authorities moved first against the forces threatening Aksu (which were allied with those of Ma Shih-ming and by extension with Ma Zhongying), sending 430 troops against them on the sixth, but they were forced back to Maral Bashi, and 600 reinforcements were dispatched around February 23. The Muslim forces entered Aksu on February 25, massacring its Han residents and seizing its armory. About 5,000 troops (300 well-armed Hui under Ma Zhancang and 4,700 ill-equipped Uyghurs under his ally Temūr) then resumed their advance on Maral Bashi and Kashgar, taking the former on April 13 and destroying a force of 1,000 retreating provincial government troops.

At this point, the government appears to have authorized reinforcements for Urumchi. In 1931, some 2,000 Chinese troops had evacuated Manchuria in the face of the Japanese invasion. They were interned in the Soviet Union and now were sent to Urumchi as the North–East National Salvation Army. They enhanced the power of the provincial government, especially its commander in chief, Sheng Shicai, a Northeasterner himself. Ma Shih-ming was forced back to Kara Shahr. On April 12, the White Russian forces overthrew Jin and installed Sheng as provincial leader.

On April 11, the old city of Yarkand fell to Uyghur forces from Khotan, Karhgalik, and Posgam; the 100 Han Chinese who remained were butchered. The Uyghurs then besieged the new city of Yarkand. In desperation, the provincial authorities attempted to use their Kirgiz levies, provoking a mutiny on April 5. Soon, Kirgiz forces and Ma Zhancang's forces were both threatening Kashgar. On May 2 the Kirgiz attacked old Kashgar, aided by thousands of local Uyghurs. The next day, the new city surrendered to Ma Zhancang. With the exception of Yarkand's new city, southern Xinjiang was now under the control of those opposed to the provincial government. An intercommunal war between Hui and Uyghur followed (see Intra-state War #715.6).

In May, Ma Zhongying's Thirty-sixth Division of the Chinese Army began its second invasion of Xinjiang. He may have had 5,000 men under his command. Sheng had a similar number at Urumchi, including the White Russians. On May 15, the Thirty-sixth Division attacked the first provincial garrison town of Kitai, which fell after bitter fighting. At this point, there was a pause in Ma Zhongying's campaign as Nanjing unsuccessfully sought peace between the two sides. But in mid-June, the main forces of the Thirty-sixth Division and the provincial leadership clashed at Tzu-ni-ch'üan, resulting in victory for the latter.

A peace emissary was flown in by the Nanjing government, but Sheng imprisoned him and shot three men whom he accused of conspiring with the emissary to overthrow him. To secure his release, the emissary recommended to Nanjing that Sheng be confirmed in his post as military leader of Xinjiang, a recommendation that the government formally adopted on September 7. Ma Zhongying was appointed garrison commander of Eastern Xinjiang. Sheng soon forced the civilian provincial leader to resign and replaced him with his own man.

The final break between Ma Zhongying and the Kumulik forces came in the summer, when Kumulik leader Khoja Niyās Ḥājī obtained provincial recognition as chief defense commissioner for Southern Xinjiang. He then moved against Ma Shih-ming, who badly defeated him at Toksun. For all practical purposes, there were three armies remaining in Xinjiang: that of the Khotanlik amirs, that of the Ma allies, and that of the provincial government. Each was soon fighting the other two.

Ma Zhongying took the opportunity opened by Ma Shih-ming to attack the provincial government once more. In December, he moved his forces across the Dawan Ch'eng to attack Urumchi. In response, Chang P'ei-yüan of Ili, who previously had remained neutral in the conflict, moved against the provincial government, attacking its forces at Wusu. The Hui of Zungharia rose up and reinforced Ma's troops. Meanwhile, the secessionist Khotanlik Amīrs of the South created a Turkish-Islamic Republic of Eastern Turkestan (TIRET), with its capital in Old Kashgar and Khoja Niyās Ḥājī as its president. But in mid-December, Khoja Niyās's forces were pushed out of Aksu by Ma Jongying, withdrawing to Old Kashgar and tightening the siege of Ma Zhancang in the new city.

Faced with these threats, Sheng turned to the Soviet Union for aid and purged his armed forces (including the leadership of the White Russian units, which were now to be commanded by Soviet officers). On January 12, Ma attacked Urumchi; its airport fell four days later. At this point, about 5,000 to 7,000 Soviet troops crossed the border into Xinjiaing, attacking rebel positions at Kulja and Chuguchak. Chang's forces were the first to be defeated, followed by those of Ma Shih-ming. Allegedly, Soviet forces used gas to defeat the troops of the latter at the Battle of the Tutun river. Both sides suffered serious losses; Ma Jongying withdrew to the Dawan Ch'eng, pursued by a motley mix of Chinese provincial troops, White Russians led by Soviet officers, and Soviet Red Army units.

Ma Jongying's forces under the command of Ma Fu-yüan now focused on destroying their Uyghur opponents (see Intra-state War #715.6), essentially destroying TIRET. Khoja Niyās Ḥājī signed an agreement with the provincial government, placing his Kumullik troops under their command and becoming civil governor of Xinjiang, while other leaders of the TIRET continued to resist at Yangi Hissar until defeated by the Mas. Meanwhile, Ma Jongying himself reached Kashgar with about 10,000 men (60 percent of them Uyghur conscripts), demoralized from Soviet bombing. He denounced Sheng as a puppet of the Soviet Union, maintaining his own loyalty to Nanjing. But during June, he negotiated with the Soviets, and on July 4 to July 6, he ordered his armies to retreat from Kashgar to Khotan (which had fallen to him without a fight). Ma Jongying then surrendered himself to the Soviet Union.

Termination and Outcome: In September 1934, the leader of the remaining Hui forces, Ma Zhongying's half-brother (or brother-in-law) Ma Hu-shan signed a truce with the provincial government, ending the war. While the Hui had been defeated in their efforts to control the provincial leadership, they had nonetheless retained significant territory in the South, soon dubbed Tunganistan by outsiders.

Coding Decisions: While figures are fragmentary, the first year of war alone killed more than 1,400 on the government side. The largest battle was fought at the West Gate of Urumchi and killed 2,000 to 6,000. Given these figures, we estimate total battle-deaths for the war at around 10,000. The real figure could be somewhat lower or higher.

Sources: Forbes (1986); Pahta (1990).[192]

INTRA-STATE WAR #712.5

Mongolian Armed Uprising of 1932 (aka Shambala War)

Participants: Mongolia and Soviet Union versus Buddhist Rebels.

Dates: Apirl 12, 1932, to October 1932.

Battle-related Deaths: Buddhist Rebels: at least 1,400;[193] Total Combatant Deaths: 2,000. (See Coding Decisions.)[194]

Initiator: Buddhist rebels.

Outcome: Mongolia wins.

War Type: Civil for local issues (suppression of religion and collectivization).

Total System Member Military Personnel: Armed Forces of Mongolia—2,000 (prewar, initial, peak).[195] Armed Forces of the Soviet Union—562,000 (prewar, initial, peak).[196]

Theater Armed Forces: Armed Forces of the Soviet Union, participating from June 1932: unknown (but see Coding Decisions);[197] Buddhist Rebels: 500 (initial); more than 6,000 (peak).[198]

Antecedents: The Soviet Union imposed a Stalinist system on Mongolia; by 1932 Mongolian policy had taken a leftist turn, particularly in the areas of agricultural collectivization and the confiscation of livestock from the lamas of the country. A minor protest by lamas with minimal armament on March 25 was crushed with great brutality and treated as a rebellion (the Tögsbuyant rebellion—in which perhaps two or three government personnel were killed) as was a similar armed protest on March 27. Many lamas tried to contact the Panchen lama in Inner Mongolia, seeking his military support for an anticommunist uprising.

Narrative: On April 12, some 100 lamas set out for the center of Rashaant in Hövsgöl *aimag*; soon their numbers reached 500. They founded a committee named Ochirbat's Ministry and began robbing collective farms, burning schools, killing Communist Party members, and committing atrocities. A man named Sambuu was appointed as commander in chief. After ten days, Orchibat's Ministry was suppressed and thirty flintlock rifles confiscated. Some fifty-four rebels were killed on the spot.

However, the revolt rapidly spread to other *aimags*, and local military troops were unable to suppress the uprising. On May 14, the government decided to send in the national army. The rebels were abysmally armed, but they had some modern weapons from captured soldiers, and it appears that some units defected to the rebel side. At least half of the rebels were ordinary people rather than lamas or lords, although the latter two categories were overrepresented grossly in the rebel ranks.

The Soviet Union sent in aircraft, armored cars, tanks, and (possibly) a detachment from Tuva to assist the government. Some authors maintain that units of the Soviet army had to be called in to repress the uprising. The results of the battles were lopsided, with the rebels suffering far higher casualties than government soldiers, with their artillery and air support. Government reports list more than 6,000 rebels; the actual number was probably higher. The main forces of the rebels were destroyed in June and July. At least 1,000 rebels were killed, and hundreds more were executed in the field.

Termination and Outcome: The revolt finally ended in October. An amnesty was promulgated, and some of the more severe sentences of imprisonment handed to rebels were quashed. The outcome of the war was a complete military victory by the government. Still, the leftist turn in policy—including collectivization of agriculture—was abandoned by the party. The campaign against the lamaseries continued, and the Church was all but extirpated by 1940.

Coding Decisions: While precise numbers are not available, the Soviet Union is included as a participant because of the substantial likelihood that it committed 1,000 or more troops to the fight. At least 1,400 rebels were killed in battle or immediately executed after capture. While Morozova claims that 10,000 died, this figure is likely to include many civilian deaths. We conservatively estimate battle-deaths at 2,000.

Sources: Baabar (1999); Bawden (1968); Kaplonski (2012); Morozova (2003).

INTRA-STATE WAR #715.6

Xinjiang Hui-Uyghur War of 1933 to 1934

Participants: Zhancang-led Hui and Ma Zhongling–led Hui versus Khotanlik Uyghurs and Temūr-led Uyghurs and Kirghiz.
Dates: May 18, 1933, to September 7, 1933, and February 6, 1934, to April 12, 1934.
Battle-related Deaths: Total Combatant Deaths: at least 1,000.[199]
Initiator: Temūr-led Uyghurs and Kirgiz.
Outcome: Hui forces win.
War Type: Intercommunal.
Theater Armed Forces: Ma Zhancang–led Hui: 300 (initial).[200] Ma Zhongling–led Hui, aka KMT Thirty-sixth Division: 5,000 (peak).[201] Khotanlik Uyghurs: up to 10,000 (peak).[202] Temūr-led Uyghurs and Kirgiz: more than 4,700 (initial).[203]

Antecedents: A revolt by Hui and Uyghurs in Xinjiang achieved some measure of success by May 1933, conquering the South of the province (see Intra-state War #711). At this point, however, the goals of the Hui leaders, who wished to overthrow the provincial government, and the Uyghur and Kirgiz provincial rebels, who feared Hui dominance in Xinjiang, came into conflict. On May 17, Hui leader Ma Zhancang attempted to place Temūr, the Uyghur leader, and "commander in chief" of anti-provincial forces, under arrest.

Narrative: The next day, the Kirgiz mounted an attack on Old Kashgar, murdering many Hui. Ma agreed to hand over administration to Temūr and his allies; the next day a tenuous truce was reached between Ma and Temūr that denied Ma Zhancang and the Hui any official position. While this halted Old Kashgar fighting, a small but well-armed force of Hui was dispatched to Yarkand, where they entered the new city and aided its defenders against the Khotanlik Uyghurs. When the city was surrendered to the Uyghurs on May 26, the Hui cavalry and noncombatants were permitted to relocate but then massacred at Kizil. At Yangi Hissar, a massacre of Hui by Uyghurs followed.

The forces of Ma Zhancang now waited inside the fortified walls of the Kashgar new city for aid from other Hui in Turfan or Kansu. The rest of the province was controlled by provincial commander Sheng Shicai's forces (the North) or by the Uyghurs and Kirgiz (the South). The Khotanlik, Temūr-led, and Kirgiz forces jockeyed for position in the South. During this intercommunal struggle, forces loyal to Ma Zhancang captured and executed Temūr. In August, Kirgiz and Kumullik forces unsuccessfully attacked Ma Zhancang's positions. At least 150 Kirgiz were killed in the fighting. On September 7, another 200 Uyghurs and Kirgiz were killed in a sortie by Ma Zhancang's forces. Soon, Kirgiz forces withdrew and the Khotanlik Amīrs became the dominant political force in the South. The siege of New Kashgar continued.

In 1934, Hui leader Ma Jongying—ally of Ma Zhacang—found himself in full retreat from Sino-Russian forces supporting the provincial government. Some of Ma Jongying's forces under the command of Ma Fu-yüan made for Old Kashgar to relieve the siege of his ally Ma Zhancang. On February 6, his 2,000 Hui and Uyghur conscripts succeeded in driving off the 10,000 besiegers. After an abortive Khotanlik attempt to recapture Old Kashgar a week later, 1,700 to 2,000 Uyghurs in the town were massacred by the Mas.

The Mas proceeded against the remnants of the Khotanlik Uyghur Turkish-Islamic Republic of East Turkestan, reaching Yangi Hissar on March 28 and committing the usual massacres. The citadel fell on April 12, at the cost of several hundred casualties among the besiegers; its garrison of 500 was put to the sword.

Termination and Outcome: The outcome of the war was a military victory for the Hui forces. After ending their revolt against the provincial government, the Hui (also known as Tungan) forces formed a statelet in south Xinjiang nicknamed Tunganistan by foreigners. It would last, despite periodic risings by Uyghurs, until destroyed by Soviet forces in 1937.

Coding Decisions: Self-explanatory from cited sources.

Source: Forbes (1986).

INTRA-STATE WAR #716

Fukien Revolt of 1933 to 1934

Participants: China versus Nineteenth Route Army.
Dates: November 20, 1933, to February 1934.
Battle-related Deaths: Total Combatant Deaths: 1,000. (See Narrative and Coding Decisions.)
Initiator: China.
Outcome: China wins.
War Type: Civil for central control.
Total System Member Military Personnel: Armed Forces of China—1,660,000 (prewar, initial, peak, final).[204]
Theater Armed Forces: Armed Forces of China: 150,000 to 200,000. Nineteenth Route Army: 40,000 (prewar, initial, peak).[205]

Antecedents: After a losing fight against the Japanese near Shanghai, the Nineteenth Route Army was redeployed to Fujian (Fukien) province in 1932. Low morale, inadequate supply, and opposition to Chiang Kai-Shek's policy of combat with the Chinese Communist Party (CCP) led the leadership to conclude an agreement with the CCP on October 26, 1933. On November 19, rebel commander Cai Tingkai imposed martial law in the province, forming a revolutionary government the next day.

Narrative: The CCP and the Nineteenth Route Army failed to coordinate with or support each other. The government responded with air strikes against the rebels and the first ground clashes occurred on December 17 and December 18. By this point, Chiang had 150,000 to 200,000 troops massed against the 40,000 rebels on a 150-mile front. Finally, in January 1934, Chiang mounted his final offensive against the rebels. Amoy fell on January 10 and the rebel capital of Foochow on January 15.

The rebel commanders did not surrender (though some defected to the government side during the fight), and mopping-up operations continued into early February.

Termination and Outcome: The outcome of the war was an unconditional military victory by the government. The Nineteenth Route Army was reintegrated into the armed forces, minus its remaining rebel commanders, who had fled to Hong Kong.

Coding Decisions: Although the fighting was desultory, the sheer number of troops engaged with modern weapons makes it plausible that 1,000 died.

Sources: Dorrill (1969); Litten (1988); Thornton (1982).

INTRA-STATE WAR #719

KMT–CCP Clashes of 1939 to 1941 (aka 1939 Clashes, Subei Crisis, and New Fourth Army Incident)

Participants: China versus Chinese Communist Party.
Dates: February 1939 to December 8, 1941.
Battle-related Deaths: Total Combatant Deaths: 31,000. (See Coding Decisions.).[206]
Initiator: China.
Outcome: Stalemate.
War Type: Civil for central control.
Total System Member Military Personnel: Armed Forces of China: 900,000 (prewar—1938 figure); 1,488,000 (initial); 2,584,000 (peak); 2,584,000 (final).[207]
Theater Armed Forces: Chinese Communist Party: 160,000 regulars and 600,000 to 700,000 irregulars (initial).[208]

Antecedents: The Second United Front between the anticommunist Guomindang (Kuomintang [KMT]) government of China and the Chinese Communist Party (CCP) reached at the end of 1936 (see Intra-state War #710) was shaky at best. Each side expected to fight the other again once the struggle against Japan was won. In 1938, Mao Zhedong (Mao Tse Tung) gained control of the CCP at its Sixth Plenum, beating out the favored candidates of the Soviet Union. From this, KMT leader Chiang Kai-shek concluded that the Soviets would be unable to restrain the CCP within the United Front. After the plenum, the CCP expanded into areas deep in the Japanese rear, growing from 40,000 to 160,000 regulars. This expansion alarmed KMT leaders, who decided to fight the communists with their own guerrillas behind Japanese lines at the Fifth Plenum of the Fifth Central Executive Committee in January 1939.

Narrative: In February 1939, the CCP authorized its forces to resist encroachments and attacks by the KMT. Combat almost immediately increased in intensity. Internal CCP figures showed that whereas there had been only a dozen KMT advances into the CCP-occupied Shaan-Gan-Ning special border district in 1938, there were fifty in 1939. Moreover, the clashes of 1938 had killed only 60 people, whereas the CCP calculated that 11,404 were killed in 1939. Moreover, there were twenty-eight KMT attacks on CCP base areas in 1939. The Eighth Route Army was heavily targeted and suffered 1,350 killed between June and December. Possibly to avoid a breach with Moscow, the CCP responded moderately to the attacks in public, refraining from scrapping the Second United Front.

Clashes continued in 1940, generally lopsided affairs in which entire government units were destroyed by the CCP: Bantanji from March 21 to March 29 (1,000 government troops destroyed against several hundred rebel casualties), Guocun from June 28 to July 4 (1,300 government battle deaths against 500 for the rebels), Beixinjie from July 28 to July 29 (nearly 2,000 government troops destroyed), Huangqiao on September 3 (two government regiments destroyed) and again on September 30 to October 6 (6,000 to 7,000 government deaths against 1,000 to 2,000 rebel casualties), and Caodian from November 29 to December 15 (more than 8,000 government casualties against 2,000 rebel casualties). During this period the fighting shifted to Subei, becoming known as the Subei Crisis.

The rebel New Fourth Army emerged from these clashes with an expanded base area. In what would become known as the New Fourth Army Incident (or Wannan Incident), government forces ambushed 10,000 marchers, inflicting 2,000 killed, 3,000 to 4,000 wounded and capturing thousands more while suffering only 3,000 to 4,000 killed or wounded itself. The rebels suffered another 4,000 casualties that spring in fighting against KMT forces led by Tang Enbo. There was another flare-up of combat in Chengdao Kou in late summer or early fall. Fighting between the KMT and CCP only definitively ceased with the Japanese attack on Pearl Harbor.

Termination and Outcome: The outcome of the war was a stalemate. Neither side achieved its objectives, but further combat was postponed until February 1945 as neither side found it in its interest to continue the civil war.

Coding Decisions: At least 13,000 were killed in 1939, perhaps 14,000 in 1940, and at least 4,000 in 1941, for a conservative total of 31,000. The real toll may have been higher.

Sources: Garver (1988); Kataoka (1974); Nathan (1976); Xiang (1998).

INTRA-STATE WAR #719.8
Ili Uprising of 1944 to 1945

Participants: China versus Army of the East Turkestan Republic.
Dates: October 8, 1944, to September 17, 1945.
Battle-related Deaths: Armed Forces of China: up to 30,000; Total Combatant Deaths: 30,000. (See Coding Decisions.)[209]
Initiator: Army of the East Turkestan Republic.
Outcome: Negotiated settlement.
War Type: Civil for local issues (secession).
Total System Member Military Personnel: Armed Forces of China: 4,228,000 (prewar); 4,228,000 (initial); 4,775,000 (peak); 4,775,000 (final).[210]
Theater Armed Forces: Armed Forces of China: 100,000 (peak). Army of the East Turkestan Republic, aka Ili National Army: 1,600 to 5,000 (initial); 30,000 (peak, final).[211]

Antecedents: In a bid to reduce Soviet influence in Xinjiang, the central government appointed its provincial strongman to a position in the Chongqing government in September 1944, creating a political vacuum in the province. Previously repressed Turkic Muslim (Uyghur) groups sought to establish a state of East Turkestan, an objective shared by Kazakh groups. The cessation of trade with the Soviet Union plunged the local economy into turmoil, and Han settlement activity exacerbated interethnic tensions. Disturbances began as early as September 11 but were minor at first. They grew in size from small riots to serious ones over the course of the month.

Narrative: The first battle of the rebellion was fought from October 8 to October 12 in Kazakh-dominated Nilka; the provincial garrison was forced to withdraw from the town by about 600 to 1,000 rebels. Then on November 7, Yining—with a garrison of 8,000 central government troops—was attacked by 400 to 500 Uyghurs, Kazakhs, and White Russians. The resulting battle left 180 government soldiers dead at the cost of only 30 rebel casualties. On November 12, the victorious rebels announced the formation of the East Turkestan Republic. The rebels steadily reduced the remaining government strongholds in Yining, and on December 25 they occupied the nearby town of Huiyan.

The string of rebel victories continued into 1945. On January 3, Suiding on the road to Jinghe was seized by the rebels, who now interdicted reinforcements sent to Jinghe. The government ordered its troops to withdraw from Yining to Jinghe, but few made it out alive. For example, of 4,000 troops that had held the airfield, only 800 remained alive when the order was given on January 29—and most of these were killed trying to escape the city. Government troops who surrendered often died of wounds, starvation, or disease. On February 17, some 3,000 rebels took the pass at Xinertai, followed by Sungshukou and Santai. Some 2,000 to 3,000 reinforcements sent to Xinertai were annihilated by the rebels. The Chinese government alleged that the Soviet Union was providing troops and arms to the rebels; whether any troops were supplied is unclear, but the rebels were probably receiving arms from Soviet sources.

By this point, up to 30,000 Chinese troops had been killed in the fighting. The government reinforced the provincial capital of Urumqi. By April, more than 100,000 government troops were in the province. They took no offensive action against the rebels, who then determined to mount an offensive of their own to seize Jinghe. After bypassing and cutting the town off from supplies, the rebels finally attacked it from September 3 to September 7, defeating at least 15,000 government troops. They also targeted Wusu (further on the road to Urumqi), to which government forces had earlier retreated, taking it on September 6. The Jinghe–Wusu campaign killed at least 2,000 government soldiers. The rebels—now 30,000 strong—advanced to the Manas River, just seventy miles from Urumqi.

Termination and Outcome: A diplomatic exchange between China and the Soviet Union followed, and on September 17 the Soviet Union offered its good offices for mediation; in an unlikely coincidence, the rebels had appealed for mediation at the same time as the government. An informal cease-fire developed, followed by negotiations. On January 3, 1946, a peace agreement was reached providing for religious and linguistic freedom for the Uyghurs, the withdrawal of government troops and secret police from the province, and a limited form of shared governance over the province. No agreement was reached on the disarmament and demobilization of rebel forces, however, until June 6. A coalition government would rule the province until mid-1947, when it was dissolved by the central government over implementation of the disarmament and demobilization provisions.

Coding Decisions: Benson estimates 30,000 government battle-deaths by the spring of 1945, but Chen simply says that the government "lost" 30,000 troops and most of their equipment to the rebels. Given the estimates for individual battles provided by Wang, It is probable that the 30,000 figure includes at least some who deserted, or were captured by the rebels, or possibly wounded as well. Rebel losses, as estimated by Wang, were much smaller—on the order of hundreds rather than thousands—but Sadri argues that rebel losses were nearly as high as government losses up to January 31, 1945 (itself a figure that may include civilians killed by massacre and disease). Given the imprecision of the sources and the distinct possibility that Benson overestimates government battle-deaths, we estimate total battle-deaths at about 30,000. The real toll could be considerably lower.

Sources: Benson (1990); Chen (1977); Wang (1997); Sadri (1984).

INTRA-STATE WAR #723.5

Chinese Civil War phase 2 of 1945 to 1950 (aka War of Liberation)

Participants: China versus Chinese Communist Party
Dates: September 10, 1945, to April 21, 1950.
Battle-related Deaths: China: 600,000; Chinese Communist Party: 600,000; Total Combatant Deaths: 1,200,000. (See Coding Decisions.)[212]
Initiator: Chinese Communist Party.
Outcome: Chinese Communist Party wins.
War Type: Civil for central control.
Total System Member Military Personnel: Armed Forces of China: 4,775,000 (prewar); 4,158,000 (initial, peak).[213]
Theater Armed Forces: Chinese Communist Party (CCP), aka People's Liberation Army: 915,538 (prewar, initial); 5 million (peak, final).[214]

Antecedents: In China, the end of World War II quickly was followed by a grab for territory occupied by the Japanese. Supported by United States air and ground transportation, the ruling Guomindang (Kuomintang [KMT]) seized control of most of the territory, especially major cities. The People's Liberation Army (PLA)—loyal to the rival Chinese Communist Party (CCP)—seized rural areas and urban centers in Manchuria, where Soviet troops initially hindered KMT movements.

The two sides underestimated each other's relative strength; whereas the communists estimated they had 915,538 regulars and 2.2 million militia against about 2 million government regulars, the government estimated that there were only 600,000 PLA regulars against 3 million government troops. Thus there was disagreement over the balance of forces, with each side undercounting its opponent while more or less correctly estimating its own strength.

Narrative: Clashes almost immediately broke out between the two sides, as the communists adopted a strategy of advance to the North and defend the South, concentrating forces to take over the Northeast and engage government troops in pitched battles while maintaining guerrilla operations in the "South" (actually North China). The first major operation was the Shandang Campaign, which kicked off on September 10. Some 31,000 rebels encircled Changzhi in Shanxi, and government general Yan Xishan sent 20,000 men to relieve the siege. On October 8, a breakout attempt failed, and local government forces surrendered two days later. The battle cost each side about 2,000 casualties, and the PLA captured and incorporated 31,000 of Yan's men.

The PLA also fought several battles in North China at Ping-Sui, Jin-Pu, and Ping-Han that autumn to delay the movement of KMT troops into Manchuria. But on November 8, five KMT divisions attacked CCP-held Shanhaiguan, forcing the PLA out of the city by November 16. The government then advanced against light or nonexistent opposition, taking control of the railways and most major cities in Manchuria before pausing to resupply on November 28. At the request of KMT leader Chiang Kai-shek (Jiang Jieshi), who feared that the PLA would seize major cities before the KMT could reinforce them, the Soviet Union delayed its withdrawal from Manchuria (initially for a month and then until March 1946).

Even as pitched battles were being fought, peace talks sponsored by the United States took place beginning on August 28. Further negotiations eventually produced a cease-fire agreement in January 1946, effective on January 13. Critically, the cease-fire did not restrict the movement of KMT troops into Manchuria. As early as January 15, the PLA counterattacked at the port of Yinkou, driving the KMT out of the port it had occupied just ten days earlier. In February, the CCP resolved to inflict heavy losses on the advancing KMT troops in a few carefully chosen engagements rather than try to hold a front line. The strategy led to a major victory at Xiushuihezi but also produced a major defeat at Shalingzi.

On the eve of the Soviet withdrawal, each side prepared to fill the vacuum with its own forces. Violence increased in March as the Soviets withdrew. For example, when the Soviets handed control over Shenyang (Mukden) to the KMT on March 15, the PLA seized Sipingjie (also known as Siping or Suping), a rail junction midway between Shenyang and Changchun, three days later. As the withdrawal con tinued into April, the PLA took control of Changchun, Harbin, and Qiqihaer. Major fighting began over Sipingjie in April, as 60,000 to 65,000 PLA attempted to hold the town against 40,000 KMT. By April 18, Sipingjie had been besieged; the rebels held off ten government assaults over the next month before withdrawing on May 18. Both sides called in reinforcements during the battle, which cost the rebels some 8,000 killed or wounded and the government 10,000. The rebels withdrew from Changchun and Jilin, losing 40,000 defectors to the government.

The CCP requested a cease-fire in Manchuria on June 3; a fifteen-day cease-fire went into effect four days later. After a unilateral government extension, it expired on June 30. Nevertheless, Manchuria remained relatively calm until October. Instead of attacking the PLA in Manchuria, the government attacked it in central China and along the coast during the summer. In July and August, the government destroyed some 20,000 of the 40,000 communist troops in the mountains between Hubei and Anhui. In Jiangsu, the PLA was able to lure KMT troops forward and then break through to their rear, leading to heavy government casualties in the South of the province. But in northern Jiangsu, 30,000 PLA soldiers were killed or wounded, and 10,000 surrendered to the government. Such defeats were replicated in other areas of the country. On October 10, Zhangjiakou—the last major city still in communist hands—was taken by the KMT.

The largest concentrations of PLA forces were now to be found in its northern and southern base areas in Manchuria. The government proceeded against the weaker southern base area first. In October, the southern Manchurian cities, including Andong (later renamed Dandong) and Tonghua, fell to the KMT. The CCP managed a victory at the battle of Xinkailing, annihilating a government brigade, but in general the rebels were forced to retreat northward. During the last six months of the year, the rebels lost control of 165 towns and huge swathes of territory.

During the winter of 1946 and 1947, the rebels adopted a strategy mixing guerrilla and mobile warfare. The goal was to force government units to disperse their strength fighting a guerrilla war, while select mobile units would then strike at them, one at a time, to deplete government strength. In what the CCP referred to as the Three Expeditions South of the [Songhua] River and Four Defenses of Linjiang, from December to March the government suffered serious casualties, and the southern base area was defended, although the government succeeded in capturing the rebel "capital" of Yan'an in Shaanxi on March 19. PLA losses in the Northeast (perhaps 12,000 men) were higher than those of the government, but the rebels could replenish their forces through local recruitment, while the government had to bring in fresh forces from the South.

Meanwhile, government forces in Shandong mounted an offensive in February that lasted until late in the summer. A single ambush on February 21 cost the government 35,000 killed, wounded, or captured, but the PLA eventually had to give up its positions in the Shandong mountains. Government forces now controlled more territory than at any other point during the war, but the bulk of their army was tied down on garrison duty, leaving few mobile reserves. In mid-May, the PLA mounted an offensive on Sipingjie, gaining initial success and inflicting thousands of casualties. By the end of the month, some 100,000 PLA were either directly besieging Sipingjie or holding blocking positions. But KMT artillery and airpower, as well as block-by-block fighting inside the town, cost the PLA heavy casualties and forced it to withdraw to the north on June 28. Rebel losses in the preceding year had been heavy: the CCP estimated it lost 357,000 killed or wounded from June 1946 to June 1947. On July 4, the government formally outlawed the CCP.

Meanwhile, initial successes on the Yellow river in the spring convinced Mao that an offensive across the river and into the Central Plains could inflict casualties on the KMT, seize territory for the CCP, and help relieve the pressure in Shandong and Shaanxi. Tens of thousands of peasants who had been displaced by the restoration of the Yellow river to its old bed flocked to the CCP; 100,000 communist soldiers advanced into the Central Plains. In three battles in July, the government lost 80,000 troops against PLA losses of only 10,500. PLA forces then marched south to the Dabie mountains, where they set up a new base area. Other, smaller CCP offensives also sought to relieve the pressure on Shandong.

The next large-scale campaign kicked off in late September in the Northeast. The PLA attacked KMT positions, annihilating the Forty-ninth Army. The PLA advanced and captured stockpiles of supplies before withdrawing in early November. In January 1948, they mounted an offensive against Shenyang. Resorting to an oft-used tactic, they surprised and routed the Fifth Army before ambushing and scattering reinforcements sent to its aid. The rebels then followed up their success with attacks to the east and west of Shenyang. The latter force captured Xinlitun and the entire division, defending it before the end of the month, while the former captured Liaoyang, Anshan, and in late February the port of Yingkou. The rebels then trapped government forces in Manchuria by attacking Sipingjie, defended by 19,000 KMT soldiers, with 100,000 troops. Armed with heavy artillery, they took the city on March 12; most of its defenders were killed or captured.

The CCP held the initiative at this stage of the war. By the middle of May, its surviving units in Shandong and Shanxi had retaken much of the ground that had been lost to the government in the first half of 1947, including Yan'an. In the Northeast, Changchun was besieged by the rebels. A campaign in Henan had cut off the provincial capital of Kaifeng by June 12; it fell to the PLA after a week of heavy fighting. The rebels soon abandoned the city but inflicted heavy casualties on the government troops sent to retake it. Altogether the campaign for Henan had involved 200,000 troops on each side and cost the government 60,000 killed or captured. Rebel losses in the preceding year had been even heavier than in 1946 and 1947; the CCP estimated that the PLA lost 542,600 dead or wounded from June 1947 to June 1948. KMT killed or wounded were estimated at 1,450,000 for the previous two years of combat against about 900,000 for the PLA.

The rebels formally established a government over their "liberated areas" on August 8. This was a political prelude to a massive military operation beginning on September 12 known as the LiaoShen (or Liaoning-Shenyang) Campaign. The PLA, whose nationwide strength had reached 2 million and now outnumbered the KMT in the Northeast (700,000 CCP to 480,000 KMT), mounted the LiaoShen offensives to destroy the remaining KMT in the region, concentrated in a triangle bounded by the cities of Changchun, Shenyang, and Jinzhou. Most of the major battles of the campaign involved sieges and assaults on these cities. In Changchun alone, 160,000 civilians perished of hunger. Total losses on the government side were staggering, according to CCP figures: 306,200 captured, 109,000 defections to the PLA, and 56,800 other casualties, but other sources estimate 65,000 government battle-deaths in and near Jinzhou alone.

At about the same time as the onset of the LiaoShen campaign, the rebels took 80,000 prisoners or defectors in Shandong. From July 1948 to November 1948, the total strength of the government forces declined by 1 million. The PLA now had nationwide numeric superiority, with 3 million troops compared to the government's 2.9 million. In total, the Manchurian fighting from 1945 to 1948 had cost the government 3 million killed, wounded, missing, or captured. Moreover, its Manchurian losses had come from its best divisions and included a great deal of heavy weaponry.

Having solidified its control of Shandong and Manchuria by early November, the CCP concentrated on seizing control of North China. In the Huai-Hai Campaign, 600,000 rebels from Henan and Shandong mounted a pincer attack against 500,000 KMT in and near the important rail center of Xuzhou (Suchow) in Jiangsu, seeking to control the railroads and roads leading south. In sixty-five days of fighting, all but one of the six KMT army groups defending the railroad were surrounded and defeated. The KMT suffered 250,000 killed or wounded and hundreds of thousands taken prisoner; PLA losses may have been about 100,000 killed or wounded. In all, the Huai-Hai Campaign probably resulted in 100,000 battle-deaths—the bloodiest campaign in the war.

Meanwhile, the PLA in Manchuria moved south, threatening Beiping (now Beijing) and Tianjin. The sides were evenly matched in the region, each committing about 500,000 troops. However, after some initial defeats, government forces' morale sank so low that few units resisted the PLA advance. Beiping surrendered without a fight on January 23, 1949. Once again, the PLA took hundreds of thousands of prisoners. The government attempted to open another round of negotiations, but the CCP demanded a communist state and the trial of government leaders. The negotiations, used by both sides to prepare for further conflict, failed in April.

By spring, the PLA was 4 million strong, including 2.1 million regulars; against this force the government could field no more than 1.8 million soldiers. Having consolidated their hold on the North, the CCP prepared to move south of the Yangtze. PLA forces crossed the river against light opposition on April 20. In June, the CCP estimated its losses over the previous year at 533,300. But the intensity of combat decreased over the final stages of the war, as entire KMT units collapsed or defected to the PLA. Soon Nanjing and Hanzhou were in communist hands; Shanghai surrendered with only minor clashes.

The government ended up moving the capital four times in its retreat from the rebels. Only near Sichuan did the KMT resistance stiffen. There the KMT allied itself with a neighboring Muslim warlord and counterattacked west of Xi'an; the rebels suffered 50,000 casualties before reinforcements could be brought in. Elsewhere, the government collapse continued into the fall. On October 1, the CCP declared the People's Republic of China with its capital in Beijing. As the PLA advanced deep into the interior, the KMT government fled to Taiwan (Formosa) on December 7. Two days later, the governor of Yunnan defected to the CCP; remnants of the KMT in his province retreated south into Burma, along with some Chinese Muslim soldiers.

In 1950, the PLA continued its offensives against peripheral areas that had escaped its control, such as Xikang, Xinjiang, and Hainan (which was taken by amphibious assault in April, costing the KMT 30,000 casualties). The capture of Hainan marked the last major engagement of the war; there, the PLA's victory was complete on April 21. The CCP estimated its own losses at just 89,600 from June 1949 to June 1950.

Termination and Outcome: The war terminated with the conquest of Hainan. The outcome of the war was an unconditional rebel military victory. While Taiwan continued to hold out, the PRC was unable to invade it without a navy or air force. Instead, the CCP concentrated on its internal enemies; the end of fighting did not mean the end of killing. While killings were first limited to hundreds and thousands, they escalated once the PRC joined the Korean War. Perhaps a million "counterrevolutionaries" were killed in bandit suppression campaigns that largely focused on former supporters of the KMT regime. In some areas of the Northwest, armed resistance continued for several years, and the KMT in Burma repeatedly mounted raids into the PRC. Neither of these conflicts rose to the level of civil war, however.

Coding Decisions: Clodfelter estimates 1,200,000 total battle-deaths, including 1,522,500 killed or wounded on the rebel side. If the usual 3:1 ratio of wounded to killed holds, then the PLA suffered just under 400,000 battle-deaths in combat, and by subtraction the government must have suffered 800,000. Another approach is to use the relative intensity of the casualties in 1948 and 1949. For the eighteen months beginning in June 1948, the government lost 571,160 killed or wounded—about 31,731 a month. For the twelve-month period of June 1948 to June 1949 the rebels lost 533,300—about 44,416 a month. This suggests higher casualties for the rebels than for the government: a ratio of about 1.4 rebel casualties for each government casualty, which would translate into 700,000 rebel battle-deaths and

500,000 government battle-deaths. Both approaches ignore deaths due to disease, deprivation, starvation, and mistreatment or execution of prisoners. Since the rebels held far more prisoners than the government, it stands to reason that government losses of captured personnel were greater than those of the rebels. For these reasons, we conclude that battle-deaths were approximately equal on each side, give or take 100,000.

Sources: Clodfelter (2008); Clubb (1957); Dikötter (2013); Lew (2009); Li (2012); Tanner (2003); Westad (2003); Worthing (2007).[215]

INTRA-STATE WAR #726
Taiwan Revolt of 1947 (aka 228 Incident)

Participants: China verses Taiwanese (Aggregate).
Dates: February 28, 1947, to March 21, 1947.
Battle-related Deaths: Armed Forces of China: 90 to 230;[216] Taiwanese: about 1,800;[217] Total Combatant Deaths: 2,000. (See Coding Decisions.)[218]
Initiator: Taiwanese.
Outcome: China wins.
War Type: Civil for local issues.
Total System Member Military Personnel: Armed Forces of China: 4,015,000 (prewar, initial, peak, final).[219]
Theater Armed Forces: Taiwanese: 2,000 to 4,000 (initial), up to 8,000 (peak).[220]

Antecedents: During the Chinese Civil War of 1945 to 1950 (see Intra-state War #725), the ruling Guomindang (more commonly known as the Kuomintang [KMT]) prepared the island province of Formosa (now Taiwan) against possible infiltration by communist rebels. The island also served as a fortress of last resort in case the war should go badly. For both reasons, the island was heavily militarized, curtailing the autonomy and economic opportunities that the Japanese-educated native Taiwanese elite had enjoyed before the war. A dispute between a vendor and the Monopoly Bureau escalated into a full-scale urban riot on February 28, 1947.

Narrative: Some 2,000 to 3,000 initial protesters took part in the riot, seizing government buildings and attacking police, soldiers, and civil servants. The riot turned into an insurrection as pitched battles between protesters and police and military units broke out across the island. In at least eight large towns and cities, committees were formed by the Taiwanese elite to mediate between the government forces and Taiwanese peasants, who quickly joined the rebellion. The most notable of these was the Committee to Settle the Monopoly Bureau Incident. The 4,000-strong Twenty-seventh Militia Corps went over to the rebels. However, there was no united rebel leadership, possibly because there was no united rationale for the uprising. Nevertheless, pro-independence factions existed, representing the most extreme rebels.

In two or three days of fighting, the rebels succeeded in taking control of the major cities. The government sent reinforcements to the island, but it was not until March 8 that the first ones arrived. What followed was a swift and brutal military campaign in which poorly armed rebels were slaughtered by government units. By March 10, the government controlled the cities, although fighting continued in the central highlands until March 21.

Termination and Outcome: The outcome of the war was a complete government military victory. The KMT imposed a reign of terror on the island, killing thousands. Even after the fall of the KMT in mainland China, it maintained a stranglehold on Taiwanese politics, prohibiting pro-independence sentiment.

Coding Decisions: Civil servants are excluded from the government's battle-deaths. Another 8,000 Taiwanese were killed by secret police in the months following the suppression of the revolt, but as these don't qualify as an immediate postwar massacre, they are not included in the battle-death total.

Sources: Phillips (2003); Roy (2003); Tse-Han et al. (1991).[221]

INTRA-STATE WAR #730.5
First Burmese War of 1948 to 1950

Participants: Burma and Sitwundan versus Communist Party of Burma, Communist Party of Burma—Red Flags, People's Volunteer

Organization—White Band, Burma Revolutionary Army, Karen National Defense Organization, Mon National Defense Organization, Karenni Rebels, Pa-O Rebels, and Kachin Rebels.

Dates: April 2, 1948, to December 10, 1950.

Battle-related Deaths: Armed Forces of Burma: 1,352;[222] Total Combatant Deaths: 3,424. (See Coding Decisions.)[223]

Initiator: Communist Party of Burma.

Outcome: Fighting fell below civil-war threshold.

War Type: Civil for central control (see Coding Decisions).

Total System Member Military Personnel: Armed Forces of Burma: 5,000 (initial); 8,000 (peak); 8,000 (final).[224]

Theater Armed Forces: The peak strength of all rebels combined was 30,000 to 60,000 in 1949.[225] Sitwundan/Peace Guerrillas—thousands (initial); 13,000 (peak).[226] Communist Party of Burma: 10,000 to 15,000 (peak).[227] Communist Party of Burma (Red Flags): 1,000 to 1,500 (peak).[228] People's Volunteer Organization (White Band), participating from July 28, 1948: 4,000 (initial, peak).[229] Burma Revolutionary Army, participating from August 8, 1949, but only allied with the CPB on August 10; was absorbed by the CPB on September 1, 1950: more than 350 (initial).[230] Karen National Defense Organization, participating from mid-August 1949: 10,000 (peak).[231] Mon National Defense Organization, participating from mid-August 1949: less than 2,000 (peak).[232] Karenni Rebels, participating from about August 10, 1949: a few hundred (initial, peak).[233] Pa-O Rebels, participating from 1949: 5,000 (peak).[234] Kachin Rebels/Pawngyawng National Defense Force, participating from February 16, 1949, to May 5, 1950: one battalion (initial); 2,000 to 3,000 (peak); 400 (final).[235]

Antecedents: Burma's postindependence constitution did not assign the Karen ethnicity the same rights of autonomy (and ability to secede after ten years) as it did for several other ethnicities. On February 5, 1947, the Karen National Union was established to advance the interest of ethnic Karens. It called for a boycott of the country's first elections and demanded an independent Karen state. On July 17, the Karen National Defense Organization (KNDO) was formed as a militia. Soon after, the Mons formed the Mon National Defense Organization (MNDO), cooperating closely with the KNDO. Both organizations stockpiled arms. The war did not initially involve the KNDO or MNDO, however. Instead, the start of the war was a communist rebellion.

The Communist Party of Burma (CPB) emerged from World War II as a divided organization. When Burma gained its independence, large portions of the party wanted to work within the system to effect change, while a splinter faction—the Red Flags—advocated revolution. Government repression began to push the entire party toward a policy of active resistance such as general strikes and mass protests. The government ordered the arrest of the party's leaders on March 27, 1948. The CPB's leadership escaped the dragnet and ordered cadres into rural areas.

Narrative: The first shots were fired at Paukkongyi on April 2. The fighting soon spread throughout central and upper Burma but was at first concentrated in the Pegu District. The CPB made gains in the first week, taking a number of villages and police stations, but lost much of the ground it had taken in the second week of fighting. It established a parallel administration at Legyamyaung and, in May, a temporary headquarters at Pyinmana. On May 25, Prime Minister U Nu announced a leftist unity political program to counter the insurgency's ideological appeal. But in mid-June, elements of the First and Sixth Burma Rifles defected to the rebels, strengthening the revolt. Communists also had penetrated the Second Burma Rifles. Indeed, the only battalion that was considered entirely reliable was Ne Win's Fourth Burma Rifles.

On July 28, the People's Volunteer Organization's White Band joined the revolt, allying themselves with the CPB. The PVO was ostensibly a veterans' organization that had functioned as a private militia. Some 60 percent of the PVO—4,000 troops—joined the White Band and rebellion rather than the Yellow Band, which was close to the Socialist Party and opted to support the government. They briefly tried to besiege Rangoon but were driven away by naval shellfire.

After Ne Win was appointed minister of defense, other military units mutinied and marched on Rangoon, only to be driven back by government airpower from August 8 to August 10. The mutineers then formed the Burma Revolutionary Army and allied themselves with the CPB. During the crisis, the government arrested and killed prominent Karenni leader Bee Tu Reh, triggering a revolt by the Karennis (not to be confused with the Karens). Moreover, the KNDO and MNDO were moving closer to open revolt. Karen military police took Twante on August 14; isolated attacks by KNDO and MNDO forces followed, as both organizations sought to acquire arms. A series of other Karen mutinies followed, and when the government tried to disarm the MNDO in Moulmein, the KNDO and MNDO promptly seized the town, relinquishing it to government forces only after U Nu promised to consider Karen autonomy.

In November, the government made some progress against the PVO, and the next month it launched an offensive against the CPB, simultaneously offering peace talks. However, a string of massacres of Christian Karens just before Christmas triggered a full-scale rebellion by the KNDO, which took Twante near Rangoon on January 1, 1949. From January 24 to January 28, elements of the First Karen Rifles mutinied and joined the rebellion; the KNDO was outlawed by the government on January 30. The next day, fighting began in Insein north of Rangoon; by February 2 it was under the control of 2,000 KNDO troops. Three days later, the Second Karen Rifles mutinied and unsuccessfully attempted an advance on Rangoon. On February 16, the First Kachin Rifles went over to the Karen rebels in its entirety. Ethnic Pa-O insurgents also joined the war on the side of the Karens.

The CPB and KNDO began working together; a joint force took Mandalay, Myitnge, and Kume on March 12 and March 13. On March 24, a People's Democratic Front (PDF), uniting the various leftist (but not nationalist) groups, was formed at Prome. They rejected peace talks, insisting that U Nu be tried by a people's tribunal. On April 20, after battles at Nyaunglebin and Daik-U, KNDO forces marched toward Rangoon. But on May 1, these forces were halted at Pegu and forced to retreat toward Toungoo. By this point, the government had recaptured all of Mandalay, and soon Insein, besieged by government forces for 112 days, fell to advancing government forces; the siege had cost nearly 1,000 killed, with casualties on the government side believed to be higher than those of the rebels. The KNDO forces retreated to Toungoo, which became their new headquarters.

Despite the government victories, more than half of the country was occupied by insurgents. The government sought and received weapons from India with which to combat the rebels. Karenni resistance to the state and the MNDO were bolstered by the KNDO; the network of insurgencies was interconnected at this stage of the war. The CPB claimed 6 million inhabitants in its liberated area. The rainy season made further offensive operations by the government impossible, and by its end the government controlled little more than Rangoon and its immediate environs. It had lost 42 percent of its manpower and 45 percent of its equipment to the insurgency (mostly in the form of defections). By midyear, the rebels outnumbered the government forces: at least 10,000 KNDO, 10,000 to 15,000 CPB, 4,000 PVO, and a few thousand other insurgents were in the field against the government army, variously estimated at 2,000 to 4,000 troops plus thousands of Sitwundan militia.

But within a few years, the massive shipments from India and recruiting among the Kachin, Chin, and even the Karennis had bolstered the army to nearly 30,000. As early as late 1949, the government had mounted limited offensives in some areas. In mid-March 1950, it began an advance on the KNDO headquarters of Toungoo. After just two days of fighting, it fell on March 19; KNDO forces retreated to the hills, establishing a new headquarters at Mawchi and then the more remote Papun. There they referred to their statelet as Kawthoolei, although there was no formal declaration of independence. Central Burma was no longer in KNDO hands.

On August 11, Karen leader Saw Ba U Gyi, some other leaders, and their bodyguards were surrounded and killed by government forces. Diseases such as typhoid, black water fever, and malaria claimed the lives of other rebels. Meanwhile, the Kachin rebels were suffering setbacks as well. After proclaiming an independent state of Pawngyawng and setting up a 2,000- to 3,000-strong Pawngyawng National Defense Force, they were locked in combat with government units in the mountains for months. On May 5, 1950, the remaining 400 hard-core insurgents crossed into China, where they were treated as refugees. The rest made their way back to their homes as best they could. The Kachin portion of the insurrection was over.

The CPB was also losing the war. In March 1950, the PDF began to fall apart as the PVO attacked CPB units and seized control of Thayetmyo. The town of Pakokku, held by the CPB for more than a year, fell to the government on April 29. On September 1, the CPB and BRA formally merged together and soon mounted a frontal assault on the urban center of Lewe. Although there were 3,000 rebels against only 1,000 defenders, the attack was repulsed with heavy losses. The CPB turned away from attacking urban centers toward rural guerrilla warfare. By the end of 1950, the government had recaptured all the towns lost in 1948 and 1949.

Termination and Outcome: The last significant combat for more than a year was at Pantanaw on December 10. Since 1951 saw little combat, we code this civil war as ending on that date, falling below the threshold of civil-war-level violence. Of course the civil conflict continued, with minor guerrilla actions taking the place of battles. But the outcome of the war was a de facto government victory; it would be almost a decade before full-scale civil war erupted once more. The government had offered an amnesty in May 1950; some 6,000 rebels took the opportunity to surrender.

Note that some combat took place between the government and the Guomindang (Kuomintang [KMT]) forces, which lost the Chinese Civil War (see Intra-state War #725). In January 1950, the first 300 KMT crossed from Yunnan to Burma. They were disarmed and interned by the Burmese military, but future waves of KMT would not surrender themselves so easily. Another 1,000 crossed into Burma and set themselves up at Mōng Pong near the border. The figure would rise to 2,000 by the end of March.

By the end of 1950, then, most insurgent groups were in full retreat, but the KMT buildup in Shan state continued. The government's preoccupation with ousting the KMT provided the rebels with breathing room in 1951. That February, the government mounted Operation Frost against the KMT. In November, the CPB even offered the government an alliance—the Peace and Coalition Government—against the KMT; the offer was rebuffed. By the end of the year, the KMT were 6,000 strong. The struggle to evict them would preoccupy the government for years to come and cost it the lives of more than 1,000 soldiers from 1951 to 1954 alone.

Coding Decisions: While the CPB sought to overthrow the government, other groups such as the KNDO sought autonomy or independence. Because the two war types are mutually exclusive in our typology and the revolt was initiated by the CPB, we code the war as being over the control of the central government. Some 60,000 died in the first two years of the war. Given the small size of the forces involved and the urban nature of much of the early fighting, this figure must include civilian deaths. Battle-deaths would be considerably smaller—we use Tinker's estimates of just 3,424 battle-deaths including 1,352 army personnel.

Sources: Bercovitch and Jackson (1997); Callahan (2003); Correlates of War Project (2010); Fredholm (1993); Lintner (1990, 1999); Tinker (1961).[236]

INTRA-STATE WAR #732.5

Telengana Rebellion of 1948 to 1950

Participants: India versus Hyderabad Communists.
Dates: October 1, 1948, to December 31, 1950.
Battle-related Deaths: Hyderabad Communists: about 2,000;[237] Total Combatant Deaths: at least 2,250. (See Coding Decisions.)[238]
Initiator: India.
Outcome: India wins.
War Type: Civil for central control.
Total System Member Military Personnel: Armed Forces of India: 321,000 (prewar, initial); 391,000 (peak, final). The latter figure includes about 40,000 home guards.[239]
Theater Armed Forces: Armed Forces of India: 46,000 to 47,000 (final). Hyderabad Communists: 12,000 (prewar); less than 12,000 (initial).

Antecedents: In September 1948, India overran Hyderabad, adding it to India (see Extra-state War #461). At the time of the takeover, the Communist Party in Hyderabad had been in rebellion for several years against feudal landowners and the armed Muslim Razakars, which were allied to Hyderabad's government. Thousands of lives were lost and thousands of villages fell to the communists. The communists had perhaps 2,000 mobile guerrillas and 10,000 in village defense squads on the eve of the intervention. During the intervention, they fought the forces of Hyderabad and the Razakars to gain weapons with which to continue the struggle against bourgeois-democratic India.

Narrative: Within two weeks of the end of the intervention (i.e., by October 1), landlords began returning to areas controlled by the communists with Indian police in tow, pointing out insurgents and others who had benefited from illegal land redistribution. The police and army arrested thousands and began a military campaign against those who didn't surrender. Within a few months, 500 party organizers and squad leaders were dead. By the end of December, the campaign had reached its full intensity. Some 50,000 people were arrested and kept for days to months. About 5,000 were imprisoned for years. Guerrillas captured in arms frequently were executed in the field.

The guerrillas most frequently targeted landlords and members of government-sponsored village militias known as home guards, although in 1950 they stepped up attacks on military and police forces. That year, 40 military and police personnel were killed and another 50 to 60 wounded in the Godavari forest region alone. In a series of brutal combing operations and encirclement campaigns, some 6,000 to 7,000 government police and soldiers killed about 2,000 insurgents by the time the fighting died down at the end of 1950.

Termination and Outcome: By the end of 1950, "only isolated guerrilla groups existed, there was little coordination among village republics, and the severe military repression had taken its toll on the population, with a huge loss of life, and the movement weakened."[240] The conflict thus dropped below war level in 1951, although the guerrillas continued to operate in small groups until October 21, when they formally ceased their armed struggle. The outcome of the war was plainly a government military victory.

Coding Decisions: Some 2,000 rebels were killed; cholera and malaria also took a toll. Government losses are unknown, but the former rebels report that during 1949, 34 were killed in the Garao and Pakhala areas alone; the total for 1950 in these areas was 100. Also in 1950 some 40 military and police personnel were killed in the Godavari forest region. And on April 22, the rebels detonated explosives on the Gangaram Road, killing up to 50 soldiers. Dozens of other actions are recorded. From these fragmentary reports, we find it plausible that the combined battle-deaths were at least 2,250 personnel during this period, which would qualify the conflict as a civil war.

Sources: Chadha (2005); Mathews (2011); Sundarayya (1972).

INTRA-STATE WAR #733

Huk Rebellion of 1950 to 1954 (aka Hukbalahap Rebellion)

Participants: Philippines versus Hukbong Mapagpalaya ng Bayan.
Dates: April 14, 1950, to May 17, 1954.
Battle-related Deaths: Armed Forces of the Philippines: up to 1578; Hukbong Mapagpalaya ng Bayan: up to 9695; Total Combatant Deaths: up to 11,273. (See Coding Decisions.)[241]
Initiator: Hukbong Mapagpalaya ng Bayan.
Outcome: Philippines wins.
War Type: Civil for local issues (agrarian reform).
Total System Member Military Personnel: Armed Forces of the Philippines—29,000 (prewar); 29,000 (initial); 34,000 (peak); 34,000 (final).[242]
Theater Armed Forces: Hukbong Mapagpalaya ng Bayan (HMB), aka People's Liberation Army: 12,800 (prewar, initial, peak); 660 (final—1956 figure).[243]

Antecedents: The Hukbalahap—an abbreviation of Hukbo ng Bayan labon sa Hapon or People's Anti-Japanese Army—formed from the remnants of 1930s left-wing peasant resistance movements during the Japanese occupation of the Philippines in the early 1940s. After the war, the peasants continued to demand agrarian reforms; many were disarmed or even arrested by American forces before the rest took to the hills. After attempting reform through the electoral process, the Huks resorted to violent means in September 1946. Renaming themselves the Hukbong Mapagpalaya ng Bayan (HMB, or People's Liberation Army), the rebels began to harass landlords and police.

Through spokesperson and future leader Luis Taruc, the Huks demanded enforcement of the bill of rights, amnesty and release of political prisoners, replacement of provincial and municipal officials in

Central Luzon, and implementation of preexisting land reform proposals. Despite its modest demands, the government formally outlawed the group in March 1948, demanding its unconditional surrender. The guerrillas adopted a defensive strategy from 1946 to 1949; one participant explained that the HMB adopted this stance because "the armed overthrow of the government was not our objective" (Lachica, 172).

The government mounted its first campaign against the guerrillas from 1946 to 1948. Its large-scale operations did little to check the growth of the movement, however. By 1948, rebel leaders estimated their strength at between 5,000 and 10,000 armed guerrillas. On April 15, 1948, President Manuel Roxas died, and his successor agreed to negotiations with the HMB. From June 21 to August 15, a national amnesty came into effect, but provincial officials continued to disarm and arrest Huks that tried to take advantage of it. The negotiations collapsed on August 14, and a new wave of military operations kicked off.

On April 28, 1949, Doña Aurora Quezon, widow of former president Manuel Quezon, was ambushed together with her guards. She was killed along with several guards and her daughter and son-in-law. Incensed, the government deployed some 4,000 troops to hunt down the insurgents who had conducted the ambush. They struck a Huk base on June 1 and June 2, and within a week some thirty-seven Huks had been killed. Fighting continued until September 11, when the last of the ambushers were thought to have been eliminated. Although this was an escalation of violence, it remained well below civil war levels until 1950, when the rebels adopted a more offensive strategy. Deciding that the time was ripe to build a conventional capacity, they assembled much larger units; the government took the same step, moving from the deployment of companies to the deployment of battalions. As a result, serious battles with many casualties took place.

Narrative: In April 1950, the rebels moved against Manila. Clashes north of the capital on April 15 and 16 killed 320 rebels. On September 1, Ramon Magsaysay was appointed as defense minister and immediately devoted more resources to both crushing the insurgency—often through ruses and other traditional guerrilla methods—and winning over the population through implementation of reforms and civilian protection. The government claimed to have killed 1,268 Huks between April and December. The following year, another 2,000 rebels were killed. Moreover, Magsaysay's Attraction Program was having an effect on civilians, who became less supportive of the Huks and more supportive of government forces. He also started a program to settle Huks who surrendered and grant them parcels of farmland—one of the Huks' original demands. The combination of aggressive patrolling and combat, reaching out to civilians, and enticing Huks to surrender gradually brought the rebellion to a halt.

Termination and Outcome: On May 17, 1954, Luis Taruc surrendered to government forces and ordered other Huks to do the same. While a few hundred continued to resist, the war was over. Despite being preceded by four months of negotiations, the surrender was unconditional. Taruc was imprisoned until 1968, when he was finally pardoned by the government. More than a decade after most Huks had surrendered, remnants of Huk forces would reemerge in the embryonic stages of the NPA Rebellion (Intra-state War #824).

Coding Decisions: The government suffered 1,578 battle-deaths from 1946 to 1955. Pre-1950 fatalities were "negligible," however.[244] The rebels suffered 9,695 battle-deaths from 1946 to 1955, most of which must have been suffered during the war period.

Sources: Kerkevliet (1977); Lachica (1971); Mullenbach (2013a, b); Valeriano and Bohannan (2006).[245]

INTRA-STATE WAR #734
South Moluccas War of 1950

Participants: Indonesia versus *Republik Maluku Selatan*.
Dates: July 13, 1950, to November 3, 1950.
Battle-related Deaths: Total Combatant Deaths: 3,000. (See Coding Decisions.)[246]
Initiator: Indonesia.
Outcome: Indonesia wins.
War Type: Civil for local issues (secession).
Total System Member Military Personnel: Armed Forces of Indonesia: 600,000 (initial, peak, final).[247]
Theater Armed Forces: Indonesia: Perhaps 15,000. *Republik Maluku Selatan*: 1,739 (prewar); 17,000 (initial, peak).[248]

Antecedents: The Moluccas, also called Maluku, are located in Northeast Indonesia. The 1949 agreements leading to Indonesia's recognition as an independent state provided the Moluccas with the right of self-determination by secession if desired. But upon independence, the Javanese-dominated central government began to incorporate East Indonesian areas such as the Moluccas by force. East Indonesia capitulated to the unitary central government on April 21, 1950. Seeing the prospect of federalism or autonomy dim, Moluccan leader Chris Soumokil declared independence four days later. A Republic of the South Moluccas (*Republik Maluku Selatan* [RMS]), including Amboina (Ambon), Buru, Ceram, and adjoining islands, was proclaimed. When negotiations failed to provide an immediate solution to the problem, the government decided to resolve the dispute by force, deploying troops to repress the "rebels."

Narrative: The government proclaimed a blockade of the RMS-controlled islands, but no serious combat occurred until government troops landed on Buru on July 13. Out of 60 defenders, 10 were killed. Government battle-deaths were greater, but rebel claims of hundreds of government soldiers killed were probably exaggerations. The government deployed 12,000 soldiers for its final offensive against rebel-held islands. On September 28, the government landed six battalions on Ambon itself to face the estimated single battalion of defenders. The resulting period of combat was the most intense of the war. About a month later, the government had to rush three more battalions to Ambon due to heavy resistance. The rebels' defenses collapsed within days, ending the war.

Termination and Outcome: The outcome of the war was an unconditional military victory by the government, which defeated the rebels on Ambon by November 3. Some rebel soldiers (former members of the pro-Dutch colonial KNIL force) were stripped of rank and discharged, but others were amnestied and integrated into the Indonesian armed forces; there were no postwar massacres. Small numbers of rebels evacuated to Ceram and continued to mount guerrilla operations until 1963. The struggle finally ended with the capture of Soumokil, who was summarily executed in 1966.

Coding Decisions: About 5,000 may have died, but this figure includes civilians and is therefore an overestimate. Perhaps 3,000 is nearer the mark, though the real figure could be somewhat higher or considerably lower.

Sources: Chauvel (2008); Higgins (2010); "Jakarta Adds to Amboina Force" (1950); Kahin (1952); Lundry (2009).[249]

INTRA-STATE WAR #736
Indonesia Darul Islam Rebellion of 1951 to 1962

Participants: Indonesia versus Negara Islam Indonesia.
Dates: January 1, 1951, to June 4, 1962.
Battle-related Deaths: Negara Islam Indonesia: 12,000;[250] Total Combatant Deaths: 20,000. (See Coding Decisions.)[251]
Initiator: Indonesia.
Outcome: Indonesia wins.
War Type: Civil for central control.
Total System Member Military Personnel: Armed Forces of Indonesia: 600,000 (prewar); 400,000 (initial and peak); 375,000 (final).[252]
Theater Armed Forces: Negara Islam Indonesia, aka Darul Islam: 5,000 (initial); 26,000 (peak—1954).[253]

Antecedents: In December 1948, Sukarmadji Maridjan Kartosuwiryo, the former leader of an Islamic political party, led an Islamic revolt against both the Republic of Indonesia (then fighting for its independence) and the Dutch colonial forces. By early 1949, a division of Indonesian troops sent into West Java, the initial area of revolt, was met with fierce resistance and heavy casualties but gained control of the area. Despite the defeat of his premature insurrection, Kartosuwirjo proclaimed Negara Islamic Indonesia (NII) encompassing all of Indonesia in August 1949.

By the time of independence, this Darul Islam (DI) movement had spread to Central Java. The government initially took a soft line toward the rebellion, seeking to entice DI forces back into the Indonesian fold. But DI attacks began as early as February 1950—after the Dutch withdrew from Tasikmalaja, southeast of Bandoeng, on February 8, the town was attacked by DI forces five days later. The attack killed fifty-two government soldiers and many rebels and was followed by nightly harassment of government columns and patrols.

Narrative: The government launched a major offensive against DI forces on January 1, 1951. Sixteen battalions were thrown into action in West Java, plus another eleven in Central Java. Near Garut, a tiny region near the West Javan capital of Bandoeng, the government killed some 200 Darul Islam fighters. The rebels killed 414 people in the last quarter of the year alone. By December, defections to the rebels were becoming a serious problem. Four companies deserted on January 7 and tried to break through an encirclement by government troops in an engagement that claimed the lives of 22 rebels and a dozen government troops. An entire battalion soon defected to the rebels.

On September 15, 1952 (earlier according to government sources), forces in South Sulawesi under Kahar Muzakkar joined the DI rebellion (Muzakkar officially proclaimed Sulawesi to be part of the NII on August 7 of the following year). This immediately added about 3,000 rebels to the DI ranks; the government responded by mounting Operation Halilintar against the rebels and by the end of the year had built up its strength in Sulawesi to nineteen battalions. That year, the government suffered 300 battle-deaths in the Javanese rebels' stronghold of Garut alone. The rebels, numbering about 5,000 armed and several thousand more unarmed followers, killed 2,000 throughout West Java (428 of them in the first three months of the year). The government had by this time deployed thirty to forty battalions against the rebellion. On September 20, 1953, the rebellion spread to Aceh on Sumatra, where 10,000 rebels under Daoud Beureueh affiliated themselves with DI. Fearful of defections, the government deployed only 3,500 non-Muslim troops and an equal number of armed police against them; within two months the government claimed to have inflicted 1,000 battle-deaths on the Acehnese rebels.

By 1954, the rebels numbered about 10,000 armed and ten times as many "recruits" awaiting weapons. Other estimates placed their strength at 20,000 to 30,000 fighters. Most of these were concentrated in Sulawesi, where fighting cost the government 336 troops killed or seriously wounded; rebel losses were 4,634, including those captured. By year's end, the most common estimate of DI strength was 26,000, including all factions—20,000 in South Sulawesi, 5,000 in West Java, and 1,000 remaining Acehnese. Moreover, the rebellion had spread (on a smaller scale) to South Kalimantan, where it would persist until 1959. The immense pool of potential recruits allowed the rebellion to persist and grow despite suffering perhaps 1,000 battle-deaths each year of the rebellion—losses of weapons were more pressing than losses of men.

The high-water mark of DI destruction was in Sulawesi, probably in 1956. Moreover, upon the rebellion of leftist elements in December (see Intra-state War #742), DI forces stepped up their attacks. In 1957, they killed 2,447 and thereafter killed more than 1,500 each year until 1961. In June 1957, the Acehnese rebels signed a cease-fire agreement with the government, but violence elsewhere continued unabated. According to one report, far more were killed in West Java in April 1958 than had been killed in all of the fighting in central Sumatra. In 1959, a new rebel offensive in West Java came at the price of 400 DI battle-deaths from mid-February to March 10, according to the government. The government countered with a series of encirclements of rebel hideouts using the strategy of forcing local civilians to cordon the mountain bases in a *pagar bettis*, or fence of legs. This increasingly constrained rebel operations and DI access to civilians. Moreover, the government reached a negotiated settlement with the Acehnese rebels that year, providing for local autonomy and thus removing Acehnese forces from DI. The NII decreased in capabilities and strength in 1960 and 1961, continuing to take heavy casualties, especially in West Java.

Termination and Outcome: The outcome of the war was an unconditional military victory by the government. Kartosuwiryo and his five top commanders were captured on June 4, 1962. From captivity, Kartosuwiryo ordered his forces to surrender, which ended the revolt in West Java. All six men were then executed, although many of their former soldiers accepted offers of amnesty and received livelihood assistance from the government. Further operations would be required to stamp out the rebellion in Sulawesi in 1965, but the rebellion was defeated functionally with Kartosuwiryo's surrender.

Coding Decisions: Lower estimates place the death toll at 15,000 to 20,000, including civilians. Higher estimates are that 40,000 people were killed over the course of the war—an average of about 1,000 per year on the rebel side and a total of 25,000 government soldiers or civilians. We estimate 12,000 rebel battle-deaths and somewhere between 3,000 and 13,000 government battle-deaths. Accordingly, we estimate total battle-deaths at 20,000 plus or minus about 5,000.

Sources: "Army Fights Deserters in Indonesia" (1951); "Communist Influence in Indonesia" (1954); "Fanatics Hold Java in Terror" (1953); "Fanatics in Indonesia" (1951); Harvey (1974); "Indonesian Army Fighting Terrorists in Java" (1952); "Indonesia's Indigesation Troubles" (1954); Jackson (1980); Mietzner (2009); Nawawi (1968); "New Violence Flares in Indonesia" (1959); Paul, Clarke, Grill, and Dunigan (2013); "'Serious' Fighting in West Java" (1950); Soebardi (1983); Tadjoeddin (2014); Van Dijk (1981); Warner (1953); Wilde (1958).[254]

INTRA-STATE WAR #740.5
Liangshan Rebellion of 1955 to 1957 (aka Lolo Rebellion)

Participants: China and Former Slaves versus Liangshan Rebels.
Dates: December 1955 to October 1957.
Battle-related Deaths: China: thousands;[255] Total Combatant Deaths: 10,000. (See Coding Decisions.)
Initiator: Liangshan rebels.
Outcome: China wins.
War Type: Civil for local issues (opium eradication and abolition of slavery).
Total System Member Military Personnel: Armed Forces of China: 3 million (prewar, initial); 3,156,000 (peak, final).[256]
Theater Armed Forces: Armed Forces of China: 15,000 (initial). Former Slaves, aka White Yi: 200,000 (peak).[257] Liangshan Rebels, aka Black Yi or Lolo Rebels: many thousands (initial, peak).[258]

Antecedents: In 1955, the People's Liberation Army returned to Liangshan to carry out its anti-feudal efforts against the semiautonomous Yi (Lolos). These efforts, which included reeducation and struggle sessions, antagonized not only the wealthy, slave-owning Yi of the area but much of the populace as well. The particular aspects of Yi society that were targeted were opium production and slaveholding. The Yi were divided into White Yi (the majority) and the slaveholding Black Yi (about 8 percent of the population). Some subgroups of White Yi were enslaved, but Han Chinese were also among slavery's victims in the area.

Large-scale opium planting began in 1910, and by 1950 the Yi were reliant upon its profits, with enslaved White Yi commonly using the proceeds to redeem themselves or even become slaveowners. Moreover, the constant feuding between clans led to high levels of militarization—perhaps 100,000 firearms for the 600,000 Liangshan Yi. In January 1955, the government decided to extend its opium eradication program to the Yi of Liangshan in Miyi county, leading to five months of disturbances, which cost the lives of more than a dozen government cadres. The government backed off of its antidrug campaign in Yi areas but returned in December to conduct an antislavery campaign. Slaveowners, consisting mostly of Black Yi, rebelled.

Narrative: There is little reliable information about the military course of the revolt. The government committed 10,000 PLA, 5,000 militia, and eventually hundreds of thousands of former slaves to suppression of the revolt. The Yi rarely surrendered or took prisoners, so the fighting was especially vicious. Government forces reportedly suffered thousands of deaths in the fighting and had to rush more divisions to the area, and the Black Yi nearly were exterminated by the brutal response. In July 1957, the government extended the prohibition of opium to Yi areas, which it could enforce by confiscating slaveowners' land and using farmland as an incentive for freed slaves to comply.

Termination and Outcome: The revolt finally was put down in October 1957. The outcome was an unconditional government victory. The government carried out mass executions among the defeated Yi. In 1958 and 1959, a campaign to suppress counterrevolutionaries resulted in thousands of additional arrests. Low-level resistance appears to have continued until 1961.

Coding Decisions: On the basis of limited information, we estimate that battle-deaths could be 10,000, give or take 5,000 or so.

Sources: Bachman (2007); Goldstein (2014); Norbu (1986); Yongming (2004).

INTRA-STATE WAR #741

Tibetan Khamba Rebellion of 1956 to 1959 (aka Tibetan Rebellion)

Participants: China versus Khamba Tibetans (Aggregate), Goloks (Aggregate), Chushi Gangdruk, and Tibetan Autonomous Region.
Dates: March 1, 1956, to April 14, 1959.
Battle-related Deaths: China: 10,000;[259] Total Rebels: 10,000; Total Combatant Deaths: 20,000. (See Coding Decisions.)[260]
Initiator: China.
Outcome: China wins.
War Type: Civil for local issues (disarmament, religion and land reform, and independence).
Total System Member Military Personnel: Armed Forces of China: 3,130,000 (prewar, initial); 3,208,000 (peak, final).[261]
Theater Armed Forces: Armed Forces of China: 150,000 (peak). Khamba Tibetans, participating through 1958, by which time most had ceased fighting or joined Chushi Gangdruk: 6,000 (initial); at least 20,000 (peak).[262] Goloks, participating through 1957: 10,000 (peak).[263] Chushi Gangdruk, participating from June 16, 1958: 5,000 (initial); 25,000 (peak).[264] Armed Forces of the Tibetan Autonomous Region, participating from March 10, 1959: 1,500 (initial, peak).[265]

Antecedents: In 1950 and 1951, the Chinese People's Liberation Army took control of Tibet, reintegrating it into China. The mechanism of this reintegration was the 17 Point Agreement, which committed China to respect the autonomy of a Tibetan Autonomous Region in return for acknowledgement of Chinese sovereignty and a commitment from the Tibetan Dalai Lama to refrain from hosting groups seeking to undermine the Chinese state. The Tibetan Autonomous Region (at the time consisting only of Inner Tibet) left out many ethnic Tibetans in neighboring provinces (Outer Tibet), who were granted no such autonomy. Most of them were in the region of Kham (Qamdo) in Xiking province—which was divided by the communist government in 1951 and partially absorbed by Sichuan in 1955—and Amdo in the province of Qinghai. It was among these Tibetans that the rebellion began as a reaction to the anti-Buddhist and anti-feudal policies of the ruling Chinese Communist Party, especially land reform and other centralization efforts.

It is difficult to know the exact date when resistance turned into war as there were many revolts in Outer Tibet after the onset of communist rule. In 1952 and 1953, there were up to 80,000 rebels, some 12,000 of whom were deserters from the former ruling Guomindang (Kuomintang [KMT]) army. In 1953, the intensity of the fighting declined as the rebels turned to guerrilla war, but thousands of Amdowas were killed in combat, executed, or sent to labor camps.[266] The area in revolt increased in 1954 as the nomadic Goloks joined the revolt after the burning of several monasteries; meanwhile, a revolt by up to 40,000 farmers was repressed by the government.

In Kham, the Kanting (Kanding) rebellion over the winter of 1955 and 1956 consisted largely of assassinations of government officials by up to 10,000 rebels (according to a pro-Chinese source) and was successfully suppressed by the government. The earliest year for which we can be sure that more than 1000 battle-deaths occurred is 1956, which saw a marked escalation of violence. Attempts to disarm the Khambas (Khampas) spread the revolt throughout Kham. Armed insurgents flocked to the monasteries for protection. By 1956, there were about 6,000 Khamba irregulars in the field against the government, in addition to the Goloks and other groups in Amdo. A government aircraft bombed Chantreng Sampheling monastery at the end of February 1956, forcing its surrender.

Narrative: In reaction to the destruction of Chantreng Sampheling, rebels in Lithang organized to protect its monastery. At the end of February (the second day of the Tibetan new year), government forces ambushed and killed its leader, provoking an uprising. Surrounding Chinese encampments were attacked, and many were killed. Meanwhile, the government's People's Liberation Army (PLA) laid siege to Lithang monastery. The rebels repeatedly ambushed the PLA at the local water supply, and the siege lasted more than a month before the government again won victory through air power. The battle cost 3,000 to 5,000 lives, mostly Tibetans.

At about the same time, rebellion broke out in Nyarang in Sichuan. The government forces had occupied the Castle of the Female Dragon (Drukmo Dzong). About 1,400 rebels under Dorje Yudan besieged the castle and then ambushed the government force sent to relieve the siege. According to Tibetan oral history, nearly 1,000 PLA were allegedly killed against only 26 rebels, but soon the government sent more forces, and the rebels were forced to split into two columns. One of these—2,000 fighters and family members—kept government forces occupied for the next year before being defeated. In all, the Nyarang fighting may have cost the government 2,000 battle-deaths.

The nomadic Goloks of Amdo also rebelled in 1956, destroying a Chinese garrison early in the year. By the following spring, they were rumored to be 20,000 strong (but were probably closer to 10,000 in number). Refugees began crossing into the Tibetan Autonomous Region (TAR) but received little encouragement from the TAR or the Dalai Lama, who urged patience. As the year progressed, the rebellion spread—by autumn, there were tens of thousands of rebels. The guerrillas became more effective at inflicting casualties as the year wore on, wiping out many isolated garrisons. Throughout 1956, the PLA may have suffered 8,000 killed and a further 2,000 maimed, their noses cut off by Golok irregulars.

Rebel groups could mobilize large numbers for limited times, but the logistical challenges were formidable. One rebel group peaked at 10,000 fighters in 1957 before splitting up due to supply difficulties. Also that year, a rebel named Gompo Tashi Andrugtsang took to the field against the government in Lhoka with a force of hundreds that had been organized the previous October as Chushi Gangdruk (Four Rivers Six Ranges, an old nickname for Kham). It quickly became the dominant Khamba organization; by June 1958 it had 20,000 to 30,000 poorly armed members. Meanwhile, the Goloks were reported to have inflicted 7,000 to 8,000 battle-deaths on the PLA during 1957, a figure that was no doubt grossly exaggerated. One hears nothing further about the Goloks in histories of the rebellion; presumably they were suppressed by the end of the year, by which time the government had 150,000 troops in eight divisions deployed against the rebels.

In 1958, the United States began covertly to arm the Tibetan rebels in Kham. It also trained selected rebels and infiltrated them back into Tibet. Meanwhile, the war spread into the orders of the TAR. As Chushi Gangdruk kept withdrawing into the TAR after mounting attacks, PLA troops would pursue. In May, fighting may have approached Lhasa itself; the government reportedly suffered 1,000 killed and partially withdrew. Chushi Gangdruk established a base south of Lhasa at Tsona, which the government pressured the Dalai Lama to close. However, the TAR had only weak forces available, which would not attack fellow Tibetans in any case. Small-unit engagements continued through the end of 1958; Norbu documents fourteen from August to January 1959, with perhaps 1,800 to 1,900 government deaths and more than 107 rebel deaths.

By the beginning of 1959, Chushi Gangdruk largely was confined to the TAR, occasionally making forays into Kham to attack isolated PLA garrisons. As government pressure on the Dalai Lama mounted, people and officials in the TAR began to fear that he would be kidnapped by the Chinese and surrounded the Norbulingka in Lhasa. Most officials took refuge there, and the crowds began to call for Tibetan independence. On March 17, the Dalai Lama fled to India. Once his absence was discovered, the PLA moved in on March 21 to seize Lhasa and the Norbulingka. Three days of bloody street fighting followed, in which the PLA was victorious. The government suffered more than 2,000 battle-deaths, but the rebels' losses were much higher at up to 12,000 killed, including civilians. Having gained control of Lhasa, the government moved against the Chushi Gangdruk base at Tsona.

Termination and Outcome: On April 14, Tsona fell to government forces, ending the high-intensity portion of the civil conflict. Guerrilla resistance would continue until the 1970s, albeit at sub-war levels. The outcome of the war was effectively an unconditional military victory by the government. There is some evidence of postwar massacres and executions; the TAR was retained and even enlarged over time to include much of Kham.

Coding Decisions: Rebel sources place their battle-deaths at between 5,000 and 10,000, probably an underestimate. On the other hand, the rebels claim grossly exaggerated figures for government battle-deaths—about 20,000 if one adds up the totals from the narrative. Taking the high estimate for the rebels and halving the estimate for the government provides a total of 20,000 battle-deaths, a figure likely to be accurate within 10,000.

Sources: Ardley (2002); Clodfelter (2008); Durham (2004); McCarthy (1997); McGranahan (2001); Norbu (1979, 2001); Richardson (1984); Shakya (1999); Smith (1996); van Schaik (2011).[267]

INTRA-STATE WAR #741.5
Naga Insurgency phase 1 of 1956 to 1957

Participants: India versus Naga Home Guard.
Dates: April 1956 to March 1957.
Battle-related Deaths: Total Combatant Deaths: 1,000. (See Coding Decisions.)[268]
Initiator: India.
Outcome: Fell below civil-war threshold.
War Type: Civil for local issues (independence).
Total System Member Military Personnel: Armed Forces of India: 400,000 (prewar, initial), 445,000 (peak, final).[269]
Theater Armed Forces: Naga Home Guard: 5,000 (prewar, initial); 15,000 (peak, final).[270]

Antecedents: India's remote Northeast is home to the state of Assam, containing many tribes with only loose historical connections to India. One of these minorities, the Nagas, sought autonomy and then independence from India less than a decade after the modern state was formed. In 1929 the first demand for autonomy was made by Nagas as a group; the Naga National Council (NNC) was formed in 1946 to follow up on the 1929 petition. They signed a ten-year agreement with the governor of Assam, but it was repudiated by the central government, and on August 14, 1947—the day before India did the same—the NNC declared its independence.

Angami Zapu Phizo was selected to lead the NNC in 1949. Under his leadership, a flawed referendum was held in some areas of the Naga Hills ratifying independence. In 1953, after the NNC organized a protest against Prime Minister Nehru, the state of Assam began to crack down on the organization. All Naga councils and courts were dismissed. On January 1, 1955, the Assam Disturbed Areas Act, which severely restricted civil liberties in the region and immunized police from prosecution for rights violations, went into effect. On March 22, 1956, the NNC formed the Naga federal government, complete with a constitution and a security force, the Naga home guard.

Narrative: The central government responded to the formation of the Naga federal government by sending in federal troops to defeat the Naga army. Fighting began in April and intensified in May. The rebels began with a hard core of 5,000 fighters, but their strength increased over time; by the end of 1956, there were 15,000 Naga rebels. By July 31, the government estimated that 68 police or army personnel had been killed against 371 rebels. Battles were fought at Tuensang and Zunheboto. The fighting was bitter, and human rights violations were routine—"no quarter was given or asked for."[271] Beginning in September, the intensity of the fighting declined. Guerrilla resistance continued, but a split between moderates and Phizo's nationalists developed, and some intra-NNC fighting took place.

Termination and Outcome: While the first year of fighting probably resulted in more than 1,000 battle-deaths (see previous discussion), it is less clear that subsequent years met this criterion. The conflict thus fell below the threshold of civil war. In the long run, the government made a peace deal with the moderate faction of the insurgents, resulting in Nagaland becoming an Indian state in 1964. It took another decade to reach a cease-fire with more radical elements.

Coding Decisions: According to Zhimoni, no systematic records exist on the casualties of both sides. The rebels claimed to have killed hundreds of Indian soldiers in ambushes by the end of 1956, while pro-rebel source Iralu writes that at least 140,000 Nagas died from 1954 to 1964, including 34,244 in Sema alone between 1952 and 1960, of which 10,358 died by bullet (the remainder perished in concentration camps or starved). Clodfelter says that the government acknowledged the deaths of 1,400 rebels and 162 Indian security personnel in 1956 and 1957, but Ali claims the statistic refers to the period from summer 1956 to summer 1958. Given that the fiercest fighting appears to have taken place in 1956, we find it plausible that 1,000 battle-deaths occurred during the year following the onset of the revolt.

Sources: Ali (1993); Horam (1988); Iralu (2009); Mankekar (1967); Yonuo (1984); Zhimoni (2004).

INTRA-STATE WAR #742
Permesta Rebellion of 1958 to 1961 (aka Indonesian Leftists)

Participants: Indonesia versus Permesta Rebels.
Dates: February 21, 1958, to August 17, 1961.
Battle-related Deaths: Armed Forces of Indonesia: 4,000; Permesta Rebels: 2,000; Total Combatant Deaths: 6,000. (See Coding Decisions.)[272]
Initiator: Indonesia.
Outcome: Indonesia wins.
War Type: Civil for central control.
Total System Member Military Personnel: Armed Forces of Indonesia: 265,000 (prewar); 282,000 (initial); 375,000 (peak); 375,000 (final).[273]
Theater Armed Forces: Permesta Rebels, aka Revolutionary Government of the Republic of Indonesia (PRRI)/Federal Government of Indonesia (RPI): thousands (initial); 15,000 (peak).[274]

Antecedents: By the mid-1950s, warlordism began to emerge in Indonesia as military commanders were left short of supplies and payment for their troops due to an economic downturn. Regional commanders increasingly turned to bartering, smuggling, and in some instances collaboration with the Darul Islam rebels (see Intra-state War #738) to finance their troops, on which their political influence rested. Abdul Haris Nasution was appointed army chief of staff on November 7, 1955, and attempted to recentralize the armed forces, rotating commanders to other regions or replacing them with loyalists. This prompted one commander due for transfer, Col. Zulkifli Lubis, to attempt a coup on November 15, 1956. The coup failed, and Lubis went into hiding, while the government began to arrest his supporters.

Alarmed at this turn of events, a group of Sumatran officers planned what amounted to another coup on December 4, setting forth a secret manifesto that called for the restoration of unity to the army, dissolving the cabinet, and weakening the parliament. This December 4 Idea would be reiterated in the demands of various regional commanders who joined the coming rebellion. On December 20, Col. Ahmad Husein seized civil power in West Sumatra; two days later, Col. Maludin Simbolon proclaimed himself governor of North Sumatra. The government responded by dismissing Simbolon in favor of a loyal subordinate, who was able to gain control of the troops. Simbolon fled to join Husein in West Sumatra.

In mid-January 1957, Lt. Colonel Barlian proclaimed the formation of a military council in South Sumatra, although he did not cut ties to the central government because there were many Javanese troops in his region. On March 9, he assumed the governorship; in response, a loyalist Javanese regimental commander attempted to depose him. The attempt failed, and Barlian called on Husein for support; the latter promised 1,200 troops in the event of central government intervention against the former. Meanwhile on March 2, Lt. Colonel "Vientje" Sumual in Sulawesi proclaimed a state of emergency in East Indonesia and instituted martial law, promulgating the Charter of Inclusive Struggle. The document—*Piagam Perjuangan Semesta Alam*—was shortened to Permesta, which became the name of the rebellion.

Nasution and the government responded to the rebellions by proclaiming autonomy for some areas of Sumatra, attempting to undercut civilian support for the rebels. In March, Nasution appointed Husein to lead one the newly created command in central Sumatra, which served to pacify him; later in the year, he would be appointed to a governorship. On March 14, President Sukarno proclaimed a state of emergency and dismissed the cabinet; the rebels were seemingly being granted most of their demands without any real fighting. However, in early April a new cabinet was formed that excluded the mutineers' favored candidate, the West Sumatran Mohamad Hatta. Negotiations followed, but Permesta leaders, whose anticommunism assured them of support by the United States (which was skeptical of Sukarno's neutralist course in the Cold War and tolerance of the Communist Party), refused any real compromise. A peace conference convened on September 10, but the government proved unwilling to meet the core demand for shared leadership between Sukarno and Hatta.

On November 30, anticommunist youth attempted to assassinate Sukarno; at trial, the suspects implicated Lubis, who had made his way to refuge among the Permesta mutineers in Sumatra. On January 9, 1958, the dissident officers began to plan for the formation of a joint government to resist the center. On February 10, Husein presented the government with an ultimatum—either appoint Hatta and dismiss the cabinet or see the formation of a rival government. When the ultimatum expired on

February 15, Husein declared the formation of the Revolutionary Government of the Republic of Indonesia (PRRI). Aside from Barlian, who declared his neutrality, most other rebel commanders joined him. The government swiftly dismissed rebel members of the cabinet and military rebels from their posts.

Narrative: On February 21, the government attacked the rebels in three locations by air, knocking out the rebels' main radio station. The bombing of the capital of North Sulawesi solidified local public support for the rebellion. From the outset, the rebels on Sumatra planned a guerrilla strategy, while the government planned to secure vital resources and only then turn to the destruction of rebel forces. On March 12, two companies of government paratroops seized Pekanbaru airfield and the nearby oil fields and refinery on Sumatra. Meanwhile, the government conducted a landing in central Sualwesi on March 31. In the face of government landings on the east coast of Sumatra, Husein withdrew his troops westward. Although there is evidence that the United States was willing to intervene directly for the rebels (it was already supplying them with weapons), Husein's failure to make a stand deprived it of a pretext for intervention. American air supply of the rebels was terminated in mid-1958. On April 17, the government mounted its offensive against West Sumatra. After several weeks of hard fighting, the rebel capital of Bukittinggi fell on May 4 and May 5. The rebels massacred 147 communist prisoners and then transferred their government to Manado in North Sulawesi, dividing their operations into northern and southern sectors.

In Sulawesi, the Permesta rebels decided to seize airfields within range of Jakarta, so they could bomb the capital. They assumed that government operations in Sumatra would take some time that they could use to build their movement in North Sulawesi. Indeed, by June they were able to raise substantial forces. Altogether, Permesta strength stood at about 15,000. It included a revolutionary air force on Sulawesi, staffed with foreign pilots. The Sulawesi rebels' first attacks took place on April 13, and soon two airfields were under rebel control. On May 8, the landing in central Sulawesi essentially was defeated, with the rebels recapturing all important towns from the government's forces. A government counteroffensive kicked off on May 14, and soon the rebels had been pushed back. Some fleeing Permesta rebels went on to join the Darul Islam rebellion in South Sulawesi (see Intra-state War #738). The government invaded the Minahasa peninsula in North Sulawesi on June 13 and Manado itself fell on June 26. North Sulawesi rebel forces withdrew to Tomohon (where 1,500 of them surrendered to government forces on August 16 rather than defend the town), and many of the recruits turned to guerrilla warfare.

For the rest of the year, initiative shifted to the Sumatran rebels, who attacked isolated outposts and overextended government supply lines almost at will. As long as predominantly Javanese troops were used by the government, the rebels could count on some support among the civilian populace. However, the government increasingly forced civilians into active participation in the war by forming Perpeda, a system of local administration and civil guards. These were assisted by some 6,000 largely communist youth in the People's Defense Organization (OPR). By the end of 1959, the rebels had been pushed back on every front in Sumatra, although Sulawesi rebels had inflicted more casualties on government forces than in 1958. On September 18, 1959, the last major rebel base in North Sulawesi, Kotamobagu, fell to government forces. The guerrillas were now trapped on the Minahasa peninsula.

What cooperation existed between Permesta and the DI waned after Sukarno abolished the Constitution of 1950, replacing it with the more pro-military revolutionary Constitution of 1945. For the PRRI, this was movement toward some of its goals, while it failed to move Indonesia toward any sort of Islamic State. The military rebels began to seek a way out of the war.

On February 8, 1960, the PRRI proclaimed a Federal Government of Indonesia (RPI), espousing the cause of federalism. This appears to have triggered another major offensive by the government. The Sumatran rebel headquarters of Kototinggi fell in July, leading to the loss of control over the RPI by its civilian leaders, but guerrilla resistance from military units continued. The rebels controlled much of the terrain apart from towns and major highways, a situation that remained true almost a year later. At the end of 1960, the government began efforts to convince the military commanders to return to the government side. These efforts paid dividends in April 1961, when the North Sulawesi rebels agreed to rejoin government forces, some 8,000 armed guerrillas surrendering with the promise of amnesty. Small units began to surrender on Sumatra. On June 21, Husein surrendered with about 100 men and ordered the rest of his followers to do the same "or he would hunt them down" (Kahin, 226). The bulk of the Sumatran insurgents—several thousand rebels—surrendered in June and July. On August 12, the last of the major commander surrendered; five days later, the rebels' civilian government ordered the complete cessation of hostilities. That same day, Sukarno announced an amnesty for all who surrendered by October 5.

Termination and Outcome: The war ended on August 17; those few commanders who held out trickled in during the amnesty period. The outcome of the war was a government victory with a promise of amnesty, which was more or less honored for enlisted men, although civilian supporters of the insurgency often were attacked and arrested by communists after the war. Officers were imprisoned upon their surrender and sent to Java at the end of the year.

Coding Decisions: Estimates of total deaths range from 13,000 to 30,000. The most specific estimate of battle-deaths is that Permesta suffered 2,000 battle-deaths and the government suffered 4,000, for a total of 6,000 battle-deaths.

Sources: Friend (2003); Harvey (1977); Kahin (1999); Kahin and Kahin (1995).[275]

INTRA-STATE WAR #746
Second Burmese War of 1958 to 1960

Participants: Burma versus Communist Party of Burma, Karen National Defense Organization, Karenni National Progressive Party, United Pa-O Organization, Kachin Independence Army, Shan Rebels, and KMT Remnants.
Dates: October 28, 1958, to April 1960.
Battle-related Deaths: Total Combatant Deaths: 1,500. (See Coding Decisions.)[276]
Initiator: Burma.
Outcome: Fighting fell below civil-war threshold.
War Type: Civil for central control (but see Coding Decisions).
Total System Member Military Personnel: Armed Forces of Burma: 56,000 (prewar); 67,000 (initial); 79,000 (peak); 79,000 (final).[277]
Theater Armed Forces: The rebels in the field may have numbered 15,000 in all (linearly interpolated from 1953 and 1962 estimates) plus the 7,000-strong KMT for a total of 22,000 troops opposing the government.[278] Communist Party of Burma: 4,000 to 5,000 (final—1960 estimate).[279] Karen National Defense Organization/Karen People's Liberation Army (Rebel Army): 5,000 (final—1963 estimate).[280] Karenni National Progressive Party: unknown. United Pa-O Organization: unknown. Kachin Independence Army, participating from about March 1960, when it finally met the 100-participant threshold for inclusion: 30 (prewar); 100 (initial).[281] Shan Rebels/Shan State Independence Army, participating from November 16, 1959: 450 (prewar); 1,000 (initial); 2,000 (peak—interpolated from 1959 and 1961 estimates).[282] KMT Remnants, participating throughout the war; although it usually sought to avoid engagements with government forces, the latter would attack it on sight: 7,000 (initial); 7000 (peak).[283]

Antecedents: By 1957, the Burmese army had been transformed into a powerful political and economic actor led by Ne Win with little real civilian control. When socialist prime minister U Nu proposed a peace initiative to transform leftist rebels into legal political parties, he was partly successful, securing the surrender of 2,000 PVO rebels who had been in arms since 1948 (see Intra-state War #732). But fears that the Burmese Communist Party would be legalized led to a military coup on September 26, 1958. The military formed a government with Ne Win at its head on October 28; the latter argued that rebel activity was increasing and that the civilian government was too divided to take action. Whatever the real reason for the coup, the military mounted a campaign against the country's insurgent groups.

Narrative: The government publicly estimated that there were 9,000 insurgents in the country in November. Though this was an underestimate, the Communist Party of Burma (CPB) had been in decline for some time, as had the Karen insurgents. By 1960—just fourteen months later—it estimated that 1,872 insurgents had been killed, 1,959 wounded, 1,238 captured, and 3,618 surrendered.

While these figures are dubious, there was clearly an uptick in fighting and some major surrenders during this period. The fighting took place between the government and a loose alliance of the CPB and an alphabet soup of ethnic resistance movements. Most of the larger groups were members of the National Democratic United Front (NDUF). In July 1959, amid growing rebel activity, the government offered amnesty to the insurgents; a number surrendered.

A new insurrection was that of the Shan, who demanded independence and numbered a few hundred at the onset of the war. Their first combat was on November 16, 1959; less than a week later, they seized the town of Yang-yan and looted its armory. They were eventually supported by the Guomindang (Kuomintang [KMT]) forces still lurking in the jungles of Shan state. Moreover, the Kachins rebelled again in March 1960, in response to U Nu's promise to make Burma a Buddhist state.

Termination and Outcome: We have no data on fatalities beyond April 1960, but that month seems to mark the end of this poorly documented phase of fighting. The government reduced the insurgents to the point that they were unable to inflict civil-war-scale casualties. The outcome of the war was a stalemate that ultimately favored the government. In December 1960 the government, with assistance from the People's Republic of China, mounted Operation Mekong against the KMT. About 3,000 KMT left Burma as a result of the offensive, joining the troops of Gen. Phoumi Nosavan in Laos. Only 4,000 remained in Burma as of mid-February 1961. Over the next two months, most of them were evacuated to Formosa (now Taiwan).

Coding Decisions: The war was fought by both rebels seeking to overthrow the state and rebels seeking to secede from it. Because the CPB seemed to be the linchpin of the rebel alliance, we code the contest as a civil war for control of the central government. Lintner calls the government's estimate of 1,872 rebels killed and 1,959 wounded to the beginning of 1960 "grossly inflated" (207). The same report claimed only 520 government battle-deaths for the same period. Despite reservations, both Clodfelter and Tinker give figures of 2,278 rebels killed and 2,351 wounded. Historians are therefore divided on the subject, and we conclude that it is possible that the high figures are correct. Still, we estimate that the government at least doubled the number of rebel fatalities; counting the government's own (doubtless underreported) losses, there may have been roughly 1,500 battle-deaths.

Sources: Clodfelter (2008); Lintner (1999), Scott (1966), Tinker (1961).[284]

INTRA-STATE WAR #748

Vietnam War phase 1 of 1960 to 1965

Participants: Republic of Vietnam and United States versus National Liberation Front and Democratic Republic of Vietnam.

Dates: January 17, 1960, to February 6, 1965.

Battle-related Deaths: Armed Forces of the Republic of Vietnam: 25,000[285]; Armed Forces of the United States: 458;[286] National Liberation Front: 41,500;[287] Total Combatant Deaths: 67,000. (See Coding Decisions.)[288]

Initiator: National Liberation Front (before it was named as such).

Outcome: Transforms into inter-state war #163.

War Type: Civil for central control.

Total System Member Military Personnel: Armed forces of the Republic of Vietnam: 160,000 (prewar, initial); 565,000 (peak, final). Armed Forces of the United States of America: 2,328,000 (prewar); 2,306,000 (initial); 2,807,000 (peak); 2,660,000 (final). Armed Forces of the Democratic Republic of Vietnam: 230,000 (prewar); 240,000 (initial); 260,000 (peak); 256,000 (final).[289]

Theater Armed Forces: Armed Forces of the Republic of Vietnam: same as system member personnel. Armed Forces of the United States of America, participating from the beginning of 1961: 1,000 (initial); 23,300 (peak); 23,300 (final).[290] National Liberation Front, aka People's Liberation Armed Forces (see Coding Decisions): 10,000 plus militia (initial); 106,700 (peak); 106,700 (final). Armed Forces of the Democratic Republic of Vietnam, aka People's Army of North Vietnam, participating from November 20, 1964: 1,000 (initial); 5,000 (peak, final). The peak and final estimates are rough interpolations between 2,500 at the end of 1964 and 8,500 in April 1965.[291]

Antecedents: Although the division of Vietnam into northern and southern halves was conceived as being temporary when it was worked out in 1954, no unifying election ever was held. Instead, the government of the Republic of Vietnam (South Vietnam) persecuted former Viet Minh in its territory, who responded with assassinations and bombings. Organized resistance to the government of South Vietnam began in October 1957 with the creation of communist rebel units in central and southwestern areas of the new state. By the end of the year, there were thirty-eight such units, and in 1958 they began to engage the Army of the Republic of Vietnam (ARVN) in combat. Propelled by the momentum of events, wishing to buttress its socialist credentials, and determined to retain control of the insurrection in the South, the government of Democratic Republic of Vietnam (North Vietnam) resolved to support revolution through low-intensity operations and assassinations in January 1959.

At this time, the would-be rebels in the South had fewer than 10,000 fighters; those who were armed carried archaic weapons. Moreover, repression by the South Vietnamese regime had decimated the ranks of communist supporters. A later official history by the North Vietnamese revealed that from 1957 to 1959, more than 10,000 communists were killed or captured in Can Tho and Soc Trang provinces alone. In Ben Tre, another 17,000 had been either killed or captured and tortured. In the Central Highlands, some 70 percent of party cell executives, 60 percent of district executives, and 40 percent of provincial executives had been captured or killed. The rebellion was weak and lacked a support base. The North responded by infiltrating up to 4,600 formerly southern cadres, technicians, and military advisors—as "volunteers"—into the South between 1959 and 1960. To facilitate the movement of advisors and supplies, North Vietnam upgraded infrastructure along the borders with Laos and Cambodia—the Ho Chi Minh Trail. Finally, Southerners responded to the North Vietnamese resolution by mounting a wave of more than 1,700 assassinations of government officials and employees from 1959 to 1960 and encouraging popular uprisings throughout 1959.

The government struck back by promulgating a law in May 1959 that mandated death sentences for those engaged in the rebellion. Within months, it had arrested half a million people and executed 68,000 of them. It quickly suppressed the popular uprisings and retook control of most villages in the second half of the year. The insurgents found themselves unable to expand or even to maintain their holdings without offensive action and new uprisings.

Narrative: On January 17, 1960, a major uprising broke out in Ben Tre province; although ARVN forces quickly squashed the uprising, its temporary success set off a chain of similar uprisings across the South. Indeed, there were hundreds of such actions over the next few months, marking the escalation of the civil conflict to civil war. The rebels continued to assassinate an average of 130 people each month and began to consolidate liberated zones at the village level, establishing popular committees and rebuilding the party's structure while engaging in land reform to win converts to the cause. At one point or another during 1960, they had exerted control over one-third of the country's population. At the end of the year, a National Liberation Front was announced, with the People's Liberation Armed Forces as its military wing, subordinated to the People's Army of Vietnam (North Vietnam's armed forces).

The PAVN aided the PLAF by infiltrating another 19,150 personnel—generally former Southerners—into the South from 1961 to 1962. During the first half of 1961, the rebels killed about 1,500 government troops and assassinated or kidnapped another 2,000 officials or government supporters. The government responded by upgrading its armed forces with American aid and by launching a strategic hamlet program to cut the NLF off from its peasant support base. By the end of the year, there were 500 strategic hamlets; the number rose to 4,000 by the end of 1962. In October 1961, the United States deployed forty helicopters and 400 troops to maintain and protect them to Saigon. The result was an increase in ARVN capabilities, especially once more aid and troops arrived in 1962, bringing the total US presence to 10,000.

In January 1963, an engagement at Ap Bac resulted in the defeat of a sizeable government force at the hands of greatly outnumbered guerrillas. The battle's outcome strengthened the hand of those in the North who favored greater intervention on behalf of the rebels. In September, further troops and advisors were sent from the North to the NLF—in all, another 7,850 PAVN "volunteers" infiltrated the South that year. On November 2, the government of South Vietnam was overthrown in a military coup. Fearing that the new regime would defeat the rebels (membership in the NLF dropped immediately after the coup), North Vietnamese leaders resolved on a policy of direct intervention in the South by January 20, 1964. They conducted a purge and then mobilized for possible war with South Vietnam and the United States. Within weeks, NLF attacks were up 40 percent in the South, and serious encounters rose by 75 percent. American intelligence detected massive buildups of supplies headed south. Though the number of American advisors rose to 23,000, the United States decided against initiating war with North Vietnam.

Following the Gulf of Tonkin incident in August, the United States conducted retaliatory bombing of North Vietnam. After this, the North decided to directly commit PAVN units to the war in the South. The first units departed for the South on November 20. Less than three weeks earlier, NLF forces had attacked an American airfield at Bien Hoa, killing four American troops and wounding another thirty. On December 6, a joint NLF–PAVN offensive kicked off with a massive attack on government forces at An Lao.

Termination and Outcome: This intra-state war ended on February 6, 1965, as it was transformed as of February 7, 1965, into an inter-state war when NLF forces attacked the American camp at Pleiku, inflicting 8 battle-deaths and 100 injuries. Three days later, a hotel bombing by the NLF killed 23 US troops. The United States responded by massively escalating its involvement in South Vietnam. Operation Rolling Thunder, an aerial attack on North Vietnam, was authorized on February 13.

On March 2, the first missions of Rolling Thunder were flown. The inter-state war that followed ultimately led to the escalation and then withdrawal of American and other allied forces, followed by the victory of North Vietnamese regulars over South Vietnam, even though the latter largely had crushed the NLF itself as an independent force by early 1969.

Coding Decisions: The government suffered 21,442 battle-deaths from 1961 to 1964. Adding in those experienced in 1960 and the first two months of 1965 probably brings the total to about 25,000. The government's estimate of about 83,000 rebel deaths during this phase was likely a gross overestimate. Generally, government estimates were 30 percent too high and included civilians, so we very roughly estimate that half of these (about 41,500) were actual battle-deaths. This yields a total of 66,500. Adding in American losses brings the total to about 67,000.

The National Liberation Front functionally participated throughout the war, although it was not named as such until December 1960. Its theater force estimates include militia and southern PAVN "volunteers" or "regroupees" who were integrated into the NLF but not PAVN units themselves.

Sources: Asselin (2013); Clodfelter (1995).[292]

INTRA-STATE WAR #749

First Laotian War of 1960 to 1968 (aka Laotian Civil War, phases 1–3)

Participants: Laos, United States, and Vang Pao–led Forces versus Neutralists, Pathet Lao, and the Democratic Republic of Vietnam.

Dates: May 24, 1960, to June 6, 1961, and January 25, 1962, to June 23, 1962, and March 19, 1963, to January 12, 1968.

Battle-related Deaths: United States of America: 172;[293] Total Combatant Deaths: at least 10,000. (See Coding Decisions.)[294]

Initiator: Pathet Lao.

Outcome: Transformed into inter-state war #170.

War Type: Civil for central control.

Total System Member Military Personnel: Armed Forces of Laos, aka Royal Lao Army: 29,000 (prewar); 29,000 (initial); 101,000 (peak—includes 8,000 more or less integrated neutralists).[295] Armed Forces of the United States of America: 2,306,000 (prewar, initial), 3,550,000 (peak, final).[296] Armed Forces of the Democratic Republic of Vietnam: 240,000 (prewar, initial); 447,000 (peak, final).[297]

Theater Armed Forces: United States of America: air campaign only. Vang Pao–led Forces, participating from late 1960: 9,000 (initial); about 35,000 (peak—early 1968 estimate).[298]

Neutralists, aka Kong Le–led Forces, participating from August 9, 1960, to the beginning of April 1963 on the rebel side and from the beginning of April 1963 to October 16, 1966, on the government side before effectively being integrated into government forces: 600 (initial); 12,000 (peak); 8,000 (final—1967 estimate).[299] Pathet Lao, aka Lao People's Liberation Army: 3,500 to 5,500 (prewar summer 1959 estimate); 8,000 (initial—interpolated from 1959 and 1962 estimates); 30,000 (peak); 30,000 (final).[300] Democratic Republic of Vietnam: up to 10,000 (initial); 25,000 (peak); 25,000 (final).[301]

Antecedents: The communist Pathet Lao participated in the rebellion against French rule and entered Laos in 1953. When the French withdrew, low-level fighting between the government and the Pathet Lao continued, eventually leading to a peace agreement and a coalition government in 1957. Integration of Pathet Lao forces stalled in 1958, and in May 1959 a disastrous attempt to integrate two Pathet Lao battalions led to a new round of fighting in which the rebels were supported by the North Vietnamese Army (NVA). The government repelled the attack in Sam Neua province, but fighting continued to escalate, and communist deputies were arrested in the capital. Communists contested the elections of April 1960, but vote rigging brought rightists affiliated with Defense Minister Phoumi Nosavan to power almost everywhere, undercutting the popular center (which was widely thought to have won the elections) and the left alike.

Narrative: After the elections, the Pathet Lao resumed attacking government garrisons. On May 23, the imprisoned communist deputies escaped and fled into the countryside. This seems to mark an escalation of the fighting, for within one year 1,000 combatants would be dead. Accordingly, we code May 24 as the first day of the full-scale civil war.

On August 9, 1960, the Second Parachute Battalion under "neutralist" Kong Le, which had been heavily involved in the fighting against the Pathet Lao, mounted a coup and offered the communists and royalists participation in a coalition government. The Pathet Lao sent forces into the capital of Vientiane, which were joined by an NVA artillery unit. Moreover, China supplied enough weapons to arm 20,000 Pathet Lao.

The right-wing royalists responded to the coup by massing forces in Savannakhet for an assault on Vientiane. On September 19, the advance guard of the rightist forces was defeated and forced to retreat by Kong Le's paratroopers. A week later, the Pathet Lao and NVA captured Som Neva. The coup led to mobilization among the ethnic Hmong (Meo), and rightist Vang Pao was able to raise about 9,000 Hmong irregulars by December. After heavy fighting, rightist forces retook the capital on December 8, with both Kong Le and the Pathet Lao forced to withdraw north. About 600 people, mostly civilians, were killed in the battle for Vientiane.

The rebel forces then moved east, taking the Plain of Jars in Xieng Khouang province on January 1, despite opposition from 9,000 rightist soldiers and an equal number of Vang Pao's guerrillas, who were soon armed by the United States. Early in 1961, North Vietnam sent infantry, artillery, and engineer battalions—up to 12,000 "advisers" in all—into Laos. In January, the NVA and Pathet Lao captured Tha Vieng and Tha Thom, beating back the government's offensive. Pathet Lao and NVA troops expanded their control, and by March central Laos and the road between Sala Phou Khoun and Vangviang lay under their control. The latter town fell to a joint Neutralist–Pathet Lao attack on April 23.

Fighting gradually subsided as the government repeatedly delayed further planned offensives against the Plain of Jars, and a cease-fire was agreed on May 3, 1961. Despite the cease-fire, the Pathet Lao soon took Sepon along the Ho Chi Minh Trail in southern Laos and the Hmong continued to fight the Pathet Lao until June 6, when they were forced to withdraw from their mountain base at Padong to new positions at Long Chieng and Sam Thong. Having secured significant ground and demonstrated their ability to conduct offensive operations at will, the rebels dramatically reduced their attacks for the rest of the cease-fire period. Negotiations began in June, and the parties agreed on a tripartite government of right, left, and neutralist elements.

However, negotiations on the details of this proposed arrangement stalled as Phoumi, acting behind the scenes, insisted on detailed portfolio assignments and disarmament plans before meeting again, and the government built up forces at Nam Tha in the Northwest, a position useless for strategic defense but potentially threatening to the communist forces. The NVA and Pathet Lao countered with a buildup of their own late in the year, and when another round of talks finally was opened on January 10, 1962, small-scale fighting already was taking place in the form of movement into buffer zones and probing attacks. On January 25, communist forces mortared Nam Tha, which the government used as a pretext for breaking off negotiations.

Communist bombardment of Nam Tha began in earnest on February 1, but the government reinforced the position, probably seeking to draw the United States into the war should it suffer defeat. These actions merely provoked the NVA and Pathet Lao, who eventually routed the government forces on May 6, 1962. Many government soldiers crossed the border into Thailand, and the United States warned that it would not tolerate a unilateral communist takeover of Laos, even as it worked to undermine the position of the intransigent Phoumi. The United States then airlifted 3,000 government soldiers from Thailand back into Laos. Meanwhile, the Americans mounted an ambitious covert effort to arm the Hmong and other ethnic minorities such as the Kha in the Pathet Lao zone of control, beginning on or after the program's February 5, 1962, authorization. The number of Hmong under arms increased from 9,000 in December 1960 to 18,000 in December 1962. The Pathet Lao began once more to attack Hmong and other minorities' positions, attacks that persisted throughout the dry season.

Talks resumed in early June, and on June 11, a coalition government was arranged; its neutralist prime minister took power on June 24, eliciting promises of cooperation from all three factions. Each side was permitted to continue administering the territory it controlled. On July 23, an international accord on the neutrality of Laos was reached, and while it contained loopholes, it reduced external involvement in the country. Most American advisors and about half the NVA in Laos withdrew, but ultimately the failure of the accords to produce a full NVA withdrawal undermined the agreement and aggravated the security dilemma between the sides. For its part, the Pathet Lao demanded that the United States stop resupply flights to isolated Hmong guerrillas in its territory. In November, an agreement to form a new national army by drawing equally from the three factions was reached, although it was never implemented.

On November 29, an American transport seeking to resupply neutralist forces on the Plain of Jars at the prime minister's request was shot down by antiaircraft fire from disaffected neutralists. An increasing rift developed within Kong Le's 4,500 neutralists and between them and the Pathet Lao. The prime minister asked for a full resupply of Kong Le's forces from the United States, and flights resumed by the middle of February 1963. Nevertheless, a leftist neutralist faction broke with Kong Le, was immediately declared to be the "true" neutralist faction by the Pathet Lao, and began to fight Kong Le's forces. By April 8, Kong Le was in full retreat, and within days Pathet Lao members of the coalition once again fled Vientiane to resume armed struggle.

The prime minister and Kong Le, alarmed by the Pathet Lao's actions, drew closer to Phoumi, and neutralism began to disappear. On May 15, NVA and Pathet Lao forces began the bombardment of Kong Le's remaining positions. Throughout the summer they mounted attacks against small, isolated Hmong and neutralist positions. After the Pathet Lao took the village of Ban Tha Tang, the United States upgraded the Laotian air force.

On November 2, the Hmong positions at Tha Lin Noi fell to the communist forces. The next month, the prime minister and the Pathet Lao signed an agreement to demilitarize and neutralize the royal capital of Luang Prabang, but the agreement was torpedoed by Phoumi, who insisted on similar concessions in Pathet Lao–held areas. The tempo of NVA-Pathet Lao operations began to quicken, taking Lak Sao and Kham Keut in central Laos late in the month. They took Nong Boua the next month after six months of bombardment and harassing attacks. And on January 29, 1964, the government army was forced from the Na Kay plateau. From Lak Sao to Nhommareth, the Pathet Lao now controlled Route 8. The NVA and Pathet Lao continued to advance, and a government effort to retake Tha Lin Noi was quickly defeated.

A new tripartite cease-fire was proclaimed, but the Pathet Lao insisted upon the neutralization and demilitarization of both Luang Prabang and Vientiane itself. On April 19, a right-wing military coup temporarily deposed the coalition government, forcing concessions from the civilians. In the ensuing political chaos, the Pathet Lao seized vital government defensive lines and a hill overlooking Route 7—the route by which the government had been resupplying the neutralists. On May 16, the Pathet Lao mounted a major attack on Kong Le's forces. Neutralist positions collapsed, and they were driven to the western edge of the Plain of Jars, only regrouping (sans most of their painstakingly stockpiled supplies) at Muong Soui. In its first direct involvement in the war, the United States covertly allowed Air America pilots to fly sorties against the Pathet Lao, besieging Muong Soui on May 22. The onset of the monsoon season then saved Kong Le's remaining forces from being pushed out of the Plain of Jars altogether.

While the NVA had been critical shock troops for the Pathet Lao earlier in the war, the rebels were now able to defeat government units on their own. Still, NVA in-country strength was perhaps 10,000 troops. Increasingly, the government depended on Vang Pao and (in coming years) American airpower to defend its position. The first US reconnaissance aircraft was shot down on June 6, its pilot captured by the Pathet Lao. The United States then shifted to armed reconnaissance flights escorted by fighter-bombers, which quickly became air strikes followed by reconnaissance and then became a mere euphemism for air strikes in Laos.

On June 8, the neutralists were forced from their positions on Phou Kout Mountain, opening the path to Muong Soui. The government mounted Operation Triangle to push the communists back and retake enough of Route 7 to supply Muong Soui by land. The neutralists, who at this point were totally dependent on government support, mounted five unsuccessful assaults to retake Phou Kout that year; the penultimate one ran into a minefield that inflicted 106 casualties. On August 18, neutralists fell back from the mountain after hearing rumors that NVA reinforcements were on the way. Aided by heavy American air strikes beginning on October 13, government forces were able to make progress along Route 7; on October 27, Operation Anniversary Victory was initiated by the government and Vang Pao's forces. Vang Pao advanced, but a joint NVA-Pathet Lao counterattack stopped him at Tha Thom. On December 14, an American bombing campaign, Operation Barrel Roll, systematically began bombing rebel-held areas, especially Route 7 on the Plain of Jars.

In January 1965, Phoumi made his final coup attempt; his forces were checked by loyalists southeast of Vientiane, and he was forced to flee. Military command fell to a jealous troika of generals, each unable to unify the armed forces under one command. A communist offensive in Samneua province took Ban Hong Non on January 20, and despite a Hmong counterattack and air strikes that killed 200 rebels, took Muong Khao, Pha Thom, and Ban Na Lieu from February 8 to February 10, and Hua Mong on February 14. Vang Pao ordered an evacuation of noncombatants as the communists closed in on the last major Hmong bases. On April 13, an additional American air operation codenamed Steel Tiger kicked off, targeting supplies flowing along the Ho Chi Minh trail to South Vietnam. While further losses were avoided, heavy fighting continued until the wet season.

In mid-July, the government and Vag Pao's troops launched a rainy-season offensive to retake the ground lost earlier in the year. At the end of the month, it took the key hill Keo Fa Mut at the cost of 4 dead and 33 wounded against more than 123 NVA killed. After months of fighting, Vang Pao's troops finally recovered Hua Muong in September, winding down their offensive at the end of October. The neutralists followed up with their own rainy-season offensive, unsuccessfully assaulting Phou Kout again on November 16. Meanwhile, the communists were threatening the rice-producing area of Thakhek and positions south of Route 9 on the Kum Kam river. Moreover, fresh NVA forces retook Hua Mong on December 23, and all hope of retaking Phou Khout was abandoned as Vang Pao's forces retreated northward in disorder.

The neutralists attempted to bypass Phou Khout in early 1966, but their drive quickly stalled and the communists pushed to capture Route 6, taking Houei Thom and other government positions despite a fierce defense and American close air support that inflicted perhaps 1,000 casualties (200 to 300 of which were killed) on the communist forces. After a few weeks' pause, the rebels and NVA approached Kong Le's headquarters at Mong Soui, triggering a counteroffensive that nearly cleared Phou Khout. However, the Pathet Lao sent two additional battalions into the fray, which retook Phou Khout on March 20. Despite suffering hundreds of fatalities from air strikes, communist forces pressed on, taking Ban Song on May 13. Vang Pao then mounted an offensive against the rebels, retaking Muong Hiem and Na Khang. American air strikes killed at least 300 communist troops.

Meanwhile, Kong Le's neutralists had become so demoralized that some were defecting to the communists. The government sought to bring the neutralists and Vang Pao's forces under its control, without success in the short term. During the rainy season, the government planned for Operation Prasane, which kicked off on July 18 and captured positions near the Ou river against negligible resistance before the monsoon prevented further operations for two months. On September 17, a communist assault carried San Tiau from Vang Pao, but it was retaken five days later.

On October 16, Kong Le was ousted from command of the neutralists by the government. Neutralist forces effectively were integrated into the government army, and Kong Le fled to Thailand. A coup attempt followed but was suppressed. The Pathet Lao attacked with two battalions at Tha Thom on November 24; four days of fighting that killed at least 37 rebels, mostly from air strikes, left the position in government hands. By the end of the year, the neutralist forces, now under government command, had some modest success, as did Vang Pao. But the government now faced an estimated 101 Pathet Lao and 18 NVA battalions in Laos, plus a dozen neutralist battalions of questionable loyalty and perhaps two Chinese battalions performing logistics work. North Vietnam had about 28,000 engineering and logistics personnel in Laos; although there were "only" 7,500 NVA infantry operating in battalions, there were another 5,000 attached as stiffeners or advisers to the Pathet Lao.

Then 1967 opened with an NVA attack on Na Khang, a key Hmong position; sixty-three NVA died in the unsuccessful operation, and another sixty-five NVA were killed in the subsequent assault on Nong Khang. On March 10, the NVA preempted a major government offensive near Nam Bac, suffering more than forty-four killed. The government's Operation Ban Kao then kicked off, taking the lightly defended Ban Mok Plai and then preparing for an assault on Muong Sai. But on March 20, the NVA counterattacked, drove the Hmong from Ban Mok Plai, and killed forty-three while wounding another sixty-four Hmong troops. It followed up by taking Nong Khang from Vang Pao's army, and when the Hmong struck back at Chik Mok Lok from March 15 to April 9, they were defeated, with about twenty killed on each side.

The government suggested a joint offensive, but Vang Pao balked at having his troops do most of the fighting, while the government forces occupied ground deep in traditionally Hmong territory. In the end, it was the communists who seized the initiative, bringing in three more North Vietnamese battalions against Nam Bac. Vang Pao was able to occupy the Muong Ngan Valley, an important source of rice in northern Laos. The government reinforced the Nam Bac garrison, bringing its strength to 4,500 troops, but the Pathet Lao soon occupied abandoned positions within the defensive perimeter, tightening the noose. Meanwhile, US air force strikes on the communist headquarters near Samneua killed 1,800 communist troops between July 30 and September 21.

Termination and Outcome: At the beginning of the dry season, North Vietnam escalated its involvement in Laos, and from 1968 to 1973, the Pathet Laos fought less, and all major battles were fought by the NVA. For example, by January 1968 there were four NVA battalions, five combined NVA–Pathet Lao battalions and just a single Pathet Lao battalion facing the defenders at Nam Bac. On January 12, North Vietnamese aircraft were employed in combat for the first time, attacking the airfield and radar site known as Lima Site 85. On January 14, 1968, the NVA and Pathet Lao took Nam Bac, killing or capturing at 1,500 to 3,000 of its garrison. It is clear that in these and subsequent engagements, the NVA did the bulk of the fighting, not the Pathet Lao. Hence, the civil war terminated, and an inter-state war between Laos (supported by the United States) and North Vietnam began. The inter-state war ended with a negotiated settlement on February 22, 1973. A coalition government was formed and remained stable for almost two years before events in Vietnam and Cambodia emboldened the Pathet Lao and NVA gradually to seize power in Laos.

Coding Decisions: COW previously coded two separate wars: October 15, 1960, to July 15, 1962, and March 19, 1963, to January 12, 1968. Since the break between them was less than 12 months, these two have been combined here. Leitenberg estimates only 12,000 military deaths between 1960 and 1973, but this figure is probably an underestimate, though his estimated ratio of one civilian death for each battle-death may be correct. For example, Vang Pao's Hmong forces alone lost up to 35,000 battle-deaths over this time period and suffered casualties of 18,000 by September 1969.[302] In addition, 15,000 other Laotians had been killed, not including deaths from aerial bombardment.[303] As thousands of soldiers were killed by aerial bombardment, the toll to September 1969 must have been at least 5,000 Hmong soldiers (given the typical 3:1 ratio of wounded to killed and rounding to the nearest thousand) and about 10,000 other soldiers. Thousands were killed in 1969 alone and likely a high number in 1968 as well. If we subtract 4,000 to 5,000 battle-deaths for those years, we arrive at a minimum total of 10,000 battle-deaths for the war period. The estimate is very imprecise, and the real toll might be considerably higher, although not much lower. Note that Vang Pao's forces, nominally a part of the government's armed forces, are listed separately because he routinely ignored government orders and exercised the highest level of command over his troops.

Sources: Clodfelter (1995); Conboy (1989); Evans (2002); Guan (2002); Hydrick and Brown (2003); Leitenberg (2005); Victor and Sexton (1993).[304]

INTRA-STATE WAR #771.5

First West Papua War of 1967 to 1968

Participants: Indonesia versus Organisasi Papua Merdeka.
Dates: January 1, 1967, to November 30, 1968.
Battle-related Deaths: Total Combatant Deaths: 3,000. (See Coding Decisions.)[305]
Initiator: Indonesia.
Outcome: Indonesia wins.
War Type: Civil for local issues (independence).
Total System Member Military Personnel: Armed Forces of Indonesia: 347,000 (initial); 348,000 (peak, final).[306]
Theater Armed Forces: Armed Forces of Indonesia: 6,000 (final). *Organisasi Papua Merdeka*, aka Arfak Tribe: 11,000 (peak); about 1000 (final).[307]

Antecedents: From 1962, West Papua was administered by Indonesia, while the United Nations prepared for a referendum on whether it should accede to Indonesia or become independent. In 1965, an armed resistance group against the Indonesian occupation called the Free Papua Movement (OPM) was formed. Among its grievances was the settlement of Javanese in the territory by Jakarta. The Arfak tribe already had attacked the Indonesians in April, suffering 200 killed and 600 captured, although its leader, Ferry Awom, escaped to continue the struggle. On July 26, the OPM began to carry out small-scale attacks on Indonesia's troops, prompting Indonesia to mount *Operasi Sadar* (Operation Consciousness), but the conflict appears to have remained below the threshold of war for several years.

Narrative: By 1967, the OPM threat had grown and Indonesia mounted *Operasi Brathayudha* (or *Baratayudha*—Struggle in the West) against the rebels led by Lodewijk Mandatjan and Awom. The offensive included bombing and strafing attacks against villages. By March 17, the government was accused of killing 1,000 "tribesmen"—it acknowledged the fighting but rejected the casualty claims as exaggerated. The offensive probably killed 3,500 "poorly armed villagers" that year alone.[308] In August, the government claimed that some 9,000 tribesmen had surrendered, and only 2,000 were left in the jungles. At the end of November 1968, the government promulgated an amnesty that enticed another 1,600 to surrender. Some 6,000 government troops then were able to continue their occupation against only light resistance.

Termination and Outcome: The outcome of the war was a government victory with the promise of amnesty. Even OPM leader Lodewijk Mandatjan took advantage of the amnesty, surrendering on January 2, 1969. Some rebels, armed with bows and arrows, nonetheless continued to resist and succeeded in killing ten to twenty Indonesian soldiers in early July 1969. But there is little evidence of war-scale violence after the amnesty.

Coding Decisions: The total number of deaths has been estimated at 30,000 for the entirety of the Indonesian occupation up to the end of 1969, while others say the estimate covers deaths from 1962 to 1973. The estimate of 3,500 poorly armed villagers (possibly rebels) killed in 1967 crops up in several sources. Indonesian fatalities are completely unknown, but on the basis of our limited evidence effective resistance was maintained in 1967 and 1968. We estimate perhaps 3,000 battle-deaths in all, a figure that could be an overestimate or underestimate.

Sources: "The Battle for West Irian Has Already Started" (1967); Elmslie (2003); "Indonesia Denies 1,000 Killed" (1967); "Indonesians Hunt Rebel Irian Chief" (1966); "Indonesians Hunt West Irian Rebels" (1968); "'Rebel' Wanted by Indonesia" (1965); "Rebels Fight Soldiers in West Irian" (1969); Simmons (2000); "West Irian Leader Quits" (1969).[309]

INTRA-STATE WAR #772
Cultural Revolution phase 1 of 1967

Participants: Red Guards versus Regional Militaries and Scarlet Guards.
Dates: January 9, 1967, to September 4, 1967.
Battle-related Deaths: Total Combatant Deaths: 10,000. (See Coding Decisions.)[310]
Initiator: Red Guards.
Outcome: War becomes civil (Intra-state War #776).
War Type: Regional.
Theater Armed Forces: Unknown.

Antecedents: By the mid-1960s, Mao Zhedong (Mao Tse Tung) found himself in a hard-line minority within the ruling Chinese Communist Party opposed by a revisionist majority. In response to his weakened status, he took measures to oust the revisionists, including the development of a mass movement to support him. By 1966 he had formed a Cultural Revolution Group to mobilize Red Guards from the student population. From August 18 to November 28, rallies in Beijing involved 13 million Red Guards. Mao himself appeared wearing a Red Guard armband to signify his support for the movement, which also had the approval of Lin Bao, commander of the People's Liberation Army (PLA). Initially, free rail travel was provided to the Red Guards to enable the spread of the Cultural Revolution.

The Red Guards immediately were beset by factionalism, with more and less radical factions emerging—some dominated by the children of party cadres and other (ironically more radical) ones dominated by the children of intellectuals and the bourgeoisie. Local leaders organized urban workers into so-called Scarlet Guards that were loyal to the existing power structure. Across China, political authority began to collapse, caught in a vicious cycle of mobilization and counter-mobilization and left without support by the central government. From June to December 1966, there were six known armed battles between factions, but it is not clear that battle-deaths were particularly high as arms were tightly controlled and Mao never authorized the armed seizure of power by mass organizations.

Narrative: On January 8, a mass rally in Beijing announced the ouster of some of Mao's political opponents. The next day, the *People's Daily* called on the Red Guards to emulate the example of Beijing and "seize power" from revisionists in the provinces. This is when the fighting assumed a primarily regional character as Red Guards attempted to overthrow municipal and provincial governments, opposed by public security forces controlled by local authorities and their Scarlet Guard allies. The violence escalated dramatically; there were 52 armed battles in the first three months of the year, 144 in the following three months, and 465 from July to September.

One reason for the proliferation of battles was that by January 23, Mao provided the opportunity for Red Guards to challenge regional authorities by ordering the PLA to intervene on behalf of the leftist factions. In the East China Bureau alone, there were 165,000 troops in regional forces (commanded by districts consisting of a province or regions consisting of several provinces) and another 275,000 in seven corps. At this point, Mao limited involvement to the regional forces, while the army corps were purged of anti-Mao or revisionist elements. In most regions, the PLA simply supported the party elements in power, unable or unwilling to identify the "genuine" leftists supported by Mao. Soon, regional and PLA representatives were purged from the Cultural Revolution Group, further radicalizing the movement. The PLA was limited largely to confirming the seizures of power that occurred in the January Revolution.

By the first week of February, only two provinces had established Maoist revolutionary committees, while fourteen others had sham committees dominated by the local party hierarchy. Armed struggle was still relatively uncommon, but it occurred over wide swathes of territory. Late in March, Mao deployed the army corps of the PLA to ensure that local commanders followed the new policy of stepping back from violence when left and revisionist groups clashed. The result was an upsurge of violence as mass organizations fought each other. By May, many of the groups were armed with sophisticated weapons and battle-deaths mounted.

As the violence threatened to tear the country apart, Mao searched for ways to end it while defeating his regional enemies; on June 7, the PLA was once again given limited powers to intervene in the fighting. In some areas, it intervened against the radicals. For example, in Wuhan some 350 were killed and more than 1,500 wounded in fighting between the Three Steels Red Guard group and the Million Heroes provincial Scarlet Guard from June 16 to June 24. When the government sent orders to reverse course, its agents were arrested by the Million Heroes—it took military intervention by loyal PLA units to secure their release.

Now concerned about the PLA's loyalty, Mao authorized the arming of the Red Guards by July 20. Raids on arsenals increased dramatically, and the PLA took significant casualties as it still was bound largely by the nonintervention policy and hence limited to self-defense actions. Turning once more to the army, Mao ordered central corps to take over eleven regional commands. Over half of China's best divisions were now committed to the Cultural Revolution, weakening external defense. The Cultural Revolution Group underwent another purge and was stacked with military loyalists.

Termination and Outcome: On September 5, the Central Committee ordered the disarmament of the Red Guards. This order terminated central government support for military action by the rebels, transforming the war into a civil one pitting the PLA against recalcitrant Red Guards (and occasionally Scarlet Guards and other armed regional and non-state actors). Although the number of battles declined, the killing would become much more intense over the next year.

Coding Decisions: Although the period witnessed up to 661 armed clashes in the countryside alone, most of them were not particularly bloody. Only toward the end of the war did large losses become more common as modern weapons replaced improvised ones. Up to 85,252 died in the countryside during the period of battles, but this figure includes civilians and is for a time period exceeding that of the war. The vast majority of the dead were victims of mass killing, including children. We conservatively estimate 10,000 battle-deaths for this phase of the Cultural Revolution. The real toll could be half or several times this figure.

Sources: Harding (1997); Thornton (1982); Walder and Su (2003).[311]

INTRA-STATE WAR #773
Third Burmese War of 1965 to 1993

Participants: Burma versus Communist Party of Burma, China, Karen National Union, Kachin Independence Army, Karreni National Progressive Party, Karreni State Nationalities People's Liberation Force, Kayan New Land Party, Communist Party of Arakan, Arakan National Liberation Party, Arakan Liberation Army, Rohingya Solidarity Organization, Arakan Rohinya Islamic Front, Shan State Army, Shan United Revolutionary Army, Shan State Revolutionary Army, Pa-O National Liberation Army, Shanland Nationalities Liberation Front, Shan State Nationalities People's Liberation Organization, Zomi National Front, Chin National Army, Palaung State Liberation Army, New Mon State Party, Kawthoolei Muslim Liberation Front, Wa National Army, Kuki National Army, Lahu State Army, Lahu National Army, Parliamentary Democracy Party, All-Burma Students' Democratic Front, Alliance for Democratic Solidarity (Union of Burma), and Mizo National Front.

Dates: May 1, 1965, to May 24, 1980, and January 1981 to April 8, 1993.

Battle-related Deaths: Total Combatant Deaths: 69,000. (See Coding Decisions.)[312]

Initiator: Burma.

Outcome: Fell below civil-war threshold.

War Type: Civil for central control (but see Coding Decisions).

Total System Member Military Personnel: Armed forces of Burma/Armed forces of Myanmar: 136,000 (prewar, initial); 322,000 (peak, final).[313] People's Republic of China: 2,400,000 (prewar, initial); 4,750,000 (peak).

Theater Armed Forces: The peak strength of the combined rebels was roughly 35,000, although 25,000 to 30,000 was a more common number.[314] Communist Party of Burma, participating until March through April 1989, when it splintered into four different ethnic armies: 1,500 (initial—1971 estimate); 23,000 (peak); 10,000 (final).[315] People's Republic of China, participating from 1968 to 1979, albeit using Red Guards and "volunteers" for the bulk of its troops, with military advisors attached to CPB units: thousands (initial); up to 9,000 (peak).[316] Karen National Union/Karen National Liberation Army: 20,000 (initial—1971 estimate); 20,000 (peak); 1,000 to 5,000 (final).[317] Kachin Independence Army: 4,500 (initial); 8,000 (peak); 8,000 (final).[318] Karreni National Progressive Party/Karreni Army: 1,000 (initial, peak), 400 (final—1987 estimate).[319] Karreni State Nationalities People's Liberation Force, participating from 1978: 300 to 400 (final). Kayan New Land Party—100 to 200 (final).[320] Communist Party of Arakan, participating to 1980, when its leader surrendered, splintering the organization; no fragment was subsequently able to muster 100 troops: 300 (initial); 300 (peak).[321] Arakan National Liberation Party: unknown. Arakan Liberation Army, participating from July 1972 to 1977, when it was virtually wiped out in Chin state: unknown. Rohingya Independence Force/ Rohingya Patriotic Front, participating until 1985, when it splintered into minor factions: unknown. Rohingya Solidarity Organization (Rebel Army), participating from 1982 to August 22, 1987, when it joined the Arakan Rohingya Islamic Front: one source lists the RSO as having 6,000 in 1992; 100 (peak).[322] Arakan Rohingya Islamic Front, participating from sometime in the late 1980s, when it crossed the 100-troop threshold for inclusion): 100 (initial); probably 500 (peak); 500 (final).[323] Shan State Army/Shan State Progress Party, participating to September 2, 1989, when it made peace with the government: 3,000 (prewar—1964); more than 7,500 (peak); 2,500 (final).[324] Shan United Army/Shan State Army/ Möng Tai Army, participating from 1972: 1,000 to 2,000 (initial); 18,000 to 20,000 but not all armed (peak); 18,000 to 20,000 but not all armed (final).[325] Shan United Revolutionary Army, participating from January 20, 1969, to April 1, 1984, when it merged with other groups to form what would eventually become the Möng Tai Army: 1,000 to 1,200 (initial); 2,000 to 3,000 (peak, final).[326] Shan State Revolutionary Army, participating from August 2, 1976: at least 200 (peak).[327] Pa-O National Liberation Army/Shan State Nationalities Liberation Organization, participating from 1968: 2,000 (initial, peak); 250 (final—1987 estimate).[328] Shanland Nationalities Liberation Front/Pa-O National Army, participating from 1973 to March 27, 1991, when it signed a peace treaty with the government: 500 (peak); 350 (final).[329] Shan State Nationalities People's Liberation Organization, participating from 1974: unknown. Zomi National Front/ Committee for the Restoration and Protection of the Sovereignty and Independence of Occupied Zoram: unknown. Chin National Army, participating from November 14, 1988: 100 (initial); 100 (peak).[330] Palaung State Liberation Army, participating from February 12, 1976, to April 21, 1991: 1,000 (peak); 400 (final—1987 estimate).[331] New Mon State Party: 1,000 (initial), 3,000 to 5,000 (peak); 2,000 (final).[332] Kawthoolei Muslim Liberation Front/ All Burma Muslim Union, participating from October 31, 1983: 500 (peak).[333] Wa National Army, participating from July 29, 1974: 600 (final—1987 estimate).[334] Kuki National Army (Rebel Army), participating from 1987: perhaps 100 (peak). Lahu State Army, participating from February 1973 to late 1983—in January 1984, its leader surrendered with only 30 troops: 1,000 (peak); 100 (final).[335] Lahu National Army, participating from August 1985: 700 (peak).[336] Parliamentary Democracy Party/Patriotic Liberation Army, participating from August 29, 1966, to about 1973, when leader U Nu left for India: 3,000 (peak).[337] All-Burma Students' Democratic Front, participating from November 5, 1988: 150 to 300 armed (initial); 4,800 members but only 500 to 600 armed (peak).[338] Alliance for Democratic Solidarity (Union of Burma)/ADS(B), participating from January 19, 1989: unknown. Mizo National Front, participating in 1966 and again in 1971, assisting the CPB: 800 (initial, peak, final); 800 (peak); 800 (final).[339]

Antecedents: Burma has been in a state of civil conflict more or less continuously since shortly after independence. But as the conflict waxed and waned over time, we code it as a series of separate civil wars. By 1963, violence was at its lowest point since the beginning of the insurrections. However, the government's attempt to negotiate with the rebels largely failed, and by 1965 violence was increasing in response to economic crises and the military government's increasingly repressive policies.

Organizations already in rebellion against the government included: the Communist Party of Burma (CPB), the Karen National Union (KNU) and its Karen National Liberation Army (KNLA), the unrelated Karenni National People's Party (KNPP), the Kachin Independence Army (KIA), the Communist Party of Arakan (CPA) and Arakan National Liberation Party (ANLP), the Rohingya Independence Front (RIF—later the Rohingya Patriotic Front), the Kayan New Land Party (KNLP), the Shan State Army (SSA), the Zomi National Front (ZNF), and the New Mon State Party (NMSP).

Narrative: On May 1, 1965, the government mounted a massive offensive against the rebels, reporting 30 rebels killed in the first two weeks. A newspaper report on August 22, 1965, claimed that "more than 6000 rebels . . . surrendered last year and early this year. About 5,000 rebels were killed or captured" ("Burma Is Forming an Antirebel Force," 28). While this report—likely to have come from the government of Burma—was no doubt an exaggeration, it demonstrated that serious fighting was once more underway. The KIA, KNPP, KNLP, ZNF, and SSA formed an alliance against the government that lasted for about a year.

By 1966, the Kachin Independence Organization and its army (the KIA) had been expanding steadily for five years; its mobile "battalions" had "penetrated as far as Myitkyina, the Hukawng valley, the Naga Hills, and the strategic Kamaing jade region" (Smith, 1999, 220). The government's armed forces responded with a scorched-earth policy later known as four cuts, and thousands were killed in the fighting.

The next year, the Pa-Os rebelled, forming the Pa-O National Liberation Army (PNLA). A new alliance of rebel groups (KNUP, KNPP, KNLP, NMSP, ZNF, and SSA) called the Nationalities United Front (NUF) was established; it would last (aside from the NMSP, which dropped out in 1969) until being supplanted by another alliance in 1975. Moreover, anti-Chinese riots in Burma—probably spread by the government itself—created intense opposition from China, which drastically increased its support for the CPB over the next months. The latter underwent a series of purges inspired by the Cultural Revolution in China but still managed to mount an offensive from July to November. Late in the year, nearly 1,000 Shan rebels switched sides and became government security forces (Ka Kwe Ye or home guards).

On January 1, 1968, the CPB established a new front against the government with the aid of China. This Northeast Command would eventually become the core of the party after it lost its old bases and leaders. More importantly, thousands of Chinese "volunteers" streamed across the border to fight alongside the CPB. In other areas, the government's four-cuts counterinsurgency policy began paying dividends; the KNU both politically and geographically was split in two, and over time the government was able to reconquer the Irrawaddy delta, leaving only the anticommunist Karen forces in the hills to the east (KNUF). July 22 saw a major battle between the CPB and the government at Tao Long. The communist attacks continued through the rest of the year, but in September a surprise government attack inflicted serious losses on the CPB. By the end of the year, CPB troop strength was at its lowest ebb since the onset of the war.

At the beginning of 1969, one Shan commander broke with the SSA and established the Shan United Revolutionary Army (SURA), supported by Guomindang (Kuomintang [KMT]) remnants under Li Wenhuan. Some 400 Kachin troops went over to the CPB. Another new entrant to the war was former prime minister U Nu's Parliamentary Democracy Party (PDP), which was formed on August 29 and immediately started fund-raising to purchase arms. However, the NMSP left the NUF, signaling fragmentation of the ethnic rebellions. The first half of 1970 was dominated by pitched battles between the CPB and the government (which captured the CPB's headquarters), but it also saw the formation of a new alliance, the Nationalities United Liberation Front (NLUF), which included the NMSP, PDP, and Karen rebels.

The latter suffered a serious defeat in early 1971, when the government finally drove the CPB and Karens alike out of the Irrawady Delta. The Karens retreated to Pegu Yoma, and the CPB retreated to new zones of operations adjacent to the Chinese border. The government dictator Ne Win went to

China for talks to try to repair relations between the two states. Late in the year, a forty-one-day battle erupted over control of Kunlong, culminating in defeat for the CPB on January 7, 1972. Soon, the Chinese ambassador, who had been recalled during the anti-Chinese riots, again took up his post in Rangoon, but Chinese support for the rebellion continued, and the CPB won a string of victories later in the year.

In January 1973, the government ended its home guards experiment and ordered them to be disarmed. Simultaneously, the Lahu of southern Shan state began their revolt, seizing towns on January 10 and January 11 and establishing the Lahu United National Party (LUNP) the following month. In May, the NLUF was supplanted by the Revolutionary Nationalities Alliance (RNA), composed of the KNU, KNPP, KNLP, and SSPP. Over time, the alliance would evolve into the Federal National Democratic Front in 1975 (including the same members minus the KNLP and plus the NMSP and ALP). This then would become the basis for the National Democratic Front (NDF), which added and subtracted some smaller parties.

Meanwhile on July 27, 1973, the PDP suffered a serious blow when U Nu was forced to leave Thailand, where he had been running a government in exile, for India. The party began to decline after this point. In December, the SSA and KNUP visited the CPB for alliance talks; they subsequently visited China, but only the SSA allied itself to the CPB. By March 1974, Chinese support for the CPB included the presence of up to 9,000 Chinese "volunteers" and military advisors. On March 19 the government offered amnesty to the rebels, but there was no mass response to the offer. Strikes and demonstrations by monks against the regime were crushed brutally, with hundreds of fatalities. The government—which just had promulgated a new constitution in March—declared martial law once more.

The next year saw the death of both the CPB leadership (in battle) and that of the KIA (by assassination). Nevertheless, new leaders simply began from where the old ones left off, and both insurgencies continued; for example, from November to December 1975 a government offensive resulted in 218 Shan and CPB battle-deaths. In March 1976, the SSA/SSPP split, with a pro-CPB faction taking over the movement. Yet another faction, the Shan State Revolutionary Army (SSRA), was formed in August. But in July the KIO and the CPB reached an alliance, ending eight years of skirmishes between the two groups. The KIA began receiving Chinese arms through the offices of the CPB. On January 17, 1977, the SSPP declared the formation of a united front with the CPB. The government mounted an offensive against Three Pagodas Pass, controlled by the Karen and Mon rebels. Later in the year, the KIA captured Namsan Yang and began operations in the surrounding valley.

In February 1978, the government mounted a major operation in Arakan state; soon, its scorched-earth tactics led to a flood of Muslim refugees (at least 200,000) entering Bangladesh, although repatriation of some refugees began in August. Moreover, the remnants of the PDP were dispersed late in the year, ending noncommunist ethnic Burmese resistance to the state. Only ethnic minorities and the CPB remained in the field against the government.

Early in 1979, the KIA made some progress against the government, wiping out a column and capturing significant quantities of arms. However, a devastating blow was coming. On July 12, the government announced that China would be supplying development assistance. Assistance to the CPB was drastically reduced, and Chinese "volunteers" were recalled; the government immediately mounted a large-scale offensive against the CPB in northern Burma. While it stopped short of capturing the CPB's "capital" of Panghsang, it established a foothold within twenty-five kilometers of the town.

The government mounted another dry-season offensive against Three Pagodas Pass in 1980. But on May 24, 1980, the government announced a ninety-day amnesty for insurgents; several prominent rebels took the opportunity to surrender, with perhaps 300 to 400 taking advantage of the amnesty. Later in the year, peace talks took place with the KIO. Fighting died down until January 1981, when the CPB mounted an offensive out of KIO-controlled areas; the attacking force was wiped out by the government. On April 10, peace talks with the KIO broke down, but talks with the CPB began on May 5—only to end after just four days. In July the SSPP backed out of its alliance with the CPB.

For much of 1982, fighting was composed purely of guerrilla actions, with no battles of note, but with increased intensity compared to 1980 and 1981. In December the government mounted another major offensive against the CPB, which failed after a month of fighting. The government then turned against the Karens in January 1983. In February both the CPB and KNLA attempted offensive operations of their own, only to have entire columns wiped out by the government. In June, the government caught the KNU by surprise with a rainy-season offensive that succeeded in gaining some ground (the strategic peak of Naw Taya, which overlooked KNLA bases along the Moel). In July the ousted leader of the SSPP/SSA surrendered to the government; his faction's bases were taken over by Chinese rebel Khun Sa's Shan United Army (SUA). In November, the government mounted a successful small-scale offensive against the KNU designed to free a French couple being held by the organization.

In January 1984, the government mounted another offensive against the KNU/KNLA from its base on Naw Taya, taking the base of Mae Tha Waw but failing to take Maw Pokay. The Lahu rebels (LUNP) surrendered. In March, the government scored a political success when Khun Sa's troops agreed to fight other rebel groups in exchange for a monopoly on the opium trade. His SUA soon attacked the Pa-O insurgents, taking their headquarters. On April 1, the SSA's Second Brigade joined with the SURA to become the Tai Revolutionary Council/Army (TRC/TRA); true to its agreement with Khun Sa, the government attacked the TRA while leaving the SUA untouched. Meanwhile, government troops had crossed into Thailand in an attempt to take Maw Pokay. By April 15, the government claimed to have killed 2,500 rebels at the cost of 528 of its own soldiers, plus 1,370 wounded. Fighting soon died down, and the last major battle of the year was fought against the KIA at Gauri Bum, which fell to the government after twenty days of heavy fighting.

On March 3, 1985, Khun Sa's SUA joined the TRC/TRA. The government mounted an offensive using 3,000 troops; by the mid-1980s, offensives against Three Pagodas Pass were annual activities. Fighting between the government and the KNU and NMSP was reported, but the most important developments were political. The CPB resolved to seek an alliance with the ethnic insurgents, even as the ethnic insurgents of the NDF were determined to seek an alliance with the CPB. On March 24, 1986, the NDF and CPB signed a military coordination agreement. They each controlled about 12,000 fighters, although the KNU denounced the agreement in August. In September, Khun Sa's forces fought the CPB in Shan State. On November 16, more than 1,000 CPB troops overran government positions on the mountain of Hsi-Hsinwan after a bloody battle. However, the CPB was forced to withdraw after three weeks of heavy bombardment by government artillery and air assets.

On December 16, the government opened a second front against the CPB near Pangyang in the South; within a month the dual offensive captured Möng Paw, Panghsai-Kyu Hkok, Khun Hai, and Man Hio. The government claimed to have killed 591 CPB from November to early January. The government followed up its successes by capturing Man Pi, the headquarters of a mixed Kachin–Shan–Palaung brigade of the NDF. In May 1987, the government mounted an offensive against Kachin bases, capturing the KIO's headquarters at Pa Jau. An offensive against the CPB led to 650 CPB killed against 175 on the government side.

On September 5, the government—apparently attempting to curtail black market inflation and rebel funding—demonetized about 75 percent of the country's circulating money. The move had little effect on either the insurgents or the black market but succeeded in alienating many Burmese, whose life savings were wiped out. Student demonstrations broke out immediately in Rangoon and spread to other parts of the country in November. Another wave of demonstrations struck Rangoon in March 1988; security forces killed scores of protesters. Yet more unrest occurred in June and July; Ne Win resigned his position as chair of the ruling BSPP. In August, hundreds were killed when police fired on demonstrators in Rangoon and Sagaing. On September 18, at least 1,000 people were killed by automatic gunfire from the newly formed State Law and Order Restoration Council (SLORC).

Thousands of students and dissidents (perhaps 10,000 students) fled to the CPB and KIA bases; on September 24, they established the National League for Democracy (NLD) political party. In the first year, the death rates among the students were horrendous due to disease. The established rebel groups took the opportunity to mount new offensives; the CPB recaptured Möng Yang for a few days (the battle cost 130 CPB battle-deaths against 48 on the government side), and the KNLA recaptured Mae Tha Waw. On November 5, students determined to fight the military regime established the All-Burma Students' Democratic Front (ABSDF) on the Thai border. About two weeks later, the Democratic Alliance of Burma (DAB) was formed between the NDF and the ethnically Burmese opposition forces. They claimed a strength of 15,000 combined and suffered 1,000 killed by June 1989. Less than a month later, a combined CPB–KIA force destroyed a government column in Khonsa, inflicting 106 killed, 17 wounded, and 15 captured; significant quantities of arms were seized by the victorious rebels.

However, on December 21 Mae Tha Waw once again fell to the forces of the SLORC. And on January 19, 1989, DAB and ABSDF headquarters Klerday fell to government forces. Then in March, the CPB disintegrated. Mutiny began on March 12 in Kokang, and soon the CPB had split into four ethnic armies. By April 17, the CPB's headquarters at Panghsang had fallen to Wa mutineers, ending CPB participation in the war. Negotiations with the government and cease-fires (the last of these on December 5) followed. However, the war against other ethnic insurgents continued. The Karen base of Maw Pokay fell on March 26; on May 20, some 400 government soldiers crossed into Thailand in an attempt to encircle the rebel base of Wangkha, burning a Thai village in the process. The government claimed 600 Karen battle-deaths and 177 government battle-deaths in its operations during the first five months of the year. Meanwhile, Israel and Belgium resupplied the government with weapons. On September 2, the SSA/SSPP entered a cease-fire with the government. By this time, the number of students in the jungle had decreased to 2,000; it would fall to 1,000 within another year.

The government mounted another offensive against the KNU/KPLA at the end of the year. An attack mounted from within Thailand captured Phalu on December 29. On January 24, 1990, government forces took the Karen base of Thay Baw Bo, capturing hundreds of Burmese students in the process. Walay fell a week later. Also that month, one brigade of the KIA went over to the government, becoming a recognized militia. Pa-O rebels followed suit in March, as did the Palaung guerrillas in April and another brigade of the KIA in December. The terms of the cease-fires allowed the former rebels to retain their arms and control of some territory as well as legitimating resource-extraction efforts in these areas. Meanwhile the government offensive turned against the Mons; the NMSP headquarters of Three Pagodas Pass was captured after a battle lasting from February 5 to February 11; one report estimated casualties at twenty government soldiers killed and forty rebels killed. Fighting against the NMSP and ABSDF led to more casualties—with forty rebels killed on March 22 alone.

Over the next year, the government would receive substantial military supplies from its former nemesis, China. In October 1991, the ABSDF split into two factions following a two-month-long meeting. Fighting resumed that month between the Karens and government forces near Bogala in the Irrawaddy Delta. After a brief interval, battles resumed in January 1992, as the government sought to capture the Karen headquarters of Manerplaw. On January 15, the government suffered 180 killed when 2,000 troops attacked Karen positions at Malebatta. Meanwhile in December 1991 the government had mounted an offensive against the Rohingya rebels in Arakan, going so far as to enter Bangladesh and attack a military post on January 21. Tens of thousands of refugees began to pour into Bangladesh once again.

On April 27, the government announced the suspension of operations against the Karens and other rebels along the Thai border. The government began to release hundreds of political prisoners, and peace appeared to be within sight. However, on June 5 the KIA seized Pangsau on the Indo-Burmese border, holding it for ten days before being forced out by government reinforcements. On September 1, the Karenni rebels recaptured their old headquarters of Hweponglaung near the border with Thailand. But on November 2, the government mounted a counteroffensive that retook the town.

Termination and Outcome: The war fell below the civil-war threshold in 1993, in what amounted to a limited government military victory. More than twelve months passed between the counteroffensive against the Karenni and the next major combat—a government offensive against Khun Sa's Möng Tai Army in December 1993, which did not appear to result in civil-war-scale casualties in any case. During this time, many groups negotiated peace with the government (the KNU being a notable exception). On January 22, the KIA—by far the most powerful rebel force still in arms—began negotiations with the government; a cease-fire was agreed upon on April 8. We use this date as the end of the war, as the remaining groups lacked the strength or (in the large but ineffective Möng Tai army's case) competence to inflict war-scale casualties in combat. Soon, many more cease-fires were reached; however, the agreements generally failed to resolve issues necessary for a true peace accord, such as political representation or disarmament. The KNU/KNLA continues to fight the government at sub-war levels; for example, it claimed to have killed 499 government troops and to have lost only 11 killed from June 1, 2007, to May 1, 2008. The cease-fire with the KIA broke down in 2011, resulting in another war (Intra-state War # 980).

Coding Decisions: There were a huge number of rebel groups, and if further data on inter-rebel coordination and disaggregated battle-deaths were available, we could separate their insurgencies, combining only those that actively coordinated with each other. But in the absence of such data, and in the presence of at least limited alliances between virtually all of the players (even the anticommunist KNU/KNLA and the CPB) at one point or another, we treat this as one civil war, initially fought for control of the central government. The Naga groups are excluded because they primarily fought in India, not Burma, while India's Mizo National Front is included when it fought against Burmese forces in Burma. Chinese "volunteers" are included in strength estimates for the CPB because they fought as members of it.

Casualty figures are spotty at best. In 1972, the BCP claimed 1,105 government battle-deaths over a ten-month period, and the government claimed to have killed 500 rebels in one battle alone. We can extrapolate this to at least 2,000 killed that year. From January 1968 to December 1973—a six-year period—the CPB estimated 11,400 government casualties, including 1,136 captured against lower CPB losses. The government claimed to have killed 3,000 rebels from June 1971 to March 1973. Using the 3:1 ratio of wounded to killed (a ratio that likely underestimates fatalities given the few known comparisons of killed to wounded in this war), these figures imply yearly averages of roughly 427 government battle-deaths against the BCP and 1,636 rebel battle-deaths per year, a far different ratio but a similar total of 2,060 killed per year.

For the 1980s, the government claimed to kill about 2,000 insurgents per year at the cost of 500 to 600 government battle-deaths each year. One specific claim was that 9,000 rebels died from August 1981 to August 1985 (an average of 2,250 per year). On the other hand, the rebels claimed more than 1,000 government battle-deaths per year on one front alone from 1980 to 1988, and the BCP claimed 1,908 government troops killed and 3,341 wounded from November 1979 to December 1980. Clodfelter states that "a typical year was 1984," reporting that rebel battle-deaths were 1,870 and government battle-deaths were 566.[340] To the extent that the year was "typical," we might expect 2,433 battle-deaths per year, on average—above the earlier estimates of about 2,000 but also more inclusive. From March 22, 1986, to March 21, 1987, the government claimed 2,538 rebel battle-deaths against 651 government battle-deaths.

In January 1992, a single battle cost 1,000 lives and 2,000 wounded, suggesting that the war was still ongoing. Therefore, we arrive at our estimate of battle-deaths by assuming an average of 2,000 to 2,500 battle-deaths per year through the termination of the war, which yields estimates in roughly the 55,000 to 69,000 range. Malaria also killed many government troops, and various diseases wreaked havoc on the 10,000 students who fled to the jungle in 1988, so these are probably low estimates. For that reason, we estimate the high figure of 69,000.

Sources: Arnold (1995); "Burma Is Forming an Antirebel Force" (1965); "Burma Opens Drive on Bands of Rebels" (1965); Degenhardt (1987); Laffin (1991); Lintner (1990, 1999); MacDonald (1999); Smith (1964); Smith (1999); Worobec (1983).[341]

INTRA-STATE WAR #776
Cultural Revolution phase 2 of 1967 to 1968

Participants: China versus Red Guards (Aggregate).
Dates: September 5, 1967, to September 5, 1968.
Battle-related Deaths: Total Combatant Deaths: 10,000. (See Coding Decisions.)[342]
Initiator: China.
Outcome: China wins.

War Type: Civil for local issues (disarmament, control of municipal, rural, and provincial power).

Total System Member Military Personnel: Armed Forces of China: 2,710,000 (prewar); 2,710,000 (initial); 2,800,000 (peak); 2,800,000 (final).[343]

Theater Armed Forces: Red Guards: while there were millions of Red Guards, only a small fraction were themselves armed combatants.

Antecedents: During the Cultural Revolution, the central government encouraged the formation of radical Red Guard organizations. For a brief time, it even armed them through the People's Liberation Army. However, the government proved unwilling to allow armed rebels actually to seize power and establish autonomous subnational governments. The central government insisted on the formation of "3 in 1" revolutionary committees composed of members of the PLA, cadres from the local government, and the Red Guards. Two problems arose. First, it was difficult for the center or even the local PLA units to identify the genuinely revolutionary mass organizations. Therefore, the local governments usually allied themselves with the PLA against radicals seeking their overthrow. Sometimes, however, the PLA would support the radicals against the local party cadres, suppressing conservative mass organizations. And sometimes, the PLA would be divided over which organizations to support. Second, there was the problem of suppressing the now-armed Red Guards, who were on the losing end of the political struggle over the composition of the revolutionary committees. Each of these problems was resolved with violence.

Narrative: The central government decisively turned against the Red Guards on September 5, 1967, when the PLA was ordered to disarm them. At this point, revolutionary committees had been established in less than half of the provinces, and the process of committee formation became increasingly violent. Because of the violence, the PLA came to dominate most committees. It formally assumed control of all public security forces in December. Soon, many more revolutionary committees had been established.

In June and July 1968, the government mounted a major campaign against remaining rebels, leading to some of the fiercest fighting of the war. In Guangxi, the process of committee formation was particularly violent. Early in the year, a Red Guard organization called the Guangxi April 22 Revolutionary Action Command faced off against the Guangxi United Command of Proletarian Revolutionaries. Central units of the PLA supported the former, and local units and cadres supported the latter. The central units of the PLA were withdrawn in the spring, and the local government mounted a military campaign against the "rebel" April 22 organization beginning on July 16. After a series of bloody battles, the April 22 rebels were overcome by August 8; out of about 10,000 rebels and supporters captured, some 2,324 were massacred. On August 20, the revolutionary committee formed by the local government, PLA units, and Guangxi United Command was recognized by the central government.

Beginning in August, Mao extracted main force units from combat against the Red Guards, leaving the task to local security forces and PLA units. This freed up the main force units for external defense at a time of heightened border tensions with the Soviet Union. The result was that provincial units, unrestrained by the main force units, completed the destruction of local rebel organizations. By the end of August, the Red Guard had been destroyed as a military force.

Termination and Outcome: The last revolutionary committees (Tibet and Xinjiang) were formed on September 5, ending the struggles between the Red Guards and the state. The outcome of the war was an unconditional military victory by the government. Red Guards were relocated to the countryside, where a wave of mass killings followed the establishment of the revolutionary committees, killing hundreds of thousands of people.

Coding Decisions: No source estimates battle-deaths during this war (although many estimate total deaths). There were 471 battles in the countryside alone. Several cities also saw severe fighting. While the overwhelming majority of those who died in the Cultural Revolution did so in waves of one-sided mass killings, we estimate that at least 10,000 combatants were killed during this phase. This is a conservative estimate; the real toll could be much higher.

Sources: MacFarquhar and Schoenhals (2006); Thornton (1982); Walder and Su (2003).[344]

INTRA-STATE WAR #778
Naxalite Rebellion of 1970 to 1971

Participants: India versus Communist Party of India (Marxist-Leninist).
Dates: March 1970 to August 1971.
Battle-related Deaths: Total Combatant Deaths: 1,400. (See Coding Decisions.)[345]
Initiator: Communist Party of India (Marxist-Leninist).
Outcome: India wins.
War Type: Civil for central control.
Total System Member Military Personnel: Armed Forces of India: 1,550,000 (prewar, initial); 1,560,000 (peak, final).[346]
Theater Armed Forces: Unknown.

Antecedents: In 1967, abuses by landlords led to peasant revolts, which were quickly taken over by the Communist Party of India (Marxist). The characteristic mode of conflict was terrorism by the Naxalite insurgents and indiscriminate violence against peasants by the state. Some 139 people, including 28 police, died in the fifty-two-day uprising. The insurgency was temporarily suppressed but grew again in 1969 after a split led to the formation of the Communist Party of India (Marxist-Leninist), led by Charu Mazumdar. The Naxalite movement spread to other parts of the country, including the states of West Bengal, Orissa, Uttar Pradesh, Bihar, and Andhra Pradesh, but was strongest in the region of Srikakulam, where within a few months they came to control a majority of the villages.

Narrative: Due to the failure of its rural base-building strategy, the CPI (ML) began an urban insurrection in Calcutta in March 1970. This became the primary theater of war. The level of violence then escalated, and in 1970 and 1971 there were more than 4,000 Naxalite-inspired violent incidents in India. In 1971 the CPI (ML) organized its military wing into a People's Liberation Army on the Chinese model. But by mid-1971, the violence had peaked, and the People's Liberation Army was on the wane. State violence culminated in Operation Steeplechase from July to August, which succeeded in crushing the insurgents.

Termination and Outcome: Using the fatality data from the Calcutta area, it appears that the killing tapered off significantly after August 1971. This marks a transition from civil war to low-intensity conflict. The Naxalites continued their rebellion, but by the middle of 1972 the movement was all but defunct, its leader killed while in government custody. Naxalite violence continues today, but the outcome of the war was clearly a government military victory.

Coding Decisions: Some 2,000 Naxalites were killed in "the early 1970s."[347] We conclude that since "1970–71 [was] a time when the movement was passing through its most explosive, violent and critical phase which ended in its ruthless suppression by the government," this figure likely refers primarily to those two years.[348] Between March 1970 and August 1971, police records indicate that 1,783 Naxalites or supporters were killed in Calcutta (now Kolkata) and its suburbs alone—the real figure may be double that. In addition, at least 41 police were killed by Naxalites in the first ten months of 1970. Accordingly, we find it plausible that at least 1,400 battle-deaths occurred, the minimum number needed for this period to qualify as a civil war.

Sources: Clodfelter (2008); Dasgupta (1978); Marwah (2009); Mukhopadhyay (2006); Ram (1971); Singh (1995).[349]

INTRA-STATE WAR #782
Pakistan–Bengal War of 1971 (aka Bangladesh Liberation War)

Participants: Pakistan versus East Pakistan Rifles, East Bengal Regiment, Mukti Bahini, Mujib Bahini, Kader Bahini, Afsar Battalion, Hemayet Bahini, and India.
Dates: March 25, 1971, to December 2, 1971.
Battle-related Deaths: Armed Forces of Pakistan: perhaps 5,000; Total Combatant Deaths: 20,000. (See Coding Decisions.)[350]
Initiator: Pakistan.
Outcome: Transformed into Inter-state War #178.
War Type: Civil for local issues (independence and secession).
Total System Member Military Personnel: Armed Forces of Pakistan: 404,000 (prewar); perhaps 350,000 (initial, peak, final).[351]
Theater Armed Forces: East Pakistan Rifles, participating until joining Mukti Bahini in

April: 8,000 (initial, peak).[352] East Bengal Regiment, participating until joining Mukti Bahini in April: 3,000 (initial, peak).[353] Mukti Bahini, aka Mukti Fauj, participating from April 17: 30,000 (initial); 110,000 to 115,000 (peak).[354] Mujib Bahini, participating from the summer: 5,000.[355] Kader Bahini, participating from the summer: 17,000 (peak).[356] Afsar Battalion, participating from the summer: 4,500 (peak).[357] Hemayet Bahini, participating from the summer: 5,000 (peak).[358] Armed Forces of India, participating from November 20 or 21, 1971: one brigade (initial).[359]

Antecedents: Since the creation of Pakistan, East Pakistan had been treated like a colony by West Pakistan. In November 1970, a tsunami killed up to 250,000 East Pakistan Bengalis. When the central government failed to respond effectively, the pro-autonomy Awami League gained popularity and did well in East Pakistan during national elections.

Narrative: On March 25, 1971, the government attacked the Awami League and its supporters, killing or arresting thousands, including league leader Sheikh Mujibur Rahman (but only after he was able to issue a statement declaring independence in the face of the attack). Some 20 percent of Pakistan's army rebelled. The 17,000-strong East Pakistan Rifles mutinied and resisted the government crackdown, but 4,000 immediately were disarmed, and many were killed. After a few days, only 8,000 remained in the field against the government. Some 2,000 police in Dhaka joined the resistance, as did the majority of provincial police. Soon, they were joined by the 3,000 (of 6,000) men of the East Bengal Regiment who escaped the surprise attack. But by mid-April the government had established control of the major cities, and resistance shifted to guerrilla warfare.

A nationalist movement declared independence on April 17 and formed the Mukti Bahini as a military force, theoretically uniting most of the rebels. In all, the resistance was able to mobilize 30,000 fighters, but rebel strength plunged by late May after Mukti Bahini was mauled by government forces. The government deployed four divisions, 25,000 support troops, 50,000 Razakar militiamen, and 20,000 of the paramilitary West Punjab Rangers. The war was brutal, with systematic victimization of civilians (especially the rape of women and mass killings of Hindus) by both the government army and the Razakars. By July, the government had lost 2,500 killed and 10,000 wounded.

Perhaps 10 million refugees crossed the border into India, which provided bases and arms to the rebels. China, North Korea, Jordan, and Saudi Arabia supplied arms to the government. With the Indian assistance, the Mukti Bahini rebels claimed to have 50,000 to 100,000 guerrillas and 10,000 to 15,000 regular troops (including the survivors of the East Pakistan Rifles and East Bengal regiment) by August; that month, the government estimated it was facing 100,000 rebels. Other rebel organizations sprang up during the summer: Kader Bahini led by Kader Siddiki (17,000 troops), the Afsar Battalion (4,500), Hemayet Bahini (5,000), and Mujib Bahini (5,000). Smaller units were set up by communists and other leftists. The Mujib Bahini were condemned by the rebel "government" but continued to fight on the same side during the civil war.

In October, the guerrillas began to win some successes, taking a few airfields. In pursuit of the rebels—who had been retreating into the nearly Indian-surrounded Boyra salient—Pakistani forces entered Indian territory several times, at Kamalpur (from October 20 to 22), Boyra (on November 22), and Hilli (from November 26 to 28). Each incursion led to minor skirmishes between India and Pakistan. By November 21, Indian infantry and artillery were intervening actively in the war on the side of the rebels. India also provided air and naval support. The first direct clash between Indian and government forces came the next day, when a government battalion attacked toward Boyra, losing thirteen tanks and suffering numerous casualties to Indian defenders.

Termination and Outcome: On December 3, Pakistan mounted a surprise attack against Indian air force bases. As with the American bombing of North Vietnam during the Vietnam War, this marked the transition from a civil war to an inter-state war, with the bulk of the fighting against Pakistan's government being taken over by the Indian armed forces. Although the rebels continued to fight the government, Bengali independence was ultimately won by the Indian army. Following the surrender of Pakistani forces in East Pakistan on December 16, the victorious rebels in Dhaka embarked on a massacre of real and suspected collaborators.

Coding Decisions: There were 5,000 to 10,000 government deaths, but some of these were suffered in the inter-state war against India. We take the lower estimate as a plausible total for the civil war period, given that the government had already lost 2,500 killed by July. Rebel battle-deaths are much harder to estimate but were surely much higher. We tentatively estimate 20,000 battle-deaths in all; the real toll could be somewhat lower or considerably higher.

Sources: Clodfelter (2008); Dunér (1985); Kasturi (2007); South Asia Terrorism Portal (2014); Zaheer (1994).[360]

INTRA-STATE WAR #783
First Sri Lanka–JVP War of 1971 (aka First JVP)

Participants: Ceylon versus Janatha Vimukthi Peramuna.
Dates: April 4, 1971, to June 30, 1971.
Battle-related Deaths: Armed Forces of Ceylon: 63;[361] Total Combatant Deaths: 2,000. (See Coding Decisions.)[362]
Initiator: Janatha Vimukthi Peramuna.
Outcome: Ceylon wins.
War Type: Civil for central control.
Total System Member Military Personnel: Armed Forces of Ceylon: 10,691 military and 12,843 police—both fought in the war for a total strength of 23,534 (initial, peak, final).[363]
Theater Armed Forces: *Janatha Vimukthi Peramuna*, aka People's Liberation Front: 10,000: 20,000 (initial); 20,000 (peak).[364]

Antecedents: The Janatha Vimukthi Peramuna (JVP) was a Marxist organization started and led by Rohana Wijeweera, which drew its strength from poor youths in rural areas and poorer universities. It was dedicated to the armed overthrow of the government, but in the 1970 elections, it supported a left-center coalition government that promised socialism. However, when these promises were not immediately fulfilled, the JVP turned against the government. It also virulently opposed government relations with India, fearing Indian domination. Warning signs of an insurrection appeared in March; the government declared a state of emergency and arrested 450 people, including Wijeweera. On April 2, the JVP command decided to mount an insurrection on April 5.

Narrative: The first attack—on the Wellawaya police station—was pulled off prematurely on the night of April 4, giving some warning to the armed forces. Then on April 5, the JVP mounted its insurrection, near-simultaneously attacking ninety-two more police stations and killing two police. Despite warnings of a potential insurrection, the attacks came as a surprise in many areas and succeeded in seizing population centers and territory in some. The government of Ceylon appealed for and received substantial aid during the war—naturally, India sent helicopters and a small number of troops, providing military assistance to government forces; the Soviet Union also provided arms to the government; the United Kingdom provided arms and aircraft to the government; even Pakistan, Yugoslavia, and the United States provided arms. The rebels may have been (poorly) armed by China and North Korea. After about a week, the government mounted a counteroffensive and drove the rebels back everywhere, first clearing the major trunk roads and then population centers.

The conflict degenerated into a guerrilla insurgency, for which the JVP was ill supplied and ill prepared. On May 1, the government announced a temporary amnesty; up to 6,000 surrendered. Three days later, the government began its offensive into the jungle. Some holdouts continued to fight past September, but the fighting was more or less over by the end of June.

Termination and Outcome: The outcome of the war was a complete military victory for the government. By the end of June, the government estimated that 16,000 rebels had been killed, captured, or surrendered. There were no postwar massacres, but 146 leaders of the revolt were tried and sentenced to long prison terms (they would be pardoned in 1978).

Coding Decisions: Figures vary widely; the government claimed 63 of its own forces killed and 305 wounded (figures generally believed to be reasonable) and 1,200 rebels killed (a figure generally believed to be a gross underestimate—2,000 to 3,000 is likely to be more accurate, and 6,000 is the maximum estimate). But not every JVP member was a combatant, so we estimate only 2,000 battle-deaths.

Sources: Arasaratnam (1972); Dunér (1985); O'Ballance (1989); Ranatunga (2009); Samarasinghe and Vidyamali (1991); Senaratne (1997).[365]

INTRA-STATE WAR #785
First Khmer Rouge War of 1971 to 1975

Participants: Cambodia, Republic of Vietnam, and the United States of America versus Khmer Rouge and Democratic Republic of Vietnam.

Dates: December 4, 1971, to April 17, 1975.

Battle-related Deaths: Armed Forces of Cambodia: 44,000;[366] United States of America: up to 185 (see Coding Decisions);[367] Khmer Rouge: 56,000 (give or take 25,000);[368] Total Combatant Deaths: about 100,000. (See Coding Decisions.)

Initiator: Khmer Rouge.

Outcome: Khmer Rouge wins.

War Type: Civil for central control.

Total System Member Military Personnel: Armed Forces of Cambodia (*Forces armées national khmères*): 80,000 (initial); 145,500 (peak).[369] Armed Forces of the Republic of Vietnam: 1,060,000 (prewar, initial); 1,100,000 (peak). Armed Forces of the United States: 2,720,000 (prewar, initial, peak); 2,098,000 (final). Armed Forces of the Democratic Republic of Vietnam: 445,000 (prewar, initial); 665,000 (peak); 643,000 (final).[370]

Theater Armed Forces: Republic of Vietnam, sporadically participating through 1974: 20,000 (peak).[371] United States of America, participating through August 15, 1973: air only. Khmer Rouge, aka *Front Uni National Ju Kampuchea*—15,000 (prewar—late 1970), 8,000 to 9,000 (initial); 60,000 (peak, final).[372] Democratic Republic of Vietnam, participating until at least mid-1973, although it retained troops in the country afterward to protect the Ho Chi Minh trail into South Vietnam: 8,000 or fewer engaged in combat, although tens of thousands were in-country (initial, peak); 3,000 combat troops and 2,000 cadres plus forces guarding the Ho Chi Minh trail (final).[373]

Antecedents: A communist party (under various names) existed in Cambodia from 1951. The government of Prince Norodom Sihanouk attempted to remain neutral as the struggle in Indochina escalated. In April 1967, leftist agitation against newly appointed, right-wing prime minister Lon Nol led to a peasant revolt in Battambag, which was suppressed brutally by government forces. Peasants and communist rebels took to the hills, allying themselves with the Khmer Loeu. On January 17, 1968, the 4,000 to 5,000 rebels that Sihanouk called the Khmer Rouge began a pinprick guerrilla campaign against the government. Sihanouk allowed North Vietnam to establish bases along the country's borders with North and South Vietnam. The following year, American bombers began attacking these border sanctuaries.

By 1970, Khmer Rouge strength had increased to 10,000 fighters. On March 11, Lon Nol mounted a coup against Sihanouk. Soon, he ordered the North Vietnamese to vacate their positions; when North Vietnam refused, he sent the Cambodian armed forces to evict them. The result was an inter-state conflict from 1970 to 1971—two major offensives against the North Vietnamese failed as "experienced North Vietnamese forces cut them to pieces" (Chandler, 206). Thousands of hastily raised Cambodian volunteers were killed by the North Vietnamese forces between April and June 1970 alone.

Meanwhile, Prince Sihanouk allied himself and about 700 men with the Communist Party of Kampuchea (CPK) to form the united *Front Uni National Ju Kampuchea* (FUNK) under a front organization called the Royal United National Government of Kampuchea (GRUNK), both allied to the NLF. The government requested South Vietnamese artillery support for its attacks on the NVA/NLF forces; the South Vietnamese ARVN mounted a full-scale military intervention with 40,000 troops and the temporary participation of 32,000 American troops. On October 9, 1970, Lon Nol proclaimed a Khmer republic. By the end of the year, the rebels numbered 15,000 with up to 60,000 militia; the NLF and NVA had about 40,000 in Cambodia and the ARVN 40,000. Just six months later, in June 1971, the United States estimated the Cambodian rebels' strength as 125,000 when (largely unarmed) irregulars were included.

The rebels had a diffuse command structure, with each district having its own commander not subordinated to the Central Committee. Occasionally, anti-Vietnamese elements of the Khmer Rouge clashed with NLF/NVA forces (Hanoi-trained cadres were purged by the KCP, which urged the expulsion of NVA forces), but others, especially the eastern zone, actively coordinated their activities with them. Because the bulk of the fighting against the government was still being borne by North Vietnam, the civil war proper did not begin until that situation changed. When Operation Chenla II was mounted by the government in October, its main targets were NVA forces, and it was the NVA that did the bulk of the fighting, killing 3,000 *Forces armées national khmères* (FANK) troops, including most of its elite units. Toward the end of 1971, the North Vietnamese concluded that Khmerization of the conflict was now feasible and withdrew large numbers of troops from combat operations, although it still maintained them in-country. At this point, the war became an internationalized civil war instead of an inter-state war.

Narrative: We date the Khmerization of the conflict to the end of Chenla II on December 3, 1971. The following day, the civil war began. NVA units continued to participate in combat, but the bulk of the fighting against the government was now assumed by FUNK forces. "The Khmer Republic was in tatters after Chenla II, and the strategy from 1972 to 1975 was purely defensive."[374] While various minor operations were mounted by the government, its forces were simply incapable of action on the previous scale. In early 1972, NVA units were distracted by the upcoming offensive in Vietnam, and the Central Committee began to assert its authority over the various zones of rebel control, purging Hanoi-trained cadres from leadership positions. The Khmer Rouge was coming into its own, with Prince Sihanouk playing only a titular role and real control exercised by the KCP. Meanwhile, Lon Nol spent his time consolidating all state power in his hands.

On January 10, Operation Prek Tha (Prek Ta) was launched by the FANK, acting in concert with ARVN units. On January 29, FANK mounted Operation Angkor Chey with 10,000 troops to clear the area surrounding Angkor Wat. After several weeks of heavy fighting in which 4,000 NVA played a major role, the offensive was stalemated; the government withdrew its forces later in the year. A lull settled in, and the next major action of the year was an ARVN offensive against NVA positions in March (best characterized as part of the inter-state Vietnam War). The NVA continued to take government-held areas and turn them over to the Khmer Rouge; fighting became nearly general across the boundaries of rebel-held and government-held areas.

In April, the NVA closed Route 1; government efforts to reestablish control were fruitless. Two FANK battalions were ambushed near Route 1 in June; only 13 of approximately 600 soldiers returned to friendly lines. A joint ARVN–FANK effort to retake Route 1 (Operation Sorya) kicked off on July 4. The Khmer Rouge and its North Vietnamese allies responded in August by committing armored forces against government-held positions along the road. The government was forced to shift its focus to relieving the five battalions trapped near Kompong Trabek (Operation Sorya II), and while it succeeded in establishing a corridor to the town, its garrison there was quickly besieged again in September, forcing three battalions to withdraw. Route 3 also came under heavy rebel pressure.

By October, the government had fallen into a pattern of mounting various small-scale offensives to reestablish control over enemy-controlled routes and critical rice-producing towns, only to see the rebels mount both local counterattacks and raids on the capital itself, forcing the withdrawal of government troops to secure the approaches to Phnom Penh. American air support significantly aided the government in some operations. On December 7, some 4,000 to 7,000 NVA and Khmer Rouge troops attacked the government's garrison of Kompong Thom. Casualties were heavy, and fighting lasted into 1973. By the end of the year, North Vietnamese forces had withdrawn from most of Cambodia. As the control of the Central Committee expanded, more pro-Vietnamese cadres were purged and in some cases massacred amid anger over the "betrayal" by North Vietnam.

As 1973 dawned, Lon Nol decided to negotiate. A unilateral cease-fire was declared, coming into effect on January 29. Sihanouk, reduced to little more than a spokesperson for the FUNK (his supporters were purged from local government offices throughout the year), declined to negotiate. Khmer Rouge units launched a major offensive along the Mekong, simultaneously mounting smaller attacks against Route 2, Route 3, and Kompong Thom. The government relied on American air support to blunt the offensives, but in March it faced new assaults near Takeo and the Mekong–Route 1 corridor. By April South Vietnamese aid convoys to Phnom Penh were being interdicted, and separate battles were waged over control of sections of Route 1. In June, the government managed to reopen Route 5, which had been closed for several months.

The rebels began to assault the environs of Phnom Penh itself. An assault along Route 4 about fifteen miles from the capital was repelled only with heavy American air support. The result was a limited government victory, and Routes 4 and 5 were soon reopened. The Khmer Rouge shifted more of its forces to direct assaults on the capital in July in an arc from the northwest to the south. The government was forced to withdraw its forces from other areas to meet the threat; the infusion of troops and US air support enabled the government to stave off collapse.

US tactical air support alone killed up to 900 Khmer Rouge in the conventional battles south and southwest of Phnom Penh from July 15 to August 7. In the northwest, US air support took an even higher toll on the Khmer Rouge. According to a US air force report,

> Between the first of July and August 15, 743 tactical air and 37 B-52 strikes reportedly killed or wounded 2,100 and forced enemy withdrawal from the immediate Phnom Penh area. . . . In all, for the last forty-five days, from July 1 to August 15 there were 1,908 B-52 sorties and 10,360 tactical air sorties.[375]

Clodfelter claims that up to 16,000 communist soldiers were killed by the American air campaign from June to August 1973.

At the end of August 15, the United States halted all combat air operations in Southeast Asia, including Cambodia. The government still controlled 60 percent of the population, but only 25 percent of the country's territory. Late that summer, many Sihanouk loyalists and cadres trained by the North Vietnamese secretly were executed by the Khmer Rouge. The remainder of 1973 was marked by struggles over the provincial capital of Kompong Cham (which may have been the largest battle of the war, with unofficial casualty estimates of up to 8,000 on both sides), Route 4, and positions along the Prek Thnaot River. The government was at least temporarily successful in the first two but suffered serious losses in the third. Additionally, some garrisons were overrun by Khmer Rouge forces elsewhere in the country.

By January 5, 1974, two regiments of Khmer Rouge had advanced to within four miles of the capital; the government repelled the attack and claimed that 300 rebels had been killed in five days of fighting and another 200 over the next twelve days. The government later admitted losses of 66 killed and 443 wounded. In February the FANK mounted limited offensives to secure the northwest and southern approaches to the capital, but rebels continued to interdict ammunition barges as they were towed near the Mekong.

Beginning in March, battles raged around the provincial capitals of Oudong (Udong) and Kampot. The rebels took the former, but the government successfully defended the latter; government-reported casualties for the two battles included 610 FUNK killed but only 208 FANK killed and 1,068 FANK wounded. Further FANK advances from Kampot cleared the surrounding area at the cost of 416 FANK killed, 2,363 wounded, and 79 missing; rebel losses were up to 2,363 killed. Meanwhile, follow-on attacks by the rebels near Oudong cost the government 600 troops unaccounted for and caused it to consolidate defenders into Lovek, where they were besieged on April 30.

By this time, a Khmer Rouge offensive along the Bassac/Mekong corridor was making steady progress northwest toward Phnom Penh. Once again, rebel units nearly reached the capital (at one point, they were stopped just three miles short of the city), and the government had to withdraw units from other fronts to prevent a breakthrough. By the end of May the situation had been stabilized by FANK, and it went over to the offensive north of the city in June.

By month's end, FANK controlled Route 5 and Kompong Luong; moreover, Lovek had been relieved and Oudong was soon retaken. Allegedly, the rebels had lost 1,366 killed in action between April 22 and July 9, while the government reported its own losses as just 104 killed and 786 wounded.

As usual, combat slackened somewhat during the wet season (August to December), but the government mounted a series of operations near the Bassac river to enlarge the defense perimeter of the capital. By October, arms and ammunition convoys from South Vietnam were once again using the Mekong route with little opposition from the rebels. On November 10, the rebels attempted a small offensive against Barrong Khnar Kar northeast of the capital to secure positions that could bombard the capital's defenses. The attack was repulsed by government air and artillery support, and Lon Nol's generals reported the unlikely figures of 558 rebels killed against only 16 FANK killed and 185 wounded. Meanwhile, rebel counterattacks near the Bassac took a heavy toll on the overextended government forces in November and December, recapturing much territory lost in the preceding months.

By the beginning of 1975, the FANK—though possibly at its peak numerical strength of 140,500 (plus at least 80,000 phantom soldiers that existed only on paper)—was thoroughly demoralized by battlefield defeats and dependent on foreign support to survive. At least 40,000 Khmer Rouge regulars were in the field against the government, now armed and supplied by China rather than North Vietnam. The noose continued to tighten around the capital and other population centers, and four separate government offers of peace talks had been rejected by the rebels over the previous year. The rebels mined the Mekong, preventing resupply convoys for reaching the capital by water, although the United States provided some supplies by air.

By March 12, most of the fighting for Phnom Penh was concentrated in a ten-mile radius around the capital. Within this perimeter, 75,000 FANK troops faced 30,000 Khmer Rouge. North and west of the capital, government divisions were cut off, their fronts broken. In the region of Takhmau, Route 1, and the Bassac, defenses were under pressure. On the east bank of the Mekong, the city of Neak Luong on Route 1 was isolated and cut off from the capital. It fell on April 1, opening the door to the capital; Lon Nol left the country in a last bid for peace, but the rebels pressed on along Route 1, while the rump government threw its last reserves into an effort to reconstitute a defense perimeter to the north. The government still held most provincial capitals, and the population living under its control probably outnumbered that living under rebel control by 6:1.

From April 3 to April 12, the defenses of the city crumbled. The next day, the military assumed formal control of the republic. But just two days later, the last defense perimeter in the city was breached. FANK units, now deprived of even aerial resupply, often fought "to the last bullet."[376] On April 16, the military government offered to turn over governance to GRUNK and FUNK in return for a cease-fire; the FANK had suffered 10,000 killed and 20,000 wounded in 1975 alone.

Termination and Outcome: Even this offer was rejected by Sihanouk, and on April 17 members of the military government ordered white flags of surrender to be hoisted by all troops. The outcome of the war was an unconditional rebel victory. Hundreds of officers and officials were immediately executed, and the people of the cities were forcibly dispersed into the countryside's killing fields, where more than a million would die over the next four years in what became known as the Cambodian Genocide.

Coding Decisions: The government suffered about 50,000 killed from 1970 to 1975.[377] Subtracting the estimate of about 6,000 dead for 1970 and 1971 provided by Deac, we conclude that the government suffered about 44,000 battle-deaths. The United States suffered 523 battle-deaths in Cambodia during the Vietnam War. Excluding the 338 deaths from the prewar Cambodian incursion leaves a maximum toll of 185 during the civil war period.[378] Others' battle-deaths are harder to estimate, but the Khmer Rouge appears to have suffered higher fatalities from overwhelming government and American firepower than those suffered by the government forces (see the battle descriptions in the Narrative). We tentatively estimate a total of 100,000 battle-deaths, which is probably correct to the nearest 25,000.

Sources: Bowra (1989); Chandler (1991, 2000); Clodfelter (1995); Deac (1997); Hartsock (1980); Kiernan (1985); Nhem (2013); Sutsakhan (1978).[379]

INTRA-STATE WAR #786
First Philippine–Moro War of 1972 to 1981 (aka MNLF Rebellion)

Participants: Philippines versus Moro National Liberation Front and New Moro National Liberation Front.
Dates: January 1, 1972, to April 19, 1991.
Battle-related Deaths: Armed Forces of the Philippines: about 12,000; Moro National Liberation Front: 20,000; Total Combatant Deaths: 32,000. (See Coding Decisions.)[380]
Initiator: Moro National Liberation Front.
Outcome: Fighting fell below civil-war threshold.
War Type: Civil for local issues (secession).
Total System Member Military Personnel: Armed Forces of the Philippines: 62,000 (initial); 156,000 (peak); 156,000 (final).[381]

Theater Armed Forces: Armed Forces of the Philippines: up to 125,000 (peak). Moro National Liberation Front/Bangsa Moro Army: 15,000 (initial); 21,200 (peak); 14,380 (final).[382] New Moro National Liberation Front, participating from January 1978: 500 (initial); more than 1,000 (peak); more than 1,000 (final).[383]

Antecedents: While the Moros (Philippine Muslims of Mindanao and the Sulu archipelago) had long supported autonomy or independence for these regions, violence only became common after a massacre of Muslim recruits in 1968. In 1969, the secessionist Nur Misuari and other secularly educated Moros formed the Moro National Liberation Front (MNLF). In 1970 and 1971, hundreds of Christians and Muslims fought each other in Mindanao as Christian settlers were attacked by Muslim militia and vice versa. Some 800 were killed in the fighting in 1971.

Narrative: Faced with this intercommunal conflict, the government troops intervened in 1972. As the violence escalated, Ferdinand Marcos declared martial law on September 21, 1972. The declaration sparked a large-scale Moro revolt, which the MNLF quickly took over.

On October 21, hundreds of Moro guerrillas stormed Marawi City but were repulsed within twenty-four hours. The government deployed units of the army to Muslim areas, marking the beginning of large-scale combat operations. The MNLF almost immediately was aided by Libya; indeed, it moved its headquarters to Tripoli. Perhaps emboldened by this foreign support, it attempted to seize and hold territory in early 1973, leading to very heavy casualties as government forces inevitably brought their superior firepower to bear. By 1974, the rebels switched to a standard guerrilla hit-and-run strategy, which reduced their own losses and increased those of the government, which suffered 1,750 killed by March 1975. Wary of casualties, government units began to effectively concede significant areas to the guerrillas.

Some major engagements of the first phase of the war included Labangan from March 22 to 24, 1973 (200 rebels and 10 government troops killed), the Zamboanga peninsula from July 14 to 21, 1973 (350 rebels and 25 government troops killed), a string of engagements near Jolo from February 4 to April 10, 1974 (516 rebels and 100 government troops killed), Sacol Island on September 1, 1974 (40 rebels killed), Jolo island on January 15, 1975 (41 government troops killed), and again on August 9 (69 rebels and 6 government troops killed), and Calucan island from September 19 to 27, 1976 (49 government troops killed). About 80 percent of government forces were deployed against the MNLF, allowing the simultaneous revolt of the communist New People's Army (NPA) to grow unchecked (see Intra-state War #824).

From December 15 to 23, 1976, the MNLF and government negotiated a cease-fire agreement, which went into effect on December 24. A subsequent (March 20, 1977) peace agreement provided autonomy for some areas of Mindanao and Sulu but only if the inhabitants of these areas (a majority of which were now Christian settlers and their descendants) voted for such in a referendum. In the end, the autonomy provision would prove to be a virtual dead letter as the MNLF boycotted the referendum. Although two nominally autonomous zones were established this action was too little and too late. Small clashes broke out following the peace agreement. In all, some 19 individuals, including 5 government soldiers, were killed in clashes between government troops and the MNLF between April 28 and May 6, 1977, including 3 on each side in a skirmish near Manila on the latter date. Still, the agreement largely held until September 17; in all, perhaps 100 people—many of them civilians—died in political violence during the cease-fire period.

From September 17 to September 21, clashes on Basilan and Jolo islands killed eighty-six. A second engagement on Basilan island killed fifty-three from October 2 to October 8; this was followed by more fighting on Jolo on October 10, which killed thirty-three government troops. Further clashes that month spilled over to Mindanao as well and killed another fifty government troops. The government mounted a campaign to win over MNLF commanders, offering them economic concessions and government posts in the autonomous regions. In March 1978, the vice chair of the MNLF, along with all of his troops, formally surrendered. Even among Moros who supported armed struggle, there was competition among different ethnic groups, with the MNLF dominated by ethnic Tausugs. In January 1978, Salamat Hashim led his primarily Maguindanaoan MNLF forces into a splinter organization he called the New MNLF, demanding real autonomy rather than independence. In the 1980s, he would rename his organization the Moro Islamic Liberation Front (MILF).

The war continued, albeit at lower intensity. In April 1978, another engagement on Basilan island killed 80 rebels and 11 government troops. The zone of conflict expanded to include southern Palawan and eastern Mindanao; fighting was particularly intense in September. Nonetheless, the MNLF had entered a period of military decline; it was simply unable to put as many guerrillas into the field and use them to inflict large-scale casualties on government forces. Surrender became common, and the movement's leadership in Libya gradually lost control of local factions. The level of violence subsided, but seems to have remained above the civil-war threshold. For the last six months of 1980, the rebels claimed to have killed 750 soldiers or MNLF defectors while suffering only 73 battle-deaths. In one MNLF attack on Pata island early the next year (February 12), the government acknowledged losing 119 troops killed; it responded by massacring hundreds of villagers who had little or nothing to do with the initial attack.

Termination and Outcome: The war ended as the level of fighting dropped below the threshold of civil war. The government reduced its military operations so that it could deal with the NPA (see Intra-state War #824), and the MNLF was unwilling or unable to mount major offensive operations of its own. The main MNLF elements did not lay down their arms until a peace agreement in 1996. War resumed in 2000 (see Intra-state War #916).

Coding Decisions: We estimate 32,000 battle-deaths. The government admitted to 11,000 battle-deaths from 1972 to 1980, which suggests a total somewhat lower than 12,000 for the entire period. Rebel battle-deaths were higher—at least 5 for every 3 government battle-deaths, or a minimum figure of 20,000. Other estimates run as high as 30,000 on the government side and 50,000 rebels, but we find the lower estimates to be more plausible.

Sources: Cline (2000); Clodfelter (2008); Machado (1979); McKenna (1998); Mullenbach (2013a, b); Noble (1981).[384]

INTRA-STATE WAR #787
Thai Communist Insurgency of 1972 to 1973

Participants: Thailand versus People's Liberation Army of Thailand.
Dates: January 1972 to October 15, 1973.
Battle-related Deaths: Armed Forces of Thailand: more than 1,254;[385] People's Liberation Army of Thailand: 649;[386] Total Combatant Deaths: about 2,000. (See Coding Decisions.)[387]
Initiator: Thailand.
Outcome: Fighting fell below civil-war threshold.
War Type: Civil for central control.
Total System Member Military Personnel: Armed Forces of Thailand: 205,000 (prewar, initial); 233,000 (peak, final).[388]
Theater Armed Forces: People's Liberation Army of Thailand: 3,500 (initial); 5,000 to 7,000 (peak, final).[389]

Antecedents: Thailand's communist insurgency began with an armed clash on August 7, 1965, although communists had been recruiting for years. It was focused in the Muslim southeast and in the northeast. The insurgency grew slowly; by 1967, 1300 or so rebels were killing or kidnapping about 20 people a month, largely government officials. The government resorted to indiscriminate bombing and attacks on villages, tactics that simply led to an escalation in rebel violence. American forces, stationed in Thailand to support intervention in the Vietnam War, became both targets and convenient scapegoats for the repressive Thai state. Communist recruiting increased dramatically, as did the effectiveness of their operations. Government losses in 1969 amounted to 300 killed and 500 wounded, figures that rose to 450 and 500, respectively, in 1970. The communist forces suffered 109 battle-deaths in 1969 and 96 in 1970. The latter year saw the government ally itself to Guomindang (Kuomintang [KMT]) remnants in Thailand against the Chinese-supported communists. A battle between the People's Liberation Army of Thailand (PLAT) and the KMT in late September left 30 dead. In 1971 the number of government battle-deaths climbed to 500; the rebels suffered 362.

Narrative: In 1972, the conflict escalated to full-scale civil war. In January, the government mounted a two-month offensive against the rebels, who simply withdrew across the border to Laos. The operation produced 60 government killed and 300 wounded, mostly from booby traps. No rebels were killed. In all, the government lost 700 killed that year; the rebels suffered 362 battle-deaths. PLAT numbers grew to up to 7,000 by March 1973, when the government mounted its largest counterinsurgency drive of the war—a drive that proved to be a complete failure.

Termination and Outcome: On October 14, Thailand's military government was overthrown by a student revolt in Bangkok. The new government pledged democracy and immediately reduced military actions against the rebels, leading to a reduction in casualties on both sides to below the civil-war level. The outcome of the war was a stalemate in which lower-level fighting continued (87 rebels and 217 government troops died in 1974), especially after the democratic government was overthrown by a coup in 1976. The conflict reached near-war levels again in 1980, when the government suffered 502 personnel (including some loyalist civilians) killed, and the rebels suffered 310 battle-deaths. But the back of the insurgency was soon broken, and by the end of the 1980s the government's victory was complete.

Coding Decisions: Although the United States of America had 50,000 troops in Thailand and its air bases were sometimes attacked by the rebels, it refrained from combat participation in the war and is not counted as a participant in our data. In 1972, 362 communist troops died; the government lost more than 700 killed. Without estimates of casualties for 1973, we assume that the intensity of the fighting was unchanged until October 15, which yields an estimate of about 287 rebel battle-deaths and more than 554 for the government. Combining these totals yields 649 rebel battle-deaths and more than 1,254 government battle-deaths, or somewhat more than 1,900 in all—an estimate of 2,000 captures the uncertainty in these figures.

Sources: Clodfelter (1995); Marks (1991); Prizzia (1985); Race (1975); Wongtrangan (1981); Worobec (1983).[390]

INTRA-STATE WAR #792

Baluchi Separatists War of 1973 to 1977

Participants: Pakistan versus Baluchistan People's Liberation Front and Popular Front for Armed Resistance (PFAK).

Dates: January 25, 1973, to May 1975, and January 1976 to July 1977.

Battle-related Deaths: Pakistan: 3,300;[391] Combined Rebel Forces: 5,300;[392] Total Combatant Deaths: 8,600.[393]

Initiator: Pakistan.

Outcome: Pakistan wins.

War Type: Civil for local issues (autonomy).

Total System Member Military Personnel: Armed Forces of Pakistan: 466,000 (prewar); 466,000 (initial); 604,000 (peak); 588,000 (final).[394]

Theater Armed Forces: Armed Forces of Pakistan: 70,000 to 80,000 (initial); 100,000 (peak). Baluchistan People's Liberation Front: 500 (initial—government estimate); 47,000 to 49,000 (peak—estimated by subtracting PFAR strength from combined peak of 55,000).[395] Popular Front for Armed Resistance: 400 (initial—government estimate); 6,000 to 8,000 (peak).[396]

Antecedents: Pakistan fought Balochi (Baluchi) guerrillas resisting incorporation into Pakistan in the late 1940s, then again in 1958. After some guerrillas surrendered in 1960, the government reneged on its promises of policy concessions and amnesty, executing five of the leaders. Skirmishes continued into the 1960s, especially after separatists elected in 1962 were dismissed from office, with significant engagements in 1964 and 1965. Operations were carried out by Parari led by Sher Muhammad Marri, and the Marri tribe proved to be the foundation of the later rebellion. Parari was transformed into the Baloch People's Liberation Front (BPLF) in the 1970s.

In November, Marri insurgents attacked settlers in Balochistan. The government deployed frontier guards on December 2 but did not succeed in engaging the insurgents. But by 1973, a political crisis between Balochistan's provincial leadership and the central government had emerged as autonomous parties in the province shut out the ruling Pakistan People's Party from power. The provincial government owed its loyalty to local tribal leaders and not to the PPP.

Narrative: On January 25, the government announced that rebellion had broken out against the provincial government of Balochistan and that the central government had deployed the army to fight the rebellion. But on February 12, the central government dismissed the provincial government, banned its largest political party, and arrested its leaders on charges of high treason. While the Marri tribe was already hostile, these actions alienated the Mengals and the Bizenjos as well. A massive insurrection by two groups—the Mengal- and Bizenjo-dominated Popular Front for Armed Resistance (PFAR) and the Marri-dominated BPLF—followed, with the rebels demanding the release of their leaders and the withdrawal of central government troops from the province.

Some 178 major engagements were fought during the war as well as 167 lesser ones. The bulk of the fighting occurred during the first two years of the war. By early April 1973, Balochi guerrillas were ambushing army convoys. An operation in May succeeded in killing eight government paramilitary troops. On November 5, the guerrillas claimed (implausibly) to have inflicted thousands of fatalities on government forces while suffering only two dozen themselves. The rebels numbered at least 7,000 by November 15. The government deployed 70,000 to 80,000 soldiers against the rebels, who numbered about 30,000 (4,500 PFAR and about 25,000 BPLF) by the end of 1973 and 55,000 by the end of 1974 (including 11,500 in hard-core units).

By July 1974, the rebels had cut most transportation links to the province, including the railroad used to transport coal to the rest of the provinces. At about this time, Iran actively began assisting the government, providing thirty attack helicopters and many pilots. The government mounted its offensive against the BPLF on August 21 and succeeded in forcing a large number of BPLF fighters—some sources say as many as 17,000—to stand and fight against the government forces with their air support. The Battle of Chamalang, fought from September 3 to September 9, resulted in a major government victory, despite heavy losses (the army claimed to have killed 125 rebels, while the rebels claimed to have inflicted 446 battle-deaths on the government). The BPLF was pushed back to its bases in Afghanistan, which supplied it with food, ammunition, and possibly Soviet arms.

The government declared an end to the fighting on October 17, some 5,000 rebels having surrendered. However, on the ground it followed up its success against the BPLF with an offensive against PFAR beginning on October 26. The offensive was a success, and violence was dramatically reduced as both rebel organizations hid out in Afghanistan. Buffardi notes:

> Indeed, by May of 1975, the Baluchi opposition had appeared to have died down. There was only one confirmed guerrilla action against the army that year. Taking advantage of amnesty, many of the Baluchi rebels surrendered. But the opposition forces maintained that the insurgents were "currently lying low, with some of them regrouping in Afghanistan. They claim the government called in 100,000 troops to suppress the rebels." (98, internal citations omitted)

If there was peace after May 1975, it did not last. The central government once again dismissed the provincial government in January 1976, this time imposing direct rule from the center. The rebels resumed their activities that spring but were incapable of large-unit engagements and confined themselves to small guerrilla attacks.

Termination and Outcome: In July 1977, the government was overthrown in a military coup. The new government decided to resolve the conflict through diplomatic means. Cases against Balochi leaders were withdrawn, they were released, and a general amnesty was proclaimed. Some low-level violence persisted, but the war was over. A new upsurge in violence short of civil war occurred in the twenty-first century.

Coding Decisions: Self-explanatory from cited sources.

Sources: Ali (1993); Buffardi (1981); Butt (2012); Cloughley (2000); Harrison (1981); Hewitt (1996).[397]

INTRA-STATE WAR #803

Second Laotian War of 1976 to 1979 (aka Chao Fa Rebellion)

Participants: Laos and the Democratic Republic of Vietnam versus Chao Fa Rebels.
Dates: January 1976 to February 1979.
Battle-related Deaths: Total Combatant Deaths: 5,000. (See Coding Decisions.)[398]
Initiator: Chao Fa Rebels.
Outcome: Laos wins.
War Type: Civil for local issues (reeducation camps, religion, and Vietnamese presence).

Total System Member Military Personnel: Armed Forces of Laos: 46,000 (initial); 47,000 (peak).[399] Armed Forces of the Democratic Republic of Vietnam: 665,000 (prewar); 637,000 (initial); 660,000 (peak); 650,000 (final).[400]

Theater Armed Forces: Armed Forces of the Democratic Republic of Vietnam: 30,000 to 40,000 (prewar, initial); 60,000 (peak).[401] Chao Fa: 400 to 500 (initial); 16,000 (peak).[402]

Antecedents: After the communist takeover of Laos during 1975, resistance to the new government quickly emerged from several quarters: Lao "maquis" of the Lao People's Revolutionary Front 21/8 (which engaged in low-level violence below the threshold of war), a Yao rebellion (crushed by Vietnamese troops in 1977 with more than 1,000 executions—a clear extra-state conflict), and a Hmong (Meo) revolt in the vicinity of the mountain of Phu Bia. The latter was triggered by the construction of a reeducation camp near Muong Ong and the death, a few days after the camp's completion, of a leader of the Chao Fa religious movement, Boua Cher Yang.

Narrative: The first action of the conflict was an ambush of government (LPLA) soldiers by Hmong forces in January 1976. The government may have responded by using some type of chemical agent or toxin against the rebels, although both the existence and nature of this response have been doubted by historians. What is clear is that government forces initially focused on other, larger rebellions, allowing the Chao Fa movement to grow. The rebels began ambushing Vietnamese troops, in some cases inflicting heavy casualties. These early successes converted many Hmong to the Chao Fa movement. A significant engagement between the LPLA and Chao Fa in March drew Vietnamese reinforcements. Chao Fa sources claimed implausible figures of only a dozen Chao Fa battle-deaths against 900 Vietnamese and LPLA killed or wounded.

While the Chao Fa's leader around Phu Bia was Tsong Zua Her, a separate Chao Fa force was raised in neighboring areas by Sai Shoua. The rebels continued their string of victories through July 1977, when Vietnam committed four regiments to their suppression. The Vietnamese move seems to have triggered disaffection among Hmong in the LPLA, some 3,000 of whom defected and fled to Thailand. In November, the government's dry season offensive kicked off. The offensive smashed Chao Fa forces, only slackening with the return of the rains in March 1978. Reporters estimated Chao Fa losses at 1,300 killed, 800 wounded, and 5,000 taken prisoner, although refugees estimated total Hmong losses at 5,000 killed. Tsong's forces all but disintegrated, although Sai's forces continued to mount pinprick attacks on the LPLA.

The rebels attempted their own counteroffensive but were easily repulsed at Ban Some. At Muong Cha, they claimed to have inflicted 150 killed on government forces but also suffered serious losses of their own, one platoon being wiped out. The government's next dry season offensive, mounted in December 1978, essentially wiped out the now-combined Chao Fa forces at Phu Bia. Tens of thousands of Hmong were killed in the assault—one questionable estimate says that 50,000 rebels were killed in poison attacks and another 45,000 were shot, starved, or executed. Certainly losses among civilians were very high. In all, the operation continued for two months, leaving the rebellion in tatters by the end of January 1979.

Termination and Outcome: The outcome of the war was a military victory by the government. The remaining rebels dispersed and became a low-level nuisance for more than a decade after the war but never again inflicted serious casualties on government forces. Many executions followed the government's victory over the Chao Fa movement.

Coding Decisions: Casualty reports are fragmentary and unreliable. Given the descriptive narrative and data on the force size of the rebels, we estimate 5,000 battle-deaths, most of which were suffered on the rebel side, particularly during the final battle at Phu Bia. This may be an underestimate, and certainly the number of Hmong civilians killed greatly outnumbered the deaths of the Chao Fa combatants.

Sources: Hamilton-Merritt (1992); *Keesing's Record of World Events* (1978); Quincy (2000).[403]

INTRA-STATE WAR #806

East Timorese War phase 3 of 1976 to 1979

Participants: Indonesia versus FRETILIN.

Dates: July 18, 1976, to May 26, 1979.

Battle-related Deaths: Armed Forces of Indonesia: more than 1250;[404] Total Combatant Deaths: 5,000. (See Coding Decisions.)[405]

Initiator: Indonesia.
Outcome: Indonesia wins.
War Type: Civil for local issues (secession).
Total System Member Military Personnel: Armed Forces of Indonesia: 257,000 (prewar, initial); 260,000 (peak); 250,000 (final).[406]
Theater Armed Forces: FRETILIN, aka East Timorese Liberation Army or FALANTIL: 20,000 (prewar—1975 figure); more than 5,000 (initial); more than 5,000 (peak); perhaps 1,000 (final—January 1979).[407]

Antecedents: East Timor was a Portuguese colony when Indonesia invaded it in 1975. After fighting a vicious extra-state war against the Timorese resistance (chiefly forces led by the FRETILIN party), Indonesia formally annexed East Timor on July 17, 1976. This action transformed the continuing war from an extra-state (imperial) war to a civil war.

Narrative: Although there was less fighting after the onset of the civil war phase than during the extra-state war phase, the violence was still war scale. FRETILIN even conducted offensive operations in the first months of the war. During the October through April rainy season, the government had difficulty with resupply and reinforcement of isolated garrisons, and the rebels were able to retake a number of villages. In November, the rebels claimed to have recaptured the villages of Fatumean, Fohorem, Fatululik, and Hatu Bulico. By the beginning of 1977, the rebels may have controlled up to 85 percent of the countryside and 80 percent of the population.

In February 1977, the government admitted that it might take a long time to crush the Timorese revolt. It offered amnesty to the rebels later that year and reported that many had surrendered (although later reports suggest that those who surrendered in 1977 were massacred in 1980). A Western source claimed that 80 Timorese were being killed each day. A rebel propaganda broadcast claimed that FRETILIN had fought a five-day battle over the village of Darolete, killing 525 government troops and losing only 9 dead and 3 wounded itself. A somewhat more plausible broadcast in April claimed that Indonesia lost 83 killed in a handful of clashes between March 17 and April 8.

In May 1978, the government moved another 15,000 troops into East Timor, giving lie to its claims that FRETILIN had been destroyed. Beginning on October 17, 1978, two months of fierce fighting took place at the bottom of the Matebian mountains. The rebels claimed to have killed 3,000 Indonesian troops during the fighting, a number that was obviously exaggerated but which suggests ongoing, large-scale resistance. In a blow to rebel morale, FRETILIN president Nicolao Lobato was gunned down in an engagement with government troops in the Maubese mountains on December 31, 1978. The government mounted a massive operation against the remaining rebels. Although FRETILIN still had more than 1,000 troops, its ability to inflict casualties declined precipitously thereafter.

Termination and Outcome: The outcome of the war was a military victory by the government with promises of amnesty. The war probably ended sometime before a report of the rebellion's defeat on May 26, 1979. Despite promises of amnesty, many rebels who surrendered were extrajudicially executed in the first half of 1980, causing hundreds of others to return to the bush. Resistance thus continued through 1980 and beyond, albeit at much lower levels.

Coding Decisions: In 1980, Indonesia conceded that 120,000 had died since the invasion. From 1976 to 1980 or so, about 50,000 were killed and another 50,000 died of privation. Of course, many of these fatalities would have occurred in the first half of 1976, and most were civilians. In 1999, Indonesia released official lists of government casualties, which amounted to about 3,600 dead and more than 2,400 wounded through 1999. These estimates included only casualties of combat, not disease, and so were likely underestimates. A review of Indonesian regular forces deaths by van Klinken—about 58 percent of the total government combat deaths—counted about 340 killed in 1976 and 190 in 1977, 325 in 1978, 80 in 1979, 50 in 1980, and somewhat fewer than 50 in 1981. If we assume that the casualties were distributed evenly throughout each year, we count about 170 in the second half of 1976, 515 from 1977 to 1978, and about 40 in 1979—a total of at least 725 regular forces killed. If we further assume that those not on the lists (i.e., members of pro-government militias) died in rough proportion to those on the list each year, then we arrive at a total of 1,250 government battle-deaths. Given the devastation inflicted by the government's forces on FRETILIN's forces and civilians alike, it is probable that rebel battle-deaths exceed this total by several times. Total battle-deaths might easily number

5,000, which is more likely to be an underestimate than an overestimate.

Sources: "China Reports on Fretilin" (1977); "E. Timor Expects 'Invasion'" (1978); "Fretilin Leader Shot" (1979); Inbaraj (1997); Jolliffe (1980); Lisbon Correspondent (1979); "Long Time to Crush Rebels" (1977); Plater (1977), "Timor Villages 'Fall.'" (1976); van Klinken (2005).[408]

INTRA-STATE WAR #806.3
Second West Papua War of 1977 to 1978

Participants: Indonesia versus Organisasi Papua Merdeka (Aggregate).
Dates: April 20, 1977, to November 1978.
Battle-Related Deaths: Total Combatant Deaths: 1,600. (See Coding Decisions.)[409]
Initiator: Organisasi Papua Merdeka.
Outcome: Indonesia wins.
War Type: Civil for local issues (secession).
Total System Member Military Personnel: Armed Forces of Indonesia: 260,000 (prewar, initial, peak); 250,000 (final).[410]
Theater Armed Forces: Armed Forces of Indonesia: 4,800 (initial, peak). Organisasi Papua Merdeka: about 500 (initial); thousands (peak).[411]

Antecedents: West Papua was incorporated into Indonesia in 1969, following a so-called Act of Free Choice. During this period, the government largely suppressed an insurrection by the Arfak tribe and Free Papua Movement (OPM). However, the movement still engaged in low-level violence, and in 1976, the OPM and its National Liberation Army (TPN) mounted operations against the government in a number of villages, including Bokondini, Kelila, and Pyramid. As Indonesian elections (scheduled for May 2, 1977) approached, the government deployed more troops to the island, which had the effect of fanning the flames of revolt.

Narrative: The first clear action of the war was the killing of an Indonesian officer at Kobakma on April 20. The next day, the OPM attacked a military post in Makki and a police station in Pyramid. There also may have been attacks on the villages of Wosilimo and Kimbim and the military base at Kasuraga. In June 1977, the Dhani tribe rose in revolt, killing six Indonesian soldiers while suffering about twenty killed. In response to the various attacks, the government shifted troops to the Central Highlands region, where the rebel activity was strongest.

The government's 1977 to 1978 campaign, *Operasi Kikis* (Operation Chipping Away), involved 4,800 military personnel (1,800 of them in the Central Highlands) and more sophisticated weapons than previous operations. Government violence was indiscriminate, killing OPM and villagers alike, especially in aerial bombing, strafing, and napalm attacks. The OPM claimed that bombings of Wamena in Jayawijaya killed 4,982 people in August and September alone. Mass shootings and mass rapes (often followed by massacres—of 4,146 named fatalities, 1,122 were women) also occurred, and villagers armed only with traditional weapons were largely powerless to resist them, although at Pyramid 10 villagers stole rifles and managed to kill 5 government soldiers.

The OPM, on the other hand, was capable of violent resistance. In April 1978, the government intensified its campaign against them, attacking OPM bases near the border with Papua New Guinea and sometimes entering the country in pursuit of them. Papua New Guinea pulled its own frontier troops back to prevent clashes with the Indonesian troops. In June, rebel press releases claimed the deaths of forty-three government troops at Yamas and thirty in the Holomba–Waris–Bewani area. The government neither confirmed nor denied the reports.

Termination and Outcome: In November 1978, the minister of defense ordered *Operasi Senyum* (Smiling Operation), which reduced the intensity of the government violence. The result of the war was a government military victory, as it would be several years before OPM could again mount a significant challenge to the state.

Coding Decisions: The overall death toll for 1977 to 1978 was around 3,000, according to a former governor of Papua. Other estimates run as high as 11,000 deaths from shooting, confinement, disease, and hunger—9,000 in the Central Highlands and 2,000 in the Eastern Highlands. The most precise estimate is 4,146 victims, which represents only those whose names could be collected by human rights workers. The number of battle-deaths was probably only a fraction of total deaths, but we regard civil-war-scale casualties (about 1,600 battle-deaths) as within the realm of possibility.

Sources: Asian Human Rights Commission (2013); van der Kroef (1978).[412]

INTRA-STATE WAR #809

Saur Revolution of 1978

Participants: Afghanistan versus People's Democratic Party of Afghanistan.
Dates: April 27, 1978, to April 28, 1978.
Battle-related Deaths: Armed Forces of Afghanistan: 1,800 (excluding non-immediate postwar executions);[413] Total Combatant Deaths: up to 2,000.[414]
Initiator: People's Democratic Party of Afghanistan.
Outcome: People's Democratic Party of Afghanistan wins.
War Type: Civil for central control.
Total System Member Military Personnel: Armed Forces of Afghanistan: 110,000 (prewar); about 2,000 plus elements of two divisions (initial, peak); 200 to 300 (final). These figures take defections to the rebels into account.[415]
Theater Armed Forces: Armed Forces of Afghanistan: about 2,000 plus elements of two divisions (initial, peak); 200 to 300 (final). People's Democratic Party of Afghanistan/ Fourth Brigade: 3,300 (initial); 3,300 (peak).[416]

Antecedents: In 1973, a bloodless coup placed Mohammed Daoud at the head of the Afghan government. While initially supported by the country's small communist movement, his autocratic rule gradually alienated most of his initial supporters. The communist People's Democratic Party of Afghanistan (PDPA) still was relatively weak in 1978, but its Khalq faction had enjoyed some success at infiltrating the armed forces. After the murder of a leftist, the PDPA organized a demonstration in Kabul. Alarmed, the Daoud arrested the PDPA's political leaders—but did not purge the military. Fearing such a purge, the Khalq and Parcham factions agreed to unite to overthrow the regime.

Narrative: On the morning of April 27, the coup began with an assault to free the PDPA's leaders. This was accomplished with little bloodshed, but then the rebels began to advance on the presidential palace. Units of the Fourth Brigade, a commando unit, and elements of the air force participated in the coup, while only the presidential (republican) guard and elements of two infantry divisions fought on behalf of the government. In fighting that lasted until early the next day, the 2,000-strong presidential (republican) guard fought nearly to the last man, with only some 200 being taken prisoner. Daoud himself was shot down along with many of his advisers and family members. Two infantry divisions also put up some resistance to the coup.

Termination and Outcome: The outcome of the war was an unconditional rebel victory. The Khalq faction assumed control. Within months, it had executed the prisoners and embarked on a reign of terror. Some 12,000 would be executed by the regime, which soon expanded its targets to include the rival Parcham faction. Its policies quickly alienated the rural population, bringing about the First Mujahideen War (see Intra-state War #812).

Coding Decisions: Self-explanatory from cited sources.

Sources: Arnold (1983); Ewans (2002); Joes (2010); Mardsen (2002); Rasanayagam (2003), Tanner (2002), Johnson (2011).[417]

INTRA-STATE WAR #812

Mujahideen Uprising of 1978 to 1980 (aka First Mujahideen War)

Participants: Afghanistan and Union of Soviet Socialist Republics versus National Liberation Front, Nuristan Front, Revolutionary Council of the Islamic Union of Afghanistan, Zadran Tribe, Islamic Party—Hekmatyar, Islamic Party—Khalis, Islamic Society of Afghanistan, Movement of the Islamic Revolution, National Islamic Front of Afghanistan, Ismail Khan–led Rebels, and Other Rebels including Mutineers (Aggregate).
Dates: July 1, 1978, to February 21, 1980.
Battle-related Deaths: Armed Forces of Afghanistan: 4,500; Soviet Union: up to 150;[418] Combined Rebel Forces: 9,000; Total Combatant Deaths: about 13,500. (See Coding Decisions.)[419]
Initiator: Nuristan Front.

Outcome: War was transformed into Extra-state War #476 due to Soviet invasion and its subsequent takeover of the bulk of the fighting on behalf of its new government.

War Type: Civil for central control.

Total System Member Military Personnel: Armed Forces of Afghanistan: 110,000 (prewar, initial, peak); 43,000 (final).[420] Armed Forces of Soviet Union: 3,900,000 (prewar, initial, peak, final).[421]

Theater Armed Forces: On the whole, the peak strength of the rebels was about 60,000 in the winter of 1979 and 1980.[422] We have strength estimates for relatively few rebel groups, listed as follows: Soviet Union, participating from March 10, 1979: 2,500 (initial); 58,000 (peak, final);[423] Nuristan Front: at least 2,000 (initial—may not have been entire force);[424] National Liberation Front, aka *Jabha-i Najat-i Milli*: unknown.[425] Revolutionary Council of the Islamic Union of Afghanistan, aka *Shura-i-Inqilab-i Ittefaq-i Islami Afghanistan*, participating from autumn 1978: unknown; Zadran Tribe, participating to at least October 1979: unknown; Islamic Party—Hekmatyar, aka *Hizb-i Islam-Hekmatyar*, participating from January 1979: at least 5,000 (peak).[426] Islamic Society of Afghanistan, aka *Jam'iat Islami-yi Afghanistan*: unknown; Islamic Party-Khalis, aka *Hizb-i Islam-Khalis*, participating from 1979: unknown; Movement of the Islamic Revolution, aka *Harakat-i Inqilab-i Islami*, participating from about the beginning of 1979: initially the strongest of the rebel groups, which implies more than 5,000 (initial, peak).[427] National Islamic Front of Afghanistan, aka *Mahaz-i-Milli Islami-yi Afghanistan*, participating from about the beginning of 1979: unknown. Ismail Khan–led Rebels, aka Elements of the Seventeenth Infantry Division, participating during March 1979: unknown.[428] Other Rebels (including other mutineers), participating from 1979: unknown.

Antecedents: After communists seized power in the Saur Revolution (see Intra-state war #810), the Khalq faction quickly took control and began a reign of terror against its political opponents, including the Parcham faction of the party. Its attempt to implement unpopular policies such as a clumsy land reform program and equal rights for women led to disaffection within the army and rural rebellions led by landowners and clergy. One source reports rebellions in Nooristan and Kunars as early as May 22 but expresses some skepticism at these claims. Certainly, Pakistan almost immediately began aiding potential rebels. A group of would-be rebels formed a National Salvation Front based in Pakistan on June 1, 1978, led by Sibghatullah Mojaddidi.

Narrative: The first clearly documented armed revolt broke out that month among the Safi tribe and surrounding Nuristanis in the Pech Valley, who eventually called themselves the Nuristan Front and declared independence. Fighting from July 1 to July 15 only cost the government two killed, but the rebellion continued, and from July 20 to July 22, an engagement at Falugi between some 400 soldiers and 2,000 poorly armed Nuristanis killed 30 government soldiers and resulted in the capture of 50 more. Around this time, the Zadran tribe led by Sher Mohammed Khan also rebelled against the government in the Zadran valley.

Soon after, the long-underground Islamic party Hizb-i Islam, led by Gulbuddin Hekmatyar, began guerrilla resistance to the government, as did a long-time splinter group, the Islamic Society, led by Burhanuddin Rabbani. Ethnic Tajiks and the Shiite Hazaras rebelled in the autumn. A Hazara rebel force, the Revolutionary Council of the Islamic Union of Afghanistan, headed by Sayyid Ali Beheshti, was formed. Tribal militias, which had been used to augment the armed forces, began to turn on the government.

By October, the government was conducting large-scale sweeps against the insurgents. When the government renegotiated and renewed a friendship treaty with the Soviet Union in December, resistance increased. By the end of 1978, the government faced uncoordinated low-level insurgency throughout the country (twenty-four of twenty-eight provinces), and Nooristan and the Hazarajat had fallen largely into rebel hands.

In 1979, the rebel movement further fragmented, even while it grew in size and extent. Maulaw Yunus Khalis left Hekmatyar's Islamic Party and formed one of his own. Meanwhile, Hekmatyar invaded the country from Pakistan with 5,000 soldiers in January; the local brigade under Abdur Rauf simply defected to the rebels. The strongest rebel group, the Movement of the Islamic Revolution, also was formed around this time by Maulaw Mohammad Nab Mohammadi. Finally, Pir Sayyed Ahmed Gailani formed the National Islamic Front of Afghanistan. The Soviet Union also increased its support of the government in 1979; by spring, it had 2,500 "advisers" in the country, although it denied the government any combat troops.

The Soviets were the target of the next major uprising. In March, demonstrations against the Soviet Union broke out in Herat. On March 10, the Seventeenth Infantry Division was sent to quell the protests, but instead elements under Ismail Khan joined the rebels. Attacks on Soviet advisers and their families killed more than 100. Further violence followed, with the government sending paratroopers from Kandahar and tanks from Soviet Turkmenistan against the rebels. In all, the fighting around Herat cost 3,000 to 5,000 lives and marked the beginning of active Soviet participation in the war. On March 27, the Khalq began its purge of the Parcham faction from the government. The government had suffered 10,000 casualties by April against 20,000 rebel casualties.

April 11 was a black day for the Afghan government. Mutiny broke out in Jalalabad, while fighting raged in Aimaq country (Daulatyar), Wardak, Uruzgan, Logar, Faryab, Badghis (where Jawand was captured), and elsewhere. The same day, the people of Wardak, who had been asked to mount a punitive expedition against the Hazaras—and who had demanded arms for the proposed expedition—turned against the government. The fighting in Jalalabad killed more Soviet advisers; by June, the government had committed an entire corps against the Jalalabad rebellion. Meanwhile, fighting against the forces of Gailani and Mujaddidi raged from April until June. In the Kunar Valley, fighting cost nearly 1,000 lives by April 20. In Kerala, the government and its Soviet advisers massacred 1,170 men and boys; a similar massacre in Suff killed at least 600.

On May 17, an entire motorized brigade of 2,000 men went over to the rebels in Khost. By July, the rebels were being supported not only by Pakistan and the People's Republic of China but also by the United States, which provided a secret shipment of arms. An abortive revolt by Shiites in Kabul was crushed, and up to 2,000 were executed by the government. The next month, a revolt broke out in the Panjsher Valley, which succeeded in looting government supplies and weapons. Leadership of the Panjsher revolt would be assumed by Ahmad Shah Masood, who allied himself to Rabanni.

By August, the Soviets were flying combat missions against the rebels. On August 5, armored units in the Kunar Valley revolted; Soviet gunships attacked the rebel tanks and the revolt was crushed by September 1. Demonstrations and then a full-scale mutiny in Kabul were repressed that month with Soviet assistance at a cost of 1,200 casualties. With substantial Soviet assistance, the government dubiously claimed it had quelled the uprising of the Zadran tribe in Paktiya during October 1979, having suffered a series of defeats when it conducted its own operations in the previous month. The rebels, government, and Soviets all suffered heavy casualties in the operation. That same month in Asmar, units went over to the rebels and executed Soviet advisers, going on to provide weapons to Hekmatyar's Hizb-i-Islami.

Increasingly, the government relied on Soviet help. This was necessary, for the government's armed forces were down to about one-third of their original effective strength by the end of September. Only half of the 8,000-strong officer corps still was available for service, the rest having defected or been killed. On September 16, a coup deposed President Nur Mohammed Taraki; fellow Khalq member Hafizullah Amin assumed the office. While the Soviet Union disapproved of the coup, it quickly accepted the new government and ordered its advisers to continue to coordinate combat operations against the various *mujahideen* rebels. Meanwhile, the Soviet Union continued its secret policy of offering sanctuary to communists purged by the Khalq regime.

October saw the mutiny of an entire infantry division outside Kabul. The total number of rebels rose to perhaps 60,000, outnumbering the 50,000 remaining government forces. The Soviet Union had been contemplating outright invasion of the country since at least mid-September. By this point, the civil ministries were being run by 1,500 Soviet advisers, while another 3,500 to 4,000 advisers practically ran the country's armed forces. Bagram air base was made into a Soviet headquarters, and on the night of December 5 to December 6, the Soviets disarmed its garrison without a fight. The government was losing its war—some twenty-three of twenty-eight provinces were in rebel hands—and the Soviet Union had decided to supplant it in an effort to defeat the insurgents.

On December 23, the Soviets arrested key officers in the Afghan armed forces and persuaded other units to remain in their barracks, while the 105th Guards Air Assault Division deployed. On December 27, the Soviets moved against Amin's government.

An initial assault on the presidential palace failed, but a second assault succeeded at the cost of heavy casualties. This was only the beginning of conflict between Afghan army units and Soviet forces.

Termination and Outcome: The Soviet invasion and takeover of the Afghan army (down to 30,000 men by August 3, 1980) transformed the civil war into an extra-state war. By January 1, 1980, there were 58,000 Soviet troops in Afghanistan, outnumbering remaining government forces. Their strength soon reached 80,000. From January 13 to January 15, the Soviets are reported to have clashed with elements of the Eighth Afghan Division and paratroopers at Balar Hisar. After this point, loyalist resistance was crushed, and many army units simply defected to the rebels. "The DRA was so subordinate to the Soviet forces during most of the fighting that it is difficult to talk about the performance of most troops."[429]

Sporadic rebellions by the army continued throughout the year: one on February 21 killed 50 Soviet troops, and the Fourteenth Division at Ghazni rebelled on July 28. When the Soviets finally withdrew in 1989, they left behind almost 14,000 dead.

Coding Decisions: There were some 10,000 government and 20,000 rebel casualties to the end of April 1979. Extrapolating from these figures, there were probably at least 8,000 more government and 16,000 more rebel casualties. Using the 3:1 rule of thumb regarding the number of wounded to killed, we estimate at least 4,500 government battle deaths and 9,000 rebel battle-deaths, for a total of 13,500 battle-deaths. The real toll could be somewhat lower or much higher.

Sources: Clements (2003); Clodfelter (2001); Cordesman and Wagner (1990a, b); Edwards (1987); Ewans (2001); Goodson (2001); Hiro (2012); Hussain (2005); Lesch (2001); Lobato (1988); Nojumi (2002); O'Ballance (1993); Rasanayagam (2003); Tanner (2002); Vogelsang (2002); Yunas (2002).

INTRA-STATE WAR #824
First Philippine–NPA War of 1981 to 1992

Participants: Philippines versus New People's Army.

Dates: January 17, 1981, to December 10, 1986, and February 8, 1987, to September 1, 1992.

Battle-related Deaths: Total Combatant Deaths: 30,000. (See Coding Decisions.)[430]

Initiator: New People's Army.

Outcome: Stalemate.

War Type: Civil for central control.

Total System Member Military Personnel: Armed Forces of the Philippines: 155,000 (prewar—1980); 156,000 (initial); 157,000 (peak—1982); 107,000 (final).[431]

Theater Armed Forces: New People's Army: 5,500 (prewar—1980); 6,000 (initial); 25,200 (peak—1987); 12,000 (final).[432]

Antecedents: The Communist Party of the Philippines—Marxist-Leninist (CPP–ML) was established by Jose Maria Sison on December 26, 1968. The first clash with government forces occurred two weeks later in Bataan province and killed 17 rebels and a single government soldier. On March 29, the New People's Army (NPA) was established as a military wing of the CPP–ML. Sporadic clashes with relatively light casualties continued through the end of the year and into 1970. Pedro Taruc, leader of the few remaining Huk rebels (see Intra-state War #735), was killed by government troops near Angeles on October 16. Repeated clashes between demonstrators and police in Manila during 1970 and 1971 convinced many radicals that electoral or popular change was impossible without the resort to arms. During this period, the NPA grew from 300 to more than 1,200 fighters.

On September 23, 1972, President Ferdinand Marcos suspended the constitution and declared martial law, ostensibly to deal with the country's various rebellions. The declaration of martial law was followed by a roundup that decimated the ranks of the NPA and its civilian sympathizers. The NPA was hard-pressed to simply maintain its numbers throughout most of the 1970s. While no exact figures are available, battle-deaths were low during this period as most engagements were between very small units, rarely involving more than ten to twenty armed rebels. The government deployed the bulk of its fighting forces against the Moro National Liberation Front in the south rather than the NPA, which it considered a mere nuisance in comparison (see Intra-state War #786).

Narrative: Testerman makes a compelling case that the conflict reached civil-war proportions beginning with the lifting of martial law on January 17, 1981:

> Bombings and assassinations in urban areas increased. . . . NPA units went on the tactical offensive in many provinces. . . . Reports of NPA units operating in company-sized groups of up to 100 soldiers in the early 1980s were punctuated by occasional encounters with battalion-strength units of more than 300 guerrillas. . . . In addition, the targets of NPA attacks had grown beyond ambushes and raids of unfortified positions to attacking government installations and occupying towns. The number of attacks also increased sharply in 1981. From 1977 to 1980, the number of "military-dissident" encounters with the NPA averaged 80 per year. In 1981, this number more than tripled to 252 and in 1982 there were 362 military engagements with the NPA. . . . [A] speech by President Marcos stated that communist guerrillas killed 4,922 Philippine soldiers and civilians from August 1981 to August 1984. (164–165, internal citations omitted)

At least 1,000 government troops died in 1984. The NPA enjoyed a tacit alliance with the Moro National Liberation Front and struck government forces in Mindanao repeatedly in 1984 and 1985. Major engagements also were reported in Luzon. The NPA suffered 2,017 battle-deaths in 1985, and nearly 1,000 more were killed in a massive internal purge. The Mindanao branch of the party declined from 9,000 to 3,000 in the space of a year.

The CPP–ML boycotted the violent and fraudulent presidential elections of February 1986, a contest that ended in a military coup against Marcos and then handed power to opposition candidate Corazon Aquino. She made peace overtures to the NPA, and on December 10, a cease-fire agreement was reached. More than 15,000 (many if not most of them civilians) died in the conflict between 1972 and the 1986 cease-fire agreements.

Negotiations broke down over the NPA's demand for a Marxist-Leninist program and administration. Hostilities resumed on February 8, 1987. The NPA was at its peak strength—25,200 fighters against the government's 105,000 soldiers (who also had to deal with the MNLF insurgency). Losses on both sides were heavy; the NPA suffered 1,500 battle-deaths in 1988, against about 1,100 government battle-deaths (another source gives totals of 1,913 and 912, respectively). Moreover, another round of purges took the lives of hundreds of NPA members in 1988. Unable to sustain such losses, the NPA declined to about 19,000 fighters by 1990 and just 13,000 by 1992. In July 1992, the new president pressed for a settlement with the NPA. Congress repealed the antisubversion law, which had outlawed the CPP–ML. In September 1992, the government and an alliance of opposition groups signed the Hague Declaration. It called for a cease-fire and negotiations, although both were phrased in the future tense.

Termination and Outcome: The Hague Declaration may have ended the war, but it was neither a cease-fire nor a negotiated settlement, and fighting continued at a lower level. The end of the war is best characterized as a stalemate. Certainly, casualties dropped below the civil-war threshold, but the insurgency continued, and once again assumed civil-war proportions in 2005 (see Intra-state War #936).

Coding Decisions: Up to 40,000 combat-related deaths may have occurred from 1969 to 2014. Most of these must have been suffered during the civil war period. About 30,000 battle-deaths are likely to be accurate to the nearest 10,000.

Sources: *Annual of Power and Conflict*, (1971–1972); Arnold (1995); Clodfelter (2008); Felter (2005); Laffin (1989, 1994); Mullenbach (2013a, b); Project Ploughshares (2014b, c); Romero (2015); Testerman (2012).[433]

INTRA-STATE WAR #835
First Sri Lanka Tamil War of 1983 to 1987 (aka Eelam War I)

Participants: Sri Lanka versus Liberation Tigers of Tamil Eelam, People's Liberation Organization of Tamil Eelam, Eelam Revolutionary Organization of Students, Tamil Eelam

Liberation Organization, and Eelam People's Revolutionary Liberation Front.

Dates: July 23, 1983, to June 18, 1985, and August 16, 1985, to July 31, 1987.

Battle-related Deaths: Armed Forces of Sri Lanka: 1,000;[434] Total Combatant Deaths: 4,000. (See Coding Decisions.)[435]

Initiator: Liberation Tigers of Tamil Eelam.

Outcome: Negotiated settlement.

War Type: Civil for local issues (secession).

Total System Member Military Personnel: Armed Forces of Sri Lanka—16,000 (prewar, initial); 22,000 (peak, final).[436]

Theater Armed Forces: Overall rebel forces peaked at about 10,000 to 15,000, although most probably lacked firearms.[437] Liberation Tigers of Tamil Eelam: 600 (initial); 3,000 to 7,500 (peak).[438] People's Liberation Organization of Tamil Eelam: several hundred claimed (initial); 6,000 to 8,000 (peak).[439] Eelam Revolutionary Organization of Students: 1,750 (peak—1986).[440] Tamil Eelam Liberation Organization: 4,500 (peak—1986).[441] Eelam People's Revolutionary Liberation Front: 2,500 (peak—1986).[442]

Antecedents: After 1956 legislation mandating a Sinhalese-only language policy, Tamil organizations became more militant. When noncooperation and civil disobedience failed, militant organizations began to spring up. In 1972, what would become the separatist Liberation Tigers of Tamil Eelam (LTTE) was founded by Veluppillai Prabhakaran. The LTTE killed twenty police, five officials, and five informers by July 1978. The Eelam Revolutionary Organization of Students (EROS) was formed in 1975 and began attacks on economic targets. Other militant organizations included the more moderate Tamil United Liberation Organization (TULF—particularly its less moderate youth wing), the Tamil Eelam Liberation Organization (TELO), and the People's Liberation Organization of Tamil Eelam (PLOTE). Among their grievances was encroachment—the settling of majority-Tamil areas by Sinhalese settlers.

In 1977, ethnic riots killed up to 300 people and displaced tens of thousands. The 1978 Constitution restored language equality and contained other provisions to increase Tamil representation, but it was rejected by the militant groups, which demanded autonomy or secession. Despite the proliferation of militant organizations, the number of active rebels remained small—the government estimated perhaps 200 full-time guerrillas by 1983 (though the LTTE alone had 600 members). Up to 300 had undergone training from the Palestine Liberation Organization (PLO) by 1982, but it is likely that most foreign support at this stage came from India.

After the Indian election of 1980, the new Indian government allowed training camps for the Tamils to be set up in its own Tamil Nadu province. The Eelam People's Revolutionary Liberation Front (EPRLF) was created and heavily supported by India; its agenda was secession followed by island-wide revolution. Led by K. Padmanabha, it initially focused less on attacks against government forces and more on actions such as jailbreaks. The would-be rebels achieved some degree of coordination by forming the Committee for Eelam Liberation (CEL) in August 1982. On July 22, 1983, Tamil MPs resigned their seats, further delegitimizing the government in the eyes of Tamil radicals.

Narrative: On July 23, an LTTE land mine killed 13 government soldiers. The response to the attack was anti-Tamil and anti-Indian riots—probably instigated by the ruling party's thugs—on July 24 and July 25 in which perhaps 1,000 were killed (nearly all of them civilians) and 100,000 displaced. Moreover, 35 Tamil prisoners held by the government were killed on July 25 and 18 more two days later. Rebel strength increased dramatically after the riots, increasing to 5,000 total within a year and to 10,000 to 15,000 in 1986. On August 3, the government banned separatist parties, forcing even the moderates to go underground. The Indian government responded to the riots and ban by arming the Tamil rebels and opening many more training camps.

Violent incidents increased in frequency in the early months of 1984, and combat became common by August. EROS focused on targets in the South and East. While it grew to 1,750 cadres by 1986, they were poorly armed, with fewer than 150 firearms among them. The EPRLF focused on the East; it, too, had many cadres (2,074 in the conflict zone in early 1986) and few arms (perhaps 150 firearms). Its greatest defeat was suffered at the hands of the LTTE in December 1986, when the LTTE overran some of its camps in Sri Lanka, killing 70 and capturing more than 500. PLOTE operated with 2,200 cadres in the Northeast, although the majority of its 6,000 to 8,000 cadres were based in India's Tamil Nadu province. Moreover, it did not initiate confrontations with security forces. TELO operated in Jaffna; a force called the Tamil Eelam Liberation Army (TELA) emerged, but its connection to TELO is still unclear. In 1986, TELO had 542 firearms, making it the second-most powerful military group next to the LTTE.

As for the LTTE, it was smaller than some organizations but better armed, making it the most powerful of the rebel groups. From the beginning of the war, it sought to marginalize other political and military groups. It first targeted the unarmed TULF and then began to turn on its military rivals. For example, on April 29, 1986, it attacked TELO; just over a week later, it killed TELO's leader. TELO cadres began to defect to the LTTE. In July an LTTE attack killed at least 200 TELO cadres and gained the surrender of many others. Late in the war, TELO began working with the government against the LTTE. Eventually, the LTTE killed more than 800 TELO, EPRLF, and PLOTE cadres. EROS and PLOTE pulled out of Jaffna in response, while the EPRLF was forced out in December 1986.

The LTTE's structure resembled that of a conventional armed force, with seven regional commands, a naval arm (the Sea Tigers), an intelligence wing, and eventually an elite suicide force (the Black Tigers). Its soldiers were equipped with cyanide capsules for use when capture was imminent. Though it had only 1,500 to 3,000 members until 1986, its fighters were highly motivated and better armed than its rivals. By 1985, it had developed the capability to manufacture its own weapons. It operated primarily in the North as it was seen as an organization of Jaffna Tamils.

In April 1985, the Eelam National Liberation Front (ENLF) was formed, nominally uniting the LTTE, TELO, EPRLF, and EROS (PLOTE refused to join). On June 18, an Indian-sponsored three-month cease-fire went into effect between the government and all five major rebel groups in preparation for a peace conference. Talks began on July 8 at Thimpu, but the cease-fire broke down on about August 16; over the next few days, both sides mounted armed actions. The Tamil leaders walked out of the talks on August 22, and large-scale fighting resumed in January 1986. In all, the government estimated that 194 security forces and 885 civilians had been killed during 1985; the rebels held these figures too low, arguing that at least 2,000 civilians had been killed by the government. Amnesty International lent credibility to the rebel claims, estimating 2,578 killed and 547 "disappeared" from March 1 to January 31, 1986.

On January 13, 1986, the rebels began to shell government positions. The government retaliated with raids on Tamil villages, and the two sides carried out small-scale operations in a tit-for-tat manner. On May 17, the government mounted Operation Short Shrift, deploying 2,000 troops to reopen the roads to Jaffna and relieve besieged garrisons and police stations. The columns quickly bogged down, and the operation sputtered to an unsuccessful end late in June. Meanwhile, India became frustrated by the rebels' unwillingness to compromise on the unification of the North and East provinces into Tamil Eelam and on the issue of self-determination. In November, India moved against the rebel bases in Tamil Nadu, disarming more than 1,000 fighters. The LTTE hastened to transfer its leadership, cadres, and weapons to Sri Lanka.

The ENLF lasted until March 1987, when it disintegrated due to infighting, especially LTTE attacks on its formal allies. A month after the alliance collapsed, the government offered a unilateral cease-fire, but LTTE attacks continued, including a horrific massacre of Sinhalese bus passengers. On May 26, the government mounted Operation Liberation using 4,300 troops, intending to retake the Jaffna peninsula. Over the next two weeks, 132 rebels, 62 soldiers, and 300 civilians were killed. Rather than fight conventionally, the LTTE opted for guerrilla tactics such as land mines and booby traps, which together accounted for 90 percent of government casualties during the operation. By May 29, the symbolically important towns of Vadamarachchi and Velvettiturai had been taken. A military solution seemed to be at hand.

Then India intervened. On June 3, India authorized fishing boats to deliver "humanitarian" aid to the Tamils; when Sri Lanka blocked the vessels, the supplies were airdropped instead. This signaled India's willingness to save the Tamil rebels from defeat and led to negotiations between the two states' governments. Operation Liberation was halted on June 10, leaving Jaffna in the hands of the LTTE, which used the reprieve to organize its forces for further attacks on the government. On July 5, the first Black Tiger drove a car bomb into a forward army camp in an attack that killed at least forty government soldiers. India called on Sri Lanka and the rebels to accept an Indian-guaranteed peace plan. Prabhakaran was lured to New Delhi, where he was held incommunicado in an effort to persuade him to assent. Prabhakaran prevaricated (sources disagree about whether he consented to the agreement at any point, but it is clear that he renounced it when released); the other four groups agreed to the proposal, as did the government.

Termination and Outcome: The Peace Accord was announced on July 28 and signed the next day. It called for a referendum on unification of the East and North provinces and a limited form of autonomy (an elected joint provincial council) be extended to them. Hostilities were to cease as of July 31, and rebels were to disarm by August 3. Sri Lankan troops were to be confined to barracks and their pre-Operation Liberation camps. Amnesty was to be extended to all detained Tamils and to the insurgents. Indian "peacekeeping" forces would guarantee the accord.

Although the accord did stop the fighting for a short time, it was never fully implemented. It did mark the end of Eelam War I because when the fighting resumed in October, it was Indian soldiers who inflicted the bulk of the casualties on the LTTE. Hence, we code this war as becoming extra-state, even though there was a two-month gap between the two wars. By July 31, there were already 3,000 Indian troops in northern Sri Lanka. TELO—with only thirty-seven armed cadres left in the North—surrendered its weapons to India. A symbolic surrender of about 300 arms by the LTTE was conducted on August 4, but it kept most of its weapons.

The Indian Peace-Keeping Force (IPKF) quickly grew in strength, but violence resumed between Tamils and Sinhalese and between the LTTE and the remaining Tamil factions. When the IPKF attempted to halt the LTTE's attacks on other militant groups, it came under fire. When it captured and moved to hand over seventeen LTTE members to the Sri Lankan police, they swallowed their cyanide pills; fifteen of them died. The suicides sparked a wave of Tamil protest and violence against the IPKF. On October 5, the LTTE announced its noncooperation with the IPKF and began attacks on Sri Lankan security forces. The IPKF attempted to suppress the LTTE by force, sparking off the extra-state war in which the bulk of the fighting against the LTTE was done by India. By October 28, 214 IPKF troops had been killed and 709 wounded; India claimed to have killed 607 LTTE, while the rebels admitted only 50 dead, the truth probably being that the LTTE suffered about as many killed as the IPKF.

While fighting continued until India finally withdrew the IPKF in 1990, the government reached an accommodation with the LTTE some time in March 1989, and combat between the two ceased completely. More than a year would pass before it resumed (Intra-state War #859). Beginning in May of the same year, the government actually began providing weapons to the LTTE to secure the departure of the IPKF, which was viewed by many if not most Sinhalese as an intrusion upon national sovereignty. On June 2, the government ordered the IPKF to leave, and a formal cease-fire agreement between the LTTE and government was signed on June 28.

Coding Decisions: Due to secrecy on both sides, casualty estimates are unreliable. Government figures for the first phase of the war were 900 killed, including 250 security forces and 650 civilians. The rebels claimed that these figures were too low and that thousands of civilians had been killed. One independent estimate is that 10,000 were killed by 1987, the majority of whom were Tamil civilians and 900 of whom were government security forces. Allowing for some deaths during the operations of the first half of 1987, we estimate 4,000 total battle-deaths—about 1,000 on the government side and possibly 3,000 (by subtraction) on the rebel side. This may be an overestimate; indeed, it is possible that the first or even second years of this period fell below the thousand battle-deaths-per-year threshold for inclusion, but we lack disaggregated yearly fatalities with which to determine this.

Source: Akhtar (2006); Bandarage (2009); Bloom (2003); Brogan (1998); Bullion (1995); Chalk (2003);

Dagmar-Hellmann (1994); O'Ballance (1989); Senaratne (1997).[443]

INTRA-STATE WAR #837

Indian Golden Temple War of 1984 (aka Operation Blue Star)

Participants: India versus Sikh Rebels (Aggregate).
Dates: June 1, 1984, to July 30, 1984.
Battle-related Deaths: Armed Forces of India: perhaps 250 battle-deaths;[444] Sikh Rebels: perhaps 750 battle-deaths;[445] Total Combatant Deaths: 1,000. (See Coding Decisions.)[446]
Initiator: India.
Outcome: India wins.
War Type: Civil for local issues (territory and autonomy).
Total System Member Military Personnel: Armed Forces of India: 1,120,000 (prewar, initial, peak); less than 1,118,000 (final).[447]
Theater Armed Forces: Sikh Rebels: a few hundred (prewar, initial); at least 2,000 to 5,000 (peak).[448]

Antecedents: By 1983, India faced growing resistance in Punjab, sympathetic to the Akali Dal nationalist movement and led by radical Sant Jarnail Singh Bhindranwale. The rebels demanded the incorporation of the federal city of Chandigarh into Punjab, an end to the quotas that limited Sikh positions in the armed forces, and forms of local autonomy (some calling for an independent Khalistan). On October 6, suspected Sikh extremists hijacked a bus and shot 6 Hindus. Indian president Indira Gandhi reacted by imposing president's rule over Punjab and arresting 4,000 suspected Sikh extremists or sympathizers. After the arrest of a prominent Sikh radical in late 1983, Bhindranwale's followers began to fortify the Golden Temple in Amritsar.

In early 1984, intercommunal violence erupted in several Punjabi cities between militant Hindus and Sikhs. Dozens of Sikhs were killed in Haryana. In the last week of February alone, 60 Sikhs and Hindus were killed in the violence. Bhindranwale's violent tactics alienated the moderates of Akali Dal, but he commanded hundreds of armed followers in the Golden Temple and appealed to a significant fraction of the populace. Concerned that Bhindranwale was going to launch an outright insurgency for the independence of Khalistan, the government moved forces into place near the Golden Temple.

Narrative: On June 1, militants in the Golden Temple exchanged fire with government security forces. On the night of June 4, the government launched Operation Blue Star to seize the temple and arrest Bhindranwale. It also entered thirty-seven other Sikh holy sites to arrest "extremists." After two days of fierce fighting in Amritsar, Bhindranwale lay dead, along with hundreds or thousands of others, including hundreds of government soldiers. Sikh villagers revolted and attempted to make their way to Amritsar, but hundreds of them were killed in the attempt. Resistance continued, producing a daily death toll from the new insurgency.

Shortly after Blue Star, at least 2,000 and as many as 5,000 Sikh soldiers mutinied; they, too, headed for Amritsar in hopes of liberating the Golden Temple. Most were arrested or killed in battles with loyalists. Violence continued throughout the Punjab for another month, including revolts by Sikh soldiers. Indira Gandhi became a victim of Sikh violence later that year.

Termination and Outcome: The mutinies were suppressed by the end of June. The war was an unconditional government victory. After the war, many Sikhs in the military were arrested, but there were no large-scale executions of the defeated. On October 31, President Gandhi was assassinated by her Sikh bodyguards, triggering anti-Sikh riots that killed 5,000 people. The massacre—and the Indian government's apparent complicity in it—widened the gulf separating Sikhs from the Indian government and gave increased impetus to secessionist efforts.

Coding Decisions: Estimates for this war are highly politicized, ranging from the hundreds to more than 5,000, with most of those killed being civilians. The official toll at Amritsar was 84 government soldiers killed and 492 "militants" killed; the latter figure presumably included the many civilians killed in the attack. But there are reasons to believe that the official toll was an underestimate. Three months after the attack, Rajiv Gandhi said that the military had suffered more than 700 battle-deaths. While he later retracted his statement, senior army officials conceded that the number of government battle-deaths was higher than the official toll. A somewhat higher estimate places government battle-deaths in Blue Star at 220 and Sikh deaths at 780. To these figures must be added the hundreds of villagers who rebelled and were killed trying to reach Amritsar as well as more than a hundred soldiers who died on both sides in the mutinies following the operation. Our best estimate is that about 1,000 actual combatants died in the war—perhaps 250 on the government side and 750 on the rebel side.

Sources: Chima (2010); Clodfelter (2008); "General Promises to Punish Sikh Mutineers" (1984).[449]

INTRA-STATE WAR #845

Second Sri Lanka–JVP War of 1987 to 1989 (aka Second JVP)

Participants: Sri Lanka versus Janatha Vimukthi Peramuna.
Dates: July 29, 1987, to December 28, 1989.
Battle-related Deaths: Armed Forces of Sri Lanka: 551;[450] Total Combatant Deaths: 10,000. (See Coding Decisions.)[451]
Initiator: Janatha Vimukthi Peramuna.
Outcome: Sri Lanka wins.
War Type: Civil for central control.
Total System Member Military Personnel: Armed Forces of Sri Lanka: 69,000 (initial); 110,000 (peak); 110,000 (final). These figures include police, who bore the brunt of the first two years of the war.[452]
Theater Armed Forces: *Janatha Vimukthi Peramuna*, aka People's Liberation Front: 2,000 (initial); a few thousand (peak).[453]

Antecedents: The leftist and nationalist Janatha Vimukthi Peramuna (JVP), which had been banned over allegations of involvement in the 1983 riots that ignited Eelam War I (see Intra-state War #835), steadily infiltrated the armed forces as they expanded during that war. By early 1987 there were isolated JVP attacks on police, military, and political targets; the JVP sought funds and arms for its coming revolt. When the Indo-Sri Lankan Peace Accord, which ended the first Eelam War, angered Sinhalese nationalists, the JVP decided to oppose the agreement by force of arms. Since the JVP's areas of operation did not overlap with those of the Tamil rebels, this assumed the form of an insurrection against the government. The insurrection was supported by students and lower-caste Sinhalese youth.

Narrative: On July 28, 1987, the terms of the accord were announced. The next day, government commandoes fired on crowds of civilians converging on the center of Colombo, preserving the ruling UNP regime. The JVP insurrection became general after this point. It was able to neutralize police intelligence through a combination of infiltration and assassination, and it mounted attacks against UNP and rival leftist politicians. The families of police were also targeted.

The movement reached its peak in late 1988, imposing heavy costs on the government through a combination of economic damage and military actions (although at no point becoming capable of sustained military operations that could lead to a victory of arms). Brutal military operations against suspected JVP, including the massacre of the lower-caste village of Menikhinna (near Kandy), only intensified the resistance and provided the JVP with more followers. The JVP even managed to establish a territorial presence in the southern districts of Matara and Hambantota. At the end of the year, the army was tasked with intelligence gathering, which had heretofore been the preserve of the police.

The JVP was defeated only when the army established sufficient intelligence to act and united against it. In January 1989, the country's new president lifted the state of emergency and released many JVP members. But by June the state of emergency was reimposed. In July an attempt to create a revolution through demonstrations against the Indian occupation of the North failed when the military fired on the civilians forced to demonstrate by the JVP. Hundreds were killed in two days. On August 1, secret talks were held; the JVP demanded an end to the IPKF, dissolution of parliament, the resignation of three ministers (including the hard-line minister of defense), and an end to the state of emergency. Unable to concede these demands, the government turned to a military solution.

Matters came to a head later that month, when the JVP ordered military personnel to leave their posts or have their families slaughtered. The military began arresting and killing people on the merest suspicion of association with the JVP. A cease-fire in September failed, and military operations continued. The government mobilized vigilante death squads against the rebels. Torture was used to extract information on the movement's leadership, which was then captured and shot by the government.

Termination and Outcome: On December 28, the government announced the death of Saman Piyasiri Fernando, the leader of the JVP's military wing (the Deshapremi Janatha Vyaparaya [DJV]). It proclaimed that the JVP terror was over. Certainly this period marks a dramatic decline in JVP and security force violence and is as good a termination date as any. The outcome of the war was a complete military victory by the government. Arrests and extrajudicial executions continued after the end of the rebellion; 1,160 disappearances were recorded in the South during the year following the end of the war.

Coding Decisions: From 25,000 to 60,000 people were killed in the uprising, the vast majority of which (80 to 90 percent) were actual or suspected JVP. The latter killed several thousand UNP cadres and thousands of civilians. Actual government battle-deaths were low—although 6,000 to 7,000 deaths are attributable to the JVP, it only managed to kill 209 security forces personnel and 342 police, according to newspaper accounts. The number of JVP killed remains unknown; most of those killed by the government were not actual JVP. Given the small size of the JVP, it is unlikely that more than 10,000 members could have been killed, and the real total is probably lower. We estimate 10,000 total battle-deaths, but the actual number may be several times higher or considerably lower.

Sources: Bandarage (2009); Behera (1995); Moore (1993); Ratnatunga (1989); "30 Rebels Arrested in Sri Lanka" (1990).[454]

INTRA-STATE WAR #851

Second Afghan Civil War of 1989 to 1992 (aka Third Mujahideen War)

Participants: Afghanistan versus Islamic Society, Islamic Party—Khalis, Islamic Party—Hekmatyar, Islamic Union for the Liberation of Afghanistan, Islamic Revolutionary Movement, National Islamic Front of Afghanistan, Afghanistan National Liberation Front, Islamic Movement, Organization of Victory, Guardians of the Islamic Holy War, Islamic Movement of Afghanistan, Invitation to the Islamic Unity of Afghanistan, Party of Islamic Thunder of Afghanistan, United Front, Council of the Islamic Revolutionary Alliance, Organization of the Holy Warriors of the Oppressed of Afghanistan, Pashrau-i-Jihad, Hezbollah, Unity Party, Islamic Alliance of Afghanistan Mujahideen, Sayyid Mansur-led Ismaili Militia, and Jauzjani Uzbeks (Aggregate).

Dates: February 16, 1989, to April 15, 1992.

Battle-related Deaths: Total Combatant Deaths: 40,000. (See Coding Decisions.)[455]

Initiator: Peshawar-based *mujiahideen* groups.

Outcome: Jauzjani Uzbeks and Islamic Society win.

War Type: Civil for central control.

Total System Member Military Personnel: Armed Forces of Afghanistan: 225,000 (prewar, initial); 228,000 (peak).[456]

Theater Armed Forces: Estimates of some *mujahideen* groups may be inflated as the US government estimated only 90,000 full-time *mujahideen* and 110,000 part time at the end of 1988.[457] *Jauzjani Uzbeks*, aka 53rd Division, participating as part of the Armed Forces of Afghanistan—counted above—until January 1992, then as a rebel army thereafter: 40,000 (before defection).[458] Sayyid Mansur-led Ismaili Militia, participating on the government side until January 1992 and then on the rebel side thereafter: 13,000 (initial).[459] Islamic Society, aka *Jamiat-i-Islami*: 24,000 to 30,000 (prewar); 20,000 (initial); 60,000 (peak).[460] *Islamic* Party—Khalis, aka *Hezb-i-Islami—Khalis*: 10,000 to 20,000 (prewar); 40,000 (initial, peak).[461] Islamic Party—Hekmatyar, aka *Hezb-i-Islami—Hekmatyar*: 16,000 to 20,000 (prewar); 50,000 (initial, peak).[462] Islamic Union for the Liberation of Afghanistan, aka *Ittehad-i-Islami*: 18,000 (initial, peak).[463] Islamic Revolutionary Movement, aka *Harakat-i-Inqilib-i Islami*: 16,000 (prewar); 25,000 (initial, peak).[464] National Islamic Front of Afghanistan, aka *Mahaz-i Milli*: more than 15,000 (prewar); 15,000 (initial, peak).[465] Afghanistan National Liberation Front, aka *Jabba-i-Nejat-i-Milli Afghanistan*: 4,500 to 6,000 (prewar); 15,000 (initial, peak).[466] Islamic Movement, aka

Harakat-i Islami: 16,000 (prewar); 20,000 (initial, peak).[467] Organization of Victory, aka *Sazaman-i Nasr*: 5,000 (prewar); 50,000 (initial, peak).[468] Guardians of the Islamic Holy War, aka *Sapaa* or *Pasdaran-i Jihad-i Islam or Sepha-e-Pasdaran*: 9,000 (prewar).[469] Islamic Movement of Afghanistan, aka *Nahzat-i Islami Afghanistan*: 4,000 (initial, peak).[470] Invitation to the Islamic Unity of Afghanistan, aka *Da'wat-i Ittehad-i Islami Afghanistan*: unknown. Party of Islamic Thunder of Afghanistan, aka *Hezb-i Islami Rad-i Afghanistan*: unknown. United Front, aka *Jebh-i Mutahed*: unknown. Council of the Islamic Revolutionary Alliance, aka *Shura-i Inqilab-I Itefaq-i Islam:* 10,000 (prewar); 30,000 (initial, peak).[471] Organization of the Holy Warriors of the Oppressed of Afghanistan, aka *Sazaman-i Mujahidin-i Mustazafin-i Afghanistan*: unknown. *Pashrau-i-Jihad*: 8,000 (initial, peak).[472] *Hezbollah*: 5,000 (prewar); 4,000 (initial, peak).[473] Unity Party, aka *Hezb-i-Wahdat*, participating from June 16, 1990, uniting most Shiite and Hazara groups: unknown. Islamic Alliance of Afghan Mujahideen: 6,000 (prewar).[474]

Antecedents: The Soviet Union fought a protracted and bloody extra-state war in Afghanistan from 1980 until its withdrawal in 1989. Resistance coalesced around seven groups based in Peshawar, Pakistan: three traditionalist parties open to a return of the monarchy and four fundamentalist parties seeking a more austere Islamic state. In the Hazarajat, Shiite groups dominated the area, with Iran-backed groups frequently clashing with more independent groups—and few groups clashing with government or Soviet forces, who more or less ignored the Hazarajat in the final years of the war. Many other regional resistance groups—perhaps thousands of them—also existed, but few had any real armed strength.

Before they withdrew, the Soviets strengthened the communist government of Mohammed Najibullah. An ethnically Uzbek militia under Abdul Rashid Dostum was added to government forces as the Fifty-third Division. The Soviets also avoided giving legitimacy to the *mujahideen* rebels by excluding them from the multilateral peace talks that preceded the withdrawal. In the end, an agreement was reached between the Democratic Republic of Afghanistan (DRA)—quickly renamed the Republic of Afghanistan by Najibullah—and Pakistan, with the Soviet Union and United States acting as guarantors.

The agreement called for an eventual halt to aid from the United States and an immediate halt to sanctuary from Pakistan for the *mujahideen*, although the Soviets were permitted to continue to provide massive financial aid to the government. Just before withdrawing, the Soviets launched an attack against the forces of Ahmed Shah Masood from January 23 to 25, 1989, killing up to 600 *mujahideen*. Thus, when the Soviets left, the government was still in a relatively strong position vis-à-vis the rebels.

Narrative: While the war began with minor guerrilla operations, the *mujahideen* soon tried their luck at conventional warfare, expecting a speedy government collapse. The seven major Peshawar-based groups formed the Mujahideen Alliance (which lacked an overall commander or effective coordination) and then besieged Jalalabad with about 14,000 troops on March 6, 1989. Government forces broke the siege in May and in mid-July recaptured a base at Samarkhel. The Jalalabad fighting cost the rebels at least 500 dead and 1,500 wounded.

The rebel alliance began to disintegrate with the failure of Jalalabad. The government was able to cut deals with some groups, and by the end of July about 90 percent of the rebel commanders were either inactive or fighting each other instead of the government. In particular, Gulbuddin Hekmatyar's Islamic Party targeted the commanders and officers of other *mujahideen* factions. Government forces also suffered from low morale. During an eleven-month period that year, the armed forces lost 67,000 personnel of whom more than half simply deserted. For the same period, government battle-deaths were 5,033. From September to December, the *mujahideen* unsuccessfully fought for control of Khost.

By 1990, the rebels had reverted largely to guerrilla warfare, and the government found that Dostum's Fifty-third Division was its only mobile reserve. On March 13, 1990, a coup attempt by the minister of defense, who had allied himself to the Islamic Party of Gulbuddin Hekmatyar, was quashed with the aid of loyal units and the bombardment of Darulaman Palace. The subsequent investigations by the secret police weakened the armed forces.

In April 1990, the government mounted an offensive against Paghman, a position near Kabul that had been captured by the *mujahideen* in 1985 and extensively fortified. The campaign lasted from April 10 to June 26, and while the government was forced to expend huge quantities of ammunition, it captured Paghman, killing 440 *mujahideen* and wounding 1,000 more—all at a cost of only 51 government dead and 330 wounded. The remainder of the year was characterized by guerrilla warfare as rebels shelled and rocketed Kabul and other cities but were unable to take well-defended positions.

By 1991, Dostum's strength had reached 40,000 men. In January, the government attempted to replace one of his political allies. Dostum rebelled, forming an alliance with Sayyid Mansur's Ismaili militia and aiding the *mujahideen*. The rebels took Khost and Mazar-e-Sharif in March, capturing several senior generals. Desertion was rampant in Afghan army units, increasing by 60 percent in 1991. By the end of the year, the collapse of the Soviet Union ended support from the north, leading the government to finance itself by printing money.

A shortage of fuel kept the country's air force, which had played a major role in the earlier battles, grounded during 1992. On April 15, aided by further defections among senior government defense officials, Dostum's militia landed at and took control of Kabul's airport. Najibullah fled and was forced to seek sanctuary in a United Nations compound.

Termination and Outcome: The outcome of the war was a complete rebel victory. Pro-government forces still possessed almost 1,000 tanks and nearly 200 aircraft, but communist resistance ceased with Najibullah's downfall. A race to Kabul began. Massoud and Dostum's forces advanced from the north, while Hekmatyar advanced from the south. Units of the Afghan army simply were absorbed into various rebel groups, with the majority aligning themselves with Dostum. From April 26 to April 28, Massoud and Hekmatyar's forces contested control of Kabul. Hekmatyar was ousted, and a new transitional government was formed. Hekmatyar's unwillingness to accept anything less than the presidency and his demand for the exclusion of Massoud sowed the seeds of the next civil war, one between the victorious *mujahideen*. Perhaps surprisingly, there was no large-scale purge of communists following the civil war, although Hindu and Sikh communities were targeted by extremists who saw India's hand behind Najibullah's regime.

Coding Decisions: The 1980–1989 war between the *mujahideen* and Soviets (Extra-state War #476) killed some 600,000 to 2.5 million people—at least 80 percent of them civilians—leaving about 120,000 to 500,000 battle-deaths, with the lower figure being the most plausible. Johnson argues that "violence did not lessen after the Soviet withdrawal," making the figures 1,100 battle-deaths per month, a useful upper bound for estimating the death toll in this thirty-eight-month conflict.[475] Government losses in major battles were substantially lower than the *mujahideen* (see Narrative), and the government lost only 5,033 (just under 460 per month) during eleven months in 1989. This lends plausibility to the estimate of 1,100 battle-deaths per month, or a total of about 40,000 battle-deaths. The real toll may be substantially higher, but it should be remembered that many casualties were caused by intra-*mujahideen* fighting; these intercommunal struggles are not included in our totals. This civil war is separated from Intra-state War #877.5 because one side in this war simply ceased to exist (as in the Mexican Revolution) leaving the victors to begin a new war among themselves.

Sources: Clodfelter (2008); Ewans (2001); Grau (2007); Johnson (2011); Laffin (1990, 1991); Maley (2002); Marshall (2006).[476]

INTRA-STATE WAR #853

Punjab Rebellion of 1989 to 1993 (aka Khalistan Insurgency)

Participants: India versus Sikh Guerrillas (Aggregate).
Dates: July 1, 1989, to June 30, 1993.
Battle-related Deaths: Armed Forces of India: about 1,500;[477] Sikh Guerrillas: 6,000 (likely an overestimate);[478] Total Combatant Deaths: up to 7,835. (See Coding Decisions.)[479]
Initiator: Sikh Guerrillas.
Outcome: India wins.
War Type: Civil for local issues (secession).

Total System Member Military Personnel: Armed Forces of India: 1,315,000 (prewar); 1,315,000 (initial); 1,370,000 (peak); 1,370,000 (final). Prewar and initial estimates include Punjabi police; peak and final estimates also include home guards and special police.[480]

Theater Armed Forces: Armed Forces of India: 70,000 (prewar); 210,000 (peak). Estimate includes home guards and special police. Sikh Guerrillas: several thousand (prewar); 6,000 (peak); 1,000 to 2,000 (final).[481]

Antecedents: After Operation Blue Star and the ensuing war in Punjab (Intra-state War #837), the leadership of rebel organizations either was killed or captured, temporarily ending the fighting. But forces calling for an independent Khalistan were strengthened by the destruction of the reformist groups. In 1985, there were only 10 battle-deaths, but then violence began to escalate. In 1986 there were 120 militant and police deaths, and that number increased to 423 in 1987 and 523 in 1988. In 1987, arms began to trickle across the border with Pakistan; soon, many rebels were armed with AK-47 assault rifles at a time when government forces were still using World War II–era equipment. Overall deaths, mostly civilians, increased rapidly.

On May 8, 1988, fighting again broke out around the Golden Temple complex. Some 30 militants were killed and 100 captured with no loss on the government side. In total, the government deployed about 70,000 personnel against the Punjab rebels that year. Rebel strength also had increased from a mere few hundred militants in 1987 to 2,000 to 3,000 by the spring of 1988.

By the fall of 1988, all of the major armed groups had moved into the secessionist camp. Separatist groups included the venerable Babbar Khalsa (founded in 1978) and newer groups such as the Bhindranwale Tiger Khalistan Force (BTKF), the Khalistan Liberation Force (KLF), and the factionalized Khalistan Commando Force (KCF). At least three different umbrella groups were formed, but each competed with each other so that there was little unity among the insurgents. Notably, these organizations lacked a political party to represent them as the major parties were dominated by moderates, radicals, or mere extremists willing to negotiate with the government on terms short of independence.

Narrative: Yearly battle-deaths increased to near-war levels (851 to 904) in 1989. At some point during this year, the conflict very likely reached civil-war levels (we code the onset as occurring on July 1, the first day of the second half of the year, when more than half the casualties were likely suffered). By this point, the rebels actually were killing more Sikhs than Hindus. The number of insurgents probably peaked at around 6,000 in 1990 or 1991.

Internecine warfare and the killing of Sikhs suspected of collaboration with the government or rival organizations eventually opened the door to a successful counterinsurgency campaign by central government and (especially) state police forces. By 1992, the Punjabi police began recruiting relatives of Sikh villagers killed by the Sikh guerrillas into commando units, which eventually would replace the armed forces of the central government in most of the fighting. The Punjab police were expanded to 70,000, not including another 40,000 home guards and special police. About 100,000 government soldiers provided additional security, particularly during the elections of 1991 and 1992. Against this, the rebels could field no more than a couple of thousand insurgents; these were reduced to just over 1,100 by November 1993.

Termination and Outcome: The war ended when casualties fell below the civil-war threshold. As is evident from the fact that only twenty-five security forces were killed in all of 1993, the government won the war militarily. The insurgency sputtered on for a few months, but in 1994 only seventy-six combatants—all reportedly militants—were killed. The government continued to hunt down leaders of the insurgency after the war ended, but "small fry" were tacitly provided with amnesty if they surrendered.

Coding Decisions: While there are a number of sources with slightly different annual figures, we estimate about 500 battle-deaths for the second half of 1989 and about the same number in the first half of 1993. The best annual estimates, internal data from India's Ministry of Home Affairs, are presented in Table 7.2. Including the 1990-to-1992 period, total battle-deaths are estimated at 7,835, which is likely an overestimate due to government forces sometimes killing noncombatants in staged "encounter killings."[482]

TABLE 7.2 **Indian Government Estimates of Battle-deaths in Punjab, 1988–1994**

Year	Rebels Killed	Government Security Forces Killed	Total Battle-Deaths
1988	373	110	483
1989	703	201	904
1990	1,320	476	1,796
1991	2,177	497	2,674
1992	2,113	252	2,365
1993	798	25	823
1994	76	0	76
Total for 1990–1992	5,610	1,225	6,835

Sources: Chima (1997, 2010); Dhillon (1998); Swami (2004); Telford (2001); Wallace (2010).

INTRA-STATE WAR #854
Second Khmer Rouge War of 1989 to 1991

Participants: Cambodia versus Khmer Rouge, Khmer People's National Liberation Front, and National Sihanoukist Army.
Dates: September 26, 1989, to October 23, 1991.
Battle-related Deaths: Total Combatant Deaths: 2,100. (See Coding Decisions.)[483]
Initiator: Khmer Rouge, Khmer People's National Liberation Front, and National Sihanoukist Army.
Outcome: Negotiated settlement.
War Type: Civil for central control.
Total System Member Military Personnel: Armed Forces of Cambodia: 146,000 (prewar, initial); 159,000 (peak, final). These totals include both the armed forces proper and the 47,000-strong police force, which also was used to fight the rebels.[484]
Theater Armed Forces: Khmer Rouge: 40,000 (initial).[485] Khmer People's National Liberation Front: 10,000 to 12,000 (initial).[486] National Sihanoukist Army, aka ANS: 15,000 to 18,000 (initial).[487]

Antecedents: After attacks on Vietnamese by the genocidal Khmer Rouge, Vietnam invaded Kampuchea (as Cambodia had been renamed by the Khmer Rouge) in 1979 (Extra-state War #475). A vicious guerrilla war soon developed, with several guerrilla groups fighting Vietnam and the puppet government it installed. In November 1987, Vietnam withdrew the first 20,000 of its troops from the country. It withdrew 50,000 more in May 1988, and on September 25, 1989, its withdrawal was nearly complete, leaving behind a civil war between the government of the newly renamed State of Cambodia (SOC) and its opponents.

Narrative: The rebels mounted offensives against the government after the withdrawal of most Vietnamese soldiers. Fighting was concentrated in the northern and western areas of the country. In October, the KPNLF besieged Sisophon, an important hub between Phnom Penh and Battambang, while the Khmer Rouge aimed at control of the gemstone mining area of Pailin, which they finally achieved at the end of the month after heavy fighting against elite government units.

The following year, the guerrillas expanded their control in the East. The Khmer Rouge attacked Battambang in January, and while they were eventually compelled to withdraw after setting the city ablaze, they mounted new offensives in the East that threatened government control of several provinces. They attacked Battambang again the following month. A peace effort in February failed to produce a cease-fire as disagreements over power-sharing formulae led to a bargaining impasse. In May, a cease-fire was arranged, but all sides violated it through the end of the year. Battambang was attacked by the Khmer Rouge again in July, using heavy weapons supplied by China. Meanwhile, the government used

Soviet-supplied aircraft to bombard rebel positions. By the end of the year, the rebels were operating in larger units and holding more territory than they had in January.

Termination and Outcome: Fighting subsided considerably in 1991, although the exact termination date is unclear. Upon consideration, we conclude that the war ended after a peace settlement was reached on October 23. The settlement established a transitional government with representatives from the SOC and the three resistance factions. It also called for a United Nations peacekeeping mission to monitor the May 1991 cease-fire and the implementation of the agreement as well as cantonment and 70 percent disarmament of each faction before supervised elections. Some important issues were left unresolved, and the various parties were permitted to continue to administer the areas under their control. Eventually, the refusal of the Khmer Rouge to disarm or proceed with elections, combined with continued infiltration of SOC-controlled areas, led the government to resume offensive operations, reigniting the conflict (see Intra-state War # 881).

Coding Decisions: We have identified no casualty estimates for this war. Given the number of combatants involved and the reported intensity of the combat, it is likely that at least 1,000 combatants died from all causes between September 26, 1989, and September 25, 1990. However, whether another 1,000 died over the next year is far from clear. We may be erring on the side of inclusion by estimating at least 2,100 battle-deaths total.

Sources: Broiwn (1992); Nhem (2013); Roberts (2001); Um (1990); van der Krof (1991).[488]

INTRA-STATE WAR #858
First Aceh War of 1990 to 1991

Participants: Indonesia versus Gerakan Aceh Merdeka.
Dates: April 1990 to July 1991.
Battle-related Deaths: Total Combatant Deaths: 1,500 (to the nearest thousand).[489]
Initiator: Gerakan Aceh Merdeka.
Outcome: Fighting fell below civil-war threshold.
War Type: Civil for local issues (secession).
Total System Member Military Personnel: Armed Forces of Indonesia: 283,000 (prewar, initial); 278,000 (peak, final).[490]
Theater Armed Forces: Armed Forces of Indonesia: 6,000 (initial); 12,000 (peak). Figures exclude the 60,000 civilians conscripted into militias, who were largely unarmed. *Gerakan Aceh Merdeka (GAM)*, aka Free Aceh Movement—1,000 (initial); one to several thousand (peak).[491]

Antecedents: On October 30, 1976, the seventy guerrillas of the Aceh Sumatra National Liberation Front (ASNLF)—better known as the Free Aceh Movement (*Gerakan Aceh Merdeka* [GAM])—mounted an insurgency against the government of Indonesia, seeking to liberate the territory from the state's control. The movement withdrew from most combat operations in 1982, and it was sustained largely by the Acehnese diaspora in Malaysia. From 1986 to 1989 Libya trained anywhere from a few hundred to thousands of GAM troops. When they returned from training in Libya, they had become notably more effective. In May 1988, the GAM resumed offensive military operations. The next year, they expanded from Pidie to Greater Aceh, Bireuen, North Aceh, and East Aceh. Their activities kept government forces on the defensive through the end of 1989.

Narrative: GAM stepped up its attacks in April 1990, escalating the violence to civil-war scale. In May 1990, GAM attacked a police station, killing several officers and seizing weapons. They also ambushed Indonesian troops. In response, the government instituted martial law and created *Kolakops Jaring Merah* (Military Operations Implementation Command Red Net), often called DOM, to crush the rebellion. In the first months of the war, up to 150 government security force personnel were killed (the government conceded 50). In July, the government deployed an additional 6,000 troops, bringing its total strength in Aceh to 12,000. The government forces retaliated against GAM and Acehnese civilians alike, killing perhaps 2,000 people by the end of the year. It also created village militias, armed only with bamboo spears, numbering about 60,000 by mid-1991. The militias were forced to participate in "fence of legs" counterinsurgency operations. A government army doctor reported that 2,000 soldiers and rebels were killed from July 1990 to July 1991, by which time the violence had begun to slow.

Termination and Outcome: The last twelve-month period for which we have evidence of more than 1,000 battle-deaths is July 1990 to July 1991. After this, it appears that the violence dipped below the civil-war threshold until a revival of GAM in 1999 (see Intra-state War #912). DOM was continued until 1998, and during that time suspected rebels were arrested, shot, or simply "disappeared."

Coding Decisions: Self-explanatory from cited sources.

Sources: "Jakarta Battles North's Rebel Reign of Terror" (1990); Kell (2010); Laffin (1994); "Rebellion: Indonesia Calls Them Migrant Workers" (1991); Schulze (2002, 2006).[492]

INTRA-STATE WAR #859

Second Sri Lanka Tamil War of 1990 to 2001 (aka Eelam Wars II and III)

Participants: Sri Lanka versus Liberation Tigers of Tamil Eelam (LTTE).
Dates: June 11, 1990, to October 13, 1994, and April 19, 1995, to December 24, 2001.
Battle-related Deaths: Total Combatant Deaths: 70,000. (See Coding Decisions.)[493]
Initiator: Liberation Tigers of Tamil Eelam.
Outcome: Negotiated agreement.
War Type: Civil for local issues (independence and territory: Eastern province).
Total System Member Military Personnel: Armed Forces of Sri Lanka: 22,000 (prewar, initial); 121,000 (peak, final).[494]
Theater Armed Forces: Liberation Tigers of Tamil Eelam: 10,000 (prewar, initial, peak); 7,000 (final).[495]

Antecedents: In Eelam War I (see Intra-state War #835), the Liberation Tigers of Tamil Eelam and four other Tamil groups fought against the government and each other. Just as the Sri Lankan military was about to capture the critical town of Jaffna, India intervened and insisted on a peace accord. The Indo-Sri Lankan Accord brought two months of peace, followed by an extra-state war between the Indian Peacekeeping Force (IPKF) and the LTTE. While the government first fought alongside the IPKF, elections in 1988 brought a new regime to power that was more concerned with asserting the country's sovereignty against India. The government reached an accommodation with the LTTE sometime in March 1989, and combat between the two ceased completely. More than a year would pass before it resumed.

Beginning in May of the same year, the government actually began providing weapons to the LTTE in order to secure the departure of the IPKF, and on June 2, the government ordered the IPKF to leave; a formal cease-fire agreement between the LTTE and government was signed on June 28. When the IPKF finally left in March 1990, the LTTE had swollen from a few thousand fighters at the onset of IPKF intervention to about 10,000. The tenuous peace between the LTTE and government held for several months, even as both sides expanded into territory vacated by the Indians. On June 7, however, a group of government soldiers refused to stop at an LTTE checkpoint; one of them was killed, and several others were wounded. Tensions rose as a second round of war appeared inevitable in the former Eastern province (now amalgamated into a single mixed Tamil–Muslim–Sinhalese Northeastern province).

Narrative: The first organized military activity of the war took place on June 11, when the LTTE assaulted the Batticoala police station in the East; soon, it seized eleven other stations in the province as well, executing some 600 surrendered police. The next day, the rebels attacked three army camps, taking Vellaveddi camp. Security forces evacuated other vulnerable camps while the LTTE continued to overrun police stations throughout the East before initiating operations against the army in the North on June 15. Jaffna Fort was besieged. The government responded to the brutality with Operation Sledge Hammer (a prepared military offensive against LTTE strongholds in the East), heavily bombing Tamil areas and arming local home guard units, which often committed atrocities in their pursuit of the LTTE. As fighting broke out between Tamils and Muslim home guard units in the Eastern province, the LTTE responded with a program of ethnic cleansing. In October, the 30,000 Muslims living in Jaffna were expelled by the LTTE.

Casualties were much higher than in Eelam War I. Within a week of the onset of Eelam War II, perhaps 200 LTTE and more than 50 government soldiers had been killed in the fighting (not including the executed police). In early July, the five-day Operation Strike Hard killed another 89 LTTE cadres, while a rebel assault overran the garrison at Kokavil Camp, killing all but 2 of its 51-strong garrison. A government ship was sunk by a rebel suicide squad on July 11. On July 17, a battle near Mankulam Junction killed 100 LTTE and wounded 50 more. For the first time, female combatants composed a significant fraction of those killed or wounded by the government forces. By the late 1990s, women would comprise 15 to 20 percent of the LTTE's field forces. Further battles in July killed perhaps 100 LTTE. Another 28 rebels died attacking Jaffna Fort, and a further 72 were wounded; government losses were light by comparison. Another 80 rebels were killed from August 3 to August 6.

On August 22, the government mounted Operation Thrividabalaya to relieve Jaffna Fort. Some 2,000 government soldiers attacked LTTE positions on the first day, and 300 LTTE died in fighting through August 27. Another 85 LTTE were killed in early September's Operation Sea Breeze against only 15 government soldiers. In heavy fighting near the town of Jaffna on September 13 and September 14, the government claimed to have killed 180 rebels at the cost of only 24 security forces killed and 130 wounded. Having removed weapons stockpiles and gold from Jaffna Fort, the government forces then evacuated the position, which fell to the rebels on September 26.

Meanwhile, the 2,000 soldiers who had spearheaded Thrividabalaya were redeployed to the East. The LTTE then besieged the Palali military base in the North, triggering a government counteroffensive named Operation Jayashakthi. In the monsoonal rains of mid-October, some 2,500 troops with heavy air support attacked rebel positions near Palali, resulting in 47 killed and 111 wounded on the government side and perhaps 150 to 200 LTTE fatalities. The government later claimed to have killed 440 LTTE between September 13 and October 22. On November 22, the LTTE mounted an attack on Mankulam camp, taking 75 fatalities on the first day of fighting. The government claimed 300 LTTE killed and 250 wounded by November 25, but the rebels took Mankulam.

On January 1, 1991, the LTTE declared a unilateral cease-fire. The government responded by insisting that the LTTE disarm for a cease-fire agreement, and fighting resumed. On March 2, a rebel car bomb attack in Colombo killed Sri Lanka's defense minister. On March 19, the rebels mounted an offensive against government forces in and around Silavatturai; the government admitted to 28 killed and 108 wounded while claiming to have killed 131 rebels. The government responded with a local counteroffensive known as Operation Tiger Chase, which was followed by other operations in April; the government reported 800 LTTE killed for the month. The government continued to mount offensives in May, while the rebels succeeded in assassinating Rajiv Ghandi, who seemed poised to regain the position of prime minister of India in upcoming elections. The LTTE had been concerned that Ghandi would redeploy the IPKF if elected.

Serious fighting continued almost without interruption from late May to late October. Pro-government sources consistently reported much higher rebel losses than government ones: Operation Wanni Wikrema 2 (275 rebels killed and over 300 wounded against 41 soldiers killed and 166 wounded), battles in and around Elephant Pass—including the amphibious rescue mission Operation Balavegaya (perhaps 1,000 to 2,450 rebel battle-deaths against somewhat more than 150 government killed and at least 482 wounded in what was the deadliest battle in the country's history at the time), Operation Ashaka Sena in Weli-Oya (129 rebels killed against 30 government killed), Operation Lighting Strike in Mullaithivu (up to 1,000 rebels killed and the same number wounded against 68 government battle-deaths and 600 wounded), and Operation Valampuri against rebel-held positions near the city of Jaffna (several hundred rebels killed against mere dozens of government troops). The government's air supremacy played a major role in these and subsequent offensives, substantially increasing rebel casualties and preventing ambushes.

The government mounted a number of limited offensives in 1992. From February to March, Operation Wanni Wickrema 3 destroyed several LTTE strongholds in the district of Vavuniya, killing 83 rebels (including 21 female combatants). In late March, Operation Hayepahara began in Mullaithivu, aiming at the bases in the Weli-Oya jungles the LTTE had managed to defend in 1991. The government was now equipped with substantial armor, and the offensive made rapid progress, killing 200 LTTE cadres at the price of perhaps 50 government soldiers. At the end of May, the government mounted offensives in the Jaffna peninsula (Operation Whirlwind) and Mullaithivu (Operation Sathbala). More than 200 rebels and 48 government troops were killed in the former, while losses in the latter were perhaps half as great.

In July, the government mounted Operation Balavegaya 2 to link up the beachhead established the year before with its camp at Elephant Pass, thereby cutting a major rebel line of supply. The government claimed 700 LTTE killed and a similar number wounded against only 38 government battle-deaths. Many of the rebel deaths were attributed to government air attacks on vehicles filled with rebel reinforcements. Military commanders planned a follow-up assault on Jaffna City itself; although top commanders opposed the plan, fearing high casualties in a direct assault, President Ranasinghe Premadasa personally approved the operation. The would-be commanders of the operation were killed by an LTTE mine, and the operation died with them. Instead, the new local commander ordered an attack west of Palali to expand government control on the Jaffna peninsula. Operation Earthquake captured the rebel camp of Madagal and then halted, having killed somewhat fewer than 100 LTTE. A minor follow-on operation named Chathuranga further expanded the zone of government control in September.

In the district of Mannar (Northern province), the government mounted a major anti-rebel drive known as Operation Seegrapahara, which captured 11 LTTE camps at a trivial cost. Meanwhile, the government effectively had blockaded the lagoon used by the rebels to supply Jaffna, destroying thirty rebel-operated boats by late October. Between Balavegaya 2 and its marine operations, the government thus severed the main rebel supply lines. Upon the onset of the monsoon season in the North, the government mounted the brief Operation Jayapahara in the East, which captured some LTTE supplies and allegedly inflicted dozens of casualties on the rebels, who retreated instead of fighting to defend their positions. Operation Jaya Ganga closed out the year, killing a few rebels and recovering substantial territory in the East. During 1992, the government admitted a total of 1,157 soldiers killed and 2,004 wounded against claims of 2,876 rebels killed.

In 1993, the government improved the coordination of its forces by placing the Joint Operations Command over all forces operating in the North and East. The first offensive of the year was Operation Black Fox 4 in Vavuniya, which captured territory and some civilians but failed to engage the LTTE. The rebels did suffer substantial casualties in the Kilali lagoon, however, as government ships continued to interdict supplies to Jaffna City, destroying more than 160 boats in the process. On February 23, a new offensive in Jaffna code-named Operation Ranabima advanced against guerrilla resistance by the rebels. The government forces returned to their original lines after destroying a number of LTTE strongholds.

Although the government continued to try to expand its territorial control in Jaffna, it increasingly focused on securing the much-less-heavily defended Eastern province from the LTTE. The bloodless Operation Sedapahara captured considerable territory in March, as did Operation Muhudusulang in June. Guerrilla resistance seemed weak, but on May 1 the LTTE assassinated President Premadasa in Colombo, and on July 25 a rebel attack killed twenty-four soldiers in Janakapura in the North. Moreover, the government began losing patrol craft in the Kilali lagoon to suicide attacks.

The government mounted a counterinsurgency operation in the East, which it claimed reduced LTTE strength in the East from 2,000 to only 50 cadres by the end of the year. Government losses were light, and its focus returned to the North, where in September it launched Operation Yal Devi to engage the rebels and destroy LTTE camps near Elephant Pass. The LTTE sent reinforcements to block government forces from taking Chavakkachcherri, and heavy combat occurred. The government losses stood at 118 killed against perhaps 355 rebels killed. Simultaneous naval operations destroyed 750 LTTE boats at piers in Kilali lagoon. The rebels prepared for an assault on Jaffna City that never came.

To divert government resources, the rebels attacked in Pooneryn sector. About 1,000 rebels attacked camps totaling 2,000 government troops on November 11 in Operation Unceasing Waves. With surprise, the rebels achieved initial successes, and the government responded by bombing Jaffna City. After two days of fighting, government losses totaled 250 soldiers killed and many more wounded. The government mounted an amphibious and air rescue mission, and by the end of the battle for Pooneryn, the LTTE acknowledged 600 rebel battle-deaths, against 525 killed or wounded on the government side. Losses for 1993 amounted to 718 government soldiers and 1,300 LTTE cadres.

In 1994, the government took advantage of the relative calm in the Eastern province to hold provincial elections. In April, government forces moved out of Vavuniya in Operation Jayamaga, capturing a number of villages; casualties were low on both sides. As it turned out, Jayamaga was the largest operation of the year. National elections were held in August, resulting in the opposition People's Alliance gaining power. Upon attaining power on August 19, the People's Alliance decided to pursue peace talks with the rebels. Sporadic fighting continued, including the sinking of a government ship by the rebels and a retaliatory government offensive near Palali that killed 75 rebels and wounded 200.

Peace talks resumed in October during a ceasefire. The LTTE demanded government withdrawal from the Poonryn camp and a lifting of the ban on fishing in blockaded areas such as the Kilali lagoon. On April 19, 1995, the peace talks collapsed as the LTTE resumed hostilities. This second phase of the conflict was known as Eelam War III. It opened with LTTE Sea Tiger suicide attacks on the Sri Lankan navy, which sank two gunboats. A dozen sailors were killed and 21 wounded. The rebels shot down a government transport aircraft on April 28, killing all 41 on board. By this point in Eelam War III government losses totaled 111 killed and 60 wounded. Another 52 were killed the next day, when another government aircraft was brought down by a rebel missile.

The government mounted a series of relatively minor operations against the rebels. Then in July Operation Leap Forward was undertaken by 10,000 government troops in Jaffna, resulting in (government claims of) 360 rebel battle-deaths and 60 government battle-deaths. Another government ship was sunk by the Sea Tigers. The rebels mounted an offensive in the Weli-Oya sector but suffered at least 182 killed (the government claimed 482), inflicting only trivial casualties on government forces.

Minor operations continued, and the government positioned its forces for an assault on Jaffna City, first cutting the links between the city and the LTTE stronghold of Vadamarachchi. The government acknowledged the deaths of 54 soldiers in this operation (123 being wounded) but claimed LTTE fatalities in excess of 500. In October, a massive offensive, Riviresa 1, kicked off with 30,000 soldiers assaulting LTTE positions in Jaffna. By November 21, government soldiers entered the outer limits of Jaffna City; the city center fell two weeks later. Government forces had suffered 493 killed and 3,379 wounded, while the government claimed that 2,063 rebels were killed and more than 6,000 wounded.

A lull in the fighting on Jaffna followed as the government carried out operations to counter LTTE infiltration into the Eastern province. In the North, major operations to clear the rest of Valigamam sector kicked off on March 29, 1996. Skirmishes that followed killed 9 government soldiers and wounded 21 against alleged losses of 153 killed on the rebel side. The government now held about 45 percent of the Jaffna peninsula. The next month, it advanced into the Thennamarachi sector of the Peninsula in Operation Riviresa 2. The government claimed that it had inflicted more than 260 fatalities on the rebels while suffering only 8 itself. The government forces then turned against Vadamarachchi in May's Operation Riviresa 3, which largely completed the government's occupation of the Jaffna peninsula.

The northern rebels regrouped near Kilinochchi to the south of the peninsula, while 4,000 LTTE in the East attacked Mullaithivu on July 18. The initial assault killed more than 100 elite government troops and sank one government gunboat. Altogether the opening stages of the battle killed 142 government soldiers and wounded 168; the government claimed more than 200 rebel deaths. By July 26, some 1,200 of the 1,400-man Mullaithivu garrison had been killed, and the rebels overran the base and gained access to stockpiles of weapons and ammunition, including heavy artillery. Perhaps 800 rebels were killed and 1,500 wounded in the battle.

On the last day of the battle, the government mounted an offensive against the LTTE's main strength in Kilinochchi. The first phase of Operation Sathjaya cost the lives of 63 government troops (88 being wounded) and more than 300 rebels (according to the government). Government forces had been stopped just short of Kilinochchi itself but relaunched the operation in late September, successfully seizing the town in a three-pronged assault. By the end of September, Operation Sathjaya had resulted in up to 1,000 LTTE and 350 soldiers killed (and 400 wounded).

Relatively minor operations closed out the year, but on January 9, 1997, the LTTE mounted major attacks against the government's base at the vital choke point of Elephant Pass. Paranthan was also attacked. In nine hours of fighting, the government lost 223 killed and 400 wounded, while the LTTE lost 171 (rebel claim) to 500 (government claim) killed. The rebels withdrew with up to 700 wounded.

The government mounted a series of operations to connect and consolidate its holdings in the North. It also attacked Sea Tiger bases along the eastern coast. Losses on both sides were relatively light until June, when Operation Jayasikuru, which had been launched on May 13 to connect Vavuniya and Jaffna via the A-9 highway, ran into heavy resistance. Battles over control of the highway claimed hundreds of lives on both sides by September, and fighting began to intensify. Jayasikuru lasted longer than any previous operation, and as it passed the one-year mark the government estimated that 3,200 LTTE had been killed and 6,000 wounded, while it put its own losses at 1,600 killed and 5,000 wounded. The government lost another 208 killed and 206 seriously wounded from May 28 to June 8, 1998; it claimed rebel losses of 225 killed and 600 wounded for the same period. A relative lull in fighting followed, but in August the battles resumed, albeit at lower intensity.

From September 27 to September 29, the LTTE and government forces were locked in combat in Paranthan and Kilinochchi. The government suffered 632 killed and 400 wounded, while the rebels admitted 513 killed and 400 wounded. In the South, the important rebel hub of Mankulam fell the next day, and by October 3 the government claimed rebel losses of 1,700 killed in fighting for Paranthan, Kilinochchi, and Mankulam. In December, Jayasikuru was terminated, and new operations against rebel strongholds east of the A-9 highway were undertaken, consolidating government gains.

Outside efforts at mediation were turned aside by the government, which believed it was winning the war. In March 1999, the government mounted Operations Ranagosha 1 and 2 to clear Vavuniya district west of the A-9. Fighting was minimal until Ranagosha 3 in May, in which nineteen government and forty-two rebel soldiers were killed. Operations Whirlwind and Ranagosha 4 followed; the former temporarily expanded government control near Paranthan, while the latter "liberated" 90 percent of the Mannar district. Losses were relatively light until the second phase of Ranagosha 4 in late June, which cost the lives of hundreds of LTTE. On August 6 the LTTE agreed to allow civilians to be resupplied along A-9. Civilians were thus able to cross between LTTE and government-controlled areas; a temporary cease-fire also allowed a polio vaccination program to proceed.

Heavy fighting resumed on September 12, when the government mounted Operation Ranagosha 5. During a four-kilometer advance and subsequent withdrawal to its starting positions, the government suffered 114 killed and 832 wounded, while it put LTTE losses at 127 killed and 423 wounded. Another attempt to secure the Wanni region was made on October 14, when Operation Watershed kicked off. Up to 69 LTTE were killed; government losses were much lighter.

On November 1, the LTTE launched its own offensive named Unceasing Waves 3. It took Oddusuddhan the next day and proceeded to recapture much of the territory it had lost since May 1997. In the opening stages of the offensive, the LTTE suffered 200 killed, while the government suffered 1,000 battle-deaths. After a two-week lull in the fighting, the LTTE resumed its offensive, this time targeting the Elephant Pass area. This attack proved to be costly—the government claimed that 480 LTTE had been killed against only 28 government troops. The rebels also attacked government positions on the Jaffna peninsula, resulting in heavy fighting through the end of the year. Battles near Paranthan killed nearly 1,200 LTTE and 150 government soldiers, according to government sources.

The year 2000 opened with the customary lull in fighting due to the seasonal rains. But in March, the LTTE renewed its efforts to take Jaffna and Elephant Pass. Thousands of LTTE were landed along the Vadamarachchi coast and proceeded to cut the supply route between Jaffna and Elephant Pass, which was retaken by government forces only after heavy fighting that killed more than 300 rebels and 121 government soldiers. On April 17, the LTTE seized the supply base of Iyakkachchi, cutting fresh water supplies to Elephant Pass. As the fighting continued, soldiers began to die of dehydration. On April 23, the army withdrew, and Elephant Pass fell to the LTTE. The government suffered at least 126 killed in the defeat.

The rebels followed up the attack on Elephant Pass by moving to recapture Jaffna City. Between

April 27 and May 18, the government claimed to have killed more than 653 rebels. But by May 10, the latter had reached the city gates. Heavy fighting cost hundreds of lives, but government forces held Jaffna and mounted a counteroffensive on May 29. LTTE losses were heavy, especially among officers; the organization admitted to 943 killed between April 1 and July 15, of whom 273 were officers.

On August 30, the government opened Operation Rivikirana to secure areas near Jaffna City. The one-day operation and immediate LTTE counterattacks killed 175 government soldiers and wounded another 247; rebel losses were estimated at 300 killed and many more wounded. The government followed up with a series of limited operations meant to secure lost territory on the Jaffna Peninsula. From September 3 through December 30, these operations reportedly cost the lives of 776 rebels and 268 on the government side. On December 24, the LTTE declared a unilateral cease-fire, but government operations continued.

Another limited government offensive began on January 16, 2001. After two days, the government reported 55 killed and 255 wounded and claimed 132 LTTE killed and 88 wounded. A lull in the fighting followed, although government air attacks against rebel positions continued, especially those in and around Elephant Pass. On April 24, the LTTE ended its unilateral cease-fire; hours later, the government began its last major offensive of the war, Operation Agni Kheela. From April 25 to April 29, the government suffered 167 killed and 1,900 wounded against perhaps 200 rebels killed and 400 wounded. Government forces were forced to retreat.

On July 25, an LTTE suicide commando team attacked Katunayake air force base and Bandaranaike international airport, not far from Columbo itself. Serious damage was inflicted on the Sri Lankan air force, and several commercial airliners were damaged or destroyed. Political recriminations followed the disaster, and in October the president, facing a no-confidence motion, dissolved parliament, and called for new elections, which were held in December. The opposition United National Front, together with the allied Sri Lanka Muslim Congress, won a majority of seats in the new parliament, which opened on January 1, 2002.

Termination and Outcome: The new government promised peace talks with the rebels; the LTTE responded with a month-long unilateral cease-fire beginning on December 24, 2001, which the government reciprocated on land (although naval interdiction of arms to the LTTE continued long after the end of the war). On February 23, 2002, the informal cease-fires, which had been observed since December 24, were formalized in a bilateral agreement. The terms of the cease-fire agreement were quite favorable to the LTTE: each side would abstain from hostile acts against the other, each side would allow unarmed civilians to enter its territory, the LTTE would open the A-9 highway, the government would lift its economic blockade of the Northeast, and the LTTE would assume transitional political control of the Northeast. Each side was permitted to recruit and arm forces to the pre-CFA level. Non-LTTE armed groups were to be disarmed.

Coding Decisions: Reliable figures are scarce; government reports tended to label all those it killed in battles and bombing as LTTE. According to data collected by Robert Oberst, 1990 to 1992 saw 31,000 deaths. Perhaps half of these (45 percent in 1990) were civilians. Losses for 1993 amounted to 718 government soldiers and 1,300 LTTE cadres, according to government reports. Battle-deaths were relatively low in 1994, judging from the same account. So a reasonable estimate of battle-deaths for Eelam War II is 18,000 to 19,000. From 1995 to 2000, some 56,000—up to 90 percent of them combatants—were killed. According to the South Asia Terrorism Portal, there were 412 government battle-deaths and 1,321 rebel battle-deaths in 2001. This suggests a toll of about 51,000 battle-deaths for Eelam War III. In all, we estimate 70,000 battle-deaths in this civil war, a figure that could be inflated by the inclusion of civilians in reported LTTE death tolls.

Sources: Akhtar (2006); Bandarage (2009); Bullion (1995); Hashim (2013); Mendis (2009); Shastri (2003).

INTRA-STATE WAR #860

Bougainville Secessionist War of 1990 to 1991

Participants: Papua New Guinea versus Bougainville Revolutionary Army.
Dates: September 22, 1990, to January 24, 1991, and June 1991 to December 1991.

Battle-related Deaths: Total Combatant Deaths: 1,000. (See Coding Decisions.)[496]
Initiator: Papua New Guinea.
Outcome: Fighting fell below civil-war threshold.
War Type: Civil for local issues (secession).
Total System Member Military Personnel: Armed Forces of Papua New Guinea: 3,000 (prewar, initial); 4,000 (peak, final).[497]
Theater Armed Forces: Bougainville Revolutionary Army: "thousands" (initial—rebel claim); 8,000—but only "hundreds" had firearms (peak).[498]

Antecedents: Bougainville is an island rich in mineral resources, which provided the government of Papua New Guinea with a substantial fraction of its export revenue. Convinced that they were not receiving their due share of the revenues, locals began to demand autonomy. In 1988, the Bougainville Revolutionary Army (BRA) was formed, demanding compensation for both environmental damage and landowners displaced by the Australian-owned copper mine that generated so much revenue.

In May 1989, a spate of violence and sabotage closed the copper mine. On June 27, the government imposed a state of emergency and began airlifting troops onto the island. In July, the government withdrew government services. The campaign against the BRA involved atrocities against civilians, and the rebels gained popular support. The government withdrew its forces from the island in March 1990 as a peace overture; the death toll was more than 100 people by the time of withdrawal, including many civilians. As peace talks foundered, the BRA unilaterally declared the island independent in May, and the government responded by blockading the island. The blockade would eventually claim thousands of lives, most of them civilians.

Narrative: In September 1990, the government retook the nearby island of Buka from the rebels. Between 50 and 200 rebels were reported to have been killed in the operation (although some reports were lower than this), which marked a notable increase in conflict intensity. For their part, the rebels claimed to have killed 30 government soldiers in the fighting. The blockade was temporarily lifted in January 1991. By this point, it had already killed about 1,700 people—700 from malaria alone—due to diseases that could have been treated absent the blockade. On January 24, the two sides signed the Honiara Declaration on Peace, Reconciliation, and Rehabilitation of Bougainville—a peace agreement that failed to address the issue of independence. In mid-April, although the government deployed 300 troops to northern Bougainville itself, the local rebels claimed to lack the offensive firepower necessary to expel them, and an uneasy peace continued.

In June, after two government soldiers were killed in a rebel ambush, the government reimposed its blockade; by December, another 1,300 had died of easily preventable diseases. On August 22, the government signed a separate peace deal with the rebels in the North, providing for an interim administration there. They reached a similar agreement with rebels in the South on October 24, although the leadership of the main BRA forces in the center did not participate in the talks. On November 3, an attack on a government camp ended in the death of 15 rebels.

Termination and Outcome: At some point, the fighting fell below 1,000 battle-deaths per year; we date this to the end of 1991 because government campaigns in 1992 failed to kill many rebels and resulted in few government losses. Of course, low-level fighting continued and higher-intensity fighting flared up again in 1996. A peace accord was finally reached in 1997.

Coding Decisions: In 1996, the government estimated that 10,000 had perished from violence or disease since the onset of the rebellion in 1989. Because much of the combat occurred during and in the year or so following September 1990, we tentatively estimate that this period saw 1,000 battle-deaths. This could be a considerable overestimate as many civilians died of malnutrition and disease in the 1989-to-1996 period.

Sources: Beatson (1991); Bercovitch and Fretter (2004); Gosman (1991); Grubel (1992); Milliken (1990); O'Callaghan (1989, 1991a, b, c); "PNG Signs Peace Pact with Rebels" (1991); Wilson-Roberts (2001).[499]

INTRA-STATE WAR #874

Kashmir Insurgency of 1992 to 2005

Participants: India versus Jammu-Kashmir Liberation Front, *Hizbul Mujahideen*,

Ikhwan-ul-Muslimeen, Al Jehad, Al Barq, *Al Umar Mujahideen*, *Jaish-e-Mohammed*, *Lashkar-e-Taiba*, and *Harkat-ul-Ansar*.

Dates: January 1, 1992, to December 31, 2005.

Battle-related Deaths: Armed Forces of India—about 5,000; Combined Rebel Forces—up to 18,476 including 4,000 foreign fighters; Total Combatant Deaths—up to 24,000. (See Coding Decisions.)[500]

Initiator: Jammu-Kashmir Liberation Front and Hizbul Mujahideen.

Outcome: Fighting fell below civil war threshold.

War Type: Civil for local issues (independence and accession to Pakistan).

Total System Member Military Personnel: Armed Forces of India—1,260,000 (prewar, initial); 1,325,000 (peak, final).[501]

Theater Armed Forces: Jammu-Kashmir Liberation Front, participating to May 20, 1994: up to 10,000 (prewar—1988 figure).[502] *Hizbul Mujahideen*: 13,000 to 20,000 (initial).[503] *Ikhwan-ul-Muslimeen*, participating on the rebel side until summer 1994 and on the government side thereafter: 1,500 armed with 400 rifles (initial); 1,500 (peak); 350 to 500 (final—2003 estimate).[504] *Al Jehad*: 1,800 (peak).[505] *Al Barq*: 500 (peak).[506] *Al Umar Mujahideen*: 300 (peak).[507] *Jaish-e-Mohammed*: 200 (peak).[508] *Lashkar-e-Taiba*, participating from December 22, 2001: 800 (initial).[509] *Harkat-ul-Ansar*, (Pakistani militant group), participating from the mid-1990s: 200 (initial, peak).[510]

Antecedents: The majority-Muslim population of the Indian state of Jammu and Kashmir generally has opposed Indian rule for decades. The state's nominally democratic institutions were fragile, and several times president's rule was imposed on the state. Moderates eventually made their peace with the Congress Party and came to dominate local elections in the 1980s. The radicals, marginalized by the political process by 1986, turned to demonstrations, which were met with arrests. After a controversial election in 1987 went heavily against the radical Muslim United Front, some began to resort to armed struggle. Demonstrations, strikes, assassinations, and bombings all increased in frequency.

The official date of the Kashmir uprising as an organized activity is July 31, 1988, with the Jammu–Kashmir Liberation Front (JKLF) mounting an armed campaign for Kashmiri independence. In the second half of the year, six attacks were mounted on security forces. The first rebel was killed in combat on September 18. Through at least April 1989, fighting remained at a very low level. That month, police stations were attacked with automatic rifles, and in one week in May, 4 people were killed in the violence. There were probably only 200 to 500 JKLF rebels at the time, although other sources put them at up to 10,000 in 1988. The first police battle-deaths didn't occur until July 13, but by the end of 1989 and beginning of 1990, police were being killed every few days, mostly by bombs. Moreover, thousands were crossing into Pakistan to receive training.

On January 21, 1990, the Indian army was deployed against the JKLF. The army quickly killed between 38 and 100 people, mostly civilians. By August, the government had lost 72 killed, while the rebels had killed hundreds of civilians. By the end of the year, most leaders of the JKLF had been killed or captured. Pakistan, which had funded and armed the secessionist insurgents from the beginning, cut off aid to the independence-minded JKLF and then began to sponsor its own pro-accession groups. These included the *Ikhwan-ul-Muslimeen* and the *Hizbul Mujahideen*, which were much more indiscriminate in their targeting of civilians than the JKLF had been. Thy also began to infiltrate armed militants from Azad Kashmir (the portion under Pakistani control) into India. At first, these infiltrators were recruits from Indian Kashmir, but soon fighters from the Afghan wars joined the struggle. Nearly 400 infiltrators were killed from January 1 to October 31. In 1990, the government suffered 132 battle-deaths, including 18 army soldiers, while 183 Indian militants were killed. The violence escalated in 1991, when 614 rebels and 185 security forces (including 44 army soldiers) were reported killed.

Narrative: The first twelve-month period for which we can establish that battle-deaths numbered more than 1,000 was calendar year 1992, which saw 1,058 battle-deaths. In February, the central government extended the period of president's rule rather than hold elections. By the end of the year, the JKLF had lost several thousand fighters since the Indian army entered the conflict in 1990, most of them killed. The government set up a unified command for military and paramilitary forces in 1993. Meanwhile, *Hizbul Mujahideen* targeted other groups in an effort to monopolize control over the insurgency, eventually killing hundreds of their fighters and otherwise neutralizing and disarming more than 7,000 of them. Infiltration increased; by the end of 1993, the number of foreign mercenaries increased to 1,200 Pakistanis, Afghanis, Sudanese, Lebanese, Turks, Arabs and other veterans of the fighting in Afghanistan.

Outmaneuvered and reduced to near-irrelevance by the Pakistan-backed groups, the JKLF's leader declared a unilateral cease-fire on May 20, 1994. A rump JKLF would struggle on until the death of its leadership in 1996. Moreover, by summer 1994 the *Ikhwan-ul-Muslimeen* had switched sides to aid the government, providing valuable information and in 1996 helping to secure the elections (although they performed very poorly in the electoral competition). There were now two major groupings of rebels: the largely Kashmiri (but Pakistan-sponsored) *Hizbul Mujahideen* and a welter of smaller groups sponsored by Pakistan and dominated by foreign fighters.

As the fighting became more intense, civilian protest activity fell. Human rights abuses by both sides became common; the use of torture was endemic in the government security forces, and illegal executions often were carried out using falsified reports of armed encounters. These encounter killings doubtless targeted civilians but were reported by the government as rebel (actually terrorist) deaths. Still, battle-deaths were unusually high for a low-intensity conflict precisely because the government rarely took prisoners; the number of arrestees was always a small fraction of the number of suspected rebels killed.

By 1995, the government estimated that there were no more than 6,000 rebels operating in Kashmir, but this estimate was so low as to strain credulity, given casualty figures for the year.

In 1996, the government allowed state elections to go forward, producing a state government whose platform insisted on maximum autonomy for Kashmir as well as economic aid. It was unable to deliver even modest concessions from the Indian government. What economic aid was provided was spent predominantly in the Kashmir Valley, alienating residents of Jammu.

By 1998, the *Ikhwan-ul-Muslimeen* were being systematically targeted by bombings and assassinations by the rebels; they suffered some 150 killed between then and 2003, when only 350 to 500 remained. By then, the government had decided that the excesses committed by pro-government groups like the Ikhwan was undermining the counterinsurgency effort.

Infiltration increased during the Kargil war, but infiltrator casualties increased dramatically once the shelling stopped. A peace process of sorts began to emerge in mid-2000 as Pakistan ordered the militants it controlled to cease taking credit for actions in Kashmir. On July 24, *Hizbul Mujahideen*—the largest rebel group by far—announced a three-month unilateral cease-fire. Four days later, India's senior commander in the area announced that he had suspended his offensive against the rebels. Contacts were established on August 1, but *Jamat-i-Islami* and elements of *Hizbul Mujahideen* who were opposed to the cease-fire simply stepped up their own attacks at the beginning of August. Indeed, various measures of casualties—including government battle-deaths—actually increased in August. On August 8, *Hizbul Mujahideen* withdrew the cease-fire, ostensibly because the government would not permit tripartite talks with Pakistan. The lack of unity on the rebel side and the insistence of Pakistan on being part of the process thus prevented serious peace negotiations.

On December 22, the Pakistan-backed *Lashkar-i-Taiba* mounted its first attack against the Indian military in Indian-controlled Kashmir. Nevertheless, the government extended its cease-fire offer to *Hizbul Mujahideen* through spring 2001. The intensity of fighting did not appreciably decline during this period. In January 12, 2002, Pakistan announced a crackdown on terrorist groups operating on its soil, including *Jaish-e-Muhammed* and *Lashkar-i-Taiba.* Hundreds of militants were arrested, but the government soon began releasing them for lack of evidence. In any case, the crackdown did not extend to *Hizbul Mujahideen.* In 2003, Pakistan further limited the activities of these groups and allowed fewer fighters to cross into India. In November 2003, an Indian general estimated that the number of rebels had decreased from 3,500 the year before to 1,800 (both figures are likely underestimates, but the number of insurgents surely declined as Pakistani support waned).

A year later, the Indian government symbolically withdrew 1,000 troops from Kashmir. Annual battle-deaths had decreased from a high of 2,825 in 2001 to 1,286 in 2004. The insurgency continued with Pakistani support, but the number of militants dropped as the level of that support dropped. By 2005, fatalities were barely above civil-war levels, and by 2006 they fell below that threshold.

Termination and Outcome: The war ended when the insurgency dropped below civil war levels. Without monthly casualty data, we can only estimate that this occurred at the very end of 2005. As illustrated by Table 7.3, fighting continued as of 2013. Nevertheless, it was the government that was left in control of Jammu and Kashmir, so this war ended with a government military victory. Human rights abuses and encounter killings continued after the end of the civil-war period.

Coding Decisions: Using Table 7.3, we calculate about 24,000 battle-deaths, but this is probably too high as many so-called rebels were really civilians killed in faked encounter killings by the security forces. Foreign fighters killed were mostly from Pakistan.

TABLE 7.3 Maximum Estimates of Battle-deaths in Kashmir, 1988–2013

Year (War Years Bolded)	Government security forces killed (army)	Rebels killed (foreign fighters)	Total combatants killed	Sources
1988	1	1 (0)	2	Joshi (1999); Swami (2007)
1989	13	0 (0)	13	Joshi (1999); Swami (2007)
1990	132 (18)	183 (0)	315	Joshi (1999); Swami (2007)
1991	185 (44)	614 (3)	799	Joshi (1999); Swami (2007)
1992	177 (50)	873 (19)	1,050	Joshi (1999); Swami (2007)
1993	216 (88)	1,328 (97)	1,544	Joshi (1999); Swami (2007)
1994	220 (139)	1,667 (125)	1,887	Joshi (1999); Swami (2007)
1995	258 (186)	1,377 (119)	1,635	Joshi (1999); Swami (2007)
1996	220 (139)	1,329 (194)	1,549	Joshi (1999); Swami (2007)
1997	227 (153)	1,329 (258)	1,556	Joshi (1999); Swami (2007)
1998	339	1,111 (394)	1,450	Swami (2005); Swami (2007)
1999	555	1,184 (348)	1,739	Swami (2005); Swami (2007)
2000	638	1,808 (403)	2,446	Swami (2005); Swami (2007)
2001	706	2,119 (488)	2,825	Swami (2005); Swami (2007)
2002	518	1,747 (516)	2,265	Swami (2005); Swami (2007)
2003	377	1,526 (554)	1,903	Swami (2005); Swami (2007)
2004	325	951 (286)	1,276	Swami (2005); Swami (2007)
2005	218	1,000 (239)	1,218	South Asia Terrorism Portal (2014a, b, c, d, e, f, g); Swami (2007)
2006	168	599	767	South Asia Terrorism Portal (2014a, b, c, d, e, f, g)
2007	121	492	613	South Asia Terrorism Portal (2014a, b, c, d, e, f, g)
2008	90	382	472	South Asia Terrorism Portal (2014a, b, c, d, e, f, g)
2009	78	242	320	South Asia Terrorism Portal (2014a, b, c, d, e, f, g)
2010	69	270	339	South Asia Terrorism Portal (2014a, b, c, d, e f, g)
2011	30	119	149	South Asia Terrorism Portal (2014a, b, c, d, e, f, g)
2012	17	84	101	South Asia Terrorism Portal (2014a, b, c, d, e, f, g)
2013	61	100	161	South Asia Terrorism Portal (2014a, b, c, d, e, f, g)

Sources: Behera (2000); Jamal (2009); Joshi (1999); Schofield (2003); South Asian Terrorism Portal (2001a, b, c, d, e, f, g); Swami (2003); Wirsing (1994).[511]

INTRA-STATE WAR #876
Tajikistan War of 1992 to 1997

Participants: Tajikistan including Tajikistan Security Ministry, Russia, and Popular Front of Tajikistan versus *Hezb-e Nahzat-e Islami*, United Tajik Opposition, and *Afghan Mujahideen* (Aggregate).
Dates: May 6, 1992, to June 27, 1997.
Battle-related Deaths: Russia: 60 among border guards;[512] Total Combatant Deaths: 10,000. (See Coding Decisions.)[513]
Initiator: *Hezb-e Nahzat-e Islami.*
Outcome: Negotiated agreement.
War Type: Civil for central control.
Total System Member Military Personnel: Armed Forces of Tajikistan (did not exist before 1993: 3,000 (initial), 10,000 (peak, final).[514] Russia: 1,900,000 (prewar, initial, peak); 1,300,000 (final).[515]
Theater Armed Forces: Tajikistan Security Ministry, participating through December 10, 1992: unknown. Russia: 14,000 to 16,500 (initial); 29,300 (peak); 29,300 (final).[516] Popular Front of Tajikistan (PFT), participating on the government side to October 24, 1992, against the government to December 10, 1992, and for the government thereafter: fewer than 8,000 (initial); 20,000 (peak).[517] *Hezb-e Nahzat-e Islami*, aka Islamic Renaissance Party of Tajikistan (IRP), participating until the formation of the UTO in 1993: 5,000 (final).[518] United Tajik Opposition, participating from 1993: 5,000 (initial); 10,000 to 12,000 (peak); 5,000 (final).[519] *Afghan Mujahideen*, participating in 1993: up to 3,000.

Antecedents: On September 9, 1991, Tajikistan declared its independence from the Soviet Union. That November, as the Soviet Union collapsed, presidential elections were held. Communist leader Rakhmon Nabiev won the elections, but the opposition charged that the elections were fraudulent and refused to acknowledge his legitimacy. He filled his government with communist elites from the Leninabad region, provoking opposition elsewhere in the country.

During the spring of 1992, opposition and pro-government protesters faced off against each other in the streets of Dushanbe, the capital. On May 1, President Nabiev handed out 1,700 to 1,800 rifles to largely untrained civilian volunteers under Sangak Safarov, creating a "National Guard." He declared a state of emergency on May 5, and the National Guard killed dozens of demonstrators. That night most guards at the presidential palace went over to the demonstrators; many interior ministry personnel followed suit. The security ministry remained loyal, but there was no national army to defend Nabiev, for the young state had yet to create unified armed forces. Instead, Nabiev and his opponents had formed militias.

Narrative: On May 6, demonstrators and interior ministry forces seized the airport. There was heavy fighting at Azadi. President Nabiev accepted a Russian offer to mediate, and on May 11 a coalition government of national reconciliation was announced, with Nabiev retaining the presidency but the opposition gaining about one-third of positions. The protesters returned home, satisfied with the arrangement, but the regions of Khujand (Nabiev's home region) and Kulyab refused to recognize the new government. The primary anti-Nabiev rebel organization was *Hezb-e Nahzat-e Islami* or the Islamic Renaissance Party (IRP), and the conflict quickly took on an intercommunal dimension as Kulyabis fought against the Gharmis of the IRP.

Fighting was initially at the village level, with each side (the communist Leninabadi and Kulyabis were one, while the southern and western resistance movements were another) arming itself with stockpiles from the former Soviet Union. On September 7, Nabiev was forced out of the government, and a new phase of violence began. The war spread from villages to towns such as Qurghonteppa, where between 4,000 and 5,000 armed farmers squared off. Some 600 to 650 Afghan Uzbeks from Dostum's forces joined the communist side, while 500 to 600 *mujahideen* joined the Islamist side. There was also a massive influx of weapons in September, further intensifying the fighting. Uzbekistan armed ethnic Uzbeks, who were still largely neutral in the conflict, but came to support the communist faction.

One group of loosely allied communist forces adopted the name Popular Front of Tajikistan (PFT). The PFT proceeded to seize power for the Leninabadi elites and Kulyabis. Armed by Uzbekistan and Russia, it captured Qurghonteppa on September 28, soon taking the rest of the Vaksh valley. On October 24, the PFT seized control of Dushanbe in an attempted coup d'état, but the Russian 201st Motorized Division expelled them within forty-eight hours. The PFT, now 8,000 strong, besieged Dushanbe, and the government agreed to negotiations in November. In the southwest, the PFT took Qabidian and then Shahr-e Tuz, routing IRP-armed civilians. A massacre of 150 to 1,000 civilian refugees at Auvaj and a vicious campaign of ethnic cleansing against Gharmis in the region followed.

On December 10, the Uzbek army and PFT troops entered Dushanbe against only weak government resistance; the government of national reconciliation fled. By the end of the year, the bulk of the rebels' armed units had been destroyed. Hundreds or thousands of civilians were killed by the victorious PFT, which provided the nucleus of the new Tajikistan armed forces. The IRP's leaders fled to Afghanistan in January, from where they mounted incursions that were fought by Russia and other CIS nations, which had assumed responsibility for Takikistan's external defenses. Between 20,000 and 60,000 people had died by February 1993.

However, resistance to the Kulyabi-dominated regime picked up again in the spring of 1993. Meanwhile, the loose coalition that made up the PFT began to splinter. Field Commander Fayzaili Saidov was killed by rivals within the organization. The PFT now had 20,000 fighters at its disposal but controlled only 40 percent of the country. Guerrilla warfare was pronounced particularly along the Afghan border, where the rebels could receive arms from the Afghan rebel organization *Hezb-i-Islam* and others. More arms came from Iran. Up to 3,000 Afghan *mujahideen* may have aided the 5,000 or so rebels.

On July 13, some 24 Russians were killed in a rebel attack near the Afghan border, along with 200 Kulyabi villagers and 60 opposition fighters. Russia responded by bombing rebel positions in Afghanistan. During 1993, the IRP and other, smaller, factions coalesced into the United Tajik Opposition, which would fight against the government until the end of the war. The government was a Leninabadi–Kulyabi coalition and partisans of the two blocs sometimes engaged in armed skirmishes with each other. The rebels continued to control 55 to 60 percent of the country's territory and about 25 percent of its population through the end of the conflict. The war declined in intensity after a June 1994 cease-fire, but fighting continued as peace talks stalled due to the government's unwillingness to make concessions. When the rebels achieved both military and political successes in 1996—and Russia refused to mount an offensive against the advancing rebels—the government position shifted, and peace talks made progress.

Termination and Outcome: On June 27, 1997, a peace treaty was signed in Moscow by the government and the UTO. It provided for integration of the UTO into the government and the armed forces. The UTO was allocated 30 percent of government positions—a similar level of representation to the one it had enjoyed in the government of national reconciliation in 1992. The agreement also provided for amnesty. Although the agreement had awarded control of the ministry of defense to the rebels, this provision was not implemented by the government. Mutinies in the armed forces followed the agreement but were suppressed without much fighting.

Coding Decisions: At least 20,000 were killed in the first nine months of the war, but thousands of these—if not most of them—were civilians. After this initial spasm of violence, casualty estimates are scarce. On the basis of very limited evidence, we estimate that about 1,000 battle-deaths were suffered each year thereafter. We conservatively estimate 10,000 battle-deaths for the entire war. Note that Kazakhstan and Kyrgyzstan each deployed 500 troops to fight the rebels in January 1993.[520] Because we have no evidence that either suffered 100 battle-deaths or deployed at least 1,000 troops, we do not include them as war participants.

Sources: Brown (1997); Jonson (2006); Kiasatpour (1998); Kılavuz (2009); Lynch (2000); Nourzhanov (2005); Poujol (1997); Serrano (2003); Whitlock (2003).[521]

INTRA-STATE WAR #877.5
Afghanistan Postcommunist Civil War of 1992 to 2001

Participants: Afghanistan, Islamic Society, Islamic Union for the Liberation of Afghanistan, Ismail Khan–led Forces, and Unity Party (Akbari) versus National Islamic Movement, Islamic Party (Hekmatyar), Unity Party (Mazari/Khalili), and Taliban.

Dates: June 28, 1992, to October 6, 2001.

Battle-related Deaths: Total Combatant Deaths: up to 40,000. (See Coding Decisions.)[522]

Initiator: Islamic Party (Hekmatyar).

Outcome: War becomes extra-state.

War Type: Civil for central control.

Total System Member Military Personnel: Armed Forces of Afghanistan—functionally nonexistent throughout the war. The government relied on the Islamic Society and (initially) the National Islamic movement (up to 125,000 combined troops at the onset of the war) for its protection.

Theater Armed Forces: Islamic Society, aka *Jamiat-i-Islami*—60,000 (prewar, initial).[523] National Islamic Movement, aka *Junbesh-i Milli Islami* or Jauzjani Uzbeks, participating on the government side—except for a clash in December 1992—until January 1, 1994, then switched sides, and then aided the government once again from October 8, 1996, to August 1, 1998: 65,000 (prewar, initial, peak), but Giustozzi maintains that "Dostum never fielded more than 20,000 men at the same time" out of his theoretical strength of 65,000.[524] Islamic Union for the Liberation of Afghanistan, aka *Ittehad-i-Islami*, participating as the government's ally from December 1992 or January 1993: 18,000 (prewar, initial).[525] Ismail Khan–led Forces, participating on the government's side from mid-March 1995 to September 1995 and again from late October 1996 to May 1997: 8,000 (peak).[526] Unity Party (Akbari), aka *Hezb-i-Wahdat Akbari* Faction, participating on the government side from mid-March 1995: perhaps 29,000 (initial—calculated as 25 percent of *Hezb-i-Wahdat* strength).[527] Islamic Party—Hekmatyar, aka *Hezb-i-Islami—Hekmatyar*, participating against the government from August 31, 1992, and again from February 8, 1993, to May or June 1996 and participating on the side of the government thereafter: 50,000 (prewar, initial).[528] Unity Party (Mazari/Khalili), aka *Hezb-i-Wahdat*, participating from early December 1992 to October 1996 on the rebel side and on the government side thereafter: up to 116,000 (initial, peak—derived from adding its component parties—but see Hafizullah, which estimates fewer than 20,000).[529] Taliban, participating against the government from March 11, 1995; before that, they fought various warlords rather than government forces: at least 12,000 (prewar, initial—February 1995); 50,000 (peak). These estimates include thousands of Pakistani volunteers.[530]

Antecedents: The origins of this civil war lay in the termination of Afghanistan's previous war and the struggle of the rebel *mujahideen* to overthrow the communist regime of Mohammed Najibullah. While fighting resumed quickly, the antagonists were different, making this a new civil war. Najibullah's communist regime and its armed forces simply had ceased to exist. According to Hussain (2005), "No military unit retained its organizational structure. The Afghan regular army had ceased to exist" (155). A tenuous alliance of Ahmad Shah Massoud's *Jamiat-i-Islami*, Abdul Rashid Dostum's Uzbek militia, Sayyaid Mansour Nadari in Baghlan province, and General Abdul Mohmin's Seventieth Brigade had brought down the government of Najibullah and now raced to establish control over Kabul.

On April 24, 1992, the Peshawar Accord between most of the largest *mujahideen* factions established an interim government under Sibghat Allah Mujaddidi of the relatively small Afghanistan National Liberation Front (*Jabba-i-Nejat-i-Milli Afghanistan*). Notably dissenting from the accord were the Shiite (and mostly Hazara) umbrella group *Hezb-i-Wahdat* (led by Abdul Ali Mazari) and fundamentalist Gulbuddin Hekmatyar's *Hezb-i-Islami*. The latter group attracted ethnic Pashtuns of the old Khalq faction of the communist party after the collapse of communism in the country.

In early June, intercommunal fighting broke out in Kabul between *Hezb-i-Wahdat* and the fundamentalist *Pashtun Ittehad-i-Islami*; about 100 people were killed. On June 28, power was handed over to Burhanuddin Rabbani, supported by Massoud, as called for by the Peshawar Accord. Almost immediately, fighting began, with Massoud in Kabul and Dostum in Mazar-i-Sharif on the government's side against a rebellion led by Hekmatyar (nominally part of the government himself until mid-August).

Narrative: While the government was technically allied to all of the Peshawar factions save Hekmatyar's, it could call upon far fewer forces to engage in actual combat against the latter. Most factions remained neutral or were removed from the zone of fighting. Between Rabbani and Dostum, the government could theoretically muster 125,000 troops against the 50,000 of *Hezb-i-Islami* (Hekmatyar). The fighting initially centered around Kabul, where Hekmatyar's forces mounted their first offensive.

On August 16, the fighting spilled out of Kabul for the first time, when the government bombed the rebel-controlled Shindand air base. By the end of August, up to 1,800 had been killed; a truce then halted the fighting for some time. But early in December, fighting resumed when first *Hezb-i-Wahdat* and then Dostum attacked the government in anticipation of a rigged *Shura* that was expected to (and in fact did) reelect Rabanni as president. The government found a ready ally in the *Ittehad-i-Islami*, Dostum returned to supporting the government, and the fighting subsided for another few months, but on February 8, 1993, the *Hezb-i-Islami* (Hekmatyar) insurrection resumed, with Hekmatyar's forces bombarding the capital. Two days later, the Hazaras of Kabul were targeted in the Afshar massacre, heavy government shelling of a Hazara district held by *Hezb-i-Wahdat* in conjunction with an attack on civilians by *Ittehad-i-Islami*.

Fresh peace talks were held in March, and another peace accord was signed. Hekmatyar was to join the government as prime minister, troops were to be merged into a national army, and a constitutional convention and elections were to be held. However, neither Massoud nor Dostum had participated in the agreement, and Hekmatyar was prevented from taking up his post. Heavy fighting resumed in May. The first year of *mujahideen* control had cost the country up to 30,000 killed, mostly civilians in Kabul.

On June 25, the government mounted an offensive in Kabul, which killed some 3,000 people and wounded 19,000 more. During the rest of 1993, there was a lull in the fighting, although intermittent shelling by Hekmatyar's forces continued, and *Hezb-i-Wahdat* and government ally *Ittehad-i-Islami* continued to fight in Kabul through summer and autumn. A minor battle was fought by Dostum's forces at Sher Khan Bander in November.

The relative calm was shattered on January 1, 1994, when Hekmatyar mounted a major assault on Kabul. As if on cue, Dostum switched sides; the two collaborated to take Kunduz in February, although Dostum's forces fell out with local *Heb-i-Islami* units and were routed. Despite these coordination problems, the combined rebel forces managed to drive the government out of Kabul in March; it was retaken by Massoud's forces in April. The fighting killed nearly 1,000 in the first two months. The country was geographically split; in the North, Dostum, *Hezb-i-Wahdat*, and Ismaeli Shiites were in rebellion. In the East, the Nangarhar Shura led by Haji Qadir ruled without serious challenge by either side. In the Southeast, Paktiya was ruled by Hekmatyar loyalist Mawlawli Haqhani. The West was held by Ismail Khan, who eventually would side with the government in the war. Finally, Kabul was controlled by Rabbani and Massoud's forces.

Meanwhile, a new military force was coalescing. In the spring, a small force under Mullah Muhammed Omar attacked the local garrison in Kandahar with 30 men sharing 16 rifles among them. By October, the Taliban had grown enough to mount a 200-man assault on a border post controlled by Hekmatyar. Only 7 of Hekmatyar's men and 1 Taliban were killed, but the rebels were able to seize 18,000 rifles in an operation that was permitted by the Pakistani government, which even may have lent cross-border artillery support.

In Kandahar, the local warlord preyed on convoys moving through the region. On November 3, the Taliban freed a Pakistani convoy, killing 11 of his troops in the process. Some 2,500 warlord troops then went over to the Taliban, allowing the latter to capture Kandahar at a cost of only 12 Taliban deaths. By December, some 12,000 Afghani and Pakistani students had joined the Taliban in Kandahar. At one point or another, between 80,000 and 100,000 Pakistani volunteers would fight with the Taliban during the war. The first Pakistani prisoners were taken in 1996, and the Pakistani press began reporting Pakistani casualties in mid-June 1997.

After Kandahar, the Taliban attacked the government-allied Akhundzadeh clan in Helmland. Confusingly, Hekmatyar's forces aided the Akhundzadehs, and the battle for Helmland cost hundreds of casualties. For a short time, the government was the indirect beneficiary of the Taliban offensive, fighting together with them against Hekmatyar in January 1995 in Ghazni—although the Taliban ruled out any sort of alliance with the government. The Taliban fought effectively against Hekmatyar's forces in early 1995, winning battles at Wardak and Mandanshar; a battle between the two insurgent groups on February 10 left 200 dead. Four days later, the Taliban evicted Hekmatyar from the vicinity of Kabul, ending his long bombardment of the city.

On March 6, Massoud's forces again attacked *Hezb-i-Wahdat*, expelling them from Kabul. Three-fourths of *Hezb-i-Wahdat* promptly allied itself to the Taliban, surrendering its positions in Kabul to avoid having them fall into Massoud's hands. One-fourth of the party, led by Ustad Akbari, allied itself to the government rather than surrender to the Taliban. On March 11, Massoud attacked Taliban positions in Kabul. After eight days of fighting and hundreds of Taliban battle-deaths, Massoud had established control over the capital and outlying areas. The Taliban executed Abdul Ali Mazari, the leader of *Hezb-i-Wahdat*, and Abdul Karim Khalil took his place. Kabul was to see little fighting until October.

Around the same time as fighting was raging in Kabul, the Taliban mounted an offensive in Herat, leading to the heaviest fighting since 1989. The government allied itself with local warlord Ismail Khan and rushed in 2,000 reinforcements and air support. The Taliban suffered at least 3,000 casualties by the end of the month. April saw hundreds more casualties on both sides. The Taliban was again checked at the Battle of Shinand on April 18 through April 20, and the government claimed to have killed 200 Taliban in a battle from April 28 to April 29.

Summer 1995 witnessed a lull in hostilities as Taliban and the government attempted to build up their forces. The Taliban increased from 15,000 to about 25,000, including more than 3,000 Pakistani volunteers. In June, peace talks among the *Hezb-i-Wahdat* factions failed, and the Akbari faction took Bamyan with government support. The Khalil faction mounted a massive offensive against government forces in the Hazarajat, taking control of the region and even driving government forces from Shikhali district and Parwan province.

In August, the government mounted a new offensive against the Taliban in the West, but late in the month a Taliban counteroffensive caught the government off guard. On September 3, Shinand was captured by the Taliban. Ismail Khan fled to Iran with some 8,000 followers, and Herat fell to the Taliban. The Taliban's new offensive against Kabul kicked off on October 25. Initially, they met stiff resistance, and more than ninety Taliban were killed. The fighting bogged down south of Kabul in November, and another lull in fighting settled over the combatants during the winter.

On May 10, 1996, the government launched an offensive against the Taliban; it inflicted serious casualties near Band-e-Ghazi. Hekmatyar also moved to consolidate his remaining positions, actually allying himself with government forces and taking up a position in the government in June. A remarkable international coalition supported the government with arms: Russia, Tajikistan, Iran, Ukraine, and possibly India. Meanwhile Pakistan and the Saudis provided assistance to the Taliban. In August, the Taliban mounted an offensive against Hekmatyar in Paktiya. Sensing the greater threat posed by the Taliban, Dostum agreed to a truce with the government. The next month, the offensive became general. Jalalabad (the residence of one Osama bin Laden, who had returned to Afghanistan in May and would raise an "Arab" legion to support the Taliban) fell on September 11, Sarobi (where Hekmatyar's few remaining units were routed) on September 24, and finally Kabul itself two days later (an event the Taliban marked by executing former communist ruler Najibullah and his brother). By this point, Taliban forces had increased to 30,000 to 35,000, while government forces had been only 25,000 in August.

Rabbani and Massoud withdrew to the North, where they allied once again with Dostum's forces against the Taliban. Dostum began fighting the Taliban on October 8. Furthermore, *Hezb-i-Wahdat* (Khalis) now switched sides and aided this new northern alliance against the Taliban, reconciling with the Akbari faction of the party. A government counteroffensive succeeded in retaking northern Kabul, but thousands of volunteers from Pakistan stiffened the Taliban, and government forces were pushed back out in the winter. Toward the end of October, Ismail Khan reentered the war against the Taliban with 2,000 men; three months of heavy fighting in Baghdis followed.

On January 16, 1997, the Taliban launched a major offensive into the Massoud-controlled Shomali Valley, to the north of Kabul, driving out many of its ethnic Tajik residents. Over the next few months, political machinations benefited the Taliban. In May, Dostum's foreign affairs spokesperson, Abdul Malik Pahlavan, went over to the Taliban, bringing many of Dostum's 50,000 militiamen with him. Fighting between the two factions was brief—it broke out in Mazar-e-Sharif on May 24, and Dostum almost immediately fled to Turkey. Around the same time, Ismail Khan was captured by the Taliban, ending his forces' resistance.

However, the Taliban then attempted to disarm Malik's forces, which led to a bloody battle in the city. Perhaps 600 Taliban were killed outright, and thousands of prisoners taken (including hundreds of Pakistani students) subsequently were suffocated by being forced into locked, steel shipping containers. That fall, Dostum returned to Mazar-e-Sharif, defeated Malik, and easily resumed command of his Uzbek forces, now numbering only 4,000.

Massoud and his forces advanced in late July, engaging the Taliban north of Kabul and inflicting hundreds of battle-deaths. From May to July, the Taliban lost more than 3,000 killed or wounded in battle and 3,600 prisoners, many if not most of whom were killed. Pakistan sent the Taliban another 5,000 recruits to make good the losses, and the war continued, albeit at reduced intensity, through the end of the year. Negotiations in September 1997 led to the release of some Taliban prisoners but not to a political settlement.

In March 1998, the Taliban quelled a revolt at Jalalabad. In July, they mounted an offensive that crushed the Uzbek forces under Dostum and retook the province of Faryab. On August 1, Dostum fled the country again; his forces stopped fighting, leaving 1,500 Hazara fighters exposed outside of Mazar-e-Sharif. The Hazaras fought until virtually the last man, being reduced to 100 by the end of the fighting. Mazar-e-Sharif fell to the Taliban, which massacred thousands of local Hazaras. Fighting from October to November cost the Taliban about 2,000 casualties. On December 7, Massoud—now virtually alone in the struggle against the Taliban—was appointed supreme commander of all anti-Taliban forces.

Fighting continued for years with roughly the same alignment of forces: the Taliban against Massoud's northern alliance. *Hezb-i-Wahdat* retook Bamian in April 1999, but the Taliban recaptured the city the following month. In July 1999, the northern alliance—still recognized as the government of Afghanistan by most countries and the United Nations—succeeded in driving back a Taliban offensive. The largest battle of the year was a victory for the northern alliance; the Taliban suffered 1,000 casualties. In August, the Taliban mounted another offensive into the Shomali Valley, conducting a scorched earth campaign to depopulate the region. In October, the UN once again rebuffed the Taliban's attempt to occupy Afghanistan's seat, and the Security Council voted to establish economic sanctions against the Taliban.

In 2000, a Taliban offensive succeeded in conquering Massoud's headquarters at Taloqan, but Taliban losses were estimated at 1,000 killed and 1,500 wounded. Massoud moved his headquarters eastward to the town of Khwaja Bahauddin. In December, UN sanctions were expanded to include a ban on military assistance to the Taliban. Nevertheless, the northern alliance continued to weaken: by September 2001, it claimed to have 15,000 troops but the real total was closer to 8,000. The Taliban had between 40,000 and 50,000 troops, plus an additional 4,000 to 5,000 Arab volunteers under Osama bin Laden.

Termination and Outcome: On September 11, 2001, terrorist attacks organized by Osama bin Laden's group al Qaeda killed thousands of Americans. The United States responded with an ultimatum to the Taliban: give up Osama and other key plotters, or face removal from power. The Taliban rejected the ultimatum, and on October 7, the American attack began. The United States took over the bulk of the fighting against the Taliban, transforming the civil war into an inter-state one (#225).

Coding Decisions: Some 50,000 people were killed in Kabul alone from 1992 to 1996. Although most were civilians, the level of violence clearly exceeded the threshold of civil war. In what may have been the war's most intense year, 1997, there were 350 combat deaths per month, excluding thousands of prisoners who were killed. From this, we estimate a maximum of 40,000 battle-deaths. The real total could be lower.

Sources: "Battles Rage for Kabul" (1992); Christia (2012); Davis (2001); Ewans (2001); Goodson (2001); Hafizullah (1997); Johnson (2004); Laffin (1997); Maley (2001a, b); Maley (2002); Mardsen (2002); *The Military Balance* (1993); Nojumi (2002); O'Ballance

(1993); Rasanayagam (2003); Rashid (2000); Tanner (2002); Towers (1992); "Truce Brings Afghans into Kabul Bazaars" (1992); Vogelsang (2002).[531]

INTRA-STATE WAR #881
Third Khmer Rouge War of 1993 to 1998

Participants: Cambodia versus Khmer Rouge.
Dates: January 1, 1993, to March 26, 1998.
Battle-related Deaths: Total Combatant Deaths: 10,000. (See Coding Decisions.)[532]
Initiator: Cambodia.
Outcome: Cambodia wins.
War Type: Civil for central control.
Total System Member Military Personnel: Armed Forces of Cambodia—102,000 (prewar, initial, peak), 60,000 (final).[533]
Theater Armed Forces: Khmer Rouge: 10,000 (initial), 13,000 (peak).[534]

Antecedents: The peace agreement that ended the Cambodian civil war of 1989 to 1991 (see Intra-state War #857) provided for elections to be held in 1993. However, as elections approached, violations of the cease-fire agreement became more common. Both the ruling Cambodian People's Party (CPP) of the State of Cambodia (SOC) and the Khmer Rouge feared the outcome of elections, and political assassinations became commonplace. The Khmer Rouge, which continued to receive support from Thailand and China, declared that it would boycott the elections, while the government attempted to manipulate them through violence. The Khmer Rouge further refused to disarm as required by the peace accord, citing the presence of Vietnamese civilians that it described as soldiers.

Narrative: The first clear action of the war was a government offensive on January 1, 1993. In one battle, fifty-one Khmer Rouge were killed and eighty-nine wounded. On February 1, the SOC mounted another brief offensive against the Khmer Rouge to prevent them from infiltrating more provinces. The offensive aimed at the rebel stronghold and gem-mining center of Pailin in the Southwest, but fighting was general. The government soon ended the offensive, but low-level fighting continued, and the rebels captured Bantey Meanchey province, giving them direct access to the Gulf of Thailand. In April, Khmer Rouge leaders left Phnom Penh as violence intensified in Siem Reap and Kompong Thom provinces.

May elections left the royalist FUNCINPEC and the CPP as the leading parties; they formed a coalition government with the CPP's Hun Sen as second prime minister and Prince Norodom Ranariddh of the FUNCINPEC as first prime minister. Prince Norodom Sihanouk became ceremonial head of state (king), and the partial demobilization and integration of non–Khmer Rouge armed forces proceeded, establishing a smaller national army.

The new army mounted an offensive against the rebels on August 18, with 6,000 government troops attacking a Khmer Rouge headquarters. Another was launched in December, killing 25 Khmer Rouge in a single day. By the end of the year, rebel-held territory had diminished from 20 to 15 percent of the country. The Khmer Rouge entered into power-sharing negotiations with the government early in 1994, demanding 15 percent of government positions as well as key military positions and the integration of its intact armed forces, but the talks foundered, and the government renewed offensive operations. One battle resulted in 135 Khmer Rouge battle-deaths and 149 wounded; the government lost only 26 killed but suffered 113 wounded. While the government was able to take key rebel positions at Pailin and Anlong Veng, the Khmer Rouge struck back, retaking both bases and threatening Battambang. The government had difficulty maintaining supply routes to its advance forces, compelling them to retreat.

The year 1995 opened with a rebel assault on Battambang, which came within a few miles of taking the provincial capital. Khmer Rouge artillery displaced many people in the province's Rattanak Mondul district. The government once again mounted dry season offensives against the rebels, this time taking and holding more ground. They were aided by numerous defections of Khmer Rouge fighters, and the rebellion suffered in the provinces of Siem Reap and Preah Vihear, although it remained strong in the West and the area surrounding Pailin. As both internal and Thai support for the rebellion declined, the Khmer Rouge stepped up violence against civilians at the village level.

An ambush in January 1996 decimated the government's elite paratroop regiment; the government captured An Sess in Preah Vinhear province, but an offensive with 14,000 troops failed to capture Pailin, and losses were high. The average casualty rate for 1996 was 150 to 300 per month, but the intensity of the fighting was often higher than this. The government suffered 22 killed and 84 wounded from March 25 to March 31 alone.

The second half of the year saw the partial fragmentation of each side in the conflict. On the government side, the CPP and FUNCINPEC became increasingly hostile toward one another as the 1998 elections loomed. Moreover, the CPP had failed to honor the terms of the alliance with FUNCINPEC, retaining important patronage positions and real political control despite the FUNCINPEC's electoral victory in 1993. Exacerbating these tensions was the September defection to the government of Ieng Sary, a Khmer Rouge commander who controlled resource-rich regions that had been funding the rebellion in the more remote areas controlled by Pol Pot. He had lost power within the Khmer Rouge as his patron China cut off its aid to the rebels. He brought with him 3,000 of the Khmer Rouge's best troops, and the CPP and FUNCINPEC vied for their loyalty. Other defections accounted for thousands of Khmer Rouge fighters. Despite these blows, the Khmer Rouge still had 4,000 to 8,000 troops in the field, half concentrated at Anlong Veng and half dispersed in the countryside as guerrillas.

The year 1997 witnessed the further fragmentation of the conflict. On January 15, some 3,700 Khmer Rouge were integrated with government forces, mostly the pro-FUNCINPAC faction. On February 10, fighting broke out in Battambang between soldiers loyal to FUNCINPEC and the CPP; at least 50 people were killed. Increasingly, Khmer Rouge defectors integrated with either pro-FUNCINPEC or pro-CPP factions of the armed forces. Amid further defections to the government, Pol Pot had his "defense minister" Son Sen executed along with his family in a sign of further divisions within the Khmer Rouge. Pol Pot's attempt to arrest Ta Mok went awry, and on June 19, it was Pol Pot himself who was arrested (he was soon sentenced to death in a show trial but died of poison or natural causes while under house arrest the following year).

The split in the governing coalition now extended to the police, and on July 5 Hun Sen mounted a coup to remove FUNCINPEC's Prince Ranariddh from power. Combat between FUNCINPEC (with its Khmer Rouge supporters) and CPP loyalists followed. While the CPP won control of the capital the next day, 3,000 pro-FUNCINPEC troops escaped Phnom Penh and established themselves at O'Smach on the border with Thailand. Loosely coordinated Khmer Rouge units in nearby Anlong Veng and in Samlot also continued to resist the CPP government.

Termination and Outcome: On March 26, 1998, Anlong Veng fell to government forces in the last large-scale fighting of the war. The outcome of the war was a government military victory, with promises of amnesty for rebels who integrated into government forces. By and large, these promises were kept. Some low-level fighting occurred after the fall of Anlong Veng, but most of the action was diplomatic as Khmer Rouge leaders were enticed to surrender and integrate.

Coding Decisions: While no estimates of overall battle-deaths are available, figures for individual years and months suggest that between 1,000 and 2,000 battle-deaths occurred each year. This yields an estimate of about 6,250 to about 12,500. We estimate 10,000 total battle-deaths, rounding to the nearest 5,000.

Sources: Arnold (1995); "Cambodia Stages Offensive Against Khmer Rouge" (1993); "Cambodians Open Offensive Against Khmer Rouge Rebels" (1993); Kevin (2000); Lizee (1996, 1997); *The Military Balance*, 1996–1997; Nhem (2013); Peou (1997); Shenon (1993); Um (1994, 1995), "UN Warns of Crisis as Fighting Follows Khmer Rouge Walkout" (1993).[535]

INTRA-STATE WAR #910

Maluku War of 1999 to 2002 (aka Moluccas Sectarian War)

Participants: Muslim "White" Forces (Aggregate) and Laskar Jihad versus Christian "Red" Forces (Aggregate).

Dates: January 19, 1999, to February 12, 2002.

Battle-related Deaths: Total Combatant Deaths: 5,000. (See Coding Decisions.)

Initiator: Christian "Red" Forces.

Outcome: Negotiated settlement.

War Type: Intercommunal.

Theater Armed Forces: Muslim Militia: unknown. Laskar Jihad: up to 3,000 (initial), up to 4,000 to 6,000 (peak).[536] Christian Militia: perhaps 5,000 (initial).[537]

Antecedents: During the 1980s and 1990s, the Christians of Maluku, who had been instrumental in the South Moluccas War of 1950 (Intra-state War #733), began to lose many of their traditional privileges. As the Indonesian government increasingly appealed to Islam for public support, intercommunal tensions between Muslims and Christians, particularly on the island of Ambon, escalated to arguments and then the formation of "self-defense" groups armed with primitive weapons.

Narrative: The violence began in Ambon, where a dispute between a bus driver and passenger brought Christian and Muslim gangs out against each other. Fighting eventually spread to other areas of central Maluku and then to northern Maluku. The opposing sides gradually became better armed and more lethal in their violence, with Christians slowly gaining the upper hand. But in May 2000, up to 3,000 Muslim Javanese fighters from Laskar Jihad arrived in Ambon and northern Maluku. These better-armed fighters quickly reversed the Christian gains. On June 26, 2000, the government of Indonesia declared a state of emergency and deployed elite troops; violence declined by early 2001 as the soldiers essentially forced communal partitions.

Termination and Outcome: The government sponsored a peace agreement, signed on February 12, 2002, which largely halted the remaining fighting.

Coding Decisions: Between 5,000 and 9,000 people may have been killed from 1999 to 2002.[538] Up to 2,000 Christian fighters may have been killed in 2001 alone.[539] Sources give conflicting accounts about which side actually fired first, but as Muslims adopted a primarily defensive strategy early in the war, we code the Christians as its initiators.

Sources: Goss (2000); Schulze (2002).

INTRA-STATE WAR #912

Second Aceh War of 1999 to 2004

Participants: Indonesia versus Gerakan Aceh Merdeka.

Dates: May 31, 1999, to December 9, 2002, and May 19, 2003, to December 26, 2004.

Battle-related Deaths: Total Combatant Deaths: 5,500. (See Coding Decisions.)[540]

Initiator: Gerakan Aceh Merdeka.

Outcome: Stalemate.

War Type: Civil for local issues (secession).

Total System Member Military Personnel: Armed Forces of Indonesia: 296,000 (prewar, initial); 302,000 (peak, final).[541]

Theater Armed Forces: Armed Forces of Indonesia—43,000 to 45,000 (peak—includes police used against rebels). *Gerakan Aceh Merdeka* (GAM), aka Free Aceh Movement: 3,000 (initial); 8,000 (peak).[542]

Antecedents: The Free Aceh Movement (*Gerakan Aceh Merdeka* [GAM]) was briefly able to wage civil war against the government of Indonesia in 1990 and 1991 (see Intra-state War #853), but its ability to inflict casualties declined, while it suffered heavy casualties itself. By the mid-1990s, it had begun targeting Javanese settlers in Aceh, seeing them as both agents of Indonesian colonialism and a potentially disloyal civilian population in the event of full-scale war. GAM operations all but disappeared by the end of the military operation (known as DOM) in 1998. Indeed, GAM attacks after DOM were routinely if incorrectly attributed to the Indonesian military itself as excuses to extend DOM or to disrupt pending elections.

At a ceremony marking the withdrawal of government troops from Lhokseumawe, the soldiers were pelted with stones and opened fire. Other instances of violence against government troops were reported in November and December, including the killing of seven Indonesian soldiers by an Acehnese mob. By January 1999, the government was again carrying out security operations, searching for two officers who had disappeared. Further instances of violence claimed 30 lives, and on May 3, the army opened fire on demonstrators in Kreung Geukueh, North Aceh, killing at least 45 people. In response to this and the earlier violence, GAM once more openly began attacking the government's forces in Aceh. While it is unclear exactly when battle-deaths reached the 1,000-per-year threshold, we risk erring on the side of inclusion by beginning the war with the intensification of violence in mid-1999.

Narrative: The first clear engagement of the war occurred on May 31, when GAM ambushed government soldiers returning from deployment, killing 9 and wounding 7. Two days later, the government announced the deployment of 1,300 additional police and soldiers to counter GAM. Violence picked up that summer; on August 21, the government offered the rebels amnesty, but there were no reported surrenders. On November 3, the government announced that it had ordered the withdrawal of all combat troops for Aceh in order to pursue a peaceful resolution of the settlement. Instead, it sent nearly a thousand riot police by the end of the month. By January 2, 2000, 51 police and 43 government soldiers had been killed since the onset of the war.

GAM sought a cease-fire and negotiations on January 30, but the government rejected the notion of a cease-fire without a peace agreement. Negotiations commenced in which GAM negotiators paid little attention to the position of the Indonesian government while instead courting foreign diplomatic support for a Timor solution, that is, a referendum on independence. The talks, held outside Indonesia, helped legitimize the GAM. Meanwhile, the violence continued; some 150 people—mostly civilians—were killed between January 1 and February 17. By May 5, the total was 300. A week later, the government and GAM reached agreement for a humanitarian pause in the fighting—essentially a cease-fire accord—to come into effect on June 2, but it was marked by violations on both sides. In fact, government casualties actually increased in 2000. From July 2000 to July 2002, an average of 100 a month died in the war, mostly civilians. In October, the rebels claimed to have had 43,000 troops—doubtless an exaggeration but reflective of an increase in rebel capabilities over time.

In late February 2001, a partial cease-fire called the Moratorium on Violence was reached, but in March more than 300 (mostly civilians) were killed. The government alone suffered 69 killed from March 12 to April 11, and the Humanitarian Pause cease-fire formally collapsed on March 10. While it already had 30,000 police and troops in Aceh, the government sent more reinforcements. The next month, it began a comprehensive counterinsurgency campaign called OKPH, but by the summer, GAM controlled 70 percent of Aceh. Overall, government casualties increased in 2001 compared with the year before.

The government scored a success on January 22, 2002, killing GAM military commander Tengku Abdullah Syafei and five of his guerrillas. The rebels largely went on the defensive, giving ground to the military, which claimed to have increased its control to 70 percent of Aceh by July and which estimated GAM at no more than 1,700 fighters. By December, the rebels were willing to make concessions, and a new cease-fire agreement was signed on December 9. It was largely effective—war-related civilian deaths dropped from a monthly average of 87 in 2002 to only 12 in the first month of the agreement. Armed clashes also were reduced to infrequent skirmishes.

Meanwhile, GAM established parallel governmental institutions. By April 2003 about 70 percent of Acehnese were said to be using GAM civil government offices rather than the state's institutions. On May 18, the peace talks broke off, the cease-fire agreement already having been broken several times. The next day, the government declared martial law and once again resorted to war to solve the Aceh problem.

The government's offensive was named Operasi Terpadu, and it destroyed much of the 5,000-strong GAM's fighting ability, forcing GAM to revert to pinprick guerrilla attacks. It also secured the population centers and restored much local governance. Even GAM's negotiators were arrested. The government now had 30,000 soldiers and 13,000 to 15,000 police deployed in Aceh, and it took the fight to the guerrillas, inflicting heavy casualties (it reported killing 262 GAM members by July 1 against only 32 government battle-deaths). Most of the fighting took place along or near the main highway, the Banda Aceh. The first phase of the operation ended in November; the government claimed to have killed 1,165 GAM members while suffering fewer than 70 battle-deaths itself.

A second phase of the operation was launched as martial law once again was declared for the province. During this second phase of Operasi Terpadu, the government claimed to have killed 798 GAM. From December 2003 to January 2004, the government raised additional "self-defense" militias from the local populace, who were assigned anti-GAM duties. Moreover, family members of suspected GAM members were used as human shields by the military in its operations during May.

Termination and Outcome: On December 26, 2004, a tsunami struck Aceh, killing an estimated 140,000 people in the province. The next day, the government and rebels declared a cease-fire. Despite isolated incidents, the cease-fire held, and violence remained low throughout 2005. The war was effectively a stalemate, although the 2003-to-2004 offensives clearly had resulted in tactical victories for the government.

Coding Decisions: The government (both the regular armed forces and the police) suffered up to 94 killed in the second half of 1999. As the war progressed, government casualties rose. Official estimates probably underestimate government battle-deaths and overestimate rebel battle-deaths. For example, the armed forces only admitted 50 killed and 8 missing between June 2000 and April 2001, but a police spokesperson stated that from March 12 to April 11, 2001, alone, the government suffered 69 killed (33 soldiers killed and 128 wounded, plus 36 police killed and 132 wounded). Similarly, in May 2004, the government claimed to have inflicted more casualties—killed, captured, or surrendered—on GAM over the previous year than the latter had members. Accordingly, our best estimate is that battle-deaths hovered just above the war level throughout this period—a total of about 5,500 battle-deaths, which may be several thousand too high or low.

Sources: "Aceh's Hopeless War" (2002); Chew (2000, 2001); Cooney (2000); Dillon (2001); Greenlees (2002); Human Rights Watch (1999); Martinkus (2003); Minorities at Risk Project (2010b); Perlez (2003); Schulze (2006); Sipress (2003).[543]

INTRA-STATE WAR #916

Second Philippine–Moro War of 2000 to 2001 (aka First MILF War)

Participants: Philippines versus Moro Islamic Liberation Front and Abu Sayyaf Group.
Dates: February 16, 2000, to June 22, 2001.
Battle-related Deaths: Philippines: up to 500; Moro Islamic Liberation Front: up to 1238; Abu Sayyaf Group: up to 390; Total Combatant Deaths: roughly 2,000.[544]
Initiator: Philippines.
Outcome: Negotiated settlement.
War Type: Civil for local issues (secession).
Total System Member Military Personnel: Armed Forces of the Philippines: 106,000 (prewar, initial); 107,000 (peak, final).
Theater Armed Forces: Moro Islamic Liberation Front: 10,800 (initial); 12,500 (peak, final).[545] Abu Sayyaf Group, participating from September 2000: 330 armed of 1,148 total (initial); 1,500 (peak, final).[546]

Antecedents: The Moro Islamic Liberation Front is the renamed New Moro National Liberation Force (see Intra-state War #786) that emerged in 1977 or early 1978, led by Salamat Hashim. Its secessionist rebellion remained a low-level affair until 1997, when a cease-fire agreement was reached. But in 2000, the MILF attacked two municipalities, and the government decided to mount a campaign against it.

Narrative: The government's campaign kicked off on February 16 and resulted in the deaths of 70 MILF fighters before the end of the month. Clashes in Lanao del Norte Province from March 15 to March 17 killed 5 government troops and 41 rebels. On March 21, President Joseph Estrada announced all-out war, and some 100,000 people were displaced by fighting on Mindanao by early May. Sporadic attempts at negotiation failed late in the month. Some 300 rebels and 200 government troops were killed between March and early July.

The government also attacked Abu Sayyaf forces in September, reportedly killing more than 100 of its fighters. As the fighting wore on, MILF began showing serious strains. More than 600 surrendered on October 5, another 850 on December 29, and more than 930 on March 14, 2001. On March 24, both sides agreed to peace talks, and on April 3 MILF declared a unilateral cease-fire. In May 2001, the government also declared a unilateral cease-fire. Negotiations led to a truce and framework peace agreement on June 22.

Termination and Outcome: The outcome of the war was a negotiated settlement. The peace agreement called for further talks on security issues (concluded on August 7), development assistance to war-ravaged areas (concluded on May 6, 2002), and the return of Muslim land occupied by government troops. At the last moment, the MILF dropped its insistence on self-determination. The cease-fire and steps to peace generally held, despite a few minor skirmishes, until February 2003.

Coding Decisions: Self-explanatory from cited sources.

Sources: Abuza (2003); Chalk (2002); May (2001); Mullenbach (2014); "Rebels in Philippines Sign Truce" (2001).[547]

INTRA-STATE WAR #921

Nepal Maoist Insurgency of 2001 to 2006 (aka Nepali People's War)

Participants: Nepal versus Maoist People's Liberation Army.
Dates: November 23, 2001, to January 29, 2003, and August 27, 2003, to April 27, 2006.
Battle-related Deaths: Nepal: 2,000; Maoist People's Liberation Army: 4,000; Total Combatant Deaths: 6,000. (See Coding Decisions.).[548]
Initiator: Maoist People's Liberation Army.
Outcome: Negotiated settlement.
War Type: Civil for central control.
Total System Member Military Personnel: Armed Forces of Nepal: 46,000 (prewar, initial); 69,000 (peak, final).[549]
Theater Armed Forces: Maoist People's Liberation Army: 5,000 (prewar, initial); 10,000 (peak, final). These do not include the poorly armed (many carried muzzle loaders) or unarmed people's militia, who numbered in the thousands—eventually in the tens of thousands—and functioned as a reserve.[550]

Antecedents: The small Communist Party of Nepal (Maoist), or CPN(M), issued an ultimatum to the monarchy on February 2, 1996. The ultimatum contained forty demands, including the reform of the central government. On February 13, the CPN(M) began armed attacks on government and police targets. About 800 were killed by December 1998, but the insurgency remained relatively low level until 2001, when a massacre wiped out most of the royal family, and then the rebels killed 40 police on King Gyanendra's birthday. Five days later, 65 more police were abducted. The new government declared a cease-fire, but after negotiations stalled the rebels abrogated it on November 23.

Narrative: For the first time, the CPN(M) targeted the nation's armed forces, leading to an escalation of violence. The next day, the rebels publicly declared the formation of the Maoist People's Liberation Army (PLA). The Royal Nepalese Army (RNA) subsequently was deployed fully against the rebels, and large-scale fighting and massacres both followed. At least 5,000 died over the next seven months, mostly civilians. Indeed, 2002 was the peak year of fighting. While the government claimed to have killed 3,992 insurgents, many if not most of these were suspected sympathizers rather than actual rebels. At least 666 security force personnel were killed. RNA district headquarters were attacked—usually successfully—in Dang, Syangja, Solukhumbu, Achham, Argakhanchi, and Jumla. Substantial caches of arms and ammunition fell into rebels' hands during these operations.

On January 29, 2003, the government declared a cease-fire; the rebels accepted the offer. The government immediately lifted the ban on the CPN(M), which then sought reintegration as a political party in a democratic government. Peace talks began on April 27 but ultimately failed amid lethal violations of the cease-fire agreement by both sides, especially the RNA. On August 27, the rebels renounced the cease-fire and returned to armed struggle.

The second phase of the war was less intense than the first. The CPN(M) combined periods of violence in the countryside with nonviolent protests in major cities to pressure the monarchy to democratize. Individual engagements remained small-unit affairs, with casualties in the dozens rather than hundreds or thousands. On November 16, 2004, the CPN(M) decided that the conflict had entered the third phase of Maoist struggle—the shift to conventional operations designed to destroy the RNA. The PLA began to mount somewhat larger attacks, but the monarchy responded on February 1, 2005, by dissolving parliament and censoring the media. This *autogolpe* triggered a call for a three-day national strike by the CPN(M).

The RNA became more aggressive, targeting concentrations of PLA troops. An engagement at Ganeshpur of Bardiya killed 34 PLA soldiers on February 28; on April 7, a large-scale PLA assault on the barracks at Khara of Rukum was repulsed with 53 PLA dead in fifteen hours of fighting. In one of the largest battles, the PLA attacked a RNA base camp at Pili in Kalikot district on August 7; the rebels claimed 159 government battle-deaths against only 26 on the rebel side. In an effort to build a broad front with other political parties opposing the king, the PLA announced a unilateral cease-fire on September 3. The government continued operations on a small scale throughout the three-month rebel cease-fire. By November 22, the CPN(M) had forged an alliance with seven other political parties calling for democratization.

On January 2, 2006, the Maoists resumed their military offensive. On January 21, an attack on a RNA camp at Jhurjhure Faparbari of Makwanpur cost the government sixty-four battle-deaths against only twenty-two on the rebel side, according to CPN(M) figures. Reported casualties crept upward as larger engagements were fought, usually ending in rebel victories. On April 6, the CPN(M) and a seven-party alliance began a general strike and blockade on the capital. The government imposed a curfew and used live ammunition against demonstrators in Kathmandu, but on April 24 King Gyanendra gave in and reinstated parliamentary rule in exchange for a promise by the seven-party alliance to end the general strike. The parliamentary parties then offered negotiations to the CPN(M), although they differed on some points (such as the continuation of the monarchy itself).

Termination and Outcome: Three days later, the CPN(M) lifted the blockade and announced a unilateral three-month truce. Peace talks began on May 26, resulting in a series of incremental peace agreements that culminated on November 21 with the Comprehensive Peace Agreement (CPA). Its terms amounted to a genuine compromise between the parliamentary parties and the CPN(M), including a transition to democracy and the integration of the PLA and RNA to form a new national army. The months following the CPA were free of fatalities, although small-scale violence flared up in March 2007. Still, the agreement held and ended organized armed conflict in the country.

Coding Decisions: From the beginning of the insurgency to the end of the first phase of the war, the government suffered 1,337 battle-deaths, about half of them after 2001. Accounting for the existence of battle-deaths in the last six weeks of 2001, we estimate 700 government battle-deaths for this phase. The rebels suffered more than 1,425 killed during the same period for a total of more than 2,125 battle-deaths in the first phase. Figures for the second phase are less reliable because the government tended to overreport rebel battle-deaths and underreport civilian deaths and government battle-deaths. The South Asian Terrorism Portal estimates about 1,250 government battle-deaths and about 4,700 rebel battle-deaths, although the latter figure is probably too high by a factor of two. This yields a combined total for both phases of the war of about 2,000 government battle-deaths and about 4,000 on the rebel side. We estimate 6,000 total battle-deaths.

Sources: Onesto (2005); Sapkota (2010); South Asia Terrorism Portal (2014c); Whelpton (2005).[551]

INTRA-STATE WAR #926

Third Philippine–Moros War of 2003 (aka Second MILF War)

Participants: Philippines versus Moro Islamic Liberation Front and Abu Sayyaf Group.
Dates: February 11, 2003, to July 19, 2003.
Battle-related Deaths: Abu Sayyaf Group: about 70;[552] Total Combatant Deaths: up to 1,000. (See Coding Decisions.)[553]
Initiator: Philippines.
Outcome: Stalemate.
War Type: Civil for local issues (autonomy).
Total System Member Military Personnel: Armed Forces of the Philippines: 106,000 (prewar, initial, peak, final).[554]
Theater Armed Forces: Moro Islamic Liberation Front: 10,760 (prewar, initial, peak, final).[555] Abu Sayyaf Group (Rebel Army), participating throughout the war: 460 (prewar, initial, peak, final).[556]

Antecedents: After its first war with the MILF (see Intra-state War #916), the government sought to negotiate a comprehensive peace agreement in rounds of talks. In the fourth such round in May 2002, the two sides agreed to cooperate against kidnapping and other criminal activities and to begin redevelopment of war-ravaged areas. However, the government was criticized for its concessions, while the MILF increasingly insisted that aid be directed through its organization.

Narrative: The 2003 round of fighting began on February 11, when the government attacked the MILF base of Buliok, near Pikit, in an effort to kill or capture MILF leader Salamat Hashim. Nearly a week of heavy fighting followed, costing the lives of 150 rebels and 8 government soldiers, and in March and April hundreds of civilians were killed in reciprocal massacres of Christians and Muslims. The government responded by charging the leadership of the MILF with the massacres, while the MILF countercharged that hawks in the government were perpetrating them. Late in May, the MILF announced a ten-day unilateral cease-fire, extending it by another ten days on June 12. President Gloria Macapagal-Arroyo refused to honor what she termed *ceasefire by installment*, insisting on a final and permanent peace plan and ordering further *punitive operations*.

Termination and Outcome: Hashim died of heart failure on July 13; six days later, the government and rebels agreed to end hostilities. Arroyo ordered a shift from punitive operations to active defense. The fighting subsided, and a round of peace talks in September produced another framework agreement, but the MILF refused further negotiations until the government honored its September commitment to withdraw its forces from Buliok. An international monitoring team eventually was dispatched to observe the cease-fire in October 2004. Fighting flared up again in 2005, but battle-deaths remained well below war levels: 265 government troops, 171 Abu Sayyaf fighters, 118 MILF rebels, and 16 fighters loyal to former MNLF leader Nur Misuari.

Coding Decisions: Other estimates place the death toll at 500 or even a mere 200 to 300, including civilians. Note that we follow the principle of inclusion on this and similar marginal cases. The government suffered up to 400 battle-deaths, although some of these may have been inflicted in separate (sub-war) fighting with the New People's Army (NPA). The MILF may have lost about 570, but this figure itself is suspect and may include Abu Sayyaf or NPA fatalities.

Sources: Abuza (2003), Buendia (2004); Mullenbach (2014); Vargas (2005).[557]

INTRA-STATE WAR #932
First Waziristan War of 2004 to 2006

Participants: Pakistan versus Mehsud Tribe, Ahmadzai Tribe, Bahadur-led Rebels, Rasool Khan-led Rebels, and Uzbek Foreign Fighters.

Dates: February 24, 2004, to February 7, 2005, to July 27, 2005, to June 25, 2006.

Battle-related Deaths: Pakistan: perhaps 1,000; Combined Rebel Forces: perhaps 1,000; Total Combatant Deaths: 2,000. (See Coding Decisions.)[558]

Initiator: Pakistan.

Outcome: Negotiated settlement.

War Type: Civil for local issues (foreign fighters and tribal autonomy).

Total System Member Military Personnel: Armed Forces of Pakistan: 619,000 (prewar, initial, peak, final).[559]

Theater Armed Forces: Mehsud Tribe: 4,000 (initial—2005 estimate); 4,000 (peak).[560] Ahmadzai Tribe: thousands (initial).[561] Bahadur-led Rebels, participating from late 2004: 1,500 (final—2010 estimate).[562] Rasool Khan–led Rebels, participating from late 2004: 120 to 150 (final—2010 estimate).[563] Uzbek Foreign Fighters: 200 to 300 (final—2007 estimate).[564]

Antecedents: North and South Waziristan are two of the seven tribal agencies of the Federally Administered Tribal Areas (FATA) region in western Pakistan. The region borders Afghanistan and what was once the Northwest Frontier Province (renamed Khyber-Pakhtunkhwa in 2010), as well as Balochistan and (barely) Punjab. After the terrorist attacks of September 11, 2001, the United States went to war with Afghanistan's Taliban and al Qaeda, transforming that country's civil war into an inter-state conflict. The Taliban retreated into Pakistan, where their fellow ethnic Pashtuns continued to assist them as they had done before the American intervention. The United States placed pressure on Pakistan to deal with the Taliban and al Qaeda, but local tribes—especially the Waziris but also other tribes—were armed heavily and unwilling to submit to central government control.

The Afghanistan wars influenced Waziristan in other ways. During the wars, radical religious leaders were provided money and weapons—both from the United States and later from Pakistan itself—to recruit *mujahideen* for the Afghan struggles. This upset the traditional power structures in the province, which had relied on secular tribal leaders to cooperate with the government and control the tribes. Now, the religious leaders built their own networks of patronage and support and were able to challenge tribal leaders' authority. Thus, American pressure on Pakistan to secure Waziristan conflicted with Pakistan's historic support for the religiously militant tribes during the Afghan wars.

In the early summer of 2002, the army was deployed in the FATA region, including Waziristan, for the first time since Pakistan became independent; its goal was to stop infiltration of Pakistan by Afghani fighters. Extensive negotiations with tribal leaders and religious figures ensured that no serious combat resulted. The government promised significant development funds for the region. But in 2003, the Akakhel (a Waziri subtribe) in North Waziristan aided al-Qaeda in an assault on United States forces in Afghanistan. The government responded with the first of a series of halfhearted offensives, mostly using frontier guards instead of the regular army. Perhaps 49 were killed in the offensive, about evenly divided between government and rebel forces. By this time there were perhaps 5,000 foreign fighters and insurgents in FATA. Persistent government demands for the handover of al Qaeda forces located in the region inflamed tensions, which led to low-level insurgency by 2004. The government set a deadline of February 20 for the handover of al Qaeda forces.

Narrative: When the militant tribes failed to hand over al Qaeda forces, the army moved in with a combination of 6,000 paramilitary and army troops, beginning on February 24. The offensive's goal was to defeat about 500 foreign fighters (Uzbeks, Chechens, and Arabs) who previously had fought with the Taliban in Afghanistan. The Uzbeks were sheltered by the Mehsud tribal forces of Baitullah Mehsud in South Waziristan. The government immediately captured 25 suspects, but resistance by the Mehsuds and Ahmadzais (southern Waziris, closely related to the Mehsuds) was unexpectedly fierce, and the demoralized government forces (most of whom were conscripts from local tribes themselves) led to heavy casualties. More than 50 government troops died in the first two weeks of the war. Government forces in the region rose to 10,000.

Rebel tribes negotiated while they fought, and on April 24, the first peace agreement was struck. Nek Muhammed of the Ahmadzai agreed to surrender 5 tribal elders to the government and promised loyalty in return for the release of 155 captured tribesmen. The agreement also provided a month for foreigners to surrender and offered them amnesty if they did so. The deal did not last—on June 9, Nek Muhammad's forces killed 25 people, including 17 security personnel. He was killed by the first known American drone strike in Pakistan nine days later, but his tribe remained in arms.

Baitullah Mehsud succeeded Nek Muhammad as leader of the resistance, and sporadic government offensives continued in South Waziristan until the next major peace agreement, reached on February 7, 2005. In a ceremony, Mehsud formally surrendered with his top circle and agreed to disarmament. He agreed to stop support to the foreign fighters and observe a cease-fire with the military. In return, he was pardoned by the government. Like the previous deal, this one broke down, although it took until July 27 for Mehsud to resume attacks on the security forces, alleging that the government was arresting his men in violation of the accord. Reported casualties for 2005 were only half those of 2004, but the government's strength in the region increased to between 70,000 and 80,000 troops.

Many foreign fighters fled northward to escape the growing pressure in South Waziristan. The focus of operations now turned to North Waziristan, where the powerful Haqqani Network of Afghanistan's Zadran tribe was headquartered at Miram Shah, near the Afghan border. The mediation of the Haqqani network led to a higher degree of coordination among the militants of the North, including a tribally mixed group of Uthmanzai Wazir and Daur fighters led by Hafiz Gul Bahadur and his deputy Maulana Sadiq Noor. A smaller group was led by Rasool Khan and allied itself to the unpopular Uzbek foreign fighters. In March 2006, rebels managed to seize government buildings in Miram Shah before being driven out by government forces. Significant military operations continued until the rebels in North Waziristan declared a unilateral cease-fire, subsequently extended, on June 25.

Termination and Outcome: The outcome of the war was a negotiated settlement. The government refrained from major military operations during the cease-fire (although it did arrest some two dozen Taliban in August). On September 5, 2006, Bahadur reached a peace agreement with the government, modeled on the 2005 accord in South Waziristan. The government essentially withdrew from North Waziristan; however, American drone strikes in the province would increase dramatically in the years after the war.

Coding Decisions: Battle-deaths in the two phases of the war are uncertain. According to Ali,

> The Pakistani military deliberately underestimates its casualties. The army claims that one thousand troops were killed during the Waziristan campaigns in 2004 through 2006. When in Peshawar in 2007, I was repeatedly told by local journalists that the real figure was over 3,000 killed and many thousands wounded. (251)

Estimates of rebel fatalities are even harder to come by. One source, the South Asia Terrorism Portal, based on press reports, estimates about 826 insurgents killed during this time, including non-Waziristan insurgents. Yet the same source estimates only 532 security force personnel killed across Pakistan during this period. Hence, whether the violence reached the threshold of civil war from 2004 to 2006 depends on how much credibility one gives to these unofficial casualty estimates. We do not know the answer, but we find it plausible that between the government and the insurgents, at least 1,900 were killed, the minimum needed to qualify these periods as a civil war. We estimate 2,000, which is admittedly little better than an informed guess. As for the ratio of casualties, the approximations we have suggest that they were very roughly evenly distributed between the government and rebels.

Sources: Boon, Huq, and Lovelace (2010); Gopal et al. (2013); Hasnat (2011); Hiro (2011); Mehsud (2013); South Asia Terrorism Portal (2014a, b, c, d, e, f, g); "25 Held in Pakistan al Qaeda Raid" (2004).[565]

INTRA-STATE WAR #936

Second Philippine–NPA War of 2005 to 2006 (aka Philippine Joint Offensive)

Participants: Philippines versus New People's Army.
Dates: January 1, 2005, to December 31, 2006.
Battle-related Deaths: Armed Forces of the Philippines: about 672;[566] New People's Army: 2,655;[567] Total Combatant Deaths: 3,327. (See Coding Decisions.)[568]
Initiator: Philippines.
Outcome: Fighting fell below civil war threshold.
War Type: Civil for central control.
Total System Member Military Personnel: Armed Forces of the Philippines: 106,000 (prewar, initial, peak, final).[569]
Theater Armed Forces: New People's Army: about 8,100 (initial); 7,100 (peak—2006); 6,000 (final).[570]

Antecedents: The communist New People's Army (NPA) began fighting the government in 1969; fighting was particularly intense during the 1980s (see Intra-state War #824). According to casualty figures, there was a dramatic uptick in violence in calendar year 2005, which escalated to war.

Narrative: We begin the war at the start of the calendar year 2005 because no battle marked the transition from low-level fighting to war-level violence. Indeed, the war had no outright battles to speak of but was rather a string of many small-unit engagements. In all, the government reported 1,255 such engagements with the NPA. The single biggest loss to government forces occurred on November 19, 2005, when a land mine killed 9 and wounded 20 in the town of Calinog. In June 2006, the president declared all-out war on the NPA. On July 25, the military announced plans to shift forces facing the Muslim rebels in the South to the fight against the NPA in the Southeast. Fighting ticked upward in the second half of the year, whereas there were only 104 government and 87 (or somewhat more—body counts did not include dead NPA taken by their comrades) NPA battle-deaths in the first half of the year; the remainder of the 1,000 or so battle-deaths must have been suffered after June.

Termination and Outcome: As there were likely just over 1,000 battle-deaths in 2006, we end the war with the end of the year. Fighting was much lighter in 2007. The war therefore terminated by falling below the threshold of civil war. As of January 2015, the insurgency continues.

Coding Decisions: In 2005, 1,810 NPA guerrillas and 458 government soldiers died in this conflict, according to the armed forces of the Philippines. The reported NPA figure for 2006 was 845 NPA; government losses were not specified. If the ratio of rebel to government deaths (about 4:1) remained constant from 2005 to 2006, government battle-deaths in 2006 would be about 214, for a total of 3,327 battle-deaths. Note that fighting against the MILF is excluded because the NPA and MILF were not coordinating their operations, and the MILF–government conflict killed far fewer than 1,000 people in each of these years.

Sources: Conde (2006); Landingin (2006); Mananghaya (2008); Osorio (2006); Vargas (2005).[571]

INTRA-STATE WAR #940
Third Sri Lanka Tamil War of 2006 to 2009 (aka Eelam War IV)

Participants: Sri Lanka and *Tamil Makkal Viduthalai Pulikal* versus Liberation Tigers of Tamil Eelam.
Dates: July 21, 2006, to May 17, 2009.
Battle-related Deaths: Armed Forces of Sri Lanka: at least 5,273;[572] Liberation Tigers of Tamil Eelam: up to 14,250;[573] Total Combatant Deaths: 20,000. (See Coding Decisions.)[574]
Initiator: Sri Lanka.
Outcome: Sri Lanka wins.
War Type: Civil for local issues (autonomy and secession).
Total System Member Military Personnel: Armed Forces of Sri Lanka: 110,000 (prewar); 151,000 (initial, peak); 160,900 (final).[575]
Theater Armed Forces: Liberation Tigers of Tamil Eelam: 8,000 to 10,000 (prewar, initial, peak).[576] *Tamil Makkal Viduthalai Pulikal*, aka Karuna Group, participated through June 2007: 500 to 600 (prewar, initial).[577]

Antecedents: This war stemmed from the breakdown of the 2002 cease-fire agreement (CFA) between the Liberation Tigers of Tamil Eelam (LTTE) and the government of Sri Lanka. Two provisions proved to be particularly controversial. First, each side was permitted to recruit and arm forces to the pre-CFA level, but the forced recruitment strategies used by the LTTE proved highly controversial among Tamils themselves. In addition, the government sank LTTE supply ships, killing dozens of LTTE cadres.

Second, non-LTTE armed groups were to be disarmed under the CFA. But when an eastern faction of the LTTE—3,000 cadres led by Vinayagamurthy Muralitharan (aka Karuna), roughly one-sixth to one-fourth of the organization's strength—split from the LTTE to (eventually) form the *Tamil Makkal Viduthalai Pulikal* (TMVP), the government refused to disarm them, substantially undermining the LTTE's position in the East. While Karuna's conventional forces soon were routed by the LTTE in the North of Batticaloa, he disbanded most of his troops and took up guerrilla operations against the LTTE with 400 to 600 former cadres. Moreover, peace talks were halted by the LTTE in April 2003 over the government's inability or unwillingness to even negotiate over de jure autonomy to the North and East provinces held by the LTTE. Slowly, the balance of capabilities shifted toward the government as it built up and trained its armed forces, while the LTTE had difficulty even maintaining its wartime numbers and discipline.

By 2005 both sides were committing systematic cease-fire violations. Mahinda Rajipaksa was elected president that year on a hard-line anti-LTTE platform. The LTTE carried out acts of terrorism, and the government responded in kind. Hundreds of pro-LTTE politicians, former cadres, and public figures were assassinated or "disappeared" by government-backed paramilitaries. In April, an LTTE suicide bomber unsuccessfully targeted the chief of the army. Rajipaksa now sought a pretext for full-scale war, which was provided on July 21 when the LTTE closed off a sluice gate in the East province, cutting off water to thousands of Sinhalese farmers in an adjoining army-controlled area.

Narrative: The government immediately mounted air strikes on LTTE targets; the LTTE responded by mounting an offensive against government forces south of the vital port of Trincomalee. In a month of fierce fighting that may have claimed the lives of 120 government troops and up to 940 LTTE (likely an exaggerated figure), the latter was defeated; the army then sent reinforcements, and gradually a full-scale campaign developed against the 4,000 LTTE rebels in the East province. On August 11, the LTTE assaulted army positions in Jaffna but were repulsed bloodily by August 26. Fighting continued in the East, albeit at lower intensity, through the end of the year, with one battle that claimed the lives of 630 security forces and up to 2,030 rebels.

Early in 2007, the Vakarai region fell into government hands after weeks of heavy fighting. In March, the LTTE main base of Kokkadicholai in Trincomalee district fell to government forces. Given Karuna's opposition and the fact that its command structure was entirely composed of northern Tamils, the LTTE was unable to trust the loyalty of eastern Tamils, and its local recruitment was limited. It conserved its northern troops in the North rather than reinforce a losing effort to retain control of the East. The eastern rebels were cut off; they retreated into the Thoppigala jungles, but by July, all of the main jungle bases of the LTTE in the East had been overrun. By the end of the year, the government firmly controlled the province.

Flush with success, the government renounced the CFA altogether in January 2008 and prepared an offensive into the North province, the heartland of the LTTE. As the LTTE in the East province were now limited to sporadic guerrilla resistance, control of the area had been given over to civil defense militias and Karuna's TMVP (which soon fractured, causing Karuna to flee the country), freeing up thousands of army troops for the coming northern campaign.

On April 23, the government's offensive got underway; nearly 160,000 troops were deployed to crush the approximately 10,000 remaining LTTE. After piercing the LTTE's frontline defenses, the government began securing significant territory. The Mannar peninsula fell to government troops in June; over the next month, four major LTTE bases, including the LTTE-controlled naval base at Viddattaltivu, were taken by the army. On September 2, Mallavi fell, and soon the government was within striking range of the rebels' de facto capital of Kilinochchi. Moving rapidly, the government took the city on January 2, 2009, bringing it closer to control of the vital north–south A-9 highway.

Soon, the rebels were hemmed in to a small area in the Northeast called the Vanni pocket. The government systematically chipped away at this territory, and while some LTTE were able to escape the onslaught by blending in with the civilians, most of the remaining rebels were trapped and killed in the operation. In March, rebel leader Veluppillai Prabhakaran and other senior leaders were killed in a skirmish. Mopping-up operations continued until May 17, when an LTTE spokesperson announced the end of armed resistance to the government.

Termination and Outcome: The war terminated with an absolute government victory. No amnesty was promised, and some prisoners were killed after May 17, possibly on orders from the central government. Some 11,000 were detained in 2009, of whom 700 to 800 were investigated for possible prosecution. Surprisingly, no low-level resistance remained; there were zero fatalities in terrorist violence in Sri Lanka for several years after the government victory.

Coding Decisions: Recent evidence suggests that from 2007 to 2009, at least 42,000 died (including civilians). By 2009 civilians comprised two-thirds of the yearly total. The army claims its casualties were 5,273 killed and 28,122 wounded, although this may be an underestimate of its own battle-deaths (the unusually high ratio of wounded to killed may suggest that some who later died of wounds are included in the wounded total). LTTE fatalities were much higher (especially given that government forces rarely took prisoners), though probably far short of government claims, which amounted to 22,000 (1,700 in 2006, 4,800 in 2007, 8,300 in 2008, and 7,200 in 2009). The figures for 2008 and 2009 may be double the true totals, with the other half being civilians falsely claimed to be LTTE. This would suggest a total of 14,250 rebel battle-deaths. Total battle-deaths would then number about 20,000.

Sources: Amnesty International (2011); DeSilva-Ranasinghe (2010); Nadarajah and Vimalarajah (2008); South Asia Terrorism Portal (2014a); Swamy (2010); Wickramasinghe (2009).[578]

INTRA-STATE WAR #942

Second Waziristan War of 2007 to present (aka Pakistani Taliban Insurgency)

Participants: Pakistan versus *Tehreek-e-Nafaz-e-Shariat-e-Mohammadi*, *Tehreek-e-Taliban Pakistan*, FATA Rebels (Aggregate), Uzbeks, and Other Foreign Fighters.
Dates: July 3, 2007, and ongoing.
Battle-related Deaths: Pakistan: 4,000 through 2013; Total Combatant Deaths: 30,000 to the end of 2014. (See Coding Decisions.)[579]
Initiator: FATA Rebels.
Outcome: Ongoing as of 2015.
War Type: Civil for local issues (*sharia* law).
Total System Member Military Personnel: Armed Forces of Pakistan: 619,000 (prewar, initial); 643,800 (peak as of 2014 and 2014 estimate).[580]

Theater Armed Forces: Armed Forces of Pakistan: 180,000 (peak to 2015). *Tehreek-e-Nafaz-e-Shariat-e-Mohammadi*, participating as an independent organization until joining the TTP from December 13, 2007: 2,000 (initial—Swat Valley only).[581] *Tehreek-e-Taliban Pakistan*, participating from December 13, 2007: 30,000 to 35,000 (initial, peak).[582] FATA Rebels (although many joined the TTP, others remained aloof from or even hostile to the organization: at least 28,000 to 33,000 (initial, peak).[583] Uzbeks and Other Foreign Fighters, participating from at least October 2009: 2,000 (initial).[584]

Antecedents: Pakistan's moves against foreign fighters backing the Afghan Taliban (led by the Quetta Shura) involved the deployment of the Pakistan armed forces and alienated many tribes in the Federally Administered Tribal Areas (FATA) region in western Pakistan (see Intra-state War #932). The region borders Afghanistan and what was the Northwest Frontier Province (NWFP, renamed Khyber-Pakhtunkhwa in 2010), and antigovernment insurgency slowly spread from Waziristan in FATA to areas of the NWFP. However, the insurgency remained at sub-war levels until 2007. There was a spike in rebel battle-deaths in March, but it was not until July that fighting clearly surpassed the civil-war threshold.

The incident that seems to have sparked civil war-level violence was the siege of Lal Masjid, the Red Mosque, in the capital of Islamabad. Lal Masjid was the largest mosque of the Deobandi sect in the city. However, Deobandis began to build additional mosques on public property in the city; the government threatened to demolish them, leading to an escalating war of words between Lal Masjid leaders (Abdul Aziz and Abdul Rashid Ghazi) and the government. At the end of March, Abdul Aziz issued a one-week ultimatum to the government to implement *sharia* law or face unspecified consequences. Deobandi vigilantes began trying to enforce *sharia* law, triggering protests by Pakistan's ally China and others. At the beginning of July, the government established a security cordon around Lal Masjid.

On July 3, a group of Deobandis attempted to overrun a neighboring government building, triggering a short engagement that left 20 dead. Some 1,200 students evacuated the mosque the next day, including Abdul Aziz (disguised in a burqa). However, negotiations with Abdul Rashid Ghazi failed, and on July 10, government security forces stormed Lal Masjid. More than 100 were killed in the assault, including civilian women and children.

Narrative: The next day, al Qaeda's second-in-command issued a call for *jihad* against the Pakistani government. Pakistani Taliban groups, including those in Waziristan, renounced their cease-fires and resumed targeting security forces. In June, there had been 52 battle-deaths; in July, there were 334.

The government responded by deploying more troops to the FATA (especially North Waziristan) and NWFP (especially the Swat valley). Government forces' morale was low; in one incident on August 30, some 20 fighters loyal to Baitullah Mehsud stopped a 300-strong army supply convoy and convinced them to surrender without a shot being fired. In a battle near the Afghan border in early September, the rebels claimed to have killed 150 government troops, while the government claimed to have killed 70 rebels; local officials confirmed only 10 government battle-deaths and 8 for the rebels. Another battle from October 6 to October 9 resulted in 250 deaths, with the rebels losing about three times as many killed as the government.

In November, 10,000 government troops mounted an offensive against the 2,000-strong *Tehreek-e-Nafaz-e-Shariat-e-Mohammadi* (TNSM), led by Mullah Maulana Fazlullah, in the Swat valley. Within the first two weeks of Operation Rah-e-Haq (Just Path), nearly 250 were killed. More than 100 were killed the following week and hundreds more the week after that. On December 9, the army claimed to have killed more than 300 rebels during the previous two weeks. Whatever the exact totals, the Swat valley campaign was a bloody one and a serious defeat for the rebels. By this point, the government offensive had driven the TNSM out of its strongholds and into the hills.

Meanwhile in FATA, the army was largely on the defensive through the end of the year. On December 13, some 30,000 to 35,000 rebels including the TNSM coalesced to form the *Tehreek-e-Taliban Pakistan* (TTP), led by Baitullah Mehsud and nominally loyal to Mullah Omar of the Afghanistan Taliban. The government responded to the threat by mounting Operation Zalzala (Earthquake) in Waziristan in January 2008. It quickly reached a peace agreement with the main insurgent groups of North Waziristan on February 17, but the TTP stronghold of South Waziristan proved a harder nut to crack.

On May 21, a peace agreement with the TNSM in the Malakand Agency of the NWFP was reached, calling for an end to attacks on security personnel and the closure of militant training centers in exchange for the withdrawal of the army and local implementation of *sharia* law. A similar agreement was reached with insurgents in Mohmand Agency a week later. During 2008, the government had some 112,000 troops in FATA and the NWFP.

On September 9, the government mounted Operation Sher Dil in Bajaur, which succeeded in driving militants out of major population centers at the cost of heavy civilian casualties and alienation of the local population through the use of bulldozers to demolish houses and aerial bombardment. The operation was a military success, however, and up to 1,000 rebels were killed against government losses of only 63 soldiers.

By 2009, government deployments in the border regions added up to 120,000 troops. In February, the three major leaders of the Pakistani Taliban—Baitullah Mehsud, Hafiz Gul Bahadur and Maulavi Nazir—formed the Council of the United Mujahideen to better coordinate anti-American and antigovernment actions. In April, the Malakand agreement collapsed as TNSM forces resumed attacks on security forces. The rebels blamed the government, which had stipulated that the *sharia* courts were to be subordinate to the secular supreme court. The next month, the government responded with an offensive in the Swat valley, Operation Rah-e-Rast (Path of Righteousness), aiming to clear the area of TNSM and other TTP elements. By the end of the month, the government had retaken Mingora, the largest city of Swat; in all, the operation resulted in the death or capture of some 7,000 militants.

In Waziristan, a drone strike killed Baitullah Mehsud; he was succeeded by Hakimullah Mehsud (who would himself die in a drone strike in November 2013), but Bahadur did not accept the succession, and the Council of the United Mujahideen fell apart. On October 17, the government began Operation Rah-e-Nijat (Path to Salvation), a three-pronged assault on TTP strongholds in South Waziristan. Some 10,000 to 15,000 militants defended the area, including 2,000 (mainly Uzbek) foreign fighters. The government forces included seven brigades shifted from the Indian border—a significant sign that the government considered the operation as vital to its security. The offensive met only light resistance as the TTP husbanded its resources for future guerrilla operations. The government declared victory on December 12, having captured the major population centers.

In 2010, the government had 160,000 troops deployed against the militants in the border regions. By mid-year, its armed forces were engaged in major operations in Swat, Bajaur–Mohmand, Khyber–Kurram–Orakzai, and South Waziristan. By the end of the year, most insurgents were bottled up in North Waziristan, where government forces held back, but American drone strikes (104 of them that year in the agency) took a steady toll on the insurgent leadership. Official figures stated that 3,000 died in the conflict in 2010, both military and civilian, but unofficial estimates that included fatalities from operational clashes were in the 10,000 to 12,000 range.

By 2011, the TTP had been reduced to 20,000 to 25,000 fighters, some 10,000 fewer than the number with which it had entered the war. Moreover, factionalism among commanders increased, with the fundamental disagreement being whether to focus on supporting operations in Afghanistan against the United States or to attack the Pakistani state. A number of non-TTP tribes and military leaders opted for the former, sometimes offering sanctuary to the TTP but refusing to conduct operations against the government. In 2012, operations were mounted in the Kurram Agency (February) and Miram Shah in North Waziristan (May).

By 2013, the government had 180,000 troops deployed against the rebels. In February, the TTP offered negotiations with the government, but the latter insisted on disarmament and acceptance of the supremacy of the state as prerequisites. In any case, the TTP renounced the offer in May after the loss of a leader in North Waziristan to an American drone strike. Meanwhile, the army continued an anti-TTP offensive into the Tirah valley in the first half of the year. Drone strikes continued to take a heavy toll on the TTP's leadership; on November 1, Hakimullah Mehsud was killed in one.

Termination and Outcome: The war was ongoing as of December 31, 2014.

Coding Decisions: We use the data on total security force personnel and militants killed, subtracting estimated battle-deaths in the distinct sub-war struggles in Sindh and Balochistan. After these calculations we arrive at about 4,300 government battle-deaths and 26,000 rebel battle-deaths through the end of 2014. Thus we estimate about 30,000 battle-deaths through 2013. Given government underreporting of its own casualties, the real total could be somewhat higher.

Sources: The Age (Australia) (2007); BBC News (2007a, b); Hasnat (2011); Jamal (2008); Jones and Fair (2010); Koprowski (2009); *The Military Balance* (2008, 2009, 2010, 2011, 2012, 2013, 2014); Reuters Alertnet (2007); Schmidt (2011); South Asia Terrorism Portal (2014a), Stratfor (2007a, b); TVNZ News (2007).

INTRA-STATE WAR #980
Kachin Rebellion of 2011 to 2013

Participants: Myanmar versus Kachin Independence Army.
Dates: June 9, 2011, to February 1, 2013.
Battle-related Deaths: Kachin Independence Army: more than 700; Total Combatant Deaths: 1,700. (See Coding Decisions.)[585]
Initiator: Myanmar.
Outcome: Stalemate.
War Type: Civil for local issues (independence).
Total System Member Military Personnel: Armed Forces of Myanmar: 406,000 (initial, peak, final).[586]
Theater Armed Forces: Armed Forces of Myanmar: 10,000 (peak). Kachin Independence Army: 8,000 to 10,000 (initial); 10,000 (peak).[587]

Antecedents: In 1994, the government of Myanmar reached a cease-fire agreement with the Kachin Independence Organization (KIO) and other Kachin groups. The cease-fire agreement began to break down in 2010, when the government insisted that the various cease-fire groups be transformed into border guards. This loss of autonomy was rejected by the KIO; the government responded by disallowing KIO participation in elections. The KIO also objected to the construction of new hydroelectric dams in the state. Late in the year, the government declared the cease-fire null and void, began referring to the group as insurgents, shut down KIO offices, and blocked KIO trade routes.

Narrative: Fighting began on June 9, 2011, partly over the control of two hydroelectric dams at Tarpein. The first skirmish was fought at Bumsen, which was then taken by government troops on June 12. The KIO placed its troops, the Kachin Independence Army (KIA), on a war footing and blew the bridges in the area. At the end of September, the government cancelled the controversial Myitsone dam project in Kachin, but the war continued. By late November, hundreds of combatants had been killed in the fighting, which spread throughout Kachin state and to northern Shan state.

On December 10, President Thein Sein called a unilateral halt to offensive military actions, but his order was either disobeyed or proved impossible to implement as fighting continued and even intensified in some areas. In 2011 and 2012, repeated attempts at peace talks foundered on the rebel demand that a nationwide peace agreement guaranteeing the rights of all ethnic minorities be reached. As of August 2012, the rebels claimed that the government had 10,000 troops in Kachin state, which implies local parity of forces (in numbers only—government forces were much better armed and equipped than their rivals).

In December 2012, the government began seriously to threaten the rebel headquarters at the town of Laiza. This time, it employed helicopter gunships and other aircraft in its attacks on rebel positions overlooking Laiza. Rebels on Hill 771 thrice ambushed military convoys passing through the area, inflicting 35 killed and 190 wounded (according to the government) or 50 killed in one of the ambushes alone (according to the rebels). The government then mounted an operation to take Hill 771, succeeding on December 30.

This was followed up in January by attacks on other posts and then on the major KIA base at Hka Ya Bum, which fell on January 26, 2013, at the cost of perhaps 120 government battle-deaths and 400 wounded. But by this point, China was insisting that a cease-fire be reached as some stray government shells had landed on Chinese territory. After the fall of Hka Ya Bum, the government ended its offensive short of taking Laiza.

Termination and Outcome: On February 1, the KIA announced it would refrain from offensive operations if the government would do the same. This proved to be a turning point in the conflict as clashes declined precipitously after the announcement. On February 4, peace talks began; a settlement eventually was reached on May 30, which stopped short of being a full cease-fire, but rather stipulated modalities for future negotiations. Some clashes have occurred since the agreement, but they have been small-scale affairs. Negotiations continue as of 2014.

Coding Decisions: The rebels admitted to losing 700 troops by September 2012, including 200 to their own minefields. A much less plausible rebel claim is that 1,000 engagements were fought in the same time frame, with an average of 5 to 7 government battle-deaths per engagement. While this is not credible, government losses were no doubt substantial. If they amounted to Kachin losses, then this conflict killed 1,400 combatants by September 2012, qualifying that period as a civil war. While we have no overall casualty estimates for the rest of the hostilities, hundreds probably died in just a few days' fighting in January 2013, leading us to estimate (on the basis of this very limited evidence) a total of 1,700 battle-deaths, a figure that is more likely to be an overestimate than an underestimate.

Sources: International Crisis Group (2013a, b, c, d); Loxton (2011); *The Military Balance* (2013).

Notes

1. Platt, 2012; Heath and Perry, 1994.
2. Correlates of War Project, 2010.
3. Heath and Perry, 1994; Platt, 2012.
4. Heath and Perry, 1994; Elleman, 2001.
5. Platt, 2012; Gray, 1990.
6. Platt, 2012.
7. Other sources used to code this war include Chu, 1966; Clodfelter, 2002; Franke, 1970; Gregory, 1959; Jen Yu-wen, 1973; Lin-le, 1866; Michael, 1957; Pelissier, 1963; Phillips and Axelrod, 2005; Spielmann, 1900; Teng, 1963; Wilson, 1868.
8. Bouthoul and Carrère, 1978; Phillips and Axelrod, 2005; Small and Singer, 1982.
9. Correlates of War Project, 2010.
10. Teng, 1961.
11. Other sources used to code this war include Clodfelter, 2002; Phillips and Axelrod, 2005.
12. Jenks, 1994; Farwell, 2001.
13. Correlates of War Project, 2010.
14. Jenks, 1994.
15. Ibid.
16. Other sources used to code this war include Clodfelter, 2002.
17. Grasso and Corrin, 1997; Atwill, 2005.
18. Correlates of War Project, 2010.
19. Atwill, 2005; Elleman 2001.
20. Atwill, 2005.
21. Ibid.
22. Other sources used to code this war include Atwill, 2003; Elleman, 2001.
23. Chu, 1966; Chesneaux, Bastid, and Bergère, 1976.
24. Correlates of War Project, 2010.
25. Chu, 1966; Dillon, 1999.
26. Other sources used to code this war include Lipman, 1984.
27. Kim, 2004.
28. Correlates of War Project, 2010.
29. Kim, 2004.
30. Other sources used to code this war include Clodfelter, 1992; Elleman, 2001; Kohn, 1999; Phillips and Axelrod, 2005.
31. Clement, 1891; Tutman, 1980.
32. Ibid.
33. Tutman, 1980.
34. Perry and Chang, 1980.
35. Correlates of War Project, 2010.
36. Perry and Chang, 1980.
37. Ibid.
38. Other sources used to code this war include Perry and Chang, 1980.
39. Kim, 2004.
40. Ibid.
41. Ibid.
42. Ibid.
43. Tsuzuki, 2000.
44. Ibid.
45. Sheldon, 1974; Tsuzuki, 2000.
46. Tutman, 1980.
47. Olitho, 1979; Tutman, 1980.
48. Other sources used to code this war include Clodfelter, 1992; Craig, 1961; Fairbank, Reischauer, and Craig, 1960; Hall, 1968; Phillips and Axelrod, 2005; Richardson, 1960a.
49. Kim, 2004.
50. Ibid.
51. Ibid.
52. Ibid.
53. Ibid.
54. Ibid.
55. Ibid.
56. Ibid., 96.
57. Ibid.
58. Correlates of War Project, 2010.
59. Elleman, 2001.

60. Other sources used to code this war include Clodfelter, 2002.
61. Mounsey, 1979; Vlastos, 1995.
62. Correlates of War Project, 2010; Jansen, 2000
63. Jansen, 2000.
64. Mounsey, 1979; Akamatsu, 1972.
65. Other sources used to code this war include Buck, 1973; Clodfelter, 1992; Richardson, 1960.
66. Sheck, 1980.
67. McCaffrey, 2011.
68. Correlates of War, 2010.
69. Sheck, 1980; McCaffrey, 2011.
70. Sheck, 1980.
71. Ibid.
72. McCaffrey, 2011.
73. Borjigin, 2004, 50.
74. Suh, 1994.
75. Correlates of War Project, 2010; Suh, 1994.
76. Correlates of War Project, 2010.
77. Kim, 1967.
78. See the Narrative.
79. Paine, 2003, 124.
80. Other sources used to code this war include "Chronology of the Peasant War," 1994; Clodfelter, 2002; Phillips and Axelrod, 2005; Young-hee, 1994.
81. Lipman, 1981, 1997.
82. Correlates of War Project, 2010.
83. Lipman, 1997.
84. Other sources used to code this war include Lipman, 1984.
85. Rhoads, 2000; Hsüeh, 1961; Dingle, 1921.
86. Correlates of War Project, 2010; Ch'en, 1972; Scalapino and Yu, 1985.
87. Ch'en, 1972; Scalapino and Yu, 1985; Jowett and Andrew, 1997.
88. Other sources used to code this war include Clubb, 1964; Elleman, 2001; Franke, 1970; Li, 1956; Lipman, 1984; MacNair 1931; McAleavy, 1968b; Mende, 1961; Phillips and Axelrod, 2005; Pritchard, 1951.
89. Rummel, 1994.
90. Correlates of War Project, 2010; Ch'en, 1972.
91. Ch'en, 1972.
92. Other sources used to code this war include Clubb, 1964; Elleman, 2001; Franke, 1970; Li, 1956; MacNair, 1931; McAleavy, 1968b.
93. Richardson, 1960.
94. Correlates of War Project, 2010.
95. Friedman, 1974.
96. Other sources used to code this war include Chesneaux, 1973; Li, 1956; Lipman, 1984; Richardson, 1960; Sheridan, 1966.
97. Sutton, 1980; Sheridan, 1966.
98. Correlates of War Project, 2010; Sutton, 1980.
99. Pierce, 1960; Sanborn, 2003; Olcott, 1995; Wheeler, 1964; Zenkovsky, 1960.
100. Correlates of War, 2010.
101. Olcott, 1995; Rywkin, 1990.
102. Olcott, 1995.
103. Other sources used to code this war include Bremer and Taras, 1993; Clodfelter, 1992; Seton-Watson, 1967; Soucek, 2000.
104. Sutton, 1980.
105. Ibid.
106. Ch'i, 1976; Bouthoul and Carrère, 1978.
107. Correlates of War Project, 2010; Sutton, 1980; Ch'i, 1976.
108. Sutton, 1980.
109. Other sources used to code this war include Linebarger, 1941; Phillips and Axelrod, 2005; Richardson, 1960.
110. Rummel, 1994.
111. Sutton, 1980.
112. Ibid.
113. Dreyer, 1995; Ch'i, 1976.
114. Ch'i, 1976.
115. McCormack, 1977.
116. Other sources used to code this war include Ch'en, 196); Chien-Nung, 1956; Elleman, 2001; Richardson, 1960; Schurmann and Schell, 1967.
117. Correlates of War Project, 2010.
118. Rywkin, 1990.
119. Rywkin, 1990; Olcott, 1981; "Dzhunaid Khan," 1965; Ritter, 1990.
120. Rywkin, 1990, 41.
121. Other sources used to code this war include Clodfelter, 2002, and Ritter, 1985.
122. Chi, 1969; Ch'en, 1979.
123. Other sources used to code this war include Chien-Nung, 1956; Sheridan, 1966.
124. Burdett, 2002; Gregorian, 1969; Bouthoul and Carrère, 1978.
125. Correlates of War, 2010.
126. Burdett, 2002; Stewart 1973.
127. Other sources used to code this war include Fletcher, 1965; Fraser-Tyler, 1967; Lenczowski, 1987.
128. Ch'i, 1976; Pye, 1971; Waldron, 1995.
129. Waldron, 1995; Ch'en, 1979.
130. Ibid.
131. Ch'en, 1979; Woodhead, 1969a, b.
132. Waldron, 1995.
133. Lipman, 1981.
134. Ibid.
135. Ibid., 248.
136. Waldron, 1995; Sheridan, 1966; Pye, 1971.
137. Woodhead, 1969a, b; Chi, 1969.
138. Dreyer, 1995.
139. McCormack, 1977.

140. Hsüan-chih, 1985.
141. Nathan, 1976, 60.
142. Other sources used to code this war include Chien-Nung, 1956; Elleman, 2001; Sheridan, 1966.
143. Ch'i, 1976.
144. Clodfelter, 2008.
145. Ch'i, 1976.
146. Bouthoul and Carrère, 1978.
147. Clodfelter, 2008.
148. Ibid.
149. Clubb, 1972; Dreyer, 1995.
150. Sheridan, 1966.
151. Other sources used to code this war include Brecher and Wilkenfeld, 1997; Chi, 1969; Chien-Nung, 1956; Clodfelter, 1992; Elleman, 2001; Johnson, 1976; McAleavy, 1968b; Richardson, 1960a; Takeuchi, 1935.
152. Wou, 1978.
153. Guillermaz, 1962.
154. Toynbee, 1929.
155. Sheridan, 1966.
156. Forbes, 1986.
157. Ritter, 1990; Gregorian, 1969.
158. Gregorian, 1969; Clodfelter, 2001.
159. Burdett 2002; Gregorian, 1969; Correlates of War Project, 2010.
160. Yunas, 2002; Gregorian, 1969.
161. Goodson, 2001.
162. Clodfelter, 2001.
163. Ritter, 1990; Gregorian, 1969.
164. Yunas, 2002.
165. Ibid.
166. Gankovsy, 1996.
167. Other sources used to code this war include Clodfelter, 1992; Fletcher, 1965; Fraser-Tyler, 1967; Lenczowski, 1987; Phillips and Axelrod, 2005; Richardson, 1960a.
168. Broomhall, 1910; Gillin, 1967; Woodhead, 1931.
169. Broomhall, 1910; Gillin, 1967.
170. Sheridan, 1966; Clubb, 1972; Broomhall, 1910; Gillin, 1967.
171. Eastman, Ch'en, Pepper, and van Slyke, 1991.
172. Sheridan, 1966.
173. Lary, 1985; Eastman et al., 1991.
174. Christopher, 1950.
175. Other sources used to code this war include Clubb, 1964; MacNair, 1931; McAleavy, 1968b.
176. Gankovsky, 1996.
177. Ibid.; Abdullaev, 1994.
178. Correlates of War Project, 2010.
179. Gankovsky, 1996.
180. Phillips and Axelrod, 2005.
181. Correlates of War Project, 2010.
182. Clodfelter, 2008; Morwood, 1980; Li, 2007.
183. Other sources used to code this war include Clubb, 1964; Elleman, 2001; Isaacs, 1961; McAleavy, 1968b; Phillips and Axelrod, 2005; T'ang, 1934; Wilson, 1971.
184. Elleman, 2001.
185. Ibid.
186. Ibid.; Sadri, 1984.
187. Ibid.
188. Ibid.
189. Ibid.
190. Ibid.
191. Ibid.
192. Other sources used to code this war include Starr, 2004; Tyler, 2004.
193. Baabar, 1999.
194. Ibid.; Morozova, 2003.
195. Correlates of War Project, 2010.
196. Ibid.
197. Bawden, 1968.
198. Baabar, 1999.
199. Forbes, 1986.
200. Ibid.
201. Ibid.
202. Ibid.
203. Ibid.
204. Correlates of War Project, 2010; Dorril, 1969.
205. Dorril, 1969.
206. Benton, 1999; Clodfelter, 2008; Garver, 1988; Xiang, 1998.
207. Correlates of War Project, 2010.
208. Kataoka, 1974.
209. Benson, 1990; Wang, 1997; Chen, 1977; Sadri, 1984.
210. Correlates of War Project, 2010.
211. Benson, 1990; Chen, 1977.
212. Clodfelter, 2008.
213. Correlates of War Project, 2010.
214. Clubb, 1957; Adelman, 1980.
215. Other sources used to code this war include Cady and Prince, 1966; Clodfelter, 1992; Clubb, 1964; Elleman, 2001; Kende, 1971; McAleavy, 1968b; Phillips and Axelrod, 2005; Taylor and Hudson, 1972; Thornton, 1982; Wright, 1965.
216. Tse-Han, 1991.
217. Phillips, 2003.
218. Westad, 2003.
219. Correlates of War, 2010.
220. Tse-Han, Myers, and Wou, 1991; Westad, 2003; Phillips, 2003.
221. Other sources used to code this war include Clodfelter, 1992; Kerr, 1965.
222. Tinker, 1961.
223. Fredholm, 1993; Tinker, 1961.
224. Callahan, 1996; Correlates of War Project, 2010.
225. Callahan, 1996.

226. Ibid.
227. Lintner, 1999.
228. Ibid.
229. Ibid.
230. Ibid.
231. Ibid.
232. Callahan, 1996.
233. Fredholm, 1993.
234. Ibid.
235. Lintner, 1999.
236. Other sources used to code this war include Cady, 1953, 1958; Cady and Prince, 1966; Ciment, 2007g; Clodfelter, 2002; Donnison, 1970; Fearon and Laitin, 2006; Phillips and Axelrod, 2005; Taylor and Hudson, 1972; Tinker, 1957; Wood, 1968.
237. Chadha, 2005.
238. Ibid.; Sundarayya, 1972.
239. Correlates of War Project, 2010; Sundarayya, 1972.
240. Mathews, 2011.
241. Beckett, 1999; Ramsey, 1973; Kerkevliet, 1977.
242. Correlates of War Project, 2010.
243. Ramsey, 1973; Lachica, 1971.
244. Valeriano and Bohannan, 2006, 92.
245. Other sources used to code this war include Bashore, 1962; Cady and Prince, 1966; Ciment, 2007g; Clodfelter, 2002; Hammer, 1962; Kohn, 1999; Phillips and Axelrod, 2005; Taylor and Hudson, 1972; Tirona, 1962; Vinacke, 1956; Wood, 1968.
246. Leitenberg, 2005.
247. Correlates of War Project, 2010.
248. Clodfelter, 2008; Lundry, 2009.
249. Other sources used to code this war include Armstrong, 2004; Clodfelter, 2002; Kosut, 1967.
250. Jackson, 1980.
251. Ramakrishna, 2009; Jackson, 1980; Van Dijk, 1981; Clodfelter, 2008.
252. Correlates of War Project, 2010.
253. "Fanatics Hold Java in Terror," 1953; Warner, 1954.
254. Other sources used to code this war include Armstrong, 2004; Cady and Prince, 1966; Cribb, 1999; Kingsbury, 2007; Kosut, 1967; Lowry, 1996; Tan, 2000.
255. Norbu, 1986.
256. Correlates of War Project, 2010.
257. Yongming, 2004.
258. Norbu, 1986.
259. McCarthy, 1997; Norbu, 1979; Clodfelter, 2008.
260. Smith, 1996; McCarthy, 1997; Clodfelter, 2008; Norbu, 1979; Ardley, 2002.
261. Correlates of War Project, 2010.
262. McCarthy, 1997; Durham, 2004.
263. McCarthy, 1997.
264. Norbu, 1979; Durham, 2004.
265. Shakya, 1999.
266. Norbu, 2001.
267. Other sources used to code this war include Clodfelter (1992); Patterson (1960a, 1960b); Richardson (1960a); Thomas (1959).
268. Zhimoni, 20044; Singh, 2004; Iralu, 2009; Clodfelter, 2008; Ali, 1993.
269. Correlates of War Project, 2010.
270. Mankekar, 1967; Horam, 1988.
271. Horam, 1988, 80.
272. Harvey, 1977; Friend, 2003; Kahin, 1999.
273. Correlates of War Project, 2010.
274. Harvey, 1977; Kahin, 1999.
275. Other sources used to code this war include Brackman, 1963; Britton and Nixon, 1975; Cady and Prince, 1966; Clodfelter, 2002; Cribb, 1999; Feith, 1964; Kohn, 1999; Kosut, 1967; Lowry, 1996; Phillips and Axelrod, 2005; Rummel, 1972; Stearns, 2001; Taylor and Hudson, 1972.
276. Lintner, 1999; Clodfelter, 2008; Tinker, 1961; Smith, 1999.
277. Correlates of War Project, 2010.
278. Callahan, 1996, 2003; Taylor, 1973.
279. Lintner, 1999.
280. Ibid.
281. Ibid.
282. Ibid.; Fredholm, 1993; Scott, 1966.
283. Taylor, 1973.
284. Other sources used to code this war include Cady, 1958; Cady and Prince, 1966; Ciment, 2007g; Clodfelter, 2002; Donnison, 1970; Fearon and Laitin, 2006; Phillips and Axelrod, 2005; Taylor and Hudson, 1972; Tinker 1957; Wood, 1968.
285. Clodfelter, 1995.
286. National Archives, 2006 (after excluding recorded deaths in Laos, Cambodia, and North Vietnam).
287. Clodfelter, 1995.
288. Ibid.
289. Correlates of War Project, 2010.
290. Clodfelter, 1995.
291. Asselin, 2013; Short, 1989.
292. Other sources used to code this war include Alcock and Lowe, 1970; Baldwin, 1972; Bourne, 1970; Buttinger, 1967; Chomsky, 1971; Ciment, 2007g; Clodfelter, 2002; Cooper, 1970; Gettleman, 1970a, b; Grant, 1970; Herr, 1977; Herring, 1979; Kahin and Lewis, 1969; Kende, 1971; Leitenberg and Burns, 1973; Phillips and Axelrod, 2005; Pike, 1966; Taylor and Hudson, 1972; Turner, 1975; U.S. Congress, 1969.
293. National Archives, 2006.
294. Clodfelter, 1995; Quincy, 1995, 2000.
295. Correlates of War Project, 2010; Mydans and Mydans, 1968.

296. Correlates of War Project, 2010.
297. Ibid.
298. Evans, 2002.
299. Clodfelter, 1995; Victor and Sexton, 1993; Mydans and Mydans, 1968.
300. Mydans and Mydans, 1968; Langer and Zasloff, 1969; Goldstein, 1973.
301. Ibid.
302. Clodfelter, 1995.
303. Quincy, 2000; Clodfelter, 1995.
304. Other sources used to code this war include Adams and McCoy, 1970; Cady and Prince, 1966; Chomsky, 1971; Clodfelter, 2002; Gettleman, 1970a, b; Issacs et al., 1987; Langer and Zaslof, 1970; Mydans and Mydans, 1968; Phillips and Axelrod, 2005; Taylor and Hudson, 1972; Wood, 1968; Zhang, 2002.
305. Armstrong, 2004; Budiardjo and Liong, 1988; Simmons, 2000; Asian Human Rights Commission, 2013.
306. Correlates of War Project, 2010.
307. "Indonesians Hunt West Irian Rebels," 1968.
308. Simmons, 2000.
309. Other sources used to code this war include Bercovitch and Fretter, 2004; Ciment, 2007g; *Facts on File World News Digest*, 1969; Minahan, 1996; Project Ploughshares, 2000.
310. Su, 2003; Walder, 2003.
311. Other sources used to code this war include An, 1972; Cheng, 1972; Clodfelter, 2002; Phillips and Axelrod, 2005; Taylor and Hudson, 1972.
312. Clodfelter, 2008; Smith, 1999; MacDonald, 1999; Degenhardt, 1987.
313. Correlates of War Project, 2010.
314. Annual of Power and Conflict, 1976; Smith, 1999.
315. Lintner, 1990, 1999; Annual of Power and Conflict, 1971.
316. Lintner, 1990, 1999; Smith, 1999; Worobec, 1983.
317. Annual of Power and Conflict, 1971; Smith, 1999; Shenan, 1993; *The Military Balance*, 1993–1994.
318. *The Military Balance*, 1984–1985; Cook, 1970; Shenan, 1993.
319. Fredholm, 1993; *The Military Balance*, 1987–1988.
320. Lintner, 1999.
321. Ibid.; Fredholm, 1993.
322. Ibid.; *The Military Balance*, 1992–1993.
323. Ibid.; *The Military Balance*, 1993–1994.
324. Ibid.; Smith, 1964; Worobec, 1983; *The Military Balance*, 1987–1988.
325. Worobec, 1983; Lintner, 1999.
326. Ibid.
327. Lintner, 1999.
328. *The Military Balance*, 1987–1988.
329. Ibid., 1985–1986, 1987–1988.
330. Lintner, 1999.
331. Fredholm, 1993; *The Military Balance*, 1987–1988.
332. South, 2003.
333. *The Military Balance*, 1987–1988.
334. Ibid.
335. Fredholm, 1993; Worobec, 1983.
336. *The Military Balance*, 1987–1988.
337. Lintner, 1999.
338. Ibid.; South, 2003.
339. Fredholm, 1993.
340. Clodfelter, 2008, 659.
341. Other sources used to code this war include Brogan, 1998; Clodfelter, 2002; Kohn, 1999; Phillips and Axelrod, 2005; Stearns, 2001.
342. Walder and Su, 2003; MacFarquhar and Schoenhals, 2006.
343. Correlates of War Project, 2010.
344. Other sources used to code this war include An, 1972; Cheng, 1972; Clodfelter, 2002; Phillips and Axelrod, 2005; Taylor and Hudson, 1972; Thornton, 1982; Walder and Su, 2003.
345. Clodfelter, 2008; Dasgupta, 1978; Mukhopadhyay, 2006.
346. Correlates of War Project, 2010.
347. Clodfelter, 2008, 641.
348. Dasgupta, 1978, 3.
349. Other sources used to code this war include Brogan, 1998; Clodfelter, 2002.
350. Arnold, 1995; Clodfelter, 2008.
351. Correlates of War Project, 2010; Zaheer, 1994.
352. Zaheer, 1994.
353. Ibid.
354. Zaheer, 1994; Clodfelter, 2008.
355. Jamal, 2008.
356. Ibid.
357. Ibid.
358. Ibid.
359. Zaheer, 1994.
360. Other sources used to code this war include Ayoob and Subrahmanyam 1972; Bercovitch and Fretter, 2004; Brogan, 1998; Clodfelter, 2002; *Facts on File World News Digest*, 1972; Payne, 1973; Phillips and Axelrod, 2005.
361. Senaratne, 1997.
362. Ibid.; Moore, 1993.
363. Clodfelter, 2008.
364. Ibid.; Senaratne, 1997; Moore, 1993; *Annual of Power and Conflict*, 1971.
365. Other sources used to code this war include Bush, 2003; Clodfelter, 2002; Gunaratna, 2001; *Keesing's Record of World Events*, 1971–1972.
366. Deac, 1997.
367. National Archives, 2008; Clodfelter, 1995.
368. Clodfelter, 1995; Kiernan, 1985; *Annual of Power and Conflict*, 1971.

369. Clodfelter, 1995; Sutsakhan, 1978. Although the Correlates of War Project (2010) records more than 200,000 government troops, other sources establish that 100,000 of these were purely fictitious paper soldiers used to inflate commanders' payrolls.
370. Correlates of War Project, 2010.
371. Kiernan, 1985.
372. Clodfelter, 1995; Kiernan, 1985; *Annual of Power and Conflict*, 1971.
373. Kiernan, 1985.
374. Nhem, 2013, 27.
375. Hartsock, 1980, 27–28.
376. Sutsakhan, 1978, 158.
377. Clodfelter, 1995.
378. National Archives, 2008; Clodfelter, 1995.
379. Other sources used to code this war include Bercovitch and Fretter, 2004; Caldwell and Tan, 1973; Clodfelter, 2002; *Far Eastern Economics Review*, 1970–1972; Isaacs et al., 1987; *Keesing's Record of World Events*, 1970–1975; Leifer, 1975; Leitenberg and Burns, 1973; Phillips and Axelrod, 2005; Rummel, 1994; Suhrke, 1971.
380. Muslim and Cagoco-Guiam, 1999; Yegar, 2002.
381. Correlates of War Project, 2010.
382. *Annual of Power and Conflict*, 1972–1973; Abinales, 1997.
383. Yegar, 2002.
384. Other sources used to code this war include Clodfelter, 2002; *Keesing's Record of World Events*, 1972–1981; Kohn, 1999; *Philippines Information Bulletin*, 1974; Muslim and Cagoco-Guiam, 2002; Phillips and Axelrod, 2005; Suhrke and Noble, 1977a, b; Tan, 2000.
385. Clodfelter, 1995.
386. Prizzia, 1985.
387. Ibid.; Clodfelter, 1995.
388. Correlates of War Project, 2010.
389. Clodfelter, 1995; Heaton and MacLeod, 1980; Dhiravegin, 1992.
390. Other sources used to code this war include Ciment, 2007g; Clodfelter, 2002; Morell, 1972.
391. Clodfelter, 2008.
392. Ibid.
393. Ibid.; Hurst, 1996.
394. Correlates of War Project, 2010.
395. Ali, 1993; *Annual of Power and Conflict*, 1974–1975.
396. Ibid.
397. Other sources used to code this war include Brogan, 1998; Clodfelter, 2002.
398. Quincy, 2000; Hamilton-Merritt, 1992; Lee, 1982
399. Correlates of War Project, 2010.
400. Ibid.
401. Quincy, 2000.
402. Lee, 1982; Hamilton-Merritt, 1992.
403. Other sources used to code this war include Brown and Zasloff, 1980; Clodfelter, 2002; *Keesing's Record of World Events*, 1975–1981; Phillips and Axelrod, 2005; Valdes, 1979.
404. van Klinken, 2005.
405. Simmons, 2000; Friend, 2003; Inbaraj, 1997; "E. Timor Expects 'Invasion,'" 1978; van Klinken, 2005.
406. Correlates of War Project, 2010.
407. "Fretilin Leader Shot," 1979; Tanter, 1977.
408. Other sources used to code this war include Armstrong, 2004; Clodfelter, 2002; Emmerson, 1999; Lowry, 1996; Xinhua General Overseas News Service, 1977.
409. Asian Human Rights Commission, 2013.
410. Correlates of War Project, 2010.
411. Van der Kroef, 1978.
412. Other sources used to code this war include Bercovitch and Fretter, 2004; Ciment, 2007g; Elmslie, 2003; Emmerson, 1999; Foster, 2003; *Keesing's Record of World Events*, 1977; Lowry, 1996; Minahan, 2002; Project Ploughshares, 2004.
413. Arnold, 1983.
414. Ibid.; Rasanayagam, 2003; Ewans, 2002; Tanner, 2002.
415. Ibid.; Correlates of War Project, 2010.
416. Johnson, 2011; Ewans, 2001.
417. Other sources used to code this war include Clodfelter, 2002; Dorronsoro (2005); *Europa Yearbook* (2005); Evans, 2002; Human Rights Watch (2001a, b); *Keesing's Record of World Events*, 1978, 1979.
418. Adamec, 2005.
419. Clodfelter, 2001.
420. Correlates of War Project, 2010.
421. Ibid.
422. Clodfelter, 2001.
423. O'Ballance, 1993; Hussain, 2005
424. Adamec, 1974.
425. Sinno, 2008.
426. Hussain, 2005.
427. Ibid.; Goodson, 2001.
428. Hiro, 2012.
429. Cordesman and Wagner, 1990a, b, 143.
430. Project Ploughshares, 2014b, c.
431. Correlates of War Project, 2010.
432. Felter, 2005; Abinales, 1997.
433. Other sources used to code this war include Clodfelter, 2002; *Keesing's Record of World Events*, 1972–1981; Phillips and Axelrod, 2005; Project Ploughshares, 2000.
434. Gunaratna, 1999.
435. Ibid.; O'Ballance, 1989; Bose, 2002.
436. Correlates of War Project, 2010.
437. Akhtar, 2006; Senaratne, 1997; O'Ballance, 1989.

438. Bloom, 2003; *The Military Balance*, 1987–1988; Akhtar, 2006.
439. Ram, 1989; Staniland, 2014; Akhtar, 2006.
440. Akhtar, 2006.
441. Ibid.
442. Ibid.
443. Other sources used to code this war include Bercovitch and Fretter, 2004; Bloom, 2003; Bush, 2003; Clodfelter, 2002; Gunaratna, 1998; Project Ploughshares, 2000, 2004; Rudolph, 2003; de Silva, 1998; World Alliance for Peace in Sri Lanka, 2005.
444. Chima, 2010.
445. Ibid.; Kaur, 1990.
446. Ibid.; Deol, 2000; Clodfelter, 2008; Kaur, 1990; Ali, 1993.
447. Ibid.; Correlates of War Project, 2010.
448. Ibid.; Kaur, 1990.
449. Other sources used to code this war include Ciment, 2007g; Clodfelter, 2002; Phillips and Axelrod, 2005.
450. Jansz, 2004.
451. Moore, 1993; de Silva, 1998; Senaratne, 1997; Jansz, 2004; Bose, 2002.
452. *The Military Balance*, 1987–1988; Matthews, 1990; Jansz, 2004.
453. Clodfelter, 2008; Matthews, 1990.
454. Other sources used to code this war include Clodfelter, 2002; Gunaratna, 2001.
455. Tanner, 2002; Johnson, 2011.
456. Grau, 2007; Tomán, 2006.
457. Cordesman and Wagner, 1990a, b.
458. Marshall, 2006.
459. Rubin, 2002.
460. Cordesman and Wagner, 1990a, b; *The Military Balance*, 1989, 1990, 1991.
461. Ibid.
462. Ibid.
463. The Military Balance, 1989, 1990, 1991.
464. Cordesman and Wagner, 1990a, b; *The Military Balance*, 1989, 1990, 1991.
465. Ibid.
466. Ibid.
467. Ibid.
468. Ibid.
469. Cordesman and Wagner, 1990a, b.
470. *The Military Balance*, 1989, 1990, 1991.
471. Cordesman and Wagner, 1990a, b; *The Military Balance*, 1989, 1990, 1991.
472. *The Military Balance*, 1989, 1990, 1991.
473. Cordesman and Wagner, 1990a, b; *The Military Balance*, 1989, 1990, 1991.
474. Cordesman and Wagner, 1990a, b.
475. Johnson, 2011, 249.
476. Other sources used to code this war include Brogan, 1998; Center for Defense Information, 2001; Clodfelter, 2002; Dorronsoro, 2005; *Europa Yearbook*, 2005; Human Rights Watch, 2001a, b; Phillips and Axelrod, 2005; Project Ploughshares, 2000; Uppsala Universitet, 2004.
477. Swami, 2004.
478. Ibid.
479. Ibid.
480. Ibid.; Correlates of War Project, 2010; Wallace, 2010.
481. Ibid.; Wallace, 2010; Telford, 2001; Dhillon, 1998.
482. Ibid.
483. Um, 1990; van der Krof, 1991; Broiwn, 1992.
484. Correlates of War Project, 2010.
485. Laffin, 1991.
486. *The Military Balance*, 1989.
487. Ibid.
488. Other sources used to code this war include Brogan, 1998; Ciment, 2007g; Clodfelter, 2002; Phillips and Axelrod, 2005.
489. McCarthy, 1991; Laffin, 1994.
490. Correlates of War Project, 2010.
491. Williams, 1990.
492. Other sources used to code this war include Clodfelter, 2002; Globalsecurity.org, 2005a, b, c, d); Kingsbury, 2007; Lowry, 1996; Mallay, 1999; Stearns, 2001; Tan, 2000.
493. Mendis, 2009; "Fatalities in Terrorist Violence in Sri Lanka 2002–2014," 2014; Oberst, 2014.
494. Correlates of War Project, 2010.
495. Akhtar, 2006; *The Military Balance*, 2002.
496. Roberts, 1996; Wilson-Roberts, 2001; O'Callaghan, 1991a, b, c.
497. Correlates of War, 2010.
498. "Rebels Prepared to Battle PNG Forces," 1990; Beatson, 1991.
499. Other sources used to code this war include Bercovitch and Fretter, 2004; Clodfelter, 2002; *Keesing's Record of World Events*, 1989, 1998, 2005.
500. Joshi, 1999; Swami, 2005, 2007; South Asia Terrorism Portal, 2014a, b, c, d, e, f, g.
501. Correlates of War Project, 2010.
502. Jamal, 2009.
503. Behera, 2000.
504. Joshi, 1999; Swami, 2003.
505. Das Gupta, 2002.
506. Ibid.
507. Ibid.
508. Aftergood, 2004.
509. Das Gupta, 2002.
510. Ibid.
511. Other sources used to code this war include Clodfelter, 2002; Evans, 2000; Hall, 2000; *Keesing's Record of World Events*, 2001–2006; Kohn, 1999; Project Ploughshares, 2000.

512. Serrano, 2003.
513. Whitlock, 2003.
514. Tomán, 2006; Correlates of War Project, 2010.
515. Correlates of War Project, 2010.
516. Poujol, 1997; Kiasatpour, 1998; Serrano, 2003.
517. Nourzhanov, 2005.
518. Poujol, 1997.
519. Ibid.; *The Military Balance*, 1997; Lynch, 2000.
520. Ibid.
521. Other sources used to code this war include Bercovitch and Fretter, 2004; Ciment, 2007g; Curtis, 1997; Dawisha, 1997; Project Ploughshares, 2000.
522. Khan, 2012; Clodfelter, 2008.
523. *The Military Balance*, 1991, 1993.
524. *The Military Balance*, 1993; Giustozzi, 2004.
525. *The Military Balance*, 1991, 1993.
526. Johnson, 2004.
527. *The Military Balance*, 1993; Magnus and Naby, 1998.
528. *The Military Balance*, 1991, 1993.
529. *The Military Balance*, 1993; Hafizullah, 1997.
530. Rasanayagam, 2003; Maley, 2001; *The Military Balance*, 1997, 2001.
531. Other sources used to code this war include Clodfelter, 2002; Phillips and Axelrod, 2005; Rummel, 1972; Taylor and Hudson, 1972.
532. Project Ploughshares, 2001.
533. Correlates of War Project, 2010.
534. "Cambodia Stages Offensive against Khmer Rouge," 1993; Lizee, 1997; Nhem, 2013.
535. Other sources used to code this war include Bercovitch and Fretter, 2004; Ciment, 2007g; Project Ploughshares, 2000.
536. Schulze, 2002.
537. Ibid.
538. Goss, 2000.
539. Schulze, 2002.
540. Schulze, 2006; Minorities at Risk Project, 2010b.
541. Correlates of War Project, 2010.
542. Schulze, 2006.
543. Other sources used to code this war include Armstrong, 2004; Ciment, 2007g; Clodfelter, 2002; Fabienne, 2002; Kingsbury, 2007; Project Ploughshares, 2004; Tan, 2000.
544. Felter, 2005.
545. Ibid.; Chalk, 2002.
546. Ibid.; May, 2001; *The Military Balance*, 2000–2001.
547. Other sources used to code this war include BBC News, 2005a, b; Ciment, 2007g; *Keesing's Record of World Events*, 2000, 2001; Project Ploughshares, 2005a.
548. Hutt, 2004; Marks, 2003; South Asia Terrorism Portal, 2014c.
549. Correlates of War Project, 2010.
550. Sharma, 2004; Vaughn, 2005; Mehta and Lawoti, 2010.
551. Other sources used to code this war include Bercovitch and Fretter, 2004; Ciment, 2007g; Human Rights Watch, 2001a, b, c; Project Ploughshares, 2004.
552. Felter, 2009.
553. Project Ploughshares, 2014b, c; Mullenbach, 2014; Felter, 2009.
554. Correlates of War Project, 2010.
555. Felter, 2009.
556. Ibid.
557. Other sources used to code this war include Ciment, 2007g; *Keesing's Record of World Events*, 2002–2003.
558. Ali, 2008; South Asia Terrorism Portal, 2014a, b, c, d, e, f, g; *The Military Balance*, 2014.
559. Correlates of War Project, 2010.
560. Mehsud, 2013.
561. Ibid.
562. Gopal, Mahsud, and Fishman, 2013.
563. Ibid.
564. Bajwa, 2013.
565. Other sources used to code this war include BBC News, 2004; International Institute for Strategic Studies, 2003; Project Ploughshares, 2005a, 2008; Roggio, 2006.
566. Vargas, 2005.
567. Vargas, 2005, 2007; Mananghaya, 2008; "Military Cites Gains against Insurgents," 2006.
568. Vargas, 2005, 2007.
569. Correlates of War Project, 2010.
570. Vargas, 2005, 2007; Mananghaya, 2008; "Military Cites Gains against Insurgents," 2006.
571. Other sources used to code this war include *Keesing's Record of World Events*, 2004–2005; Project Ploughshares, 2008.
572. DeSilva-Ranasinghe, 2010.
573. Ibid.; *The Military Balance*, 2007; Oberst, 2014.
574. Oberst, 2014; DeSilva-Ranasinghe, 2010; South Asia Terrorism Portal, 2014a.
575. *The Military Balance*, 2006–2010.
576. DeSilva-Ranasinghe, 2010; *The Military Balance*, 2007; Oberst, 2014.
577. DeSilva-Ranasinghe, 2010.
578. Other sources used to code this war include BBC News, 2006a, b; International Institute for Strategic Studies, 2006; *Keesing's Record of World Events*, 2006; Project Ploughshares, 2005a, 2008; Refugees International, 2006.

579. Roggio, 2006; South Asia Terrorism Portal, 2014a, c, d; South Asia Terrorism Portal, 2013a, b.
580. Correlates of War Project, 2010; *The Military Balance*, 2009–2015.
581. Koprowski, 2009.
582. Hiro, 2011.
583. Ibid.; Koprowski, 2009.
584. Jones and Fair, 2010.
585. "Time for Thein Sein to Come Clean about Burmese Losses in Kachin State," 2012; International Crisis Group, 2013a, b, c, d.
586. *The Military Balance*, 2012, 2013, 2014.
587. Loxton, 2011; *The Military Balance*, 2012.

CHAPTER EIGHT

Intra-state Wars in Sub-Saharan Africa

Below is the list of the intra-state wars that took place in Sub-Saharan Africa. Each war will then be described individually with the pertinent basic data provided.

TABLE 8.1 **List of Intra-state Wars in Sub-Saharan Africa**

(Continued)

TABLE 8.1 **List of Intra-state Wars in Sub-Saharan Africa** (Continued)

Individual Descriptions of Intra-state Wars in Sub-Saharan Africa

INTRA-STATE WAR #675.5

Negus Mikael Revolt of 1916 to 1917

Participants: Ethiopia versus Rebels led by Negus Mikael.
Dates: October 7, 1916, to August 27, 1917.
Battle-related Deaths: Ethiopia: [ ]; Rebels led by Negus Mikael: [ ]; Total Combatant Deaths: about 10,000. (See Coding Decisions.)[1]
Initiator: Rebels led by Negus Mikael.
Outcome: Ethiopia wins.
War Type: Civil for central control.
Total System Member Military Personnel: Armed Forces of Ethiopia: 250,000 (prewar, initial, peak, final).[2]
Theater Armed Forces: Armed Forces of Ethiopia: 3,000 (initial); more than 50,000 (peak).[3] Rebels led by Negus Mikael: 80,000 to 100,000 (peak).[4]

Antecedents: The victory of Ethiopia, led by Menelik II, over the Italian forces in the Second Italian–Ethiopian War of 1895 to 1896 (see Extra-state War #407), led to the general acknowledgement of Ethiopian independence. Menelik II was able to forge Ethiopia into a cohesive state and brought many of the modern techniques for farming and trade into the country. In 1906, Menelik suffered a stroke, and the issue of succession to the throne gained importance. Lij Iyasu (Lij Iassu), Menelik's grandson, was designated as Menelik's successor. When Menelik had an incapacitating stroke in 1908, the thirteen-year-old Lij Iyasu assumed power under a regency until he took power as Iyasu V upon Menelik's death in December 1913. Two other contenders to the throne were Menelik's widow, Empress Taitu, and one of Menelik's distant relative's sons, Tafari, who was a young member of the pro-modernization faction. Empress Taitu appointed Tafari as governor of Harar, but ultimately her scheming led to her banishment by Iyasu's ministers. Because of Iyasu's youth, his father, Negus Mikael, served as the power behind the throne. Iyasu's rule was disastrous. He dismantled many of Menelik's reforms, tended to side with Germany and Turkey, thereby alienating Britain and France, and devoted his time to a debauched lifestyle. As Iyasu increasingly aligned himself with Muslims against the Christian leadership, opposition to Iyasu grew. Iyasu perceived Tafari to be a threat to his regime and thus removed him as governor of Harar. The power brokers within the government, led by Fitawrari Habtegiorgis responded, and Iyasu was overthrown on September 27, 1916. The new government was headed by Menelik's daughter, Empress Zewditu, with Tafari as chief executive and heir and Habtegiorgis as minister of war.

Narrative: Negus Mikael set out immediately to have this son restored to the throne. On October 7, he gathered his army of 80,000 to 100,000 men and marched to meet Zewditu's forces. The first clash of the war occurred on October 8, resulting in 500 battle-deaths. On October 17, the rebels overran the 11,000 government troops in Ankobar, almost completely wiping them out and killing their commander, Ras Lul Segad. The next day, the rebels defeated a government column of 3,000 at Menz and then marched to engage the major government force (of 25,000 to 35,000) commanded by Ras Tafari at the Battle of Segale on October 27. The rebels attacked the aligned government gunners (who were armed with a shipment of French machine guns) and were mowed down, suffering heavy casualties. Iyasu arrived with his 6,000 reinforcements too late. In all, the government suffered 3,000 to 12,000 casualties in the battle against 8,000 to 20,000 rebel casualties. The empress's army was victorious, and Negus Mikael was captured. Iyasu and his army, accompanied by rebel survivors, fled northward. Iyasu and some of his followers were besieged at Maqdala in 1917. Escaping the siege, Iyasu was able to lead a peasant revolt that was defeated by troops led by Habtegiorgis on August 27, 1917.

Termination and Outcome: The outcome was a government victory. Iyasu escaped into the desert, where he was captured 1921. Iyasu was imprisoned, though Zewditu ensured that the conditions were luxurious. Zewditu continued to reign along with Ras Tafari Makonnen, who would become Emperor Haile Selassi I. After the empress's death in 1930, Iyasu escaped but was recaptured and died in prison in 1936.

Coding Decisions: Simply adding up the battle-deaths in major engagements (500 on October 8, 1916, about 5,000 from October 15 to 17, and between 2,750 and 8,000 on October 27) generates an estimate of 8,000 to 13,500. Therefore, we estimate 10,000 combined battle-deaths, which could be somewhat higher or considerably lower than the true toll.

Sources: Dilebo (1974); Greenfield (1965); Marcus (1975, 1987, 2002); Nelson (1981); Sandford (1946); Selassie (2014); Shinn and Ofcansky (2004).

INTRA-STATE WAR #703

Ethiopian Northern Resistance of 1928 to 1930 (aka the Raya–Azebo Rebellion)

Participants: Ethiopia versus Northern Resistance.
Dates: October 15, 1928, to April 30, 1930.
Battle-related Deaths: Ethiopia: [ ]; Northern Resistance: [ ]; Total Combatant Deaths: 2,000.
Initiator: Northern Resistance.
Outcome: Ethiopia wins.
War Type: Civil for local issues.
Total System Member Military Personnel: Armed Forces of Ethiopia: 100,000 (prewar, initial, peak, final).[5]
Theater Armed Forces: Armed Forces of Ethiopia: 35,000 (peak, final).[6] Armed Forces of the Northern Resistance: 2,000 (initial); 32,000 (peak); 10,000 (final).[7]

Antecedents: Ethiopia's ruler, Lij Iyasu, had angered many of his subjects by siding with the central powers in World War I (Inter-state War #106). Lij Iyasu (a grandson of Emperor Menelik II) was overthrown in 1916, and power was transferred to Empress Zewditu (a daughter of Menelik II), with Ras Tafari Makonnen (the future Haile Selassie) as regent. Lij Iyasu's father, Negus Mikael, immediately launched an attack on the government in an attempt to restore his son to the throne (Intra-state War #676.5: the Negus Mikael Revolt of 1916 to 1917). The revolt failed, Negus Mikail was captured, and Iyasu and his army, accompanied by a few rebel survivors, fled northward. Iyasu and some of his followers were besieged at Maqdala in 1917. Escaping the siege, Iyasu conducted a peasant revolt that was defeated by troops led by Minister of War Fitawrari Habtegiorgis on August 27, 1917.

Northern Ethiopia was the bastion of the conservatives: it was the homeland of the traditional ruling elites who had supported Emperor Menelik II and Empress Zewditu and who wished to resist foreign attempts to modernize or reform Ethiopia. In the North, the conservative opposition centered around the empress's estranged husband, Ras Gugsa Wale, and the leaders of the Tigrean people. In contrast Ras Tafari represented the growing reformist faction that was more educated and wanted to utilize ties with foreign countries to strengthen the central government and develop the coffee economy in the South. In 1926, when Minister of War Habtegiorgis died, Tafari assumed control of the army and his governate in the South. As Tafari began to extend his control into the North, the empress and her conservative supporters attempted a coup against Tafari. The attempt failed, enabling Tafari to demand the title of *negus* (or king) in compensation. The empress crowned Tafari on September 22, 1928.

Meanwhile, the summer of 1928 had been disastrous in the North, with a swarm of locusts depleting the harvest. Consequently, groups of armed Oromo men in the Raya—Azebo district of Tigray—began making forays into the neighboring areas to steal livestock and food.

Narrative: In mid-October, one of these raids involving 2,000 armed men was confronted by troops of the local governor, leading to a skirmish that caused 500 casualties. The raids escalated, involving attacks against caravans and the stealing of weapons by the Oromo and warriors from the Amhara and Tigrean highlands, with local leaders involved in organizing the raids. Perceiving these clashes as a threat to the central government, Tafari decided to act and sent an expedition against the Oromo and Tigreans. The first expedition failed. A second expedition led by Tafari's son-in-law began with the assumption that the raids were politically motivated, and thus initially he arrested local political leaders. Yet attacks against government troops continued. The violence engulfed the eastern Tigray, and refugees began fleeing into Eritrea. The second expedition ended in June 1929 but had accomplished little.

That summer Tafari decided to adopt a new tactic and appointed the empress's estranged husband, Ras Gugsa Wale (one of Tafari's opponents), as the governor of Yajju (perhaps as a test of his loyalty). On September 17, 1929, Gugsa was ordered to march to Northwest Yajju to suppress the rebels. On October 1, Tafari ordered other governors in the North to suppress the raids as well. On October 22 and October 23, 1929, the rebels surrounded and destroyed a government army at Wajja. Meanwhile, Gugsa arrived at the rebel stronghold of Zobel, and instead of attacking the rebels, Gugsa had meetings and celebrations with them. As the rebellion continued to expand, Tafari continued to call upon the local governors to attempt to suppress it. Tafari attempted to recall Gugsa, but when Gugsa refused to meet, Tafari issued the call to recruit and assemble an imperial army. On January 15, 1930, Tafari ordered Gugsa and the northern governors to join the imperial army, but they refused, uniting behind Gugsa instead. The army departed the capital on January 23, 1930, led by the minister of war, Ras Mulugeta. Ras Mulugeta advanced to Dase, where he was joined by two additional imperial armies. In contrast, Gugsa's allies began to desert him. Gugsa's forces met the imperial army on March 30, 1930, at Aynchem. The government had a three-to-one advantage in the number of soldiers, and it could (and did) conduct aerial bombing. In the ensuing battle, the rebels suffered devastating casualties, including the death of Gugsa. Government forces then advanced in pursuit of other rebel groups.

Termination and Outcome: The war ended as a government victory. Empress Zewditu died, apparently of natural causes, a day or two after her husband. Tafari was crowned as Emperor Haile Selassie in November. Haile Selassie was named man of the year for 1930 by *Time Magazine.* Five years later, Ethiopia was invaded and conquered by Italy (Inter-state War #127: the Conquest of Ethiopia of 1935 to 1936). Haile Selassie was restored to the throne in 1941 by World War II allies. Opposition continued in the North and would lead to another war involving Tigray and Eritrea in 1982 (Intra-state War #826).

Coding Decisions: Though the fighting at Aynchem was the last major battle, armed conflict between the government and the northern opposition continued for the next month as the government seized the rebel capital and the local governor reasserted his control.

Source: McCann (1985).

INTRA-STATE WAR #719.6
Weyane Rebellion of 1943

Participants: Ethiopia versus Weyane rebels.
Dates: September 12, 1943, to October 17, 1943.
Battle-related Deaths: Ethiopia: more than 473; Weyane Rebels: more than 400; Total Combatant Deaths: 1,000. (See Coding Decisions.)[8]
Initiator: Weyane rebels.
Outcome: Ethiopia wins.
War Type: Civil for local issues.
Total System Member Military Personnel: Armed Forces of Ethiopia: [ ] (prewar, initial, peak, final).
Theater Armed Forces: Weyane Rebels: 20,000 (initial, peak); 10,000 (final).[9]

Antecedents: After the overthrow of Emperor Iyasu V (see Intra-state War #676.5), Ethiopia was ruled by Empress Zewditu, with Ras Tafari Makonnen serving as her chief executive and heir. After the death of Empress Zewditu, Tafari assumed the throne as Emperor Haile Selassie on November 2, 1930. In 1935 Ethiopia again became the object of Italian colonial ambitions (see Inter-state War #127). As a result of the Italian victory, Ethiopia was combined with Eritrea and Italian Somaliland to form Italian East Africa. During World War II (Inter-state War #139), British and South African troops conquered Ethiopia and restored Emperor Haile Selassie to his throne in 1941. Haile Selassie continued his efforts to modernize Ethiopia, including a new regional government system and further efforts to abolish slavery in 1942. These efforts were opposed by the privileged class, whose status was being decreased by the moves to increase central control. Consequently, a number of revolts spread throughout the country. The most significant of these was the Weyane rebellion that began in the northernmost province of Tigray. Clashes between the weyane (or *woyane,* meaning warriors) were suppressed by a four-month government campaign in 1942 and an attack against Wejerat in May 1943. Resistance continued in eastern Tigray, where in 1943, rebel groups began to band together under the leadership of Haile Mariam Redda, who espoused a goal of liberating Tigray from Ethiopian control. The rebels began to create local administrative structures, with their headquarters at the central town of Wokro.

Narrative: On September 12, 1943, the weyane rebels, under the leadership of Fitawrari Yeebio Woldai and Dejazmach Neguise Bezabih, attacked the government garrison at Quiha. Their campaign initially met with success, with the rebels scoring another victory in a battle against a government column at the village of Sergien, where the rebels seized a number of weapons. A second government offensive at Ara also ended in a rebel victory, with the rebels capturing numerous government commanders. The rebel force of 20,000 then advanced northward, capturing the provincial capital of Makelle. The rebels were again victorious in Enderta, defeating a government army that was aided by British air power.

Meanwhile, Haile Selassie sent his minister of war, Ras Abebe Aregai, with an army northward to advance into Tigray. The government army, aided by British advisers, arrived on September 17 and engaged the rebels in a series of battles over the next three weeks. Though the rebel forces were numerically superior, the government forces had the advantage of British weaponry and air support. In the decisive battle on October 6 and October 7, a three-pronged attack by a rebel army of 10,000 led by Haile Mariam was initially successful in crushing the government army, including a number of British fatalities. However, British airpower produced the final government victory. Haile Selassie approved subsequent British bombing raids, which killed thousands of civilians and scattered rebel forces. Government troops then advanced northward, capturing Makelle on October 14 and Worko on October 17. Ras Abebe Aregai was named governor of Tigray, and he conducted a brutal pacification campaign, capturing most of the rebel leaders.

Termination and Outcome: The war ended with the government victory. Haile Mariam did not surrender until 1946, after which he was sent into exile for twenty years. Haile Mariam's son, Mengistu Haile Mariam, would be involved in the successful overthrow of Emperor Haile Selassie in 1974 and the war in Eritrea in 1975 (Intra-state War #798).

Coding Decisions: Though British forces participated in the war, it does not appear that their participation reached the requisite level to be coded as a war participant. Adding up the fatalities from major engagements provides an estimate of at least 400 rebel battle-deaths and at least 473 government battle-deaths, but these figures are almost certainly underestimates. We therefore estimate 1,000 battle-deaths combined, which is a relatively conservative number.

Sources: Greenfield (1965); Henze (1985).

INTRA-STATE WAR #750

First DRC War of 1960 to 1963

Participants: Democratic Republic of the Congo (DRC) and United Nations Operation in the Congo (ONUC) versus Anti-Lumumba Coalition (Disaffected Soldiers, Katanga, Kasai, Belgium and European Mercenaries).

Dates: July 4, 1960, to January 14, 1963.

Battle-related Deaths: DRC: [ ]; ONUC: 126;[10] Katanga: [ ]; Kasai: [ ]; Belgium: 50.[11]

Initiator: Disaffected Soldiers.

Outcome: Democratic Republic of the Congo wins.

War Type: Civil for local issues.

Total System Member Military Personnel: Armed Forces of the DRC: [ ] (prewar); 25,000 (initial, peak, final) including 1,100 Belgian officers.[12] Armed Forces of Belgium: 108,000 (prewar); 110,000 (initial); 115,000 (peak, final).[13]

Theater Armed Forces: Armed Forces of the DRC: 19,982 (peak, final).[14] Armed Forces of ONUC (Pro-government Intervener), participating from March 1, 1961: 19,982 (initial, peak); 16,000 (final).[15] Armed Forces of Katanga: 10,000 (initial, peak).[16] Armed Forces of Kasai: [ ]. Armed Forces of Belgium (Pro-rebel Intervener): 800 (prewar, initial); 9,400 (peak); 600 (final).[17] European Mercenaries (Pro-rebel Intervener): 230 (initial); 625 (peak).[18]

Antecedents: The Belgian Congo was one of the most misruled colonies in Africa, and little had been done to prepare it for independence. Belgian rule collapsed after riots in 1959, and the Congo was granted independence on June 30, 1960, though

Belgium still stationed troops in the country. Prior to independence, parliamentary elections had been held, and the Congolese National Movement (MNC) of leftist Patrice Lumumba won a plurality of the seats, though Belgium was reluctant to let Lumumba form a government. Premier Lumumba and President Joseph Kasavubu became the leaders of the new Democratic Republic of the Congo (DRC). The two men had radically different political agendas and were not entirely prepared to lead the new state. Conflict began almost immediately.

Narrative: On July 4, 1960, soldiers of the DRC's army, the *Force Publique*, mutinied against their officers (who were almost uniformly Belgian) and the Lumumba government, which had not moved to restructure the armed forces to remove foreign officers. The revolt spread, and the soldiers began to attack their officers and Europeans in general throughout the country. Within days, Belgium moved almost 10,000 troops into the DRC, primarily to evacuate Belgian nationals, but they soon began fighting against the newly configured *Armée Nationale Congolaise* (ANC). The civil war expanded on July 11, 1960, when the head of Katanga province, Moise Tshombe, encouraged by Belgium and Belgian business interests, declared Katanga's independence from the DRC. Tshombe then requested that Belgium's forces restore order on its behalf. Belgium ordered its troops into action: to disarm the Congolese army and expel it from Katanga; to seize key points in the capital; and to ferry European refugees out of the country. Lumumba broke diplomatic relations with Belgium and appealed to the United Nations (UN) for peacekeeping forces. The UN dispatched almost 20,000 peacekeepers from a number of countries in an attempt to stabilize the new government. Meanwhile, Belgian troops continued to attack government forces. Lumumba sought additional assistance from the UN, and on July 14, he warned that if the West and the UN would not pressure Belgium to withdraw, he would seek Soviet help. UN secretary general Daj Hammarskjöld agreed to visit the DRC to promote discussions but was unable to persuade Belgium to withdraw. Furthermore, Tshombe was not inclined to negotiate, and he warned the UN that its troops would meet armed resistance. The Security Council finally decided to send troops to Katanga, but they were ordered to maintain neutrality in terms of Katanga's separatist movement, which only increased Lumumba's disenchantment with the UN. On August 15, 1960, Lumumba asked the Soviet Union for assistance, and soon Soviet military supplies began to enter DRC. Using Soviet vehicles, the ANC launched a limited foray in Katanga that month, though it was repulsed by the mercenary-led Katanga army. By August, Belgium concentrated its army within Katanga, and both Belgium and the United States encouraged President Kasavubu to get rid of Lumumba. Also that month, the province of Kasai, led by Albert Kalonji, declared its independence from the DRC, and there was increasing talk of the creation of an anti-Lumumba federation. Lumumba responded by sending troops into Kasai, and following a massacre, Kalonji fled.

The UN finally was able to negotiate an agreement by which virtually all Belgian troops would be removed by September 9, 1960. Approximately 600 Belgian troops officially remained in Katanga, though some of the Belgian troops who were to have been removed stayed behind and served as private mercenaries for the Katanga government. The withdrawal of Belgian troops merely fueled the conflict between President Kasavubu and Premier Lumumba, both of whom attempted to remove the other from office. Both sides also began to organize and arm their supporters, with each gaining supporters from the ANC. In the meantime, Chief of Staff Joseph Mobuto seized power on September 14, 1960 (with connivance of the UN and the CIA). Mobuto formed an interim government with Kasavubu. The United States and Belgium schemed with them to have Lumumba removed, and the CIA launched an assassination attempt. Lumumba was captured by Mobutu's forces on December 1, 1960. Lumumba's supporters created a new government at Stanleyville, the Free Republic of the Congo. It augmented its army, and by late December, it controlled eastern Congo, having repulsed an offensive by Congolese forces. Pro-Lumumba forces attacked into Katanga and Kivu in December 1960, and the heavy fighting through January 1961 forced the UN troops from the region. Meanwhile, Lumumba was moved into Katanga, where he was tortured and killed in February 1961. The extent of the involvement of Belgium in Lumumba's murder was only revealed in 2000.[19] The pro-Lumumba government continued under the leadership of Antoine Gizenga.

A number of UN peacekeepers had been attacked and killed, and Hammarskjöld appealed to the UN for additional assistance. On February 21, 1961, a new UN resolution expanded the authorization for UN soldiers to use force not only in self-defense but also to prevent civil war and to arrest mercenaries. At the end of February, the anti-Lumumba coalition of Tshombe, Kalonji, and the new Congolese premier, Joseph Ileo, announced the formation of a common front against the UN. In early March, fighting broke out between Katangan troops and a UN contingent (which marks the beginning of the ONUC as a war participant).

Later that month, the anti-Lumumba coalition met and developed a plan for a new Congolese federation, a plan that was rejected by Gizenga. Fearing that the Congo was on the verge of collapse, UN officials met with President Kasavubu in mid-April and negotiated an agreement for the withdrawal of foreign troops. At that point, the anti-Lumumba coalition began to collapse. Mobutu briefly arrested Tshombe on April 24, 1961, though Tshombe later reneged on a promise to end his revolt. In August 1961, the UN facilitated talks among the various factions, leading to the creation of a new government of conciliation led by Prime Minister Cyrille Adoula (who assumed office from Ileo on August 2, 1961). The new government included both anti- and pro-Lumumba factions: Gizenga pledged his loyalty to the Kasavubu–Mobuto–Adoula government, disbanded the government in Stanleyville, and ultimately accepted the position as vice prime minister.

In August 1961, the UN decided to enforce the April 1961 UN–Kasavubu agreement to remove foreign forces from DRC. On August 28, 1961, the UN launched Operation Rumpunch to remove foreign troops from Katanga and began arresting foreign mercenaries. The UN also tried to persuade Tshombe to expel the foreign officers, though he refused. These efforts fueled opposition to the UN, and on September 12, a UN contingent of 150 Irish troops was attacked by the Katanga forces and ultimately forced to surrender. A subsequent UN effort, Operation Morthor, was designed to end Katanga's secession by seizing key Katangan government buildings (including the bases of the gendarmes) and by capturing government officials. The operation began on September 13 and was met by a coordinated attack by the Katangan military. In battles over the next eight days, 11 UN soldiers and 50 Katanga troops were killed (along with some civilians). Within days, Hammarskjöld flew to Katanga to try to work out a settlement, but Hammarskjöld was killed in a plane crash on September 18. On October 30, the Congolese army invaded Katanga but was repulsed. Fighting in Katanga also continued with UN forces (now under the direction of UN secretary general U Thant). A Security Council vote on November 21, 1961, reaffirmed the UN's mandate to use force to apprehend mercenaries and political advisors, which prompted further attacks on UN personnel. On December 5, an Indian UN contingent near Elizabethville, in Katanga, engaged in combat, including artillery fire and aerial attacks, against Katangan forces for almost two weeks, leading to 21 UN and 206 Katangan deaths. On December 17, the UN sent reinforcements to Elizabethville and soon gained control of the city. The Katangan government fled.

On December 20, 1961, the UN was able to facilitate a meeting between Tshombe and Congolese prime minister Cyrille Adoula. Tshombe stalled in accepting the agreement, and a political stalemate ensued for most of 1962. During the year, both the DRC and Katanga augmented their forces, and the UN created its own air force. The DRC engaged in sporadic attacks upon Tshombe's troops. In December 1962, the ONUC launched Operation Grand Slam, whereby its air force destroyed Katanga's aircraft and its ground forces scattered Katanga's mercenary troops. The ONUC captured Jadotville on January 1, 1973, and Tshombe surrendered on January 21, 1963.

Termination and Outcome: The outcome of the war was a DRC victory, in which the forces of the UN actively intervened to defeat Tshombe and reunify the Congo. The role of the UN during this war and its impact has been hotly contested. Unfortunately, two wars would begin the following year (Intra-state Wars #761 and #762). Tshombe initially went into exile but was subsequently invited by Kasavubu to form a Congolese government in July 1964.

Coding Decisions: As Patrice Lamumba was premier (chief executive) at the start of the war, he and his supporters are considered to be the government until the period after August 1961, when they reunited with the Kasavubu–Mobutu–Adoula Congolese government. Though Gizenga later instigated a mutiny of pro-Lumumba troops in the army, this quickly was suppressed, and Gizenga was arrested.

Though UN forces entered DRC in July 1960, they did not engage in organized combat until their role was strengthened, and they were attacked in March 1961.

Information concerning fatality statistics for this war is scarce. A commonly cited figure is that 100,000 to 110,000 people were killed in the conflict, though the vast majority of these would have been civilian deaths.[20]

Kisangani, Ndikumana, and Kisangani consider the Katanga war of secession and the Kasai secession to be two separate wars; however, because of the anti-Lumumba focus of the two wars and Kalonji's cooperation with Tshombe in the anti-Lumumba negotiations, these conflicts are included together in this broader war.

Sources: Bercovitch and Fretter (2004); Cady and Prince (1966); Ciment (2007a–h); Clodfelter (2002); Cutter (2007); Hoskyns (1965); Kisangani (2012); Lefever (1965, 1972); Meredith (2005); Mydans and Mydans (1968); Ndikumana and Kisangani (2005); Oliver and Atmore (2004); Phillips and Axelrod (2005); Stapleton (2013); Stearns (2001); Taylor and Hudson (1972); Van Nederveen (2001).

INTRA-STATE WAR #757
First Ogaden War of 1963 to 1964

Participants: Ethiopia versus Ogaden Liberation Front (OLF) and Somalia.
Dates: June 1963 to March 30, 1964.
Battle-related Deaths: Ethiopia: [ ]; Ogaden: [ ]; Somalia: [ ].
Initiator: OLF.
Outcome: Compromise.
War Type: Civil for local issues.
Total System Member Military Personnel: Armed Forces of Ethiopia: 30,000 (prewar); 55,000 (initial); 60,000 (peak, final).[21] Armed Forces of Somalia, participating from November 1963); 4,000 (prewar); 9,000 (initial); 11,000 (peak, final).[22]
Theater Armed Forces: Ogaden Liberation Army: 3,000 (peak).

Antecedents: The Somali people inhabit not only Somalia but also areas of Djibouti, the eastern Ogaden region of Ethiopia, and northern Kenya. After attaining its independence from Britain in 1960, Somalia's instigation led to armed conflict between the Ogaden Somalis and the Ethiopian army in 1960 and 1961, which strained relations between the two countries. In 1963, a group of Somalis, led by Muktel Dahir, created the Ogaden Liberation Front (OLF) and began to create a government structure for the Ogaden in preparation for seeking independence from Ethiopia. The OFL also created the Ogaden Liberation Army (OLA), which received military support from Somalia. Ethiopia emperor Haile Selassie refused.

Narrative: In June 1963, the OLF began a rebellion against Ethiopia by attacking government installations and police outposts throughout the Ogaden. The OLA was successful in basically restricting Ethiopia's Third Army to its garrisons, and the OLF had virtual control of the region. However, in August, Somalia charged the Ethiopian army with inflicting severe reprisals on the Somalis in Ogaden. In November, Somalia sent troops to directly assist the rebels. In early 1964, Ethiopian–OLA clashes increased along the Ethiopia–Somalia border, leading to a direct armed conflict between Somalia and Ethiopia. Haile Selassie sent the Ethiopian Third Division, armed by the United States, into Ogaden, where it defeated OLA forces. An attack by Somalia against an Ethiopian post prompted Ethiopia to retaliate with air strikes, both in the Ogaden and against Somalian posts and villages on February 7, 1964. Ethiopia then declared a state of emergency and launched a brief invasion of Somali territory from February 27 to February 29. Sporadic fighting continued between Ethiopia and the OLA through March.

The Organization of African Unity (OAU) had called for a cease-fire as early as February 14, 1964. Even though Ethiopia generally was winning the war, its American military advisers were interested in reducing the conflict with the Soviet-supported Somali regime. Consequently both Ethiopia and Somalia accepted Sudan's offer to mediate. Talks were held in Khartoum from March 25 to March 30, which addressed both the Ethiopia–Somali conflict and the attacks by Somalis in Kenya. The mediation produced an agreement for both Ethiopia and Somalia to pull back their troops from the border area.

Termination and Outcome: Muktal Dahir announced that the OLF would not abide by the cease-fire and would continue its attacks. However, without Somali support, the OLF reduced its efforts significantly. The Ethiopian government launched a pacification program in the Ogaden that entailed providing services, such as wells and schools, to the region.

Coding Decisions: Because Ethiopia and Somalia accepted the mediated cease-fire agreement, the civil war is coded a compromise. The issue of the Ogaden was not resolved, however, and war would resume in 1976 (Intra-state War #806).

In terms of battle-deaths, Stapleton claimed that the war claimed 2,000 lives. In terms of the attacks and air raids on February 7, 1964, alone, Lefever cites Ethiopian figures of 30 Ethiopian deaths and 400 Somali deaths, contrasted to Somali reports of 350 Ethiopian and 307 Somali deaths. As it is unclear whether these numbers include civilian deaths, they are not reported here. However, they do indicate that this conflict likely caused more than 1,000 battle-deaths.

Sources: Alker (1995); Bercovitch and Fretter (2004); Ciment (2007a–h); Cordesman (1993a, b); Lefever (1970); Meredith (2005); Stapleton (2013).

INTRA-STATE WAR #760
First Rwanda War of 1963 to 1964

Participants: Rwanda versus Tutsi (Watusi) Rebels.
Dates: December 21, 1963, to July 1964.
Battle-related Deaths: Tutsi (Watusi) Rebels: [ ]; Rwanda: [ ]; Total Combatant Deaths: 1,000.
Initiator: Tutsi (Watusi) Rebels.
Outcome: Rwanda wins.
War Type: Civil for central control.
Total System Member Military Personnel: Armed Forces of Rwanda: 1,000 (prewar, initial); 2,000 (peak, final).[23]
Theater Armed Forces: Tutsi (Watusi) Armed Forces (*Inyenzi*): 200 (initial); 5,000 (peak).[24]

Antecedents: During the final years of Belgium's control over Rwanda, a social revolution broke out between the Hutu and the Tutsi peoples (Non-state War #1574, 1959 to 1962). The Tutsi (constituting 15 percent of the population) had dominated the majority Hutu (85 percent), and Tutsi feelings of superiority had been reinforced by the colonial powers. However, as anticolonial sentiment spread, the Tutsi were attracted by the policies of communist regimes. Seeing the Hutu as less threatening and potentially more pliable, Belgium and other Western powers began to shift their support to the Hutus. In the war, the Hutu prevailed, the Tutsi king was deposed, and Rwanda became a republic under the leadership of President Kayibanda when it attained its independence from Belgium in July 1962. Conflict between the two peoples continued, and approximately 140,000 Tutsi fled to the nearby countries of Burundi, Uganda, Congo, and Tanganyika. Among the Tutsis, refugees and the 250,000 Tutsis who remained in Rwanda, those who couldn't accept their current status formed a rebel group, called *inyenzi*, which aimed to restore Tutsi rule in Rwanda. The *inyenzi* were trained primarily in the refugee camps in Burundi into a relatively effective fighting force. In 1963, the Tutsi émigrés began several attempts to return to Rwanda: a raid into Rwanda by the *inyenzi* in Uganda on July 5, 1963, prompted Uganda to end its practice of being a welcoming sanctuary for the Tutsi. In the Congo (DRC), the Tutsi were welcomed in the areas controlled by the leftist MNC-L (pro-Lumumba) faction, and the two groups established an informal alliance that entailed cooperation in each other's conflicts. Burundi was the primary sanctuary for the Tutsi leadership, which operated within the two refugee camps close to the Burundi–Rwanda border. On November 25, 1963, a march of 1,500 armed Tutsi from Burundi toward Rwanda was spotted by UN officials and turned back at the border. However, the Burundi regime continued to be supportive of the Tutsis, a position that was enhanced in December 1963 with the establishment of diplomatic relations between Burundi and the People's Republic of China.

Narrative: The Bugesera (a region in southern Rwanda) invasion was planned by the *inyenzi* to be coordinated attacks into Rwanda from four directions: from Congo, Tanzania, Burundi, and Uganda. The initial raids on December 21 and December 22, 1983, came from Congo and were repulsed by the Rwandan army, which subsequently executed its 90 prisoners. At the same time, a force of 200 to 300 *inyenzi*, accompanied by Congolese mercenaries and armed with spears and sticks, crossed from Burundi into Rwanda and overran a Rwanda military post at Gako, where they seized a jeep and some weapons. They then marched toward the capital Kigali but stopped to make contact with local Tutsis at Nyamata, where their numbers increased to well over 1,000. Within twelve miles of Kigali, the rebels were intercepted by the Rwanda Garde Nationale, which was armed with automatic weapons and led by Belgian officers. In the ensuing battle, the rebels suffered heavy losses (several hundred Tutsi and a small number of Congolese) before retreating. The Rwanda government responded to the threat by arresting prominent Tutsis. Twenty of those whose names had been found on an *inyenzi* list of the members of a proposed Tutsi government were executed. The government then created a series of Hutu local defense militias, which then engaged in widespread massacres of the Tutsi population, killing an estimated 10,000 to 14,000. On December 24, a group of 6,000 Tutsis fled into Uganda, while thousands of others took refuge in Catholic churches.

Nonetheless, the *inyenzi* raids continued. On December 27, a force of 600 well-armed Tutsis entered Rwanda from Uganda and was met by the Rwandan army. In a brief battle, 300 of the rebels were killed, and others were captured. The planned attacks from Tanzania did not materialize. Meanwhile the Tutsi leadership appealed to the UN for assistance, but no action was taken. On January 22, 1964, Rwandan forces entered Burundi and killed a number of Tutsi there, prompting Burundi to appeal to the UN. *Inyenzi* raids from the Congo continued from March to April and from June to July 1964.

Termination and Outcome: The war ended as a victory for the Rwandan government. By the summer of 1964, tensions had moderated somewhat, and Tutsi refugees were allowed to return.

During the war, 10,000 to 13,000 Tutsi were killed, the majority of whom were civilians massacred by the local Hutu militias and the Rwandan army. The conflict between the Hutu and Tutsi would reignite in the second Rwanda war (Intra-state War #886) and the ensuing genocide of 1994.

Coding Decisions: Combatant fatality information for this war is spotty at best, and we have not located any mention of Rwandan army deaths. Based upon the limited information provided about Tutsi deaths, we are convinced that the conflict reached the war-level threshold of 1,000 combatant deaths.

Sources: "Atlantic Report Rwanda" (1964); Bhavnani and Backer (2000); Ciment (2007a–h); Clodfelter (2002); Lemarchand (1970); Meredith (2005); Phillips and Axelrod (2005); Scherrer (2002); Taylor and Hudson (1972); Twagilimana (2003).

INTRA-STATE WAR #761

Second DRC War of 1964 to 1965 (The *Jeunesse* War or the Kwilu Rebellion)

Participants: Democratic Republic of the Congo (DRC) versus *Jeunesse* warriors.

Dates: January 6, 1964, to December 31, 1965.

Battle-related Deaths: Congo: [ ]; *Jeunesse* warriors: [ ]; Total Combatant Deaths: 3,500 to 9,000.[25]

Initiator: *Jeunesse* warriors.

Outcome: DRC wins.

War Type: Civil for local issues.

Total System Member Military Personnel: Armed Forces of DRC: 20,000 (prewar); 25,000 (initial, peak, final).[26]

Theater Armed Forces: *Jeunesse* warriors: 10,000 (initial, peak, final).[27]

Antecedents: Immediately upon gaining its independence from Belgium, the Democratic Republic of Congo (DRC) confronted a number of internal disturbances. The first DRC war (Intra-state War #750), which ended in January 1963, had involved the southeastern province of Katanga's attempt to secede from the DRG. Katanga's endeavor was defeated by the DRC with the assistance of forces from the United Nations (UN). During the war, the UN had promoted the reconciliation of the pro-Lumumba and anti-Lumumba factions, and a government of conciliation had been formed in August 1961 under the leadership of Prime Minister Cyrille Adoula, who included the leader of the Lumumba faction, Antoine Gigenza, as vice prime minister. However, not all of the Lumumbists accepted reconciliation: Pierre Mulele, who had served as Lumumba's minister of education and as secretary general of the radical wing of the *Parti Solidaire African* (PSA), preferred exile to selling out to the interests of the West. While in exile in Egypt and China, Mulele developed further his theories of peasant rebellion, which he began to implement upon his return to the DRC in 1963. Mulele began his efforts among his Mbunda ethnic group in the southwest Kwilu province, which saw itself as being marginalized by the central government. In July 1963, Mulele began to organize the *Jeunesse* (young warriors, age fifteen to twenty-three), using the training in guerrilla tactics that he had received in China. By December 1963, Mulele had 10,000 soldiers.

Narrative: In 1964, the *Jeunesse*, who operated under a rigid code of conduct based on that of Mao Zedong combined, began guerrilla attacks against government forces. The initial attack on January 6, 1964, led to the burning of the administrative center of Mungindu, and by the end of the month, attacks had spread to the Idiofa and Gungu territories. On January 21, the Adoula government declared a state of emergency and sent additional troops into the region. The rebellion's ethnic focus limited the scope of the rebellion to a relatively small area; however, within a few months the *Jeunesse* controlled most of the province. Even though the rebels were poorly armed, their fervor and their ferocity frequently persuaded the Congolese soldiers to flee. It took the government two years to crush their revolt.

Termination and Outcome: The war ended as a government victory in December 1965. Mulele fled to Congo-Brazzaville. In 1968, DRC president Joseph-Désiré Mobutu offered an amnesty program. Mulele returned to DRC and was initially feted, but then Mobutu announced that Mulele did not qualify for amnesty. Mulele was captured, tried, tortured, and killed. In response, Congo-Brazzaville broke diplomatic relations with the DRC.

Coding Decisions: Because of the limited size and scope of this war, a number of scholars include it in the more-widespread Simba rebellion (Intra-state War #762). However, because of the geographic distance between the two, the difference in goals, and the lack of evidence of coordination between the rebellions, they are coded here as separate wars.[28]

Sources: Clodfelter (2002); "The Congo: Death of a Rebel" (1968); Kisangani (2012); Ndikumana and Kisangani (2005).

INTRA-STATE WAR #762
Third DRC Rebellion of 1964 to 1965 (aka the Simba War, the Eastern Rebellion, or the Uvira-Fizi Rebellion)

Participants: Democratic Republic of the Congo (DRC) and Belgium versus Gbenye-led CNL.
Dates: April 15, 1964, to September 30, 1965.
Battle-related Deaths: CNL (Simbas): 4,500; DRC: 250; Pro-government Mercenaries: 50; Belgium: 5. (See Coding Decisions.)
Initiator: Gbenye-led CNL.
Outcome: DRC and Belgium win.
War Type: Civil for central control.
Total System Member Military Personnel: Armed Forces of DRC: 25,000 (prewar, initial, peak, final).[29] Armed Forces of Belgium: 115,000 (prewar, initial, final, peak).[30]
Theater Armed Forces: Armed Forces of the CNL (Simbas): 6,000 (initial).[31] Belgian Armed Forces, participating from August 7, 1964: 1,700 (initial); 2,250 (peak); 1,700 (final).[32] Foreign Mercenaries (Pro-government Interveners), participating from August 20, 1964: 400 (initial); 1,500 (peak).[33]

Antecedents: In the aftermath of the first rebellion in the Democratic Republic of the Congo (DRC) (Intra-state War #750 from 1960–1963), instability continued, and the DRC was confronted with two rebellions early in 1964: the first was a limited war by the *Jeunesse* (young warriors) in the Southwest Kwilu province (Intra-state War #761); the second was this larger revolution that broke out in the East and would soon involve almost half of the country.

A by-product of the 1960-to-1963 conflict was an increasing rivalry within the *Mouvement National Congolais/Patrice* Lumumba (MNC/L), whose more moderate members had joined the government of reconciliation (of President Joseph Kasavubu and Prime Minister Cyrille Adoula), created with the assistance of the UN in August 1961. The moderates then were perceived by the more radical and nationalist members of MNC/L as having been coopted by a pro-Western government. In July 1963, Adoula dismissed the more radical members of his cabinet, and on September 29, 1963, President Joseph

Kasavubu adjourned the parliament. These measures served to unify and motivate the radical opposition. The radicals met in the capital from September 29 to October 3 and created the Union of Nationalist Parties. This group left the country, crossing the Congo river into the Republic of Congo (or Congo-Brazzaville), which was ruled by President Alphonse Massamba-Débat, who was creating a system of government based on scientific socialism. Here the radicals created the *Conseil National de Libération* (National Council of Liberation [CNL]) with the aim of overthrowing the Adoula government and removing Western influence from the country. The leader of this movement was Christophe Gbenye (who had served as minister of the interior under Lumumba), aided by Gaston Soumialot and Laurent Kabila.

Narrative: In February 1964, Gbenye sent Soumialot and Laurent Kabila to the eastern DRC to organize military action against the government. There they established the CNL (with aid from communist and leftist governments) and began to encourage the young men of the tribes in the Uvira and Fizi areas (which generally were opposed to the government) to join the rebel army, the *Armée Populaire de Libération* (Popular Liberation Army of APL), also called the Simbas (Lions). The rebellion began on April 15, 1964, with rebel attacks as several points in the Uvira-Fizi region. The Simbas, led by Gen. Nicolas Olenga, rapidly advanced (encouraged by a belief that bullets fired against them would turn into water), capturing towns and defeating two battalions of the Congolese army (the ANC). The DRC government of President Kasavubu (apparently pressured by the United States and Belgium) responded to the growing threat by dismissing Prime Minister Adoula and recalling Moïse Tshombe (the former Katangan secessionist leader—see Intra-state War #750) from exile to form a new government on July 10, 1964. Tshombe and the ANC were incapable of dealing with the rebel threat, and to prevent the DRC from disintegrating, Tshombe began to both recruit his own group of foreign mercenaries (a group of about 300 soldiers, mostly from South Africa, led by Irishman Michael Hoare) and to seek the assistance of the United States and Belgium. The United States, fearing the possible creation of a communist government in the DRC, had sent a military advisory team to the DRC in 1962 and had created the United States Military Mission, Congo (COMISH) in July 1963. The CIA had also created a Congolese air force in 1962, initially with seven Cuban exiles piloting the American planes. As the situation in the DRC had deteriorated in early 1964, the CIA had added weapons to the planes. During the summer of 1964, the CIA obtained additional planes and expanded the Cuban exile force to more than 100 to fly and maintain the planes.[34] Belgium also was willing to provide assistance to the DRC government. On August 6, 1964, Belgium dispatched Colonel Frédéric Vanderwalle, a mechanized brigade, and six logistics units to the DRC (which marks Belgium's entry into the war as a state participant). The mercenaries, the Cuban exiles, and the Belgian troops (totaling about 2,100 men) would provide critical military support to the DRC government efforts in fighting the Simba rebellion.

The rebels had three fronts in the eastern DRC, which were receiving military supplies individually from China, the Soviet Union, Cuba, and other socialist states. The rebels were able to advance, often against little government resistance. The rebels had captured Kalemie, on the western shore of Lake Tanganyika, and Hoare developed a plan for the foreign troops to spearhead the effort to retake the city by coupling bombing raids by the Cuban exile air force with coordinated attacks by the mercenaries and the ANC. The plan succeeded on August 30. However, the rebels continued to advance elsewhere, and they soon had control over the Northeast, capturing Stanleyville (also known as Kisangani) in August. There they proclaimed the establishment of a rebel government (a People's Republic of the Congo) led by Gbenye on September 5, 1964. The CNL soon controlled the eastern half of the DRC. The rebels engaged in massacres of civilians perceived to be counterrevolutionaries.[35] They also seized more than 2,000 Western hostages in Stanleyville. The CIA-developed air force began to strafe rebel positions there in September. However, the CIA and Belgian armed forces finally concluded that direct military action was going to be necessary to rescue the Westerners trapped in the rebel zone. Belgium offered to provide paratroopers to parachute into Stanleyville, if the United States could provide training and transportation. The United States agreed, and operation Dragon Rouge was launched on November 15, 1964. The first group of

Belgian paratroopers landed into DRC on November 24, 1964, and their efforts were coordinated with the Belgian and mercenary ground troops. About 1,955 of the Western hostages were rescued, while a large number were killed.

Stanleyville marked a turning point in the war. Gradually the ANC and Western troops began to advance against the rebels, establishing government control in the East in early 1965. An interesting development was the April 19, 1965, deployment of a Cuban contingent of 120 to 200 soldiers led by Che Guevara to support the rebels. The war continued with both the rebels and the government scoring victories. The final battle took place at Baraka, on the shore of Lake Tanganyika. The foreign mercenaries, the Cuban exiled air force, and an ANC contingent confronted 2,000 rebels, including the Cubans led by Che. The battle lasted for five days, and the government forces finally recaptured the town on September 30, 1965.

Termination and Outcome: The war ended in a government victory. Even though the DRC had regained control of the eastern sector, Prime Minister Tshombe's reputation had been damaged by his reliance on foreign troops. Thus, on October 13, 1965, President Kasavubu removed Tshombe from office. Six weeks later, on November 24, 1965, the ANC commander, Joseph-Désiré Mobutu, staged a coup, removing Kasavubu from power and establishing a U.S.-supported anticommunist regime that would last for thirty-two years.

Coding Decisions: Though the United States was heavily involved in this war, the number of troops committed to the war effort did not reach the level necessary for it to be considered a war participant. The same is also true of the Cuban involvement.

Battle-death statistics for this war are limited and contradictory. Clodfelter concludes that through April 1965, there were 200 ANC, 35 mercenary, 4 Belgian, and 4,000 Simba deaths. These numbers seem low in comparison to the claim that an estimated 10,000 Simba warriors were killed in the Stanleyville rescue operation.[36] Because we code fighting as continuing through September 1965, we are reporting rounded-up versions of Clodfelter's statistics but are cognizant of the fact that these may underestimate the combatant fatalities. Clodfelter also reports that 18,000 civilians were killed in the massacres during this war.

Sources: Clodfelter (2002); Kisangani (2012); Meredith (2005); Ndikumana and Kisangani (2005); Stapleton (2013); Van Nederveen (2001); Villafaña (2009).

INTRA-STATE WAR #768

First Uganda War of 1966

Participants: Uganda versus Buganda.
Dates: May 23, 1966, to June 1, 1966.
Battle-related Deaths: Uganda: [ ]; Buganda: [ ]; Total Combatant Deaths: 1,000.
Initiator: Uganda.
Outcome: Uganda wins.
War Type: Civil for local issues.
Total System Member Military Personnel: Armed Forces of Uganda: 6,000 (prewar); 11,000 (initial, peak, final).[37]
Theater Armed Forces: Armed Forces of Buganda: 120 (initial—palace guards); thousands of warriors (peak, final).[38]

Antecedents: Uganda attained its independence from Britain in 1962. At that point, Milton Obote became prime minister, with Mutesa II, the traditional Kabaka or king of the Buganda tribe, as a ceremonial president. The Buganda (in the South) was Uganda's largest, wealthiest, most educated kingdom, and the tribe had been a favored group under British colonial rule. In contrast, Obote had been a herds boy in the Langi tribe. Obote initially tried to develop a government that would encourage cooperation among the disparate tribes in Uganda; yet Obote ultimately established a government that was increasingly autocratic. As opposition to his rule grew, Obote focused on supporting the military. By 1965, he had increased Ugandan military spending by 400 percent. He entered into one agreement by which Israel provided military training and another through which the Soviet Union also supplied training and weaponry. Even so, the military became internally divided along regional lines, with the northern, more senior officers, including Idi Amin, supporting Obote, and the more southern junior officers supporting Brigadier Shaban Opolot. Opolot became involved in several coup attempts against Obote between October 1965 and February 1966. That month, Obote had several of the government ministers involved in the plots arrested, and leadership of the opposition shifted to Mutesa II. Mutesa and Opolot began planning a military coup, including amassing weapons and seeking assistance from a foreign power (probably Britain). Obote finally announced that he was abrogating the constitution, suspending the parliament, and assuming all government powers himself. These measures entailed removing Mutesa II from the presidency and installing his confederate, Idi Amin, as the army commander. In April, Obote announced a new constitution under which he assumed the office of executive president. On May 19, the Buganda parliament rejected Obote's reforms, ordered the government to leave the kingdom (that included the capital Kampala), and prepared to defend the Kabaka's palace.

Narrative: Obote interpreted the demands to be a declaration of secession by Buganda and the beginning of a rebellion. On May 23, 1966, Obote ordered the army under Amin to attack the Kabaka's palace and crush the Buganda resistance. A state of emergency was declared, and security forces were deployed throughout the capital and in other areas of Buganda. Amin and units of the Ugandan army advanced to the palace on Mengo Hill, where a battle against the palace guards ensued. Fighting was intense, and Amin had to call up reinforcements to capture the palace during the twelve-hour battle. Mutesa II was able to escape, though the government troops set fire to the palace, burning a trove of historical documents and cultural treasures. The Kabaka also called upon the people to come to the defense of the government. Thousands of Buganda warriors and armed citizens marched against the government troops. Though fighting was periodically intense, the Baganda were no match for the government's automatic weapons. On May 26, a number of the leaders of the rebellion were arrested. Guerrilla attacks against government installations in the kingdom continued over the next week, as did the killings of Baganda civilians by government troops.

Termination and Outcome: The war ended in a government victory. The Kabaka went into exile in London, where he died three years later. In September 1967, Obote imposed a new constitution that formally abolished all of the kingdoms.

Coding Decisions: Fatality statistics for this war are limited and somewhat contradictory because the government attempted to conceal the numbers of Baganda killed. Brogan reports that 2,000 Baganda were killed, though this figure presumably includes the deaths of noncombatants but not the deaths experienced by government forces. Given the intensity of the initial fighting and the involvement of thousands of warriors, it is likely that the number of combatant deaths reached the threshold of 1,000 for war.

Sources: Adhola (2014); Brogan (1998); Ciment (2007a–h); Edgerton (2002); Gukiina (1972); Meredith (2005); Stapleton (2013); Taylor and Hudson (1972); "Uganda: The Battle of Mengo Hill" (1966); Young (1966).

INTRA-STATE WAR #771

First Chad Rebellion of 1966 to 1971 (aka the FROLINAT Rebellion)

Participants: Chad and France versus FROLINAT Rebels.
Dates: November 1966 to June 16, 1971.
Battle-related Deaths: FROLINAT Rebels: 3,000; Chad: 500; France: 50.[39]
Initiator: FROLINAT Rebels.
Outcome: Chad and France win.
War Type: Civil for local issues.
Total System Member Military Personnel: Armed Forces of Chad: 4,000 (prewar); 5,000 (initial); 8,000 (peak, final).[40] Armed Forces of France: 585,000 (prewar); 580,000 (initial); 595,000 (peak); 565,000 (final).[41]
Theater Armed Forces: FROLINAT Rebels: 5,000 (initial).[42] Armed Forces of France (Pro-government Intervener), participating from August 28, 1968: 2,000 (initial); 3,500 (peak).[43]

Antecedents: Chad, one of the poorest nations in the Sahelian region of Africa (just south of the Sahara Desert), has a population that is split between Christians and animist blacks in the South and Muslims in the North. Chad was a colony of France from 1913 until it gained its independence on August 11, 1960. Strife, either political or military, was endemic in Chad since independence. The first president, François Tombalbaye, was from the South. Opposition to his rule grew as the economic conditions deteriorated. In response to rioting in 1963, Tombalbaye declared a state of emergency and outlawed all political parties except his own, the Chadian Progressive Party (PPT). He gradually removed all the Northerners (Muslims) from the government. The worsening economic situation prompted rioting in November 1965 in which more than 500 people died. Several groups were formed by Chadian Muslims in Sudan and Libya with the goal of exerting control over the opposition groups in Chad. The most important of these was the National Liberation Front of Chad (FROLINAT), which was created in June 1966 in Sudan (though it later moved to Algiers). FROLINAT's goal was to remove Tombalbaye from power, which garnered it support from Libya.

Narrative: In November 1966, FROLINAT launched a rebellion in the North. Its successes in defeating government forces in the Muslim areas within the first two years led Tombalbaye to request French assistance. France agreed to intervene to support the government, and French forces arrived in August 1968. By May 1970, the French military had reversed the Chadian government's earlier loses. Sporadic fighting continued until June 1971, when France then removed its forces.

Termination and Outcome: Chad, aided by France, won the war. The French had encouraged Tombalbaye to liberalize his regime by releasing political prisoners and adding Muslims to his government. These efforts ceased in August 1971, when Tombalbaye claimed that his forces had defeated a coup attempt by Chadians, aided by Libya. Tombalbaye was killed during another coup on April 13, 1975.

Coding Decisions: France became an outside intervener in the war in August 1968. The French operated in conjunction with the Chadian army and do not appear to have taken over the bulk of the fighting, though their participation was instrumental in changing the course of the war.

Sources: Azevedo and Nnadozie (1998); Bercovitch and Fretter (2004); Ciment (2007a–h); Clodfelter (2002); Cutter (2007); Meredith (2005); Nolutshungu (1996).

INTRA-STATE WAR #775
Biafra War of 1967 to 1970

Participants: Nigeria versus Biafrans.
Dates: July 6, 1967, to January 13, 1970.
Battle-related Deaths: Nigeria: [ ]; Biafrans: [ ]; Total Combatant Deaths: 45,000.[44]
Initiator: Nigeria.
Outcome: Nigeria wins.
War Type: Civil for local issues.
Total System Member Military Personnel: Armed Forces of Nigeria: 30,000 (prewar); 35,000 (initial); 200,000 (peak, final).[45]
Theater Armed Forces: Biafrans: 3,000 (initial); 30,000 (peak).[46]

Antecedents: The country of Nigeria was a creation of British colonial policies that united three major tribal groups: the Yoruba (in the West), the Hausa-Fulani (in the North), and the Ibo (or Igbo in the East). Thus, when Nigeria attained its independence in 1960, politics involved the rivalry among these three groups. The East and West tended to be more prosperous, while the Muslim North was relatively poorer. Most of the government officials were Catholic Ibo. In January 1966, a coup d'état brought another Ibo leader, Gen. Johnson Aguiyi-Ironsi, to power, but within months a counter-coup, on July 29, 1966, installed a northern Christian, Lt. Col. Yakuba Gowon, as a military ruler. Many of the Southern military officers were killed, and in September more than 10,000 Ibo living in the North were massacred by the predominantly Muslim Hausa, precipitating a flood of thousands of Ibo into the East. During talks in Ghana in January 1967, both sides agreed to a peaceful settlement of the conflict. However, both sides soon reneged on the agreement. Furthermore, in May 1967, the government announced a redistricting plan that would have reduced the relative influence of the Ibo. Consequently, on May 30, 1967, the Ibos in three eastern states, under the leadership of Col. Chukwuemeka Odumggwu Ojukwu, declared the independence of the Republic of Biafra.

Narrative: Initially Nigeria, led by Gowon, established a quarantine around the breakaway region, but on July 6, 1967, Nigerian troops invaded Biafra in a pincer movement that initially made slow progress. The Biafrans responded by sending three battalions in a counteroffensive toward the capital of Lagos. The Biafrans almost reached the capital before being repulsed. The government then dispatched an additional army into Biafra, and Biafra was soon surrounded. Only four African countries recognized the independence of Biafra, though France, Rhodesia, and South Africa secretly sent it supplies. Meanwhile, the Nigerian government received assistance from both Britain and the Soviet Union, enabling it to increase its army to 70,000 men. A new Nigerian offensive in June 1968 served to further reduce Biafran territory, and the government instituted a blockade to force the Biafrans to surrender. As the size of the Nigerian army continued to grow, the Biafrans began to utilize foreign mercenaries, predominantly French pilots. The Nigerians also benefitted from the participation of British mercenaries. After peace talks failed, the government gradually ground down the Biafran resistance, capturing Amichi, the last Biafran-controlled town, on January 13, 1970.

Termination and Outcome: The outcome was a complete military victory for the Nigerian government.

Coding Decisions: The costs of this war were horrific. It is estimated that between 500,000 and 3 million civilians died, mostly from starvation or disease. Stapleton estimates that total combat casualties range from 90,000 to 120,000.[47] In this instance, the term *casualties* seems to refer to deaths in combat, but it is unclear whether those figures also include civilians killed in armed conflict. Clodfelter reports that a total of 45,000 combatants were killed, and that is the number reported here, though it may well be an underestimate.

Sources: Arnold (2009); Carrère (1972); Ciment (2007a–h); Clendenen (1972); Clodfelter (2002); Cutter (2007); Edgerton (2002); Meredith (2005); Phillips and Axelrod (2005); Stapleton (2013); Taylor and Hudson (1972).

INTRA-STATE WAR #788
Eritrean Split of 1972 to 1974

Participants: Eritrean Liberation Front (ELF) versus Popular Liberation Forces (PLF).
Dates: February 1972 to October 13, 1974.
Battle-related Deaths: ELF: [ ]; PLF: [ ]; Total Combatant Deaths: 3,000.[48]
Initiator: ELF.
Outcome: Stalemate.
War Type: Intercommunal.
Theater Armed Forces: ELF: 10,000 (initial);[49] PLF: [ ].

Antecedents: At the end of World War II (Inter-state war #139), Italy was stripped of its colonial possessions in the Horn of Africa, including Eritrea. In 1952, Ethiopia accepted control of Eritrea from Great Britain, and Eritrea became a province of Ethiopia. In 1962 the Eritrean parliament formally voted in favor of union with Ethiopia. However there were others who opposed union and sought Eritrean independence. In 1961, the Eritrean Liberation Front (ELF) began a low-level guerrilla war against the Ethiopian government. In 1970, sectors of the ELF membership split from the group and created a rival organization, the Popular Liberation Forces (PLF), which included the PLF-Dankalia and PFL-Ala. Though both the ELF and the PLF shared a Marxist orientation and the goal of independence, the ELF tended to consist of well-educated Muslims, while the more left-wing PLF drew its membership from Christians in the highlands. The two organizations soon began fighting skirmishes against each other as the ELF tried to reassert its control, and on December 16, 1970, Ethiopia declared a state of emergency in Eritrea.

Narrative: The conflict reached war level in 1972 as fighting spread along the Red Sea coast. The ELF and the PLF stopped their infighting as the war with Ethiopia approached.

Termination and Outcome: Villagers had appealed to the ELF and PLF to stop their fighting and concentrate on the effort to gain independence from Ethiopia. The war against Ethiopia, in which both the ELF and the PLF would participate, began in 1975 (Intra-state War #798: the Eritrean War of 1975 to 1978). In the midst of that war, three rebel groups (the PLF-Dankalia, the PFL-Ala, and the Obel group) formally united to form the Eritrean People's Liberation Front (EPLF) in January 1977. The EPLF soon became the primary Eritrean revolutionary organization.

Coding Decisions: The war is coded as ending in a stalemate, though some scholars have referred to it as an EPFL victory in that the ELF was unsuccessful in achieving its goal of eliminating its rival. Armed conflict between the ELF and the EPLF would emerge in 1980 and 1981, at which time the EPLF would defeat the ELF.

Sources: Brogan (1998); Clodfelter (2002); Lefebvre (1996).

INTRA-STATE WAR #789
First Burundi War of 1972

Participants: Burundi versus Hutu.
Dates: April 29, 1972, to May 25, 1972.
Battle-related Deaths: Hutu (Rebels, Soldiers, and Leaders): 1,500; Burundi: [ ].[50]
Initiator: Hutu.
Outcome: Burundi wins.
War Type: Civil for central control.
Total System Member Military Personnel: Armed Forces of Burundi: 3,000 (prewar, initial, peak, final).[51]
Theater Armed Forces: Hutu Rebels: 3,000 (initial, peak).[52]

Antecedents: Like Rwanda to the North, Burundi became independent in 1962 when the Belgian Trusteeship of Ruanda–Urundi was divided. Also as in Rwanda, postindependence politics was dominated by the Tutsi–Hutu rivalry. In contrast, however, a Tutsi kingdom had taken over in Burundi from the departing Belgians, while a republic under Hutu control had been created in Rwanda. Massacres of the Tutsi by the Hutu in Rwanda prompted many of the Tutsi to flee into Burundi, where two refugee camps were established. War broke out in 1963 and 1964 entailing raids by the Tutsi *inyenzi* rebels from Burundi, Congo, and Uganda into Rwanda in an attempt to overthrow the government (Intra-state War #760).

The example of Rwanda had an impact within Burundi, inspiring the Hutu who captured most of the parliamentary seats in Burundi's first election in May 1965. Despite their victory, the Tutsi king failed to appoint a Hutu prime minister, leading to a coup attempt in October 1965 that forced the king to flee the country. Tutsi army units then arrested and killed many of the leading Hutu politicians. Another coup in 1966 brought the army to power. Once in office (on November 28, 1966), Tutsi officer Capt. Michel Micombero established a republic with himself as president and began to remove the Hutus from the government. These developments further alienated many of the Hutu, including three university students affiliated with the militant *Parti du Peuple* (PP).

Narrative: On April 29, 1972, attacks instigated by the PP students against government installations and three towns in the South were launched by the Hutu, who were joined by a few rebels from Tanzania. As they advanced, some of the rebels were strafed by government aircraft. After seizing control of two local armories, the rebels killed all of the local military and civilian authorities. Some of the insurgents engaged in brutal attacks against Tutsi civilians. The rebels then advanced to Vyanda, where they proclaimed a *République de Martyazo.* Within ten days, government troops advanced to Vyanda, dispersing the rebel republic. The Tutsi government troops also attacked the Hutu soldiers in their midst, killing 150 to 500 of them.

Termination and Outcome: The civil war ended as a government victory by May 25. On May 30, 1972, the government ordered the army to conduct a coordinated slaughter of Hutu civilians. Approximately 150,000 to 200,000 people (including Christians) were killed.[53] Conflict between the Hutu and Tutsi continued periodically for the next twenty years, when a second civil war broke out in 1993 (Intra-state War #883).

Coding Decisions: The difficulty in coding this war comes from trying to disentangle the elements of the civil war between the leftist Hutu rebels and the Burundi government from the more widespread attacks against civilians by both sides. Yet, it is clear that an attempt to overthrow the central government was the precipitant of the chain of violence.

Sources: Bentley and Southall (2005); Carrêre (1972); Ciment (2007a–h); Clodfelter (2002); Cutter (2007); Edgerton (2002); Eggers (1997); Lemarchand (1975, 1994, 2004); Marchak (2003); Melady (1974); Meredith (2005); Ndarubagiye (1996); Phillips and Axelrod (2005); Rwantabagu (2001); Scherrer (2002).

INTRA-STATE WAR #791
Rhodesia War of 1972 to 1979

Participants: Rhodesia versus Patriotic Front.
Dates: December 28, 1972, to December 28, 1979.
Battle-related Deaths: Patriotic Front: 10,000; Rhodesia: 950.[54]
Initiator: Patriotic Front.
Outcome: Patriotic Front wins.
War Type: Civil for central control.
Total System Member Military Personnel: Armed Forces of Rhodesia: 11,000 (prewar); initial); 38,000 (peak, final).[55]

Theater Armed Forces: Armed Forces of Rhodesia: 58,700 (peak, including police and reserves).[56] Foreign Volunteers (Pro-government Interveners): 1,500 (peak).[57] Armed Forces of the Patriotic Front (ZIPRA and ZANLA): 20,000 (peak).[58]

Antecedents: In November 1965, the white-controlled Rhodesian Front declared unilateral independence from Britain to maintain white domination of what had been the British colony of Southern Rhodesia. The new government under the leadership of Prime Minister Ian Smith established a system whereby Rhodesia's 240,000 whites ruled over its 4 million blacks. The blacks already had begun to create resistance organizations: the more moderate group was the Zimbabwean African People's Union (ZAPU), led by Joshua Nkomo; while the Zimbabwean African National Union (ZANU), led by Ndabaningi Sithole, favored a more radical approach and tactics. Opposition efforts had begun in the early 1960s, and as the groups began to realize that nonviolent protest was going to be insufficient, they formed military wings: ZAPU created the Zimbabwe People's Revolutionary Army (ZIPRA), and ZANU created the Zimbabwe African National Liberation Army (ZANLA). The military organizations were based in Zambia, where they received assistance from Eastern bloc countries, while Rhodesia received aid from South Africa, Mozambique, and covertly from the Western bloc countries. Advance contingents of the rebel armies entered Rhodesia in 1967 and 1968, but they generally were detected by Rhodesia's security forces and killed or captured. Most of the leaders of both rebel organizations were arrested and spent the next ten years imprisoned. In the 1970s, the two rebel groups began to diverge with ZAPU–ZIPRA adopting a Soviet-Leninist revolutionary strategy, while ZANU–ZANLA focused more on a Chinese model of mobilizing the peasants.

Narrative: The war began in 1972, after ZANLA moved its base of operations to Mozambique, where it collaborated with FRELIMO (which had been fighting against the Portuguese) and where the geography allowed them to funnel troops into eastern Rhodesia more easily. ZIPRA remained in Zambia, where the terrain made raids into Rhodesia more difficult. During the next few years, the rebels conducted relatively limited and unsuccessful raids into Rhodesia. The intensity of the war increased after 1975, after the Portuguese abandoned Mozambique, and FRELIMO took control of the country (see Extra-state War #471). ZANLA was then able to expand its operations, and Rhodesia increasingly faced rebel attacks on two fronts. The Rhodesian military was successful in most direct engagements but gradually lost control of the countryside. Robert Mugabe was released from prison and took control of ZANU, which became linked to ZAPU in the Popular Front. At this point, Rhodesia prime minister Smith and the rebels all faced international pressure to reach a negotiated settlement to the war. Smith compromised by creating a moderate black government under Bishop Abel Muzorewa, but because the rebels were not included, the fighting continued.

Termination and Outcome: The war ended as a victory for the Patriotic Front with the creation of black rule in Rhodesia. In 1980, Robert Mugabe was elected prime minister in what had become Zimbabwe.

Coding Decisions: Self-explanatory from cited sources.

Sources: Clodfelter (2002); Edgerton (2002); Meredith (2005); *New York Times* (1972–1980); Phillips and Axelrod (2005); Preston (2004); Stapleton (2013).

INTRA-STATE WAR #798
Eritrean War of 1975 to 1978

Participants: Ethiopia and Cuba versus Eritrean People's Liberation Front (PLF/EPLF) and Eritrean Liberation Front (ELF).
Dates: January 31, 1975, to December 31, 1978.
Battle-related Deaths: EPLF and ELF: 6,000; Ethiopia: 7,100; Cuba: [ ]. (See Coding Decisions.)
Initiator: ELF and EPLF.
Outcome: Ethiopia and Cuba win.
War Type: Civil for local issues.
Total System Member Military Personnel: Armed Forces of Ethiopia: 45,000 (prewar); 50,000 (initial); 233,000 (peak, final).[59] Armed Forces of Cuba: 140,000 (prewar); 120,000 (initial); 210,000 (peak, final).[60]
Theater Armed Forces: Armed Forces of Ethiopia: 25,000 (initial); 120,000 (peak, final).[61]

Ethiopian Militia, participating in late 1976: 100,000.[62] Armed Forces of Cuba (Pro-government Intervener), participating from May 1977: 2,000 (initial, peak). Armed Forces of the ELF (including ELF–Popular Liberation Front): 24,000 (initial).[63] Armed Forces of the PLF (the EPFL after January 1977): 12,000 (initial); 15,000 (final).[64]

Antecedents: Eritrea and Ethiopia had been colonial possessions of Italy. After World War II (Inter-state War #139), the UN decided to create a federation between the two, which lasted until Eritrea voted to become part of Ethiopia in 1962. Resistance to Ethiopian rule led to the development of the two rival Eritrean rebel groups, the ELF and PLF, which went to war against each other in 1972 (Intra-state War #788). The war ended as a stalemate as villagers appealed to the two groups to stop fighting and fight for independence from Ethiopia instead.

In 1974, Emperor Haile Selassie was overthrown by a Marxist military coup by the Dergue (Derg or Dirgue) led by Col. Haile Mariam Mengistu. The Dergue was a group of about 120 lower-ranking military personnel from the army, air force, navy, imperial guards, territorial army, and the police, which was initially formed to deal with military grievances and corruption in the military. The Dergue gathered power as that of the central government and Emperor Haile Selassie declined, and the Dergue finally seized power on September 12, 1974. The Dergue initially appointed Lt. Gen. Aman Andom (an Eritrean) as the acting head of state. Subsequent disagreements within the Dergue led the Dergue to remove him from power and execute him on November 23, 1974 (along with some of his supporters and former imperial officials). Brigadier Gen. Tafari Benti became the new head of state, with Haile Mariam Mengistu and Atnafu Abate as the vice chairs. The new regime was confronted with opposition from the nobility, landowners, Afar tribesmen, the Tigray People's Liberation Front, the Oromo Liberation Front, and the Western Somali Liberation Front. The Eritreans decided to take advantage of Ethiopia's internal disorder to launch a struggle for independence.

Narrative: In early 1975, the Eritrean rebels from the ELF and PLF launched a massive offensive against the government. The Ethiopian government responded immediately, with a bombing campaign that drove the rebels from Eritrea's capital, Asmara. However, the rebels were successful in gaining control of 85 percent of Eritrea, with the government controlling only Asmara and the ports of Massawa and Assab. In an attempt to augment its armed forces, Ethiopia recruited a peasant army of 100,000 men that it sent against the Eritreans. In May 1976, the poorly armed peasants were routed easily at the Eritrean border.

Meanwhile, in July 1976, the secessionists in Ogaden also launched a bid for independence (Intra-state War #805: the Second Ogaden War phase 1 of 1976 to 1977). This war was transformed in 1977 into the Second Ogaden War phase 2 (Inter-state War #187) as Somalia invaded and took over the bulk of the fighting in pursuit of its goal to unite the Somali people of Ogaden within Somalia. Somalia occupied most of the Ogaden and advanced into Ethiopia. The Ethiopian government was saved only by the intervention of Cuban troops and the arrival weapons from the Soviet Union. Ethiopia and Cuba defeated Somalia on March 9, 1978, though the civil war continued against the Ogaden (Intra-state War #808).

While the Ethiopian army was engaged in the Ogaden, the ELF and EPFL launched a major offensive, capturing the centrally located city of Keren in heavy fighting on July 9, 1977. The rebels moved southward, besieging Asmara and the ports of Assab and Massawa. After March 9, 1978, the situation changed radically as the war with Somalia ended (Inter-state War #197), and the Ethiopian troops with the assistance of Cuba were able to refocus on Eritrea. In early May, the Ethiopian-Cuban army launched a three-pronged offensive against the Eritreans. The eight-month campaign pitted 120,000 Ethiopians and 2,000 Cubans against 40,000 rebels. The rebels were forced to retreat to their stronghold in the mountains at Nakfa.

Termination and Outcome: The war ended in a victory for the Ethiopian-Cuban forces. The civilian fatalities were also significant, with estimates of 250,000 killed during this war.[65] The ELF and the EPLF would fight against each other in 1981, leading to the defeat and demise of the ELF. The Eritreans would go to war again against Ethiopia in 1982 (Intra-state War #827) in conjunction with the Tigrean independence movement.

Coding Decisions: In November 1977, the Soviet Union mounted an airlift and sealift operation to bring tanks, fighter aircraft, artillery, and hundreds of military advisors into Ethiopia.[66] Though the impact of this effort was significant, an insufficient number of Soviet troops were involved in armed combat for the Soviet Union to be considered a war participant.

There is limited information about the fatalities in this war. Combining the few figures provided in Clodfelter, and using the standard ratio within casualties of 3 wounded to 1 killed, produces 7,100 combatant deaths for the government and 6,000 for the rebels. We are reporting those here, in spite of the fact that they are undoubtedly underestimates due to the amount of missing data. Civil deaths were also high; Brogan cites a figure from Colin Legum that 250,000 Ethiopians died in fighting between 1974 and 1983.[67]

Sources: Brogan (1998); Clodfelter (2002); Cordesman (1993a, b); *Keesing's Record of World Events* (1974–1980); Lefebvre (1996); Meredith (2005); Skutsch (2007a, b); Tareke (2002).

INTRA-STATE WAR #804
Angolan Control War of 1976 to 1991

Participants: Angola and Cuba versus Union for the Total Independence of Angola (UNITA) and South Africa.
Dates: February 13, 1976, to May 15, 1991.
Battle-related Deaths: Angola: [ ]; UNITA: [ ]; Cuba: [ ]; South Africa: [ ].
Initiator: UNITA.
Outcome: Compromise.
War Type: Civil for central control.
Total System Member Military Personnel: Armed Forces of Angola: 30,000 (prewar); 35,000 (initial); 150,000 (peak, final).[68] Armed Forces of Cuba: 120,000 (prewar); 125,000 (initial); 297,000 (peak, final).[69] Armed Forces of South Africa: 50,000 (prewar); 59,000 (initial); 102,000 (peak); 80,000 (final).
Theater Armed Forces: Armed Forces of UNITA: 65,000 (peak). Armed Forces of Cuba (Pro-government Intervener), participating to August 5, 1988: 4,000 (initial); 100,000 (peak); 40,000 (final).[70] Armed Forces of South Africa (Pro-rebel Intervener), participating to August 5, 1988: 5,000 (initial); 10,000 (peak).[71]

Antecedents: Angola had been a Portuguese colony for almost 400 years, from 1575. After World War II (Inter-state War #139), Portugal had resisted giving up its colonial empire and was the last major European power with colonies in Africa. In 1961, Angola launched a war against Portugal seeking its independence (Extra-state War #469: the Angola–Portuguese War of 1961 to 1974). The war was launched by two rebel groups: the Popular Movement for the Liberation of Angola (MPLA) and the National Front for the Liberation of Angola (FNLA). A third rebel group, the Union for the Total Independence of Angola (UNITA), joined the war in 1966. The war against Portugal was hampered by the infighting among these groups. In 1974, a group of army officers overthrew the Portuguese government and then appealed to the Angolan groups to cease hostilities. The Portuguese entered signed accords with the rebels in October 1974, with the last one signed on October 14, 1975. This marked the end of the extra-state war, which was then transformed into a non-state war (War #1581 from October 17, 1974, to October 22, 1975) with cold war overtones as the fighting continued, with FLNA and UNITA (aided by the United States and South Africa) fighting against MPLA (which was aided by Cuba and the Soviet Union). By September 1975, the MPLA was winning, and a turning point occurred on October 23, when South Africa and Cuba entered the war and took over the bulk of the fighting, thereby transforming the war into an inter-state war (War #186: the War over Angola of 1975 to 1976). Neither side was immediately victorious. Consequently, when Angola's independence day arrived on November 11, 1975, there were declarations of two separate governments: the People's Republic of Angola, formed by the MPLA in Luanda (on the northwest coast), and the Social Democratic Republic of Angola, formed by FNLA and UNITA in the centrally located Huambo. The MPLA government was recognized as the new government of Angola. As Angola was now a member of the interstate system, it entered the inter-state war on the side of Cuba. The Angolan and Cuban troops went on the offensive in January and February 1976, capturing most of the provincial capitals, forcing UNITA to retreat to the south, and driving the South African troops out of the country. The departure of South Africa as a war participant thus ended the inter-state war on February 12, 1976. The Angolan government declared the end of the Second Liberation War, and a few Cuban troops began leaving the country. The fighting nonetheless continued. Because Angola was now strong enough to do the bulk of the fighting, the war thus became the civil war of Angola versus the UNITA and FNLA rebels.

Narrative: The war (beginning on February 13, 1976) was internationalized immediately as the Cuban troops continued to assist the government in combatting guerrilla attacks by UNITA. South Africa also became reengaged in conflict with Angola as a by-product of its war in Namibia (Extra-state War #473: the Namibian War of 1975 to 1988). Namibia was a colony of South Africa, and the war against South African control had been launched in 1975 by the Southwest African People's Organization (SWAPO). Angola provided diplomatic and military support to SWAPO. As northern Namibia became a war zone, housing 15,000 to 45,000 South African troops, in early February1976, South Africa carved out an eighty-five-mile-wide buffer zone in Angola along the Namibia border, patrolled by 4,000 to 5,000 South African troops, into which it would launch incursions against SWAPO troops. On February 23, the weakened FNLA announced that it would forego large military offensives in favor of guerrilla warfare, though several thousand of its troops were incorporated into the South African Defence Force (SADF), which launched attacks into Angola against SWAPO and Angolans. South Africa also used the region as a means of funneling assistance to UNITA, whose fighting capacity was increased significantly in 1976 and 1977. Thereafter, the war degenerated into a lengthy guerrilla conflict, with Jonas Savimbi, the UNITA leader, continuing the war in the South.

The level of hostilities increased in 1978. On May 4, South Africa launched a ground and air attack against SWAPO forces in Angola. Operation Reindeer targeted the Cassinga camp (in Angola, 250 kilometers north of the Namibian border), with South Africa claiming that it was both a refugee camp and a SWAPO military base. More than 1,200 people were killed, including 60 Cuban military advisers. In September 1978, South African president P. W. Botha announced his total strategy that would include military operations in both Namibia and in Angola to destabilize the Angolan regime. South Africa forces launched twelve major operations into Angola over the next ten years. UNITA forces would follow the South African forces, occupying the "liberated" territory and defending it against the Angolan troops. After the election of Ronald Reagan as US president, American material aid to UNITA increased markedly. South Africa also increased its activities in support of UNITA, conducting 1,000 bombing missions in 1981. South Africa also sent a 5,000-strong force into the province of Cunene, though Angolan and Cuban forces soon stopped its advance. In 1983, South African forces again invaded the Cassinga camp. Operation Askari was intended to seize the camp and from there to advance on Luanda and overthrow the government. However, the Soviet Union was able to provide Angola with satellite data about the mission, forcing South Africa to reduce the scale of the invasion. UNITA was continuously active, launching strikes in all of Angola's provinces.

In 1984, the Reagan administration urged the parties in the war to engage in peace talks in Lusaka, Zambia. Though the parties signed the cease-fire accord, it was not honored, and the war continued, with both sides adopting increasingly brutal practices. In 1987 and 1988, major battles were conducted at Mavinga and Cuito Cuanavale. Angola attempted to defeat UNITA by launching a major offensive against UNITA-controlled Mavinga (north of its headquarters at Jamba) on September 10, 1987. The Angolan army had received sophisticated weapons from the Soviet Union and was accompanied by 45,000 to 50,000 Cuban troops. UNITA, with weapons from the United States and aided by South Africa, was able to repel the Angolan advance in fighting that lasted until October 2. The Angolan-Cuban army retreated to Cuito Cuanavale, where it established defensive positions. The UNITA–South African forces advanced but were unable to capture the government positions and besieged the town instead. Subsequent UNITA–South African attacks from January through March 1988 also failed. South Africa's losses persuaded it to enter negotiations with Angola in 1988, leading to an August 1988 cease-fire agreement involving pledges that foreign forces would withdraw. The New York Accord, signed by Angola, Cuba, and South Africa on December 22, 1988, included commitments by Cuba to withdraw its troops from Angola and for South Africa to withdraw from Namibia (though a small number of Cuban troops remained till 1991).

Though Angola had hoped that the withdrawal of South Africa would lead to the collapse of UNITA, in 1989 and 1990, the United States increased its assistance to UNITA substantially.

Fighting between Angola and UNITA continued, despite several mediation attempts. A cease-fire finally was negotiated in talks held in Portugal, and fighting ended on May 15, 1991.

Termination and Outcome: Finally, on May 31, 1991, UNITA and the MPLA-led government negotiated a power-sharing arrangement. Savimbi lost the first multiparty election in 1992, and UNITA returned to armed conflict (Intra-state War #880).

Coding Decisions: Many scholars describe the Angolan conflict from 1975 to 1991 as one war, however COW's coding of wars based upon which parties are doing the bulk of the fighting leads to the coding of three separate wars: a non-state war, an inter-state war, and this intra-state war.

The battle-deaths for this war are unknown. Estimates of the total number of Angolan fatalities range from 60,000 to 500,000. James reports estimates of Cuban deaths ranging from 2,100 to 15,000.

Sources: Bercovitch and Fretter (2004); Ciment (2007a–h); Clodfelter (2002); Human Rights Watch (1994a, b, c); James (2011); *Keesing's Record of World Events* (1975–1980); Malaquias (2007); Phillips and Axelrod (2005); Stapleton (2003); Valdez (1979); Wallace (2011).

INTRA-STATE WAR #805

Second Ogaden War phase 1 of 1976 to 1977

Participants: Ethiopia versus Western Somali Liberation Front (WSLF) and Somalia.
Dates: July 1, 1976, to July 22, 1977.
Battle-related Deaths: WSLF: [ ]; Ethiopia: [ ]; Somalia: 300.
Initiator: WSLF.
Outcome: Transformed into Inter-state War #189.
War Type: Civil for local issues.
Total System Member Military Personnel: Armed Forces of Ethiopia: 50,000 (prewar); 65,000 (initial); 225,000 (peak, final).[72] Armed Forces of Somalia: 30,000 (prewar); 31,000 (initial); 53,000 (peak, final).[73]
Theater Armed Forces: Armed Forces of WSLF: 3,000 (initial, peak).[74] Armed Forces of Somalia: 3,000 (initial, peak); 2,700 (final).[75]

Antecedents: In 1963, a group of Somalis, led by Muktel Dahir, created the Ogaden Liberation Front (OLF) and its related Ogaden Liberation Army (OLA) in preparation for seeking Ogaden's independence from Ethiopia. The OLF received assistance from Somalia as Somalia had begun efforts to liberate the Somalis living in Ethiopia to bring them into Somalia. In the First Ogaden War (Intra-state War #757, June 1963 to March 1964), the OLA and Somali troops fought against the Ethiopian army, commanded by Emperor Haile Selassie. The Organization of African Unity (OAU) mediated an end to the war as both Ethiopia and Somalia agreed to pull back their troops. The end of the war did not resolve Ogaden's desire for independence. In 1969, Major Gen. Mohammed Siad Barre came to power in Somalia as the result of a military coup. He and the Supreme Revolutionary Council (SRC) established the socialist Somali Democratic Republic that continued the emphasis on Somali nationalism and desire to incorporate Somali-inhabited areas into Somalia. In 1973, President Siad Barre met Yusuf Dheere, a young Somali. Siad Barre provided limited support to Dheere to create the Western Somali Liberation Front (WSLF) in Ogaden, and Dheere immediately recruited 3,000 soldiers.

Meanwhile, Ethiopian emperor Haile Selassie was overthrown by a Marxist military coup by the Dergue (Derg or Dirgue) led by Col. Haile Mariam Mengistu on September 12, 1974. Attempting to take advantage of dissention within the government, Ethiopia's province of Eritrea launched its bid for independence, which led to war in 1975 (Intra-state War #798: the Eritrean War of 1975 to 1978). The WSLF also decided to take advantage of Ethiopia's focus elsewhere and (with the encouragement of Somalia) launch a revolt against Ethiopia. The second Ogaden war, which started in July 1976, had three distinct phases, which basically consisted of two periods of intra-state war that bracket an inter-state war.

Narrative: In early 1976, President Siad Barre concluded an alliance with the Ogaden clan that promised Somalian support for any Ogaden independence moves. Somalia provided training and weapons to the WSLF, and the WSLF leadership remained in Mogadishu. The WSLF launched its war for independence in July 1976 with attacks on Ethiopian government installations in Ogaden. Though the WSLF initially made some military gains, when its advance stalled, Somalia decided to provide more direct support and sent 3,000 of its troops (disguised as guerrillas) into the Ogaden. The augmented rebel army soon had control over 60 percent of the Ogaden. However, a rebel attack on an Ethiopian garrison at Gode in May 1977 was repulsed. The Somali forces suffered 300 combat deaths, which persuaded Somalia that a full-scale invasion was necessary.

Termination and Outcome: As Somalia invaded and took over the bulk of the fighting on July 23, 1977, this civil war was ended, and the conflict was transformed into an inter-state war (#187).

Coding Decisions: The conflict would revert to a civil war again in 1978 (Intra-state War #808).

Sources: Africa's Watch (1991); Cordesman (1993a, b); Cutter (2007); *Keesing's Record of World Events* (1975–1980); Meredith (2005); Nelson and Kaplan (1981); Stapleton (2013).

INTRA-STATE WAR #806.8
Chad–FAP War of 1977 to 1978

Participants: Chad and France versus People's Armed Forces (FAP) and Libya.
Dates: June 22, 1977, to June 1978.
Battle-related Deaths: Chad: 2,000; France: [ ]; FAP: 2,000; Libya: [ ].[76] (See Coding Decisions.)
Initiator: FAP.
Outcome: Chad wins.
War Type: Civil for central control.
Total System Member Military Personnel: Armed Forces of Chad: 11,000 (prewar); 9,000 (initial, peak); 5,000 (final).[77] Armed Forces of France: 585,000 (prewar); 584,000 (initial, peak); 581,000 (final).[78] Armed Forces of Libya: 25,000 (prewar); 30,000 (initial); 50,000 (peak, final).[79]
Theater Armed Forces: Armed Forces of FAP: 2,500.[80] Armed Forces of France (Pro-government Intervener): 2,000 (initial); 2,500 (peak, final).[81] Armed Forces of Libya (Pro-rebel Intervener), participating from January 29, 1978: 4,000 (peak, final).

Antecedents: The population of Chad is divided into the Muslims in the North and the Christians and animist blacks in the South. After achieving independence from France, Chad's first president was a Southerner, François Tombalbaye. Opposition to his rule grew among the Muslims, who in 1966 created the National Liberation Front of Chad (FROLINAT) with the goal of removing Tombalbaye from power. In November 1966, FROLINAT launched a rebellion in the northern part of the country (Intra-state War #771). France intervened to support the government, and Chad aided by France won the war in 1971. In neighboring Libya, Col. Muammar al-Gadhafi had come to power in a coup in 1969. In 1971, Tombalbaye accused Libya and Egypt of supporting a coup attempt against him and broke diplomatic ties. Gadhafi responded by recognizing FROLINAT as the legitimate government of Chad.

The acrimonious relations were ended the next year as Chad and Libya signed a treaty of friendship. Gadhafi withdrew his support from FROLINAT, forcing it to move its headquarters from Libya to Algeria. Supposedly, Tombalbaye signed a secret agreement with Gadhafi, ceding to Libya the Aouzou strip (a 100-kilometer-wide strip of land in Chad along the Libyan border) in exchange for financial compensations. Libyan troops occupied the Aouzou in 1973. Partly in response to the Aouzou deal, Tombalbaye was removed from office and killed in 1975. The new Chadian head of state was Gen. Félix Malloum, who expelled the French troops. Gadhafi resumed his opposition to the Chadian government and his support of FROLINAT. The issue of ties with Libya split FROLINAT into two factions in 1976: the minority anti-Libya became the Armed Forces of the North (FAN) led by Hissène Habré; the majority became the People's Armed Forces (FAP), under the leadership of Goukouni Oueddei (Gukuni Wedei). In 1977, Libya began supplying weapons to the FAP.

Narrative: On June 22, 1977, the FAP attacked the Chadian Armed Forces (FAT) in Northwest Chad and besieged Bardaï. Government forces retreated, and Bardaï surrendered on July 4. The rebel advance on Ounianga was repelled on June 20 by government forces aided by France. As President Malloum began to realize the weakness of his military situation, he formed an alliance with Habré's FAN in September 1977 (formalized in the Khartoum Agreements of September 1977 and January 1978). Gadhafi saw the alliance as threatening his influence in Chad, and thus he decided to send Libyan forces to aid Goukouni's FAP. A joint offensive was launched against government troops in northern Chad on January 29, 1978; the rebels seized control of most of the BET Prefecture, which constituted almost half of Chad's territory. A force of 2,500 rebels (aided by 4,000 Libyans) captured the BET capital of Faya-Largeau from 5,000 government troops on February 18. International pressure forced Chad and the rebels to sign (on March 27, 1978) the Benghazi accord, which included a cease-fire and commitment for French forces to leave Chad.

Within days, Goukouni's forces began a new offensive toward N'Djamena, Chad's capital. Malloum sought the return of French troops, and in April 2,500 French troops arrived to secure the capital. The rebel advance was stopped at the town of Ati, and the government's garrison of 1,500 soldiers was attacked on May 19. The arrival of Chadian and French reinforcements, including French planes, ensured the Chadian victories on May 21 and in June.

Termination and Outcome: The war ended as a government victory. Malloum appointed Habré as prime minister on August 29, 1978. The appointment was a mistake in that the two leaders had divergent agendas. The failure of the rebel offensive also led to dissension within FROLINAT and the rebel expulsion of Libyan forces from Chad. Meanwhile, the integration of FAN and the Chad national army (FAT) was not accomplished. Another war, this time pitting FAN against the Chadian government, would break out within two years (Intra-state War #820: 1980 to 1984).

Coding Decisions: France is coded as an intervener for the total period of the war. Though there was a period of less than a month (from March 27 to early April 1978) when French forces agreed to leave Chad, a change of status of that short a period is not coded as a break in participation. Information on the fatalities suffered in this war is limited. Azevedo and Nnadozie mention 2,000 total fatalities suffered by Chad during the war, and Stapleton mentions FAP fatalities of 2,000 in just one battle. Based upon these two figures, the conflict meets the war threshold. The FAP fatalities are reported previously, with the realization that the figure is a minimum for war.

Sources: Azevedo and Nnadozie (1998); Bercovitch and Fretter (2004); Ciment (2007a–h); Clodfelter (2002); Mays (2003); Meredith (2005); Nolutshungu (1996); Stapleton (2013).

INTRA-STATE WAR #808
Second Ogaden War Phase 3 of 1978 to 1980

Participants: Ethiopia and Cuba versus Ogaden Independence Movement (WSLF, SALF, OLF, IFLOSLF, and Echat) and Somalia.
Dates: March 10, 1978, to December 3, 1980.
Battle-related Deaths: Ogaden Independence Movement: 20,000; Ethiopia: 2,000; Cuba: [ ].[82]
Initiator: Ogaden independence movement.
Outcome: Ethiopia and Cuba win.
War Type: Civil for local issues.
Total System Member Military Personnel: Armed Forces of Ethiopia: 225,000 (prewar); 233,000 (initial); 250,000 (peak, final).[83] Armed Forces of Cuba: 200,000 (prewar); 210,000 (initial); 220,000 (peak, final).[84] Armed Forces of Somalia: 53,000 (prewar), 54,000 (initial, peak, final).
Theater Armed Forces: Armed Forces of Ethiopia (plus Air Force and Peasant Militia): 60,000 (peak).[85] Armed Forces of the Ogaden Independence Movement, a rebel aggregate consisting of:

Western Somali Liberation Front (WSLF): 12,000 (initial);[86]
Somali Abo Liberation Front (SALF): 6,000 (initial);[87]
Oromo Liberation Front (OLF): 6,000 (initial);[88]
Islamic Front for the Liberation of Oromia (IFLO): 3,000 (initial);[89]
Sidama Liberation Front (SLF) (participated until March 1979): 500 (initial);[90]
Ethiopian Oppressed Peoples' Struggle (Echat), participating until March 1979: 500 (initial).[91]
Armed Forces of Cuba (Pro-government Intervener): [ ]. Armed Forces of Somalia (Pro-rebel intervener), participating from May 1980: [ ].

Antecedents: The overall conflict over the Ogaden between 1976 and 1980 is coded into three distinct phases and wars. It began as the Second Ogaden War phase 1, #805, a civil war between Ethiopia and the Ogaden WSLF rebels (July 1, 1976, to July 22, 1977). The war was then transformed into an inter-state war (#187) between Ethiopia and Cuba against Somalia by the invasion of Somali troops (July 23, 1977, to March 9, 1978). Finally, the inter-state war was transformed into this civil war by the withdrawal of Somalia from the conflict in March 1978, while Ethiopia and the WSLF continued fighting. In this war, the scope of the conflict was widened, moving into four provinces (Hararghe, Bale, Sidamo, and Arussi) a region collectively described as Western Somalia (which is larger than the area referred to as the Ogaden). Conflict also involved troops from a wider array of rebel groups. In particular, the population of Bale is 75 percent Oromo people, and so the participating rebel groups represented both the Somali and Oromo people. At this point there were six independent organizations operating in the region, often with overlapping territories and sometimes with competing goals. Of these, the Western Somali Liberation Front (WSLF) was the largest and oldest. The largest of the Oromo groups was the Oromo Liberation Front, founded in 1973. The other rebel groups were: Somali Abo Liberation Front (SALF), Islamic Front for the Liberation of Oromia (IFLO), Sidama Liberation Front (SLF), and Ethiopian Oppressed Peoples' Struggle (Echat).

Narrative: In 1978, Ethiopia still was engaged in the war against Eritrea (Intra-state War #798), thus the Ogaden independence movement decided to take advantage of Ethiopia's lack of interest to continue to advance its cause despite the withdrawal of Somalia's troops. The rebel armies carried on with attacks against Ethiopian and Cuban troops and engaged in fierce battles. For its part, Ethiopia, which had been significantly strengthened during the war with Somalia by an infusion of military hardware from the Soviet Union, decided to focus upon defeating the rebellion in Eritrea first before devoting too many resources to the war in Ogaden. Thus over the next six months, the rebels regained control over most of the Ogaden, with the WSLF dominant in the lowlands and the OLF controlling the highlands. The war in Eritrea ended in December 1978 as the rebels were forced to retreat to their stronghold at Nakfa.

Starting in February 1979, the Ethiopian government shifted its focus back to the Ogaden and began a series of offensives in the four provinces: the SLF and Echat soon were defeated. The larger rebel groups proved to be more difficult to defeat because of their ties to the communities into which they could retreat. Thus the government began a program of villagisation, whereby peasants were relocated into settlements controlled by the government. This maneuver (applied especially in Bale, where 586,000 villagers had been relocated by the end of 1979)[92] gradually forced the rebel groups to concentrate in province of Hararghe. The Ethiopian government also was involved in attempts to overthrow the government on Somalia. In May and June 1980, Ethiopia launched five attacks against the rebels, who then retaliated with counterstrikes by a joint WSLF–Somalia army, as Somalia entered the war. Finally, Ethiopia launched a major offensive, Operation Lash, on August 28, 1980. Approximately 60,000 Ethiopian troops, aided by the air force, thousands of the peasant militia, and Cuban-mechanized brigades and troops advanced against the rebel forces, primarily targeting the WSLF. SALF soon was defeated, OLF retreated to the South, and the WSLF moved toward Somalia. Subsequent offensives between September 20 and November 19 forced many of the rebels into Somalia, though the OLF claimed to have engaged the Ethiopians in forty major battles during this period. Somalia intervened briefly in November, sending troops into Somalia to attempt to assist the faltering rebels. An Ethiopian offensive on November 22, 1980, forced the Somalis and rebels out of the country by December 3, 1980.

However, the war continued in early 1981, mostly in Bale and Sidamo against the Oromo. The SLF revived as the government's attacks targeted civilians, with thousands fleeing as 1,000 to 2,000 were killed by a wall of flame created by gas ignited by a bombing raid from March 19 to March 21, 1981. Major conflict ends at this point, though attacks at below-war levels continued.

Termination and Outcome: The war ended as a government victory. Approximately 25,000 civilians were killed, and 800,000 fled the country. The rebels did not reconstitute a threat, though there were a few attacks in early 1981 with government retaliatory bombing raids. Ethiopia shifted much of its army to the North, where it would soon confront a rebellion in Tigray and Eritrea (Intra-state War #826 in 1982). The government did create the Somali National Movement that engaged in conflict with the WSLF in 1981.

Coding Decisions: Specific fatality information for combatants seems to be unavailable. Most sources discuss the deaths of civilians and the fate of the refugees.

Sources: Africa's Watch (1991); Clodfelter (2002); Correlates of War (2010); Henze (1985); Tareke (2002).

INTRA-STATE WAR #810

Zaire–FNLC War of 1978 (aka Shaba War, Shaba II, or the Fourth DRC War)

Participants: Zaire (formerly Democratic Republic of Congo—DRC), Belgium, and France versus *Front de Liberation Nationale* (FNLC)
Dates: May 11, 1978, to June 14, 1978.
Battle-related Deaths: FNLC: [ ]; Zaire: [ ]; France: 11; Belgium: 1; Total Combatant Deaths: 1,000. (See Coding Decisions.)
Initiator: FNLC.
Outcome: Zaire, Belgium, and France win.
War Type: Civil for central control.
Total System Member Military Personnel: Armed Forces of Zaire: 53,000 (prewar, initial, peak, final).[93] Armed Forces of Belgium: 107,000 (prewar); 109,000 (initial, peak, final).[94] Armed Forces of France: 584,000 (prewar); 581,000 (initial, peak, final).[95]
Theater Armed Forces: Armed Forces of Zaire: 8,000 (initial).[96] Armed Forces of FNLC: 4,000 (initial, peak).[97] Armed Forces of France, participating from May 19, 1978: 2,000 (initial, peak, final).[98] Armed Forces of Belgium, participating from May 20, 1978: 1,171 (initial, peak, final).[99]

Antecedents: In the previous war in the Democratic Republic of Congo (Intra-state War #762: the Third DRC Rebellion of 1964 to 1965), the *Conseil National de Libération* (National Council of Liberation, or CNL) attempted to create the People's Republic of the Congo in the eastern half of the DRC (including Southeastern Katanga province). The rebellion was defeated by the DRC army (ANC) with the assistance of Belgium. Six weeks later, on November 24, 1965, the ANC commander, Joseph-Désiré Mobutu, staged a coup, removing President Kasavubu from power and establishing a US-supported anticommunist regime. As part of his program to restore national authenticity, Mobutu changed the Congo's name to Zaire in 1971; the following year he changed his own name to Mobutu Sese Seko; and in 1978, the province where the rebellion had begun was renamed from Katanga to Shaba. A number of rebels from the war fled into Angola, where they created the *Front Nationale pour la Libération du Congo* (FNLC). In 1975, when the DRC/Zaire sent troops to intervene in the war in Angola (Inter-state War #186), the FNLC was roused into action. There were two ensuing Shaba conflicts, referred to as Shaba I and Shaba II, though Shaba I does not qualify as a war under COW coding.

Narrative: On May 11, 1978, the FNLC entered the Shaba province. Numbering about 4,000 soldiers under the leadership of General Mbumba, the army was divided in two, with one directed to cut the railroad and the other to capture the important southern mining city of Kolwezi. The Zairian armed forces (FAZ) had 8,000 troops in Shaba, but they were along the Angolan border, while the rebels mostly infiltrated along the unguarded border with Zambia. The smaller FNLC contingent captured Mutshatsha. The larger FNLC force attacked Kolwezi on May 13, and though some of the FAZ forces guarding the city put up a stiff resistance, others retreated. The rebels captured the airport, destroying FAZ planes, and soon seized the city of Kolwezi. Kolwezi housed at least 3,000 foreigners (mostly Belgians), and once word of the attacks had spread, the ambassadors of France, Belgium, and the United States began consultations on their options. Though the FNLC had not explicitly threatened the foreigners, the French ambassador considered them to be hostages and called on his government to intervene. President Mobutu also issued an appeal for foreign intervention. In the meantime, Zaire began to airlift additional troops into the area. Belgium initially declined to militarily intervene, though the United States began to send military supplies to the Zairian government. Mobutu decided to act without the Europeans and ordered a company to parachute into Kolwezi to link up with the advancing ground troops. On May 16, sixty paratroopers dropped near Kolwezi, though many were killed before they hit the ground by FNLC troops. A second drop suffered the same fate. Unnerved by the events, many of the FAZ forces in the area fled. The angered FLNC troops began killing foreign civilians and FAZ prisoners.

On May 17, a force of 200 FAZ troops arrived at Kolwezi after surviving several encounters with FNLC rebels, and they were able to recapture the airfield. Meanwhile, most of the Americans in the area, employees of Morris-Knudsen, had been evacuated by company helicopters and trucks, thus reducing the American motivation for involvement. The French and Belgians continued to plan a hostage-rescue mission, for which the United States would provide transportation. Ultimately, the French and Belgians were unable to cooperate, and two separate offensives were launched. On May 19, Operation Leopard was launched, and French paratroops were dropped at Kolwezi; most arrived safely despite fire from the rebels. Most of the rebels had begun to evacuate the city on May 18, though 500 had been left to confront the allies. Despite sporadic exchanges with the rebels, the French forces soon occupied most of the city. The Belgians launched Operation Bean the next day, May 20, unloading paratroopers and vehicles into the area. The Belgian focus was on evacuating the remaining 2,000 foreigners (120 to 131 had been killed). The French continued to exchange fire with the rebels, and on May 20, French troops captured Metalkat. The French and Belgians gained control over the entire area until they were relieved on June 14 by an inter-African Force of 2,000 soldiers (mostly from Morocco and Senegal).

Termination and Outcome: The war ended in a victory by Zaire, aided by France and Belgium. The FNLC retreated back into Angola.

Coding Decisions: There were insufficient battle-deaths for Shaba I to be coded as a war. As there was a period of over a year between the end of Shaba I and the beginning of Shaba II (April 1977 to May 1988), during which there was no armed combat between the FNLC and Zaire, these two conflicts are considered as separate conflicts. Though the United States provided transportation for the French and Belgian forces, the American did not engage in combat and thus are not included as a war participant.

Battle-deaths of this war are a matter of disagreement. Ndikumana and Kisangani report a death toll of 1,000 to 3,500.[100] It is unclear whether this includes civilian deaths. A number of sources refer to about 600 combatant deaths at Kolwezi. Because these figures apparently do not include the conflict at Mutshatsha, nor the initial Zaire paratroopers, nor deaths suffered by the ambushed Zaire troops advancing by land, we think it is likely that total combatant deaths reached 1,000.

Sources: Brogan (1998); Clodfelter (2002); Ndikumana and Kisangani (2005); Odom (1993); Stapleton (2013); Stearns (2001); Van Nederveen (2001).

INTRA-STATE WAR #820
Chad–FAN War of 1980 to 1984 (aka Habre Revolt)

Participants: Chad, *Forces Armées Populaires* (FAP), and Libya versus *Forces Armées du Nord* (FAN), France, and Zaire.

Dates: March 22, 1980, to January 1984.

Battle-related Deaths: Chad: 3,500; FAN: 1,500; Libya: 1,000; France: 200.

Initiator: FAN.

Outcome: FAN and France win.

War Type: Civil for local issues.

Total System Member Military Personnel: Armed Forces of Chad: 5,000 (prewar); 3,000 (initial); 16,000 (peak, final).[101] Armed Forces of Libya: 51,000 (prewar); 53,000 (initial); 90,000 (peak, final).[102] Armed Forces of France: 578,000 (prewar, initial, peak); 571,000 (final).[103] Armed Forces of Zaire: 40,000 (prewar); 42,000 (initial); 60,000 (peak, final).[104]

Theater Armed Forces: Armed Forces of *Forces Armées Populaires* (FAP): 6,800 (initial).[105] Armed Forces of *Forces Armées du Nord* (FAN): 5,000 (initial); 22,000.[106] Armed Forces of Libya (Pro-government Intervener), participating from August 1980 to November 1981 and from May 1983): 4,000 (initial); 14,000 (peak).[107] Armed Forces of France: (Pro-rebel Intervener), participating from August 9, 1983: 2,700 (initial, peak).[108] Armed Forces of Zaire (Pro-rebel Intervener), participating from July 1983: 2,000 (initial, peak).[109]

Antecedents: In 1966, Chad was confronted by the FROLINAT rebellion (Intra-state War #771). Chad, with the assistance of France, defeated the rebels in 1971. However, FROLINAT continued to be a major force in Chadian politics. FROLINAT split in two in 1976 over the issue of accepting assistance from Libya: the smaller faction led by Hissène Habré formed the *Forces Armées du Nord* (FAN), while the majority became the People's Armed Forces (FAP), under the leadership of Goukouni Oueddei (Gukuni Wedei). In 1977, Libya, led by Muammar Gadhafi, began supplying weapons to FAP. On June 22, 1977, FAP went to war against Chad (Intra-state War #806.8). During the war, Chad's President Malloum began to realize the weakness of his military situation, and he formed an alliance with Habré's FAN in September 1977 (formalized in the Khartoum Agreements of September 1977 and January 1978). Gadhafi saw the alliance as threatening his influence in Chad, and thus he decided to send Libyan forces to aid Goukouni's FAP. A joint FAP–Libya offensive was launched against government troops in northern Chad on January 29, 1978. However, Chad, aided by French reinforcements, defeated FAP and Libya in June.

In the aftermath of the war, President Malloum appointed Habré as prime minister on August 29, 1978. The appointment was a mistake in that the two leaders had very divergent agendas. The integration of FAN and the Chad national army (FAT) was not accomplished as anticipated in the Khartoum Accords. Meanwhile, the failure of the FAP offensive also led to dissension among the rebels. Gadhafi backed a failed attempt to overthrow FAP's Oueddei, which then led to the rebel expulsion of Libyan forces from Chad. In February 1979, fighting between Habré FAN and Malloum's FAT erupted in the capital. Oueddei and FAP forces entered the fray in support of FAN, and the FAT forces fled amid intercommunal violence between the North and South that killed and displaced thousands of civilians. International mediation efforts made several unsuccessful attempts to resolve the crisis until they finally created a coalition government formed among representatives of the South along with ten of the northern Muslim organizations in November 1979. The *Gouvernement d'Union Nationals de Transition* (the Transitional Government of National Unity, or GUNT) included Oueddei as a Southerner president, Wadel Abdelkader Kamougué (leader of the armed forces) as vice president, and Habré as defense minister. The coalition was unstable because the members distrusted one another. Each faction retailed its armed forces, with Kamougué rebuilding the Chadian army with recruits from the South. The coalition started to collapse as Oueddei and Kamougué created an informal alliance against Habré's FAN. Oueddei organized more than 5,000 FAP partisans.

Narrative: On March 22, 1980, Habré's soldiers attacked the remainder of GUNT (FAP troops of President Oueddei and those of his ally Kamougué's FAT) in the capital N'Djamena. FAP and FAT were soon on the defensive as FAN advanced. Fighting raged for ten days during which 3,000 people were killed. FAP's forces were decimated, and the losses within Kamougué's FAT persuaded him to leave the capital and flee south. France withdrew its last 1,100 troops in April 1980. Fighting continued throughout the spring, despite several international mediation attempts. Oueddei appealed to Libya for assistance, and the two parties signed a treaty on June 15, 1980. The OAU considered involvement in the war in Chad but decided in July 1980 not to intervene. As FAP was on the verge of surrender, Libya sent an army of 4,000 south from the Aouzou strip and into N'Djamena. The arrival of the Libyan troops tipped the balance of power against FAN, which retreated to the East as Oueddei and the Libyans took control of N'Djamena on December 15, 1980. Habré retreated to Cameroon and Sudan, though he vowed to continue the war. Sporadic fighting continued in the North, and despite the arrival of Libyan troops into the region, 2,000 FAN soldiers were able to move into Sudan. Bath Sudan and Egypt promised to assist in arming FAN.

On January 7, 1981, Libya and Chad revealed their plan for a union of their two countries, an announcement that produced widespread African opposition. Libya increased its troops' strength in Chad to 14,000 by February 1981, and Libyan troops remained in control in Chad until the OAU refused to send in a peacekeeping force until Libyan troops were removed. Oueddei asked the Libyans to withdraw, which they did by mid-November 1981. The 3,300 peacekeepers (mostly Nigerian) were deployed between December 17, 1981, and January 1982. The OAU troops took over security functions that did not involve combat, allowing GUNT to focus on FAN. Meanwhile, Habré's FAN forces had regained the offensive, winning a few engagements between November 19, 1981, and January 1982, while seizing arms that the Libyans had left behind. Despite President Oueddei's request for the OAU peacekeepers to become involved in defending his regime, the OAU decided to withdraw its forces by June 30, 1982. Significant fighting between Chad/FAP and FAN resumed March 21, 1982, and ended with the overthrow of Oueddei on June 8, 1982. President Oueddei fled to Cameroon and Libya, and Habré established a government in N'Djamena. Habré then went on the offensive against Kamougué's army in the South. Habré captured Kamougué's headquarters, and Kamougué escaped in October 1982 to join Oueddei in Libya. Oueddei and Kamougué, aided by Libya, established a new government at Bardaï.

On January 7, 1983, Habré's forces merged FAN with some of the remaining FAT soldiers into the *Forces Armées Nationales Tchadiennes* (FANT). Oueddei again raised an army in the North and, with Libyan logistical support, seized Faya-Largeau on June 24, 1983. FANT counterattacked in July and was able to recapture two cities that FAP had seized. Oueddei then attempted to retake Faya-Largeau with Libyan aerial support. Libya's involvement prompted the United States to increase logistical support for FAN. In July, Zaire sent 2,000 troops to aid Habré in the defense of the capital, and France announced its decision to intervene militarily on August 9, 1983. The international interventions stabilized the situation, with Chad divided along the Red Line, or Fifteenth parallel, into zones ruled by two rival governments. France called for a cease-fire on August 17, 1983. OAU negotiations made little progress. GUNT and Libyan forces attacked FANT troops along the Red Line in January 1984 but were turned back by the French air force. France brought in more troops and moved the Red Line to the Sixteenth parallel.

Termination and Outcome: The battle in January 1984 seems to mark the end of the fighting, and thus the end of the war. The war ended as a victory for Habré and FAN as they remained in control of the capital. In September 1984, France and Libya negotiated a mutual agreement to withdraw their forces. However, Libyan forces remained and began to expand their presence in the Aouzou strip. This set the stage for the war over the Aouzou strip between Chad and Libya in 1986 (Inter-state War #207).

Coding Decisions: Though France had troops in Chad at the beginning of the war, they do not appear to have participated in the early fighting in March 1980. French troops were withdrawn in April 1980 and did not return until August 1983, when France is coded as a war participant.

Sources: Amoo (2003); Azevedo and Nnadozie (1998); Bercovitch and Fretter (2004); Brogan (1998); Burr and Collins (1999); Ciment (2007a–h); Clodfelter (2002); Cordesman (2004); Meredith (2005); Nolutshungu (1996); Phillips and Axelrod (2005); Stapleton (2013).

INTRA-STATE WAR #823

Nigeria–Muslim War of 1980 to 1981 (aka the 1980 Maitatsine Uprising in Kano)

Participants: Nigeria versus Muslim Fundamentalists.
Dates: December 8, 1980, to January 1, 1981.
Battle-related Deaths: Muslim Fundamentalists: 1,000; Nigeria: 55.[110] (See Coding Decisions.)
Initiator: Nigeria.
Outcome: Nigeria wins.
War Type: Civil for local issues.
Total System Member Military Personnel: Armed Forces of Nigeria: 164,000 (prewar); 150,000 (initial, peak); 144,000 (final).[111]
Theater Armed Forces: The Maitatsine: 3,000 (initial); 10,000 (peak, final).[112]

Antecedents: On October 1, 1960, Nigeria had obtained its independence from Britain, and in 1963, it was established as a federal republic. The republic lasted for only three years till a military junta seized power in 1966. The country went to war the following year as the eastern area of Biafra sought its independence (Intra-state War #775). After general elections in July 1979, Nigeria briefly was returned to civilian rule under President Alhaji Shehu Shagari. However, popular rule did not end the many conflicts within society, in particular those involving religion. Nigeria was divided almost evenly between the Muslims and Christians, with the Muslims living mostly in the North. The Al Masifu sect (or Maitatsine), led by Alhaji Muhammadu Marwa Maitatsine, wanted to purify Islam, and starting in 1966 the Marwa began inciting his followers and intimidating citizens in the North-central Kano province. Marwa was arrested on numerous occasions for preaching that incited his followers to violence. Marwa claimed that killing was a means to get to heaven, and thus his followers received military training. The Maitatsine soldiers were always armed and were scattered throughout the audience at all the Marwa's gatherings. The Al Masifu spiritual center was also a heavily armed fortress. By 1980, Marwa had 6,000 followers in Kano and a total of 8,000 to 12,000 overall.[113] The governor finally ordered the sect to leave the province, but the Al Masifu sect refused.

Narrative: On December 8, 1980, the Kano police decided to confront the Maitatsine. The force of 150 men occupied the Shahoci Playing Ground where the Marwa was scheduled to speak. As the Maitatsine arrive, the police discharged smoke bombs, and the 3,000 Maitatsine attacked with arrows and machetes. The police responded with gunfire, but were outnumbered and overpowered. Four police were killed and the rest fled. A rampage ensued for the next eleven days. On December 19, 1980, the Maitatsine attacked a group of Muslims praying in a mosque and seized the police station. Fighting continued, and a week later, the Maitatsine attacked the residence of the governor of Kano. The governor then called for military assistance from the national army. On December 28, the army sealed off the area in which the sect lived, and then the army and air force opened fire. At least 1,000 members of the sect were killed, including the Marwa (some reports put the number as high as 7,000). The local populace joined in, killing any suspected sect members on sight. The attack forced the remaining members of Al Masifu to flee from Kano city. The poorly armed sect members captured weapons from the government, and fighting continued in a nearby village through January 3, 1981.

Termination and Outcome: The war ended in a government victory, though smaller riots involving the Maitatsine continued in 1982 and 1984. The government established a tribunal to investigate the events in Kano. The tribunal concluded that 10,000 Maitatsine had participated in the conflict.

Coding Decisions: Reports of fatalities during this war range from 1,000 to 10,000, and government deaths (police and army) are mentioned only in a few confrontations. It seems likely that a large percentage of the deaths would have been civilians killed by the Maitatsine. Clodfelter concludes that 1,000 of the Maitatsine were killed, including the Marwa. Police deaths were 5 the first day and 50 on December 18 and 19, for a total of 55. These numbers are reported here, though they may well be underestimates.

Sources: Agi (1998); Clark (1987); Clodfelter (2002); Falola (1998); Falola and Heaton (2008); Udoidem (1997).

INTRA-STATE WAR #825
Mozambique War of 1981 to 1992 (aka the Mozambican Civil War)

Participants: Mozambique, Zimbabwe, and Tanzania versus *Resistência Nacional Moçambicana* (RENAMO).

Dates: April 10, 1981, to October 4, 1992.

Battle-related Deaths: Mozambique: [ ]; RENAMO: [ ]; Zimbabwe: 500; Tanzania: 50; Total Combatant Deaths: 20,000. (See Coding Decisions.)[114]

Initiator: RENAMO.

Outcome: Mozambique, Zimbabwe, and Tanzania win.

War Type: Civil for central control.

Total System Member Military Personnel: Armed Forces of Mozambique: 25,000 (prewar); 30,000 (initial); 65,000 (peak); 50,000 (final).[115] Armed Forces of Zimbabwe: 24,000 (prewar); 38,000 (initial); 94,000 (peak); 48,000 (final).[116] Armed Forces of Tanzania: 63,000 (prewar); 53,000 (initial); 84,000 (peak); 46,000 (final).[117]

Theater Armed Forces: Armed Forces of RENAMO: 2,000 (initial); 20,000 (peak).[118] Armed Forces of Zimbabwe (Pro-government Intervener), participating from 1983: 2,000 (initial); 20,000 (peak).[119] Armed Forces of Tanzania (Pro-government Intervener), participating from 1982: 2,000 (initial); 7,000 (peak).[120]

Antecedents: In 1975 Mozambique became independent under the control of the Marxist Front for the Liberation of Mozambique (FRELIMO) and President Samora Machel. The one-party regime imposed nationalization, and as a result rampant discontent grew during the late 1970s. The FRELIMO government established a policy of supporting opposition movements in neighboring countries (ZANLA insurgents against Rhodesia and ANC rebels against South Africa could use Mozambique territory). In response, the Rhodesia Central Intelligence Organization (CIO) created an opposition group within Mozambique, the anti-communist *Resistência Nacional Moçambicana* (RENAMO), which was formed in 1975 (initially as the Mozambican National Resistance) with the goal of destabilizing the government in Mozambique. The group initially had about 1,000 members, and its activities were relatively limited. However, as the war in

Rhodesia came to an end in 1979 with the creation of black rule in 1980 as Zimbabwe (Intra-state War #791), sponsorship of RENAMO and its 2,000 rebels was transferred to South Africa, and a new RENAMO training center was created in the Transvaal. Zimbabwe switched to supporting the FRELIMO government. Armed conflict between RENAMO and Mozambique remained at below-war levels until 1981.

Narrative: By 1981, with South African assistance RENAMO had grown to 10,000 warriors.[121] South Africa would ferry RENAMO rebels into Mozambique, and in April 1981, fierce fighting began as RENAMO attacked the Cahora hydroelectric power lines and government forces. By the end of 1981, FRELIMO was forced to create armed people's militias to aid the government in its fight against the rebels. The next year, RENAMO increased the scope of its activities, and President Machel appealed to Zimbabwe for assistance and to Tanzania to increase its forces already in Mozambique. A defense agreement between Zimbabwe and Mozambique in 1982 led to the deployment of several thousand Zimbabwean troops in 1983 to protect the railroad. That year, RENAMO was active in nine of the ten provinces, and the government responded by launching two major operations against the rebels.

Mozambique's declining military situation persuaded the government to enter into an agreement with South Africa on March 16, 1984: the Nkomati Accords committed each party to prevent opposition groups from operating within its territory. South Africa did not comply with the accord, and later in 1984, RENAMO increased the intensity of its attacks with assistance from South Africa (by August 1984, RENAMO was active in all ten provinces). The government responded with a counteroffensive in November that destroyed 100 RENAMO bases and killed 1,000 rebels. A June 1985 meeting among the leaders of Mozambique, Zimbabwe, and Tanzania produced a commitment by Zimbabwe to increase its efforts in Mozambique. A subsequent offensive by FREMILO and Zimbabwe troops captured the RENAMO headquarters at Casa Banana in August 1985.

The worst year of the war was 1986: Casa Banana was recaptured by the rebels and then seized by the government again. The forces of Mozambique, Zimbabwe, and Tanzania cooperated to defeat a RENAMO offensive designed to cut Mozambique in two. In 1987, the US intelligence community created Freedom Inc, which became a new source of support for RENAMO. By 1987, there were 4 million Mozambicans facing starvation. Splits emerged within RENAME between Paulo Oliveira (who advocated peace) and leader Afonso Dhlakama (who favored continuing the war), prompting Oliveira to defect to the government. Nonetheless, peace negotiations began in 1989, and more than 3,000 rebels accepted a government amnesty. The end of the Cold War contributed to the resolution of the war as Mozambique moved further into the West, and Eastern bloc support declined.

Termination and Outcome: On October 4, 1992, a cease-fire was signed, ending the war as RENAMO moved to join Mozambique's political process. In March 1994, UN peacekeeping troops began moving into the demilitarized zone. In the October 1994 elections, RENAMO received 33 percent of the presidential vote and 38 percent of the seats in the parliament, and it accepted its role as the opposition within the government. In 2012 and 2013, RENAMO was involved in attacks against the government, though conflict did not reach war level.

Coding Decisions: There is disagreement among scholars about when the conflict in Mozambique became an actual civil war. RENAMO began attacks against the government in 1976, but they were of limited intensity. Uppsala University Conflict Data codes May 6, 1977, as the first use of armed force. An earlier version of COW data coded the start of the war as October 21, 1979, with the government's attack against the main RENAMO base. However, work by Weinstein and Francisco argues that conflict dropped to almost null in 1980 before rebounding in 1981.[122] Thus we now code the start of the war as the attack on the Cabora Basso hydroelectric power plant in April 1981.

Though Zimbabwe initially sent 600 troops to assist Mozambique in 1982, Zimbabwe could not be considered a war participant until it had committed more than 1,000 troops, which happened the next year. South African forces participated in attacks and bombing raids into Mozambique (despite South African denials); however, there is no indication that its participation reached the level of a war participant.

While exact battle-death figures are not available, tens of thousands were killed in the fighting; our estimate of 20,000 battle-deaths is therefore a conservative one. Total war-related deaths (including disease and malnutrition) may have numbered up to 600,000. Millions of people were displaced by the war, internally and into other countries.

Sources: Arnold (2009); Brogan (1998); Ciment (2007a–h); Clodfelter (2002); Conciliation Resources (1998); Cutter (2007); Meredith (2005); Phillips and Axelrod (2005); Stapleton (2013); Uppsala Universitet (2004); Weinstein and Francisco (2005).

INTRA-STATE WAR #826

Tigrean and Eritrean War of 1982 to 1991

Participants: Ethiopia versus Tigray People's Liberation Front (TPLF), Eritrean People's Liberation Front (EPLF), and Ethiopian People's Revolutionary Democratic Front (EPRDF).
Dates: January 23, 1982, to May 28, 1991.
Battle-related Deaths: Ethiopia: 150,000; TPLF: 10,000; EPLF: 70,000; EPRDF: [ ].[123]
Initiator: Eritrean People's Liberation Front (EPLF).
Outcome: EPLF, TPLF, and EPRDF win.
War Type: Civil for local issues.
Total System Member Military Personnel: Armed Forces of Ethiopia: 240,000 (prewar, initial); 300,000 (peak); 120,000 (final).[124]
Theater Armed Forces: Armed Forces of Ethiopia (includes Militia): 136,540 (initial); 430,000 (peak).[125] Armed Forces of TPLF: 2,500 (initial); 20,000 (peak).[126] Armed Forces of EPLF: 19,500 (initial); 26,000 (in 1987); 100,000 (peak, final).[127] Armed Forces of Ethiopian People's Revolutionary Democratic Front (EPRDF), participating from February 1991: [ ].

Antecedents: The Eritrean independence movement was defeated by Ethiopia with the assistance of Cuba in 1978 (Intra-state War #798). The Eritrean resistance survived (partially in their mountain stronghold of Nafka) because the government of Ethiopia also had to confront rebellions elsewhere. The desire of Somalis living in the eastern Ogaden region to leave Ethiopia and unite with Somalia led to a series of three wars: Intra-state War #805 from 1976 to 1977; Inter-state war #187 from 1977 to 1978 against Somalia; and Intra-state War #808 from 1978 to 1980, which involved both the Somali and Oromo people. The latter war ended after Ethiopia launched Operation Lash, which also targeted the civilian population, killing approximately 25,000 civilians and forcing 800,000 to flee the country.

Meanwhile, groups within the northern province of Tigray (adjacent to Eritrea) also sought independence. The Tigray People's Liberation Front (TPLF) was created in 1975 in Mekelle, and it established a military base in the West at Dedebit. The TPLF, with support and weapons from the Eritrean People's Liberation Front (EPLF), engaged in low-level attacks against government installations after 1976. There also was fighting between the TPFL and other rival Tigrayan movements during this period. After Ethiopia's success against the Ogaden in 1980, the government turned its attention to confronting the rebellions in the North, and in 1982, the Ethiopian Dergue government decided to develop a plan to finally eliminate the rebels.

Narrative: A preemptive attack by the EPLF against government forces at Asmara started the war on January 23, 1982. On February 15, the government launched Operation Red Star, an offensive planned with Soviet assistance, to advance on three fronts against the rebellions in Tigray and Eritrea, with a focus on the Eritrean rebel stronghold at Nakfa. The rebels were seriously outnumbered as the government deployed almost 137,000 troops to rebels numbering 22,000 (including four brigades of TPLF soldiers, which represented half its strength at the time). Early government advances finally were halted by the rebels in fierce fighting that cost 15,000 rebel and 37,176 government casualties.[128] The EPLF and TPLF claimed the victory because the government offensive had been halted. The rebels launched a counteroffensive on March 5. Between March and April, government reinforcements arrived, enabling a government offensive in the South in May and June, which also failed to attain its objectives. Though the campaign destroyed the morale of the Ethiopian forces, it also had significant costs for the rebels as well. Due to its heavy losses, the TPLF concentrated on guerrilla attacks for the next few years rather than major offensives to capture and hold territory like the EPLF. The EPLF also had suffered significant losses, and thus it soon had to widen its recruitment efforts: by the mid-1980s women constituted one-third of its army, and in 1987 the EPLF began conscripting young men and women, which enabled it to establish a small naval contingent.

During the first six months of 1983, the government launched another offensive into Eritrea, which similarly produced few results. The war stagnated in the mid-1980s during a famine in the country, partially caused by the government's counterinsurgency measures in Tigray that included burning of crops. Soviet support to the Ethiopian government began to decline significantly after 1985, limiting the government's efforts and allowing the rebels to make gains. The EPLF continued launching raids against government and military installations, which increased after December 1986. In December 1987, an EPLF offensive captured an Ethiopian brigade. Better harvests in 1987 enabled TPLF to expand its efforts to gain control of portions of its countryside.

The year 1988 saw several major campaigns. The EPLF launched a major offensive on March 17, 1988, and it secured its greatest victory when it killed 18,000 Ethiopian troops and captured 6,000 more at the Ethiopian headquarters at Afabet. Thereafter the EPLF gained control of most of Eritrea. The TPLF launched a major offensive in May 1988, forcing government troops to retreat from western Tigray to the capital of Mekele in the Southeast. Mengistu then mounted a massive counteroffensive in August 1988, involving 150,000 troops that recaptured all of the major Tigrean towns and massacred thousands of civilians. In response, in February 1989, the TPLF, aided by the EPLF, again went on the offensive and were successful in pushing Ethiopian forces out of most of Tigray by March. In February 1990, the EPLF launched Operation Fenkil, which pitted 100,000 EPLF soldiers in successful attacks against Ethiopian positions at Semhar and the port of Massawa. During the battle of Massawa alone, 3,000 Eritreans and 9,000 Ethiopian troops were killed. In April and May, the government responded with an intense aerial bombing campaign that destroyed the port and killed hundreds of civilians.

Meanwhile, in February 1989, the TPLF created a new organization, consisting of a coalition of anti-Mengistu rebels, known as the Ethiopian People's Revolutionary Democratic Front (EPRDF), which included the Oromo People's Democratic Organization (OPDO). In late February 1991, the EPRDF and the TPLF launched operation Tewodros, which expelled government forces to the West. The government army was collapsing. Between February and May 1991, the EPLF advanced its control of the coastline, blocking Ethiopian access to the sea. In late May 1991, the EPLF staged its final offensive. In May, Mengistu fled to Zimbabwe, and later that month, the EPRDF and TPLF captured the Addis Ababa. With the fall of the Mengistu regime, Ethiopian forces in Eritrea fled, allowing the EPLF to take control of Eritrea without a fight.

Termination and Outcome: The war ended as a victory for the EPLF, the TPLF, and the EPRDF. The EPRDF and the Oromo Liberation Front formed a provisional government, pending a UN-supervised referendum in late April 1993, while the EPLF took control of Eritrea. The April vote overwhelmingly supported Eritrean independence and Eritrea achieved independence in May 1993.

The loss of life during this war included the deaths of 100,000 Eritrean civilians.[129] Conflict was not entirely ended, however, and Eritrea and Ethiopia would become involved in a border dispute in 1998 (Inter-state War #219: the Badme Border War of 1998 to 2000).

Coding Decisions: Though some authors (including Stapleton) describe the insurgencies in Eritrea and Tigre as separate conflicts, they are coded here as one war due to the coordination, cross-training of recruits, and joint military operations by the TPLF and the EPLF. In contrast, Clodfelter has one long entry for the Eritrean War—1961 to 1991—that includes not only the Eritrean wars but the Tigrayan one as well.

Sources: Arnold (2009); Brogan (1998); Clodfelter (2002); Laffin (1989); Phillips and Axelrod (2005); Skutsch (2007b); Stapleton (2013); Tareke (2002).

INTRA-STATE WAR #828.3

Second Uganda War of 1982 to 1986 (aka the Ugandan Bush War, the Luwero War, or the Ugandan Civil War)

Participants: Uganda versus National Resistance Army (NRA).
Dates: June 1982 to March 19, 1986.
Battle-related Deaths: Uganda: 39,516; National Resistance Army: 6,000.[130]
Initiator: National Resistance Army.

Outcome: National Resistance Army wins.
War Type: Civil for local issues.
Total System Member Military Personnel: Armed Forces of Uganda: 6,000 (prewar, initial); 15,000 (peak, final).[131]
Theater Armed Forces: National Resistance Army: 4,000 (in 1983); 10,000 (peak, final).[132]

Antecedents: During the First Uganda war in 1966 (Intra-state War #768), Uganda's President Milton Obote with his army commander, Idi Amin, defeated a secession attempt by the kingdom of Buganda. In 1971, Idi Amin overthrew Obote, and he then established one of the world's most repressive regimes. Faced with growing opposition, Amin tried to garner popular support by invading Tanzania in 1978 (Inter-state War #190: October 1978 to April 1979). Not only was Tanzania able to repel the invasion, but it then launched a counterattack into Uganda, which overthrew Amin. The Uganda National Liberation Army (UNLA) had fought alongside Tanzania against Amin, and the Uganda National Liberation Front (UNLF) was created in March 1979 to serve as a temporary Ugandan government pending elections in December 1980. Yusuf Lule was installed as the UNFL leader, with Yuweri Museveni serving as defense minister. The UNLF soon was wracked with infighting, and Lule and Museveni were removed from office by Godfrey Binaisa in June 1979. In turn, in May 1980, Binaisa was removed from office by a military commission that included Museveni.

In December 1980, Obote was returned to the presidency through what some claimed was a rigged election. Several resistance groups immediately formed, including the National Resistance Army (NRA), led by Lule and Museveni. The NRA began attacks against the government (but at below-war level). Between February and March 1981, Museveni led 35 men in a string of guerrilla attacks on government locations. He devoted the following two months to recruiting an army of 200 fighters. The NRA continued to expand, soon forming six units that were based in different parts of the country, one of which was located in the Luwero Triangle, northwest of Kampala, where the revolt emerged.

Narrative: By 1982, Obote's UNLA numbered 10,000 men, and in June 1982 the government launched Operation Bonanza, the UNLA's first major offensive against the NRA in the Luwero Triangle. Despite its superior numbers, the UNLA's offensive failed as the NRA was able to attack isolated units. A second operation was launched in January 1983 that aimed to encircle the NRA. The NRA, lacking weapons for its 4,000 guerrillas, retreated northward in March 1983, and 1.5 million refugees accompanied the NRA, fleeing atrocities being committed by the UNLA's soldiers.

In February 1984 the NRA regrouped and now included 1,500 Tutsi Rwandan refugees who had lived in Uganda since the early 1960s and 3,000 child soldiers. An NRA contingent attacked the Masindi barracks north of the triangle in a battle in which five rebels died, while 200 government personnel were killed. In January 1985 the government launched a new highly trained brigade, led by Lieut. Col. John Ogole, against the NRA. The brigade, accompanied by North Korean soldiers wielding rocket launchers, was defeated by the NRA in major clashes. In June the special brigade fell into an NRA trap and was routed after suffering heavy losses. Later that month the NRA launched simultaneous attacks against a variety of UNLA targets, and the UNLA responded by massacring suspected rebel sympathizers. By the middle of 1985 about 300,000 people had been killed, and another 200,000 had fled into neighboring countries.

As the NRA continued to make gains, the government's UNLA began to splinter, primarily along tribal lines of the Langi versus the Acholi officers. On July 27, 1985, Obote, who was a Langi, was removed from office in a coup by a group of Acholi officers, who then ruled the country through a military council. NRA efforts to come to terms with the new regime failed, so the NRA launched a new offensive in the West. Subsequent operations in September through November led to UNLA retreats, and the NRA soon controlled the West and South. At the end of November, the government launched a new offensive with 10,000 UNLA troops, divided into two columns to advance toward the West and South. In heavy fighting, the NRA was able to stop the advances. The NRA then received major shipments of foreign weapons. In January 1986, an NRA army of 10,000 advanced toward Kampala, which was defended by 15,000 UNLA soldiers. After heavy fighting, the UNLA was forced back, and it ultimately fled north. The NRA followed in pursuit, capturing major cities along the way during February and March. Finally, the UNLA retreated into Sudan. Museveni assumed the presidency on January 29, 1986.

Termination and Outcome: The exodus of most of the UNLA in March ended the war. Within five months, the new government would face a challenge from the Holy Spirit Movement (Intra-state War #843).

Coding Decisions: Though many scholars date the start of this war in February 1981, combatant fatality rates were below-war level until the offensive in June 1982, which is coded here as the start of the war. It is estimated that as many as 800,000 Ugandans died during this war.[133]

Sources: Ciment and Nichter (2007); Clodfelter (2002); Edgerton (2002); Jackson (2002); Katumba-Wamala (2000); Stapleton (2013).

INTRA-STATE WAR #843

Holy Spirit Movement War of 1986 to 1987

Participants: Uganda versus the Holy Spirit Movement/Mobile Force (HSMF).
Dates: August 1986 to October 1987.
Battle-related Deaths: HSMF: 5,000; Uganda: 2,000.[134]
Initiator: HSMF.
Outcome: Uganda wins.
War Type: Civil for central control.
Total System Member Military Personnel: Armed Forces of Uganda: 15,000 (prewar, initial); 25,000 (peak, final).[135]
Theater Armed Forces: Armed Forces of HSMF: 10,000 (peak).[136]

Antecedents: In December 1980, elections returned Milton Obote to the presidency of Uganda. Some saw the elections as fraudulent, and a number of groups formed in opposition to Obote's government, including the National Resistance Army (NRA), led by Yusuf Lule and Yuweri Museveni. The NRA began attacks against the government's Uganda National Liberation Army (UNLA) in 1981, but a war began in June 1982, when the UNLA launched an offensive against the NRA (Intra-state War #828.3: the Second Uganda War of 1982 to 1986). During the war, the government's UNLA began to splinter, primarily along tribal lines of the Langi versus the Acholi officers. On July 27, 1985, Obote, who was a Langi, was removed from office in a coup by a group of Acholi officers, who then ruled the country through a military council. Tribal affiliations continued to play a role as the UNLA was predominantly Acholi, while the NRA represented the Southern and Western groups. Ultimately, the NRA offensives were successful, and the UNLA retreated into Sudan. Museveni assumed the presidency on January 29, 1986.

A number of the Acholi former UNLA soldiers began to return to northern Uganda, where they created the Uganda People's Democratic Army (UPDA). One of the major factions within the UPDA was the Holy Spirit Movement, which was a religious sect in North Uganda headed by Alice Lakwena (an Acholi). Alice was convinced that she had to overthrow the government of Museveni to remove wrongdoing from society. Alice recruited an army, the Holy Spirit Mobile Force (HSMF), which ultimately had approximately 10,000 soldiers, who were organized into four large companies. The warriors were coated with special oils to protect them from bullets, and the HSMF battle strategy was channeled by the spirits through Alice.

Narrative: The HSMF began attacks against the NRA in August 1986. In November, Alice persuaded the UPDA to put 150 of its soldiers under her command. The HMSF fought conventional battles against the NRA. After a couple of victories, including winning a battle at Kilak Corner in November 1986, the HMSF decided to undertake its march toward Kampala in August 1987. The HMSF was defeated in heavy fighting at Jinja, just fifty miles from Kampala.

Termination and Outcome: After the defeat of the HSMF, Alice fled into Kenya. The Holy Spirit message was adopted by a number of similar groups, one of which would become the Lord's Resistance Army, which would terrorize the civilian population in and around Uganda from 1987 on.

Sources: Ciment and Nichter (2007); Cline (2003, 2013); Clodfelter (2002); Dunn (2007); Edgerton (2002); Jackson (2002).

INTRA-STATE WAR #846

Inkatha–ANC War of 1987 to 1994

Participants: Inkatha versus African National Congress (ANC).
Dates: December 20, 1987, to April 26, 1994.
Battle-related Deaths: Inkatha: [ ]; ANC: [ ]; Total Combatant Deaths: 13,000.[137]

Initiator: Inkatha.
Outcome: Stalemate.
War Type: Intercommunal.
Theater Armed Forces: Armed Forces of Inkatha: 10,000 (peak). Armed Forces of the ANC: [ ].

Antecedents: In 1961, South Africa became a republic with a parliamentary system. The government continued the apartheid system that privileged the white minority over the black majority. The major opposition group was the African National Congress (ANC), which had initially advocated a nonviolent end to apartheid. After the Sharpeville massacre (March 21, 1960), the ANC was banned in South Africa (on April 5, 1960), and on December 16, 1961, the ANC dropped its commitment to nonviolence and announced the creation of the *Umkhonto we Sizwe* (Spear of the Nation, or MK) as the ANC's armed wing. From 1961 to 1976, South Africa saw increasing levels of violence as *Umkhonto* conducted guerrilla attacks against the government. In 1963 and 1964, Nelson Mandela and other ANC leaders were arrested and sentenced to long prison terms. The Soweto Uprising (June 16, 1976), in which black youth battled police, represented the growing black frustration with the apartheid system. Subsequently, a number of black youth fled the country and joined the ANC. Between 1976 and 1991, the ANC ran military camps in Angola, where MK combatants were trained and armed by Soviet advisers.

The year 1976 also saw the development of an alternative black organization. Zulu Chief Gatsha Mangosuthu Buthelezi was a traditionalist who believed that blacks should work within the governmental system. In 1976, he founded the Black Unity Front and the Inkatha movement, which soon had a membership of 200,000. The ANC and Inkatha competed for control of the black population: the more rural Zulus tended to support Inkatha, while the urban Zulus tended to side with ANC. United Democratic Front (UDF), which was a cover for the banned ANC, emerged in 1983 and accompanied an increasing number of boycotts and strikes. Inkatha wanted to ensure that the leftist UDF/ANC would not come to power once apartheid ended.

Narrative: In 1985, the South African government began Operation Marion, by which the South African Defense Force (SADF) Special Forces trained members of the Inkatha militia at one of their camps in the Caprivi Strip in Namibia. The South African government then encouraged Inkatha in its opposition to the ANC. The intercommunal war began in 1987, with attacks by the Inkatha militia against the ANC/UDF in the eastern Kwa-Zulu-Natal region, though the fighting spread throughout the country, with more than 3,000 partisans killed by March 1990. Violence between the two groups continued even after the ANC was unbanned and Mandela was released from prison in 1990.

Termination and Outcome: The intercommunal attacks finally ceased after the presidential election in 1994, in which the ANC's Nelson Mandela was elected.

Coding Decisions: The war is coded as a stalemate in that fighting ceased, while neither side attained its objectives.

Sources: Arnold (2009); Berkeley (2001); Clodfelter (2002); *Keesing's Record of World Events* (1987–1994); Kohn (1999); Meredith (2005); Ottaway (1993); Thompson (2001).

INTRA-STATE WAR #848
First Somalia War of 1988 to 1991 (aka the Overthrow of Siad Barre, or the Somalian Civil War)

Participants: Somalia versus Somali National Movement (SNM), United Somali Congress (USC), and Somali Patriotic Movement (SPM).
Dates: May 26, 1988, to January 26, 1991.
Battle-related Deaths: Somalia: [ ]; USC: [ ]; Total Combatant Deaths: [ ].
Initiator: Somali National Movement (SNM).
Outcome: Somali National Movement (SNM), United Somali Congress (USC), and Somali Patriotic Movement (SPM) win.
War Type: Civil for central control.
Total System Member Military Personnel: Armed Forces of Somalia: 50,000 (prewar); 47,000 (initial); 47,000 (peak); 7,000 (final).[138]
Theater Armed Forces: Armed Forces of the SNM: 18,000 (initial).[139] Armed Forces of the USC: [ ]. Armed Forces of the SPM: [ ].

Antecedents: Somalia had been ruled since 1969 by Muhammad Siad Barre. Siad Barre originally had the support of the Soviet Union. However, after

Somalia tried to capture the Ogaden from Ethiopia (Intra-state War #805 of 1976 to 1977 and Inter-state War #187 of 1977 to 1978), the Soviet Union switched to supporting Ethiopia. Somalia's loss in that war in 1978, coupled with Ethiopia's victory in the subsequent war between Ethiopia and a coterie of Somali and Oromo independence organizations (Intra-state War #808 of 1978 to 1980), led to a flood of refugees from the Ogaden into Somalia. The refugees also included a number of Somalis who opposed the Somali government, including the Somali National Movement (SNM). The SNM had been formed in 1981 in London by a group of Somalis of the Isaaq clan, who were motivated by the perceived lack of representation of Western Somalis within the Siad Barre government. The SNM aimed to overthrow Siad Barre's dictatorship and had had a base in Ethiopia, from where it had launched guerrilla raids into Somalia from 1982 to 1987. To reduce tensions along the border, on April 4, 1988, the presidents of Ethiopia and Somalia signed an agreement whereby they each agreed to end subversive activities by organizations within their borders against each other. Facing the cessation of Ethiopian assistance, the SNM moved its operations into North Somalia in May 1988.

Narrative: The SNM launched its revolt against the Somali government with an attack at Hargeisa on May 26, 1988. Over the next month, the SNM briefly would control the provincial capitals of Hargeisa and Burao in fighting that would kill 1,000. The early successes prompted thousands of Somalis to join the SNM. The government responded in June with an aerial bombardment campaign that heavily damaged both cities, killed 5,000 civilians, and forced hundreds of thousands of civilians to flee into Ethiopia. Over the next few years, the SNM would control most of Northwest Somalia, besieging the major cities that remained under government control. The SNM also encouraged the formation of other rebel movements, including: the United Somali Congress (USC), which was active in central Somalia, and the Somali Patriotic Movement (SPM), which operated in southern Somalia. As the revolution spread, the SNM, the USC, and the SPM signed an agreement on November 24, 1990, to unify to facilitate a common military strategy. By the end of the year each of the rebel organizations had made advances against the government.

On January 26, 1991, the USC gained control of Mogadishu by seizing the presidential palace and ending the war; Siad Barre fled the country.

Termination and Outcome: The SNM–USC–SPM agreement failed to survive after the rebel victory, and Somalia was left in a state of near anarchy. The USC formed an interim government, led by Ali Mahdi Muhammad, though conflict over control of the capital erupted between Muhammad and USC General Mohamed Farah Aideed. The SNM refused to recognize the USC government and declared the Northwest to be an independent Republic of Somaliland. The SPM remained dominant in the South. Conflict among the rebel groups that won this war would lead to a new war in November 1991 (Intra-state War #865.8).

Coding Decisions: The war is coded as a victory for all three rebel organizations (SNM, USC, and SPM) in that their collective efforts led to the disintegration of the Siad Barre regime, even though the USC succeeded in creating the new government.

It is estimated that 50,000 Somalis lost their lives during this war. The vast majority of these would have been civilians. Even though combatant deaths are not available, the level of fighting indicates that this conflict can be coded as a war.

Sources: Arnold (2009); Bercovitch and Fretter (2004); Brogan (1998); Clodfelter (2002); Cordesman (1993a, b); Cutter (2007); Duyvesteyn (2004); Project Ploughshares (2000).

INTRA-STATE WAR #852

Chad–Déby War of 1989 to 1990 (aka the Déby Coup)

Participants: Chad versus rebels led by Idriss Déby April 1 Movement and *Mouvement Patriotique du Salut* (MPS).
Dates: April 1, 1989, to December 2, 1990.
Battle-related Deaths: Chad: 3,000; Déby-led Rebels: 800.[140] (See Coding Decisions.)
Initiator: Déby-led Rebels.
Outcome: Déby-led Rebels win.
War Type: Civil for central control.
Total System Member Military Personnel: Armed Forces of Chad: 33,000 (prewar, initial); 50,000 (peak, final).[141]

Theater Armed Forces: Armed Forces of Déby-led Rebels (April 1 Movement and MPS): 74 (initial); 2,000 (peak, final).[142]

Antecedents: Hissène Habré (the leader of the *Forces Armées du Nord* [FAN]), came to power in June 1982 during a war against Chad's president (and leader of the *Forces Armées Populaires* [FAP]) Goukouni Ouddei (Intra-state War #820 in 1980–1984). Libya, France, and Zaire had intervened in that war, and at the conclusion of the fighting, both France and Libya agreed to remove their military personnel. However Libyan forces remained and expanded their presence in the Aouzou strip, which led to the war between Libya and Chad (Inter-state War #207 in 1986 to 1987). Libya lost the war in 1987, partially due to the leadership of Habré's chief military advisor, Idriss Déby. Déby was a long-time ally of Habré, having served as the chief of staff for FAN. After Habré had come to power, he named Déby commander-in-chief of the army. However, Habré had become concerned about Déby's growing popularity, so in 1985, Habré sent him for advanced training in France. Déby's success in 1987 served only to heighten the growing rift between the two men.

Narrative: After the conclusion of the war with Libya, Habré's government still faced internal opposition, much of it ethnically related to Chad's split between the Muslims in the North, and the Christians and animist blacks in the South. Habré (from the North) responded to the opposition by launching a terror campaign in the South. Habré also faced opposition from those who were concerned by the growing concentration of power in Habré's hands. On April 1, 1989, Habré accused three of his senior advisors, Déby, Hassan Djamous (commander in chief of the army), and Mahamat Itno (minister of the interior) of plotting a coup against him. The three supposed rebels gathered a column of seventy-four loyal soldiers, fought their way out of the capital (N'Djamena), and fled toward Sudan, pursued by a contingent of Habré's troops. The record is unclear whether Djamous was killed on the night of April 1 or in the subsequent battle. The rebels fled into East Chad, where they hoped to organize a rebellion among the Zaghawa people who lived there and in South Sudan, with the goal of toppling Habré (with Sudan's assistance). However, the rebels, now referred to as the April 1 Movement, were found in Sudan by Habré's soldiers (of FANT), and a fierce battle ensued on April 12, which caused heavy casualties on both sides. Of the three leaders, only Déby survived. Déby continued to gather support and soldiers for his army, even traveling to Libya, where he received a pledge of assistance.

Meanwhile, Habré, who received significant assistance from the United States and France, was under international pressure to create a process for reconciliation and involving the opposition in the government. In June 1989, he instead put forward a draft constitution that created a strong presidency and one-party legislature. Subsequent elections affirmed the constitution and gave Habré a new seven-year term of office. This served to convince many of Habré's opponents that he would have to be removed from office by force. In October of that year, the April 1 Movement advanced back into Chad and launched attacks at government positions there. Chad then launched Operation Rezzou, in which FANT forces advanced into Darfur and engaged the MPS and Islamic Legion in a weeklong battle. After suffering heavy casualties, the legion retreated back to Libya

Acting upon a suggestion from Libya's Muammar al-Gadhafi, Déby created the *Mouvement Patriotique du Salut* (Patriotic Salvation Movement, or MPS), by combining the April 1 Movement, Chadian army defectors, Arab mercenaries, and elements of Libya's Islamic Legion. The MPS began making raids into Chad from its base in Sudan. In March 1990, an MPS incursion in Chad overwhelmed the FANT soldiers near the border. On November 10, 1990, Déby led his 2,000-strong MPS army against the 30,000-strong Chadian army. The rebels seized the town of Abéché on November 30, with FANT soldiers fleeing or defecting to the MPS. The MPS then marched westward, and Déby's forces succeeded in capturing the capital, N'Djamena. Déby assumed the presidency on December 2, 1990.

Termination and Outcome: The war is coded as a victory for the Déby rebels in that they accomplished their goal of overthrowing Habré. Déby would later be challenged by a revolt (Intra-state War #906) in 1998.

Coding Decisions: We have coded this war as an intra-state civil war because both the start of the war and most of the major combat takes place within Chad. Though there are extra-state war elements as

Chad conducts armed conflict with non-state actors outside its borders, these events are not of sufficient intensity or duration to merit the transformation of the whole war into an extra-state war. Though Libya commits soldiers of the Islamic Legion to this war, they are not of a sufficient number for Libya to be coded as a war participant.

Keesing's reports the battle-death numbers cited as deaths just during the November 10 to 30, 1990, period. We report them here in the absence of alternative data to give a sense of the overall fatalities of this war, though they are, needless to say, underestimates.

Sources: Arnold (2009); Brogan (1998); Cutter (2007); Dougueli (2014); Hall (2000); *Keesing's Record of World Events* (1989, 1990); Nolutshungu (1996); Skutsch and Shantz (2007); Stapleton (2013).

INTRA-STATE WAR #857
First Liberian War of 1989 to 1990

Participants: Liberia, Nigeria, Ghana, and Guinea versus the National Patriotic Front of Liberia (NPFL) and Independent National Patriotic Front (INPFL).
Dates: December 24, 1989, to November 28, 1990.
Battle-related deaths: Liberia: [ ]; Nigeria: [ ]; Guinea: [ ]; NPFL: [ ]; INPFL: [ ]; Total Combatant Deaths: [ ]. (See Coding Decisions.)
Initiator: NPFL.
Outcome: Stalemate.
War Type: Civil for central control.
Total System Member Military Personnel: Armed Forces of Liberia (AFL): 7,000 (prewar, initial); 8,000 (peak, final).[143] Armed Forces of Nigeria: 107,000 (prewar); 94,000 (initial, peak, final).[144] Armed Forces of Guinea: 15,000 (prewar, initial, peak, final).[145] Armed Forces of Ghana: 16,000 (prewar); 9,000 (initial, peak, final).[146]
Theater Armed Forces: Armed Forces of Liberia (AFL): 6,000 (initial, peak); 2,000 (final).[147] Armed Forces of NPFL: 200 (initial); 10,000 (peak, final).[148] Armed Forces of INPFL, participating from July 1990: 500 (initial); 6,000 (peak, final).[149] Armed Forces of Nigeria, participating from August 24, 1990): 1,000 (initial), 2,600 (peak, final).[150] Armed Forces of Guinea, participating from August 24, 1990: 1,000 (initial, peak, final).[151] Armed Forces of Ghana, participating from August 24, 1990): 700 (initial); 2,000 (peak, final).[152]

Antecedents: A number of freed slaves from the United States settled in Liberia in the mid-nineteenth century. After becoming a republic in 1847, Liberia was controlled by this relatively small group of Americo-Liberians for more than 130 years. The situation changed in 1980, when Samuel K. Doe (of the indigenous Krahn tribe) seized power in Liberia through a coup that killed President William R. Tolbert Jr. and most of the ruling elite. Doe, who became a ruthless dictator, was elected president in 1985 in what many claimed were rigged elections. This mobilized the antigovernment opposition, and there was a failed coup attempt against Doe that year.

Charles Taylor had been an official in the Doe administration. When he was removed from office, he fled to the United States, where he was arrested. Facing extradition, Taylor escaped from prison (perhaps with the assistance of the CIA) and fled to Libya to receive guerrilla training. There Taylor became a protégé of Libya's Muammar Qaddafi. Taylor moved on to Côte d'Ivoire, and while there he founded the National Patriotic Front of Liberia (NPFL) in conjunction with Ellen Johnson Sirleaf and Tom Woewiyu. With the backing of Libya, Taylor began to raise an army among those in North Liberia who had been persecuted by Doe's government.

Narrative: On December 24, 1989, Taylor and his 200-strong NPFL army invaded Liberia, where thousands rushed to join him, including many child soldiers. Doe responded by sending two battalions of the Liberian army (AFL) against the rebels. The indiscriminate fighting by both sides killed thousands of civilians. By May 1990, Taylor's forces controlled much of the country, and in June they besieged the capital Monrovia. At the end of July, the rebel army was divided as Prince Yormie Johnson split from the NPFL to form the Independent National Patriotic Front (INPFL). Both rebel organizations continued to fight against the government.

Taylor's advance was halted by the intervention of the Economic Community of West African States (ECOWAS). On August 20, 1989, ECOWAS was instrumental in creating an interim government under the presidency of Amos Sawyer. Despite the weakness of President Doe's position, he refused to resign and accept the new government, as did Taylor and Johnson, who both made claims to the presidency. ECOWAS also decided to send a peacekeeping force, referred to as Economic Community of West African States Monitoring Group (ECOMOG), to Liberia. ECOMOG initially dispatched 3,000 troops from Nigeria, Ghana, Guinea, and Sierra Leone, which arrived in Liberia on August 24, 1990. Unlike usual peacekeeping missions, ECOMOG became involved in peacemaking efforts as it attempted to separate the participants. As ECOMOG forces began to establish positions at Monrovia's port, they were attacked by the NPFL. In fighting over the next two days, the ECOMOG forces attacked and disabled the NPFL's only ship.

When Doe visited the ECOMOG headquarters on September 9, 1990, he was captured by an INPLF force and taken to an INPFL base where he was tortured and killed. On September 29, ECOMOG doubled the size of its army with the arrival of additional brigades from Ghana and Nigeria. ECOMOG then became actively involved in the war, fighting on the side of the Liberian government against the rebels. It was successful in forcing the NPFL to retreat from its positions around the capital.

Termination and Outcome: At this point, the rebel forces and the government agreed to participate in ECOWAS-sponsored negotiations in Gambia. The agreement, the Bamako Accord, included a ceasefire and an agreement to peacefully resolve their disagreements concerning the interim government. The accord, signed on November 28, 1990, ended the fighting in a stalemate as the fundamental issues were not resolved. Warfare would resume two years later (Intra-state War #879).

Coding Decisions: The ECOMOG forces were composed of troops from Nigeria, Guinea, Ghana, and Sierra Leone. Of these, only Sierra Leone is not considered as a participant in this war because its contingent of 700 is below the 1,000 troop requirement for a state system member participation.[153]

In terms of battle-related deaths, a number of scholars mention that there were 10,000 deaths in Liberia during this war (1989 to 1990). It is unclear whether this figure includes the deaths of civilians, though as it presumably does, it is not cited in terms of combatant deaths.

A number of scholars refer to one civil war in Liberia encompassing the period of 1989 to 1997. COW coding rules divide this long period into two distinct wars based on the level of armed conflict. There is one distinct period, 1990 to 1992, during which combat generally ceased and fatality levels fell below war level, thus ending this war. The new war (Intra-state War #879: the Second Liberia War of 1992 to 1996) begins when fighting at war level resumes.

Sources: Adebajo (2002); Arnold (2008); Ciment (2007b); Clodfelter (2002); GlobalSecurity.org (2005a, b, d, e); Human Rights Watch (1993); Hutchful (1999); Meredith (2005); *The Military Balance* (1995); Olonisakin (2003); SIPRI (1995); Stapleton (2013); Uppsala Universitet (2004).

INTRA-STATE WAR #863
First Sierra Leone War of 1991 to 1996

Participants: Sierra Leone, Nigeria, United Liberation Movement for Democracy in Liberia (ULIMO), and Executive Outcomes versus the Revolutionary United Front (RUF) and National Patriotic Front of Liberia (NPFL).
Dates: March 23, 1991, to April 23, 1996.
Battle-related Deaths: Sierra Leone: [ ]; Nigeria: [ ]; ULIMO: [ ]; Executive Outcomes: [ ]; RUF: [ ]; NPFL: [ ].
Initiator: RUF.
Outcome: Compromise.
War Type: Civil for central control.
Total System Member Military Personnel: Armed Forces of Sierra Leone: 5,000 (prewar, initial); 8,000 (peak); 5,000 (final).[154] Armed Forces of Nigeria: 94,000 (prewar); 94,000 (initial, peak); 80,000 (final).[155]
Theater Armed Forces: Armed Forces of Sierra Leone (SLA): 14,000 (peak).[156] Armed Forces of RUF: 100 (initial).[157] Armed Forces of National Patriotic Front of Liberia (NPFL, Pro-rebel Intervener): [ ]. Armed Forces of Nigeria (Pro-government Intervener) participating from May 1991: 1,200 initial.[158] Armed Forces of ULIMO (Pro-government Intervener) participating from July 1991: 1,000 (initial, peak, final).[159] Armed Forces of Executive Outcomes (EO, Pro-government Intervener) participating from March 1995: 3,500 (initial, peak, final).[160]

Antecedents: Siaka Stevens came to power in the former British colony of Sierra Leone in a coup in 1968. Stevens ruled for seventeen years and created a one-party system (of the All People's Congress [APC]), which was known for its repression and its exploitation of the diamond industry to enrich the ruling elite. The collapse of Sierra Leone's economy contributed to the informal coup that brought Gen. Joseph Saidu Momoh to power in 1985 through an election in which he was the only candidate. Momoh tried unsuccessfully to implement an economic reform program with the World Bank, yet Sierra Leone's economy continued to disintegrate. Complaints about the economy and government corruption led to protests and strikes, and Momoh responded by curtailing political activity even more in late 1987.

Opposition to Momoh coalesced on a couple of fronts. In 1991, a rebel movement known as the Revolutionary United Front (RUF) was created under the leadership of Foday Sankoh. Sankoh had served in Sierra Leone's army before being imprisoned for seven years for taking part in a 1971 mutiny. Sankoh and his colleagues began gathering supporters for an armed conflict against the government. They traveled to neighboring Liberia, where they worked and trained with revolutionary leader Charles Taylor, the founder of the National Patriotic Front of Liberia (NPFL). Having similar goals, Taylor helped to train and arm the RUF recruits.

Another sector that was unhappy with Momoh was a segment of Sierra Leone's military. Soldiers were poorly supplied and rarely paid on time, and some of the soldiers wanted to inform the government of their grievances. Both RUF and the soldiers would confront Momoh in 1991 and 1992.

Narrative: On March 23, 1991, the RUF crossed from Liberia into Sierra Leone and began a war to overthrow the government. RUF advanced into the countryside: one of its targets was the diamond mining region, and the rebels hoped to use its proceeds to finance both RUF and Taylor's NPFL. The NPFL sent a contingent into Sierra Leone to assist RUF. As RUF occupied the mining towns, it gained the support of the illegal diamond diggers and forcibly recruited child soldiers. In response to the uprising, President Momoh sent a force of 2,150 troops to confront the NPFL incursions along the border. He also substantially increased the size of Sierra Leone's army and appealed to Nigeria and Guinea for assistance. In May 1991, Nigeria sent 1,200 troops, and Guinea contributed 300 soldiers to help stabilize the situation in Sierra Leone.

Momoh also encouraged Liberian refugees living in Sierra Leone to create their own antirevolutionary group (the United Liberation Movement for Democracy in Liberia [ULIMO]), both to help the Sierra Leone armed forces (SLA) in the fight against RUF and to become involved in the fight against the NPFL in Liberia (see Intra-state War #879). RUF and NPFL soon occupied significant portions of Southeast Sierra Leone. In November 1991, the SLA, Guinea, Nigeria, and ULIMO launched an offensive against the rebels. They were successful in recapturing some territory but were unable to destroy RUF. Another offensive in January 1992 had similar results.

At this point, resentment within the military was growing because the government did not have the resources to pay or provide for the new recruits. A group of young officers including Capt. Valentine Strasser drove to the capital to report their grievances on April 29, 1992. When President Momoh saw them, he fled, at which point the officers declared themselves as the new government (the National Provisional Ruling Council [NPRC]) under the leadership of Strasser.

Ultimately, both Strasser and the RUF's Sankoh seemed primarily interested in exploiting Sierra Leone's diamond wealth. Conflict over the next three years focused upon gaining control of the diamond mines and removing the diamonds to fund the military operations. Each side had successful operations, though RUF gradually extended its control toward the capital, Freetown. By that point, the fighting had displaced 750,000 people. In March 1995, Strasser did use some of his diamond wealth to hire a South African mercenary army, Executive Outcomes (EO), to drive the RUF back from the capital. EO was successful in that mission in April 1995. EO assistance also enabled the government coalition to regain control over most the country, though it was unable to completely destroy the RUF. RUF's Sankoh did begin to make peace overtures.

Sierra Leone's military was becoming frustrated by the government's inability to devise a strategy to defeat the RUF. Consequently, a group of soldiers within the ruling NPRC, led by Strasser's deputy, Brigadier Gen. Julius Maada-Bio, ousted Strasser from office on January 16, 1996. Under international pressure, Maada-Bio scheduled an election, in which Ahmad Tejan Kabbah was elected, taking office on March 29, 1996.

Termination and Outcome: Ahmed Tejan Kabbah immediately entered into peace negotiations. A compromise agreement was signed in early April 1996, which stopped the civil war, though RUF continued terrorizing citizens. A second agreement was signed in November 1996, which stipulated ending the contract with EO. Its departure precipitated another coup and a countercoup, which led to the involvement of the UN in returning Kabbah to power. War would resume in 1998 (Intra-state War #902).

Coding Decisions: Though Guinean forces engaged in combat alongside Nigeria in support of the government, the size of its contingent (300 soldiers) is insufficient for it to be considered a state system member war participant.[161] Britain also sent 1,000 troops, but they seem mostly to have been involved in providing technical assistance, rather than combat, and thus Britain is not coded as a war participant.[162]

Combatant fatalities are unknown.

Sources: Adebajo (2002); Arnold (2009); Ciment and Cuthbertson (2007); Clodfelter (2002); Edgerton (2002); Meredith (2005); Oliver and Atmore (2004); Stapleton (2013).

INTRA-STATE WAR #865.8
Second Somalia War of 1991 to 1997

Participants: Somalia (Ali Mahdi Faction), Canada, France, Italy, Nigeria, Pakistan, and the United States versus Aideed Faction and the Somali National Front (SNF).

Dates: September 3, 1991, to December 22, 1997.

Battle-related Deaths: Somalia USC: [ ]; Aideed Faction: [ ]; Total Somali Combatant Deaths: 32,000; United States: 44; Pakistan: 24; France: 2.

Initiator: Aideed Faction.

Outcome: Stalemate.

War Type: Civil for central control.

Total System Member Military Personnel: Armed Forces of Somalia: 47,000 (prewar); 4,000 (initial); 7,000 (peak); [ ] (final).[163] Armed Forces of Canada: 86,000 (prewar), 82,000 (initial, peak); 75,000 (final).[164] Armed Forces of France: 554,000 (prewar, initial, peak); 475,000 (final).[165] Armed Forces of Italy: 493,000 (prewar); 473,000 (initial, peak); 419,000 (final).[166] Armed Forces of Nigeria: 94,000 (prewar, initial, peak); 76,000 (final).[167] Armed Forces of Pakistan: 550,000 (prewar); 565,000 (initial); 610,000 (final, peak).[168] Armed Forces of United States: 2,180,000 (prewar); 2,110,000 (initial, peak); 1,530,000 (final).[169]

Theater Armed Forces: Armed Forces of Somalia (Ali Mahdi faction): 5,000 (initial).[170] Armed Forces of Aideed Faction: 10,000 (initial).[171] Armed Forces of Canada (Pro-government Intervener), participating from December 15, 1992, to May 4, 1993: 1,500 (initial, peak, final). Armed Forces of France (Pro-government Intervener), participated from December 25, 1992, to March 21, 1994: 2,100 (initial, peak). Armed Forces of Italy (Pro-government Intervener), participating from December 14, 1992, to March 21, 1994: [ ]. Armed Forces of Nigeria (Pro-government Intervener): [ ]. Armed Forces of Pakistan (Pro-government Intervener), participating from September 14, 1992, to March 5, 1995: 500 (initial); 7,200 (peak). Armed Forces of United States (Pro-government Intervener), participating from December 9, 1992, to March 25, 1994: 25,000 (initial, peak); 4,000 (final).

Antecedents: The disintegration of Somalia began with Somalia's 1978 loss in the Ogaden War (Intra-state War #805 and Inter-state War #187). Violence spilled into Somalia itself, precipitating a civil war in 1988 (Intra-state War #848), which ended in the defeat of the government of Siad Barre on January 26, 1991. Somalia was left in a state of near anarchy as the various rebel groups took control of different parts of the country. Factional fighting within the winning coalition soon broke out: the United Somali Congress (USC), which controlled the capital, proclaimed Ali Mahdi Mohammed (of the Abgal group) as president, though he faced competition from Gen. Mohamed Farah Aideed. The Somali National Movement (SNM) refused to recognize the USC government, seized control of the North, and in May 1991 declared it to be an independent Republic of Somaliland. The Somali Patriotic Movement (SPM) remained dominant in the South. Siad Barre briefly remained in the South, where he rallied his followers into the Somali National Front (SNF). However, he was soon forced to flee to Kenya, where he died in 1995.

Narrative: In July 1991, a meeting of the United Somali Congress (USC) attempted to resolve the conflict between the Aideed and Mahdi factions. The compromise solution was that Aideed was elected as chair, while

Mahdi would remain as president. The attempt to create a unity government failed as conflict between the two groups continued, precipitating conflict at war level at the beginning of September. The Mahdi faction controlled the capital and the remaining institutions of government and thus is considered to be the government. In the South, the Somali National Front (SNF), a group loyal to former president Siad Barre continued to oppose the USC government. As the fighting between the Aideed and Mahdi factions became more intense, another attempt at forming a unity government was made in October, which also failed. Heavy fighting between November 1991 and March 1992 killed an estimated 14,000 people in the capital. Aideed was able to advance and to take control of large sectors of Mogadishu. In February 1992, the UN launched a failed attempt to broker a cease-fire, and some of the most serious combat of the war took place in 1992.

The growing humanitarian crisis (with almost a million Somali refugees outside the country and 25 percent of the remaining population facing starvation) prompted the UN to launch a peacekeeping mission in April 1992. The goal of UNOSOM was to halt the fighting; however, its initial deployment of 50 peace-monitors and 500 armed guards could do little. In November, Aideed demanded that the UN forces leave. The following month, the United States, with UN approval, launched Operation Restore Hope (or United Task Force—UNITAF), which entailed sending 37,000 troops (21,000 from the United States) to Somalia. UNITAF's mission was different from UNOSOM's, shifting to peacemaking and using all necessary means to restore peace and security. UNOSOM was ended at this point, and the American troops began to arrive on December 9, 1992. UN Secretary General Boutros Boutros-Ghali felt that UNITAF should prioritize disarming the Somali factions, which was not the US focus, and this difference of opinion hindered the mission's success. UNITAF launched an amphibious assault into Mogadishu and went on to seize Mogadishu's airport, the airport at Baidoa, and the port city of Kismayo to enable the delivery of humanitarian relief. On March 24, 1993, the UN authorized a task force (UNOSOM II) to assume the tasks of the U.S. coalition, and by May 4, 1993, the coalition had been transferred to UN authority. Though the United States withdrew most of its troops, it continued to maintain a rapid response force on ships off the Somali coast. On October 3, a U.S. force of 160 soldiers was dispatched by helicopter to capture Aideed, and two helicopters were shot down and 18 soldiers killed. In March 1994 the United States withdrew the last of its land forces from Somalia, and UNOSOM II was evacuated in March 1995.

Though the international interventions had difficulties, they did have several successes. Not only did they deliver humanitarian assistance that saved lives, but their withdrawal ultimately weakened the factions. Though conflict continued, it became much narrower, over local political and economic interests rather than countrywide political control. Meanwhile, Aideed was killed in battle in 1996, and control of his faction passed to his son, Hussein Mohamed Farrah. In December 1997, at a meeting in Cairo, the leaders of the Aideed and Mahdi factions (along with twenty-six other factional leaders) agreed to the terms of a peace accord, which ended the war.

Termination and Outcome: The outcome of the war is coded as a stalemate. The fundamental issues were not resolved, and low-level conflict persisted among the factions. Somalia entered what some have called a failed state phase. War would return in 2006 (Intra-state War #940.8).

Coding Decisions: Though some scholars discuss a Somali civil war that lasts from 1968 to 2013, we code three wars (1988 to 1991, 1991 to 1997, and 2006 to 2008) as either the level of fatalities falls below war level or the participants in the conflict change between phases.

There were more participants in UNITAF than those listed, however. For a system member to be considered a war participant, it has be engaged in armed combat and either allocate more than 1,000 troops to a conflict or suffer more than 100 battle-related deaths.

Sources: Australian War Memorial (1992); Bercovitch and Fretter (2004); Ciment (2007a–h); Clodfelter (2002); Cordesman (1993a, b); Cutter (2007); Human Rights Watch (1994a, b, c); INS Resource Information Center (1993); Kieh (2002); Menkhaus (2010); "Operation Deliverance" (2009); Project Ploughshares (2005); Prunier (1997, 2004); Saalax and Xildhiban (2010); Saleem (2011); Stapleton (2013); United Nations (1997); "US Plans to Leave Troops to Back UN Somalia Unit" (1993).

INTRA-STATE WAR #868
Jukun–Tiv War of 1991 to 1992

Participants: Jukun versus Tiv.
Dates: October 1991 to March 1992.

Battle-related Deaths: Jukun: [ ]; Tiv: [ ]; Total Combatant Deaths. (See Coding Decisions.)
Initiator: Unclear.
Outcome: Stalemate.
War Type: Intercommunal.
Theater Armed Forces: Armed Forces of the Jukun: [ ]. Armed Forces of the Tiv: [ ].

Antecedents: The Jukun are an ethnic group clustered in the Taraba province of East Nigeria. In the Southwest lies the adjacent province of Benue, where many Tiv live. The conflict between the two groups partially can be traced to their experience with British colonial rule. The British decided to rule by relying on local authorities, and they chose the Jukun king (Aku Uka) to rule over both peoples. As Nigeria prepared for independence, conflict emerged between the two groups because the minority Jukun, who dominated politics in the region, feared the potential political power of the more numerous Tiv, who might use elections to strip the Jukun of their power. Their fear was reinforced in an election for the House of Representatives in 1959, when the Tivs cooperated with the majority Hausa people to ensure the election of a Tiv candidate. After Nigeria gained its independence in 1960, the Jukun and Tiv peoples engaged in periodic skirmishes, as both sides increasingly resorted to armed force to determine elections.

Narrative: Conflict began in 1990 between Jukun and Tiv political factions, but it reached intercommunal war level in October 1991 as a result of government plans to create a new administrative district that would be placed either within an area dominated by the Jukun or one populated by the Tiv. The Tiv apparently did not want to accept the authority of the Aku Uka to control the distribution of land. From the perspective of the Tiv's leader (the Tor Tiv), the issue was more the pattern of discrimination against the Tiv exercised by the Jukun. The election campaign for the state governor precipitated combat between armed partisans of both communities.

Both communities blame the other for starting the conflict. The Jukuns portray the war as part of a Tiv plan to seize political power. According to the Tiv perspective, the Jukun had launched a program referred to as Operation PATSWI, meaning an operation to recover land. The operation included recruiting and training warriors to strike against the Tiv.[172] Furthermore, the Tiv claimed that the local police sided with the Jukun fighters and that the government would not take action to stop the killing. Clearly, villages were attacked and burned in both communities, and thousands of refugees fled the area. Yet, by some measures, the Tiv suffered more (as a result of the violence, twenty-nine Tiv primary schools were closed, whereas this was true for only six Jukun schools), and virtually all the Tiv villages were burned.[173] Accounts also seem to agree that the conflict escalated further on February 12, 1992, when the Jukuns attacked the Hausa town of Bantaji.

On February 14, Nigeria's Vice President Augustus Aikhomu sponsored a meeting between the Tor Tiv and the Aku Uka in the capital, but the attempt to get the leaders to stop the fighting failed. Finally in March, the presence of government forces was successful in ending the war.

Termination and Outcome: The war ended as a stalemate in that the fundamental sources of conflict were not resolved. Armed conflict at below-war level would emerge in 1998 and 2002.

Coding Decisions: The decision to code this conflict as a war was difficult. The media reports generally referred to it as a war, but the lack of specific information makes this terminology suspect. There were a significant number of deaths caused during this brief period, with an estimate of 5,000 killed as the most common. However, there is no indication of how many of these would have been combatant deaths, which is a common feature of intercommunal wars.

Sources: Akombo (2005); Facts on File (1991–1992); *Keesing's Record of World Events* (1991–1992); Maier (2000).

INTRA-STATE WAR #879
Second Liberian War of 1992 to 1996

Participants: Liberia, Nigeria, Ghana, Guinea, Senegal, United Liberation Movement for Democracy in Liberia (ULIMO), Liberian Peace Council (LPC) versus the National Patriotic Front of Liberia (NPFL).
Dates: October 15, 1992, to August 19, 1995, and April 5, 1996, to August 20, 1996.

Battle-related Deaths: Liberia: [ ]; NPFL: [ ]; Nigeria: [ ] Ghana: [ ]; Guinea: [ ]; Senegal: [ ]; ULIMO: [ ]; LPC: [ ].
Initiator: NPFL.
Outcome: Compromise.
War Type: Civil for central control.
Total System Member Military Personnel: Armed Forces of Liberia: 5,000 (prewar); 2,000 (initial, peak); [ ] (final).[174] Armed Forces of Nigeria: 94,000 (prewar); 76,000 (initial); 80,000 (peak, final).[175] Armed Forces of Guinea: 15,000 (prewar); 15,000 (initial, peak); 12,000 (final).[176] Armed Forces of Ghana: 9,000 (prewar); 7,000 (initial, peak, final).[177] Armed Forces of Senegal: 18,000 (prewar, initial, peak, final).[178]
Theater Armed Forces: Armed Forces of Liberia (AFL): 3,000 (initial, peak, final).[179] Armed Forces of NPFL: 10,000 (initial); 12,000 (peak, final).[180] Armed Forces of ULIMO (combined ULIMO-J and ULIMO-K, Pro-government Intervener): 7,000 (peak, final).[181] Armed Forces of the LPC (Pro-government Intervener), participating from October 1993): 800 (initial); 2,000 (peak, final).[182] Armed Forces of Nigeria (Pro-government Intervener): 2,600 (initial); 10,000 (peak); 6,000 (final).[183] Armed Forces of Guinea (Pro-government Intervener): 1,000 (initial, peak, final).[184] Armed Forces of Ghana (Pro-government Intervener): 2,000 (initial, peak, final).[185] Armed Forces of Senegal (Pro-government Intervener), participating to January 1993: 1,500 (initial, peak, final).[186]

Antecedents: The previous intra-state war in Liberia (War #857) involved a 1989 attempt to overthrow the government of Samuel K. Doe by Charles Taylor's National Patriotic Front of Liberia (NPFL). As the NPFL surrounded the capital of Monrovia, the NPFL split, and Prince Yormie Johnson withdrew from the NPFL in late July 1990 to form the Independent National Patriotic Front (INPFL). Both rebel organizations continued to fight against the government.

Taylor's offensive was stopped by the intervention of Economic Community of West African States (ECOWAS). ECOWAS both created an interim government for Liberia under the presidency of Amos Sawyer (which was not accepted by Doe, Taylor, and Johnson), and it dispatched a peacekeeping force, the Economic Community of West African States Monitoring Group (ECOMOG), with troops from Nigeria, Ghana, Guinea, and Sierra Leone. The ECOMOG troops, which arrived in Liberia on August 24, 1990, immediately became involved directly in the war as combatants on the side of the Liberian government. President Doe was captured and killed by the INPFL in September 1990. The ECOMOG forces gradually pushed Taylor's troops away from the capital Monrovia. The combatants accepted the ECOWAS proposals for negotiations, and the resulting agreement, the Bamako Accord, included a cease-fire and an agreement to resolve their disagreements peacefully concerning the interim government. The accord, signed on November 28, 1990, ended the war.

The cease-fire lasted for almost two years, though there was some low-level fighting. ECOMOG and interim president Amos Sawyer controlled the area around the capital Monrovia, while the NPFL dominated in most of the rest of the country. During that two-year period, a number of changes occurred. A broader peace agreement, the Lome Agreement, was signed in February 1991, though disarmament of forces was delayed. The INPFL divided and faded as a resistance army, while a new group appeared: the United Liberation Movement of Liberia for Democracy (ULIMO) was created in May 1991 by followers of former president Doe who had served in the Liberian Armed Forces (ALF). ULIMO fought briefly at the side of Sierra Leone in its war against the Revolutionary United Front (RUF, see Intra-state War #863) before entering Liberia in September 1991. Taylor's NPFL continued to be wary of disarmament and turning over territory to ECOMOG, especially as rumors emerged about an ECOMOG–ULIMO alignment. ECOMOG increased its forces with the addition of troops from Senegal. ULIMO–NPFL violence escalated as ULIMO seized a diamond-mining center.

Narrative: This war started on October 15, 1992, when the NPFL launched Operation Octopus, in an attempt to seize control of the capital Monrovia from ECOMOG, the Liberian government (ALF), and ULIMO. The Nigerian air force bombed NPFL positions, and the NPFL offensive was stopped by forces from ECOMOG, ALF, and ULIMO. Fighters from all sides engaged in looting throughout the city. In January 1993, ECOMOG launched an offensive against the NPFL and made major gains. Soon thereafter Senegal withdrew its troops from ECOMOG.

Taylor decided to participate in a series of talks brokered by the UN, the Organization of African Unity (OAU), and ECOWAS representatives to reach a settlement. A new accord (the Contonou Agreement) was signed by the NPFL, ULIMO, and Sawyer on July 23, 1993. This accord differed from earlier agreements in that it included provisions for a new interim government for Liberia, the Liberia National Transition Government, which was to include all the major parties. However, the implementation of the agreement was delayed continuously, while fighting continued. In October 1993, a new group emerged: the Liberian Peace Council, an offshoot of the AFL, headed by George Boley, a former minister of education in the Doe government and a former member of ULIMO. The LPC joined the government in the fight against the NPFL.

The years 1994 and 1995 included attempts at negotiated settlements, interspersed with continued fighting. On May 16, 1994, the new transitional government (which included the interim government, NPFL, and ULIMO) was formed, yet disarmament was sidelined as fighting was renewed, including an ECOMOG attack on the NPFL in July that caused heavy casualties. Widespread atrocities against civilians increased as ULIMO split into two rival ethnic factions. The LPC gained control of areas of the Southeast from the NPFL, yet the NPFL still controlled the bulk of the country, and no one side ever was able to win militarily. The war was evolving into a general stalemate.

By the middle of 1995, ECOMOG was growing tired of the war, and yet another peace accord, the Abuja Accord, was signed on August 19, 1995, creating a six-member council of state, which included representatives from all the factions, to replace the transitional government. A new timetable of disarmament and elections was set. This agreement brought a general cessation in hostilities that lasted for almost eight months. However, on April 6, 1996, Taylor tried one more assault against the capital, where he met fierce resistance from ULIMO and the AFL. The fighting was the worst in three years. Another 80,000 people were displaced, and fighters looted millions of dollars' worth of equipment from the UN and humanitarian nongovernmental organizations. By late July, ECOMOG retained control of the capital after the factions' leaders ordered their forces to withdraw.

Termination and Outcome: The war ended as a compromise as a new peace accord was signed in August 1996. The peacekeeping forces began disarming the combatants in November. The militia leaders agreed to form their groups into political parties that would compete in an upcoming election. On July 19, 1997, Charles Taylor and his National Patriotic Party won a clear victory. Taylor was declared the president on July 23, 1997, and took office on August 2, 1997.

Taylor was able to remain in power, partially due to his control of the diamond trade. However, his administration began to falter in 2002. Fighting began as his regime was challenged by the Liberians United for Reconciliation and Democracy (LURD, Intra-state War #922). On August 11, 2003, Taylor resigned the presidency and fled to Nigeria.

Coding Decisions: The period of August 20, 1995, to April 4, 1996, is coded as a break in the war due to the reduction in hostilities as a result of the Abuja Accord. Combatant battle-death figures apparently are unavailable, but the level of killing among the population was horrendous. It has been mentioned that 200,000 to 300,000 people died in the war.

Sources: Adebajo (2002); Arnold (2008); Bercovitch and Fretter (2004); Ciment (2007b); Clodfelter (2002); DeGeorge (2001); GlobalSecurity.org (2005a, b, c, d, e); Human Rights Watch (1993); Human Rights Watch (1994a, b, c); Hutchful (1999); Meredith (2005); *The Military Balance* (1995); Olonisakin (2003); SIPRI (1995); Stapleton (2013); Uppsala Universitet (2004).

INTRA-STATE WAR #880
Angolan War of the Cities of 1992 to 1994

Participants: Angola versus Union for the Total Independence of Angola (UNITA).
Dates: October 28, 1992, to November 15, 1994.
Battle-related Deaths: Angola: [ ]; UNITA: [ ].
Initiator: UNITA.
Outcome: Stalemate.
War Type: Civil for central control.
Total System Member Military Personnel: Armed Forces of Angola: 150,000 (prewar); 128,000 (initial, peak); 120,000 (final).[187]
Theater Armed Forces: Armed Forces of UNITA: 55,000 (peak, final).[188]

Antecedents: Angola's first civil war (Intra-state War #804) had lasted for fifteen years (1976 to 1991).

It ended in a power-sharing arrangement between the Popular Movement for the Liberation of Angola (MPLA) government and the UNITA rebels led by Jonas Savimbi. The agreement stipulated that the UN would oversee the cease-fire and the transition to a multiparty democracy, which would involve elections within a year. The government held elections in 1992, and when UNITA lost by a narrow margin, it launched another war.

Narrative: In contrast to the earlier war, in this war, most of the fighting took place in the cities. At first, in October 1992, UNITA was driven out of the capital of Luanda. During the next two months, UNITA continued fighting in the North, capturing an air base and the city of Uige and much of the diamond region in the Northeast. Starting in January 1993, the rebels launched a nationwide offensive, taking the fighting to fifteen of Angola's eighteen provinces. The rebels made gains in the central part of the country as well, capturing the provincial capital (and Angola's second largest city) of Huambo in March 1993 after a two-month siege. UNITA soon controlled two-thirds of the country.

The tide then began to turn against UNITA. The UN imposed a trade embargo, and the United States ended its support. South African mercenaries joined the war on the side of the government and helped it stop the rebel advance. In 1994, the Angolan army (FAA) went on the offensive, recapturing Huambo and reducing the rebel-controlled territory to less than half of the country. Consequently, UNITA was persuaded to enter into another peace agreement.

Termination and Outcome: The negotiations in Lusaka, Zambia, produced an agreement on November 15, 1994, to stop fighting and enter into a coalition government. The agreement (the Lusaka Protocol) was overseen by a commission including UN representatives and 7,000 UN troops. Nonetheless, neither side was too scrupulous about adhering to the agreement's terms, and Savimbi procrastinated in complying so that he could rebuild his coffers with the mining profits. Finally in April 1977, a coalition government with UNITA ministers (though not Savimbi) was created. It did not last long, and fighting at war level would resume with a government offensive in December 1998 (Intra-state War #903).

Coding Decisions: Because of its urban focus, this war caused horrendous destruction. The estimates of the number of civilians killed range from 80,000 to 300,000, with at least 10,000 dying in the siege of Huambo. However, it is unclear how many of these were combatant deaths.

Sources: Bercovitch and Fretter (2004); Clodfelter (2002); *Keesing's Record of World Events* (1993, 1994); Malaquias (2007); Meredith (2005); *The Military Balance* (1995); Phillips and Axelrod (2005); Stapleton (2013).

INTRA-STATE WAR #883
Second Burundi War of 1993 to 1998

Participants: Burundi Government and Hutu Militias versus Tutsi Army and Tutsi Militias.
Dates: October 21, 1993, to July 20, 1998.
Battle-related Deaths: Burundi: [ ]; Hutu Militias: [ ]; Tutsi Army: [ ]; Tutsi Militias: [ ]. (See Coding Decisions.)
Initiator: Tutsi army factions.
Outcome: Conflict continues at below-war level.
War Type: Civil for central control.
Total System Member Military Personnel: Armed Forces of Burundi: 13,000 (prewar, initial); 35,000 (peak, final).[189]
Theater Armed Forces: Hutu Militias (a Rebel Aggregate), consisting of:

National Forces of Liberation (FNL): [ ].
Intagoheka, participating from April 1994): [ ].
Forces for the Defense of Democracy (FDD), participating from June 1994: [ ].
Tutsi Militia: [ ].

Antecedents: The First Burundi war (Intra-state War #789 in 1972) concerned an attack by the Hutus against the Tutsi government, which then led to widespread violence against the Hutu. Conflict between the Hutu and Tutsi continued periodically for the next twenty years. In 1987, Pierre Buyoya, a Tutsi military officer, led a coup that overthrew the government of Jean-Baptiste Bagaza. Though he promised reconciliation between the Hutu and the Tutsi, Buyoya's regime was dominated by Tutsi. In 1988, the Hutu, who were angered by the enduring Tutsi domination and fearing a Tutsi attack, brutally killed Tutsi. The Tutsi responded, killing about 15,000 Hutu. Unlike the earlier incident, this conflict appears to have been more the murder and massacre of peasants rather than organized attacks by combatants. Under international pressure, Buyoya brought more Hutu into his government and attempted to liberalize the practices of the regime. In June 1993, Buyoya conducted an open election. The Hutu candidate was Melchior Ndadaye. Ndadaye had fled Burundi during the 1972 war, going to Rwanda, where he was involved in the creation of the Burundi Workers' Party. He returned to Burundi in 1983, and he and his followers created the Front for Democracy in Burundi (FRODEBU), which remained underground until before the 1993 elections. In the election, Ndadaye represented FRODEBU, though he had the support of other Hutu parties as well. Ndadaye won the presidency (taking office on July 10) and the Hutu won the majority of parliamentary seats. Even though Ndadaye tried to incorporate Tutsi in his government, his reform efforts threatened entrenched Tutsi interests.

Narrative: On October 21, 1993, President Ndadaye and a number of Hutu government officials were murdered in a coup attempt by Tutsi army officers. The initial coup failed in that Ndadaye's civilian government maintained control. Prime Minister Sylvie Kinigi (a Tutsi woman) was named acting president. The ensuing violence involved both a war of army forces loyal to the civilian government and Hutu militias fighting against Tutsi-dominated factions of the military and Tutsi militias (in what has been called a creeping coup)[190] and violence against civilians, which killed 50,000 civilians in the next few months alone. The focus here is on the war or sustained combat between the organized, armed combatants, while the more well-known massacres of civilians are discussed only peripherally.

The civil war aspects became more clarified as the opposing groups solidified in 1994. On February 5, 1994, a coalition government was formed by the Hutu party FRODEBU and the Tutsi *Union pour le Progrès national* (Union for National Progress, or UPRONA) that included a Hutu president, Cyprien Ntaryamira, and a Tutsi prime minister, Anatole Kanyenkiko. Ntaryamira's presidency was brief: he and Rwanda's president, Juvenal Habyarimana, met in Tanzania to discuss ways to end the conflict, and both were killed on April 6, 1994, when their plane was shot down. The Burundi coalition appointed Sylvestra Ntibantunganya as the new president on April 8. The murder of Habyarimana also led to another war next door in Rwanda (Intra-state War #886). The events in Rwanda, where extremist Hutus killed hundreds of thousands of Tutsi, prevented a cessation of hostilities in Burundi. After the Rwandan Tutsi-led army defeated the Hutu government, Rwandan Hutu refugees poured into Burundi, aggravating the conflict there.

Since 1980, the primary Hutu organization had been the Party for the Liberation of the Hutu People (PALIPHEHUTU) with its armed wing, the National Forces of Liberation (FNL). In April 1994, another Hutu group emerged; a militia called Intagoheka began attacks against the Tutsi army. Then in June, the *Conseil National Pour la Défense de la Démocratie* (National Council of the Defense of Democracy, or CNDD) was formed as a Hutu organization with a military wing, the *Forces pour la Défense de la Démocratie* (Forces for the Defense of Democracy [FDD]). The FDD (with forces drawn from throughout Burundi) joined the war, launching attacks in the northwest provinces of Cibitoke and Bubanza in 1995, where they created local governments. Meanwhile, from March to June, the Tutsi army launched a campaign in the capital of Bujumbura, forcing the Hutu to flee—many to the West into Zaire. That fall, attacks by the FNL in Cibitoke prompted a Tutsi offensive there as well. In early 1996, the National Liberation Front (FROLINA), an offshoot of the FNL, began attacks on military posts in the South and Southwest. In response, the army began to move the population into resettlement camps to deprive the Hutu militias of their support. By the middle of 1996, the war had spread to eleven of the fifteen provinces, and the Ntibantunganya government was unable to act.

The army staged a coup on July 25, 1996, against Ntibantunganya, and former Tutsi president, Pierre Buyoya, was installed as president. The fighting continued in Bujumbura as the government described all Hutu males to be the enemy. Conflict also increased in the South as a by-product of the war in Zaire (Intra-state War #895).

Termination and Outcome: In June 1998, a Transitional Constitutional Act was passed that gave the Hutu greater representation in the parliament. The related cease-fire, negotiated as part of the Arusha Peace talks facilitated by Tanzania's former president Julius Nyerere, took effect on July 20, 1998, and reduced the level of fighting below war levels, thus ending this war. The armed wings of the Hutus (the FDD and FNL) did not accept the agreement and continued their attacks. Economic sanctions imposed on Burundi by neighboring states were lifted in 1999. Fighting at war levels would resume in 2001 (Intra-state War #918).

Coding Decisions: The government of Burundi is considered to be headed by the president. The major opponent was the Burundi Tutsi-dominated armed forces. During most of this period, the government exercised limited control over the army; the forces considered to be fighting on the side of the government include the various Hutu militias.

Estimates of the number of Burundins killed during this war range from 100,000 to 300,000. The overwhelming majority of these were civilians. However, significant numbers of combatants were reportedly killed, though specific numbers are unavailable.

Sources: Bercovitch and Fretter (2004); Cutter (2007); Clodfelter (2002); Dougherty (2004); GlobalSecurity.org (2014a, b, c, d, e); Home Office (2004); Lemarchand (2004); Phillips and Axelrod (2005); Project Ploughshares (2000); Skutsch and Allan (2007); Stapleton (2013); Tripp (2005).

INTRA-STATE WAR #886
Second Rwanda War of 1994

Participants: Rwanda and Hutu Militias versus Rwanda Patriotic Front (RPF).
Dates: April 6, 1994, to July 18, 1994.
Battle-related Deaths: Rwanda: [ ]; RPF: [ ].
Initiator: Rwanda.
Outcome: Patriotic Front wins.
War Type: Civil for central control.
Total System Member Military Personnel: Armed Forces of Rwanda: 30,000 (prewar, initial, peak, final).[191]
Theater Armed Forces: Rwanda Patriotic Front (RPF): 25,000 (initial, final).[192] Hutu Militias (Pro-government Intervener, consisting of the *Impuzamugambi* and *Interahamwe*): 40,000 (final).[193]

Antecedents: The Rwanda Patriotic Front (RPF) had been organized in Uganda to represent Tutsis who had been driven there by the civil war in 1963 (Intra-state War #760) and the subsequent killings of Tutsi civilians by the Hutu majority. Starting in 1990, the RPF began a low-level guerrilla war against Rwanda, which the RPF accused of conducting a genocide against the Tutsi. In 1992, the Hutu organizations began forming their own paramilitary wings: the ruling National Republican Movement for Democracy and Development (MRNDD) created the *Interahamwe*; and the extremist Coalition for the Defense of the Republic (CDR) created the *Impuzamugambi*, which was trained by France and served as one of the major Hutu death squads. In January 1993, the killing of 300 Tutsi civilians in North Rwanda precipitated an RPF offensive in February that advanced on the capital while also engaging in the murder of Hutu civilians. The intervention of 600 French troops with artillery helped stop the RPF advance, though low-level guerrilla attacks continued. Under international pressure, Rwanda's Hutu President Habyarimana signed the 1993 Arusha Accords with the RPF, by which Rwanda's Hutu government was to cede some power to the Tutsi. Implementation of the accord was to be supervised by the UN Assistance for Rwanda (UNAMIR), and troops from Belgium and Ghana began arriving in October 1993, while most French troops were to be withdrawn.

Meanwhile, the first Hutu president, Melchior Ndadaye, had been elected in Burundi, and his assassination by Tutsi army officers on October 21, 1993, precipitated a war there (Intra-state War #883). In April 1994, Rwanda's President Habyarimana and Burundi's President Cyprien Ntaryamir had attended a conference in Tanzania to addresses ways to diffuse the Hutu–Tutsi conflicts, and they were killed on April 6, when their plane was shot down, apparently by the extremely anti-Tutsi element of the Hutu palace guard, who opposed any compromise with the Tutsi (though the Tutsi RPF was initially blamed). This incident served both to increase the level of conflict in Burundi and to launch this new conflict in Rwanda. Refugees moving across their common border posed challenges to both governments.

Narrative: The armed conflict that began on April 6, 1994, was in essence two conflicts: a well-planned killing spree by the Rwandan Hutu army (FAR) and Hutu militia (*Impuzamugambi* and *Interahamwe*) squads against Tutsi civilians and a civil war between the FAR and the Tutsi RPF. The focus here is on the war, and the more well-known massacre of civilians will be addressed only peripherally.

A Rwandan military committee, led by Col. Theoneste Bagosora, immediately took control of the country, and the presidential guard and the *Interahamwe* began killing leading Tutsi figures (including Prime Minister Agathe Uwilingiyimana, who was killed alongside her ten Belgian UNAMIR guards). The RPF, under the command of Lt. Col. Charles Kayonga, left the parliament building and took a position north of the city where they repelled an FAR attack. The killing of Tutsi civilians spread. The main RFP forces were located outside the city, and on April 8, the RPF (commanded by Paul Kagame) began a three-pronged offensive from the North. One branch moved west, one east, and the largest contingent moved south toward the centrally located capital of Kigali. The RPF steadily advanced, increasing the size of its forces along the way. By April, the southern contingent had begun to encircle Kigali, and the Rwandan government relocated to Gitarama and later to Gisenyi. An international contingent (including French, Belgian, and Italian paratroopers) took control of the Kigali airport to evacuate European citizens. On May 22, the RPF captured the airport. By June 3, the RPF encircled Kigali, and heavy fighting continued there until July. The RPF captured Gitarama on June 13. Ten days later, France launched Operation Turquoise, whereby 2,500 French troops and 500 troops from African countries landed in Rwanda, supposedly to prepare a haven for the refugees along the Burundi border. The French mission also had an unannounced goal of stopping the RPF from gaining control of the country. They had seen the Hutu as the persecuted party, but when they encountered evidence of the Hutu massacres of Tutsi, the French mission changed to a more neutral posture. The RPF ultimately captured Kigali on July 4, 1994, and by July 18 captured Gisenyi.

Termination and Outcome: The Rwandan government and *Interahamwe* soldiers fled into Zaire, ending the war. The new Rwandan government was established along the lines of the Arusha Accords, though former president Habyarimana's party was banned. The military wing of the RPF became the new Rwandan army. Paul Kagame was assigned the roles of vice president and minister of defense. Pasteur Bizimungu, a Hutu who had joined the RPF was appointed. Kagame was the de facto ruler of the country, and he became president on March 24, 2000.

The end of the war precipitated a flood of about 2 million Hutu refugees into neighboring countries, creating a humanitarian crisis. The international community that had ignored the genocide then rushed aid to the refugee camps. The refugees included many of the FAR and Hutu militia soldiers who had committed the attacks against the civilians, and thus the international community aided the Hutu to organize in preparation for another war. The Hutu *Ressamblement Dèmocratique pour la Rwanda* (RDR) began to organize guerrilla contingents in the refugee camps, especially those in Zaire, to oppose the new Rwandan government. Rwanda responded by sponsoring a revolution by the Alliance of Democratic Forces of Congo (AFDL) led by Laurent-Désiré Kabila against Zaire (Intra-state War #895). War would return to Rwanda in 1997 (Intra-state War #896).

Coding Decisions: A number of scholars discuss a Rwandan Civil War lasting from 1990 to 1994. Yet it appears that the 1990-to-1994 period was more attacks against civilians (that killed 10,000 people) than a civil war. The 1994 war, which lasted only 100 days, covered a period during which 500,000 and 1,000,000 Rwandans were killed (mostly Tutsi victims of the government and militias). It is estimated that more than 75 percent of the Tutsi living in Rwanda were killed.[194] Deaths suffered by the combatants are unknown.

Sources: Browne (2001); Ciment and Quinn (2007); Clodfelter (2002); International Crisis Group (2001); *Keesing's Record of World Events* (2000); Kisangani (2012); Longman (2010); Meredith (2005); Phillips and Axelrod (2005); Stapleton (2013); Tripp (2005); Twagilimana (2003); United States Institute of Peace (2002).

INTRA-STATE WAR #895

Zaire–AFDL War of 1996 to 1997 (aka the First Congo War of 1996–1997)

Participants: Zaire, UNITA, and Mercenaries versus Alliance of Democratic Forces for the Liberation of Congo (AFDL), Rwanda (Rwanda Patriotic Army [RPA]), Uganda, Angola, and Mai Mai.

Dates: October 17, 1996, to May 15, 1997.

Battle-related Deaths: Zaire: [ ]; UNITA: [ ]; AFDL: [ ]; Rwanda: [ ]; Uganda: [ ]; Angola: [ ]; Burundi: [ ]; Mai Mai: [ ]; Total DRC Combatant Deaths: 4,000.

Initiator: Zaire.
Outcome: AFDL coalition wins.
War Type: Civil for central control.
Total System Member Military Personnel: Armed Forces of Zaire (FAZ): 40,000 (prewar); 50,000 (initial, peak); 30,000 (final).[195] Armed Forces of Rwanda: 30,000 (prewar); 55,000 (initial, peak); 40,000 (final).[196] Armed Forces of Uganda: 51,000 (prewar); 50,000 (initial, peak, final).[197] Armed Forces of Angola: 100,000 (prewar); 95,000 (initial, peak, final).[198] Armed Forces of Burundi: 22,000 (prewar); 25,000 (initial); 35,000 (peak, final).[199]
Theater Armed Forces: Armed Forces of Rwanda (RPA): 2,000 (initial); 10,000 (final).[200] *Interahamwe* (Pro-government Intervener including former FAR Soldiers), participating from November 1996: [ ]. Armed Forces of Rwanda UNITA (Pro-government Intervener), participating from April 1997: [ ]. Mercenary Armed Forces (Pro-government Intervener): 300 (initial); 3,000 (peak).[201] Armed Forces of AFDL: 2,000 (initial).[202] Armed Forces of Rwanda (Pro-rebel Intervener): [ ]. Armed Forces of Uganda (Pro-rebel Intervener): [ ]. Armed Forces of Burundi (Pro-rebel Intervener), participating from November 15, 1996: [ ]. Armed Forces of Angola (Pro-rebel Intervener, mainly the Katanga Tigers), participating from February 15, 1997: 3,000 (initial).[203] Armed Forces of the Mai Mai: (Pro-rebel Intervener), participating from December 20, 1996: 16,000 (initial); 25,000 (peak).[204]

Antecedents: Armed conflict in Zaire (formerly the Democratic Republic of Congo) tended to spill into other countries and vice versa. In a war from 1964 to 1965, rebels had attempted to create People's Republic of the Congo in the eastern half of the DRC (Intra-state War #762).

The rebellion was defeated by Zaire with assistance of Belgium. A number of rebels from the war fled into Angola, where they created the *Front Nationale pour la Libération du Congo* (FNLC). In 1975, after Zaire sent troops to intervene in the war in Angola (Inter-state War #186), the FNLC was roused into action and recrossed the border in 1978 in an attempt to overthrow the Zaire regime (Intra-state War #810). The war ended in a victory by Zaire, aided by France and Belgium. The FNLC retreated back into Angola. The 1980s were a period of general stability in Zaire, with the exception of the activities of Laurent Kabila. Kabila had been one of the leaders of the 1964 and 1965 war, and after defeat he had fled east, establishing a base in the eastern area of South Kivu province. Here his Party of Popular Revolution (PRP) created a secessionist Marxist state. In 1984 a contingent of PRP forces engaged in a brief conflict with the government army in North Katanga.

With the collapse of the Soviet Union, Zaire's President Mobutu Sese Seko came under pressure from the West to liberalize his regime, which led to a period of instability in the early 1990s as there was a reduction in foreign aid, a proliferation of political parties, and disenchantment within the military. In East Zaire, ethnic conflict broke out in Nord-Kivu province in March 1993. By the end of August, between 7,000 and 16,000 people had been killed, and 200,000 were internally displaced.[205] The situation was aggravated the following year as more than a million Hutu refugees fled from the 1994 genocide in Rwanda (see Intra-state War #886). Among the refugees were 20,000 to 25,000 former members of the Rwandan armed forces (FAR) and 30,000 to 40,000 warriors of the Hutu militias that had massacred the Tutsi population. The Tutsi Rwanda Patriotic Front (RPF) had defeated Rwanda's Hutu government, taking office in mid-July 1994. The Hutu refugees created the *Ressamblement Dèmocratique pour la Rwanda* (RDR) and began launching incursions back into Rwanda.

The flood of refugees also led to increasing unrest in Zaire as it altered the ethnic mix in Kivu. By 1996, there were attempts to remove citizenship from the Congolese Tutsi (Banyamulenge) population. Politicians used the fear of the creation of a Hutu homeland to incite conflict between the Tutsi and other ethnic groups in Nord-Kivu. The result was two periods of ethnic conflict (July to December 1995 and April to October 1996) in which about 30,000 people were killed. Meanwhile, on October 6, based upon a federal directive, a local government in Sud-Kivu asked the Tutsi Banyamulenge to leave. The Tutsi refused and turned to the governments of Rwanda and Uganda for assistance. Rwanda's RPA began providing military training to the Banyamulenge and organized RPA forces to be prepared to intervene. Uganda's President Yoweri Museveni collaborated with Rwanda's Gen. Paul Kagame. Museveni was instrumental in persuading Kagame that their efforts in Zaire needed local leadership and in promoting Laurent-Désiré Kabila, even though Kabila's PRP had ceased to exist. Kabila became the leader of the Alliance of Democratic Forces for the Liberation of Congo (AFDL or ADFLC), which brought the Banyamulenge together with three opposition groups. Kabila was the AFDL's spokesperson, though André Kisase Ngandu was the head of AFDL's military wing, the National Resistance Council (CNRD).

Narrative: The war began in Sud-Kivu on October 17, 1996, when the government of Zaire sent an army against the Banyamulenge and the AFDL. Rwanda and Uganda immediately sent troops into Zaire to support the ADFL. The ADFL repulsed the government army and went on the offensive. The AFDL marched north, capturing Uvira and the provincial capital of Bukavu. On November 1, the AFDL reached Goma, which was near one of the major Hutu refugee centers, Mugunga camp, housing 600,000 refugees. Here Kabila announced that the AFDL's ultimate goal was to overthrow Mobutu. The AFDL attacked on the camp, joined by RPA forces who marched across from Gisenyi or crossed the lake in boats. The rebels engaged in fighting with the Hutu *Interahamwe* and precipitated more ethnic conflict (and massacres of civilians by both the AFDL and the Zairean soldiers). News reporting in France and Britain focused upon the humanitarian crisis in an attempt to persuade the West to intervene in support of Mobutu. On November 8, 1996, the UN Security Council did pass a resolution to create a multinational force to intervene for humanitarian purposes. To forestall international intervention, the RPA closed the major refugee camps in Zaire, leading to the migration of perhaps as many as 700,000 refugees, either back into Rwanda or further into Zaire.

Meanwhile, the AFDL continued its advance north and was joined by Ugandan troops in an attack on Bunia, and they soon had captured much of eastern Zaire. Mobutu was under treatment for cancer and unable to exert much control over his government. The French could not intervene openly to support him but did hire a group of 300 mercenaries to assist the Zairean army to little avail. The Rwandan Hutu *Interahamwe* also provided limited assistance in resisting the AFDL. In contrast, the rebel army was gaining strength. In December, a force of 25,000 Mai Mai (many child soldiers) joined the rebels. Angolan President José Eduardo dos Santos and Zaire's Prime Minister Léon Kengo wa Dondo met in early December 1996 and reached an agreement that Zaire would dismantle the UNITA bases in its country in exchange for which Angola would prevent the Katanga Tigers from entering the war in Zaire. When it appeared that Zaire was unable or unwilling to restrain UNITA, Angola decided to enter the war. In mid-February, Angolan troops (including the Katanga Tigers—or Zairean soldiers from Katanga who had fled into Angola in 1978) were sent to assist the AFDL: they were flown to Kigali and then marched into Zaire, where they joined the rebels in the Northeast. The reinforced rebels then turned westward and advanced toward the provincial capital of Kisangani, which they captured on March 15, 1997, in a fight in which the Tigers played a decisive role. They continued their advance toward the capital. The rebel successes prompted Angola to augment its contribution, and in April, additional Angolan forces crossed into Zaire in the Southwest, capturing towns, such as Tshikapa and Kikwit, as they advanced northward. The two rebel contingents met at Kenge (in Bandundu province—east of Kinshasha), where they defeated a UNITA–FAZ defense in the last major battle of the war. That month American negotiators tried to persuade Mobutu to resign. After an unsuccessful meeting with Kabila, Mobutu finally left the country on May 15, 1997, and the rebels entered the capital, ending the war.

Termination and Outcome: The result of the war was a rebel victory, ending Mobutu's thirty-two-year rule. Kabila assumed the office of president on May 17, 1997. Kabila switched the name of the country back to the Democratic Republic of the Congo. Mobutu died in Rabat, Morocco, on September 7, 1997. A new war in DRC would begin in 1998 (Intra-state War #905). Kabila stayed in office until January 16, 2001, when he was assassinated.

It is estimated that 100,000 Congolese died during this war, most of whom were civilians.

Coding Decisions: There is some question about the extent of the role of Rwanda during this war. Pottier has argued that the media incorrectly portrayed the war as a civil war, a rebellion by the AFDL and its allies, all of whom had common goals, against the government of Zaire. This narrative downplayed the role that Rwanda in particular played in organizing and conducting the war, which (Pottier claims) is what the Rwandan government wanted. Yet, subsequently Kagame claimed that Rwanda was the key actor: "Everywhere it was our forces, our troops."[206] Determining how this war is coded is dependent partially upon evaluating which perspective most closely fits reality. Turner also provides a discussion of the implications of the various descriptions of the type of war this is. If Rwanda were the key actor, then the war would be an interstate war of Rwanda against Zaire instead of a civil war. In determining the key actor, Pottier focused upon the composition of the rebel alliance, the motivations for the war, and degree of unity among the rebels. For COW, the key factor is determining which parties are doing the bulk of the fighting. Though it is true that Rwanda was a key participant in the war, it is not clear that it conducted the bulk of the fighting on behalf of the rebels.

Sources: Bercovitch and Fretter (2004); Brogan (1998); Ciment (2007d); Clodfelter (2002); Kisangani (2012); Meredith (2005); Pitsch (2001); Pottier (2002); Project Ploughshares (2000); Prunier (2004); Reed (1999); Stapleton (2013); Stearns (2001); Turner (2002, 2007).

INTRA-STATE WAR #896

Third Rwanda War of 1997 to 1998

Participants: Rwanda versus Army for the Liberation of Rwanda (ALiR).
Dates: March 17, 1997, to October 30, 1998.
Battle-related Deaths: ALiR rebels: 3,000; Rwanda: 300. (See Coding Decisions.)
Initiator: ALiR.
Outcome: Rwanda wins.
War Type: Civil for central control.
Total System Member Military Personnel: Armed Forces of Rwanda (Rwandan Patriotic Army [RPA]): 55,000 (prewar); 40,000 (initial, peak, final).[207]
Theater Armed Forces: Army for the Liberation of Rwanda (ALiR): 15,000 (initial); 40,000 (peak, final).[208]

Antecedents: The Hutu people of Rwanda had gained control of the country in 1962 after a war with the Tutsi ruling elite (Non-state War #1574, 1959 to 1962). Tutsi efforts to recapture the government failed in 1964 (Intra-state War #760). Rwandan Tutsi exiles who had fled into Uganda created the Rwandan Patriotic Front (RPF), which returned and captured control of Rwanda in 1994 (Intra-state War #886). During the war, Rwanda endured a period of genocide, in which the Rwandan army and Hutu militias murdered thousands of civilians, mostly Tutsis. As the Tutsi RPF took control of Rwanda, at least 1 million Hutus, including the remnants of the Rwandan army (20,000 to 25,000 FAR soldiers) and 30,000 to 40,000 members of the Hutu militias, fled into the Zaire, contributing to the war there in 1996 (Intra-state War #895).[209] During that war, the predominantly Tutsi AFDL launched attacks near several of the major Hutu refugee camps, prompting thousands of Hutu to flee back into Rwanda. In the Zaire camps, the remaining FAR and Hutu militia joined together with local Hutus in 1997 to create the Army for the Liberation of Rwanda (ALiR), which began launching raids into Rwanda with the aims of killing as many Tutsi as possible and overthrowing the government of Paul Kagame in Kigali.

Narrative: On March 17, 1997, when Rwandan forces were involved in the final offensive in the war to unseat President Mobuto, the ALiR launched a significant series of raids from the camps in Zaire against the Tutsi in Northwest Rwanda (marking the start of this war). Conflict continued throughout the year, often involving the killing of thousands of civilians. The new president of the Democratic Republic of Congo (formerly Zaire), Laurent Kabila, signed security agreements with his eastern neighbors, Rwanda and Uganda, who had helped in the war that brought him to power. Yet, Rwanda and Uganda did not feel that Kabila was doing enough to stop the refugee attacks from DRC into their countries. Significant rebel offensives occurred in Rwanda in December 1997 and January 1998. The attack on Gitarama (just west of the capital) in February 1998 proved that the rebels could advance almost to Kigali. An attack on a jail in Gitarama on March 1, 1998, involved 2,000 rebels. Later that month, the ALiR strikes spread to Southeast Rwanda. The rebels themselves also were moving gradually back into Rwanda, though support bases in the DRC continued to provide weapons and training. The ALiR also was receiving assistance from the Hutus in Burundi. In July 1998, the alliance among Kabila, Rwanda, and Uganda had broken down, prompting Rwanda and Uganda to form another group, the Rally for Congolese Democracy (RCD), to overthrow Kabila.

Termination and Outcome: The civil war in the DRC, which would become known as Africa's World War, erupted in August 1998. Though fighting in Rwanda continued through October 1998, fatality levels tapered off as focus shifted to the DRC, thus this month marks the end of the war. Since the ALiR was unable to overthrow the Tutsi government, this war is coded as a government victory. Fighting resumed in 2001 (Intra-state War #920).

Coding Decisions: Data concerning combatant battle-deaths during this war is limited. By adding together the fatalities reported for some of the individual engagements, we derive estimates of 3,000 rebel and 300 Rwandan combatant deaths. Given the amount of missing information, especially concerning government deaths, these figures may well be underestimates. Overall, it is estimated that 10,000 Rwandans died during this war.

Sources: Bercovitch and Fretter (2004); Cutter (2007); Human Rights Watch (2001a, b, c); Jackson (2004); *Keesing's Record of World Events* (1997, 1998); Kisangani (2012); Reyntjens (2000).

INTRA-STATE WAR #897
First Congo-Brazzaville War of 1997

Participants: Republic of the Congo (or Congo-Brazzaville), Cocoye Militia, and Ninja Militia versus Cobra Militia and Angola.
Dates: June 5, 1997, to October 14, 1997.
Battle-related Deaths: Congo: [ ]; Cobra Militia: [ ]; Cocoye Militia: [ ]; Ninja Militia: [ ]; Angola: [ ]; Total Combatant Deaths: [ ]. (See Coding Decisions.)
Initiator: Cocoye Militia.
Outcome: Cobra Militia and Angola win.
War Type: Civil for central control.
Total System Member Military Personnel: Armed Forces of Congo (*Forces Armées Congolaises*), or FAC: 10,000 (prewar, initial, peak, final).[210] Armed Forces of Angola: 95,000 (prewar, initial, peak, final).[211]
Theater Armed Forces: Armed Forces of Cocoye Militia (Pro-government Intervener): [ ]. Armed Forces of Ninja Militia (Pro-government Intervener), participating from September 1997: [ ]. Armed Forces of Cobra Militia: 8,000 (peak).[212] Armed Forces of Angola (Pro-rebel Intervener), participating from October 1997): 1,500 (initial, peak, final).[213]

Antecedents: From 1970 to 1991, the Republic of Congo (or Congo-Brazzaville) was a Marxist-Leninist, one-party state (The People's Republic of the Congo). The left-wing military regimes frequently supported revolutionary movements in the region and generally maintained good relations with both the Soviet Union and its former colonial power, France. Denis Sassou Nguesso served as president from 1979 to 1992, representing the Congolese Party of Labour (PCT). With the collapse of the Soviet Union, and with the encouragement of France, Sassou Nguesso began moving Congo-Brazzaville toward a capitalist economy and a multiparty political system. In the June and July 1992 elections, Sassou Nguesso was eliminated in the first round, and the final contest pitted Pascal Lissouba of the Pan-African Union for Social Democracy (UPADS) against Bernard Kolelas of the Congolese Movement for Democracy and Integral Development (MCDDI). Lissouba won, taking office on August 31, 1992.

Each of the major political parties had created its own armed militia. Nguesso had the Cobra militia, Kolelas created the Ninja militia, and Lissouba had the Cocoye (or Zulu) militia. As a result of perceived electoral irregularities, armed conflict broke out in 1993 and 1994 that pitted the Ninjas and the Cobras against the Cocoyes and government forces, though the major victims were civilians. Widespread war was averted when Gabon and the Organization of African Unity (OAU) intervened. In 1994, Sassou Nguesso left the country for Paris. He returned to the Congo in January 1997 with the intention of participating in the July 1997 presidential election. As the election approached, conflict between the militias increased. In May 1997, the war in Zaire (Intra-state War #895) came to an end with the overthrow of the government of President Mobutu. Soldiers from Angola's UNITA rebels had fought in Zaire on the side of the government, and when it fell, a number of UNITA soldiers fled into neighboring Congo-Brazzaville. The UNITA soldiers were welcomed by Lissouba, and some were incorporated into his Cocoyes. This decision earned Lissouba the enmity of the Angolan government.

Narrative: On June 5, 1997, President Lissouba decided to implement a December 1995 agreement to disarm and demobilize the militias. Lissouba started the process by moving against Sassou

Nguesso's Cobra militia. He sent a contingent of his Cocoyes militia (Aubevilleois) to Sassou Nguesso's headquarters (in the Mpila section of Brazzaville), and the Cobras resisted. Conflict between the two groups expanded, and Brazzaville was soon divided into three zones: one controlled by Lissouba; another dominated by Sassou Nguesso; and the third the base of Bernard Kolélas (the former presidential contender and current mayor of Brazzaville). The intensity of the fighting increased as the Congolese armed forces (FAC) became involved; the air force began bombing Mpila on August 27, 1997. The fighting soon spread northward out of the capital.

Realizing the seriousness of his situation, Lissouba tried to bring his opponents into a coalition government. In September, Kolélas accepted the position of prime minister in a new government of national unity, though Sassou Nguesso rejected the plan. Kolélas's Ninja militia joined the fighting on the side of the government: their alliance was formalized with the creation of the *Mouvement National pour la Liberation du Congo* (MNLC). In early October, Angola decided to intervene and dispatched ground troops and air force planes to assist Sassou Nguesso. The ground troops advanced to Pointe Noire, where they seized the port, preventing its destruction.

Termination and Outcome: With the assistance of Angola, Sassou Nguesso's forces seized the capital on October 14, ending the war in the rebel victory. Lissouba fled to Kinshasa and Kolélas to Mali and then to France. The Cobras engaged in widespread looting. Sassou Nguesso assumed the presidency on October 25, 1997. Fighting resumed a little more than a year later (Intra-state War #908).

Coding Decisions: Stearns notes that 1,000 to 3,000 people were killed in June and July, Stapleton concludes that 8,000 people were killed during the war, while Clodfelter estimates that 10,000 lives were lost in the war, though it is unclear how many of those were civilians,

Sources: Ali-Dinar (1999); Bercovitch and Fretter (2004); Ciment (2007c); Clodfelter (2002); Project Ploughshares (2000); Stapleton (2013); Stearns (2001); Sundberg (1999, 2000); United States Bureau of Citizen and Immigration Services (2000).

INTRA-STATE WAR #898
Second Sierra Leone War of 1998 to 2000 (aka Sierra Leone Civil War)

Participants: Sierra Leone versus Kabbah Faction, *Kamajors*, Economic Community of West African States Monitoring Group (ECOMOG), and the United Kingdom.

Dates: February 6, 1998, to July 7, 1999, and May 2000 to November 10, 2000.

Battle-related Deaths: Sierra Leone: [ ]; Kabbah Faction: [ ]; Nigeria: [ ]; Ghana: [ ]; Guinea: [ ]; United Kingdom: 9.

Initiator: *Kamajors* and ECOMOG.

Outcome: Kabbah Faction, *Kamajors*, ECOMOG, and United Kingdom win.

War Type: Civil for central control.

Total System Member Military Personnel: Armed Forces of Sierra Leone (SLA): 5,000 (prewar); 4,000 (initial, peak); 3,000 (final).[214] Armed Forces of Ghana: 7,000 (prewar, initial, peak, final).[215] Armed Forces of Guinea: 12,000 (prewar, initial, peak); 10,000 (final).[216] Armed Forces of Nigeria: 76,000 (prewar, initial); 77,000 (peak); 76,000 (final).[217] Armed Forces of United Kingdom: 218,000 (prewar, initial, peak); 212,000 (final).[218]

Theater Armed Forces: Armed Forces of Sierra Leone (the People's Army of the AFRC/RUF Coalition), consisting of the AFRC (referred to as ex-SLA after March 10, 1998), participating until January 31, 1999, and RUF: 15,000 (initial); 45,000 (peak).[219]

Kabbah Faction's portion of the Sierra Leone Army (SLA):

Kamajors (Pro-Kabbah Intervener): 20,000.
Economic Community of West African States Monitoring Group (ECOMOG, Pro-Kabbah Intervener): 4,600 (initial); 15,000.[220]
Armed Forces of Ghana: [ ].
Armed Forces of Guinea: [ ].
Armed Forces of Nigeria: 10,000.[221]
Armed Forces of United Kingdom (Pro-Kabbah Intervener), participating from May 2000: 1,300 (initial).[222]

Antecedents: In 1991, the Revolutionary United Front (RUF) began a rebellion in Sierra Leone (Intra-state War #863). RUF initially was formed to oppose the ruling elite and to try to provide more benefits to the majority of the population, but instead it soon became known for its cruelty to the populace as it attempted to gain control of the diamond mines. Because this was also true of the Sierra Leone armed forces (SLA), many civilians created private militias, known as the *Kamajors*, for their protection. Toward the end of the war, Sierra Leone, under international pressure, held an election, which Ahmad Tejan Kabbah won, and he assumed the presidency on March 29, 1996. Kabbah immediately entered into peace negotiations with RUF. A compromise agreement was signed in early April 1996, which stopped the civil war. All foreign troops had to leave Sierra Leone, which deprived the government of its major defenders. Thus Kabbah began to rely more on the *Kamajors*. The *Kamajors* were structured into the Civil Defense Forces (CDF), which soon had 20,000 troops, thus dwarfing the Sierra Leone Army (SLA). President Kabbah was ousted in May 1997 by a military faction led by Maj. Paul Koroma. The coup leaders created the Armed Forces Revolutionary Council (AFRC) and invited the RUF to join the new military government. The coup and the AFRC/RUF coalition were condemned by the UN, the Organization for African Unity (OAU), the Economic Community of West African States (ECOWAS), and Nigeria. In June 1997, Nigeria (under the auspices of ECOWAS and its military affiliate ECOMOG) moved troops into Freetown and attacked the government, but the offensive was pushed back by the new People's Army of AFRC and RUF. The government also faced opposition from the *Kamajors*, who supported the Kabbah government. After ECOWAS tightened sanctions against Sierra Leone in August 1997, low-level attacks against the government by the *Kamajors* and Nigeria continued for the remainder of the year. A British security firm, Sandline, helped to arm and train the Nigerian and *Kamajors* forces.

Narrative: This war began in February 1998, when the *Kamajors* and ECOMOG troops (from Guinea, Ghana, and Nigeria) undertook direct military action against the AFRC/RUF government on behalf of former president Kabbah. ECOMOG forces entered Freetown against entrenched AFRC/RUF positions and fought house-to-house battles for the next month. The *Kamajors* were particularly involved in offensives in the South, where they attempted to seize the diamond mines. By March ECOMOG and the *Kamajors* controlled the capital, and the AFRC/RUF government withdrew. The civilian Kabbah government was returned to power on March 10, 1998. The war continued, now with AFRC and RUF fighting against the pro-Kabbah faction (including remnants of the Sierra Leone army, *Kamajors*, and the ECOMOG troops). Kabbah began to purge the army of soldiers who had supported the AFRC/RUF government. Nigeria, which had had RUF leader Foday Sankoh imprisoned in Nigeria, returned him to Sierra Leone for trial. In October, Sankoh was convicted and sentenced to death. RUF had warned that unless Sankoh were released, it would launch a terrorist campaign against the civilian population; its Operation No Living Thing produced massacres and mutilations of civilians. RUF received military supplies from Liberia and Burkina Faso, enabling it to again march against Freetown in an attempt to free Sankoh. On January 6, 1999, RUF and AFRC forces broke through the lines of the 25,000 pro-Kabbah troops (ECOMOG, *Kamajors*, and pro-Kabbah SLA).[223] In fierce fighting, much of Freetown was destroyed. Facing defeat, the ECOMOG forces retreated.

The Kabbah government and the leadership of the RUF entered tentative cease-fire discussions. The two parties reached a peace agreement in Lomé, Togo, on July 7, 1999. The agreement freed Sankoh and gave him the position of vice president. RUF troops and the *Kamajors* were supposed to demobilize, with amnesty for the RUF. ECOMOG was replaced by a UN peacekeeping force, UNAMSIL. Fighting ceased, marking a break in the war. However, disagreements continued over control of the countryside because RUF controlled the Kono diamond field. When UNAMSIL planned to enter the diamond field, RUF seized 500 peacekeepers as hostages. The peace agreement collapsed in May 2000 as conflict resumed. Britain dispatched an expeditionary force to Freetown, and as the troops arrived, a group of citizens marched to Sankoh's house, demanding the release of the peacekeepers. Sankoh's bodyguards fired on the crowd as Sankoh escaped. Sankoh was later captured and imprisoned. Fighting resumed as the British took control of key points throughout the city in aid of the Kabbah government. On the other hand, RUF had begun to fragment. On September 10, 2002, a force of 150 British paratroopers attacked the base of an RUF affiliate, the West Side Boys, who had been holding six British soldiers hostage. In the operation, 1 British soldier was killed as were 25 of the West Side Boys. By November 2000, a new cease-fire agreement, brokered by ECOWAS, was signed in Abuja, Nigeria on November 11, 2000, ending the war.

Termination and Outcome: Though the Abuja agreement ended the war-level fighting, a second agreement in May 2001 was more successful in implementing the terms of the agreement by disarming and demobilizing thousands of former combatants. President Kabbah formally announced a declaration of peace in Sierra Leone in January 2002.

Coding Decisions: Because the AFRC and RUF coalition was in control of the institutions of government at the start of the war, it is coded as the government for the remainder of the war, even though the Kabbah regime was returned to power in the midst of the war. As the Lomé Accord stopped the fighting for more than a month, the period from July 1999 to May 2000 is coded as a break in the war.

Between 1990 and 2000 (including both Intra-state Wars #863 and #898), more than 100,000 people were killed.[224] Estimates of the number of people killed in this war range from 14,000 to 50,000.[225] Battle-death figures for the combatants are incomplete.

Sources: Arnold (2009); Bercovitch and Fretter (2004); BBC News (1999a, b, c, d, 2000); Ciment and Cuthbertson (2007); Clodfelter (2002); Edgerton (2002); Ero (2000); *Keesing's Record of World Events* (1998, 1999); Khobe (2000); Meredith (2005); Project Ploughshares (2002); Stapleton (2013).

INTRA-STATE WAR #902

Guinea-Bissau Military War of 1998 to 1999

Participants: Guinea-Bissau, Guinea, and Senegal versus Mané Junta.

Dates: June 7, 1998, to August 26, 1998; October 17, 1998, to November 1, 1998; February 3, 1999, to February 17, 1999; and May 8, 1999, to May 10, 1999.

Battle-related Deaths: Guinea-Bissau: [ ]; Mané Junta: [ ]; Senegal: [ ]; Guinea: [ ]; Total Guinea-Bissau Combatant Deaths: 2,000.

Initiator: Mané Junta.

Outcome: Mané Junta wins.

War Type: Civil for central control.

Total System Member Military Personnel: Armed Forces of Guinea-Bissau: 1,000 (prewar, initial, peak, final).[226] Armed Forces of Guinea: 12,000 (prewar, initial, peak, final).[227] Armed Forces of Senegal: 14,000 (prewar); 14,000 (initial, peak, final).[228]

Theater Armed Forces: Armed Forces of Mané Junta: 5,400. Armed Forces of Guinea (Pro-government Intervener): 700 (initial); 1,500.[229] Armed Forces of Senegal (Pro-government Intervener): 1,300 (initial); 2,000.[230]

Antecedents: Portugal granted independence to Guinea-Bissau on September 10, 1974. A coup in 1980 brought João Bernardo Vieira to the presidency, an office he continued to hold despite several coups against him. Vieira won Guinea-Bissau's first presidential election representing the African Party for the Independence of Guinea and Cape Verde (PAIGC), and he won a second term in voting in 1998. Guinea-Bissau was one of the poorest countries in the world, and Vieira was perceived by many to have sold the country to foreign economic interests. Vieira also faced public discontent over government corruption and military opposition to the government's policies concerning a rebellion in Senegal. On June 6, 1998, Vieira dismissed his military chief of staff, Gen. Ansumane Mané. When Vieira's troops arrived to arrest Mané, Mané's supporters launched a revolt. Mané formed a junta that called for President Vieira to resign. Vieira refused, and civil war broke out between elements in the army loyal to Vieira and those supporting Mané's junta. The junta soon had the support of 90 percent of the military.

Narrative: Fighting began June 7, 1998, and lasted for almost a year. Both Senegal and Guinea sent in troops to assist the faltering government. The government, Senegalese, and Guinean troops launched offensives against the rebels, seizing Mansoa on July 3 and attacking rebel positions in the capital on July 5. Thousands of civilians fled into Guinea. Mediation efforts by the Community of Portuguese-speaking Countries (CPLP) and the Economic Community of West African States (ECOWAS) led to cease-fire agreements on August 26, 1998; November 1, 1998; and February 17, 1999. The August agreement was broken in October over rebel complaints about the government's use of foreign troops. The troops from Senegal and Guinea kept the Vieira regime alive, but they were insufficient to defeat the rebels. The November 1998 cease-fire agreement created a coalition government between Vieira and Mané, though fighting between the two revived in February. After the February cease-fire, the troops from Senegal and Guinea departed in March after peacekeepers from the Economic Community of West African States (ECOWAS) had arrived. Under the terms of the cease-fire, President Vieira was supposed to reduce substantially the size of his presidential guard, and when he refused, fighting began again on May 8, 1999. Soon Mané controlled the entire country, and Vieira was persuaded to resign on May 10, 1999, ending the war.

Termination and Outcome: Mané's victory led to a brief period of military rule by the junta, followed by elections in November 1999. Vieira went to exile in Portugal but returned to Guinea-Bissau in 2005, when he won the election and reassumed the presidency. He was assassinated by the military in 2009.

Coding Decisions: The cease-fire agreements on August 24, 1998, on November 1, 1998, and in March 1999 each lasted for more than a month and thus are coded as breaks in the war.

Sources: Cutter (2007); IRIN (1998); *Keesing's Record of World Events* (1998, 1999); Neumann (2007); Project Ploughshares (2004); Stapleton (2013); Uppsala Universitet (2003, 2006).

INTRA-STATE WAR #905
Africa's World War of 1998 to 2002

Participants: Democratic Republic of Congo, Angola, Namibia, Zimbabwe, Chad, Sudan, Central African Republic and Hutu Militia versus Congolese Rally for Democracy (RCD), Congo Liberation Movement (MLC), Rwanda, Uganda, and Burundi.
Dates: August 2, 1998, to December 17, 2002.
Battle-related Deaths: Democratic Republic of Congo: [ ]; Hutu Militias: [ ]; RCD: [ ]; MLC: [ ]; Angola: [ ]; Namibia: [ ]; Zimbabwe: [ ]; Chad: [ ]; Sudan: [ ]; Rwanda: [ ]; Uganda: [ ]; Burundi: [ ]; Total Combatant Deaths: 145,000.[231] (See Coding Decisions.)
Initiator: RCD and Rwanda.
Outcome: Compromise.
War Type: Civil for central control.
Total System Member Military Personnel: Armed Forces of DRC: 30,000 (prewar); 50,000 (initial); 81,000 (peak, final).[232] Armed Forces of Angola: 95,000 (prewar); 100,000 (initial); 130,000 (peak); 100,000 (final).[233] Armed Forces of Namibia: 8,000 (prewar); 3,000 (initial); 9,000 (peak, final).[234] Armed Forces of Zimbabwe: 40,000 (prewar, initial, peak); 26,000 (final).[235] Armed Forces of Chad: 35,000 (prewar); 30,000 (initial, peak, final).[236] Armed Forces of Sudan: 105,000 (prewar, initial); 117,000 (peak, final).[237] Armed Forces of Central African Republic: 5,000 (prewar); 4,000 (initial, peak); 3,000 (final).[238] Armed Forces of Rwanda: 40,000 (prewar, initial); 70,000 (peak, final).[239] Armed Forces of Uganda: 50,000 (prewar, initial); 55,000 (peak, final).[240] Armed Forces of Burundi: 35,000 (prewar, initial); 46,000 (peak, final).[241]
Theater Armed Forces: Armed Forces of RCD: [ ]. Armed Forces of MLC: 15,000 (initial).[242] Armed Forces of Rwanda (Pro-rebel Intervener): 15,000 (initial); 35,000 (peak); 23,000 (final).[243] Armed Forces of Uganda (Pro-rebel Intervener): 1,000 (initial); 10,000 (peak); 6,000 (final).[244] Armed Forces of Burundi (Pro-rebel Intervener): 2,000 (August 1999). Armed Forces of Angola (Pro-government Intervener), participating from August 23, 1998: 1,000 (initial); 7,000 (peak); 2,500 (final).[245] Armed Forces of Namibia (Pro-government Intervener), participating from August 1998): 2,000 (initial, peak, final).[246] Armed Forces of Zimbabwe (Pro-government Intervener), participating from August 21, 1998: 900 (initial); 16,000 (peak); 5,000 (final).[247] Armed Forces of Chad: (Pro-government Intervener), participating from September 18, 1998, to May 1999: 1,000 (initial); 2,000 (peak, final).[248] Armed Forces of Sudan (Pro-government Intervener), participating from September 1998): 2,000 (initial); 10,000 (peak, final).[249] Armed Forces of Central African Republic (Pro-government Intervener), participating from September 1998: 2,000 (initial, peak, final).[250] Hutu Militias (Pro-government Intervener, including *Interahamwe* and ex-FAR soldiers): 15,000 (initial, peak, final).[251]

Antecedents: A cluster of intra-state wars occurred in the Great Lakes region of Africa during the 1990s, affecting Uganda, Rwanda, Burundi, and the Democratic Republic of the Congo (Zaire or DRC) individually and frequently collectively. In the latest series of these, the Tutsis came to power in Rwanda in 1994 (Intra-state War #886), as a result of which Hutu refugees fled into Zaire. The Rwandan government (joined by Uganda and Burundi) then proceeded to attack the Rwandan Hutus in Zaire as part of their effort to support the Alliance of Democratic Forces for Liberation (ADFL), led by Laurent Kabila, in its successful drive to overthrow Zaire's Mobutu Sese Soko (Intra-state War #895). Kabila assumed the office of president on May 17, 1997, and he switched the name of the country from Zaire back to the Democratic Republic of the Congo (DRC). By July 1998, the alliance among Kabila, Rwanda, Burundi, and Uganda had broken down, and Kabila ordered his Rwandan and Ugandan advisers and their troops to leave the DRC (possibly to deter a coup attempt). Kabila shifted his alliance to ties with Angola, Namibia, and Zimbabwe, with whom he signed a mutual defense pact. Some of Kabila's former allies, including Rwanda and Uganda, along with local disaffected groups, united to form the Congolese Rally for Democracy (RCD), with the goal of unseating Kabila. The RCD was created in the eastern town of Goma, on August 1, and was headed by former professor Ernest Wamba dia Wamba.

Narrative: The war began on August 2, 1998, with a mutiny within the DRC government military (FAC) in Goma, and an invasion of Rwandan troops. The FAC soldiers of the Tenth battalion (who were Banyamulenge, ethnically Tutsi) accused President Kabila of corruption and of inciting ethnic conflict and, in cooperation with the RCD, expressed the goal of removing Kabila from office. The rebel FAC soldiers then launched attacks against government garrisons at nearby Bukavu and Uriva. Partially due to the preceding conflicts, the Kabila government had limited capacity to confront a new uprising. Yet, the DRC armed forces counterattacked Tutsi garrisons in other parts of the country. The ethnic ramifications of the emerging conflict encouraged a number of the government's Tutsi soldiers to join the RCD, while Hutu militias including the *Interahamwe* and ex-FAR soldiers (soldiers of the previous Rwandan Hutu government who had fled from Rwanda to Zaire in 1994) rushed to join the government. The Congolese rebels flew soldiers across country to the Bas Congo province, west of Kinshasa, where they recruited troops and seized a hydroelectric complex and the port of Matadi. At a meeting of the South African Development Community (SADC) on August 17, Zimbabwe, Angola, Zambia, and Namibia announced their decision to send troops to aid the government of the DRC. Angola moved troops into Congo's coastal towns on August 23, regaining control of Matadi. As the rebels advanced on the capital, troops from Zimbabwe arrived at the Kinshasa airport on August 21 and began bombarding rebel positions on August 26. The intervention of Angola, Zimbabwe, and Namibia prevented the speedy coup that the rebels had intended, and within a month nine neighboring countries became involved in the most widespread war in the continent's modern history. The DRC government was supported by Angola, Zimbabwe, Namibia, Chad, Sudan, and the Central African Republic, while the rebels were aided by Rwanda, Uganda, and Burundi. Rwanda and Uganda soon divided their efforts: Rwanda's forces (RPA) still acted in conjunction with RCD, while Uganda's army (UPDF) created its own rebel movement, the Congo Liberation Movement (MLC).

The defeat of the rebel moves in the West, around Kinshasa, forced them to concentrate their efforts in the East, and there the rebel forces had military success. In February, the rebels launched their first (and only) major combined offensive: a two-pronged attack involving 60,000 soldiers from the MLC, UPDF, RCD, and RPA. The MLC and UPDF advanced in the North to Gbadolite and Mbandaka, while the RCD and RPA moved in the East to seize Mbuji-Mayi and head toward Lubumbashi. By March 1999, the rebel groups already controlled one-third of the country. The DRC soon became divided into three main regions: Kabila controlled Kinshasa and the southern tier; the North was controlled by the MLC, led by Jean-Pierre Bemba, and Uganda; and the Rwanda RPA/RCD coalition controlled the huge central zone from the eastern Kivu westward, including parts of Katanga. Fighting continued in each of the regions as the rebels continued their offensive and as the government tried to respond. In the North, MLC-Uganda army forced government troops to retreat into the Central African Republic as they captured Mobutu's hometown of Gbadolite along the northern border. In the center, the DRC air force bombed Goma in May, while the RCD/RPA forces began a battle against Zimbabwean troops defending Kabil's hometown of Manono in the Southeast, which ended in a rebel victory in June. However, the rebel advance toward the diamond mines at Mbuji-Mayi stalled. However, May 1999 also saw divisions within the RCD, which split into several factions: the main organization became known as RCD–Goma; Wamba headed what became known as the RCD–Kisangani (RCD–K); and Mbusa Nyamwisi headed the RCD–ML. In July 1999, Rwandan/RCD forces launched a two-pronged offensive westward, and it looked like Kinshasa might fall. However international pressure was applied to all the parties, prompting them to sign the Lusaka cease-fire agreement (July to August 1999).

The agreement was soon broken by all of the parties. Sudan aircraft bombed two cities held by the rebels in northern DRC on August 4, 1999. The MLC with Ugandan support advanced westward toward Mbandaka. Kabila's forces (FAC) with the aid of Zimbabwe tried moving northeast into South Kivu, where they hoped to assist the Burundi Hutu rebels of the *Forces de la Défense de la* Démocratie (FDD) to infiltrate back into Burundi. The RCD and Rwandan troops counterattacked, forcing a FAC retreat, and then advanced to capture the strategic town of Pweto, from which they could threaten the Katangan capital of Lubumbashi. The victory at Pweto produced significant losses for the DRC (of advanced weapons and of FAC forces who fled to Zambia) but also led to tensions within the rebel community over how to take advantage of the victory. Fighting erupted among the rebels: between RCD–Goma and RCD–K as well as among Rwandan-backed RCD–Goma, Uganda, and the MLC in December 1999.

Efforts to find a negotiated settlement to the conflict continued, though some scholars have claimed that peace efforts were halfhearted at best since some of the participants wanted to continue to exploit DRC's natural resources. In November 1999, the UN Organization Mission in the Democratic Republic of Congo (MUNUC) was established with 5,500 peacekeepers to be sent to the DRC (though they were delayed). Yet the fighting continued. On January 16, 2001, Kabila was assassinated by one of his bodyguards (perhaps with Angolan involvement) and was succeeded as president by his son Joseph Kabila. The new president Kabila put a greater emphasis on the peace process, appealing to the UN to dispatch peacekeepers. The fighting continued but began to wind down as a number of countries, including Uganda and Rwanda, began to reduce or withdraw their troops. From August 20 to August 24, 2001, peace talks were conducted in the Botswana capital of Gaberone, attended by representatives of all the countries and factions fighting in DRC as well as civil society and interest group representatives. Yet despite these, and a number of subsequent efforts, fighting continued.

Termination and Outcome: The war ended with a compromise agreement. On December 16, 2002, a cease-fire agreement was signed, along with a plan to create a new shared government, with Kabila remaining as president and the armed groups to be integrated into a new military force.

A final peace accord was signed on April 2, 2003, in Sun City in South Africa. The new government was created June 30, 2003. The war produced a humanitarian crisis of untold proportions. In addition to the deaths of combatants, widespread violence against civilians, disease, and starvation are estimated to have killed 2.5 million people by 2002, with the total growing to 3.9 million by 2006, and 5.4 million by 2007.[252]

The end of this war did not stop all the fighting in the DRC. A separate war continued in DRC's North Ituri district between the Hemda and Lindu peoples, which spread into neighboring Uganda, making it a non-state war (Non-state War #1594 from 1999 to 2005).

Coding Decisions: The primary coding decision for this war was the determination of whether it was an intra-state civil war or an inter-state war among the DRC and its allies against Rwanda, Uganda, and Burundi. Turner provides a summary of the various ways in which this war could be categorized, emphasizing the perspective that the war was externally induced. In COW's determination of the coding of a war, the concern is to identify which parties were conducting the bulk of the fighting. The consensus within COW was that it was the Congolese themselves (the FAC, RCD, and MLC) who engaged in most of the armed combat, though they all received significant outside support. Thus the war is an intra-state war internationalized by the involvement of the nine neighboring countries.

As noted, the fatalities during this war were horrendous. Given the magnitude of the carnage, there is little information available about the specific deaths of combatants.

Sources: Afoaku (2002); BBC News (1998–2002); Bercovitch and Fretter (2004); Ciment (2007e); Clodfelter (2002); Coghlan et al. (2004); Crossette (2000); Cutter (2007); Edgerton (2002); GlobalSecurity.org (2005a, b, c, d, e); Hara (2002); International Rescue Committee (2004, 2008); Kisangani (2012); *New York Times* (2000, 2001); O'Ballance (2000); Pitsch (2001); Project Ploughshares (2004); Prunier (2004, 2009); Robinson and Walt (2006); Rupiya (2002); Stapleton (2013); Swarns (2001); Tripp (2005); Tull (2007); Turner (1998, 2002, 2007); Uppsala Universitet (2004).

INTRA-STATE WAR #906
Chad–Togoimi Revolt of 1998 to 2000

Participants: Chad versus the Movement for Democracy and Justice in Chad (MDJT).
Dates: October 16, 1998, to July 18, 2000.
Battle-related Deaths: Chad: [ ]; MDJT: [ ]; Total Combatant Deaths: [ ].
Initiator: MDJT.
Outcome: Conflict continues at below-war level.
War Type: Civil for central control.
Total System Member Military Personnel: Armed Forces of Chad: 35,000 (prewar); 30,000 (initial, peak, final).[253]
Theater Armed Forces: Armed Forces of MDJT: [ ]. Armed Forces of MDD: [ ].

Antecedents: Idriss Déby and his *Mouvement Patriotique du Salut* (MPS) came to power in Chad in 1990 as a result of the previous war (Intra-state War #852). Déby, who had been President Hissène Habré's chief military adviser, was concerned about the growing concentration of power in Habré's hands. When Habré accused Déby of disloyalty, Déby fled and launched a rebellion with assistance of Libya and Sudan. After overthrowing Habré, Déby was able to establish a government that gradually solidified its control over Chad, though it did face discontent from Habré supporters and from discontented Christians and animist blacks in the South. A significant sore spot was resolved in 1994, when Libya finally removed its forces from the Aouzou Strip, returning control of the territory to Chad as the result of a finding by the International Court of Justice. In July 1996, Déby won the presidency in Chad's first multiparty election, and the following year he began to sign peace agreements with a number of the opposition groups. In October 1998, Déby was confronted with a revolt in the North led by Youssouf Togoïmi, who had served the Déby government in several positions, including defense minister. Togoïmi resigned from the government in June 1997 over what he perceived to be the government's moves toward dictatorship. In 1998 Togoïmi founded the *Mouvement pour la démocratie et la justice au Tchad* (MDJT). The MDJT claimed that it launched the war as a means of restoring democracy to Chad and announced its willingness to ally with other similar movements.

Narrative: The war began with attacks by MDJT on October 16, 1998, against military personnel in the Northwest Tibesti region, during which 100 government soldiers were reportedly killed. The area was home to the Toubou tribe, of which Togoimi was a member. The war was conducted mostly as a guerrilla war, where the rebels attacked government military installations and placed land mines in strategic locations. Fighting became more intense in early 1999, with a string of about fifteen attacks in January through March. In one attack, on March 4, Deputy Chief of Staff Abderahim Bahar was killed, and two army garrisons were captured. The MDJT claimed to have captured the towns of Zoumri and Omou. Though the government continued to deny that the revolt was significant, it did dispatch an additional 3,000 troops into Tibesti at the end of March.

In April 1999, the Movement for Democracy and Development (MDD), led by Moussa Medella Manamat, announced an agreement for MDD to merge with MDJT and the Democratic Revolutionary Council, led by Acheikh ibn Oumar. The MDD originally had conducted attacks against the Déby regime in 1991 and wanted now to join in the current revolt. However, on July 3, 1999, Chad announced that it had reached an agreement with the MDD during talks in Sudan, thus MDD does not appear to have participated in the conflict.

There was an upsurge of fighting in Tibesti during the summer of 1999, and the MDJT claimed it now controlled all the tracks leading to the area. The government continued to launch excursions into the area, during which some of the soldiers reportedly defected to the rebels. Fighting continued in November and December, and the rebels shot down a government plane on December 2. The rebels advanced on the town of Yebbi-Bou in Tibesti on January 23, 2000, where they encountered a government counterattack. In February, 2000, the MDJT again attempted to form a rebel alliance. The former armed wing of MDD had now been renamed as the Movement for Unity and the Republic (MUR) under the leadership of Gaeled Bourkou Manda, and it allied with MDJT and the Democratic Revolutionary Council. Neither of the other groups appears to have participated in the fighting.

There was another upsurge of fighting between the government and MDJT in February and March 2000. On March 6, the MDJT launched a major offensive against the garrison at the major city of Bardai, killing 126 government troops while losing 15 rebels. The MDJT accused the government of poisoning wells and burning oases in Tibesti. The rebels launched another offensive in April. The rebels then captured Bardai in fierce fighting on July 18, 2000.

Termination and Outcome: July 18, 2000, marks the end of the fighting at war level. After that, the conflict continued but at below-war-level fatalities. At a December 2001 meeting in Libya, the MDJT announced its willingness to enter into peace negotiations. Libya was able to mediate a peace settlement that was signed in January 2002, and some of the rebels were integrated into Chad's army. Parliament approved an amnesty for the rebels in February, and the political prisoners were released that month. However, talks about integrating the MDJT into the army ultimately faltered, and fighting (at below-war level) resumed in March 2002. Another peace agreement was signed in December 2003. Togoimi died in September 2002 after his vehicle hit a land mine. Déby won reelection in 2001 but was faced by a rebellion in 2005 (Intra-state War #937).

Coding Decisions: Fatality statistics for this war are limited, and the MDJT claimed that the government consistently underestimated fatalities in an attempt to downplay the significance of the revolt. The available limited information seems to suggest that the battle-deaths for both combatants would be just above war level.

Sources: BBC News (1998–2002); Cutter (2007); Frère (2007); Immigration and Refugee Board of Canada (1999); *Keesing's Record of World Events* (1998–2003); Project Ploughshares (2000, 2005); Skutsch and Shantz (2007).

INTRA-STATE WAR #907
Third Angolan–UNITA War of 1998 to 2002

Participants: Angola versus Union for the Total Independence of Angola (UNITA).
Dates: December 4, 1998, to February 22, 2002.
Battle-related Deaths: Angola: [ ]; UNITA: [ ]; Total Combatant Deaths: [ ].
Initiator: Angola.
Outcome: Angola wins.
War Type: Civil for central control.
Total System Member Military Personnel: Armed Forces of Angola (FAA): 95,000 (prewar); 100,000 (initial); 130,000 (peak); 100,000 (final).[254]
Theater Armed Forces: Armed Forces of UNITA: 44,000 (prewar); 35,000 (initial); 70,000 (final).[255]

Antecedents: The first civil war in Angola (Intra-state War #804) between the Angola's MPLA government (People's Movement for the Liberation of Angola) and the Union for the Total Independence of Angola (UNITA) rebels ended on May 31, 1991, when UNITA and the MPLA government negotiated a cease-fire and a power-sharing arrangement, which entailed multiparty elections. The elections were held on September 29 and 30, 1992, and pitted MPLA's President José Eduardo dos Santos against Jonas Savimbi of UNITA and nine other candidates. In the first round dos Santos officially received 49.57 percent of the vote and Savimbi won 40.6 percent. Because none of the candidates had a majority, a second round was scheduled, but claiming that the election had not been fair, Savimbi refused to participate. The second round was never held because UNITA launched a second civil war (Intra-state War #880 from 1992 to 1994). This war ended with a November 15, 1994, agreement negotiated in Lusaka, Zambia. The Lusaka Protocol committed the parties to stop fighting and to enter into a coalition government, whereby UNITA members would be integrated into the armed forces and national police. The agreement was overseen by the UN. President dos Santos and Savimbi negotiated about the coalition but procrastinated as each side continued to stockpile weapons. The unity government was created in April 1977, which included UNITA ministers (though not Savimbi). It did not last long: in August, the UN decided that UNITA was obstructing the peace process and voted to impose sanctions. The sanctions were strengthened in June 1998, and the MPLA expelled the UNITA members from the government over UNITA's refusal to disarm and increasing incidents of armed conflict. In August 1998, Angola became involved in Africa's World War in the Democratic Republic of Congo (DRC, Intra-state War #905), partially as a means of trying to cut off UNITA's flow of weapons and money. By the end of the year, the MPLA government felt it was in a strong enough position to launch an offensive against UNITA directly.

Narrative: The Angolan armed forces launched an attack against UNITA on December 4, 1998 (starting this war). At a conference of the MPLA the next day, President dos Santos explained that war was the only way to achieve peace, rejected the Lusaka Protocol, and asked the UN forces to leave the country. The government's major offensive in March 1999 was designed to destroy UNITA's strongholds of Bailundo and Andulo, located in Angola's central highlands southeast of the capital of Luanda. Initially UNITA was strong enough to repulse the government offensive and with its new weaponry was able to launch a counterattack and advanced toward the capital in early 1999. On July 20, UNITA launched an attack at Catete, just 60 kilometers from the capital. Yet, UNITA was unable to sustain a campaign over such a distance for long. Meanwhile, Angola's armed forces (FAA) were fortifying their bases in the center of the country in anticipation of their next offensive.

On September 14, 1999, the Angolan military, with support from the United Kingdom and the United States, launched a massive offensive, Operation Restore, which captured Bailundo and Andulo by October 20. The rebels retreated eastward, leaving behind stores of weapons and supplies. Savimbi moved to a base in East Moxico and prepared for a final battle. By early 2000, the military estimated that it had destroyed 80 percent of UNITA's forces and now controlled 92 percent of Angola. The government's offensive had sapped UNITA's strength, and UNITA was reduced to utilizing guerrilla tactics in 2000 and 2001. However, in April 2000, UNITA was bolstered by the arrival of weapons despite the UN sanctions and was able to launch a series of attacks along the eastern borders. The government retaliated with a new offensive in May involving ground forces and air strikes. The operation heightened tensions between Angola and Zambia as Zambia accused Angola of dropping incendiary bombs on a Zambian village. To isolate UNITA, Angola forced the citizens to relocate to major cities, which had severe humanitarian consequences. Government offensives continued, and FAA forces killed Savimbi on February 22, 2002, which essentially ended the fighting and thus ended the war.

Termination and Outcome: Negotiations between government and UNITA military commanders began, and they agreed to a cease-fire, which was expanded on April 4 into a peace agreement as an addendum to the Lusaka Protocol. UNITA's new leadership declared that UNITA was becoming a political party and demobilized its armed forces in August 2002.

The war created a humanitarian crisis as it displaced an estimated 400,000 Angolans into neighboring countries and created more than 3 million internally displaced persons (IDPs). Both Angola's government and UNITA used child soldiers during this war, and it is estimated that over the total twenty-seven years of war, 100,000 children were orphaned. Another 70,000 to 200,000 people were disabled by land mines.

Coding Decisions: During the entire period of Angola's civil war (encompassing three COW wars), it is estimated that more than 500,000 Angolans were killed, most of them civilians. The Uppsala Universitet Conflict Data Project reports almost 16,000 war-related fatalities during this war, though that figure also includes civilians killed in combat.

Sources: Bercovitch and Fretter (2004); Ciment (2007f); Clodfelter (2002); Cutter (2007); Harden (2001); *Keesing's Record of World Events* (1997–1999, 2002); Kohn (1999); Malaquias (2007); Meredith (2005); Phillips and Axelrod (2005); Project Ploughshares (2003); Uppsala Universitet (2002).

INTRA-STATE WAR #908
Second Congo-Brazzaville War of 1998 to 1999

Participants: Congo-Brazzaville, Angola, and Cobra Militia versus Ninja Militia, Ntsiloulous Militia, and Cocoye Militia.
Dates: December 15, 1998, to November 16, 1999.
Battle-related Deaths: Congo-Brazzaville: [ ]; Angola: [ ]; Cobra Militia: [ ]; Ninjas and Cocoye Militias: [ ]; Total Combatant Deaths: 2,500.[256]
Initiator: Ninja and Cocoye Militias.
Outcome: Congo-Brazzaville wins.
War Type: Civil for central control.
Total System Member Military Personnel: Armed Forces of Congo-Brazzaville: 10,000 (prewar, initial, peak, final).[257] Armed Forces of Angola: 95,000 (prewar); 100,000 (initial, peak, final).[258]
Theater Armed Forces: Armed Forces of Angola (Pro-government Intervener): 1,500 (initial, peak, final).[259] Armed Forces of Cobra Militia (Pro-government Intervener): [ ]. Armed Forces of Ninja Militia: [ ]. Armed Forces of Cocoye Militia: [ ]. Armed Forces of Ntsiloulous Militia: [ ].

Antecedents: From 1970 to 1991, the Republic of Congo (or Congo-Brazzaville) was a Marxist-Leninist, one-party state (the People's Republic of the Congo). Denis Sassou Nguesso served as president from 1979 to 1992. With the collapse of the Soviet Union, Sassou Nguesso began moving Congo-Brazzaville toward a capitalist economy and a multiparty political system. The 1992 presidential election involved candidates from three major political parties: Denis Sassou Nguesso represented the Congolese Party of Labour (PCT), Pascal Lissouba the Pan-African Union for Social Democracy (UPADS), and Bernard Kolelas the Congolese Movement for Democracy and Integral Development (MCDDI). Each political party had its own associated militia. Sassou Nguesso had the Cobra militia, Kolelas created the Ninja militia, and Lissouba had the Cocoye (or Zulu) militia. Lissouba won the election, taking office on August 31, 1992. As a result of perceived electoral irregularities, armed conflict broke out among the militias in 1993 and 1994 and intensified as the 1997 presidential election approached. War erupted in 1997 (Intra-state War #897). The Cobra militia assisted by Angola gained control of the government, and Denis Sassou Nguesso assumed the presidency on October 25, 1997.

Lissouba fled to Kinshasa and Kolélas to Mali and then France, while their militias, the Ninjas and the Cocoye, fled to the south to regroup. During 1998 a new militia group, the Ntsiloulous, split from the Ninjas. In October 1998, a court indicted former government officials, including Lissouba and Kolélas for human rights abuses.

Narrative: The war began in December 1998 as the Ninjas, Ntsiloulous, and Cocoye militias launched a major strike trying to regain control over Southeast Brazzaville and ultimately to overthrow the Sassou Nguesso government. Though the rebels made gains in early 1999, in May 1999, the government, with Cobra and Angolan support, launched a major offensive and captured rebel bases in the center of the country. During the summer, the rebels continued to ambush members of the armed forces and to conduct attacks against the civilian population throughout the Pool region that surrounds the capital. The rebels were unable to defeat the government, and the conflict began to decline toward the end of the year.

Termination and Outcome: On November 16, 1999, the Pointe-Noire Peace agreement was signed by all the parties. In December 1999, further discussions in Gabon involved a new umbrella organization for the Cocoye–Ninja–Ntsiloulou organization, the *Conseil National de la Résistance* (CNR). The agreement included a commitment to develop a new constitution. The process of disarming the militias began in early 2000. During the war, the use of heavy weapons in urban areas meant that there were a significant number of civilian fatalities.

Coding Decisions: Estimates of total fatalities during this brief war range from 7,000 to 11,000, many of whom were civilians.[260]

Sources: Ali-Dinar (1999); Bercovitch and Fretter (2004); Cutter (2007); *The Military Balance* (1999, 2000); Project Ploughshares (2006); Stapleton (2013); Stearns (2001); United States Bureau of Citizenship and Immigration Services (2000); Uppsala Universitet (2002).

INTRA-STATE WAR #913
Oromo Liberation War of 1999

Participants: Ethiopia versus Oromo Liberation Front.
Dates: May 30, 1999, to August 18, 1999.
Battle-related Deaths: Oromo Liberation Front: [ ]; Ethiopia: [ ]. (See Coding Decisions.)
Initiator: Oromo Liberation Front.
Outcome: Conflict continues at below-war level.
War Type: Civil for local issues.
Total System Member Military Personnel: Armed Forces of Ethiopia: 200,000 (prewar); 300,000 (initial, peak, final).[261]
Theater Armed Forces: Armed Forces of OLF (OLA): 17,000 (final).[262]

Antecedents: The Oromo are the largest ethnic group in Ethiopia, approximately 33 to 40 percent of the population, though they frequently have seen themselves as targets of government discrimination. Consequently, the Oromo Liberation Front (OLF) was formed in 1973, seeking Oromo independence. The OLF and its armed wing, the Oromo Liberation Army (OLA), joined with the Somalis seeking independence from Ethiopia in the third phase of the Ogaden war (Intra-state War #808: Second Ogaden War phase 3 of 1978 to 1980), which was won by Ethiopia. During the final phase of the war, Ethiopia launched a punitive campaign against Oromo civilians, burning farms and forcing many to flee. Ethiopia was soon confronted by the nine-year war against liberation movements in Tigray and Eritrea (Intra-state War #826 from 1982 to 1991). As Ethiopia lost the military assistance of the Soviet Union and Cuba from 1989 to 1991, it became unable to contain the rebellion. In late May 1991, the rebels captured the capital, Addis Ababa, and the Mengistu regime collapsed. Eritrea achieved its independence in May 1993, after a UN-supervised referendum in late April 1993.

During the war, a variety of the ethnic-based political groups created an umbrella group, the Ethiopian People's Revolutionary Democratic Front (EPRDF), which included the Oromo People's Democratic Organization (OPDO) as the representatives of the Oromo. The OPDO had been created in 1982 in opposition to the OLF. At the end of the war, a national conference was held that created a transitional government that gave dominant roles to the EPRDF and the OLF. The new government supported greater autonomy for the Tigreans and the Oromo but not independence. By 1992, it had become clear that the OLF and the OPDO could not work together: skirmishes broke out between their respective military wings. When the OLF announced it was leaving the government, the government immediately arrested 20,000 OLF soldiers. Much of the OLF leadership fled the country, though remnants of the OLF waged a low-level guerrilla campaign against the government, some from bases in Kenya. Units also fled to Somalia and Eritrea, both of which have utilized the OLF to destabilize the Ethiopian government. In April 1998, the OLF elected a more militant leadership, leading to an increased focus on military activities. As Ethiopia and Eritrea fought a border war (Inter-state War #219: the Badme Border War of 1998 to 2000), Eritrea armed and trained the OLA for attacks into Ethiopia.

Narrative: Clashes between the Ethiopian government and the OLF reached war status at the end of May 1999, fueled by a May 6 delivery of weapons and money from Eritrea. The shipment, which also included 500 to 700 newly trained OLA fighters, arrived in Somalia for distribution to the OLF and other Oromo groups with affiliates in Somalia. The appearance of the rebel groups in Baidoa prompted calls from Somali politicians appealing for foreign intervention to deal with the militias. In June, there was an increase in attacks by the OLA against Ethiopian positions along the Kenyan border, and Kenya became increasingly concerned about OLA and Ethiopian activities within Kenyan territory. That month, 3,000 Ethiopian troops, along with their Somali ally, the Rahanweyn Resistance Army (RRA), occupied Baidoa as they pursued the OLA. Conflict was particularly fierce in August 1999, when there were repeated clashes between the Ethiopian army and the OLF along Ethiopia's southeast borders. On August 11, the Ethiopian government claimed to have killed or captured 1,000 OLA rebels during recent encounters in the East. The following day, the OLA reported that it had scored major victories in the South, leading to thousands of casualties on the government side. Later that month, the Ethiopian government announced that it had destroyed the OLA, a claim the OLF denied. However, war-level conflict appears to have ceased at that point, though low-level conflict continued.

Termination and Outcome: Fighting between the OLF and Ethiopian army continued at lower levels throughout the year. The OLF suffered a setback when Somalia closed the OLF office in Mogadishu on December 1, 1999. The OLF shifted some of its personnel to Eritrea. In March 2000, OLF signed cooperation agreements with the United Oromo People's Liberation Front (UOPLF) and the Oromo People's Liberation Organization. Fighting flared along the Sudanese border in 2002.

Coding Decisions: Fatality estimates for this war are fairly unreliable. The OLF claimed that Ethiopia downplayed the numbers of engagements and the levels of casualties it suffered, while others claimed that the OLF exaggerated the fatalities they inflicted. Yet overall it appears that total combatant deaths were more than 1,000.

Sources: ABO/OLF (2005); BBC News (1999); Cordesman (1993a, b); International Crisis Group (2009); *IRIN News Reports* (1999); *Keesing's Record of World Events* (1999); Sandberg (2001); Skutsch (2007b).

INTRA-STATE WAR #917
Guinean War of 2000 to 2001

Participants: Guinea versus Rally of Democratic Forces of Guinea (RFDG).
Dates: September 4, 2000, to May 8, 2001.
Battle-related Deaths: Guinea: [ ]; RDFG: [ ].
Initiator: RDFG.
Outcome: Stalemate.
War Type: Civil for central control.
Total System Member Military Personnel: Armed Forces of Guinea: 12,000 (prewar); 10,000 (initial, peak, final).[263]
Theater Armed Forces: Armed Forces of RFDG: [ ].

Antecedents: Col. Lansana Conté came to power in Guinea through a bloodless coup in 1984. Conté shifted away from the previous administration's socialist policies and made gradual moves toward moving to civilian rule. In December 1993, the country's first multiparty presidential was held, which Conté won, and in 1995 Conté's party, the Party of Unity and Progress, won the majority of the seats in the parliament. Yet Conté's rule was basically authoritarian and ushered in a period of civil unrest (including a coup attempt in 1996) and government repression. The situation in Guinea was destabilized further by its proximity to Liberia and Sierra Leone, whose civil wars (Intra-state Wars #892 and #902) led to the presence of approximately 500,000 refugees living in Guinea. Furthermore, Guinea harbored a Liberian rebel group.

Narrative: The war began on September 4, 2000, with an armed attack against a Guinean town near its border with Liberia in which several Guinean soldiers were killed. Similar attacks occurred during the next few days in towns along the Guinean border with Sierra Leone. A Guinean rebel group, the Rally of Democratic Forces of Guinea (RFDG), claimed responsibility for the attacks. The RFDG had been formed by dissidents within the Guinean military, some of whom had participated in the 1996 coup attempt against President Conté. However, Conté blamed the attacks on Liberia and rebels in Sierra Leone, which prompted Guineans to attack and harass the Liberian and Sierra Leonean refugees in their midst, ultimately causing a humanitarian crisis as the refugees were moved to other camps or deported. Meanwhile, the rebel attacks continued, some near Macenta in the diamond district. In December, rebel attacks moved further afield, including a battle at Guekedou in which the government claimed to have killed 150 rebels and an attack against a Guinean army garrison at Pamalap, closer to the Guinean capital of Conakry. In January 2001, ECOWAS announced a plan to dispatch 1,676 ECOMOG peacekeepers to Guinea, and fighting continued around Guekedou. Conté had purchased new artillery and helicopter gunships for his military, and these were used in February in attacks against suspected RUF (Revolutionary United Front) bases in Sierra Leone, causing a number of civilian fatalities. The same month, Guinean troops were able to recapture Guekedou after four days of heavy fighting. On May 8, the Guineans again used the helicopter gunships and artillery to attack rebel bases in Sierra Leone. At that point, major attacks generally ceased.

Termination and Outcome: The war is coded as ending in a stalemate: the ECOMOG forces could restrain the conflict but could not resolve the sources of the conflict. Conté remained in power until his death in 2008.

Coding Decisions: The primary difficulty in coding this war was determining who the combatants were.

The Guinean government initially insisted on portraying the conflict in international terms as an attempt by Liberia to overthrow the Guinean government with the aid of the RUF in Sierra Leone while discounting involvement of domestic dissidents. Subsequently, the RDFG claimed responsibility for the attacks, and the pattern of the RDFG in moving from Guinea to training camps in Liberia and then into Sierra Leone as a base for their attacks became clearer. Though RDFG was trained and assisted by Liberia's President Charles Taylor and Taylor's RUF allies (or proxies), it is unclear to what extent Liberian or RUF soldiers were involved in the fighting, though there were reports that the attacks around the diamond area of Macenta involved Liberians.

Fatality information for this war is missing for most of the engagements. However, in just three of the major battles, the Guineans claim to have killed 700 rebels, so it seems likely that total combatant fatalities would exceed 1,000.[264]

Sources: BBC News (2005b); Bercovitch and Fretter (2004); International Crisis Group (2010a); *IRIN News Reports* (2000, 2001); *Keesing's Record of World Events* (2000, 2001); Onishi (2001); Project Ploughshares (2004).

INTRA-STATE WAR #918
Third Burundi War of 2001 to 2003

Participants: Burundi and Rwanda versus Force Nationale de Liberation (FNL) and Forces for the Defense of Democracy (FDD).
Dates: March 1, 2001, to October 8, 2003.
Battle-related Deaths: FNL and FDD: 3,000; Burundi: 150; Rwanda: [ ].
Initiator: FNL.
Outcome: Compromise.
War Type: Civil for central control.
Total System Member Military Personnel: Armed Forces of Burundi: 40,000 (prewar); 46,000 (initial); 50,000 (peak, final).[265] Armed Forces of Rwanda: 70,000 (prewar, initial, peak); 50,000 (final).[266]
Theater Armed Forces: Armed Forces of Rwanda: 3,000.[267] Armed Forces of FNL: 1,000 to 2,000 (initial); 3,000 (peak, final).[268] Armed Forces of FDD: 25,000 (final).[269]

Antecedents: In the midst of the last war in Burundi (Intra-state War #883 from 1993 to 1998), the army staged a coup in 1996, replacing the Hutu president with a Tutsi, Pierre Buyoya. The fighting continued with the Hutu National Council for the Defense of Democracy (CNDD) and its military wing, the Forces for the Defense of Democracy (FDD), along with the National Forces of Liberation (FNL) leading the attacks against the government. In June 1998, a compromise agreement gave the Hutu greater representation in the parliament, and the related cease-fire reduced the level of fighting below war levels. The more comprehensive Arusha Peace and Reconciliation Agreement was signed on August 28, 2000, between the two political parties, Buyoya's Union for National Progress (UPRONA) and the Front for Democracy in Burundi (FRODEBU), which was the major party of the Hutu. The agreement was not accepted by the Hutu armed forces (the FDD and the FNL). Consequently, violence continued but at below-war level. Meanwhile, Burundi's military still believed that a military resolution to the conflict was preferable; and the FNL and FDD wanted to emphasize the limited value of any agreement that did not include them. Thus toward the end of 2000, the level of conflict started to escalate.

Narrative: Fighting at war level resumed on February 8, 2001, when the FNL began a new set of attacks. Heavy fighting took place first in the southern provinces, and on February 16, the rebels attacked a military position in the capital, Bujumbura. The government responded with an offensive that attempted to reverse the rebel gains. On April 11, the army used mortars to attack the FNL in central Burundi. In September, fifty rebels were killed as the navy sank their boat on Lake Tanganyika. The rebels launched additional attacks around the capital of Bujumbura in December in fighting that would continue for the next two years. During 2002, the government scored a number of significant victories against the rebels, occasionally by utilizing its helicopter gunships. Additional troops from Rwanda were also instrumental. In March and April, the FNL lost its positions in Mbare and began retreating from Bujumbura. In mid-July 2002, the FDD launched a counteroffensive on all three major fronts (the East, South, and Center), and at the end of the month, the FNL shelled Bujumbura as fighting erupted in the capital's suburbs.

The fighting continued in 2003, and in the Central Gitega province, clashes between FDD and the government persuaded 60,000 people to flee. Meanwhile, the government continued its efforts toward a new peace agreement, and a preliminary cease-fire agreement was reached with the FDD, which continued fighting nonetheless. On October 8, 2003, the government and the FDD signed a cease-fire accord.

Termination and Outcome: The October cease-fire led to a reduction in hostilities, as did the subsequent November 16 agreement that brought many of the rebel forces into the Burundi armed forces. The FNL refused to join the peace process and continued its attacks upon the government at a below-war level for the next three years. In 2006, the FNL finally signed a peace agreement.

Coding Decisions: In addition to the combatants, thousands of civilians were killed in the war. Reliable combatant fatality data for this war is not available.

Sources: Cutter (2007); Home Office (2004); International Crisis Group (2002b, c); IRIN (2001); Phillips and Axelrod (2005); Project Ploughshares (2004); Reyntjens (2000); Stapleton (2013).

INTRA-STATE WAR #920
Fourth Rwanda War of 2001

Participants: Rwanda versus Army for the Liberation of Rwanda.
Dates: May 21, 2001, to September 4, 2001.
Battle-related Deaths: Army for the Liberation of Rwanda (ALiR): 1,800;[270] Rwanda: [ ].
Initiator: ALiR.
Outcome: Rwanda wins.
War Type: Civil for central control.
Total System Member Military Personnel: Armed Forces of Rwanda (RPA): 70,000 (prewar, initial, peak, final).[271]
Theater Armed Forces: Armed Forces of ALiR: 40,000 (initial, peak).[272]

Antecedents: Toward the end of Rwanda's earlier war (Intra-state War #886 in 1994), a number of Hutu militia (the *Interahamwe*) and soldiers of Rwanda's Hutu army (the FAR) fled into Zaire along with 2 million Hutu civilians as Rwanda's Hutu government was being overthrown by the Tutsi Rwanda Patriotic Front (RPF). In refugee camps in Zaire the *Interahamwe* and ex-FAR joined together with Hutu volunteers in 1997 to create the Army for the Liberation of Rwanda (ALiR), which began launching raids into Rwanda with the aims of killing as many Tutsi as possible and overthrowing the government of Paul Kagame in Kigali. These strikes expanded into another war (Intra-state War #896 of 1997 to 1998). In this war, the Hutu were unable to overthrow the Tutsi RPF government, and fatality levels in the fighting declined below war level at the end of October 1998 as Rwanda shifted its focus to the Democratic Republic of Congo (DRC) and its role in the emerging Africa's World War (Intra-state War #905 of 1998 to 2002). Toward the end of that war, the DRC encouraged and coerced the Rwandans in the camps to return to their country.

Narrative: Many of the Hutu (including ALiR guerrillas) crossed from the DRC into Rwanda's Northwest Ruhengeri area. On May 21, as seventy members of the ALiR crossed the border, they were intercepted; forty were killed, and the rest captured by the Rwandan army, thus starting this brief war. Fighting spread in Ruhengeri as the RPA announced that it was confronting one of the biggest attacks on the country in years. ALiR guerrillas crossed into Rwanda at several different points along the border. Over the next two months, the RPA and the ALiR engaged in almost daily clashes. For instance, on June 6, a major engagement involved several hundred ALiR combatants who were detected crossing the border. Both sides suffered fatalities, and a helicopter was forced down. The RPA, using infantry, artillery, and helicopter gunships, attacked the rebels in Rwanda and in the DRC as well. The RPA quickly defeated the rebel forces, with most killed or captured. Rwanda opened several detention camps for the prisoners.

Termination and Outcome: By the end of July, the RPF had succeeded in decimating the ALiR forces. Some of the survivors retreated into the Vininga volcano range on the border with Uganda. Uganda and Rwanda reached an agreement to cooperate in efforts to curb instability along their common border.

Coding Decisions: There have been competing portrayals of which party was the initiator in this war. Rwanda portrayed the ALiR as invading its territory in attacks similar to those in the preceding war. Other reports conclude that the ALiR was driven into Rwanda, where it was attacked by the RPA. Because so many of the ALiR remained in the DRC, from which future attacks were launched, the RPA version seems plausible, thus the ALiR is coded as the initiator.

Similarly, there are contrasting estimates of the size of the ALiR forces. There were apparently approximately 40,000 ALiR members in the DCR, though somewhere in the vicinity of 4,000 of them crossed into Rwanda. Human Rights Watch characterizes this as being different from its predecessors in that only limited numbers of civilians were killed.

Sources: Arnold (2009); Cutter (2007); Human Rights Watch (2001b); Project Ploughshares (2004).

INTRA-STATE WAR #922
Liberia–LURD War of 2002 to 2003

Participants: Liberia versus Liberians United for Reconciliation and Democracy (LURD) and Movement for Democracy in Liberia (MODEL).
Dates: May 2002 to August 4, 2003.
Battle-related Deaths: Liberia: [ ]; LURD and MODEL: [ ]; Total Combatant Deaths: 3,000.
Initiator: LURD.
Outcome: LURD and MODEL win.
War Type: Civil for central control.
Total System Member Military Personnel: Armed Forces of Liberia (ALF): 15,000 (prewar, initial, peak, final).[273]
Theater Armed Forces: Armed Forces of LURD: 3,000 (initial).[274] Armed Forces of MODEL, participating from April 2003: [ ].

Antecedents: Charles Taylor's desire to rule Liberia had contributed to two earlier wars in Liberia (Intra-state Wars #857 and #879). The latter war ended as a compromise when a new peace accord was signed in August 1996. The militia leaders agreed to form their groups into political parties that would compete in an upcoming election. On July 19, 1997, Charles Taylor and his National Patriotic Party (NPP) won a clear victory. Taylor was declared the president on July 23, 1997, and took office on August 2, 1997. During his term in office, Taylor was accused of fueling wars in neighboring Sierra Leone and Guinea. In the Sierra Leone war of 1998 to 2000 (Intra-state War #898), Taylor is accused of aiding the Revolutionary United Front (RUF), which engaged in massacres and mutilations of civilians as it attempted to stay in power. Two years later, Taylor was charged with aiding rebels trying to overthrow the government of Guinea (Intra-state War #917 of 2000 to 2001).

Meanwhile, opposition to Taylor within Liberia had emerged as well. The Liberians United for Reconciliation and Democracy (LURD) began attempts to oust Taylor from power in 1999 with the assistance of Guinea. Fighting was below war level at this point. Taylor was able to remain in power, partially due to his control of the diamond trade. The UN had imposed sanctions on Liberia, and Taylor argued that these constrained his ability to fight the rebels. As a result, his administration began to falter in 2002.

Narrative: The rebels of LURD launched a major offensive in May 2002, which marks the start of the war. The LURD forces advanced to within twenty-five kilometers of the capital. Government forces counterattacked, and by October 2002, Taylor had reoccupied most of the country's territory. By November 2002, the conflict had created nearly 130,000 internally displaced persons (IDPs) as well as 230,000 refugees in bordering states. In April, a second rebel group, the Movement for Democracy in Liberia (MODEL), entered the war aided by Côte d'Ivoire. LURD advanced in the North toward Monrovia, while MODEL occupied the South and East. By May 2003, the rebel forces neared the capital, where heavy fighting lasted for weeks. A preliminary cease-fire was arranged for June but collapsed within days. In Late July, MODEL captured the port town of Buchanan, southeast of the capital.

Termination and Outcome: On August 4, 2003, the first contingent of ECOWAS peacekeeping forces arrived, and the fighting subsided, marking the end of the war. On August 11, 2003, Taylor relinquished power and was granted asylum in Nigeria. A peace agreement was signed on August 18 in Accra. Eager to end the fighting in West Africa, the UN dispatched a contingent of 15,000 peacekeepers to Liberia in February 2004. The country began to prepare for elections. In 2005, Ellen Johnson-Sirleaf was elected, taking office on January 16, 2006. Johnson-Sirleaf ultimately engineered Taylor's extradition from Nigeria, and he was sent to stand trial at The Hague, where he was convicted of war crimes and crimes against humanity.

Coding Decisions: There is very little information available about battle-deaths during this war.

Sources: Arnold (2009); BBC News (2003); Bercovitch and Fretter (2004); Ciment (2007f); GlobalSecurity.org (2002, 2003, 2004, 2006); International Crisis Group (2002b, c); *Keesing's Record of World Events* (2003–2004); Meredith (2005); Project Ploughshares (2005); Reno (2007); Stapleton (2013).

INTRA-STATE WAR #925
Côte d'Ivoire Military War of 2002 to 2003 (aka First Ivoirian Civil War)

Participants: Côte d'Ivoire, France, and Front for the Liberation of the Great West (FLGO) versus Patriotic Movement of Ivory Coast (MPCI), Ivorian Popular Movement for the Far West (MPIGO), and Movement for Justice and Peace (MJP).

Dates: September 19, 2002, to October 17, 2002, and November 27, 2002, to May 3, 2003.

Battle-related Deaths: MPCI, MPIGO, MJP: [ ]; Côte d'Ivoire: [ ]; France: [ ]; FLAGO: [ ]; Total Combatant Deaths: 3,000.[275]

Initiator: MPCI.

Outcome: Compromise.

War Type: Civil for central control.

Total System Member Military Personnel: Armed Forces of Côte d'Ivoire (FANCI): 14,000 (prewar); 17,000 (initial, peak, final).[276] Armed Forces of France: 274,000 (prewar); 260,000 (initial, peak); 256,000 (final).[277]

Theater Armed Forces: Armed Forces of France, participating from December 21, 2002: 2,500 (initial, peak, final).[278] Front for the Liberation of the Great West (FLGO): several thousand (peak, final).[279] Anti-government Rebels (later called New Forces, or FDS-FN): 35,000 (peak, final);[280] also consisting of Armed Forces of MPCI, participating September 19, 2002, to October 17, 2002: 800 (initial);[281] Armed Forces of MPIGO (Pro-rebel Intervener), participating from November 27, 2002: 6,000 (peak, final); and Armed Forces of MJP (Pro-rebel Intervener), participating from November 27, 2002: [ ].

Antecedents: When Côte d'Ivoire attained its independence from France in 1960, it was considered to be one of West Africa's most prosperous countries. Félix Houphouët-Boigny was its first president, and he aligned Côte d'Ivoire with France and the West and against the Soviet Union and the People's Republic of China. This position put him into conflict with the Marxist regimes in Africa and into collaboration with South Africa and conservative regimes. Houphouët-Boigny was instrumental in persuading France to aid Charles Taylor in his efforts to come to power in Liberia (Intra-state War #857 in 1989 to 1990), partially in the hopes of augmenting his personal wealth. As Côte d'Ivoire's economy began to falter in the 1980s, opposition to Houphouët-Boigny's government began to spread. One of the leaders of student demonstrations at that time was Laurent Gbagbo, who with his wife would found the Ivorian Popular Front (FPI). As Houphouët-Boigny was dying, he selected the president of the national assembly, Aimé Henri Konan Bédié, to be his successor (upon his death in 1993).

Bédié's government was perceived to be corrupt, and Bédié espoused a vision of *Ivoirité* (or being a true Ivoirian) that privileged the Christian South against the immigrant population of the North (many from Burkina Faso). Bédié was overthrown in a military coup led by Gen. Robert Guéï in 1999. Guéï promised open elections, but he refused to allow opposition candidates Alassane Ouattara or Henri Konan Bédié to participate, claiming that Ouattara (who represented the Muslim North) was not a true Ivoirian. Gbagbo was the only opposition candidate who participated. Guéï declared himself the victor in the election of October 22, 2000. However, when investigations revealed that Gbagbo had in fact won, Guéï fled as Gbagbo installed himself as president. Gbagbo's party, FPI, gained a plurality of seats in the parliamentary election in December. Meanwhile, Ouattara was demanding a new presidential election in which he could be a candidate.

Narrative: As the government began plans to demobilize a large segment of its military, a military coup started this war on September 19, 2002. The rebels launched a three-pronged offensive against the capital, Abdijan, and other cities. In the first few days of fighting between rebel and loyalist military in the capital, hundreds were killed, including Guéï. As the initial coup failed, the main rebel group, the Patriotic Movement of Ivory Coast (MPCI), retreated to the North. Heavy fighting took place at the end of September around Bouaka, Côte d'Ivoire's second-largest city, where French troops evacuated foreign nationals.

France initially had about 1,000 troops in Côte d'Ivoire, and it began to increase the number of its forces (ultimately to 4,000) through Operation Unicorn. France conceived of its troops as peacekeeping forces that would separate the two armies. France's stance was controversial and would evolve through the course of the war. Côte d'Ivoire's Prime Minister Pascal Affi N'Guessan suggested that France should provide active military assistance to Côte d'Ivoire based on an earlier defense pact, and the Economic Community of West African States (ECOWAS) proposed that France provide logistical support. France had been criticized for providing sanctuary to government opponent Ouattara in September and would be again in October for firing tear gas at crowds of demonstrators. Yet, the presence of French troops near Yamoussoukro did deter rebel advances southward. Meanwhile, ECOWAS tried to negotiate a cease-fire and to stop Ivoirian citizens from attacking the immigrant population. The worldwide price of cocoa soared as rebels captured Vavoua near the cocoa-producing region. In fighting on October 12, the rebels captured Daloa in the Northwest, giving them control of the northern half of the country. As cease-fire efforts faltered, a flood of West African immigrants began to leave the country, many to Ghana and to Burkina Faso (which President Gbagbo claimed was the source of the rebellion). Government forces recaptured Daloa on October 15. Meanwhile, the rebels established a capital at Bouake. On October 17, an ECOWAS-mediated cease-fire was signed in Bouake, and it was successful in stopping the fighting. At the end of the month, negotiations between the government and the rebels began in Togo. Key rebel demands were the removal of Gbagbo and the reintegration of the rebels into the Ivoirian army.

Fighting resumed on November, 27, 2002, as two new rebel groups emerged, the Ivorian Popular Movement for the Far West (MPIGO) and the Movement for Justice and Peace (MJP), and they captured towns in the western part of the country. MPIGO and MJP claimed to be acting to avenge the death of General Guéï (who was from that region). MPIGO was rumored to have been established by Liberia's President Charles Taylor and contained both Ivoirian and Liberian guerrillas. In opposition, the Front for the Liberation of the Great West (FLGO) was created as a militia (including foreign mercenaries and Patriotic Youth) to fight with the government forces when the government launched an attempt to retake rebel-held areas in the West on November 30. Government forces engaged MPIGO and MJP forces in heavy fighting around the city of Man, which the government captured and then lost in December. The fighting drove 30,000 refugees to flee to Liberia and Guinea. In December, French augmented its peacekeeping forces, and ECOWAS deployed 1,500 peacekeepers to work alongside the French. France also sponsoring a new round of peace talks in Paris. On December 21, 2002, France was brought into the war as a combatant as French forces were attacked by the western rebels. Though the rebels initially claimed that the attacks were mistakes, and France argued that they were merely defending French nationals, the skirmishes were perceived widely as indicating that France was intervening on the side of the government. French and rebel forces engaged in fighting throughout January 2003 as well.

On January 15, 2003, peace talks between the government of Côte d'Ivoire and the three rebel groups began in Paris. By the January 24, an agreement for a power-sharing government was reached: Gbagbo would remain president, though most of the power would be held by Prime Minister Seydou Diarra (a Muslim from the North); the groups would share cabinet positions; and the rebels would end the conflict and disarm. The agreement was implemented gradually, and the rebels began assuming government positions in April. Yet, fighting continued in the western region. A new cease-fire agreement took effect on May 3, 2003. The UN also sent seventy-five peacekeepers (MINUCI) to assist France and ECOWAS in separating the combatants and to monitor the human rights situation.

Termination and Outcome: In May, the war ended in a compromise as the parties formed a unity government and created a cease-fire that stopped the fighting. In early July, the unity government signed an agreement ending the war. However, rebel disarmament was not complete. A dispute over how to fill the positions of minister of defense and minister of security prompted the rebels (now allied together as the New Forces) to withdraw from the unity government on September 23, 2003. The rebels returned to their capital at Bouake, and both sides began rearming. A period of political stalemate ensued.

On February 27, 2004, the UN established a new peacekeeping force (UNOIC) and attempted to encourage compromise. Fighting resumed between the government and the rebels in June 2004 but ended within two days. Most of the casualties of those bombing raids were civilians. With UN encouragement, the

Accra Agreement was signed on July 31, 2004, in an attempt to restart the peace process. There was a brief period of armed conflict in November 2004. South African President Thabo Mbeki conducted talks in Pretoria from April 3 to April 6 in 2005, leading to the Pretoria Agreement, which officially ended the war.

Coding Decisions: The October 17, 2002, cease-fire between the government and MPCI represents an agreement between the two parties in the war at that point to stop fighting. Because armed conflict ceased for a period longer than a month, that date is coded as the end date of the participation of MPCI in the war. As war participation for the government began again with the attacks by the western rebels on November 27, 2002, the period between October 17 and November 27 is coded as a break in the fighting for the government.

Sources: Arnold (2009); Baégas and Marshall-Fratani (2007); BBC News (2006b); Bercovitch and Fretter (2004); GlobalSecurity.org (2002, 2003, 2004); *IRIN News Reports* (multiple reports 2002–2004); Marshall (2014); Project Ploughshares (2004); Safer Access (2007).

INTRA-STATE WAR #933
Second Nigeria Christian–Muslim War of 2004

Participants: Christian Tarok versus Muslim Fulani.
Dates: March 2004 to September 16, 2004.
Battle-related Deaths: Christian Tarok: [ ]; Muslim Fulani: [ ]; Total Combatant Deaths: 1,650.[282]
Initiator: Muslim Fulani.
Outcome: Stalemate.
War Type: Intercommunal.
Theater Armed Forces: Christian Tarok Militia: Muslim Fulani Militia: [ ].

Antecedents: The Muslims constitute about 48 percent of the population of Nigeria and the Christians about 36 percent. Nigeria generally is divided into a Muslim-dominated North and a Christian South, though there are enclaves of each religious group in each other's territory.

As Nigeria shifted to a more democratic government in 1999, tensions between the Christians and Muslims were heightened as Muslims tried to take advantage of the increased governmental flexibility to begin to apply *sharia* law. Religious differences also were intertwined with differences in ethnicity, and in this case the Christian Tarok people of Nigeria's central highland tended to be an agricultural society, while the Muslim Fulani tended to be more pastoral. The situation also was exacerbated by money coming into the country, which produced a flow of weapons to local militias, increasing the probability of armed conflict.

In 2000, the adoption of *sharia* law in the state of Kaduna precipitated rioting and reprisal attacks between the Christians and Muslims, in which hundreds of civilians were killed and thousands displaced throughout the central states of the North. The Plateau state received the largest share of displaced persons, and their movements fueled conflict between the Christian farmers and the Muslim herders. However, the conflict in 2004 differed from 2000 in that each of the ethno-religious groups had an armed militia, and so the conflict took the form of clashes between the militias rather than riots.

Narrative: Violence broke out in March 2004 as a result of a dispute over a piece of land and whether it should be used for farming or grazing. The Christian and Muslim militias, armed with guns, bows, and machetes, clashed in the Plateau state over the next couple of months. In an attempt to stem the rising intercommunal conflict, Nigeria's government declared a state of emergency and outlawed the extremist Muslim group, the Council of Ulamma. The government's measures reduced the level of violence and ended this war in September 2004.

Termination and Outcome: In addition to the fatalities within the Muslim and Christian militias, as many as 57,000 civilians may have been displaced in the fighting since 1999.

Coding Decisions: Self-explanatory from cited sources.

Sources: Ciment and Schofield (2007); GlobalSecurity.org (2002, 2003, 2004); Project Ploughshares (2004).

INTRA-STATE WAR #937
Chad–United Opposition War of 2005 to 2008

Participants: Chad versus the United Opposition (Armed Forces of Rally for Democracy and Freedom, or RDL; Front for Democratic

Change, or FUC; and Union of Forces for Democracy and Development, or UFDD).

Dates: December 18, 2005, to December 12, 2006, and November 26, 2007, to February 3, 2008.

Battle-related Deaths: United Opposition: [ ]; Chad: [ ]; Total Combatant Deaths: 2,500.[283]

Initiator: RDL and Platform for Change, Unity, and Democracy (SCUD).

Outcome: Conflict continues at below-war level.

War Type: Civil for central control.

Total System Member Military Personnel: Armed Forces of Chad: 30,000 (prewar, initial, peak); 23,000 (final).[284]

Theater Armed Forces: Armed Forces of United Opposition: 1,500 (initial);[285] Rebel Aggregate consisting of:

Armed Forces of Platform for Change, Unity, and Democracy (SCUD): 600 (initial).[286]

Armed Forces of Rally for Democracy and Liberty (RDL): [ ].

Armed Forces of United Front for Democratic Change (FUC): [ ].

Armed Forces of United Forces for Development and Democracy (UFDD): 3,000 (peak).

Armed Forces of Rally of the Forces for Change (RFC): 800 (peak).

Armed Forces of National Accord of Chad: [ ].

Antecedents: In 2000, Chad's President Idriss Déby and his *Mouvement Patriotique du Salut* (MPS) defeated a revolt by former defense minister Youssouf Togoimi, who led the *Mouvement pour la démocratie et la justice au Tchad* (MDJT, Intra-state War #906). Opposition to Déby continued, partially influenced by events in neighboring Sudan. Groups seeking independence for Sudan's Darfur region launched a war against the Sudanese government (Intra-state War #927 of 2003 to 2006). In the course of the war, Sudan utilized the Janjaweed to attack rebel bases. The Janjaweed began indiscriminate attacks against civilians, creating a humanitarian crisis that involved a flood of 200,000 (later 400,000) refugees coming into East Chad. Many of the refugees were of the Zaghawa ethnic group, as were Déby and a number of his military officers. Déby was caught between trying to maintain cordial relations with Chad's powerful neighbor (Sudan) and supporting the refugees. The judgment that Déby was not doing enough of the latter contributed to an attempted coup against Déby by military officers in 2004. The growing opposition to Déby's rule led to the desertion of hundreds of military personnel (including most of Déby's presidential guard and two of his nephews), many of whom fled to East Chad, where they created a number of rebel groups, two of which were the Platform for Change, National Unity and Democracy (SCUD) and the Rally for Democracy and Liberty (RDL). In 2005, Déby engineered constitutional reforms that increased the power of the president and allowed him to run for a third presidential term. This produced calls from SCUD and RDL for Déby's resignation and led to an emerging consensus among the opposition group toward the necessity of armed action against Déby.

Narrative: The war began on December 18, 2005, as SCUD and RDL attacked the Chadian border town of André. The attack was repulsed by Chadian forces in an engagement that cost 300 lives. The Chadian troops chased the rebels into Sudan and destroyed a base there, prompting Déby to claim that Sudan was supporting the rebels (which Sudan denied). The leader of the RDL, Mahamat Nour Abdelkarim (who had served in Déby's cabinet), then announced that the rebels had more grandiose plans for the future. By the end of the month, Nour had engineered an alliance among eight of the rebel groups under the umbrella of the Front for Democratic Change (FUC), with Nour as one of its presidents. In April, the rebels launched a coordinated offensive against the Chadian capital, N'Djaména. FUC troops drove westward across country from the East, while a second rebel group advanced from the South. France, which had 1,200 troops stationed in Chad, provided the logistical support that enabled the Déby government to defeat the rebels on April 13. Déby was reelected in the presidential election in May.

In the fall, a new rebel coalition appeared, also under Nour's leadership. The Union of Forces for Democracy and Development (UFDD) became the largest of the rebel groups by uniting the FUC with two additional rebel armies. In September 2006, Chad's armed forces launched attacks against the rebels in Abéché, and Déby personally piloted a helicopter so that he could oversee the army's progress. In October, UFDD entered Chad from Sudan in a convoy of sixty to eighty vehicles and attacked the towns of Goz Beida on October 22 and Am Timan on October 23. Then on October 30, forces from Chad and the UFDD engaged in a battle at Marche Borgo in which the rebels were defeated, losing 100 men to the government's loss of 4, including Gen. Moussa Sougui, head of Chad's armed forces. A similar battle at Bobok on December 12, 2006, led to the deaths of 50 to 100 rebels and 30 to 300 government troops.

Later that month, Déby attempted to ameliorate some of the opposition to his regime by negotiating a deal with UFDD/FUC leader Nour, whereby Nour joined Déby's government as minister of defense, and thousands of FUC soldiers would be integrated into the Chadian military. The UFDD fragmented: though a few additional UFDD leaders accepted government positions, others rejected the agreement and vowed to continue fighting against the government, either within UFDD or other groups. Yet there was little conflict between the government and the rebels through the first nine months of Nour's tenure as minister of defense in 2007. Déby signed a cease-fire agreement with other rebel groups in October. Nouri's stint as minister of defense lasted less than a year, during which time he ordered the FUC fighters to join Chad's army. The integration did not go well, leading to the defection in October 2007 of many of the FUC rebels, some of whom returned to the FUC base in East Chad and rejoined UFDD. At the end of November, the UFDD and the Rally of the Forces for Change (RFC) each launched operations in East Chad entailing significant fighting with Chad's forces. At that point, Déby dismissed Nour from his position on December 1, 2007, and Nour returned to the UFDD. Lack of coordination between the UFDD and RFC contributed to heavy rebel losses in what was the most serious fighting of the war.

By early 2008, there were a dozen different rebel groups operating along the border between Chad and Sudan. On January 28, 2008, the rebels (this time with a united military command) launched another offensive against N'Djaména with 3,000 troops. In fighting on February 2 and February 3, the rebels were able to advance into the capital and surround the presidential palace. However, the Chadian armed forces were ready for them. The air force, commanded by Déby (a trained helicopter pilot) bombed rebel positions, forcing them to retreat. More than 20,000 civilians fled the city.

Termination and Outcome: Major armed combat declined after the rebels were pushed back from N'Djaména in 2008. Conflict at below-war level continued after February 3. In January 2010, the governments of Chad and Sudan signed an agreement to cease aiding rebels in their territory.

Coding Decisions: The period between December 12, 2007, and November 26, 2007, is coded as a break in the fighting brought on by the Déby–Nour agreement.

Sources: Arnold (2009); BBC News (2005b); Boguslaw (2010); *Chicago Tribune* (2008); Cutter (2007); Erikson and Hagströmer (2004); GlobalSecurity.org (2005d, e); Immigration and Refugee Board of Canada (2009); International Crisis Group (2011); *IRIN News Reports* (2007, 2009, 2011); *Keesing's Record of World Events* (2005); Maliti (2008); Marshall (2014); NationMaster (2005, 2006); *The New York Times* (2008); Project Ploughshares (2008, 2013); Stapleton (2013).

INTRA-STATE WAR #940.8
Third Somalia War of 2006 to 2012

Participants: Somalia, Ethiopia, Uganda, Burundi, Kenya, United States, Puntland, and *Ahlu Sunna Waljama'a* versus Islamic Courts Union (ICU) and Eritrea.

Dates: December 20, 2006, to June 11, 2008, and February 8, 2009, to September 29, 2012.

Battle-related Deaths: Total Combatant Deaths: [ ]. (See Coding Decisions.)

Initiator: ICU.

Outcome: Somalia, Ethiopia, Uganda, Burundi, Kenya, United States, Puntland, and *Ahlu Sunna Waljama'a* win.

War Type: Civil for central control.

Total System Member Military Personnel: Armed Forces of Somalia, combining forces of Transitional Federal Government (TFG), Puntland, and Somaliland: 2,000, 15,000, and 7,500 equal 24,500 (initial, peak).[287] Armed Forces of Ethiopia: 182,000 (prewar); 183,000 (initial, peak); 135,000 (final).[288] Armed Forces of United States: 1,473,000 (prewar); 1,546,000 (initial, peak); 1,580,000 (final).[289] Armed Forces of Uganda: 45,000 (prewar, initial).[290] Armed Forces of Burundi: 20,000 (prewar, initial).[291] Armed Forces of Kenya: 24,000 (prewar).[292] Armed Forces of Eritrea: 202,000 (prewar, initial, peak, final).[293]

Theater Armed Forces: Armed Forces of Somalia (Transitional Federal Government [TFG]):

8,000 (in 2010).[294] Armed Forces of United States (Pro-government Intervener): [ ]. (See Coding Decisions). Armed Forces of autonomous region of Puntland (Pro-government Intervener): [ ]. Armed Forces of Ethiopia (Pro-government Intervener), participating from January 25, 2009, and May 20, 2010: 4,000 (initial); 8,000 (peak).[295] Armed Forces of Ahlu Sunna Waljama'a: 2,000 (in 2010).[296] Armed Forces of Kenya (Pro-government Intervener), participating from October 16, 2011, till integrated into AMISOM in June 2012: 3,000 (initial).[297] AMISOM (Pro-government Intervener), participating as a war participant after July 22, 2010: 5,300 (initial); 21,500 (peak, final)[298] as aggregate consisting of:

Armed Forces of Uganda (Pro-government Intervener), participating from July 22, 2010: 1,500 (initial); 6,223.[299]

Armed Forces of Burundi (Pro-government Intervener), participating from July 22, 2010): 1,700 (initial); 5,432.[300]

Armed Forces of Kenya (Pro-government Intervener), participating as part of AMISOM from February 22, 2012: 4,512 (peak).[301]

Armed Forces of Islamic Courts Union (ICU, Rebel Aggregate), participating until January 31, 2009: 8,000.

Armed Forces of Al-Shabaab, participating independently after February 8, 2009: 3,000 to 7,000.[302]

Armed Forces of Hizbul Islam, participating independently from February 8, 2009, to December 20, 2010): [ ].

Armed Forces of Eritrea (Pro-rebel Intervener): 500 (initial);[303] 2,000.

Antecedents: Between 1991 and 1997, Somalia suffered through an internationalized civil war (Intra-state War #865.8) during which the United Somali Congress (USC) split into an Aideed faction and the Mahdi faction, which struggled for control of the capital. In December 1997, the leaders of the Aideed and Mahdi factions agreed to the terms of a cease-fire, which ended the war, though some low-level conflict persisted among the other clans. Somalia entered a phase in which it was referred to as a failed state because even though there were two governments formed, they had virtually no control. International efforts led to the 2000 creation of a Somali Intergovernmental Authority on Development (IGAD) in Djibouti, which created a transitional national government (TNG), which transformed in 2004 into the transitional federal government (TFG), which was based in Nairobi, Kenya. TFG was under the leadership of Col. Abdullah Yusuf Ahmed, who had served in the Somali National Army but later became involved in the movement to create an autonomous Puntland, ultimately serving as its first president from 1998 to 2004, when he was elected as president of Somalia. Ahmed pledged to promote reconciliation with the various clans and factions.

In the meantime, the Islamic Courts Union (ICU, later known as the Supreme Council of Islamic Courts [SCIC]) had gained control over most of South Somalia, including the capital, Mogadishu, and it imposed *sharia* law. In 2005 the TFG moved its base to Baidoa and Jawhar (near Mogadishu) and began the process of gaining control in Somalia. That project would entail unifying the clans; disarming 50,000 militia guerrillas; and reincorporating the semiautonomous areas of Somaliland and Puntland into Somalia. However, it was confronted by the ICU, which also wanted to establish control over the entire country. In 2006, the warlords in Mogadishu formed the Alliance for the Restoration of Peace and Counter-Terrorism (ARPCT), funded by the American CIA. In March, the ICU and ARPCT engaged in armed conflict over control of Mogadishu. Initially it was perceived that the conflict was between TFG and the ICU, but TFG denied involvement. By June, the ICU had gained control of the city, and the warlords fled as the ICU spread its control further outside the capital in September. This war began in December 2006 as the ICU confronted the TFG.

Narrative: In late December 2006, the ICU, joined by troops from Eritrea, began an offensive against the TFG at Baidoa. The TFG was saved by the intervention of Ethiopia, which already had a few troops in Somalia, and encouraged by the United States, it sent a large contingent of land forces, helicopters, and fighter planes to assist the TFG. The TFG also mobilized forces from Puntland that advanced from the North, and soon the TFG controlled the capital as the IUC retreated. The TFG–Ethiopian forces continued to advance southward, while the United States conducted air strikes against the IUC along the Somali border with Kenya. US warships also launched operations along the Somali coast.

In January 2007, the African Union (AU) created the African Union Mission in Somalia (AMISOM), which was established to support the TFG, and 1,500 forces from Uganda arrived in March, though their mission was peacekeeping (not combat). In June, US warships pounded IUC positions as a new front was opened in Puntland in the Northeast. Throughout 2007, the TFG was successful in extending its control, and a cease-fire on June 11, 2008, ended most of the fighting (this marks a break in the war). The practice of piracy increased during this period. On December 29, 2008, President Ahmed announced his resignation from the TFG presidency. He was succeeded by Aden "Madobe" Mohamed, the speaker of the parliament. In January 2009, the TFG absorbed a relatively moderate IUC faction (Alliance for the Re-liberation of Somalis [ARS]), led by Sharif Sheikh Ahmed. Sheikh Ahmed was then elected president of the TFG on January 31. The withdrawal of Ethiopian troops that month meant a loss of territory for the TFG as the fighting resumed.

At the beginning of February 2009, a number of the Islamic factions (united as Hizbul Islam) and the extreme youth faction, Al-Shabaab, vowed to continue the fight against the TFG and the AU peacekeepers. On February 8, 2009, fighting broke out in Mogadishu and spread northwest to Baidoa, where TFG forces had been gathering. Al-Shabaab led heavy fighting in the central region and around Mogadishu in May and June 2009. On June 5, Al-Shabaab and Hizbul Islam captured Wabho (in Galgudud) in heavy fighting from the *Ahlu Sunna Waljama'a*, a pro-government militia. The government's losses prompted President Sharif Ahmed to appeal for foreign assistance on June 19 and to declare a state of emergency on June 22. TFG officials and forces began to defect to the Islamic groups.

In October 2009, fighting erupted between Al-Shabaab and Hizbul Islam over a power-sharing agreement. Battles between the two groups continued throughout 2010, with Al-Shabaab generally victorious, and on December 20, 2010, Hizbul Islam formally surrendered to Al-Shabaab and disbanded. During this period, armed conflict between Al-Shabaab and the TFG declined. However, Al-Shabaab advanced, gaining control over most of South Somalia by January 2010, while the TFG was limited to the area around the capital. In response to the TFG's appeal for foreign assistance, Ethiopia reentered the war in May 2010. Its forces made incursions from Ethiopian bases along the border into West Somalia throughout the rest of the year, and they were able to capture several towns from Al-Shabaab. The AU also acted to meet the growing threat: a meeting of AU ministers on July, 22, 2010, agreed that the AU forces could take on a more active role, moving to peace enforcement, which could involve preemptive strikes against Al-Shabaab. The involvement of foreign forces became critical for the success of Somali operations in 2011. In early 2011, AMISOM engaged in attacks against Al-Shabaab in what it called the Battle of Gashandiga, and by March TFG and AMISOM had gained control of more of Mogadishu. AMISOM forces were increased by another 1,000 to a total of 9,000, and by August 6, TFG and AMISOM had recaptured the capital. Fighting continued in Puntland in the North and in the South. In October 2011, government troops and forces from Kenya and Ethiopia launched Operation Linda Nchi with the goal of crippling Al-Shabaab. The offensives lasted through February 2012 as the united forces bombed and attacked Al-Shabaab facilities and forces in the South. A significant success was the recapturing of Baidoa in February. Kenyan forces were absorbed subsequently into AMISOM.

Termination and Outcome: The final battle of the war took place when TFG and Kenya (with support of the United States and France) bombarded the Al-Shabaab port of Kismayo on September 28, 2012, and the city was attacked and captured by TFG and AMISOM forces the following day. Kismayo was Al-Shabaab's last stronghold, and the rebels retreated and dispersed. This victory on September 29, 2012, marked the end of the war.

Coding Decisions: This case raises an issue that has become more problematic over the years in terms of what armed conflict means. With the advances in modern weaponry, the classical picture of armed combatants confronting each other individually has given way to more remote methods of killing by artillery, planes, long-range missiles, and now drones, whereby someone sitting at a desk in a remote location surely can be killing opponents yet not be in danger oneself. This issue impacts the coding of the number of combatants engaged in a war. Though support personnel generally have been considered part of the armed forces engaged in a war, the number of people in combat-related positions seems to be an ever-widening circle. This particularly relates to the coding of the United States as a war participant and the number of combatants involved. A number of sources do not include the United States as a war participant, while others mention that the United States only had 100 military advisers in Somalia, yet the United States conducted approximately twenty-four separate attacks between 2001 and 2014 utilizing naval and air power.[304]

The fatality information available for this war is incomplete and somewhat contradictory. A number of sources report variations of figures similar to the best guess figures utilized by the Uppsala Universitet Conflict Data Program (UCDP), which for the period 2006 to 2012 total 11,816.[305] UCDP coding includes combatant and civilian deaths in their calculations, yet similar numbers are said to reflect total deaths, combatant deaths, deaths for Somalia (both sides), or deaths of Al-Shabaab. If sources specifically identify deaths for the AMISOM forces, they are generally quite low, yet a UN official has indicated that the fatality figure should be closer to 3,000.[306] Consequently, we consider an accurate counting of the combatant battle-deaths for this war to still be unknown.

Sources: African Union (2014); Charbonneau (2013); *Chicago Tribune* (2006–2014); Ciment and Poljarevic (2007); Cloud (2007); Cutter (2007); DronesTeam (2012); Gettleman (2006); Harnisch (2010); *Keesing's Record of World Events* (2006); Mbaria (2007); Menkhaus (2010); Pettersson (2014); Project Ploughshares (2008); Stapleton (2013); Tekle (2013).

INTRA-STATE WAR #963
Boko Haram War of 2013, ongoing in Nigeria

Participants: Nigeria versus Boko Haram.
Dates: May 7, 2013, and ongoing.
Battle-related Deaths: Nigeria: 200; Boko Haram: 1,600. (See Coding Decisions.)
Initiator: Boko Haram.
Outcome: War ongoing.
War Type: Civil for central control.
Total System Member Military Personnel: Armed Forces of Nigeria: 80,000 (prewar).[307]
Theater Armed Forces: Boko Haram: 500 to 9,000.[308]

Antecedents: Muslims constitute about 48 percent of the population of Nigeria, and the Christians are about 36 percent. Nigeria generally is divided into a Muslim-dominated North and a Christian South, though there are pockets of each religious group in the other's zone. Conflict between the two groups led to war in 1980 (Intra-state War #823). Nigeria had been ruled by a military dictatorship from the North, and it shifted to a more democratic government in 1999 with the election of a southern Christian, former general Olusegun Obasanjo, as president in May. Obasanjo began taking steps to reduce the power of Muslims within the military. Tensions between the two religious groups heightened as the Muslims took advantage of the more flexible system to increasingly apply *sharia* law, leading to Muslim–Christian conflicts in 1999, 2000, and 2004.

The most recent major religion-based actor to emerge in Nigeria is the Boko Haram. Boko Haram is an Islamist terrorist group founded by Mohammed Yusuf in Northeast Nigeria in 2002. Boko Haram began fairly peacefully as an Islamic school but became increasingly militant in 2009. The arrest of 9 Boko Haram members on July 26, 2009, led to riots in which 700 people were killed. Yusuf was arrested and died in custody. Boko Haram was then led by Abubakar Shekau, who has developed ties to al-Qaida through their shared goal of creating an Islamic state. Boko Haram gradually shifted to conducting terrorist attacks against groups and organizations that did not share its Islamic beliefs: churches, banks, schools, and Western organizations, including the United Nations. From 2009 to 2011, Boko Haram conducted 140 attacks, though the vast majority was against civilian targets and caused civilian casualties.[309] The pattern of attacking civilians continued till May 2013.

Narrative: The war began as Boko Haram shifted from attacking civilian targets to an increased emphasis on attacking the government and its military and security forces. On May 7, 2013, Boko Haram launched coordinated strikes in Barna in Northeast Borno state: government and security service buildings were burned, and 150 prisoners were freed. On May 14, President Goodluck Jonathan declared a state of siege in the northeastern states. He deployed additional troops to the region, who were able to force Boko Haram out of many of the villages. In response, Boko Haram declared war against the government and launched a series of retaliatory raids. After this point, fatalities included a greater proportion of combatant deaths (both government and Boko Haram). This pattern continued for the remainder of 2013 and all of 2014.

Termination and Outcome: The war was apparently still ongoing at the end of 2014.

Coding Decisions: To determine the start date of this war (as opposed to one-sided attacks against civilians), we had to determine at what point the battle-deaths among combatants attained war level, more than 1,000 within a twelve-month period. A preliminary summation of news reports that mention combatant deaths from the period of May 7, 2013, to the end of 2014 yields an estimate of 1,600 Boko Haram and 200 government fatalities. Those figures are reported here, though they are probably underestimates. The government tends to report the killing of Boko Haram guerrillas but is less likely to mention government fatalities. Plus, it is unlikely that all of the engagements are reported in the press.

Sources: BBC News (2012–2014); Forest (2012); *Global Terrorism Index* (2014); International Crisis Group (2014); *Keesing's Record of World Events* (2014); Stapleton (2013); Wilkenfeld (2014).

INTRA-STATE WAR #973
Second Côte d'Ivoire War of 2011

Participants: Côte d'Ivoire, Front for the Liberation of the Greater West, Young Patriots, and Liberian Mercenaries versus New Forces, France, United Nations, and Invisible Commando.

Dates: February 21, 2011, to April 11, 2011.

Battle-related Deaths: Total Combatant Deaths: 1,000. (See Coding Decisions.)

Initiator: Côte d'Ivoire.

Outcome: New Forces, France, United Nations, and Invisible Commando win.

War Type: Civil for central control.

Total System Member Military Personnel: Armed Forces of Côte d'Ivoire (FANCI): 17,000 (prewar, initial).[310] Armed Forces of France: 353,000 (prewar).[311]

Theater Armed Forces: Armed Forces of Côte d'Ivoire: 9,000 (prewar, initial); 50,000 (peak); 2,000 (final).[312] Armed Forces of the Front for the Liberation of the Greater West (Pro-government Intervener): 10,000 (initial).[313] Young Patriots (Pro-government Intervener): [ ]. Liberian Mercenaries (Pro-government Intervener): [ ]. Armed Forces of New Forces (the Republican Forces): [ ]. Armed Forces of France (Pro-rebel Intervener): 900 (prewar); 1,500 (peak).[314] Armed Forces of the United Nations (UNOIC, Pro-rebel Intervener): 8,650 (prewar); 10,650 (initial).[315] Armed Forces of Invisible Commando (Pro-rebel Intervener): 5,000 (peak); 1,000 (final).[316]

Antecedents: The first civil war in Côte d'Ivoire (Intra-state War #925 of 2002 to 2003) ended with a May 3, 2003, cease-fire agreement that stopped the fighting and led to the creation of a national unity government later that year. The power-sharing government included Côte d'Ivoire's president, Laurent Gbagbo, who would remain president, though most of the power would be held by Prime Minister Seydou Diarra (a Muslim from the North); the rebel groups and the government would share cabinet positions. However, the disarming of the rebel groups proved to be problematic, and a dispute erupted between the government and the rebels (now allied together as the New Forces) over how to fill the positions of minister of defense and minister of security. The disagreements prompted the rebels to withdraw from the unity government on September 23, 2003. The rebels returned to their capital at Bouake, and both sides began rearming. A period of political stalemate ensued, which was finally broken by the 2005 Pretoria Agreement, which officially ended the war.

Prime Minister Seydou Diarra originally had been seen as a neutral figure, yet when he did not take a strong stand against the refusal of the rebels to disarm, he was criticized by the supporters of President Gbagbo who demanded his resignation. African Union mediators decided that Diarra would be replaced by former banker Charles Konan Banny on December, 7, 2005. After an accord between the rebels and the government was signed on March 4, 2007, Guillaume Soro (originally the leader of the rebel Patriotic Movement of Côte d'Ivoire, or MPCI, and subsequently secretary general of the united rebel group, New Forces) became prime minister. He and Gbagbo began a process of reconciliation: Gbagbo visited the North; Soro, and Gbagbo participated in a peace flame, a ceremonial burning of weapons; the New Forces and the government began dismantling the zone that the peacekeepers had created to divide the country.

Meanwhile, Gabagbo's term as president had been set to expire in October 2005, but because of the disagreements over disarmaments and the government's lack of preparedness, it was extended to 2006, 2007, and then later to 2010. In October 2010, fourteen candidates vied for the presidency, though three were primary: Gbagbo, former president Aimé Henri Konan Bédié, and Alassane Ouattara (the government's refusal to allow Ouattara to be a presidential contender in 2000 had been one of the causes of the war). The results of the election were: Gbago received 38 percent of the vote; Ouattara had 32 percent; and Bédié got 25 percent. As none of the candidates received an absolute majority, a second round of elections was scheduled for November 28, 2010. Bédié, who would not run in the second round, gave his support to Ouattara. Within days, two different election results were announced. On December 2, the Independent Election Commission (CEI) announced that Ouattara was the winner with 54 percent of the vote to Gbagbo's 46 percent. On December 3, the constitutional council reported that Gbagbo had won the elections with 51 percent as the results of several northern departments were invalid due to voter fraud. Both candidates were sworn in as president in competing ceremonies. Ouattara was recognized as the winner by the international community (the United Nations, the African Union, ECOWAS, and the European Union), the prime minister, and the former rebel groups; the government's armed forces backed Gbagbo. Clashes between the supporters of the two candidates erupted in December, prompting the fear of the resurgence of the civil war, and thousands of refugees began leaving the country.

Narrative: Violence escalated as government security officers began to attack and arrest Ouattara's supporters. Ouattara took refuge in a hotel, where he was protected by international peacekeepers; peacekeepers from France and the United Nations (UNOIC) had been in the country since the previous war. Violence increased as Côte d'Ivoire security police began attacking and arresting supporters of the opposition. On December 18, 2010, Gbagbo asked the French and UN peacekeepers to leave the country, and the UN, which did not recognize Gbagbo as the president, refused. The UN was accused of having ties to the former rebels who had controlled the North of the country since the last war. Sporadic attacks by the government's armed forces (FANCI) against Ouattara's army and the UNOIC were reported. Gbagbo resisted international pressure to resign and continued the harassment and killing (by death squads) of Ouattara's civilian supporters while blockading Ouattara's hotel headquarters. In January 2011, the UN voted to add 2,000 troops to its contingent in Côte d'Ivoire.

The war began on February 21, 2011, as conflict shifted from attacks on civilians to conflict between two armed forces. Government forces, armed with rocket launchers, advanced into neighborhoods of the southeastern city of Abidjan (the former capital), where they were ambushed, and ten of Gbagbo's soldiers were killed by commandos claiming loyalty to Ouattara. Clashes continued around Abidjan over the next few days, while rebels from the North launched a successful offensive against the town of Zouan-Hounien along the border with Liberia. The rebels continued their advance in the North, capturing two more towns, including Toulépleu, at the beginning of March, contributing to the flood of 70,000 refugees into Liberia. The conflict around Abidjan continued between government security forces and the rebel group Invisible Comando, though it also led to the involvement of Gbago's Young Patriots, who looted the homes of Ouattara supporters. Between 700,000 and 1,000,000 of Abidjan's citizens fled the city.

At the end of March, the rebels advanced toward Côte d'Ivoire's centrally located capital of Yamoussoukro (where Gbago's forces were gathering) in a two-pronged pincer movement: one from the rebel capital of Bouaka, northeast of Yamoussoukro, the other from the West, where the New Forces recently had captured the town of Daloa. Gbagbo's increasingly demoralized troops abandoned the city with hardly a fight on March 30, and a number defected to the rebels. The rebels then advanced toward Abidjan, Côte d'Ivoire's largest city and business capital. As FANCI soldiers increasingly defected, the pro-government militias (the Liberian mercenaries and the Young Patriots) played a greater role in defending the city. Sustained fighting took place around the president's palace. Meanwhile, UN officials uncovered the bodies of hundreds of people killed in Duékoué, though it was unclear how many were civilians and how many were combatants.

On April 3, French and UN forces took control of Abdijan's airport to evacuate civilians. The next day, UN and French forces launched military action against Gbagbo in attacks against his palace and offices to destroy the government's heavy weapons and thereby protect civilians. Fighting continued as Gbagbo, protected in his bunker, refused to surrender. In the following week, government forces went on the offensive, attacking Ouattara's Republican Forces at his hotel headquarters and throughout Abdijan. French forces responded on April 10 with missile attacks against the palace.

Termination and Outcome: Gbagbo surrendered on April 11, 2011, and was taken into custody. Sporadic fighting between Gbagbo and Ouattara's supporters continued through the next month. At the end of November 2011, Gbagbo was handed over to the International Criminal Court for trial.

Coding Decisions: Even though President Gbagbo was not recognized as the president of Côte d'Ivoire by the United Nations, he was in control of the national institutions at the start of the war, and thus he and his forces (FANCI) are coded as representing the government of Côte d'Ivoire during this war.

The most commonly cited figure is 3,000 deaths during this war; however, this figure apparently includes civilian deaths that were common especially during the beginning states of the war.[317] We thus report an estimate of 1,000 combatant fatalities.

Sources: GlobalSecurity.org (2010, 2011); Human Rights Watch (2011); International Crisis Group (2011); *IRIN News Reports* (multiple dates, 2010–2011); Marshall (2014); Perry (2012); Stapleton (2013).

INTRA-STATE WAR #985

North Mali War of 2012 to 2013 (aka the Tuareg Independence War)

Participants: Mali, France, Chad, and Nigeria versus the Northern Opposition (National Movement for the Liberation of Azawad, or MNLA), Ansar Dine, Movement for Oneness and Jihad in West Africa (MOJWA), Boko Haram, and Al-Qaeda in Islamic Maghreb (AQIM).

Dates: January 16, 2012, to March 2, 2013.

Battle-related Deaths: Mali: 320; France: 9; Chad: 38; Nigeria: 4; MNLA: 84; Islamic groups: 625. (See Coding Decisions.)

Initiator: MNLA.

Outcome: Mali, France, Chad, and Nigeria win.

War Type: Civil for local issues (independence).

Total System Member Military Personnel: Armed Forces of Mali: 7,350 (prewar); 7,000 (initial).[318] Armed Forces of France: 218,200 (initial).[319] Armed Forces of Chad: [ ]. Armed Forces of Nigeria: [ ].

Theater Armed Forces: Armed Forces of National Movement for the Liberation of Azawad (MNLA): 3,000 (initial); 4,000 (peak).[320] Armed Forces of Ansar Dine, participating from March 15, 2012): [ ]. Armed Forces of Boko Haram (Pro-rebel Intervener), participating from January 8, 2013): [ ]. Armed Forces of MOJWA (Pro-rebel Intervener), participating from January 8, 2013): [ ]. Armed Forces of AQIM (Pro-rebel Intervener), participating from January 8, 2013: [ ]. Armed Forces of France (Pro-government Intervener), participating from January 11, 2013: 3,000 ground troops and unknown air support. Armed Forces of Chad (Pro-government Intervener), participating from January 29, 2013: 2,000. Armed Forces of Nigeria (Pro-government Intervener), participating from January 29, 2013: 1,200.

Antecedents: Mali gained its independence from France in 1961. Soon thereafter, the Tuareg people began agitating for their own homeland in territory that was currently within North Mali, North Niger, and South Algeria. There was an armed uprising (at below-war level) in 1964, easily suppressed by the Mali army, that had weapons from the Soviet Union. The brutality of that suppression led to the radicalization of a larger segment of the Tuareg population. Another Tuareg uprising in 1990 ended in a compromise settlement, which started to unravel in 1994. At that point, northern non-Tuareg peoples formed their own organization, the Malian Patriotic Movement (or Ganda Kai), which engaged in skirmishes with the Tuaregs. Tuareg conflict broke out again from 2006 to 2009 in North Niger (at below-war level) that spilled over into Mali, though the government drove many of the rebels into Algeria in 2009. Many of the Tuareg fighters also had gone into the Libyan army, and as the Libyan regime of Muammar Gadaffi fell apart, a number of the armed

Tuareg soldiers returned to Mali, where in October 2011, they formed a new nationalist organization, the National Movement for the Liberation of Azawad (MNLA). The MNLA's goal was to create an autonomous or independent secular homeland for the Tuareg in Azawad, which is (as defined by the MNLA) a region that encompasses Northeast Mali and constitutes about 60 percent of current Mali territory. The MNLA attracted members from the previous Tuareg insurgencies as well as from other groups disenchanted with the government of President Amadou Toumani Touré. Touré had won a second term in 2007 and was thus scheduled to leave office in 2012.

Narrative: The war began on January 16, 2012, when the MNLA attacked government forces at the small town of Ménaka in the East. The rebels soon gained control of two nearby towns, though the government claimed to regain control the next day. Fighting over control of the area continued for the rest of the month. On January 24, the MNLA defeated government forces at Aguelhok in a battle in which 160 Malian soldiers were killed when they ran out of ammunition (a situation that led to anti-government protests in the capital, Bamako). The government launched air and ground attacks to retake some of the territory, but on February 1, they began a strategic retreat. In operations throughout the region, MNLA captured control of towns from Malian forces. The rebels had besieged the town of Tessalit. Despite an airlift of supplies by the United States to the government troops, the army abandoned its efforts to lift the siege and fled on March 11. The MNLA continued its advance eastward, heading toward the historic city of Timbuktu. At this point (the middle of March 2012), a second rebel group joined the war: Ansar Dine was an Islamic Tuareg group seeking to create an Islamic state in North Mali. Though substantially smaller than the MNLA, Ansar Dine began taking control of areas along Mali's eastern border. The two groups soon began operations together. In offensives at the end of March, MNLA and Ansar Dine won control of the regional capitals of Kidal and Gao, along with their military bases. On April 1, the rebels captured Timbuktu, and at this point the rebels had captured all of the major cities in northern Mali.

Meanwhile, the situation had changed in the capital. On March 22, 2012, President Touré was ousted in a military coup (led by Captain Amadou Sanogo) over his handling of the war. The coup was condemned widely throughout the region. Mediation efforts by the Economic Community of West African States (ECOWAS) led to an agreement on April 6, whereby a new civilian government, led by national assembly speaker Diouncounda Traoré, was created. Taking office on April 12, Traoré vowed to continue war against rebels. The rebels had decided to take advantage of the confusion in the capital to advance their cause. On April 6, 2012, the MNLA declared the independence of Azawad, though the declaration was not recognized by other countries. On May 26, the MNLA and Ansar Dine announced a pact to merge as the MNLA accepted the goal of creating an Islamic state.

The rebel accord soon collapsed, and what ensued was a period in which there was conflict within both the government and rebel camps. The government's military was divided internally into factions that supported the coup and those who supported former president Touré; armed conflict broke out between the two. The rebels split into secular and Islamic groups, and fighting began between MNLA and Ansar Dine. Ansar Dine had been strengthened by the arrival of fighters from two Islamic groups—Movement for Oneness and Jihad in West Africa (MOJWA) and Boko Haram—bringing the allied Islamic groups' strength closer to that of the MNLA. Conflict between the MNLA and the Islamic faction began on June 8 at Goa, and in the Battle of Goa on June 27, the Islamic groups took control of the city, driving out the MNLA. The Islamic groups continued their offensive, taking control of Timbuktu on July 12, 2012, where they began to destroy historic tombs and shrines. Fighting continued through the fall, and though the MNLA tried to launch a counteroffensive to capture Gao in November, it was defeated. Though this fighting within either the government or the northern opposition is not included as part of the civil war against the government, it did have the result of forcing the MNLA to withdraw from the civil war. In December 2012, MNLA withdrew its demand for Azawad's independence in talks with the government (though a peace accord was not signed until June 2013).

The civil war of the Mali government against the northern opposition, now represented by the Islamic groups, reemerged in January 2013. Fearing that the capital of Bamako was likely to fall to the Islamic groups, in October 2012, Mali appealed for international assistance. The UN Security Council approved a resolution for an African-led contingent (an African-led International Support Mission in Mali [AFISMA]) and requested plans from the African Union (AU) and ECOWAS. However, while the African plans were delayed, the Islamic groups captured government troops on January 8, 2013, and on January 10, they captured the strategic town of Konna. France decided to act, and on January 11, it launched Operation Serval, whereby airpower from French forces based in Chad attacked the Islamic insurgents at Konna. The bombing paved the way for a Malian army to advance and recapture the town. Britain provided planes to transport a French force of 3,000 soldiers into Mali. The bombing raids continued, attacking Islamic rebel bases throughout the central area. The French special forces joined the Malian army as it advanced northward, gaining control of the towns from the Islamic groups. Timbuktu was recaptured on January 28. The next day, armed troops from Chad and Nigeria joined the fighting as part of the AFISMA mission. As the rebels retreated toward the eastern highlands, on February 19, the French launched a new offensive, Operation Panther, to destroy them there, sometimes by parachuting troops in. The French–Chad forces defeated Islamic forces in mountain engagements on February 28 and March 2, 2013, killing two of the primary leaders of the Islamic forces. These deaths were a significant blow to the rebels, and major fighting between Mali and the Islamic forces ceased at that point.

Termination and Outcome: The war ended as a victory of Mali and its allies over the northern rebels. A peace agreement was signed on June 28, 2013. Periodic clashes between the government and Islamic forces and the MNLA began again in September 2013 (but at below-war level), after the government opened fire on a group of protestors.

Coding Decisions: Though there were twelve other countries that contributed to AFISMA, they did not commit the prerequisite number of troops (1,000) to be coded as war participants. Estimates of combined rebel strength during this war range from 3,000 to 15,000. Estimates of fatalities also vary, with Project Ploughshares citing a range of 1,500 to 3,524. Adding up fatality estimates of combatants killed for a number of the major battles (excluding the period of fighting among the rebels) yields the totals listed, which may be underestimates.

Sources: Arieff (2013); Gaasholt (2013); *IRIN News Reports* (2012–2013); Keenan (2012); Primo (2013); Project Plowshares (2014a); Reuters (2012–2013); Stapleton (2013).

INTRA-STATE WAR #990

Central African Republic War of 2012 to 2013

Participants: The Central African Republic (CAR) versus Séléka.
Dates: December 10, 2012, to March 25, 2013.
Battle-related Deaths: CAR: [ ]; Séléka: [ ]. (See Coding Decisions.)
Initiator: Séléka.
Outcome: Séléka wins.
War Type: Civil for central control.
Total System Member Military Personnel: Armed Forces of Central African Republic (FACA): 2,150 (initial).[321] Armed Forces of Chad: 25,350 (initial).[322]
Theater Armed Forces: Armed Forces of Chad (Pro-government Intervener), participating from December 18, 2012: 2,000 (initial, peak, final). Armed Forces of Séléka: 5,000 (peak, final).[323]

Antecedents: In 2003, former military chief of staff François Bozizé seized the presidency in the Central African Republic (CAR) with the support of troops from Chad. Over the next several years, Bozizé was confronted by two rebellions: one in the Northwest conducted by the Popular Army for the Restoration of Democracy (APRD) and the Democratic Front for the Central African People (FDPC) and one in the Northeast led by the Union of Democratic Forces for Unity (UFDR), which was an alliance of smaller opposition groups. Hundreds (mostly civilians) were killed in fighting between the CAR army and the rebel groups. In late 2006, France intervened, and French troops assisted the CAR armed forces (FACA) in a battle at Birao. Starting in 2007, the various rebel groups began signing peace agreements with the government, culminating in the Libreville Comprehensive Peace Agreement on June 21, 2008, which provided for a cessation of hostilities, the recognition of the UFDR as a political party, and the integration of the rebel soldiers into FACA. Additional agreements provided for a unity government and elections to be held in 2010. Limited conflict continued between some of the rebel groups over control of the western diamond fields.

In 2011, Bozizé was reelected in an election that many saw as rigged. The following September, a number of the rebel groups (including UFDR, FDPC, and Patriots for Justice and Peace, or CPJP) united to form Séléka (meaning coalition), a predominantly Muslim group. Arguing that Bozizé had failed to implement the earlier agreements, Séléka launched a rebellion.

Narrative: The war began on December 10, 2012, when Séléka rebels attacked government forces at N'Dele and two other towns in the North of CAR. Throughout the rest of the month, Séléka gained control of the major towns in the North. Séléka troops then began an advance on the capital, seizing Bria, at the center of the diamond district, along the way. FACA proved incapable of halting the rebel advance. Bozizé appealed for assistance, and Chad pledged to send a contingent of 2,000 troops, the first of which arrived on December 18, 2012. The Chadian troops were dispatched to assist FACA forces in the North for a planned assault to recapture N'Dele. Demonstrations at the French embassy persuaded France to increase its garrison at Bangui (the capital) to facilitate the evacuation of civilians. Further rebel advances toward Damara prompted CAR to request international assistance on December 27. Though France and the United States declined Bozizé's request to provide direct military assistance, the Economic Community of Central African States (ECCAS) augmented its Multinational Force for Central Africa (FOMAC) peacekeeping forces in CAR to about 1,720.

FACA forces launched a counterattack at Bambari on December 28. After heavy fighting there, the rebel advance continued. FOMAC stationed 700 of its troops at Damara, about seventy kilometers north of Bangui. Not wanting to risk conflict with FOMAC, the rebels stopped their advance. On January 11, 2013, the rebels and the Bozizé government reached an agreement that included a cease-fire, in exchange for which a new coalition government would be formed in which Bozizé would remain as president, though a new prime minister would be appointed from the opposition, Nicolas Tiangaye. Séléka would continue to control the towns pending a new election.

The cease-fire soon dissolved with armed conflict on January 23. The rebels resumed their advance toward Damara. Fighting at Damara began on March 22, with both sides alternating control, though an aerial attack initially turned back a move toward Bangui. The next day, the rebels shot down a helicopter and continued their advance on the capital. Amidst heavy fighting on March 24, the rebels reached the presidential palace, but Bozizé had already fled. The rebels also advanced against the Bangui airport, where they attacked the base housing 200 South African soldiers. In heavy fighting, the South Africans killed approximately 500 rebels while sustaining 13 fatalities.

Termination and Outcome: On March 25, 2013, the rebels were victorious, and the Séléka leader, Michael Djotodia, took over as president. Nicolas Tiangaye remained as prime minister, and the new government was established on March 31, 2013. However, limited fighting continued between Séléka forces and forces loyal to Bozizé. In September 2013, Djotodia disbanded Séléka, but some of the rebels continued fighting. The conflict took on religious overtones as the former Séléka's Muslim fighters splintered into multiple factions that increasingly fought against Christian militias called anti-balaka. A humanitarian crisis erupted as the fighting targeted civilians (killing more than 5,000) and created 400,000 internally displaced persons (IDPs).

Coding Decisions: Though South Africa had 200 soldiers who participated in the fighting on behalf of the CAR government, the number of their troops (less than 1,000) precludes South Africa from being coded as a state participant in the war. Reports on fatalities in the CAR have focused on the civilian deaths after the war. However, even reports from a few engagements suggest that total combatant battle-deaths exceed 1,000.

Sources: International Crisis Group (2013a, c, d); *Keesing's Record of World Events* (2014); Larson (2014); Project Ploughshares (2014a); Stapleton (2013).

NOTES

1. Marcus, 1975; Shinn and Ofcansky, 2004; Sandford, 1946; Dilebo, 1974.
2. Correlates of War Project, 2010.
3. Marcus, 2002, 116.
4. Ibid.
5. Correlates of War Project, 2010.
6. McCann, 1985, 609, 618.
7. Ibid.
8. Tareke, 1991.
9. Henze, 1985, 23.
10. Bercovitch and Fretter, 2004, 64; Clodfelter, 2002, 620.
11. Bercovitch and Fretter, 2004, 64.
12. Correlates of War Project, 2010; Lefever, 1965, 9.
13. Correlates of War Project, 2010.
14. Lefever, 1965, 104
15. Ibid., 97, 104; Stapleton, 2013, 157.
16. Lefever, 1965, 75.
17. Van Nederveen, 2001, 7, 20; Clodfelter, 2002, 619.
18. Lefever, 1965, 90.
19. Meredith, 2005, 114.
20. Bercovitch and Fretter, 2004, 64.
21. Correlates of War Project, 2010.
22. Ibid.
23. Ibid.
24. Meredith, 2005, 487; Brecher, Wikenfeld, and Moser, 1988, 268.
25. Ndikumana and Kisangani, 2005, 64; Clodfelter, 2002, 62.
26. Correlates of War Project, 2010.
27. Kisangani, 2012, 69.
28. Ibid., 66.
29. Correlates of War Project, 2010.
30. Ibid., 2010.
31. Kisangani, 2012, 69.
32. Estimated from Villafaña, 2009, 77, 97.
33. Villafaña, 2009, 85; Stapleton, 2013, 158.
34. Villafaña, 2009, 197–200.
35. Meredith, 2005, 114.
36. Villafaña, 2009, 104.
37. Correlates of War Project, 2010.
38. "Uganda: The Battle of Mengo Hill," 1966.
39. Bercovitch and Fretter, 2004, 72.
40. Correlates of War Project, 2010.
41. Ibid.
42. Ibid., 613.
43. Bercovitch and Fretter, 2004, 72.
44. Clodfelter, 2002, 622.
45. Correlates of War Project, 2010.
46. Stapleton, 2013, 53.
47. Ibid., 53.
48. Brogan, 1998, 56.
49. Lefebvre, 1996, 393.
50. Calculated from Lemarchand, 2004, 324–25.
51. Correlates of War Project, 2010.
52. Melady, 1974, 99.
53. Lemarchand, 2004, 325; Meredith, 2005, 488.
54. Edgerton, 2002, 93.
55. Correlates of War Project, 2010.
56. Clodfelter 2002, 624.
57. Ibid.
58. Ibid.
59. Correlates of War Project, 2010.
60. Ibid.
61. Ibid.
62. Clodfelter 2002, 612.
63. Ibid.
64. Ibid; Skutsch, 2007a, 158.
65. Brogan, 1998, 56.
66. Meredith, 2005, 247.
67. Brogan, 1998, 56.
68. Correlates of War Project, 2010.
69. Ibid.
70. Stapleton, 2013, 250; Ciment, 2007a, 90; James, 2011, 218.
71. Ciment, 2007a, 88, 89.
72. Correlates of War Project, 2010.
73. Ibid.
74. Nelson and Kaplan, 1981, 269.
75. Africa's Watch, 1991, 75.
76. Azevedo and Nnadozie, 1998, 52; Stapleton, 2013, 172.
77. Correlates of War Project, 2010.
78. Ibid.
79. Ibid.
80. Stapleton, 2013, 172.
81. Nolutshungu, 1996, 101; Stapleton, 2013, 172.
82. Tareke, 2002, 472.
83. Correlates of War Project, 2010.
84. Ibid.
85. Tareke, 2002, 471.
86. Ibid., 468.
87. Ibid.
88. Ibid.
89. Ibid.
90. Ibid., 469.
91. Ibid.
92. Africa's Watch, 1991, 84.
93. Correlates of War Project, 2010.
94. Ibid.
95. Ibid.
96. Odom, 1993, 27.
97. Ibid., 26.
98. Ibid., 66.
99. Van Nederveen, 2001, 50.

100. Ndikumana and Kisangani, 2005, 64.
101. Correlates of War Project, 2010.
102. Ibid.
103. Ibid.
104. Ibid.
105. Clodfelter, 2002, 613.
106. Burr and Collins, 1999, 132.
107. Ibid., 133; Nolutshungu, 1996, 153.
108. Nolutshungu, 1996, 189.
109. Azevedo and Nnadozie, 1998, 149.
110. Clodfelter, 2002, 628.
111. Correlates of War Project, 2010.
112. Falola, 1998, 153, 159.
113. Ibid., 143.
114. Africa Watch/Human Rights Watch, 1992.
115. Correlates of War Project, 2010.
116. Ibid.
117. Ibid.
118. Arnold, 2009, 247.
119. Ibid., 248; Conciliation Resources, 1998, location 2956.
120. Arnold, 2009, 243, 248; Conciliation Resources, 1998, location 3007.
121. Stapleton, 2013, 278.
122. Weinstein and Francisco, 2005, 164.
123. Stapleton, 2013, 98; Clodfelter, 2002, 613.
124. Correlates of War Project, 2010.
125. Tareke, 2002, 478; Stapleton, 2013, 96; Clodfelter, 2002, 612.
126. Tareke, 2002, 478; Skutsch, 2007b, 177.
127. Tareke, 2002, 478; Stapleton, 2013, 97.
128. Stapleton, 2013, 96.
129. Ibid., 98.
130. Clodfelter, 2002, 628.
131. Correlates of War Project, 2010.
132. Stapleton, 2013, 139, 141.
133. Ciment and Nichter, 2007, 316
134. Cline, 2003, 117.
135. Correlates of War Project, 2010.
136. Cline, 2013, 10
137. Arnold, 2009, 349–50.
138. Correlates of War Project, 2010.
139. Duyvesteyn, 2004, 44.
140. *Keesing's Record of World Events*, 1990, 37907.
141. Correlates of War Project, 2010.
142. Dougueli, 2014; *Keesing's Record of World Events*, 1990.
143. Correlates of War Project, 2010.
144. Ibid.
145. Ibid.
146. Ibid.
147. Adebajo, 2002, 58.
148. Uppsala Universitet Conflict Data Project, multiple years; Clodfelter, 2002, 629.
149. Adebajo, 2002, 58.
150. *The Military Balance*, 1995, 247.
151. Ibid.
152. Adebajo, 2002, 82.
153. *The Military Balance*, 1995, 247.
154. Correlates of War Project, 2010.
155. Ibid.
156. Stapleton, 2013, 61.
157. Meredith, 2005, 562.
158. Adebajo, 2002, 82.
159. Stapleton, 2013, 60.
160. Ibid., 62.
161. *The Military Balance*, 1995, 255.
162. Oliver and Atmore, 2004, 352.
163. Correlates of War Project, 2010.
164. Ibid.
165. Ibid.
166. Ibid.
167. Ibid.
168. Ibid.
169. Ibid.
170. Stapleton, 2013, 105.
171. Ibid.
172. Akombo, 2005, 287.
173. Ibid., 299, 300, 303.
174. Correlates of War Project, 2010.
175. Ibid.
176. Ibid.
177. Ibid.
178. Ibid.
179. *The Military Balance*, 1995, 247.
180. Uppsala Universitet Conflict Data Project, multiple years; Clodfelter, 2002, 629.
181. *The Military Balance*, 1995, 247.
182. Human Rights Watch, 1994a, b, c; *The Military Balance*, 1995, 247.
183. *The Military Balance*, 1995, 247.
184. Ibid.
185. Adebajo, 2002, 82.
186. Ibid., 89.
187. Correlates of War Project, 2010.
188. *The Military Balance*, 1995, 234.
189. Correlates of War Project, 2010.
190. Stapleton, 2013, 190.
191. Correlates of War Project, 2010.
192. Stapleton, 2013, 1181; Kisangani, 2012, 28.
193. Kisangani, 2012, 28.
194. Browne, 2001, 233.
195. Correlates of War Project, 2010.
196. Ibid.
197. Ibid.
198. Ibid.
199. Ibid.
200. Pottier, 2002, 88; Meredith, 2005, 535.
201. Meredith, 2005, 535; Reed, 1999, 18.
202. Bercovitch and Fretter, 2004, 109.

203. Clodfelter, 2002, 630; Turner, 2002, 82.
204. Kisangani, 2012, 117, 138.
205. Ibid., 27.
206. Meredith, 2005, 536.
207. Correlates of War Project, 2010.
208. Bercovitch and Fretter, 2004, 103; Human Rights Watch, 2001b, 4.
209. Kisangani, 2012, 28.
210. Correlates of War Project, 2010.
211. Ibid.
212. Ali-Dinar, 1999, 2.
213. Ciment, 2007c, 149.
214. Correlates of War Project, 2010.
215. Ibid.
216. Ibid.
217. Ibid.
218. Ibid.
219. Clodfelter, 2002, 629; Edgerton, 2002, 168.
220. Arnold, 2009, 321; Clodfelter, 2002, 629.
221. BBC News, May 31, 1999d, http://news.bbc.co.uk/2hi/africa/357601.stm.
222. *Keesing's Record of World Events*, 2000.
223. Clodfelter, 2002, 629.
224. Bercovitch and Fretter, 2004, 104.
225. Clodfelter, 2002, 630; Meredith, 2005, 572.
226. Correlates of War Project, 2010.
227. Ibid.
228. Ibid.
229. *Keesing's Record of World Events*, 1998; Uppsala Universitet Conflict Data Project, multiple years.
230. *Keesing's Record of World Events*, 1998; Uppsala Universitet Conflict Data Project, multiple years.
231. *The Military Balance*, 2002.
232. Correlates of War Project, 2010.
233. Ibid.
234. Ibid.
235. Ibid.
236. Ibid.
237. Ibid.
238. Ibid.
239. Ibid.
240. Ibid.
241. Ibid.
242. O'Ballance, 2000.
243. Afoaku, 2002; Hara, 2002, 1; Tull, 207, 125.
244. Uppsala Universitet, 2004, 10; Clodfelter, 2002, 630.
245. O'Ballance, 2000; Stapleton, 2013, 209; Turner, 2002, 87.
246. *New York Times*, 2001, 2; Stapleton, 2013, 208.
247. Swarns, 2001, 2; Rupiya, 2002, 94.
248. Prunier 2004, 378; *BBC News Summary of World Broadcasts*, October 1, 1998.
249. Uppsala Universitet Conflict Data Project, 2004, 4.
250. BBC News Summary of World Broadcasts, October 1, 1998.
251. Clodfelter, 2002, 630.
252. Robinson and Walt, 2006, 38;
253. Correlates of War Project, 2010.
254. Ibid.
255. *Keesing's Record of World Events*, 1997, 41722; Harden, 2001, 7; Malaquais, 2007, 218.
256. *The Military Balance*, 1999, 2000.
257. Correlates of War Project, 2010.
258. Ibid.
259. Ali-Dinar, 1999, 3.
260. Ploughshares, 2000, 3.
261. Correlates of War Project, 2010.
262. Sandberg, 2001, 17.
263. Correlates of War Project, 2010.
264. *IRIN News Reports* December 12, 2000; February 5, 2001; February 7, 2001.
265. Correlates of War Project, 2010.
266. Ibid.
267. International Crisis Group, 2002a, 4.
268. Reyntjens, 2000, 21; Home Office, 2004, 12.
269. Home Office, 2004, 12.
270. Human Rights Watch, 2001b, 5.
271. Correlates of War Project, 2010.
272. Human Rights Watch, 2001b, 5.
273. Correlates of War Project, 2010.
274. Reno, 2007, 77.
275. Marshall, 2014, 7.
276. Correlates of War Project, 2010.
277. Ibid.
278. *IRIN News Reports* (December 30, 2002), 1.
279. Baégas and Marshall-Fratani, 2007, 98.
280. *IRIN News Reports* (January 19, 2004), 1; Safer Access, 2007, 3; Baégas and Marshall-Fratani, 2007, 94.
281. GlobalSecurity.org, 2002, 2003, 2004, 1; Baégas and Marshall-Fratani, 2007, 93.
282. Project Ploughshares, 2000, 5.
283. NationMaster, 2005, 2006.
284. Correlates of War Project, 2010; *The Military Balance*, 2009, 294.
285. *Chicago Tribune*, 2008, sect. 1, 9.
286. *IRIN News Reports* (October 28, 2005).
287. *The Military Balance* 2009, 318; 2010, 324–25.
288. Correlates of War Project, 2010; *The Military Balance*, 2010, 307.
289. Correlates of War Project, 2010.
290. *The Military Balance* 2009, 324; 2010, 330.
291. *The Military Balance* 2009, 291; 2010, 297.
292. *The Military Balance*, 2010, 312.
293. Correlates of War Project, 2010.
294. Harnisch, 2010, 2.
295. *Chicago Tribune* (December 27, 2006), sect. 1, 13; Tekle, 2013, 1.
296. Harnisch, 2010, 4.
297. Project Plowshares, 2014a, 4.

298. Harnisch, 2010, 3; Project Plowshares, 2014a, 8; African Union, 2014.
299. Stapleton, 2013, 108; African Union, 2014.
300. Ibid.
301. African Union, 2014.
302. Project Plowshares, 2014a, 5.
303. Stapleton, 2013, 107.
304. DronesTeam, 2012, 2.
305. Pettersson, 2014.
306. Charbonneau, 2013, 1.
307. *The Military Balance*, 2010, 319.
308. *Global Terrorism Index*, 2014, 53.
309. Forest, 2012, 68.
310. *The Military Balance*, 2010, 302.
311. Ibid., 129.
312. *The New York Times* (December 19, 2010); Stapleton, 2013, 67; *Times Live* (April 1, 2011). It is unclear if the peak figure includes the pro-government militias.
313. *New York Times* (March 6, 2011).
314. *The Military Balance*, 2010, 133; *New York Times* (April 4, 2001).
315. *New York Times* (December 20, 2010; January 12, 2011).
316. *New York Times* (April 20, 2011; April 23, 2011).
317. Marshall, 2014, 8; International Crisis Group, 2011, 1.
318. *The Military Balance*, 2010, 316; Arieff, 2013, 2.
319. NationMaster, 2005, 2006.
320. Keenan, 2012, 1.
321. *The Military Balance*, 2012.
322. Ibid.
323. Project Plowshares, 2014a, 2.

APPENDIX

List of All Intra-state Wars in Chronological Order

Year	War Number	War Title	Region
1818	#500	First Caucasus War of 1818 to 1822	Europe
1820	#502	First Two Sicilies War of 1820 to 1821	Europe
1820	#502.1	Ali Pasha Rebellion of 1820 to 1822	Europe
1821	#503	Sardinian Revolt of 1821	Europe
1821	#504	Greek Independence War of 1821 to 1828	Europe
1821	#504.3	Sidon–Damascus War of 1821 to 1822	Middle East
1821	#505	Spanish Royalists War of 1821 to 1823	Europe
1824	#507	Egypt–Mehdi War of 1824	Middle East
1825	#507.5	Greater Chechnya Revolt of 1825 to 1826	Europe
1826	#508	Janissary Revolt of 1826	Middle East
1828	#510	Miguelite War of 1828 to 1834	Europe
1830	#511	First Murid War of 1830 to 1832	Europe
1830	#512	First Albanian Revolt of 1830 to 1832	Europe
1830	#513	First French Insurrection of 1830	Europe
1830	#515	Belgian Independence War of 1830	Europe
1831	#516	Egyptian Taka Expedition of 1831	Middle East
1831	#517	First Polish War of 1831	Europe
1831	#518	First Syrian War of 1831 to 1832	Middle East
1832	#520	First Mexican War of 1832	N. America
1832	#520.3	Cabanada War of 1832 to 1835	S. America
1834	#521	Palestinian Anti-conscription Revolt of 1834	Middle East
1834	#522	First Carlist War of 1834 to 1840	Europe
1834	#523	Second Murid War of 1834	Europe
1835	#525	Cabanos Revolt of 1835 to 1837	S. America
1835	#525.5	Zacatecas Rebellion of 1835	N. America
1835	#526	Farroupilha War of 1835 to 1845	S. America
1835	#527	Texan War of 1835 to 1836	N. America
1836	#528	First Bosnian War of 1836	Europe
1836	#530	Third Murid War of 1836 to 1852	Europe
1837	#531	Sabinada Rebellion of 1837 to 1838	S. America
1837	#532	Druze Rebellion of 1837 to 1838	Middle East

Year	War Number	War Title	Region
1838	#532.5	Tampico Revolt of 1838 to 1839	N. America
1838	#532.7	Balaiada Revolt of 1838 to 1841	S. America
1839	#533	Second Syrian War of 1839	Middle East
1840	#535	Lebanon Insurgency of 1840	Middle East
1840	#536	First Colombian War of 1840 to 1842	S. America
1840	#537	Third Syrian War of 1840 to 1841	Middle East
1841	#538	First Argentina War phase 2 of 1841 to 1842	S. America
1841	#539	Nish Uprising of 1841	Europe
1841	#540	Second Bosnian War of 1841	Europe
1841	#541	Triangular Revolt of 1841	N. America
1841	#541.2	First Maronite–Druze War of 1841	Middle East
1842	#542	Karbala Revolt of 1842 to 1843	Middle East
1845	#543	Second Maronite–Druze War of 1845	Middle East
1847	#545	Mayan Caste War phase 1 of 1847 to 1848	N. America
1847	#546	Second Carlist War of 1847 to 1849	Europe
1848	#547	Second Two Sicilies War of 1848 to 1849	Europe
1848	#548	First Venezuela War of 1848 to 1849	S. America
1848	#549	Second French Insurrection of 1848	Europe
1848	#550	Viennese Revolt of 1848	Europe
1848	#551	Milan Five Day Revolt of 1848	Europe
1848	#553	Mayan Caste War phase 2 of 1848 to 1855	N. America
1848	#554	Hungarian War of 1848 to 1849	Europe
1850	#554.3	Third Bosnian War of 1850 to 1851	Europe
1850	#554.5	Aleppo Revolt of 1850	Middle East
1851	#555	First Chilean War of 1851 to 1852	S. America
1852	#556	First Turco-Montenegrin War of 1852 to 1853	Europe
1853	#557	First Peru War of 1853 to 1855	S. America
1854	#557.1	Epirus Revolt of 1854	Europe
1854	#557.2	Greek Nationalists of Macedonia War of 1854	Europe
1854	#557.3	Colombia's Barracks Rebellion of 1854	S. America
1854	#557.8	Barquisimeto Rebellion of 1854	S. America
1855	#557.9	Libyan Insurrection of 1855 to 1856	Middle East
1855	#558	Puebla War of 1855 to 1856	N. America
1856	#560	Second Peru War of 1856 to 1858	S. America
1858	#561	Mexican Reform of 1858 to 1861	N. America
1858	#562	Second Turco-Montenegrin War of 1858	Europe
1859	#562.5	Constituent Revolution of 1859	S. America
1859	#563	Second Venezuela War of 1859 to 1863	S. America
1860	#565	Second Colombian War of 1860 to 1862	S. America
1860	#566	Third Maronite–Druze War of 1860	Middle East
1860	#567	Taiping Rebellion phase 2 of 1860 to 1866	Asia & Oceania
1860	#568	Second Nien Revolt of 1860 to 1868	Asia & Oceania

(Continued)

Year	War Number	War Title	Region
1860	#570	Miao Rebellion phase 2 of 1860 to 1872	Asia & Oceania
1860	#571	Panthay Rebellion phase 2 of 1860 to 1874	Asia & Oceania
1861	#572	US Civil War of 1861 to 1865	N. America
1861	#573	Third Buenos Aires War of 1861 to 1862	S. America
1861	#575	Third Turco-Montenegrin War of 1861 to 1862	Europe
1862	#576	Tungan Rebellion of 1862 to 1873	Asia & Oceania
1862	#577	Sioux–Minnesota War of 1862	N. America
1862	#578	Bolivian Perez Rebellion of 1862	S. America
1863	#579	Second Polish War of 1863 to 1864	Europe
1863	#580	Second Argentina War of 1863	S. America
1863	#580.5	Bandit War of 1863	Europe
1864	#581	Sahil Revolt of 1864 to 1865	Middle East
1864	#582	Xinjiang Muslim Revolt of 1864 to 1866	Asia & Oceania
1864	#582.3	Kanto Insurrection of 1864 to 1865	Asia & Oceania
1865	#582.5	Constitutionalist Rebellion of 1865 to 1866	S. America
1866	#583	First Cretan War of 1866 to 1868	Europe
1866	#585	Yellow Cliff Revolt of 1866	Asia & Oceania
1866	#586	Third Argentina War of 1866 to 1867	S. America
1867	#586.5	Kashgar–Khotan War of 1867	Asia & Oceania
1867	#587	Queretaro War of 1867	N. America
1867	#587.8	Third Venezuela War of 1867 to 1868	S. America
1868	#588	Meiji Restoration of 1868 to 1869	Asia & Oceania
1868	#591	Spanish Liberals War of 1868	Europe
1868	#592	Guerre des Cacos of 1868 to 1869	N. America
1869	#592.5	Yellow Revolution of 1869 to 1872	S. America
1870	#592.7	First Kashgarian–Tungan War of 1870	Asia & Oceania
1870	#593	Fourth Argentina War of 1870 to 1871	S. America
1870	#595	Bolivia–*Criollos* War of 1870 to 1871	S. America
1871	#596	Paris Commune War of 1871	Europe
1871	#596.7	Second Kashgarian–Tungan War of 1871 to 1872	Asia & Oceania
1872	#597	Third Carlist War of 1872 to 1876	Europe
1873	#597.5	Entre Rios War of 1873	S. America
1873	#598	Catonalist Uprising of 1873 to 1875	Europe
1874	#600	Fifth Argentina War of 1874	S. America
1875	#601	Bosnia and Bulgaria Revolt of 1875 to 1876	Europe
1876	#602	Díaz Revolt of 1876	N. America
1876	#603	Defeat of Xinjiang Muslims of 1876 to 1878	Asia & Oceania
1876	#605	Third Colombian War of 1876 to 1877	S. America
1876	#606	Ecuador's Veintemilla Revolt of 1876	S. America
1877	#607	Satsuma Rebellion of 1877	Asia & Oceania
1878	#608	Argentine Indians War of 1878 to 1879	S. America
1879	#609	Revindication War of 1879	S. America

(Continued)

Year	War Number	War Title	Region
1880	#610	Fourth Buenos Aires War of 1880	S. America
1881	#610.5	Mahdist Rebellion phase 1 of 1881 to 1882	Middle East
1883	#611	Haitian Civil War of 1883 to 1884	N. America
1884	#612	Fourth Colombian War of 1884 to 1885	S. America
1885	#613	Peru's National Problem of 1885	S. America
1890	#616	First Yemeni Imamate Rebellion of 1890 to 1892	Middle East
1890	#616.5	Campos Mutiny of 1890	S. America
1891	#617	Second Chilean War of 1891	S. America
1891	#618	Zaili–Jinden Revolt of 1891	Asia & Oceania
1892	#619	Venezuela's Legalist Revolution of 1892	S. America
1893	#620	Brazil Federalists War of 1893 to 1894	S. America
1893	#621	Brazil Naval War of 1893 to 1894	S. America
1894	#623	Tonghak Rebellion phase 1 of 1894	Asia & Oceania
1894	#625	Third Peru War of 1894 to 1895	S. America
1895	#626	Fifth Colombian War of 1895	S. America
1895	#627	Ecuador Liberals War of 1895	S. America
1895	#628	First Gansu Muslim Revolt of 1895 to 1896	Asia & Oceania
1895	#630	Druze Rebellion of 1895 to 1896	Middle East
1895	#630.2	Second Zeitun Uprising of 1895 to 1896	Middle East
1896	#631	Second Cretan War of 1896 to 1897	Europe
1896	#631.5	Ecuadorian Conservative Revolt of 1896	S. America
1896	#632	Third Brazil War of 1896 to 1897	S. America
1898	#632.3	*Revolución de Queipa* of 1898	S. America
1898	#632.6	Second Yemeni Imamate Rebellion of 1898 to 1899	Middle East
1899	#633	Fourth Venezuelan War of 1899	S. America
1899	#635	Second Yaqui War of 1899 to 1900	N. America
1899	#636	Sixth Colombian War of 1899 to 1902	S. America
1899	#637	Quintana Roo War of 1899 to 1901	N. America
1901	#638	Fifth Venezuelan War of 1901 to 1903	S. America
1902	#639	Third Yemeni Imamate Rebellion of 1902 to 1906	Middle East
1902	#640	Ilinden War of 1902 to 1903	Europe
1904	#641	First Uruguay War of 1904	S. America
1904	#641.5	Saudi Revolt of 1904	Middle East
1905	#643	Bloody Sunday War of 1905 to 1906	Europe
1907	#645	Romanian Peasant Revolt of 1907	Europe
1907	#646	Hafiziyya Uprising of 1907 to 1908	Middle East
1908	#647	Iranian Constitution War of 1908 to 1909	Middle East
1909	#647.5	Asir–Yemen Revolt of 1909 to 1911	Middle East
1909	#649	Bluefields Insurrection of 1909 to 1910	N. America
1910	#650	Second Albanian Revolt of 1910 to 1912	Europe
1910	#650.8	Hawran Druze Rebellion of 1910	Middle East
1910	#652	Third Mexican War of 1910 to 1914	N. America

(Continued)

Year	War Number	War Title	Region
1911	#656	Paraguay War of 1911 to 1912	S. America
1911	#657	First Nationalist Revolution of 1911	Asia & Oceania
1912	#657.3	War of the Ecuadorian Generals of 1912	S. America
1912	#658	Cuban Black Uprising of 1912	N. America
1913	#665	Second Nationalist Revolution of 1913	Asia & Oceania
1913	#667	Ecuadorian Civil War of 1913 to 1916	S. America
1914	#672	China Pai Ling (White Wolf) War of 1914	Asia & Oceania
1914	#672.5	Contestado Rebellion of 1914 to 1915	S. America
1914	#673	Fourth Mexican War of 1914 to 1920	N. America
1915	#674	Anti-monarchy War of 1915 to 1916	Asia & Oceania
1916	#675	Russian Turkestan Revolt of 1916 to 1917	Asia & Oceania
1916	#675.5	Negus Mikael Revolt of 1916 to 1917	Africa
1917	#676	First Yunnan–Sichuan War of 1917	Asia & Oceania
1917	#676.5	Southern China Revolt of 1917 to 1918	Asia & Oceania
1917	#677	Russian Civil War of 1917 to 1920	Europe
1918	#680	Finnish Civil War of 1918	Europe
1918	#681	Western Ukrainian War of 1918 to 1919	Europe
1919	#682	Sparticist Rising of 1919	Europe
1919	#683	Hungary's Red and White Terror War of 1919 to 1920	Europe
1920	#684	Second Yunnan–Sichuan War of 1920	Asia & Oceania
1920	#684.5	Gilan Marxist Rebellion of 1920 to 1921	Middle East
1920	#685	Zhili–Anfu War of 1920	Asia & Oceania
1920	#686	Green Rebellion of 1920 to 1921	Europe
1920	#687	Bashmachi Rebellion of 1920 to 1924	Asia & Oceania
1920	#688	Italian Fascist War of 1920 to 1922	Europe
1921	#689	Simko Rebellion of 1921 to 1922	Middle East
1921	#690	Kronstadt Rebellion of 1921	Europe
1922	#692	First Zhili–Fengtien War of 1922	Asia & Oceania
1923	#693	Agrarian Rising of 1923	Europe
1923	#695	De La Huerta Rebellion of 1923 to 1924	N. America
1924	#696	Honduran Conservative War of 1924	N. America
1924	#697	First Afghan Anti-reform War of 1924 to 1925	Asia & Oceania
1924	#697.3	Second Zhili–Fengtien War of 1924	Asia & Oceania
1925	#697.6	Shaikh Said's Rebellion of 1925	Middle East
1925	#697.8	Labrang War of 1925 to 1926	Asia & Oceania
1925	#698	Anti-Fengtien War of 1925 to 1926	Asia & Oceania
1926	#700	Chinese Northern Expedition of 1926 to 1928	Asia & Oceania
1926	#701	*Cristeros* Revolt of 1926 to 1929	N. America
1927	#702	First KMT–CCP War of 1927	Asia & Oceania
1928	#702.5	Second Gansu Muslim Revolt of 1928 to 1929	Asia & Oceania
1928	#703	Ethiopian Northern Resistance of 1928 to 1930	Africa
1928	#705	Second Afghan Anti-reform War of 1928 to 1929	Asia & Oceania

(Continued)

Year	War Number	War Title	Region
1929	#707	Escobar Rebellion of 1929	N. America
1929	#707.3	Ikhwan Revolt of 1929 to 1930	Middle East
1929	#707.5	Central Plains War of 1929 to 1930	Asia & Oceania
1930	#708	Ararat Revolt of 1930	Middle East
1930	#709	Campaign against Ibrahim Beg of 1930 to 1931	Asia & Oceania
1930	#710	Chinese Civil War phase 1 of 1930 to 1936	Asia & Oceania
1931	#711	Xinjiang Muslim Revolt of 1931 to 1934	Asia & Oceania
1932	#712	Matanza War of 1932	N. America
1932	#712.5	Mongolian Armed Uprising of 1932	Asia & Oceania
1932	#713	Aprista Revolt of 1932	S. America
1932	#715	Paulista Rebellion of 1932	S. America
1933	#715.6	Xinjiang Hui–Uyghur War of 1933 to 1934	Asia & Oceania
1933	#716	Fukien Revolt of 1933 to 1934	Asia & Oceania
1934	#717	Spain–Miners War of 1934	Europe
1936	#718	Spanish Civil War of 1936 to 1939	Europe
1937	#718.5	Dersim Revolt of 1937 to 1938	Middle East
1939	#719	KMT–CCP Clashes of 1939 to 1941	Asia & Oceania
1941	#719.3	First Forest Brethren War of 1941	Europe
1943	#719.6	Weyane Rebellion of 1943	Africa
1944	#719.8	Ili Uprising of 1944 to 1945	Asia & Oceania
1944	#720	Greek Civil War of 1944 to 1945	Europe
1945	#721	Polish Ukrainians War of 1945 to 1947	Europe
1945	#722	Ukrainian Partisans War of 1945 to 1947	Europe
1945	#723	Forest Brethren War of 1945 to 1949	Europe
1945	#723.5	Chinese Civil War phase 2 of 1945 to 1950	Asia & Oceania
1946	#724	Greek Civil War—Round Three—of 1946 to 1949	Europe
1947	#726	Taiwan Revolt of 1947	Asia & Oceania
1947	#727	Paraguay War of 1947	S. America
1948	#728	Sanaa Revolt of 1948	Middle East
1948	#730	Costa Rica War of 1948	N. America
1948	#730.5	First Burmese War of 1948 to 1950	Asia & Oceania
1948	#731	Seventh Colombian *La Violencia* War of 1948 to 1953	S. America
1948	#732.5	Telengana Rebellion of 1948 to 1950	Asia & Oceania
1950	#733	Huk Rebellion of 1950 to 1954	Asia & Oceania
1950	#734	South Moluccas War of 1950	Asia & Oceania
1951	#736	Indonesia Darul Islam Rebellion of 1951 to 1962	Asia & Oceania
1952	#737	Bolivian War of 1952	S. America
1955	#739	*La Violencia* Second Wave of 1955 to 1962	S. America
1955	#740	Argentine Military War of 1955	S. America
1955	#740.5	Liangshan Rebellion of 1955 to 1957	Asia & Oceania
1956	#741	Tibetan Khamba Rebellion of 1956 to 1959	Asia & Oceania
1956	#741.5	Naga Insurgency phase 1 of 1956 to 1957	Asia & Oceania

(Continued)

Year	War Number	War Title	Region
1958	#742	Permesta Rebellion of 1958 to 1961	Asia & Oceania
1958	#743	First Lebanese War of 1958	Middle East
1958	#745	Cuban Revolution of 1958 to 1959	N. America
1958	#746	Second Burmese War of 1958 to 1960	Asia & Oceania
1959	#747	Mosul Revolt of 1959	Middle East
1960	#748	Vietnam War phase 1 of 1960 to 1965	Asia & Oceania
1960	#749	First Laotian War of 1960 to 1968	Asia & Oceania
1960	#750	First DRC War of 1960 to 1963	Africa
1961	#752	First Iraqi Kurds War of 1961 to 1963	Middle East
1962	#753	Algerian Revolution of 1962	Middle East
1962	#755	North Yemen War of 1962 to 1970	Middle East
1963	#757	First Ogaden War of 1963 to 1964	Africa
1963	#758	First South Sudan War of 1963 to 1972	Middle East
1963	#760	First Rwanda War of 1963 to 1964	Africa
1964	#761	Second DRC War of 1964 to 1965	Africa
1964	#762	Third DRC Rebellion of 1964 to 1965	Africa
1965	#765	Second Iraqi Kurds War of 1965 to 1966	Middle East
1965	#766	Dominican Republic War of 1965	N. America
1966	#768	First Uganda War of 1966	Africa
1966	#770	First Guatemala War of 1966 to 1968	N. America
1966	#771	First Chad Rebellion of 1966 to 1971	Africa
1967	#771.5	First West Papua War of 1967 to 1968	Asia & Oceania
1967	#772	Cultural Revolution phase 1 of 1967	Asia & Oceania
1965	#773	Third Burmese War of 1965 to 1993	Asia & Oceania
1967	#775	Biafra War of 1967 to 1970	Africa
1967	#776	Cultural Revolution phase 2 of 1967 to 1968	Asia & Oceania
1968	#777	Third Iraqi Kurds War of 1968 to 1970	Middle East
1970	#778	Naxalite Rebellion of 1970 to 1971	Asia & Oceania
1970	#780	Black September War of 1970	Middle East
1970	#781	Second Guatemala War of 1970 to 1971	N. America
1971	#782	Pakistan–Bengal War of 1971	Asia & Oceania
1971	#783	First Sri Lanka–JVP War of 1971	Asia & Oceania
1971	#785	First Khmer Rouge War of 1971 to 1975	Asia & Oceania
1972	#786	First Philippine–Moro War of 1972 to 1981	Asia & Oceania
1972	#787	Thai Communist Insurgency of 1972 to 1973	Asia & Oceania
1972	#788	Eritrean Split of 1972 to 1974	Africa
1972	#789	First Burundi War of 1972	Africa
1972	#791	Rhodesia War of 1972 to 1979	Africa
1973	#792	Baluchi Separatists War of 1973 to 1977	Asia & Oceania
1973	#793	Chilean Coup of 1973	S. America
1974	#797	Fourth Iraqi Kurds War of 1974 to 1975	Middle East
1975	#798	Eritrean War of 1975 to 1978	Africa

(Continued)

Year	War Number	War Title	Region
1975	#800	Argentine Leftists War of 1975 to 1976	S. America
1975	#801	Second Lebanese War of 1975 to 1976	Middle East
1976	#803	Second Laotian War of 1976 to 1979	Asia & Oceania
1976	#804	Angolan Control War of 1976 to 1991	Africa
1976	#805	Second Ogaden War phase 1 of 1976 to 1977	Africa
1976	#806	East Timorese War phase 3 of 1976 to 1979	Asia & Oceania
1977	#806.3	Second West Papua War of 1977 to 1978	Asia & Oceania
1977	#806.8	Chad–FAP War of 1977 to 1978	Africa
1978	#808	Second Ogaden War phase 3 of 1978 to 1980	Africa
1978	#809	Saur Revolution of 1978	Asia & Oceania
1978	#810	Zaire–FNLC War of 1978	Africa
1978	#811	Third Guatemala War of 1978 to 1983	N. America
1978	#812	Mujahideen Uprising of 1978 to 1980	Asia & Oceania
1978	#815	Sandinista Rebellion of 1978 to 1979	N. America
1978	#815.5	Iranian Islamic Revolution of 1978 to 1979	Middle East
1979	#816	Anti-Khomeini Coalition War of 1979 to 1983	Middle East
1979	#817	El Salvador War of 1979 to 1992	N. America
1980	#820	Chad–FAN War of 1980 to 1984	Africa
1980	#823	Nigeria–Muslim War of 1980 to 1981	Africa
1981	#824	First Philippine–NPA War of 1981 to 1992	Asia & Oceania
1981	#825	Mozambique War of 1981 to 1992	Africa
1982	#826	Tigrean and Eritrean War of 1982 to 1991	Africa
1982	#826.5	Hama Uprising of 1982	Middle East
1982	#827	Shining Path War of 1982 to 1992	S. America
1982	#828	Contra War of 1982 to 1988	N. America
1982	#828.3	Second Uganda War of 1982 to 1986	Africa
1983	#833	Fourth Lebanese War of 1983 to 1984	Middle East
1983	#834	Second South Sudan War of 1983 to 2002	Middle East
1983	#835	First Sri Lanka Tamil War of 1983 to 1987	Asia & Oceania
1984	#837	Indian Golden Temple War of 1984	Asia & Oceania
1985	#840	Fifth Iraqi Kurds War of 1985 to 1988	Middle East
1986	#842	South Yemen War of 1986	Middle East
1986	#843	Holy Spirit Movement War of 1986 to 1987	Africa
1987	#845	Second Sri Lanka–JVP War of 1987 to 1989	Asia & Oceania
1987	#845.5	Fourth Guatemala War of 1987 to 1990	N. America
1987	#846	Inkatha–ANC War of 1987 to 1994	Africa
1988	#848	First Somalia War of 1988 to 1991	Africa
1988	#849	Eighth Colombian War of 1988 to present	S. America
1989	#850	Fifth Lebanese War of 1989 to 1990	Middle East
1989	#851	Second Afghan Civil War of 1989 to 1992	Asia & Oceania
1989	#852	Chad–Déby War of 1989 to 1990	Africa
1989	#853	Punjab Rebellion of 1989 to 1993	Asia & Oceania

(Continued)

Year	War Number	War Title	Region
1989	#854	Second Khmer Rouge War of 1989 to 1991	Asia & Oceania
1989	#856	Romania War of 1989	Europe
1989	#857	First Liberian War of 1989 to 1990	Africa
1990	#858	First Aceh War of 1990 to 1991	Asia & Oceania
1990	#859	Second Sri Lanka Tamil War of 1990 to 2001	Asia & Oceania
1990	#860	Bougainville Secessionist War of 1990 to 1991	Asia & Oceania
1991	#861.8	Georgia–South Ossetia War of 1991 to 1992	Europe
1991	#862	Iraqi–Shiite Rebellion of 1991	Middle East
1991	#862.1	Sixth Iraqi Kurds Rebellion of 1991	Middle East
1991	#863	First Sierra Leone War of 1991 to 1996	Africa
1991	#864	Croatian Independence War of 1991 to 1992	Europe
1991	#865	Turkey–PKK War of 1991 to 1999	Middle East
1991	#865.8	Second Somalia War of 1991 to 1997	Africa
1991	#866	SPLM/A Division (Dinka-Nuer) War of 1991 to 1992	Middle East
1991	#868	Jukun–Tiv War of 1991 to 1992	Africa
1991	#871	Georgia War of 1991 to 1992	Europe
1991	#872	Nagorno-Karabakh War of 1991 to 1993	Europe
1991	#873	Dniestrian Independence War of 1991 to 1992	Europe
1992	#874	Kashmir Insurgency of 1992 to 2005	Asia & Oceania
1992	#875	Algeria's Islamic Front War of 1992 to 2002	Middle East
1992	#876	Tajikistan War of 1992 to 1997	Asia & Oceania
1992	#877	Abkhazia Revolt of 1992 to 1994	Europe
1992	#877.5	Afghanistan Postcommunist Civil War of 1992 to 2001	Asia & Oceania
1992	#878	Bosnian-Serb Rebellion of 1992 to 1995	Europe
1992	#879	Second Liberian War of 1992 to 1996	Africa
1992	#880	Angolan War of the Cities of 1992 to 1994	Africa
1993	#881	Third Khmer Rouge War of 1993 to 1998	Asia & Oceania
1993	#883	Second Burundi War of 1993 to 1998	Africa
1994	#885	South Yemeni Secessionist Revolt of 1994	Middle East
1994	#886	Second Rwanda War of 1994	Africa
1994	#887	First Iraqi Kurds Internecine War of 1994 to 1995	Middle East
1994	#888	First Chechnya War of 1994 to 1996	Europe
1995	#891	Croatia–Krajina War of 1995	Europe
1996	#893	Seventh Iraqi Kurds War of 1996	Middle East
1996	#895	Zaire–AFDL War of 1996 to 1997	Africa
1997	#896	Third Rwanda War of 1997 to 1998	Africa
1997	#897	First Congo-Brazzaville War of 1997	Africa
1997	#897.5	Second Iraqi Kurds Internecine War of 1997	Middle East
1998	#898	Second Sierra Leone War of 1998 to 2000	Africa
1998	#900	Kosovo Independence War of 1998 to 1999	Europe
1998	#902	Guinea-Bissau Military War of 1998 to 1999	Africa
1998	#905	Africa's World War of 1998 to 2002	Africa

(Continued)

Year	War Number	War Title	Region
1998	#906	Chad–Togoimi Revolt of 1998 to 2000	Africa
1998	#907	Third Angolan–UNITA War of 1998 to 2002	Africa
1998	#908	Second Congo-Brazzaville War of 1998 to 1999	Africa
1999	#910	Maluku War of 1999 to 2002	Asia & Oceania
1999	#912	Second Aceh War of 1999 to 2004	Asia & Oceania
1999	#913	Oromo Liberation War of 1999	Africa
1999	#915	Second Chechen War of 1999 to 2003	Europe
2000	#916	Second Philippine–Moro War of 2000 to 2001	Asia & Oceania
2000	#917	Guinean War of 2000 to 2001	Africa
2001	#918	Third Burundi War of 2001 to 2003	Africa
2001	#920	Fourth Rwanda War of 2001	Africa
2001	#921	Nepal Maoist Insurgency of 2001 to 2006	Asia & Oceania
2002	#922	Liberia–LURD War of 2002 to 2003	Africa
2002	#925	Côte d'Ivoire Military War of 2002 to 2003	Africa
2003	#926	Third Philippine–Moro War of 2003	Asia & Oceania
2003	#927	Darfur Rebellion of 2003 to 2006	Middle East
2004	#932	First Waziristan War of 2004 to 2006	Asia & Oceania
2004	#933	Second Nigeria Christian–Muslim War of 2004	Africa
2004	#935	First Al-Houthi Rebellion of 2004 to 2005	Middle East
2005	#936	Second Philippine–NPA War of 2005 to 2006	Asia & Oceania
2005	#937	Chad–United Opposition War of 2005 to 2008	Africa
2006	#940	Third Sri Lanka Tamil War of 2006 to 2009	Asia & Oceania
2006	#940.8	Third Somalia War of 2006 to 2012	Africa
2007	#941	Second Al-Houthi Rebellion of 2007 to 2008	Middle East
2007	#942	Second Waziristan War of 2007 to present	Asia & Oceania
2009	#960	Nigeria War of 2009	Africa
2009	#963	Boko Haram War of 2013, ongoing in Nigeria	Africa
2010	#971	Iraqi–Sunni Revolt of 2010 to present	Middle East
2011	#973	Second Côte d'Ivoire War of 2011	Africa
2011	#976	Libyan Civil War of 2011	Middle East
2011	#978	Sudan Revolutionary Front Rebellion of 2011 to present	Middle East
2011	#980	Kachin Rebellion of 2011 to 2013	Asia & Oceania
2011	#982	Syrian Arab Spring War of 2011 to present	Middle East
2012	#985	North Mali War of 2012 to 2013	Africa
2012	#990	Central African Republic War of 2012 to 2013	Africa
2013	#991	South Sudan War of 2013 to present	Middle East
2014	#991.5	ISIS–al Nusra Front War of 2014	Middle East
2014	#992	Third Al-Houthi Rebellion of 2014 to present	Middle East
2014	#993	Ukraine Separatists War of 2014 and ongoing	Europe
2014	#996	IS–YPG War of 2014 to present	Middle East
2014	#997	Rada'a War of 2014 to present	Middle East

Bibliography

Abaad Studies & Research Center. "Abaad Report: 7,000 Yemenis Killed in 2014, Houthis Control 70% of the State Army Capabilities." 2015. http://www.abaadstudies.org/?p=1837&lang=en.

Abd-Allah, Umar F. *The Islamic Struggle in Syria*. Berkeley, CA: Mizan Press, 1983.

Abdullaev, Kamol. "Central Asian Emigres in Afghanistan: First Wave (1918–1932)." *Central Asia Monitor* 5 (1994): 16–27.

Abinales, Patricio N. "State Building, Communist Insurgency, and Cacique Politics in the Philippines." In *The Counter-Insurgent State: Guerilla Warfare and State Building in the Twentieth Century*, edited by Paul B. Rich and Richard Stubbs, 26–49. New York: St. Martin's, 1997.

ABO/OLF. "A Losing Bet in Ethiopia." *Oromo Liberation Front*. 2005. http://www.oromoliberationfront.org.

Aboluhom, Ali. "Houthis Killed in Rada'a Explosion." *Yemen Times*, January 21, 2015. http://www.yementimes.com/en/1853/news/4818/Houthis-killed-in-Rada%E2%80%99a-explosion.htm.

Abraham, A. J. *Lebanon at Mid-Century: Maronite–Druze Relations in Lebanon 1840–1860*. Washington, DC: University Press of America, 1981.

______. *The Lebanon War*. Westport, CT: Praeger, 1996.

Abrahamian, Ervand. *The Iranian Mojahedin*. New Haven, CT: Yale University Press, 1989.

Abu-Odeh, Adnan. *Jordanians, Palestinians, and the Hashemite Kingdom in the Middle East Peace Process*. Washington, DC: United States Institute of Peace Press, 1999.

Aburish, Said K. *The Rise, Corruption and Coming Fall of the House of Saud*. New York: St. Martin's Press, 1995.

Abuza, Zachary. *Militant Islam in Southeast Asia: Crucible of Terror*. Boulder, CO: Lynne Rienner, 2003.

Academia de História Miltar Terrestre do Brazil. "A Balaida no Maranhão 1838–1840." n.d. http://www.ahimtb.org.br/c3i.htm.

"Aceh's Hopeless War." *Straits Times*, January 26, 2002.

Acevedo, Eduardo. *Anales Historicos del Uruguay*. Vols. 3–5. Montevideo: Barreiro y Ramos, 1934.

Adám, Magda. *The Little Entente and Europe (1920–1929)*. Budapest, Hungary: Akadémiai Kiadó, 1993.

Adamec, Ludwig. *Afghanistan's Foreign Affairs to the Mid-twentieth Century: Relations with the USSR, Germany, and Britain*. Tucson: University of Arizona Press, 1974.

______. *Historical Dictionary of Afghan Wars, Revolutions, and Insurgencies*. Lanham, MD: Scarecrow Press, 2005.

______. *Historical Dictionary of Afghanistan*. Lanham, MD: Scarecrow Press, 1997.

Adams, N. S., and A. W. McCoy, eds. *Laos: War and Revolution*. New York: Harper, 1970.

Adebajo, Adekeye. *Liberia's Civil War: Nigeria, ECOMOG, and Regional Security in West Africa*. Boulder, CO: Lynne Rienner, 2002.

Adelman, Jonathan R. *The Revolutionary Armies: The Historical Development of the Soviet and Chinese People's Liberation Armies*. Westport, CT: Greenwood Press, 1980.

Adhola, Yoga. "ÚPC: From Independence to the 1966 Revolution." n.d. http://www.upcparty.net/memboard/independenceto1966.

Adshead, S. A. M. "Salt and Warlordism in Szechwan 1914–1922." *Modern Asian Studies* 24, no. 4 (1990): 729–43.

Afary, Janet. *The Iranian Constitutional Revolution, 1906–1911*. New York: Columbia University Press, 1996.

Afoaku, Osita. "Congo's Rebels: Their Origins, Motivations, and Strategies." In *The African Stakes of the Congo War*, edited by John F. Clark, 109–28. New York: Palgrave Macmillan, 2002.

Africa Watch/Human Rights Watch. *Conspicuous Destruction: War, Famine, and the Reform Process in Mozambique*. New York: Human Rights Watch, 1992.

African Union. "AMISOM: African Mission in Somalia." 2014. http://amisom-au.org.

Africa's Watch. *Evil Days: Thirty Years of War and Famine in Ethiopia.* New York: Human Rights Watch, 1991.

Aftergood, Steven. "Jaish-e-Mohammed (JEM)." *Federation of American Scientists Intelligence Resource Program.* 2004. http://www.fas.org/irp/world/para/jem.htm.

The Age (Australia). "Bomber Kills 15 Pakistani Soldiers." September 14, 2007.

Agence France-Presse. "Ocalan Issues Warning, as Turkish Army Rejects Offers." September 28, 1999.

Agi, S. P. I. *The Political History of Religious Violence in Nigeria.* Calabar, Nigeria: Pigasiann and Grace, 1998.

"Agrarians Seize Town in Mexico." *Montreal Gazette,* November 27, 2002, 8.

Agwani, M. S., ed. *The Lebanon Crisis, 1958: A Documentary Study.* London: Asia Publishing House, 1965.

Akamatsu, Paul. *Meiji 1868: Revolution and Counter-Revolution in Japan.* Translated by Miriam Kochan. New York: Harper and Row, 1972. Originally published 1968.

Akers, Charles Edmond. *A History of South America.* London: John Murray, 1930.

______. *A History of South America, 1854–1902.* New York: E. P. Dutton and Co., 1912.

Akhtar, Shaheen. "Ethnic Conflict in Sri Lanka: Domestic, Regional and International Linkages (1983–1993)." PhD diss., Quaid-i-Azam University, Department of International Relations, 2006.

Akol, Lam. *SPLM/SPLA: The Nasir Declaration.* Lincoln, NE: iUniverse, 2003.

Akombo, Elijah Ityavkase. "Jukun–Tiv Relations since 1850: A Case Study of Inter-Group Relations in Wukari Local Government Area of Taraba State." Doctoral diss., University of Jos, 2005.

Aksan, Virginia H. *Ottoman Wars 1700–1870: An Empire Besieged.* Harlow, UK: Pearson Education, 2007.

Al Jazeera. Multiple items concerning war in Yemen. January–April, 2007. http://www.aljazeera.net.

Al Rasheed, Madawi. *Politics in an Arabian Oasis: The Rashidi Tribal Dynasty.* London: I. B. Tauris, 1991.

Al-Abdin, A. Z. "The Free Yemeni Movement (1940–48) and Its Ideas on Reform." *Middle Eastern Studies* 15, no. 1 (1979): 36–48.

Al-Aiban, Bandar Mohammed. "United States Policy in the Middle East and Its Intervention in Lebanon, 1955–1958." PhD diss., Johns Hopkins University, 1996.

Albrecht-Carrié, René. *A Diplomatic History of Europe since the Congress of Vienna.* New York: Harper and Row, 1958.

Alcock, Norman Z., and Keith Lowe. "The Vietnam War as a Richardson Process." *Journal of Peace Research* 7 (1970): 105–12.

Alec-Tweedie. *The Maker of Modern Mexico: Porfirio Diaz.* New York: John Lane, 1906.

Alessio Robles, Vito. *Coahuila y Texas.* 2 vols. Mexico City: Antigua Librereoa Robredo, 1945–46.

Alexander, Rani T. *Yaxcabá and the Caste War of Yucatán, an Archaeological Perspective.* Albuquerque: University of New Mexico Press, 2004.

Alexander, Robert J. *The Bolivian National Revolution.* New Brunswick, NJ: Rutgers University Press, 1958.

______. *Juan Domingo Perón: A History.* Boulder, CO: Westview Press, 1979.

______. *The Tragedy of Chile.* Westport, CT: Greenwood Press, 1978.

Ali, S. Mahmud. *The Fearful State: Power, People, and Internal War in South Asia.* London: Zed Books, 1993.

Ali, Tariq. *The Duel: Pakistan on the Flight Path of American Power.* New York: Scribner, 2008.

Aličić, Ahmed S. *Herzegovina.* Privredni Vjesnik, 1981.

Ali-Dinar, Ali B. "Congo-Brazzaville: Background on Militia Groups." *African Studies Center, University of Pennsylvania,* 1999. http://www.africa.upenn.edu/Hornet/irin_21799.html.

Alker, Hayward. "Somali Borders, 1962–1967." *Prototype Action Recommending Information System (PARIS in LA).* Los Angeles: University of Southern California, 1995. http://www.usc.edu/dept/anctr/Paris-in-LA/Database.

Allen, W. E. D., and Paul Muratoff. *Caucasian Battlefields.* Cambridge, UK: Cambridge University Press, 1953.

Al-Marashi, Ibrahim, and Sammy Salama. *Iraq's Armed Forces: An Analytical History.* New York: Routledge, 2008.

Al-Moshki, Ali Ibrahim. "Clashes in Rada'a between Houthis and AQAP." *Yemen Times,* December 11, 2014. http://www.yementimes.com/en/1841/news/4674/Clashes-in-Rada%E2%80%99a-between-Houthis-and-AQAP.htm.

Alvarado, Lisandro. *Historia de la Revolucion Federal en Venezuela.* Caracas, Venezuela: Oficina Central de Informacion, 1975.

Americas Watch. "Closing the Space: Human Rights in Guatemala, May 1987–October 1988." Washington, DC: Americas Watch, 1988.

Ameringer, Charles D. *The Caribbean Legion.* University Park: Pennsylvania State University Press, 1996.

______. *Don Pepe: A Political Biography of José Figueres of Costa Rica.* Albuquerque: University of New Mexico Press, 1978.

Amin, Mohamed. "Over 100 Soldiers Killed in Sudan Govt, Rebel Clashes." *Daily Nation (Kenya),* June 10, 2014.

Amnesty International. "Annual Report 2011: Sri Lanka." 2011. http://www.amnesty.org/en/region/sri-lanka/report-2011.

______. "Croatia: A Shadow on Croatia's Future: Continuing Impunity for War Crimes and Crimes against Humanity." EUR 64/005, 2004.

______. *Militias Threaten Hopes for New Libya.* London: Amnesty International Publications, 2012.

Amoo, Sam G. "Frustrations of Regional Peacekeeping: The OAU in Chad, 1977–1982." *Carter Center Working Paper Series* (2003).

An, Tai Sung. *Mao Tse-Tung's Cultural Revolution.* Indianapolis, IN: Bobbs-Merrill, 1972.

Anastasoff, Christ. *The Bulgarians.* Hicksville, NY: Exposition Press, 1977.

______. *The Tragic Peninsula: A History of the Macedonian Movement for Independence since 1878.* St. Louis, MO: Blackwell Wiebendy, 1938.

Anatolia News Agency. "Kurdish Rebel Movement Will Abandon Those Who Ignore Withdrawal." *BBC Summary of World Broadcasts,* December 14, 1999.

Andermann, Jens. "Argentine Literature and the 'Conquest of the Desert.'" n.d. http://www.bbk.ac.uk/ibamuseum/texts/Andermann02.htm.

Anderson, G. Norman. *Sudan in Crisis: The Failure of Democracy.* Gainesville: University Press of Florida, 1999.

Anderson, James M. *The History of Portugal.* Westport, CT: Greenwood Press, 2000.

Anderson, Mary. *Do No Harm. How Aid Can Support Peace—or War.* Boulder, CO: Lynne Rienner Publishers, 1999.

Anderson, R. C. *Naval Wars in the Levant.* Princeton, NJ: Princeton University, 1952.

Anderson, Thomas P. *Matanza.* Lincoln: University of Nebraska Press, 1971.

______. *Matanza: The 1932 "Slaughter" That Traumatized a Nation, Shaping US–Salvadoran Policy to This Day.* 2nd ed. Willimantic, CT: Curbstone Press, 1992.

______. *Politics in Central America: Guatemala, El Salvador, Honduras, and Nicaragua.* Westport, CT: Praeger, 1988.

Andrijasevic, Zivko M. "Montenegro from Ancient Times to the Balkan Wars." In *The History of Montenegro from Ancient Times to 2003,* edited by Zivko M. Andrijasevic and Serbo Rastoder, 9–135. Podgorica, Montenegro: Diaspora Centre, 2006.

Angel, Barbara A. "Choosing Sides in War and Peace: The Travels of Herculano Balam among the Pacificos del Sur." *The Americas* 53, no. 4 (1997): 525–49.

______. "The Reconstruction of Rural Society in the Aftermath of the Mayan Rebellion of 1847." *Journal of the Canadian Historical Association* 4 (1993): 33–53.

Angell, Alan. "Chile since 1958." In *The Cambridge History of Latin America. Volume VIII,* edited by Leslie Bethell. Cambridge, UK: Cambridge University Press, 1984.

Annual of Power and Conflict. London: Institute for the Study of Conflict, multiple years.

The Annual Register, or a View of the History, Politics and Literature of the Year 1836. London: Baldwin and Cradock, 1837.

Annual Register of World Events. London: Longmans, 1758–.

Anscombe, Frederick F. *The Ottoman Gulf: The Creation of Kuwait, Saudi Arabia, and Qatar.* New York: Columbia University Press, 1997.

Appleton's Annual Cyclopaedia and Register of Important Events of the Year 1883. New York: D. Appleton and Company, 1886.

Aranzaes, Nicanor. *Las Revoluciones de Bolivia.* La Paz, Bolivia: Casa EditoraTallerres Graficos "La Prensa," 1886.

Aras, Ramazan. "Political Violence, Fear and Pain: The Formation of Kurdishness in Turkey." PhD diss., University of Western Ontario, Department of Anthropology, 2010.

Arasaratnam, S. "The Ceylon Insurrection of April 1971: Some Causes and Consequences." *Pacific Affairs* 4, no. 3 (1972): 356–71.

Arbrahamian, Ervand. *Iran Between Two Revolutions.* Princeton, NJ: Princeton University Press, 1982.

Arbuthnot, G. *Herzegovina; or Omer Pacha and the Christian Rebels.* London: Longman, Green, Longman, Roberts and Green, 1862.

Archer, Christon I. "Fashioning a New Nation." In *The Oxford History of Mexico,* edited by Michael C. Meyer, and William H. Beezley. Oxford, UK: Oxford University Press, 2000.

Ardley, Jane. *The Tibetan Independence Movement: Political, Religious and Ghandian Perspectives.* London: Routledge Curzon, 2002.

Arens, Olavi, and Andrew Ezergailis. "The Revolution in the Baltics: Estonia and Latvia." In *Critical Companion to the Russian Revolution, 1914–1921,* edited by Edward Acton, Vladimir Iu. Cherniaev, and William G. Rosenberg, 667–78. London: Arnold, 1997.

Arfa, Hassan. *Under Five Shahs.* London: John Murray, 1964.

"Argentina Country at War." In Political Papers, No. 11 (January–March, 1977): 87–102. Centro do Documentaci6n de los Movememtos Armados. http://www.cedema.org.

Arguedas, Alcides. *Los Caudillos Bárbaros.* Barcelona, Spain: Editorial Viuda de Luis Tasso, 1929.

Arieff, Alexis. "Crisis in Mali." *CRS Report for Congress.* Congressional Research Service, January 14, 2013. http://www.fas.org/sgp/crs/row/R42664.pdf.

Arjomand, Said Amir. *The Turban for the Crown: The Islamic Revolution in Iran.* New York: Oxford University Press, 1988.

Armour, Ian D. *A History of Eastern Europe 1740–1918: Empires, Nations, and Modernisation.* New York: Bloomsbury Academic, 2006.

Arms Control and Disarmament Agency. *The Control of Local Conflict: Case Studies.* Vol. III. Brown and Shaw International Studies Division. Waltham, MA: Bolt Beranek and Newman Inc., 1969.

Armstrong, David. "The Next Yugoslavia? The Fragmentation of Indonesia." *Diplomacy and Statecraft* 15, no. 4 (2004): 783–808.

"Army Fights Deserters in Indonesia." *The Mercury (Hobart, Tasmania)*, December 12, 1951, 11.

Arnold, Anthony. *Afghanistan's Two-Party-Communism: Parcham and Khalq.* Stanford, CA: Hoover Institution Press, 1983.

Arnold, Guy. *The A to Z of Civil Wars in Africa.* Lanham, MD: The Scarecrow Press, 2009.

______. *Wars in the Third World since 1945.* 2nd ed. London: Cassell, 1995.

Aron, Raymond. *Peace and War, a Theory of International Relations.* Abridged. Garden City, NY: Anchor Books, 1973.

Arrabyee, Nasser. "Peninsula on the Brink." *Al Ahram Weekly*, November 12–18, 2009. http://weekly.ahram.org.eg/2009/972/re5.htm.

Arreche, Mariano. "A 32-Year Fall in Combat Commander Mario Roberto Hitórica Santucho and Address of PRT-ERP." *Centro do Documentación de los Movememtos Armados*, July 13, 2008. http://www.cedema.org.

Arslan, Humbaraci. *Algeria: A Revolution That Failed.* New York: Frederick Praeger, 1964.

Ascher, Abraham. *The Revolution of 1905, a Short History.* Stanford, CA: Stanford University Press, 2004.

Ashmead-Bartlett, Ellis. *The Passing of the Shereefian Empire.* Edinburgh, Scotland: William Blackwood, 1910.

Ashwell, Washington. *Concepcion 1947: Cincuenta Años Después.* Asunción, Paraguay: Edipar S. R. L., 1998.

Asian Human Rights Commission. *The Neglected Genocide: Human Rights Abuses against Papuans in the Central Highlands, 1977–1978.* Hong Kong: Asian Human Rights Commission, 2013.

Assefa, Hizkias. *Mediation of Civil Wars: Approaches and Strategies—The Sudan Conflict.* Boulder, CO: Westview Press, 1987.

Asselin, Pierre. *Hanoi's Road to the Vietnam War, 1954–1965.* Berkeley: University of California Press, 2013.

Assunção, Matthias Röhrig. "Elite Politics and Popular Rebellion in the Construction of Post-colonial Order, the Case of Maranhão, Brazil (1820–41)." *Journal of Latin American Studies* 31 (1999): 1–38.

Atabaki, Touraj. *Azerbaijan: Ethnicity and Autonomy in Twentieth-century Iran.* London: British Academic Press, 1993.

Atamian S. *The Armenian Community.* New York: Philosophical Library, 1955.

Atherley-Jones, Llewellyn Archer, and Hugh Hale Leigh Bellot. *Commerce in War.* New York: D. Appleton and Company, 1907.

Atkin, Ronald. *Revolution: Mexico 1910–1920.* London: Macmillan and Co., 1969.

Atkins, G. Pope, and Larman Curtis Wilson. *The Dominican Republic and the United States: From Imperialism to Transnationalism.* Athens: University of Georgia Press, 1988.

"Atlantic Report: Rwanda." *The Atlantic Monthly*, June 1964. http://www.theatlantic.com.

"Attack on Abu Karshola Leaves 411 Sudan Soldiers Dead–Rebels." *Africa News Service*, May 15, 2013.

Attié, Caroline. *Struggle in the Levant: Lebanon in the 1950s.* New York: I. B. Tauris, 2004.

Atwill, David G. "Blinkered Visions: Islamic Identity, Hui Ethnicity, and the Panthay Rebellion in Southwest China, 1856–1873." *The Journal of Asian Studies* 62, no. 4 (2003): 1079–108.

______. *The Chinese Sultanate: Islam, Ethnicity, and the Panthay Rebellion in Southwest China, 1856–1873.* Stanford, CA: Stanford University Press, 2005.

______. "Islam in the World of Yunnan: Muslim Yunnanese Identity in Nineteenth Century Yunnan." *Journal of the Institute of Muslim Minority Affairs* 17 (1997): 9–30.

Australian War Memorial. "United Nations Operation in Somalia (UNOSOM) 1992." n.d. http://www.awm.gov.au.

Axelrod, Alan. *Political History of America's Wars.* Washington, DC: CQ Press, 2007.

Ayers, R. William. "Chechnya and Russia: A War of Succession." In *History Behind the Headlines: The Origins of Conflicts Worldwide*, vol. 1, edited by Sonia G. Benson, Nancy Matuszak, and Meghan Appel O'Meara. Detroit, MI: Gale Group, 2001.

Ayoob, Mohammed, and K. Subrahmanyam. *The Liberation War.* New Delhi: S. Chand, 1972.

Azevedo, Mario J., and Emmanuel U. Nnadozie. *Chad, a Nation in Search of Its Future.* Boulder, CO: Westview Press, 1998.

Baabar (Bat-Erdene Batbayar). *Twentieth-century Mongolia.* Translated by D. Sühjargalmaa, S. Burenbayar, H. Hulan, and N. Tuya. Cambridge, UK: White House Press, 1999.

Bachman, David. "Aspects of an Institutionalizing Political System: China, 1958–1965." In *The History of the People's Republic of China, 1949–1976*, edited by Julia Strauss, 79–104. Cambridge, UK: Cambridge University Press, 2007.

Baddeley, John F. *The Russian Conquest of the Caucasus.* New York: Longmans, Green, 1908.

Baégas, Richard, and Ruth Marshall-Fratani. "Côte d'Ivoire: Negotiating Identity and Citizenship." In *African Guerrillas, Raging against the Machine*, edited by Morten Bøås and Kevin C. Dunn. Boulder, CO: Lynne Rienner, 2007.

Baerlein, Henry. *The March of the Seventy Thousand.* London: Leonard Parsons, 1971.

Bağçeci, Yahya. "1895 Zeytun Ermeni İsyani." *Turkish Studies* 3, no. 2 (2008): 123–49.

Bagley, Bruce Michael. "Drug Trafficking, Political Violence, and US Policy in Colombia under the Clinton Administration." In *Elusive Peace: International, National, and Local Dimensions of Conflict in Colombia*, edited by Cristina Rojas and Judy Meltzer, 21–52. New York: Palgrave Macmillan, 2005.

Bailey, David C. *¡Viva Cristo Rey!* Austin: University of Texas Press, 1974.

Bajwa, Abu Bakr Amin. *Inside Waziristan: Journey from War to Peace.* Lahore, Pakistan: Vanguard Books, 2013.

Bakhash, Shaul. *The Reign of the Ayatollahs: Iran and the Islamic Revolution.* New York: Basic Books, 1984.

Baldry, John. "Al-Yaman and the Turkish Occupation 1849–1914." *Arabica* 23, no. 2 (1976): 156–96.

______. "The History of the Tihamah from 1800 to the Present." In *Studies on the Tihāmah: The Report of the Tihāmah Expedition 1982 and Related Papers*, edited by Francis Stone, 45–50. Essex, UK: Longman, 1985.

Baldwin, Frank. "Patrolling the Empire: Reflections on the USS *Pueblo.*" *Bulletin of Concerned Asian Scholars* 4, no. 2 (1972): 54–74.

Ball, Patrick, Paul Kobrak, and Herbert F. Spirer. *State Violence in Guatemala, 1960–1996: A Quantitative Reflection.* Washington, DC: American Association for the Advancement of Science, 1999. http://shr.aaas.org/guatemala/ciidh/qr/english/index.html.

Balogh, Eva S. "Nationality Problems of the Hungarian Soviet Republic." In *Hungary in Revolution, 1918–1919: Nine Essays*, edited by Iván Völgyes. Lincoln: University of Nebraska Press, 1971.

Banac, Ivo, John G. Ackerman, and Roman Szporluk, eds. *Nation and Ideology, Essays in Honor of Wayne S. Vucinich.* Boulder, CO: East European Monographs, 1981.

Bancroft, Hubert Howe. *History of Mexico.* San Francisco, CA: A. L. Bancroft, 1885.

Bancroft, Hubert Howe, William Nemos, Thomas Savage, and Joseph Joshua Peatfield. *History of Mexico: 1824–1861.* San Francisco, CA: The History Company, 1886.

______. *History of Mexico: 1861–1887.* San Francisco, CA: The History Company, 1888.

Bandarage, Asoka. *The Separatist Conflict in Sri Lanka: Terrorism, Ethnicity, Political Economy.* New York: Routledge, 2009.

Bang, Anne K. "'This Is an Announcement to the People:' The Bayān of 1912 by Muḥammad B. 'Alī al-Idrīsi in 'Asīr." In *New Arabian Studies 4*, edited by J. R. Smart, Gerald Rex Smith, and Brian R. Pridham, 1–38. Devon, UK: Exeter Press, 1997.

______. *The Idrīsī State in 'Asīr 1906–1934.* Bergen, Norway: Center for Middle Eastern and Islamic Studies, 1996.

Baracco, Luciano. "Sandinista Anti-imperialist Nationalism and the Atlantic Coast of Nicaragua: Sandinista-Miskito Relations, 1979–1981." *Nationalism and Ethnic Politics* 10, no. 4 (2004): 625–55.

Barber, Ben. "Guatemala's Ex-rebels Hope Peace Will Hold: McLarty Visits Them to Bolster the Transition." *The Washington Times*, March 18, 1997, 17.

Barbieri, Katherine, Omar M. G. Keshk, and Brian Pollins. "TRADING DATA: Evaluating our Assumptions and Coding Rules." *Conflict Management and Peace Science* 26, no. 5 (2009): 471–91.

Barclay, Glen. *Struggle for a Continent: The Diplomatic History of South America, 1917–1945.* London: Sidgwick and Jackson, 1971.

Barltrop, Richard. *Darfur and the International Community: The Challenges of Conflict Resolution in Sudan.* London: I. B. Tauris, 2011.

Barman, Roderick J. *Brazil, the Forging of a Nation, 1798–1852.* Stanford, CA: Stanford University Press, 1988.

Barnouin, Barbara, and Changgen Yu. *Zhou Enlai: A Political Life.* Hong Kong: Chinese University Press, 2006.

Barrett, John Gilchrist. *The Civil War in North Carolina.* Chapel Hill: University of North Carolina Press, 1963.

Barry, Tom. *Central America Inside Out: The Essential Guide to Its Societies, Politics, and Economies.* New York: Grove Weidenfeld, 1991.

Bartlett, William. *Croatia: Between Europe and the Balkans.* London: Routledge, 2002.

Basadre, Jorge. *Historia de la Republica del Peru.* Lima, Peru: Editorial Cultura Anartica S.A., 1970. Originally published 1940.

"Bashir Gives Rare Toll." *Al-Arab (London)*. July 14, 2014.

Bashiriyeh, Hossein. *The State and Revolution in Iran, 1962–1982*. New York: St. Martin's, 1984.

Bashore, Maj. Boyd T. "Dual Strategy for Limited War." In *Modern Guerrilla Warfare*, edited by F. Osanka. Glencoe, IL: Free Press, 1962.

Bassouni, M. Cherif. *Final Report of the UN Commission of Experts, Annex III and Annex III.A*. New York: United Nations Commission of Experts, 1992.

"The Battle for West Irian Has Already Started." *The Canberra Times*, December 9, 1967, 2.

"Battles Rage for Kabul." *Guardian Weekly*, August 30, 1992, 15.

Baumann, Robert F. *Russian-Soviet Unconventional Wars in the Caucasus, Central Asia, and Afghanistan*. Leavenworth Papers, Number 20. Fort Leavenworth, KS: Combat Studies Institute, US Army Command and General Staff College, 1993.

Bawden, C. R. *The Modern History of Mongolia*. New York: Frederick A. Praeger, 1968.

Bayat, Kaveh. "Rizah Shah and the Tribes: An Overview." In *The Making of Modern Iran: State and Society under Riza Shah, 1921–1941*, edited by Stephanie Cronin, 213–19. London: Routledge Curzon, 2003.

Bayat, Mangol. *Iran's First Revolution: Shi'ism and the Cultural Revolution of 1905–1909*. New York: Oxford University Press, 1991.

Bazaz, Sahar. "Challenging Power and Authority in Pre-Protectorate Morocco: Shaykh Muhammad al-Kattānī and the Tarīqa Kattāniya." PhD diss., Harvard University, History and Middle Eastern Studies, 2002.

BBC News. "Britain's Role in Sierra Leone." September 10, 2000. http://news.bbc.co.uk.

______. "Counting Kosovo's Dead." November 12, 1999a. http://.bbc.co.uk/1/hi/world/europe/517168.stm.

______. "Country Profile: Chad." January 5, 2006a. http://news.bbc.co.uk.

______. "Country Profile: Guatemala." July 20, 2002. http://news.bbc.co.uk.

______. "Deaths Mount in Liberian Capital." July 22, 2003. http://newsvote.bbc.co.uk.

______. "Guide to the Philippines Conflict." February 10, 2005a. http://newsvote.bbc.co.uk.

______. "Horrors of Kosovo Revealed." December 6, 1999b. http://news.bbc.co.uk/1/hi/world/europe/551875.stm.

______. "Kurdish PKK Rebels 'Begin Leaving Turkey' after Truce." May 8, 2013. http://www.bbc.co.uk/news/world-europe-22448118.

______. "Many Killed Near Pakistani Border." September 13, 2007a.

______. May 31, 1999d, http://www.bbc.co.uk.

______. Multiple news items, 1999–2014.

______. "Q&A: Ivory Coast's Crisis." January 17, 2006b. http://newsvote.bbc.co.uk.

______. "Sierra Leone's Hostages." August 10, 1999. http://news.bbc.co.uk.

______. "Swat Battle Tests Pakistan's Resolve." November 21, 2007b.

______. "Timeline: Guinea." December 12, 2005b. http://newsvote.bbc.co.uk.

______. "UN Gives Figure for Kosovo Dead." November 10, 1999c. http://news.bbc.co.uk/1/hi/world/europe/514828.stm.

______. "World: Africa." Multiple stories concerning Chad, 1998–2002. http://news/bbc/co/uk.

BBC News Summary of World Broadcasts. October 1, 1998. http://www.bbc.co.uk.

BCI Eclipse. *The Great Indian Wars 1540–1890*. (DVD.) New Hope, MN: Navarre Corporation, 2005.

Beach, Vincent W. *Charles X of France*. Boulder, CO: Pruett, 1971.

Beatson, Jim. "Papua New Guinea Squeezes Breakaway Island." *The Guardian (London)*, May 10, 1991.

Beckett, Ian F. W. *Encyclopedia of Guerilla Warfare*. Santa Barbara, CA: ABC–CLIO, 1999.

______. *Modern Insurgencies and Counter Insurgencies: Guerrillas and Their Opponents since 1750*. New York: Routledge, 2001.

Behera, Ajay Darshan. "Insurgency in South Asia: A Study of the Janatha Vimukthi Peramuna (JVP) in Sri Lanka." PhD diss., Jawaharlal Nehru University, Centre for South, Central, Southeast Asian and Southwest Pacific Studies, School of International Studies, 1995.

Behera, Navnita Chadha. *State, Identity, and Violence: Jammu, Kashmir, and Ladakh*. New Delhi: Manohar Publishers, 2000.

"Beja Congress Joins Sudan Revolutionary Front." *Radio Dabanga*, November 16, 2012. http://www.radiodabanga.org/node/21016.

Bell, John Patrick. *Crisis in Costa Rica: The 1948 Revolution*. Austin: University of Texas, 1971.

Bello, Jose Maria. *A History of Modern Brazil, 1889–1964*. Stanford, CA: Stanford University Press, 1966.

Bennison, Amira. "The 1847 Revolt of 'Abd al-Qadir and the Algerians against Mawlay Abd al-Rahman, Sultan of Morocco." *Maghreb Review* 22, nos. 1–2 (1997): 109–23.

Benson, Linda. *The Ili Rebellion: The Moslem Challenge to Chinese Authority in Xinjiang 1944–1949.* Armonk, NY: M. E. Sharpe, 1990.

Bentley, Kristina A., and Roger Southall. *An African Peace-Process.* Cape Town, South Africa: Nelson Mandela Foundation, 2005.

Bento, Cláudio Moreira. "Compêndio de História Militar Terrestre Do Brasil." 2002. http://www.resenet.com.br/ahimtb/brasillutint.htm.

Benton, Gregor. *New Fourth Army: Communist Resistance Along the Yangtze and the Huai, 1938–1941.* Berkeley: University of California Press, 1999.

Benvenuti, Francesco. "The Red Army." In *Critical Companion to the Russian Revolution, 1914–1921,* edited by Edward Acton, Vladimir Iu. Cherniaev, and William G. Rosenberg, 403–15. London: Arnold, 1997.

Bercovitch, Jacob, and Judith Fretter. *Regional Guide to International Conflict and Management from 1945 to 2003.* Washington, DC: CQ Press, 2004.

Bercovitch, Jacob and Richard Jackson. *International Conflict: A Chronological Encyclopedia of Conflicts and Their Management 1945–1995.* Washington, DC: CQ Press, 1997.

Berghold, Rev. Alexander. *The Indians' Revenge or Days of Horror.* Roseville, MN: Edinborough Press, 2007. Originally published 1891.

Bergquist, Charles. *Coffee and Conflict in Columbia, 1886–1910.* Durham, NC: Duke University Press, 1978.

Berkeley, Bill. *The Graves Are Not Yet Full.* New York: Basic Books, 2001.

Berkeley, George F. H. *Italy in the Making 1815–1846.* Vol. 1. Cambridge, UK: Cambridge University Press, 1932.

______. *Italy in the Making: January 1st 1848 to November 19th 1848.* Cambridge, UK: Cambridge University Press, 1940.

Bernstein, Harry. *Modern and Contemporary Latin America.* New York: Russell and Russell, 1965.

Berthe, P. A. *Garcia Moreno: President of Ecuador, 1821–1875.* Translated by Lady Herbert. London: Burnes and Oates, 1889.

Bertier de Sauvigny, Guillaume de. *La Restauration.* Paris: Flammarion, 1955.

Best, Felix. *Historia de las Guerras Argentinas.* 2 vols. Buenos Aires: Peuser, 1960.

Bethell, Leslie. *Brazil: Empire and Republic, 1822–1930.* New York: Cambridge University Press, 1989.

Bethell, Leslie and José Murilo de Carvalho. "1822–1850." In *Brazil Empire and Republic 1822–1930,* edited by Leslie Bethell. Cambridge, UK: Cambridge University Press, 1989.

______, ed. *Cuba: A Short History.* Cambridge, UK: Cambridge University Press, 1993.

Betts, Robert Benton. *The Druze.* New Haven, CT: Yale University Press, 1988.

Bhavnani, Ravi, and David Backer. "Localized Ethnic Conflict and Genocide." *Journal of Conflict Resolution* 44, no. 3 (2000): 283–306.

Bickford-Smith, Ronden Albert Henry. *Cretan Sketches.* London: Richard Bentley and Son, 1898.

Bidwell, Robin, ed. *The Affairs of Arabia, 1905–1906.* Frank Cass, 1971.

______. *The Two Yemens.* Essex, UK: Longman Group, 1983.

Billingsley, Phil. *Bandits in Republican China.* Stanford, CA: Stanford University Press, 1988.

Bird, Leonard. *Costa Rica: The Unarmed Democracy.* London: Sheppard Press, 1984.

Bisher, Jamie. *White Terror: Cossack Warlords of the Trans-Siberian.* London: Routledge, 2005.

Black, Ian. "Libyan Revolution Casualties Lower Than Expected, Says New Government." *The Guardian,* January 8, 2013. http://www.guardian.co.uk/world/2013/jan/08/libyan-revolution-casualties-lower-expected-government.

Blakemore, Harold. "The Chilean Revolution of 1891 and Its Historiography." *Hispanic American Historical Review* 45 (August 1965): 393–421.

Blank, Stephen J., and Earl H. Tilford Jr. "Russia's Invasion of Chechnya: A Preliminary Assessment." *Strategic Studies Institute,* January 13, 1995.

Blanksten, George I. *Ecuador: Constitutions and Caudillos.* Vol 3. Berkeley: University of California Press, 1951.

Blasier, Cole. "The United States and the Revolution." In *Beyond the Revolution: Bolivia since 1952,* edited by James M. Malloy and Richard S. Thorn, 53–110. Pittsburgh, PA: University of Pittsburgh Press, 1971.

Bloom, Mia M. "Ethnic Conflict, State Terror and Suicide Bombing in Sri Lanka." *Civil Wars* 6, no. 1 (2003): 54–84.

Board of Commissioners. *Minnesota in the Civil and Indian Wars, 1861–1865.* Vol. 1. St. Paul: Minnesota Historical Society Press, 2005. Originally published 1890.

Bodart, Gaston. *Losses of Life in Modern Wars.* Oxford: Clarendon Press, 1916.

______. *Militär-historiches Kriegs-Lexikon, 1618–1905.* Wien: C. W. Stern, 1908.

Bodart, Gaston, and Vernon Lyman Kellog. *Losses of Life in Modern Wars and Race Deterioration.* London: Clarendon Press, 1916.

Boguslaw, Pacek. "The European Union Military Operation in Chad and Central African Republic." *Military Review* 90, no. 1 (2010): 26–33.

Boland, B. J. *The Struggle of Islam in Modern Indonesia.* The Hague, Netherlands: Martinus Nijhoff, 1971.

Bollaert, William. *The Wars of Succession of Portugal and Spain from 1826 to 1840.* 2 vols. London: Edward Stanford, 1870.

Bonachea, Ramón L., and Marta San Martín. *The Cuban Insurrection, 1952–1959.* New Brunswick, NJ: Transaction Publishers, 1974.

Boon, Kristen E., Aziz Huq, and Douglas C. Lovelace Jr. *Narco-terrorism.* Vol. 105 of *Terrorism: Commentary on Security Documents.* Oxford, UK: Oxford University Press, 2010.

Boorstein, Edward. *Allende's Chile: An Inside View.* New York: International Publishers, 1977.

Boot, Max. *The Savage Wars of Peace.* New York: Basic Books, 2002.

Booth, John A., "A Guatemalan Nightmare: Levels of Political Violence, 1966–1972." *Journal of Interamerican Studies and World Affairs* 22, no. 2 (1980): 195–225.

Booth, John A., and Thomas W. Walker. *Understanding Central America.* Boulder, CO: Westview Press, 1999.

Borjigin, Burensain. "The Complex Structure of Ethnic Conflict in the Frontier: Through the Debates around the 'Jindandao Incident' in 1891." *Inner Asia* 6, no. 1 (2004): 41–60.

Bose, Sumantra. "Flawed Mediation, Chaotic Implementation: The 1987 Indo-Sri Lankan Peace Agreement." *In Ending Civil Wars: The Implementation of Peace Agreements,* edited by Stephen John Stedman, Donald Rothchild, and Elizabeth M. Cousens, 631–59. Boulder, CO: Lynne Rienner, 2002.

Bourne, Peter G. *Men, Stress, and Vietnam.* Boston, MA: Little, Brown, 1970.

Bournoutian, George A. *A Concise History of the Armenian People (from Ancient Times to the Present).* 2nd ed. Costa Mesa, CA: Mazda Publishers, 2003.

Bouron, N. "The Druze of al-Atrash." In *Druze History.* Translated by Ed. F. Massey, 111–114. Detroit, MI, 1952. Originally published 1927.

Bouthoul, Gaston. *War.* New York: Walker and Company, 1962.

Bouthoul, Gaston, and René Carrère. "A List of the 366 Major Armed Conflicts of the Period 1740–1974." *Peace Research* 10, no. 3 (1978): 83–108.

Bowei, Lu, and Wang Guoping. *The Revolution of 1911: Turning Point in Modern Chinese History.* Translated by He Fei. Beijing: Foreign Languages Press, 1991.

Bowra, Ken. *The War in Cambodia 1970–1975.* Oxford, UK: Osprey, 1989.

Bracamonte, José Angel Moroni, and David E. Spencer. *Strategy and Tactics of the Salvadoran FMLN Guerrillas.* Westport, CT: Praeger, 1995.

Bracey, Audrey. *Resolution of the Dominican Crisis, 1965: A Study in Mediation.* Washington, DC: Institute for the Study of Diplomacy, School of Foreign Service, Georgetown University, 1980.

Brackman, Arnold C. *Indonesian Communism.* New York: Praeger, 1963.

Bradley, John. *Allied Intervention in Russia.* New York: Basic Books, 1963.

Bravo Ugarte, José. *Historia de México: Independencia, caracterización política e integración socia.* Vol. 3. Mexico City: Editorial Jus, 1962.

Brecher, Michael, and Jonathan Wilkenfeld. *Crises in the Twentieth Century.* New York: Pergamon Press, 1988.

______. *A Study of Crisis.* Ann Arbor: University of Michigan Press, 1997.

Brecher, Michael, Jonathan Wilkenfeld, and Sheila Moser. *Handbook of International Crises.* Vol. 1 of *Crises in the Twentieth Century.* New York: Pergamon Press, 1988.

Brecke, Peter. "The Characteristics of Violent Conflict since 1400 A.D." Paper presented at the annual meeting of the International Studies Association, Washington, DC, February 17–20, 1999, and associated dataset.

Bremer, Ian, and Ray Taras, eds. *Nations and Politics in the Soviet Successor States.* Cambridge, UK: Cambridge University Press, 1993.

Bremer, Stuart A. "Dangerous Dyads: Conditions Affecting the Likelihood of Interstate War, 1816–1965." *The Journal of Conflict* 56, no. 2 (1992): 309–41.

Bremer, Stuart A., with Faten Ghosn. "Defining States: Reconsiderations and Recommendations." *Conflict Management and Peace Science* 20, no. 1 (2003): 24.

Brewer, David. *The Flame of Freedom: The Greek War of Independence, 1821–1833.* London: John Murray, 2001.

Brewster, Keith. "Militarism and Ethnicity in the Sierra de Puebla, Mexico." *The Americas* 56, no. 2 (1999): 253–75.

Brewster, Keith, and Claire Brewster. "Ethereal Allies: Spiritism and the Revolutionary Struggle in Hidalgo." In *Faith and Impiety in Revolutionary Mexico,* edited by Matthew Butler, 93–109. New York: Palgrave Macmillan, 2007.

Brill, William H. *Military Intervention in Bolivia: The Overthrow of Paz Estenssoro and the MNR.* Washington, DC: Institute for the Comparative Study of Political Systems, 1967.

Brinkley, George A. *The Volunteer Army and Allied Intervention in Southern Russia, 1917–1921.* South Bend, IN: University of Notre Dame Press, 1966.

Britton, Peter, and Richard Nixon. "Indonesia's NeoColonial Armed Forces." *Bulletin of Concerned Asian Scholars* 7, no. 3 (1975): 14.

Broadley, A. M. *The Last Punic War: Tunis, Past and Present.* Edinburgh, UK: William Blackwood and Sons, 1882.

Brockett, Charles D. *Political Movements and Violence in Central America.* New York: Cambridge University Press, 2005.

Brockett, L. P. *The Cross and the Crescent.* Philadelphia, PA: Hubbard Bros., 1887.

Brogan, Patrick. *World Conflicts.* 3rd ed. London: Bloomsbury Publishing, 1998.

Broiwn, Frederick Z. "Cambodia in 1991: An Uncertain Peace." *Asian Survey* 32, no. 1 (1992): 99–6.

Broomhall, Marshall. *Islam in China: A Neglected Problem.* London: Morgan and Scott, 1910.

Broussard, Ray F. "The Puebla Revolt: First Challenge to the Reform." *Journal of the West* 18, no. 1 (1979): 52–57.

Brovkin, Vladimir N. *Behind the Front Lines of the Civil War: Political Parties and Social Movements in Russia, 1918–1922.* Princeton, NJ: Princeton University Press, 1994.

Brown, Bess A. 1997. "The Civil War in Tajikistan, 1992–1993." In *Tajikistan: Trials of Independence*, edited by Mohammed-Reza Djalili, Frédéric Grare, and Shirin Akiner, 86–96. New York: St. Martin's Press.

Brown, Gordon L. "Guatemala: The Origins and Development of State Terrorism." In *Revolution and Counterrevolution in Central America and the Caribbean*, edited by Donald E. Schulz and Douglas Graham, 269–99. Boulder, CO: Westview Press, 1984.

Brown, Macalister, and Joseph J. Zasloff. "Laos 1973: Wary Steps toward Peace." *Asian Survey* 14, no. 2 (February 1974): 166–74.

______. "Laos in 1975: People's Democratic Revolution–Lao Style," *Asian Survey* 16, no. 2 (February 1976): 193–99.

______. "Laos 1979: Caught in Vietnam's Wake." *Asian Survey* 20, no. 2 (February 1980): 103–11.

______. *War in Shangri-La, a Memoir of Civil War in Laos.* New York: Radcliffe Press, 2001.

Brown, Mervyn. *A History of Madagascar.* Princeton, NJ: Markus Wiener Publisher, 2001.

Brown, Michael E., Owen R. Coté Jr., Sean M. Lynn Jones, and Steven E. Miller, eds. *Nationalism and Ethnic Conflict.* Cambridge, MA: MIT Press, 1997.

Brown, Timothy C. *The Real Contra War: Highlander Peasant Resistance in Nicaragua.* Norman: University of Oklahoma Press, 2001.

Browne, Dalls L. "Rwanda and Burundi: Culture, History, Power, and Genocide." In *History Behind the Headlines: The Origins of Conflicts Worldwide*, vol. 1, edited by Sonia G. Benson, Nancy Matuszak, and Meghan Appel O'Meara. Detroit, MI: Gale Group, 2001.

Browne, Edward G. *The Persian Revolution of 1905–1909.* London: Frank Cass, 1966.

______. *The Persian Revolution of 1905–1909.* Washington, DC: Mage Publishers, 1995. Originally published 1910.

Broxup, Marie Benningsen. "The Last Ghazawat: The 1920–1921 Uprising." In *The North Caucasus Barrier: The Russian Advance towards the Muslim World*, edited by Marie Bennigsen Broxup, 112–45. New York: St. Martin's, 1992.

Bruce, George. *Harbottle's Dictionary of Battles.* 3rd ed. New York: Van Nostrand Reinhold, 1981.

Brzozowski, Marie. *La Guerre de Pologne en 1831.* Leipzig: Brockhaus, 1833.

Buck, James H. "The Satsuma Rebellion of 1877: From Kagoshima through the Siege of Kumamoto Castle." *Monumenta Nipponica* 28, no. 4 (Winter 1973): 427–46.

Budiardjo, Carmel and Liem Soei Liong. *The War against East Timor.* New York: Zed Books, 1984.

______. *West Papua: The Obliteration of a People.* London: Tapol, 1988.

Buendia, Rizal G. "The GRP-MILF Peace Talks: Quo Vadis?" In *Southeast Asian Affairs*, 205–21. 2004.

Buffardi, Louis Nicholas. "Soviet Strategy in South Asia 1953–1977. Focus: Baluchistan." PhD diss., Georgetown University, Russian Area Studies, 1981.

Bullion, Alan J. *India, Sri Lanka, and the Tamil Crisis 1976–1994: An International Perspective.* London: Pinter, 1995.

Bunkley, Allison W. "Sarmiento and Urquiza." *Hispanic American Historical Review* 30, no. 2 (May 1950): 176–94.

Burdett, A. L. P. *Afghanistan Strategic Intelligence: British Records 1919–1970.* Archive Editions, 2002.

______. *Iraq: Defence Intelligence 1920–1973.* Vol. 5. Archive Editions, 2005.

______, ed. *King Abdul Aziz: Diplomacy and Statecraft 1902–1953.* Vol. 1. Archive Editions, 1998.

______, ed. *Records of the Hijaz 1798–1925.* Archive Editions, 1996.

Burke, Edmund. "Pan-Islam and Moroccan Resistance to French Colonial Penetration, 1900–1912." *The Journal of African History* 13, no. 1 (1972): 97–118.

______. *Prelude to Protectorate in Morocco.* Chicago, IL: University of Chicago, 1976.

"Burma Is Forming an Antirebel Force." *New York Times,* August 22, 1965, 28.

"Burma Opens Drive on Bands of Rebels." *New York Times,* May 22, 1965, 6.

Burns, E. Bradford. *A History of Brazil.* New York: Columbia University Press, 1980.

______. *A History of Brazil.* 3rd ed. New York: Columbia University Press, 1993.

______. *Revolutionary Sudan: Hasan Al-Turabi and the Islamist State, 1989–2000.* Leiden, Netherlands: Brill, 2003.

Burrell, R. M., ed. *Iran Political Diaries 1881–1965.* Vols. 4 and 6. Archive Editions, 1997.

Burrowes, Robert D. *Historical Dictionary of Yemen.* New York: Rowman and Littlefield, 2010.

______. *The Yemen Arab Republic: The Politics of Development.* Boulder, CO: Westview Press, 1987.

Burt, Jo-Marie. *Political Violence and the Authoritarian State in Peru.* New York: Palgrave Macmillan, 2007.

Bush, Kenneth. *The Intra-Group Dimensions of Ethnic Conflict in Sri Lanka.* New York: Palgrave Macmillan, 2003.

Bushnell, David. *The Making of Modern Colombia.* Berkley: University of California Press, 1993.

Butler, Matthew. *Popular Piety and Political Identity in Mexico's Cristero Rebellion: Michoacán, 1927–29.* Oxford, UK: Oxford University Press, 2004.

Butt, Ahsan Ishaq. "Goodbye or See You Later: Why States Fight Some Secessionists but Not Others." PhD diss., University of Chicago, Department of Political Science, 2012.

Buttinger, Joseph. *Vietnam: A Dragon Embattled.* Vol. 2. London: Pall Mall Press, 1967.

Bpås, Morten, and Kevin C. Dunn, eds. *African Guerrillas; Raging against the Machine.* Boulder, CO: Lynne Rienner, 2007.

Caballero Jurado, Carlos, and Nigel Thomas. *Central American Wars, 1959–89.* London: Osprey Publishing, 1990.

Cady, John F. *Foreign Intervention in the Rio de la Plata, 1838–50.* Philadelphia: University of Pennsylvania Press, 1929.

Cady, John F. *A History of Modern Burma.* Ithaca, NY: Cornell University Press, 1958.

______. "The Situation in Burma." *Far Eastern Survey* 22, no. 5 (April 22, 1953): 49–54.

Cady, Richard H., and William Prince. *Political Conflicts, 1944–1966.* Ann Arbor, MI: Bendix Social Sciences Division, 1966. Data available from ICPSR at the University of Michigan.

Calcott, Welfrid Hardy. *Santa Anna.* Hamden, CT: Archon, 1964.

Calderón de la Barca, Madame (Frances). *Life in Mexico, during a Residence of Two Years in That Country.* Vol. 1. Boston, MA: Charles C. Little and James Brown, 1843.

Caldwell, Malcolm, and Lek Hor Tan. *Cambodia in the Southeast Asian War.* New York: Monthly Review, 1973.

Call, Charles T. "Assessing El Salvador's Transition from Civil War to Peace." In *Ending Civil Wars: The Implementation of Peace Agreements,* edited by Stephen John Stedman, Donald Rothchild, and Elizabeth M. Cousens, 383–420. Boulder, CO: Lynne Rienner, 2002.

Callahan, Mary Patricia. *Making Enemies: War and State-Building in Burma.* Ithaca, NY: Cornell University Press, 2003.

______. "The Origins of Military Rule in Burma." PhD diss., Cornell University, Department of Political Science, 1996.

Callcott, Wilfred Hardy. *Santa Anna.* Norman: University of Oklahoma Press, 1936.

Calogeras, João Pandiá. *A History of Brazil.* Chapel Hill: University of North Carolina Press, 1939.

______. *A History of Brazil.* Translated and edited by Percy A. Martin. New York: Russell and Russell, 1963.

Calvert, Peter. "Paraguay–History." In *South America, Central America and the Caribbean 2002,* edited by Jacqueline West, 630–31. London: Europa Publications, 2001.

"Cambodia Stages Offensive against Khmer Rouge." *New York Times,* August 19, 1993, A7.

"Cambodians Open Offensive against Khmer Rouge Rebels." *New York Times,* December 23, 1993, A4.

Camín, Hécton Aguilar, and Lorenzo Meyer. *In the Shadow of the Mexican Revolution.* Translated by Luis Alberto Fierro. Austin: University of Texas Press, 1993.

Campos y Serrano, Martinez de. *Espana Belica: El Siglo XIX.* Madrid, Spain: Aguilar, 1961.

Caplan, Karen Deborah. "Local Liberations: Mexico's Indigenous Villagers and the State, 1812–1857." PhD diss., Princeton University, Department of History, 2001.

Cardoza, Efraim. *Paraguay Independiente.* Vol. 21 in *Historia de America,* edited by A. Ballesteros y Beretta. Barcelona, Spain: Salvat, 1949.

Carey, James C. "The Latin American Legacy: The Background for Civil War." In *Civil Wars in the Twentieth Century,* edited by Robin Higham. Lexington: University Press of Kentucky, 1972.

Carley, Kenneth. *The Sioux Uprising of 1862.* St. Paul: The Minnesota Historical Society, 1961.

Carment, David, and Patrick James, eds. *Wars in the Midst of Peace: The International Politics of Ethnic Conflict.* Pittsburgh, PA: University of Pittsburgh Press, 1997.

Carr, Raymond. *Spain: 1808–1939.* Oxford, UK: Oxford University Press, 1966.

______. *Spain: 1808–1975.* Oxford, UK: Oxford University Press, 1982.

Carrêre, Rene. "1870–1871, Guerre Ancienne ou Guerre Moderne?" *Etudes Polemologiques* 5 (July 1972): 23–4.

Carriedo, Robert. "The Man Who Tamed Mexico's Tiger: General Joaquin Amaro and the Professionalization of Mexico's Revolutionary Army." PhD diss., University of New Mexico, 2005.

Carroll, Rory. "Argentinian Founding Father Recast as Genocidal Murder." *The Guardian,* January 13, 2011.

Castellan, Georges. *History of the Balkans from Mohammed the Conqueror to Stalin.* Boulder, CO: East European Monographs, 1992.

Cattaui, Rene, and Georges Cattaui. *Mohamed Aly et L'europe.* Paris, France: Libraire Orientaliste, 1950.

Catton, Bruce. *The Army of the Potomac: A Stillness at Appomattox.* Vol. 3. Garden City, NY: Doubleday & Company, Inc., 1953.

______. *The Army of the Potomac: Glory Road.* Vol. 2. Garden City, NY: Doubleday & Company, Inc., 1952b.

______. *The Army of the Potomac: Mr. Lincoln's Army.* Vol. 1. Garden City, NY: Doubleday & Company, Inc., 1952a.

Catudal, Honore M., Jr. "The War in Kurdistan: End of a Nationalist Struggle?" *International Relations* 5 (1976): 1024–44.

Cayley, Edward. *The European Revolutions of 1848.* 2 vols. London: Smith, Elder, 1856.

Cbe, Najib Alamuddin. *Turmoil: The Druzes, Lebanon and the Arab–Israeli Conflict.* London: Quarter Books, 1993.

Center for Balkan Development. "History of the War in Bosnia." 1996. http://www.friendsofbosnia.org.

Center for Defense Information. "Afghanistan: Re-Emergence of a State." December 21, 2001a. http://www.cdi.org.

______. "Forces in Play." October 26, 2001b. http://www.cdi.org.

Central Intelligence Agency. *Balkan Battlegrounds: A Military History of the Yugoslav Conflict, 1990–1995.* Vol.1. Washington, DC: Central Intelligence Agency, 2002.

______. "El Salvador: Evaluation of the Perquin Operation." July 15, 1982. http://www.foia.cia.gov/browse_docs.asp?doc_no=0000809898.

CERAC (Centro de Recursos para el Análisis de Conflictos). Colombia Conflict Database. Release 8, January 11, 2008. http://www.cerac.org.co.

Chadha, Vivek. *Low Intensity Conflicts in India.* New Delhi, India: SAGE, 2005.

Chalk, Peter. "Militant Islamic Extremism in the Southern Philippines." In *Islam in Asia,* edited by Jason F. Isaacson and Colin Rubinstein, 187–222. New Brunswick, NJ: Transaction Publishers, 2002.

Chandler, David P. *A History of Cambodia.* 3rd ed. Boulder, CO: Westview Press, 2000.

______. *The Tragedy of Cambodian History: Politics, War, and Revolution since 1945.* New Haven, CT: Yale University Press, 1991.

Chandler, James A. "Spain and Her Moroccan Protectorate 1898–1927." *Journal of Contemporary History* 10, no. 2 (April 1975): 301–22.

Chapman, Tim. *Imperial Russia: 1801–1905.* London: Routledge, 2001.

Chaqueri, Cosroe. *The Soviet Socialist Republic of Iran, 1920–1921, Birth of the Trauma.* Pittsburgh, PA: University of Pittsburgh Press, 1995.

Charbonneau, Louis. "Up to 3,000 African Peacekeepers Killed in Somalia since 2007: UN." *Reuters,* May 9, 2013. http://www.reuters.com/article/2013/05/09/us-somalia-peacekeepers-killed-in-Sonalia-since-2007.

Chasteen, John Charles. "Cabanos and Farrapos: Brazilian Nativism in Regional Perspective, 1822–1850." *Locus* 7, no. 1 (1994): 31–46.

______. *Heroes on Horseback: The Life and Times of the Last Gaucho. Caudillos.* Albuquerque: University of New Mexico Press, 1995.

Chauvel, Richard. *Nationalists, Soldiers and Separatists: The Ambonese Islands from Colonialism to Revolt, 1880–1950.* Leiden, Netherlands: Brill, 2008.

Chebabi, H. E. "Iran and Lebanon in the Revolutionary Decade." In *Distant Relations: Iran and Lebanon in the Last 500 Years,* edited by H. E. Chebabi and Rula Abasaab, 201–30. London: I. B. Tauris, 2006.

Cheeseboro, Anthony Q. "Sudan: Slavery and Civil War." In *History Behind the Headlines: The Origins of Conflicts Worldwide,* vol. 1, edited by Sonia G. Benson, Nancy Matuszak, and Meghan Appel O'Meara. Detroit, MI: Gale Group, 2001.

Chelala, César. "Sudan: A War against the People." *The Lancet* 359, no. 9301 (2002, January 12): 162–63.

Chen, Jack. *The Sinkiang Story.* New York: MacMillan Publishing Co., 1977.

Ch'en, Jerome. "Defining Chinese Warlords and Their Factions." *Bulletin of the School of Oriental and African Studies, University of London* 31, no. 3 (1968): 563–600.

______. *The Military-Gentry Coalition: China under the Warlords.* Downsview, Ontario: University of Toronto–York University Joint Centre on Modern East Asia, 1979.

______. *Yuan Shi-K'ai.* 2nd ed. Stanford, CA: Stanford University Press, 1972.

Chen, Leslie H. Dingyan. *Chen Jiongming and the Federalist Movement: Regional Leadership and Nation Building in Early Republican China.* Ann Arbor: University of Michigan Center of Chinese Studies, 1999.

Cheng, Peter. *A Chronology of the People's Republic of China.* Totowa, NJ: Rowman & Littlefield, 1972.

Chesneaux, Jean, Marianne Bastid, and Marie-Claire Bergère. *China from the Opium Wars to the 1911 Revolution.* Translated by Anne Destenay. New York: Pantheon Books, 1976.

Chew, Lee Kim. "'Harsh' Govt Helps Rebels Win Hearts." *Straits Times*, October 26, 2000.

______. "More Troops Won't Solve Aceh Problem." *Straits Times*, March 22, 2001.

Chi, Hsi-hseng. *The Chinese Warlord System: 1916 to 1928.* Washington, DC: American University Center for Research in Social Systems, 1969.

Ch'i, Hsi-Sheng. *Warlord Politics in China, 1916–1928.* Stanford, CA: Stanford University Press, 1976.

Chiang Siang-Tseh. *The Nien Rebellion.* Seattle: University of Washington Press, 1954.

Chicago Tribune. Multiple articles, 2006–2014.

Chien-Nung, Li. *The Political History of China, 1840–1928.* Translated by Ssu-Yu Teng and Jeremy Ingalls. Princeton, NJ: D. Van Nostrand Co., 1956.

Chilcote, Ronald H., ed. *Protest and Resistance in Angola and Brazil.* Berkley: University of California Press, 1972.

Chima, Judgep S. *The Sikh Separatist Insurgency in India: Political Leadership and Ethnonationalist Movements.* Los Angeles, CA: Sage, 2010.

______. "Why Some Ethnic Insurgencies Decline: Political Parties and Social Cleavages in Punjab and Northern Ireland Compared." *The Journal of Commonwealth & Comparative Politics* 35, no. 3 (1997): 1–26.

"China Reports on Fretilin." *The Canberra Times*, April 25, 1977, 5.

"Chinese Position." *The Straits Times*, April 22, 1926, 9.

Ching, Erik, and Virginia Tilley. "Indians, the Military and the Rebellion of 1932 in El Salvador." *Journal of Latin American Studies* 30 (1998): 121–56.

Chomsky, Noam. *At War with Asia.* London: Fontana, 1971.

______. "East Timor: The Press Coverup." *Inquiry* (1979, February 14): 16–20.

Christgau, John. *Birch Coulie, The Epic Battle of the Dakota War.* Lincoln: University of Nebraska Press, 2012.

Christia, Fotini. *Alliance Formation in Civil Wars.* New York: Cambridge University Press, 2012.

Christopher, James William. *Conflict in the Far East.* Leiden, Netherlands: Brill, 1950.

Chronicle of the 20th Century. Mount Kisco, NY: Chronicle Publications, 1987.

"Chronology of the Peasant War." *Korea Journal* (Winter 1994): 125–26.

Chu, Wen-Chang (Wen-Djang Chu). *The Moslem Rebellion in Northwest China 1862–1878.* Paris, France: Mouton and Co., 1966.

Chu, Wen-Djang. "The Moslem Rebellion in Northwest China, 1862–1878." *Central Asiatic Studies* 5 (1966).

Churchill, Charles Henry. *The Druzes and the Maronites under the Turkish Rule from 1840 to 1860.* London: Berbard Quaritch, 1862.

"CIA Says IS Numbers Underestimated." *Al Jazeera*, September 12, 2014. http://www.aljazeera.com/news/middleeast/2014/09/cia-triples-number-islamic-state-fighters-201491232912623733.html.

Ciccarelli, Orazio A. *Militarism, Aprismo, and Violence in Peru: The Presidential Election of 1931.* Buffalo: Council on International Studies, State University of New York at Buffalo, 1973.

Cimbala, Stephen J., and Peter K. Forster. *Multinational Military Intervention: NATO Policy Strategy and Burden Sharing.* Burlington, VT: Ashgate Publishing, 2010.

Ciment, James. *Algeria: The Fundamentalist Challenge.* New York: Facts on File, 1997.

______. "Angola: First War with UNITA, 1975–1992." In *Encyclopedia of Conflicts since World War II*, vol. 1, edited by James Ciment, 86–92. Armonk, NY: Sharpe Reference, 2007a.

______. "Angola: Second War with Unita, 1992–2002." In *Encyclopedia of Conflicts since World War II*, vol. 1, edited by James Ciment, 93–6. Armonk, NY: Sharpe Reference, 2007f.

______. "Congo, Democratic Republic of: Invasions and Internal Strife, 1998–." In *Encyclopedia of Conflicts since World War II*, vol. 1, edited by James Ciment, 142–46. Armonk, NY: Sharpe Reference, 2007e.

______. "Congo, Democratic Republic of: Kabila Uprising, 1996–1997." In *Encyclopedia of Conflicts since World War II*, vol. 1, edited by James Ciment, 136–41. Armonk, NY: Sharpe Reference, 2007d.

______. "Congo, Republic of: Civil Conflict, 1997." In *Encyclopedia of Conflicts since World War II*, vol. 1, edited by James Ciment, 147–51. Armonk, NY: Sharpe Reference, 2007c.

______, ed. *Encyclopedia of Conflicts since World War II*. 2nd ed. Vols. 1–4. Armonk, NY: Sharpe Reference, 2007g.

______. "Liberia: Anti-Taylor Uprising, 1998–2003." In *Encyclopedia of Conflicts since World War II*, vol. 1, edited by James Ciment. Armonk, NY: Sharpe Reference, 2007f: 208–11.

______. "Liberia: Civil War, 1989–1997." In *Encyclopedia of Conflicts since World War II*, vol. 1, edited by James Ciment, 202–7. Armonk, NY: Sharpe Reference, 2007b.

Ciment, James, and Daniel F. Cuthbertson. "Sierra Leone: Civil Conflict, 1990–Present." In *Encyclopedia of Conflicts since World War II*, vol. 1, edited by James Ciment, 269–73. Armonk, NY: Sharpe Reference, 2007.

Ciment, James, and Luke Nichter. "Uganda: Civil Conflict since 1980." In *Encyclopedia of Conflicts since World War II*, vol. 1, edited by James Ciment, 315–18. Armonk, NY: Sharpe Reference, 2007.

Ciment, James, and Emin Poljarevic. "Somalia: Civil War since 1991." In *Encyclopedia of Conflicts since World War II*, vol. 1, edited by James Ciment, 274–81. Armonk, NY: Sharpe Reference, 2007.

Ciment, James, and Erika Quinn. "Rwanda: Civil War and Genocide since 1991." In *Encyclopedia of Conflicts since World War II*, vol. 1, edited by James Ciment, 258–68. Armonk, NY: Sharpe Reference, 2007.

Ciment, James, and Julian Schofield. "Nigeria: Coups and Ethnic Unrest since 1966." In *Encyclopedia of Conflicts since World War II*, vol. 1, edited by James Ciment, 251–57. Armonk, NY: Sharpe Reference, 2007.

Cioffi-Revilla, Claudio. "Ancient Warfare: Origins and Systems." In *Handbook of War Studies II*, edited by Manus Midlarsky, 59–89. Ann Arbor: University of Michigan Press, 2000.

______. "The Long-Range Analysis of War." *The Journal of Interdisciplinary History* 21, no. 4 (Spring 1991): 603–29.

______. *The Scientific Measurement of International Conflict*. Boulder, CO: Lynne Rienner, 1990.

Clark, A. Kim. *The Redemptive Work: Railway and Nation in Ecuador, 1895–1930*. Wilmington, DE: Scholarly Resources Inc., 1998.

Clark, Peter. "The Maitatsine Movement in Northern Nigeria in Historical and Current Perspective." In *New Religious Movements in Nigeria*, edited by Rosalind I. J. Hackett. Lewiston, NY: Edwin Mellen Press, 1987.

Clarke, Henry Butler. *Modern Spain, 1815–1898*. Cambridge, UK: Cambridge University Press, 1906.

Clausewitz, Carl Von. *On War*. Translated by Michael Howard and Peter Paret. New York: Alfred A. Knopf, 1993. Originally published 1832.

Clayton, Anthony. *Frontiersmen: Warfare in Africa since 1950*. London: UCL Press, 1999.

Clayton, Govinda. "Quantitative and Econometric Methodologies." In *The Routledge Handbook of Civil Wars*, edited by Edward Newman and Karl DeRouen, Jr., 28–40. London: Routledge, 2014.

Clement, E. W. 1891. "The Mito Civil War." In *Transactions of the Asiatic Society of Japan*. Vol. XIX, 393–419. Tokyo: The Hakubunsha.

Clements, Frank. *Conflict in Afghanistan: A Historical Encyclopedia*. Santa Barbara, CA: ABC–CLIO, 2003.

Clendenen, Clarence C. "Tribalism and Humanitarianism: The Nigerian-Biafran Civil War." In *Civil Wars in the Twentieth Century*, edited by Robin Higham. Lexington: University Press of Kentucky, 1972.

Clessold, Stephen, ed. *A Short History of Yugoslavia*. Cambridge, UK: Cambridge University Press, 1966.

Cleveland, William L. *A History of the Modern Middle East*. Boulder, CO: Westview Press, 1994.

Cline, Lawrence. "The Islamic Insurgency in the Philippines." *Small Wars & Insurgencies* 11, no. 3 (2000): 115–38.

______. *The Lord's Resistance Army*. Santa Barbara, CA: Praeger, 2013.

______. "Spirits and the Cross: Religiously Based Violent Movements in Uganda." *Small Wars and Insurgencies* 14, no. 2 (Summer 2003): 113–30.

Clodfelter, Micheal. *The Dakota War, the United States Army versus the Sioux, 1862–1865*. Jefferson, NC: McFarland & Company, Inc., 1998.

______. *Warfare and Armed Conflicts: A Statistical Encyclopedia of Casualty and Other Figures, 1494–2007*. 3rd ed. Jefferson, NC: McFarland, 2008.

______. *Warfare and Armed Conflicts: A Statistical Reference to Casualty and Other Figures, 1500–2000*. 2nd ed. Jefferson, NC: McFarland and Co., 2001.

______. *Warfare and Armed Conflicts: A Statistical Reference to Casualty and Other Figures, 1618–1991*. Vols. I and II. Jefferson, NC: McFarland and Co., 1991.

Close, David H. "The Changing Structure of the Right, 1945–1950." In *Greece at the Crossroads, the Civil War and Its Legacy*, edited by John O. Iatrides and Linda Wrigley. University Park: The Pennsylvania State University Press, 1995.

Close, David H., and Thanos Veremis. "The Military Struggle, 1945–9." In *The Greek Civil War, 1943–1950*, edited by David H. Close. New York: Routledge, 1993.

Cloud, David S. "US Airstrike Aims at Qaeda Cell in Somalia." *New York Times*, January 9, 2007. http://www.nytimes.com.

Cloughley, Brian. *A History of the Pakistan Army: Wars and Insurrections*. 2nd ed. New York: Oxford Press, 2000.

Clubb, O. Edmund. *20th Century China*. 2nd ed. New York: Columbia University Press, 1972.

______. "Manchuria in the Balance, 1945–1946." *Pacific Historical Review* 26, no. 4 (1957): 377–89.

______. *Twentieth Century China*. New York: Columbia University Press, 1964.

CNN. "In-Depth Specials—Focus on Kosovo—A Timeline of Tensions." 1998. http://www.cnn.com/SPECIALS/1998/10/kosovo/timeline.

______. "KLA Goes from Splinter Group to Potential Giant-Killer." 1999. http://www.cnn.com/WORLD/europe/9903/24/kla.history.

Coatsworth, John H. "Patterns of Rural Rebellion in Latin America: Mexico in Comparative Perspective." In *Riot, Rebellion, and Revolution, Rural Social Conflict in Mexico*, edited by Friedrich Katz. Princeton, NJ: Princeton University Press, 1988.

Coghlan, Benjamin, Valeria Nkamgang Bemo, Pascal Ngoy, Tony Stewart, Flavien Mulumba, Jennifer Lewis, Colleen Hardy, and Richard Brennan. *Mortality in the Democratic Republic of Congo, an Ongoing Crisis*. New York: International Rescue Committee, 2004.

Colaresi, Michael P., Karen Rasler, and William Thompson. *Strategic Rivalries in World Politics: Position, Space and Conflict Escalation*. New York: Cambridge University Press, 2007.

Cole, Juan I. R., and Moojah Momen. "Mafia, Mob, and Shiism in Iraq: The Rebellion of Ottoman Karbala 1824–1843." *Past & Present* 112 (August 1986): 112–43.

Collier, Paul, V. L. Elliott, Havard Hegre, Anke Hoeffler, Marta Reynal-Querol, and Nicholas Sambanis. *Breaking the Conflict Trap, Civil War and Development Policy*. Washington, DC: World Bank and Oxford University Press, 2003.

Collier, Simon. *Chile: The Making of a Republic, 1830–1865*. Cambridge, UK: Cambridge University Press, 2003.

Collier, Simon, and William F. Sater. *A History of Chile, 1808–1994*. Cambridge, UK: Cambridge University Press, 1996.

______. *The History of Chile, 1808–2002*. 2nd ed. Cambridge, UK: Cambridge University Press, 2004.

Collins, Charles D., Jr. *Atlas of the Sioux Wars*. 2nd ed. Fort Leavenworth, KS: Combat Studies Institute Press, 2006.

Collins, Robert O. "Africans, Arabs, and Islamists: From the Conference Tables to the Battlefields in the Sudan." *African Studies Review* 42, no. 2 (September 1999): 105–23.

______. *A History of Modern Sudan*. Cambridge, UK: Cambridge University Press, 2008.

______. *The Southern Sudan in Historical Perspective*. Tel Aviv, Israel: University of Tel Aviv Students Association, 1975.

"Colombia." In *The American Cyclopaedia*. Vol. 5, 2nd rev. ed. New York: D. Appleton and Co., 1879.

"Colombia ELN Rebels Edge Toward Peace Process." *Colombia Report*. November 12, 2012. http://colombiareports.com/colombia-news/peace-talks/26956-colombia-eln-rebels-edge-toward-peace-process.html.

"Colombia Tries Again to End Drug-Fed War." *New York Times*, October 18, 2012, 1.

The Columbia Encyclopedia. 5th ed. New York: Columbia University Press, 1993.

Comisão Executiva Central do Sesquicentenário sa Indepenêndencia do Brasil. *História do Exército Brasilieiro*. Vol. 2. Rio de Janeiro, Brazil: Edicão do Estado-Majoe do Exército, 1972.

"Communist Influence in Indonesia." *Morning Bulletin (Rockhampton, Australia)*, July 1, 1954, 11.

Conboy, Kenneth. *Shadow War: The CIA's Secret War in Laos*. Boulder, CO: Lynne Rienner, 1995.

______. *The War in Laos, 1960–75*. London: Osprey 1989.

Conciliation Resources. "Mozambican Peace Process in Perspective." *Accord, an International Review of Peace Initiatives* 3 (1998). http://www.c-r.org.

Conde, Carlos H. "Philippines Again Declares 'All-Out War' against Rebels." *International Herald Tribune*, June 20, 2006, 3. InfoTrac Newsstand, EBSCOhost.

"The Congo: Death of a Rebel." *Time*, October 18, 1968. http://content.time.com/time.

Congressional Quarterly. *The Middle East*. 8th ed. Washington, DC: Congressional Quarterly, 1994.

Congressional Research Service. "Kosovo: US and Allied Military Operations." Washington, DC: Library of Congress, 2000.

______. "Kosovo Conflict Chronology: January–August 1998." Washington, DC: Library of Congress, 1998.

Conquest, Robert. *The Harvest of Sorrow.* Oxford: Oxford University Press, 1987.

Contreras, E. Lopez. *Paginas Para la Historia Militar de Venezuela.* Caracas, Venezuela: Tipografia Americana, 1944.

Cook, C. P. "The Era of Ne Win." *The World Today* 26, no. 6 (1970): 259–66.

Cooke, James J. "Lyautey and Etienne: The Soldier and the Politician in the Penetration of Morocco, 1904–1906." *Military Affairs* 36, no. 1 (February 1972): 14–8.

Cooney, Daniel. "Indonesia and Rebels Agree to a Cease-Fire." *Contra Costa Times (California)*, May 13, 2000.

Cooper, Chester. *The Lost Crusade.* New York: Dodd, Mead, 1970.

Cooper, John. "Yemen: Brutal End to a Bitter Dispute." *Middle East Economic Digest*, December 23, 1994.

Cordesman, Anthony H. *After the Storm: The Changing Military Balance in the Middle East.* Boulder, CO: Westview Press, 1993a.

______. *Bahrain, Oman, Qatar, and the UAE: Challenges of Security.* Boulder, CO: Westview Press, 1997.

______. *The Lessons of Modern War Volume III: The Afghan and Falklands Conflicts.* Boulder, CO: Westview, 1990b.

______. *The Military Balance and Arms Sales in Yemen and the Red Sea States: 1986–1992.* Washington, DC: Center for Strategic and International Studies, 1993b.

______. *A Tragedy of Arms: Military and Security Developments in the Maghreb.* Westport, CT: Praeger, 2004.

Cornell, Svante E. *Small Nations and Great Powers: A Study of Ethnopolitical Conflict in the Caucasus.* Surrey, UK: Curzon Press, 2001.

Correia de Andrade, Manuel. "The Social and Ethical Significance of the War of the Cabanos." In *Protest and Resistance in Angola and Brazil*, edited by Ronald H. Chilcote, 91–107. Berkeley: University of California Press.

Correlates of War Project. *National Material Capabilities Dataset.* Version 3.02. 2009. http://cow.la.psu.edu/Datasets.htm.

______. *National Material Capabilities Dataset.* Version 4.0. 2010. http://cow.la.psu.edu/Datasets.htm.

Cortés, Carlos E. "Armed Politics in the Rio Grande do Sul." In *Perspectives on Armed Politics in Brazil*, edited by Henry H. Keith and Robert A. Hayes, 113–38. Tempe: Arizona State University, 1976.

______. *Gaúcho Politics in Brazil: The Politics of Rio Grande do Sul, 1930–1964.* Albuquerque: University of New Mexico Press, 1974.

Corum, James S. "Guatemala's Protracted War—The Role of the Guatemalan Air Force." *Air & Space Power Journal (Español).* Terce Trimestre (2004). http://www.airpower.au.af.mil/apjinternational/apj-s/2004/3trimes04/corumeng.htm.

Costello, Patrick. "Guatemala: Historical Background." *Accord* (2002).

Costeloe, Michael P. "The Triangular Revolt in Mexico and the Fall of Anastasio Bustamante, August–October 1841." *Journal of Latin American Studies* 20, no. 2 (November 1988): 337–60.

"Country Profile: Guatemala." *BBC News: Americas*, July 20, 2002. http://news/bbc.co.uk/1/hi/world/americas/country_profiles/1215758.stm.

Cousin, Tracey L. "Eritrean and Ethiopian Civil War." In *ICE Case Studies.* Washington, DC: American University, November 1997.

Coverdale, John F. *Italian Intervention in the Spanish Civil War.* Princeton, NJ: Princeton University Press, 1975.

Cowell, Alan. "War Deaths in Syria Said to Top 100,000." *New York Times (Late ed.)*, June 27, 2013, 6.

Coyle, James John. "Nationalism in Iranian Kurdistan." PhD diss., George Washington University, 1993.

Craig, Albert M. *Chōshū in the Meiji Restoration.* Cambridge, MA: Harvard University Press, 1961.

Crain, David A. "Guatemalan Revolutionaries and Havana's Ideological Offensive of 1966–1968." *Journal of Interamerican Studies and World Affairs* 17, no. 2 (May 1975): 175–205.

Crampton, R. J. *Eastern Europe in the Twentieth Century and After.* 2nd ed. London: Routledge, 1997.

______. *A Short History of Modern Bulgaria.* Cambridge, UK: Cambridge University Press, 1987.

Crandall, Russell. "Requiem for the FARC?" *Survival: Global Politics and Strategy* 53, no. 4 (2011): 233–40.

Crassweller, Robert D. *Perón and the Enigmas of Argentina.* New York: W. W. Norton, 1987.

Crawley, Charles William. *The Question of Greek Independence.* Cambridge, UK: Cambridge University Press, 1930.

______. *The Question of Greek Independence.* New York: Howard Fertig, 1973.

Creasy, Edward S. *History of the Ottoman Turks. Beirut:* Khayats, 1961. Originally published 1878.

Cribb, Robert. "Nation: Making Indonesia." In *Indonesia Beyond Suharto: Polity, Economy, Society, Transition*, edited by Donald K. Emmerson. Armonk, NY: M. E. Sharpe, 1999.

Crichfield, George Washington. *American Supremacy: The Rise and Progress of the Latin American Republics and Their Relations to the United States under the Monroe Doctrine.* New York: Brentano's, 1908.

Crocker, Chester A., Fen Osler Hampson, and Pamela Aall, eds. *Grasping the Nettle: Analyzing Cases of Intractable Conflict.* Washington, DC: United States Institute of Peace Press, 2005.

Croissant, Michael P. *The Armenia–Azerbaijan Conflict: Causes and Implications.* Westport, CT: Praeger, 1998.

Cronin, Stephanie. *The Army and the Creation of the Pahlavi State in Iran, 1910–1926.* New York: Tauris Academic Studies, 1997.

Crossette, Barbara. "War Adds 1.7 Million Deaths in Eastern Congo, Study Finds." *New York Times*, June 9, 2000. http://www.nytimes.com.

Crow, John A. *The Epic of Latin America.* Garden City, NY: Doubleday, 1971.

Cumberland, Charles C. *The Mexican Revolution: The Constitutionalist Years.* Austin: University of Texas Press, 1972.

______. *Mexico: The Struggle for Modernity.* New York: Oxford University Press, 1968.

Cummins, Joseph. *The War Chronicles: From Flintlocks to Machine Guns.* Beverly, MA: Fair Winds Press, 2009.

______. *Why Some Wars Never End: The Stories of the Longest Conflicts in History.* Beverly, MA: Fair Winds, 2010.

Cunha, Euclides Da. *Rebellion in the Backlands (Os Sertoes).* Chicago, IL: University of Chicago Press, 1944.

Curtis, Glenn E. *Kazakstan, Kyrgyzstan, Tajikistan, Turkmenistan, and Uzbekistan: Country Studies.* Washington, DC: Library of Congress, 1997.

Curtiss, John Shelton. *The Russian Army under Nicholas I.* Durham, NC: Duke University Press, 1965.

Cushman, John R., Jr. "The Endless Battle, Iraq, the Kurds and the United States." *New York Times*, September 4, 1996.

Cutter, Charles H. *Africa.* 42nd ed. Harpers Ferry, WV: Stryker-Post Publications, 2007.

Daalder, Ivo H., and Michael E. O'Hanlon. *Winning Ugly; NATO's War to Save Kosovo.* Washington, DC: Brookings Institution Press, 2000.

Dadrian, Vahakn N. *The History of the Armenian Genocide: Ethnic Conflict from the Balkans to Anatolia to the Caucasus.* 4th rev. ed. Oxford, NY: Berghan Books, 2004.

Dagmar-Hellmann, Rajanayagam. "The 'Groups' and the Rise of Militant Secessionism." In *The Sri Lankan Tamils: Ethnicity and Identity*, edited by Chelvadurai Manogaran and Bryan Pfaffenberger, 169–207. Boulder, CO: Westview Press, 1994.

Dakin, Douglas. *The Greek Struggle for Independence 1821–1833.* Berkeley: University of California Press, 1973.

______. *The Greek Struggle in Macedonia, 1897–1913.* Thessaloniki, Greece: Institute for Balkan Studies, 1966.

______. *The Unification of Greece 1770–1923.* New York: St. Martin's Press, 1972.

Dallas Morning News. "Revolution in Honduras Breaks Anew." August 8, 1924, 1.

Daneshvar, Parviz. *Revolution in Iran.* New York: St. Martin's, 1996.

Dann, Uriel. *Iraq under Qassem: A Political History, 1958–1963.* New York: Praeger, 1969.

DaPonte, Beth Osborne. "A Case Study in Estimating Casualties from War and Its Aftermath: The 1991 Persian Gulf War." *The PSR Quarterly* 3, no. 2 (1993): 57–66.

Darlow, Michael, and Barbara Bray. *Ibn Saud: The Desert Warrior Who Created the Kingdom of Saudi Arabia.* New York: Skyhorse Publishing, 2012.

Das Gupta, J. B. *Islamic Fundamentalism and India.* Kolkata, India: Maulana Abdul Kalam Azad Institute of Asian Studies, 2002.

Dasgupta, Biplab. "The Naxalite Movement: An Epilogue." *Social Scientist* 6, no. 12 (1978): 3–24.

Dau, Butros. *History of the Maronites: Religious, Cultural, and Political.* Lebanon: Butros Dau, 1984.

Davenport, Richard A. *The Life of Ali Pasha of Tepebni, Vizier of Epirus.* London: Thomas Tegg and Son, 1837.

Davis, Anthony. "How the Taliban Became a Military Force." In *Fundamentalism Reborn? Afghanistan and the Taliban*, rev. ed., edited by William Maley, 43–71. Washington Square: New York University Press, 2001.

Davis, H. P. *Black Democracy, the Story of Haiti.* New York: Biblo and Tannen, 1967.

Davis, Harold F. *History of Latin America.* New York: Ronald Press, 1968.

Davis, John A. *Naples and Napoleon: Southern Italy and the European Revolutions (1780–1860).* New York: Oxford University Press, 2006.

Davis, Paul K. *Encyclopedia of Invasions and Conquests from Ancient Times to the Present.* Millerton, NY: Grey House, 2006.

Davis, William C. *Lone Star Rising: The Revolutionary Birth of the Texas Republic.* New York: Free Press, 2004.

Dawisha, Karen. *Conflict, Cleavage and Change in Central Asia and the Caucasus.* Cambridge, UK: Cambridge University Press, 1997.

Dawson, Thomas Cleland. *The South American Republics.* 2 vols. New York: Knickerbocker Press (G. P. Putnam's Sons), 1903.

"The Day the Katiba Fell." *Al Jazeera English*, March 1, 2011. http://english.aljazeera.net/indepth/spotlight/libya/2011/03/2011317584018962O.html.

De Beauchamp, Alph. *The Life of Ali Pacha, of Jannina.* 2nd ed. London: S. and R. Bentley, 1823.

de la Fuente, Ariel. "Federalism and Opposition to the Paraguayan War in the Argentine Interior." In *I Die with My Country: Perspectives on the Paraguayan War, 1864–1870*, edited by Hendrik Kraay and Thomas L. Whigham, 140–53. Lincoln: University of Nebraska Press, 2004.

De La Peña, Guillermo. "Rural Mobilizations in Latin America since c. 1920." In *The Cambridge History of Latin America*, vol. VI, part 2, edited by Leslie Bethell, 379–482. Cambridge, UK: Cambridge University Press, 1994.

de Mesa, Jose, Teresa Gisbert, and Carlos D. Mesa Gisbert. *Historia de Bolivia.* 4th ed. La Paz, Bolivia: Editorial Gisbert y Cia S. A., 2001.

de Silva, K. M. *Reaping the Whirlwind: Ethnic Conflict, Ethnic Politics in Sri Lanka.* New Delhi: Penguin Books India, 1998.

de Waal, Alex. "The Politics of Destabilization in the Horn, 1989–2001." In *Islamism and Its Enemies in the Horn of Africa*, edited by Alex de Waal, 182–230. Bloomington: Indiana University Press, 2004.

Deac, Wilfred P. *Road to the Killing Fields: The Cambodian War of 1970–75.* College Station: Texas A&M University Press, 1997.

Deans, William. *History of the Ottoman Empire.* London: A. Fullerton, 1854.

DeAtkine, Norvell B. "The Arab as Insurgent and Counterinsurgent." In *Conflict and Insurgency in the Contemporary Middle East*, edited by Barry M. Rubin, 24–45. New York: Taylor & Francis, 2009.

DeFronzo, James. *Revolutions and Revolutionary Movements.* Boulder, CO: Westview Press, 1996.

Degenhardt, Henry W., ed. *Revolutionary and Dissident Movements: An International Guide.* UK: Longman Group, 1987.

DeGeorge, Barbara. "Liberia in Civil War: Haven for Freed Slaves Reduced to Anarchy." In *History Behind the Headlines: The Origins of Conflicts Worldwide*, vol. 1, edited by Sonia G. Benson, Nancy Matuszak, and Meghan Appel O'Meara. Detroit, MI: Gale Group, 2001.

Delpar, Helen. "Aspects of Liberal Factionalism in Colombia, 1875–1885." *The Hispanic American Historical Review* 51, no. 2 (1971): 250–74.

Delupis, Ingrid Detter. *The Law of War.* 2nd ed. Cambridge, UK: University of Cambridge Press, 2000.

Demarest, Geoffrey. "War of the Thousand Days." *Small Wars and Insurgencies* 12, no. 1 (Spring 2001): 1–30.

Demetriou, Spyros. "Rising from the Ashes? The Difficult (Re)Birth of the Georgian State." *Development and Change* 33, no. 5 (2002): 859–83.

"Denial by Indonesia." *The Canberra Times*, November 2, 1977, 11.

Deol, Harnik. *Religion and Nationalism in India: The Case of the Punjab.* London: Routledge, 2000.

DePalo, William A., Jr. *The Mexican National Army, 1822–1852.* College Station: Texas A&M University Press, 1997.

Deployment Health Clinical Center. "Operation Allied Force." 2006. http://www.pdhealth,mil/508/deployments/alliedforce/background.asp.

DeRouen, Karl, and Uk Heo. *Civil Wars of the World.* Vols. 1 and 2. Santa Barbara, CA: ABC–CLIO, 2007.

DeSilva-Ranasinghe, Sergei. "Strategic Analysis of Sri Lankan Military's Counter-Insurgency Operations." *Future Directions International*, February, 12, 2010. http://www.futuredirections.org.au/files/1266992558-FDIStrategicAnalysisPaper-12February2010.pdf.

Destani, B. *Minorities in the Middle East: Druze Communities 1840–1974.* Vol. 3. London: Archive Editions, 2006.

Detter, Ingrid. *The Law of War.* New York: Cambridge University Press, 2000.

Deutsch, Karl W. "Quincy Wright's Contribution to the Study of War, a Preface to the Second Edition." In *A Study of War*, 2nd ed., by Quincy Wright. Chicago, IL: University of Chicago Press, 1965.

Dhillon, K. S. "A Decade of Violence, 1983–92." In *Punjab in Prosperity and Violence: Administration, Politics, and Social Change, 1947–1997*, edited by J. S. Grewal and Indu Banga. Chandigarh, India: Institute of Punjab Studies, 1998.

Dhiravegin, Likhit. *Demi Democracy: The Evolution of the Thai Political System.* Singapore: Times Academic Press, 1992.

Diacon, Todd A. *Millenarian Vision, Capitalist Rebellion: Brazil's Contestado Rebellion, 1912–1916.* Durham, NC: Duke University Press, 1991.

Digital National Security Archive. Chronology: Results from January 1, 1979, to December 31, 1994. (Collections: El Salvador 1977–1984; El Salvador 1980–1994.)

______. Chronology: Results from January 1, 1980, to December 31, 1996. (Collection: Guatemala and the United States.)

Dikötter, Frank. *The Tragedy of Liberation: A History of the Chinese Revolution 1945–1957.* New York: Bloomsbury Press, 2013.

Dilebo, Getahun. "Emperor Menelik's Ethiopia, 1865–1916: National Unification or Amhara Communal Domination." PhD diss., Howard University, Department of History, 1974.

Dillon, Michael. *China's Muslim Hui Community: Migration, Settlement, and Sects.* Sydney, Australia: Curzon Press, 1999.

Dillon, Paul. "Strategy of Provocation That Keeps Aceh's War in Public Eye." *The Scotsman*, May 17, 2001.

Dingle, Edwin J. *China's Revolution*. New York: McBride, Nast and Company, 1912.

Dinstein, Yoram. *War, Aggression, and Self-Defence*. 4th ed. New York: Cambridge University Press, 2005.

Dirlik, Arif. "The Guangzhou Uprising (11–13 December 1927) in Workers' Perspective." *Modern China* 23, no. 4 (1997): 363–97.

Dix, Robert H. *The Politics of Colombia*. New York: Praeger Publishers, 1987.

Dixon, J. "Suggested Changes to the COW Civil War Dataset 3.0." Paper presented at the annual meeting of the International Studies Association, Portland, Oregon, February 25–March 1, 2003.

______. "What Causes Civil Wars? Integrating Quantitative Research Findings." *International Studies Review* 11, no. 4 (2009): 707–35.

Dixon, Jeffrey, and Meredith Reid Sarkees. "Intervention, Recognition, and War Transformation: A Consistent Standard for Distinguishing Inter-state, Extra-state, and Intra-state Wars." Paper presented at the annual meeting of the International Studies Association, Honolulu Hawaii, March 1–5, 2005.

Djilas, Milovan. *Wartime*. New York: Harcourt, 1977.

Djordjevic, Dimitrije, and Stephen Fischer-Galati. *The Balkan Revolutionary Tradition*. New York: Columbia University Press, 1981.

Dodwell, Henry. *The Founder of Modern Egypt: A Study of Muhammad Ali*. Cambridge, UK: Cambridge University, 1931.

Donia, Robert, and John Fine. *Bosnia and Hercegovina*. New York: Columbia University Press, 1994.

Donnison, Frank S. V. *Burma*. New York: Praeger, 1970.

Dontas, D. N. *Greece and the Great Powers*. Thessaloniki, Greece: Institute for Balkan Studies, 1966.

Dorril, William F. "The Fukien Rebellion and the CCP: A Case of Maoist Revisionism." *China Quarterly* 37, no. 1 (1969): 31–53.

Dorronsoro, Gilles. *Revolution Unending, Afghanistan: 1979 to the Present*. New York: Columbia University Press, 2005.

Dougherty, Carter. "Burundi Inching Closer to Ending Long Civil War." *World and I* 19, no. 11 (November 2004).

Douglas, J. Leigh. *The Free Yemeni Movement 1935–1962*. Beirut: American University of Beirut, 1987.

Dougueli, Georges. "Chad: Habré and the Ghost of Hassan Djamous." *Jeune Afrique*, April 25, 2014.

Doyle, Kate. "The Final Battle: Ríos Montt's Counterinsurgency Campaign." *National Security Archive, Electronic Briefing Book No. 425*. May 9, 2013. http://www2.gwu.edu/~nsarchiv/NSAEBB/NSAEBB425.

______. "Operation Sofia: Documenting Genocide in Guatemala." *National Security Archive Electronic Briefing Book No. 297*. December 2, 2009. http://www2.gwu.edu/~nsarchiv/NSAEBB/NSAEBB297/index.htm.

Doyle, Kate, and Carlos Osario. "US Policy in Guatemala, 1966–1996." *National Security Archive Electronic Briefing Book No. 11*. n.d. http://www.nsarchiv.gwu.edu.

Dresch, Paul. *A History of Modern Yemen*. Cambridge, UK: Cambridge University Press, 2000.

Dreyer, Edward L. *China at War: 1901–1949*. New York: Longman, 1995.

DronesTeam. "Somalia: Reported US Covert Actions 2001–2015." *The Bureau of Investigative Journalism*, February 22, 2012. http://www.thebureauinvestigates.com/2012/02/22.

Droz, Jacques. *Les Revolutions Allmandes de 1848*. Paris, France: Presses Universitaires de France, 1957.

Duarte, Maria Amalia. *Tiempos de Rebellion: 1870–1873*. Bueno Aires, Argentina: Academia Nacional de la Historia, 1988.

Dubois, Jules. *Fidel Castro: Rebel–Liberator or Dictator?* Indianapolis, IN: Bobbs-Merrill, 1959.

Duggan, Christopher. *The Force of Destiny: A History of Italy since 1796*. Boston, MA: Houghton Mifflin Company, 2008.

Duke, Simon, Hans-Georg Ehrhart, and Matthias Karadi. "The Major European Allies: France, Germany and the United Kingdom." In *Kosovo and the Challenges of Humanitarian Intervention*, edited by Albrecht Schnabel and Ramesh Thakur. New York: United Nations University Press, 2000.

Dulles, John W. F. *Yesterday in Mexico: A Chronicle of the Revolution, 1919–1936*. Austin: University of Texas Press, 1961.

Dumas, Samuel, and Knud Otto Vedel-Peterson. *Losses of Life Caused by War*. London: Oxford University Press, 1923.

Dumond, Don E. *The Machete and the Cross, Campesino Rebellion in Yucatan*. Lincoln: University of Nebraska Press, 1997.

Dumont, Jean, ed. *Les Coups d'État*. Paris: Hachette, 1963.

Dunér, Bertil. *Military Intervention in Civil Wars: The 1970s*. London: Gower Publishing Co., 1985.

Dunkerley, James. *Rebellion in the Veins: Political Struggle in Bolivia, 1952–82*. London: Verso Editions, 1984.

Dunn, Kevin C. "Uganda: The Lord's Resistance Army." In *African Guerrillas: Raging against the Machine*, edited by Morten BpÅs and Kevin C. Dunn. Boulder, CO: Lynne Rienner, 2007.

Dunn, Ross E. "The Bu Himara Rebellion in Northeast Morocco: Phase I." *Middle Eastern Studies* 17, no. 1 (1981): 31–48.

______. *Resistance in the Desert: Moroccan Responses to French Imperialism, 1881–1912.* Madison: University of Wisconsin Press, 1977.

Dupuy, R. Ernest, and Trevor N. Dupuy. *The Encyclopedia of Military History from 3500 B.C. to the Present.* New York: Harper and Row, 1970.

______. *The Harper Encyclopedia of Military History from 3500 B.C. to the Present.* 4th ed. New York: HarperCollins, 1993.

Dupuy, Trevor N. *Attrition: Forecasting Battle Casualties and Equipment Losses in Modern War.* Fairfax, VA: Hero Books, 1990.

Durham, Mike. *Buddha's Warriors: The Story of the CIA-Backed Tibetan Freedom Fighters, the Chinese Invasion, and the Ultimate Fall of Tibet.* New York: Jeremy P. Tarcher/Penguin, 2004.

Durham, Whitney Dylan. "The 1920 Treaty of Sèvres and the Struggle for a Kurdish Homeland in Iraq and Turkey Between World Wars." PhD diss., Oklahoma State University, 2000.

Dutt, Vidya Prakash. "The First Week of Revolution: The Wuchang Uprising." In *China in Revolution: The First Phase 1900–1913*, edited by Mary Clabaugh Wright, 383–418. New Haven, CT: Yale University Press, 1968.

Duyvesteyn, Isabelle. *Clausewitz and African War: Politics and Strategy in Liberia and Somalia.* New York: Routledge, 2004.

Dyer, Frederick H. *Number and Organization of the Armies of the United States.* Vol. 1 of *A Compendium of the War of the Rebellion.* New York: Thomas Yoseloff, 1959.

"Dzhunaid-Khan, 'King of the Karakum Desert.'" *Central Asian Review* 13 (1965): 216–26.

"E. Timor Expects 'Invasion.'" *The Canberra Times*, June 7, 1978, 11.

Earle, Rebecca. "The War of the Supremes: Border Conflict, Religious Crusade or Simply Politics By Other Means?" In *Rumors of Wars: Civil Conflict in Nineteenth-century Latin America*, edited by Rebecca Earle, 119–34. London: Institute of Latin American Studies, 2000.

Eastman, Lloyd E., Jerome Ch'en, Suzanne Pepper, and Lyman P. van Slyke. *The Nationalist Era in China, 1927–1949.* Cambridge, UK: Cambridge University Press, 1991.

Eberwein, Wolf Dieter, and Sven Chojnacki. "Scientific Necessity and Political Utility: A Comparison of Data on Violent Conflicts." Discussion paper P01–304. Berlin, Germany: Arbeitsgruppe: Internationale Politik, 2001.

Echenique, Rafael. *Catálogo Alfabético y Cronológico de los Hechos de Armas.* Mexico: Oficina Tipográfica de la Secretaría de Fomento, 1894.

Edgerton, Robert B. *Africa's Armies, from Honor to Infamy.* Boulder, CO: Westview Press, 2002.

Edmonds, Martin. "Civil War and Arms Sales: The Nigerian-Biafran War and Other Cases." In *Civil Wars in the Twentieth Century*, edited by Robert Higham, 203–16. Lexington: University of Kentucky Press, 1972.

Edwards, David Busby. "Origins of the Anti-Soviet Jihad." In *Afghan Resistance: The Politics of Survival*, edited by Grant M. Farr and John G. Merriam, 21–50. Boulder, CO: Westview, 1987.

Edwards, H. Sutherland. *The Private History of a Polish Insurrection.* London: Saunders, 1865.

Eggers, Ellen K. *Historical Dictionary of Burundi.* Lanham, MD: Scarecrow Press, 1997.

Ekinci, Mehmet Ugur. "The Origins of the 1897 Ottoman-Greek War: A Diplomatic History." Master's thesis, Bilkent University, Ankara, 2006.

El Khazen, Farid. *The Breakdown of the State in Lebanon, 1967–1976.* London: I. B. Tauris, 2000.

______. "Ending Conflict in Wartime Lebanon: Reform, Sovereignty and Power, 1976–88." *Middle Eastern Studies* 40 no. 11 (2004): 65–84.

"El Salvador Leftists Take Refuge on University Campus." *St. Petersburg Times*, January 4, 1980, 2A.

"El Salvador Officials Resign." *St. Petersburg Times*, January 4, 1980, 2A.

"El Salvador 30 Day Truce Is Declared." *Kentucky New Era*, November 7, 1979, 16.

"El Salvador Violence." *The Pittsburgh Press*, October 23, 1979, A-4.

El-Khattabi, Elizabeth. "Prelude to the Riffian War: Nineteenth and Early Twentieth Century Patterns of Precolonial Protest and Resistance in the Sharifian Empire." PhD diss., Princeton University, Department of History, 1998.

Elleman, Bruce A. *Modern Chinese Warfare, 1795–1989.* London: Routledge, 2001.

Elliadi, M. N. *Crete, Past and Present.* London: Heath Cranton Ltd., 1933.

Ellis, John. *A Short History of Guerilla Warfare.* New York: St. Martin's, 1976.

Elmslie, Jim. *Irian Jaya under the Gun: Indonesian Economic Development versus West Papuan Nationalism.* Honolulu: University of Hawaii Press, 2003.

Emerson, Edwin, Jr. *A History of the Nineteenth Century, Year by Year.* Vol 2. New York: P. F. Collier and Son, 1902.

Emmerson, Donald K. *Indonesia Beyond Suharto: Polity, Economy, Society, Transition.* Armonk, NY: M. E. Sharpe, 1999.

England, Shawn Louis. "The Curse of Huitzilopochtli: The Origins, Process, and Legacy of Mexico's Military Reforms, 1920–1946." PhD diss., Arizona State University, 2008.

Ensalaco, Mark. *Chile under Pinochet: Recovering the Truth.* Philadelphia: University of Pennsylvania Press, 2000.

Eprik, Cecil. *War and Peace in the Sudan: 1955–1972.* London: David Charles, 1972.

Erikson, Hans, and Björn Hagströmer. *Chad: Towards Democratisation or Petro-Dictatorship?* Uppsala, Sweden: Nordiska Afrikainstitutet, 2004.

Ero, Comfort. "ECOMOG: A Model for Africa?" In *Building Stability in Africa: Challenges for the New Millennium.* Monograph 46, February 2000.

Escott, Paul D., Lawrence N. Powell, James I. Robertson, Jr., and Emory M. Thomas. *Encyclopedia of the Confederacy.* Vol. 1. New York: Simon & Schuster, 1993.

Esherick, Joseph W. *Reform and Revolution in China: The 1911 Revolution in Hunan and Hubei.* Berkeley: University of California Press, 1976.

Estado Mayor General del Ejercito. *Historia del Ejercito de Chile.* Santiago, Chile: Estado Mayor General del Ejercito, 1980.

Estep, Raymond. "Mexia, Jose Antonio." In *Handbook of Texas Online.* Texas State Historical Association. http://www.tshaonline.org/handbook/online/articles/fme34.

Europa Yearbook, 2005. New York: Freedom House, 2005.

Evans, Alexander. "The Kashmir Insurgency: As Bad as It Gets." *Small Wars and Insurgencies* 11, no. 1 (Spring 2000): 69–81.

Evans, Grant. *A Short History of Laos: The Land in Between.* Crows Nest, Australia: Allen & Unwin, 2002.

Eversley, Lord. *The Turkish Empire from 1288 to 1914.* London: Adelphi Terrace, 1924.

Ewans, Martin. *Afghanistan: A New History.* Surrey, UK: Curzon, 2001.

______. *Afghanistan: A Short History of Its People and Politics.* New York: HarperCollins, 2002.

Ewell, Judith. *Venezuela: A Century of Change.* Stanford, CA: Stanford University Press, 1984.

Ezergailis, Andrew. *The Latvian Impact on the Bolshevik Revolution.* Boulder, CO: East European Monographs, 1983.

Facts on File World News Digest. New York: Facts on File, multiple years (weekly since 1940).

Fagg, John Edwin. *Latin America: A General History.* New York: Macmillan, 1963.

Fahmy, Khaled. *All the Pasha's Men: Mehmed Ali, His Army, and the Making of Modern Egypt.* Cambridge, UK: Cambridge University Press, 1997.

______."The Era of Muhammad 'Ali Pasha, 1805–1848." In *The Cambridge History of Egypt,* vol. 2, edited by M. W. Daly, 139–79. Cambridge, UK: Cambridge University Press, 1998.

______. "Mutiny in Mechmed Ali's New Nizami Army, April–May 1824." *International Journal of Turkish Studies* 8, nos. 1–2 (2002): 129–38.

Fairbank, John K. Edwin O. Reischauer, and A. M. Craig. *East Asia: Tradition and Transformation.* New York: Houghton Mifflin, 1989. Also published 1958 and 1960.

Falola, Toyin. *Violence in Nigeria: The Crisis of Religious Politics and Secular Ideologies.* Rochester, NY: University of Rochester Press, 1998.

Falola, Toyin, and Matthew Heaton. *A History of Nigeria.* New York: Cambridge University Press, 2008.

"Fanatics Hold Java in Terror." *Newcastle Morning Herald and Miners' Advocate,* March 14, 1953, 2.

"Fanatics in Indonesia." *The Northern Miner (Australia),* December 1, 1951, 1.

Far Eastern Economic Review. *Asia Yearbook.* Hong Kong: Far Eastern Economic Review, 1970–72, 1974.

Farah, Caesar E. "The Anglo-Ottoman Confrontation in Yemen, 1840–1849." *International Journal of Turkish Studies* 3, no. 2 (Winter 1985/86): 69–93.

______. "The Lebanese Insurgence of 1840 and the Powers." *Journal of Asian History* 1, no. 2 (1967): 105–32.

______. *The Politics of Interventionism in Ottoman Lebanon, 1830–1861.* London: I. B. Tauris, 2000.

______. "Reaffirming Ottoman Sovereignty in Yemen, 1825–1840." *International Journal of Turkish Studies* 3, no. 1 (Winter 1984/85): 101–116.

______. *The Sultan's Yemen: Nineteenth-century Challenges to Ottoman Rule.* London: I. B. Tauris, 2002.

Fariní, Juan Angel. *Cronologia de Mitre, 1821–1906.* Buenos Aires, Argentina: Institucion Mitre, 1970.

Farouk-Sluglett, Marion, and Peter Sluglett. *Iraq since 1958: From Revolution to Dictatorship.* Rev. ed. London: I. B. Tauris, 2001.

Farwell, Byron. *The Encyclopedia of Nineteenth-century Land Warfare.* New York: W. W. Norton, 2001.

FAS Intelligence Resource Program. "Kosovo Liberation Army (KLA)." 2005. http://www.fas.org/irp/world/para/kla.htm.

Fathi, Ashgar. "The Role of the 'Rebels' in the Constitutional Movement in Iran." *International Journal of Middle East Studies* 10, no. 1 (1979): 55–66.

Fausto, Boris. *A Concise History of Brazil.* Cambridge, UK: Cambridge University Press, 1999.

Fawaz, Leila Tarazi. *An Occasion for War: Civil Conflict in Lebanon and Damascus in 1860.* London: I. B. Tauris, 1994.

Fearon, James D., and David D. Laitin. "Burma." *Ethnicity, Insurgency and Civil War Research Project,* July 7, 2006. http://www.stanford.edu/group/ethnic/random narratives.

Fedyshyn, Oleh S. *Germany's Drive to the East and the Ukrainian Revolution, 1917–1918.* New Brunswick, NJ: Rutgers University Press, 1971.

Fehrenbach, T. R. *Fire and Blood, a History of Mexico.* New York: Macmillan Publishing Co. Inc., 1973.

Feith, Herbert. "Indonesia." In *Government and Politics in Southeast Asia,* edited by G. Kahin. Ithaca, NY: Cornell University Press, 1964.

Felter, Joseph H., III. "Taking Guns to a Knife Fight: A Case for the Empirical Study of Counterinsurgency." PhD diss., Stanford University, Political Science, 2005.

Fermoselle, Rafael. *The Evolution of the Cuban Military, 1492–1986.* Miami, FL: Ediciones Universal, 1987.

Ferris, Cornelius Jr. "Report on the Insurrection in Paraguay in February and March, 1911." In *Papers Relating to the Foreign Relations of the United States 1912,* 1265–1267. Washington, DC: Government Printing Office.

Feuerwerker, Albert. *Rebellion in Nineteenth-century China.* Ann Arbor: University of Michigan Center for Chinese Studies, 1975.

Fields, Lanny B. *Tso Tsung-T'ang and the Muslims: Statecraft in Northwest China, 1868–1880.* Kingston, Ontario: Limestone Press, 1978.

Figes, Orlando. *A People's Tragedy, The Russian Revolution: 1891–1924.* New York: Penguin Books, 1996.

"Fighting in Paraguay." *Poverty Bay Herald (New Zealand)* XXXIX, no. 12721 (March 25, 1912): 5.

Financial Times (London), January 30, 2001, 13.

Finkel, Caroline. *Osman's Dream: The Story of the Ottoman Empire, 1300–1923.* New York: Basic Books, 2005.

Finlay, George. *History of the Greek Revolution.* Edinburgh, UK: William Blackwood and Sons, 1861.

Firro, Kais M. *A History of the Druzes.* New York: E. J. Brill, 1992.

Fisher, Howard T., and Marion Hall Fisher, eds. *Life in Mexico, the Letters of Fanny Calderón de la Barca.* Garden City, NY: Anchor Books, 1970. With new material from the author's private journals.

Fitchen, E. "Self-Determination or Self-Preservation? The Relations of Independent Yucatán with the Republic of Texas and the United States 1847–1849." *Journal of the West* 18, no. 1 (January 1979).

"Five Killed in Clash Between Northern Soldiers, Southern Villagers." *Agence France-Presse,* November 19, 1993.

Flandrau, Charles E. "The Indian War of 1862–1864 and Following Campaigns in Minnesota." In *Board of Commissioners, Minnesota in the Civil and Indian Wars.* Vol. II. St. Paul, MN: Pioneer Press, 1890. http://www.openlibrary.org.

Fletcher, Arnold. *Afghanistan: Highway of Conquest.* Ithaca, NY: Cornell University Press, 1965.

Florinsky, Michael T. *Russia: A History and an Interpretation.* Vol. 2. New York: Macmillan, 1953.

Fluharty, Lee Vernon. *Dance of the Millions: Military Rule and the Social Revolution in Colombia, 1930–1956.* Pittsburgh, PA: University of Pittsburgh Press, 1957.

Folwell, William Watts. *A History of Minnesota.* Saint Paul: Minnesota Historical Society, 1924.

Foote, Shelby. *Fort Sumter to Perryville.* Vol. 1 of *The Civil War, a Narrative.* New York: Vintage Books, 1986a.

______. *Fredericksburg to Meridian.* Vol. 2 of *The Civil War, a Narrative.* New York: Vintage Books, 1986b.

______. *Red River to Appomattox.* Vol. 3 of *The Civil War, a Narrative.* New York: Vintage Books, 1986c.

Forbes, Andrew D. W. *Warlords and Muslims in Chinese Central Asia.* Cambridge, UK: Cambridge University Press, 1986.

Ford, Peter. "Contra's Lament." *The Telegraph,* February 13, 1987, 6–9.

Forest, James J. F. *Confronting the Terrorism of Boko Haram in Nigeria.* MacDill Air Force Base, FL: Joint Special Operations University, 2012.

Forster, Edward Seymour. *A Short History of Modern Greece, 1821–1956.* London: Methuen & Co., 1958.

Fortoul, Jose Gil. "Santa Ines y La Cople." In *La Federacion y La Guerra Historiografia,* edited by Ezequiel y su tiempo Zamora. Caracas, Venezuela: Oficina Central de Informacion, 1976.

Foster, Charles. "Indonesia and West Papua." *Contemporary Review* 282, no. 1645 (February 2003): 73–6.

Fowler, Will. "Civil Conflict in Independent Mexico, 1821–57 an Overview." In *Rumours of Wars: Civil Conflict in Nineteenth-Century Latin America,* edited by Rebecca Earle. London: Institute of Latin American Studies, 2000a.

______. *Malcontents, Rebels, and Pronunciados: The Politics of Insurrection in Nineteenth-century Mexico.* Lincoln: University of Nebraska Press, 2012.

______. *Santa Anna of Mexico.* Lincoln: University of Nebraska Press, 2007.

______. *Tornel and Santa Anna: The Writer and the Caudillo, Mexico, 1795–1853.* Westport, CT: Greenwood Press, 2000b.

Franke, Wolfgang. *A Century of Chinese Revolution, 1851–1949.* Oxford, UK: Blackwell, 1970.

Fraser-Tyler, William K. *Afghanistan.* London: Oxford University Press, 1967.

Fredholm, Michael. *Burma: Ethnicity and Insurgency.* Westport, CT: London, 1993.

Freeman, Colin, Barney Henderson, and Mark Oliver. "Al Qaeda Map." *The Telegraph,* June 12, 2014. http://www.telegraph.co.uk/news/worldnews/al-qaeda/10893889/Al-Qaeda-map-Isis-Boko-Haram-and-other-affiliates-strongholds-across-Africa-and-Asia.html.

Freeman-Grenville, F. S. P. *A Chronology of African History.* London: Oxford University Press, 1973.

Freij, Hanna Yousef. "Tribal Identity and Alliance Behaviour among Factions of the Kurdish National Movement in Iraq." *Nationalism and Ethnic Politics* 3, no. 3 (1997): 86–110.

Frère, Marie-Soleil. *The Media and Conflicts in Central Africa.* Boulder, CO: Lynne Rienner, 2007.

"Fretilin Leader Shot." *The Canberra Times,* January 3, 1979, 4.

Friedman, Edward. *Backward Toward Revolution.* Berkeley, CA: University of California Press, 1974.

Friend, Theodore. *Indonesian Destinies.* Cambridge, MA: Belknap Press of Harvard University Press, 2003.

Frilley, G., and Jovan Wlahovitj. *Le Monténégro Contemporain.* Paris, France: E. Plon et Cie, Imprimeurs-Éditeurs, 1876.

Frost, John. *The History of Mexico and Its Wars.* New Orleans, LA: Armand Hawkins, 1882.

Frundt, Henry J. "Guatemala in Search of Democracy." *Journal of Interamerican Studies and World Affairs* 32, no. 3 (1990): 24–74.

G. G. D. V. (Vaudoncourt, Frédéric Baron Guillaume de). *Letters on the Internal Political State of Spain During the Years 1821, 22, & 23.* London: Lupton Relfe, 1824.

Gaasholt, Ole Martin. "Northern Mali 2912: The Short-lived Triumph of Irredentism." *Strategic Review for Southern Africa* 35, no. 2 (November 2013): 68+.

Gagnon. V. P., Jr. *The Myth of Ethnic War, Serbia and Croatia in the 1990s.* Ithaca, NY: Cornell University Press, 2004.

Galbraith, W. O. *Columbia.* London: Royal Institute of International Affairs, 1953.

Gambill, Gary. "The Pivotal Role of Lebanon's Armenian Christians." *Tayyar (Beirut),* September, 18, 2009.

Gambone, Michael D. *Capturing the Revolution: The United States, Central America, and Nicaragua, 1961–1972.* Westport, CT: Praeger, 2001.

Gambra, Rafael. *La Primera Guerra Civil de Espana (1821–1823).* Madrid, Spain: Esceliecer, 1972.

Gammer, Moshe. *The Lone Wolf and the Bear, Three Centuries of Chechen Defiance of Russian Rule.* Pittsburgh, PA: University of Pittsburgh Press, 2006.

______. *Muslim Resistance to the Tsar: Shamil and the Conquest of Chechnia and Daghestan.* London: Frank Cass, 2003.

______. "Was General Klüge-von-Klugenau Shamil's Desmichels?" *Cahiers du monde russe et soviétique* 33, no 2–3 (Avril–Septembre 1992): 207–21.

Ganguly, Rajat, and Raymond C. Taras. *Understanding Ethnic Conflict.* New York: Longman, 1998.

Gankovsky, Yuri V. "Ibrahim Beg Lakai: An Outstanding Leader of the Basmachi Movement in Central Asia." *Journal of South Asian and Middle Eastern Studies* 16 (1993): 1–8.

______. "Ibrahim Beg Lokai (1899–1932)." *Pakistan Journal of History and Culture* 17 (1996): 105–14.

Gao, James Z. *Historical Dictionary of Modern China (1800–1949).* Lanham, MD: Scarecrow Press, 2009.

Garcia, Gabriel Cevallos. *Historia del Ecuador.* Segunda parte. Cuenca, Ecuador: Editorial Von Bosco, 1979.

García-Pérez, Gladys Marel *Insurrection & Revolution, Armed Struggle in Cuba, 1952–1959.* Translated by Juan Ortega. Boulder, CO: Lynne Rienner Publishers, 1998.

Gardner, Paul F. *Shared Hopes, Separate Fears: Fifty Years of US-Indonesian Relations.* Boulder, CO: Westview, 1977.

Garner, Paul. *Porfirio Díaz.* New York: Longman, 2001.

Garthwaite, Gene R. *Khans and Shahs: A Documentary Analysis of the Bakhtiyari in Iran.* Cambridge, UK: Cambridge University Press, 1983.

Garver, John W. *Chinese-Soviet Relations, 1937–1945.* Oxford, UK: Oxford University Press, 1988.

Gavin, Robert. "The Ottoman Reconquest of Arabia 1871–73." *History Today* 13 (1963): 774–84.

Gawrych, George W. *The Crescent and the Eagle: Ottoman Rule, Islam and the Albanians, 1874–1913.* New York: I. B. Tauris, 2006.

Gediminas, Vitkus. "'Forest Brothers' and the Consequences of the Metropole-periphery Distinction

Elimination in the 'Correlates of War' Typology." *Journal of Baltic Studies* 43, no. 4 (2012): 515–27.

______, ed. *Wars of Lithuania, a Systematic Quantitative Analysis of Lithuania's Wars in the Nineteenth and Twentieth Centuries.* Vilnius, Lithuania: EUGRIMAS, 2014.

Geller, Daniel S., and J. David Singer. Nations at War: A Scientific Study of International Conflict. Cambridge, UK: Cambridge University Press, 1998.

Gemie, Sharif. *French Revolutions, 1815–1914.* Edinburgh, Scotland: Edinburgh University Press, 1999.

"General Promises to Punish Sikh Mutineers." *New York Times*, July 2, 1984. http://www.nytimes.com/1984/07/02/world/general-promises-to-punish-sikh-mutineers.html.

"General Rafael Franco Reported Leading Paraguay Rebels." *News and Courier (Charleston, SC, morning edition)*, March 24, 1947, 3.

Georgieva, Valentina, and Sasha Konechni. *Historical Dictionary of the Republic of Macedonia.* Lanham, MD: Scarecrow Press, 1998.

Gerolymatos, André. *The Balkan Wars: Conquest, Revolution, and Retribution from the Ottoman Era to the Twentieth Century and Beyond.* New York: Basic Books, 2002.

Gerome, Frank A. "Race and Politics in Cuba and the US Intervention of 1912." *SECOLAS Annals: Journal of the Southeastern Council on Latin American Studies* 28 (1997): 5–26.

Gerrard, Craig. "The Foreign Office and British Intervention in the Finnish Civil War." *Civil Wars* 3, no. 3 (Autumn 2000): 87–100.

Gettleman, Jeffrey. "Somalia Forces Retake Capital from Islamists." *New York Times,* December 29, 2006. http://www.nytimes.com.

Gettleman, Marvin, ed. *Vietnam.* New York: Fawcett, 1970a.

Gettleman, Marvin, S., L. Kaplan, and C. Kaplan, eds. *Conflict in Indochina.* New York: Vintage, 1970.

Gewehr, Wesley M. *The Rise of Nationalism in the Balkans, 1800–1930.* Hamden, CT: Archon Books, 1967.

Ghalib, Abbas. "South Says Northern Units Resisting Withdrawal to Barracks." *Associated Press Worldstream,* March 2, 1994.

Ghareeb, Edmund. *The Kurdish Question in Iraq.* Syracuse, NY: Syracuse University Press, 1981.

Ghattas, Samir. "Government Says It Controls Last Southern Strongholds." *Associated Press,* July 10, 1994.

Ghosn, Faten, Glenn Palmer, and Stuart Bremer. "The MID3 Data Set, 1993–2001: Procedures, Coding Rules, and Description." *Conflict Management and Peace Science* 21 (2004): 133–54.

Giaffo, Lou. *Albania: Eye of the Balkan Vortex.* Bloomington, IN: Xlibris Corporation, 2000.

Gibbs, Brian H., and J. David Singer. *Empirical Knowledge on World Politics: A Summary of Quantitative Research, 1970–1991.* Westport, CT: Greenwood Press, 1993.

Gibler, Douglas M., and Meredith Reid Sarkees. "Measuring Alliances: The Correlates of War Formal Interstate Alliance Dataset, 1816–2000." *Journal of Peace Research* 41, no. 2 (March 2004).

Giglio, Mike. "Hezbollah Comes Clean." *Newsweek Global* 161, no. 20 (May 29, 2013).

Gillin, Donald G. *Warlord: Yen Hsi-shan in Shansi Province 1911–1949.* Princeton, NJ: Princeton University Press, 1967.

Gilmore, Robert L. *Caudillism and Militarism in Venezuela, 1810–1910.* Athens: Ohio University Press, 1964.

Girling, J. L. S. "Laos: Falling Domino?" *Pacific Affairs* 43, no. 3 (Autumn 1970): 370–83.

Giustozzi, Antonio. "The Demodernisation of an Army: Northern Afghanistan, 1992–2001." *Small Wars & Insurgencies* 15, no. 1 (2004): 1–18.

Gleditsch, N. P., P. Wallensteen, M. Eriksson, M. Sollenberg, and H. Strand. "Armed Conflict 1946–2001: A New Dataset." *Journal of Peace Research* 39, no. 5 (2002): 615–37.

Gleijeses, Piero. *The Dominican Crisis.* Baltimore, MD: Johns Hopkins University Press, 1978.

Glenny, Misha. *The Balkans: Nationalism, War, and the Great Powers 1804–1999.* New York: Penguin Books, 1999.

Glickson, Roger C. "Counterinsurgency in Southern Sudan: The Means to Win?" *Journal of Conflict Studies* 15, no. 1 (2005). http://journals.hil.unb.ca/index.php/JCS/article/view/4594.

Global Terrorism Index, 2014. New York: Institute for Economics and Peace, 2014.

GlobalSecurity.org. "Burundi Civil War." 2006. http://www.globalsecutiry.org/military/world/war/burundi.htm.

______. "Congo Civil War." 2005a. http://www.globalsecurity.org.

______. "Free Aceh (Aceh Merdeka) Free Aceh Movement [Gerakin Aceh Merdeka (GAM)] Aceh Security Disturbance Movement (GPK)." 2005b. http://www.globalsecurity.org.

______. "Insurgency in Nepal." 2005c. http://www.globalsecurity.org.

______. "Ivory Coast Conflict." 2002, 2003, 2004. http://www.globalsecurity.org/military/world/war/ivory-coast.htm.

______. "Ivory Coast Conflict." 2010, 2011. http://www.globalsecurity.org/military/world/war/ivory-coast.htm.

______. "Liberia—First Civil War—1989–1996." 2005d. http://www.globalsecurity.org.

______. "Liberia—Second Civil War—1997–2003." 2005e. http://www.globalsecurity.org.

Gnorowski, S. B. *Insurrection of Poland.* London: James Ridgeway, 1839.

Gochman, Charles S., and Zeev Moaz. "Militarized Interstate Disputes, 1916–1976." In *International War: An Anthology and Study Guide*, edited by Melvin Small and J. David Singer, 27–36. Homewood, IL: Dorsey Press, 1985.

Godechot, Jacques. *Les Revolutions de 1848.* Paris, France: Albin Michel, 1971.

Gohdes, A., and Price, M. "First Things First: Assessing Data Quality Before Model Quality." *Journal of Conflict Resolution* (November 15, 2012).

Gold, Eva. "Military Encirclement." In *Reagan Versus the Sandinistas*, edited by Thomas W. Walker. Boulder, CO: Westview Press, 1987.

Goldschmidt, Arthur J. *A Concise History of the Middle East.* Boulder, CO: Westview Press, 1991.

Goldstein, Joshua S. *War and Gender.* Cambridge, UK: Cambridge University Press, 2001.

Goldstein, Martin. *American Policy Toward Laos.* Cranbury, NJ: Associated University Presses, 1973.

Goldstein, Melvyn C. *The Storm Clouds Descend. 1955–1957.* Vol. 3 of *A History of Modern Tibet.* Berkeley: University of California Press, 2014.

Goldstone, Jack A. *The Encyclopedia of Political Revolutions.* Washington, DC: Congressional Quarterly, 1998.

Gonçalves de Magalthhaes, Domingos José. "Uprising in Maranhão, 1839–1840." In *The Brazil Reader*, edited by Robert M. Levine and John J. Crocitti. Durham, NC: Duke University Press, 1999.

Gonzales, Michael J. *The Mexican Revolution, 1910–1940.* Albuquerque: University of New Mexico Press, 2002.

______. "Neo-colonialism and Indian Unrest in Southern Peru, 1867–1898." *Latin American Research* 6, no. 1 (1987): 1–26.

Goodhand, Jonathan. *Aiding Peace? The Role of NGOS in Armed Conflict.* Boulder, CO: Lynne Rienner Publishers, 2006.

Goodsell, James Nelson. "'Viet War' Growing in Argentina." *The Baltimore Sun*, January 18, 1976.

Goodson, Larry P. *Afghanistan's Endless War: State Failure, Regional Politics, and the Rise of the Taliban.* Seattle: University of Washington Press, 2001.

Gopal, Anand, Mansur Khan Mahsud, and Brian Fishman. "The Taliban in North Waziristan." In *Talibanistan: Negotiating the Borders Between Terror, Politics, and Religion*, edited by Peter Bergen and Katherine Tiedemann, 128–63. New York: Oxford University Press, 2013.

Gopčević, Spiridion. *Le Monténégro et les Monténégrins.* Paris, France: Octare Doin, 1877.

Goria, Wade R. *Sovereignty and Leadership in Lebanon 1943–1976.* London: Ithaca Press, 1985.

Górka, Olgierd. *Outline of Polish History, Past and Present.* London: M. I. Kolin, Ltd., 1942.

Gorleri, Claudio Morales. *Luis María Campos: "El General Petit."* Buenos Aires, Argentina: Edivérn S. R. L., 2003.

Gorman, John. "Bulldog's Bite." In *Sea Classics* 35, no. 1 (January 2002).

Gosman, Keith. "Fear for Children in PNG Blockade." *Sun Herald (Sydney)*, December 1, 1991, 29.

Goss, Jon. "Understanding the "Maluku Wars:" Overview of Sources of Communal Conflict and Prospects for Peace." *Cakalele: Maluku Research Journal* 11 (2000): 7–39.

Graham, Richard. *Patronage and Politics in Nineteenth-century Brazil.* Stanford, CA: Stanford University Press, 1990.

Gramizzi, Claudio, and Jérôme Tubiana. *New War, Old Enemies: Conflict Dynamics in South Kordofan.* Geneva, Switzerland: Small Arms Survey, 2013.

Grant, Jonathan, Jonathan Unger, and Laurane A. G. Moss, eds. *Cambodia: The Widening War in Indochina.* New York: Simon and Schuster, 1970.

Grasso, June, Jay Corrin, and Michael Kort. *Modernization and Revolution in China.* Armonk, NY: M. E. Sharpe, 1997.

Grau, Lester. "Breaking Contact Without Leaving Chaos: The Soviet Withdrawal from Afghanistan." *Journal of Slavic Military Studies* 20, no. 2 (2007): 235–61.

Gray, Jack. *Rebellions and Revolutions: China from the 1800s to the 1980s.* Oxford, UK: Oxford University Press, 1990.

Green, Stanley C. *The Mexican Republic: The First Decade, 1823–1832.* Pittsburgh, PA: Pittsburgh University Press, 1987.

Greenfield, Richard. *Ethiopia, a New Political History.* New York: Frederick A. Praeger, 1965.

Greenlees, Don. "Army Wants to Crush Stricken Aceh Rebels." *The Weekend Australian*, July 13, 2002.

Greentree, Todd. *Crossroads of Intervention: Insurgency and Counterinsurgency Lessons from Central America.* Westport, CT: Praeger Security International, 2008.

Greenwood, Christopher. "The Concept of War in Modern International Law." *International and Comparative Law Quarterly* 36, no. 2 (1987): 283–306.

Gregorian, Vartan. *The Emergence of Modern Afghanistan.* Stanford, CA: Stanford University Press, 1969.

Gregory, John S. "British Intervention against the Taiping Rebellion." *Journal of Asian Studies* 19 (November 1959): 11–24.

Grenier, Yvonne. "Understanding the FMLN: A Glossary of Five Words." *Conflict Quarterly* XI, no. 2 (1991): 51–75.

Gross, Liza. *Handbook of Leftist Guerrilla Groups in Latin America and the Caribbean.* Boulder, CO: Westview Press, 1995.

Grubel, James. "More PNG Troops Land on Island." *The Advertiser*, May 21, 1992.

Grunwald, Constantin de. *Tsar Nicholas I.* Translated by Brigit Patmore. New York: Macmillan, 1955.

Grynspan, Dévora. "Nicaragua: A New Model for Popular Revolution in Latin America." In *Revolutions of the Late Twentieth Century*, edited by Jack A. Goldstone, Ted Robert Gurr, and Farrokh Moshiri, 88–115. Boulder, CO: Westview Press, 1991.

Guan, Ang Chen. *The Vietnam War from the Other Side: The Vietnamese Communists' Perspective.* London: Routledge Curzon, 2002.

Guáqueta, Alexandra. "The Colombian Conflict: Political and Economic Dimensions." In *The Political Economy of Armed Conflict: Beyond Greed and Grievance*, edited by Karen Ballentine and Jake Sherman, 73–106. Boulder, CO: Lynne Rienner, 2003.

Guarak, Mawut Achiecque Mach. *Integration and Fragmentation of the Sudan: An African Renaissance.* Bloomington, IL: AuthorHouse, 2011.

"Guatemalan Guerrillas Admit They Are Retreating." *United Press International*, April 15, 1983.

Güell y Mercader, José. *Guzmán Blanco y Su Tiempo.* Caracas, Venezuela: Imprenta de "La Opinion Nacional," 1883.

Guevara, Che. *Guerrilla Warfare.* Lincoln: University of Nebraska Press, 1985.

Guha-Sapir, Debarati, and Olivier Degomme. *Darfur: Counting the Deaths.* Brussels, Belgium: Centre for Research on the Epidemiology of Disasters, 2005.

Guillermaz, J. "The Nanchang Uprising." *The China Quarterly* 11 (July–September 1962): 160–68.

Gukiina, Peter M. *Uganda: A Case Study in African Political Development.* Notre Dame, IN: University of Notre Dame Press, 1972.

Gunaratna, Rohan. "Burning Bright." *Himāl* (April 1999). http://old.himalmag.com/himal-feed/53/2217-Burning-bright.html.

______. *Sri Lanka, a Lost Revolution? The Inside Story of the JVP.* Kandy, Sri Lanka: Institute of Fundamental Studies, 2001.

______. *Sri Lanka's Ethnic Crisis and National Security.* Colombo, Sri Lanka: South Asian Network on Conflict Research, 1998.

Gunson, Phil, Greg Chamberlain, and Andrew Thompson. *The Dictionary of Contemporary Politics of Central America and the Caribbean.* New York: Routledge, 1991.

Gunter, Michael M. "The KDP-PUK Conflict in Northern Iraq." *Middle East Journal* 50, no. 2 (Spring 1996): 225–41.

______. "The Kurds Struggle for 'Kurdistan.'" In *Encyclopedia of Modern Ethnic Conflicts*, edited by Joseph R. Rudolph. Westport, CT: Greenwood Press, 2003.

Gurr, Ted Robert. *Minorities at Risk: A Global View of Ethnopolitical Conflict.* Washington, DC: United States Institute of Peace Press, 1993.

Gurr, Ted Robert, and Barbara Harff. *Ethnic Conflict in World Politics.* Boulder, CO: Westview Press, 1994.

Gvosdev, Nikolas K. *Imperial Policies and Perspectives towards Georgia, 1760–1819.* Oxford, UK: St. Antony's College, 2000.

Haber, Stephen, Armando Razo, and Noel Maurer. *The Politics of Property Rights: Political Instability, Credible Commitments, and Economic Growth in Mexico, 1876–1929.* Cambridge, UK: Cambridge University Press, 2003.

Habib, John S. *Ibn Sa'uds Warriors of Islam.* Leiden, Netherlands: E. J. Brill, 1978.

Haddad, George M. *Part I: Iraq, Syria, Lebanon and Jordan.* Vol. II of *Revolution and Military Rule in the Middle East: The Arab States.* New York: Robert Speller and Sons, 1971.

Hadid, Diaa, and Bassem Mroue. "West-backed Syria Rebels Shaken on Multiple Fronts." *Tulsa World*, November 15, 2014.

Hadžiselimovic', Omer. *At the Gates of the East: British Travel Writers on Bosnia and Hercegovina from the Sixteenth to the Twentieth Centuries.* Boulder, CO: East European Monographs, 2001.

Hafez, Mohammed M. *Why Muslims Rebel: Repression and Resistance in the Islamic World.* Boulder, CO: Lynne Rienner, 2003.

Hafizullah, Emadi. "The Hazaras and Their Role in the Process of Political Transformation in Afghanistan." *Central Asian Survey* 16, no. 3 (1997): 363–87.

Haglund, David G., and Allen Sens. "Kosovo and the Case of the (Not So) Free Riders: Portugal, Belgium, Canada, and Spain." In *Kosovo and the Challenges of Humanitarian Intervention*, edited by Albrecht Schnabel and Ramesh Thakur. New York: United Nations University Press, 2000.

Halaf, Samir. *Civil and Uncivil Violence in Lebanon: A History of the Internationalization of Communal Conflict.* New York: Columbia University Press, 2002.

Hale, Charles R. *Resistance and Contradiction: Miskitu Indians and the Nicaraguan State, 1894–1987.* Stanford, CA: Stanford University Press, 1996.

Haley, Edward P., and Lewis W. Snider, eds. *Lebanon Crisis.* Syracuse, NY: Syracuse University Press, 1979.

Hall, D. G. E. *A History of South-East Asia,* 4th ed. New York: St. Martin's Press, 1981.

Hall, John Whitney. *Japan: From Prehistory to Modern Times.* Ann Arbor: University of Michigan Press, 1968.

Hall, Richard Andrew. "Theories of Collective Action and Revolution: Evidence from the Romanian Transition of December 1989." *Europe–Asia Studies* 52, no. 6 (September 2000): 1069–93.

Halleck, Henry Wager. *Elements of International Law and Laws of War.* Philadelphia, PA: J. B. Lippincott Company, 1885.

Hallenbeck, Ralph A. *Military Force as an Instrument of US Foreign Policy: Intervention in Lebanon, August 1982–February 1984.* New York: Praeger, 1991.

Hamilton, Richard E. "German Revolution (1918)." *The Encyclopedia of Political Revolutions,* edited by Jack A. Goldstone. Washington, DC: Congressional Quarterly, Inc., 1998.

Hamilton-Merritt, Jane. *Tragic Mountains: The Hmong, the Americans, and the Secret War for Laos, 1942–1992.* Bloomington: Indiana University Press, 1992.

Hammer, Kenneth M. "Huks in the Philippines." In *Modern Guerrilla Warfare,* edited by F. Osanka. Glencoe, IL: Free Press, 1962.

Hamnett, Brian. *A Concise History of Mexico.* Cambridge, UK: Cambridge University Press, 1999.

______. "Mexican Conservatives, Clericals, and Soldiers: The 'Traitor' Tomás Mejía through Reform and Empire, 1855–1867." *Bulletin of Latin American Research* 20, no. 2 (2001): 187–209.

Hancock, Anson Uriel. *A History of Chile.* Chicago, IL: Charles H. Sergel and Co., 1893.

______. *A History of Chile.* Indiana: Repressed Publishing, 2014.

Handy, Jum. *Revolution in the Countryside: Rural Conflict and Agrarian Reform in Guatemala, 1944–1954.* Chapel Hill: University of North Carolina Press, 1994.

Hannum, Hurst. *Autonomy, Sovereignty, and Self-Determination: The Accommodation of Conflicting Rights.* Philadelphia: University of Pennsylvania Press, 1996.

Hansis, Randall. "The Political Strategy of Military Reform: Álvaro Obregón and Revolutionary Mexico, 1920–1924." *The Americas* 36, no. 2 (1979): 199–233.

Hara, Fabienne. "Hallow Peace Hopes in Shattered Congo." *International Crisis Group: D.R. Congo,* July 7, 2002. http://www.crisisweb.org/projects/showreport.cfm?reportid=695.

Harbottle, Thomas Benfield, and George Bruce. *Dictionary of Battles.* New York: Stein and Day, 1971.

Harcave, Sidney. *The Russian Revolution of 1905.* London: Collier-Macmillan, 1964.

Harden, Blaine. "Africa's Diamond Wars." *New York Times (Outlook),* 2001. http://www.nytimes.com/library/world/africa.

Harding, Harry. "The Chinese State in Crisis: 1966–9." In *The Politics of China,* 2nd ed., edited by Roderick MacFarquhar, 148–247. Cambridge, UK: Cambridge University Press, 1997.

Harff, Barbara. "Cambodia: Revolution, Genocide, Intervention." In *Revolutions of the Late Twentieth Century,* edited by Jack A. Goldstone, Ted Robert Gurr, and Farrokh Moshiri, 218–34. Boulder, CO: Westview Press, 1991.

Harik, Iliya. *Politics and Change in a Traditional Society: Lebanon, 1711–1845.* Princeton, NJ: Princeton University Press, 1968.

Harmer, Tanya. *Allende's Chile and the Inter-American Cold War.* Chapel Hill: University of North Carolina Press, 2011.

Harnisch, Chris. "Operation Briefer: The Upcoming Battle for Mogadishu." *AEI: Critical Threats.* April 1, 2010. http://www.criticalthreats.org.

Harris, David. *A Diplomatic History of the Balkan Crisis of 1875–1878: The First Year.* Stanford, CA: Stanford University Press, 1936.

Harris, Mark. *Rebellion on the Amazon: The Cabanagem, Race, and Popular Culture in the North of Brazil, 1798–1840.* Cambridge University Press, 2010.

Harris, Walter B. *France, Spain, and the Rif.* London: Arnold, 1927.

______. *A Journey through the Yemen.* London: William Blackwood and Sons, 1893.

Harris, William W. *Faces of Lebanon: Sects, Wars, and Global Extensions.* Princeton, NJ: Markus Wiener, 1997.

______. *Lebanon: A History, 600–2011.* New York: Oxford University Press, 2012.

Harrison, Selig S. *In Afghanistan's Shadow: Baluch Nationalism and Soviet Temptations.* New York: Carnegie Endowment for International Peace, 1981.

Hart, John Mason. *Empire and Revolution: The Americans in Mexico since the Civil War.* Berkeley: University of California Press, 2002.

Hartsock, E. H. *The Air Force in Southeast Asia: The End of the US Involvement, 1973–1975.* Arlington, VA: Office of Air Force History, Headquarters USAF, 1980. http://www.afhso.af.mil/shared/media/document/AFD-110323–032.pdf.

Hartzell, Caroline. "The Role of an Implementation Regime in Nicaragua." In *Ending Civil Wars: The Implementation of Peace Agreements,* edited by Stephen John Stedman, Donald Rothchild, and Elizabeth M. Cousens, 353–82. Boulder, CO: Lynne Rienner, 2002.

Harvey, Barbara Sillers. *Permesta: Half a Rebellion.* Monograph series—Publication No. 57. Ithaca, NY: Cornell Modern Indonesia Project, 1977.

______. *Tradition, Islam, and Rebellion: South Sulawesi, 1950–1965.* New York: Cornell University, Department of Political Science, 1974.

"Has Fortified Position." *Montreal Gazette,* December 4, 1923, 17.

Hasbrouck, Alfred. "The Argentine Revolution of 1930." *Hispanic American Historical Review* 18 (August 1938): 285–321.

______. "The Conquest of the Desert." *Hispanic Historical Review* 15, no. 2 (May 1935): 195–228.

Hashim, Ahmed S. *When Counterinsurgency Wins: Sri Lanka's Defeat of the Tamil Tigers.* Philadelphia: University of Pennsylvania Press, 2013.

Hasnat, Syed Farooq. *Global Security Watch—Pakistan.* Santa Barbara, CA: Praeger, 2011.

Hazard, Samuel. *Santo Domingo, Past and Present; With a Glance at Hayti.* New York: Harper and Brothers, 1873.

Headley, P. C. *The Life of Louis Kossuth.* Auburn, NY: Derby and Miller, 1852.

Heard, Isaac V. D. *History of the Sioux War and Massacres of 1862 and 1863.* New York: Harper & Brothers, 1864.

Hearder, H., and P. Waley. *A Short History of Italy: From Classical Times to the Present Day.* Cambridge, UK: Cambridge University Press, 1963.

Hearder, Harry. *Italy in the Age of the Risorgimento 1790–1870.* New York: Routledge, 2014.

Heath, Ian, and Michael Perry. *The Taiping Rebellion, 1851–66.* London: Osprey, 1994.

Heaton, William R., and Richard MacLeod. "People's War in Thailand." In *Insurgency in the Modern World,* edited by Bard E. O'Neill, William R. Heaton, and Donald J. Alberts. Boulder, CO: Westview Press, 1980.

Heflin, Jean. Unpublished notes about major power conflicts, memo to R. C. North, January 19, 1970.

Hehn, Paul. "Capitalism and the Revolutionary Factor in the Balkans and Crimean War Diplomacy." *East European Quarterly* XVIII, no. 2 (June 1984): 155–84.

Heidler, David S., and Jeanne T. Heidler. *Encyclopedia of the American Civil War, a Political, Social, and Military History.* Vol. 1. Santa Barbara, CA: ABC–CLIO, 2000.

Heinl, Robert Debs, and Nancy Gordon Heinl. *Written in Blood: The Story of the Haitian People 1492–1971.* Boston, MA: Houghton Mifflin Company, 1978.

Heinl, Michael, Nancy Gordon Heinl, and Michael Heinl. *Written in Blood: The Story of the Haitian People 1492–1995.* Lanham, MD: University Press of America, 1996.

______. *Written in Blood.: The Story of the Haitian People 1492–1995.* Lanham, MD: University Press of America, 2005.

Helg, Aline. *Our Rightful Share: The Afro-Cuban Struggle for Equality, 1886–1912.* Chapel Hill: University of North Carolina Press, 1995.

Hellenic Resources Network. "Summary Data." February 24, 2006. http://www.hri.org/docs/nato/summary.html.

Henao, Jesus Maria, and Gerardo Arrubla. *Historia de Colombia.* Tomo 2. Bogota, Colombia: Plaza & Jones, 1910. Originally published 1984.

______. *History of Colombia.* Chapel Hill: University of North Carolina Press, 1938.

Henderson, Errol A. *Democracy and War: The End of an Illusion.* Boulder, CO: Lynne Rienner, 2002.

Henderson, Errol, and J. David Singer. "New Wars and Rumors of New Wars." *International Interactions* 28 (2002): 165–90.

Henderson, James D. *When Columbia Bled: A History of the Violencia in Tolima.* University: University of Alabama Press, 1985.

Henderson, Timothy J. *The Worm in the Wheat: Rosalie Evans and Agrarian Struggle in the Puebla–Tlaxcala Valley of Mexico, 1906–1927.* Durham, NC: Duke University Press, 1998.

Hentea, Călin. *Brief Romanian History.* Lanham, MD: Scarecrow Press, 2007.

Henze, Paul. *Rebels and Separatists in Ethiopia.* Santa Monica, CA: Rand Corporation, 1985.

Herr, Michael. *Dispatches.* New York: Knopf, 1977.

Herring, George. *America's Longest War.* New York: Wiley, 1979.

Herring, Hubert. *A History of Latin America from the Beginnings to the Present.* New York: Knopf, 1966.

Hewitt, Vernon. "Ethnic Construction, Provincial Identity, and Nationalism in Pakistan: The Case of Baluchistan." In *Subnational Movements in South Asia,* edited by Subrata K. Mitra and R. Alison Lewis, 43–67. Boulder, CO: Westview, 1996.

Hey, Hilda. *Gross Human Rights Violations: A Search for Causes.* The Hague, Netherlands: Kluwer Law International, 1995.

"Hezbollah Braces for Big Syria Battle, But Takes Losses" UPI.com. n.d. http://www.upi.com/Top_News/Special/2013/06/25/Hezbollah-braces-for-big-Syria-battle-but-takes-losses/UPI-44791372183587/#ixzz2XgJwVkSH.

Hicks, Elahé Sharifpour, and Neil Hicks. "The Human Rights of Kurds and the Islamic Republic of Iran." In *Kurdish Identity: Human Rights and Political Status,* edited by Charles MacDonald and Carole O'Leary, 201–12. Gainesville: University Press of Florida, 2007.

Higgins, Noelle. *Regulating the Use of Force in Wars of National Liberation: The Need for a New Regime.* Leiden, Netherlands: Brill, 2010.

Higgonet, Etelle, and Marcie Mersky. *Quiet Genocide: Guatemala 1981–1983.* New Brunswick, NJ: Transaction Publishers, 2009.

Higham, Robin, ed. *Civil Wars in the Twentieth Century.* Lexington: University Press of Kentucky, 1972.

Hill, Richard Leslie. *On the Frontiers of Islam: Two Manuscripts concerning the Sudan under Turco-Egyptian Rule, 1822–1841.* Oxford, UK: Clarendon Press, 1970.

Hillman, James. *A Terrible Love of War.* New York: Penguin Press, 2004.

Hiro, Dilip. *Apocalyptic Realm: Jihadists in South Asia.* New Haven, CT: Yale University Press, 2001b.

______. *Apocalyptic Realm: Jihadists in South Asia.* New Haven, CT: Yale University Press, 2011.

______. The Essential Middle East: A Comprehensive Guide. New York: Basic Books, 2003.

______. *Iran under the Ayatollahs.* London: Routledge and Kegan Paul, 1985.

______. *Lebanon: Fire and Embers.* London: Weidenfeld and Nicolson, 1993.

______. *The Middle East.* Phoenix, AZ: Oryx Press, 1996.

______. *Neighbors, Not Friends: Iraq and Iran after the Gulf Wars.* London: Routledge, 2001a.

"Historia de Venezuela Para Nostros." July 9, 2008. http://web.archive.org/web/20080709051629/http://www.fpolar.org.ve/nosotros/educacional/instituc/guzbgobi.html.

Hitchens, Keith. *Rumania, 1866–1947.* Oxford, UK: Clarendon Press, 1994.

Hitti, Philip Khuri. *A History of the Arabs.* New York: St. Martin's Press, 1970.

______. *Lebanon in History from the Earliest Times to the Present.* London: Macmillan, 1962.

Ho, Ping-ti. *Studies on the Population of China, 1368–1953.* Cambridge, MA: Harvard University Press, 1959.

Hobbes, Thomas. *Leviathan.* Rev. student ed. New York: Cambridge University Press, 1996. Originally published 1651.

Hodges, Donald C. *The Legacy of Che Guevara: A Documentary Study.* London: Thames and Hudson, 1977.

Hoensch, Jörg K. *A History of Modern Hungary, 1867–1994.* London: Longman, 1996.

Holsti, Kalevi J. *The State, War, and the State of War.* Cambridge, UK: Cambridge University Press, 1996.

Holt, Edgar. *The Carlist Wars in Spain.* Chester Springs, PA: Dufour Editions, 1967.

Holt, P. M. *The Mahdist State in the Sudan, 1881–1898.* Oxford, UK: Clarendon Press, 1958.

______. *A Modern History of the Sudan, from the Funj Sultanate to the Present Day.* New York: Grove Press, 1961.

Holt, P. M., and M. W. Daly. *The History of the Sudan from the Coming of Islam to the Present Day.* 3rd ed. London: Weidenfeld and Nicolson, 1979.

______. *The History of the Sudan from the Coming of Islam to the Present Day.* 5th ed. Harlow, Essex: Pearson Education, 2000.

Holub, Norman. "The Brazilian Sabinada (1837–38) Revolt of the Negro Masses." *The Journal of Negro History* 54, no. 3 (1969): 275–83.

Home Office. "Burundi Country Report." *Country Information and Policy Unit* (April 2004).

Honey, Martha. *Hostile Acts: U.S. Policy in Costa Rica in the 1980s.* Gainesville: University Press of Florida, 1994.

Hoole, Francis W., and Dina A. Zinnes, eds. *Quantitative International Politics.* New York: Praeger Publishers, 1976.

Horam, M. *Naga Insurgency: The Last Thirty Years.* New Delhi, IN: Cosmo Publications, 1988.

Hordynski, Joseph. *History of the Late Polish Revolution.* Boston, MA: Carter and Hendle, 1832.

Horne, Alastair. *A Savage War of Peace.* New York: Viking Press, 1977.

Horton, Lynn. *Peasants in Arms: War and Peace in the Mountains of Nicaragua, 1979–1994.* Athens: Ohio University Center for International Studies, 1998.

Hösch, Edgar. *The Balkans.* New York: Crane, Russak & Company, 1972.

Hoskyns, Catherine. *The Congo since Independence, January 1960–December 1961.* London: Oxford University Press, 1965.

Howard, Douglas A. *The History of Turkey.* Westport, CT: Greenwood Press, 2001.

Howe, Herbert. "Lessons of Liberia: ECOMOG and Regional Peacekeeping." In *Nationalism and Ethnic Conflict*, edited by Michael E. Brown, Owen R. Coté Jr., Sean M. Lynn-Jones, and Steven E. Miller. Cambridge, MA: MIT Press, 1997.

Hozier, Henry Montague. *The Russo-Turkish War.* 2 vols. London: W. Mackenzie, 1878.

Hsüan-chih, Tsai. *The Red Spears, 1916–1949.* Translated by Ronald Suleski. Ann Arbor: University of Michigan Center for Chinese Studies, 1985.

Hsüeh, Chün-tu. *Huanh Hsing and the Chinese Revolution.* Stanford, CA: Stanford University Press, 1961.

Hubbard, Ben. "Syrian Rebels Eject Qaeda Extremists." *International New York Times*, January 10, 2014, 4.

Hu-DeHart, Evelyn. *Yaqui Resistance and Survival: The Struggle for Land and Autonomy, 1821–1920.* Madison: University of Wisconsin Press, 1984.

Hudson, Miles. *Intervention in Russia 1918–1920: A Cautionary Tale.* South Yorkshire, UK: Leo Cooper, 2004.

Hudson, Rex A. *Brazil a Country Study.* Washington, DC: Library of Congress, 1997.

Human Rights Watch. "Abducted and Abused: Renewed Conflict in Northern Uganda." *Human Rights Watch* 15, no. 12(A) (July 2003b).

______. "Afghanistan: Crisis of Impunity." *Human Rights Watch* 13, no. 3 (July 2001a).

______. *Angola: Arms Trade and Violations of the Laws of War since the 1992 Elections.* New York: Human Rights Watch, 1994a.

______. *Angola: Violations of the Laws of War by Both Sides.* New York: Human Rights Watch, April 1989b.

______. "Annual Report 1989, Guatemala." 1989a. http://www.hrw.org/reports/1989/WR89/Guatemala .htm.

______. "Civilian Deaths in the NATO Air Campaign." 2000a. http://www.hrw.org/reports/2000/nato/natbm200–01.htm.

______. "Human Rights Abuses by the Liberian Peace Council and the Need for International Oversight," *Reports* 6, no. 3 (May 17, 1994c).

______. "Hundreds of Lives Lost on Ivory Coast Amidst Slow International Response." March 25, 2011. http://www.hrw.org/news/2022/03/25.

______. "Indonesia: Aceh under Martial Law: Inside the Secret War." *Human Rights Watch* 15, no 10(C) (December 2003b).

______. *Indonesia: The May 3, 1999 Killings in Aceh.* New York: Human Rights Watch, 1999. http://www.hrw .org/legacy/campaigns/indonesia/aceh0515.htm.

______. "Ituri: Bloodiest Corner of Congo." 2003a. http://www.hrw.org/campaigns/congo/ituri/ituri.htm.

______. "Pentagon Report Whitewashes Civilian Deaths in Yugoslavia." In *HRW World Report.* 2000b. http://www.hrw.org/press/2000.

______. "Rwanda, Observing the Rules of War?" *Human Rights Watch* 13, no. 8 (December 2001b).

______. "Somalia, Human Developments." 1994b. www.hrw.org/reports/1994.

______. "Under Orders: War Crimes in Kosovo—2. Background." 2001c. http://www.hrw.org/reports/2001/kosovo/underword-01.htm.

______. "Waging War to Keep the Peace: The ECOMOG Intervention and Human Rights," *Reports* 5, no. 6 (June 1993). http://www.hrw.org.reports/1993/liberia.

Human Security Centre. *Human Security Report 2005: War and Peace in the 21st Century.* Oxford, UK: Oxford University Press, 2005.

Human Security Project. *Human Security Report 2009/2010.* Oxford, UK: Oxford University Press, 2011.

Hume, Martin A. S. *Modern Spain, 1788–1898.* London: Putnam, 1900.

Hunt, Jeffrey William. *The Last Battle of the Civil War: Palmetto Ranch.* Austin: University of Texas Press, 2002.

Hunt, Steve. "Rethinking a Model for Peace in Guatemala." *Reports, Science from the Developing World* (September 20, 2002).

Huntington, Samuel. "Patterns of Violence in World Politics." In *Changing Patterns of Military Politics*, edited by Samuel Huntington. New York: Free Press, 1962.

Hupchick, Dennis P. *The Balkans: From Constantinople to Communism.* New York: Palgrave, 2002.

Hupchick, Dennis, and Harold Cox. *The Palgrave Concise Historical Atlas of Eastern Europe.* Rev. and upd. ed. New York: Palgrave, 2001.

Hurst, Christopher O. "Pakistan's Ethnic Divide." *Studies in Conflict & Terrorism* 19 (1996): 179–98.

Hussain, Rizwan. *Pakistan and the Emergence of Islamic Militancy in Afghanistan.* Hampshire, UK: Ashgate, 2005.

Hussein, Tahiri. *Structure of Kurdish Society and the Struggle for a Kurdish State.* Costa Mesa, CA: Mazda Publishers, 2007.

Hutchful, Eboe. "The ECOMOG Experience with Peacekeeping in West Africa." *Wither Peacekeeping in Africa?* Monograph No. 36, April 1999.

Hutchinson, Sharon E. "A Curse from God? Religious and Political Dimensions of the Post-1991 Rise of Ethnic Violence in South Sudan." *The Journal of Modern African Studies* 39, no. 4 (2001): 307–31.

Hutt, Michael. "Introduction." In *Himalayan People's War: Nepal's Maoist Rebellion*, edited by Michael Hutt, 1–20. Bloomington: Indiana University Press, 2004.

Hydrick, Blair, and Barbara Brown. *A Guide to the Microfilm Edition of Confidential US State Department Central Files: Laos, 1960–January 1963*. Bethesda, MD: Lexis-Nexis, 2003.

Hylton, Forrest. *Evil Hour in Colombia*. London: Verso, 2006.

Immigration and Refugee Board of Canada. "Chad: Leadership of the United Front for Democratic Change (*Front uni pour le changement*, FUC) in 2005–2006." April 29, 2009. http://www.refworld.org/docid/4b20f02e3chtml.

______. "The Movement for Democracy and Justice in Chad (MDJT)." December 1999. http://www.ecoi.net/local_link/196298/314974_de.html.

"The Implications of the Iran–Iraq Agreement." Joint Intelligence Analysis by the U.S. State Department, CIA, and DIA. May 1, 1975. http://www.gwu.edu/~nsarchiv/NSAEBB/NSAEBB167/01.pdf.

Inbaraj, Sonny. *East Timor: Blood and Tears in ASEAN*. Rev. ed. Chiang Mai, Thailand: Silkworm Books, 1997.

Independent International Commission on Kosovo. *The Kosovo Report*. Oxford, UK: Oxford University Press, 2000.

"Indonesia Denies 1,000 Killed." *The Canberra Times*, March 17, 1967, 5.

"Indonesia's Indigesation Troubles." *Cairns Post*, June 12, 1954, 9.

"Indonesian Army Fighting Terrorists in Java." *The West Australian (Perth)*, March 21, 1952, 4.

"Indonesians Hunt Rebel Irian Chief." *The Canberra Times*, August 27, 1966, 3.

"Indonesians Hunt West Irian Rebels." *The Canberra Times*, December 5, 1968, 2.

Ingram, Doreen, and Leila Ingram, eds. *Records of Yemen, 1798–1960*. Vols. 4–5. 1993.

Ingrams, Harold. *The Yemen*. London: John Murray, 1963.

INS Resource Information Center. "Somalia, Things Fall Apart." In *Alert Series*. Department of Justice, January 1993.

"Insurgents Crushed, Ben Bella Reports." *Dallas Morning News*, December 12, 1962, 16.

Integrated Regional Information Networks (IRIN). "Yemen: The Conflict in Saada Governorate—Analysis." 2008. http://www.refworld.org/docid/488f180d1e.html.

International Crisis Group. "Aceh: A Slim Chance for Peace." *Indonesia Briefing* (March 27, 2002a): 1–15.

______. "The Burundi Rebellion and the Ceasefire Negotiations." *Africa Briefing* (August 6, 2002c).

______. "Central African Republic: Better Late Than Never." *Africa Briefing* 96 (December 2, 2013a).

______. "CrisisWatch Database: Central African Republic." 2012–2014. http://www.crisisgroup.org/en/publication-type/crisiswatch.aspx.

______. "CrisisWatch Database: Nigeria," 2011–2015. http://www.crisisgroup.org/en/publication-type/crisiswatch.aspx.

______. "A Critical Period for Ensuring Stability in Côte d'Ivoire." *Africa Report*, 176 (August 1, 2011).

______. "Curbing Violence in Nigeria (II): The Boko Haram Insurgency." *Africa Report* 216 (April 4, 2014).

______. "Ethiopia: Ethnic Federalism and Its Discontents." *Africa Report* 153 (September 3, 2009).

______. "Guinea: Reforming the Army." *Africa Report* 164 (September 23, 2010a).

______. "Liberia Unravelling." August 2002b. http://www.crisisweb.org/projects.

______. "Northern Nigeria: Background to Conflict." *Africa Report* 168 (December 20, 2010b).

______. "Rwanda/Uganda: A Dangerous War of Nerves." *Africa Briefing* (December 21, 2001): 1–15.

______. "Sudan's Spreading Conflict (I): War in South Kordofan." *Africa Report* 198 (February 14, 2013c). http://www.crisisgroup.org/~/media/Files/africa/horn-of-africa/sudan/198-sudans-spreading-conflict-i-war-in-south-kordofan.pdf.

______. "Sudan's Spreading Conflict (II): War in Blue Nile." *Africa Report* 204 (June 18, 2013d). http://www.crisisgroup.org/~/media/Files/africa/horn-of-africa/sudan/204-sudans-spreading-conflict-ii-war-in-blue-nile.

______. "A Tentative Peace in Myanmar's Kachin Conflict." *Crisis Group Asia Briefing* 140 (June 12, 2013b). http://www.crisisgroup.org/~/media/Files/asia/south-east-asia/burma-myanmar/b140-a-tentative-peace-in-myanmars-kachin-conflict.pdf.

International Institute for Strategic Studies. "International Terrorism." Armed Conflict Database, 2003. http://acd/iiss.org/armedconflict.

______. "Sri Lanka (LTTE)" Armed Conflict Database, 2006. http://acd/iiss.org/armedconflict.

International Rescue Committee. "The IRC in Democratic Republic of Congo." December 2004. http://www.theirc.org/drc.

______. "Mortality in the Democratic Republic of Congo: An Ongoing Crisis." 2008.

Iorio, Anthony di. "Italy and Rumania in 1914: The Italian Assessment of the Rumanian Situation, 1907 to 1914." In *Rumanian Studies, an International Annual of the Humanities and Social Sciences, 1976–1979*, vol. IV, edited by Keith Hitchens. Leiden, the Netherlands: E. J. Brill, 1979.

IPS—Inter-Press Service. "Guatemala: Government, Army Spurn Rebel Offer to Dialogue." January 26, 1990.

Iralu, Kaka D. *The Naga Saga*. 3rd ed. Kohima, India: ACLS Offset Press, 2009.

Iraq Body Count. "Iraq 2014: Civilian Deaths Almost Doubling Year on Year." 2015. https://www.iraqbodycount.org/analysis/numbers/2014/.

______. "Iraqi Deaths from Violence 2003–2011." 2012. http://www.iraqbodycount.org/analysis/numbers/2011/.

______. "Iraqi Deaths from Violence in 2010." 2010. http://www.iraqbodycount.org/analysis/numbers/2010/.

______. "Iraqi Deaths from Violence in 2012." 2013. http://www.iraqbodycount.org/analysis/numbers/2012/.

IRIN (Integrated Regional Information Networks). "Burundi: IRIN Focus on Rebel Movements." UN Office for the Coordination of Humanitarian Affairs, November 2001.

______. "DRC: Ituri Conflict Linked to Illegal Exploitation of Natural Resources." UN Office for the Coordination of Humanitarian Affairs, September 3, 2004.

______. "DRC: Who's Who in Ituri–Militia Organizations, Leaders." UN Office for the Coordination of Humanitarian Affairs, April 29, 2005.

______. "West Africa Update 224." UN Office for the Coordination of Humanitarian Affairs, June 6–8, 1998.

IRIN News Reports. Multiple stories 1999–2013. http://www.irinnews.org/reports.

Irwin, Domingo, and Ingrid Micett. *Caudillos, Militares y Poder: Una Historia del Pretorianismo en Venezuela*. Caracas, Venezuela: Universidad Católica Andrés Bello, 2008.

Isaacs, Arnold R., Gordon Handy, Macalister Brown, and the Editors of Boston Publishing Company. *Pawns of War: Cambodia and Laos*. Boston, MA: Boston Publishing Company, 1987.

Isaacs, Harold R. *The Tragedy of the Chinese Revolution*. Stanford, CA: Stanford University Press, 1961.

"ISIL Says It Faces War with Nusra in Syria." *Al Jazeera*, March 8, 2014. http://www.aljazeera.com/news/middleeast/2014/03/isil-says-it-faces-war-with-nusra-syria-20143719484991740.html.

"ISIS Attack on Northern Syria Continues—Turkish Daily." *BBC Monitoring Europe—Political*. July 14, 2014.

"ISIS, Islamist Rebels Clash over Eastern Oil Fields." *The Daily Star (Lebanon)*, March 28, 2014.

"Islamic State Faces War of Attrition in Syria Border Town." *Al-Arab*, November 15, 2014.

Ismael, Tareq Y., and Jacqueline S. Ismael. *PRD Yemen, Politics, Economic, and Society*. London: Frances Pinter, 1986.

Iyob, Ruth, and Gilbert M. Khadiagala. *Sudan, the Elusive Quest for Peace*. Boulder, CO: Lynne Rienner, 2006.

Jack, Freeman. "The al Houthi Insurgency in the North of Yemen: An Analysis of the Shabab al Moumineen." *Studies in Conflict & Terrorism* 32, no. 11 (2009): 1008–19.

Jackson, Karl D. *Traditional Authority, Islam, and Rebellion: A Study of Indonesian Political Behavior*. Berkeley: University of California Press, 1980.

Jackson, Paul. "Legacy of Bitterness: Insurgency in North West Rwanda." *Small Wars and Insurgencies* 15, no. 1 (Spring 2004): 19–37.

______. "The March of the Lord's Resistance Army: Greed or Grievance in Northern Uganda?" *Small Wars and Insurgencies* 13, no. 3 (Autumn 2002): 29–52.

Jackson, Richard. "Critical Perspectives." In *The Routledge Handbook of Civil Wars*, edited by Edward Newman and Karl DeRouen, Jr., 79–90. London: Routledge, 2014.

Jackson, Wanda Faye. *The Diplomatic Relationship Between the United States and Haiti 1862–1900*. PhD diss., University of Kentucky, Department of History, 1999.

Jacques, Tony, ed. *Dictionary of Battles and Sieges: A Guide to 8,500 Battles from Antiquity through the Twenty-first Century*. Westport, CT: Greenwood, 2006.

Jae-gen, Cho. "The Connection of the Sino-Japanese War to the Peasant War of 1894." *Korea Journal* 34, no. 4 (1994): 45–58.

"Jakarta Adds to Amboina Force." *New York Times*, October 30, 1950, 2.

"Jakarta Battles North's Rebel Reign of Terror." *Sunday Herald Sun (Melbourne)*, July 29, 1990.

Jamal, Ahmed Abdullah. "Mukti Bahini and the Liberation War of Bangladesh: A Review of Conflicting Views." *Asian Affairs* 30, no. 4 (2008): 5–17.

Jamal, Arif. *Shadow War: The Untold Story of Jihad in Kashmir*. Brooklyn, NY: Melville House, 2009.

James, W. Martin, III. *A Political History of the Civil War in Angola*. Rev. ed. New Brunswick, NJ: Transaction Publishers, 2011.

Jane's Defense. "Kosovo: Background to Crisis (March 1999)." 1999. http://www.janes.com/defence/news/kosovo/misc990301_03_n.shtml.

Jankauskienė, Edita. "Chapter 4, the 1944–1953 Lithuanian Partisan War with the Soviet Union." In *Wars of Lithuania, a Systematic Quantitative Analysis of Lithuania's Wars in the Nineteenth and Twentieth Centuries*, edited by Gediminas Vitkus. Vilnius, Lithuania: EUGRIMAS, 2014.

Jansen, Marius B. *The Making of Modern Japan*. Cambridge, MA: Belknap Press of Harvard University Press, 2000.

______. "The Meiji Restoration." In *The Emergence of Meiji Japan*, edited by Marius B. Jansen, 144–202. Cambridge, UK: Cambridge University Press, 1995.

Jansz, Frederica. "Haunting Memories of the JVP that Linger." *The Sunday Leader (Colombo, Sri Lanka)* 36, no. 10 (March 21, 2004). http://www.thesundayleader.lk/archive/20040321/spotlight.htm.

Jaques, Tony. *Battles and Sieges: A Guide to 8,500 Battles from Antiquity through the Twenty-first Century*. Vols. 1–3. Westport, CT: Greenwood Press, 2007.

Jasci, Oscar. *Revolution and Counter-revolution in Hungary*. New York: Howard Fertig, 1969.

Jawad, Sa'ad. *Iraq & the Kurdish Question 1958–1970*. London: Ithaca Press, 1981.

Jeffrey, William H. *Mitre and Argentina*. New York: Library Publishers, 1952.

Jelavich, Barbara. *History of the Balkans: Eighteenth and Nineteenth Centuries*. Cambridge, UK: Cambridge University Press, 1983.

Jelavich, Charles, and Barbara Jelavich. *The Establishment of the Balkan National States, 1804–1920*. Seattle: University of Washington Press, 1977.

Jen Yu-Wen. *The Taiping Revolutionary Movement*. New Haven, CT: Yale University Press, 1973.

Jendia, Catherine. *The Sudanese Civil Conflict: 1969–1985*. New York: Peter Long, 2002.

Jenks, Robert D. *Insurgency and Social Disorder in Guizhou: The "Miao" Rebellion, 1854–1873*. Honolulu: University of Hawaii Press, 1994.

Jensen, Amy Elizabeth. *Guatemala*. New York: Exposition, 1955.

______. *The Makers of Mexico*. Philadelphia, PA: Dorrance, 1953.

Jochmus, Augustus. *The Syrian War and the Decline of the Ottoman Empire*. 2 vols. Berlin, Germany: Albert Cohn, 1883.

Joes, Anthony. *Victorious Insurgencies: Four Rebellions That Shaped Our World*. Lexington: University Press of Kentucky, 2010.

Joffé, George. "National Reconciliation and General Amnesty in Algeria." *Mediterranean Politics* 13 no. 2 (2008): 213–28.

Johnson, Donald. *The Northern Expedition*. Honolulu: University of Hawaii Press, 1976.

Johnson, Douglas H. *The Root Causes of Sudan's Civil Wars*. Oxford, UK: James Currey, 2003.

______. *The Root Causes of Sudan's Civil Wars*. Bloomington: Indiana University Press, 2004.

Johnson, Douglas H., and Gerard Prunier. "The Foundation and Expansion of the Sudan Peoples' Liberation Army." In *Civil War in the Sudan*, edited by M.W. Daly and Ahmad Alawad Sikainga, 117–41. London: British Academic Press, 1993.

Johnson, Robert. *The Afghan Way of War: How and Why They Fight*. Oxford, UK: Oxford University Press, 2011.

Johnson, Thomas H. "Ismail Khan, Herat, and Iranian Influence." *Strategic Insights* 3, no. 7 (2004). http://www.dtic.mil/cgi-bin/GetTRDoc?AD=ADA485209.

Johnston, Katie A. "Transformations of Conflict Status in Libya." *Journal of Conflict and Security Law* 17 no. 1 (2012): 81–115.

Jok, Jok Madutm, and Sharon Elaine Hutchinson. "Sudan's Prolonged Second Civil War and the Militarization of Nuer and Dinka Ethnic Identities." *African Studies Review* 42, no. 2 (1999): 125–45.

Jolliffe, Jill. "Timor: Resistance Goes On." *The Canberra Times*, May 23, 1980, 7.

Jonas, Susanne. *The Battle for Guatemala, Rebels, Death Squads, and US Power*. Boulder, CO: Westview Press, 1991.

______. "Dangerous Liaisons: The US in Guatemala." *Foreign Policy* 103 (Summer 1996): 144+.

______. *Of Centaurs and Doves: Guatemala's Peace Process*. Boulder, CO: Westview Press, 2000.

Jones, Adam. "Kosovo: Orders of Magnitude." *IDEA–A Journal of Social Issues* 5, no. 1 (2000). http://www.ideajournal.com/articles.php?Id=24.

Jones, Daniel M., Stuart A. Bremer, and J. David Singer. "Militarized Interstate Disputes, 1816–1992: Rationale, Coding Rules, and Empirical Patterns." *Conflict Management and Peace Science* 15, no. 2 (1996): 163–213.

Jones, Gregg R. *Red Revolution: Inside the Philippine Guerilla Movement*. Boulder, CO: Westview Press, 1989.

Jones, Seth G., and Christine Fair. *Counterinsurgency in Pakistan*. Santa Monica, CA: RAND Corporation, 2010.

Jonson, Lena. *Tajikistan in the New Central Asia: Geopolitics, Great Power Rivalry and Radical Islam*. London: I. B. Tauris, 2006.

Jordan, Karl G. *Der Aegyptisch-Turkische Krieg, 1839*. Zurich, Germany: Borsig, 1923.

Joshi, Manoj. *The Lost Rebellion: Kashmir in the Nineties.* New Delhi, India: Penguin Books India, 1999.

Jowett, Philip, and Stephen Andrew. *Chinese Civil War Armies 1911–1949.* Oxford, UK: Osprey, 1997.

"Juan Cristosomo Falcon." n.d. http://www.efemerides-venezolanas.com/html/falcon.htm.

Juba-Based Observer. "The Military Dynamics of South Sudan's Civil War." Enough Forum. July 21, 2014. http://www.enoughproject.org/reports/enough-forum-military-dynamics-south-sudan%E2%80%99s-civil-war.

Judah, Tim. *Kosovo: War and Revenge.* New Haven, CT: Yale University Press, 2000.

Jung, Harald. "Behind the Nicaraguan Revolution." In *Revolution in Central America,* edited by Stanford Central America Action Network. Boulder, CO: Westview Press, 1983.

Jurado, Carlos Caballero, and Nigel Thomas. *Central American Wars 1959–89.* Oxford, UK: Osprey Publishing, 1990.

Jurado, Jonni Alexander Giraldo. *La Guerra Civil de 1860 en el Estado de Antioquia.* Medellin, Colombia: Universidad de Antioquia. 2003. http://biblioteca-virtual-antioquia.udea.edu.co/pdf/11/11_604352368.pdf.

Jureidini, Paul A., R. D. McLaurin, and James M. Price. *Military Operations in Selected Lebanese Built-Up Areas, 1975–1978.* Aberdeen Proving Ground, MD: US Army Human Engineering Laboratory, 1979.

Jwaideh, Wadie. "The Kurdish Nationalist Movement: Its Origins and Development." PhD diss., Syracuse University, Political Science, International Law and Relations, 1960.

Kagan, Robert. *A Twilight Struggle: American Power and Nicaragua, 1977–1990.* New York: Free Press, 1996.

Kahin, Audrey R., and George McTuman Kahin. *Rebellion to Integration: West Sumatra and the Indonesian Polity.* Amsterdam, Netherlands: Amsterdam University Press, 1999.

______. *Subversion as Foreign Policy: The Secret Eisenhower and Dulles Debacle in Indonesia.* New York: New Press, 1995.

Kahin, George. *Nationalism and Revolution in Indonesia.* Ithaca, NY: Cornell University Press, 1952.

Kahin, George, and John Lewis. *The United States in Vietnam.* New York: Dial, 1969.

Kaiser, Daniel R. "The Regional Response to the Crisis in Colombia." Master's thesis, Naval Postgraduate School, Monterey, CA, 2003.

Kaldor, Mary. *New and Old Wars.* Stanford, CA: Stanford University Press, 2001.

Kallendar, George. *Tonghak Heterodoxy and Early Modern Korea.* Honolulu: University of Hawaii Press, 2013.

Kalyvas, Stathis N. *The Logic of Violence in Civil War.* Cambridge, UK: Cambridge University Press, 2006.

Kant, Immanuel. *The Metaphysics of Morals.* Translated by Mary Gregor. New York: Cambridge University Press, 1996. Originally published 1797.

______. *Perpetual Peace and Other Essays.* Translated by Ted Humphrey. Indianapolis, IN: Hackett Publishing Company, 1983. Originally published 1795.

Kaplonski, Christopher. "Resorting to Violence: Technologies of Exception, Contingent States and the Repression of Buddhist Lamas in 1930s Mongolia." *Ethnos: Journal of Anthropology* 77, no. 1 (2012): 72–92.

Kapp, Robert Alexander. "Szechwanese Provincial Militarism and Central Power in Republican China." PhD diss., Yale University, Department of History, 1970.

Karpat, Kemal. "The Transformation of the Ottoman State, 1789–1908." *International Journal of Middle East Studies* 3, no. 3 (July 1972): 243–81.

Kasturi, Bhashyam. *The State of War with Pakistan. A Military History of India and South Asia.* Edited by Daniel P. Marston and Chandar S. Sundaram. Westport, CT: Praeger Security International, 2007.

Kaszeta, Daniel J. "Lithuanian Resistance to Foreign Occupation, 1940–1952." *Lituanus* 34, no. 3 (1988): 5–32.

Kataoka, Tetsuya. *Resistance and Revolution in China: The Communists and the Second United Front.* Berkeley: University of California Press, 1974.

Katra, William H. *The Argentine Generation of 1837: Echeverría, Alberdi, Sarmiento, Mitre.* Cranbury, NJ: Associated University Presses, 1996.

Katumba-Wamala, Edward. "The National Resistance Army (NRA) as a Guerrilla Force." *Small Wars and Insurgencies* 11, no. 3 (Winter 2000): 160–71.

Katz, Friedrich, ed. *Riot, Rebellion, and Revolution, Rural Social Conflict in Mexico.* Princeton, NJ: Princeton University Press, 1988.

Katz, Mark N., ed. *Revolution: International Dimensions.* Washington, DC: CQ Press, 2001.

Katzman, Kenneth. "Iraq's Opposition Movements." Congressional Research Service. June 27, 2000.

Kaufman, Stuart J. *Modern Hatreds: The Symbolic Politics of Ethnic War.* Ithaca, NY: Cornell University Press, 2001.

______. "Spiraling to Ethnic War: Elites, Masses and Moscow in Moldova's Civil War." In *Nationalism and Ethnic Conflict,* edited by Michael E. Brown, Owen R. Coté Jr., Sean M. Lynn-Jones, and Steven E. Miller. Cambridge, MA: MIT Press, 1997.

Kaur, Harminder. *Blue Star over Amritsar.* Delhi: Ajanta Publications, 1990.

Kazemi, Farhad, and John Waterbury, ed. *Peasants and Politics in the Modern Middle East.* Miami: Florida International University Press, 1991.

Keenan, Jeremy. "Mali's Tuareg Rebellion: What's Next?" *Al Jazeera,* March 20, 2012. http://www.aljazeera.com/indepth/opnion/2012/03/20.

Keenan, Jerry. *The Great Sioux Uprising, Rebellion on the Plains, August–September 1862.* Cambridge, MA: Da Capo Press, 2003.

Keesing's Contemporary Archives. London, multiple years.

Keesing's Record of World Events (formerly *Keesing's Contemporary Archives: Weekly Diary of World Events*). 60, no. 5 (May 2014).

______. "Developments in Bosnia-Hercegovina." March 1992.

______. London, multiple years.

Keleher, William Aloysius. *Turmoil in New Mexico, 1846–1868.* Santa Fe, NM: Sunstone Press, 2008. Originally published 1952.

Kell, Tim. *The Roots of Acehnese Rebellion, 1989–1992.* Singapore: Equinox Press, 2010.

Kempster, Norman. "US Copters Fly Guatemala Combat Troops." *Los Angeles Times,* May 6, 1987. http://articles.latimes.com/print.1987–05–06/news/mn-2413_1_guatemala.

Kende, Istvan. "Twenty-Five Years of Local Wars." *Journal of Peace Research* 8 (1971): 5–22.

Kenez, Peter. *Civil War in South Russia 1919–1920.* Berkeley: University of California Press, 1977.

Kerkevliet, Benedict J. *The Huk Rebellion: A Study of Peasant Revolt in the Philippines.* Berkeley: University of California Press, 1977.

Kerr, George H. *Formosa Betrayed.* Boston, MA: Houghton Mifflin, 1965.

Kerr, Malcolm. "The Lebanese Civil War." In *The International Regulation of Civil Wars,* edited by Evan Luard, 65–90. New York: New York University Press, 1972.

Kessel, William B., and Robert Wooster, eds. *Encyclopedia of Native American Wars and Warfare.* New York: Facts on File, 2005.

Kessler, Glenn. "Sudanese Rebels Sign Peace Plan for Darfur." *Washington Post,* May 6, 2006, A01.

Kessler, Richard J. *Rebellion and Repression in the Philippines.* New Haven, CT: Yale University Press, 1989.

Kevin, Tony. "Cambodia's International Rehabilitation, 1997–2000." *Contemporary Southeast Asia* 22, no. 3 (2000): 594–612.

"A Key Battle Cheers Syrian Capital." *Los Angeles Times,* June 7, 2013, part A, 1.

Khalid, Mansour. *The Government They Deserve: The Role of the Elite in Sudan's Political Evolution.* New York: Kegan Paul International, 1990.

Khalidi, Walid. *Conflict and Violence in Lebanon: Confrontation in the Middle East.* Cambridge, MA: Center for International Affairs at Harvard University, 1979.

Khan, Imtiyaz Gul. "Afghanistan: Human Cost of Conflict since the Soviet Invasion." *Perceptions* 17, no. 4 (2012): 209–24.

Khobe, Mitikishe Maxwell. "The Evolution and Conduct of ECOMOG Operations in West Africa." *Boundaries of Peace Support Operations.* Monograph no. 44, February 2000.

Kiasatpour, Soleiman M. "Regime Transition in Post-Soviet Central Asia: The Cases of Tajikistan and Kyrgyzstan." PhD diss., University of California, Riverside, 1998.

Kieh, George Klay, Jr. "The Somali Civil War." In *Zones of Conflict in Africa: Theories and Cases,* edited by George Klay Kieh Jr. and Ida Rousseau Mukenge. Westport, CT: Praeger, 2002.

Kiernan, Ben. *How Pol Pot Came to Power: A History of Communism in Kampuchea, 1930–1975.* London: Verso, 1985.

Kieser, Hans-Lukas. "Alevis, Armenians and Kurds in Unionist-Kemalist Turkey (1908–1938)." In *Turkey's Alevi Enigma: A Comprehensive Overview,* edited by Paul J. White and Joost Jongerden, 177–96. Leiden, Netherlands: Brill, 2003.

Kifner, John. "Newsmen Reaching Aden Get Story of Civil War." *Milwaukee Journal,* January 31, 1986, 14.

Kılavuz, İdil Tunçer. "The Role of Networks in Tajikistan's Civil War: Network Activation and Violence Specialists." *Nationalities Papers* 37, no. 5 (2009): 693–717.

Kim, Eugene C. I. *Korea and the Politics of Imperialism 1876–1910.* Berkeley: University of California Press, 1967.

Kim, Hodong. *Holy War in China: The Muslim Rebellion and State in Chinese Central Asia, 1864–1877.* Stanford, CA: Stanford University Press, 2004.

Kim, Jinwung. *A History of Korea: From "Land of the Morning Calm" to States in Conflict.* Bloomington: Indiana University Press, 2012.

Kimmerling, Baruch S., and Joel Samuel Migdal. *The Palestinian People: A History.* Cambridge, MA: Harvard University Press, 2003.

King, Bolton. *A History of Italian Unity.* Vol. 1. London: James Nisbet, 1899.

King, Charles. *Ending Civil Wars.* Adelphi Paper 308. London: International Institute for Strategic Studies, 1997.

______. *The Ghost of Freedom: A History of the Caucasus.* Oxford, UK: Oxford University Press, 2008.

______. *The Moldovans: Romania, Russia, and the Politics of Culture.* Studies of Nationalities. Stanford, CA: Hoover Institution Press, 2000.

Kingsbury, Damien. "The Free Aceh Movement: Islam and Democratisation." *Journal of Contemporary Asia* 37, no. 2 (2007): 166–89.

Kirişci, Kemal, and Gareth M. Winrow. *The Kurdish Question and Turkey: An Example of a Trans-State Ethnic Conflict.* Portland, OR: Frank Cass, 1997.

Kirkpatrick, Frederick A. *A History of the Argentine Republic.* Cambridge, UK: Cambridge University Press, 1931.

______. *Latin America: A Brief History.* New York: Macmillan, 1939.

Kisangani, Emizet François. *Civil Wars in the Democratic Republic of Congo, 1960–2010.* Boulder, CO: Lynne Rienner Publishers, 2012.

Kisirwani, Maroun. "Foreign Interference and Religious Animosity in Lebanon." *Journal of Contemporary History* 15, no. 4 (October 1980): 685–700.

Klaiber, Jeffrey L. *Religion and Revolution in Peru, 1824–1976.* Notre Dame, IN: University of Notre Dame Press, 1977.

Klarén, Peter F. *Modernization, Dislocation, and Aprismo: Origins of the Peruvian Aprista Party, 1870–1932.* Austin: University of Texas Press, 1973.

______. *Peru: Society and Nationhood in the Andes.* New York: Oxford University Press, 2000.

Klein, Herbert S. *Parties and Political Change in Bolivia 1880–1952.* Cambridge, UK: Cambridge University Press, 1969.

Klein, Herbert S., and Francisco Vidal Luna. *Slavery in Brazil.* New York: Cambridge University Press, 2010.

Kline, Harvey F. *State Building and Conflict Resolution in Colombia, 1986–1994.* Tuscaloosa: University of Alabama Press, 1999.

Knight, Alan. *The Mexican Revolution.* Cambridge, UK: Cambridge University Press, 1986.

Koblas, John. *Fire.* Vol. II in *Let Them East Grass, the 1862 Sioux Uprising in Minnesota.* St. Cloud, MN: North Star Press of St. Cloud, Inc., 2006.

Kochan, Lionel. *Russia in Revolution 1890–1918.* London: Weidenfeld and Nicolson, 1966.

Kohn, George Childs. *Dictionary of Wars.* New York: Facts on File, 1986.

______. *Dictionary of Wars,* Rev. ed. New York: Facts on File, 1999.

______. *Dictionary of Wars,* 3rd ed. New York: Checkmark Books, 2007.

Kolinski, Charles J. *Historical Dictionary of Paraguay.* Metuchen, NJ: Scarecrow Press, 1973.

______. *Independence or Death.* Gainesville: University of Florida Press, 1965.

König, Marietta. "The Georgian-South Ossetian Conflict." Instutut für Friedensforschung und Sicherheitspolitik (IFST) an der Universität Hamburg, 2014.

Koprowski, Mike. "Defeating the FATA Insurgency." *Yale Journal of International Affairs* 4, no. 2 (2009): 66–86.

Korb, Richard K. "Cold War along the 'Cactus Curtain.'" *VFW Magazine* 86, no. 5 (January 1999): 36+. http://www.Questia.com.

Korbani, Agnes G. *US Intervention in Lebanon, 1958 and 1982: Presidential Decisionmaking.* New York: Praeger, 1991.

Kornbluh, Peter. *Chile and the United States: Declassified Documents Relating to the Military Coup, September 11, 1973.* National Security Archive Electronic Briefing Book No. 8. http://www2.gwu.edu/~nsarchive on October 23, 2014.

______. "The Covert War." In *Reagan Versus the Sandinistas,* edited by Thomas W. Walker. Boulder, CO: Westview Press, 1987.

Koschmann, J. Victor. "The Mito Ideology: Discourse, Reform, and Insurrection in Late Tokugawa Japan, 1790-1864." *Monumenta Nipponica* 43, no. 2 (Summer 1988): 241–43.

Kostakos, Georgios. "The Southern Flank: Italy, Greece, Turkey." In *Kosovo and the Challenges of Humanitarian Intervention,* edited by Albrecht Schnabel and Ramesh Thakur. New York: United Nations University Press, 2000.

Kostiner, Joseph. *Yemen: The Tortuous Quest for Unity, 1990–94.* London: Royal Institute of International Affairs, 1996.

Kosut, Hal, ed. *Indonesia: The Sukarno Years.* New York: Facts on File, 1967.

Koth, Karl B. *Waking the Dictator: Veracruz, the Struggle for Federalism, and the Mexican Revolution, 1870–1927.* Calgary, Alberta: University of Calgary Press, 2002.

Kraay, Hendrik. "'As Terrifying as Unexpected': The Bahian Sabinda, 1837–1838." *Hispanic American Historical Review* 72, no. 4 (November 1992): 501–27.

Krauze, Enrique. *Mexico: Biography of Power: A History of Modern Mexico, 1810–1996.* New York: HarperCollins, 1997. (Kindle version)

Kubijovych, Volodymyr E. *Ukraine: A Concise Encyclopedia.* Vol. 1. Toronto, Ontario: University of Toronto Press, 1963.

Kudryashev, Sergei. "The Central Asian Revolt of 1916." In *Arming the State: Military Conscription in the Middle*

East and Central Asia 1775–1925, edited by Erik Jan Zürcher, 79–94. New York: I. B. Tauris, 1999.

Kuhnke, LaVerne. *Lives at Risk: Public Health in Nineteenth-Century Egypt.* Berkeley: University of California Press, 1990.

Kuneralp, Sinan. "Military Operations During the 1904–1905 Uprising in the Yemen." *Studies on Turkish Arab Relations* 2 (1987): 63–70.

Kuodytė, Dalia, and Rokas Tracevskis. *The Unknown War: Armed Anti-Soviet Resistance in Lithuania in 1944–1953.* Vilnius: Genocide and Research Centre of Lithuania, 2006.

"Kurdish People's Protection Unit YPG." 2015. GlobalSecurity.org. http://www.globalsecurity.org/military/world/para/ypg.htm.

"Kurds Enter Northern Syria to Protect Kobane: NGO." *NGO Daily News*, July 16, 2014.

Kurzman, Charles. *The Unthinkable Revolution in Iran.* Cambridge, MA: Harvard University Press, 2004.

Kutschera, Chris. "Mad Dreams of Independence: The Kurds of Turkey and the PKK." *Middle East Report*, 189 (July–August 1994): 12–15.

Lacey, Marc. "Sudan Government and Rebels Agree to Cease-Fire." *New York Times* (late edition), October 16, 2002, A6.

Lacey, Robert. *The Kingdom of Arabia and the House of Saud.* New York: Avon, 1981.

Lachica, Eduardo. *The Huks: Philippine Agrarian Society in Revolt.* New York: Praeger, 1971.

Lacina, B., and N. P. Gleditsch. "Monitoring Trends in Global Combat: A New Dataset of Battle Deaths." *European Journal of Population/Revue Européenne de Démographie* 21, no. 2 (2005): 145–66.

______. "The Waning of War Is Real: A Response to Gohdes and Price." *Journal of Conflict Resolution* (November 15, 2012).

Lacina, B., N. P. Gleditsch, and B. Russett. "The Declining Risk of Death in Battle." *International Studies Quarterly* 50, no. 3 (2006): 673–80.

Lafeber, Walter. *Inevitable Revolutions: The United States in Central America.* New York: W. W. Norton, 1993. Originally published 1983.

Laffin, John. *War Annual 3.* London: Brassey's Defence Publishers, 1989.

______. *War Annual 4.* London: Brassey's Defence Publishers, 1990.

______. *War Annual 5.* London: Brassey's Defence Publishers, 1991.

______. *War Annual 6.* London: Brassey's Defence Publishers, 1994.

______. *War Annual 7.* London: Brassey's Defence Publishers, 1996.

______. *War Annual 8.* London: Brassey's Defence Publishers, 1997.

Lake, David A., and Donald Rothchild, eds. *The International Spread of Ethnic Conflict.* Princeton, NJ: Princeton University Press, 1998.

Lampe, John R. *Yugoslavia as History: Twice There Was a Country.* 2nd ed. Cambridge, UK: Cambridge University Press, 2000.

Landau, Saul. *The Guerilla Wars of Central America.* London: Weisenfield and Nicolson, 1993.

Landingin, Roel. "Manila Focuses on Maoist Threat." *Financial Times (USA Edition)*, July 24, 2006, 5.

Lang, David Marshall. *A Modern History of Soviet Georgia.* New York: Grove Press, 1962.

Langer, Paul F. "Laos: Search for Peace in the Midst of War." *Asian Survey* 8, no. 1 (January 1968): 80–86.

Langer, P. F., and J. J. Zasloff. *North Vietnam and Laos.* Cambridge, MA: Harvard University Press, 1970.

______. *Revolution in Laos: The North Vietnamese and the Pathet Lao.* Santa Monica, CA: RAND Corporation, 1969.

Langer, William L., ed. *An Encyclopedia of World History.* Boston, MA: Houghton Mifflin, 1952. Originally published 1948.

______. *European Alliances and Alignments, 1871–1890.* New York: Alfred A. Knopf, 1931.

Langley, Lester D., and Thomas Schoonover. *The Banana Men: American Mercenaries and Entrepreneurs in Central America, 1880–1930.* Lexington: University Press of Kentucky, 1995.

Laps, Leo. "Os Camponeses do Contestado." *A Nova Democracia* 1, no. 9 (2003). http://www.anovademocracia.com.br/09/15.htm.

Larrosa, Augusto Solza. "Relación Histórica de la Medicina y Cirugía Militares en el Uruguay, 1811–1904." *Salud Militar* 25, no. 1 (2003). http://www.dnsffa.gub.uy/revista/Vol25/P97a128V25.htm.

Larson, Krista. "More than 5,000 Dead in C. African Republic." *AP*, September 12, 2014.

Lary, Diana. *Warlord Soldiers: Chinese Common Soldiers, 1911–1937.* Cambridge, UK: Cambridge University Press, 1985.

Latimer, Elizabeth Wormeley. *Spain in the Nineteenth Century.* Chicago, IL: A. C. McClurg & Co., 1898.

Lattimore, Owen. *Pivot of Asia: Sinkiang and the Inner Afghan Frontiers of China and Russia.* Boston, MA: Little, Brown and Co., 1950.

Lauderbaugh, George M. *The History of Ecuador.* Santa Barbara, CA: Greenwood Press, 2012.

Lawson, Fred H. "Rural Revolt and Provincial Society in Egypt, 1820–24." *International Journal of Middle East Studies* 13, no. 2 (1981): 131–53.

Lear, Jody B., Diane Macaulay, and Meredith Reid Sarkees, eds. *Advancing Peace Research: Leaving Traces, Selected articles by J. David Singer.* London: Routledge, 2012.

Lederer, Edith. "Is Death Estimate for Darfur Too Low?" *AP*, March 28, 2008.

LeDonne, John P. *The Grand Strategy of the Russian Empire, 1650–1831.* New York: Oxford University Press, 2004.

______. *The Russian Empire and the World, 1700–1917: The Geopolitics of Expansion and Containment.* New York: Oxford University Press, 1997.

Lee, Gary Y. "Minority Policies and the Hmong." In *Contemporary Laos: Studies in the Politics and Society of the Lao People's Democratic Republic*, edited by Martin Stuart-Fox, 199–219. St. Lucia: University of Queensland Press, 1982.

Lee, Ki-baik. *A New History of Korea.* Translated by Edward W. Wagner. Cambridge, MA: Harvard University Press, 1984.

Leezenberg, Michiel. "Chapter 12: The Anfal Operations in Iraqi Kurdistan." In *A Century of Genocide: Critical Essays and Eyewitness Accounts*, edited by Samuel Totten, William S. Parsons, and Israel W. Charny. New York: Routledge, 2004.

Lefebvre, Jeffrey A. "Middle East Conflicts and Middle Level Power Intervention in the Horn of Africa." *Middle East Journal* 50, no. 3 (Summer 1996): 387–404.

LeFefvre, Edith E. "Jane Addams: Peace Activist, Intellectual, and Nobel Prize Winner." In *Women Who Speak for Peace*, edited by Colleen E. Kelley and Anna L. Eblen. Lanham, MD: Rowman & Littlefield Publishers, Inc., 2002.

Lefever, Ernest W. *Crisis in the Congo, a United Nations Force in Action.* Washington: The Brookings Institution, 1965.

______. "Peacekeeping by Outsiders: The UN Congo Expeditionary Force." In *Civil Wars in the Twentieth Century*, edited by Robin Higham. Lexington: University Press of Kentucky, 1972.

______. *Spear and Scepter: Army, Police, and Politics in Tropical Africa.* Washington: Brookings Institution, 1970.

"Leftists Free 276 Hostages." *The Tuscaloosa News*, October 30, 1979, 1.

"Leftists Revolution Seen in Future of El Salvador." *Lodi News-Sentinel*, October 15, 1979, 3.

Leger, J. N. *HAITI, Her History and Her Detractors.* Westport, CT: Negro Universities Press, 1970. Originally published 1907.

Legion de los Andes. "Batallas y Combates de la Historia de Chile." n.d. http://legionarios.webhispana.net/33%20Batallas%20y%20Combates/index%20Batallas%20y%20Combates.htm.

Leifer, Michael. "The International Dimensions of the Cambodian Conflict" *International Affairs (Royal Institute of International Affairs 1944* 51, no. 4 (October 1975): 531–43.

Leitenberg, Milton. "Deaths in Wars and Conflicts Between 1945 and 2000." In *Peace Studies: Critical Concepts*, edited by Matthew Evangelista, 88–141. New York: Routledge, 2005.

Leitenberg, Milton, and Richard Dean Burns, comps. *The Vietnam Conflict.* Santa Barbara, CA: ABC–CLIO, 1973.

Leitman, Spencer Lewis. "The Black Ragamuffins: Racial Hypocrisy in Nineteenth Century Southern Brazil." *Americas* 33, no. 3 (1977): 504–18.

______. "Cattle and Caudillos in Brazil's Southern Borderland, 1828 to 1850." *Ethnohistory* 20, no. 2 (1973): 188–98.

______. "Socio-Economic Roots of the Ragamuffin War: A Chapter in Early Brazilian History." PhD diss., University of Texas at Austin, 1972.

Lemarchand, René. *Burundi, Ethnocide as Discourse and Practice.* Cambridge, UK: Cambridge University Press, 1994.

______. "Chapter 10: The Burundi Genocide." In *A Century of Genocide: Critical Essays and Eyewitness Accounts*, edited by Samuel Totten, William S. Parsons, and Israel W. Charny. New York: Routledge, 2004.

______. "Ethnic Genocide." *Society* 12, no. 2 (January–February 1975): 50–60.

______. *Rwanda and Burundi.* New York: Praeger, 1970.

Lenczowski, George. *The Middle East in World Affairs.* 4th ed. Ithaca, NY: Cornell University Press, 1987.

______. *Russia and the West in Iran, 1918–1948: A Study in Big-Power Rivalry.* New York: Greenwood Press, 1968.

Leng, Russell, and J. David Singer. "Militarized Interstates Crises: The BCOW Typology and Its Applications," *International Studies Quarterly* 32 (1988): 115–74. Reprinted in J. David Singer and Paul Diehl, eds. *Measuring the Correlates of War.* Ann Arbor: University of Michigan Press, 1990.

Lesch, Ann Mosely. *The Sudan: Contested National Identities.* Bloomington: Indiana University Press, 1998.

Lesch, David W. *1979: The Year That Shaped the Modern Middle East.* Boulder, CO: Westview Press, 2001.

______. *Syria: The Fall of the House of Assad.* New Haven, CT: Yale University Press, 2012.

Leslie, R. F. *Polish Politics and the Revolution of November.* London: London University, 1956. Originally published 1930.

______. *Reform and Insurrection in Russian Poland.* London: London University, 1963.

"Lessons of Nicaragua's Revolt Don't Quite Fit in El Salvador." *New York Times*, September 16, 1979, 4.

Levene, Ricardo. *A History of Argentina.* Chapel Hill: University of North Carolina Press, 1963. Originally published 1937.

Levine, Robert M. *The History of Brazil.* Westport, CT: Greenwood Press, 1999.

______. "'Mud-Hut Jerusalem': Canudos Revisited." *Hispanic American Historical Review* 68, no. 3 (August 1988): 525–72.

______. *Vale of Tears: Revisiting the Canudos Massacre in Northeastern Brazil.* Berkeley: University of California Press, 1992.

Lew, Christopher R. *The Third Chinese Revolutionary Civil War, 1945–49: An Analysis of Communist Strategy and Leadership.* New York: Routledge, 2009.

Lew, Christopher R., and Edwin Pak-wah Leung. *Historical Dictionary of the Chinese Civil War.* 2nd ed. Lanham, MD: Scarecrow Press, 2013.

Lewis, Paul H. *Guerrillas and Generals: The "Dirty War" in Argentina.* Westport, CT: Praeger, 2002.

______. *Political Parties and Generations in Paraguay's Liberal Era, 1869–1940.* Chapel Hill: University of North Carolina Press, 1993.

Leys, M. D. R. *Between Two Empires.* London: Longmans, Green, 1955.

Li, Chien-Nung. *The Political History of China, 1840–1928.* Princeton, NJ: Van Nostrand, 1956.

Li, Xiaobing. *A History of the Modern Chinese Army.* Lexington: University Press of Kentucky, 2007.

Li, Xiaoxiao. "Fourth Field Army (1948–1955)." In *China at War: An Encyclopedia*, edited by Xiaobing Li, 126–28. Santa Barbara, CA: ABC–CLIO, 2012.

Library of Congress (Federal Research Division). *Lebanon: A Country Study.* Washington, DC: Government Printing Office, 1989.

Liebman, Marcel. *The Russian Revolution.* New York: Vintage, 1970.

Linantud, John L. "Backs against the Wall: War, Dictatorship, and Democracy in the Philippines, South Korea, and Thailand." PhD diss., Arizona State University, 2000.

Lincoln, W. Bruce. *Red Victory: A History of the Russian Civil War.* New York: Simon and Schuster 1989.

Linebarger, Paul M. A. *The China of Chiang K'ai-Shek.* Boston, MA: World Peace Foundation, 1941.

Ling, Dwight L. *Tunisia: From Protectorate to Republic.* Bloomington: Indiana University Press, 1967.

Linke, Lilo. *Ecuador, Country of Contrasts.* London: Oxford University Press, 1960.

Lin-Le. *Ti Ping Tien-Kwoh: The History of the Ti-Ping Revolution.* London: Day and Son, 1866.

Lintner, Bertil. *Burma in Revolt: Opium and Insurgency since 1948.* 2nd ed. Chiang Mai, Thailand: Silkworm Books, 1999.

______. *The Rise and Fall of the Communist Party of Burma (CPB).* Ithaca, NY: Southeast Asian Program, Cornell University, 1990.

Lipman, Jonathan Neaman. "The Border World of Gansu, 1895–1935." PhD thesis, Stanford University, 1981.

______. "Ethnicity and Politics in Republican China: The Ma Family Warlords of Gansu." *Modern China* 10, no. 3 (July 1984): 285–316.

______. *Familiar Strangers: A History of Muslims in Northwest China.* Seattle: University of Washington Press, 1997.

Lisbon Correspondent. "East Timor." *The Economist*, May 26, 1979.

Litten, Frederick S. "The CCP and the Fujian Rebellion." *Republican China* 14, no. 1 (1988): 57–74.

Little, Michael R. *A War of Information: The Conflict Between Public and Private US Foreign Policy on El Salvador, 1979–1992.* Lanham, MD: University Press of America, 1994.

Livermore, H. V. *A New History of Portugal.* 2nd ed. New York: Cambridge University Press, 1966.

Livermore, Thomas L. *Numbers and Losses in the Civil War in America: 1861–65.* Bloomington: Indiana University Press, 1957. Originally published 1900.

Lizee, Pierre P. "Cambodia in 1995: From Hope to Despair." *Asian Survey* 36, no. 1 (1996): 83–88.

______. "Cambodia in 1996: Of Tigers, Crocodiles, and Doves." *Asian Survey* 37, no. 1 (1997): 65–71.

Llano, Alonso Valencia. "Tomás Cipriano de Mosquera y la Guerra en el Cauca Entre 1859 y 1862." In *Las Guerras Civiles Desde 1830 y su Proyección en el Siglo XX*, edited by Ernesto Restrepo Tirado, 91–104. Bogotá, Colombia: Museo Nacional de Colombia, 1997.

Lobato, Chantal. "Chronology (1977–1987)." In *Afghanistan: The Terrible Decade 1978–1988*, edited by Curtis Cate, 9–42. New York: American Foundation for Resistance International, 1988.

Locke, John. *Second Treatise of Government.* Indianapolis, IN: Hackett Publishing Company, 1980. Originally published 1690.

Loeb, Vernon. "Yugoslav Military Is Formidable Foe." *Washington Post*, April 3, 1999, A9. http://www.washingtonpost.com/wp-srv/inatl/daily/april99/ forces040399.htm.

London Times. Issues from July 1, 1875, to June 30, 1876.

"Long Time to Crush Rebels on Timor, Malik Says." *The Canberra Times*, February 21, 1977, 3.

Longman, Timothy. *Christianity and Genocide in Rwanda.* New York: Cambridge University Press, 2010.

Lorimer, John Gordon. *Gazetteer of the Persian Gulf, 'Omān, and Central Arabia.* Vol. I, Part 1B. Westmead, England: Gregg International Publishers Limited, 1970. Originally published 1915.

Love, Joseph. *Rio Grande do Sul and Brazilian Regionalism, 1882–1930.* Stanford, CA: Stanford University Press, 1971.

Loveman, Brian, and Thomas M. Davies Jr. "Che on Guerrilla Warfare." In *Guerrilla Warfare*, by Che Guevara. Lincoln: University of Nebraska Press, 1985a.

______. "Colombia." In *Guerrilla Warfare*, by Che Guevara. Lincoln: University of Nebraska Press, 1985b.

Lowry, Robert. *The Armed Forces of Indonesia.* St. Leonards, NSW: Allen and Unwin, 1996.

Loxton, Edward. "Hundreds Die in Obscure War on Burma's border with China." *The Week (UK)*, November 25, 2011. http://www.theweek.co.uk/world-news/42982/hundreds-die-obscure-war-burmas-border-china.

Luciak, Ilya A. *After the Revolution: Gender and Democracy in El Salvador, Nicaragua, and Guatemala.* Baltimore, MD: Johns Hopkins University Press, 2001.

Luckett, Richard. *The White Generals: An Account of the White Movement and the Russian Civil War.* London: Longman Group Ltd., 1971.

Lundry, Chris. "Separatism and State Cohesion in Eastern Indonesia." PhD diss., Arizona State University, Department of Political Science, 2009.

Lynch, Dov. *Russian Peacekeeping Strategies in the CIS: The Cases of Moldova, Georgia & Tajikistan.* New York: Palgrave-Macmillan, 2000.

Lynch, John. *Caudillos in Spanish America, 1800–1850.* Oxford, UK: Clarendon Press, 1992.

Ma'oz, Moshe. *Ottoman Reform in Syria and Palestine, 1840–1861.* Oxford, UK: Clarendon Press, 1968.

______. *Syria and Israel: From War to Peacemaking.* Oxford, UK: Oxford University Press, 1995.

Macartney, C. A. *The Hapsburg Empire, 1790–1918.* London: Weidenfeld and Nicolson, 1968.

MacDonald, Martin. *Kawthoolei Dreams, Malaria Nights.* Bangkok, Thailand: White Lotus Press, 1999.

MacFarquhar, Roderick, and Michael Schoenhals. *Mao's Last Revolution.* Cambridge, MA: Belknap Press, 2006.

MacGahan, J. A. *The Turkish Atrocities in Bulgaria.* London: Bradbury, Agnew, and Co., 1876.

Machado, Kit G. "The Philippines in 1978: Authoritarian Consolidation Continues." *Asian Survey* 19, no. 2 (1979): 131–40.

Machado, Manuel A. "The United States and the de la Huerta Rebellion." *Southwestern Historical Quarterly* 75, 3 (1972): 303–24.

Mackenna, Benjamín Vicuña. *Historia de los Diez Años de la Administracion de Don Manuel Montt.* Tomo I. Santiago, Chile: Imprenta Chilena, 1862.

MacKenzie, David. *The Serbs and Russian Pan-Slavism, 1875–1878.* Ithaca, NY: Cornell University Press, 1967.

Mackie, J. Milton. *Life of Schamyl and Narrative of the Circassian War of Independence against Russia.* Boston, MA: John P. Jewett and Company, 1856.

Mackowski, Joanne. "Table of Military Assets." In *Short War, Long Shadow: The Political and Military Legacies of the 2011 Libya Campaign*, edited by Adrian Johnson and Saqeb Mueen, ix–xii. London, UK: Royal United Services Institute for Defence and Security Studies, 2012.

MacNair, Harley F. *China in Revolution.* Chicago, IL: University of Chicago, 1931.

MacQueen, Benjamin. *An Introduction to Middle East Politics: Continuity, Change, Conflict and Co-operation.* London: Sage, 2013.

Madden, Lori. "The Canudos War in History." *Luso-Brazilian Review* 30, no. 2 (1993): 5–22.

Mafinezam, Alidad, and Aria Mehrabi. *Iran and Its Place Among Nations.* Westport, CT: Praeger, 2008.

Magnus, Ralph H., and Eden Naby. *Afghanistan: Mullah, Marx and Mujahid.* Boulder, CO: Westview Press, 1998.

Magocsi, Paul R. *A History of Ukraine.* Seattle: University of Washington Press, 1996.

Maier, Karl. *This House Has Fallen: Midnight in Nigeria.* New York: Public Affairs, 2000.

Maillart, Ella K. *Forbidden Journey: From Peking to Kashmir.* London: William Heinemann Ltd., 1937.

Makdisi, Ussama. "Corrupting the Sublime Sultanate: The Revolt of Tanyus Shahin in Nineteenth-century

Ottoman Lebanon." *Comparative Studies in Society and History* 42, no. 1 (January 2000): 180–208.

Makino, Valerie. "Kosovo Conflict Chronology: January–August 1998." *CRS Report for Congress*. Washington, DC: Congressional Research Service, 1998.

Malamud, Carlos. "The Origins of Revolution in Nineteenth-century Argentina." In *Rumors of Wars: Civil Conflict in Nineteenth-Century Latin America*, edited by Rebecca Earle, 29–48. London: Institute of Latin American Studies.

Malaquias, Assis. "Angola: How to Lose a Guerrilla War." In *African Guerrillas; Raging against the Machine*, edited by Morten BρÅs and Kevin C. Dunn. Boulder, CO: Lynne Rienner, 2007.

Malcolm, Noel. *Bosnia, A Short History*. London: Macmillan, 1994.

Maley, William. *The Afghanistan Wars*. New York: Palgrave Macmillan, 2002.

______. "Interpreting the Taliban." In *Fundamentalism Reborn? Afghanistan and the Taliban*, rev. ed., edited by William Maley, 1–28. Washington Square: New York University Press, 2001a.

______. "Preface." In *Fundamentalism Reborn? Afghanistan and the Taliban*, rev. ed., edited by William Maley, v–ix. Washington Square: New York University Press, 2001b.

Malian Ministry of Foreign Affairs and International Cooperation. "Mapping of Non-State Armed Groups in the ECOWAS Region." Paper presented at the 6th Ministerial Meeting of the Human Security Network, Bamako, Mali, May 27–29, 2004.

Maliti, Tom. "Rebels, Troops Clash in Chad Capital." *Chicago Tribune*, February 3, 2008, 1, 15.

Mallay, Michael. "Regions: Centralization and Resistance." In *Indonesia Beyond Suharto: Polity, Economy, Society, Transition*, edited by Donald K. Emmerson. Armonk, NY: M. E. Sharpe, 1999.

Mallin, Jay, Sr. *Cuba's Armed Forces: From Colony to Castro*. Reston, VA: Ancient Mariners Press, 2000.

Mallon, Florencia E. "Nationalist and Antistate Coalitions in the War of the Pacific: Junín and Cajamarca, 1879–1902." In *Resistance, Rebellion, and Consciousness in the Andean Peasant World, 18th to 20th Centuries*, edited by Steve J. Stern, 232–79. Madison: University of Wisconsin Press, 1987.

Malloy, James M. *Bolivia: The Uncompleted Revolution*. Pittsburgh, PA: University of Pittsburgh Press, 1970.

Mamdani, Mahmood. *When Victims Become Killers: Colonialism, Nativism, and the Genocide in Rwanda*. Princeton, NJ: Princeton University Press, 2002.

Man, W. K. Che. *Muslim Separatism: The Moros of the Southern Philippines and the Malays of Southern Thailand*. New York: Oxford University Press, 1990.

Mananghaya, James. "AFP: Communist Influence Weakens." *Philippine Star*, January 1, 2008.

Mankekar, D. R. *On the Slippery Slope in Nagaland*. Bombay, India: Manaktalas, 1967.

Manwaring, Max G. "Nonstate Actors in Colombia: Threat and Response." Strategic Studies Institute, May 2002.

Manz, Beatriz. *Refugees of a Hidden War*. Albany: State University of New York Press, 1988.

Maoz, Zeev. "The Controversy over the Democratic Peace: Rearguard Action or Cracks in the Wall?" *International Security* 22 (1997).

Maoz, Zeev, and Errol A. Henderson. "The World Religion Dataset, 1945–2010: Logic, Estimates, and Trends." *International Interactions* 39, no. 3 (2013).

Marchak, M. Patricia. *Reigns of Terror*. Montreal: McGill-Queen's University Press, 2003.

Marchak, Patricia, and William Marchak. *God's Assassins: State Terrorism in Argentina in the 1970s*. Montreal, Québec: McGill-Queen's University Press, 1999.

Marcus, Harold G. *A History of Ethiopia*. Updated ed. Berkley: University of California Press, 2002.

______. *Haile Selassie I*. Lawrenceville, NJ: Red Sea Press, 1987.

______. *The Life and Times of Menelik II: Ethiopia 1844–1913*. Oxford: Clarendon Press, 1975.

Mardsen, Peter. *The Taliban: War and Religion in Afghanistan*. Rev. ed. London: Zed Books, 2002.

Marett, Robert. *Peru*. New York: Praeger, 1969.

Markham, Clements R. *A History of Peru*. Chicago: Charles H. Sergel, 1892.

______. "Travels in Peru and India." *Eclectic Magazine of Foreign Literature, Science, and Art* LIX, no. 1 (1868): 1–20.

Marks, Thomas Andrew. "Insurgency in Nepal." Strategic Studies Institute, December 2003.

______. "Making Revolution: The Insurgency of the Communist Party of Thailand (CPT) in Structural Perspective." PhD diss., University of Hawaii: Political Science, 1991.

Marks, Thomas P. *Insurgency in Nepal*. Carlisle, PA: Strategic Studies Institute, US Army War College, 2003.

Marley, David M. *Wars of the Americas: A Chronology of Armed Conflicts in the New World, 1492 to the Present*. Santa Barbara, CA: ABC-CLIO, 1998.

Marples, David R. *Heroes, and Villains. Creating National History in Contemporary Ukraine*. New York: Central European University Press, 2007.

______. *Stalinism in Ukraine in the 1940s*. New York: St. Martin's Press, 1992.

Márquez, Rafael Angel Rondón. *Crespo y la Revolución Legalista.* Caracas, Venezuela: Ediciones de la Contraloria, 1973.

Marsans-Sakly, Sylvia. Personal correspondence regarding Tunisian Archives, 2003.

Marshall, A. "Phased Withdrawal, Conflict Resolution and State Reconstruction." Master's thesis, Conflict Studies Research Center, Defence Academy of the United Kingdom, 2006.

Marshall, Monty G. "Major Episodes of Political Violence 1946–2013." Center for Systemic Peace, 2014. http://systemicpeace.org/warlist.htm.

Marsland, William D., and Amy L. Marsland. *Venezuela through Its History.* New York: Thomas Y. Crowell Company, 1954.

Martell, Peter. "50,000 and Not Counting: South Sudan's War Dead." *Agence France-Presse,* November 15, 2014.

Martin, B. G. "Ghūma bin Khalīfa, a Libyan Rebel, 1795–1858." In *Studies on Ottoman Diplomatic History V: The Ottomans and Africa,* edited by Selim Deringil and Sinan Kuneralp, 57–73. Istanbul, Turkey: Isis Press, 1990.

Martin, Michael R., and Gabriel H. Lovett. *Encyclopedia of Latin American History.* Indianapolis, IN: Bobbs-Merrill, 1968.

Martin, Percy Falcke. *Maximilian in Mexico: The Story of the French Intervention (1861–1867).* New York: Charles Scribner's Sons, 1914.

Martinez, Luis. *The Algerian Civil War 1990–1998.* Translated by John Derrick. New York: Columbia University Press, 2000.

______. "Why the Violence in Algeria?" In *Islam, Democracy and the State in Algeria,* edited by Michael Bonner, Megan Reif, and Mark Tessler, 14–27. London: Routledge, 2005.

Martinkus, John. "Aceh a Forbidden Province as Military Step up War on Rebels." *New Zealand Herald,* July 2, 2003.

Marwah, Ved. *India in Turmoil: Jammu & Kashmir, the Northeast and Left Extremism.* Kolkata, India: Rupa & Company, 2009.

Mason, T. D., J. P. Weingarten Jr., and P. J. Fett. "Win Lose, or Draw: Predicting the Outcomes of Civil Wars." *Political Research Quarterly* 52, no. 2 (1999): 239–68.

Mason, Thomas David. *Caught in the Crossfire: Revolutions, Repression, and the Rational Peasant.* Lanham, MD: Rowman & Littlefield, 2004.

Masters, Bruce. "The 1850 Events in Aleppo: An Aftershock of Syria's Incorporation into the Capitalist World-System." *International Journal of Middle East Studies* 13, no. 2 (1990): 251–57.

Masterson, Daniel M. *Militarism and Politics in Latin America: Peru from Sánchez Cerro to Sendero Luminoso.* Westport, CT: Greenwood Press, 1991.

Mathews, Rohan D. "The Telengana Movement: Peasant Protests in India, 1946–51." *Ritimo,* July 1, 2011. http://www.ritimo.org/article885.html Last Accessed on May 14, 2014.

Mathieu, Henri. *La Turquie.* Paris, France: E. Dentu, 1856.

Matthews, Bruce. "Sri Lanka in 1989: Peril and Good Luck." *Asian Survey* 30, no. 2 (1990): 144–49.

Matthews, Matt M. *The US Army on the Mexican Border: A Historical Perspective.* Fort Leavenworth, KS: Combat Studies Institute Press, 2007.

Maullin, Richard L. *Soldiers, Guerrillas and Politics in Colombia.* Lexington, MA: D. C. Heath, 1973.

Maurice, C. Edmund. *The Revolutionary Movement of 1848–49 in Italy, Austria-Hungary, and Germany.* New York: Putnam, 1887.

May, R. J. "Muslim Mindanao: Four Years after the Peace Agreement." In *Southeast Asian Affairs,* 263–75. Singapore: Institute of Southeast Asian Studies, 2001.

May, Rachel A. "'Surviving All Changes is Your Destiny': Violence and Popular Movements in Guatemala." *Latin American Perspectives* 26, no. 2 (March 1999): 68–91.

______. *Terror in the Countryside, Campesino Responses to Political Violence in Guatemala, 1954–1985.* Athens: Ohio University Center for International Studies, 2001.

Mays, Terry M. *Africa's First Peacekeeping Operation: The OAU in Chad, 1981–1982.* Westport, CT: Praeger, 2003.

Mbaria, John. "Exit of the Islamists Will See a Revival of Clan Conflicts." *Analysis,* January 9, 2007. http:// allafrica .com.

McAleavy, Henry. *Black Flags in Vietnam.* New York: Macmillan, 1968a.

______. *The Modern History of China.* London: Weidenfield and Nicholson, 1968b.

McBeth, Brian S. *Gunboats, Corruption, and Claims: Foreign Intervention in Venezuela, 1899–1908.* Westport, CT: Greenwood Press, 2001.

McCaa, Robert. "Missing Millions: The Demographic Costs of the Mexican Revolution." *Mexican Studies/Estudios Mexicanos* 19, no. 2 (Summer 2003): 367–400.

McCaffrey, Cecily. "From Chaos to a New Order: Rebellion and Ethnic Regulation in Late Qing Inner Mongolia." *Modern China* 37 no. 5 (2011): 528–61.

McCann, Frank D. *Soldiers of the Pátria: A History of the Brazilian Army, 1889–1937.* Stanford, CA: Stanford University Press, 2004.

McCann, James. "The Political Economy of Rural Rebellion in Ethiopia: Northern Resistance to Imperial Expansion, 1928–1935." *The International Journal of African Historical Studies,* 18, no. 4 (1985): 601–23.

McCarthy, Justin. *Death and Exile: The Ethnic Cleansing of Ottoman Muslims 1821–1922.* Princeton, NJ: Darwin Press Inc., 1995.

______. *The Ottoman Turks, An Introductory History to 1923.* New York: Longman, 1997.

McCarthy, Roger E. *Tears of the Lotus: Accounts of Tibetan Resistance to the Chinese Invasion, 1950–1962.* Jefferson, NC: McFarland and Co., 1997.

McCarthy, Terry. "Indonesian Soldiers Accused of Brutality against Separatists." *The Independent (London),* January 21, 1991.

McClain, James L. *Japan: A Modern History.* New York: W.W. Norton and Co., 2002.

McCleary, Rachel M. *Dictating Democracy: Guatemala and the End of Violent Revolution.* Gainesville: University Press of Florida, 1999.

McCord, Edward A. *Military Force and Elite Power in the Formation of Modern China.* New York: Routledge, 2014.

______. *The Power of the Gun: The Emergence of Modern Chinese Warlordism.* Berkeley: University of California Press, 1993.

McCormack, Gavin. *Chang Tso-lin in Northeast China, 1911–1928: Japan and the Manchurian Idea.* Stanford, CA: Stanford University Press, 1977.

McCoy, James W. *Secrets of the Viet Cong.* New York: Hippocrene Books, 1992.

McDermott, Jeremy. "Colombian Death Squads Cut Down 100 'Rebels.'" *The Scotsman,* January 11, 1999, 7.

McDowall, David. *A Modern History of the Kurds.* New York: I. B. Tauris, 1996.

McGranahan, Carole. "Arrested Histories: Between Empire and Exile in 20th Century Tibet." PhD diss., University of Michigan, Anthropology and History, 2001.

McGregor, Andrew. *A Military History of Modern Egypt.* Westport, CT: Praeger Security International, 2006.

McHenry, J. Patrick. *A Short History of Mexico.* Garden City, NY: Doubleday, 1962.

McKenna, Thomas M. *Muslim Rulers and Rebels: Everyday Politics and Armed Separatism in the Southern Philippines.* Berkeley: University of California Press, 1998.

McKiernan, Kevin. "Turkey's War on the Kurds." *Bulletin of the Atomic Scientists* (March–April 1999): 26–37.

McLaughlin, Sean J. "Ivory Coast: Civil Disorder since 1999." In *Encyclopedia of Conflicts since World War II,* vol. 1, edited by James Ciment, 190–94. Armonk, NY: Sharpe Reference, 2007.

McLynn, F. J. "The Montonero Risings in Argentina during the Eighteen-Sixties." *Canadian Journal of History* 15, no. 1 (1980): 49–66.

______. *Villa and Zapata, a History of the Mexican Revolution.* New York: Basic Books, 2000.

McPherson, James. *The Illustrated Battle Cry of Freedom: The Civil War.* New York: Tess Press, 2008.

McQuerry, Elizabeth. "Central American Women's Organizations: Two Case Studies of Political Participation." Master's thesis, University of Arizona, 1988.

Mehsud, Mansur Khan. "The Taliban in South Waziristan." In *Talibanistan: Negotiating the Borders between Terror, Politics, and Religion,* edited by Peter Bergen and Katherine Tiedemann, 164–201. New York: Oxford University Press, 2013.

Mehta, Ashok, and Mahendra Lawoti. "Military Dimensions of the 'People's War': Insurgency and Counterinsurgency in Nepal." In *The Maoist Insurgency in Nepal: Revolution in the Twenty-first Century,* edited by Mahendra Lawoti and Anup Pahari, 175–94. New York: Routledge, 2010.

Meiselas, Susan. *Kurdistan: In the Shadow of History.* New York: Random House, 1997.

Mejia, Alvaro Tirado. *Aspectos Sociales de las Guerras Civiles en Colombia.* Instituto Colombiano de Cultura, 1976.

Melady, Thomas Patrick. *Burundi: The Tragic Years.* Maryknoll, NY: Orbis, 1974.

"Memoria de la Direccion General de Estadistica al Presidente de los Estados Unidos de Venezuela en 1873." 1873. http://books.google.com/books?id=vc8TAAAAYAA.

Mende, Tibor. *The Chinese Revolution.* London: Thames and Hudson, 1961.

Méndez, Juan E. *Political Murder and Reform in Colombia: The Violence Continues.* New York: Human Rights Watch, 1992.

Mendis, L. M. H. *Assignment Peace in the Name of the Motherland: Eelam War I, IPKF Operations, Eelam War II, Eelam War III, and the Undeclared Eelam War IV.* Colombo, Sri Lanka: Social Scientists' Organization, 2009.

Mendoza, Hugo Andrés Arenas. *¿Estado Irresponsable o Responable?: La Reponsabilidad Patrimonial del Estado Colombiano Luego de la Guerra Civil de 1876–1877.* Bogotá, Colombia: Editorial Universidad del Rosario, 2008.

Menendez Pidal, Ramon. *Historia de Espana.* Vol. 26. Madrid, Spain: Espasa-Calpe, 1968.

Menkhaus, Ken. "Non-state Actors and the Role of Violence in Stateless Somalia." In *Violent Non-state Actors in World Politics*, edited by Klejda Mulaj. New York: Columbia University Press, 2010.

Mennecke, Martin. "Genocide in Kosovo?" In *Century of Genocide*, 2nd ed., edited by Samuel Totten, William S. Parsons, and Israel W. Charny. New York: Routledge, 2004.

Meo, Leila. "The War in Lebanon." In *Ethnic Conflict in International Relations*, edited by Astri Suhrke and Lela Garner Nobel. New York: Praeger, 1977.

Mercer, John. "The Cycle of Invasion and Unification in the Western Sahara." *African Affairs*, 75, no. 301 (October 1976): 498–510.

Meredith, Martin. *The Fate of Africa: From the Hopes of Freedom to the Heart of Despair*. New York: Public Affairs, 2005.

Merrill, Tim, ed. *Honduras: A Country Study*. Washington, DC: GPO for the Library of Congress, 1995. http://countrystudies.us/honduras/17.htm.

Merritt, Richard L., and Dina A. Zinnes, "Foreword." In *Measuring the Correlates of War*, edited by J. David Singer and Paul F. Diehl. Ann Arbor: University of Michigan Press, 1990.

Metz, Helen Chapin. *Persian Gulf States: Country Studies*, 3rd ed. Washington, DC.: Library of Congress, 1994.

Meyer, Jean. *La Cristiada: La Guerra de los Cristeros*. 22nd ed. Mexico City: Siglio XXI. 2005. Originally published 1973.

Meyer, Michael C. *Mexican Rebel: Pascual Orozco and the Mexican Revolution, 1910–1915*. Lincoln: University of Nebraska Press, 1967.

Meyer, Michael C., and William H. Beezley, eds. *The Oxford History of Mexico*. Oxford, UK: Oxford University Press, 2000.

Meyer, Michael C., William L. Sherman, and Susan M. Deeds. *The Course of Mexican History*. 6th ed. New York: Oxford University Press, 1999.

______. *The Course of Mexican History*. 7th ed. New York: Oxford University Press, 2003.

Michael, Franz. "T'ai Ping T'ien-Kuo." *Journal of Asian Studies* 17, no. 1 (November 1957): 67–76.

______. *The Taiping Rebellion: History and Documents*. Vol. I. Seattle: University of Washington Press, 1966.

Michno, Gregory F. *Encyclopedia of Indian Wars: Western Battles and Skirmishes, 1850–1890*. Missoula, MT: Mountain Press Publishing Co., 2003.

Middle East Watch. *Genocide in Iraq: The Anfal Campaign against the Kurds*. New York: Human Rights Watch, 1993.

______. *Syria Unmasked: The Suppression of Human Rights by the Asad Regime*. New Haven, CT: Yale University Press, 1991.

Midlarsky, Manus. *On War: Political Violence in the International System*. New York: Free Press, 1975.

Mietzner, Marcus. *Military Politics, Islam, and the State in Indonesia: From Turbulent Transition to Democratic Consolidation*. Singapore: Institute for Southeast Asian Studies, 2009.

Milani, Mohsen M. *The Making of Iran's Islamic Revolution: From Monarchy to Islamic Republic*. 2nd ed. Boulder, CO: Westview Press, 1994.

The Military Balance. London: International Institute for Strategic Studies, year as provided.

"Military Cites Gains against Insurgents." *Manila Standard*, December 29, 2006.

Miller, Benjamin. *States, Nations, and the Great Powers*. Cambridge, UK: Cambridge University Press, 2007.

Miller, Robert Ryan. *Mexico: A History*. Norman: University of Oklahoma Press, 1985.

Miller, William. *The Balkans: Romania, Bulgaria, Servia, and Montenegro*. Freeport, NY: G. P. Putnam's Sons, 1972.

______. *The Ottoman Empire, 1801–1913*. Cambridge, UK: Cambridge University Press, 1913.

______. *The Ottoman Empire and Its Successors, 1801–1927*. Cambridge, UK: Cambridge University Press, 1927.

______. *The Ottoman Empire and Its Successors, 1801–1927, with an Appendix, 1927–1936*. Cambridge, UK: Cambridge University Press, 1936.

Millett, Richard L. *Colombia's Conflicts: The Spillover Effects of a Wider War*. Carlisle, PA: Strategic Studies Institute, US Army War College, 2002.

Milliken, Robert. "How Papua New Guinea Terrorised Rebel Island." *The Independent (London)*, November 27, 1990, 9.

Minahan, James. *Encyclopedia of the Stateless Nations: Ethnic and National Groups around the World*. 4 vols. Westport, CT: Greenwood Press, 2002.

______. *Nations without States: A Historical Dictionary of Contemporary National Movements*. Westport, CT: Greenwood Press, 1996.

Ministère de La Défense. "'OPÉRTION LÉOPARD,' Une intervention humanitaire Kolwezi 17 mai–16 juin 1978." n.d. http://www.defense.gouv.fr.

Ministerio de Defense Nacional. "Avance de la Politica de Defensa y Seguridad: Información de Criminalidad, Resultados Operacionales, Afectación de las Propias Tropas y Pie de Fuerza. Año Corrido." 2012. http://www.mindefensa.gov.co/irj/go/km/docs/Mindefensa/Documentos/descargas/estudios%20sectoriales/info_estadistica/Avance%20de%20la%20Politica%20de%20Defensa%20y%20Seguridad.pdf.

Minnesota Historical Society. *Minnesota in the Civil and Indian Wars, 1861–1865*. Vol. 1. Minneapolis: Minnesota Historical Society Press, 2005.

Minorities at Risk Project. "Chronology for Acehnese in Indonesia." 2010b. http://www.cidcm.umd.edu/mar/chronology.asp?groupId=85006.

______. "Chronology for Kurds in Iraq." 2010a. http://www.cidcm.umd.edu/mar/chronology.asp?groupId=64504.

______. "Chronology for Kurds in Turkey." 2013. http://www.cidcm.umd.edu/mar/chronology.asp?groupId=64005 Last accessed 6/23/2013.

Miranda, Roger, and William Ratliff. *The Civil War in Nicaragua: Inside the Sandinistas*. New Brunswick, NJ: Transaction Publishers, 1993.

Mishāqa, Mikhāyil. *Murder, Mayhem, Pillage, and Plunder: The History of the Lebanon in the 18th and 19th Centuries*. Translated by Wheeler M. Thackston Jr. Albany: State University of New York Press, 1988.

______. *The Baltic States: Years of Dependence, 1940–1990*. Exp. and upd. ed. London: Hurst and Co., 1993.

Mobley, Richard A. "US Joint Military Contributions to Countering Syria's 1970 Invasion of Jordan." *Joint Force Quarterly* 55 (2009): 160–67.

Møller, Bjørn. "The Nordic Countries: Whither the West's Conscience?" In *Kosovo and the Challenges of Humanitarian Intervention*, edited by Albrecht Schnabel and Ramesh Thakur. New York: United Nations University Press, 2000.

Montgomery, Tommie Sue. *Revolution in El Salvador: From Civil Strife to Civil Peace*. Boulder, CO: Westview Press, 1995.

______. *Revolution in El Salvador, Origins and Evolution*. Boulder, CO: Westview Press, 1982.

Moore, Mick. *Thoroughly Modern Revolutionaries: The JVP in Sri Lanka*. Modern Asian Studies 27, no. 3 (1993): 593–642.

Moore, Perry. *Stamping Out the Virus: Allied Intervention in the Russian Civil War 1918–1920*. Atglen, PA: Schiffer Military History, 2002.

Moorehead, Alan. *The Russian Revolution*. New York: Harper, 1958.

Moosa, Matti. *The Maronites in History*. Syracuse, NY: Syracuse University Press, 1986.

Mora, Enrique Ayala. *Historia de la Revolución Liberal Equatoriana*. Quito, Ecuador: Corporacion Editora Nacional, 1994.

Morales, Waltraud Q. *A Brief History of Bolivia*. New York: Facts on File, 2003.

Morell, David. "Thailand: Military Checkmate." *Asian Survey* 12, no. 2 (February 1972): 156–67.

Moreno, Pedro Carlos Verdugo. *La Guerra Civil de 1876–77 y el Ocaso del Liberalismo Radican en los Estados Unidos de Colombia*. San Juan de Pasto, Colombia: Impresos la Castellana, 2001.

Moreno, Segundo Luis. "La Campaña de Esmereldas de 1913–1916." *Revista: Del Centro de Estudios Historicos y Geograficos* IX, no 33 (1939): 1–49.

Morfill, William R. *Poland*. Freeport, NY: Books for Libraries Press, 1972. Reprint of 1893.

Morón, Guillermo. *A History of Venezuela*. London: George Allen and Unwin Ltd., 1964.

Morozova, Irina. "Revolutionary Mongols, Lamas, and Buddhism (1921–1941)." *IIAS Newsletter* 31 (July 2003): 24.

Morris, Richard B., ed. *Encyclopedia of American History*. New York: Harper, 1970.

Mortensen, Inge Demont. *Nomads of Luristan*. London: Thames and Hudson, 1993.

Mortimer, Robert. "Islamists, Soldiers, and Democrats: The Second Algerian War." *Middle East Journal* 50, no. 1 (Winter 1996): 18–39.

Morwood, William. *Duel for the Middle Kingdom: The Struggle Between Chiang Kai-shek and Mao Tse-tung for Control of China*. New York: Everest House, 1980.

Moseley, Edward H. "Chapter 6: The United States and Mexico, 1810–1850." In *United States–Latin American Relations, 1800–1850: The Formative Generations*, edited by Shurbutt, T. Ray. Tuscaloosa: University of Alabama Press, 1991.

Mosley, Melinda M. "Operation Deliberate Force." *Air Force Library* (March 2000). http://www.au.af.mil.

Mounsey, Augustus H. *The Satsuma Rebellion: An Episode of Modern Japanese History*. Washington, DC: University Publishers of America, 1979. Reprint of 1879.

Mowafi, Reda. *Slavery, the Slave Trade, and Abolition Attempts in Egypt and the Sudan 1820–1882*. Stockholm, Sweden: Esselte Studium, 1981.

Mukhopadhyay, Ashoke Kumar. "Through the Eyes of the Police: Naxalites in Calcutta in the 1970s." *Economic and Political Weekly* 41, no. 29 (2006): 3227–233.

Mullenbach, Mark. DADM—Intrastate Dispute Narratives: Asia/Pacific Region: 15. Philippines (1946–Present). 2013a. http://uca.edu/politicalscience/dadm-project/asiapacific-region/philippines-1946-present/.

______. DADM—Intrastate Dispute Narratives: Asia/Pacific Region: 16. Philippines/Moro National Liberation Front (1946–Present). 2013b. http://uca.edu/politicalscience/dadm-project/asiapacific-region/philippinesmoro-national-liberation-front-1968-present/.

______. DADM—Intrastate Dispute Narratives: Asia/Pacific Region: 16. Philippines/Moro Islamic Liberation Front (1977–Present). 2014. http://uca.edu/politicalscience/dadm-project/asiapacific-region/philippinesmoro-islamic-liberation-front-1978-present/.

______. DADM—Intrastate Dispute Narratives: Middle East/North Africa/Persian Gulf Region: 8. Kingdom of Nadj-Hijaz (1916–1932). n.d. http://uca.edu/politicalscience/dadm-project/middle-eastnorth-africapersian-gulf-region/kingdom-of-nadj-hijaz-1916–1932/.

Munro, Dana Gardner. *Intervention and Dollar Diplomacy in the Caribbean 1900–1921*. Princeton, NJ: Princeton University Press, 1964.

______. *The Latin American Republics*. New York: Appleton-Century-Crofts, 1942.

______. *The Latin American Republics: A History*. New York: D. Appleton-Century-Crofts, 1960.

______. *The United States and the Caribbean Republics 1921–1933*. Princeton, NJ: Princeton University Press, 1974.

Murdoch, James. *A History of Japan*. Vol. III, part 2, rev. ed. Edited by Joseph H. Longford. New York: Frederick Ungar Publishing Co., 1964.

Murray, William Smith. *The Making of the Balkan States*. New York: Columbia University, 1910.

Muslim, Macapado A., and Rufa Cagoco-Guiam. "Mindanao: Land of Promise." *Accord* (1999). http://www.c-r.org/sites/default/files/Accord%2006_2Mindanao%20land%20of%20promise_1999_ENG.pdf.

______. "Mindanao: Land of Promise." *Accord* (2002). http://www.c-r.org/accord.

Mydans, Carl, and Shelly Mydans. *The Violent Peace*. New York: Atheneum, 1968.

Nachmani, Amikam. *Turkey: Facing a New Millennium, Coping with Intertwined Conflicts*. Manchester, UK: Manchester University Press, 2003.

Nadarajah, Suthaharan, and Luxshi Vimalarajah. *The Politics of Transformation: The LTTE and the 2002–2006 Peace Process in Sri Lanka*. Berlin, Germany: Berghof Research Center for Constructive Conflict Management, 2008.

Nahaylo, Bohdan, and Victor Swoboda. *Soviet Disunion: A History of the Nationalities Problem in the USSR*. New York: Free Press, 1990.

Nantet, Jacques. *Histoire du Liban*. Paris, France: Editions de Minuit, 1963.

Nathan, Andrew J. *Peking Politics, 1918–1923: Factionalism and the Failure of Constitutionalism*. Berkeley: University of California Press.

National Archives. *Defense Casualty Analysis System (DCAS) Public Use File, 1950–2005, June 28, 1950–May 28, 2006*. 2006. http://aad.archives.gov/aad/series-list.jsp?cat=WR28.

______. *Statistical Information about Fatal Casualties of the Vietnam War*. 2008. http://www.archives.gov/research/military/vietnam-war/casualty-statistics.html.

NationMaster. "Chad Military Stats." 2005, 2006. http://www.nationmaster.com/country-info/profiles/Chad/Military.

NATO. "NATO's Role in Relation to the Conflict in Kosovo." 1999. http://www.nato.int/kosovo/history.htm.

______. "Operation Deliberate Force." *NATO-OTAN AF SOUTH Fact Sheets* (December 16, 2002). http://www.afsouth.nato.int/factsheets.

Nawawi, Mohammed Ansori. "Regionalism and Regional Conflicts in Indonesia." PhD diss., Princeton University, Department of Political Science, 1968.

Nazzal, Nafez Y., and Laila A. Nazzal. *Historical Dictionary of Palestine*. Lanham, MD: Scarecrow Press, 1997.

Ndarubagiye, Léonce. *Burundi: The Origins of the Hutu–Tutsi Conflict*. Nairobi, Kenya: Léonce Ndarubagiye, 1996.

"NDC Extends Hadi's Term for One Year on a Day Marked by an Assassination." *Yemen Times*, January 23, 2014.

Ndikumana, Léonce, and Emizet F. Kisangani. "The Case of the Democratic Republic of Congo." In *Understanding Civil War: Evidence and Analysis*, vol. 1, edited by Paul Collier and Nicholas Sambanis, 63–88. Washington: World Bank, 2005.

Nelson, Harold D., and Irving Kaplan. *Ethiopia, a Country Study*. Washington, DC: Department of the Army, 1981.

Neumann, Caryn E. "Guinea-Bissau: Civil War, 1998–2000." In *Encyclopedia of Conflicts since World War II*, vol. 1, edited by James Ciment, 186–89. Armonk, NY: Sharpe Reference, 2007.

"New Violence Flares in Indonesia." *Canberra Times*, March 10, 1959, 3.

New York Times, July 15, 1868, 1.

New York Times, September 24, 1869, 1.

New York Times, November 24, 1869, 1.

New York Times, January 21, 1870. 5.

New York Times, February 17, 1870, 1.

New York Times, June 18, 1870, 1.

New York Times, August 28, 1870, 1.

New York Times, October 23, 1870, 1.

New York Times, November 24, 1870, 1.

New York Times, February 5, 1924, 14.

New York Times, February 9, 1924, 8.

New York Times, February 28, 1924, 23.

New York Times, March 10, 1959, 1, 7.

New York Times, March 11, 1959, 1, 34.

New York Times, December 7, 1986, 28.

New York Times. Multiple articles, 2010, 2011. http://www.nytimes.com.

New York Times, multiple years.

New York Times Index, 1909, 1947.

Newman, Edward. *Understanding Civil Wars: Continuity and Change in Intrastate Conflict*. London, Routledge, 2014.

Newman, Edward, and Karl DeRouen, Jr., eds. *The Routledge Handbook of Civil Wars*. London: Routledge, 2014.

Newman, Stephen Morrell. *America: An Encyclopedia of Its History and Biography*. Chicago, IL: G. W. Borland, 1881.

Nhem, Boraden. *The Khmer Rouge: Ideology, Militarism, and the Revolution That Consumed a Generation*. Santa Barbara, CA: Praeger, 2013.

Nickson, R. Andrew. *Historical Dictionary of Paraguay*. 2nd ed. Metuchen, NJ: Scarecrow Press, 1993.

Nietupski, Paul Kocot. *Labrang: A Tibetan Buddhist Monastery at the Crossroads of Four Civilizations*. Ithaca, NY: Snow Lion Publications, 1999.

Nkundabagenzi, Félix. "Ethnicity and Intra-State Conflict: Types, Causes and Peace Strategies—A Survey of Sub-Saharan Africa." In *Ethnicity and Intra-State Conflict*, edited by Håkan Wiberg and Christian P. Scherrer, 280–98. Brookfield, VT: Ashgate, 1999.

Noble, Lela G. "Muslim Separatism in the Philippines, 1972–1981: The Making of a Stalemate." *Asian Survey* 21, no. 11 (1981): 1097–114.

Nodal, Roberto. "The Black Man in Cuban Society: From Colonial Times to the Revolution." *Journal of Black Studies* 16, no. 3 (March 1986): 251–67.

Nofi, Albert A. *A Civil War Treasury: Being a Miscellany of Arms and Artillery, Facts and Figures, Legends and Lore, Muses and Minstrels, Personalities and People*. De Capo Press, 1995.

Nojumi, Neamatollah. *The Rise of the Taliban in Afghanistan: Mass Mobilization, Civil War, and the Future of the Region*. New York: Palgrave, 2002.

Nolutshungu, Sam C. *Limits of Anarchy: Intervention and State Formation in Chad*. Charlottesville: University Press of Virginia, 1996.

Norbu, Dawn. "The 1959 Tibetan Rebellion: An Interpretation." *The China Quarterly* 77 (1979): 74–93.

Norbu, Jamyang. "The Tibetan Resistance Movement and the Role of the CIA." In *The History of Tibet*, vol. 3, edited by Alex McKay, 610–618. London: Routledge Curzon.

______. *Warriors of Tibet: The Story of Aten and the Khampas' Fight for the Freedom of their Country*. London: Wisdom Publications, 1986.

Norden, Deborah L. *Military Rebellion in Argentina: Between Coups and Consolidation*. Lincoln: University of Nebraska Press, 1996.

Nourzhanov, Kirill. "Saviours of the Nation or Robber Barons? Warlord Politics in Tajikistan." *Central Asian Survey* 24 (2005): 109–30.

Nunn, Frederick M. *The Military in Chilean History*. Albuquerque: University of New Mexico Press, 1976.

"Nusra Front Kills 90 ISIL Militants in Syria." *FARS News Agency*, May 25, 2014.

Nzongola-Ntalaja, G. *The Congo: From Leopold to Kabila: A People's History*. London: Zed Books, 2002.

O'Ballance, Edgar. *Afghan Wars, 1839–1992*. New York: Brassey's, 1993.

______. *Arab Guerilla Power, 1967–1972*. London: Faber and Faber, 1974.

______. *Civil War in Lebanon 1975–1992*. New York: St. Martin's Press, 1998.

______. *The Cyanide War: Tamil Insurrection in Sri Lanka, 1973–88*. London, UK: Brassey's, 1989.

______. *The Greek Civil War, 1944–1949*. New York: Praeger, 1966.

______. *Islamic Fundamentalist Terrorism, 1979–95: The Iranian Connection*. Washington Square: New York University Press, 1997.

______. *The Kurdish Struggle, 1920–94*. New York: St. Martin's Press, 1996.

______. *Sudan, Civil War, and Terrorism 1956–99*. New York: St. Martin's, 2000.

______. *The War in the Yemen*. Hamden, CT: Archon Books, 1971.

Oberst, Robert C. "Sri Lanka: The Levels of Violence during the War & After." *The Sri Lanka Guardian*, August 19, 2014. http://www.srilankaguardian.org/2014/08/sri-lanka-levels-of-violence-during-war.html.

O'Brien, Thomas F. *The Revolutionary Mission: American Enterprise in Latin America, 1900–1945*. Cambridge, UK: Cambridge University Press, 1999.

O'Callaghan, Mary-Louise. "Attack on Army Camp Leaves 15 Dead, 6 Injured." *Sydney Morning Herald*, November 5, 1991a, 9.

______. "Painful Peace in Paradise." *Sydney Morning Herald*, February 23, 1991b, 45.

______. "PNG Gives Self-rule to Island." *Sydney Morning Herald*, October 24, 1991c, 7.

______. "Troops Poised to Launch Assault on Jungle Rebels." *Sydney Morning Herald*, June 26, 1989, 9.

Ocampo, Antonio Vélez. *Cartago, Pereira, Manizales: Cruce de Caminos Históricos*. Pereira, Colombia: Editorial Papiro, 2007. http://www.banrepcultural.org/blaavirtual/modosycostumbres/crucahis/indice.htm.

Odom, Thomas P. *Shaba II: The French and Belgian Intervention in Zaire in 1978*. Fort Leavenworth, KS: Combat Studies Institute, 1993.

Oehler, C. M. *The Great Sioux Uprising*. New York: Oxford University Press, 1959.

Ofransky, Thomas P. "Warfare and Instability along the Sudan-Uganda Border: A Look at the 20th Century." In *While Nile, Black Blood: War, Leadership, and Ethnicity from Khartoum to Kampala*, edited by Jay Spaulding and Stephanie Beswick. Lawrenceville, NJ: Red Sea Press, 2000.

O'Kane, Trish. *Guatemala in Focus: A Guide to the People, Politics, and Culture*. Northampton, MA: Interlink Books, 2006.

Olarte, Guillermo Plazas. "El Ejército y Los Conflictos del Siglo XIX." In *Historia de las Fuerzas Militares de Colombia*, edited by Alvaro Valencia Tovar, 147–278. Bogotá: Planeta Colombia Editorial S.A., 1993.

Olcott, Martha B. "The Basmachi or Freemen's Revolt in Turkestan, 1918–24." *Soviet Studies* 33, no. 3 (July 1981): 352–68.

______. *The Kazakhs*. 2nd ed. Stanford, CA: Stanford University Press, 1995.

Olitho, Harold. "The Echigo War, 1868." *Monumenta Nipponica* 34, no. 3 (1979): 259–77.

Oliver, Robert T. *A History of the Korean People in Modern Times: 1800 to the Present*. Newark, NJ: University of Delaware Press, 1993.

Oliver, Roland, and Anthony Atmore. *Africa since 1800*. Cambridge, UK: Cambridge University Press, 2004. Originally published 1972, 1994.

Oliveira, A. R. *Politics, Economics and the Men of Modern Spain*. London: Victor Gollancz, 1946.

Olonisakin, Funmi. "Liberia." In *Dealing with Conflict in Africa: The United Nations and Regional Organizations*, edited by Jane Boulden. New York: Palgrave Macmillan, 2003.

Olson, Robert. *The Emergence of Kurdish Nationalism and the Sheikh Said Rebellion, 1880–1925*. Austin: University of Texas Press, 1989.

______. *Imperial Meanderings and Republican By-Ways: Essays on Eighteenth Century Ottoman and Twentieth Century History*. Istanbul, Turkey: Isis Press, 1996.

______. "The Kurdish Rebellions of Sheikh Said (1925), Mt. Ararat (1930), and Dersim (1937–8): Their Impact on the Development of the Turkish Air Force and on Kurdish and Turkish Nationalism." *Die Welt Des Islams* 40, no. 1 (2000): 66–94.

Onacewicz, Wlodzimierz. *Empires by Conquest*. Fairfax, VA: HERO Books, 1985.

"One Step Forward, Two Steps Back." *Al-Ahram Weekly*, February 28, 2014.

"One Thousand Die in Fierce Battle." *Rome News Tribune*, November 9, 1962, 1.

Onesto, Li. *Dispatches from the People's War in Nepal*. London: Pluto Press, 2005.

Onishi, Norimitsu. "Guinea in Crisis as Area's Refugees Pour In." *New York Times*, February 24, 2001.

"Operation Deliverance." *Details/Information for Canadian Forces (CF)*, Canada National Defense Operations Database, November 28, 2009. http://www.cmp-cpm.forces.gc.ca.

Oppenheim, Lassa. *International Law: A Treatise*. New York: Longmans, Green, and Co., 1906.

Oquist, Paul. "Colombia's 'La Violencia.'" In *The Encyclopedia of Political Revolutions*, edited by Jack A. Goldstone. Washington, DC: Congressional Quarterly, 1998.

______. *Violence, Conflict, and Politics in Colombia*. New York: Academic Press, 1980.

Orend, Brian. *The Morality of War*. Peterborough, Canada: Broadview Press, 2006.

Orsi, Pietro. *Cavour and the Making of Modern Italy*. New York: Putnams', 1914.

Ortega, Enrique Montalvo. "Revolts and Peasant Mobilizations in Yucatán: Indians, Peons, and Peasants from the Caste War to the Revolution." In *Riot, Rebellion, and Revolution, Rural Social Conflict in Mexico*, edited by Katz, Friedrich. Princeton, NJ: Princeton University Press, 1988.

Ortiz, Venancio. "Historia de la Revoluci6n del 17 de Abril de 1854." 2004. Originally published 1855. http://www.lablaa.org/blaavirtual/historia/histrevo/indice.htm.

Osorio, Elisa. "AFP Casualty Tally Exceeds NPA's." *BusinessWorld (Philippines)*, June 29, 2006, S1/12.

Ottaway, David, and Marina Ottaway. *Algeria: The Politics of a Socialist Revolution*. Berkeley: University of California Press, 1970.

Ottaway, Marina. *South Africa: The Struggle for a New Order*. Washington, DC: Brookings Institution Press, 1993.

Páez, Rámon. *Wild Scenes in South America, or, Life in the Llanos of Venezuela.* New York: Charles Scribner, 1862.

Page, Joseph F. *Perón: A Biography.* New York: Random House, 1983.

Page, Stanley W., and Andre Ezergailis. "The Lenin-Latvian Axis in the November Seizure of Power." *Canadian Slavonic Papers* 19, no. 1 (1977): 32–49.

Pahta, Ghulamuddin. "Soviet-Chinese Collaboration in Eastern Turkestan: The Case of the 1933 Uprising." *Journal of the Institute of Muslim Minority Affairs* 11 (1990): 243–53.

Paige, Jeffery M. "Social Theory and Peasant Revolution in Vietnam and Guatemala." *Theory and Society* 12, no. 6 (November 1983): 699–736.

Paine, S. C. M. *The Sino-Japanese War of 1894–1895: Perceptions, Power, and Primacy.* Cambridge, UK: University of Cambridge Press, 2003.

Palacio, Ernesto. *Historia de la Argentina.* Tomo IV. Argentina: Editorial Revisi6n, 1975.

Palacios, Marco. *Between Legitimacy and Violence: A History of Colombia.* Translated by Richard Stoller. Durham, NC: Duke University Press, 2006.

Palmer, Alan. *The Decline and Fall of the Ottoman Empire.* New York: Barnes and Noble Books, 1992.

Palmer, David Scott. "The Revolutionary Terrorism of Peru's Shining Path." In *Terrorism in Context.* Edited by Martha Crenshaw. University Park: Pennsylvania State University Press, 1995.

Papageorgiou, Stephanos P. "The Army as an Instrument for Territorial Expansion and for Repression by the State: The Capodistrian Case." *Journal of the Hellenic Diaspora* 12, no. 4 (1985): 21–34.

Papers Relating to Foreign Affairs, Accompanying the Annual Message of the President to the Second Session, Thirty-Eighth Congress. Part IV. Washington, DC: Government Printing Office, 1865.

Papers Relating to the Foreign Relations of the United States. Vol. 19, part 2. Washington, DC: Government Printing Office, n.d.

Paquin, Lyonel. *The Haitians: Class and Color Politics.* Brooklyn, NY: Multi-Type, 1983.

"Paraguay Rebels Routed." *New York Times,* May 14, 1912.

"Paraguay Revolution." *Thames Star (New Zealand)* XLVII, no. 10310 (March 4, 1911): 2.

"Paratroopers in Sheba's City." *The Glasgow Herald,* December 6, 1962, 8.

Pardo-Maurer, Rogelio. *The Contras, 1980–1989: A Special Kind of Politics.* Westport, CT: Greenwood Publishing Group, 1990.

Park, Alexander G. *Bolshevism in Turkestan 1917–1927.* New York: Columbia University Press, 1957.

Park, James William. *Rafael Núñez and the Politics of Colombian Regionalism, 1863–1886.* Baton Rouge: Louisiana State University Press, 1985.

Parkes, Henry Bamford. *A History of Mexico.* 3rd ed. Boston, MA: Houghton Mifflin Company, 1966.

Parsa, Misagin. *Social Origins of the Iranian Revolution.* New Brunswick, NJ: Rutgers University Press, 1989.

Parsons, Laila. *The Druze Between Palestine and Israel, 1947–49.* New York: St. Martin's Press, 2000.

Pǎrvanova, Zorka. "Changes in the Political Status of the Island of Crete 1894–1899." *Etudes Balkaniques* 25, no. 4 (1989): 64–84.

Patterson, George N. "China and Tibet: Background to the Revolt." *The China Quarterly* 1 (January–March 1960b): 87–102.

______. *Tibet in Revolt.* London: Faber and Faber, 1960a.

Paul, Christopher, Colin P. Clarke, Beth Grill, and Molly Dunigan. *Paths to Victory: Detailed Insurgency Case Studies.* Santa Monica, CA: RAND, 2013.

Paul, Matthew Robert, Jr. "Rural Violence and Social Unrest in Venezuela, 1840–1858: Origins of the Federalist War." PhD diss., New York University, Department of History, 1974.

Payne, James L. *Patterns of Conflict in Colombia.* New Haven, CT: Yale University Press, 1968.

Payne, Robert. *The Civil War in Spain, 1936–1939.* New York: Capricorn, 1970.

______. *Massacre.* New York: Macmillan, 1973.

Payne, Stanley G. *The Franco Regime 1936–1975.* Madison: University of Wisconsin Press, 1987.

Payno, Manuel. "Compendio de la Historia de México, Cuarte Part, Leccíon XXXVII." n.d. http://www.antorcha.net/biblioteca_virtual/historia/compendio/4_37.html.

Pearson, Owen. *Albania and King Zog.* Vol 1 of *Albania in the Twentieth Century: A History.* London: I. B. Tauris, 2004.

Pelissier, Roger. *The Awakening of China, 1793–1949.* London: Secker and Warburg, 1963.

Pelletiere, Stephen C. *The Kurds: An Unstable Element in the Gulf.* Boulder, CO: Westview Press, 1984.

Peña, Mario Aguilera. *Insurgencia Urbana en Bogotá: Motín, Conspiración y Guerra Civil, 1893–1895.* Bogotá: Instituto Colombiano de Cultura, 1997.

Pennell, C. R. *Morocco since 1830: A History.* London: Hurst & Co., 2000.

Pennington, A. Stuart. *The Argentine Republic.* New York: Frederick A. Stokes Co., 1910.

Peou, Sorpong. "Cambodia: A Ray of Hope?" *Southeast Asian Affairs* (1997): 83–103.

Peralta, Gabriel Aguilera, and John Beverly. "Terror and Violence as Weapons of Counterinsurgency in Guatemala." *Latin American Perspectives* 7, no. 2/3 (Late Spring–Summer, 1980): 91–113.

Pérez, Antonio García. *Estudio Político-Militar de la Campaña de Mejico 1861–67.* Madrid, Spain: Imprenta de Avrial, 1901.

Perez, Louis A., Jr. "Cuba, c. 1930–1959." In *Cuba: A Short History*, edited by Leslie Bethell. New York: Cambridge University Press, 1993.

Perkins, Kenneth J. *Tunisia: Crossroads of the Islamic and European Worlds.* Boulder, CO: Westview Press, 1986.

Perlez, Jane. "Indonesian Province Enjoying First Signs of Peace." *New York Times*, January 15, 2003, A3.

Pernell, Jennie. "Cristero Rebellion." In *Concise Encyclopedia of Mexico*, edited by Michael Werner, 146–50. Chicago, IL: Fitzroy Dearborn Publishers, 2001.

Perovic, Jeronim. "The North Caucasus on the Brink." *International Relations and Security Network* (August 29, 2006). http://www.isn.ethz.ch.

Perris, George Herbert. *The Eastern Crisis of 1897 and British Policy in the Near East.* London: Chapman and Hall, 1897.

Perry, Alex. "Bitter Divide Remains in Ivory Coast a Year after Civil War." *Time* (June 11, 2012). http://world.time.com/2012/06/11.

Perry, Elizabeth J. "Social Banditry Revisited: The Case of Bai Lang, a Chinese Brigand." *Modern China* 9, no. 3 (1983): 355–82.

Perry, Elizabeth J., and Tom Chang. "The Mystery of Yellow Cliff: A Controversial 'Rebellion' in the Late Qing." *Modern China* 6, no. 2 (April 1980): 123–60.

Perry, Laurens Ballard. *Juárez and Díaz: Machine Politics in Mexico.* DeKalb: Northern Illinois University Press, 1978.

Perry, Richard O. "Warfare on the Pampas in the 1870s." *Military Affairs* 36, no. 2 (April 1972): 52–58.

Petersen, Alexander. "The 1992–93 Georgia-Abkhazia War: A Forgotten Conflict." *Caucasian Review of International Affairs* 2, no. 4 (Autumn 2008): 188–99.

Petran, Tabitha. *The Struggle over Lebanon.* New York: Monthly Review Books, 1987.

Petras, James. "Revolution and Guerrilla Movements in Latin America: Venezuela, Guatemala, Colombia, and Peru." In *Latin America: Reform or Revolution?*, edited by J. Petras and M. Zeitlin. Greenwich, CT: Fawcett, 1968.

Petrovich, Michael Boro. *A History of Modern Serbia: 1804–1918.* Vol. II. New York: Harcourt Brace Jovanovich, 1976.

Petterson, Donald. *Inside Sudan: Political Islam, Conflict, and Catastrophe.* Rev. ed. Boulder, CO: Westview Press, 2003.

Pettersson, Therése. "UCDP Battle-Related Deaths Dataset, version 5.0." 2014. http://www.pcr.uu.se/research/ucdp/datasets/ucdp_battle-related_deaths_dataset.

Philipp, Thomas. *Acre: The Rise and Fall of a Palestinian City, 1730–1831.* NY: Columbia University Press, 2001.

Philippines Information Bulletin 2, no. 2 (April 1974).

Phillips, Charles, and Alan Axelrod. *Encyclopedia of Wars.* Vols. 1–3. New York: Facts on File, 2005.

Phillips, Christopher. "Syria's Torment." *Survival* 54, no. 4 (2012): 67–82.

Phillips, Steven E. *Between Assimilation and Independence: The Taiwanese Encounter Nationalist China, 1945–1950.* Stanford, CA: Stanford University Press, 2003.

Phillips, Walter Alison. *The War of Greek Independence.* London: Smith, Elder, 1897.

Phisterer, Frederick. *Statistical Record of the Armies of the United States.* New York: Charles Scribner's Sons, 1868.

Pholsena, Vatthana, and Ruth Banomyong. *Laos: From Buffer State to Crossroads.* Chiang Mi, Thailand: MeKong Press, 2006.

Picard, Elizabeth. *Lebanon: A Shattered Country.* Rev. ed. Holmes & Meier Pub., 2002.

Picon, Alirio Gomez. *El Golpe Militar del 17 de Abril de 1854.* Bogotá, Colombia: Editorial Kelly, 1972.

Pierce, Richard A. *Russian Central Asia 1867–1917: A Study in Colonial Rule.* Berkeley, CA: University of California Press, 1960.

Pike, Douglas. *Viet Cong.* Cambridge, MA: MIT Press, 1966.

Pike, Frederick. *The Modern History of Peru.* New York: Praeger, 1967.

Pineo, Ronn F. *Social and Economic Reform in Ecuador: Life and Work in Guayaquil.* Tallahassee: University Press of Florida, 1996.

Pinson, Mark. "Ottoman Bulgaria in the First Tanzimat Period: The Revolts in Nish (1841) and Vidin (1850)." *Middle Eastern Studies* 11, no. 2 (1975): 103–46.

Pitsch, Anne. "The Democratic Republic of Congo (Congo-Kinshasa): The African World War." In *History Behind the Headlines: The Origins of Conflicts Worldwide*, vol. 1, edited by Sonia G. Benson, Nancy Matuszak, and Meghan Appel O'Meara. Detroit, MI: Gale Group, 2001.

Plater, Diana. "Ken Fry Believes in Timor's Dream." *The Canberra Times*, May 26, 1977, 23.

Platt, Stephen R. *Autumn in the Heavenly Kingdom: China. The West, and the Epic Story of the Taiping Civil War.* New York: Alfred A. Knopf, 2012.

"PNG Signs Peace Pact with Rebels." *Herald Sun*, August 22, 1991.

Poggi, Rinaldo Alberto. *Crisis en el Ejército de Operaciones en Entre Rios, 1870.* Buenos Aires, Argentina: Editorial Dunken, 2004.

Polites, Athanase G. *Le Conflict Turko-Egyptien.* Cairo, Egypt: Institut Francaise d'Archeologie Oriental du Caire, 1931.

Polk, William R. *The Opening of South Lebanon, 1788–1840: A Study of the Impact of the West on the Middle East.* Cambridge, MA: Harvard University Press, 1963.

Pollack, Kenneth M. *Arabs at War: Military Effectiveness, 1948–1991.* Lincoln: University of Nebraska Press, 2004.

Pollo, Stefanaq, and Arben Puto. *The History of Albania from Its Origins to the Present Day.* London: Routledge & Kegan Paul, 1981.

Polo, Marco, Jr. "Ibrahim Pacha, the Conqueror of Syria." *New Monthly Magazine* XXXVII, no. CXLVI (February 1833): 153–54.

Porch, Douglas, and María José Rasmussen. "Demobilization of Paramilitaries in Colombia: Transformation or Transition?" *Studies in Conflict and Terrorism* 31 (2008): 520–40.

Posada-Carbo, Eduardo. "Elections and Civil Wars in Nineteenth-century Colombia: The 1875 Presidential Campaign." *Journal of Latin American Studies* 26, no. 3 (October 1994): 621–49.

Pottier, Johan. *Re-imagining Rwanda: Conflict, Survival and Disinformation in the Late Twentieth Century.* Cambridge, UK: Cambridge University Press, 2002.

Poujol, Catherine. "Some Reflections on Russian Involvement and Interests in Tajikistan: The Role of Afghanistan, Pakistan, and Iran." In *Tajikistan: Trials of Independence*, edited by Shirin Akiner, Mohammad-Reza Djalili, and Frederic Grare. New York: Routledge, 1997.

Prazmowska, Anita. *A History of Poland.* New York: Palgrave Macmillan, 2004.

Preston, Matthew. "Stalemate and the Termination of Civil War: Rhodesia Reassessed." *Journal of Peace Research* 41, no. 1 (2004): 65–83.

Preston, Paul. *The Coming of the Spanish Civil War: Reform, Reaction, and Revolution in the Second Republic.* New York: Routledge, 1994.

______. *Revolution and War in Spain, 1931–1939.* New York: Routledge, 1993.

Prevost, Gary. "The 'Contra War' in Nicaragua." *Conflict Quarterly* VII, no. 3 (1987): 5–21.

Price-Mars. *Jean-Pierre Boyar Bazelais et la Drame de Miragoane.* Port-au-Prince, Haiti: Imprimerie de l'Etat, 1948.

Priestley, Herbert Ingram. *The Mexican Nation, a History.* New York: The Macmillan Company, 1926.

Primo, Nicholas. "No Music in Timbuktu: A Brief Analysis of the Conflict in Mali and Al Qaeda's Rebirth." *Pepperdine Policy Review* 6 (January 1, 2013): F1+.

Prisk, Max G. Manwaring Court. *El Salvador at War: An Oral History of Conflict from the 1979 Insurrection to the Present.* Washington, DC: National Defense University Press, 1988.

Pritchard, Earl H. "Political Ferment in China, 1911–1947." *Annals* 277 (September 1951).

Prizzia, Ross. *Thailand in Transition: The Role of Oppositional Forces.* Honolulu: University of Hawaii Press, 1985.

Project Ploughshares. "Armed Conflict Report." 2000. www.ploughshares.ca/content.

______. "Armed Conflict Report." 2004. www.ploughshares.ca/content.

______. "Armed Conflict Report." 2005a. www.ploughshares.ca/libraries.

______. "Armed Conflict Report." 2008. www.ploughshares.ca/libraries.

______. "Cambodia (1978–2000)." 2001. http://ploughshares.ca/pl_armedconflict/cambodia-1978–2000/.

______. "Central Africa Republic." 2014a. www.ploughshares.ca/pl_armedconflict/central-african-republic-update.

______. "Chad 1965–2013." 2013. www.ploughshares.ca/pl_armedconflict/chad-1965-first-combat-deaths/.

______. "Iraq–Kurds (1961–2004)." 2005b. http://ploughshares.ca/pl_armedconflict/iraq-kurds-1961–2004/.

______. "Philippines-CPP/NPA (1969—First Combat Deaths)." 2014b. http://ploughshares.ca/pl_armedconflict/philippines-cppnpa-1969-first-combat-deaths/.

______. "Philippines-Mindanao (1971—First Combat Deaths)." 2014c. http://ploughshares.ca/pl_armedconflict/philippines-mindanao-1971-first-combat-deaths/.

______. "Yemen (2004—First Combat Deaths)." 2014d. http://ploughshares.ca/pl_armedconflict/yemen-2004-first-combat-deaths.

Prunier, Gérard. *Africa's World War: Congo, the Rwandan Genocide, and the Making of a Continental Catastrophe.* New York: Oxford University Press, 2009.

______. *Darfur: The Ambiguous Genocide.* London: Hurst and Company, 2005.

______. "The Experience of European Armies in Operation Restore Hope." In *Learning from Somalia: The Lessons of Armed Humanitarian Intervention,* edited by Walter M. Clarke and Jeffrey M. Herbst. Boulder, CO: Westview Press, 1997.

______. "Rebel Movements and Proxy Warfare: Uganda, Sudan and the Congo (1986–99)." African Affairs 103, no. 412 (2004): 359–83.

______. "Somalia: Civil War, Interventions and Withdrawal, 1990–1995." *WRITENET,* July 1, 1995. http://www.refword.org/docid/3ae6a6c98.html.

Purnell, Jennie. *Popular Movements and State Formation in Revolutionary Mexico: The Agraristas and Cristeros of Michoacán.* Durham, NC: Duke University Press, 1999.

Pushkarev, Sergei. *The Emergence of Modern Russia, 1801–1917.* New York: Holt Rinehart and Winston, 1963.

Puzyrewsky, Alexander. *Der Polnisch-Russische Krieg, 1831.* 3 vols. Vienna, Austria: Kreisel and Groger, 1893.

Pye, Lucian W. *Warlord Politics: Conflict and Coalition in the Modernization of Republican China.* New York: Praeger, 1971.

Quataert, Donald. *The Ottoman Empire, 1700–1922.* Cambridge, UK: Cambridge University Press, 2000.

Quatriglio, Giuseppe. *Thousand Years in Sicily.* Mineola, NY: Legas, 1997.

Quincy, Keith. *Harvesting Pa Chay's Wheat: The Hmong and America's Secret War in Laos.* Spokane: Eastern Washington University Press, 2000.

______. *Hmong: History of a People.* 2nd ed. Cheney: Eastern Washington University Press, 1995.

Quintana, Alejandro. "The President That Never Was: Maximino Ávila Camacho and the Taming of Caudillismo in Early Post-revolutionary Mexico." PhD diss., City University of New York, 2007.

Rabinovich, Itamar. *The War for Lebanon.* Ithaca, NY: Cornell University Press, 1985.

Rabinowitch, Alexander. *The Bolsheviks Come to Power.* New York: W. W. Norton, 1976.

Race, Jeffrey. "Thailand: 1973: 'We Certainly Have Been Ravaged by Something . . .'" *Asian Survey* 14, no. 2 (February 1974).

______. "Thailand in 1974: A New Constitution." *Asian Survey* 15, no. 2 (February 1975): 157–65.

Raleigh, Donald J. *The Emperors and Empresses of Russia: Rediscovering the Romanovs.* Armonk, NY: M. E. Sharpe, 1996.

Ram, Mohan. "Shift in Naxalite Tactics." *Economic and Political Weekly* 6, no. 34 (1971): 1798–799.

______. *Sri Lanka: The Fractured Island.* New Delhi, India: Penguin Books, 1989.

Ramakrishna, Kumar. *Radical Pathways: Understanding Muslim Radicalization in Indonesia.* Westport, CT: Praeger Security International, 2009.

Ramet, Sabrina P. *Thinking about Yugoslavia, Scholarly Debates about the Yugoslav Breakup and the Wars in Bosnia and Kosovo.* Cambridge, UK: Cambridge University Press, 2005.

Ramsey, Russell W. *Revolución Campesina, 1950–1954.* 1st ed. en Española. Versión de María Restrepo Castro. Bogotá, Colombia: Ediciones Libros de Colombia, 1973.

Ramsey, Russell Wilcox. "The Modern Violence in Colombia,1946–1965." PhD diss., University of Florida, 1970.

Ranatunga, Cyril. *Adventurous Journey: From Peace to War, Insurgency to Terrorism.* Colombo, Sri Lanka: Vijjitha Yapa Publications, 2009.

Ranke, Leopold. *The History of Serbia.* London: Bohn, 1853.

Ranstorp, Magnus. *Hizb'allah in Lebanon: The Politics of the Western Hostage Crisis.* New York: St. Martin's Press, 1997.

Rapport, Michael. *1848: Year of Revolution.* New York: Basic Books, 2009.

Rasanayagam, Angelo. *Afghanistan: A Modern History.* London: I. B. Tauris, 2003.

Rashid, Ahmed. *Taliban: Militant Islam, Oil, and Fundamentalism in Central Asia.* New Haven, CT: Yale University Press, 2000.

Rastoder, Šerbo. "A Short Review of the History of Montenegro." In *Montenegro in Transition,* edited by Florian Bieber, 107–37. Baden-Baden, Germany: Nomos Verlagsgesellschaft, 2003.

Ratnatunga, Sinha. "Terror of JVP 'Ended.'" *The Guardian (London),* December 29, 1989.

Rauch, George V. *The Argentine Military and the Boundary Dispute With Chile, 1870–1902.* Westport, CT: Greenwood Publishing Group, 1999.

Raun, Toivo U. *Estonia and the Estonians.* Stanford, CA: Hoover Institution Press, 1987.

Ray, James Lee, and J. David Singer. "Measuring the Concentration of Power in the International System." *Sociological Methods and Research* 1 (1973): 403–37; reprinted in J. David Singer and Associates *Explaining War.* Beverly Hills, CA: Sage, 1979, and in J. David Singer and Paul Diehl, eds. *Measuring the Correlates of War.* Ann Arbor: University of Michigan Press, 1990.

Read, Christopher. *From Tsar to Soviets: the Russian People and their Revolution.* New York: Oxford University Press, 1996.

Reano, Mariella. *The Origin of Peruvian Professional Militarism.* Baton Rouge: Louisiana State University, 2002.

"Rebel Chief Defects, Quiets Yemen War." *Miami News*, January 16, 1969, 9A.

"'Rebel' Wanted by Indonesia." *The Canberra Times*, September 6, 1965, 1.

"Rebellion: Indonesia Calls Them Migrant Workers but They May Be Refugees, Fleeing from Trouble." *Globe and Mail (Canada)*, May 24, 1991.

"Rebels Defeat Federals." *Reading Eagle*, December 12, 1923, 10.

"Rebels Fight Soldiers in West Irian." *The Canberra Times*, July 11, 1969, 1.

"Rebels in Philippines Sign Truce." *The Sunday Times (Perth)*, June 24, 2001.

"Rebels Prepared to Battle PNG Forces." *Courier-Mail*, October 11, 1990.

"Recent Disturbances in Morocco." *The American Journal of International Law* 1, no. 4 (October 1907): 975–78.

Rector, John L. *The History of Chile.* Westport, CT: Greenwood Press, 2003.

Reddaway, W. F., et al., eds. *The Cambridge History of Poland.* Cambridge, UK: Cambridge University Press, 1941.

Reed, Nelson. A. *The Caste War of Yucatan.* Stanford, CA: Stanford University Press, 1964.

______. *The Caste War of Yucatán.* Rev. ed. Stanford, CA: Stanford University Press, 2001.

Reed, W. Cyrus. "Patronage, Reform, and Public Policy: The Role of Zaire in the Great Lakes Crisis." Unpublished manuscript, March 8, 1999.

Refugees International. "Sri Lanka: Renewed Conflict Displacing Thousands." *Bulletin* (July 10, 2006). http://www.refugeesinternational.org.

Regan, P. "Conditions of Successful Third-party Intervention in Intrastate Wars." *Journal of Conflict Resolution* 40, no. 2 (1996): 336–59.

Regan, Patrick M. *Civil Wars and Foreign Powers: Outside Intervention in Intrastate Conflict.* Ann Arbor: University of Michigan Press, 2000.

Reid, Brian Holden. *The American Civil War and the Wars of the Industrial Revolution.* London: Cassell, 1999.

Reid, James J. *Crisis of the Ottoman Empire.* Stuttgart, Germany: Franz Steiner Verlag, 2000.

Rempe, Dennis. *Past as Prologue? A History of US CI Policy in Colombia, 1958–66.* Carlisle, PA: Strategic Studies Institute, 2002.

Reno, William. "Liberia: The LURDs of the New Church." In *African Guerrillas; Raging against the Machine*, edited by Morten BρÅs and Kevin C. Dunn. Boulder, CO: Lynne Rienner, 2007.

______. "Sierra Leone: Warfare in a Post-State Society." In *State Failure and State Weakness in a Time of Terror*, edited by Robert I. Rotberg, 71–100. Cambridge, MA: World Peace Foundation, 2003.

Research Directorate, Immigration and Refugee Board, Canada. "The Role of the Military." January 1, 1991. http://www.refworld/org/docid/3ae6a80f28.html.

Restrepo, Jorge, Michael Spagat, and Juan F. Vargas. "The Dynamics of the Colombian Civil Conflict: A New Data Set." Paper presented at the conference Revolutions, Old and New, Villa Gualino, Italy, June 2003.

______. "The Severity of the Columbian Conflict: Cross-Country Datasets versus New Micro Data." Unpublished manuscript, 2004.

Reuters. Multiple articles, 2012–2013. http://www.reuters.com.

Reuters Alertnet. "Pakistani Troops Attack Militants in Scenic Valley." November 15, 2007.

"Revolt in Mexico Extending to Six States." *The Victoria Advocate*, December 7, 1923, 1.

"Revolução Farroupilha." n.d. http://www.pampasonline.com.br/tradicao/tradicao_revolucaofarroupilha.htm.

Reyntjens, Filip. *Small States in an Unstable Region—Rwanda and Burundi, 1999–2000.* Uppsala, Sweden: Nordic African Institute, 2000.

Rezun, Miron. *Intrigue and War in Southwest Asia.* New York: Praeger, 1992.

Rhoads, Edward J. M. *Manchus and Han: Ethnic Relations and Political Power in Late Qing and Early Republican China, 1861–1928.* Seattle: University of Washington Press, 2000.

Riall, Lucy. *Sicily and the Unification of Italy: Liberal Policy and Local Power.* Oxford, UK: Clarendon House, 1998.

Ribetti, Marcella Marisa. "Some Conflicts May Not End: The Stability of Protracted Violence." PhD diss., University of Texas at Austin, 2002.

Rice, Edward. *Wars of the Third Kind.* Berkeley: University of California Press, 1988.

Rice, Michael David. "Nicaragua and the United States: Policy Confrontations and Cultural Interactions, 1893–1933." PhD diss., University of Houston, Department of History, 1995.

Richani, Nazih. "Caudillos and the Crisis of the Colombian State: Fragmented Sovereignty, the War System and the Privatisation of Counterinsurgency in Colombia." *Third World Quarterly* 28 (2007): 403–17.

______. *Systems of Violence: The Political Economy of War and Peace in Colombia.* Albany: State University of New York Press, 2002.

______. "Third Parties, War Systems' Inertia, and Conflict Termination: The Doomed Peace Process in Colombia, 1918–2002." *The Journal of Conflict Studies* 25, no. 2 (Winter 2005).

Richard, Carlos Macías. "El Territorio de Quintana Roo. Tentativas de Colonización y Control Militar en la Selva Maya." *Historia Mexicana* XLIX, no. 1 (1999): 5–54.

Richardson, Hugh. *Tibet and Its History.* Boulder, CO: Shambala Publications, 1984.

Richardson, Lewis F. *Statistics of Deadly Quarrels.* Pittsburgh, PA: Boxwood Press, 1960.

Richmond, Douglas A. *Carlos Pellegrini and the Crisis of the Argentine Elites, 1880–1916.* Westport, CT: Praeger, 1989.

Rieber, Alfred J. "Civil Wars in the Soviet Union." *Kritika: Explorations in Russian and Eurasian History* 4, no. 1 (2003): 129–62.

Ripley, George, and Charles Dana. *The New American Cyclopaedia: A Popular Dictionary of General Knowledge.* New York: D. Appleton and Company, 1861.

Rippy, J. Fred. *The Caribbean Danger Zone.* New York: G. P. Putnam's Sons, 1940.

Ritter, William S. "The Final Phase in the Liquidation of Anti-Soviet Resistance in Tadzhikistan: Ibrahim Bek and the Basmachi, 1924–1931." *Soviet Studies* 37, no. 4 (October 1985): 484–93.

______. "Revolt in the Mountains: Fazail Maksum and the Occupation of Garm, Spring 1929." *Journal of Contemporary History* 25 (1990): 547–80.

Roberts, David W. *Political Transition in Cambodia 1991–99: Power, Elitism and Democracy.* Richmond, Surrey, UK: Curzon, 2001.

Roberts, Elizabeth. *Realm of the Black Mountain: A History of Montenegro.* Ithaca, NY: Cornell University Press, 2007.

Roberts, Greg. "PNG's Agony: 10,000 Dead." *Sydney Morning Herald,* July 13, 1996, 1

Robertson, Priscilla. *Revolutions of 1848: A Social History.* Princeton, NJ: Princeton University Press, 1952.

Robins, Nicholas. *Native Insurgencies and the Genocidal Impulse in the Americas.* Bloomington: Indiana University Press, 2005.

Robinson, Fay. *Mexico and the Military Chieftains from the Revolution of Hidalgo to the Present Time.* Glorieta, NM: The Rio Grande Press, Inc., 1847.

Robinson, Simon, and Vivienne Walt. "The Deadliest War in the World." *Time,* June 5, 2006, 38–53.

Rochlin, James F. *Vanguard Revolutionaries in Latin America: Peru, Colombia, Mexico.* Boulder, CO: Lynne Rienner, 2003.

Rock, David. *Argentina, 1516–1982.* Berkley: University of California Press, 1985.

______. "The Collapse of the Federalists: Rural Revolt in Argentina 1863–1876." *Estudios Interdisciplinarios de America Latina y el Caribe* 9, no. 2 (July–December 1998). http://www.tau.ac.il/eial/IX_2/rock.html.

______. *State Building and Political Movements in Argentina, 1860–1916.* Stanford, CA: Stanford University Press, 2002.

Rodman, Selden. *Haiti: The Black Republic, The Complete Story and Guide.* New York: Devin-Adair, 1954.

Rodriguez Herrero, Enrique. *Campana Militar de 1904.* Montevideo, Uruguay: n.p., 1934.

Rogan, Eugene L. *The Frontiers of the State in the Late Ottoman Empire.* Cambridge, UK: Cambridge University Press, 1999.

Roggio, Bill. "The Fall of Northwestern Pakistan: An Online History." *The Long War Journal* (September 13, 2006). http://www.longwarjournal.org.

Rolandson, Øystein H. *Guerilla Government: Political Changes in the Southern Sudan During the 1990s.* Sweden: Almquist and Wiksell Tryckeri AB, 2005.

Rollman, Wilfrid J. "The 'New Order' in a Precolonial Muslim Society: Military Reform in Morocco, 1844–1904." PhD diss., University of Michigan, Department of History, 1983.

Romero, Alexis. "AFP-NPA Ceasefire Ends at Midnight." *Philippine Star,* January 19, 2015. http://www.philstar.com/headlines/2015/01/19/1414591/afp-npa-ceasefire-ends-midnight.

Rondon Marquez, R. A. *Guzman Blanco.* Caracas, Venezuela: Garrido, 1944.

Rood, Judith Mendelsohn. "Mehmed Ali as Mutinous Khedive: The Roots of Rebellion." *International Journal of Turkish Studies* 8, nos. 1, 2 (Spring 2002): 115–28.

Rosales, Manuel Landaeta. *Guerra de Venezuela en 1898.* Caracas, Venezuela: Imprenta Federación, 1898.

Rose, Gregory F. "The Post-Revolutionary Purge of Iran's Armed Forces: A Revisionist Assessment." *Iranian Studies* 17, no. 2/3 (1984): 153–94.

Rosello, Victor M. "Lessons From El Salvador." *Parameters* XXIII (Winter 1993): 101–8.

Rosenau, James N., ed. *International Politics and Foreign Policy.* New York: Free Press, 1969.

Ross, Daniel James Jonathan. *The Honduran Revolution of 1924 and American Intervention.* Master's thesis, University of Florida, 1969.

Ross, Edward Alsworth. *The Russian Soviet Republic.* New York: The Century Co., 1923.

Rotberg, Robert I. *Haiti, The Politics of Squalor.* Boston, MA: Houghton Mifflin Company, 1971.

Rourke, Thomas. *Gómez: Tyrant of the Andes.* New York: Greenwood Press, 1969. Originally published 1936.

Rousseau, Jean-Jacques. *The Noble Savage.* Translated by Maurice Cranston. New York: Penguin Books, 1968. Originally published 1762.

Roxborough, Ian, Philip O'Brien, and Jackie Roddick. *Chile: The State and Revolution.* New York: Holmes and Meier Publishers Inc., 1977.

Roy, Denny. *Taiwan: A Political History.* Ithaca, NY: Cornell University Press, 2003.

Royle, Charles. *The Egyptian Campaigns 1882 to 1885.* Rev. ed. London: Hurst and Blackett Ltd., 1900.

Ruay, Deng. *The Politics of Two Sudans: The South and the North, 1821–1969.* Sweden: Nordiska Afrikainstitutet, 1994.

Rubin, Avshalom H. "Abd al-Karim Qasim and the Kurds of Iraq: Centralization, Resistance and Revolt, 1958–63." *Middle Eastern Studies* 43 (2007): 353–82.

Rubin, Barnett R. *The Fragmentation of Afghanistan: State Formation and Collapse in the International System.* 2nd ed. New Haven, CT: Yale University Press, 2002.

Rudolph, Donna Keyse, and G. A. Rudolph. *Historical Dictionary of Venezuela.* Metuchen, NJ: Scarecrow Press, 1971.

Rudolph, James D. *Peru: The Evolution of a Crisis.* Westport, CT: Praeger, 1992.

Rudolph, Joseph R., ed. *Encyclopedia of Modern Ethnic Conflicts.* Westport, CT: Greenwood Press, 2003.

Rugeley, Terry. *Rebellion Now and Forever: Mayas, Hispanics, and Caste War Violence in Yucatán, 1800–1880.* Stanford, CA: Stanford University Press, 2009.

______. *Yucatán's Maya Peasantry and the Origins of the Caste War.* Austin: University of Texas Press, 1996.

Ruiz, Bert. *The Colombian Civil War.* Jefferson, NC: McFarland and Co., 2001.

Rummel, Rudolph J. *Death by Government.* New Brunswick, NJ: Transaction, 1994.

______. *The Dimensionality of Nations.* Beverly Hills, CA: Sage, 1972.

______. *Statistics of Democide: Genocide and Mass Murder since 1900.* Münster, Germany: Lit Verlag, 1998.

Rupiya, Martin R. "A Political and Military Review of Zimbabwe's Involvement in the Second Congo War." In *The African Stakes of the Congo War,* edited by John F. Clark. New York: Palgrave Macmillan, 2002.

Russell, Tom. "A Lebanon Primer." *MERIP Reports* 133 (1985): 17–9.

Russett, Bruce. *Grasping the Democratic Peace.* Princeton, NJ: Princeton University Press, 1994.

Russett, Bruce, J. David Singer, and Melvin Small. "National Political Units in the Twentieth Century: A Standardized List." *American Political Science Review* LXII, no. 3 (September 1968): 932–51.

Rustum, Asad J. *The Royal Archives of Egypt and the Disturbances in Palestine, 1834.* Beirut, Lebanon: American Press, 1938.

Rwantabagu, Hermeneglide. "Explaining Intra-state Conflicts in Africa: The Case of Burundi." *International Journal on World Peace* 18, no. 2 (2001): 41–46.

Rywkin, Michael. *Moscow's Muslim Challenge: Soviet Central Asia.* Rev. ed. Armonk, NY: M. E. Sharpe Inc., 1990.

Saalax, Warsan Cismaan, and Abdulaziz Ibrahim Xildhiban. "Somali Peace Agreements: Fuelling Factionalism." [Whose Peace Is It Anyway? Connecting Somali and International Peacemaking]. *Accord* 21 (2010): 32–3.

Sabahi, Houshang. *British Policy in Persia, 1918–1925.* Portland, OR: Frank Cass, 1990.

Sabry, M. *L'Empire Egyptien Sous Mohamed-Ali et la Question d'Orient.* Paris, France: Librairie Orientaliste, 1930.

Sadri, Roostam. "The Islamic Republic of Eastern Turkestan: A Commemorative Review." *Journal of the Institute of Muslim Minority Affairs* 5 (1984): 294–320.

Safer Access. "A Summary of Armed Groups and Political Parties in Côte d'Ivoire." January 17, 2007. http://www.geneva-academy.ch/rulac/pdf_state/Summary-of-Armed-Groups-and-Political-Parties-in-Côte-d'ivoire.pdf.

Safford, Frank, and Marco Palacios. *Colombia: Fragmented Land, Divided Society.* New York: Oxford University Press, 2002.

Saleem, Adnan. "United Nations Operations in Somalia (UNOSOM, UNITAF, UNOSOM II)." *Pakistan Urdu IT,* 2011. http://pakistanurduit.blogspot.com.

Salibi, Kamal S. *Crossroads to Civil War.* Delmar, NY: Caravan, 1976.

______. *The Modern History of Jordan.* New York: St. Martin's, 1993.

Salih, Shakeeb. "The British-Druze Connection and the Druze Rising of 1896 in the Hawran." *Middle Eastern Studies* 13, no. 2 (1977): 251–57.

Salmoni, Barak A., Bryce Loidolt, and Madeleine Wells. *Regime and Periphery in Northern Yemen: The Houthi Phenomenon*. Santa Monica, CA: RAND, 2010.

Samarasinghe, S. W. R. de A. and Vidyamali Samarasinghe. *Historical Dictionary of Sri Lanka*. Lanham, MD: Scarecrow Press, 1991.

San Miguel, Pedro L. *The Imagined Island: History, Identity, and Utopia in Hispaniola*. Chapel Hill: University of North Carolina Press, 2005.

"Sanaa Falls to Rebels." *Al-Ahram Weekly*, September 25, 2014.

Sanborn, Joshua A. *Drafting the Russian Nation: Military Conscription, Total War, and Mass Politics, 1905–1925*. DeKalb: Northern Illinois University Press, 2003.

Sánchez, Gonzalo, and Donny Meertens. *Bandits, Peasants, and Politics: The Case of "La Violencia" in Colombia*. Translated by Alan Hynds. Austin: University of Texas Press, 2001.

Sanchez, Justo. *Efemérides Militares de la República Argentina*. Buenos Aires, Argentina: Talleres Gráficos–Arsenal Principal de Guerra, 1906.

Sandberg, Peter. "Oromo–the Forgotten People?" *New African* (July–August 2001): 17.

Sanders, James E. *Contentious Republicans: Popular Politics, Race, and Class in Nineteenth-century Colombia*. Durham, NC: Duke University Press, 2004.

Sandford, Christine. *Ethiopia under Hailé Selassié*. London: J. M. Dent and Sons Ltd., 1946.

Sandole, Dennis J. D. *Capturing the Complexity of Conflict*. New York: Pinter, 1999.

Sante, Angela Delli. *Nightmare or Reality: Guatemala in the 1980s*. Amsterdam, Netherlands: Thela Publishers, 1996.

Santos, Richard G. *Santa Anna's Campaign against Texas 1835–1836*. 2nd ed., rev. Salisbury, NC: Texian Press/ Documentary Publications, 1982.

Santovenia, Emeterio S. *Eloy Alfaro* (Translation of "Eloy Alfaro y Cuba"). Academy of History, Cuba, 1935.

Sapkota, Dipak. *Ten Years of Upheaval: Reportage of the Decade Long Maoist People's War in Nepal*. Kathmandu, Nepal: Revolutionary Journalist Association–Central Committee, 2010.

Saray, Mehmet. *The Russian, British, Chinese, and Ottoman Rivalry in Turkestan*. Ankara: Turkish Historical Society Printing House, 2003.

Sarkees, Meredith Reid. "Assessing Trends in War." Presented on the panel Grand Strategy in the 21st Century at the joint meeting of International Security Studies Section and International Security and Arms Control, US Army War College, Carlisle, PA. October 30–November 1, 2003.

______. "The Correlates of War Data on War: An Update to 1997." *Conflict Management and Peace Science* 18, no. 1 (Fall 2000): 123–44.

______. "The COW Typology of War: Defining and Categorizing Wars (Version 4 of the Data)." 2011. http:// www.correlatesofwar.org.

______. "Data Bases of War Available to Researchers: The Correlates of War Project." *Peace Psychology Newsletter* 4, no. 3 (Fall 1995): 4, 8.

______. "Defining and Categorizing Wars." In *Resort to War: A Data Guide to Inter-state, Extra-state, Intra-state, and Non-state Wars, 1816–2007*, by Meredith Reid Sarkees and Frank Whelon Wayman, 39–73. Washington, DC: CQ Press, 2010a.

______. "Inter-state, Intra-state and Extra-state Wars: A Comprehensive Look at Their Distribution over Time, 1816–1997." In *War*, edited by Paul Diehl, Thousand Oaks, CA: Sage, 2004.

______. "The Intra-state Wars." In *Resort to War: A Data Guide to Inter-state, Extra-State, Intra-state, and Non-State Wars, 1816–2007*, by Meredith Reid Sarkees and Frank Whelon Wayman, 337–484. Washington, DC: CQ Press, 2010b.

______. "Intra-state Wars (Version 4.0): Definitions and Variables." 2009, http://www.correlatesofwar.org.

______. "J. David Singer and the Democratic Peace." In "Reflections and Reassessments on the Early Work and Ideas of J. David Singer" by Daniel S. Geller and Paul F. Diehl, *International Studies Review* 15, no. 2 (June 2013): 259–84.

______. "Old Wars, New Wars, and an Expanded War Typology." Paper presented at the joint meeting of the International Studies Association and the Japan Association of International Relations, Tokyo, September 20–23, 1996.

______. "Patterns of Civil Wars in the Twenty-first Century: The Decline of Civil War?" In *The Routledge Handbook of Civil Wars*, edited by Edward Newman and Karl DeRouen, Jr., 236–56. London: Routledge, 2014.

______. "Response to the 'Forest Brothers' and the Consequences of the Metropole-Periphery Distinction Elimination in the 'Correlates of War' Typology." *Journal of Baltic Studies* 43, no. 4 (2012): 528–38.

______. "Trends in Intra-state (Not Ethnic) Wars." Presented at the international joint meetings of International Studies Associations, Hong Kong, July 26–28, 2001.

______. "What Do We Know about War." In *Resort to War: A Data Guide to Inter-state, Extra-state, Intrá-state, and Non-state Wars, 1816–2007*, by Meredith Reid Sarkees and Frank Whelon Wayman, 541–77. Washington, DC: C Q Press, 2010c.

Sarkees, Meredith Reid, and J. David Singer. "Armed Conflict Past and Future: A Master Typology?" Paper presented at the European Union Conference on Armed Conflict Data Collection, Uppsala, Sweden, June 2001.Sarkees, Meredith, Frank Wayman, and J. David Singer. "Inter-state, Intra-state, and Extra-state Wars: A Comprehensive Look at their Distribution over Time, 1816–1997." *International Studies Quarterly* 77 (2003): 49–70.

Sarkees, Meredith Reid, and Frank Whelon Wayman. *Resort to War 1816–2007*. Washington, DC: CQ Press, 2010.

Saudi Arabia: Secret Intelligence Records, 1926–1939. Vol. I: 1926–1931, archive ed. 2003.

Saunders, M. G. *The Soviet Navy*. New York: Praeger, 1958.

"Savage War Raging Among Paraguayans." *New York Times*, December 26, 1911.

Say, Shaul. *The Red Sea Terror Triangle: Sudan, Somalia, Yemen, and Islamic Terror*. Piscataway, NJ: Transaction Publishers, 2005.

Scalapino, Robert A., and George T. Yu. *Modern China and Its Revolutionary Process*. Berkeley: University of California Press, 1985.

Schaefer, Robert W. *The Insurgency in Chechnya and the North Caucasus From Gazavat to Jihad*. Denver, CO: Praeger, 2011.

Schafer, Phil. "States, Nations, and Entities from 1492 to 1992." Ann Arbor: University of Michigan Terminal System, for the Correlates of War Project, 1995.

Scheidel, Walter. *Death on the Nile: Disease and the Demography of Roman Egypt*. Leiden, Netherlands: Brill, 2001.

Scheina, Robert L. *The Age of the Caudillo, 1791–1899*. Vol 1 of *Latin America's Wars*. Washington, DC: Brassey's, 2003a.

______. *The Age of the Professional Soldier, 1900–2001*. Vol 2 of *Latin America's Wars*. Washington, DC: Brassey's, 2003b.

______. *Santa Anna, A Curse upon Mexico*. Washington, DC: Brassey's Inc., 2002.

Scherrer, Christian P. *Genocide and Crisis in Central Africa*. Westport, CT: Praeger, 2002.

Schevill, Ferdinand. *History of the Balkan Peninsula*. New York: Frederick Ungar Publishing, 1966.

Schiemann, Theodor. *Geschichte Russlands Unter Kaiser Nikolaus I*. Vol. 3. Berlin, Germany: George Reimer, 1913.

Schilcher, Linda Schatkowski. "Violence in Rural Syria in the 1880s and 1890s: State Centralization, Rural Integration, and the World Market." In *Peasants and Politics in the Modern Middle East*, edited by Farham Kazemi and John Waterbury, 50–84. Miami: Florida International University Press, 1991.

Schirmer, Jennifer. *The Guatemalan Military Project: A Violence Called Democracy*. Philadelphia: University of Pennsylvania Press, 1998.

Schlarman, Joseph. *Mexico: A Land of Volcanoes*. Milwaukee: Bruce, 1951. Originally published 1950.

Schlesinger, Stephen, and Stephen Kinzer. *Bitter Fruit, the Untold Story of the American Coup in Guatemala*. Garden City, NY: Doubleday & Company, Inc., 1982.

Schmid, Alex P. *Soviet Military Interventions since 1945*. New Brunswick, NJ: Transaction Books, 1985.

Schmidt, Dana Adams. *Yemen: The Unknown War*. London: The Bodley Head, 1968.

Schmidt, John R. *The Unraveling: Pakistan in the Age of Jihad*. New York: Farrar, Straus, and Giroux, 2011.

Schneider, Ronald M. *Latin American Political History*. Boulder, CO: Westview Press, 2007.

______. *"Order and Progress" A Political History of Brazil*. Boulder, CO: Westview Press, 1991.

Schodt, David W. *Ecuador: An Andean Enigma*. Boulder, CO: Westview Press, 1987.

Schofield, Victoria. *Kashmir in Conflict: India, Pakistan, and the Unending War*. New York: I. B. Tauris, 2003.

Schulz, Donald E. "Ten Theories in Search of Central American Reality." In *Revolution and Counter Counterrevolution in Central America and the Caribbean*, edited by Donald E. Schulz and Douglas H. Graham, 3–64. Boulder, CO: Westview Press, 1984.

Schulze, Kristen. "Insurgency and Counter-insurgency: Strategy and the Aceh Conflict, October 1976–May 2004." In *Veranda of Violence: The Background to the Aceh Problem*, edited by Anthony Reid, 225–71. Singapore: Singapore University Press, 2006.

______. "Laskar Jihad and the Conflict in Ambon." *Brown Journal of World Affairs* 9, no. 1 (2002): 57–69.

Schurmann, Franz, and Orville Schell. *Republican China*. Vol. 2 of *The China Reader*. New York: Vintage Books, 1967.

Scobell, Andrew. *China's Use of Military Force: Beyond the Great Wall and Long March*. Cambridge, UK: Cambridge University Press, 2003.

Scobie, James R. "The Aftermath of Pavon." *Hispanic American Historical Review* 35, no. 2 (May 1955): 153–74.

Scott, Richard C., Jr. *Case Studies in the Termination of Internal Revolutionary Conflict*. Vol. VIII. Cambridge, MA: ABT Associates Inc., 1966.

Selassie, Bereket Habte. *Emperor Haile Selassie.* Athens: Ohio University Press, 2014.

Selbin, Eric. *Modern Latin American Revolutions.* Boulder, CO: Westview Press, 1993.

Seligson, Mitchell A., and Vincent McElhinny. "Low-intensity Warfare, High Intensity Death: The Demographic Impact of the Wars in El Salvador and Nicaragua." *Canadian Journal of Latin American and Caribbean Studies* 21, no. 42 (1996): 211–41.

Senaratne, Jagath P. *Political Violence in Sri Lanka, 1977–1990: Riots, Insurrections, Counterinsurgencies, Foreign Intervention.* Amsterdam, Netherlands: VU University Press, 1997.

Senese, Paul D., and John A. Vasquez. *The Steps to War, and Empirical Study.* Princeton, NJ: Princeton University Press, 2008.

"'Serious' Fighting in West Java." *The West Australian (Perth),* February 22, 1950, 1.

Serrano, Andres Smith. "CIS Peacekeeping in Tajikistan." In *Regional Peacekeepers: The Paradox of Russian Peacekeeping,* edited by John MacKinlay and Peter Cross, 156–82. United Nations University Press, 2003.

Seton-Watson, Hugh. *The Decline of Imperial Russia, 1855–1914.* London: Methuen, 1952.

______. *The Russian Empire 1801–1917.* Oxford, UK: Oxford University Press, 1967.

"Severe Fighting in Paraguay." *Evening Post (New Zealand)* LXXXI, no. 67 (March 21, 1911): 7.

Shakya, Tsering. *The Dragon in the Land of Snows: A History of Modern Tibet since 1947.* London: Pimlico, 1999.

Shantz, Jeffrey A. "Zimbabwe: Anti-Mugabe Struggle." In *Encyclopedia of Conflicts since World War II,* vol. 1, edited by James Ciment, 333. Armonk, NY: Sharpe Reference, 2007.

Sharma, Sudheer. "The Maoist Movement: An Evolutionary Perspective." Translated by Jyoti Thapa. In *Himalayan People's War: Nepal's Maoist Rebellion,* edited by Michael Hutt, 38–57. Bloomington: Indiana University Press.

Shastri, Amita. "Sri Lanka in 2002: Turning the Corner?" *Asian Survey* 43, no. 1 (2003): 215–21.

Shek, Richard. "The Revolt of the Zaili, Jindan Sects in Rehe (Jehol), 1891." *Modern China* 6, no. 2 (1980): 161–96.

Sheldon, Charles. "Review: The Boshin War by Haraguchi Kiyoshi; a History of the Boshin War by Hirao Michio." *The Journal of Asian Studies* 33, no. 2 (1974): 314–16.

Shenan, Philip. "Burmese Rebel Army Seeks End to 40-Year War." *New York Times,* December 5, 1993, 28.

Sheng, Hu. *From the Opium War to the May Fourth Movement.* Vol. I. Translated by Dun J. Li. Beijing: Foreign Language Press, 1991.

Shenon, Phillip. "Cambodia Attacks Khmer Rouge." *New York Times,* February 2, 1993, A7.

Sheridan, James E. *China in Disintegration.* New York: Free Press, 1975.

______. *Chinese Warlord: The Career of Feng Yü-hsiang.* Stanford, CA: Stanford University Press, 1966.

Shetterly, Aran. *The Americano: Fighting with Castro for Cuba's Freedom.* Chapel Hill, NC: Algonquin Books, 2007.

Shinn, David H., and Thomas P. Ofcansky. *Historical Dictionary of Ethiopia.* New ed. Lanham, MD: Scarecrow Press, 2004.

Shinn, Rinn S. *Italy, A Country Study.* Washington, DC: American University, 1985.

Shoham, Dany. "The Evolution of Chemical and Biological Weapons in Egypt." ACPR Policy Paper 46. 1998.

Short, Anthony. *The Origins of the Vietnam War.* New York: Routledge, 1989.

Shrader, Charles R. *The Withered Vine: Logistics and the Communist Insurgency in Greece, 1945–1949.* Westport, CT: Praeger, 1999.

Shulze, Kirsten E. "The Struggle for an Independent Aceh: The Ideology, Capacity, and Strategy of GAM." *Studies in Conflict and Terrorism* 26, no. 4 (2003): 241–71.

Siaroff, Alan. "Democratic Breakdown and Democratic Stability: A Comparison of Interwar Estonia and Finland." *Canadian Journal of Political Science/Review Canadienne de Science Politique* 32, no. 1 (March 1999): 103–24.

Sicker, Martin. *Reshaping Palestine: From Muhammad Ali to the British Mandate, 1831–1922.* Westport, CT: Praeger, 1999.

Silverfarb, Daniel. "Great Britain, Iraq, and Saudi Arabia: The Revolt of the Ikhwan, 1927–1930." *The International History Review* 4, no. 2 (1982): 222–48.

Silverlight, John. *The Victor's Dilemma.* New York: Weybright and Talley, 1970.

Simmonds, Stuart. "Laos and Cambodia: The Search for Unity and Independence." *International Affairs (Royal Institute of International Affairs 1944–)* 49, no. 4 (October 1973): 574–83.

Simons, Geoff. *Colombia: A Brutal History.* London: SAQI, 2004.

______. *Indonesia: The Long Oppression.* New York: St. Martin's Press, 2000.

Şimşir, Bilâl N. İngiliz Belgeleriyle Türkiye'de "Kürt Sorunu" (1924–1938): Şeyh Sait, Ağri ve Dersim, Ayaklanmalari. Ankara, Turkey: Türk Tarih Kurumu Üyesi, 1991.

Singer, J. David. "Alliance Aggregation and the Onset of War, 1815–1945." In *Quantitative International Politics, Insights and Evidence*, edited by J. David Singer, New York: Free Press, 1968a.

______, ed. *Correlates of War I: Research Origins and Rationale.* New York: Free Press, 1979b.

______, ed. *Correlates of War II: Testing Some Realpolitik Models.* New York: Free Press, 1980.

______, ed. *Explaining War: Selected Papers from the Correlates of War Project.* Beverly Hills, CA: Sage Publications, 1979a.

______. "J. David Singer—Parent of the Field." George Mason University, School for Conflict Analysis & Resolution (videotaped interview), 2003. https://scar.gmu.edu/parents-of-field/david-singer.

______. "The Making of a Peace Researcher." In *Journeys through World Politics*, edited by Joseph Kruzel and James N. Rosenau, 213–29. Lexington, MA: Lexington Books.

______. "One Man's View: A Personal History of the Project." In *Prisoners of War?* (Festchrift for Correlates of War Project), edited by Charles S. Gochman and Alan N. Sabrosky, 11–27. Lexington, MA: Lexington Books, 1990.

______, ed. *Quantitative International Politics*, Insights and Evidence. New York: Free Press, 1968b.

______. "Reconstructing the Correlates of War Dataset on Material Capabilities of States, 1816–1985." *International Interactions*, 14 (1987): 115–32; reprinted in J. David Singer and Paul Diehl, eds. *Measuring the Correlates of War.* Ann Arbor: University of Michigan Press, 1990.

______. "Variables, Indicators, and Data: The Measurement Problem in Macro-political Research." *Social Science History* 6 (1982): 181–217; reprinted in J. David Singer and Paul Diehl, eds. *Measuring the Correlates of War*, Ann Arbor: University of Michigan Press, 1990; and in J. David Singer, ed. *Models, Methods, and Progress in World Politics: A Peace Research Odyssey*, Boulder, CO: Westview, 1990.

______. *The Wages of War, 1816–1965: A Statistical Handbook.* New York: Wiley, 1972.

______. "The War Proneness of Democratic Regimes, 1816–1965." *Jerusalem Journal of International Relations* (1976): 49–69.

______. "Who Is This Fellow?" In *Advancing Peace Research: Leaving Traces, Selected Articles by J. David Singer*, edited by Jody B. Lear, Diane Macaulay, and Meredith Reid Sarkees, 1–16. London: Routledge, 2012.

Singer, J. David, Stuart Bremer, and John Stuckey. "Capability Distribution, Uncertainty, and Major Power War, 1820–1965." In *Peace, War, and Numbers*, edited by Bruce Russett, 19–48. Beverly Hills, CA: Sage, 1972; reprinted in J. David Singer, ed. *The Correlates of War I: Research Origins and Rationale*, Free Press, 1979; and in J. David Singer and Associates, *Explaining War*, Beverly Hills, CA: Sage, 1979.

Singer, J. David, and Paul F. Diehl, eds. *Measuring the Correlates of War.* Ann Arbor: University of Michigan Press, 1990.

Singer, J. David, and Melvin Small. "The Composition and Status Ordering of the International System 1815–1940." *World Politics* 18, no. 2 (January 1966): 236–82.

Singh, Chandrika. *North-East India: Politics & Insurgency.* New Delhi, India: Manas Publications, 2004.

Singh, Kelvin. "Big Power Pressure on Venezuela During the Presidency of Cipriano Castro." *Revista/Review Interamericana* 29, nos. 1–4 (1999): 125–43.

Singh, Prakash. *The Naxalite Movement in India.* Kolkata, India: Rupa Publications, 1995.

Singleton, Fred. *A Short History of Finland.* Cambridge, UK: Cambridge University Press, 1989.

Sinno, Abdulkader. *Organizations at War in Afghanistan and Beyond.* Ithaca, NY: Cornell University Press, 2008.

Sipress, Alan. "Indonesia Extends Martial Law in Unsettled Province." *Washington Post*, November 4, 2003, A22.

SIPRI (Stockholm International Peace Research Institute). *SIPRI Yearbook, 1995.* New York: Oxford University Press, 1995.

Sirriah, Hussein. "Lebanon: Dimensions of Conflict." Adelphi Paper 243. IISS, 1989.

"Six Guerilla Leaders in Colombia Surrender." *Prescott Evening Courier*, June 17, 1953, 3.

Sjamsuddin, Nazaruddin. *The Republican Revolt: A Study of the Acehnese Rebellion.* Singapore: Institute of Southeast Asian Studies, 1985.

Skidmore, Thomas E., and Peter H. Smith. *Modern Latin America.* New York: Oxford University Press, 2004.

Sklar, Holly. *Washington's War on Nicaragua.* Cambridge, MA: South End Press, 1988.

Skorupsky, Bolko Josef. "The Etiology of Protracted and Criminally Sustained Internal Wars in the Post-Cold War: The Continuation and Termination of the FARC, KLA, and EZLN Insurgencies." PhD diss., University of Virginia, Department of Politics, 2012.

Skutsch, Carl. "Eritrea: War for Independence, 1958–1991." In *Encyclopedia of Conflicts since World War II*, vol. 1, edited by James Ciment, 155–164. Armonk, NY: Sharpe Reference, 2007a.

______. "Ethiopia: Civil War, 1978–1991." In *Encyclopedia of Conflicts since World War II*, vol. 1, edited by James Ciment, 174–79. Armonk, NY: Sharpe Reference, 2007b.

Skutsch, Carl, and Charles Allan. "Burundi: Ethnic Strife since 1962." In *Encyclopedia of Conflicts since World War II*, vol. 1, edited by James Ciment, 101–7. Armonk, NY: Sharpe Reference, 2007.

Skutsch, Carl, and Jeffrey A. Shantz. Chad: Civil Wars, 1960s-1990s." In *Encyclopedia of Conflicts since World War II*, vol. 1, edited by James Ciment, 114–18. Armonk, NY: Sharpe Reference, 2007.

Slade, Adolphus. *Turkey, Greece and Malta*. London: Saunders and Otley, 1837.

______. "Formal Alliances, 1816–1965: An Extension of the Basic Data." *Journal of Peace Research* 3 (1969): 257–82; reprinted in J. David Singer and Paul Diehl, eds. *Measuring the Correlates of War*, Ann Arbor: University of Michigan Press, 1990.

Small, Melvin. "History and the Correlates of War Project." In *Prisoners of War? Nation-states in the Modern Era*, edited by Charles S. Gochman and Alan Ned Sabrosky. Lexington, MA: Lexington Books, 1990.

______, eds. *International War: An Anthology and Study Guide*. Homewood, IL: Dorsey Press, 1985.

______, eds. *International War: An Anthology and Study Guide*, 2nd ed. Homewood, IL: Dorsey Press, 1989a.

______. "Patterns in International Warfare, 1816–1980." In *International War: An Anthology*, 2nd ed. Chicago, IL: Dorsey Press, 1989b.

______. *Resort to Arms: International and Civil War, 1816–1980*. Beverly Hills, CA: Sage, 1982.

Small, Melvin, and J. David Singer. "Diplomatic Importance of States, 1816–1970: An Extension and Refinement of the Indicator." *World Politics*, 25 (1973): 577–99; reprinted in J. David Singer, ed. *The Correlates of War I: Research Origins and Rationale*, New York: Free Press, 1979; and in J. David Singer and Paul Diehl, eds., *Measuring the Correlates of War*, Ann Arbor: University of Michigan Press, 1990.

Small Arms Survey Sudan. "Timeline of Recent Intra-Southern Conflict." 2014. http://www.smallarmssurveysudan.org/fileadmin/docs/documents/HSBA-South-Sudan-Crisis-Timeline.pdf.

Smith, C. Jay Jr. *Finland and the Russian Revolution, 1917–1922*. Athens: University of Georgia Press, 1958.

Smith, Denis Mack. *A History of Sicily: Modern Sicily after 1713*. New York: Viking Press, 1968.

Smith, Hedrick. "Burmese Separatists Intensify Fight against Ne Win's Regime." *New York Times*, February 23, 1964, 1–2.

Smith, Joseph. "Britain and the Brazilian Naval Revolt of 1893–4." *Journal of Latin American Studies* 2, no. 2 (November 1970): 175–98.

Smith, Martin. *Burma: Insurgency and the Politics of Ethnicity*. 2nd ed. New York: Zed Books Ltd., 1999.

Smith, Michael Llewellyn. *The Great Island: A Study of Crete*. London: Longmans, 1965.

Smith, Ole L. "The Greek Communist Party, 1945–9." In *The Greek Civil War, 1943–1950*, edited by David H. Close. New York: Routledge, 1993.

Smith, Rhea Marsh. *Spain: A Modern History*. Ann Arbor: University of Michigan Press, 1965.

Smith, Warren W., Jr. *Tibetan Nation: A History of Tibetan Nationalism and Sino-Tibetan Relations*. Boulder, CO: Westview, 1996.

Smithsonian Institution. *The Civil War, A Visual History*. New York: DK Publishing, 2011.

Smyth, William Henry. *Sketch of the Present State of the Island of Sardinia*. London: John Murray, 1828.

Snow, Peter G. *Argentine Radicalism*. Iowa City: University of Iowa Press, 1965.

Snow, Peter J. *Hussein*. Washington, DC: Luce, 1972.

Soebardi, S. "Kartosuwiryo and the Darul Islam Rebellion in Indonesia." *Journal of Southeast Asian Studies* 14, no. 1 (1983): 109–33.

Soguel, Dominique. "US Airstrikes in Syria." *Christian Science Monitor*, September 23, 2014.

"Soldiers Kill Leftists in El Salvador Shooting." *Times-News (Hendersonville, NC)*, December 19, 1979, 3.

Solmi, Arrigo. *The Making of Modern Italy*. Port Washington, NY: Kennikat Press, 1970.

Sonyel, Salahi R. "How the Turks of the Peloponnese Were Exterminated during the Greek Rebellion." *Belleten* 62, no. 233 (1998): 121–35.

Sorokin, Pitirim A. *Fluctuation of Social Relationships, War and Revolution*. Vol. 3 of *Social and Cultural Dynamics*. New York: American Book, 1937.

Soto, Enrique Chirinos. *Historia de la Republica (1821–1930)*. Tomo I. Lima, Peru: Ediatores Importadores S.A., 1985.

Soucek, Svat. *A History of Inner Asia*. Cambridge, UK: Cambridge University Press, 2000.

South, Ashley. *Mon Nationalism and Civil War in Burma: The Golden Sheldrake*. London: Routledge Curzon, 2003.

South Asia Terrorism Portal. "Annual Fatalities in Terrorist Violence 1988–2014." 2014a. http://www.satp.org/satporgtp/countries/india/states/jandk/data_sheets/annual_casualties.htm.

______. "Balochistan Assessment—2014." 2014b. http://www.satp.org/satporgtp/countries/pakistan/Balochistan/index.html.

______. "Fatalities in Maoist Insurgency, 2000–2014." 2014c. http://www.satp.org/satporgtp/countries/nepal/database/fatalities.htm.

______. "Fatalities in Terrorist Violence in Pakistan 2003–2014." 2014f. http://www.satp.org/satporgtp/countries/pakistan/database/casualties.htm.

______. "Fatalities in Pakistan Region Wise: 2011." 2013a. http://www.satp.org/satporgtp/countries/pakistan/database/fatilities_regionwise2011.htm.

______. "Fatalities in Pakistan Region Wise: 2012." 2013b. http://www.satp.org/satporgtp/countries/pakistan/database/fatilities_regionwise2012.htm.

______. "Fatalities in Pakistan Region Wise: 2013." 2014d. http://www.satp.org/satporgtp/countries/pakistan/database/fatilities_regionwise2013.htm.

______. "Fatalities in Terrorist Violence in Sri Lanka 2002–2014." 2014e. http://www.satp.org/satporgtp/countries/shrilanka/database/annual_casualties.htm.

______. "Monthly Break-up of Casualties in Terrorist Violence—1998–2001." 2001. http://www.satp.org/satporgtp/countries/india/states/jandk/data_sheets/monthwise_killing_1998_00.htm.

"South Sudan: 'White Army' Militia Marches to Fight." *USA Today*, December 28, 2013. http://www.usatoday.com/story/news/world/2013/12/28/south-sudan-white-army-militia/4231213/.

"South Sudan's Army Advances on Rebels in Bentiu and Bor." *BBC News*, January 10, 2014. http://www.bbc.com/news/world-africa-25671847.

Southall, Aidan. "Social Disorganization in Uganda: Before, During and after Amin." *Journal of Modern African Studies* 18, no. 4 (December 1980): 627–56.

Spence, James Mudie. *The Land of Bolivar, or War, Peace, and Adventure in the Republic of Venezuela*. London: Sampson Low, Marston, Searle, & Rivington, 1878.

Spencer, Edmund. *Travels in European Turkey in 1850*. London: Colburn and Co., 1851.

Spicer, Edward H. *The Yaquis: A Cultural History*. Tucson: University of Arizona Press, 1980.

Spielmann, Christian. *Die Taiping-Revolution (1850–1864)*. Halle, Germany: Hermann Gesenius, 1900.

Spindler, Frank. *Nineteenth Century Ecuador*. Fairfax, VA: George Mason University Press, 1987.

Stanford Central America Action Network, ed. *Revolution in Central America*. Boulder, CO: Westview Press, 1983.

Staniland, Paul. *Networks of Rebellion: Explaining Insurgent Cohesion and Collapse*. Ithaca, NY: Cornell University Press, 2014.

Stansfield, Gareth. *Iraqi Kurdistan: Political Development and Emergent Democracy*. New York: Routledge/Curzon, 2003.

Stapleton, Timothy J. *The Era of Independence: From the Congo Crisis to Africa's World War (ca. 1963–)*. Vol. 3 of *A Military History of Africa*. Santa Barbara, CA: Praeger, 2013.

Starr, S. Frederick. *Xinjiang: China's Muslim Borderland*. Armonk, NY: M. E. Sharpe, 2004.

Stašaitis, Arûnas. "Lithuania's Struggle against Soviet Occupation 1944–1953." *Baltic Defence Review*, no. 3 (2000): 115–22.

Stavrianos, Leften. *The Balkans since 1453*. New York: Holt, Rinehart and Winston, 1958.

______. *The Balkans since 1453*. New York: New York University Press, 2000.

Steans, Jill. *Gender and International Relations*. 2nd ed. New York: Polity, 2006.

Stearns, Peter N., ed. *Encyclopedia of World History: Ancient, Medieval, and Modern, Chronologically Arranged*. Wilmington, MA: Houghton Mifflin, 2001.

Stein, Steve. *Populism in Peru*. Madison: University of Wisconsin Press, 1980.

Steinberg, David I. "International Rivalries in Burma: The Rise of Economic Competition." *Asian Survey* 30, no. 6 (June 1990): 587–601.

Stempel, John. *Inside the Iranian Revolution*. Bloomington: Indiana University Press, 1981.

Stephen, John J. *The Russian Far East: A History*. Stanford, CA: Stanford University Press, 1994.

Stephenson, Nathaniel W. *Texas and the Mexican War*. New Haven, CT: Yale University Press, 1921.

Stevens, Richard P. "Historical Setting." In *Ethiopia, a Country Study*, 3rd ed., edited by Harold D. Nelson and Irving Kaplan. Washington, DC: Department of the Army, 1981.

Stevenson, Francis Seymour. *A History of Montenegro*. New York: Arno Press/New York Times, 1971.

Stevenson, Sara Yorke. *Maximilian in Mexico: Reminiscences of the French Intervention 1862–1867*. New York: Century Co., 1899.

Stewart, George. *The White Armies of Russia*. London: Macmillan, 1933.

Stewart, Rhea Talley. *Fire in Afghanistan, 1914–1929*. Garden City, NY: Doubleday and Co., 1973.

Stillman, W. J. *American Consul in a Cretan War*. Austin, TX: Center for Neo-Hellenic Studies, 1966. Originally published 1874.

______. *The Autobiography of a Journalist*. Vol. 2. Boston, MA: Houghton, Mifflin, and Co., 1901.

______. *The Union of Italy.* Cambridge, UK: University Press, 1898.

Stinnett, Douglas M., Jaroslav Tir, Philip Schafer, Paul F. Diehl, and Charles Gochman. "The Correlates of War Project Direct Contiguity Data, Version 3." *Conflict Management and Peace Science* 19, no. 2 (2002): 58–66.

Stoll, David. *Between Two Armies in the Ixil Towns of Guatemala.* New York: Columbia University Press, 1993.

Stoll, Richard. "An Attempt to Scale Major Power Disputes, 1816–1965: The Use of a Method to Detect Development Processes." Presented at the annual meeting of the International Studies Association, 1977.

Stone, Daniel. *A Military History of Russia.* Westport, CT: Praeger Security International, 2006.

Stone, Martin. *The Agony of Algeria.* New York: Columbia University Press, 1997.

Stora, Benjamin. *Algeria 1830–2000: A Short History.* Translated by Janc Marie Todd. Ithaca, NY: Cornell University Press, 2001.

Stratfor. "Pakistan: Heavy Fighting Continues." October 9, 2007a.

______. "Pakistan: Musharraf Asserts Himself With a Bombing." October 9, 2007b.

Stuart-Fox, Martin. *A History of Laos.* Cambridge, UK: Cambridge University Press, 1997.

______. "National Defence and Internal Security in Laos." In *Contemporary Laos: Studies in the Politics and Society of the Lao People's Democratic Republic,* edited by Martin Stuart-Fox, 220–44. St. Lucia, Queensland: University of Queensland Press, 1982.

Su, Yang. "Tumult from Within: State Bureaucrats and Chinese Mass Movement, 1966–71." PhD diss., Stanford University, Sociology, 2003.

Subtelny, Orest. *Ukraine, a History.* Buffalo, NY: University of Toronto Press, 1988.

"SUDAN: Special Report II: Chad and the Darfur Conflict." IRIN, February 16, 2004. http://www.irinnews.org/report/48590/sudan-special-report-ii-chad-and-the-darfur-conflict.

"Sudan Revolutionary Front." 2013. http://www.smallarmssurveysudan.org/fileadmin/docs/facts-figures/sudan/darfur/armed-groups/opposition/HSBA-Armed-Groups-SRF.pdf.

Suh, Young-hee. "Tracing the Course of the Peasant War of 1894." *Korea Journal* 34, no. 4 (1994): 17–30.

Suhrke, Astri. "Smaller-Nation Diplomacy: Thailand's Current Dilemmas." *Asian Survey* 11, no. 5 (May 1971): 429–44.

Suhrke Astri, and Lela Garner Nobel, eds. *Ethnic Conflicts in International Relations.* New York: Praeger, 1977a.

______. "Muslims in the Philippines and Thailand." In *Ethnic Conflicts in International Relations,* edited by Astri Suhrke and Lela Garner Nobel. New York: Praeger, 1977b.

Sullivant, Robert S. *Soviet Politics and the Ukraine, 1917–1957.* New York: Columbia University Press, 1962.

Sumner, Benedict H. *Russia and the Balkans 1870–1880.* Oxford, UK: Oxford University Press, 1937.

______. *Russia and the Balkans, 1870–1880.* London: Archon Books, 1962 [reprint].

Sundarayya, Putchalapalli. *Telangana People's Struggle and Its Lessons.* Calcutta, India: Communist Party of India (Marxist), 1972.

Sundberg, Anne. "The Problem of Change and Reorganization of the One-Party Dictatorship in Congo." *African Journal of Political Science* 4, no. 2 (1999): 181–213.

______. "The Struggle for Kingship: Moses or Messiah—Ethnic War and the Use of Ethnicity in the Process of Democratization in Congo-Brazzaville." In *Ethnicity Kills?: The Politics of War, Peace, and Ethnicity in Subsaharan Africa,* edited by Einar Braathen, Morton Bøås, and Gjermund Saether. Houndmills, UK: Macmillan Press, 2000.

Sutsakhan, Sat. "The Khmer Republic at War and the Final Collapse." Indochina Refugee Authored Monograph Program. Washington, DC: Department of the Army, 1978. http://www.vietnam.ttu.edu/virtualarchive/items.php?item=2390505001.

Sutton, Donald S. *Provincial Militarism and the Chinese Republic: The Yunnan Army, 1905–1925.* Ann Arbor: University of Michigan Press, 1980.

Swami, Praveen. "Failed Threats and Flawed Fences: India's Military Responses to Pakistan's Proxy War." *India Review* 3, no. 2 (2004): 147–170.

______. *India, Pakistan and the Secret Jihad: The Covert War in Kashmir, 1947–2004.* London: Routledge, 2007.

______. "India's Forgotten Army." *The Hindu,* September 14, 2003. http://www.hindu.com/thehindu/2003/09/14/stories/2003091406170800.htm Last accessed May 28, 2014.

______. "Quickstep or Kadam Taal? The Elusive Search for Peace in Jammu and Kashmir." *United States Institute of Peace, Special Report #133* (March 2005): 1–12.

Swamy, M. R. Narayan. *The Tiger Vanquished: LTTE's Story.* New Delhi, India: SAGE, 2010.

Swarns, Rachel L. "Zimbabwe Says It Stands by Congo in Conflict." *New York Times,* January 20, 2001. http://www.nytimes.com.

Swietochowski, Tadeusz. *Russian Azerbaijan, 1905–1920.* Cambridge, UK: Cambridge University Press, 1985.

Swire, J. *Albania: The Rise of a Kingdom.* London: Williams and Norgate Ltd., 1929.

______. *Albania: The Rise of a Kingdom.* New York: Smith, 1950.

Sylvester, Christine. *Feminist International Relations, an Unfinished Journey.* Cambridge, UK: Cambridge University Press, 2002.

"Syria: What Really Happened in Jisr al-Shughour?" *BBC News,* June 7, 2011. http://www.bbc.co.uk/news/world-middle-east-13679109.

Syrian Observatory for Human Rights. "About 2 Million People Killed and Wounded in 47 Months, and It Is Still Not Enough . . ." 2015. http://syriahr.com/en/2015/02/about-2-millions-killed-and-wounded-in-47-months-and-it-is-still-not-enough/.

"Syria's Homs under a Military Siege, Activists Say." CNN, December 24, 2011. http://articles.cnn.com/2011–12–24/middleeast/world_meast_syria-unrest_1_bab-amr-security-forces-local-coordination-committees?_s=PM:MIDDLEEAST.

Taagepera, Rein. *Estonia, Return to Independence.* Boulder, CO: Westview Press,1993.

Tabeau, Ewa, and Jakub Bijak. "War-related Deaths in the 1992–1995 Armed Conflicts in Bosnia and Herzegovina: A Critique of Previous Estimates and Recent Results." *European Journal of Population* 21 (2005): 187–215.

Tadjoeddin, Mohammad Zulfan. *Explaining Collective Violence in Contemporary Indonesia: From Conflict to Cooperation.* New York: Palgrave Macmillan, 2014.

Takeuchi, Tutsuni. *War and Diplomacy in the Japanese Empire.* Garden City, NY: Doubleday, 1935.

Tallmer, Jerry. "37 Years Later, Elizabeth Butson's Guatemalan Rebel Photo Article Remains the Definitive Account." *The Villager* 73, no. 33 (December 17–23, 2003). http://www.thevillager.com/villager_33/37yearslater.html.

Tallon, James N. "The Failure of Ottomanism: The Albanian Rebellions of 1909–1912." PhD diss., University of Chicago, Department of Near Eastern Languages and Civilizations, 2012.

Tan, Andrew. "Armed Muslim Separatist Rebellion in Southeast Asia: Persistence, Prospects, and Implications." *Studies in Conflict & Terrorism* 23 (2000): 267–88.

T'ang Leang-Li, ed. *Suppressing Communist Banditry in China.* Shanghai: China United Press, 1934.

Tanner, Harold M. "Guerrilla, Mobile, and Base Warfare in Communist Military Operations in Manchuria, 1945–1947." *The Journal of Military History* 67, no. 4 (2003): 1177–222.

Tanner, Stephen. *Afghanistan: A Military History From Alexander the Great to the Fall of the Taliban.* New York: Da Capo Press, 2002.

Tanner, Victor, and Jérôme Tubiana. *Divided They Fall: The Fragmentation of Darfur's Rebel Groups.* Geneva, Switzerland: Small Arms Survey, 2007.

Tanter, Richard. "The Military Situation in East Timor." *Pacific Research* 8, no. 2 (1977): 1–6.

Tappe, E.D. "The 1821 Revolution in the Rumanian Principalities." In *The Struggle for Greek Independence,* edited by Richard Clogg, 135–55. Hamden, CT: Archon Press, 1973.

Tapper, Richard. *Frontier Nomads of Iran: A Political and Social History of the Shahsevan.* Cambridge, UK: Cambridge University Press, 1997.

Tareke, Gebru. *Ethiopia: Power and Protest, Peasant Revolts in the Twentieth Century.* Cambridge, UK: Cambridge University Press, 1991.

______. "From Lash to Red Star: The Pitfalls of Counter-insurgency in Ethiopia, 1980–82." *Journal of Modern African Studies* 30, no. 3 (2002): 465–98.

Tarver, H. Michael, and Julia C. Frederick. *The History of Venezuela.* Westport, CT: Greenwood Press, 2005.

Tatsios, Theodore George. *The Megali Idea and the Greek-Turkish War of 1897.* Boulder, CO: East European Monographs, 1984.

Taylor, Charles Lewis, and Michael C. Hudson. *World Handbook of Political and Social Indicators.* New Haven, CT: Yale University Press, 1972.

Taylor, John G. *East Timor: The Price of Freedom.* New York: Zed Books, 1999.

Taylor, Lewis. *Shining Path: Guerilla War in Peru's Northern Highlands, 1980–1997.* Liverpool, UK: Liverpool University Press, 2006.

Taylor, Robert H. *Foreign and Domestic Consequences of the KMT Intervention in Burma.* Ithaca, NY: Southeast Asia Program, Department of Asian Studies, Cornell University, 1973.

Tekle, Tesfa-Alem. "Somalia: Ethiopia Decides to Join Amisom Force in Somalia." *Allafrica,* November 13, 2013. http://allafrica.com/stories/201311131037.html.

Telford, Hamish. "Counter-Insurgency in India: Observations from Punjab and Kashmir." *Journal of Conflict Studies* 21, no. 1 (2001). http://journals.hil.unb.ca/index.php/jcs/article/view/4293/4888.

Temperly, Harold. *England and the Near East.* Hamden, CT: Archon Books, 1964.

Teng Ssu-Yti. *Historiography of the Taiping Rebellion.* Cambridge, MA: East Asia Research Center, Harvard University, 1963.

______. *The Nien Army and Their Guerrilla Warfare, 1851–1868.* The Hague, Netherlands: Mouton, 1961.

______. *The Taiping Rebellion and the Western Powers.* London: Oxford University Press, 1971.

Teplitz, Benjamin I. "The Political and Economic Foundations of Modernization in Nicaragua: The Administration of José Santos Zelaya 1893–1909." PhD diss., Howard University, 1973.

Terrill, W. Andrew. "Understanding the Strengths and Vulnerabilities of ISIS." *Parameters* 44, no. 3 (2014): 13–23.

Testerman, Matthew A. "Rebel Financing in Civil Wars: A Quantitative Analysis with Three Case Studies of Civil Wars in the Philippines." PhD diss., University of Rochester–Department of Political Science, 2012.

"Thirty Rebels Arrested in Sri Lanka." *Xinhua News Service*, January 5, 1990.

Thomas, Hugh. *Cuba: The Pursuit of Freedom.* New York: Harper, 1971.

______. *The Spanish Civil War.* New York: Harper, 1961.

Thomas, Jeffrey. "President Puntin's North Caucasus Challenge." Center for Strategic & International Studies, March 8, 2001.

Thomas, Lowell, Jr. *The Silent War in Tibet.* Garden City, NY: Doubleday, 1959.

Thompson, Ewa M. *Imperial Knowledge: Russian Literature and Colonialism.* Westport, CT: Greenwood Press, 2000.

Thompson, Leonard. *A History of South Africa.* 3rd ed. New Haven, CT: Yale University Press, 2001.

Thompson, William R., and David R. Dreyer. *Handbook of International Rivalries,1494–2010.* Washington DC: Congressional Quarterly Press, 2011.

Thomson, Guy P. C., and David G. LaFrance. *Patriotism, Politics, and Popular Liberalism in Nineteenth-century Mexico.* Wilmington, DE: S. R. Books, 1999.

Thornton, Richard C. *China, A Political History, 1917–1980.* Boulder, CO: Westview Press, 1982.

Thurner, Mark. "Atusparia and Caceres: Rereading Representations of Peru's Late Nineteenth-century 'National Problem.'" *Hispanic American Historical Review* 77, no. 3 (August 1997): 409–41.

Tickner, J. Ann. *Gender in International Relations.* New York: Columbia University Press, 1992.

Tillema, Herbert K. *International Armed Conflict since 1945: A Bibliographic Handbook of Wars and Military Interventions.* Boulder, CO: Westview Press, 1991.

Tilman, Robert O. "Burma in 1986: The Process of Involution Continues." *Asian Survey* 27, no. 2 (February 1987): 254–63.

Timberg, Craig. "Sudan's Offensive Comes at Key Time." *Washington Post,* September 5, 2006, A01.

"Time for Thein Sein to Come Clean about Burmese Losses in Kachin State." Kachinnews.com. September 22, 2012. http://kachinnews.com/news/2408-time-for-thein-sein-to-come-clean-about-burmese-losses-in-kachin-state.html.

"Timeline: Libya's Civil War Nears End." *Reuters.* October 20, 2011. http://www.reuters.com/article/2011/10/20/us-libya-events-idUSTRE79J24N20111020.

The Times (London), January 30, 1860, 7a.

The Times (London), August 1, 1885, 10d.

Times Live. "Rebelswonder: Where Did Gbagbo Go? April 1, 2011. http://www.timeslive.co.za/africa/2011/04/01/rebels-wonder-where-did-gbagbo-go.

"Timor Villages 'Fall.'" *The Canberra Times*, November 10, 1976, 15.

Tinker, Clifford A. "Occupation of Haiti and Santo Domingo." In *Selected Articles on Intervention in Latin America.* Vol. 5. Compiled by Lamar T. Beman. New York: The H. W. Wilson Company, 1928.

Tinker, Hugh. *The Union of Burma.* London: Oxford University Press, 1957.

______. *The Union of Burma.* 3rd ed. New York: Oxford University Press, 1961.

Tir, Jaroslav, Philip Schafer, Paul Diehl, and Gary Goertz. "Territorial Changes, 1816–1996: Procedures and Data." *Conflict Management and Peace Science* 16, no. 1 (1998): 89–97.

Tirona, Tomas C. "The Philippine Anti-communist Campaign." In *Modern Guerrilla Warfare*, edited by F. Osanka. Glencoe, IL: Free Press, 1962.

Tlemcani, Rachid. *State and Revolution in Algeria.* Boulder, CO: Westview, 1986.

Toft, Monica Duffy. *The Geography of Ethnic Violence.* Princeton, NJ: Princeton University Press, 2003.

Tokarski, Fernando. "Pluralidades e Singularidades Entre Canudos e o Contestado." *Pharos: Revista Semestral de la Universidad de las Americas* 9, no. 2 (2002): 151–53.

Tomán, René De La Pedraja. *Wars of Latin America, 1899–1941.* Jefferson, NC: McFarland Press, 2006.

Tombs, Robert. *France, 1814–1914.* New York: Longman, 1996.

______. "Paris Commune (1871)." In *The Encyclopedia of Political Revolutions*, edited by Jack A. Goldstone. Washington, DC: Congressional Quarterly, 1998.

Topik, Steven C. *Trade and Gunboats: The United States and Brazil in the Age of Empire.* Stanford, CA: Stanford University Press, 2000.

Torres-Rivas, Edelberto. "The Origins of Crisis and Instability in Central America." In *Democracy in Latin America: Visions and Realities*, edited by Susanne Jonas and Nancy Stein, 53–64. New York: Bergin & Garvey Publishers, 1990.

Towers, Roy. "Afghan Lion's Roar Is Toned Down to Disconsolate Growl." *The Herald (Glasgow)*, December 14, 1992, 20.

Toynbee, Arnold. *Survey of International Affairs 1928.* London: Oxford University Press, 1929.

Toyos, Sergio. "Campañas de Pacificación del Interior (1861 y 1867)." n.d. http://www.rs.ejercito.mil.ar/Contenido/Nro648/Revista/histomilitar.htm.

Tozer, Henry. *Researches in the Highlands of Turkey.* London: John Murray, 1869.

Traboulsi, Fawwaz. *History of Modern Lebanon.* London: Pluto Press, 2007.

"Travelers Thrown into Sanaa Battle." *Herald-Tribune (FL)*, June 2, 1968, 6A.

Treadway, John D. *The Falcon and the Eagle: Montenegro and Austria-Hungary, 1908–1914.* West Lafayette, IN: Purdue University Press, 1983.

Treece, David. *Exiles, Allies, Rebels: Brazil's Indianist Movement, Indigenist Politics, and the Imperial Nation-state.* Westport, CT: Greenwood Press, 2000.

Treptow, Kurt, ed. *A History of Rumania.* Jaşi, Romania: East European Monographs/Center for Romanian Studies, 1996.

Tripp, Aili Mari. "Women, Violence, and Peacebuilding in the Great Lakes Region." Unpublished manuscript, 2005.

Tripp, Charles. *A History of Iraq.* Cambridge, UK: Cambridge University Press, 2000.

"Troops in Bloodbath–400 Killed or Injured in Yemen." *Daily Record (Scotland)*, April 30, 1994.

"Truce Brings Afghans into Kabul Bazaars." *New York Times*, August 31, 1992, A3.

Tschebotarioff, Gregory P. "The Cossacks and the Revolution of 1917." *Russian Review* 20, no. 3 (1961): 306–16.

Tse-Han, Lai, Ramon H. Myers, and Wei Wou. *A Tragic Beginning: The Taiwanese Uprising of February 28, 1947.* Stanford, CA: Stanford University Press, 1991.

Tsing, Yuan. "Yakub Beg (1820–77) and the Moslem Rebellion in Chinese Turkestan." *Central Asiatic Journal* 2 (June 1961): 154–67.

Tsuzuki, Chushichi. *The Emergence of Power in Modern Japan, 1825–1995.* Oxford, UK: Oxford University Press, 2000.

Tuck, Jim. *The Holy War in Los Altos: A Regional Analysis of Mexico's Cristero Rebellion.* Tucson: University of Arizona Press, 1982.

Tucker, Spencer C., ed. *A Global Chronology of Conflict: From the Ancient World to the Modern Middle East.* Vol. III. Santa Barbara, CA: ABC–CLIO, LLC., 2010.

Tull, Denis M. "The Democratic Republic of Congo: Militarized Politics in a 'Failed State.'" In *African Guerrillas, Raging against the Machine*, edited by Morten Bøås and Kevin C. Dunn. Boulder, CO: Lynne Rienner, 2007.

Turkish Ministry of Foreign Affairs. "A Report on the PKK and Terrorism." 1995. http://www.fas.org/irp/world/para/docs/mfa-t-pkk.htm.

Turner, John W. *Continent Ablaze: The Insurgency Wars in Africa, 1960 to the Present.* London: Arms and Armour, 1998.

Turner, Robert T. *Vietnamese Communism: Its Origins and Development.* Stanford, CA: Hoover Institution Press, 1975.

Turner, Thomas. "Angola's Role in the Congo War." In *The African Stakes of the Congo War*, edited by John F. Clark. New York: Palgrave Macmillan, 2002.

______. *The Congo Wars: Conflict, Myth and Reality.* New York: Zed Books, 2007.

Tuson, Penelope, and Anita Burdett, eds. *Records of Saudi Arabia: Primary Documents, 1902–1960.* Vols. 1 and 2. Archive Editions, 1992.

Tutman, Conrad. *The Collapse of the Tokugawa Bakufu 1862–1868.* Honolulu: University of Hawaii Press, 1980.

TVNZ News. "Bomb Kills Pakistani Soldiers." November 29, 2007.

Twagilimana, Aimable. *The Debris of Ham: Ethnicity, Regionalism, and the 1994 Rwandan Genocide.* Lanham, MD: University Press of America, 2003.

"Twenty-five Held in Pakistan al Qaeda Raid." *CNN*, February 24, 2004. http://www.cnn.com/2004/WORLD/asiapcf/02/24/pakistan.alqaeda.

"Twenty-four Killed in Yemen Clashes." *Iran Daily*, February 28, 2014.

"Two Thousand Ten Iraq Death Toll Tops 2009: Government." *Agence Presse France*, January 1, 2011.

Tyler, Christian. *Wild West China: The Taming of Xinjiang.* Piscataway, NJ: Rutgers University Press, 2004.

Udoidem, Sylvanus I. "Religion in the Political Life of Nigeria." In *New Strategies for Curbing Ethnic and Religious Conflicts in Nigeria*, edited by F. U. Okafor. Enugu, Nigeria: Fourth Dimension, 1997.

Ufford, Letitia. *The Pasha: How Mehemet Ali Defied the West, 1839–1841.* Jefferson, NC: McFarland, 2007.

"Uganda: The Battle of Mengo Hill." *Time*, June 3, 1966. http://content.time.com/time.

Uhalley, Stephen, Jr. "The Controversy Over Li Hsiu-ch'eng: An Ill-Timed Centenary." *The Journal of Asian Studies* 25, no. 2 (1966): 305–17.

Ukraine Defense Ministry. "Heroes Pantheon." http://www.mil.gov.ua/multimedia/panteon-geroiv/spisok-zagiblih-vijskovosluzhbovcziv-zsu-v-hodi-vedennya-ato.html.

Ulam, Adam B. *The Bolsheviks.* Toronto: Collier-Macmillan, 1965.

______. *The Bolsheviks: The Intellectual and Political History of the Triumph of Communism in Russia.* Toronto, Ontario: Collier Books, 1968.

Um, Khatharya. "Cambodia in 1989: Still Talking but No Settlement." *Asian Survey* 30, no. 1 (1990): 96–104.

______. "Cambodia in 1993: Year Zero Plus One." *Asian Survey* 34, no. 1 (1994): 72–81.

______. "Cambodia in 1994: The Year of Transition." *Asian Survey* 35, no. 1 (1995): 76–83.

"UN Warns of Crisis as Fighting Follows Khmer Rouge Walkout." *The Guardian (London)*, April 15, 1993, 11.

United Nations. "Somalia–Unosom I." Department of Public Information, March 21, 1997, 1–4.

United States Bureau of Citizenship and Immigration Services. "Republic of Congo (Brazzaville): Information on the Human Rights Situation and the Ninja Militia." November 2000. http://www.refworld.org/docid/3dedffab4.html.

United States Department of Defense. "Operation New Dawn (OND) US Casualty Status." 2013. http://www.defense.gov/news/casualty.pdf.

United States Institute of Peace. "Civil Society under Siege in Colombia." *Special Report* 114, February 2004, 1–16.

______. "Rwanda: Accountability for War Crimes and Genocide." Report on a United States Institute of Peace Conference, 2002.

"United States of Colombia." *New York Times*, March 7, 1862.

Uppsala Universitet Conflict Data Project. "Afghanistan—Detailed Information—Whole Conflict." 2004. http://www.pcr.uu.se.

______. "Angola." 2002. http://www.pcr.uu.se/database.

______. "Azerbaijan." 1997. http://www.pcr.uu.se/database.

______. "Bosnia-Hercegovina." 1995a. http://www.pcr.uu.se/database.

______. "Congo, Democratic Republic of (Zaire)." 2003. http://www.pcr.uu.se.

______. "Congo—Detailed Information—Whole Conflict." 2006. http://www.pcr.uu.se.

______. "Croatia." 1995b. http://www.pcr.uu.se/database.

______. "Liberia." 2005. http://www.pcr.uu.se/database.

Urlanis, Boris T. *Voini I Narodo-Nacelenie Evropi (Wars and the Population of Europe).* Moscow, Russia: Government Publishing House, 1960.

Urquhart, D. *Spirit of the East.* London: Henry Colburn, 1838.

"U.S. Plans to Leave Troops to Back U.N. Somalia Unit." *The New York Times*, April 30, 1993. http://www.nytimes.com.

US Congress, Senate Committee on Foreign Relations. *Hearings Before a Subcommittee on US Security Agreements Abroad.* 91st Cong., 1st sess., part 2, October, 20, 21, 22, 28, 1969.

US Library of Congress. "The Finnish Civil War." January 3, 2008. http://countrystudies.us/finland/15.htm.

Usborne, C. V. *The Conquest of Morocco.* London: Stanley Paul, 1936.

"US-led Coalition Hits Jihadist Positions with 39 Air Strikes." *Al-Arab*, December 27, 2014.

Valdes, Nelson P. "Revolutionary Solidarity in Angola." In *Cuba in the World*, edited by Cole Blasier and Carmelo Mesa-Lago. Pittsburgh, PA: University of Pittsburgh Press, 1979.

Valentino, Benjamin A. *Final Solutions: Mass Killing and Genocide in the 20th Century.* Ithaca, NY: Cornell University Press, 2004.

Valeriano, Napoleon D., and Charles T. R. Bohannan. *Counter-guerrilla Operations: The Philippine Experience.* Westport, CT: Praeger Security International, 2006.

Van Bruinessen, Martin. *Agha, Shaikh, and State: The Social and Political Structures of Kurdistan.* London: Zed Books, Ltd., 1992.

______. "Kurdish Tribes and the State of Iran: The Case of Simko's Revolt." *The Conflict of Tribe and State in Iran and Afghanistan*, edited R. Tapper, 364–400. New York: St. Martin's, 1983.

______. "The Kurds Between Iran and Iraq." *Middle East Report* 141 (July–August 1986): 14–27.

Van Dam, Nikolaos. *The Struggle for Power in Syria.* New York: I. B. Taurus, 1996.

van de Ven, Hans J. *War and Nationalism in China, 1925–1945.* London: Routledge Curzon, 2003.

van der Kroef, Justin M. "Cambodia in 1990: The Elusive Peace." *Asian Survey* 31, no. 1 (1991): 94–102.

______. "Irian Jaya: The Intractable Conflict." *Asian Affairs* 6, no. 2 (1978): 119–33.

Van Dijk, C. *Rebellion under the Banner of Islam: The Darul Islam in Indonesia.* The Hague, Netherlands: Martinus Nijhoff, 1981.

van Klinken, Gerry. "Indonesian Casualties in East Timor, 1975–1999: Analysis of an Official List." *Indonesia* 80 (2005): 109–22.

Van Nederveen, Gilles K. "USAF Airlift into the Heart of Darkness, the Congo 1960–1978, Implications for Modern Air Mobility Planners." Airpower Research Institute Paper #2001–04, September 2001, 1–31.

van Schaik, Sam. *Tibet: A History.* New Haven, CT: Yale University Press, 2011.

Vanderwood, Paul J. "Betterment for Whom? The Reform Period: 1855–1875." In Meyer, Michael C. and William H. Beezley, eds. *The Oxford History of Mexico.* Oxford, UK: Oxford University Press, 2000.

______. "Response to Revolt: The Counter-guerilla Strategy of Porfirio Diaz." *Hispanic American Historical Review* 66 (1976): 509–39.

Vanger, Milton I. *José Batlle y Ordoñez of Uruguay.* Cambridge, MA: Harvard University Press, 1963.

Vargas, Anthony. "AFP Claims It's Winning War vs. Insurgent Groups." *Manila Times*, January 1, 2007.

______. "Govt Winning War on Rebellion, Terror." *Manila Times*, December 31, 2005.

Vasques, John A. "The Steps to War: Toward a Scientific Explanation of Correlates of War Findings." *World Politics* 40, no. 1 (1987): 108–145.

Vasquez, John A., and Marie T. Henehan, eds. *The Scientific Study of Peace and War, a Text Reader.* New York: Lexington Books, 1992.

______. *The War Puzzle.* New York: Cambridge University Press, 1993.

Vassiliev, Alexei. *The History of Saudi Arabia.* London: Saqi Books, 1998.

Vaughn, Bruce. "Nepal: Background and US Relations." *Congressional Research Service* (June 8, 2005).

Vazquez-Gomez, Juana. *Dictionary of Mexican Rulers, 1325–1997.* Westport, CT: Greenwood Press, 1997.

Vickers, Miranda. *The Albanians: A Modern History.* London: I. B. Taurus, 1995.

______. *The Albanians: A Modern History.* Rev. ed. London: I. B. Tauris, 1999.

Victor, Anthony B., and Richard R. Sexton. *The War in Northern Laos.* Washington, DC: United States Air Force Center for Air Force History, 1993.

Vicuña, Elias Muñoz. *Primero Entre Iguales.* Guayaquil, Ecuador: Litografia e Imprenta de la Universidad de Guayaquil, 1984.

"Villa Force Defeated." *New York Times*, November 3, 1914.

Villafaña, Frank R. *Cold War in the Congo, the Confrontation of Cuban Military Forces, 1960–1967.* New Brunswick, NJ: Transaction Publishers, 2009.

Villalobos, Marty. "Counter-insurgency and the People's War in El Salvador." *Kasarinlan: Philippine Journal of Third World Studies* 3, no. 1 (1987): 37–54.

Vinacke, Harold M. *Far Eastern Politics in the Post War Period.* New York: Appleton-Century-Crofts, 1956.

Vines, Alex. *RENAMO: Terrorism in Mozambique.* Bloomington: Indiana University Press, 1991.

"Violence Rips Salvador; Two Newspapers Bombed." *The Bulletin (Bend, OR)*, October 29, 1979,: 12

Vira, Varun, and Anthony H. Cordesman. "The Libyan Uprising: An Uncertain Trajectory." Center for Strategic and International Studies. June 20, 2011. http://csis.org/files/publication/110620_libya.pdf.

Vitkus, Gediminas, ed. *Wars of Lithuania, a Systematic Quantitative Analysis of Lithuania's Wars in the Nineteenth and Twentieth Centuries.* Vilnius, Lithuania: EUGRIMAS, 2014.

Vitug, Marites Dañguilan, and Glenda M. Gloria. *Under the Crescent Moon: Rebellion in Mindanao.* Quezon City, Philippines: Ateneo Center for Social Policy and Public Affairs, 2000.

Vives, Enrique Mendez. *El Uruguay de la Modernización 1876–1904.* Historia Uruguaya. Tomo 5. Montevideo, Uruguay: Ediciones de la Banda Oriental, 1975.

Vlastos, Stephen. "Opposition Movements in Early Meiji, 1868–1885." In *The Emergence of Meiji Japan*, 203–267, edited by Marius B. Jansen. Cambridge, UK: Cambridge University Press, 1995.

Vogelsang, William. *The Afghans.* Oxford, UK: Blackwell Publishers, 2002.

Volgyes, Ivan, ed. *Hungary in Revolution, 1918–19: Nine Essays.* Lincoln: University of Nebraska Press, 1971.

Volpi, Frédéric. *Islam and Democracy: The Failure of Dialogue in Algeria.* Sterling, VA: Pluto Press, 2003.

Von Moltke, Helmuth. *Darstellung des Turkisch-Aegyptischen Feldzugs in Sommer 1839.* Berlin, Germany: Junker and Dunnhaupt, 1935.

Von Sax, Carl Ritter. *Geschichte des Machtverfalls der Torkel.* Vienna, Switzerland: Manziche K. U. K. Hof Verlags and Universitätsbuchhandlung, 1913.

Von Sternegg, J. K. *Schlacten-Atlas des XIX Jahrhunderts: Der Russisch-Turkische Krieg, 1877–1878.* Leipzig, Germany: P. Bauerle, 1866–1899.

Wade, Rex A. *The Bolshevik Revolution and Russian Civil War.* Westport, CT: Greenwood Press, 2001.

______. *The Russian Revolution, 1917.* Cambridge, UK: Cambridge University Press, 2000.

Walder, Andrew G., and Yang Su. "The Cultural Revolution in the Countryside: Scope, Timing and Human Impact." *The China Quarterly* (2003): 74–99.

Waldman, Eric. *The Spartacist Uprising of 1919 and the Crisis of the German Socialist Movement: A Study of the Relation of Political Theory and Party Practice.* Milwaukee, WI: Marquette University Press, 1958.

Waldron, Arthur. *From War to Nationalism: China's Turning Point, 1924–1925.* Cambridge, UK: Cambridge University Press, 1995.

______. "War and the Rise of Nationalism in Twentieth-century China." *Journal of Military History* 57 (October 1993): 87–104.

Wallace, Marion. *A History of Namibia.* New York: Columbia University Press, 2011.

Wallace, Michael, and J. David Singer. "Intergovernmental Organization in the Global System, 1816–1964: A Quantitative Description." *International Organization* 24 (1970): 239–87.

Wallace, Paul. Political "Violence and Terrorism in India: The Crisis of Identity." In *Terrorism in Context*, edited by Martha Crenshaw, 353–410. University Park: Penn State University Press, 2010.

Waller, Michael, Kyril Drezov, and Bülent Gökay. "Introduction." In *Kosovo: The Politics of Delusion*, edited by Michael Waller, Kyril Drezov, and Bülent Gökay. Portland, OR: Frank Cass, 2001.

Walsh, Rodolfo. "Intelligence Office Analysis, Montoneros." Centro do Documentación de los Movememtos Armados, January 2, 1977. http://www.cedema.org.

Walter, Barbara F. "Introduction." In *Civil Wars, Insecurity, and Intervention*, edited by Barbara F. Walter and Jack Snyder, 1–12. New York: Columbia University Press, 1999.

Walzer, Michael. *Just and Unjust Wars: A Moral Argument with Historical Illustrations.* 2nd ed. New York: Basic Books, 1992.

Wang, David. "The Xinjiang Question of the 1940s: The Story Behind the Sino-Soviet Treaty of August 1945." *Asian Studies Review* 21 1997: 83–105.

Warner, Denis. "Indonesian Government Harried—Rebels Tie Army Down." *Newcastle Morning Herald and Miners' Advocate*, December 8, 1954, 7.

______. "Stalemate in Sumatra Uprising." *Newcastle Morning Herald and Miners' Advocate*, November 17, 1953, 3.

Warner, Philip. *Dervish: The Rise and Fall of an African Empire.* London: MacDonald, 1973.

"Warnings of War." *Al-Ahram Weekly*, July 17, 2014.

Warren, Harris Gaylord. *Paraguay.* Norman: University of Oklahoma Press, 1949.

Watts, Nicole. "Relocating Dersim: Turkish State-building and Kurdish Resistance, 1931–1938." *New Perspectives on Turkey* 23 (2000): 5–30.

Wayman, Frank, and Atsushi Tago. "Explaining the Onset of Mass Political Killing, 1949–87." *Journal of Peace Research* 46, no. 6 (2009).

Weinberg, Phil. *Homage to Chiapas: The New Indigenous Struggles in Mexico.* Verso, 2000.

Weinberger, Naomi Joy. *Syrian Intervention in Lebanon: The 1975–76 Civil War.* New York: Oxford University Press, 1986.

Weinstein, Jeremy M. *Inside Rebellion: The Politics of Insurgent Violence.* Cambridge, UK: Cambridge University Press, 2007.

Weinstein, Jeremy M., and Laudemiro Francisco. "The Civil War in Mozambique, the Balance Between Internal and External Influences." In *Understanding Civil War: Evidence and Analysis*, vol. 1, edited by Paul Collier ad Nicholas Sambanis, 157–92. Washington, DC: World Bank, 2005.

Wells, Allen, and Gilbert M. Joseph. *Summer of Discontent, Seasons of Upheaval: Elite Politics and Rural Insurgency in Yucatan, 1876–1915.* Stanford, CA: Stanford University Press, 1996.

Wenner, Manfred W. "The Civil War in Yemen, 1962–1970." In *Stopping the Killing*, edited by Roy Licklider, 95–124. New York: New York University Press, 1993.

______. *The Yemen Arab Republic.* Boulder, CO: Westview Press, 1991.

Werenfels, Isabelle. *Managing Instability in Algeria: Elites and Political Change since 1995.* New York: Routledge, 2007.

Wert, Michael. "Tokugawa Loyalism: Boshin War." In *Japan at War: An Encyclopedia*, edited by Louis G. Perez, 438–39. Santa Barbara, CA: ABC-CLIO, 2013.

"West Irian Leader Quits." *The Canberra Times*, January 3, 1969, 3.

Westad, Odd Arne. *Decisive Encounters: The Chinese Civil War, 1946–1950.* Stanford, CA: Stanford University Press, 2003.

Westwood, J. N. *Endurance and Endeavor: Russian History, 1812–1992.* Oxford, UK: Oxford University Press, 1993.

Westwood, Kathleen. "The Libyan Rebels: Evolution of a Fighting Force." Civil Military Fusion Centre, July 2011. http://www.operationspaix.net/DATA/DOCUMENT/6408~v~The_Libyan_Rebels__Evolution_of_a_Fighting_Force.pdf.

Whealey, Robert H. *Hitler and Spain, the Nazi Role in the Spanish Civil War 1936–1939.* Lexington: The University Press of Kentucky, 1989.

Wheatcroft, Andrew. *The Ottomans.* New York: Viking, 1993.

Wheeler, Geoffrey. *The Modern History of Soviet Central Asia.* New York: Frederick A. Praeger Publishers, 1964.

Whelpton, John. *A History of Nepal.* Cambridge, UK: Cambridge University Press, 2005.

Whitaker, Arthur P. *Argentine Upheaval.* New York: Praeger, 1956.

White, Alistair. *El Salvador.* New York: Praeger, 1973.

White, Andrew Dickson. *Autobiography of Andrew Dickson White.* Vol. 1. New York: Century, 1905.

White, G. F. *A History of Spain and Portugal.* London: Methuen, 1909.

White, Paul. *Primitive Rebels or Revolutionary Modernizers? The Kurdish National Movement in Turkey.* London: Zed Books, 2000.

Whitehead, Lawrence. "Bolivia since 1930." In *The Cambridge History of Latin America,* Vol. VIII, edited by Leslie Bethell, 509–86. Cambridge, UK: Cambridge University Press, 1984.

Whitlock, Monica. *Land Beyond the River: The Untold Story of Central Asia.* New York: St. Martin's Press, 2003.

"Who's Who Among Syria's Rebel Groups, For Now." *San Jose Mercury News,* January 10, 2014.

Wickham-Crowley, Timothy P. *Guerillas and Revolution in Latin America: A Comparative Study of Insurgents and Regimes since 1956.* Princeton, NJ: Princeton University Press, 1992.

______. "The Rise (and Sometimes Fall) of Guerrilla Governments in Latin America." *Sociological Forum* 2, no. 3 (Summer, 1987): 473–99.

______. "Terror and Guerrilla Warfare in Latin America, 1956–1970." *Comparative Studies in Society and History* 32, no. 2 (April, 1990): 201–37.

Wickramasinghe, Nira. "Sri Lanka in 2007: Military Successes, but at Humanitarian and Economic Costs." *Asian Survey* 48, no. 1 (2008): 191–97.

______. "Sri Lanka in 2008: Waging War for Peace." *Asian Survey* 49, no. 1 (2009): 59–65.

Wicks, Daniel H. "Dress Rehearsal: United States Intervention on the Isthmus of Panama, 1885." *Pacific Historical Review* 49, no. 4 (1980): 581–605.

Wilbur, C. Martin. *The Nationalist Revolution in China, 1923–1928.* Cambridge, UK: Cambridge University Press, 1983.

Wilbur, Donald N. *Contemporary Iran.* New York: Praeger, 1963.

Wilde, James. "Mystery Man of Indonesia." *Canberra Times,* May 1, 1958, 2.

Wilkenfeld, Jonathan. "Profiles of Active Armed Conflicts." In *Peace and Conflict 2014,* edited by David A. Backer, Jonathan Wilkenfeld, and Paul K. Huth. Boulder, CO: Paradigm Publishers, 2014.

Wilkinson, Endymion. *Chinese History: A Manual.* Rev. and enlarged. Cambridge, MA: Harvard-Yenching Institute, 2000.

Wilkinson, John Gardner. *Modern Egypt and Thebes: Being a Description of Egypt, Including the Information Required for Travellers in That Country.* London: John Murray, 1843.

Williams, Devin O'Neal. "Violence Upon Seizing the Railroad: Qing Policy in Creating the Suchuan Railway Movement." Master's thesis, University of Utah, Department of History, 2013.

Williams, Henry Smith. *The Historians' History of the World.* Vols. 21–22. New York: Encyclopaedia Britannica Company, 1907.

Williams, Kristen P. *Despite Nationalist Conflicts: Theory and Practice of Maintaining World Peace.* New York: Praeger, 2001.

Williams, Louise. "Savage Scimitars of Sumatra." *Sydney Morning Herald,* September 22, 1990.

Williams, Mary W. *The People and Politics of Latin America.* Rev. ed. Boston, MA: Ginn and Co., 1945.

Williams, Mary W., Ruhl J. Bartlett, and Russell E. Miller. *The People and Politics of Latin America.* Boston, MA: Ginn, 1955.

Williamson, Edwin. *The Penguin History of Latin America (Revised).* London: Penguin Books, 2009.

Wilson, Andrew. *The "Ever Victorious Army."* Edinburgh, Scotland: Blackwood, 1868.

______. *Ukrainians: Unexpected Nation.* New Haven, CT: Yale University Press, 2000.

Wilson, Bruce M. *Costa Rica: Politics, Economics, and Democracy.* Boulder, CO: Lynne Rienner Publishers, 1998.

Wilson, Dick. *The Long March: The Epic of Chinese Communism's Survival, 1935.* New York: Viking, 1971.

Wilson-Roberts, Guy. "The Bougainville Conflict: An Historical Overview." In *Peace on Bougainville,* edited by Rebecca Adams, 23–32. Wellington, New Zealand: Victoria University Press, 2001.

Wingate, Francis Reginald. *Mahdism and the Egyptian Sudan.* London: Macmillan and Co., 1891.

Winslow, Charles. *Lebanon: War and Politics in a Fragmented Society.* New York: Routledge, 2003.

Winstone, H. V. F. *The Illicit Adventure: The Story of Political and Military Intelligence in the Middle East From 1898 to 1926.* Frederick, MD: University Publishers of America, 1982.

Wirsing, Robert G. *India, Pakistan, and the Kashmir Dispute.* New York: St. Martin's, 1994.

Wise, George S. *Caudillo: A Portrait of Antonio Guzmán Blanco.* New York: Columbia University Press, 1951.

Wise, George S. *Caudillo: A Portrait of Antonio Guzmán Blanco.* Westport, CT: Greenwood Press, 1970 [reprint].

Wise, George Schneiweis. "Antonio Guzman Blanco: A Study of Caudillismo." PhD diss., Columbia University, Department of Political Science, 1950.

Wolf, Paul. "Anti-Communist Programs." 2002–2004a. http://www.icdi.com/~paul wolf.

______. "CIA Survey Teams." 2002–2004b. http://www.icdi.com/~paul wolf.

______. "Movimento Revolucionario Liberal." 2002–2004d. http://www.icdi.com/~paul wolf.

______. "Plan Lazo and the Alliance for Progress." 2002–2004c. http://www.icdi.com/~paul wolf.

______. "Political Dissidents and Rural Unrest." In *Bandits Peasants and Politics: The Case of "La Violencia" in Colombia*, edited by Gonzalo Sánchez and Donny Meertens, 160–66. Translated by Alan Hynds. Austin: University of Texas Press, 2001.

Wolf, Sue Rabbitt. *Timor's Anschluss: Indonesian and Australian Policy in East Timor 1974–1976*. Lewiston, NY: Edwin Mellen Press, 1992.

Womble, Theresa Liane. "Early Constitutionalism in Tunisia, 1857–1864: Reform and Revolt." PhD diss., Princeton University, 1997.

Wongtrangan, Kanok. "Communist Revolutionary Process: A Study of the Communist Party of Thailand." PhD diss., Johns Hopkins University, 1981.

Wood, David. "Conflict in the Twentieth Century." *Adelphi Papers 48*. London: Institute of Strategic Studies, June 1968.

Wood, Elisabeth Jean. *Insurgent Collective Action and Civil War in El Salvador*. Cambridge, UK: Cambridge University Press, 2003.

Woodhead, H. G. W., ed. *The China Year Book 1925/26. Part II*. Nendeln, Liechtenstein: Kraus Reprint, 1969a.

______, ed. *The China Year Book 1929/30. Part II*. Nendeln, Liechtenstein: Kraus Reprint, 1969b. Originally published 1930.

______, ed. *The China Year Book 1931*. Shanghai: North-China Daily News and Herald, 1931.

Woodhouse, C. M. *The Greek War of Independence*. New York: Hutchinson, 1952.

Woodward, Ralph Lee, Jr. *Rafael Carrera and the Emergence of the Republic of Guatemala, 1821–1871*. Athens: University of Georgia Press, 1993.

Worcester, Donald E. *Brazil from Colony to World Power*. New York: Scribner's, 1973.

World Alliance for Peace in Sri Lanka. *Peace in Sri Lanka, Obstacles and Opportunities*. London: World Alliance for Peace in Sri Lanka, 2005.

"World News Briefs." *Daily News* (Bowling Green, KY), January 27, 1969, 10.

Worobec, Stephen Francis. "International Narcotics Control in the Golden Triangle of Southeast Asia." PhD diss., Claremont Graduate School, International Relations, 1983.

Worthing, Peter. *A Military History of Modern China: From the Manchu Conquest to Tian'anmen Square*. Westport, CT: Praeger Security International, 2007.

Wortzel, Larry M. *Dictionary of Contemporary Chinese Military History*. Westport, CT: Greenwood Press, 1999.

Wou, Odoric Y. K. *Militarism in Modern China: The Career of Wu Pei-fu, 1916–39*. Folkestone, UK: Dawson, 1978.

Wright, John F. R., Suzanne Goldenberg, and Richard Schofield, eds. *Transcaucasian Boundaries*. London: UCL Press, 1996.

Wright, Mary Clabaugh. *The Last Stand of Chinese Conservatism: The T'ung-chih Restoration, 1862–1874*. 2nd printing. Stanford, CA: Stanford University Press, 1962.

Wright, Quincy. *A Study of War*. Rev. ed. 2 vols. Chicago, IL: University of Chicago Press, 1965.

Wright, Thomas C. State *Terrorism in Latin America: Chile, Argentina, and International Human Rights*. Lanham, MD: Rowman & Littlefield, 2007.

Wuorinen, John H. *A History of Finland*. New York: Columbia University Press, 1965.

Xiang, Lanxin. *Mao's Generals: Chen Yi and the New Fourth Army*. Lanham, MD: University Press of America, 1998.

Xinhua General Overseas News Service. "East Timor." March–December, 1977.

Yadav, Stacey Philbrick. "Political Conflicts." In *Yemen*, edited by Steven A. Caton, 270–83. Santa Barbara, CA: ABC-CLIO, 2013.

Yanaga, Chitoshi. *Japan since Perry*. New York: McGraw-Hill, 1949.

Yapp, M. E. *The Making of the Modern Near East 1792–1923*. New York: Longman, 1987.

Yarrington, Doug. *A Coffee Frontier: Land, Society, and Politics in Duaca, Venezuela, 1830–1936*. Pittsburgh, PA: University of Pittsburgh Press, 1997.

Yavuz, M. Hakan. "Five Stages of the Construction of Kurdish Nationalism in Turkey." In *Kurdish Identity: Human Rights and Political Status*, edited by Charles MacDonald and Carole O'Leary, 56–76. Gainesville: University Press of Florida, 2007.

______. "Five Stages of the Construction of Kurdish Nationalism in Turkey." *Nationalism & Ethnic Politics* 7, no. 3 (Autumn 2001): 1–24.

Ycaza, Julio Estrada. "La Campaña de Esmereldas 1913–1916." *Revista del Archivo Historico del Guayas* 9, no. 17 (1980): 5–128.

Yegar, Moshe. *Between Integration and Secession: The Muslim Communities of the Southern Philippines, Southern Thailand, and Western Burma/Myanmar.* Lanham, MD: Lexington Books, 2002.

Yekelchyk, Serhy. *Ukraine, Birth of a Modern Nation.* New York: Oxford University Press, 2007.

"Yemen Rebel Surrender Forecast." *The Age*, November 27, 1962, 4.

"Yemen Rebels, Royalists Both Claim Victory." *The Times-News (NC)*, October 6, 1962, 1.

"Yemen Ruler Reported Out." *Tuscaloosa News*, June 4, 1969, 3.

"Yemen Times' Publishes Maps Showing Troop Deployments by Salih and Bid Forces." *BBC Summary of World Broadcasts* (orig. *Agence France-Presse*), March 10, 1994.

"Yemen Troops Defy Orders Despite Reconciliation Efforts." *Associated Press Worldstream*, January 23, 1994.

"Yemeni Leaders Sign Deal to End Intermilitary Clashes." *The Globe and Mail (Canada)*, February 28, 1994.

"Yemeni Socialists Expel Former Leader." *Agence France-Presse*, October 9, 1994.

Yildiz, Kerim. *The Kurds in Iraq: The Past, Present, and Future.* London: Pluto Press, 2004.

Yongming, Zhou. "Suppressing Opium and 'Reforming' Minorities: Antidrug Campaigns in Ethnic Communities in the Early People's Republic of China." In *Dangerous Harvest: Drug Plants and the Transformation of Indigenous Landscapes*, edited by Michael K. Steinberg, Joseph J. Hobbs, and Kent Matthewson, 232–45. New York: Oxford University Press, 2004.

Yonuo, Asoso. *The Rising Nagas: A Historical and Political Study.* Delhi, India: Manas Publications, 1984. Originally published 1974.

Young, Jordan M. *The Brazilian Revolution of 1930 and the Aftermath.* New Brunswick: Rutgers University Press, 1967.

Young, M. Crawford. "The Obote Revolution." *African Report* 11 (June 1966): 8–14.

Young-hee, Suh. "Tracing the Course of the Peasant War of 1894." *Korea Journal* (Winter 1994): 17–30.

Youngs, Tim, Mark Oakes, and Paul Bowers. "Kosovo: Operation 'Allied Force.'" Research Paper series 99, no. 48. London: House of Commons Library, 1999.

"YPG Releases Balance-Sheet of 2014." *BestaNûçe*, December 28, 2014. http://www.bestanuce1.com/haber/160643/ypg-releases-balance-sheet-of-2014-nearly-5000-isis-members-killed&dil=en.

Yu-Chang, Wu. *The Revolution of 1911: A Great Democratic Revolution of China.* Peking, China: Foreign Languages Press, 1964.

Yuk-fun, Law. "Xi'an (Sian) Incident." In *China at War: An Encyclopedia*, edited by Xiaobing Li, 496–97. Santa Barbara, CA: ABC–CLIO, 2012.

Yunas, S. Fida. *Afghanistan: A Political History.* Hayatabad, Pakistan, 2002.

Zackrison, James L. "*La Violencia* in Colombia: An Anomaly in Terrorism." *Conflict Quarterly* (1989): 5–18.

Zahar, Marie Joëlle. "Peace by Unconventional Means: Lebanon's Ta'if Agreement." In *Ending Civil Wars: The Implementation of Peace Agreements*, edited by Stephen John Stedman, Donald Rothchild, and Elizabeth M. Cousens, 567–97. Boulder, CO: Lynne Rienner, 2002.

Zaheer, Hasan. *The Separation of East Pakistan: The Rise and Realization of Bengali Muslim Nationalism.* Karachi, Pakistan: Oxford University Press (Mas Printers), 1994.

Zeitlin, Maurice. *The Civil Wars in Chile (or the Bourgeois Revolutions That Never Were).* Princeton, NJ: Princeton University Press, 1984.

Zelkina, Anna. *In Quest for God and Freedom: the Sufi Response to the Russian Advance in the North Caucasus.* London: Hurst & Company, 2000.

Zenkovsky, Serge A. *Pan-Turkism and Islam in Russia.* Cambridge, MA: Harvard University Press, 1960.

Zhang, Xiaoming. "China's Involvement in Laos during the Vietnam War, 1963–1975." *The Journal of Military History* 66, no. 4 (October 2002): 1141–166.

Zhimoni, Kukoi. *Politics and Militancy in Nagaland.* New Delhi, India: Deep & Deep Publications, 2004.

Zürcher, Christoph. *The Post-Soviet Wars.* New York: New York University Press, 2007.

Zürcher, Erik Jan. "The Ottoman Conscription System in Theory and Practice." In *Arming the State: Military Conscription in the Middle East and Central Asia 1775–1925*, edited by Erik Jan Zürcher, 79–94. New York: I. B. Tauris, 1999.

Index

Page references followed by *t* indicate a table of information.